Explore Australia

Viking
A division of Penguin Books Australia Ltd
487 Maroondah Highway, PO Box 257
Ringwood, Victoria 3134, Australia
Penguin Books Ltd
Harmondsworth, Middlesex, England
Viking Penguin, A division of Penguin Books USA Inc.
375 Hudson Street, New York, New York 10014, USA
Penguin Books Canada Limited
10 Alcorn Avenue, Toronto, Ontario, Canada M4V 3B2
Penguin Books (N.Z.) Ltd
182–190 Wairau Road, Auckland 10, New Zealand

This sixteenth edition published by Penguin Books Australia Ltd, 1997
First published by George Philip & O'Neil Pty Ltd, 1980
Second edition 1981   Fourth edition 1985
Third edition 1983   Fifth edition 1986
Reprinted 1984
Sixth edition published by Penguin Books Australia, 1987
Seventh edition 1988   Twelfth edition 1993
Eighth edition 1989   Thirteenth edition 1994
Ninth edition 1990   Fourteenth edition 1995
Tenth edition 1991   Fifteenth edition 1996
Eleventh edition 1992

Copyright © Penguin Books Australia Ltd, 1997

ISBN 0 670 87507 4

Printed in Hong Kong through Bookbuilders Ltd

Publisher's Note: Every effort has been made to ensure that the
information in this book is accurate at the time of going to press.
The publisher welcomes information and suggestions for corrections
or improvement. e-mail: abrowne@penguin.com.au.
A Suggestion Form is provided on page 599.

Disclaimers: The publisher cannot accept responsibility for any
errors or omissions. The representation on the maps of any road
or track is not necessarily evidence of public right of way.
The population figures given in *Explore Australia* have been taken
from the most recent Census results available. They are intended to
provide only an approximate idea of the size of the various cities
and towns. Accommodation listed is a guide to accommodation
available in each town.

Shortly after the Victorian section of this book went to print, there were a number
of changes to government agencies mentioned in the text. The Alpine Resorts
Commission was disbanded and replaced with separate boards of management.
The National Parks Service merged with Melbourne Parks and Waterways to form
Parks Victoria (Vault 11, Banana Alley, Melbourne 3000; 13 1963;
Web Site address http://parks.vic.gov.au).

HALF-TITLE PAGE: Coastline north of Derby, Western Australia
  (Bill Bachman/Stock Photos)

TITLE PAGE: Old shearing shed near the Grampians, Victoria
  (David Scaletti/Stock Photos)

ON THE ROAD?

THE COMPLETE COMPANION
TO FOUR-WHEEL DRIVING

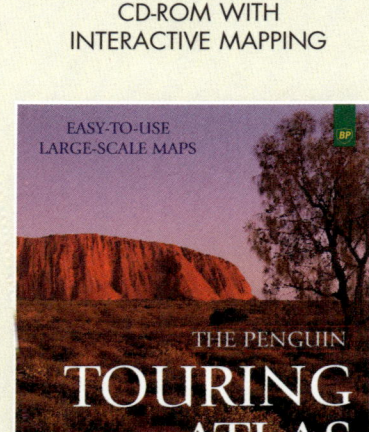

CD-ROM WITH
INTERACTIVE MAPPING

AUSTRALIA'S BEST-SELLING
TRAVEL GUIDE

THE COMPLETE GUIDE TO TOURING
NEW SOUTH WALES AND THE ACT

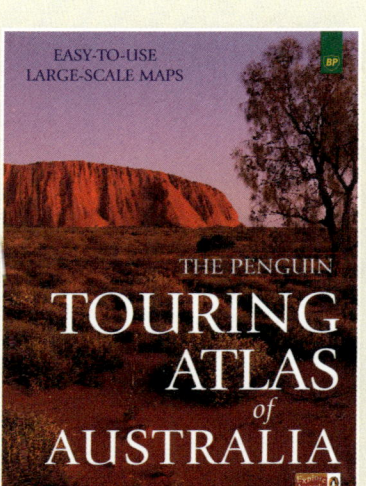

EASY-TO-USE LARGE-SCALE MAPS

THE ESSENTIAL GUIDES TO FISHING
IN NEW SOUTH WALES, VICTORIA
& QUEENSLAND

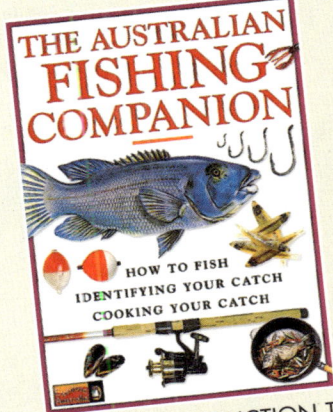

THE IDEAL INTRODUCTION TO
FISHING IN AUSTRALIA

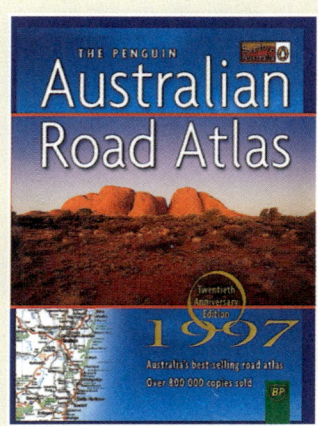

AUSTRALIA'S
MOST COMPREHENSIVE
ROAD ATLAS

SHEET MAPS FOR ALL STATES,
TERRITORIES AND CAPITAL CITIES

ALWAYS TRAVEL WITH PENGUIN BOOKS

Major Inter-city Routes

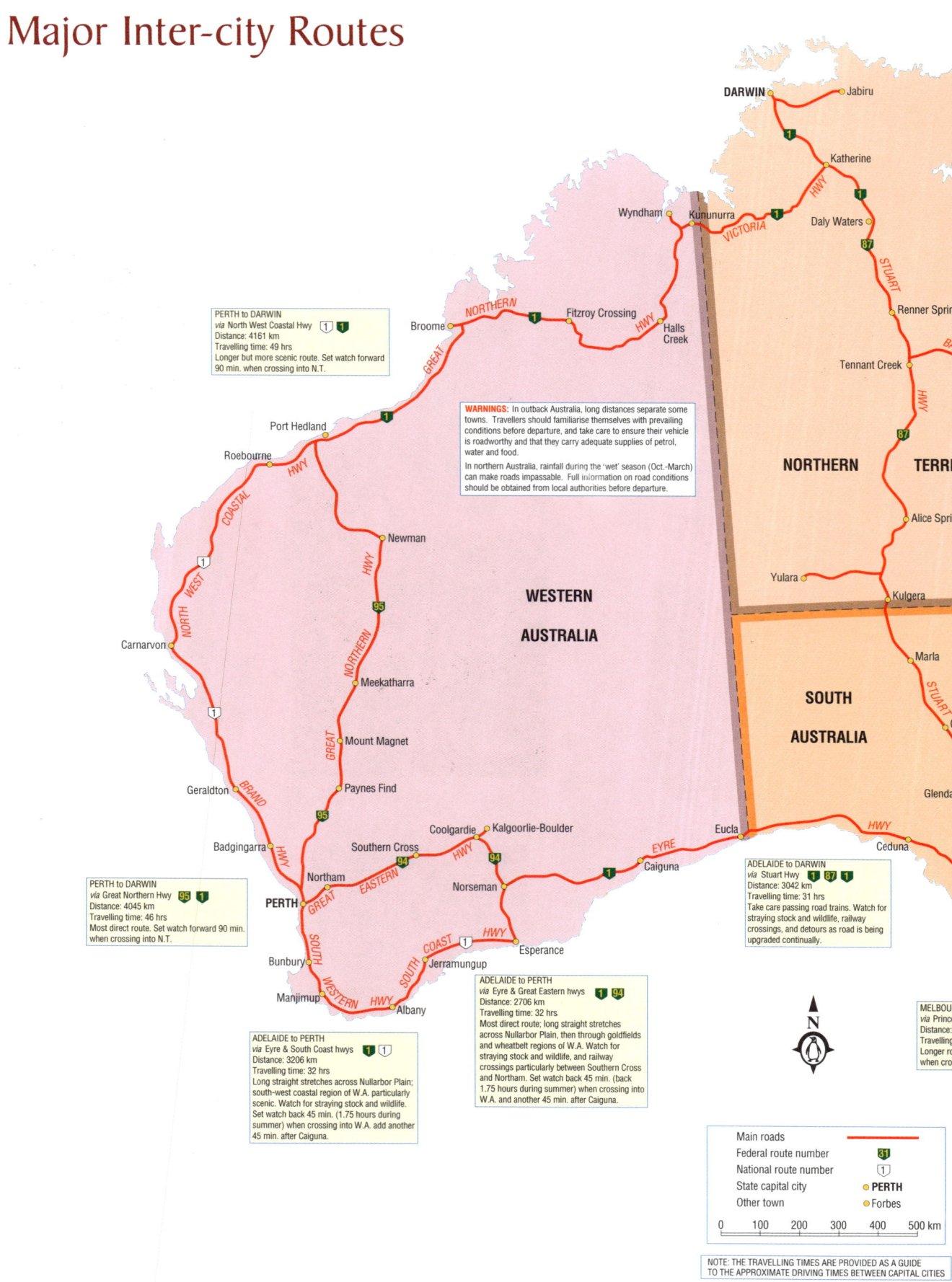

PERTH to DARWIN
via North West Coastal Hwy ① ①
Distance: 4161 km
Travelling time: 49 hrs
Longer but more scenic route. Set watch forward
90 min. when crossing into N.T.

WARNINGS: In outback Australia, long distances separate some
towns. Travellers should familiarise themselves with prevailing
conditions before departure, and take care to ensure their vehicle
is roadworthy and that they carry adequate supplies of petrol,
water and food.

In northern Australia, rainfall during the 'wet' season (Oct.-March)
can make roads impassable. Full information on road conditions
should be obtained from local authorities before departure.

PERTH to DARWIN
via Great Northern Hwy 95 ①
Distance: 4045 km
Travelling time: 46 hrs
Most direct route. Set watch forward 90 min.
when crossing into N.T.

ADELAIDE to DARWIN
via Stuart Hwy ① 87 ①
Distance: 3042 km
Travelling time: 31 hrs
Take care passing road trains. Watch for
straying stock and wildlife, railway
crossings, and detours as road is being
upgraded continually.

ADELAIDE to PERTH
via Eyre & Great Eastern hwys ① 94
Distance: 2706 km
Travelling time: 32 hrs
Most direct route; long straight stretches
across Nullarbor Plain, then through goldfields
and wheatbelt regions of W.A. Watch for
straying stock and wildlife, and railway
crossings particularly between Southern Cross
and Northam. Set watch back 45 min. (back
1.75 hours during summer) when crossing into
W.A. and another 45 min. after Caiguna.

ADELAIDE to PERTH
via Eyre & South Coast hwys ① ①
Distance: 3206 km
Travelling time: 32 hrs
Long straight stretches across Nullarbor Plain;
south-west coastal region of W.A. particularly
scenic. Watch for straying stock and wildlife.
Set watch back 45 min. (1.75 hours during
summer) when crossing into W.A. add another
45 min. after Caiguna.

MELBOURN
via Princes
Distance: 92
Travelling ti
Longer rout
when crossi

Main roads
Federal route number 31
National route number ①
State capital city ● **PERTH**
Other town ○ Forbes

0   100   200   300   400   500 km

NOTE: THE TRAVELLING TIMES ARE PROVIDED AS A GUIDE
TO THE APPROXIMATE DRIVING TIMES BETWEEN CAPITAL CITIES

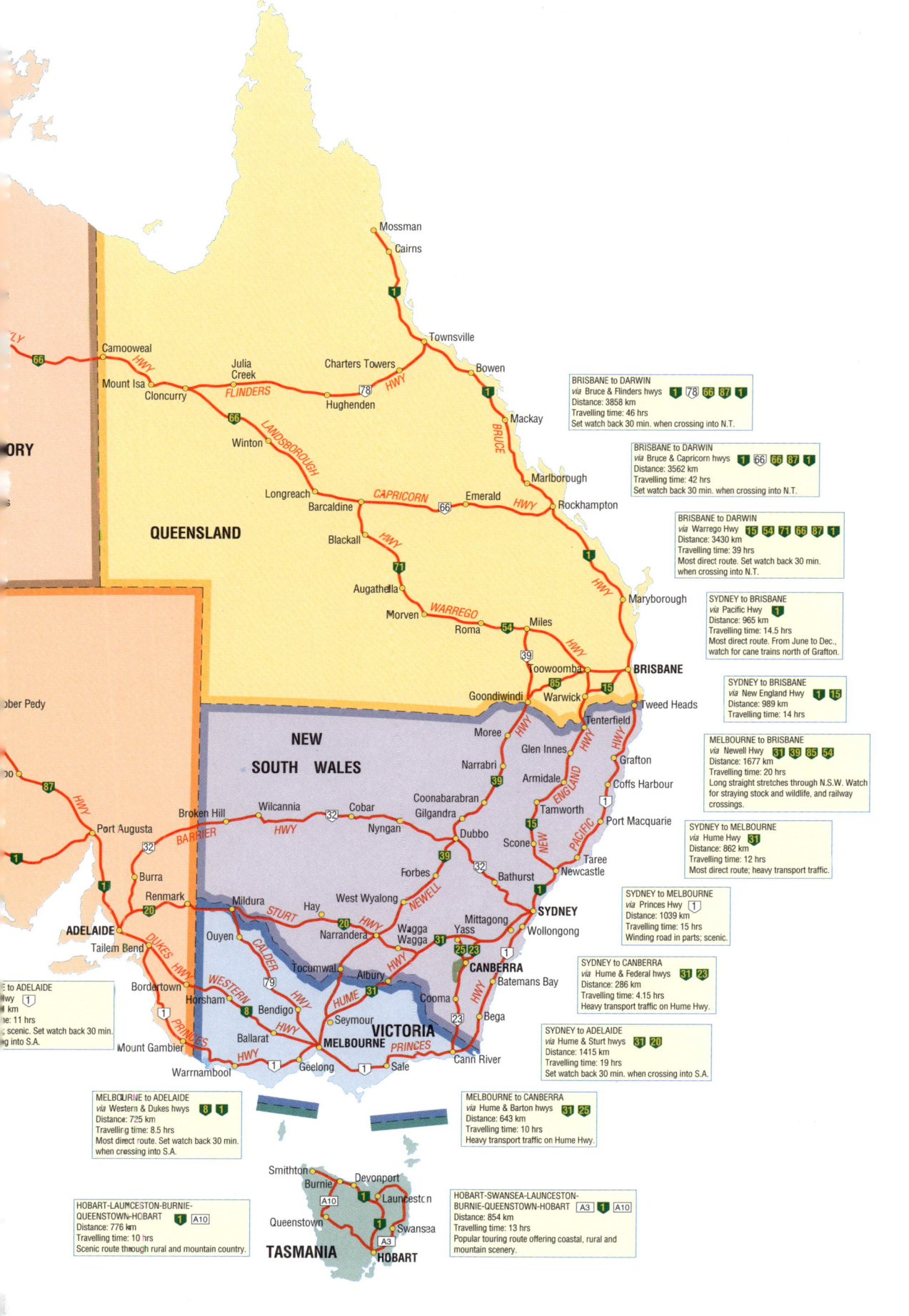

Mossman
Cairns
1
Townsville
Camooweal
66
Charters Towers
Bowen
Julia Creek
HWY
Mount Isa
FLINDERS
78
HWY
Cloncurry
Hughenden
BRUCE
Mackay
1
LANDSBOROUGH
66
Winton
Marlborough
CAPRICORN
Longreach
Emerald
HWY
Rockhampton
Barcaldine
66
Blackall
HWY
71
Augathella
1
Maryborough
Morven
WARREGO
Miles
54
Roma
HWY
QUEENSLAND

BRISBANE to DARWIN
via Bruce & Flinders hwys **1** **78** **66** **87** **1**
Distance: 3858 km
Travelling time: 46 hrs
Set watch back 30 min. when crossing into N.T.

BRISBANE to DARWIN
via Bruce & Capricorn hwys **1** **66** **66** **87** **1**
Distance: 3562 km
Travelling time: 42 hrs
Set watch back 30 min. when crossing into N.T.

BRISBANE to DARWIN
via Warrego Hwy **15** **54** **71** **66** **87** **1**
Distance: 3430 km
Travelling time: 39 hrs
Most direct route. Set watch back 30 min.
when crossing into N.T.

SYDNEY to BRISBANE
via Pacific Hwy **1**
Distance: 965 km
Travelling time: 14.5 hrs
Most direct route. From June to Dec.,
watch for cane trains north of Grafton.

SYDNEY to BRISBANE
via New England Hwy **1** **15**
Distance: 989 km
Travelling time: 14 hrs

MELBOURNE to BRISBANE
via Newell Hwy **31** **39** **85** **54**
Distance: 1677 km
Travelling time: 20 hrs
Long straight stretches through N.S.W. Watch
for straying stock and wildlife, and railway
crossings.

SYDNEY to MELBOURNE
via Hume Hwy **31**
Distance: 862 km
Travelling time: 12 hrs
Most direct route; heavy transport traffic.

SYDNEY to MELBOURNE
via Princes Hwy **1**
Distance: 1039 km
Travelling time: 15 hrs
Winding road in parts; scenic.

SYDNEY to CANBERRA
via Hume & Federal hwys **31** **23**
Distance: 286 km
Travelling time: 4.15 hrs
Heavy transport traffic on Hume Hwy.

SYDNEY to ADELAIDE
via Hume & Sturt hwys **31** **20**
Distance: 1415 km
Travelling time: 19 hrs
Set watch back 30 min. when crossing into S.A.

MELBOURNE to CANBERRA
via Hume & Barton hwys **31** **25**
Distance: 643 km
Travelling time: 10 hrs
Heavy transport traffic on Hume Hwy.

MELBOURNE to ADELAIDE
via Western & Dukes hwys **8** **1**
Distance: 725 km
Travelling time: 8.5 hrs
Most direct route. Set watch back 30 min.
when crossing into S.A.

ober Pedy
87
HWY
Port Augusta
1
BARRIER
Broken Hill
Wilcannia
32
Cobar
Coonabarabran
Gilgandra
Moree
HWY
Glen Innes
Grafton
32
Nyngan
Narrabri
Armidale
39
Coffs Harbour
NEW
Tamworth
ENGLAND
Port Macquarie
1
SOUTH WALES
Dubbo
Scone
PACIFIC
Burra
39
Forbes
Bathurst
Taree
Renmark
West Wyalong
32
Newcastle
20
Mildura
Hay
NEWELL
ADELAIDE
STURT
20
Narrandera
Wagga
Mittagong
SYDNEY
Tailem Bend
HWY
Wagga
Yass
Wollongong
Ouyen
Tocumwal
31
1
CALDER
Albury
25 **23**
Bordertown
79
31
CANBERRA
Horsham
WESTERN
Tumut
HUME
Cooma
Batemans Bay
1
8
Bendigo
HWY
23
Bega
DUKES HWY
Seymour
VICTORIA
PRINCES
Mount Gambier
Ballarat
HWY
MELBOURNE
PRINCES
Cann River
HWY
Warrnambool
1
Geelong
1
Sale

to ADELAIDE
Hwy **1**
km
e: 11 hrs
scenic. Set watch back 30 min.
ng into S.A.

Smithton
Devonport
Burnie
A10
1
Launceston
Queenstown
1
Swansea
A3
TASMANIA
HOBART

HOBART-LAUNCESTON-BURNIE-
QUEENSTOWN-HOBART **1** **A10**
Distance: 776 km
Travelling time: 10 hrs
Scenic route through rural and mountain country.

HOBART-SWANSEA-LAUNCESTON-
BURNIE-QUEENSTOWN-HOBART **A3** **1** **A10**
Distance: 854 km
Travelling time: 13 hrs
Popular touring route offering coastal, rural and
mountain scenery.

MAP SYMBOLS

ROAD MAP SYMBOLS

F3	Freeway, with Freeway Route Number
	Freeway under construction
31	Highway, sealed, with Federal Route Number
1	Highway, sealed, with National Route Number
5	Highway, sealed, with Metroad Route Number
A10	Highway, unsealed, with Tasmania Route Number
	Highway under construction
26	Main road, sealed, with State Route Number
	Main road, unsealed, with Tourist Route
	Main road under construction
	Secondary road (suburbs maps only)
	Secondary road, unsealed (suburbs maps only)
	Other road, with traffic direction arrow
	Other road, unsealed
	Mall
	Vehicle track
	Walking track
Paratoo	Railway, with station
Flagstaff	Underground railway, with station
114	Total kilometres between two points
45	Intermediate kilometres
	State border
	Fruit Fly Exclusion Zone Boundary
SYDNEY	State capital city
GEELONG	Town, over 50 000 inhabitants
Bundaberg ⊙	Town, 10 000–50 000 inhabitants
Katherine ⊙	Town, 5 000–10 000 inhabitants
Narrogin ⊙	Town, 1 000–5 000 inhabitants
Robe ⊙	Town, 200–1 000 inhabitants
Tharwa ○	Town, under 200 inhabitants
Strickland	Locality
GLENORCHY	Suburb, on state and region maps
Glenorchy	Suburb, on suburban maps
Alroy Downs □	Pastoral station homestead
Murgenella ○	Closed Aboriginal town
Fortesque Roadhouse ▦	Roadhouse
✈	Commercial airport
•∎	Place of interest
•	Landmark feature
∎	General interest feature
∎	Accommodation
+	Hill, mountain
⚒	Minesite
★	Lighthouse
	River, waterfall
	Lake
	Intermittent lake
TO GOULBURN	Route destination
294	Adjoining page number
	National park
	Other reserve
	Other named area
	Aboriginal land
	Prohibited area
❏	Text entry in A to Z listing

WILDLIFE-WATCHING SYMBOLS

Wildlife symbols indicate fauna found in particular areas which may be of interest to visitors.
The symbols are used on the wildlife-watching maps that appear on the following pages:
71 (NSW), 182 (Vic.), 273 (SA), 339 (WA), 404 (NT), 480 (Qld), 538 (Tas.).

	bandicoots/quolls		kangaroos/wallabies
	bats		koalas
	birds		lizards
	Bogong moths		penguins
	butterflies		platypuses
	crocodiles		possums
	dingoes		quokkas
	dolphins		seals
	dugongs		snakes
	echidnas		Tasmanian devils
	fish		tree kangaroos
	flying foxes		turtles
	frogs		whales
	gliders		wombats
	glow-worms		

Explore Australia

The Complete Touring Companion

VIKING

Acknowledgements

Cartography and research
Penguin Cartographic, a division of Penguin
Books Australia Ltd

Copy editors
Fran Church, EdInk Pty Ltd; Frith Luton

Desktop publishing
P.A.G.E. Pty Ltd

Photographers
George Bareth; Ross Barnett; Canberra Tourism;
Andrew Chapman; Cowra Tourism; Stuart Grant;
Richard I'Anson; Alex Julius; Lochman
Transparencies: Brian Downs, David Hancock,
Jiri Lochman, Marie Lochman, Dennis Sarson,
Len Stewart, Geoff Taylor; Ern Mainka; Peter
McNeill; PD Munchenberg; Pajinka Wilderness
Lodge; Nick Rains; Don Skirrow; Robin Smith;
South Australian Tourism Commission; Ken
Stepnell; Warren Steptoe; Bruce Stewart; Stock
Photos: Kevin Aitken, Bill Bachman, David
Basset, Diana Calder, John Carr, Trevern Dawes,
Robert Della-Piana, Roger Du Buisson, Peter
Elliston, Robert Fox, Ron Gale, Robert Gray,
Owen Hughes, John Jenkins, Noeline Kelly,
Russell Kord, Mark Laricchia, Gary Lewis,
Pauline Madden, Lance Nelson, Bruce Peebles,
Otto Rogge, David Scaletti, David Simmonds,
Don Skirrow, Paul Steel, Ken Stepnell,
Stocktake, James Walshe, Michael Wennrich,
Paul Wilson.

Text
For the preparation of this edition, each tourist
information centre for the towns described was
contacted and the information for each town
checked. The revision of this edition could not
have occurred without their assistance. As well,
assistance was received from the following
individuals and organisations:

New South Wales
Sydney Visitors and Convention Bureau
National Parks and Wildlife Service
Geographical Names Board
Australian Capital Territory
Canberra Tourism
ACT Parks and Conservation Service
Nomenclature Committee
Victoria
Tourism Victoria
Melbourne Convention and Marketing Bureau
Department of Natural Resources and
Environment
Place Names Committee

South Australia
South Australian Tourism Commission
Adelaide Convention and Tourism
Authority
Department of Environment and Natural
Resources
Geographical Names Advisory Committee
Western Australia
Western Australia Tourism Commission
Department of Conservation and Land
Management
Geographic Names Committee
Northern Territory
Central Australian Tourism Industry Association
Darwin Region Tourism Association
Australian Nature Conservation Agency
Parks and Wildlife Commission of the Northern
Territory
Northern and Central land councils
Place Names Committee
Queensland
Queensland Tourist and Travel Corporation
Brisbane Visitors and Convention Bureau
Department of Environment
Department of Natural Resources (place names)
Great Barrier Reef Marine Park Authority
Tasmania
Department of Tourism, Sport and Recreation
Tasmanian Parks and Wildlife Service
Nomenclature Board of Tasmania
The Quill Consultancy
Wildspot Tours Tasmania
Priscilla Park

Maps
The publisher wishes to acknowledge the
assistance of over 500 rural local government
offices in checking and updating map details for
this edition.
Assistance was also received from the various
regional tourism authorities, place name
committees, Aboriginal communities and land
councils, and the following individuals –
Christopher Crook, Bruce Whitehouse and
Michael Vella.

The publisher also wishes to acknowledge Geoff
Rasmussen of Edutech Productions for
preparation of the indexing software, the Bureau
of Meteorology for the Climate Guides and St
John Ambulance Australia for Accident Action
illustrations and information.

CONTENTS

Redbank Gorge, Northern Territory

Warrumbungle National Park, New South Wales

Rocky outcrop, Pilbara, Western Australia

Palms and eucalypts overhead, Palm Cove, Queensland

Floriade, Canberra, Australian Capital Territory

Ghost gum, East McDonnell Ranges, Northern Territory

INTRODUCTION

Exploring Australia by motor vehicle provides the traveller with the opportunity to venture into remote areas, tropical rainforests, coastal regions and inland deserts, and to visit large cosmopolitan cities and tiny outback settlements.

Black Spur, Victoria

Australia is a land of contrast and wonder. It offers many opportunities for exploration and adventure: from dusty outback towns to sandy beaches, from rainforest hinterland to breathtaking alpine vistas. The entire continent is crisscrossed by a combination of bitumen highways, sealed roads and rough bush tracks, almost all navigable in the modern motor car, although some require 4WD vehicles.

Australia comprises an area of approximately 8.5 million square kilometres. This vast continent covers a distance of 3700 kilometres from north to south, and 4000 kilometres east to west. Within these boundaries there is an extraordinary range of flora and fauna, and a vast array of geological wonders.

It is a land of extremes. Australia's temperatures vary from an average 36°C in the midsummer of the Red Centre to an average of 6°C in the highlands in winter. The parched deserts of central Australia may be totally dry for years until flooding rains produce a short-term sea. Sydney has a population of approximately 4 million, whereas Innamincka in South Australia has only 9 permanent residents.

Australia has been the home of Aborigines for over 40 000 years and evidence of their early occupation abounds, particularly in cave paintings and rock carvings made thousands of years ago and found at numerous locations across the continent.

The predominant colours of the Australian landscape are red, blue and green. Inland, the stark red of the Simpson Desert sand dunes contrasts dramatically with the deep azure blue of the noonday sky. Dotted here and there are clumps of velvet-green scrub and, after rain, Sturt's desert pea blooms scarlet.

The superb monolith Uluru (Ayers Rock) is sited almost in the centre of this island continent. This area, known as the Red Centre, features red sand dunes, rocky tors and hardy bush scrub which have a forbidding beauty all their own, even in times of drought. After rain, gardens of brilliant wildflowers are added to the landscape. Across the Far North, from Cape York Peninsula in the east to the Kimberleys in the west, tropical rainforests are of a green so luxuriant as to rival the colour from an artist's paintbrush.

Almost all Australia is accessible to the exploring traveller. It is possible to drive from Melbourne in the south of the mainland to Cooktown in the Far North. The intrepid can plan a trip from the Pacific to the Indian Ocean; from the rainforests in the north to the temperate beaches of the southern coast. And for the traveller seeking peace and tranquillity, there are the green pasturelands and rugged, splendidly scenic mountain areas of Tasmania, the Island State.

Simply put, Australia is a wonderland. And in order to discover what it has to offer, either for a one-day tour or as a full-year, once-in-a-lifetime adventure, *Explore Australia* is an invaluable travelling companion. It is designed to be of assistance with every facet of your travel itinerary. It is an encouragement and an almanac; a manual and a tour guide. It is recommended that you read it as part of your travel planning, particularly for long-distance journeys. For experienced road travellers, it will reinforce knowledge acquired in the past; for less experienced road travellers, it can ensure the utmost pleasure from the holiday you have planned, and help to make it trouble-free.

Have a good trip – and remember to drive carefully!

PLANNING Ahead

A network of sealed roads ensures pleasant touring

There is so much of Australia to see and so many ways to see it. Today, even the most remote sections of this vast continent are accessible, particularly to 4WD vehicles designed for use on bush tracks and unmade roads.

For some, exploring Australia will mean touring the made highways and staying in motels, Bed & Breakfasts and farm-stays. Others will tow their accommodation behind them in the form of a caravan or camper trailer, and probably, as a result, stay mainly on made roads. Still others will opt for a mobile home with sleeping and cooking facilities, and yet another group, perhaps the true adventurers, will load a tent into the back of a 4WD and go bush. In all cases, some careful planning will enhance the journey immeasurably.

Obviously a one-, two- or three-day tour will not require the time and effort necessary for a round-Australia jaunt; but in any case, advance planning of the route and of overnight stopping-points, and a careful estimate of travel time, make for safety, comfort and enjoyment. So, indeed, will the roadworthiness of the vehicle. While as a matter of course your travel vehicle will be properly maintained and in reliable condition, some extra attention will not go astray, especially for long journeys. More of that later.

Advance Information

Any journey will benefit from careful advance planning. The idea of throwing a bag in the back and taking off is attractive in theory but creates complications in practice. Try to gather as much information as possible as far ahead of your planned departure as you can. Remember, the planning is half the fun. Research will confirm, or perhaps deny, your original choice of destination; it also will reveal ways and means, and problems where they exist. And bear in mind that although information sources are extensive, there is nothing like local 'on-the-spot' knowledge.

The first places to obtain information are: **State tourist bureaus** and **motoring organisations** (**see**: Useful Information). They are excellent sources for travel brochures, regional maps and accommodation guides, and they usually have up-to-date knowledge of local conditions. For details of specific areas, they can put you in touch with the appropriate tourist authority.

Travel agencies, **airline travel centres** and the **main railway booking offices** in each State can help if you are planning a fly/drive holiday, or intend to combine rail and motor travel.

This book. The introductions to each State provide information on main tourist areas. Once you have decided on your destination, check it out by consulting the A–Z entries for specific towns and the feature articles for the major tourist regions. Do note that while the capital cities and towns have been covered quite comprehensively in this book, the fine detail will be available at local information centres.

How Far Ahead to Start

It can be a major disappointment to decide on a certain destination and then discover that motels, caravan parks and camping grounds in the area are booked out. In some regions at certain times of the year – Christmas, Easter, and school holiday periods – accommodation can be booked out a year in advance. Explore all possibilities and, on long journeys, remember the travel-time factor. When booking accommodation in advance, always remember to allow enough time to travel comfortably to your destination. Your trip will lose a great deal of its charm if you have to rush from one point to the next (**see**: Itineraries).

While all popular destinations are likely to be busy at holiday peak times, some will be booked out around the time of special events: Melbourne at Melbourne Cup time; Adelaide at the time of the Adelaide Festival of Arts, for example. Always check ahead for the

Useful Information

MOTORING ORGANISATIONS

There are motoring organisations in all Australian States and territories. All are affiliated under the Australian Automobile Association and reciprocal rights are available to their members. Membership can consist of service and social membership or service membership only.

• **Service membership.** When planning a trip it would be advisable for you to take out service membership of the motoring organisation in your home State. Not only will this ensure that you receive service in that State, but by producing your membership card you can request assistance from the equivalent organisation in other States.

The advantages of service membership of a motoring organisation are wide-ranging. They include emergency breakdown and towing services, vehicle inspection and 'approved repairer' services; tuition in safe and defensive driving for licensed drivers; legal advice on matters such as the procedure to be followed after motor vehicle accidents or traffic charges, and the possible penalties; and motor vehicle insurance cover.

Service membership also provides touring information and advice for motoring holidays, including guides, maps and reports on road conditions, accommodation and travel bookings, package holidays, accommodation at concessional rates and a variety of car accessories.

• **Social membership.** Social or 'club' membership entitles members to the use of club facilities and accommodation, including reciprocal use in some 50 clubs throughout Australia.

The following lists the main office for each State's motoring organisation:

New South Wales
National Roads & Motorists' Association (NRMA)
151 Clarence St, Sydney 2000
13 2132 Fax: (02) 9292 8058

Australian Capital Territory
National Roads & Motorists' Association (NRMA)
92 Northbourne Ave, Braddon 2601
13 2132 Fax: (02) 6240 4689

Victoria
Royal Automobile Club of Victoria Ltd (RACV)
360 Bourke St, Melbourne 3000
(03) 9790 3333, 1800 335566; Fax: (03) 9790 3063

South Australia
Royal Automobile Association of SA Inc. (RAA)
41 Hindmarsh Sq., Adelaide 5000
(08) 8202 4600; Fax: (08) 8202 4520

Western Australia
Royal Automobile Club of WA Inc. (RAC)
228 Adelaide Tce, Perth 6000
(08) 9421 4444; Fax: (08) 9221 1887

Northern Territory
Automobile Association of NT Inc. (AANT)
AANT Building
79–81 Smith St, Darwin 0800
(08) 8981 3837; Fax: (08) 8941 2965

Queensland
Royal Automobile Club of Queensland (RACQ)
300 St Pauls Tce, Brisbane 4000
(07) 3361 2444; Fax: (07) 3257 1863

Tasmania
Royal Automobile Club of Tasmania (RACT)
cnr Patrick and Murray sts, Hobart 7000
(03) 6232 6300; Fax: (03) 6234 8784

For Motorcyclists

Motorcycle Riders' Association of Australia Inc.
380 Elizabeth St, Melbourne 3000
(03) 9663 2164

TOURIST BUREAUS

New South Wales
Countrylink NSW Travel Centre
11–31 York St, Sydney 2000
13 2077; Fax: (02) 9224 4513

Australian Capital Territory
Canberra Visitor Centre
Northbourne Ave, Dickson 2602
(02) 6205 0044, 1800 026166; Fax: (02) 6205 0776

Victoria
Victoria Visitor Information Centre
Melbourne Town Hall,
cnr Little Collins and Swanston sts,
Melbourne 3000
(03) 9658 9949; Fax: (03) 9650 6168

South Australia
SA Travel Centre
1 King William St, Adelaide 5000
(08) 8212 1505, 1800 882092; Fax: (08) 8303 2249

Western Australia
WA Tourist Centre
Albert Facey House
cnr Forrest Pl. and Wellington St, Perth 6000
(08) 9483 1111, 1800 812808; Fax: (08) 9481 0190

Northern Territory
Darwin Region Tourism Association
Beagle House, cnr Mitchell and Knuckey sts,
Darwin 0800
(08) 8981 4300; Fax: (08) 8981 0653

Central Australian Information and Interpretive Centre
Gregory Tce, Alice Springs 0871
(08) 8952 5800; Fax: (08) 8953 0295

Queensland
Queensland Government Travel Centre
cnr Adelaide and Edward sts, Brisbane 4000
13 1801; Fax: (07) 3221 5320

Tasmania
Tasmanian Travel and Information Centre
20 Davey St, Hobart 7000
(03) 6230 8233; Fax: (03) 6224 0289

ACCOMMODATION

VIP Backpackers Resorts of Australia
PO Box 600, Cannon Hill, Brisbane 4170
(07) 3268 5733; Fax: (07) 3268 4066

Bed and Breakfast Australia
PO Box 408, Gordon NSW 2072
(02) 9498 5344; Fax: (02) 9498 6438

Farm holidays
The following is a list of contact addresses in each State if you wish to arrange a farm holiday.

• **New South Wales**
Australian Farm Host Holidays Pty Ltd
PO Box 65, Culcairn 2660
(02) 6029 8621; Fax: (02) 6029 8770
(Properties available Australia-wide)

• **Victoria**
Host Farms Association Inc.
6th Floor, 230 Collins St, Melbourne 3000
(03) 9650 2922; Fax: (03) 9650 9434

• **South Australia**
SA Farm and Country Holidays Inc.
PO Box 74, Burra North 5417
(08) 8892 2755; Fax: (08) 8892 2383

• **Western Australia**
WA Farm and Country Holidays Association
Evedon Park, Burekup 6227
(08) 9726 3012; Fax: (08) 9726 3397

• **Northern Territory**
NT Holiday Centre
PO Box 2532, Alice Springs 0871
1800 621336; Fax: (08) 8951 8581

• **Queensland**
Queensland Host Farm Association
RACQ Travel Service
PO Box 537, Fortitude Valley 4006
(07) 3361 2390, 1800 777888;
Fax: (07) 3257 1504

• **Tasmania**
Homehost Tasmania Pty Ltd
PO Box 780, Sandy Bay 7005
(03) 6224 1612; Fax: (03) 6224 0472

YHA Australia
422 Kent St, Sydney NSW 2000
(02) 9261 1111; Fax (02) 9261 1969

Emergency (for all States)
For police, ambulance and fire-brigade services, dial 000.

The Ghan journeys between Adelaide and Alice Springs

timing of local special events (**see**: Calendar of Events in the introduction to each State).

If you wish to go to a favourite hotel or try a special type of accommodation – a farm homestead, a houseboat or charter boat – book well ahead. Other holiday-makers will have the same interests. And remember, a number of national parks require advance notice to give permission for camping within their boundaries.

When to Go

With a few exceptions you can travel Australia at any time of the year. The exceptions include parts of the Far North between October and May, that is, in the 'wet' or tropical monsoon season (this applies particularly if you plan to use bush tracks and unmade roads, many of which are impassable for months). Tropical cyclones are random summer hazards between November and March. In the New South Wales and Victorian high country, from about May to August many roads will be snow-bound. The Red Centre is not especially inviting in midsummer, when daytime temperatures can reach 45°C, while it can be bitterly cold at night.

Otherwise, remember the holiday peaks. If you can avoid travelling in the dense traffic during these major vacation periods, do so.

Which Way to Go

If you flinch at the thought of driving seemingly endless kilometres, you should consider an alternative: both fly/drive

packages and MotoRail facilities eliminate time-consuming travel and allow for concentration on areas of interest. Given fuel costs, neither of these is necessarily an extravagance. Cost them out against the expenses involved in using your own car for the entire trip.

█ Fly/drive. Contact a travel agent or airline travel centre for advice and information on fly/drive packages.

█ MotoRail. For information on this easy way of covering long distances, contact the State tourist bureaus (**see**: Useful Information) or the main State railway offices (see below). Inquire about discount fares; a reduction in rail fare is available on some interstate services if travel is booked and paid for in advance. For all Rail-travel reservations and inquiries phone 13 2232. For the price of a local call you will reach your nearest capital city, where operators will give you Australia-wide information. The following lists MotoRail services:

• Perth–Sydney–Perth
Indian–Pacific
Crosses the continent from ocean to ocean; over the Blue Mountains and across the Nullarbor Plain. Two services a week each way: leaves Sydney Mon. and Thurs., leaves Perth Fri. and Mon.; 66 hours.

• Perth–Adelaide–Perth
Indian–Pacific
Two services a week each way: leaves Adelaide Tues. and Fri., leaves Perth Mon. and Fri.; 38 hours. This service connects with *The Overland* to Melbourne.

• Melbourne–Adelaide–Melbourne
The Overland
Daily, each way (overnight); 12 hours.

• Adelaide–Alice Springs–Adelaide
The Ghan
A classic and historic journey. Travel in luxury across the desert May–October, 2 services a week each way; November–April, 1 service a week each way; 22 hours.

• Brisbane–Townsville–Cairns–Townsville–Brisbane
The Queenslander
One service a week each way: leaves Brisbane Sun., leaves Cairns Tues.; 33 hours.

• Brisbane–Longreach
Spirit of the Outback
Two services a week each way: leaves Brisbane Tues. and Fri., leaves Longreach Thurs. and Sun.

Note: There are no MotoRail services between Melbourne–Sydney and Sydney–Brisbane.

For further information contact the following main State railway offices:
New South Wales
Country Link NSW Travel Centre
11–31 York St, Sydney 2000
(02) 9224 4744 (for timetables only; reservations have to be made in person or by calling 13 2232)
Victoria
V/Line Reservations and Information
Level 2, Transport House
589 Collins St, Melbourne 3000
(03) 9619 5000

South Australia
Australian National Passenger
Reservations and Enquiries
1 Richmond Rd, Keswick 5035
(08) 8217 4111
Western Australia
Westrail Centre
West Pde, East Perth 6000
(08) 9326 2222
Queensland
Queensland Rail
305 Edward St, Brisbane 4000
(07) 3235 2222

Other Touring Possibilities

▍ **Spirit of Tasmania.** This passenger and car ferry makes three return voyages weekly across Bass Strait between Melbourne and Devonport, northern Tasmania. Bookings can be made through the TT Line Tasmania at Port Melbourne and at Dockside, Devonport, or through your local Tasmanian Travel Centre or travel agent.

▍ **Campervan rental.** Available in all States and most cities and major towns, the campervans are fully equipped and vary in size and level of luxury. Costs vary accordingly and also with the season. There are often restrictions on where you can take a campervan; so check first.

▍ **Escorted group trips.** If you are interested in a full-on adventure tour, but are intimidated by the thought of doing it alone, motoring organisations and many private tour operators provide escorted group trips into more remote areas, Cape York for example. These tag-along tours save you the worry of navigation and planning (except for your vehicle) and also provide expert help and backup in case of a mechanical breakdown. Some of the tours require a 4WD vehicle.

Spirit of Tasmania, a car and passenger ferry between Melbourne and Devonport

▍ **Other ideas.** You also could leave your vehicle behind and tour in a 4WD coach, take a camel trek or try a canoe adventure – or travel almost any way you choose. Check with your travel agent or tourist bureau (**see:** Useful Information).

Where to Stay

State motoring organisations, tourist bureaus and booksellers – all have accommodation guides; some include information on camping and caravan parks. Travel agents and airline travel centres can also provide information.

▍ **Resorts, hotels and motels.** Contact the relevant State tourist bureau, motoring organisation (**see:** Useful Information), your travel agent or airline travel centre for details and bookings. Major motel chains, such as Best Western and Flag, cover most of the country and have head offices in each capital city. Brochures detailing accommodation are available from these head offices.

▍ **Serviced or self-service holiday flats.** If you are planning a stay in a city or at any holiday destination for a length of time, this provides a sensible family alternative to motel or hotel accommodation. The relevant tourist bureau (**see:** Useful Information) will provide you with the details.

▍ **House swapping.** This is yet another possibility for a lengthy stay. This can be arranged through organisations such as Latitudes Home Exchange, PO Box 436, South Perth WA 6951; (08) 9367 9412. In addition, advertisements for those seeking a house-swapping holiday often appear in the classified sections of the newspapers. Make sure you are totally satisfied with the arrangements made concerning your commitments and that you are happy with the people with whom you are dealing. Also check that your householder's insurance covers you in such circumstances (**see:** Insurance).

▍ **Host farms.** Such accommodation varies from spartan to luxurious and, in some

Campervans are available for rental in all States

Other Information

Houseboats at Lake Eildon, Victoria

Pets

Do not forget: whether you are leaving your pets behind or taking them with you, you will need to make arrangements for them.

Leaving them behind

- Pet care services (see *Yellow Pages* telephone book): provide care of pets in their own environment. They will also care for plants and property, etc.
- Dog boarding kennels and catteries (see *Yellow Pages*): provide care and accommodation. Some have pickup and delivery services.
- Animal welfare organisations and veterinary surgeons (see *Yellow Pages*): for advice and information.

Taking them with you

- Make sure, in advance, that the accommodation or mode of travel booked permits animals. Many caravan parks and most national parks do not admit animals.
- During the trip, carry additional water and stop at regular intervals for toileting and exercise.
- Do not leave an animal unattended in a vehicle for any length of time; always provide fresh air.

- Allow sufficient room in the vehicle to comfortably accommodate the animal.
- Do not transport an animal in a moving caravan.
- Consider purchasing a dog harness for your vehicle to protect yourself and the animal in case of sudden braking.

Before Departure

- Cancel newspapers, mail deliveries.
- Make arrangements for the garden to be watered and lawns mowed. Board out your indoor plants or place them in the sink, surround with damp peat and water thoroughly. Encasing each pot in a sealed polythene bag also helps retain moisture.
- If you have a pet, arrange for its safekeeping well in advance (**see:** Pets).
- Arrange for a neighbour to keep an eye on the house. Contact your local police and inform them of your absence. Alternatively, consult a professional home security service (see *Yellow Pages*).
- Valuable items, such as jewellery, are best left for safekeeping at your bank.
- Turn the electricity off at the mains and leave the fridge door open. If you have equipment that must operate in your absence, for example a stocked freezer, leave power on and remove plugs from all other power points. Make sure that everything else that should be turned off is off.
- Check that all windows and doors are locked; then check again.
- Always leave a contact address with a friend or neighbour.

Carrying a Camera

You probably will want to preserve the highlights of your trip on film. Check the following points:

- If you have recently bought a camera, take at least one test film before departure so that you know how the equipment reacts to different light conditions.
- As weather conditions may vary, it is a good idea to carry film with a range of speeds. If you are not an expert, talk to your local dealer about the varieties of film available.
- Before you leave, have a good supply of film, fresh batteries and a lens brush. Other useful accessories are a close-up lens, lens hood, filters and a tripod.
- Keep your equipment in a plastic bag inside a camera bag to protect it from water, heat, sand

and dust. It can get very hot in a closed car, so always keep the camera in the shade. The best place is on the floor, on the side opposite the exhaust pipe. Make sure, however, that the bag cannot rattle around.

- High temperatures and humidity can damage colour film. Store your film in the coolest spot available and do not break the watertight vapour seal until just before use. Once the film is used, remove it from the camera, mark it with an E for 'exposed' and send it for processing as soon as possible.
- When using the camera in bright conditions, even with automatic exposure, it may be necessary to allow one stop or half of a stop down to compensate for the brilliance of the light. If in doubt, consult the instruction sheet included with the film.
- Check that your personal property insurance covers the loss of cameras and photographic equipment while travelling (**see:** Insurance).

Time Zones

Australia has 4 time zones:

- **Eastern Standard Time** (EST), in Queensland, Australian Capital Territory, New South Wales, Victoria and Tasmania. (Note: Broken Hill, in central western New South Wales, operates on CST, half an hour behind the rest of New South Wales.)
- **Central Standard Time** (CST is half an hour behind EST), in South Australia and Northern Territory.
- **Western Standard Time** (WST is 2 hours behind EST), in Western Australia.
- **Central Western Time** (CWT is 45 minutes ahead of WST), a local time zone operating from 3 km east of Caiguna in Western Australia to the South Australian border.

Daylight saving is adopted by some States in summer. In New South Wales, Victoria, Tasmania, Australian Capital Territory and South Australia, clocks are put forward 1 hour at the beginning of summer. Northern Territory, Western Australia and Queensland do not have daylight saving.

Quarantine Regulations

Throughout Australia, State quarantine regulations prohibit the transport by travellers of certain plants and foods, and even soil, across State borders. Further information is available from offices of agricultural departments in all States.

Backpacker accommodation in Kings Cross, Sydney

be forgotten. Travel insurance is a wise precaution (**see**: Insurance).

▌ **Accommodation.** Accommodation costs can be estimated when you book, but you might simply average the figure. If you do, estimate high rather than low.

▌ **Food.** This is a matter of personal choice: you may eat out every night or prepare all or some of your meals yourself. Be realistic when budgeting the cost of eating out or preparing meals: allow for the unexpected, and for the higher cost of food and meals in popular holiday destinations or in remote areas. Budget for snacks and recreational treats, if you are travelling with children.

▌ **Fuel.** Once you know your vehicle's fuel consumption you can work out your fuel costs in advance. The usual method is based on litres per 100 kilometres. If your vehicle uses 16 litres per 100 kilometres and your journey distance works out at 5000 kilometres, you will use 50 times 16 litres of fuel, or 800 litres. Allow for rises in the cost of petrol and other vehicle expenses, and also for the fact that fuel is more expensive in remote areas.

▌ **Entertainment and other costs.** When budgeting, allow for such 'budget biters' as admission charges, postcards, camera film, chemist's items, tips, bridge tolls and car repairs. Remember also that accommodation, travel and rental charges rise during peak periods.

cases, guests are invited to take part in farm life. Associations in each State (**see**: Useful Information) or tourist authorities will provide details.

▌ **Bed and breakfast accommodation.** Contact Bed & Breakfast Australia (**see**: Useful Information) for information on bed and breakfast accommodation in homestay or farmstay environments throughout Australia.

▌ **Backpacker accommodation.** This type of accommodation is provided at budget rates in a communal environment and is becoming very popular amongst younger travellers. Note, however, that the accommodation offered is not always suitable for children. During the holiday season, some hostels may not accept telephone reservations without payment and it is advisable to book well in advance. To obtain information on the range of accommodation available, contact VIP Backpackers Resorts of Australia (**see**: Useful Information). A Backpackers VIP Discount Kit costing $25 (add $5 for postage and handling,

if purchasing by mail), valid in 24 countries with an accommodation guide (free) to 140 hostels Australia-wide, is available from this organisation.

▌ **Youth hostels.** For the young at heart, there are over 100 youth hostels throughout Australia open to YHA members. For information, contact YHA Australia (**see**: Useful Information).

▌ **Floating accommodation.** If you are into staying afloat, consider hiring a houseboat on the Hawkesbury River or Eildon Weir, taking a paddle wheeler cruise on the Murray, or even chartering a yacht to cruise in the Whitsundays. Obtain details from your travel agent or State tourist bureau (**see**: Useful Information).

Dividing Up the Dollars

Very few people can afford the 'money-no-object' approach to holidays, no matter what the length of stay. Your planning should include budgeting. You will need principally to consider accommodation, food, fuel and entertainment, although emergency funds should not

Carrying large amounts of cash with you is not a good idea, hence credit cards, EFTPOS and Automatic Teller Machines are a good alternative. It is advisable to carry more than one card in case a card is 'eaten' by an ATM or damaged during use.

Car Maintenance Courses

If you plan to tour in the remoter areas, you should acquire basic mechanical knowledge and skills. In general you should have a broad understanding of the technology of your vehicle and know how much roadside repair is possible in the event of a breakdown (**see**: Breakdowns). You should also have some specific knowledge; for example how to change a tyre on the vehicle you will be using; and whether you can use jumper leads to start your car and if so, how it is done. Car care and basic car-maintenance courses are run by Adult Education centres, TAFE Colleges and motoring organisations in all States. The courses vary widely in content and

Shark Bay, near Monkey Mia in Western Australia

INTRODUCTION

length. A call to these organisations will ascertain which course is available and appropriate. Test your knowledge by reading through the Trouble Shooting flow-charts and the Tools and Spare Parts list (**see:** Breakdowns).

Insurance

The benefits of a comprehensive insurance policy on your vehicle, caravan or trailer are obvious. As well as cover against loss or damage due to accident, theft and vandalism, your personal effects are covered against loss or damage when they are in the insured vehicle. Additional policies will cover such eventualities as, for example, the cost of temporary accommodation should your caravan become uninhabitable. Short-term travel insurance is available from several companies to cover loss of luggage or cancellation of accommodation bookings, etc. Information and advice can be obtained from the various motoring organisations (**see:** Useful Information), insurance companies and travel agents.

Itineraries

Some people make itineraries and stick to them; others do not. At the very least, a rough schedule to ensure a good mixture of travel and sightseeing time is essential. Allow some flexibility. You never know what might detain you: the weather (frequent rest breaks are necessary in extreme heat), or children, who have a low tolerance for long periods without a break (**see:** Child's Play).

Clothing

Be strict with yourself and the family when you are packing and travel as lightly as you can. It is better to spend an hour at a laundromat than overburden your vehicle with clothing you probably will not wear.

Essentials are a jumper or jacket, even in summer; sensible comfortable shoes; and a wide-brimmed hat to protect yourself from the sun at all times. Non-irons are practical. Carry items like swimwear, towels, spare socks and jumpers in a bag that can be kept within easy reach. Gumboots are a handy item also.

First-aid Kit

A first-aid kit is essential. Include band-aids, antiseptic, bandages, headache tablets, extra blockout, sunburn cream, insect repellent and a soothing lotion for bites. Eye drops are a good idea, as is a thermometer and a tourniquet. Kits are available from various suppliers including St John Ambulance Australia, which also conducts basic courses in first aid. As car sickness is often a problem on long journeys, particularly with young children, include medication to counter this. Your chemist or a doctor will advise you.

Useful Extras

Depending on the length and nature of your tour, some items are valuable, some essential (**see:** Tools and Spare Parts). Carry picnic and barbecue equipment, tissues, toilet paper and a container or plastic bag for rubbish – and take it with you rather than leaving it behind, at least until you can find a legitimate rubbish tip. Rugs or blankets are a necessary extra, as is a large sheet of plastic, which can be used as an emergency windscreen. Having a mobile phone may be useful if you are travelling within signal range; check the coverage before departure. If you are going to the outback, a necessary item is some type of shade cover, such as a tarpaulin, as sun protection in case of an emergency stop (**see:** Outback Motoring).

Accidents do happen; the right insurance prevents financial disaster

Inter-city Route Maps

The following inter-city route maps will help you plan your route between major cities. As well, you can use the maps during your journey, since they provide information on distances between towns along the route, roadside rest areas, road conditions and which towns are described in the A–Z listings. The map below provides an overview of the routes mapped.

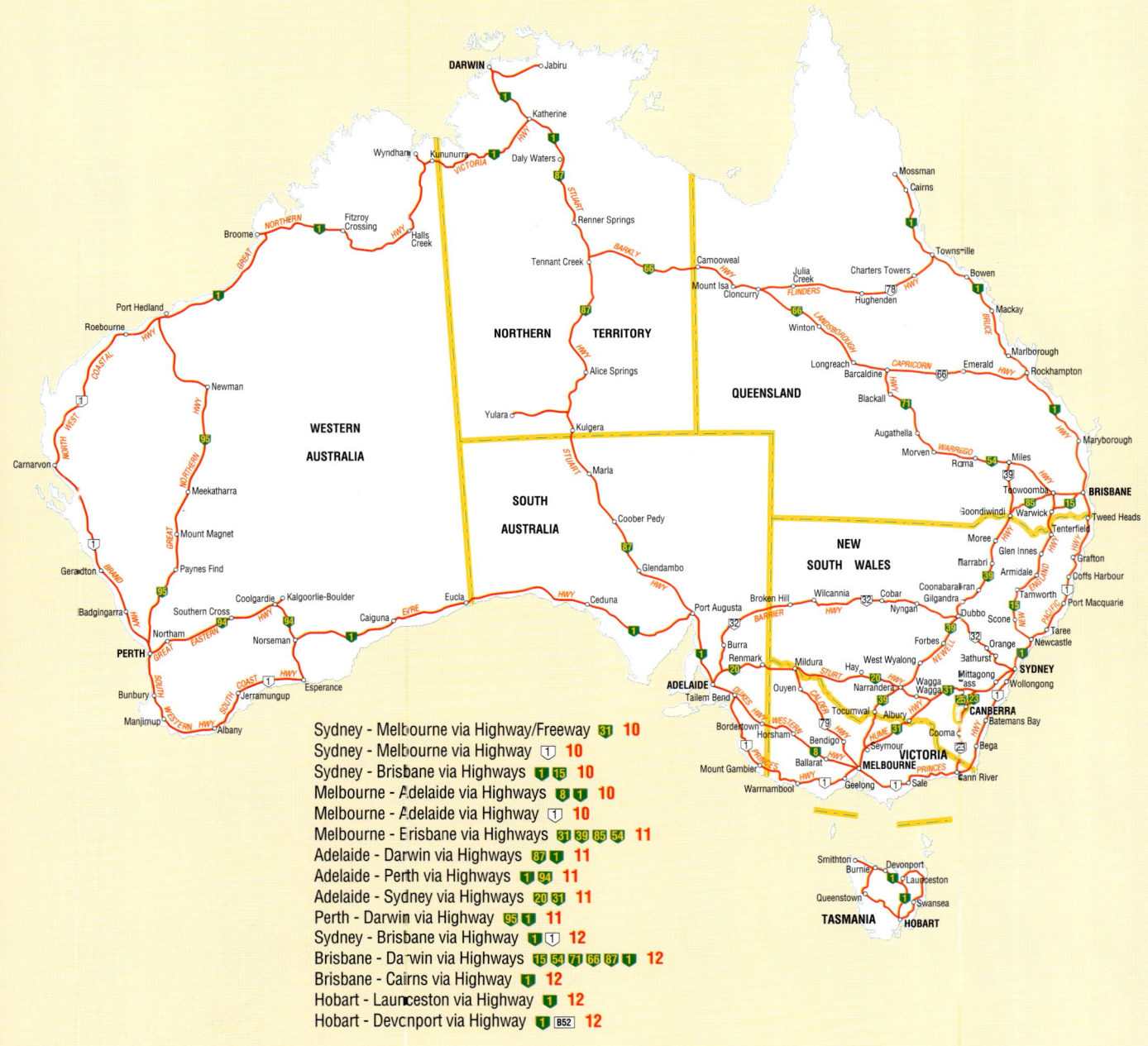

Sydney – Melbourne via Highway/Freeway 31 **10**
Sydney – Melbourne via Highway 1 **10**
Sydney – Brisbane via Highways 1 15 **10**
Melbourne – Adelaide via Highways 8 1 **10**
Melbourne – Adelaide via Highway 1 **10**
Melbourne – Brisbane via Highways 31 39 85 54 **11**
Adelaide – Darwin via Highways 87 1 **11**
Adelaide – Perth via Highways 1 94 **11**
Adelaide – Sydney via Highways 20 31 **11**
Perth – Darwin via Highway 95 **11**
Sydney – Brisbane via Highway 1 1 **12**
Brisbane – Darwin via Highways 15 54 71 66 87 1 **12**
Brisbane – Cairns via Highway 1 **12**
Hobart – Launceston via Highway 1 **12**
Hobart – Devonport via Highway 1 B52 **12**

SYDNEY - MELBOURNE
via HUME HIGHWAY/FREEWAY

Legend
- Freeway
- Main highway
- Divided highway
- Other highway
- Town ○
- Rest area ®
- Federal route number
- National route number
- State route number
- Distance between towns *23*
- Distance to Sydney ▲422 / Melbourne ▼440
- *Not drawn to scale*

SYDNEY ▲0 ▼862
- *32* Liverpool
- *19* Campbelltown
- *55* Mittagong 106/756
- *35* Berrima
- To Wollongong 89 km *48*
- *54* Marulan
- Goulburn 206/656
- *11* *21* *24* Breadalbane
- *28* To Canberra 98 km — Gunning
- *25* Yass 280/582 18, To Canberra 61 km
- Bowning
- Bookham
- *49* Jugiong *21*
- Coolac
- Gundagai
- *54* To Wagga Wagga 45 km, Tarcutta — Cooma 223 km, ▲422 ▼440
- *68* Holbrook ▲490 ▼372
- *15* Woomargama
- NEW SOUTH WALES
- *51* Albury 556/306
- Wodonga — VICTORIA
- Rutherglen 28 km
- *78* Mt Beauty 87 km
- Wangaratta — Glenrowan, Bright 77 km
- *36* To Shepparton 66 km, Benalla
- Euroa 718/144, Mansfield 59 km
- Shepparton 83 km
- *52* Seymour, Yea 42 km — Bendigo 115 km
- *50* Beveridge
- *42* Kalkallo
MELBOURNE ▲862 ▼0

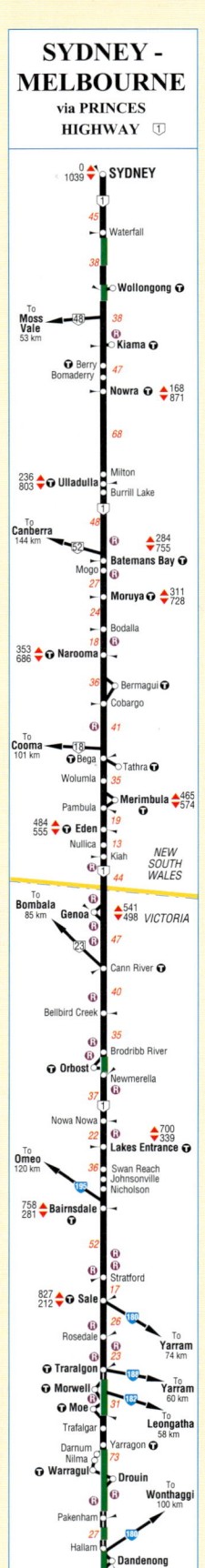

SYDNEY - MELBOURNE
via PRINCES HIGHWAY

SYDNEY ▲0 ▼1039
- *45* Waterfall
- *38* Wollongong
- Kiama *38*
- *47* Berry, Bomaderry — Nowra ▲168 ▼871
- *68* Milton 236/803, Ulladulla, Burrill Lake
- *48* Mogo — Batemans Bay ▲284 ▼755
- *27* Moruya ▲311 ▼728
- *24* Bodalla
- *18* Narooma 353/686
- *36* Bermagui
- Cobargo
- *41* Bega — Cooma 101 km
- Tathra
- *35* Wolumla — Merimbula ▲465 ▼574
- Pambula
- Eden 484/555 *19*
- *13* Nullica, Kiah
- *44* NEW SOUTH WALES / VICTORIA
- Bombala 85 km — Genoa ▲541 ▼498
- *47* Cann River
- *40* Bellbird Creek
- *35* Brodribb River
- Orbost — Newmerella
- *18* *37* Nowa Nowa
- *20* *22* Lakes Entrance ▲700 ▼339
- Omeo 120 km — Swan Reach, Johnsonville, Nicholson
- *36* Bairnsdale 758/281
- *52* Stratford
- Sale 827/212 *17*
- *26* Rosedale — Yarram 74 km
- *23* Traralgon — Yarram 60 km
- Morwell — Leongatha 58 km
- Moe *31*
- Trafalgar, Darnum, Nilma
- Yarragon *73* Warragul — Drouin
- Wonthaggi 100 km
- Pakenham *27*
- Hallam — Dandengong
- *32* MELBOURNE ▲1039 ▼0

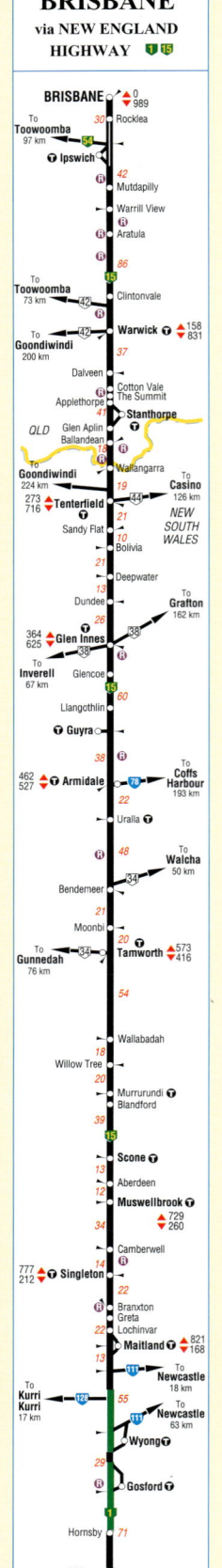

SYDNEY - BRISBANE
via NEW ENGLAND HIGHWAY

BRISBANE ▲0 ▼989
- *30* Rocklea
- To Toowoomba 97 km — Ipswich
- *42* Mutdapilly
- Warrill View
- Aratula
- *86* To Toowoomba 73 km — Clintonvale
- To Goondiwindi 200 km — Warwick ▲158 ▼831
- *37* Dalveen — Cotton Vale, The Summit
- Applethorpe — Stanthorpe
- Glen Aplin, Ballandean — QLD
- Goondiwindi 224 km — Wallangarra
- *19* To Tenterfield 273/716 — Casino 126 km
- *21* Sandy Flat — NEW SOUTH WALES
- *10* Bolivia
- Deepwater
- *13* Dundee — Grafton 162 km
- *26* Glen Innes 364/625 — Glencoe
- *60* Inverell 67 km — Llangothlin
- Guyra
- *38* — Coffs Harbour 462/527 193 km
- Armidale *22* — Uralla
- *48* Walcha 50 km
- Bendemeer *34*
- *21* Moonbi
- *20* Gunnedah 76 km — Tamworth ▲573 ▼416
- *54* Wallabadah
- Willow Tree
- *20* Murrurundi, Blandford
- *39* Scone
- Aberdeen *13*
- Muswellbrook ▲729 ▼260
- *34* Camberwell
- Singleton 777/212 *14*
- *22* Branxton, Greta, Lochinvar
- *22* Maitland ▲821 ▼168
- *13* — Newcastle 18 km
- Kurri Kurri 17 km *55* — Newcastle 63 km
- Wyong
- *29* Gosford
- Hornsby *71*
- SYDNEY ▲989 ▼0

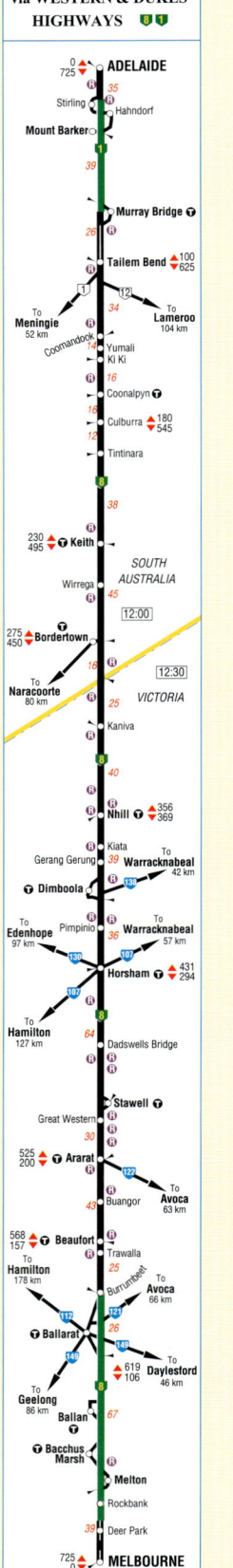

MELBOURNE -ADELAIDE
via WESTERN & DUKES HIGHWAYS

ADELAIDE ▲0 ▼725
- *35* Stirling — Hahndorf
- Mount Barker *39*
- Murray Bridge
- Tailem Bend ▲100 ▼625
- To Meningie 52 km — Lameroo 104 km
- Coomandook, Yumali, Ki Ki
- *16* Coonalpyn
- Culburra ▲180 ▼545
- Tintinara
- *38* Keith 230/495
- Wirrega
- *45* Bordertown 275/450 — SOUTH AUSTRALIA *12:00*
- *16* Naracoorte 80 km — *12:30* VICTORIA
- *25* Kaniva
- *40* Nhill ▲356 ▼369
- Kiata
- Gerang Gerung — Warracknabeal 42 km
- Dimboola
- Edenhope 97 km, Pimpinio — Warracknabeal 57 km
- *36* Horsham ▲431 ▼294
- Hamilton 127 km *64* — Dadswells Bridge
- Stawell
- Great Western
- *30* Ararat 525/200
- Buangor — Avoca 63 km
- *43* Beaufort 568/157
- Trawalla
- Hamilton 178 km — Burrumbeet, Avoca 66 km
- *26* Ballarat
- Geelong 86 km, Ballan
- *67* Bacchus Marsh
- Melton
- Rockbank
- *39* Deer Park
MELBOURNE ▲725 ▼0

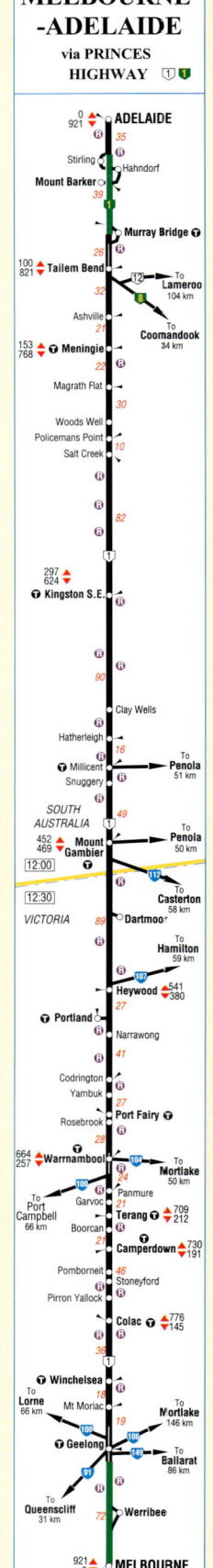

MELBOURNE -ADELAIDE
via PRINCES HIGHWAY

ADELAIDE ▲0 ▼921
- *35* Stirling — Hahndorf
- Mount Barker *39* — Murray Bridge
- *26* Tailem Bend 100/821 — Lameroo 104 km
- *32* Ashville — Coomandook 34 km
- Meningie 153/768
- *30* Magrat Flat
- Woods Well — Policemans Point, Salt Creek
- *82* Kingston S.E. 297/624
- Clay Wells
- *90* Hatherleigh
- Millicent — Penola 51 km
- Snuggery
- SOUTH AUSTRALIA
- *49* Mount Gambier 452/469 — Penola 50 km
- *12:00* / *12:30* VICTORIA
- *89* Dartmoor
- Casterton 58 km
- Hamilton 59 km
- Heywood ▲541 ▼380
- *27* Portland — Narrawong
- *41* Codrington, Yambuk, Rosebrook
- *28* Warrnambool 664/257 — Mortlake 50 km
- Port Campbell 66 km, Panmure, Garvoc — Terang ▲709 ▼212
- Boorcan — Camperdown ▲730 ▼191
- *46* Pomborneit, Stoneyford, Pirron Yallock
- Colac ▲776 ▼145
- Winchelsea — Mortlake 146 km
- Lorne 66 km, Mt Moriac
- *19* Geelong — Ballarat 86 km
- Queenscliff 31 km — Werribee
MELBOURNE ▲921 ▼0

MELBOURNE -BRISBANE
via HUME, NEWELL GORE & WARREGO HIGHWAYS

BRISBANE 0 / 1677
30 Rocklea
25 Ipswich — Warwick 128 km
To Esk 55 km
Marburg / Minden / Hatton Vale / Plainland
37
Crows Nest 44 km / Gatton / Grantham
35
Toowoomba ▲127 / ▼1550
42
Dalby 83 km — Warwick 52 km
Southbrook / Pittsworth
44
41 Brookstead / Pampas / Millmerran
Miles 198 km — Inglewood 90 km
122
39 Goondiwindi ▲352 / ▼1325
Boggabilla
QUEENSLAND
NEW SOUTH WALES
127
479/1198 Moree — Inverell 140 km
38
To Walgett 209 km
97
576/1101 Narrabri
37 Gunnedah 99 km
To Gunnedah 100 km
34
118
Coonabarabran ▲694 / ▼983
94
Warren 85 km
34 Gilgandra ▲788 / ▼889
Eumungerie
65
Narromine 40 km
32 Dubbo — Wellington 50 km
853/824
53
18 Tomingley
25 Peak Hill
24 Alectown
Parkes ▲973 / ▼704
33
Forbes
68
39 Cowra 124 km
Marsden
37
Wyalong
West Wyalong ▲1111 / ▼566
67
Hay 257 km
Mirrool / Ardlethan
67
Grong Grong
Narrandera ▲1245 / ▼432
Hay 175 km — Wagga Wagga 101 km
NEW SOUTH WALES
110
Jerilderie
Deniliquin 58 km / Finley — Albury 145 km
Tocumwal
21
Echuca 93 km — Wodonga 131 km
Strathmerton / Numurkah / Wunghnu
Tallygaroopna / Cengunta
Shepparton ▲1498 / ▼179
VICTORIA
56
Nagambie
Euroa 47 km
Bendigo 115 km
Seymour
Yea 39 km
1677 / 0
MELBOURNE

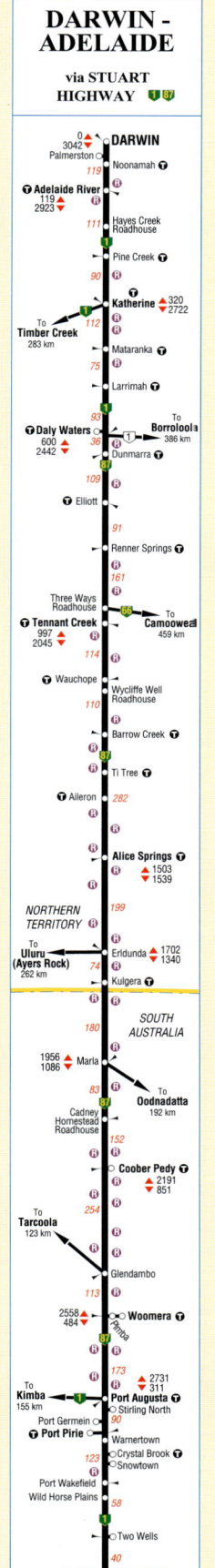

DARWIN - ADELAIDE
via STUART HIGHWAY

DARWIN 0 / 3042
Palmerston
Noonamah
Adelaide River 119 / 2923
Hayes Creek Roadhouse
Pine Creek
90
Katherine ▲320 / ▼2722
Timber Creek 283 km
112
Mataranka
75
Larrimah
93
Daly Waters 600 / 2442 — Borroloola 386 km
36 Dunmarra
109
Elliott
91
Renner Springs
161
Three Ways Roadhouse
Tennant Creek 997 / 2045 — Camooweal 459 km
114
Wauchope
110
Wycliffe Well Roadhouse
Barrow Creek
Ti Tree
282
Aileron
Alice Springs ▲1503 / ▼1539
NORTHERN TERRITORY
199
Uluru (Ayers Rock) 262 km — Erldunda ▲1702 / ▼1340
74 Kulgera
SOUTH AUSTRALIA
180
Marla 1956 / 1086
83
Cadney Homestead Roadhouse
152
Coober Pedy ▲2191 / ▼851
254
Tarcoola 123 km
Glendambo
113
Woomera 2558 / 484
Pimba
173
Kimba 155 km — Port Augusta ▲2731 / ▼311
Port Germein / Stirling North
Port Pirie
Warnertown / Crystal Brook / Snowtown
123
Port Wakefield
Wild Horse Plains
58
Two Wells
40
ADELAIDE 3042 / 0

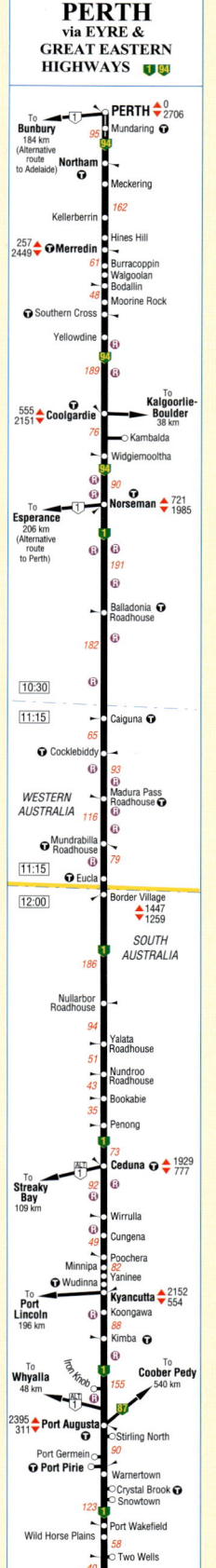

ADELAIDE - PERTH
via EYRE & GREAT EASTERN HIGHWAYS

PERTH 0 / 2706
95 Mundaring
To Bunbury 184 km (Alternative route to Adelaide) — Northam
94
Meckering
162
Kellerberrin
257 / 2449 Merredin — Hines Hill
61
Burracoppin / Walgoolan / Bodallin / Moorine Rock
Southern Cross
Yellowdine
189
555 / 2151 Coolgardie — Kalgoorlie-Boulder 38 km
76 Kambalda
Widgiemooltha
90
Esperance 206 km (Alternative route to Perth) — Norseman ▲721 / ▼1985
191
Balladonia Roadhouse
182
10:30
11:15
65
Caiguna
Cocklebiddy
93
Madura Pass Roadhouse
116
Mundrabilla Roadhouse
79
11:15
Eucla
12:00
Border Village ▲1447 / ▼1259
SOUTH AUSTRALIA
186
Nullarbor Roadhouse
94
Yalata Roadhouse
51
Nundroo Roadhouse
43
Bookabie
35
Penong
73
Ceduna ▲1929 / ▼777
92
Streaky Bay 109 km — Wirrulla
Cungena
Poochera
82
Minnipa / Yaninee
Wudinna
Kyancutta ▲2152 / ▼554
Koongawa
88
Kimba
To Whyalla 48 km / Iron Knob
155
Coober Pedy 540 km
Port Lincoln 196 km
2395 / 311 Port Augusta
90 Stirling North
Port Germein
Port Pirie
Warnertown / Crystal Brook / Snowtown
123
Port Wakefield
Wild Horse Plains
58
Two Wells
40
ADELAIDE 2706 / 0

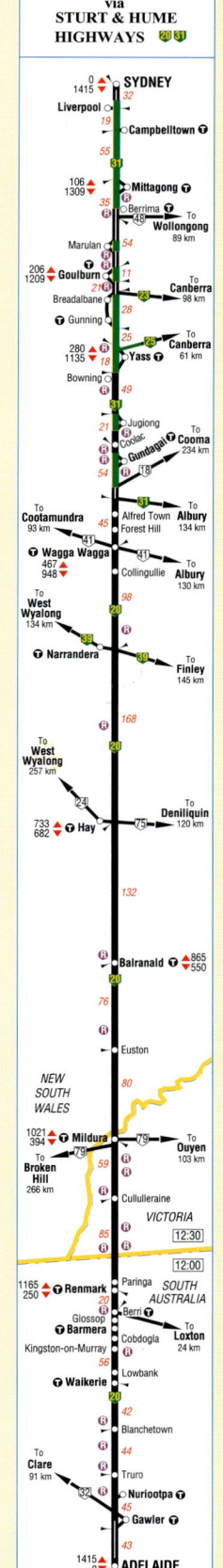

ADELAIDE - SYDNEY
via STURT & HUME HIGHWAYS

SYDNEY 0 / 1415
32 Liverpool
19 Campbelltown
55
106 / 1309 Mittagong — Berrima
35 Wollongong 89 km
54 Marulan
206 / 1209 Goulburn — Canberra 98 km
28 Breadalbane
Gunning
25
280 / 1135 Yass — Canberra 61 km
18 Bowning
49
31 Jugiong / Coolac
54 Gundagai — Cooma 234 km
18
Alfred Town / Forest Hill — Albury 134 km
41
Cootamundra 93 km
45
Wagga Wagga 467 / 948 — Albury 130 km
Collingullie
98
West Wyalong 134 km
39 Narrandera — Finley 145 km
168
West Wyalong 257 km
24 — Deniliquin 120 km
733 / 682 Hay 75
132
Balranald ▲865 / ▼550
76
Euston
80
NEW SOUTH WALES
1021 / 394 Mildura — Ouyen 103 km
To Broken Hill 266 km — 79 / 59
Cullulleraine
85
VICTORIA
12:30
12:00
1165 / 250 Renmark — Paringa
20 Berri
Glossop
Barmera — Loxton 24 km
Kingston-on-Murray / Cobdogla
56
Waikerie / Lowbank
44 Blanchetown
Clare 91 km — Truro
32 Nuriootpa
Gawler
1415 / 0
ADELAIDE

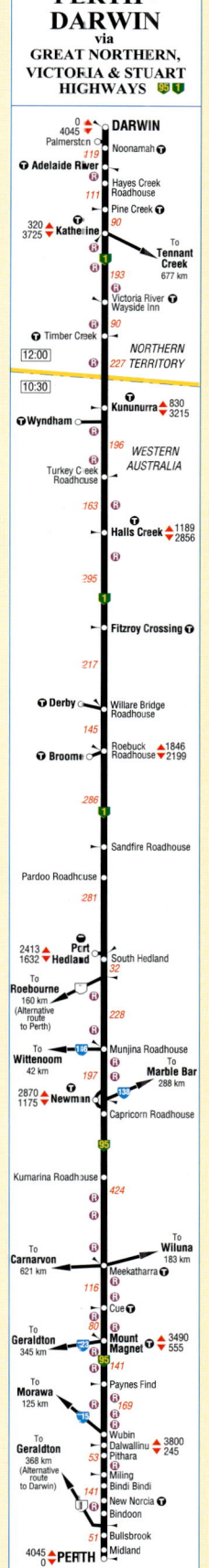

PERTH - DARWIN
via GREAT NORTHERN, VICTORIA & STUART HIGHWAYS

DARWIN 0 / 4045
Palmerston
Noonamah
Adelaide River 320 / 3725
Hayes Creek Roadhouse
Pine Creek
90
Katherine — Tennant Creek 677 km
193
Victoria River Wayside Inn
90
Timber Creek
12:00
NORTHERN TERRITORY
227
10:30
Kununurra ▲830 / ▼3215
Wyndham
196
WESTERN AUSTRALIA
Turkey Creek Roadhouse
163
Halls Creek ▲1189 / ▼2856
295
Fitzroy Crossing
217
Derby — Willare Bridge Roadhouse
145
Broome — Roebuck Roadhouse ▲1846 / ▼2199
286
Sandfire Roadhouse
Pardoo Roadhouse
281
2413 / 1632 Pt Hedland — South Hedland
32
Roebourne 160 km (Alternative route to Perth)
228
Wittenoom 42 km — Munjina Roadhouse
197
2870 / 1175 Newman — Marble Bar 288 km
Capricorn Roadhouse
Kumarina Roadhouse
424
Carnarvon 621 km — Wiluna 183 km
Meekatharra
116
Cue
80
Geraldton 345 km — Mount Magnet ▲3490 / ▼555
141
Morawa 125 km
169
Geraldton 368 km (Alternative route to Darwin) — Wubin ▲3800 / ▼245
53 Dalwallinu / Pithara
Miling / Bindi Bindi
141
New Norcia
Bindoon
51 Bullsbrook
Midland
PERTH 4045 / 0

SYDNEY - BRISBANE
via PACIFIC HIGHWAY

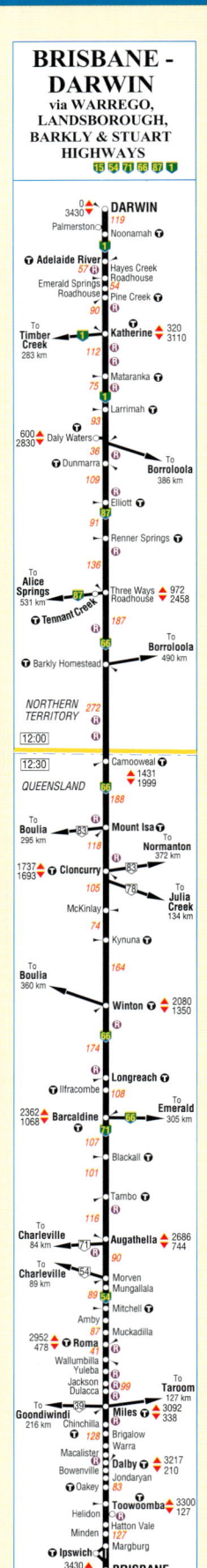

0 / 965	BRISBANE
Loganholme	
Beenleigh	
Yatala	
Ormeau	
Oxenford	
Nerang	Main Beach
Mudgeeraba	Surfers Paradise
35	Coolangatta
90	
QUEENSLAND	Tweed Heads / 106 / 859
NEW SOUTH WALES	24
	Murwillumbah
Burringbar	33
Ocean Shores	
	Brunswick Heads / 163 / 802
Bangalow	48
Lismore 35 km	Newrybar
	Ballina / 211 / 754
Wardell	36
Broadwater	
Woodburn	
	53
Chatsworth	
Maclean	
Tyndale	
Glen Innes 162 km	41
Ulmarra	
	Grafton / 341 / 624
	57
398 / 567	Woolgoolga
	Emerald Beach
Moonee Beach	29
	Coffs Harbour / 423 / 542
Sawtell	24
	Urunga
Valla Beach	38
485 / 480	Nambucca Heads
	56
Fredrickton	
	Kempsey / 541 / 424
Kundabung	25
Walcha 166 km	Telegraph Point
	16
Kew	Port Macquarie / 24
	49
	Coopernook
655 / 310	Taree / 24
	Nabiac
	49
	Bulahdelah / 728 / 237
	39
Karuah	
	26
Maitland 13 km	Raymond Terrace / 793 / 172
	26
Kurri Kurri 17 km	To Newcastle 18 km
	46
	To Newcastle 63 km
	Wyong
	29
	Gosford
Hornsby	71
965 / 0	SYDNEY

BRISBANE - DARWIN
via WARREGO, LANDSBOROUGH, BARKLY & STUART HIGHWAYS

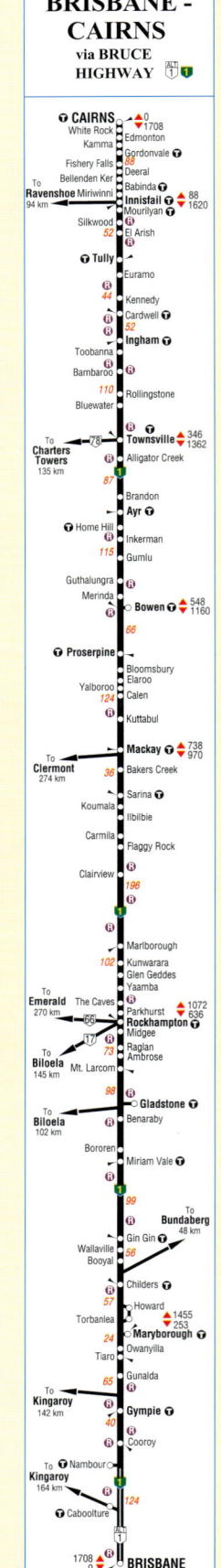

0 / 3430	DARWIN
Palmerston	119
	Noonamah
Adelaide River	57
Emerald Springs Roadhouse	54
Timber Creek 283 km	Pine Creek
	112
	Katherine / 320 / 3110
	Mataranka
	75
	Larrimah
600 / 2830	93
Daly Waters	
	36
Dunmarra	
	109
Borroloola 386 km	
Elliott	
	91
Renner Springs	
	136
Alice Springs 531 km	Three Ways Roadhouse / 972 / 2458
Tennant Creek	187
Barkly Homestead	Borroloola 490 km
NORTHERN TERRITORY	272
12:00	
12:30	Camooweal / 1431 / 1999
QUEENSLAND	188
Boulia 295 km	Mount Isa
	118
	Normanton 372 km
1737 / 1693	Cloncurry
	105
McKinlay	Julia Creek 134 km
	74
	Kynuna
Boulia 360 km	164
	Winton / 2080 / 1350
	174
Ilfracombe	Longreach
	108
2362 / 1068	Barcaldine
	71 / Emerald 305 km
	107
Blackall	
	101
Tambo	
	116
Charleville 84 km	Augathella / 2686 / 744
	90
Charleville 89 km	Morven / Mungallala
	89
Amby	Mitchell
	87
	Muckadilla
2952 / 478	Roma
Wallumbilla / Yuleba	41
Jackson / Dulacca	Taroom 127 km
Goondiwindi 216 km	Miles / 3092 / 338
Chinchilla	39
Macalister	128
Brigalow / Warra	
Bowenville	Dalby / 3217 / 210
Jondaryan	83
Oakey	
Helidon	Toowoomba / 3300 / 127
Minden	Hatton Vale
	127
	Margburg
Ipswich	
3430 / 0	BRISBANE

BRISBANE - CAIRNS
via BRUCE HIGHWAY

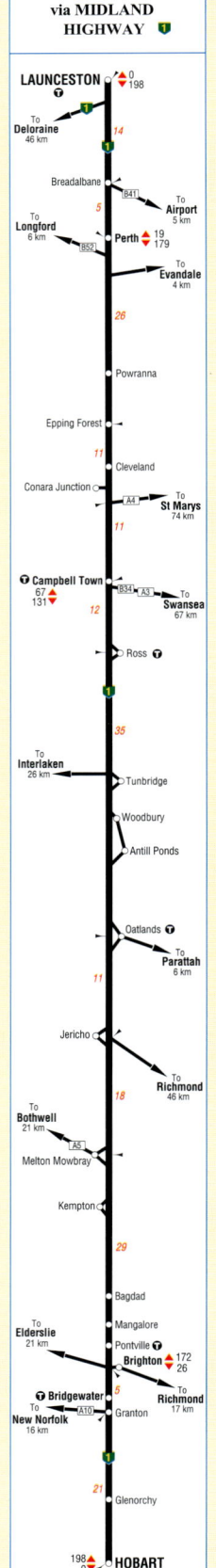

0 / 1708	CAIRNS
White Rock	Edmonton
Kamma	Gordonvale
Fishery Falls	Deeral
Bellenden Ker	Babinda
Ravenshoe 94 km / Miriwinni	Innisfail / 88 / 1620
	Mourilyan
Silkwood	52 / El Arish
	Tully
	Euramo
	44 / Kennedy
	Cardwell
	52 / Ingham
Toobanna	
Bambaroo	110
	Rollingstone
Bluewater	
	Townsville / 346 / 1362
Charters Towers 135 km	78 / Alligator Creek
	87 / Brandon
	Ayr
Home Hill	Inkerman
	Gumlu
	115
Guthalungra	
Merinda	Bowen / 548 / 1160
	66
Proserpine	
	Bloomsbury / Elaroo
Yalboroo	Calen
	124 / Kuttabul
	Mackay / 738 / 970
Clermont 274 km	36 / Bakers Creek
	Sarina
Koumala	Ilbilbie
Carmila	Flaggy Rock
Clairview	
	196
	Marlborough
	102 / Kunwarara
Emerald 270 km / The Caves	Glen Geddes / Yaamba
	Parkhurst / 1072 / 636
	Rockhampton / Midgee
Biloela 145 km	17 / Raglan / Ambrose
	73 / Mt. Larcom
	98
	Gladstone
Biloela 102 km	Benaraby
	Bororen
	Miriam Vale
	99
	Bundaberg 48 km
	Gin Gin
Wallaville / Booyal	56
	Childers
	57 / Howard / 1455 / 253
Torbanlea	
	24 / Maryborough
	Owanyilla
Tiaro	65
	Gunalda
Kingaroy 142 km	Gympie / 40
	Cooroy
	Nambour
Kingaroy 164 km	124
	Caboolture
1708 / 0	BRISBANE

HOBART - LAUNCESTON
via MIDLAND HIGHWAY

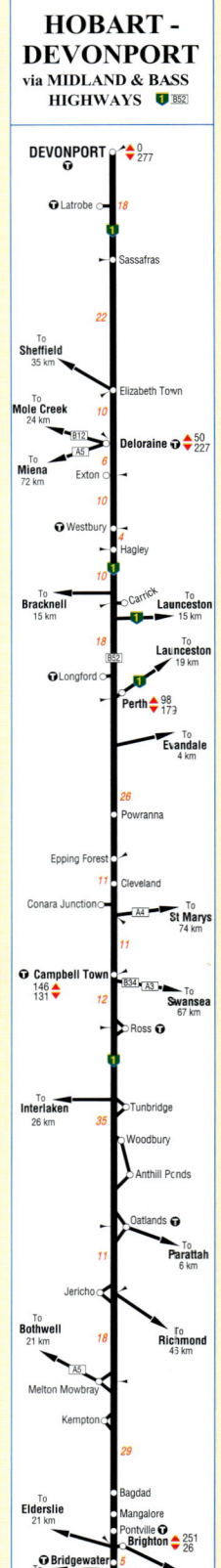

0 / 198	LAUNCESTON
Deloraine 46 km	14
Breadalbane	
Longford 6 km	5 / To Airport 5 km
	Perth / 19 / 179
	Evandale 4 km
	26
Powranna	
Epping Forest	11
Conara Junction	Cleveland
	11 / St Marys 74 km
Campbell Town / 67 / 131	11 / Swansea 67 km
	Ross
	35
Interlaken 26 km	
	Tunbridge
	Woodbury
	Antill Ponds
	11
	Oatlands
	Parattah 6 km
	11
Jericho	
	18 / Richmond 46 km
Bothwell 21 km	
Melton Mowbray	
Kempton	29
	Bagdad
	Mangalore
Elderslie 21 km	Pontville
	Brighton / 172 / 26
	5 / Richmond 17 km
Bridgewater	
New Norfolk 16 km	Granton
	21
	Glenorchy
198 / 0	HOBART

HOBART - DEVONPORT
via MIDLAND & BASS HIGHWAYS

0 / 277	DEVONPORT
Latrobe	18
	Sassafras
	22
Sheffield 35 km	
	Elizabeth Town
Mole Creek 24 km	10
	Deloraine / 50 / 227
Miena 72 km	6 / Exton
	10
	Westbury
	Hagley / 4
	10
Bracknell 15 km	Carrick / To Launceston 15 km
	18 / To Launceston 19 km
Longford	Perth / 98 / 173
	Evandale 4 km
	26
	Powranna
Epping Forest	11 / Cleveland
Conara Junction	St Marys 74 km
	11
Campbell Town / 146 / 131	12 / Swansea 67 km
	Ross
Interlaken 26 km	35 / Tunbridge
	Woodbury
	Anthill Ponds
	Oatlands
	11 / Parattah 6 km
Jericho	
Bothwell 21 km	18 / Richmond 43 km
Melton Mowbray	
Kempton	29
Elderslie 21 km	Bagdad
	Mangalore
	Pontville / Brighton / 251 / 26
Bridgewater	5 / Granton
New Norfolk 16 km	Richmond 7 km
	21
	Glenorchy
277 / 0	HOBART

Have a **GOOD TRIP**

Checking the Car

All the care that you devote to your own comfort can be for nothing if you do not make sure that the car checks out too.

For a one-, two- or three-day tour, you could simply fuel up, check the tyre pressures, clean all the windows and head off; if you maintain your vehicle at all times in reasonable condition – as indeed you should – probably little further preparation is required. However, a vacation of a week or more, or any time involving long-distance driving, will need more thorough preparation. If you intend travelling through remote areas, for example, you should first check that your vehicle is able to handle off-road conditions. The service department of your State motoring organisations (**see:** Useful Information) will give advice and will make a preliminary inspection of your vehicle.

Regardless of the length of your tour, you should check the wheelbrace, jack and under-vehicle jacking points, in case you have to change a tyre.

Unless you are able to service your vehicle yourself, this preparation should be left to your mechanic. To avoid breakdowns and to confirm the reliability of safety-related items, ask the mechanic to include a check of the fuel supply, electrics, brakes, tyres and certain ancillary equipment, as follows.

▌ **Fuel supply.** Check fuel pump for flow. Check carburettor for wear and potential blockages or check condition of electronic or mechanical fuel injection. When the tank is almost empty, remove the drain plug and drain the tank, to check that the remaining fuel is perfectly clean. Check fuel-supply lines for cracks and poor connections, and make sure no fuel line is exposed to damage by rocks or low-clearance projections.

▌ **Electrics.** Check battery output and condition (including terminals), alternator/generator output and condition, spark plugs, condenser, coil, distributor and all terminals and cables. If the vehicle is fitted with electronic ignition it should be checked in the prescribed manner.

▌ **Lights.** Check all lights, not just to see that they work, but to make sure that

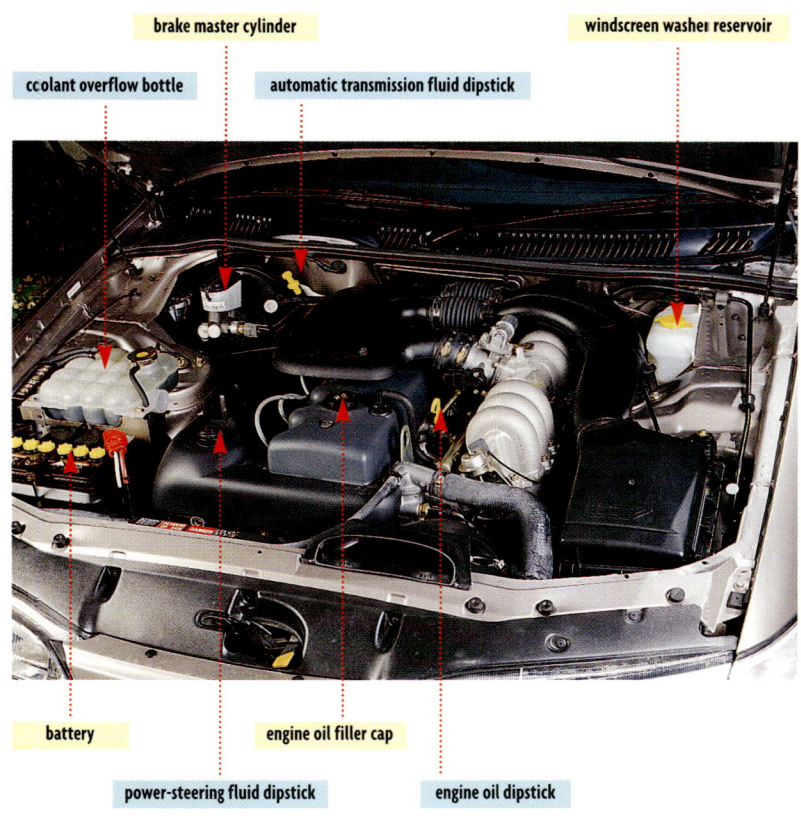

brake master cylinder

windscreen washer reservoir

coolant overflow bottle

automatic transmission fluid dipstick

battery

engine oil filler cap

power-steering fluid dipstick

engine oil dipstick

they are aligned correctly and are likely to continue working. It can be very, very dark at night in outback Australia.

▌ **Brakes.** Check wear of pads and/or linings, check discs for runout and drums for scoring. Brake dust should be cleaned off. Check brake lines and hoses for cracks and wear. Make sure brake lines are not liable to be damaged by rocks or low projections. Check parking brake for adjustment and cable stretch.

▌ **Tyres.** Check for uneven or excessive wear. Check walls for cracks and stone or kerb fractures. Check pressures. Include spare (or spares) in all checks. Make sure that the spare wheel matches those on the car, and uses the same kind of wheel nuts.

▌ **Windscreen-wiper blades.** Check for wear and proper contact, and washers

for direction and effectiveness. Include rear wiper and washer, where fitted.

▌ **Windscreen glass.** Check for cracks and replace if necessary.

▌ **Seat mountings and adjustments.** Check.

▌ **Lubricant levels.** Check (including brake and clutch fluid) and either top up or drain and refill.

▌ **Wheel bearings.** Check for play and adjust or replace.

▌ **Universal and constant velocity joints.** Check, where appropriate, and replace if necessary.

▌ **Dust and water sealing.** A pre-run test in appropriate conditions will reveal any problems. What you do not need is dust, exhaust fumes or water inside the vehicle.

▌ **Roof rack.** Check mounts and welds for weaknesses and cracks.

▌ **Seat belts.** Check for tears or

Hazards

Flood

In some remote areas, floods can occur without warning. Do not camp in dry river beds or close to the edges of creeks or streams. Always exercise extreme caution when approaching flooded roads or bridges. Floodwaters are deceptive; always check the depth before attempting to cross. If you do find yourself stranded in deep water:

* Do not panic.
* Wind up all the windows, to slow down or prevent water entering. (You should have closed all the windows before you tried to cross.)
* When the car has stabilised, undo the seatbelts.
* Turn the headlights on to help rescuers locate the car.
* If the car does not sink, but drifts (which is often the case with a well–sealed car), wait until it reaches shallow water or is close to the bank, then open the door or windows and climb out.
* Form a human chain and help children to keep their heads above water.
* If the car is sinking, it will be necessary to wait for the water pressure to equalise before you can open the doors or windows. As a last resort, kick out the windscreen or rear window.

Bushfire

If you have to travel on days of critical fire danger (that is, total fire ban days), make sure you carry some woollen blankets and a filled water container. If you are trapped as a bushfire approaches:

* Do not panic.
* Stop the car in the nearest cleared area.
* Wind up all the windows.
* Turn on the hazard lights to warn any other traffic.
* DO NOT GET OUT OF YOUR CAR. The temperature may become unbearably hot, but it is still safer to stay in the car.
* Lie on the car floor, below window level, to avoid radiant heat.
* Cover yourself and your passengers with blankets.

The car will not explode or catch fire, and a fast-moving wildfire will pass quickly overhead.

Animals

Although some species of Australia's unique wildlife are immensely appealing, some species are extremely dangerous.

Exercise extreme caution when crossing flooded areas

Marine life

* **Box jellyfish (or marine stingers).** These are found in the coastal waters of Queensland and northern Australia in the summer months (from October–May). A sting from their many long tentacles can be lethal, and for that reason swimming on coastal beaches north of Rockhampton is prohibited at this time. Also, walking or paddling in a few centimetres of water is equally as dangerous as swimming.
* **Stonefish.** Among Australia's several species of poisonous stinging fish, the stonefish, found all around the northern coastline, is particularly dangerous. Walking gently in the water, wearing sandshoes and not turning over coral and rocks will reduce the likelihood of a sting.
* **Blue-ringed octopuses.** Common in rock pools in all Australian States, their bite can paralyse in 15 minutes resulting in death. Do not handle in any circumstances and warn children of the potential hazard. Unless provoked, the distinctive blue rings of this dangerous octopus may not be evident.
* **Sharks.** Sharks are common in Australian waters. Do not swim where sharks have been seen or are known to congregate. Do not swim near dogs or other domestic pets. Do not swim at dusk or after dark, or at locations where water becomes abruptly deeper. Avoid areas of low visibility and turbid water.
* **Freshwater and saltwater crocodiles.** These are found throughout northern Australia. The saltwater crocodile is particularly dangerous and may be found in both salt water (including the sea) and fresh water. The freshwater crocodile will also bite, thus caution is necessary for both

species. Neither species is easy to see in the water. Heed local warning signs and do not swim or paddle in fresh or salt water or allow children or animals near the water's edge. People standing in or near water while feeding or cleaning fish are particularly vulnerable, as are shore-based anglers and small-boat operators.

Snakes

As a rule, snakes are timid and generally do not attack unless threatened. However, several species are highly venomous.

Spiders

Funnel-web spiders and **red-back spiders.** The bite from both species can be deadly. The funnel-web is found in southern and eastern States. The red-back is found in all Australian States.

Insects

Wasps, bees, ants (particularly **bull-ants**), **scorpions, centipedes** and **mosquitoes.** These insects are found throughout Australia. Their sting or bite normally is not harmful, except to those people who are allergy-prone, but it may cause pain and discomfort. Mosquitoes are of more serious concern in areas affected by Ross River virus. **Ticks** are a serious health threat, especially for children. When located, a tick should be removed promptly with tweezers, keeping the body intact. Do not compress the body.

Study Australia's wildlife and learn to identify dangerous species. Remember also that some plant species are poisonous. When visiting a new area, check with local authorities to ascertain which dangerous species, if any, are found there.

An early start, Mt Rowland in Tasmania

sun-hardening. Replace if necessary. Also check inertia reels.

▌ **Radiator water level and condition.** Check; drain and flush if necessary. Check radiator for leaks and radiator pressure cap for pressure release accuracy. Check water-pump operation. Check radiator and heater hoses for cracks and general condition, and replace if necessary. Check hose clamps.

▌ **Fan belt.** Check for tension and fraying.

▌ Check anything else you might think is worthwhile.

All this should be done as near as practicable to your departure date. Allow time for unexpected work or part replacement, and for a return to the garage if a particular problem persists. Note: *Nothing should be overlooked* – lives may be at stake.

Packing the Car

First and most important, you should carry only those items that are absolutely necessary with you in the passenger compartment. In a sedan this is not difficult. You have a boot, and that is where most items should be carried; but in a station wagon it is much more difficult. Loose items in the passenger compartment get under your feet (especially hazardous for the driver), interfere with your comfort and become dangerous projectiles if you have a collision. So for your station wagon, buy or rig up a safety net, which can be fitted behind the rear seat to separate you from the objects that could otherwise harm you.

This rule applies also to food and drink. Empty bottles and cartons should be stowed out of the way in a rubbish bag, until you are able to dispose of them properly.

And if you are short of space, cull some non-essential items.

In order to provide extra space, many drivers fix a roof rack to their vehicle. This is not recommended. Laden roof racks upset the balance of the vehicle by changing its centre of gravity, making it top-heavy. They disturb the air flow, which can destabilise the vehicle, and they certainly increase fuel consumption by interfering with the aerodynamics. In some circumstances they can snag on overhanging limbs of trees.

If you must use a roof rack, carry as little on it as possible and keep the maximum loading height as low as you can. Protect the load by wrapping it in a tarpaulin or groundsheet and, if possible, create a sharp (aerofoil) leading edge on the load to improve air flow.

A better alternative to a roof rack is a small, strong, lightweight trailer, but there are times when this will be a disadvantage also.

If you are towing a caravan, some items can be carried inside the van on the floor, preferably strapped down (anything loose will be flung about) and located over the axle (or axles). In some States, caravans must be fitted with a fire extinguisher. (And remember, no people or animals are to be transported in a towed caravan.)

Once your vehicle is loaded, and preferably with the passengers aboard, check the tyre pressures (yes, even as you leave home on day one). The additional load will mean higher pressures are needed. The tyre placard or owner's handbook can be used as a guideline. The tyre will bag if it is under-inflated and destabilise the car. It also will offer a baggy sidewall to rocks and stones, encouraging wall fractures and potential blowouts. Laden-tyre pressure requirements vary with tyre size and design, but the pressure is important. If in any doubt contact the tyre manufacturer.

When to Set Off

There is evidence to suggest that people drive best during the hours in which they are accustomed to being awake, and probably at work. As drowsiness is deadly in drivers, this is worth noting. Leaving home, for example at 1 a.m., might avoid the heat of the day and beat the traffic to a large extent, but somewhere between 3 and 5 a.m. you may find yourself wanting to doze off again.

Plan to share long-distance driving as much as possible. Depart around or just before sunrise and stop no later than sundown. Allow regular stops, not just to stretch your legs but to take nourishment as well. Food helps keep the energy levels up. You might care to leave later if you are travelling east, to avoid the rising sun shining in your eyes, and finish earlier if you are travelling west, for the converse reason.

Leaving Home

Everyone knows the feeling that usually comes when you are a good distance from home: did I lock all the windows, turn off the electricity at the meter, cancel the newspaper and mail delivery? Usually all is well, but it is reassuring to double-check everything before you leave (**see:** Before Departure).

Better **DRIVING**

Take extra care on icy roads

In skilful driving, the two most important ingredients are concentration and smoothness.

Concentration. Find a position that is comfortable position and stay comfortable; discomfort destroys concentration. Lack of concentration is the biggest single cause of road accidents.

Wear the right clothes: loose-fitting, cool or warm as appropriate, but capable of being changed (not while you are driving!) as temperatures change. Lightweight shoes are better than boots. (There are such things as driving shoes, which are excellent.) Wear good quality antiglare sunglasses. Sit comfortably: neither too close to the steering wheel and cramped, nor too far back and stretching; and be sure you can reach the foot controls through the entire length of their movement. Drive with both hands all the time. No one can control a car properly with one hand.

Driving gloves are recommended. Make all seat, belt and rear-view mirror adjustments before you drive off (particularly if you share the driving with someone not your size).

Concentration means *no distractions*. It is probably unrealistic to suggest that no conversation takes place while you are driving, but do not allow conversations to interfere with your concentration. Aim to keep the children quiet and amused (**see:** Child's Play). If an important issue needs to be resolved, first stop the car and then sort it out.

Smoothness. Smoothness is vital for the vehicle's safe, effective operation, but unfortunately many people are not smooth drivers. A vehicle in motion is a tonne or so of iron, steel and plastic sitting atop a set of springs. It is inherently unstable and prone to influences such as pitch and roll. This is difficult enough to control in normal motion, but worse when the driver exaggerates these instabilities by stabbing at the brakes, jerking the steering wheel and crashing the gears. Two things derive from being a smooth driver. The first is passenger comfort; on a long trip, everyone will arrive much fresher and more relaxed if the driver has provided a smooth and therefore pleasant journey. The second is increased safety; the vehicle will react better to smooth driving than it will to hamfisted driving. Smooth driving brings even further benefits: less wear and tear and lower fuel consumption.

However, to define better driving as a combination of concentration and smoothness only would not be wholly accurate. There are other factors:

Know your vehicle. Understand its breaking capacities, especially in emergencies – some cars move around a lot, or become directionally unstable under harsh braking. Be aware of its usable power and its limitations. And drive well within the cornering and road-holding limits of the vehicle's suspension and tyre combination.

Drive defensively. It is worth assuming that a proportion of road users are inattentive or devoid of skill. It is remarkable how your driving awareness is increased by such an attitude.

Do not be impatient. Advance planning should have provided you with ample time for the day's journey.

Do not drive with an incapacitating illness or injury. Something as simple as a bruised elbow might restrict rapid arm movement when you most need it.

Driving Emergencies

Of course, the best way to handle emergencies is to avoid them. However, to suggest one problem or another will never occur is unrealistic. A course in defensive driving is an advantage; contact your local motoring organisation to obtain more information (**see:** Useful Information).

Skidding. The possibility of skidding worries most drivers, as well it should. There are a number of causes of a skid, some of them composite. Essentially skidding occurs when the tyres lose their grip on the road.

The most common form is a front-wheel (or sometimes all-wheel) skid caused by over-braking. When the wheels stop rolling, the vehicle will no longer react to steering input. If you avoid jumping on the brake pedal, (that is, drive smoothly), you will avoid this type of skid. However if you do skid, quickly ease just sufficient pressure off the brake pedal to allow the wheels to roll again. The steering will come back, which at least will allow you to take avoiding action as well as to slow down.

A rear-wheel skid also may occur as a result of harsh braking, usually while turning at the same time (for example if corner entry speed is too high, or braking too harsh). In slippery conditions the tail of the car may also fishtail because you have entered a corner too fast or, in rear-wheel drive vehicles, because too much power has been applied too soon, causing the rear tyres to break traction. A rear-wheel skid of any kind requires some reverse steering, often only briefly. It is not enough to advise turning the steering in the direction of the skid: the question is, by how much? Turn the steering wheels to point them in the direction you wish to travel and, at the same time, try to recognise what you did to cause the skid in the first place. If it was because of excessive acceleration, back off a little and re-apply the accelerator more gently. If it was because you entered the corner too fast or because of your braking (or both at the same time), ease the brakes and let your corrective steering realign the car and then, smoothly, increase the power again by gently applying the accelerator.

Skids can be complex and difficult to control. Over-correction is common, with the result that the vehicle swings into another skid in the opposite direction. It is important not to panic, and to be smooth in your reaction. Easy to say – not so easy to do!

▌ **Aquaplaning.** This is a form of skidding where the tyres roll a layer of water up in front of the vehicle and then ride on to it, breaking contact with the road surface. What you sense is a sudden loss of driving 'feel'. Slow down, very smoothly, until the tyres come off the layer of water and then proceed more carefully. Watch out for deep puddles: they are the danger.

Driving in snow, ice and mud also produces adhesion problems. Once again, smooth, steady progress, while 'feeling' the vehicle and staying on top of its movements, is the only answer.

▌ **Icy roads.** For a visit to the snow, your vehicle should be fitted with chains. If it is not and the car's back wheels begin to spin wildly on packed and rutted snow or ice:
- Stop the car.
- Look for and remove any obstructions under the car.
- Pack loose gravel, sticks or vegetation under the driving wheels.
- Remember that on a level surface a gentle push sometimes will get the car moving again.

Because it cannot be seen, ice can be more dangerous than snow.

▌ **Foggy conditions.** When driving in fog:
- Switch on dipped headlights, or fog-lights if your car is fitted with them.
- Use front and back demisters.
- If visibility is reduced to such an extent that driving becomes an ordeal, pull as far off the road as you can, switch on your emergency lights and wait until the fog lifts and you feel able to continue.

The advice in this section applies equally to driving in the cities and in the outback. The techniques are the same; only the conditions vary (**see:** Outback Motoring for more detail on driving in the outback).

Safe Driving

Basic Traffic Laws

There are variations in road traffic laws from State to State throughout Australia. Some affect the traveller, some do not. Drivers are expected to know and observe those rules that apply to a vehicle's operation; however, specific State laws that affect the registration of vehicles, trailers or caravans, for example, are not enforced between States.

The city of Melbourne, which is the last stronghold of the tram, has its unique hook turn, where at some inner-city intersections a vehicle making a righthand turn must move to the far left of the intersection and wait until the traffic clears and the traffic lights change before completing the turn. Overtaking on the right of a tram is forbidden and no vehicle may pass a stationary tram at a recognised tram stop.

Drink-driving laws are extremely strict in all States and drivers can be pulled up at random and be required to take a blood alcohol test.

Speed regulations vary in each State. In some States, the use of cameras to catch speeding drivers, both in the city and country, is widespread; as well, cameras are positioned at traffic lights on many intersections to record drivers who do not stop at the red light.

In most other respects, the road traffic laws are essentially the same from State to State. However, legislation is subject to change and the cautious driver will check first with the relevant State motoring organisation (**see:** Useful Information) for answers to any questions raised on specific regulations.

Positioning

Positioning is vital on any road.
- Try to stagger the position of your car in the line of traffic so that you can see well ahead.

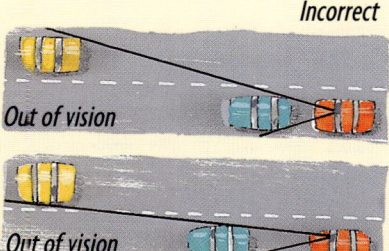

Incorrect

Out of vision

Out of vision

Correct

- When turning right on a two-lane highway, do not angle the car; keep it square to the other traffic so that cars can pass on the left.

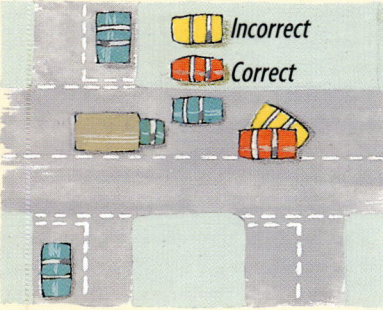

Incorrect

Correct

In Case of Accident

In all States of Australia, any accident in which someone is injured or killed *must* be reported to police at once, or within 24 hours. In Western Australia, all car accidents must be reported.

It is highly advisable to report to police any accident that involves substantial property damage. Police may or may not decide to attend the scene, but they at least will have your report on record, which may well be useful should there be legal proceedings or insurance claims.

When involved in an accident and if required by police, you *must* give your name and address and produce your driver's licence. If you do not have it with you, you may be liable for an on-the-spot fine. It is advisable to obtain the insurance details of the other parties involved.

All parties involved in the accident should exchange names and addresses, and insurance details. *Do not volunteer any other information.* In particular, do not discuss the accident. Should court action result, you may find something said in the stress of the aftermath of the accident used against you. Above all, *do not admit you are at fault in any way.*

You are not obliged to make a statement to police. If you are disturbed and upset, wait until you can think clearly.

An accident that involves damage to persons or property should be reported to your insurance company as soon as possible.

TOWING

Touring near the Hamersley Range, Western Australia

Towing your accommodation behind you will provide the advantage of low-budget touring and flexibility with stopovers. It can be a disadvantage also, in that it may restrict access to some areas. You can, however, use the caravan for most sections of your journey and park it somewhere while you go off in the car and explore the more difficult tracks.

▌ **Obtain advice.** If you are new to towing, the first thing you must do is to get expert advice from your local motoring organisation (**see:** Useful Information) on your towing hitch. It is very important that the rig (that is, car and caravan, boat or trailer) is balanced and the weight over the tow ball is not excessive. An adjustable height hitch with spring bars is best.

▌ **Learn to reverse.** Once you have decided on the hitch and you have learned how to hook up and unhook, you must learn to reverse the rig. Find a wide open area, an empty car park for example, and practise. Get the feel of the rig and aim to be proficient at reversing before you depart.

▌ **Allow for added length.** On the road, remember to make allowances for the added overall length and give yourself extra space for turning and extra distance for overtaking. The added weight will obviously affect the towing vehicle's performance with regard to acceleration and braking.

▌ **Know the speed limit.** In most States there are speed limits on articulated vehicles and you should know what they are before departure and abide by them (**see:** Basic Traffic Laws). High-speed towing of vans and trailers can cause major difficulties, magnifying driving problems substantially.

▌ **Avoid trailer sway.** Cross-winds can be a problem when towing a caravan; the van's slab sides acting like sails. The combination of high speed and cross-winds can cause trailer sway, a dangerous characteristic that dramatically destabilises both towing vehicle and caravan. You probably will feel it happening before you see it, but checking in the rear-view mirrors will confirm it. Should the trailer begin to move about, ease back on your speed, braking if necessary, but very gently. Harsh or sudden braking will compound the problem. When the caravan stabilises, resume speed, perhaps very gradually if you are continuing in a cross-wind area.

▌ **Fit good-quality towing mirrors on your vehicle.** It is very important that your rear view down both sides of the trailer or caravan is not obscured.

▌ **Be courteous.** If, because of the relative slowness of your progress, you observe in the rear-view mirror a line of vehicles banking up behind you, be courteous and pull over when and where you can, to allow vehicles to overtake.

▌ **Locate load correctly.** The carrying of goods and equipment in a caravan has been mentioned, but it is worth repeating that such items should be located as much as possible over and just to the front of the caravan axle (or axles); never behind, as this will lift the front of the caravan and the tow ball.

▌ **Check the rig.** Before setting off and every day of the trip, whatever the vehicle, always check and double-check that the hitch is secure, that the safety chains are correctly fitted, and that the electrical connections are working so that indicator lights function at the rear of the towed vehicle.

▌ **Allow extra time.** Remember to allow extra time for each day's travel, and remain alert.

Checklist

When towing anything:

- Check the hitch for security. The law in most States demands that tow bars are fitted with safety chains.
- Check that the tail and stop lights, marker lights and signal lights are working.
- Remember to check the air pressure in the caravan or trailer tyres.
- If towing a boat, check the lashings.
- Check that caravan doors, windows and roof vents are closed before departure.
- If the caravan or trailer is fitted with separate brakes, check these as soon as you start to move.

OUTBACK Motoring

A 4WD vehicle negotiating bulldust

Australia's size and remoteness deter many people from exploring it. However, properly set up and equipped, and armed with common sense and a little background knowledge, every intending traveller can explore the country's huge open spaces.

If you intend travelling in the outback, planning ahead is vital, for it is possible to travel in some sections of the Australian outback and not see another vehicle or person for several days. (The Canning Stock Route is a good example.)

It is possible to travel in some areas of the outback in a 2WD vehicle, but it is safer and much more practical to do so in a 4WD vehicle suited to off-road conditions. Remember that if you rent a vehicle, there may be restrictions on insurance if you drive on unclassified roads; seek advice before you make any plans.

Your vehicle should be fitted with air conditioning to counteract high inland daytime temperatures and to allow you to drive with all the windows closed through dusty areas. You should be able to carry out small running repairs and must carry an owner's manual for the vehicle, tools and spare parts (**see:** Tools and Spare Parts).

Driving Conditions

Outback driving conditions vary greatly. The deserts are usually dry; conditions change after rain. Many parts of the tropics are accessible only in the 'dry' season, and even then there are streams to ford and washaways to contend with.

Pre-reading road conditions is vital. Recognising that a patch of different colour may represent a change in surface is an example. Sand can give way to rock; rock may lead to mud; hard surfaces become bulldust with little warning.

Soft sand, bulldust and mud. These are best negotiated at the highest reasonable speed and in the highest possible gear *and* in 4WD. However, examine the road surface first. Never enter deep mud or mud covered with water without first establishing the depth of either or both.

Deep sand. Requires low tyre pressures. Carry a tyre pressure gauge and drop pressures to about 10 psi. Reinflate when on gravel or bitumen roads again, because the soft tyres will perform very badly and may blow out as a result of stone fractures on hard surfaces.

Crossing a creek or stream. Stop to check the track across for clear passage and water depth. If the water is deep but fordable, cover the front of the vehicle with a tarpaulin and remove the fan belt to stop water being sprayed over the engine electrics. Drive through in low range second gear or high range first gear, and clear the opposite embankment before stopping again. If it has rained, beware of flash flooding.

Dips. Dips are common on outback roads and can break suspension components if you enter too fast. To cross a dip, brake on entry to drop the vehicle's nose, and hold the brake on until just before the bottom of the depression. Then accelerate again to lift the nose and therefore the suspension, as you exit. This will prevent the springs from bottoming out and will also give maximum clearance.

Cattle grids. Also a potential hazard, as they are often neglected, with broken approaches and exits. If a grid appears to be in disrepair, stop and check first, before attempting to cross.

Road trains. These multi-trailered, long trucks are difficult and often dangerous to overtake, particularly on dusty roads. Wait for a chance to get the front of your vehicle out to a position where the road-train driver can see you in the rear-view mirror, but even then do not try to overtake until the driver has signalled acknowledgement that you are there. Sometimes it is prudent to stop and take a break, rather than try to overtake a road train. If you meet an oncoming road train, pull over and stop until it has passed.

Animals. There are vast areas of unfenced property in the outback where stock roam free. A bullock or a large kangaroo can seriously damage your vehicle. Be especially wary around sunrise and sunset when animals are more active. A bull-bar or roo-bar provides limited protection at low speeds only, especially against larger animals. Driver concentration should be at as high a level as in city peak hours.

Surviving in the Outback

You might be stranded in a remote area with a major mechanical breakdown, or if your vehicle becomes bogged. For this eventuality you should be equipped to wait at that spot until you are found. Always carry a week's supply of spare water, minimum 21 litres per head.

Keep it for an emergency. Emergency supplies of dry biscuits and canned food will keep hunger at bay, but body evaporation and thirst is the vital factor. Do not drink radiator coolant. Often it is not water but a chemical compound, and even if it is water, usually it has been treated with chemicals (**see:** How to Obtain Water).

Do not try to walk out of a remote area. You are going to survive only if you wait by the car. Before entering a remote area, check with police or a local authority, and tell them where and when you are going, and when you expect to arrive. When you reach your destination, telephone and advise of your arrival. This is important as failure to do so causes unneccessary and expensive searches.

If stranded, set up some type of shelter and, in the heat of the day, remain in its shade as motionless as possible. Movement accelerates fluid loss (**see:** How to Obtain Water).

Direction Finding

Clever electronic hand-held navigation devices, using the Global Positioning System (GPS), are now available from bushwalking shops and outdoor centres. These can be used with or without a map and are much more sophisticated and accurate than a magnetic compass.

If you cannot read a map or use a compass – or if you have no navigational device with you – it is vital to have some means of orientating yourself if you are lost.

A simple method of finding north is to use a conventional wristwatch.

Place the 12 on the watch in line with the sun and bisect the angle between it and the hour hand. This will give a fairly accurate indication of north.

At night, the Southern Cross can be used to determine south.

When exploring a side track off the main road, be sure to make a rough sketch of the route you are following, noting all turnoffs and distances between them (using the speedometer), together with any prominent landmarks. When you return, reconcile your return route with the sketch, point by point.

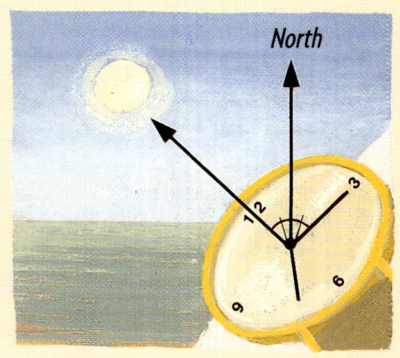

North

How to Obtain Water

Less than 24 hours without water can be fatal in outback heat.
- It is essential to conserve body moisture. Take advantage of any shade that can be found.
- **DO NOT LEAVE your vehicle**. It may be the only effective shade available.
- Ration your drinking water. Do not drink your car's radiator coolant.

Although a river or creek bed may be dry, there is often an underground water source. A hole dug about a metre deep may produce a useful soak.

Making an Arizona Still

Where there is vegetation, it is possible to extract water from it using an Arizona still.
- Before the heat of the day, dig a hole about one metre across and a little more than half a metre deep.
- Put a vessel of some kind in the hole's centre to collect the water.
- Surround the vessel with cut vegetation. (Fleshy

plants hold more moisture than drier saltbush.)
- Cover the hole with a plastic sheet held down by closely packed rocks, so that the hole is sealed off.
- Put a small stone in the centre of the sheet, directly above the collection vessel.

The sun's heat will evaporate moisture from the plants. This moisture will condense on the inside

of the plastic, run down the cone formed by the weight of the stone and drip off into the vessel. In uninterrupted sunlight, with suitable plants, about one litre of water should be collected about every six hours. The Arizona still takes about three hours to start producing and it will become less efficient as the ground moisture dries out. A new hole will need to be dug at intervals.

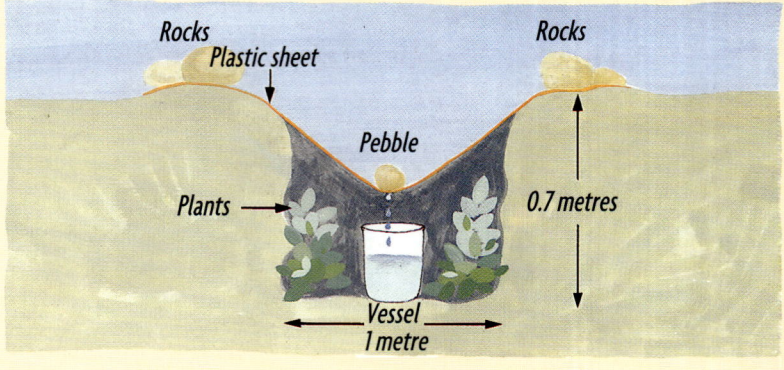

Rocks
Plastic sheet
Rocks
Pebble
Plants
Vessel
1 metre
0.7 metres

INTRODUCTION

Outback Advice

Critical Rules for Outback Motoring

- Check intended routes carefully.
- Check the best time of year to travel.
- Check that your vehicle is suited to outback conditions.
- Check your load; keep it to a minimum.
- Check ahead for local road conditions, weather forecasts and fuel availability.
- Check that you have advised someone of your route, destination and arrival time.
- Check that you have essential supplies: water, food, fuel, spare parts.
- Carry detailed maps.
- Carry an extra supply of food and water in case of emergency; four to five litres of water per person per day in hot areas.
- Always remain with your vehicle if it breaks down.

Warning. When driving on desert roads remember:

- There is no water, except after rains.
- Unmade roads can be extremely hazardous, especially when wet.
- Traffic is almost non-existent, except on main roads.

Outback Advice Service

The Royal Flying Doctor Service of Australia (RFDS) provides emergency outback assistance. The service was the brain-child of Reverend John Flynn, whose dream of a 'mantle of safety' in the outback resulted in the service's first flight in 1928. RFDS bases and visitors centres provide advice on outback safety, communications and proper emergency procedures. Bases at Broken Hill (NSW), Charleville (Qld) and Jandakot (WA) also hire out transceiver sets with a fixed emergency call button in case of accident or sickness, at a very reasonable cost. Some bases that do not hire out sets can suggest local outlets for them.

New South Wales
Broken Hill: Broken Hill Airport 2880
(08) 8088 0777 (base)
(08) 8088 1188 (emergency assistance)

South Australia
Port Augusta: 4 Vincent St 5700
(08) 8642 2044

Western Australia
Emergency assistance for all of WA:
1800 625800

Sign beside the Eyre Highway in South Australia

Derby: Clarendon St 6728
(08) 9191 1211
Jandakot: 3 Eagle Dr., Jandakot Airport 6164
(08) 9414 1200
Kalgoorlie: Kalgoorlie-Boulder Airport 6430
(08) 9093 1500

Northern Territory
Alice Springs: Stuart Tce 0870
(08) 8952 1129 (base)
(08) 8952 1033 (emergency assistance)

Queensland
Brisbane: Casuarina St, Eagle Farm 4007
(07) 3860 5388 (base)
(07) 3364 1311 (emergency assistance)
Cairns: 1 Junction St 4870
(070) 53 1952 (base)
(070) 53 5419 (emergency assistance)
Charleville: Old Cunnamulla Rd 4470
(076) 54 1233 (base)
(076) 54 1443 (emergency assistance)
Mount Isa: Barkly Highway 4825
(077) 43 2800 (base)
(077) 43 2802 (emergency assistance)

For general information relating to the services offered by the Royal Flying Doctor Service, contact: The Australian Council of the Royal Flying Doctor Service of Australia, Level 5, 15–17 Young St, Sydney 2000; (02) 9241 2411, fax (02) 9247 3351.

Sharing the Outback

As you travel through the outback, remember you are sharing the land with its traditional Aboriginal owners, pastoralists, other tourists – and even nature itself. In order to protect and preserve the outback for future visitors:

- Respect Aboriginal sacred and cultural sites, and heritage buildings and pioneer relics.
- Protect native flora and fauna; take photographs not specimens.
- Follow restrictions on the use of firearms. These restrictions protect wildlife and stock.
- Carry your own fuel source (for example a portable gas stove), to avoid lighting fires in fire-sensitive areas.
- When lighting a campfire (if you must), keep it small and use any fallen wood sparingly. Never leave a fire unattended; extinguish completely before you move on.
- Do not drive off-road.
- Do not camp immediately adjacent to water sources (for example on riverbanks or by dams). Allow access for stock and native animals.
- Do not bury your rubbish; carry out everything you take in.
- Dispose of faecal waste by burial.
- Leave gates as you find them: open or shut.
- Do not ignore signs warning of dangers or entry restrictions. These are there for your protection.

BREAKDOWNS

Roadside repairs in northern Queensland

There are many causes of motor vehicle breakdown, but fortunately modern vehicle technology has vastly reduced the possibility of being stuck by the roadside. Breakdowns that do occur can sometimes be cured with a roadside 'fix'; but this is often less possible with today's computer-driven vehicles. Inexpert or makeshift repairs may lead to further complications and a bigger repair bill.

Proper vehicle preparation and maintenance should at least reduce the possibility of roadside breakdowns and, on long journeys, the regular vehicle-service schedule should be maintained.

In areas where you have access to service through a motoring organisation, it is better to leave even slightly complicated repairs to the specialist. (Remember to carry your membership card, which entitles you to assistance in other States; see: Useful Information.) If you are driving a rental car, most rental companies list their recognised repair organisations in the manual supplied. (Before you drive the car, you should check that these details are provided.) If your rental vehicle cannot be repaired immediately, you should request an exchange vehicle.

If you plan to journey into remote areas, it is a good idea to first take a basic course in vehicle maintenance (see: Car Maintenance Courses). As well, you should carry a range of tools and spare parts (see: Tools and Spare Parts).

Modern Vehicles

Most modern vehicles are fitted with electronic engine-management systems, or with electronic ignition and fuel injection. Generally these are more reliable than older systems and usually, in case of partial failure of the system, they have a 'limp home' mode, which enables travelling a limited distance at limited speed. However, total failure of such a system is difficult or impossible to remedy at the roadside without expert knowledge and equipment. This means that travel into remote areas is rendered much safer by travelling with at least one other vehicle, and by installing or hiring an appropriate long-range radio transmitter, receiver and aerial (see: Outback Advice).

Earlier-model Vehicles

For those who drive earlier-model vehicles with less complex electrics and fuel systems, the trouble-shooting flow-charts are designed to be of assistance (see: Trouble Shooting). But first, always remember to:

▍ **Watch warning gauges.** These have been installed to warn that things *may* be going wrong. A flickering battery warning light will suggest all is not well with the generator/alternator charge rate and should be attended to promptly. A fluctuating temperature gauge *may* suggest the onset of a problem with the cooling system. Act on the warning at the earliest opportunity.

▍ **Make a daily check** of fluid levels. Check fuel, water and oil (including spare supplies); also tyre pressures, and fan-belt tension and condition.

▍ **Make a regular check** of brake-fluid and battery-acid levels, and pressure of spare tyre.

If the vehicle develops an unexplained sound, move to the side of the road as soon as possible. Park on flat ground if you can. You may have to spend some time under the bonnet, so look for shade or shelter. A loud, 'serious' sound usually indicates a major problem. Try to locate the source of the sound. If it is coming from the engine, do nothing and seek help.

When the Engine Stops

When the engine either splutters to a stop, constantly misfires or stops suddenly but was otherwise running smoothly, the problem is probably in one of two areas: fuel supply or electrics. Use the Trouble Shooting flow-charts to establish where the problem lies. If the problem is within the drive-train – the gearbox, drive-shaft or differential – once again, seek help.

Tools and Spare Parts

Be prepared when travelling in remote areas

Remote-area travelling requires that someone in the vehicle knows, at least, the basics of breakdown repairs (**see:** Breakdowns). This means carrying emergency tools, spare parts and spare fuel, and the *vehicle owner's manual*. The following is a guide to what may be appropriate for your vehicle:

Tools

- Set of screwdrivers (blade and Phillips head)
- Small set of socket spanners
- Set of open-end/ring combination spanners
- Small and medium adjustable wrenches
- Small ball pein (engineer's) hammer
- Pliers and wire-cutters
- Hand drill and bits
- Workshop scissors
- Aerosol puncture repair can
- Tyre pump
- Puncture repair kit
- Tyre-pressure gauge
- Wheel brace
- Jack with supplementary wide base for sand or mud (block of wood, approximately the size of an A4 sheet of paper and 3 cm thick)
- Jumper leads (capacitor-type if for EFL engine)
- Hydrometer
- Small spade
- Vice grips
- Good quality tow-rope
- Heavy duty torch, spare batteries and globe
- Pocket knife
- Fire extinguisher(s)

Spare Parts

- Epoxy resin bonding 'goo' (for repair of punctured fuel tank)
- Plastic insulating tape
- Spare radiator and heater hoses
- Engine accessory belts (fan, alternator, power steering, etc.)
- Roll of cloth adhesive tape
- 1 metre fuel line (reinforced plastic)
- Insulated electric wire
- Spare electrical connections (range)
- Spare hose-clips (range)
- Distributor cap
- Set of high tension leads
- Condenser (where appropriate)
- Rotor
- Set of spark plugs
- Can of dewatering spray
- Set of points
- Spare fuel, air and oil filters
- Fuel pump kit, water pump kit
- Small-diameter plastic tubing
- Range of spare light globes and fuses
- Nuts, bolts, washers, split pins
- Lubricants: automatic transmission and power steering fluid
- Radiator sealant
- Tube of hand cleaner, clean rags

Fuel

- Spare fuel (40 litres minimum) in steel jerry cans. (Do *not* use non-approved plastic containers; some plastics react with fuel.) Also check fuel range, and the distance between refuelling points.
- At least one spare wheel (slightly over-inflated to allow for some air loss). If travelling in remote areas, consider additional tyres/tubes.

Trouble Shooting (for earlier-model vehicles)

King Leopold Range in the Kimberley, Western Australia

INTRODUCTION

Engine will not turn over

Check battery for charge.

If flat...
recharge or replace, or tow-start (if manual transmission vehicle) until next service opportunity. (If automatic, check handbook. Most autos cannot be tow- or clutch-started.)

▼

If battery OK...
check if battery terminals and straps are loose, broken or dirty. If so, clean, repair or replace.

▼

If terminals OK...
check for jammed starter motor. For manual vehicle, put in top gear and rock back and forth to try to free pinion. An indication that starter may be jammed is an audible click when you try to start the engine and it will not turn over. With an automatic vehicle, try to turn engine back and forth

with a spanner on crankshaft pulley to free pinion. Put gearbox into 'N' first.

▼

If the starter motor is free...
it is possible a solenoid has failed. Unless you are an auto electrician and carry a spare, seek help.

Starter motor whirrs but will not turn engine

Very likely, you have stripped a starter ring-gear, which means major repair work. But check to see that the starter motor is fully bolted to its mounting bracket, and tighten if not.

Engine turns over but will not fire, or fires but will not run cleanly, or misfires regularly, or runs and stops

Problem may be electrics or fuel supply. If unsure, begin with electrics.

Electrics

1 Check that spark is getting to spark plugs. Remove high tension (HT) lead from No. 1 plug and remove No. 1 plug. Reattach HT lead to plug and hold plug body with pliers 1 mm from cylinder-head bolt or similar and turn engine over. Spark plug should produce strong blue spark at regular intervals.

▼

2 If not...
the simplest and fastest way to deal with an electrical problem is to replace parts, either at once or progressively, with spares (**see:** Tools and Spare Parts). Replace coil and all HT leads and try engine. If problem persists, remove distributor cap and replace condenser and points. Re-set points and fit new rotor and distributor cap. Engine should start and run cleanly.

▼

3 If you carry no spare parts, you can still confirm electrics as the problem by a process of elimination. If there is no spark at the spark plugs, the problem has to be between battery and plug. Check that low tension lead at side of distributor is connected properly and tightly mounted. If so, remove distributor cap and check for cracks. If there is a crack, repair with an epoxy glue/filler until it can be replaced. Check that condenser is tightly mounted and its LT wire is connected. Check that points open and close properly by turning engine over by hand slowly and watching for a spark between points. Points may be burned or deeply pitted. If so, remove points and use nail-file to clean up faces, then replace and re-set. If, however, you have established an electrical problem and you have no spares, seek assistance.

▼

4 If you have a spark at the plugs, most likely you have a fuel-supply problem.

Fuel supply

Check fuel tank for fuel, despite gauge reading. (It may be faulty.)

1 If fuel OK...
check accelerator cable connection and for free operation, and check choke cable and operation. For vehicle with automatic choke, remove air-cleaner carrier and element, and look down choke tube. If

choke butterfly is not fully open, open it and check to see if it stays open. If it closes again, engine is flooding, and may not run for that reason. A faulty auto choke cannot be repaired at the roadside.

▼

2 If accelerator and choke cables are operating correctly...
do not replace air cleaner; remove fuel line to carburettor and turn engine over. Fuel should flow freely. If so, check it is not contaminated by pumping small amount into clear glass or plastic container and examine for water and/or dirt.

▼

3 If water or dirt are apparent...
check and replace fuel filter and remove and check fuel pump. Examine glass for contamination. If none or very little, replace fuel line to carburettor and try engine again.

▼

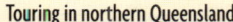

Touring in northern Queensland

4 If there is substantial contamination...
it may be coming from fuel tank. Tank will need to be drained and perhaps flushed. Drained fuel should be saved and strained back. If you are travelling a long way before next fuel stop, be careful not to waste fuel.

▼

5 If no fuel at fuel line and no apparent blockage...
fuel pump has failed for some reason. If you are carrying a spare, replace pump. If not, seek mechanical assistance.

▼

6 If fuel is clean and running freely...
blockage may be inside carburettor. Carefully remove top and then main jet and float. Clear main jet and clean out float bowl. Be careful not to interfere with float level. Replace parts and try engine again.

Overheating in a water-cooled engine

(Occurs when coolant level falls or circulation is interrupted. Dash gauge gives warning, but vehicle also will lose power.)

1 Stop vehicle. Do not remove radiator cap. Check hoses and hose connections for signs of leakage, or steam if system is boiling. Any identified leak can be cured temporarily with spare hoses or binding with cloth tape.

▼

2 If no sign of leakage...
after about 10 minutes and holding radiator cap with a thick cloth, slowly remove cap, letting out steam under pressure at same time. Top up radiator while engine is running and car's heater is on hot setting. Do not add cold water until engine is running.

▼

3 Check again for leaks.

▼

4 If there is a slow drip from radiator core itself...
fix with an internal chemical sealant or externally with an epoxy filler or adhesive.

▼

5 If no leak is apparent...
check fanbelt for tension. It may be slipping and not driving water pump. If so, tighten by releasing bolts on generator/alternator and increasing tension and re-tightening.

▼

**6 If you cannot account for overheating by any of the preceding, you may have a failed water-pump, a blocked system, a failed pressure cap or a combination of all three. Seek help as soon as possible, but you may drive on if you can continue topping up.

Child's **PLAY**

Everyone in the family looks forward to a holiday, but most parents dread a long car trip when children travelling in the back seat can become bored and irritable passengers.

Most children are good travellers, but there are some car journeys that are inappropriate for small children (say, under the age of 10). Usually, however, children will consider every trip an adventure and start looking forward to it for weeks ahead. A little thought and planning by parents will avoid the boredom of a long drive and ease the strain on all concerned, particularly the driver, who needs to be able to apply total concentration.

Dos and Don'ts

Several days before setting out, make a list of 'dos' and 'don'ts' for the children and explain, seriously, why their cooperation is necessary. Make it quite clear that you expect them to observe the rules because they are safety measures, and reinforce this message at the time of departure. For example:

▌ DO NOT fight or yell while the car is in motion. This distracts the driver and can cause a collision or a serious mishap, which might bring the holiday to an abrupt end.

▌ DO NOT play with door handles or locks. (Set the child-proof locks on rear doors before departure.)

▌ DO keep head, arms and hands inside the car. DO NOT lean out of the windows, ever.

▌ DO NOT unbuckle seat belts or restraints while the car is in motion.

Handy Hints

▌ Any long car trip, even with frequent stops, can be tiring. Make sure the children are as cool and comfortable as possible. Curtains (or substitutes, for example a towel) or sun screens on rear windows are advisable. Babies and pre-school children may need their security blankets or favourite soft toys. These items can save the day if the children are upset or sleepy.

▌ Pack a small bag – a cosmetic bag is ideal – along with packets of moist towelettes or a damp face cloth.

▌ Make sure your first-aid kit contains some junior aspirin and supplies of any other medication taken by the children. It is important to carry some insect repellent and sunblock, since children tend to get bitten easily, and their skin must be protected from the sun. Also bring a mosquito net to cover your baby's bassinette when you are outdoors.

▌ Make up a 'busy box' for the children to take on the trip. Use a small box – a shoe box is best – and keep it on the back seat where the children can reach it easily. Fill the box with small note-pads, crayons or felt-tipped pens (pencils break and need to be sharpened) and activity books. Choose activity books for each child's age group. Do not forget to include your children's favourite storybooks.

▌ If your car has a radio and cassette player, include some tapes of stories for entertainment, and children's songs for 'quiet times'. Music soothes and lulls children to sleep.

▌ Although your primary concern will be to keep the children happy and occupied during the car trip, it is also important to take along some games, such as Snakes and Ladders, pocket-sized video games or a pack of cards, to keep them amused in the evenings and on rainy days. Also encourage older children to keep a diary. A rubber ball and skipping rope will be welcomed by young children who enjoy playing outdoors.

▌ If you have room, breakfast trays can be used as book supports for drawing or colouring-in. If not, a clipboard will serve as well.

▌ When travelling with young children, make sure that you stop the car every hour or so, so that they can stretch their legs and let off steam. Try to stop at a park or an area with some play equipment. If it is raining, stop at a newsagent or bookshop where the children can browse and perhaps buy something to read.

▌ If children complain of feeling sick, stop the car as soon as possible and let them out for some fresh air. Sit with them for a while and persuade them

to take a sip of water before returning to the car and continuing the trip.

▌ When approaching a rest area, a garage or a small town, offer the children a toilet stop. Do not delay until they get desperate and cannot wait.

▌ Even though you plan to stop for meals and snacks on your journey, you should still pack some food and drink. Children become very hungry and thirsty when travelling and it is important that they eat little but often. Pack small snacks in their own lunch boxes. Avoid chocolate, which is messy and can make children feel sick, and potato chips which are almost as messy and encourage thirst. Avoid greasy foods. Sultanas, nuts (for older children only), bananas, grapes, cheese cubes, celery and carrot sticks, and boiled sweets are good for snacks. For lunches, pack easy-to-eat meals like chicken drumsticks or bite-size rolled-up pieces of cold meat with crackers on the side. Children can find large sandwiches difficult to handle, so remember to cut their sandwiches small. Sandwich fillings require some thought, avoid anything moist or runny.

▌ Avoid spills and breakages by buying milk or fruit juice in small cartons and making sure you have a good supply of drinking straws. If you carry drinks in a flask, take training cups for younger children. For older children use paper or styrofoam cups with tight-fitting lids and with straws, and recycle as much as possible.

▌ Have plastic bags for waste paper and empty drink cartons in the cars.

▌ When eating out, choose places that have fast service – or have meals sent to your room.

Child Restraints

Note that the law in each State and Territory is very specific when it comes to child restraints in cars. As the law differs from State to State, it is important to check with the State motoring organisation (**see:** Useful Information) when travelling with children. Under certain ages and weights, children in passenger cars are required to be seated in the rear seat, and in an approved child restraint.

Games

To while away the long hours you will spend in the car with your children, here are some games for them to play.

For younger children

▮ **Colour contest:** Each child selects one colour, then tries to spot cars of that colour. The first with ten cars wins.

▮ **Spot the mistake in the story:** Either you or an older child tells a story with obvious mistakes. For example, 'Once upon a time, there was a little boy called Goldilocks, and he visited the house of the seven dwarfs.'

▮ **Scavenger:** Make a list of 10 things you are likely to come across during your trip. For example: farmhouse, bus stop, cow, lamb, chemist shop, woman with a hat. Ask the children to spot them, one at a time. Older children cross the objects off the list as they are seen.

▮ **Alphabet game:** Select a letter and ask the children to spot as many things as possible beginning with that particular letter of the alphabet.

For older children

▮ **Rhyme stories:** One child starts a story, and the next has to take up the story with a line that rhymes. The second child also continues the story with a line of new rhyme. For example:
1st child: 'I know a man called Sam.'
2nd child: 'He loves to eat ham.
The more he eats the more he wants.'

▮ **Cliff-hangers:** One child begins a story and stops at the most exciting part, leaving the next child to continue.

▮ **I packed my bag...** A good memory game in which each player has to name one object she or he puts into a bag. As each child takes a turn, she or he lists all the objects in order and adds a new item to the list. For example:
1st child: 'I packed my bag and put an apple in it.'
2nd child: 'I packed my bag and put an apple and a comb in it.'
3rd child: 'I packed my bag and put an apple, a comb and a key in it.'
4th child: 'I packed my bag and put an apple, a comb, a key and a ball in it.'

▮ **What am I?** This is an old favourite. One player thinks of an object or an animal and keeps it secret. The others take turns to ask questions, which must be answered only by 'Yes' or 'No', for clues to the identity of the object or animal.

▮ **Number-plate messages:** Note the letters of the number plate on a nearby car and ask the children to make up a message or conversation from them. For example:
WFL: 'What's for lunch?'

▮ **Navigation:** All you need is a spare road-map covering the route you are taking. The children can follow your progress with a coloured marker.

▮ **Word scramble:** Prepare a list of words with jumbled letters and get the children to unscramble them.

▮ **Crossword:** Draw crossword squares on several note-pads. During the trip, play the crossword game by calling out letters at random. The children write the letters in any square they wish and try to make up words.

Safety

Note the following safety hints:

Safe Swimming, Surfing

• Swim or surf only at those beaches patrolled by lifesavers.
• Swim or surf within the area indicated by the red and yellow flags. (An amber flag indicates that the surf is dangerous. A red flag and sign 'Danger – closed to bathing' indicates the beach is unsafe; do not swim or surf in this area.)
• Do not enter the water directly after a meal or under the influence of alcohol.
• If you are caught in a rip or strong current, swim diagonally across it. If you tire or cannot avoid the current, do not panic. Straighten, raise one arm as a distress signal and float until help arrives.
• If seized with a cramp, keep the affected part perfectly still, raise one arm as before and float until help arrives.

Safe Skiing

Skiing is fun, but like any sport, there is the risk of injury. It is also strenuous. If possible, train beforehand, and avoid overdoing it on the slopes. All ski resorts have instructors if you need to take lessons.

• Choose slopes that suit your ability.
• Wear clothing suited to the conditions.
• Check equipment before setting out.
• Avoid skiing alone; if you must, then tell someone where you are going.
• If lost, stay where you are; only retrace your tracks if they are very clear.

Cross-country skiing requires careful planning.
• Tell someone in authority of your intended route.
• Travel in a group.
• Take plenty of food and adequate equipment for your survival.
• Protect yourself against sunburn.
• Watch the weather.
• Be alert for signs of exposure (hypothermia): tiredness, reluctance to carry on, clumsiness, loss of judgement and collapse.

Safe Boating

• Tell someone where you are going.
• Check the weather forecast.
• Carry adequate equipment.
• Carry effective life jackets.
• Carry enough fuel and water.

• Ensure engine reliability.
• Guard against fire.
• Do not overload the craft.
• Know the boating rules and local regulations; also distress signals.
• Watch the weather.
• Do not drink alcohol while boating.

For safety, swim in a patrolled area

New South Wales

Founding State

New South Wales is a State of contrasts, covering an area of 801 428 square kilometres, with extremes of country ranging from subtropical to alpine. The State's capital, Sydney, is Australia's largest city.

In 1770 Captain Cook took possession for the British of all Australian territories east of the 135th meridian of east longitude and named them New South Wales. Today the founding State has shrunk somewhat and occupies just 10 per cent of the continent. The settlement at Sydney Cove, established as the site of a penal colony in 1788, was developed under the guiding hand of Governor Arthur Phillip. Following his departure in 1792, however, much of Phillip's initial planning was negated, owing to the influence of the infamous New South Wales Corps, until 1810 heralded the arrival of the redoubtable Governor Macquarie.

In 1813 Blaxland, Lawson and Wentworth discovered the lands to the west of the Blue Mountains. Further exploration quickly followed and settlement fanned out from Sydney. Sydney itself thrived and its citizens agitated against the stigma of the penal presence, with the result that transportation of convicts ended in 1840. The goldrushes of the 1850s swelled the population and led to much development throughout the State. In 1856, with the granting of responsible government, the founding State was well on its way.

Today New South Wales is the most populous State and its central region, around Sydney, Newcastle and Wollongong-Port Kembla, has been described as 'the heart of industrial Australia'. New South Wales produces two-thirds of the nation's black coal, and the silver-lead-zinc mines of Broken Hill are a major source of mineral wealth. Primary production is diversified and thriving – New South Wales is the nation's main wheat producer and has more than one-third of the nation's sheep population.

The State is divided naturally into four regions: the sparsely-populated western plains, which take up two-thirds of the State; the high tablelands and peaks of the Great Dividing Range; the pastoral and farming country of the Range's western slopes; and the fertile coastal region. The climate varies with the landscape: subtropical along the north coast, temperate on the south coast. The north-west has dry summers, and the high country has brisk winters with extremes of cold in the highest alpine areas. Sydney has a midsummer average of 25.7°C, a midwinter average of 15.8°C and boasts sunshine for an average of 342 days a year.

Lively and sophisticated, Sydney offers the shopping, restaurants and nightlife expected of a great cosmopolitan city, yet within a 200-kilometre radius is much of the best country in New South Wales: superb beaches, the myriad of intricate bays and inlets of Pittwater, the Hawkesbury River, Tuggerah Lakes and the breathtaking Illawarra coastline. The scenic Blue Mountains and the Jenolan Caves can be reached in a day trip. Most of the State's highways

NOT TO BE MISSED in New South Wales	Map Ref.
Berrima – historic town in the beautiful Southern Highlands	116 B6
Fossicker's Way – scenic drive from Nundle through the New England region	123 K12
Hill End – once a boom town, now a fascinating ghost town	104 A1
Hunter Valley – good food and good wine in delightful country surroundings	113
Jenolan Caves – magnificent limestone caves within a flora and fauna reserve	104 F8
Katoomba Scenic Railway – hair-raising ride down cliff face into Jamison Valley	104 H7
Riverboat Postman – an unusual way to cruise the Hawkesbury River	108 E11
Skitube – an exciting train ride through Thredbo Valley in the Snowy Mountains	118 D11
Warrumbungle National Park – spectacular scenery with gorges, rocky outcrops and freshwater springs	122 E11
Western Plains Zoo – where landscaped parklands provide natural habitats for the animals and walking trails for visitors	120 E2

Blue Mountains National Park, a major holiday destination

Mudgee, an attractive town west of the Hunter Valley

lead out from the capital. The Pacific Highway runs north via the industrial city of Newcastle and the popular resort town of Port Macquarie. Diverting inland, you can sample the products of the rich Hunter Valley vineyards, considered to be one of the most important wine-growing areas in the country. Further north, the highway passes through country that is hilly and subtropical, with irresistible golden beaches to the east and to the west the New England tablelands – high mountain and grazing country, at its best in autumn.

NEW SOUTH WALES

CALENDAR OF EVENTS

Note: The information given here was accurate at the time of printing. However, as the timing of events held annually is subject to change and some events may extend into the following month, it is best to check with the local tourism authority or event organisers to confirm the details. The calendar is not exhaustive. Most towns and regions hold sporting competitions, arts and craft exhibitions, agricultural and flower shows, music festivals and other such events annually. Details of these events are available from local tourism outlets.

JANUARY
Public holidays: New Year's Day; Australia Day. **Sydney:** Sydney Festival (includes Opera in the Park; Ferry Boat Race). **Bermagui:** Blue Water Fishing Classic. **Bombala:** Wool and Wood Festival. **Brunswick Heads:**

Fish and Chips Festival. **Byron Bay:** Arts and Music Festival. **Condobolin:** Rodeo. **Cooma:** Rodeo. **Corowa:** Federation Festival. **Culburra:** Open Fishing Carnival. **Deniliquin:** Sun Festival. **Forbes:** Jazz Festival; Flatlands Hang-Gliding. **Gunnedah:** National Tomato Competition. **Guyra:** Lamb and Potato Festival (includes Hydrangea Festival). **Lake Cargelligo:** Bowling Festival. **Nelligen:** Country Music Festival. **Newcastle:** National Maritime Regatta. **Parkes:** Elvis Revival. **Picton:** Rodeo. **Port Macquarie:** Golden Lure Tournament. **Quirindi:** Wallabadah New Year's Day Cup Meeting. **Tamworth:** Australasian Country Music Festival. **Taree:** Aquatic Festival. **The Entrance:** Australia Day Family Concert and Fireworks. **Thredbo:** Blues Festival. **Tumbarumba:** New Year's Day Rodeo.

Walcha: Australia Day Breakfast in the Park. **Wingham:** Rodeo.

FEBRUARY
Sydney: Gay and Lesbian Mardi Gras. **Adaminaby:** Race Meeting. **Albury:** Festival of Sport. **Bega:** Far South Coast National Show. **Bermagui:** International Dog Show. **Berry:** Agricultural Show. **Camden:** Heritage Wine and Food Fair. **Cessnock:** Vintage Festival. **Gunning:** Agricultural Show. **Katooma:** Blue Mountains Folk Festival. **Kiama:** Jazz Festival; Seven-a-Side Rugby Competition. **Nelson Bay:** Game-fishing Tournament. **Orange:** Banjo Paterson Festival. **Rylstone-Kandos:** Show. **Temora:** Golden Gift. **Tweed Heads:** Tweed Valley Triathlon. **Walcha:** Agricultural Show. **Wentworth Falls:** Regatta Day.

MARCH
Albury: Festival of Sport (contd). **Alstonville:**

Tibouchina Festival. **Armidale:** Autumn Festival. **Bega:** Cheese Pro-Am. **Bermagui:** Tag and Release Game-fishing Tournament. **Blayney:** Agricultural Show. **Eden:** Amateur Fish Club Competition. **Grenfell:** Picnic Races. **Hay:** Riverina Stud Merino Field Days. **Inverell:** Art Exhibition. **Jamberoo:** Illawarra Folk Festival. **Jindabyne:** Strzelecki Polish Festival. **Lismore:** Square Dance Festival. **Medlow Bath:** Blue Mountains Herb Fest. **Moss Vale:** Agricultural Show. **Murrumburrah:** Grain Festival. **Narooma:** Festival. **Narrandera:** John O'Brien Folk Festival. **Newcastle:** Surfest; Beaumont Street Jazz Arts Fair. **Orange:** Banjo Paterson Festival (contd). **Raymond Terrace:** Oz Ski. **Robertson:** Agricultural Show. **Thirlmere:** Festival of Steam. **Tocumwal:** Pioneer Skills Day. **Wagga Wagga:** Australian

Veterans Games. **Wauchope:** Lasiandra Festival. **Wellington:** The Wellington Boot; Vintage Fair. **Wingham:** Agricultural Show. **Wyong:** Festival of Arts. **Yass:** Agricultural Show.

EASTER
Public holidays: Good Friday; Easter Monday. **Sydney:** Royal Easter Show. **Balranald:** Homebush Gymkhana. **Bermagui:** Victorian Game-fishing Tournament; Four Winds Easter Concerts. **Berridale:** Fair. **Bingara:** Gold Rush Festival; Easterfish. **Brunswick Heads:** Blessing of the Fleet; Fishing Competition. **Byron Bay:** East Coast Blues Festival. **Canowindra:** Model Aircraft Championships. **Coonabarabran:** Carnival. **Deniliquin:** Jazz Festival. **Gilgandra:** Goat Races; Rodeo. **Grenfell:** Guinea Pig Races. **Griffith:** Festival of Griffith. **Holbrook:** Ultra Fly-In (biennial, even-

numbered years). **Huskisson:** White Sands Carnival. **Leeton:** Sunrice Country Festival (biennial, even-numbered years). **Lightning Ridge:** Great Goat Races. **Maclean:** Highland Gathering. **Moree:** Carnival of Sport. **Moulamein:** Yabby Races. **Narooma:** Tilba Festival. **Parkes:** Sports Festival. **Tocumwal:** Festival of Family Fun. **Ulladulla:** Blessing of the Fleet.

APRIL
Public holiday: Anzac Day. **Sydney:** AJC Autumn Racing Carnival (includes Sydney Cup Week). Australian International Dragon Boat Festival. **Batlow:** Apple Harvest Festival. **Bourke:** Fred Hollows Foot Race (to Sydney). **Braidwood:** Heritage Festival. **Brewarrina:** Agricultural Show. **Bundanoon:** Bundanoon is Brigadoon Annual Highland Gathering. **Campbelltown:** Show.

The State's extreme north-west is still frontier territory and has limited tourist facilities. If you enjoy getting off the beaten track, and if you and your car are well prepared, the region can be very rewarding. Highlights include the spectacular Nandewar and Warrumbungle ranges, Lightning Ridge and the green oasis of Broken Hill, the State's storehouse of mineral wealth. The best time for touring is between March and November when the temperature is relatively cool and the winter days are clear and dry, but remember, if you break down in the 'outback' areas, stay with your vehicle.

Many relics of the early goldmining and agricultural history of the State can be seen in and around such inland towns as Bathurst, Dubbo, Wellington, Griffith and Wagga Wagga. Towards the Victorian border, where the Murray River forms a natural State boundary, irrigation greens the countryside and supports many vineyards and citrus groves. The Murray River towns retain much of the history of the riverboat era when the Murray was a major transport route.

CLIMATE GUIDE

SYDNEY

	J	F	M	A	M	J	J	A	S	O	N	D
Maximum °C	26	26	25	22	19	17	16	18	20	22	24	25
Minimum °C	19	19	17	15	11	9	8	9	11	13	16	17
Rainfall mm	104	113	134	126	121	131	101	80	69	79	83	78
Raindays	12	12	13	12	12	12	10	10	11	12	11	12

COFFS HARBOUR REGION

	J	F	M	A	M	J	J	A	S	O	N	D
Maximum °C	27	27	26	24	21	19	19	20	22	23	25	26
Minimum °C	19	19	18	15	11	9	7	8	11	14	16	18
Rainfall mm	197	221	241	180	161	119	73	90	67	97	125	150
Raindays	16	15	17	13	11	10	8	8	9	12	11	14

ALPINE REGION

	J	F	M	A	M	J	J	A	S	O	N	D
Maximum °C	21	21	18	14	10	6	5	6	9	13	16	19
Minimum °C	7	7	6	2	0	-3	-4	-2	-1	2	3	5
Rainfall mm	110	90	122	131	183	146	144	184	200	220	161	113
Raindays	11	10	11	13	15	16	16	17	17	17	15	12

MERIMBULA REGION

	J	F	M	A	M	J	J	A	S	O	N	D
Maximum °C	24	25	23	21	19	16	16	17	18	20	21	23
Minimum °C	15	15	14	11	8	6	4	5	7	9	12	14
Rainfall mm	80	71	95	71	70	64	37	45	52	77	85	65
Raindays	10	9	10	9	10	9	7	9	10	11	12	11

Condobolin: Centre Trek. **Dungog:** Rodeo. **Gulgong:** Foundation Day (biennial, odd-numbered years). **Holbrook:** Beef Fest. **Kempsey:** Agricultural Show. **Macksville:** Nambucca River Show. **Maitland:** Hunter Valley Steamfest; Indoor Equestrian Dressage Championships. **Molong:** Cabonne Country Day. **Murrurundi:** Sheepdog Trials. **Muswellbrook:** Agricultural Show. **Narrabri:** Agricultural Show. **Nyngan:** Anzac Day Race Meeting. **Shellharbour:** Sunshine Festival. **Taree:** Taree and District Eisteddfod. **Tenterfield:** Oracles of the Bush. **Tumut:** Festival of the Falling Leaf. **Wee Waa:** Agricultural Show. **Wentworth Falls:** Autumn Festival.

MAY
Casino: Beef Week Festival. **Cobar:** Agricultural Show. **Dubbo:** Agricultural Show.

Gilgandra: Agricultural Show. **Glen Innes:** Celtic Festival. **Hay:** Sheep Show. **Lismore:** Trinity Arts Festival. **Macksville:** Egg-throwing Championships. **Merriwa:** Polocrosse Carnival. **Nyngan:** Agricultural Show. **Scone:** Horse Festival. **Sussex Inlet:** Fishing Carnival. **Tamworth:** Gold Cup Race Meeting. **Taree:** Taree and District Eisteddfod (contd). **Thredbo:** Jazz Festival. **Tumut:** Festival of the Falling Leaf (contd). **Warialda:** Agricultural Show. **Warren:** Golden Fleece Race Day. **White Cliffs:** Gymkhana and Rodeo. **Windsor:** Bridge to Bridge Power Boat Classic. **Wingham:** Manning Valley Beef Week. **Woy Woy:** Motor Show. **Yanco:** Murrumbidgee Farm Fair.

JUNE
Public holiday: Queen's Birthday. **Sydney:** Film Festival; Food and Wine Festival (at Manly). **Blue Mountains:** Yulefest. **Bourke:** Bourke to B-Bash. **Bryon Bay:** Whale Watch Weekend. **Coonamble:** Rodeo. **Dubbo:** Eisteddfod. **Grenfel :** Henry Lawson Festival of Arts. **Gulgong:** Henry Lawson Festival. **Katoomba:** Winter Magic Festival. **Kiama:** Folk Music Festival. **Lake Cargelligo:** Blue Water Art and Craft Festival. **Lightning Ridge:** Pistol Shoot. **Manilla:** Lake Keepit Kool Sailing Regatta. **Merimbula:** Jazz Festival. **Merriwa:** Festival of Fleeces. **Nambucca Heads:** Ken Howard Memorial Bowls Competition. **Parkes:** Central West Jazz Triduum. **Snowy Mountains Region:** Opening of Ski Season (long weekend). **Southern Highlands Region:** Christmas in June. **Tibooburra:** Festival (sometimes held in July). **Tocumwal:** Country Craft Fiesta.

JULY
Boggabri: Wean Picnic

Races. **Blue Mountains:** Yulefest (contd). **Iluka:** Amateur Fishing Classic. **Kempsey:** Off-road Race. **Kyogle:** Rodeo. **Lightning Ridge:** Opal and Gem Expo. **Port Macquarie:** Lifestyle. **Stroud:** International Brick and Rolling-pin Throwing. **Pitt Town:** Fun Run. **Urunga:** Bowling Club Carnival. **White Cliffs:** Royal Flying Doctor Ball.

AUGUST
Sydney: Sun City to Surf (fun run to Bondi Beach). **Bellingen:** Jazz Festival. **Blue Mountains:** Yulefest (contd). **Casino:** Gold Cup. **Condobolin:** Agricultural Show. **Cootamundra:** Wattle Festival. **Evans Head:** Bowling Carnival. **Forster:** Australian Veteran Cycling Championships. **Gunnedah:** Ag Quip Agricultural Field Days. **Lismore:** Street Festival. **Menindee:** Burke and Wills Fishing Challenge. **Murwillumbah:** Banana

Festival. **Nambucca Heads:** VW Spectacular (biennial, odd-numbered years). **Narrandera:** Camellia Show. **Newcastle:** Jazz Festival. **Nundle:** Camp Drafting and Dog Trials. **Shellharbour:** Shellcove Aquatic and Outdoor Expo. **Snowy Mountains Region:** FIS Australian Championships; Continental Cup (both snow skiing). **Tweed Heads:** Bowls Tournament. **Wellington:** Eisteddfod. **Wollongong:** South Coast Youth Arts and Skills Festival.

SEPTEMBER
Sydney: Rugby League Grand Final; Festival of the Winds (kite flying, held at Bondi). **Armidale:** Arts Festival. **Barham:** Pro-Am Golf Tournament. **Batlow:** Daffodil Show. **Bega:** Festival. **Bingara:** Veterans Golf Tournament. **Blue Mountains (Blaxland, Glenbrook, Leura):** Legacy Gardens Festival. **Bourke:**

Mateship Festival. **Bowral:** Tulip Time Festival; District Art Society Exhibition. **Broke:** Village Fair. **Broken Hill:** Silver City Show. **Camden:** Camden Park House Open Weekend. **Canowindra:** Agricultural Show. **Coffs Harbour:** Garden Competition. **Cowra:** World Peace Day. **Dungog:** Spring Festival. **Finley:** Agricultural Show. **Forbes:** Show Day. **Glen Innes:** Minerama Gem Festival. **Gloucester:** Mountain Man Triathlon. **Gosford:** Springtime Flora Festival. **Gunnedah:** Vintage Car Club Swap Meet. **Henty:** Machinery Field Days. **Kempsey:** Country Music Festival. **Lake Cargelligo:** Lake Show. **Lismore:** Cup Day. **Maclean:** Cane Harvest Festival. **Merimbula:** Country Music Festival. **Mudgee:** Wine Festival. **Mullumbimby:** Chincogan Fiesta. **Murrumburrah:** Agricultural Show. **Nambucca Heads:** Septemberfest Carnival.

Shoalhaven River at Nowra on the Illawarra Coast

The Princes Highway leads south from Sydney down the Illawarra Coast, famous for its panoramic views, excellent beaches and numerous national parks. Good fishing of all kinds can be enjoyed here and there is splendid bushwalking and climbing in the nearby foothills of the Southern Highlands. Nearby, the Snowy Mountains area includes well-equipped snow resorts, the natural grandeur of Kosciusko National Park and the wonder of the Snowy Mountains hydro-electric scheme.

Linked by a network of freeways, highways and roads, New South Wales offers a wide variety of regions to explore.

NEW SOUTH WALES

CALENDAR OF EVENTS

Nimbin: Show. **Nundle:** Camp Drafting and Dog Trials (contd). **Richmond:** Hawkesbury District Orchid Spring Show. **Stroud:** Rodeo. **Toukley:** Azalea Festival. **Wagga Wagga:** National Festival of the Voice. **West Wyalong:** Agricultural Show. **Yamba:** Family Fishing Festival.

OCTOBER
Public Holiday: Labour Day. **Armidale:** Arts Festival (contd). **Bathurst:** Bathurst 1000 Car Races. **Bega:** Bega Valley Art Awards. **Bellingen:** World Music, Dance and Art Festival. **Berrigan:** Agricultural Show. **Bingara:** Country Music Talent Quest. **Blue Mountains:** (Blaxland, Glenbrook, Leura): Legacy Gardens Festival (contd). **Bourke:** Back o' Bourke Stampede. **Bowral:** Tulip Time Festival (contd). **Broken Hill:** Country Music Festival. **Bundanoon:** Gullies Gallop Fun Run. **Casino:** Agricultural Show. **Cessnock:** Jazz Concerts.

Cobar: Back to Cobar. **Condobolin:** Art Exhibition. **Cooma:** Cooma Fest. **Coonabarabran:** Cooma Cup Racing Carnival. **Coonamble:** Gold Cup Race Meeting; Western Sandfly Supercross Motorbike Race. **Cowra:** Sakura Matsuri; Japanese Cultural Exhibition. **Dubbo:** Festival of the Red Earth. **Eden:** Whale Festival. **Forster:** Oyster Festival. **Gilgandra:** Coo-ee Festival. **Gosford:** Mangrove Mountain District Country Fair; City Arts Festival. **Grafton:** Jacaranda Festival; Bridge to Bridge Ski Race. **Grenfell:** Iris Festival. **Griffith:** Festival of Gardens. **Gulgong:** Heritage Weekend. **Gundagai:** Spring Flower Show. **Inverell:** Sapphire City Floral Festival. **Kundabung:** Australasian Bull-riding Titles. **Kiama:** Seaside Festival. **Kyogle:** Show. **Leura:** Garden Festival; Village Fair; Greystanes Spring Gardens. **Lismore:** Folk

Festival; North Coast National Show. **Lithgow:** National Go-Kart Championships. **Macksville:** Pro-Ag Field Day. **Manilla:** Festival of Spring Flowers. **Milton:** Settlers Fair. **Moonan Flat:** Jazz Festival. **Murrurundi:** Bushman's Carnival. **Muswellbrook:** Spring Wine Festival. **Nambucca Heads:** Show'n'Shine Hot Rod Exhibition. **Narrabri:** Spring Festival. **Narrandera:** Tree-mendous Festival. **Narromine:** Festival of Sport. **Nowra:** Spring Festival. **Parkes:** Country Music Spectacular. **Port Macquarie:** Discovery Concert (held 13 km w at Cassegrain Winery). **Raymond Terrace:** Twin Rivers Festival. **Singleton:** Festival of Wine and Roses. **Stroud:** Rodeo (contd). **Tathra:** Amateur Fishing Competition. **Tenterfield:** Federation Festival; Spring Wine Festival; Highland Gathering. **Tibooburra:** Gymkhana and Rodeo. **Toukley:** Cycle Classic.

Walgett: Weekend Extravaganza. **Wauchope:** Colonial Carnival. **West Wyalong:** Highways Festival (biennial, odd-numbered years). **Windsor:** Bridge to Bridge Canoe Classic. **Wyong:** Cycle Classic. **Yamba:** Family Fishing Festival (contd).

NOVEMBER
Adaminaby: Trout Festival. **Armidale:** Arts Festival (contd). **Barraba:** Fine Music Festival. **Batemans Bay:** Clyde River Carnival. **Blackheath:** Rhododendron Festival. **Braidwood:** Music at the Creek. **Bulahdelah:** Show and Rodeo. **Campbelltown:** Festival of Fisher's Ghost. **Cooma:** Cooma Fest (contd); Snowy Mountains Chainsaw Classic. **Glen Innes:** Land of the Beardies Bush Festival. **Glenbrook:** Spring Festival. **Grafton:** Jacaranda Festival (contd); Bridge to Bridge Sailing Classic. **Grenfell:** Grenfell Guineas. **Gundagai:** Dog on the Tuckerbox Festival.

Guyra: Rodeo. **Holbrook:** Agricultural Show. **Jindabyne:** Snowy Mountains Trout Festival. **Kyogle:** Festival; Golf Tournament. **Lake Windamere** (19 km w of Rylstone): Fishing Festival. **Lithgow:** Festival of the Valley (biennial, even-numbered years). **Macksville:** Macksville Gift. **Merimbula:** Spring Carnival. **Moree:** Golden Grain Festival. **Picton:** Village Fair. **Queanbeyan:** Queanbeyan Celebrations; Agricultural Show. **Scone:** Rodeo. **Stroud:** Branch Picnic Races. **Tenterfield:** Australian Line-dancing Exhibition. **The Channon:** Music Bowl Live Band Concert. **The Entrance:** Celtic Festival. **Tumbarumba:** Heritage Week. **Wagga Wagga:** Festival. **Warren:** Cotton Cup Racing Carnival. **Wentworth:** Wentworth Cup. **Windsor:** Bridge to Bridge Water Ski Classic. **Wingham:** Rodeo. **Woy Woy:** Oyster and Wine

Festival. **Yass:** Rodeo. **Young:** National Cherry Festival.

DECEMBER
Public holidays: Christmas Day; Boxing Day. **Sydney:** World Series Cricket; Carols by Candlelight (in the Domain); Sydney–Hobart Yacht Race. **Abercrombie Caves:** Carols in the Caves. **Adelong:** Boat Regatta. **Balranald:** Christmas Festival. **Bingara:** Country Christmas Carnival. **Corowa:** National Skydiving Championships. **Jindabyne:** Lake Jindabyne Sailing Club Hobie Cat Races. **Moulamein:** Horseracing Cup. **Nundle:** Camp Drafting and Dog Trials. **Queanbeyan:** Country Music Festival. **The Entrance:** Tuggerah Lakes Mardi Gras Festival. **Wollongong:** Junior Surf Lifesaving Championships. **Young:** National Cherry Festival (contd).

SYDNEY

Australia's First City

The Opera House and Harbour Bridge

Sydney, a thriving harbourside metropolis populated by almost 4 million people, is Australia's largest and best-known city. It was the first site of European settlement on the Australian continent – one vastly different from today's cosmopolitan showcase.

Command of the first colonial expedition was entrusted to Captain Arthur Phillip. On his arrival at Botany Bay in 1788, Phillip was not impressed with this proposed settlement site and decided to look further afield. On 26 January he sailed into a beautiful natural harbour, where he dropped anchor, named the area Sydney Cove, hoisted the flag and proclaimed the colony of New South Wales.

Sydney Cove, now Circular Quay, saw those First Fleet convicts toiling to clear a site for the settlement that was to become the city of Sydney. Testament to their endeavours is **The Rocks**, an area of winding lanes and sandstone buildings situated near the Harbour Bridge. An integral part of Sydney's history, providing rich memories of how the city was forged, today The Rocks features outdoor cafes, art and craft centres, weekend markets, museums, curio shops and rollicking pubs. Nearby the **Sydney Observatory**, a group of colonial buildings, houses a

museum of astronomy with some hands-on displays.

In the sandstone building alongside Circular Quay is the **Museum of Contemporary Art**, which houses splendid collections of Australian and Aboriginal art. It is Australia's first major museum dedicated to the contemporary visual arts.

Sydney Cove has remained the gateway to Australia, situated in calm waters some 11 kilometres from the towering bluffs that flank the harbour mouth: **North Head** and **South Head**. Both headlands command a breathtaking view back along the harbour to the shimmering city skyline and its highlights the **Harbour Bridge**, the **Opera House** and **Sydney Tower**.

While these three structures may be the city's best known landmarks, it is **Sydney Harbour** itself that is the city's pride and joy. Its innumerable waterways extend in all directions, the product of a drowned valley system that finds bottom in the depths of the Pacific Ocean. Its surface is a glistening blue aquatic playground for Sydneysiders.

With the harbour as its heart, the city proper is bounded by water to the north and west, and fringed to the east by the extensive green parklands of the Botanic

Gardens and the Domain. Hyde Park, in the middle of the city, provides areas of tranquil, verdant delight in a bustling central business district. Within these boundaries, Sydney is an exciting and rewarding city to explore.

In line with Sydney's boundaries, the city's bus services terminate at three main points: **Circular Quay** in the north, **Wynyard Square** in the west and, in the south, **Central Railway Station**, the grand, domed building that is the outlet for all country and interstate train services. An underground train service travels on the ground outside the central business area and connects the city with outlying suburbs. The **Sydney Explorer** tourist bus loops around 28 kilometres of the city daily, stopping at 27 leading attractions and allowing passengers to alight and rejoin following buses at will.

Where Phillip's First Fleet dropped anchor, the shoreline has become a neat U-shaped area, with wharves on either arm and harbour-ferry terminals at its base. **Circular Quay** was built in the nineteenth century to handle overseas shipping and, in the final great era of sail, the days of the superb clipper ships, Sydney Cove was a forest of majestic masts. Today it boasts a huge international shipping terminal with anchorage for ships of 40 000 tonnes and is the hub of Sydney's water traffic: its ferries, JetCats, cruise boats and water taxis. Circular Quay is a bright, colourful part of town where buskers play for the entertainment of strolling lunchtime shoppers, and where there are a variety of restaurants offering superb harbour views while you dine.

Located on an island in the heart of the harbour is **Fort Denison**, built during the Crimean War to discourage invasion. The fort is now a fascinating museum; guided tours depart daily from Circular Quay.

Across the water from the Quay, the Harbour Bridge disgorges its congested traffic into Sydney's mini-twin **North Sydney**, a high-rise, high-density satellite of the 1960s. The **Harbour Tunnel**, which runs beneath the harbour, also links both business districts. **Mary MacKillop Place** museum, commemorating the life of Australia's first saint, is in Mount Street, North Sydney.

Under the shadow of the Bridge on the city side of the harbour is **Pier One**, a complex of shops, restaurants (specialising in seafood) and a tavern decorated in Old Sydney style. It was once a disembarkation point for immigrants. Further along is **Pier Four**, which has been converted into a permanent home for the Sydney Theatre Company. The Wharf Theatre is the venue for the Sydney Theatre Company's year-round calendar, while the Wharf Restaurant commands one of Sydney's best views.

Standing sentinel at the eastern end of Sydney Cove is the **Sydney Opera House**, a building whose aspect is breathtaking against the blue of the harbour. Its white arches seem to rise out of the water like sails scudding up from the waves. At weekends, the Opera House promenade is the venue for several outdoor markets and a variety of free outdoor concerts.

The Quay is typically waterfront. **Circular Quay Plaza** and the Rocks area are the home of some of the city's oldest pubs, many of which are early openers, catering for night-shift workers from 6 a.m. Detached from these, and from its high-rise neighbours, the old **Customs House,** in the centre of the Plaza, continues to preside over the scene, a monument in sandstone to nineteenth-century Sydney. Its time-honoured clock is surrounded by tridents and dolphins, and the coat of arms above the entrance is one of the best stone carvings in Australia.

Immediately behind Circular Quay Plaza, a series of maritime-flavoured laneways and narrow streets culminates in **Macquarie Place** and its sheltering canopies of giant Moreton Bay fig trees. An anchor and a cannon from Phillip's flagship HMS *Sirius* are preserved in the park, which they share with gas lamps, an 1857 drinking fountain, an ornate Victorian 'gents' (classified by the National Trust) and a weathered obelisk from which distances to all points in the colony used to be measured. In the surrounding laneways look for one of the

world's smallest churches, the tiny **Marist Chapel** at 5 Young Street, run by the Marist Fathers. Further east on the corner of Bridge and Phillip streets is the impressive **Museum of Sydney**, on the site of the first Government House, an innovative contemporary museum examining Sydney from 1788 to 1850.

The present **Government House** is an imposing neo-Gothic sandstone mansion of the 1840s, not open to the public but easily admired from the adjacent Botanic Gardens. Between the entrances to both, the fortress-like lines of the **NSW Conservatorium of Music** successfully conceal the building's origin as stables, designed in 1816 by the renowned convict architect Francis Greenway, and completed in 1821 as part of an earlier Government House on the site. During teaching terms there are free lunchtime concerts here on Wednesdays and Fridays.

The **Royal Botanic Gardens**, more than 24 hectares of formal landscaping, occupy a prime position on the shores of Farm Cove. Originally dedicated in 1816, today they are a perennial landscape of colour where more than 17 000 native and exotic plants bloom throughout the year. In one small corner there is a stone wall, over 200 years old, marking the original plot of the colony's first vegetable garden, planted at the direction of Governor Phillip. Within the gardens the Tropical Centre re-creates Australian and international tropical ecosystems. The National Herbarium displays plants collected and dried by Sir Joseph Banks, who accompanied Captain Cook on his voyage of discovery in 1770. Free guided walks of the gardens are available at 10.30 a.m. daily, except public holidays.

An imposing sandstone building on the eastern side of Macquarie Street, the **State Library of New South Wales**, overlooks the Botanic Gardens. In the library's Mitchell wing is one of the world's great repositories of national archives and memorabilia, a priceless collection of Australiana and historical records. The new wing of the State Library is sited between the old building and Parliament House. This high-tech building features the latest technology, including study aids for the disabled. A brochure for a self-guide tour of the library is available.

Adjacent to the Library are two of Sydney's oldest buildings: the **New South Wales Parliament** which has regular guided tours when Parliament is not

City on the Water

In the arid continent of Australia, Sydney is a cosmopolitan, subtropical oasis, set around the bays and inlets of Port Jackson, and extending north and south along the coast. The foreshore stretching over 250 kilometres is scalloped with white sandy beaches, while the South Pacific Ocean caresses the shores of sheltered coves and thunders in on some of the best surf beaches in the country. The climate is mild, the water warm enough for swimming most of the year.

Australia's best-known city sits majestically on the shores of its beautiful natural **harbour** – a harbour bustling with commuter ferries and JetCats, small tugs and massive container ships, and visiting luxury liners. Sydneysiders are rightly proud of their city. It is the cradle of Australian history and, industrially and commercially, the focal point of the South Pacific. The people are relaxed yet sophisticated. The water that surrounds them has a major impact on their lifestyle; many office workers commute by ferry and spend their lunch hours by the foreshore, enjoying the cool sea breeze in hot summer months. At weekends Sydneysiders collectively stretch out on the beaches or set sail.

Sydney owes a lot to its harbour. Its first European discovery was in 1770 by Captain James Cook, who named it Port Jackson, and in 1788 Captain Arthur Phillip declared it 'the finest harbour in the world'. Today, due to its vast size, its protection from storms, its uniform depth, small tides, freedom from silting, and lack of navigational hazards, together with its wharves conveniently situated close to the city's business centre – it is arguably the world's best natural harbour. It embraces more than 55 square kilometres of water and caters for more than 6000 vessels each year.

At weekends sailing boats, speedboats, yachts and launches join the busy harbour traffic. Sydney Harbour is also the venue for many boating classics, including the Sydney to Hobart Yacht Race which starts on Boxing Day, and the Festival of Sydney's Ferry Boat Race in January.

Between Sydney's two most famous landmarks, the Opera House and the Harbour Bridge, is Sydney Cove – the birthplace of the city, State and nation. In 1788, Captain Arthur Phillip chose this inlet for the first colony because of its deep bay and running stream of fresh water. Its foreshore,

Ferry passing the Opera House on Sydney's beautiful harbour

now **Circular Quay**, in the heart of the city, is dwarfed by skyscrapers, with the City Circle Railway passing immediately overhead and the Cahill Expressway forming a canopy over the railway.

Circular Quay is the nucleus of a network of ferry services that links the city to its waterfront suburbs (Manly, Mosman, Neutral Bay, Balmain and Parramatta), beaches, Darling Harbour and Taronga Zoo. Most ferry routes pass close to **Fort Denison**, also known as Pinchgut, where convicts were once imprisoned on a diet of bread and water. Today this fortress island can be hired for special functions. It is possible also to hire an aqua cab (water taxi) to take you to any point around the harbour.

The ferry service to **Manly** dates back to 1854. This waterfront suburb took as its slogan around the turn of the century: 'seven miles from Sydney and a thousand miles from care', and it stands as true today. Named by Captain Phillip after the 'manly' behaviour of the Aborigines, Manly can be reached by a 35-minute ferry ride or a 15-minute journey in a JetCat. Each summer, Manly's population doubles, thanks to the mild climate and the popularity of the harbour and ocean beaches nearby.

Between Grotto Point and Middle Head is the fishing and boating haven of **Middle Harbour**. Here the Spit Bridge opens for vessels visiting the area's many bays, small coves and beaches.

Along the **northern shore** of Port Jackson are several well-known beaches. These include Chowder Bay, where American whalers concocted their famous dish using Sydney rock oysters; Neutral Bay, where ships from foreign countries once anchored; and the picturesque Mosman Bay and Chinamans Beach.

On the **southern foreshore**, there are almost 100 hectares of parkland in the Domain and Royal Botanic Gardens. City workers flock to the gardens for a quiet lunch break, a stroll or jog along the foreshore, or a quick game of cricket.

Sydney is also renowned for its fine **surf beaches**. The scenic northern beaches stretch from Manly to Palm Beach. To the south, Bondi, just 7 kilometres from the General Post Office, is the most popular and most famous metropolitan beach. Coogee and Cronulla are also popular. The smaller beaches at Clovelly, Tamarama and Bronte offer quiet seclusion. Sydney's 34 surfing beaches are patrolled by volunteer lifesavers, who stage colourful large-scale carnivals throughout the summer. Lady Jane and Reef beaches on the harbour cater for nude sunbathers. Surfers should take heed of warning flags placed on the sand, which mark the areas safe for surfing on that day. Rock pools are abundant and are ideal for children. It is not advisable to swim in the harbour.

The 'city on the water' has a pronounced maritime character, its appearance dominated by the many bays and inlets of its harbour, and its white sandy beaches.

The Strand Arcade

sitting, and the **Colonial Mint** (1816) which houses the fascinating **Sydney Mint Museum**. The museum tells the story of gold in Australia and there is a shop selling a range of gold items and coins. As well, there is a magnificently designed collection of jewellery, ornaments and trophies inspired by Australian flora and fauna.

Parliament House and the former Mint were once a part of the original colonial hospital, which was known as the Rum Hospital. When there was a shortage of coinage in the colony and rum was the currency, the builders were paid in casks of the spirit. Standing between them, in all its dour Victorian splendour, is the **Sydney Hospital**, a city institution, which opened in 1879. Behind the buildings, the **Domain** – location for such annual events as Opera in the Park (part of the Sydney Festival held in January) and Carols by Candlelight – separates the rear of Macquarie Street from the **Art Gallery of New South Wales**. During January, when the annual **Sydney Festival** is in full swing, the Domain becomes a giant outdoor concert hall where hundreds of thousands of Sydneysiders and tourists flock to hear jazz, opera and symphonies in the park.

Macquarie Street leads to **Queens Square**, arguably one of Sydney's most elegant precincts. The square is encircled by Hyde Park, the towering **Law Courts** building and Francis Greenway's pre-1820 masterpieces, **St James's Church** and **Hyde Park Barracks** (now a social history museum with unique relics from Sydney's convict origins). Flowing harmoniously on from the old barracks are two great neo-Gothic triumphs of the nineteenth century: the **Registrar-General's Building** and **St Mary's Roman Catholic Cathedral**.

Hyde Park is divided in two by Park Street. One half is dominated by the **Archibald Fountain** – a legacy to the city from the first publisher of the *Bulletin* – and the other by a **Pool of Remembrance** and the **Anzac War Memorial**. At night, Hyde Park's avenues of huge fig trees are lit with thousands of fairy lights. On the park's eastern boundary, in College Street, stand the **Australian Museum**; one of Sydney's oldest colleges, **Sydney Grammar School**; and two high-rise neighbours, the **Returned Servicemen's League** headquarters and the **NSW Police Department** administration building.

On the city side of Hyde Park runs **Elizabeth Street**. No longer the major city artery it once was, it now serves as a vital, almost continuous, bus feeder route, particularly where two underground railway stations, **St James** and **Museum**, disgorge. It is still, however, noteworthy for one of Sydney's historic buildings, the **Great Synagogue**, and for the headquarters of one of Australia's great retailing empires, **David Jones**. David Jones, with its liveried doormen, marble floors and title of 'the most beautiful store in the world', stands on the corner of Elizabeth Street and Market Street and is a Sydney landmark. 'I'll see you on DJ's corner' was, and still is, a regular Sydney rendezvous. From here, Elizabeth Street continues north to the spacious semicircle of **Chifley Square**, named in honour of former Prime Minister J.B. Chifley.

In a wedge-shaped sector of blocks made by Bent, Bridge, Young, Phillip and Loftus streets stand the office buildings of colonial New South Wales, constructed from Sydney's superb Hawkesbury sandstone, on which the city is built. Mostly late Victorian, the buildings still serve their original purpose as housing for State government departments.

The disordered pattern of the surrounding streets is a product of the complete lack of planning in the period after Governor Phillip's recall from Sydney. Bullock tracks and cow paths determined the town plan until Governor Macquarie attempted to impose order some 20 years later. Today the result contributes to Sydney's charm.

Castlereagh Street, parallel to Elizabeth Street, also loses itself in the tangle of colonial office blocks above the Quay. In **Martin Place**, a traffic-free plaza running from Elizabeth Street through Castlereagh and Pitt streets and finishing at George Street, lunchtime

SYDNEY ON FOOT

There are numerous walking tours around Sydney and the following list is a small selection. All are guided tours organised by private companies; bookings are essential and a charge applies.

- **Aboriginal Australia:** Aboriginal exhibits at the Art Gallery and the Australian Museum.
- **Art galleries:** tour of Sydney's contemporary art scene.
- **Behind the scenes:** of the Australian Broadcasting Commission, the Law Courts, NSW Parliament House and other institutions.
- **China Town:** discover this colourful area of Sydney.
- **Coffee houses of Darlinghurst:** guided tour with plenty of caffeine!
- **Fish Markets:** see fish auctions and eat fish and chips.
- **Kings Cross:** discover the historical side of this somewhat raffish area.
- **The Rocks:** numerous guided tours available.
- **Sydney city and Opera House:** includes the city's major attractions.
- **Sydney Harbour Bush Walk:** follows shoreline around Middle Harbour.

For further information contact Countrylink NSW Travel Centre, 11–31 York St, Sydney; 13 2077.

office workers attend outdoor concerts in the amphitheatre, flower sellers hawk their wares from colourful barrows, and cut-price theatre and concert tickets are on sale at a Halftix booth. The **GPO** sits in Martin Place, between Pitt and George streets. South of Martin Place the character of the area changes from a merchant belt to a shopping mecca. The **MLC Centre** dominates almost a whole block and contains suites of luxurious offices, and at ground level, some exclusive shops, mostly jewellers and fashionable boutiques. The complex also houses a cinema (the Dendy) with bar and bistro, and, for the theatre-goer, Sydney's prestigious **Theatre Royal**. The King and Castlereagh streets crossroads, with its collection of elite retail traders such as Chanel and Gucci, has been compared to New York's Fifth Avenue and London's Bond Street.

Only two of Sydney's north-south arteries actually make a complete journey from Circular Quay to Central Railway Station: Pitt Street and George Street. As Pitt Street is a pedestrian mall between King and Market streets, traffic must make this journey using George Street only. Sydney has several well-known shopping arcades that run off Pitt and George streets. One of these, **The Strand**, is particularly noteworthy, having been restored to its 1892 splendour and housing some of Australia's leading fashion designers, jewellers and craftspeople.

In both Pitt and George streets there is little trace of colonial Sydney, although handsome turn-of-the-century commercial buildings are carefully watched over by devoted citizens and the National Trust, lest developers' ambitions exceed their sense of history and good taste. Of the two streets, **Pitt Street** is probably the more exciting in terms of shops, cafes and street hawkers. The monorail beside Pitt Street winds through the city above street level, linking it to the Darling Harbour complex.

Between King and Park streets is **Pitt Street Mall** with department stores, including **Grace Bros** and **Centrepoint**; a popular sporting club, **City Tattersalls**; the Pitt Street side of the Methodist Church's Wesley headquarters; cinemas; and, dominating the two blocks, the soaring **Sydney Tower**, the tallest building in Sydney. This 300-metre golden tower has two revolving restaurants and from the observation decks at its summit, high-powered binoculars and a video television camera enhance the spectacular views

which on a clear day include Terrigal to the north, Wollongong to the south and the Blue Mountains to the west.

Pitt Street becomes rather nondescript as it heads south, with its secondhand stores, cheap accommodation places, and a laneway that leads to a nineteenth-century police headquarters building, now a city watchhouse and serving as cells for the grim **Central Criminal Court** building on one of the cross-streets, Liverpool Street.

On carnival-thronged evenings along the entertainment section of **George Street**, cinema complexes, fast-food houses, pin-ball alleys, all-night bookshops and erotic movie houses – all compete for the jostling crowd's attention. Apart from its entertainment area that makes its nights so boisterous, George Street boasts a number of Sydney's most important and interesting buildings, both old and new. Twenty years ago, Sydney's and Australia's tallest building was the **Australia Square Tower**. Tall and circular in shape, it has an observation platform on the forty-eighth floor and a revolving restaurant. These days the tower is dwarfed by more recent buildings on Sydney's ever-changing skyline.

South from here are the Wynyard underground railway station and the remarkable **Queen Victoria Building** (QVB), which monopolises an entire block. The restoration of the QVB included the refurbishing of its enormous copper dome, which once loomed over the older city skyline. The building now houses many restaurants and over 160 shops; free tours of the complex are available daily. A landmark of the city's earlier

days is to be found opposite the Queen Victoria Building, through the George Street entrance to the Hilton Hotel. In the hotel's basement, restored to its original ornate detail, is the superb **Marble Bar** of the old Adams Hotel, which once stood on the site of the Hilton. On the next corner stands the spiralling blue **Coopers and Lybrand tower**. With its art deco design, it has been dubbed the Superman Building because of its similarity to the fictitious Daily Planet building depicted in film and comic strip.

The **Town Hall**, now dwarfed but not overshadowed by a modern council administration block, is Italian Renaissance in style. Built of mellow brown sandstone, it was completed in 1889. Within the Town Hall, the Treasury Club Bar offers alcoholic and other refreshments in a grand setting. A graceful, shaded pedestrian plaza, **Sydney Square** borders the Town Hall and separates it from Sydney's Anglican Cathedral, **St Andrew's**.

Further west is the impressive **Darling Harbour** complex, which includes: the **Chinese Garden** (incorporating the Garden of Friendship, a Bicentennial gift from the people of Quandong province in China), the **Sydney Convention and Exhibition Centre**, waterside walks, a variety of eating places, 7-day-a-week shopping, and splendid parklands around a busy harbour inlet that was once a dull industrial port. Sydney's temporary **Casino** is on the northern arm of Darling Harbour. At the western end of the National Trust-classified Pyrmont Bridge is the **National Maritime Museum** which focuses on Australia's maritime

ACCOMMODATION

HOTELS

Hotel Nikko Darling Harbour
161 Sussex St, Darling Harbour
(02) 9299 1231

The Observatory
89–113 Kent St, The Rocks
(02) 9256 2222

Quay West
98 Gloucester St, The Rocks
(02) 9240 6000

Regent, Sydney
199 George St, Sydney
(02) 9238 0000

Renaissance Sydney Hotel
30 Pitt St, Sydney
(02) 9372 2233

Ritz Carlton
93 Macquarie St, Sydney
(02) 9252 4600

Sebel of Sydney
23 Elizabeth Bay Rd, Elizabeth Bay
(02) 9358 3244

Sheraton on the Park
161 Elizabeth St, Sydney
(02) 9286 6000

Sydney Hilton
259 Pitt St, Sydney
(02) 9266 0610

FAMILY AND BUDGET

Russell Hotel
143a George St, The Rocks
(02) 9241 3543

The York
5 York St, Sydney
(02) 9210 5000

YWCA
5–11 Wentworth Ave, Darlinghurst
(02) 9264 2451

MOTEL GROUPS: BOOKINGS

Best Western 13 1779

Flag 13 2400

Travelodge 1300 363300

This list is for information only; inclusion is not necessarily a recommendation.

NEW SOUTH WALES

Modern city skyscrapers contrast with historic buildings at the Rocks

The Rocks

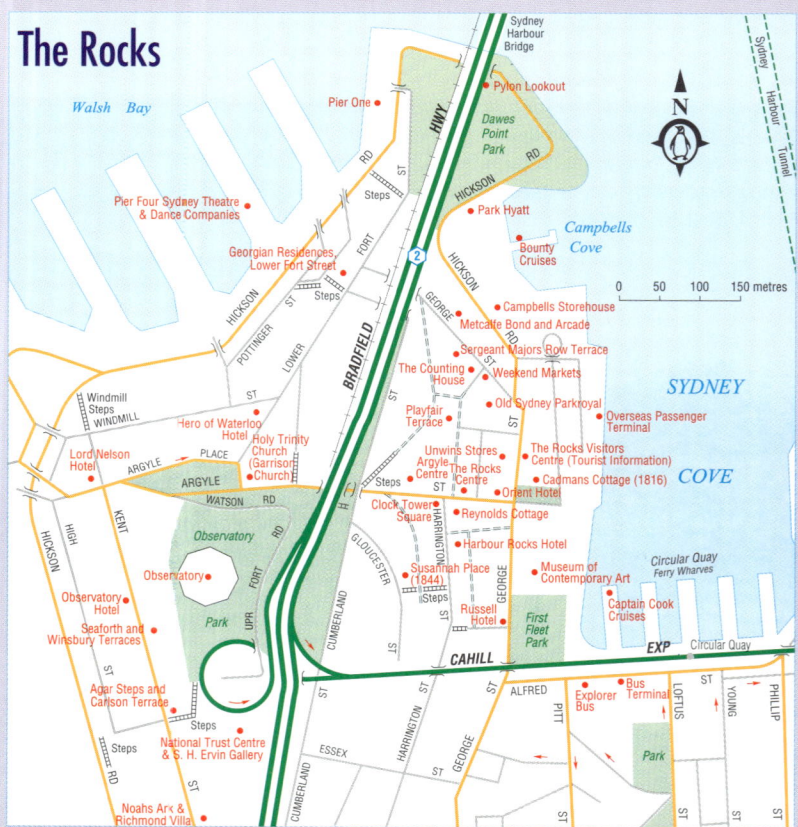

A Colonial Past

At the first settlement at Sydney Cove, Captain Watkin Tench of the Marines wrote: 'to proceed on a narrow, confined scale in a country of the extensive limits we possess, would be unpardonable . . . (the) extent of Empire demands grandeur of design'.

Such grand design began in 1810, when the vision of the new Governor, Lachlan Macquarie, was put into practice by the convict architect Francis Greenway, resulting in a heritage of splendid buildings, many of which are landmarks today. It continued through nearly a century of growth and lofty ideals to create a prosperous and busy metropolis – a great symbol of colonial aspirations.

As Sydney developed, it was both 'mean and princely', a mixture of broad, tree-lined avenues and narrow streets and alleys, grand buildings and crowded cottages and terraces. Its switchback, craggy hills around the indented harbour made orderly Georgian-style planning impossible, and the grand outlines of earlier days soon became blurred by the city's growth from first settlement to colonial seat, to State capital to modern city.

In modern Sydney with its gleaming towers, its crowds and its traffic, substantial remnants of old Sydney can still be seen. Some parts of the city, like **The Rocks** area adjacent to Circular Quay, are almost pure history. The Rocks were the site of the first encampment of convicts and soldiers in 1788, and the site of Sydney's first dwellings. Later it played host to a lively community of seamen, early entrepreneurs, emancipist traders, publicans, prostitutes and street gangs. Here the old hotels and bandstands, sandstone cottages and terrace houses, the Argyle Cut and Agar Steps, the Garrison Church and the village green form an oasis separated from the bustling city by Flagstaff Hill, where the old Observatory stands, and the approaches to the Harbour Bridge are seen.

There are many other inner suburban areas that are reminiscent of the feeling of old Sydney. **Paddington** is the showplace historic suburb, with its picturesque terraces and cottages, most superbly restored. Established in the 1840s, it is now a National Trust conservation area. The narrow streets winding through steep hillsides of this once working-class suburb provide an intimate, neighbourly feeling. Perhaps the most striking example of colonial architecture in Sydney is Victoria Barracks (1841) in Paddington. This two-storeyed building of severe Georgian style, 74 metres long with cream-painted upper and lower verandahs, is a model of elegance. (Visit on Thursday at 10 a.m., watch the changing of the guard and be entertained by the Australian Army Band, Sydney, and follow with a guided tour of this historic group of buildings.)

The suburbs of Balmain, Leichhardt and Redfern are also popular as the advantages of inner-suburban living attract owners who are conscious of the aesthetic quality of the old sandstone cottages.

In the city itself, the street that best reflects the past is probably **Macquarie Street**, which overlooks both the Botanic Gardens and the Domain, where Government House, the Conservatorium of Music, the State Library and the Art Gallery of NSW are situated. Governor Macquarie planned for the east side of the street to be occupied by official buildings and for the west to contain the town houses of wealthy citizens; the west side is now occupied mainly by medical practitioners.

Other interesting buildings in Macquarie Street are: Parliament House (1816), a verandahed sandstone building, originally one wing of the Rum Hospital; the adjoining Mint Building, restored from the other wing of the original Rum Hospital; Sydney Hospital, whose buildings replaced the central block of the Rum Hospital; the Royal College of Physicians; and the Hyde Park Barracks (1819), now a museum. In nearby Queens Square is the classical St James's Church (1882), Sydney's oldest church.

At the harbour end of Mrs Macquarie's Road is a reminder of the Macquarie era – a sandstone shell known as Mrs Macquarie's Chair. The Governor's wife is said to have sat here and gazed upon the great harbour, now one of the world's busiest and most picturesque waterways.

There are a number of other **major buildings** in or near the city, including Elizabeth Bay House (1835), a Regency mansion, now restored and a showplace for the rich furnishings of the time when it looked over a harbour backed by cliff and woodland; the General Post Office in Martin Place, completed in 1887 in classic Renaissance style; the Great Hall at Sydney University, and St Andrew's Cathedral, both designed by Edmund Blacket; St Mary's Cathedral, designed by William Wardell; the Greek Revival court house in Taylor Square, designed by Mortimer Lewis; and Vaucluse House, the former home of William Charles Wentworth, father of the NSW Constitution.

As settlement extended from the harbourside colony, villages were established, first in the upper **Hawkesbury region** to the north-west, then to the south and finally, as the Blue Mountains were breached, out to the western plains and throughout New South Wales.

In the upper Hawkesbury valley are the sister towns of Windsor and Richmond, two of the Macquarie Towns both beautifully sited on the river and retaining the peaceful charm, as well as many of the buildings, of earlier days. Windsor has a number of fine buildings: Claremont Cottage, St Matthew's Anglican Church, the Macquarie Arms, Tebbutt's Observatory, the Doctor's House and the Toll House, to name a few. At Richmond are Belmont, Hobartville, Toxana House, the School of Arts and St Peter's Anglican Church.

In the **Southern Highlands**, the settlements of Mittagong, Moss Vale, Berrima and Bowral are full of historic interest. The Berrima Village Trust is responsible for the preservation of the village as it was in the 19th century. Sited in a valley, Berrima contains a number of fine sandstone buildings grouped around a central common, among them the gaol and court house, the Surveyor-General Inn, the Church of the Holy Trinity, Harper's Mansion and Allington. New South Wales has many other historic towns and properties bearing the hallmarks of the nation's foundation.

The Historic Houses Trust of New South Wales manages nine historic properties in or near Sydney. These are, in central Sydney: Museum of Sydney (cnr Phillip and Bridge sts), Hyde Park Barracks Museum (Macquarie St), Justice and Police Museum (Albert St), Susannah Place (Gloucester St); in Sydney's suburbs: Elizabeth Bay House (Onslow Ave, Elizabeth Bay), Vaucluse House (Wentworth Rd, Vaucluse), Elizabeth Farm (Alice St, Parramatta), Rose Seidler House (Clissold Rd, Wahroonga); and south of Sydney: Meroogal (cnr West and Worrigee sts, Nowra). Visitors can purchase a Ticket Through Time which allows admittance to all nine attractions and is valid for three months. This ticket is sold at all properties.

For further information on colonial towns and buildings, contact the National Trust New South Wales, Observatory Hill Sydney; (02) 9258 0123.

Picturesque terraces at Paddington, an inner-city suburb

Chinatown in Dixon St

history from Aboriginal settlement onwards. Near the eastern end of this one-time traffic carrier, now used as a walkway, is the fascinating **Sydney Aquarium** featuring giant sharks, large saltwater crocodiles and fur seals.

The **Powerhouse Museum** on the southern edge of the Darling Harbour Complex is also well worth a visit. Its size is such that it can exhibit aeroplanes, trams, boats and steam engines, plus many equally fascinating smaller exhibits. Opposite is the **Sydney Entertainment Centre,** a major venue for concerts and conventions. Nearby lies **Dixon Street**, the pedestrianised heart of Sydney's **Chinatown**, a traditional area of restaurants, warehouses, specialty stores and Chinese grocers, where even banks and service stations are labelled in Chinese script. At its southern end the visitor will find **Paddy's Markets**, which reopened in 1994.

Not far from Darling Harbour is Australia's largest fish market, the **Sydney Fish Market** at Pyrmont; it has retail stores, coffee shops, Doyle's seafood restaurant, sushi bars, souvenir outlets and Australia's first seafood school. A pleasant, informal way to dine here is to purchase some seafood and a bottle of wine, and enjoy your meal at one of the umbrella-covered tables on the board-walk. Walking tours are available.

Of the city's cross-streets, two handsome boulevards are noteworthy: **Park Street** and **Martin Place**. The authentic heart of the city, Martin Place, with its memorial **Cenotaph** to Australia's war dead, is the annual stage for the city's Anzac Day March on April 25. It is also the venue for a variety of free lunch-time entertainment.

Park Street ambles east splitting Hyde Park in two before turning into William Street which leads to **Kings Cross,** Sydney's version of Soho and Greenwich Village. Yet the Cross has its unique flavour: the breath of a Sydney Harbour breeze and a glimpse of blue water are a delight. Whatever the Cross has borrowed from other cities in its strip joints, gaudy nightspots and colourful characters, it has its own bohemian traditions. In its backyard are **Garden Island** dockyard, where the Fleet is nearly always in, and the encircling apartment houses of select **Elizabeth Bay**. Located on its boundaries are the lively suburbs of Darlinghurst and Woolloomooloo.

The once notorious **Darlinghurst,** a long-time haunt of pimps, prostitutes and gangsters, boasts the historic Darlinghurst Gaol (where bushrangers were hanged) as one of its attractions. Today, however, the face of Darlinghurst has changed dramatically. Its main artery, **Oxford Street**, with its adult bookshops, pubs, clothing stores and restaurants, is the gay capital of Australia. Nearby in Surry Hills, **Brett Whiteley's studio** displays a range of the late artist's work.

Woolloomooloo has seen its cramped houses and narrow streets skyrocket in price as the desire for trendy inner-city living escalates. Individual restaurants and bars are many and various. Trendy brasseries compete amid the leftovers of 'sleaze' on Bayswater Road and Kellett Street, where the gentrification of the Cross is most apparent. But, even so, there are a great number of erotic movie houses and specialty bookshops still left in the Cross. A less controversial landmark is the dandelion-shaped **El Alamein Fountain** commemorating the World War II battle.

In the other direction, Darlinghurst Road and Bayswater Road lead to **Paddington**, a suburb of steep hills, unplanned streets and picturesque terrace houses, hardly one without ornate Victorian wrought-iron railings and fences and lots of trees. The old-fashioned pubs are now terribly chic, the result of Paddington's fashionable revival back in the late fifties. Next door to 'Paddo' is **Centennial Park**, Sydney's equivalent to New York's Central Park and London's Regent Park, where horseriding, cycling and picnicking are weekend activities.

Paddington's counterpart on the other side of Sydney, **Glebe** (bordering historic **Sydney University**) is not quite so leafy or picturesque, and certainly not as expensive. Nearby **Balmain** with its

harbour frontage has also undergone a fashionable revival.

At every turn these inner suburbs reveal something old and handsome in weathered sandstone: a church, a cottage, a school from Sydney's past. They have also given rise to a Sydney phenomenon: village markets, usually held on Saturdays and featuring colourful identities plying their wares at open-air stalls in the grounds of schools or churches, or in local parks. The colourful **Paddington Markets** and the **Balmain Market** each Saturday are Sydney's most popular.

From Paddington's neighbours, **Woollahra** and **Rushcutters Bay**, through the harbourside suburbs of exclusive **Double Bay**, **Rose Bay** and **Vaucluse**, to **The Gap** and **South Head**; or across the harbour by ferry, JetCat, Harbour Bridge or Harbour Tunnel to **Manly** and the long line of ocean beaches stretching north to beautiful **Palm Beach** – each competes in terms of wealth and privilege with the precipitous bush gorges and superior heights of the elegant **North Shore** suburbs. A floatplane service at Rose Bay has flights between Sydney and Palm Beach, Gosford and Newcastle; and there are charter cruises from Circular Quay up the coast into Broken Bay and the Hawkesbury River.

The **Olympic Games site**, west of the city at Homebush Bay, is a hive of activity in preparation for the games due to be held here in the year 2000. Here and beyond lies the metropolitan heartland of Sydney's great urban sprawl – 75 kilometres from the harbour across the vast, flat western suburbs to the foothills of the **Blue Mountains**.

In Sydney one can dine out on the cuisines of almost every nation in the world. (However, it should be mentioned that Sydney is famous for its rock oyster and the Balmain Bug – an odd-looking but tasty crustacean.) The choice of cinema, live theatre and live-theatre restaurants, and jazz and blues clubs, is just as wide.

For further information on Sydney, contact the Countrylink NSW Travel Centre, 11–31 York St, Sydney; 13 2077. For information regarding public transport, contact the Transport Infoline 131500. A Sydney Pass provides unlimited travel for 3, 5 or 7 days on all public buses, harbour ferries, the Manly JetCat and Parramatta RiverCat, Sydney Explorer bus, Bondi and Bay Explorer buses, and the Airport Express.

TOURS from Sydney

Monument at Captain Cook's Landing Place, Kurnell

Sydney's range of available day tours out and about is almost unrivalled for the variety of scenic and recreational attractions on offer. In the frantic rush to get out of the city, however, it is easy to overlook two of Sydney's greatest assets: Royal National Park, little more than an hour's drive south from the GPO, and Ku-ring-gai Chase National Park, 40 km north; both offer good bushwalking.

Harbour Cruises

An ideal way to view Sydney and its harbour is by boat. Sydney ferries criss-cross the harbour as a means of public transport; as well, several cruises are available. State Transit run three cruises; all depart from Wharf 4 at Circular Quay: a one-hour Morning Harbour Cruise (departs 10 a.m. and 11.15 a.m. daily) through the main reach of the harbour then west along the Parramatta River; a two-and-a-half hour Afternoon Harbour Cruise (departs 1 p.m. weekdays and 1.30 p.m. weekends) down the main harbour and Middle Harbour; and an Evening Harbour Lights Cruise (departs 8 p.m. Mon.–Sat.), a one-and-a-half hour cruise of the main harbour at

night offering splendid views of the city's lights. Bookings are not necessary.

Captain Cook Cruises offer a wide variety of cruises (which depart from Wharf 6 at Circular Quay) including the *Sydney Harbour Explorer* which stops at six harbourside attractions enabling passengers to disembark, explore then catch the next *Explorer;* coffee cruises, which run twice daily through Main and Middle harbours; luncheon cruises travel to Cockatoo Island; and the *John Cadman* makes a dinner cruise nightly. Captain Cook Cruises also conduct tours daily to Fort Denison. Built on an island in the middle of the harbour during the Crimean War to discourage invasion, the fort is now a fascinating museum managed by the NSW National Parks and Wildlife Service.

Matilda Cruises offer a range of harbour discovery cruises of one-and-a-half or two-hour duration, departing from the Aquarium Wharf at Darling Harbour and Circular Quay. As well they offer cruises aboard the *Solway Lass,* a restored sailing-ship. Another Tall Ship, the *Bounty* departs from Campbells Cove at The Rocks for lunch and dinner cruises. Sail Venture Cruises use large sailing catamarans for their sightseeing, lunch, cocktail

or dinner cruises. Departure is from the Aquarium Wharf at Darling Harbour or the East Pontoon at Circular Quay.

Taronga Zoo

12 minutes by ferry from Circular Quay, Wharf 2

Taronga is set in 30 ha of harbourside bushland, giving it a magnificent and unique setting; the views back to the city are splendid. Of particular interest are the displays of Australian native animals and the nocturnal house. Children will enjoy meeting the tame animals at the Friendship Farm.

Manly

Manly ferry or JetCat from Circular Quay

Manly on the north side of the harbour has traditionally been a popular day trip for both locals and visitors. The historic Manly Wharf and modern Harbourside Centre offer specialty shops, restaurants, a ferris wheel and a merry-go-round. For a first-hand look at the ocean's creatures, take a short walk from Manly Wharf along West Esplanade to Oceanworld. The Corso, a pedestrian walkway, links the harbour side of Manly to the famous ocean beach with its Norfolk Pines.

Palm Beach

48 km from Sydney via Pittwater Road

This beautiful beach in bush surroundings offers swimming and boating facilities, and a choice of ocean or Pittwater beaches. The drive from Sydney reveals many of Sydney's lovely northern beaches and it is tempting to stop at every one. The Mona Vale Road provides a shorter route if you are based in the northern suburbs; allow time to visit Waratah Park, a fauna reserve at Namba Rd, Duffy Forest.

Captain Cook's Landing Place, Kurnell

35 km from Sydney via Princes Highway and Captain Cook Bridge

The site of the first recorded landing by Europeans on the east coast of Australia

The Blue Mountains

The famous rock formation the Three Sisters is a major attraction near Katoomba

For more than a century, the Blue Mountains have been a favourite holiday resort for Sydneysiders. Rising from the coastal plain 65 kilometres west of Sydney, they combine a unique blend of superb mountain scenery, outstanding geographical features, beautiful gardens and highly developed tourist attractions.

The towering cliffs of the Blue Mountains presented a seemingly impassable barrier to the early European settlers until Blaxland, Lawson and Wentworth made their historic crossing in 1813 – thus opening up much-needed pasture-land beyond. In the late 1870s the well-to-do of Sydney discovered the area's charms as a resort, and started to build elaborate holiday houses to escape the summer heat of the coast. At first they travelled by Cobb & Co. coach, later by train. Now the mountains are less than two hours from Sydney by road or rail. One-day round-trip coach tours run daily between Sydney and Katoomba.

The Blue Mountains are justly famous for their spectacular scenery of high precipices rising from densely wooded valleys. Their highest point is about 1100 metres above sea level. Bushwalking is a very popular pastime in the mountains and several self-guide brochures are available from tourist information centres with details of routes, highlights and grades of walks. Deep gorges and high rocks in this area make some of the terrain accessible only to skilled bushwalkers and mountaineers. Climbing schools offer rock-climbing weekends for beginners, and there are day courses in beginners' abseiling.

The panoramic **Blue Mountains National Park**, which covers an area of 218 100 hectares, is the fourth largest national park in the State. The park protects some of the best-known scenery in New South Wales.

The City of Blue Mountains incorporates 26 towns and villages, the main towns being **Katoomba**, Leura, Blackheath, Wentworth Falls, Springwood and Glenbrook. All these towns depend on tourism and are geared for the holiday trade. They offer a wide range of accommodation, from bed and breakfast at old-style guest houses to luxury living at modern resorts.

The Blue Mountains' reputation for natural wonders is rapidly being rivalled by its popularity as a gastronomic centre. Wining and dining to suit all tastes and budgets is available.

For further information, contact the Blue Mountains Tourism Authority (BMTA), PO Box 8, Glenbrook 2773; (02) 4739 6299, or visit the information centres at Echo Point, Katoomba or Glenbrook on the Great Western Hwy. *The Blue Mountains Holiday Book*, produced by the BMTA, also details accommodation and activities in the area. **See also:** National Parks and text entry for Katoomba in A–Z listing. **Map references:** 104 I6, 106-107, 116 A1, 119 H1, 120 I8.

Why are the Blue Mountains so blue? The whole area is heavily timbered with eucalypts, which constantly disperse fine droplets of oil into the atmosphere. These droplets cause the blue light-rays of the sun to be scattered more effectively, thus intensifying the usual light refraction phenomenon (Rayleigh Scattering), which causes distant objects to appear blue.

NEW SOUTH WALES

Winery in the Hunter Valley region

in 1770 is set aside as an historic site on a pleasant reserve. The Discovery Centre displays items related to Captain James Cook's life and discoveries. A short historical walk takes visitors past several points of interest. There are picnic/barbecue facilities in the grounds.

Parramatta

22 km from Sydney via Great Western Highway

Although it is now a city within Sydney, Parramatta retains its individuality and has some interesting buildings. Pick up a *Historic Houses* self-guide leaflet from Tourist information, cnr Church and Market sts; (02) 9630 3703. Elizabeth Farm (1793), at 70 Alice St, contains part of the oldest surviving European building in Australia and, as the home of Elizabeth and John Macarthur, was for the first 40 years of the colony the social, political and agricultural centre – do not miss the audiovisual presentation and the period gardens (1830s). Hambledon Cottage (1824) in Hassall St was part of the original Elizabeth Farm property. Experiment Farm Cottage in Ruse St was the site of James Ruse's 'experiment' to support himself from the land in the early years of the colony. Closer to the centre of the city are two historic sites: Old Government House and St John's Cathedral. Old Government House in attractive Parramatta Park, has been beautifully restored from its 1799 beginnings (enlarged 1815) and is maintained by the National Trust. A guided tour is available Tues.–Sun. St John's Cathedral (1855), in the heart of the shopping district, is open Thurs. and Fri.; guides are on duty Fri. St John's cemetery is a block away from

the church itself and contains the oldest headstone in the colony, dated January 1791. A short trip north along Pennant Hills Rd leads to the Koala Park Sanctuary (Castle Hill Rd, West Pennant Hills) where koalas are on show all day.

Historic Camden and Campbelltown

60 km from Sydney via Liverpool, on Hume Highway

Liverpool, situated 32 km from Sydney and a major retail and commercial centre, has many buildings of historic interest: St Luke's Church (1818), designed by Francis Greenway; Liverpool Hospital (1820s), now the Liverpool College of TAFE; and Glenfield Farm (1817). The ultra-modern Liverpool Regional Museum, built as a bicentennial project, fronts Collingwood Cottage, built in 1810 for Ebor Bunker, a whaling captain. A good stopping-point is Chipping Norton Lakes, a reclaimed area with picnic and barbecue facilities, and walking tracks. Further down the highway, lovers of history can enjoy a relaxed stroll around the streets of two early towns of New South Wales, Camden and Campbelltown. **See also:** Text entries for Camden and Campbelltown in A–Z listing.

Windsor and Richmond

60 km from Sydney via Great Western Highway and Windsor Road

These two towns near the Hawkesbury River are reminders of the earliest days of settlement in New South Wales, and are a must for lovers of history and early architecture. **See:** Text entries for Windsor and Richmond in A–Z listing.

Katoomba and the Blue Mountains via Penrith

104 km from Sydney via Western Motorway

The Blue Mountains are a favourite destination for both tourists and Sydneysiders. They offer superb mountain scenery, outdoor activities such as bushwalking, and a wide range of accommodation and restaurants.

The gateway to the Blue Mountains is the historic town of Penrith, 57 km from Sydney. The town dates back to the opening of the Blue Mountains road in 1815, when a court house and a small gaol were built there. Today it makes a pleasant stopover en route to the Blue Mountains. Penrith's attractions include the Museum of Fire in Castlereagh Rd, paddle-boat cruises on the *Nepean Belle* through the Nepean Gorge, the Lewers Bequest and Penrith Regional Art Gallery at Emu Plains, and Vicary's Winery south of the town.

If time permits, it is worth diverting from the motorway before Penrith to Featherdale Wildlife Park in Kildare Rd, Doonside to see the extensive fauna collection and to visit their souvenir shop. Another diversion off the motorway (take the Wallgrove Rd exit) is the popular Australia's Wonderland and Wildlife Park at Eastern Creek. **See also:** The Blue Mountains and Katoomba entry in A–Z listing.

The Hunter Valley Vineyards

160 km from Sydney via Pacific Highway

Although it is possible to do this trip in a day, this certainly would not do the area justice – and it is definitely not a good idea if you plan to do any wine-tasting! The best time to visit the Hunter Valley is at vintage time, when you can see the grapes being fermented in great open vats. Picking starts any time from the end of January, but this can vary considerably, and sometimes does not start until well into February. Tyrrell's and Drayton's wineries were established within a few years of each other in the 1850s. At Tyrrell's you can still see the classic hand-presses which were used during vintage and fermentation. Most of the wineries are open daily and welcome visitors. Visits can be arranged with the wineries direct or at Wine Country Tourism, Turner Park, Aberdare Rd, Cessnock; (02) 4990 4477. **See also:** Vineyards and Wineries, and Cessnock entry in A–Z listing.

NEW SOUTH WALES from A to Z

NEW SOUTH WALES

Lake Eucumbene, near Adaminaby, renowned for its excellent fishing

Adaminaby
Pop. 375

MAP REF. 118 H5, 119 D8, 142 E9, 243 L1

This small town was moved in the 1950s to its present site; the old town site was flooded to form Lake Eucumbene as part of the Snowy Mountains Scheme. Located on the Snowy Mountains Hwy it is a good base for cross-country skiers and anglers. The ski area of Mt Selwyn is nearby. Adaminaby is the stepping-off point for Lake Eucumbene, where there are a range of lakeside holiday resorts and excellent fishing. **Of interest:** World's largest trout, Baker St. Feb.: Race Meeting. Nov.: Trout Festival (fishing competition). **In the area:** Fishing-boat hire at: Old Adaminaby (8 km SW), Anglers Reach (16 km W) and Buckenderra (44 km S). Horseriding and alpine horseback safaris available, contact Tourist information for details. Yarrangobilly Caves and thermal pool, 53 km NW off Snowy Mountains Hwy. **Tourist information:** Post Office, 3 Denison St; (02) 6454 2303. **Accommodation:** 1 hotel/motel, 2 motels, 1 cara./camp. park.

Adelong
Pop. 795

MAP REF. 119 B5, 120 D13

Both fossickers and goldfields historians are attracted to this picturesque tablelands town on the Snowy Mountains Hwy. Adelong became a thriving community following the discovery of reef gold in the area in 1857. **Of interest:** National Trust-classified Tumut St, from Campbell to Neil sts; some buildings, such as old Bank of NSW (now a B&B), of great historical interest. Also in Tumut St: Gold Fields Galleries, for art and craft; restored Old Pharmacy (now a guest house and restaurant). Village Walk, includes police station (1861) in Campbell St, St James Catholic Church (1868) in Gundagai St, and ends at Adelong Falls Reserve; brochures at Tourist information. Dec.: Boat Regatta ('boats' raced along street). **In the area:** Adelong Falls Reserve, 1 km N on Tumblong–Gundagai Rd, where famous Reefer Battery operated until 1910 driven by water from falls (ruins still visible); at reserve: scenic picnic area, 3 marked walking trails, gold fossicking. **Tourist information:** York's Newsagency, Tumut St; (02) 6946 2051. **Accommodation:** 2 hotels, 4 B&B, 1 cara./camp. park.

Albury
Pop. 39 975

MAP REF. 127 Q13, 241 P4, 242 C1

Albury-Wodonga is situated beside the Murray River, 572 km SW of Sydney. Once the meeting-place for local Aboriginal groups, today the Albury region makes a convenient stopover for motorists driving via the Hume Hwy between Sydney and Melbourne. The building of the Hume Weir in 1936 created Lake Hume, one of the most extensive and beautiful artificial lakes in Australia. **Of interest:** Albury Regional Museum, in former Turk's Head Hotel, Wodonga Pl. Botanical Gardens (1871), cnr Wodonga Pl. and Dean St. The Parklands (comprising Hovell Tree Reserve, Noreuil and Australia parks), on western side of Wodonga Pl. at town entrance, for riverside walks, river swimming, kiosk and picnic areas. PS *Cumberoona* offers Murray River cruises; embarkation points within parks. Albury Regional Art Centre, Dean St, features extensive Sir Russell Drysdale collection. 360° views from Albury Monument Hill at end of Dean St. Performing Arts Centre, Civic Centre, Swift St. Frog Hollow Leisure Park, Olive St, offers maze, theatre and mini-golf. Sales of local dairy products at Haberfield's Milk Dairy Shop, Hovell St (tours during business hours). Feb.-Mar.: Festival of Sport. **In the area:** Ettamogah Wildlife Sanctuary, 12 km NE on Hume Hwy. Nearby, cartoonist Ken Maynard's Ettamogah Pub, worth photographing. Cooper's Ettamogah Winery, 3 km further along hwy. Australian Newsprint Mill, 15 km N (tours by appt). Jindera Pioneer Museum, 14 km NW, featuring Wagner's Store, a general store restored to its original old-world charm. Hume and Hovell Walking Track from Albury to Gunning, 370 km NE; the track offers a 20-day trek for long distance walkers but design caters for half-day, one-day and weekend walks along the way; contact the Department of Lands, 22–23 Bridge St, Sydney; (02) 9228 6111. A section of this track together with some other trails are part of the Albury-Wodonga Trail System; for further information contact Albury-Wodonga Regional Parklands Committee, (02) 6023 8007. Day trips to wineries of Rutherglen, 47 km W, and into Mad Dan Morgan (the infamous bushranger) country. Bogong Mountains, gateway to Victorian snowfields and high country, 130 km S. Hume Weir, 14 km E, a paradise for anglers, canoeists, swimmers, sailors, water-skiers, speedboat enthusiasts and wind-surfers. Hume Weir Trout Farm, nearby, offers trout feeding and fishing. Upstream of weir, Wymah Ferry, still in operation, carries two cars at a time 800 m across river. **Tourist information:** Choices Information Centre, Hume Hwy, Ettamogah (12 km NE near Table Top); (02) 6040 2114; accommodation booking line, 1800 64 0699. **Accommodation** (in Albury-Wodonga): 2 hotels, 55 motels, 1 hostel, 13 cara./camp. parks.

Alstonville   Pop. 3678

MAP REF. 123 Q3, 505 Q12

The village of Alstonville nestles in lush surroundings at the top of the Ballina Cutting between Ballina and Lismore. Famous for the beautiful purple Tibouchina tree, the town holds a Tibouchina Festival during blossom time in Mar. Surrounding properties produce potatoes, sugarcane, tropical fruits, macadamia nuts and avocados. **Of interest:** Prize-winning town in 'Tidy Towns' competition since 1986. Lumley Park, Bruxner Hwy, features open-air pioneer transport museum. In Budgen Ave: Kolinda Gallery and Ward's Antiques for local art and craft. Elizabeth Ann Brown Park, Main St, a rainforest park with picnic facilities. Mar.: Tibouchina Festival. **In the area:** House With No Steps, 10 km S, a unique enterprise with nursery, crafts, fruit sales and tearooms run by disabled people. Nearby, Victoria Park features a boardwalk and picnic area. **Tourist information:** Ballina Tourist Information Centre, Las Balsas Plaza, Ballina; (02) 6686 3484. **Accommodation:** 1 motel.

Armidale   Pop. 21 605

MAP REF. 123 L9

Situated midway between Sydney and Brisbane in the New England Ranges (altitude 980 m), this university city is the centre of the New England district and an attractive tourist centre, with more than 30 National Trust-classified buildings. **Of interest:** In Kentucky St: New England Regional Art Museum, contains Hinton Collection, Australia's most valuable provincial art collection; Aboriginal Centre and Keeping Place, a museum, education centre and Aboriginal craft displays. Folk Museum in National Trust-classified building, cnr Faulkner and Rusden sts, displays pioneer relics.

Railway Museum, adjacent to station in Brown St (open Mon., Wed. and Fri.). In Dangar St: St Mary's Roman Catholic Cathedral (1912), magnificent Gothic revival structure; St Peter's Anglican Cathedral (1875), built of 'Armidale blues' bricks. The Stables (1872), Moore St, now craft shop. Court house (1860) and Imperial Hotel (1889) in Beardy St. Central Park, Dangar St, pleasant city park with useful relief map of area. Self-guide heritage walk (3 km) and heritage drive (25 km) of city, and numerous self-drive scenic drives of area; pamphlets available at Tourist information. Markets in Mall, last Sun. each month. Mar.: Autumn Festival. Sept.–Nov.: Arts Festival. **In the area:** Excellent trout fishing. University of New England, 5 km NW, features historic Booloominbah homestead, now administration building, Antiquities Museum, Zoology Museum, and kangaroo and deer park. Mt Yarrowyck Nature Reserve, 23 km NW off Bundarra Rd, has Aboriginal rock-art site and cultural walk. Dumaresq Dam, 15 km NE, features walking tracks, non-power boating, swimming and fishing for trout (Oct.–June). At ghost town of Hillgrove, 31 km E: Rural Life and Industry Museum with exhibits of gold-mining equipment; self-guide town walk through old town site (brochure at Tourist information). Oxley Wild Rivers National Park, 39 km E, includes Wollomombi Falls, one of the highest falls in the State, plunging 220 m, Dangars Falls and Mihi Falls. Fine views of Bellinger Valley from Point Lookout (1500 m) and excellent walking trails in World Heritage-listed New England National Park, 80 km E; on road into park, L.P. Dutton Trout Hatchery. Cathedral Rock National Park, 80 km E, features magnificent granite tors, bushwalking and 360° views from top of Cathedral Rock. National Trust-owned Saumarez Homestead (1888), 5 km S, guided tours of house and self-guide farm and garden tours available (homestead closed mid June–end Aug.). **Tourist information:** Visitors Centre & Coach Station, 82 Marsh St; (02) 6772 4655; freecall 1800 627736. **Accommodation:** 5 hotels, 21 motels, 3 B&B, 2 cara./camp. parks. **See also:** New England.

Ashford   Pop. 567

MAP REF. 123 K4, 505 L13

This small New England town is the centre of a tobacco-growing district. **In**

the area: Network of limestone caves and spectacular Macintyre Falls, 36 km NW. Pindari Dam, 20 km S, offers swimming and fishing, and camping, bushwalking, picnic/barbecue facilities in surrounds. **Tourist information:** Shire Tourism Committee, Water Towers Complex, Campbell St, Inverell; (02) 6722 1693. **Accommodation:** 1 hotel, 1 cara./camp. park. **See also:** New England.

Ballina   Pop. 14 554

MAP REF. 123 Q3, 505 R12

Ballina is a fishing town at the mouth of the Richmond River in northern NSW. Ideal year-round temperatures, golden beaches, picturesque farmlands and friendly rural atmosphere make the area a popular family holiday destination. Cedar cutters were among the first European settlers, attracted by the red cedar trees along the shores of the river. Farmers followed and by 1900 a dairy-farming industry was established alongside sugarcane plantations. **Of interest:** Naval Museum, adjacent to Tourist information, features a restored Las Balsas Expedition raft that sailed from South America in 1973. Kerry Saxby Walkway, begins behind Tourist information and follows river to its mouth (brochure available at Tourist information). B Framed Gallery, River St. Outdoor Entertainment Reserve, Canal Rd. The Big Prawn Complex, Pacific Hwy, features fresh seafood, antiques, opal and gem museum, and art and craft. *Richmond Princess* river cruises. Markets at Outdoor Entertainment Reserve, Canal Rd, 3rd Sun. each month. **In the area:** MacKay Harrison Galleries, 2 km N on The Coast Rd. Freshwater Lake Ainsworth, 12 km N, at Lennox Head. Thursday Plantation Tea Tree Oil, 3 km W; guided tours available. **Tourist information:** Las Balsas Plaza, cnr River and Norton sts; (02) 6686 3484. **Accommodation:** 23 motels, 4 B&B, 1 hostel, 12 cara./camp. parks.

Balranald   Pop. 1327

MAP REF. 126 H8, 239 N6

On the Murrumbidgee River, Balranald is 438 km NW of Melbourne, in a wool, cattle, wheat, fruit and timber area. **Of interest:** Historical Museum and Heritage Park, Market St, includes gaol, Murray pine school house, museum with local history displays (open by appt) and Tourist information centre. Lions Park has picnic/barbecue facilities and playground. Picturesque Memorial Drive. Easter: Homebush Gymkhana. Dec.: Christmas Festival (on Christmas Eve). **In the area:** Balranald (low-level) Weir for picnics, barbecues and fishing. Yanga Lake, 7 km SE, offers good fishing and water sports. Historic Homebush Hotel (1878), 25 km N. Redbank Weir, 58 km N, for barbecues and picnics. Mungo National Park, 150 km NW within Willandra Lakes World Heritage Region, features the Walls of China; the lakes preserve record of 40 000 years of Aboriginal life. **Tourist information:** Market St; (03) 5020 1599. **Accommodation:** 1 hotel/ motel, 5 motels, 1 cara./camp. park.

Bangalow   Pop. 819

MAP REF. 123 Q2, 505 Q12

Bangalow is a delightful village, with rustic charm and set amid magnificent scenery, 10 km SW of Byron Bay. **Of**

interest: Art, craft and antique shops. Byron Creek walking track, off Deacon St, through splendid rainforest to picnic area. Market at Showgrounds, Market St, 4th Sun. each month. **In the area:** Beaches at Byron Bay, 12 km E. **Tourist information:** 80 Jonson St, Byron Bay; (02) 6685 8050. **Accommodation:** 1 hotel, 1 motel.

Barham   Pop. 1217

MAP REF. 126 I12, 237 Q2, 239 Q13, 240 B1

Barham and its twin town Koondrook, on the other side of the Murray River, are centres for the timber, cattle, fat-lamb, dairying and tourism industries. **Of interest:** Barham Lakes Complex, Murray St, includes artificial lakes, walking track, picnic/barbecue and swimming facilities. Bonum Red Gum Saw Mill, Moulamein Rd. Sept.: Pro-Am Golf Tournament. **In the area:** Around Koondrook: Shannkirst Park Zoological Reserve; Gannawarra Wetlander Cruises, 15 km S; Kerang

Ibis Rookery, 28 km SW on Murray Valley Hwy; State Forest, East Barham Rd; Red-gum woodcraft at Brady's Burls, 2½ km NW on Murrabit Rd. At Murrabit, 20 km NW: Karaweena Alpacas (open Sun. and public holidays); market, 1st Sat. each month. **Tourist information:** 25 Murray St; (03) 5453 3100. **Accommodation:** 3 hotels, 6 motels, 3 cara./camp. parks.

Barooga   Pop. 843

MAP REF. 127 M13, 241 J3

A small but rapidly-growing town near the Victorian town of Cobram, Barooga's beautiful setting and abundant wildlife make it a popular holiday town. **Of interest:** Sandy beaches along Murray River. In Vermont St: Dalveile Gallery, features antique oil lamp collection; Botanical Gardens. Binghi Boomerang Factory, Tocumwal Rd. Market, Vermont St, 3rd Sun. each month. Jan., Easter, June, Aug.: major golf events. **In the area:** Citrus- and

The Hawkesbury

The Hawkesbury River, north of Sydney, is one of the most attractive rivers in Australia and also played an important role in Sydney's early colonial history. The first European settlers arrived in 1794 to establish farming settlements to help feed the starving colony. In 1810 Governor Macquarie founded the towns of **Windsor**, **Richmond**, Castlereagh, Wilberforce and **Pitt Town** in the upper Hawkesbury valley. Today much of this land is still used for agriculture and there are many oyster leases on the lower river.

Although farming has been pursued since the late 18th century, the charm of the Hawkesbury lies mainly in the fact that the river is still surrounded by large areas of untouched bushland. Four national parks front the river: upstream the **Dharug National Park**, noted for its Aboriginal rock carvings; Marramarra National Park, noted for its flora; downstream the **Ku-ring-gai Chase National Park**, a bushland haven; and **Brisbane Water National Park**, with its Aboriginal rock engravings and colourful displays of waratahs and Christmas bush.

Car ferry crossing the river at Berowra Waters

The Hawkesbury River is a popular recreational waterway, particularly at its lower and wider reaches between Brooklyn and Pittwater. One of the best ways of exploring the Hawkesbury is by boat. Craft of all types are available for hire at Brooklyn, Bobbin Head, Berowra Waters and **Wisemans Ferry**. A delightful way to see the river is to join the Riverboat Postman, a mailboat run which leaves Brooklyn on weekdays and takes about 3 hours. Cruises on the river are also available, from 2 hours to a full day, on the *Deerubbun* and other craft, departing from the wharf at Brooklyn.

If you are travelling north from Sydney by road, the Newcastle–Sydney Freeway crosses the

Hawkesbury and its tributary, Mooney Mooney Creek. Here, the freeway cuts through magnificent sandstone cliffs and offers spectacular views. Further upstream, the convict-built Old Great North Road, a major nineteenth-century engineering feat, can be explored on foot or mountain bike (closed to traffic).

For further information, contact Tourism Hawkesbury, Ham Common Bicentenary Park, Richmond Rd, Clarendon; (02) 4588 5895. **See also:** National Parks and individual text entries in A–Z listing for those parks and towns indicated by bold type. **Map references:** 105 M4, 108 C10, 121 K6.

grape-growing. Brentwood Fruit Juices, 6 km E, tours available (contact Tourist information). **Tourist information:** The Old Grain Store, cnr Station St and Punt Rd, Cobram; (03) 5872 2132. **Accommodation:** 1 hotel, 10 motels, 1 B&B, 2 cara./camp. parks.

Barraba   Pop. 1427

MAP REF. 122 I8
Surrounded by magnificent mountain scenery on the Manilla River in the Nandewar Ranges, Barraba is an agricultural and pastoral centre, and an ideal base for exploring the eastern section of the Nandewar Mountains. **Of interest:** Nandewar Historical Museum, Queen St (open by appt). Clay Pan Fuller Gallery, Queen St, for art, craft and pottery. Beautiful old organ in St Laurence's Anglican Church, Fitzroy St. Nov.: Fine Music Festival. **In the area:** Adam's Lookout, 4 km N, for views of town. Elembee Fine Fibre Farm, 32 km W on Horton Falls Rd, a goat stud in 500 ha of bushland offering walks, fossicking for jasper and petrified wood, and wildlife. Horton River Falls, 38 km W towards Mt Kaputar National Park. At Mt Kaputar National Park, walk to summit (18 km return). Split Rock Dam Recreation Area, 25 km SE. **Tourist information:** 116 Queen St; (02) 6782 1255. **Accommodation:** 3 hotels, 1 motel, 2 cara./camp. parks. **See also:** New England.

Batemans Bay   Pop. 8320

MAP REF. 119 H7, 143 N7
Crayfish and oysters are the specialty of this attractive holiday town on the Princes Hwy 285 km S of Sydney. Located at the estuary of the Clyde River, Batemans Bay provides convenient access to both the Pacific Ocean and the safe waters of the Clyde. **Of interest:** *Clyde Princess* and MV *Merinda*, for river cruises (depart Ferry Wharf). On Beach Rd: 27-hole golf course; Birdland Animal Park, featuring a rainforest trail. Houseboats available for hire. Fishing charters available. Markets, each 2nd and 4th Sun. Nov.: Clyde River Carnival. **In the area:** Excellent fishing. Murramarang National Park, 10 km NE, a coastal park noted for its mostly undisturbed coastline and kangaroos on beach. Durras Lake, 8 km NE, for fishing and swimming. Historic Nelligen, 10 km NW, on Clyde River; has Country Music

Festival each Jan. Araluen, old goldmining town, 82 km W. At Mogo, 8 km S: art and craft outlets; Mogo Goldfields Park, featuring working goldmine; Old Mogo Town, 19th-century re-created goldmining town; Mogo Zoo. Calligraphy Gallery, 12 km SE, for local art. Surfing at Malua Bay, 14 km SE. **Tourist information:** Eurobodalla Coast Visitors Centre, cnr Princes Hwy and Beach Rd; (02) 4472 6900. **Accommodation:** 18 motels, 3 B&B, 1 hostel, 8 cara./camp. parks. **See also:** The South Coast.

Bathurst   Pop. 24 682

MAP REF. 104 B4, 120 H6
Bathurst, 210 km W of Sydney on the Macquarie River, and the centre of a pastoral and fruit- and grain-growing district, has many historic connections. The birthplace of former Prime Minister, J.B. Chifley, it is better known today for its famous motor-racing circuit, Mount Panorama. **Of interest:** Self-guide historic walking tour and Fossicker's self-drive tour (leaflets at Tourist information). Ben Chifley's Cottage, Busby St. In Russell St: Historical Society Museum in East Wing of court house; Miss Traill's house (c. 1845), containing items collected by one family over 100 years, which record history of town and reflect family's passion for horse-breeding and racing. Bathurst Regional Art Gallery, Keppel St. Oct.: Bathurst 1000 Car Races. **In the area:** South-west of city centre at Mt Panorama on Panorama Ave: Bathurst Goldfields, a reconstruction of historic goldmining area; Bathurst Motor Racing Hall of Fame, at Mt Panorama Circuit; magnificent views from summit of Mt Panorama; nearby, McPhillamy Park features Sir Joseph Banks Nature Reserve. Abercrombie Caves, 72 km S on Bathurst–Goulburn Rd, limestone cave system containing Arch Cave, considered one of finest natural arches in world and larger than Grand Arch at Jenolan Caves (Carols in the caves held in Dec.). Abercrombie House (1870s), 6 km W on Ophir Rd, baronial-style Gothic mansion. Hill End Historic Site, 86 km NW, former goldfield with many original buildings; Visitor centre in old Hill End Hospital (equipment for panning and fossicking available for hire). Other old gold towns nearby include Rockley, O'Connell, Trunkey Creek and Sofala. Bathurst Sheep and Cattle Drome at Rossmore

Park, 6 km NE on Limekilns Rd, features performing sheep and cattle, and milking, shearing and sheepdog demonstrations. **Tourist information:** 28 William St; (02) 6332 1444. **Accommodation:** 9 hotels, 12 motels, 29 B&B, 1 cara./camp. park.

Batlow   Pop. 1143

MAP REF. 119 B6, 120 D13, 142 A4
This timber-milling and former goldmining town, situated in the Great Dividing Range 33 km S of Tumut, is located in a district renowned for its apples, pears and berry fruits. **Of interest:** Historical Society Museum, Mayday Rd. Mountain Maid Cannery, off Kurrajong Ave. Batlow Fruit Packing Complex, Forest Rd. Cascade Fuschia Nursery, Fosters Rd (open Oct.–Apr.). Superb views of town and peaks of Snowy Mountains from Weemala Lookout Flora and Fauna Reserve on H.V. Smith Dr. Apr.: Apple Harvest Festival. Sept.: Daffodil Show. **In the area:** Hume and Hovell Lookout, 6 km E, for views over Lake Blowering; picnic area at site where explorers paused in 1824. Lake Blowering, 20 km E. Springfield Orchard, 6 km N on Tumut Rd, grows 16 apple varieties; picnic/barbecue facilities available. Pick-your-own berry fruits and cherries at farms on Tumut Rd. Access points for shorter section walks on 370-km Hume and Hovell Walking Track, which runs from Gunning to Albury. Batlow District Drive, south of town, links various walks and forest parks in Bago State Forest (brochure available at Tourist information). Spectacular Buddong Falls, 25 km S; accessible during fine weather only. **Tourist information:** Fitzroy St (Snowy Mtns Hwy), Tumut; (02) 6947 1849. **Accommodation:** 1 hotel, 1 motel, 1 B&B, 1 cara./camp. park.

Bega   Pop. 4202

MAP REF. 117 F7, 119 G10, 243 Q6
It is possible to surf and ski on the same day from Bega, set as it is between the beach and the Kosciusko snow resorts. The town is near the junction of the Princes and Snowy Mountains hwys, which link Sydney, Melbourne and Canberra. **Of interest:** Bega Family Historical Museum, cnr Bega and Auckland sts. Feb.: Far South Coast National Show. Mar.: Cheese Pro-Am. Sept.: Bega Festival. Oct.: Bega Valley

Art Awards. **In the area:** Fine views from Dr George Lookout (8 km NE) and Bega Valley Lookout (2 km N). Bega Cheese Heritage Centre, 3 km N, restored original cheese factory with displays of old cheese-making techniques, also has art and craft gallery. See cows being milked at Brogo Valley Rotolactor, 18 km N. Mumbulla Falls picnic area with beautiful rock pools and natural waterslide, 15 km NE. Grevillea Estate Winery, 5 km W on Buckajo Rd. Historic village of Candelo, 23 km SW, with its old-world charm untouched by time; market (largest on south coast) held 1st Sun. each month. Tathra, 18 km SE, has beautiful beaches, historic wharf, Mimosa Rocks National Park to the north, and Wallagoot Lake and Bournda National Park to the south. **Tourist information:** Gipps St; (02) 6492 2045. **Accommodation:** 4 hotels, 5 motels, 1 hostel, 1 cara./camp. park. **See also:** The South Coast.

Bellingen   Pop. 2298

MAP REF. 123 P8

Bellingen is an attractive tree-lined town on the banks of the Bellinger River in the rich dairylands of the Bellinger Valley. In pioneer days it was a timber-getting and ship-building centre. **Of interest:** Much of town classified by Heritage Commission. Restored Hammond and Wheatley Emporium, Hyde St, now houses Sweetwater Gallery. Local art and craft at Yellow Shed, cnr Hyde and Prince sts, and at Butter Factory Complex, Dopel La. Canoe hire available. Markets at Bellingen Park, Church St, 3rd Sat. each month. Aug.: Jazz Festival. Oct.: World Music, Dance and Arts Festival. **In the area:** River-side walks and canoeing on Bellinger River. Bike tours into surrounding forest areas, contact Tourist information. Scenic island in river, with flying fox colony. Picnicking at Thora, 14 km NW, at foot of the Dorrigo Plateau. State forests for bushwalking and horseriding. Trout fishing in streams on Dorrigo Plateau. Scenic drive north-east through farmlands and wooded valleys, across Never Never Creek to the Promised Land; swimming holes and picnic areas along the way; road continues to Dorrigo National Park. Gambaarri Aboriginal Cultural Tours offer a tour to same area with Aboriginal guide. **Tourist information:** Bellingen Travel, 42 Hyde St; (02) 6655 2055.

Accommodation: 1 hotel, 1 motel, 8 B&B, 1 hostel, 1 cara./camp. park.

Bermagui   Pop. 1166

MAP REF. 117 H4, 119 H9, 143 M13, 243 R4

Fishing in all forms – lake, estuary, deep-sea and big-game – is excellent in this delightful small port, 13 km from the Princes Hwy. It was much publicised for its fishing by American novelist-sportsman Zane Grey in the 1930s. Because of its close proximity to the Continental Shelf, the town plays host to numerous game-fishing tournaments from Nov.–June. The town's harbour is the safest on the south coast. **Of interest:** Charter boats offer diving, deep sea and game-fishing trips; depart from harbour. Fresh fish and prawns for sale at Fish Co-op at harbourside. Humpback, southern right and dolphin watching cruises depart from harbour Sept.–Nov. Craft market, last Sun. each month. Jan.: Blue Water Fishing Classic. Feb.: International Dog Show. Mar.: Tag and Release Game-fishing Tournament. Easter: Four Winds Easter Concerts. **In the area:** Beautiful rock pools, particularly Blue Pool, rugged coastline and unspoiled countryside. Safe swimming at Horseshoe Bay Beach. Good surfing at Beares, Mooreheads, Cuttagee and Haywards beaches. Coastal walk (8 km) to Wallaga Lake passing through wetland flora and fauna reserves, and remnants of Montreal Goldfields. At Wallaga Lake, 8 km N: Camel Rock, unusual rock formation on shoreline; Umbarra Cultural Centre, offering Aboriginal cultural tours; Wallaga Lake National Park, for boating, fishing, swimming, bushwalking and picnicking, and walking trail to summit of Mt Dromedary. Central Tilba historic village, a National Trust-classified town, 14 km N. Montague Island, 23 km NE, has seal colony and fairy penguins; surrounding waters a mecca for anglers. Cobargo, 19 km W on Princes Hwy, an unspoiled old working village with several art galleries, wood and leather crafts, iron forge, pottery and tearooms; country market held 3rd Sun. each month in grounds of Co-op. Mimosa Rocks National Park, 20 km S. **Tourist information:** BP Bermagui, 8 Coluga St; (02) 6493 4174. **Accommodation:** 1 hotel, 5 motels, 1 hostel, 5 cara./camp. parks. **See also:** The South Coast.

Berridale   Pop. 949

MAP REF. 118 I10, 119 D9, 142 E12, 243 L4

This small town is located near Lake Eucumbene, Lake Jindabyne and the ski fields of southern NSW. **Of interest:** St Marys Church (1860), off Kosciusko Rd. Berridale School (1883), Oliver St. Berridale Inn (1863) and Berridale Store (1863), both in Exchange Sq. Easter: Fair. **In the area:** On Old Dalgety Rd: Snowy River Winery, 12 km S, has restaurant and tastings; Snowy River Ag Barn and Fibre Centre, 15 km S. At Dalgety, 19 km S, historic Buckley's Crossing Hotel (1889) marks the place where cattle used to be driven across the Snowy River. Eucumbene Trout Farm, 19 km N, has sales, and offers horseriding and tours. **Tourist information:** Berridale Store, 64 Jindabyne Rd; (02) 6456 3206. **Accommodation:** 1 hotel, 5 motels, 1 cara./camp. park.

Berrigan   Pop. 949

MAP REF. 127 N12, 241 K1

A traditional country town with many old buildings reflecting a bygone era, Berrigan is best known for its connections with horseracing. **Of interest:** Historic buildings. Berrigan Racecourse and Kilfenora Racing Stables. Sojourn Station Art Studio. Oct.: Agricultural Show. **Tourist information:** River Foreshore, Tocumwal; (03) 5874 2131. **Accommodation:** 3 hotels, 1 hotel/motel, 1 motel, 1 cara./camp. park.

Berrima   Pop. 723

MAP REF. 116 B6, 119 H3, 121 J10

A superbly preserved 1830s Australian town, Berrima is on the Old Hume Hwy in the Southern Highlands. **Of interest:** Self-guide historic walking tour, contact Tourist information. Many old buildings restored as craft and antique shops, restaurants and galleries. In Market Pl.: White Horse Inn (1832), now a restaurant; historical museum; Australian Alpaca Centre, selling knitwear. Australia's oldest continually licensed hotel the Surveyor General (1835), Old Hume Highway. Gaol (1839), still in use; Argyle St. Court house (1838), finest building in the town, first trial by jury in Australia held here in 1841, Wilshire St, now a museum with displays and an excellent video of early Berrima. Harper's Mansion (1830s) cnr Wilkinson St and Old Hume Hwy. **In the area:**

NEW SOUTH WALES

Joadja Winery, 8 km NW, (open for tastings, weekends and school holidays). Amber Park Emu and Ostrich Farm, 11 km NW. **Tourist information:** Southern Highlands Visitor Information Centre, 62–70 Main St, Mittagong; (02) 4871 2888; freecall, 1800 656176. **Accommodation:** 1 hotel, 2 motels, 6 B&B. **See also:** Southern Highlands.

Berry   Pop. 1570

MAP REF. 116 F11, 119 I4, 121 K11

Old English trees add to the charm of this town on the Princes Hwy, 18 km NE of Nowra. In rich dairying country, it was founded by David Berry, whose brother Alexander was the first European settler in the Shoalhaven area. **Of interest:** Many National Trust-classified buildings including Historical Museum, Queen St. Impressive variety of antique shops and galleries. Market at Showgrounds, 1st Sun. each month. Feb.: Agricultural Show. **In the area:**

Cambewarra Lookout, 14 km SW. Coolangatta, 11 km SE, a group of convict-built cottages, restored to historic village, winery and resort on site of first European settlement in area in 1822. Wineries open for tastings and sales: Jasper Valley Wines, 4 km S; The Silos Winery; 6 km S; Coolangatta Estate, 11 km SE; Cambewarra Estate (open weekends and public holidays), 14 km SW. **Tourist information:** Princes Hwy, Bomaderry; (02) 4421 0778. **Accommodation:** 1 hotel, 1 hotel/ motel, 1 motel, 3 B&B.

Bingara   Pop. 1231

MAP REF. 122 I6

Sapphires, tourmalines and gold may be found in the creeks and rivers around this fascinating town. **Of interest:** Stamper battery at site of former All Nations Gold Mine, top of Hill St. National Trust-classified Museum (1860), in slab building thought to be

town's first hotel, displays furniture and photographs from last-century settlement, gems and minerals, and has a working smithy. Murray Cod Hatchery, Bandalong St (open by appt). Gwydir River Rides (trail rides), Maitland St. Easter: Gold Rush Festival; Easterfish. Sept.: Veterans Golf Tournament. Oct.: Country Music Talent Quest. Dec.: Country Christmas Carnival. **In the area:** Rocky Creek glacial area, 37 km SW. Sawn Rocks, 70 km SW, pipe-shaped volcanic rock formations. At Upper Bingara 24 km S: remains of old gold and copper mines; Three Creeks Tourist Goldmine, a working mine where visitors can pan for gold. Copeton Dam, 42 km E, ideal for fishing and boating, also has two waterslides. Alongside dam golf course where kangaroos graze at dusk. Nearby, excellent camping and accommodation. **Tourist information:** Museum, Maitland St; (02) 6724 1726. **Accommodation:** 2 hotels, 1 motel, 1 cara./camp. park. **See also:** New England.

Southern Highlands

When Governor Lachlan Macquarie visited the area to the south of Sydney that came to be known as the Southern Highlands, he recorded in his diary for that year, 1820: 'the situation of the New Settlers, four miles southwest of Throsby Park, is particularly beautiful and rich, resembling a fine extensive pleasure ground in England'.

Located within the Sydney-Canberra-Melbourne transport corridor formed by the Hume Freeway and the main railway between Sydney and Melbourne, the Southern Highlands is easily accessible, with Canberra to the south (170 kilometres from Bowral), Wollongong and the coast to the east (50 kilometres from Bowral) and Sydney to the north (130 kilometres from Bowral).

The thriving towns of **Mittagong, Bowral, Berrima, Moss Vale, Robertson** and **Bundanoon** are surrounded by the gentle softness of a rural landscape varied by the changing colours of the seasons.

The crisp mountain air has long attracted visitors. The area offers colourful gardens, and in

Moss Vale, one of the major centres in the Southern Highlands

the towns and villages the visitor will find galleries, antiques, and arts and crafts. There are also rugged mountain ranges, rolling green hillsides, plunging waterfalls and marvellous bushwalks.

The landscape ranges from gently undulating to rugged, at 650–860 metres above sea level. The eastern side of the region is bounded by the cliffs and ravines of the Illawarra escarpment and **Morton National Park**. There are small sections of remnant rainforest in the vicinity of Robertson.

The major natural attraction in the region is the picturesque Fitzroy Falls, part of Morton National Park. Wombeyan Caves, 67 kilometres north-west of Mittagong, are remarkable for their limestone formations. Budderoo National Park is

small, but noted for its views and excellent walking tracks. Other popular attractions include the Alpaca Centre at Berrima, the Highlands Equestrian Centre at Sutton Forest (14 kilometres south-west of Moss Vale), the Tulip Time Festival, held in late September, early October at Bowral and 'Christmas in June' held in towns and villages throughout the region.

For further information, contact the Southern Highlands Visitor Information Centre, 62–70 Main St, Mittagong; (02) 4871 2888; freecall, 1800 656175. **See also:** National Parks and individual text entries in A–Z listing for those parks and towns indicated by bold type. **Map reference:** 116.

NEW SOUTH WALES

Blayney
Pop. 2652

MAP REF. 120 G6

A progressive country town with a growing goldmining industry on the Mid Western Hwy between Cowra and Bathurst, and close to the historic villages of Carcoar and Millthorpe. **Of interest:** Buildings classified by National Trust. Avenues of deciduous trees, particularly beautiful in autumn. In Adelaide St: Forever Country, for local crafts; Heritage Park. Carrington Park, Church St. Mar.: Agricultural Show. **In the area:** Carcoar Dam, 12 km SW, for water sports; camping and picnic/barbecue facilities nearby. National Trust-classified village of Carcoar, 14 km SW, scene of NSW's first bank hold-up in 1863. At Newbridge, 20 km E, historic buildings and craft outlets. Local art and craft at Taroona Wool Pack (5 km NE) and Cottesbrook Gallery (15 km NE), both on Mid Western Hwy. Millthorpe, 11 km NW, a National Trust-classified village featuring Golden Memories Museum and craft shops. **Tourist information:** Mid West Mini Market, 20 Adelaide St; (02) 6368 2570. **Accommodation:** 4 hotels, 2 motels, 1 B&B, 1 cara./camp. park.

Boggabri
Pop. 751

MAP REF. 122 H9

Situated 115 km NW of Tamworth, this town is the centre of a wool, wheat and cotton area. **Of interest:** Historical Museum, Brent St. Honey factory, Lynn St (open by appt). July: Wean Picnic Races. **In the area:** Fishing. Gin's Leap, 4 km N, a rock formation. **Tourist information:** Narrabri Information Centre, Newell Hwy, Narrabri; (02) 6792 3583. **Accommodation:** 3 hotels, 1 motel, 1 cara./camp. park.

Bombala
Pop. 1404

MAP REF. 117 A9, 119 E11, 243 N7

This small town on the Monaro Hwy, 89 km S of Cooma, is the centre for the surrounding wool, beef cattle, sheep, vegetable and timber-producing area. The area is also renowned for its rich trout fishing, particularly the Bombala River. **Of interest:** Self-guide historical walk (1 hr) includes court house, cnr High and Dickinson sts; School of Art, Caveat St (leaflet from Tourist information). Toorallie Knitting Mill, Maybe St (check opening times at Tourist information).

In Caveat St: White House Gallery (c.1835); Endeavour Reserve, featuring 2-km return walking track. In Mahratta St: Folk Museum, displaying local artifacts and farm implements; Bicentennial Park, with pleasant river walk. Jan.: Wool and Wood Festival. **In the area:** On Monaro Hwy: Burnima historic homestead, 6 km N (open by appt). Bibbenluke Lodge Lavender Nursery, 13 km N (usually open spring and summer). Early Settlers Hut at Delegate, 36 km SW. Scenic drive (gold fossicking along route, with landowners' permission) to Bendoc Mines in Vic., 57 km SW. Coolumbooka Nature Reserve, 15 km NE. **Tourist information:** Mobil Service Station, 125 Maybe St; (02) 6458 3047. **Accommodation:** 3 hotels, 1 motel, 1 B&B, 1 cara./camp. park.

Bourke
Pop. 2976

MAP REF. 125 N5

Anything 'Back o' Bourke' is the real outback. Bourke itself is the service centre of a vast area of sheep country that produces up to 55 000 bales of wool a year. It is claimed to be the largest centre for wool shipment in the world. Crops in the area including cotton have been successful due to irrigation provided by the weir on the Darling River. **Of interest:** Many colonial buildings; self-guide historical tour available, contact Tourist information. Tourist information in Old Railway Station, Anson St, has displays of Aboriginal artifacts, products of local industries and local history. In Cobar Rd: Fred Hollows' grave and memorial in cemetery; Cotton Gin, open for tours. Fishing for cod, Darling River. Bridge (1883) over Darling River, first lift-up bridge in NSW. Lock, only lock on Darling. Replica of historic wharf, Sturt St, a reminder of days when Bourke was a busy paddlesteamer port. Apr.: Fred Hollows Foot Race (to Sydney). June: Bourke to B-Bash (charity car rally, different destination each year, always starting with 'B'). Sept.: Mateship Festival (includes paddleboat regatta). Oct.: Back o' Bourke Stampede (rodeo). **In the area:** Replica of Fort Bourke Stockade, 20 km SW, testament to early explorer Major Thomas Mitchell. Mt Gunderbooka, 74 km S, wildlife sanctuary featuring caves with Aboriginal art. Mt Oxley, 40 km E, views of plains from summit. **Tourist information:** Old Railway Station, 45 Anson Street; (02)

6872 2280. **Accommodation:** 6 hotels, 5 motels, 1 hostel, 3 cara./camp. parks.

Bowral
Pop. 7929

MAP REF. 116 C6, 119 I3, 121 J10

The friendly township of Bowral nestles below Mount Gibraltar, 114 km S of Sydney. Originally a popular summer retreat for wealthy Sydney residents, who left a legacy of stately mansions and beautiful gardens, Bowral today is the commercial centre of the Southern Highlands region. **Of interest:** Corbett Gardens, Merrigang St, showpiece of Tulip Time Festival (Sept.–Oct.). Bradman Oval, near house where cricketer Sir Donald Bradman spent his youth, and Bradman Museum, St Jude St. Historic buildings, mostly in Wingecarribee and Bendooley sts. Specialty shopping in antiques, especially in Bong Bong St. Sept.–Oct.: Tulip Time Festival; District Art Society Exhibition. **In the area:** Lookout on Mt Gibraltar, 2 km N; also bushwalking trails. **Tourist information:** Southern Highlands Visitor Information Centre, 62–70 Main St, Mittagong; (02) 4871 2888; freecall, 1800 656176. **Accommodation:** 3 hotels, 7 motels, 4 B&B.

Braidwood
Pop. 976

MAP REF. 119 G6, 120 H13, 143 L4

This old town, 84 km S of Goulburn, has been declared an historic village by the National Trust. Gazetted in 1838, Braidwood was a pastoral centre prior to the discovery of gold in the area in 1851, after which it developed as the principal town of the southern goldfields. Much of the architecture from this period has survived. *Ned Kelly* (1969), *The Year My Voice Broke* (1986) and *On Our Selection* (1994) – all filmed here. **Of interest:** Museum, Wallace St, displays of local Aboriginal history, Chinese settlement and goldmining artifacts (open Thurs.–Mon., daily during school holidays). Historic buildings include: St Andrews Church, Elrington St; St Bedes, and Royal Mail Hotel with its beautiful iron lacework, both in Wallace St. Self-guide tour of historic buildings, leaflets from Tourist information. Galleries; craft and antique shops. Apr.: Heritage Festival. Nov.: Music at the Creek. **In the area:** Scenic drives, contact Tourist information for brochure. The Big Hole, a large sink hole, and the Marble Arch rock formation, 45 km S. **Tourist information:**

Museum, Wallace St; (02) 4842 2310. **Accommodation:** 1 hotel, 3 motels, 5 B&B, 1 hostel.

Brewarrina   Pop. 1168

MAP REF. 125 Q5

Located 95 km E of Bourke, this town takes its name from an Aboriginal word meaning 'place of the fishery'; it is still an ideal base for the keen angler. The main industries include wool and wheat production. **Of interest:** Ancient Aboriginal stone fish-traps in Darling River, once a major food source for local Aborigines. Aboriginal Cultural Museum, Bathurst St, displays aspects of Aboriginal life from Dreamtime to present (open Mon.–Fri.). Many 19th-century buildings, built when town was

a thriving river port. Self-guide drive, contact Tourist information. Wildlife park, Doyle St. Apr.: Agricultural Show. **In the area:** Narran Lake, 40 km NE, features native birdlife and other fauna. **Tourist information:** Shire Offices, Bathurst St; (02) 6839 2106. **Accommodation:** 2 hotels, 1 motel, 1 cara./camp. park.

Broken Hill   Pop. 23 263

MAP REF. 124 B12

This artificial oasis in the vast arid lands of far western NSW was created to serve the miners working in the rich silver-lead-zinc mines of the Barrier Range. The mines produce 2 million tonnes of ore annually. The green parks and colourful gardens, 1170 km NW of

Sydney, seem unreal in the semi-desert setting. The city's water supply comes from local storage schemes and the Menindee Lakes on the Darling River. Note that Broken Hill operates on Central Standard Time, half an hour behind the rest of NSW. **Of interest:** Self-guide heritage trails, contact Tourist information for pamphlets. National Trust-classified historic streetscape, Argent St. Railway, Mineral and Train Museum, cnr Blende and Bromide sts. Geo Centre Museum, cnr Crystal and Bromide sts. White's Mineral Art and Mining Museum, Allendale St. Joe Keenan's Lookout, Marks St, for view of town and mine dumps, and information boards displaying town history. Many art galleries, including City Art Gallery, cnr Blende and Chloride sts, which features

Port Stephens

The white volcanic sand and aquamarine waters of the beaches of Port Stephens have a distinctly tropical look, and the annual average temperature is within about 2°C of that of the Gold Coast. This large deep-water port, less than an hour's drive from Newcastle, is one of the most unspoiled and attractive seaside holiday areas on the New South Wales coast. Two-and-a-half times the size of Sydney Harbour, and almost enclosed by two volcanic headlands, the harbour is fringed by sheltered white sandy beaches backed by stretches of natural bushland. In spring, wildflowers grow in profusion.

The deep, calm waters of the harbour are ideal for boating and there is excellent beach and estuary fishing for the keen angler. You can hire a range of boats, from aquascooters and catamarans to sailing and power boats. Various cruises are available, including cruises to watch bottlenose dolphins, Myall River cruises, lake cruises and whale-watch cruises (June, July to see humpbacks; end Sept.–early Nov. to see humpbacks and minke whales). Excellent game-fishing waters are within reach outside the harbour, but local fishing clubs warn against going outside the heads unless you are an experienced sailor with a two-motor boat. The best way to reach these waters is aboard one of the many professional charter boats licensed to take anglers and sightseers outside the heads. Early in the afternoon you can watch the local fishing fleet coming into **Nelson Bay**, the main anchorage of the port.

One of the many sheltered inlets at Port Stephens

Restaurants in the area – not surprisingly – offer fresh seafood as a specialty. Sample a superb lobster supreme, washed down by a fine Hunter Valley or Port Stephens wine. For dedicated oyster lovers, a trip to Moffat's Oyster Barn, Swan Bay, is a must. As well as viewing oyster cultivation and learning about their 4-year life cycle, you can also enjoy a delicious meal of oysters. If you go by boat, keep within the well-marked channel to avoid oyster leases.

For surfing, you can visit the spectacular ocean beaches outside the harbour. Within about 6 kilometres of Nelson Bay are Zenith, Wreck and Box beaches, Fingal Bay and One Mile Beach. Always popular is the Coastal Explorer 4WD tour along Stockton Beach, a huge sand-dune expanse – you can view Aboriginal shell middens, the *Sygna* wreck and World War II lines of defence. There are also camel rides available along Stockton Beach.

Other local attractions include: art galleries; craft markets; Aussie Ewe and Lamb Centre, Anna Bay; the toboggan run at Toboggan Hill Park, Salamander Bay; Oakvale Farm and Fauna World; and Fighter World, RAAF Base Williamtown. There is a wide variety of accommodation available in the area, including caravan and camping parks. The main towns, apart from Nelson Bay, are Shoal Bay, Fingal Bay, Anna Bay, Tanilba Bay, Lemon Tree Passage and Soldiers Point on the south shore, and Tea Gardens and Hawks Nest on the north shore.

For further information about the area, including such nearby attractions as the Myall Lakes National Park, contact the Port Stephens Visitors Centre, Victoria Pde, Nelson Bay; (02) 4981 1579. **See also:** text entry for Nelson Bay in A–Z listing. **Map references:** 112 H2, 121 O4.

NEW SOUTH WALES

Silver Tree commissioned by Charles Rasp, discoverer of Broken Hill orebody in 1883. Broken Hill is home of Brushmen of the Bush, a group of artists that includes Pro Hart and Jack Absalom. School of the Air, cnr McCulloch and Lane sts (open by appt, book at Tourist information). Mine tours to Delprat's Mine, off Crystal St. Moslem Mosque (1891), Buck St, built by Afghan community then living in town. Zinc Twin Lakes, off Wentworth Rd, South Broken Hill. Sept.: Silver City Show. Oct.: Country Music Festival. **In the area:** Royal Flying Doctor Service, 10 km S (open by appt, book at Tourist information). Water sports, fishing and camping at Menindee Lakes, 110 km SE. Mootwingee National Park, 130 km NE, features magnificent scenery and Aboriginal historic site, rich in rock art and stencils (access to site limited, contact Tourist information); visitors are advised to be fully self-sufficient in food, water and fuel. Fred Hollows Sculpture Symposium and The Living Desert, 6 km N on Nine Mile Rd; leaflet from Tourist information. Excellent viewing of wildlife on Sundown Nature Trail (2.8 km return), begins 9 km N on Tibooburra Rd; contact Tourist information for leaflet (take water). Silverton, 23 km NW, where silver chlorides were discovered in 1883; town has been location for films *Wake in Fright*, *Mad Max 2* and *A Town Like Alice*; tours of Day Dream Mine; heritage walking trail; several galleries featuring work of resident artists; Silverton Hotel (c. 1880); Old Gaol Museum displaying historic items; camel rides available. Mundi Mundi Plains Lookout, 4 km further N, and a further 9 km N, Umberumberka Reservoir Lookout. **Tourist information:** cnr Blende and Bromide sts; (08) 8087 6077. **Accommodation:** 12 hotels, 13 motels, 2 hostels, 3 cara./camp. parks.

Brunswick Heads   Pop. 1662

MAP REF. 123 Q2, 505 Q12

This town at the mouth of the Brunswick River is well known for its outstanding fishing, and is the base for a large commercial fishing fleet. **Of interest:** Canoe and paddleboat hire at the *Pirate Ship* on the river off Mullumbimby St. Surfing and swimming. Market at Banner Park, Fawcett St, 1st Sat. each month. Jan.: Fish and Chips (wood chop) Festival. Easter: Blessing of the Fleet; Fishing

Competition. **In the area:** New Brighton Hotel, an old pub with character 7 km NW at Billinudgel. **Tourist information:** 80 Jonson St, Byron Bay; (02) 6685 8050. **Accommodation:** 1 hotel, 4 motels, 4 cara./camp. parks.

Bulahdelah   Pop. 1097

MAP REF. 121 O3

Situated on the Pacific Hwy at the foot of Alum Mountain, Bulahdelah is a good base for a bushwalking or houseboating holiday. The town is surrounded by State forests and the beautiful Myall Lakes. Nov.: Show and Rodeo. **In the area:** Bulahdelah Mountain Park, a lovely park with picnic/barbecue facilities, remains of machinery used for alunite mining, rare orchids and walking track. In Bulahdelah State Forest, 14 km N off the Lakes Way, is State's tallest known tree, a flooded gum *Eucalyptus grandis*. At Wootton, 15 km N, historical railway walk along a reconstructed timber railway, ends at an historic trestle bridge with picnic/barbecue facilities nearby. Bulahdelah Logging Railway, 19 km N, offers full-size steam train rides Fri., Sat. and school holidays. Myall Lakes National Park, 12 km E, contains one of State's largest networks (10 000 ha) of coastal lakes, ideal for water sports, houseboats available for hire; bushwalking and camping in surrounding rainforest. Beaches and camping at Seal Rocks, 40 km E. **Tourist information:** Little St, Forster; (02) 6554 8799. **Accommodation:** 1 hotel, 4 motels, 2 cara./camp. parks.

Bundanoon   Pop. 1513

MAP REF. 116 A9, 119 H3, 121 J10

This town is 32 km SW of Mittagong. The area is famous for its deep gullies and views over the rugged mountains and gorges of Morton National Park. Walk or drive to lookouts. Bundanoon was once a honeymoon resort; today it boasts an English-style pub, delightful guest houses and a health resort. The train stops in the heart of town. Apr.: Bundanoon is Brigadoon Annual Highland Gathering. Oct.: Gullies Gallop Fun Run. **In the area:** Exeter, a small village 6 km N; the surrounding area boasts some of the finest horse studs in the country. Bundanoon section of Moreton National Park, 4 km S, is particularly scenic with spectacular lookouts, walking tracks and the famous glow

worms visible at night in Glow Worm Glen (access is via the end of William St, a 25-minute walk, or Riverview Rd, a 40-minute walk). **Tourist information:** Southern Highlands Visitor Information Centre, 62–70 Main St, Mittagong; (02) 4871 2888; freecall 1800 656176. **Accommodation:** 1 hotel, 2 motels, 1 cara./camp. park, 1 camp. ground.

Byron Bay   Pop. 5001

MAP REF. 123 R2, 505 R12

Surfers from near and far gravitate to Wategos Beach, on Cape Byron. Its northerly aspect makes it one of the best beaches for surfboard riding on the east coast. Visitors can go bushwalking, horseriding, fishing, swimming, scuba diving, trikeflying or skydiving, or just enjoy the delightful climate and relaxing lifestyle of this idyllic spot. Dairy products, bacon, beef and tropical fruits are produced locally. Market, 1st Sun. each month. Jan.: Arts and Music Festival. Easter: East Coast Blues Festival. June: Whale Watch Weekend (date varies according to individual season). **In the area:** On Cape Byron, most easterly point on Australian mainland, 3 km SE: Cape Byron Lighthouse, Australia's most powerful lighthouse; Byron Bay Whale Centre, in old lighthouse keeper's cottage, celebrates majesty of whales with educational displays and spectacular audio/visual 'Journey with the Whales'; humpback whales pass the Cape May–Dec. (the Whale Centre is a good whale-watching spot), dolphins can be seen in the area all year. Ocean Shores Golf Course, 1½ km N, considered to be best in State. **Tourist information:** 80 Jonson St; (02) 6685 8050. **Accommodation:** 2 hotels, 23 motels, 6 hostels, 7 cara./ camp. parks.

Camden   Pop. 8440

MAP REF. 105 K10, 116 F1, 119 I1, 121 K8

In 1805 John Macarthur was granted 5000 acres (2023 ha) at what was known as the Cowpastures which he called Camden Park. It was here his wife Elizabeth conducted her famous sheep-breeding experiments. The town of Camden dates from 1840, and is 60 km SW of Sydney on Camden Valley Way. **Of interest:** Many historic buildings, including Belgenny Farm (1819) and Camden Park House (1834), (open one weekend in Sept. only), both part of Macarthur's Camden Estate, Elizabeth

Macarthur Ave; Church of St John the Evangelist (1840–49), John St; Camelot, designed by J. Horbury Hunt, and Kirkham Stables (1816), both in Kirkham La. Camden History Museum, John St. Self-guide walk and scenic drive available, contact Tourist information. Feb.: Heritage Wine and Food Fair. Sept.: Camden Park House Open Weekend. **In the area:** Mt Annan Botanic Garden, just north-east of town on Narellan Rd. At Narellan, 3 km NE, Museum of Aviation. Struggletown Fine Arts Complex, 3 km N. Historic Gledswood Homestead and winery, 10 km N on Camden Valley Way, presents a unique opportunity for visitors to experience a working colonial farm; craft market held last Sun. each month. Vicarys Winery, 25 km N (open weekends). Camden Aerodrome, 3 km NW, for ballooning and gliding; vintage aircraft on display. Markets held at Cobbitty, 11 km NW, 1st Sat. each month. Cowell's Camellia Nursery, 12 km NW at Terry Rd, Theresa Park. Oran Park Raceway, 4 km W, venue for bike, car and truck racing. Wollondilly Heritage Centre and slab-built St Matthew's Church (1838) at The Oaks, 16 km W. Burragorang Lookout, 24 km W, for views over Lake Burragorang. Further west, Yerranderie, fascinating but remote old silver-mining town; reached by 6-hour 4WD journey from Camden or 30-min. plane flight. **Tourist information:** Oxley Cottage, Camden Valley Way; (02) 4658 1370. **Accommodation:** 1 hotel, 4 motels, 1 B&B, 1 cara./camp. park. **See also:** Vineyards and Wineries.

Campbelltown   Pop. 10 004

MAP REF. 105 L10, 116 G1, 121 K8

Founded and named by Governor Macquarie in 1820 after his wife's maiden name, Campbelltown is now a rapidly growing city 50 km SW of Sydney. It is also the location for the legend of Fisher's ghost. In 1826 an ex-convict Frederick Fisher disappeared. The ghost of Fisher is alleged to have pointed to the place where his body was subsequently found and as a result the murderer was brought to justice. **Of interest:** Campbelltown City Bicentennial Art Gallery and Japanese Gardens, Art Gallery Rd, cnr Camden and Appin rds. Historic buildings: Glenalvon (1840) and Richmond Villa (1830–40), Lithgow St; Colonial Houses, 284–298 Queen St; St Peter's

Church (1823), Cordeaux St; Old St John's Church, cnr Broughton and George sts, with grave of James Ruse; Emily Cottage (1840), cnr Menangle and Camden rds; and Campbelltown Art and Craft Society (licensed as Farrier's Arms Inn in 1843) and Fisher's Ghost Restaurant, formerly Kendall's Millhouse (1844), both in Queen St. Self-guide heritage walks, leaflet available at Tourist information. Apr.: Show. Nov.: Festival of Fisher's Ghost. **In the area:** Eschol Park House (1820), 15 km N. Steam and Machinery Museum, 5 km SW on Menangle Rd. Menangle House (1839) and St James' Church at Menangle, 9 km SW. **Tourist information:** Council Offices, 91 Queen St; (02) 4620 1510. **Accommodation:** 4 motels.

Canowindra   Pop. 1721

MAP REF. 120 E7

Bushranger Ben Hall and his gang commandeered this township in 1863. Canowindra today is known as the 'Balloon Capital of Australia' as more balloon flights take place here annually than anywhere else in Australia. Fish fossils of world significance, 360 million years old were discovered in 1956, 9 km SW, and another major dig took place in 1993. Situated on the Belubula River, Canowindra is noted for its curving main street and notable buildings; the entire commercial section in Gaskill St has been classified by the National Trust as a Heritage Conservation Area. **Of interest:** In Gaskill St: Research and Learning Centre has displays of fish fossils (open 11 a.m.–3 p.m. Sat. and Sun. or by appt, contact Tourist information); museum, exhibits local memorabilia (Sun. p.m.); antique shops. Gondwana Dreaming Fossil Tours, 2nd weekend each month. Hot-air balloon rides, Mar.–Nov. (weather permitting). Easter: Model Aircraft Championships. Sept.: Agricultural Show. **Tourist information:** Canowindra Bakery, Gaskill St; (02) 6344 1399. **Accommodation:** 3 hotels, 1 motel, 1 B&B, 1 cara./camp. park.

Casino   Pop. 10 850

MAP REF. 123 P3, 505 P12

This important commercial centre beside the Richmond River is a typical country town with its wide streets and verandahed hotels. It is the centre for the surrounding beef-cattle region. **Of interest:** Casino Folk Museum, Walker

St (open Wed. p.m. and Sun. p.m.). Many fine buildings including public school and court house, both in Walker St; St Mark's Church of England, West St; and Cecil Hotel, post office and Tattersall's Hotel, all in Barker St. Mini railway, West St, operates 1st Sat. and 3rd Sun. each month. Eight parks in town and attractive picnic spots beside Richmond River. Tours of meat works by appt only. May: Beef Week Festival. Aug.: Gold Cup (horserace). Oct.: Agricultural Show. **In the area:** Freshwater fishing on Cooke's Weir and Richmond River. Aboriginal rock carvings, 20 km W on Tenterfield Rd. **Tourist information:** Memorial Baths Centre, Centre St; (02) 6662 3566. **Accommodation:** 4 hotels, 7 motels, 2 cara./camp. parks.

Cessnock   Pop. 17 506

MAP REF. 112 B10, 113 E12, 121 M4

Many excellent Hunter River table wines are produced in the Cessnock district. The economy of the city, formerly based on coal mining, is now centred on wine and tourism. **Of interest:** Galleries, antique and craft shops. Feb.: Vintage Festival. Oct.: Jazz Concerts. **In the area:** More than 55 quality wineries in Pokolbin area, most open for tastings and cellar-door sales (see Lower Hunter Vineyards map). Hot-air ballooning at Rothbury, 11 km N. Local art at Branxton Inn and Gallery, 22 km N at Branxton. Rusa Park Zoo, an exotic wildlife park at Nulkaba, 7 km NW. Picturesque village of Wollombi, 29 km SW, has wealth of historic buildings, including beautiful St John's Anglican Church; court house, now Endeavour Museum (open weekends); old-style combined general store and post office; Aboriginal cave paintings; tours. Watagan Mountains and State Forest, 33 km SE; splendid views and picnic/barbecue facilities at Heaton, Hunter's and McLean's lookouts. Bimbadeen Lookout over Hunter Valley, 10 km E. At Pelaw Main, 17 km E, Richmond Main Mining Museum offers steam-train rides. German Tourist and Holiday Estate, 10 km NE, has pottery, art gallery, Windarra Winery and restaurant. Richmond Vale Mining Museum, 13 km NE (open 1st, 2nd and 3rd Sun. each month). Local art at Butterflies Gallery and Cafe, 17 km NE. **Tourist information:** Turner Park, Aberdare Rd; (02) 4990 4477. **Accommodation:** 7 hotels, 68 motels, 3 cara./camp. parks.

Cobar   Pop. 4138

MAP REF. 125 N10

A progressive copper, gold, silver, lead and zinc mining town with wide tree-lined streets, Cobar is 723 km NW of Sydney. The town is on the Barrier Hwy, used by travellers to visit outback areas of NSW, Qld and NT. Since the opening of the CSA copper mine in the mid-1960s, and the introduction of a channel water supply, the town has been transformed from an arid landscape to a green oasis. There is an abundance of native flora and fauna in the area. The CSA mine has an annual output of 600 000 tonnes of copper and copper-zinc ores. The Elura silver-lead-zinc mine opened in 1983 and the Peak gold-mine in 1992. Wool is the main local primary industry. **Of interest:** Great Cobar Outback Heritage Centre, Barrier Hwy, features pastoral, mining and technological displays. Fine early architecture, including court house and police station, Barton St; St Laurence O'Toole Catholic Church, Prince St; Great Western Hotel, Marshall St, with longest iron-lace verandah in NSW. Heritage walk, heritage bus tour of town (2½ hours) and bus tour of town and surroundings available, details at Tourist information. Commonwealth Meteorological Station, Louth Rd (open by appt). May: Agricultural Show: Oct.: Back to Cobar. **In the area:** Mt Grenfell Aboriginal cave paintings, turn-off 40 km W on Barrier Hwy, near Mt Grenfell Homestead; picnic area nearby. Historic, deserted mining town of Mt Drysdale, 34 km N; tours available, contact Tourist information. **Tourist information:** Great Cobar Outback Heritage Centre, Barrier Hwy; (02) 6836 1452. **Accommodation:** 2 hotels, 1 hotel/motel, 7 motels, 1 B&B, 1 cara./camp. park.

Coffs Harbour   Pop. 20 326

MAP REF. 123 P8

One of the larger centres on the Holiday Coast, this subtropical holiday town is 580 km N of Sydney on the Pacific Hwy. The surrounding district produces timber, bananas, vegetables, dairy products and fish. Coffs Harbour is really two towns – one on the highway and the other near the harbour and railway station. **Of interest:** In High St: Historic Pier Hotel (rebuilt 1920s); jetty (1892); Coffs Harbour Museum. The Marina, departure point for fishing charters and scuba-diving trips to the Solitary Islands. A walk along northern sea wall of harbour leads to Muttonbird Island Nature Reserve, a great vantage point to view annual migration of humpback whales (June–Nov.) and to view short-tailed shearwaters (muttonbirds) (Aug.–Apr.). North of jetty, Pet Porpoise Pool, Orlando St, features performing porpoises and seals; also has research and nursery facilities. Aquajet Waterslide, Park Beach Rd. North Coast Regional Botanical Gardens complex, Hardacre St, noted for its splendid rainforest and prolific birdlife. Coffs Harbour Explorer offers bus tours around town and surrounding area (contact Tourist information for more details). Sept.: Garden Competition. **In the area:** White-water rafting (on Nymboida River), canoeing, game-fishing, scuba diving, horseriding through lush rainforest, Harley rides and 4WD tours; Gambaari Aboriginal Cultural Tour of coastal area; self-guide tours through Wedding Bells State Forest and the Dorrigo Region (4WD only) – for further information, contact Tourist information. Coastline views from surrounding area. Clog-making and Dutch village at Clog Barn on Pacific Hwy, 2 km N. The Big Banana, 4 km N along Pacific Hwy, an unusual concrete landmark in form of huge banana with displays illustrating banana industry; alongside, Big Banana Theme Park features Aboriginal Dreamtime Cave experience and 'realistic' bunyip. World of Horticulture, with monorail, is nearby. Coffs Harbour Zoo, 14 km N. Bruxner Park Flora Reserve, Korora, 9 km NW, a dense tropical jungle area of vines, ferns and orchids; bushwalking tracks and picnic area at Park Creek. Georges Gold Mine tours, 38 km W, contact Tourist information. **Tourist information:** Visitors and Convention Bureau, Pacific Hwy; (02) 6652 1522. **Accommodation:** 8 resorts, 9 hotels, 37 motels, 6 cara./ camp. parks.

Coleambally   Pop. 580

MAP REF. 127 N9

This recently established town, officially opened in June 1968 and the centre of the Coleambally Irrigation Area, is south of the Murrumbidgee River. Rice is the main crop of the 87 600 ha under irrigation; vegetables, grain, sorghum, safflower and soya beans are also grown. The town has a modern shopping centre and a rice mill. **Of interest:** Wineglass Water Tower, Brolga Pl. **Tourist information:** Kingfisher Family Park, Kingfisher Ave; (02) 6954 4100. **Accommodation:** 1 hotel, 1 motel, 1 cara./camp. park.

Condobolin   Pop. 3163

MAP REF. 120 A5

On the Lachlan River, 475 km W of Sydney, Condobolin is the centre of a red-soil plains district producing wheat, wool, beef cattle, fat lambs, fruit and mixed farm products. The town is the southernmost point to which road trains operate from NT and Qld. Jan.: Rodeo. Apr.: Centre Trek (car rally). Aug.: Agricultural Show. Oct.: Art Exhibition. **In the area:** Aboriginal relics, 40 km W, including monument marking burial place of one of the last Lachlan tribal elders. Gum Bend Lake, 5 km W, good for fishing and watersports. Agricultural research station, 10 km E (open Mon.–Fri.). Mt Tilga, 8 km N, said to be geographic centre of NSW; stiff climb to summit but view is worth it. **Tourist information:** Shire Offices, 62–64 Molong St; (02) 6895 2377. **Accommodation:** 1 hotel/motel, 2 motels, 1 cara./ camp. park.

Cooma   Pop. 7385

MAP REF. 117 A2, 119 E9, 142 G11, 243 M3

This lively, modern tourist centre at the junction of the Monaro and Snowy Mountains hwys, on the Southern Tablelands of NSW, was once dubbed Australia's most cosmopolitan town. Thousands of migrants from many different countries worked in the region on the Snowy Mountains Scheme. It is a busy tourist centre year-round, and the jumping-off point for the Snowies. Motorists are advised to check their tyres and stock up on petrol and provisions before setting off for the snow country. **Of interest:** Self-guide Town Walk views National Trust-classified buildings in Lambie St, a street lined with huge oaks, pines and elms (brochure available from Tourist information). In Vale St: Old Gaol Museum; court house (1887), designed by noted colonial architect James Barnet. Cooma Hospital (1867), Bombala St. St Paul's Church, Commissioner St, was constructed with local alpine ash and granite and has a number of beautiful stained-glass windows; first service held here in 1869. In Centennial Park, Sharp St: International Avenue of Flags, with flags of 27 countries unfurled in 1959 to commemorate 10th anniversary of Snowy Mountains Hydro-electric Authority and in recognition of nationalities of people who worked on project; The Time Walk, a Bicentennial project presenting district history in 40 ceramic mosaics. Also in Sharp St, Southern Cloud Park, features Southern Cloud Memorial, a display (with audiotape) of remains of *Southern Cloud* aircraft, which crashed here in 1931 and found in 1958 Snowy Mountains Authority Information Centre, Monaro Hwy, has displays and films on Snowy Mountains Scheme. Alongside, Snowy Memorial, commemorating the 121 people who lost their lives working on the scheme. Nanny Goat Hill Lookout, Massie St, offers views of town. Local art and craft at Loegoss Gallery and The Little Gallery, both in Sharp St. Raglan Gallery and Cultural Centre, Lambie St, has works by local artists and a permanent local history display. Bike track between Lambie St and Rotary Oval follows Cooma Creek. Market, 3rd Sun. each month in Centennial Park. Jan.: Rodeo. Oct.–Nov.: Cooma Fest. Nov.: Snowy Mountains Chainsaw Classic. **In the area:** Clog Maker, 2.5 km W on Snowy Mountains Hwy, features clog-making demonstration by Dutch artisans. Mt Gladstone Lookout, 3 km W, for spectacular views; also mountain-bike trails here. Llama World, 13 km W on Snowy Mountains Hwy (open weekends and school holidays). Kosciusko Memorial, 2.5 km N, donated in 1988 by the Polish Government, commemorating Tadeuz Kosciuszko, champion of the underprivileged and after whom Australia's highest mountain was named. **Tourist information:** 119 Sharp St; (02) 6450 1742; freecall, 1800 636525. **Accommodation:** 6 hotels, 21 motels, 2 hostels, 3 cara./camp. parks.

Coonabarabran   Pop. 2959

MAP REF. 122 F11

A tourist-conscious town in the Warrumbungle Mountains on the Castlereagh River, 465 km NW of Sydney, near Warrumbungle National Park. **Of interest:** Wool 'n' Yarn Co., Dalgarno St, has displays of local wool industry and range of woollen products. Crystal Kingdom, Oxley Hwy, exhibits unique collection of minerals from Warrumbungle Range. At Tourist information, Australian Megafauna Exhibition, featuring prehistoric animal remains from local area including a diprotodon skeleton. Easter: Carnival (includes market on Easter Sat.). Oct.: Cooma Cup Racing Carnival. **In the area:** Aboriginal cultural and ecological tours in surrounding area, details at Tourist information. Skywatch Night 'n' Day Observatory, 2 km NW on National Park road, has interactive display and planetarium. Pilliga Pottery, 34 km NW, off Newell Hwy, mudbrick workshop and showrooms in bushland setting. Pilliga Scrub 'A million wild acres' near Baradine, 44 km NW, a 450 000-ha forest (biggest in NSW) mainly white cypress pine and ironbark plains of dense heath and scrub; location of picnic areas, forest drives and walking tracks from Baradine Forestry Office or Tourist information. Miniland, 8 km W, life-size models of prehistoric animals displayed in bushland setting, as well as an historical museum, children's fun park and water-slide, kiosk and picnic/barbecue facilities. Siding Spring Observatory, 24 km W, has largest optical telescope (3.9 m) in Australia (open day annually in Oct.), and permanent hands-on exhibition 'Exploring the Universe'. Warrumbungle National Park, 35 km W, features 'The Breadknife' a volcanic plug and offers bushwalking, rock climbing, colourful wildflowers, nature study and camping facilities (guided walks available at school holidays or by appt). **Tourist information:** Newell Hwy; (02) 6842 1441. **Accommodation:** 3 hotels, 12 motels, 2 B&B, 2 hostels, 2 cara./camp. parks.

The Illawarra Coast

Magnificent panoramic views along the rugged Illawarra Coast more than compensate for the often winding route of the Princes Highway, which runs the length of it. 'Illawarra' is a corruption of an Aboriginal word appropriately meaning 'high and pleasant place by the sea'. Stretching from Sydney south to Batemans Bay, the Illawarra Coast is bounded on the west by the Southern Highlands.

Fine surf beaches stretch along Illawarra's craggy coast, which is liberally dotted with mountain streams, waterfalls, inlets and lakes. Fauna and colourful wildflowers abound in the many reserves along the coast, and the distinctive vegetation includes cabbage palms, tree ferns and giant fig trees. This is the setting for the State's third largest city, **Wollongong**, which

View from Stanwell Park near Wollongong

has many tourist attractions, scenic lookouts and beautiful beaches.

The other main towns on the coast are **Shellharbour**, a popular holiday and residential town south of Lake Illawarra; **Kiama**, the centre of a prosperous dairying and mixed-farming district; **Nowra**, the main town of the fascinating Shoalhaven River district; and **Ulladulla**, a picturesque little fishing town and popular summer holiday destination.

For further information, contact Tourism Wollongong, 93 Crown St, Wollongong; (02) 4228 0300. **See also:** individual text entries in A–Z listing for those towns indicated by bold type. **Map references:** 116 G13, 119 I7, 121 K12.

Japanese Garden, just north of Cowra

NEW SOUTH WALES

Coonamble
Pop. 2886

MAP REF. 122 C10

This town on the Castlereagh Hwy is situated on the Western Plains, 518 km NW of Sydney. It serves a district that produces wheat, wool, lamb, beef, cypress pine and hardwood timber. **Of interest:** Historical Museum, in former police station and stables, Aberford St. June: Rodeo. Oct.: Gold Cup Race Meeting; Western Sandfly Supercross Motorbike Race. **In the area:** Warrana Creek Weir, on southern outskirts of town, for boating and swimming. Macquarie Marshes, 80 km NW, a breeding-ground for waterbirds. Swimming at Hollywood Bore, 45 km NE. **Tourist information:** Historical Museum, Aberford St; (02) 6822 3040. **Accommodation:** 5 hotels, 3 motels, 1 cara./camp. park.

Cootamundra
Pop. 6386

MAP REF. 119 B3, 120 D10

This town on the Olympic Way, 427 km SW of Sydney, is less than 2 hours' drive from Canberra, and is well known for the Cootamundra wattle (*Acacia baileyana*). It has a strong retail sector and is a large stock-selling centre for the surrounding pastoral and agricultural rural holdings. **Of interest:** Self-guide 'Two Foot Tour' around town, contact Tourist information for brochure. Local crafts available at Tourist information and at the Art and Craft Centre, Hovell St. Birthplace of Sir Donald Bradman, town's most famous son, at 89 Adams St. Cootamundra Public School Museum, Cooper St (check opening times). Rotary markets at Albert Park, Bourke St, last Sun. each month. Aug.: Wattle Festival (includes garden fair). **In the area:** Wineries in the Harden area, 78 km E. Inglenook Deer Farm at Wallendbeen, 19 km NE. Yandilla Mustard Seed Oil, 26 km N (tours by appt). **Tourist information:** Railway station, Hovell St; (02) 6942 4212. **Accommodation:** 4 hotels, 4 motels, 1 B&B, 1 cara./camp. park.

Corowa
Pop. 5064

MAP REF. 127 O13, 241 M3

Birthplace of Australia's Federation, Corowa took its name from *Currawa*, an Aboriginal word describing the pine trees that once grew there in profusion. A typical Australian country town, Corowa's wide main street, Sanger St, lined with turn-of-the-century verandahed buildings, runs down to the banks of the Murray River. Tom Roberts' painting *Shearing of the Rams* displayed in the National Gallery of Victoria, was completed at Brocklesby Station, just out of town, in 1889. **Of interest:** Federation Museum, Queen St. Self-guide historic walk (guide available on request for groups), contact Tourist information. Gliding joyflights at aerodrome off Redlands Rd (weekends, weather permitting). Market in Sanger St, 1st Sun. each month. Jan.: Federation Festival. Dec.: National Skydiving Championships. **In the area:** Rutherglen wineries, begin 4 km S, only a short drive or bicycle ride away. **Tourist information:** Railway station building, John St; (02) 6033 3221. **Accommodation:** 6 hotels, 17 motels, 4 cara./camp. parks.

Cowra
Pop. 8422

MAP REF. 120 F8

The peaceful air of this busy country town on the Lachlan River belies its dramatic recent history. On 5 August 1944, over 1000 Japanese prisoners attempted to escape from a nearby POW camp. Four Australian soldiers and 231 Japanese prisoners died in the ensuing struggle. **Of interest:** Australia's World Peace Bell, Darling St. Cowra Rose Garden, adjacent to Tourist information centre. Lachlan Valley Railway and Steam Museum, Campbell St, has displays and train rides (check times). Colemane's Country Corner, cnr Mulyan and Cooyal sts, a country music museum. Cowra Mill Winery, Vaux St, winery and restaurant in former flour mill (1861). Sept.: World Peace Day (ceremony at Peace Bell). Oct.: Sakura Matsuri (Cherry Blossom Festival); Japanese Cultural Exhibition. **In the area:** Australian and Japanese War Cemeteries, 5 km N, beside Cowra-Canowindra Rd (Australian soldiers who died are buried in Australian War Cemetery; Japanese soldiers who died during escape, and Japanese internees who died in Australia during World War II, are buried in Japanese War Cemetery). Sakura Ave, 5 km of flowering cherry trees, links site with POW camp, Breakout Walking Track and Japanese Garden which includes Cultural Centre, traditional teahouse, bonsai house, pottery and display of Japanese artifacts. Historic Croote Cottage, 25 km NW at Gooloogong, built by convicts and raided by bushrangers (open by appt). Conimbla

National Park, 27 km W. Quarry Cellars winery, 4 km S, on Boorowa Rd. Darby Falls Observatory, 25 km SE, where amateur astronomer has a series of telescopes available to the public nightly. Wyangala Waters State Recreation Area, 40 km SE, a mecca for watersports and fishing enthusiasts. Cowra museums (war, rail and rural museums in one complex), 5 km E on Sydney Rd. **Tourist information:** Olympic Park, junction Boorowa, Grenfell and Young rds; (02) 6342 4333. **Accommodation:** 4 hotels, 2 hotel/ motels, 8 motels, 18 B&B, 3 cara./camp. parks.

Crookwell Pop. 1966

MAP REF. 119 F2, 120 H10

Located 45 km NW of Goulburn, Crookwell is the centre of a rich agricultural and pastoral district, producing wool, beef, fat lambs, apples, pears and cherries, and is the State's major supplier of certified seed potatoes. **Of interest:** Stevensons Mill, Roberts St, a flour mill restored by local historians (open Wed. or by appt). Weaving Mill and Gallery, Denison La. (open Wed.–Sun.). Self-drive bushranger trails, contact Tourist information. Market at Uniting Church, Goulburn St, 1st Sat. each month. **In the area:** Many quaint historic villages associated with gold and copper mining, as well as bushranging, including Tuena, Peelwood, Laggan, Bigga, Binda (all north of town) and Roslyn (south, and birthplace of poet Dame Mary Gilmore). Redground Lookout, 8 km NE. Willow Vale Mill, 9 km NE at Laggan, restored flour mill with restaurant and accommodation. Wombeyan Caves, 60 km NE, has five caves open to public. Abercrombie Caves, 64 km N along Bathurst Rd, set in a 220-hectare reserve featuring the largest natural arch in the southern hemisphere (tours available). Snowy Mountain Lookout, 42 km NE. Upper reaches of Lake Wyangala and Grabine State Recreation Area, 65 km NW, for water-skiing, picnicking, fishing, bushwalking and camping. **Tourist information:** Crookwell Promotion Centre, 44 Goulburn St; (02) 4832 1988. **Accommodation:** 4 hotels, 2 motels, 1 cara./ camp. park.

Culburra Pop. 3145

MAP REF. 116 G13, 121 K11

Famous for its prawning and fishing, this town is situated 23 km SE of Nowra near Wollumboola Lake. **Of interest:** Surfing, swimming, and lake, shore and rock fishing. The beach is patrolled in summer holidays. Jan.: Open Fishing Carnival. **Tourist information:** Shoalhaven Tourist Centre, 254 Princes Hwy, Bomaderry; (02) 4421 0778. **Accommodation:** 1 motel, 2 cara./camp. parks.

Culcairn Pop. 1175

MAP REF. 127 Q12, 241 Q1

Dating back to 1880 and planned to service the railway between Sydney and Melbourne, Culcairn today reflects the district's rural prosperity. Bushranger Dan Morgan began his life of crime at Round Hill Station, with a hold-up on 19 June 1864. The town owes its picturesque tree-lined streets and parks to its unlimited underground water supply (discovered in 1926). **Of interest:** Historic Culcairn Hotel (1891), Railway Pde. Many National Trust-classified buildings on Railway Pde and Olympic Way Also in Railway Pde, French's Furniture, for rustic Australian-style furniture. Local crafts at N & H Crafts, Balfour St. Centenary Mural, Main St. Artesian pumping station, Gordon St. **In the area:** John McLean's Grave, 3 km E; a price was put on Morgan's head after he shot McLean. Round Hill Station, Holbrook Rd. At Walla Walla, 18 km W: Old Schoolhouse (1875), museum and largest Lutheran church (1924) in NSW. Morgan's Lookout, 4 km N. Premier Yabbies, 7 km S. Pioneer Museum at Jindera, 42 km S. **Tourist information:** Post office, 33a Balfour St; (02) 6029 8521. **Accommodation:** 1 hotel, 1 motel, 1 cara./camp. park.

Deniliquin Pop. 7895

MAP REF. 127 L11

At the centre of the largest irrigation complex in Australia, Deniliquin has the largest rice export mill in the world; it services the Japanese market. The town is located beside the Edward River, 750 km SW of Sydney. The northern part of the district is famed for its merino sheep studs, including Wanganella and Boonoke. **Of interest:** Sunrice Visitors Centre, at rice mill in Ricemill Rd. Peppin Heritage Centre (1879), George St, a museum dedicated to the development of merino sheep industry by the Peppin family last century. Waring

Gardens, Cressy St. Island Sanctuary, off Cressy St footbridge, features free-ranging kangaroos and prolific birdlife. River beaches, including McLean and Willoughby's beaches. Market, 4th Sat. each month. Jan.: Sun Festival. Easter: Jazz Festival. **In the area:** Pioneer Tourist Resort and Garden Centre, 6 km N, features antique steam and pump display. Bird Observatory Tower at Mathoura, 34 km S. Irrigation works at Lawsons Syphon, 6 km E and Stevens Weir, 26 km W. **Tourist information:** Peppin Heritage Centre, George St; (03) 5881 2878; freecall, 1800 650712. **Accommodation:** 6 hotels, 3 hotel/ motels, 8 motels, 1 hostel, 5 cara./ camp. parks.

Dorrigo Pop. 1135

MAP REF. 123 O8

This important timber town is surrounded by magnificent river, mountain and forest scenery. **Of interest:** Old railway station, Tallowood St, has large collection of locomotive and rolling stock. For local crafts: Calico Cottage, Hickory St, and The Art Place, Cudgery St. Market at Showground, Armidale Rd, 1st Sat. each month. **In the area:** Excellent trout fishing in district. Dangar Falls, 2 km N. Dorrigo Pottery, 8 km W on Tyringham Rd. Dutton Trout Hatchery near Ebor, 63 km W. Nearby, Ebor Falls, favourite with photographers. Point Lookout, 60 km W, in New England National Park, for stunning views over head of Bellinger Valley across to ocean; claimed to be one of best views on the east coast. Dorrigo National Park, 5 km E, features luxuriant rainforest; wide variety of birds including bowerbirds and lyrebirds; a Skywalk (begins at Rainforest Centre) offering birds' eye views over canopy of World Heritage-listed rainforest; and a Walk with the Birds Birdwalk. **Tourist information:** Hickory St; (02) 6657 2486. **Accommodation:** 2 hotel/motels, 1 cara./camp. park.

Dubbo Pop. 28 064

MAP REF. 120 E2

This pleasant city on the banks of the Macquarie River, 420 km NW of Sydney, is recognised as the regional capital of western NSW, and supports many agricultural and secondary industries. **Of interest:** In Macquarie St: Old Dubbo Gaol, featuring original gallows and solitary confinement cells, and animatronic robots telling story of convicts; Dubbo Museum. Dubbo Regional Art Gallery, Darling St. Indoor Kart Centre, Mountbatten Dr. May: Agricultural Show. June: Eisteddfod. Oct.: Festival of the Red Earth (community festival). **In the area:** Western Plains Zoo, 5 km S, Australia's first open-range zoo with over 300 ha of landscaped park and animals from six continents, some roaming in natural surroundings. Military Museum, 8 km S, with open-air exhibits; 4 km further S, Yarrabar Pottery. Restored Dundullimal Homestead (1840s), 7 km SE on Obley Rd. Golfworld, 3 km N in Fitzroy St, has driving range and minigolf course. Jinchilla Gardens and Gallery, 12 km N, off Gilgandra Rd. **Tourist information:** cnr Erskine and Macquarie sts; (02) 6884 1422. **Accommodation:** 6 hotels, 33 motels, 1 B&B, 1 hostel, 6 cara./camp. parks.

Dungog   Pop. 2187

MAP REF. 112 A1, 121 N3

These days an ideal base for bushwalking enthusiasts, Dungog was established in 1838 as a military post to prevent bushranging in the area. Situated on the upper reaches of the Williams River, it is on one of the main access routes to Barrington Tops National Park. Apr.: Rodeo. Sept.: Spring Festival. **In the area:** Chichester Dam, 23 km N, in picturesque mountain setting; nearby Duncan Park is ideal for picnicking. Telegherry Forest Park, 30 km N, with walking trails to waterfalls along Telegherry River and picnic, swimming and camping spots. Barrington Tops National Park, 40 km N, noted for its unusual native flora and rich variety of wildlife; good bushwalking and forest drives. Superb views from Mt Allyn (1100 m), 40 km NW. Clarence Town historic village, 25 km S. Paterson historic village, 34 km SW. **Tourist information:** cnr Brown and Dowling sts; (02) 4992 2212. **Accommodation:** 3 hotels, 1 motel.

Eden   Pop. 3277

MAP REF. 117 F11, 119 G11, 243 Q8

Eden is a quiet former whaling town on Twofold Bay, 512 km S of Sydney, with an outstanding natural harbour. Fishing and timber-getting are the main industries. **Of interest:** Eden Killer Whale Museum, Imlay St, features skeleton of

notorious 'Tom the killer whale'. Bay cruises available. Mar.: Amateur Fish Club Competition. Oct.: Eden Whale Festival. **In the area:** Whale-watching, particularly humpbacks, Oct.–Nov.; whale-watch cruises available. Ben Boyd National Park, extending 8 km N and 19 km S of Eden, has outstanding scenery and is ideal for fishing, swimming, camping and bushwalking; prominent park features include Boyd's Tower (1840s) at Red Point, and the red and white earth formations, the Pinnacles, located 8 km N. On perimeter of park, 9 km S, at Nullica Bay, former rival settlement of Boydtown has convict-built Seahorse Inn (still licensed), safe beach and excellent fishing. Davidson Whaling Station Historic Site on Kiah Inlet, 14 km S. Harris Daishowa Chipmill Visitors Centre, Jews Head, 26 km S (other side of Twofold Bay), has video and static displays on logging and milling operations (tours, Thurs. 10.30 a.m.). Good fishing at Wonboyn Lake, 40 km S; scenic area in between Ben Boyd National Park and Nadgee Nature Reserve. **Tourist information:** Princes Hwy; (02) 6496 1953. **Accommodation:** 2 hotels, 10 motels, 1 B&B, 6 cara./camp. parks. **See also:** The South Coast.

Eugowra   Pop. 572

MAP REF. 120 E6

It was near this small town on the Orange–Forbes road that 'the great gold-escort robbery' occurred in 1862. **Of interest:** Eugowra Museum, displaying Aboriginal artifacts, gemstones, early farm equipment and wagons. Nangar Gems, Norton St, for sapphires, opals, emeralds and garnets. **In the area:** Escort Rock, 3 km E, where bushranger Frank Gardiner and gang hid before ambush of Forbes gold escort; rock is on private property, but plaque on road gives details, unlocked gate allows entry. **Tourist information:** Visitors Centre, Civic Gardens, Byng St, Orange; (02) 6361 5226. **Accommodation:** 2 hotels.

Evans Head   Pop. 2375

MAP REF. 123 Q4, 505 Q13

This holiday and fishing town, and centre of the NSW prawning industry, is situated off the Pacific Hwy via Woodburn. It has safe surf beaches and sandy river flats. Rock, beach and ocean fishing, boating and windsurfing are

popular activities. Aug.: Bowling Carnival. **In the area:** Bundjalung National Park, just south, renowned for its fishing; also Aboriginal relics. Broadwater National Park, 5 km N, for bushwalking, birdwatching, fishing and swimming. At Woodburn, 10 km NW, Riverside Park beside Richmond River; further 14 km S at New Italy, monument and remains of settlement, result of ill-fated Marquis de Rays' expedition in 1880. **Tourist information:** The Professionals Real Estate, 9 Oak St; (02) 6682 4611. **Accommodation:** 1 hotel, 1 motel, 1 cara./ camp. park.

Finley   Pop. 2220

MAP REF. 127 M12, 240 I1

This town on the Newell Hwy, 20 km from the Victorian border, is the centre of the Berriquin irrigation scheme. **Of interest:** Mary Lawson Log Cabin (replica) and museum, Murray St (Newell Hwy), has display of rural heritage. Finley Lake, Newell Hwy, for boating and sailing, picnic areas on lake banks. Sept.: Agricultural Show. **Tourist information:** Mary Lawson Log Cabin, Murray St; (03) 5883 2195. **Accommodation:** 3 hotels, 5 motels, 1 cara./camp. park.

Forbes   Pop. 7552

MAP REF. 120 D6

Noted bushranger Ben Hall is buried in this former goldmining town, 386 km W of Sydney beside the Lachlan River. He was shot by police just outside the town in 1865. Today the town's industries include an abattoir, feed lots, pet food manufacture, and export of beef and hay. **Of interest:** Many historic buildings, especially in Camp and Lachlan sts. Historic town walk, brochure at Tourist information. Historic museum, Cross St, featuring relics associated with Ben Hall. Forbes Cemetery, Bogan Gate Rd, has graves of Ben Hall, Ned Kelly's sister, Kate Foster, and Captain Cook's niece, Rebecca Shields. Memorial in King George V Park, Lawler St, where 'German Harry' discovered gold in 1861. In small park in Dowling St, memorial marks spot where explorer John Oxley first passed through Forbes. Jan.: Jazz Festival; Flatlands Hang-gliding. Sept.: Show Day. **In the area:** Sandhills Vineyard, 6 km E on Eugowra Rd. Lachlan Valley Wines, 5 km SE. Lachlan Vintage Village, 1 km S, a re-creation of gold-rush era with emphasis on lifestyles. Gum Swamp Sanctuary for native fauna, 4 km w. **Tourist information:** Old Railway Station, Union St; (02) 6852 4155. **Accommodation:** 7 hotels, 7 motels, 3 B&B, 4 cara./camp. parks.

Forster   Pop. 14 578

MAP REF. 121 P2

Forster is connected by a bridge to its twin town Tuncurry on the opposite side of Wallis Lake, a holiday area in the Great Lakes district. The area is well known for its fishing and is a major producer of oysters. Launches and boats may be hired for lake and deep-sea fishing. **Of interest:** Forster Art and Craft

Centre, Breese Pde. Dolphin-watch cruises and lake cruises available. Toburabba Walking Tour, visits sites of Aboriginal cultural significance in town; inquire at Tourist information. Apr.: Australian Iron Man Triathlon. Aug.: Australian Veteran Cycling Championships. Oct.: Oyster Festival. **In the area:** Curtis Collection of vintage cars, 3 km s. The Green Cathedral, an unusual 'open-air cathedral' at Tiona on shores of Wallis Lake, 13 km s. Booti Booti National Park, 17 km s. Sugar Creek Toymakers, 22 km s at Bungwahl. Wallingat State Forest, 25 km s. Myall Lakes National Park, 35 km s; houseboat hire available. Camping and beaches at Seal Rocks, 40 km s, site of a whale

rescue in 1991. **Tourist information:** Great Lakes Tourism, Little St; (02) 6554 8799. **Accommodation:** 2 hotels, 19 motels, 1 hostel, 12 cara./camp. parks.

Gerringong   Pop. 2478

MAP REF. 116 G10, 121 K11

Spectacular views of white sand and rolling breakers can be seen from this town, 11 km s of Kiama on the Illawarra Coast. **Of interest:** Heritage museum, Blackwood St (check opening times). Market, 2nd Sun. each month. **In the area:** Surfing, fishing and swimming at local beaches. Gerroa and Seven Mile beaches, 3 km s, world-famous as windsurfing locations. Memorial to pioneer

The South Coast

The southern coast of New South Wales, from Batemans Bay to the Victorian border, is an angler's paradise. Hemmed by the Great Dividing Range, it is one of the finest areas for fishing in southern Australia. It is also a haven for anyone who enjoys swimming, surfing or bushwalking in an unspoiled setting.

One of the attractions of this stretch of coast is the variety of country: superb white surf beaches and crystal-clear blue sea against a backdrop of craggy mountains, gentle hills, lakes, inlets and forests. The coast is dotted with quaint little fishing and holiday towns, offering a wide range of accommodation, including caravan parks. These towns are not highly commercialised, although many of them triple their population in the peak summer months. Boats of all kinds can be hired at the major towns.

Peaceful **Batemans Bay**, at the estuary of the Clyde River, is very popular with the landlocked residents of Canberra, the national capital. **Narooma**, Montague Island and **Bermagui** are well known for their game-fishing. Black marlin, blue fin and hammerhead sharks are the main catch. Narooma also boasts an 18-hole cliff-side golf course where you tee off from the third hole across a narrow canyon.

Bega, to the south, is the unofficial capital of the area and is an important dairying and cheese-making centre. As Bega is about 10 minutes inland from the coast and 2 hours from the snow fields, the town's proud boast is that you can ski in the

Coast near Merimbula

Snowies and surf in the Pacific on the same day. Further south is the popular holiday resort of **Merimbula** and its sister village of Pambula.

The southernmost town of the region is the quaint old fishing village of **Eden**, and its former rival settlement, Boydtown, both reminders of the colourful whaling days of the last century. Whale-watching is popular in Eden in the months of October and November.

Fishing is excellent all along the coast. You can catch a variety of fish, including rock cod, bream and jewfish, from the beach or net crayfish off the

rockier parts of the coast. Prawning is good in the scattered inlets, and trout and perch can be caught in the many rivers draining from the mountains.

The region's all-year-round mild climate has made it a favourite with visitors, but you must book well ahead in the peak holiday period.

For further information, contact Sapphire Coast Tourism, 2/163 Auckland St, Bega; (02) 6492 3313. **See also:** individual entries in A–Z listing for those towns indicated by bold type. **Map references:** 117, 119 H12, 143.

Jacarandas in full bloom at Grafton

NEW SOUTH WALES

aviator Sir Charles Kingsford Smith and lookout at northern end of Seven Mile Beach, site of his takeoff to New Zealand in the *Southern Cross* in 1933. Bushwalks through Seven Mile Beach National Park, 13 km S; camping and picnic areas available. Wild Country Park in natural rainforest setting at Foxground, 8 km W. **Tourist information:** Visitors Centre, Blowhole Pt, Kiama; (02) 4232 3322. **Accommodation:** 1 hotel, 3 motels, 1 hostel, 3 cara./camp. parks.

Gilgandra   Pop. 2890

MAP REF. 122 D13

An historic town at the junction of three highways, Gilgandra is the centre for the surrounding wool and farming country. It was the home of the famous 'Coo-ee March', which left from Gilgandra for Sydney in 1915 in a drive to recruit more soldiers for World War I. The area is also known for its windmills, which once provided sub-artesian water. **Of interest:** Museum at Tourist information, on the Newell Hwy, displays memorabilia from 'Coo-ee March'. Film *The Chant of Jimmy Blacksmith* was based on Breelong Massacre, which took place near Gilgandra; related items in museum. Australian Collection, Miller St, features Aboriginal artifacts, display of minerals, fossils and marine specimens, and Gwen Collison watercolours. The Observatory and Display Centre, cnr Wamboin and Willie sts. On Newell Hwy: Orana Cactus World; Rural Museum, featuring antique farm machinery (open Sat., Sun., school holidays or by appt). Coo-ee Tourist Walk, historic walk based on 1915 march; tourist drive around town and to Flora Reserve (brochures available at Tourist information). Easter: Goat Races; Rodeo. May: Agricultural Show. Oct.: Coo-ee Festival. **In the area:** Gilgandra Flora Reserve, 14 km NE, has wildflowers in spring. Warrumbungle National Park, 82 km NE. **Tourist information:** Coo-ee March Memorial Park, Newell Hwy; (02) 6847 2045. **Accommodation:** 3 hotels, 11 motels, 3 cara./camp. parks.

Glen Innes   Pop. 6140

MAP REF. 123 L6

Gazetted in 1852, this mountain town was the scene of many bushranging exploits. In a beautiful setting, at an elevation of 1073 m, it is now the centre of a lush farming district where sapphire mining is an important industry. **Of interest:** Many historic public buildings, particularly in Grey St; self-guide walks available, contact Tourist information for brochures. Centennial Parklands with Martin's Lookout, Meade St, now site of Celtic monument 'Australian Standing Stones'. Land of the Beardies History House, cnr Ferguson St and West Ave, a folk museum housed in town's first hospital and set in extensive grounds, with reconstructed slab hut, period room settings and pioneer relics. May: Celtic Festival. Sept.: Minerama Gem Festival. Nov.: Land of the Beardies Bush Festival. **In the area:** Scenic mountain and riverside country. Good fishing for trout, perch and cod. Fossicking for sapphire, topaz and quartz, within 45-km radius of town. Horse treks, with accommodation at historic bush pubs available, contact Tourist information. Convict-carved tunnel, halfway between Glen Innes and Grafton, on Old Grafton Rd. Gibraltar Range National Park, 70 km NE, has impressive falls, and The Needles and Anvil Rock granite formations. World Heritage-listed Washpool National Park, 75 km NE, a rainforest wilderness area. Fishing safaris at Deepwater, 25 km N. Fossicking at old mining town, Emmaville, 38 km NW. Fossicking and unique rock formations at Torrington, 66 km NW. Gem fossicking and unusual balancing rock formation, 18 km S. Guy Fawkes River National Park, 77 km SE, wild river area ideal for bushwalking, canoeing and fishing. **Tourist information:** Church St; (02) 6732 2397. **Accommodation:** 4 hotels, 10 motels, 6 cara./camp. parks. **See also:** New England.

Gloucester   Pop. 2465

MAP REF. 121 N1

This town lies at the foot of a range of monolithic hills, The Bucketts. It is at the junction of three tributaries of the Manning River, which has excellent trout and perch fishing. **Of interest:** Heritage walk, brochure at Tourist information. Gloucester District Park, outstanding sporting complex. Market at Billabong Park, Denison St, Sat. of each long (public holiday) weekend. Sept.: Mountain Man Triathlon (kayaking, mountain-biking and running). **In the area:** The Bucketts Walk (1½ hours return), just west of town, leads up Bucketts Mountain Range offering good views. Scenic flights from aerodrome, 4 km S. Views from Mograni Lookout (5 km E), Kia-ora Lookout (4 km N) and Berrico Trig Station (14 km W). Mountain Maid Gold Mine at Copeland, 16 km W. Excellent bushwalking and forest drives in Barrington Tops National Park, 60 km W. **Tourist information:** cnr Church and Denison sts; (02) 6558 1408. **Accommodation:** 1

hotel, 1 hotel/ motel, 2 motels, 2 B&B, 1 cara./camp. park.

Gosford   Pop. 38 205

MAP REF. 105 P4, 108 F6, 121 M6

Gosford, part of the scenic Central Coast, is 85 km N of Sydney on the beautiful Brisbane Water. Sept.: Springtime Flora Festival. Oct.: Mangrove Mountain District Country Fair; Gosford City Arts Festival. **In the area:** Henry Kendall Cottage (1838), 3 km SW in Henry Kendall St, where poet lived 1874–5; picnic/barbecue facilities in pleasant grounds. Australian Reptile Park and Wildlife Sanctuary, 9 km SW, features a snake house with taipans and pythons, goannas and a platypus. Adjacent is Old Sydney Town, a reconstruction of an early pioneer settlement. Somersby Falls, near Old Sydney Town, ideal picnic spot. Aboriginal engraving site Bulgandry, 10 km SW in Brisbane Water National Park; also spectacular waratahs here in spring. Bouddi National Park, 17 km SE, for bushwalking, camping, fishing and swimming. Central Coast Winery, 11 km NE, open for tastings and cellar-door sales. Elizabeth's Berry Farm, 12 km NE, a blueberry farm with tearooms. Award-winning Forest of Tranquillity at Ourimbah, 14 km NW. **Tourist information:** 200 Mann St; (02) 4325 2835; freecall, 1800 806258. **Accommodation:** 3 hotels, 10 motels, 2 B&B, 1 cara./camp. park.

Goulburn   Pop. 21 451

MAP REF. 119 G3, 120 H11

This provincial city, steeped in history (proclaimed a city in 1833), can be accessed from the Hume Hwy bypass some 209 km SW of Sydney. It is the centre of a wealthy farming district at the junction of the Wollondilly and Mulwarry rivers beyond the Southern Highlands. **Of interest:** National Trust-classified coaching-house Riversdale (1840), Maud St. St Clair History House (c.1843), Sloane St, a 20-room mansion restored by local historical society. Garroorigang, Braidwood Rd, South Goulburn (1857), private home in almost original condition (open by appt). Old Goulburn Brewery Hotel, Bungonia Rd. Goulburn Court House, Montague St. In Bourke St: Regional Art Gallery; Cathedral of St Saviour. Cathedral of St Peter and St Paul, cnr

Bourke and Verner sts. Two-foot Walking Tour (2 hours) of historic town buildings, brochure available at Tourist information. Goulburn Yurt Works, Copford Rd, tours (by appt) of factory making prefabricated round houses. Fibre Designs gallery, Montague St. The Big Merino, a 15-m sculptured relief, Hume Hwy, has displays of wool products and Australiana items for sale. South Hill, Garoorigang Rd, features woollen art. Excellent picnic/ barbecue facilities on Wollondilly River at Marsden Weir. Rocky Hill War Memorial, Memorial Dr., city's best-known landmark, built in memory of local World War I soldiers. **In the area:** Shearing and sheepdog demonstrations (by appt) at Pelican Sheep Station, 10 km S. Geologically interesting Bungonia State Recreation Area, 35 km E; range of walks available, including one through the spectacular Bungonia Gorge (information about walks available from Tourist information). Wombeyan Caves, 70 km NE, open daily for cave tours. **Tourist information:** 6 Montague St; (02) 4823 0492. **Accommodation:** 7 hotels, 1 hotel /motel, 13 motels, 3 cara./camp. parks.

Grafton   Pop. 16 642

MAP REF. 123 P6

A garden city, famous for its riverbank parks and the jacaranda, wheel and flame trees lining its wide streets, Grafton is situated at the junction of the Pacific and Gwydir hwys, 665 km N of Sydney. **Of interest:** Numerous National Trust buildings. Schaeffer House (1900), Fitzroy St, now district historical museum. Stately Prentice House, Fitzroy St, one of Australia's finest regional art galleries. Susan Island in Clarence River, a recreation reserve covered with rainforest and home to large fruit-bat colony. Oct.: Bridge to Bridge Ski Race. Oct.–Nov.: Jacaranda festival. Nov.: Bridge to Bridge Sailing Classic. **In the area:** Four major national parks within hour's drive: Yuraygir (50 km E), Bundjalung (70 km N), Washpool (88 km NW) and Gibraltar Range (92 km NW). National Trust-classified Ulmarra village, 12 km NE, a fine example of turn-of-the-century river port. Houseboat hire at Brushgrove, 20 km NE. Weekend gliding at Eatonsville, 18 km NW. Canoeing and rafting on wild-river systems in surrounding area; also many scenic drives. **Tourist information:** cnr Spring St and Pacific Hwy, South

Grafton; (02) 6642 4677. **Accommodation:** 17 hotels, 14 motels, 4 B&B, 1 hostel, 3 cara./camp. parks.

Grenfell   Pop. 2037

MAP REF. 119 B1, 120 D8

The birthplace of poet and short-story writer Henry Lawson, this small town is 377 km W of Sydney, on the Mid Western Hwy. **Of interest:** Henry Lawson Obelisk, next to Lawson Park on road south to Young, on site of house where poet is believed to have been born in 1867. Historic George St, has many buildings dating back to 1860s. Historic Building Walk, Tour of Grenfell Town (drive) (brochures available at Tourist information). Museum, Camp St (open weekends). Off Camp St, O'Brien's Lookout, where gold was discovered, has walkway and picnic facilities. Mar.: Picnic Races. Easter: Guinea Pig Races. June: Henry Lawson Festival of Arts. Oct.: Iris Festival. Nov.: Grenfell Guineas (horse-race). **In the area:** Weddin Mountains National Park, 18 km SW, for bushwalking, camping and picnicking (drive/walk available, contact Tourist information); area used as hideout by bushrangers Ben Hall, Frank Gardiner, Johnnie Gilbert and others; easy walk to Ben Hall's Cave and to Seaton's Farm, an historic homestead within park. Lirambenda Riding School and Animal Farm, 20 km S. Cypress Valley Ostrich Facility, 30 km NE on Peaks Creek Rd, offers tours. Old Richmond Cottage, 30 km W at Quandialla, for tours of cottage gardens, bush stories, poetry readings and devonshire teas (by appt only). **Tourist information:** CWA Craft Centre, 68 Main St; (02) 6343 1612. **Accommodation:** 5 hotels, 1 motel, 1 B&B, 1 hostel, 1 cara./camp. park.

Griffith   Pop. 13 296

MAP REF. 127 N7

A thriving city developed as a result of the introduction of irrigation, Griffith was designed by Walter Burley Griffin, architect of Canberra, and named after Sir Arthur Griffith, the first Minister for Public Works in the NSW government. Of a diversity of industries, rice is the most profitable, followed by citrus fruits, grapes, vegetables, eggs and poultry. Griffith is also well known as a wine-producing area; there are over a dozen wineries in the district. The Murrumbidgee Irrigation Area produces

NEW SOUTH WALES

Dog on the Tucker Box near Gundagai

80 per cent of the State's wines. **Of interest:** Two Foot Tour walk around town, brochure available at Tourist information. Koala Gourmet Foods, Whybrow St (tours available). In Banna Ave: Regional Theatre has stage curtain designed and created by efforts of 300 residents to reflect city, surrounding villages and industries; Regional Art Gallery, has monthly exhibitions. Griffith Cottage Gallery, Bridge Rd. Crafty Spot, Benerembah St. Market, each Sun. in Wakaden St. Easter: Festival of Griffith. Oct.: Festival of Gardens. **In the area:** Pioneer Park Museum, set in 18 ha of bushland 2 km N, features drop-log buildings, memorabilia from early 20th century and Bagtown village, re-created to give insight into development of area. Lake Wyangan, 10 km NW, for water sports. Bagtown Cemetery, 5 km S, a reminder of pioneering days. Catania Fruit Salad Farm, 6 km S on Cox Rd at Hanwood, a horticultural farm offering demonstrations of processes (open weekdays p.m., weekends by appt). Cocoparra National Park, 25 km NE. Many wineries in area, most open for tastings and sales (for details contact Tourist information). **Tourist information:** cnr Banna and Jondaryan aves; (02) 6962 4145. **Accommodation:** 2 hotels, 1 hotel/motel, 8 motels, 1 hostel, 2 cara./camp. parks. **See also:** Vineyards and Wineries.

Gulgong
Pop. 2042

MAP REF. 120 H2

This old goldmining town, 29 km NW of Mudgee, is known as 'the town on the

(original) $10 note'. In its heyday in the 1870s it was packed with fortune hunters from all over the world. Some of its glory remains in the many restored buildings; the town's narrow streets are lined with clapboard and iron buildings decorated with their original iron lace. **Of interest:** Henry Lawson Centre, Mayne St, boasts largest collection of Lawson memorabilia outside Sydney's Mitchell Library. Historic buildings on self-guide Town Trail (brochures available from Tourist information) include Prince of Wales Opera House, Mayne St; Ten Dollar Town Motel (formerly Royal Hotel), cnr Mayne and Medley sts; American Tobacco Warehouse and Fancy Goods Emporium, Mayne St; Pioneers Museum, cnr Herbert and Bayly sts. Red Hill, off White st, site of original gold strike, features restored stamper mill, poppet head, memorial and statue of Henry Lawson. Apr.: Foundation Day (odd-numbered years). June: Henry Lawson Festival. Oct.: Heritage Weekend (at Pioneer Museum). **In the area:** Ulan Coal Mine, viewing areas overlook this large open-cut mine; Hands on the Rock, rock paintings; The Drips, curtains of water dripping through rocks alongside Goulburn River – all 25 km N. **Tourist information:** 109 Herbert St; (02) 6374 1202. **Accommodation:** 4 hotels, 3 motels, 1 B&B, 1 cara./camp. park.

Gundagai
Pop. 2069

MAP REF. 119 B5, 120 D12

Much celebrated in song and verse, this town on the Murrumbidgee River at the foot of Mt Parnassus, 398 km SW of Sydney, has become part of Australian folklore. Its history includes Australia's worst flood disaster in 1852 when 89 people drowned, nearby gold rushes, and many bushranging attacks. Today it is the centre of a rich pastoral and agricultural district that produces wool, wheat, fruit and vegetables. **Of interest:** Marble carving of cathedral, comprising over 20 000 pieces, by Frank Rusconi (sculptor of tucker box dog) on display in Tourist Information Centre, Sheridan St. Also in Sheridan St: Gabriel Gallery, with its outstanding collection of early photographs, letters and possessions of poet Henry Lawson; National Trust-classified court house (1859), scene of many historic trials, including that of notorious bushranger Captain Moonlite; National Trust-classified Prince

Alfred Bridge (1866), longest timber viaduct in Australia. Historical museum, Homer St. National Trust-classified St John's Anglican Church (1861), cnr Otway and Punch sts. Excellent views from Mt Parnassus Lookout, Hanley St, and Rotary Lookout, Luke St, South Gundagai. Oct.: Spring Flower Show. Nov.: Dog on the Tucker Box Festival. **In the area:** Dog on the Tuckerbox, 'five miles from' or 8 km N, monument to pioneer teamsters and their dogs, celebrated in song by Jack O'Hagan; nearby larger-than-life copper statues of Dad and Dave characters from an old radio serial; kiosk; fern-house; and ruins of Five Mile Pub. Asparagus plantation at Jugiong, 21 km NE (open daily for sales Oct.–Dec.). **Tourist information:** Sheridan St; (02) 6944 1341. **Accommodation:** 4 hotels, 6 motels, 1 B&B, 2 cara./camp. parks.

Gunnedah
Pop. 8874

MAP REF. 122 H10

A prosperous town on the banks of the Namoi River, Gunnedah is the centre of rich pastoral and agricultural country, and is one of the largest stock-marketing and killing centres in NSW. Other industries include a brickworks, a tannery, flour mills and open-cut and underground coal mines. **Of interest:** In Anzac Park, South St: Water Tower Museum; Dorothea MacKellar Memorial statue (MacKellar was an Australian poet and author of 'My Country'. Opposite at Tourist information, collection of Dorothea MacKellar's memorabilia. Rural Museum, Mullaley Rd. Red Chief Memorial to an Aboriginal warrior of Gunn-e-dar group, State Office building in Abbott St. Old Bank Gallery, Conadilly St. Creative Arts Centre, Chandos St. Eighth Division Memorial Avenue of flowering gums. Self-drive town tour; self-guide Bindea Town Walk (brochures available from Tourist information). Market, 3rd Sat. each month in Wolsely Park, Conadilly St. Jan.: National Tomato Competition. Aug.: Ag Quip (Agricultural Field Day). Sept.: Vintage Car Swap Meet. **In the area:** Porcupine Lookout, 3 km SE, offers views over town and surrounding agricultural area. Lake Keepit Dam and State Recreation Centre, 34 km NE, for water sports, bushwalking, gliding club, picnicking, camping, caravan park. 150° East Time Meridian, 28 km W. **Tourist** information: Anzac Park, South St; (02) 6742 4300. **Accommodation:** 6 hotels, 7 motels, 1 cara./camp. park.

Gunning   Pop. 497

MAP REF. 119 E4, 120 G11

This town, on the Old Hume Hwy between Goulburn and Yass, is in the centre of pastoral country. **Of interest:** In Yass St: Pye Cottage, a slab-style pioneer cottage; historic post office; Telegraph Hotel; old court house; Do Duck Inn. Feb.: Agricultural Show. **In the area:** Greendale Pioneer Cemetery, Gunning–Boorowa Rd. Hume and Hovell Walking Track extends from Gunning to Albury, a distance of 370 km and a 20-day trek for long distance walkers, but half-day, one-day and weekend walks at various points along the route (for information on this walking track contact the Department of Land and Water Conservation, 23–33 Bridge St, Sydney; (02) 9228 6111). **Tourist information:** Gunning Motel, Yass St; (02) 4845 1191. **Accommodation:** 1 hotel, 1 motel, 1 B&B.

Guyra   Pop. 1942

MAP REF. 123 L8

Guyra is Aboriginal for 'fish may be caught', and the local streams are excellent for fishing. At 1300 m, this small town in the Great Dividing Range is one of the highest in NSW. Guyra is the centre of a highly productive area known for fat lambs, beef, wool and potatoes. **Of interest:** In Bradley St: Historical Society Museum (open Sun. or by appt); Railway station, with large display of antique machinery. Waterbirds at Mother of Ducks Lagoon, McKie Pde. Jan.: Lamb and Potato Festival (includes Hydrangea Festival). Nov.: Rodeo. **In the area:** Chandler's Peak, 20 km E, for spectacular views. Llangothlin Handcraft Hall on Hwy, 10 km N. Thunderbolt's Cave, 10 km S. Ebor Falls and picnic reserve, 75 km SE. **Tourist information:** Penns Art Gallery, New England Hwy; (02) 6779 1206. **Accommodation:** 2 hotels, 2 motels, 1 cara./camp. park. **See also:** New England.

Hartley   Pop. 5

MAP REF. 104 G5, 120 I7

This historic village just off the Great Western Hwy, 134 km NW of Sydney, was an important stopover for travellers in the early colonial days. Situated in the Hartley Valley, it is now administered by the National Parks and Wildlife Service. **Of interest:** Self-guide leaflet (from Tourist information) introduces several historic buildings, including convict-built court house (1837), designed by colonial architect Mortimer Lewis; Royal Hotel (early 1840s); Old Trahlee Cottage; post office (1846); St Bernard's Church and Presbytery (1842); Farmer's Inn; Ivy Cottage; and Shamrock Inn. **Tourist information:** 285 Main St, Lithgow; (02) 6351 2307. **Accommodation:** 1 cara./camp. park.

Hay   Pop. 2817

MAP REF. 127 K8

Hay, established in 1859, was named after the politician and pastoralist, Sir John Hay. It is the commercial centre for a huge area of semi-arid grazing country, and is located on the banks of the Murrumbidgee River at the junction of the Cobb, Mid Western and Sturt hwys. Increasing irrigation from the Murrumbidgee has led to an expansion in vegetable- and fruit-growing. There is a beef industry and many world-famous sheep studs, including Mungadal, Uardry and Cedar Grove, are in the area. **Of interest:** In Lachlan St: historic buildings, including post office (1881), Shire office (1877) and Lands office (1896) an early example of a government building designed specifically for the harsh outback environment; Witcombe Fountain (1883) and plaque, commemorating journey of explorer Charles Sturt along Murrumbidgee and Murray rivers in 1829-30; coach house in main shopping area, featuring original Cobb & Co. coach that plied Deniliquin–Hay–Wilcannia run until 1901. Hay Gaol Museum, Church St, has pioneer relics. Restored court house, Moppett St. Restored railway station (1882), Murray St. Hay Park, cnr of Moppett and Pine sts. Signposted scenic drive around town. Nature walk along banks of river, southern end of town off Brunker St. Sandy river beaches along Murrumbidgee for swimming, boating and fishing. Birdwatching area close to town; breeding ground for many inland species. Bishop's Lodge, South Hay (1888), restored as museum, exhibition gallery and conference centre; market day held here in Oct. Mar.: Riverina Stud Merino Field Day. May: Sheep Show. **In the area:** Ruberto's Winery, Sturt Hwy, South Hay. Sunset viewing area, 16 km N on Booligal Rd. John Oxley Memorial at Booligal, 78 km N on Lachlan River; town mentioned in Banjo Paterson's poem 'Hay and Hell and Booligal'. Weir on Murrumbidgee River, 12 km W. Villages of Maude (53 km W), with its attractive picnic areas near weir, and Oxley (87 km NW), with its river red gums along river and prolific wildlife (best seen at dusk). **Tourist information:** 407 Moppett St; (02) 6993 4045. **Accommodation:** 6 hotels, 7 motels, 3 cara./camp. parks.

Henty   Pop. 840

MAP REF. 120 A13, 127 Q11

The historic pastoral township of Henty is in the heart of Morgan Country, so called because of the infamous but ill-fated bushranger Dan Morgan. Almost midway between Albury-Wodonga and Wagga Wagga, Henty can be reached by the Olympic Way or by the Hume Hwy and Boomerang Way. **Of interest:** Headlie Taylor Header Memorial, Henty Park, off Allen St, a tribute to machine (invented 1914) that revolutionised the grain industry. Sept.: Machinery Field Days. **In the area:** Sergeant Smith Memorial Stone, 2 km W on Pleasant Hills Rd, marks site where Dan Morgan fatally wounded a policeman. Doodle Cooma Swamp (2000 ha), breeding area for waterbirds, is visible from memorial stone. Buckingingah Woolshed, built of chocks and logs (no nails), 11 km E on Cookardinia Rd. Squatters Arms Inn (1848) at Cookardinia, 24 km E. **Tourist information:** Doodle Cooma Arms Hotel, Sladen St; (02) 6929 3013. **Accommodation:** 2 hotels.

Holbrook   Pop. 1369

MAP REF. 127 R12, 241 R1

This small town is a well known stock-breeding centre, 521 km SW of Sydney, on the Hume Hwy. **Of interest:** Bronze statue of Commander Holbrook as well as his submarine in Holbrook Park, Hume Hwy; submarine is a scaled model of one in which Commander N. D. Holbrook won VC in World War I; town (formerly Germonton) was renamed in his honour. Adjacent to park, 30 m submarine formerly called the Otway, decommissioned in 1995. Woolpack Inn Museum, in former hotel (1860), features 20 rooms furnished in

National Parks

The national parks of New South Wales encompass areas ranging from World Heritage-listed rainforests to unspoiled beaches. Tourists return time and time again to these popular scenic retreats, which offer a wide range of activities for holidaymakers. Many of the State's parks are found along the coast, their rugged headlands, quiet inlets and sweeping beaches pounded by the crashing surf. The easy accessibility of these coastal parks accounts for their popularity.

Around Sydney

Sydney Harbour National Park is made up of pockets of bushland encircling Sydney Harbour and is the closest national park to the city. Daily visits to Fort Denison leave from Circular Quay.

Just south of Sydney is **Botany Bay National Park** which is divided into two sections: the northern section contains the sandy beaches of La Perouse and a maritime museum (guided tours available), while the southern section at Kurnell protects the site of Captain Cook's first Australian landing in 1770. Here the Discovery Centre features exhibitions of the history of the area.

The **Royal National Park**, just 32 kilometres south of Sydney, was the first national park to be proclaimed in Australia. It was established in 1879, and has over 16 000 hectares of sandstone plateau country, broken here and there by fine surf beaches, including Wattamolla and Garie. The Hacking River runs almost the entire length of the park. Boats may be hired at Audley and visitors can row in leisurely fashion along the river, following its twisting course.

Lane Cove National Park, located within the northern urban area of Sydney, offers good walks and is extremely popular with families. There are many picnic areas next to the river, some of which can be reserved. The river is good for boating (non-powered only), and visitors can enjoy a ride on a paddlewheeler. A wildlife shelter and wildlife shop are popular features of the park.

Further inland, to the west of Sydney, are splendid parks nestling in the mountains that overawed the early explorers. Year after year, innumerable visitors return to the **Blue Mountains National Park**, where mysterious blue mists shroud the immense valleys of the Grose and Coxs rivers, creating ever-changing patterns of green, blue and purple. At Katoomba, pillars of weathered sandstone rise abruptly like isolated church spires: these are the Three Sisters, the most popular tourist attraction in the Blue Mountains. The Grose and Jamison valleys offer many walks with spectacular views.

Just north of Sydney are two prominent national parks, on the southern and northern shores of the Hawkesbury River: **Ku-ring-gai Chase** and **Brisbane Water national parks**, which offer sheltered creeks and inlets, ideal for

Patonga and headlands in Brisbane Water National Park

boating, and bushland walking tracks adorned with colourful wildflowers.

Ku-ring-gai Chase, established in 1894 and only 24 kilometres from Sydney, hugs the shores of Cowan Creek, Broken Bay and Pittwater. Comprising 15 000 hectares of eucalypt forest, scrub and heath, it is the home of a wide range of animal life, including the shy swamp wallaby, the elusive lyrebird, honeyeaters, waterbirds, colourful parrots and lorikeets. A network of walking tracks leads to Aboriginal hand stencils and rock engravings.

Brisbane Water also has sandstone landscapes rich in Aboriginal art. There are scenic views from Warrah Trig and Staples Lookout, while Somersby Falls and Girrakool picnic areas mark the beginning of rainforest walks.

Nearby on the coast is **Bouddi National Park** which protects the coast and bush at the eastern entrance to Broken Bay and on the coastal foreshore from Killcare Heights to McMasters Beach; it also covers a large offshore area near the beautiful Maitland Bay. An extensive network of walking tracks leads to secluded, unspoiled beaches and pockets of rainforest.

Upstream along the Hawkesbury River is **Dharug National Park,** its sandstone cliffs rising high above the meandering river. A network of walking tracks includes a section of the convict-built Old Great North Road.

In the north-east of the State

The largest coastal lake system in New South Wales is protected by the **Myall Lakes National Park,** an important waterbird habitat. Water is the focus of tourist activities: you can enjoy sailing and canoeing on the quiet lake waters, or surfing and beach fishing off the shores of the Pacific Ocean.

Barrington Tops, one of the State's most popular national parks, is a World Heritage Area with a section set aside as wilderness. It has a mountainous plateau (1600 metres), providing spectacular views of the surrounding Hunter Valley and, in the distance, the Pacific Ocean, but visitors should be prepared for sudden bad weather. The stands of snow gums here give way, at about 1000 metres, to forests of Antarctic beech, with lichens, mosses and tree ferns. The lowest areas of the park feature subtropical rainforests, rivers, waterfalls and rapids. Many of the walking tracks in the park are suitable for families. Longer walks, ranging from 4–5 hours to overnight, are suitable for more experienced bushwalkers.

The World Heritage **New England National Park**, which preserves one of the largest remaining areas of rainforest in New South Wales, is 576 kilometres north-east of Sydney. Its 29 985 hectares cover three distinct zones: subalpine with tall snow gums; temperate forests of ancient moss-covered Antarctic beeches; and true subtropical rainforests, rich in ferns, vines and orchids. The park has a diverse range of flora and fauna, including the rare rufous scrub-bird. Some 20 kilometres of walking tracks reveal to visitors the charm of the rainforest, while the trackless wilderness attracts more experienced bushwalkers. Nearby, the World Heritage **Dorrigo National Park** protects some of the rainforests of northern New South Wales. At the Dorrigo Rainforest Centre, visitors can experience the sights, sounds and smells of rainforests. The Skywalk provides magnificent views over the rainforest canopy to the Bellinger Valley and Pacific Ocean beyond.

Yuraygir and **Bundjalung national parks**, to the south and north respectively of the Clarence River on the far north coast, are a water wonderland with isolated beaches, quiet lakes and striking scenery. The parks deserve their reputation as prime areas for fishing. Surfing is also popular; waterways invite exploration by canoe; and the estuaries offer safe swimming. Heathwalking offers opportunities for birdwatching and nature photography, particularly in spring when both parks explode in a spectacle of colour.

In the far north of the State, **Border Ranges**, **Mount Warning** and **Nightcap national parks** offer the visitor vistas of World Heritage-listed rainforest. The 31 508-hectare Border Ranges National Park includes the rim of the ancient volcano once centred on Mt Warning to the east. The best access is via the spectacular Tweed Range Scenic Drive. Stunning escarpments, waterfalls, and walking tracks from picnic areas abound in the eastern part.

Known to the Aborigines as 'Wollumbin', the cloud-catcher, Mt Warning (1157 metres) dominates the landscape and catches the first rays of the rising sun on the continent. A walk through Breakfast Creek rainforest leads to a steep climb and the summit viewing platform. Nightcap National Park is part of the volcanic remnants of Mt Warning and includes the popular summit viewing platform and Protector Falls.

Further inland are two well-known national parks: Warrumbungle and Mount Kaputar. **Warrumbungle National Park**, on the western

NEW SOUTH WALES

side of the Great Divide, is 491 kilometres north-west of Sydney. Here is some of the most spectacular scenery in the nation: sheltered gorges, rocky spires and volcanic peaks. At Warrumbungle, east meets west: the dry western plains and moist eastern coast combine to give high peaks covered with gums and lower forests filled with fragrant native trees and shrubs. Walking trails lead to lookout points where hikers are rewarded with magnificent views. In the spring and summer months the colourful displays of wildflowers and the calls of brightly plumaged birds lure many visitors. There are also easy access tracks for families and the disabled.

Mount Kaputar National Park, near Narrabri, is one of Australia's most accessible wilderness areas. Several lookouts can be reached by car or are only a short walk from your car. Its vegetation ranges from dry sclerophyll forest to subalpine, and the park is rich in flora and fauna. One of the highlights of the park is Sawn Rocks, a 40-metre-high rock formation resembling a series of organ pipes. This is some of the finest columnar jointing in the country and represents one of the various volcanic formations found in the park. Limited cabin accommodation is available within the park.

In the south-east of the State
There are a number of national parks in the southern part of the State, including **Morton National Park**, particularly known for the Fitzroy and Belmore falls, and **Budderoo National Park**, which includes the award-winning Minnamurra Rainforest Centre, where an elevated boardwalk takes you into the rainforest canopy.

Over 9000 hectares of rocky but beautiful coastline flanking Twofold Bay make up **Ben Boyd National Park**. Flowering heaths and colourful banksias add to the area's attraction. Boyd's Tower, constructed in the 1840s, is a prominent feature of the park.

The largest national park in New South Wales is **Kosciusko**. Its 647 097 hectares include mainland Australia's only glacial lakes, as well as limestone caves, grasslands, heaths and woodlands. Situated 450 kilometres south-west of Sydney, this park is of particular significance because it embraces a large area of the continent's largest alpine region and contains Australia's highest mountains as well as the sources of the important Murray, Snowy and Murrumbidgee rivers. The most extensive snowfields of the nation are located here, centred around Thredbo, Perisher, Smiggin Holes, Mt Blue

The remarkable Walls of China in Mungo National Park

Cow, Mt Selwyn and Charlotte Pass. There are easy grades for beginners and slopes for expert skiers. Although Kosciusko is associated with winter sports, it is also a superb summer retreat with its crisp, clean air, crystal-clear lakes and a wonderful display of alpine wildflowers. It is a popular venue for those who enjoy camping, fishing, boating and bushwalking. Yarrangobilly Caves are a feature of the park and are open all-year round, subject to winter road conditions. Yarrangobilly boasts five tourist caves – one with wheelchair access – a naturally heated thermal pool, nature trails and picnic facilities.

In the west of the State
In the far west of New South Wales are four outstanding national parks. **Kinchega**, 110 kilometres south-east of Broken Hill, contains the beautiful saucer-shaped overflow lakes of the Darling River. The lakes provide a most important breeding ground for a wide variety of waterbirds, including herons, ibises, spoonbills and black swans. Walking tracks pass through forests of river red gums, and scenic drives follow the course of the river and the lake shores.

North-east of Wentworth is the World Heritage-listed **Mungo National Park**, part of the Willandra Lakes World Heritage Area. The shores of the now dry lake hold a continuous record of Aboriginal life dating back more than 40 000 years. The remarkable Walls of China, a great crescent of dunes, stretches along the eastern shore of the lake bed. Visitors can enjoy the park on a day

trip or take advantage of the shearers' quarters accommodation or camping facilities. Self-guide walking tracks and a 60-kilometre self-guide drive tour provide visitors with the opportunity to see and learn about the many attractions of the park.

Mootwingee National Park, covering an area of 68 912 hectares and 130 kilometres north-east of Broken Hill, offers breathtaking scenery and a rich heritage of Aboriginal art.

The most remote national park in the State is **Sturt**, 1400 kilometres from Sydney and 330 kilometres north of Broken Hill. This is an ideal place for those who want to get away from it all and experience the real Australian outback. The park's 310 634 hectares comprise scenic red sand dunes, rocky ridges, ephemeral lakes and Mitchell grass plains. Visitors must come well prepared but may camp in the park and enjoy bushwalking over the sandplains. Wildflowers, which include the scarlet and black Sturt's desert pea, are abundant in good seasons. Fort Grey, where Sturt and his party built a stockade to protect their supplies, is worth a visit, even though there is little evidence of his occupation today.

For further information about the national parks of New South Wales, contact the National Parks and Wildlife Service, 43 Bridge St (PO Box 1967), Hurstville, NSW 2220; (02) 9585 6333. National Parks and Wildlife Service has produced an excellent brochure *Visitor Guide to National Parks in NSW* which can be obtained from its centres or by mail.

turn-of-the-century style, the complete plant of old cordial factory, bakery, horse-drawn vehicles and farm equipment. Ten Mile Creek, behind museum, attractive area for picnics and walks. Easter: Ultra Fly-in (biennial, even-numbered years). Apr.: Beef Fest. Nov.: Agricultural Show. **In the area:** Ultralight Centre, 3 km N at Holbrook airport; flights and instruction available. **Tourist information:** Woolpack Inn Museum, 83 Albury St (Hume Hwy); (02) 6036 2131. **Accommodation:** 2 hotels, 7 motels, 1 cara./camp. park.

Huskisson   Pop. 900

MAP REF. 119 I5, 121 K12, 143 R1

A thriving town, Huskisson is 24 km SE of Nowra, on the shores of Jervis Bay. **Of interest:** Lady Denman Heritage Complex, Dent St, provides history of wooden shipbuilding at Huskisson (check opening times); also in Complex, Laddie Timbery's Aboriginal Art and Craft Centre, artifacts made on site by Aboriginal artisans; Museum of Jervis Bay Science and the Sea, with its fine maritime and surveying collections. Several antique and craft shops. Diving and dolphin-watch cruises available. Market, 2nd Sun. each month at White Sands Park. Easter: White Sands Carnival. **In the area:** At Jervis Bay: water sports, particularly scuba diving, also excellent fishing; Bay renowned for its clean water and is frequently used to film underwater sequences; Barry's Bushtucker Tours (contact Tourist information for details). **Tourist information:** Shoalhaven Tourist Centre, 254 Princes Hwy, Bomaderry; (02) 4421 0778. **Accommodation:** 4 motels, 2 cara./camp. parks.

Iluka   Pop. 1795

MAP REF. 123 Q5

A coastal resort alongside the mouth of the Clarence River, Iluka is well known for its fishing. A deep-sea fishing fleet operates from the harbour. **Of interest:** Daily passenger ferry services to Yamba. River cruises available from Boatshed, Wed. & Fri. 11.45 a.m. July: Amateur Fishing Classic. **In the area:** World Heritage-listed Iluka Rainforest, at northern edge of town, for excellent walks. Further north, Bundjalung National Park, a beautiful coastal park offering excellent fishing, swimming, surfing, canoeing, walking and camping. Woombah Coffee Plantation, 14 km W,

world's southernmost coffee plantation (tours by appt). **Tourist information:** Lower Clarence Visitors Centre, Ferry Park, Pacific Hwy, Maclean; (02) 6645 4121. **Accommodation:** 1 motel, 3 cara./camp. parks.

Inverell   Pop. 9736

MAP REF. 123 K6

Known as 'Sapphire City', this town, 67 km W of Glen Innes, is in fertile farming land also rich in minerals. Industrial diamonds, zircons, tin and sapphires are mined in the area. **Of interest:** National Trust-classified court house, Otho St. Pioneer Village, Tingha Rd, has buildings dating from 1840, moved from their original sites, including Grove Homestead, Paddy's Pub and Mt Drummond Woolshed. Tourist Centre and Mining Museum in Water Towers Complex, Campbell St. Art Society Gallery, Evans St. Gem Centre, Byron St. Town Stroll, a self-guide walk (contact Tourist information). Sapphire City market, 3rd Sun. each month. Mar.: Art Exhibition. Oct.: Sapphire City Floral Festival. **In the area:** Fossicking. Lake Inverell Reserve, 3 km E. Draught Horse Centre, Fishers Rd, 4 km E, with six breeds, has display of harness and memorabilia. See working sapphire mine at DeJon Sapphire Centre, 19 km E on Glen Innis Rd. Goonoowigall Bushland Reserve, 5 km S. Gilgai Winery, 12 km S. Green Valley Farm and museum, 35 km S. Copeton Dam State Recreation Area, northern foreshore 17 km S, for boating, water-skiing, swimming, fishing, bushwalking, rock climbing, adventure playgrounds, waterslides and picnic/barbecue facilities. Honey Farm and Bottle Museum, 8 km W. Gwydir Ranch 4WD Park, 28 km W. **Tourist information:** Water Towers Complex, Campbell St; (02) 6722 1693. **Accommodation:** 4 hotels, 6 motels, 3 B&B, 3 cara./camp. parks. **See also:** New England.

Jamberoo   Pop. 704

MAP REF. 116 G9, 121 K10

Jamberoo, 10 km W of Kiama, is in one of the most picturesque areas of the NSW coast, with lush pastures surrounded by towering escarpments. The district has been well-known for the quality of its dairy products since early European settlement days. **Of interest:** Jamberoo Hotel, Allowrie St, features

bush bands Sun. p.m. Market in hotel carpark, last Sun. each month. Mar.: Illawarra Folk Festival. **In the area:** Jamberoo Recreation Park, 3 km N. Saddleback Lookout, 7 km S, for 180° views of coast and starting point for Hoddles Trail, a one-hour walk to Barren Grounds escarpment. Jamberoo Pass, 8 km SW, for excellent views. Walking trails and bird-watching in Barren Grounds Bird Observatory and Nature Reserve, 10 km SW; various wildlife-watching activities and workshops available (bookings essential). Breathtaking State-award-winning Minnamurra Rainforest Centre, 4 km W, features elevated timber boardwalk through rainforest area. **Tourist information:** Kiama Visitors Centre, Blowhole Point, Kiama; (02) 4232 3322. **Accommodation:** 1 hotel, 1 motel/lodge, 1 B&B.

Jerilderie   Pop. 898

MAP REF. 127 M11

This town on the Newell Hwy was held by the Kelly gang for two days in 1879 when they captured the police station, cut the telegraph wires and robbed the bank. Today it is the centre of the largest merino stud area in NSW and also supports an expanding vegetable industry. **Of interest:** Telegraph Office Museum, Powell St; next door, The Willows historic home, for crafts, Devonshire teas and light lunches. Original court house, now library, Newell Hwy. Doll World, Bolton St, displays large collection from around the world. Lake Jerilderie for water sports; adjacent, Luke Park features Steel Wings, one of largest windmills in southern hemisphere; park has shady picnic areas. **In the area:** Tomato and onion factory, 2 km E (tours by appt). **Tourist information:** The Willows, Powell St; (03) 5886 1666. **Accommodation:** 1 hotel/motel, 3 motels, 1 cara./camp. park.

Jindabyne   Pop. 4601

MAP REF. 118 G11, 119 D9, 142 C12, 243 K4

Now on the shores of Lake Jindabyne at the foothills of the Snowy Mountains, the original township was on the banks of the Snowy River. From 1962, residents of the old town moved to the new site chosen by the Snowy Mountains Hydro-electric Authority. This made way for the damming of the Snowy River to form a water storage as part

NEW SOUTH WALES

of the Snowy Mountains Scheme. At an altitude of 930 m and situated in the heart of the Snowy Mountains, Jindabyne attracts skiers in winter and anglers, water-sports enthusiasts and bushwalkers in summer. **Of interest:** Kosciusko National Park Headquarters and Visitor Centre, Kosciusko Rd. Walkway/cycleway around lake's foreshore, from Banjo Paterson Park on Kosciusko Rd to Snowline Caravan Park. Mar.: Strzelecki Polish Festival. Nov.: Snowy Mountains Trout Festival. Dec.: Lake Jindabyne Sailing Club Hobie Cat Races. **In the area:** Lake Jindabyne, well stocked with trout, also ideal for boating, water-skiing and other water sports. Crackenback Cottage, 12 km SW, has craft shop, timber maze and restaurant. Winter shuttle-bus service to Bullocks Flat and Thredbo. At Bullocks Flat, 20 km SW, terminal for Skitube, a fascinating train ride to Perisher and Mt Blue Cow (operates daily, winter, Easter and Christmas holidays). After snow has melted, 50-min. drive south-west from Jindabyne leads to Charlotte Pass and 300-m boardwalk to view main range; 16-km return walk to summit of Mt Kosciusko. At Thredbo, 37 km SW, chairlift operates all year; in summer provides easy walking access over steel-mesh track to summit of Mt Kosciusko, 12-km round trip. Wallace Craigie Lookout, 40 km SW, for excellent views of Snowy River Valley. Gaden Trout Hatchery, 10 km NW (daily tours offered between 10 a.m. and 4 p.m.; barbecues available alongside Thredbo River). Kunama Galleries, 7 km NE. **Tourist information:** Snowy Region Visitor Centre, Kosciusko Rd; (02) 6456 2444. **Accommodation:** 2 hotel/motels, 5 motels, 1 hostel, 2 cara./camp. parks.

Junee
Pop. 3673

MAP REF. 119 A4, 120 C11, 127 R9

Junee is an important railhead town and commercial centre 482 km SW of Sydney on the Olympic Way. **Of interest:** Monte Cristo Homestead, overlooking town, a restored colonial mansion with carriage collection. Roundhouse Museum, Harold St, features 32-m turntable for swivelling train engines to attach to carriages, 42 repair bays, original workshop, locomotives and memorabilia (open Tues., Thurs., Sat., Sun. and public holidays). Hobbin Pond, Peel St. **In the area:** Historic Hotel Shirley, 30 km NE at Bethungra.

Turnoff at Bethungra for Bethungra Dam, ideal for canoeing and sailing. Bethungra Rail Spiral 33 km NE, a unique engineering feat. **Tourist information:** Tourism Wagga Wagga, Tarcutta St, Wagga Wagga; (02) 6923 5402. **Accommodation:** 4 hotels, 1 motel, 1 cara./camp. park.

Katoomba
Pop. 16 927

MAP REF. 104 H7, 106 E9, 121 J7

Katoomba is the highly developed tourism centre of the Blue Mountains area which attracts 3 million people each year. Nearby, the smaller towns of Leura and Wentworth Falls have many interesting features as well as superb mountain scenery. Originally developed as a coal mine last century, it was not long before Katoomba was attracting wealthy Sydney holidaymakers. The coal mine foundered, but Katoomba continued to develop as a tourist destination. Markets at Civic Centre, Katoomba St, 1st and 3rd Sat. each month. Feb.: Blue Mountains Folk Festival. June: Winter Magic Festival. Yulefest held during June, July and Aug. throughout the region. **In the area:** Excellent bushwalking, 4-wheel driving, cycling and scenic flights; contact Tourist information for details. *Around Katoomba:* Echo Point, best place to view the famous Three Sisters rock formation (floodlit at night) within Blue Mountains National Park. Orphan Rock and Katoomba Falls, also floodlit at night. Scenic Skyway and Railway Complex, Violet St/Cliff Dr: Skyway, first horizontal passenger-carrying ropeway in Australia, travels 350 m across mountain gorge above Cooks Crossing providing magnificent views of Katoomba Falls, Orphan Rock and Jamison Valley; the Scenic Railway, built in late 1800s by founder of Katoomba coal mine to bring out coal and transport miners, is reputed to be world's steepest railway descending into Jamison Valley at an average incline of 45°, through a sunlit, tree-clad gorge approximately 445 m in length. The Edge Maxvision Cinema, Great Western Hwy, a six-storey high screen showing brilliantly clear images of the Blue Mountains (several screenings daily). Explorers Tree, west of town off highway, remains of tree which once had early explorers' initials carved into it. *East of Katoomba: At Leura, 3 km E,* Leura Mall, tree-lined main street and

gardens (beautiful in spring and autumn) with many specialty shops, galleries and restaurants. Everglades Garden, Everglades Ave, one of Australia's great gardens built in 1930s, includes a gallery devoted to its creator, Danish master gardener Paul Sorenson. Leuralla, Olympian Pde, a historic art deco mansion with major collection of 19th-century Australian art and one of Australia's largest collections of toys, dolls, trains and railway memorabilia, as well as memorial museum to well-known politician Dr H. V. Evatt. Cascades, just south of town, where Leura Creek cascades into the valley. Dramatic views from Sublime Point; Cliff Drive following cliff tops around Katoomba-Leura region offers spectacular views at many lookouts and picnic spots. Walking tracks along cliff tops and descending into Jamison Valley. Market at public school, Great Western Hwy, 1st Sun. each month. Sept.–Oct.: Legacy Gardens Festival. Oct.: Leura Garden Festival; Leura Village Fair; Greystanes Spring Gardens. *At Wentworth Falls, 7 km E,* Yester Grange (1870s), a colonial homestead-museum on 4.7-ha site, has been restored and furnished to late-Victorian splendour. Conservation Hut Cafe, an eco-designed cafe with splendid views. Feb.: Regatta Day (on Wentworth Falls Lake). Apr.: Autumn Festival. *At Linden, 23 km E,* Kings Cave; Caleys Repulse Cairn, commemorating an early surveyor. *At Faulconbridge, 27 km E,* Corridor of Oaks, oak trees planted by recent Australian Prime Ministers; grave of Sir Henry Parkes, the 'father' of Federation. Norman Lindsay Gallery and Museum, north-east of town (open Wed.–Mon.). *At Springwood, 31 km E,* market at Civic Centre, Macquarie Rd, 2nd Sat. each month; Twilight Market at public school in Macquarie Rd, 4th Sat. each month (not Jan. or Feb.). *Near Hawkesbury Heights, 30 km NE,* Hawkesbury Lookout and Yellow Rock Lookout offer views across plains to Penrith. *At Glenbrook, 43 km E,* Lapstone Zig Zag Walking Track, follows cutting for original Zig Zag railway; lookouts; monument to John Whitton, who had a key role in the development of the railway line; convict-built Lennox Bridge, oldest surviving bridge on mainland; Wascoe Sliding Miniature Railway (1st Sun. each month). South of town is Euroka Clearing, for camping; also a good spot to see eastern grey kangaroos.

Market, 1st Sun. each month (not Jan.); Stamp and Coin Fair, 2nd Sun. each month (not Oct.); both at Community Hall, Great Western Hwy. Sept.–Oct.: Legacy Gardens Festival. Nov.: Spring Festival. ***West of Katoomba:*** *At Medlow Bath, 5 km* NW, Hydro Majestic Hotel, once a health resort; Shipley Tea Rooms, for art exhibitions (open weekends). Mar.: Blue Mountains Herb Fest. *Around Blackheath, 8 km* NW, Jemby-Rinjah Lodge on edge of Blue Mountains National Park, includes environmental studies centre. Evans Lookout, east of town. On Govetts Leap Rd, National Parks and Wildlife Heritage Centre, starting point for Fairfax Heritage Track walk; Govetts Leap Lookout. Pulpit Rock Reserve and Lookout north-east of town. North of town, rhododendrons and azaleas at Bacchante Gardens. South-west of town, statue commemorating the legend of Govett, a daring bushranger; Mt Blackheath Lookout. Pleasant walk to Mermaid cave, south of town. Market at Community Centre, Great Western Hwy, 3rd Sun. each month. Nov.: Rhododendron Festival. Horseriding at Werriberri Trail Rides in Megalong Valley. Nearby, Megalong Valley Farm, a tourist farm. *Mount Victoria, 6 km* NW, a historic village with craft shops, museum and Mt Vic Flicks historic cinema (open Thurs.–Sun. and school holidays). ***South of Katoomba:*** Jenolan Caves, some of the most splendid underground caves and above-ground arches in Australia, in flora and fauna reserve 76 km SW of Katoomba. Yerranderie, a silver-mining ghost town surrounded by 2430-ha wildlife reserve, 200 km S of Katoomba via Oberon (4WD access only), features several historic buildings including museum and quaint hostel-style accommodation. **Tourist information:** Great Western Hwy, Glenbrook; (02) 4739 6266. **Accommodation:** 3 hotels, 8 motels, numerous lodges and guesthouses, 2 B&B, 3 hostels, 1 cara./camp. park. **See also:** The Blue Mountains.

Kempsey   Pop. 9049

MAP REF. 109 G3, 123 O11

Kempsey, situated in the Macleay River Valley, 428 km N of Sydney, is the commercial centre of a growing district of dairying, horticulture, tourism and light industry, including the Akubra hat factory. The town celebrated its sesquicentenary in 1986. **Of interest:** Macleay

Cascades at Leura, in the Blue Mountains

River Historical Society Museum and Settlers Cottage, Pacific Hwy, South Kempsey. Number of 19th-century buildings in Kemp, Elbow, Sea and Belgrave sts, West Kempsey. Free video of the Akubra hat-making process can be seen at Tourist information. Markets at racecourse, North St, 1st Sat. each month. Apr.: Agricultural Show. July: Off-road Race. Sept.: Country Music Festival. **In the area:** At South West Rocks, 35 km NE: good beach; handfeeding of fish at Everglades Aquarium; nearby, Trial Bay Gaol, built by prisoners in 1880s; Smoky Cape Lighthouse (1891) and restored Boatmans Cottage (1902). Hat Head National Park, 32 km E, a coastal park with magnificent sand dunes and unspoiled beaches. Crescent Head, 20 km SE, popular seaside holiday town. Limeburners Creek Nature Reserve, 34 km SE. Fish Rock Cave, noted for scuba diving, just off Smoky Cape. At Kundabung, 12 km S, Australasian bull-riding titles held each Oct. Ronbara Equestrian Park, 36 km NW, offers horseriding, gig rides, canoeing; also tearooms and overnight accommodation. Bellbrook, 47 km NW, a National Trust-classified village. **Tourist information:** Pacific Hwy, South Kempsey; (02) 6563 1555. **Accommodation:** 5 hotels, 12 motels, 5 cara./camp. parks.

Khancoban   Pop. 416

MAP REF. 118 A9, 119 B9, 242 I3

Set in the lush green Murray Valley at the western end of the Alpine Way, 109 km

NW of Jindabyne, this small modern town was built by the Snowy Mountains Authority. **Of interest:** Lady Hudson Rose Garden, Mitchell Ave. National Parks and Wildlife Service, Scott St, have videos of the Snowy Mountains Scheme and Kosciusko National Park. **In the area:** Trout fishing, water sports and whitewater rafting; fishing tours available, contact Tourist information. Permit required for vehicles entering National Park; contact Tourist information. Murray 1 Power Station 10 km SE on Alpine Way; guided tours daily. Excellent picnic and rest areas along Alpine Way; brilliant roadside displays of wildflowers in spring and autumn. Spectacular mountain views from Scammel's Spur Lookout, 20 km SE. **Tourist information:** National Parks and Wildlife Service, Scott St; (02) 6076 9373. **Accommodation:** 1 hotel/motel, 4 B&B, 2 hostels, 1 cara./camp. park.

Kiama   Pop. 10 631

MAP REF. 116 H9, 121 K10

The spectacular blowhole is the best known attraction of this holiday town. Discovered by explorer George Bass in 1797, it sprays water up to heights of 60 m and is floodlit each evening. Kiama is the centre of a prosperous dairying and mixed farming district. **Of interest:** Terrace houses, specialty and craft shops in Collins St. Family History Centre, Railway Pde, contains world-wide collection of records for tracing family history. Heritage walk, contact Tourist

Wildlife-Watching

The rich variety of wildlife in New South Wales includes eastern grey kangaroos and lyrebirds, along with inquisitive dolphins, basking sea lions and huge humpback whales which navigate the State's coast each year.

In Sydney

Australia's largest city is not the perfect environment for native animals, though several species have found a niche. For a colourful and noisy spectacle visit the seaside suburb of **Manly,** where thousands of raucous rainbow lorikeets arrive each evening to roost in the Norfolk pines along the ocean-beach foreshore.

Sydney's other winged residents are somewhat quieter. A large colony of flying-foxes — up to 50 000 in summer months — lives in Ku-ring-gai Flying Fox Reserve in Sydney's northern suburbs. The reserve itself is not open to the public though the bats can still be seen. After spending the day hanging in trees, they take to the air at dusk along particular 'flight paths' to feed on flowering trees. The best vantage point to view this exodus is the Rosedale Road bridge in **Gordon**.

Around Sydney

Royal National Park south of Sydney provides a green buffer against the city's southern suburbs, and many birds thrive among the park's wide range of plant communities. Sulphur-crested cockatoos are happy to make their presence known, though it is worth keeping an eye out for less boisterous birds, such as heath wrens, satin bowerbirds, lyrebirds and top-knot pigeons. Diamond pythons, eastern water dragons and lace monitors can also be seen by observant reptile-watchers.

The famous **Blue Mountains National Park** is a prime location for eastern grey kangaroos. A large mob lives around Euroka Clearing at the eastern-end of the park near Glenbrook. While they are most active at dawn and dusk, there are usually eastern greys about at any time of day. Also in the park are tiny iridescent glow-worms. They are actually the larvae of the fungus gnat, and can be found in the darkness of a disused railway tunnel near Lithgow known as the Glow Worm Tunnel. A kilometre-long walk will take you to the entrance, after which you will need a torch to

Sulphur-crested cockatoo, a Royal National Park resident

negotiate the uneven and sometimes slippery ground inside. To see their gentle glow, turn off your torch and wait quietly for a few minutes. Tiny blue spots of light will gradually become visible on the damp walls of the tunnel.

In the North-East of the State

Cape Byron, next to the township of Byron Bay, is the most popular land based whale-watching spot on the New South Wales coast. Humpback whales are once again regular visitors to the waters off Cape Byron following the demise of the east-coast whaling industry in 1963. Between two and three thousand now migrate peacefully from Antarctica to their northern breeding grounds, passing the Cape in June and July. They return either pregnant or with newborn calves between September and October. A calm ocean and a pair of binoculars will increase your chances of witnessing humpback whale acrobatics. The Whale Centre at the Cape provides a good introduction to the life-cycle and behaviour of these whales, and each year towards the end of June the Whale Watch Weekend Festival celebrates their arrival.

Further south is **Muttonbird Island Nature Reserve**. The island, linked to the city of Coffs Harbour by bridge, has a sizeable population of short-tailed shearwaters (muttonbirds), between August and April each year. Dawn and dusk are the best times to look skywards as the shearwaters fly out and return from fishing excursions. Also keep an eye on the ocean for passing humpback whales in season.

Just inland from Coffs Harbour is the stunning rainforest of **Dorrigo National Park**. Brush turkeys are a common sight around the park's picnic areas; these bald-headed ground dwellers are brash characters, very much at home among human visitors. The Walk with the Birds Boardwalk is a good way to see other forest birds, including yellow robins, thornbills and riflebirds. The Lyrebird Link Track often lives up to its name by providing an opportunity to come across one of Dorrigo's numerous lyrebirds. A unique park resident is the regent bowerbird; the male of the species is well-known for its habit of collecting objects to decorate its bower in the hope of attracting a mate.

On the Central Coast

Bottlenose dolphins are a favourite amongst wildlife-lovers, and the deep, clean waters around **Port Stephens** are a great place to see these marine mammals at play. Fortunately the 60 or so resident dolphins seem to enjoy some 'people-watching' themselves. They will often ride on bow waves of dolphin-spotting boats, turning on their side to glance at the excited humans aboard. If they are in a playful mood, they will also barrel-roll and swim upside down. And with the right combination of tide and swell, they can be seen surfing the breakers at Port Stephens, cutting across the face of waves and launching themselves through the air.

A sail-powered catamaran operates out of Nelson Bay, within Port Stephens, to view migrating humpback whales in season (June, July, September and October). Watching these marine entertainers as they tail-slap, pectoral fin-wave and launch their 30-tonne bodies clear of the water is a memorable experience. Turtles, dolphins, sea eagles and shearwaters (muttonbirds) are also likely to make an appearance. Later in the season minke whales arrive in the area as they follow shoals of pilchards along the coast.

On the South Coast

Thirty minutes by boat from the coastal town of Narooma is **Montague Island Nature Reserve**, home to hundreds of Australian fur seals. August

CAPE BYRON

MUTTONBIRD ISLAND
NATURE RESERVE

DORRIGO NATIONAL PARK

PORT STEPHENS

MANLY & GORDON

BARREN GROUNDS
NATURE RESERVE

MONTAGUE ISLAND
NATURE RESERVE

BLUE MOUNTAINS
NATIONAL PARK

ROYAL NATIONAL PARK

Eastern grey kangaroo with joey

to December are the best times to view and photograph large numbers of these protected sea mammals as they sun themselves on the rocks. Montague Island is one of the few 'haul-out' sites for these seals on the Australian coastline; boat tours operate to the colony daily.

A second boat tour heads for the nightly penguin parade. Each evening at dusk the island's penguins return from their daily fishing excursion at sea. June to March are the best times to see the birds emerge from the waves and waddle up the beach to their burrows. Between August and November the tour-boat skippers watch for migrating whales as there is a good chance of spotting a humpback at this time of year.

In the Southern Highlands

Within **Barren Grounds Nature Reserve** near Jamberoo is a bird observatory which offers some unique wildlife-watching experiences. This non-profit environmental education venture, set up by the Royal Australian Ornithologists Union, hosts regular nature-based day and weekend activities.

Popular workshops include a lyrebird-watching weekend in winter, when the birds' courtship displays and songs are at their finest. The Birds for Beginners days combine bird-watching with useful information, while the Slither and Croaker weekend concentrates on searching for reptiles and

frogs. There is also a bird-banding workshop where visitors can watch birds being trapped, banded, measured and released. Phone (02) 4236 0195 for bookings. The observatory has several good walking tracks for bird-watchers to view yellow-tailed black cockatoos, beautiful firetails and yellow robins.

For more information on wildlife-watching in national parks contact the National Parks and Wildlife Service, 43 Bridge St (PO Box 1967), Hurstville NSW 2220; (02) 9858 6333. For more information on bird-watching contact the Bird Observers Club of Australia, 183 Springvale Rd, Nunawading, Victoria 3131; (03) 9877 5342.

WILDLIFE-WATCHING ETHICS

- Do not disturb wildlife or wildlife habitats. Keep the impact of your presence to a minimum. Use available cover or hides wherever possible.
- Do not feed wildlife, even in urban areas. (Note: supervised feeding is allowed at some locations)
- Be careful not to introduce exotic plants and animals – definitely no pets.
- Stay on defined trails.

information. At Blowhole Point: Blowhole; Pilots Cottage Historical Museum. Kiama Beach for surfing, swimming and fishing. Market, 3rd Sun. each month. Feb.: Jazz Festival; Seven-a-Side Rugby Competition. June: Folk Music Festival. Oct.: Seaside Festival. **In the area:** Little Blowhole, 2 km S, off Tingira Cres. Cathedral Rocks, 3 km N at Jones Beach, a scenic rocky outcrop, best at dawn. **Tourist information:** Blowhole Point Rd; (02) 4232 3322. **Accommodation:** 2 hotels, 6 motels, 1 B&B, 2 hostels, 4 cara./camp. parks. **See also:** The Illawarra Coast.

Kyogle
Pop. 2912

MAP REF. 123 P2, 505 P12

Kyogle makes a good base for exploring the mountains nearby. It is also the centre of a lush dairy and mixed-farming area on the upper reaches of the Richmond River near the Qld border. July: Rodeo. Oct.: Show. Nov.: Festival; Golf Tournament. **In the area:** World Heritage-listed Border Ranges National Park, 27 km N, with forestry road access, walking tracks, camping facilities and views of Mt Warning and Tweed Valley; in eastern section, Tweed Range Scenic Drive (64 km) through pristine rainforest with deep gorges and waterfalls plunging into crystal-clear creeks. Rodeo in Mar. at Wiangaree, 15 km N. Scenic forest drive via Mt Lindesay, 45 km NW on NSW-Qld border, offers magnificent views; Toonumbar Dam, 31 km W, with bushwalking and picnic/barbecue facilities nearby; at Bell's Bay, 2 km from dam, excellent bass fishing and camping. Picnic spots include Roseberry Nursery, 23 km N; Sheepstation Creek, in Border Ranges National Park. **Tourist information:** Geneva St; freecall, 1800 685579. **Accommodation:** 2 hotels, 1 motel, 3 cara./camp. parks.

Lake Cargelligo
Pop. 1256

MAP REF. 127 O4

A small township, 586 km W of Sydney, with the same name as the lake alongside, Lake Cargelligo serves the surrounding agricultural and pastoral district. **Of interest:** The lake, 8 km long and 3.5 km wide, ideal for fishing (silver perch, golden perch and redfin), boating, sailing, water-skiing and swimming. The lake is also home to many species of bird, including at times, the

rare black cockatoo. Tourist information centre, Foster St, has a large gem collection and information on Harley Davidson motorbike tours of surrounding area. Jan.: Bowling Festival. June: Blue Water Art and Craft Festival. Sept.: Lake Show. **Tourist information:** Foster St; (02) 6898 1501. **Accommodation:** 3 hotels, 2 motels, 1 cara./camp. park.

Laurieton
Pop. 4385

MAP REF. 109 F10, 123 O12

The villages of Laurieton, North Haven and Dunbogan are scattered around the foreshore of a large inlet formed by the Camden Haven River at its mouth, 44 km S of Port Macquarie. This tidal inlet is ideal for estuary fishing. **Of interest:** Historical Museum, in old post office, Laurie St (open by appt). **In the area:** Oysters, lobsters, crabs, bream and flathead in local rivers and lakes. Seafront well-known fishing spot. Delightful bushwalks along seafront and around lakes. River cruises available. Crowdy Bay National Park, 5 km S, renowned for its prolific birdlife and magnificent ocean beach; walking tracks provide spectacular ocean view. Panoramic views from North Brother Mountain, 6 km SW. Big Fella Gum Tree, 18 km SW, one of three exceptionally large trees in Middle Brother State Forest. At Kendall, 10 km W, several art and craft galleries including Craft Co-op in railway station; markets in Logans Crossing Rd, 1st and 3rd Sun. each month. Rainforest with waterfalls, 60 km W at Comboyne Plateau. **Tourist information:** Pacific Hwy, Kew; (02) 6559 4400. **Accommodation:** 1 hotel, 3 motels, 2 cara./camp. parks.

Leeton
Pop. 6245

MAP REF. 127 O8

Located 560 km SW of Sydney, Leeton is the first of the planned towns in the Murrumbidgee Irrigation Area and was designed by American architect Walter Burley Griffin. The town is an important administrative and processing centre for the surrounding intensive cultivation of fruit, rice and wine-grapes. **Of interest:** Art Deco streetscape including Roxy Theatre and historic Hydro Hotel (1919) at Chelmsford Pl. Tours weekdays at Sunrice Country Visitors Centre at rice mill, Calrose St and Sunburst Juice Factory, Brady Way. Riverina Cheese Factory,

Massey Ave, has sales outlet in Acacia Ave. Easter: Country Festival, 10-day festival culminates Easter Mon. (biennial; even-numbered years). **In the area:** Wine tastings at Toorak and Lillypilly Estate wineries, both near town. Fivebough Swamp, 2 km N, a waterbird sanctuary. Gliding, hot-air ballooning at Brobenah airfield, 9 km N. Whitton Court House Museum, 23 km W. Gogeldrie Weir, 23 km SW. Yanco Weir, 7 km S. Murrumbidgee State Forest, 12 km S. **Tourist information:** Yanco Ave; (02) 6953 2832. **Accommodation:** 2 hotels, 4 motels, 2 cara./parks. **See also:** Vineyards and Wineries.

Lennox Head
Pop. 3036

MAP REF. 123 R3, 505 R12

Just north of Ballina, Lennox Head has a charming seaside village atmosphere. The area is famous for its surfing beaches. **Of interest:** Freshwater Lake Ainsworth, 50 m from surfing beach, popular with windsurfers. Market, 2nd Sun. each month. **In the area:** Swimming, surfing and snorkelling. Many scenic walks and rainforests a short drive away. Pat Morton Lookout, 1 km S; whale-watching from here May–Sept. **Tourist information:** Ballina Tourist Information Centre, Las Balsas Plaza, cnr River and Norton sts, Ballina; (02) 6686 3484. **Accommodation:** 3 motels, 1 hostel, 1 cara./camp. park.

Lightning Ridge
Pop. 1522

MAP REF. 122 B5

Lightning Ridge is a small opal-mining town in the famous opal fields, 74 km N of Walgett, via the Castlereagh Hwy. The valuable black opal found in the area attracts gem enthusiasts worldwide. **Of interest:** Many displays of art and craft, including opal jewellery and gem opals. Underground mine tours available, contact Tourist information. In Opal St: Bottle House Museum, has collection of bottles, minerals and mining relics; paintings and photographs at John Murray Art. In Pandora St: Gemopal, for local pottery; Goondee Aboriginal Keeping Place, featuring Aboriginal artifacts re-created bush shelter and educational tours of premises. Local craft market at Morilla St, each Fri. Easter: Great Goat Races. June: Pistol Shoot. July: Opal and Gem Expo. **In the area:** Bush Moozeum at Simms Hill opal field, eastern outskirts of town off Pandora St. Opal-cutting demonstrations and daily underground working-mine tours at Big Opal on the Three Mile Field, southern outskirts of town. Self-guide drives, contact Tourist information. Nature reserves, fossicking. Cactus Nursery, 2 km N, off Bald Hill Rd. Fauna Orphanage, Opal St, 3 km S. Hot Artesian Bore Baths (free), 2 km NE. **Tourist information:** Morilla St; (02) 6829 1466. **Accommodation:** 4 motels, 5 cara./ camp. parks.

Lismore
Pop. 27 246

MAP REF. 123 Q3, 505 Q12

Regional centre of the Northern Rivers district of NSW, a closely settled and intensively cultivated rural area, Lismore is situated beside the Wilsons River (formerly the north arm of the Richmond River), 821 km N of Sydney. It is best known for its rainforest heritage, including the Rotary Rainforest Reserve in the residential area of the city. **Of interest:** Indoor rainforest walk and displays of local art and craft at Tourist information. Picnic areas and mini steam train rides in surrounding Heritage Park, cnr Ballina and Molesworth sts. Cedar Log Memorial, Ballina St. Richmond River Historical Museum and Lismore Regional Art Gallery, both in Molesworth St. Robinson's Lookout, Robinson Ave. Claude Riley Memorial Lookout, New Ballina Rd. Wilsons Park, Wyrallah St, East Lismore. River cruises on MV *Bennelong*, The Wharf, Magellan St. Car boot market, 1st and 3rd Sun. each month at Lismore Shopping Square. Heritage Park market, 3rd Sun. each month. Mar.: Square Dance Festival. May: Trinity Arts Festival. Aug.: Lismore Street Festival. Sept.: Cup Day. Oct.: Folk Festival; North Coast National Show. **In the area:** At Alphadale, 11 km E: Macadamia Magic, a macadamia processing plant and tourist complex; Stephen Morris Glassware. Boatharbour Reserve, 5 km N on Bangalow Rd. Rocky Creek Dam, 25 km N. Minyon Falls and Peates Mountain Lookout in Whian Whian State Forest, 25 km N. Three World Heritage-listed areas in vicinity: Border Ranges National Park, 40 km N of Kyogle, Nightcap National Park, 25 km N of Nimbin, with its spectacular Protestor Falls and Mt Warning National Park near Murwillumbah, 105 km NE. Lismore Lake, 3 km S, good lagoon for swimming with picnic/

barbecue facilities and adventure park on foreshore. Tucki Tucki Koala Reserve, 15 km S, adjacent to Lismore–Woodburn Rd; Aboriginal ceremonial ground nearby. **Tourist information:** cnr Ballina and Molesworth sts; (02) 6622 0122. **Accommodation:** 9 hotels, 12 motels, 8 B&B, 3 hostels, 6 cara./camp. parks.

Lithgow
Pop. 11 968

MAP REF. 104 G5, 120 I6

This important coal-mining city on the north-west fringes of the Blue Mountains is a must for railway enthusiasts. The city itself is highly industrialised with two power stations and several large factories; the surrounding countryside is beautiful. **Of interest:** Eskbank House, Bennett St, built 1841 by Thomas Brown, who discovered Lithgow coal seam, now museum with fine collection of 19th-century furniture and vehicles, and displays depicting industrial history of area (open Sat.-Sun.). Blast Furnace Park, a wetland restoration area off Inch St, with ruins of Australia's first blast furnace complex. State Mine Railway Heritage Park, State Mine Gully Rd, features mining and railway equipment, and historic mining buildings (open Sat., Sun., public and school holidays). Small Arms Museum, Methven St (open Sat., Sun. and public holidays). Art and Craft in the Park at Queen Elizabeth Park, one Sat. each month, Aug.–May (contact Tourist information for dates). Oct.: National Go-Kart Championships. Nov.: Festival of the Valley (biennial, even-numbered years). **In the area:** Zig Zag Steam Railway, 10 km E via Bells Line of Road, a breathtaking stretch of railway built in 1869 and later restored, offers train trips. Mt Tomah Botanic Gardens at Berambing, 35 km E. Glow Worm Tunnel, 37 km N within Blue Mountains National Park; 1-km walk to glow-worms in disused rail tunnel (take a torch). Lake Wallace at Wallerawang, 11 km NW, for sailing and trout fishing. Mt Piper Power Station, 21 km NW (guided tours available, admission free). Archvale Rainbow Trout Farm, 7 km W, for fishing and trout sales. Lake Lyell, 9 km W, for power boating, water-skiing and trout fishing. Hassans Walls Lookout, 5 km S via Hassans Walls Rd. Hartley historic village, outstanding architecturally and historically, 12 km SE, off Great Western Hwy, features convict-built court house

(1837). Jenolan Caves, 60 km SE. **Tourist information:** 285 Main St; (02) 6351 2307. **Accommodation:** 7 hotels, 5 motels, 1 hostel, 1 cara./camp. park.

Lockhart
Pop. 887

MAP REF. 127 P10

This pleasant historic town, situated 65 km SW of Wagga Wagga, was originally known as Green's Gunyah and was renamed Lockhart in 1897. **Of interest:** National Trust-classified Green St, a fine turn-of-the-century streetscape, with wide, shady, shop front verandahs. **In the area:** Galore Hill, 8 km S, features caves where bushranger Mad Dog Morgan hid; also walking tracks, lookouts and picnic/barbecue facilities. **Tourist information:** Tarcutta St, Wagga Wagga; (02) 6923 5402. **Accommodation:** 2 hotels, 1 motel, 1 cara. park.

Macksville
Pop. 2869

MAP REF. 123 P9

Macksville is an attractive town beside the Nambucca River, south of Nambucca Heads. **Of interest:** In River St: Mary Boulton Pioneer Cottage, replica of pioneer home with furniture, costumes and museum of horse-drawn vehicles; Star Hotel (1885). Craft markets on riverbank, 4th Sat. each month. Apr.: Nambucca River Show. May: Egg-throwing Championships. Oct.: Pro-Ag Field Day. Nov.: Macksville Gift (Australia's second oldest footrace). **In the area:** Forest drives, contact Tourist information. Nambucca Valley Crafters Cottage co-op, 4 km N. More than 4000 dolls at Flo's House of Dolls, 4 km N. At Bowraville (the 'verandah-post town'), 16 km NW: Joseph and Eliza Newman Folk Museum; Sat. markets (a.m.); regular racedays at picturesque racecourse; Blues Festival each April. Bakers Creek Station, 30 km W, for horseriding, fishing, rainforest walking, canoeing and picnicking; accommodation available. Cosmopolitan Hotel (1903), the 'pub with no beer', made famous by song, at Taylors Arm, 26 km SW. Yarahappini Mt Lookout, 10 km S, for 360° views. Quantum Creations, 15 km S at Eungai Creek, for pottery and sculpture. Horseriding in Way Way State Forest, 10 km SE (contact Tourist information for details). Scotts Head, 18 km SE, has excellent surfing, swimming and fishing; dolphins often seen offshore. **Tourist**

Hunter Valley Steamfest held at Maitland in April

NEW SOUTH WALES

information: 4 Pacific Hwy, Nambucca Heads; (02) 6568 6954. **Accommodation:** 2 hotels, 3 motels, 2 cara. parks.

Maclean   Pop. 2890

MAP REF. 123 P5

Fishing and river-prawning fleets are based at Maclean, on the Clarence River, about 740 km N of Sydney. Professional anglers from this pretty town and from the nearby towns of Yamba and Iluka catch about 20 per cent of the State's seafood. Sugarcane, maize and mixed farm crops are grown in the area. **Of interest:** In River St: Scottish Corner; Civic Hall (1903). Free Presbyterian Church (1864), cnr Wharf and River sts. Self-guide historic buildings walk, contact Tourist information. Bicentennial Museum and adjacent Stone Cottage (1879), Wharf St, top of Maclean Lookout and Pinnacle Rocks. Arts and crafts at Ferry Park. Rainforest walking track from High School. Market, 2nd Sun. each month. Easter: Highland Gathering. Sept.: Cane Harvest Festival. **In the area:** Houseboat hire at Brushgrove, 21 km SW. Yuraygir National Park, 24 km SE. **Tourist information:** Lower Clarence Visitors Centre, Ferry Park, Pacific Hwy; (02) 6645 4121. **Accommodation:** 3 hotels, 2 motels, 1 B&B, 2 cara./camp. parks.

Maitland   Pop. 45 209

MAP REF. 112 C7, 121 M4

On the Hunter River, 28 km NW of Newcastle, Maitland dates back to early colonial days. The city's winding High St has been recorded by the National Trust as a Conservation Area and most of the buildings date back to the 1800s. First settled in 1818, when convicts were put to work as cedar-cutters, it was a flourishing township by the 1840s. **Of interest:** National Trust properties Grossmann House (1862), Georgian-style folk museum, and Brough House (1870), containing city's art collection, are mirror images; both in Church St. Cintra, Regent St, a Victorian mansion offering weekend B&B. Self-guide heritage walks: East Maitland, Maitland Central Precinct and one designed for children; brochures available at Tourist information. Poetry in the Pub, Queens Arms, High St (last Mon. each month). Market, 1st Sun. each month at Showground. Apr.: Hunter Valley Steamfest; Indoor Equestrian Dressage Championships. **In the area:** At Morpeth, 5 km NE: historic buildings with superb iron lace; craft shops open Thurs.–Sun.; heritage walk, contact Tourist information. Scenic drive (inquire at Tourist information) to Walka Waterworks, 3 km N, former pumping station, now excellent recreation area. Scenic drive north-west to historic settlements of Tocal and Paterson. At Lochinvar, 13 km W, Windermere Colonial Homestead, a private residence built of sandstone brick by convict labour in 1820s, was favourite residence of William Charles Wentworth and has museum in dungeons where convicts were housed (open by appt, contact Tourist information for details). Also at Lochinvar, NSW Equestrian Centre (open to bus tours only). **Tourist information:** cnr New England Hwy and High St; (02) 4933 2611. **Accommodation:** 4 hotels, 6 motels, 2 B&B, 1 cara./camp. park.

Manilla   Pop. 2110

MAP REF. 123 J9

This small town, located 42 km NW of Tamworth, is renowned for its meadery, one of only two meaderys in the State. **Of interest:** Dutton's Meadery, Barraba St, has tastings and sales of fresh honey and mead. In picturesque Manilla St: antique and coffee shops; Royce Cottage Historical Museum. June: Lake Keepit Kool Sailing Regatta. Oct.: Festival of Spring Flowers. **In the area:** Manilla Ski Gardens on Lake Keepit, 20 km SW. Warrabah National Park, 40 km NE, a peaceful riverside retreat. Swimming, fishing and canoeing on Namoi and Manilla rivers. **Tourist information:** cnr Murray and Peel sts, Tamworth; (02) 6766 9422. **Accommodation:** 4 hotels, 1 motel, 1 cara./camp. park. **See also:** New England.

Menindee   Pop. 467

MAP REF. 124 E13, 126 E1

It was at this small town, 110 km SE of Broken Hill, that the ill-fated Burke and Wills stayed in 1860 on their journey north. **Of interest:** Maiden's Hotel (where they lodged). Ah Chung's Bakehouse Gallery, Menindee St. Menindee Lakes Lookout. Aug.: Burke and Wills Fishing Challenge. **In the area:** Yachting, fishing and swimming on lakes in area. Menindee Lake, 1 km NW, part of water-storage scheme that guarantees an unfailing water supply to Broken Hill; they provide an interesting contrast to the surrounding semi-arid country. Copi Hollow, 12 km E, attracts water-skiers and power-boat enthusiasts. Kinchega National Park, 1 km W, has prolific wildlife, Visitors Centre (15 km W), wreck of paddlesteamer *Providence* on Darling River (10 km W), and restored shearers' quarters. **Tourist information:** Yartla St; (08) 8091 4274. **Accommodation:** 2 hotels, 1 motel, 3 cara./camp. parks.

Merimbula
Pop. 4259

MAP REF. 117 F9, 119 G11, 243 Q7

Excellent surfing, fishing and prawning at this small sea and lake town. Its sister village of Pambula also offers fine fishing and surfing. **Of interest:** Aquarium at Merimbula Wharf, Lake St. Old School Museum, Main St. June: Jazz Festival. Sept.: Country Music Festival. Nov.: Spring Carnival. **In the area:** Lake cruises; boat hire available. Magic Mountain Family Recreation Park, 5 km N on Sapphire Coast Dr. Tura Beach, 5 km NE. Yellow Pinch Wildlife Park, 5 km E. Pambula, 7 km SW, historic village; market held 2nd Sun. each month. Walking track and lookout at nearby Pambula Beach, 10 km S; kangaroos and wallabies can be seen on foreshore early morning and late afternoon. **Tourist information:** Beach St; (02) 6495 1129. **Accommodation:** 1 hotel, 17 motels, 1 hostel, 4 cara./camp. parks. **See also:** The South Coast.

Merriwa
Pop. 962

MAP REF. 121 J2

This small town in the western Hunter region is noted for its many historic buildings. **Of interest:** Self-guide historic walks, brochures from Tourist information. Historical Museum in store cottage (1857), Bettington St. Bottle Museum, Vennacher St. May: Polocrosse Carnival. June: Festival of Fleeces (includes fireworks). **In the area:** The Drips (curtains of water dripping through rocks) picnic area, at Goulburn River National Park, 35 km S. Convict-built Flags Rd, runs from town to Gungal, 25 km SE. Old gold-boom town of Cassilis, 45 km NW, has several historic sandstone buildings. Official gem-fossicking area, 27 km SW. **Tourist information:** Historical Museum, Bettington St; (02) 6548 2607. **Accommodation:** 2 hotels, 1 motel, 1 B&B, 1 cara./camp. park.

Mittagong
Pop. 5666

MAP REF. 116 C6, 119 I2, 121 J10

The gateway to the Southern Highlands, Mittagong is 110 km S of Sydney.

Of interest: Historic cemeteries and many gracious old buildings. Natural wonders of Lake Alexandra, Queen St. **In the area:** Well-planned walk through nearby hills at Box Vale, turnoff 4 km SW. Loopline Scenic Drive north-east includes Thirlmere Lakes National Park, Thirlmere Railway Museum, potteries and orchards. Wombeyan Caves, 60 km NW; reached by scenic but narrow road (not suitable for caravans). **Tourist information:** 62–70 Main St; (02) 4871 2888; freecall, 1800 656176. **Accommodation:** 2 hotels, 6 motels, 1 B&B, 1 cara./camp. park. **See also:** Southern Highlands.

Molong
Pop. 1563

MAP REF. 120 F5

Molong is a small rural town on the Mitchell Hwy, 35 km NW of Orange. **Of interest:** Yarn Market, Craft Cottage and Coach House Gallery, Bank St. Apr.: Cabonne Country Day. **In the area:** Grave of Yuranigh, Aboriginal guide of explorer Sir Thomas Mitchell, 2 km E; grave marked by a headstone that pays tribute to his courage and fidelity. Mitchell's Monument, 21 km S, marks site of explorer's base camp. **Tourist information:** Visitors Centre, Civic Gardens, Byng St, Orange; (02) 6361 5226 or Railway Station Complex, Mitchell Hwy, Molong. **Accommodation:** 2 hotels, 1 motel, 2 B&B, 1 cara./camp. park.

Moree
Pop. 10 062

MAP REF. 122 G5

Situated on the Mehi River, 640 km NW of Sydney, this town is the nucleus of a large cotton and wheat region. It is best known for its artesian spa baths, said to relieve arthritis and rheumatism. **Of interest:** Spa complex, Anne St. Mary Brand Park, Gwydir St. National Trust-classified Moree Lands Office (1894), cnr Frome and Heber sts. Moree Plains Regional Gallery, Heber St. Historic walk, contact Tourist information. Yurundiali Aboriginal Corporation, Endeavour Lane, a screen-print clothing factory. The Big Plane, Amaroo Dr., a DC3 transport plane at Amaroo Tavern. Market, 1st Sun. each month at Jellicoe Park, Balo St. Easter: Carnival of Sport. Nov.: Golden Grain Festival. **In the area:** Pecan nut farm, 35 km E (tours available). Inspection of cotton gins during harvesting season

(Apr.–July), contact Tourist information. **Tourist information:** Lyle Houlihan Park, Newell Hwy; (02) 6752 7479. **Accommodation:** 4 hotels, 1 hotel/motel, 17 motels, 3 cara./camp. parks.

Moruya
Pop. 2520

MAP REF. 119 H7, 143 M8

Many well known old dairying estates were founded near this town, which was once a gateway to the Araluen and Braidwood goldfields. Situated on the Moruya River, 322 km S of Sydney, it is now a dairying and oyster-farming centre. Granite used in the pylons of the Sydney Harbour Bridge was quarried in the district. **Of interest:** Eurobodalla Historic Museum, in town centre, depicts discovery of gold at Mogo and general history of district. Court house (1880), Princes Hwy. Catholic Church (1889), Queen St. Markets in Main St, each Sat. Mar.: Music Festival. **In the area:** Good fishing, surfing and water sports. Black swan and sea-eagle colonies located up-river at Yarragee. Deua National Park, 20 km W, for a variety of flora and fauna; Hanging Mountain and Mt Wanderer lookouts located in park. Nerrigundah, 44 km SW, former goldmining town. At Bodalla, 24 km S: Coomerang House, home of 19th-century industrialist and dairy farmer Thomas Sutcliffe Mort; Mort Memorial Church and historic cemetery. **Tourist information:** cnr Princes Hwy and Beach Rd, Batemans Bay; (02) 4472 6900, and Narooma; (02) 4476 2881. **Accommodation:** 1 hotel, 1 hotel/motel, 2 motels, 2 B&B, 2 cara./camp. parks.

Moss Vale
Pop. 5690

MAP REF. 116 B7, 119 I3, 121 J10

The industrial and agricultural centre of the Southern Highlands, this town stands on part of the 1000-acre parcel of land granted to Charles Throsby in 1819. **Of interest:** Leighton Gardens, Main St. Historic walk, contact Tourist information for details. Mar.: Agricultural Show. **In the area:** Cecil Hoskins Nature Reserve, 3 km NE, has abundance of birdlife. At Sutton Forest, 6 km SW, A Little Piece of Scotland, for all things Scottish. Exeter, 4 km further S. Fitzroy Falls in Morton National Park, 20 km SE. **Tourist information:** Southern Highlands Visitor Information Centre,

62–70 Main St, Mittagong; (02) 4871 2888; freecall, 1800 656176. **Accommodation:** 3 hotels, 2 motels, 4 B&B, 1 cara./camp. park. **See also:** Southern Highlands.

Moulamein   Pop. 459

MAP REF. 126 I10, 239 P9

This is the oldest town in the Riverina, already well established in the 1870s as a prosperous inland port on the Edward River. Today the town is noted for its river fishing. **Of interest:** Old wharf, Morago St. Restored court house, Nyang St (obtain key from Tourist information). Riverside picnic areas. Lake Moulamein, Brougham St. Easter: Yabby Races. Dec.: Horseracing Cup. **Tourist information:** 25 Murray St, Barham; (03) 5453 3100. **Accommodation:** 2 hotels, 1 cara./camp. park.

Mudgee   Pop. 7447

MAP REF. 120 H3

This attractively-designed town is the centre of a productive agricultural area on the Cudgegong River, 264 km NW of Sydney. Wine grapes, fine wool, sheep, cattle and honey are among the local produce. There are also many horse studs in the area. **Of interest:** Many fine buildings. In Market St: St John's Church of England (1860); St Mary's Roman Catholic Church; railway station; town hall; Colonial Inn Museum (open Sun. and public holidays). Judy's Doll Museum, Gladstone St. Mt Vincent Meadery, Common Rd. Honey Haven, cnr Hill End and Gulgong rds, and Mudgee Honey, Robertson St. Market, 1st and 2nd Sat. each month. Sept.: Wine Festival. **In the area:** Henry Lawson's boyhood home memorial, 6 km N, plaque on remains of demolished cottage. Cudgegong River Park, 39 km W, on eastern foreshores of Burrendong Dam, for water sports and excellent fishing. Pick-Your-Own Farm, 12 km S, has variety of fruit and vegetables (open Oct.–May). Water sports and trout fishing at Windamere Dam, 24 km SE; camping facilities on shore. Eighteen local wineries, including Craigmoor, Montrose, Huntington Estate, Botobolar; contact Tourist information for details. **Tourist information:** 84 Market St; (02) 6372 5875. **Accommodation:** 5 hotels, 10 motels, 22 B&B, 4 cara./camp. parks. **See also:** Vineyards and Wineries.

Mullumbimby   Pop. 2612

MAP REF. 123 Q2, 505 Q12

Situated in lush subtropical country, Mullumbimby is some 850 km NE of Sydney. **Of interest:** Art Gallery, cnr Burringbar and Stuart sts. Restored Cedar House, Dalley St, is National Trust-classified and antiques gallery. Brunswick Valley Historical Museum, in old post office (1907), Stuart St. Brunswick Valley Heritage Park, Tyagarah St, features rainforest plants. Market, 3rd Sat. each month at museum. Sept.: Chincogan Fiesta. **In the area:** Wanganui Gorge, 20 km W. Crystal Castle, 7 km SW, large display of natural quartz. Skydiving and paragliding at airstrip at Tyagarah, 13 km SE on Pacific Hwy. **Tourist information:** 80 Jonson St, Byron Bay; (02) 6685 8050. **Accommodation:** 2 hotels, 2 motels.

Mulwala   Pop. 1330

MAP REF. 127 N13, 241 L3

On the foreshores of Lake Mulwala, the town is a major aquatic centre. Lake Mulwala is an artificial lake of over 6000 ha, formed by the damming of the Murray River at Yarrawonga Weir in 1939 to provide water for irrigation. **Of interest:** Yachting, water-skiing, sailboarding, swimming, canoeing and fishing. Linley Animal Park, Corowa Rd, has native and exotic animals, and horse and pony rides. Tunzafun Amusement Park, Melbourne St, for mini-golf, mini-train and dodgem cars. Cruises available on Lake Mulwala. **Tourist information:** Irvine Pde, Yarrawonga; (03) 5744 1989. **Accommodation:** 2 hotels, 13 motels, 1 B&B, 6 cara./camp. parks.

Murrumburrah   Pop. 1018

MAP REF. 119 C3, 120 E10

Murrumburrah, 357 km SW of Sydney, with its twin town Harden were settled in 1830. The surrounding area is rich grain and stock country. **Of interest:** In Albury St: Harden-Murrumburrah Historical Museum (open weekends); Which Craft and Coffee Cottage for local crafts; Coddington Park for good picnic areas. Mar.: Grain Festival. Sept.: Agricultural Show. **In the area:** Newson Park, in Albury St Harden, has picnic/barbecue facilities. Barwang Vineyard, 20 km N (open by appt). **Tourist information:** Which Craft and

Coffee Cottage, Albury St; (02) 6386 2343. **Accommodation:** 4 hotels, 1 motel, 1 B&B, 1 cara./camp. park.

Murrurundi   Pop. 983

MAP REF. 123 J13

This picturesque town on the New England Hwy, set in a lush valley on the Pages River, is overshadowed by the Liverpool Ranges. **Of interest:** St Joseph's Catholic Church, Polding St, contains altar made of 1000 pieces of Italian marble. Historic town walk, brochure available at Tourist information. Murrurundi Museum, Main St (check at Tourist information for opening times). Paradise Park, Paradise Rd, is horseshoe-shaped and surrounded by mountains; kangaroos visit in evening. Just behind park, walk called 'Through the Eye of the Needle' referring to two large rocks with small gap to squeeze through (not an easy walk); excellent view from top of rock formation. Apr.: Sheepdog Trials. Oct.: Bushman's Carnival. **In the area:** Chilcott's Creek, 15 km N, where huge diprotodon remains, now in Sydney Museum, were found. Wallabadah Rocks, 26 km NE, a large plug of an extinct volcano (959-m high); flowering orchids seen here in Oct. Brick and Bottle Museum, 10 km E. Burning Mountain, 20 km S at Wingen, a deep coal seam that has been smouldering at least 1000 years. Timor Limestone Caves, 43 km E. **Tourist information:** Council Offices, 47 Mayne St; (02) 6546 6205. **Accommodation:** 3 hotels, 2 motels, 1 B&B, 1 cara./camp. park.

Murwillumbah   Pop. 8003

MAP REF. 123 Q1, 505 Q11

Situated on the banks of the Tweed River, 31 km S of the Qld border in the beautiful Tweed Valley, Murwillumbah's local industries include cattle-raising and the growing of sugarcane, tropical fruits, tea and coffee. **Of interest:** Tweed River Regional Art Gallery, Tumbulgum Rd. Museum, cnr Queensland Rd and Bent St, has displays of local history (open Wed. and Fri., 11 a.m.–3 p.m.). Market in Main St, 1st Sat. each month. Aug.: Banana Festival. **In the area:** Tweed River houseboat hire, on Pacific Hwy, 1 km N of Tourist information. Condong sugar mill, 5 km N (open July–Dec.). Tropical Fruitworld, 15 km N. Treetops Environment

NEW SOUTH WALES

The Snowy Mountains

The Snowy Mountains are a magnet to tourists all year round. The combination of easily accessible mountains, alpine heathlands, forests lakes, streams and dams is hard to beat. In winter, skiers flock to the snug, well-equipped snow resorts in the area. When the snow melts it is time for fishing, bushwalking, cycling, horse-riding, water-skiing and boating.

The creation of the Snowy Mountains Hydro-electric Scheme was indirectly responsible for boosting tourism. The roads built for the scheme through the previously difficult and sometimes inaccessible mountain country helped to open up the area, which is now used for a range of recreational activities year-round.

All the ski resorts of the Snowy Mountains are within Kosciusko National Park, which is the largest national park in the State and includes the highest plateau in the Australian continent. Mt Kosciusko (2228 m) is its highest peak. The major ski areas are: Thredbo, Perisher, Smiggin Holes, Mt Blue Cow, Guthega and Charlotte Pass in the southern part of Kosciusko National Park; and Mt Selwyn in the northern part of the park.

The resorts are easily accessible and the major centres have first-class amenities such as motels, hotels, restaurants, lodges, apres-ski entertainment, chairlifts, ski-tows and expert instruction. The snow sports season officially begins on the long weekend in June and continues until the October long weekend.

Thredbo, 98 kilometres from Cooma at the foot of the Crackenback Range. Thredbo hosted the World Cup ski race in 1989, and has facilities for skiers at all levels, including ski hire and instruction. The chairlift to the summit of Mt Crackenback operates year-round. The village has a wide range of amenities, restaurants, cultural entertainment and outdoor recreation for every season.

Charlotte Pass, 104 kilometres from Cooma and 8 kilometres from the summit of Mt Kosciusko. A convenient base for ski tours to some of Australia's highest peaks and most spectacular ski runs.

Perisher, 94 kilometres from Cooma. One of the highest and most popular ski resorts in the area; all the facilities of a small town. Caters for both downhill and cross-country skiers. The Nordic Centre caters especially for cross-country skiers. Ski hire and instruction available.

Smiggin Holes, 92 kilometres from Cooma. Linked to Perisher by ski-lifts and a free shuttle bus service. Essentially for beginners and intermediate skiers. Ski hire and instruction available.

Mt Blue Cow can be reached by Skitube underground railway which runs from Bullocks Flat Terminal (20 kilometres from Jindabyne) up to Perisher and on to Mt Blue Cow, by road from Guthega, or from Perisher by the 'Interceptor' quad chair lift. Limited overnight accommodation at Guthega. No overnight accommodation at Mt Blue Cow. Ski hire and instruction available at Mt Blue Cow and Guthega.

A wide variety of accommodation is available at Perisher and Smiggin Holes. However, overnight parking is limited; overnight visitors are advised to use Skitube from Bullocks Flat on the Alpine Way. Perisher, Smiggin Holes, Mt Blue Cow and Guthega resorts have merged to become Perisher Blue Ski Resort.

Mt Selwyn, now called **Selwyn Snowfields**, at the northern end of Kosciusko National Park. has been designed for beginners, families and school groups. It is one of the main centres for cross-country skiing. There is no overnight accommodation; accommodation is available in nearby towns including Adaminaby. Ski hire and instruction available.

For further information on the Snowy Mountains, contact the Snowy Region Visitor Centre in Jindabyne; (02) 6456 2444. **See also:** Safe Skiing. **Map reference:** 118.

Snow scene at Three Mile Dam on the Kiandra–Cabramurra road

Centre, 8 km NE, features furniture crafted from salvaged timber. Madura Tea Estates, 12 km NE. Hare Krishna Community Farm at Eungella, 10 km W; visitors welcome. Pioneer Plantation, 25 km SE, a banana plantation with farm animals, native gardens and wide variety of nectar-feeding birdlife (tours available). World Heritage-listed areas within radius of 50 km W include Nightcap National Park (road access to Mt Nardi, one of highest peaks in park), Border Ranges National Park (featuring walking tracks to Pinnacle Lookout with views of Mt Warning and Tweed Valley, Tweed Valley Lookout and Antarctic Beech Picnic area) and Mt Warning National Park. **Tourist information:** cnr Pacific Hwy and Alma St; (02) 6672 1340. **Accommodation:** 4 hotels, 4 motels, 1 cara./camp. park.

Muswellbrook   Pop. 10 140

MAP REF. 121 K2

In the Upper Hunter Valley, Muswellbrook is the centre for the surrounding agricultural area. There is also a large open-cut coal-mining industry. **Of interest:** Art Gallery in old town hall, Bridge St. Historical town walk, contact Tourist information for brochure. Apr.: Agricultural Show. Oct.: Spring Wine Festival. **In the area:** Seven local wineries open for tastings and sales, including Rosemount Estate (35 km SW) and Arrowfield Wines (28 km S). Wollemi National Park, 30 km SW, features Aboriginal carvings and paintings. Bayswater Power Station, 16 km S (tours available). Goulburn River National Park, 50 km W. **Tourist information:** Old Teahouse, 208 Bridge St; (02) 6543 3599. **Accommodation:** 3 hotel/ motels, 9 motels, 2 cara./camp. parks.

Nambucca Heads   Pop. 5683

MAP REF. 123 P9

At the mouth of the Nambucca River, 552 km N of Sydney, this beautifully-sited town is ideal for boating, fishing, surfing and swimming. **Of interest:** Nambucca Historical Museum, Headland Reserve. Model Train Museum, Pelican Cres. Stringer Art Gallery, Ridge St, for local art. Mosaic sculpture, Bowra St. V Wall Gallery, Wellington Dr., where you can add your own 'postcard' (i.e., graffiti) on the rocks at the wall. Stuart Island Golf Club, in middle of river, Australia's only island set aside for a golf course.

Water-skiing and several rainforest walks available, contact Tourist information. Market, 2nd Sun. each month at Nambucca Plaza. June: Ken Howard Memorial Bowls Competition. Aug.: VW Spectacular (odd-numbered years). Sept.: Septemberfest Carnival. Oct.: Show 'n' Shine Hot Rod Exhibition. **In the area:** Breathtaking views from several local lookouts. Wooden toys at Swiss Toymaker, 5 km N on Pacific Hwy (closed Sun.). At Valla Beach, 10 km N: Worm Farm, featuring educational worm displays; Australiana Workshop. **Tourist information:** 4 Pacific Hwy; (02) 6568 6954. **Accommodation:** 1 hotel, 12 motels, 1 B&B, 1 hostel, 6 cara./camp. parks.

Narooma   Pop. 3443

MAP REF. 117 I2, 119 H9, 143 N11, 243 R2

This popular fishing resort situated at the mouth of the Wagonga Inlet on the Princes Hwy, 360 km S of Sydney, is well known for its rock oysters. **Of interest:** Cruises on *Wagonga Princess* (Wed., Fri.–Sun.), depart Riverside Dr. adjacent to Taylors Boat Shed; whale-watching tours (mid Sept.–early Dec.); details at Tourist information. Mar.: Festival. Easter: Tilba Festival. **In the area:** Excellent golf course on scenic cliff top, Ballingalla St. Mystery Bay near Lake Corunna, south of town, haunt of lapidary collectors with its coloured sands and strange rock formations. Other inlets and lakes north and south of town. Central Tilba, a heritage area (founded 1895), 17 km SW just off Princes Hwy, classified as 'unusual mountain village' by National Trust, has old buildings in original 19th-century condition and new buildings to National Trust specifications; well-known as well for its high quality arts and crafts. Nearby, Deer Park and Tilba Valley Vineyard. Montague Island, a wildlife sanctuary 5.7 nautical miles offshore, has large colony of little (fairy) penguins and Australian fur seals (tours available, contact Tourist information for best times). Umburra Cultural Tours in surrounding area, contact tourist information. **Tourist information:** Princes Hwy; (02) 4476 2881. **Accommodation:** 1 hotel, 13 motels, 5 B&B, 4 cara./camp. parks. **See also:** The South Coast.

Narrabri   Pop. 6694

MAP REF. 122 G8

Situated between the Nandewar Range,

including Mt Kaputar National Park and the extensive Pilliga scrub country, Narrabri is a phenomenally successful cotton-producing centre. **Of interest:** Historic buildings including court house (1886), Maitland St. Self-guide town tour, contact Tourist information. Riverside picnic area, Tibbereena St. Apr.: Agricultural Show. Oct.: Spring Festival. **In the area:** Tours of cotton fields and gin processing plants (Apr.–June, inquire at Tourist information). Plant Breeding Institute, 9 km N, on Newell Hwy. CSIRO Observatory, 25 km W, has six giant radio telescopes; Visitors Centre (open Mon.–Fri.). Yarrie Lake, 32 km W. Pilliga State Forest, 23 km SW. Salt Caves, 90 km SW. Mt Kaputar National Park, 53 km E in dramatic, volcanic mountain country; 360° views from peak take in one-tenth of NSW; Sawn Rocks, wilderness area in northern section (via Bingara Rd), has spectacular basaltic formation. **Tourist information:** Newell Hwy; (02) 6792 3583. **Accommodation:** 6 hotels, 2 hotel/motels, 8 motels, 4 cara./camp. parks.

Narrandera   Pop. 4649

MAP REF. 127 P9

This historic town on the Murrumbidgee River, at the junction of the Newell and Sturt hwys, has been declared an urban conservation area with several buildings classified or listed by the National Trust. Located 570 km SW of Sydney, it is the gateway to the Murrumbidgee Irrigation Area. **Of interest:** Lake Talbot Aquatic Playground, Lake Dr. Antique shops in Larmer and East sts. NSW Forestry Tree Nursery, Broad St. On Newell Hwy: Tiger Moth Memorial; Parkside Cottage Museum; Tourist information centre with 5.8 m-long, playable guitar at Narrandera Park. My Dolls, Dangar Dr., a doll and teddy-bear collection. Two Foot town heritage tour; Bundidgerry Walking Track through Nature Reserve, Blue arrow scenic drive (pamphlets available at Tourist information). Mar.: John O'Brien Folk Festival. Aug.: Camellia Show. Oct.: Tremendous Festival. **In the area:** Inland Fisheries Research Station, 6 km SE, has visitors centre (open Mon.–Fri.). Berembed Weir, 40 km SE. Craig Top Deer Farm, 8 km NW (tours daily). **Tourist information:** Big Guitar Tourist Information Centre, Narrandera Park, Newell Hwy; (02) 6959 1766.

Accommodation: 5 hotels, 9 motels, 1 B&B, 2 cara./camp. parks. See also: Vineyards and Wineries.

Narromine   Pop. 3378

MAP REF. 120 D2

On the Macquarie River, 457 km NW of Sydney, the area surrounding Narromine is well-known for quality agricultural products, including citrus fruit, tomatoes, corn, lamb, beef and cotton It is also regarded as a good gliding area. Of interest: On Mitchell Hwy: Waterslide, at eastern edge of town; gliding and ultralight flying at airport, western side of town. Oct.: Festival of Sport. In the area: Swane's Rose Production Nursery, 5 km W. Tourist information: 37 Burraway St; (02) 6889 4596. Accommodation: 3 hotels, 1 hotel/motel, 2 motels, 3 cara./camp. parks.

Nelson Bay   Pop. 6766

MAP REF. 112 H2, 121 O4

The beautiful bay on which this town is sited is the main anchorage of Port Stephens, about 60 km N of Newcastle. Of interest: Restored Inner Lighthouse, Nelson Head, includes museum highlighting early history of area. Contact Tourist information for details of: self-guide heritage walk extending from Dutchmans Bay to Little Beach; dolphin-watch cruises; whale-watch cruises on catamaran (June–July, Sept.–Oct. approx.); cruises on harbour, on Myall River and to Broughton Island (Sun. only); dive charters; 4WD tours along coastal dunes; canoe, aquabike and boat hire. Shell Museum, Sandy Point Rd, Corlette. Feb.: Game-fishing Tournament. In the area: Native Flora Reserve at Little Beach, 1 km E. Gan Gan Lookout, 2 km SW on Nelson Bay Rd. Toboggan Hill Park at Salamander Bay, 5 km SW, has toboggan runs, mini-golf course, indoor wall-climbing and fun shed. On Nelson Bay Rd: Port Stephens Wines, 10 km SW; Oakvale Farm and Fauna World, 16 km SW at Salt Ash. Tomago House, 30 km SW on Tomago Rd, Tomago (open 1st Sun. each month). Convict-built Tanilba House (1831), 37 km W (open Wed., Sat. and Sun.). Tomaree National Park, along coastline from Shoal Bay, 3 km NE, to Anna Bay, 10 km SW; within park, excellent coastal walks, Fort Tomaree Lookout for 360° views (signposted walkway to top). Across bay (70 km by road) Yacaaba Lookout also offers 360° views. Tourist information: Port Stephens Visitors Centre, Victoria Pde; (02) 4981 1579. Accommodation: 12 motels, 1 cara./camp. park. See also: Port Stephens.

Newcastle   Pop. 262 331

MAP REF. 110, 112 G7, 121 N4

Australia's largest industrial city, located 158 km N of Sydney is encircled by some of the finest surfing beaches in the world and overlooks a huge, spectacular harbour. Rebuilding in some areas followed the 1989 earthquake. Newcastle is experiencing a boom in tourism as visitors are attracted to the wineries and vineyards, and picturesque

New England

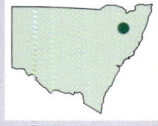

Despite the scenery, it is worth keeping your eyes on the ground if you pull over for a rest in the New England area. Some of the best fossicking specimens in the district have been found by the roadside. All kinds of quartz, jaspers, serpentine, crystal and chalcedony are found in this area – not to mention sapphires, diamonds and gold, though these are harder to find.

The round trip from Nundle, through Tamworth, Manilla, Barraba, Bingara, Warialda, then on to the New England towns of Inverell and Glen Innes and back, is known as 'The Fossickers' Way' and tourist signs have been placed at intervals to guide the motorist. Nearby is the Copeton Dam, which holds two-and-a-half times as much water as Sydney Harbour, with part of its foreshores forming Copeton State Recreational Area.

Glen Innes and Inverell have nearby sapphire reserves where fossickers may hire tools and try their luck; anything you find is yours. The largest find to date in the Nullamanna Fossicking Reserve, near Inverell, is a 70-carat blue, valued at $3000.

The New England district is the largest area of highlands in Australia, and has plenty to offer

Lookout in Boonoo Boonoo National Park, north-east of Tenterfield

bes des gemstones. The countryside is varied and lovely, with magnificent mountains, and streams cascading into spectacular gorges, contrasting with the rich blacksoil plains of wheat and cotton to the west. Some of the State's most outstanding national parks and World Heritage features are found in New England, and the southern hemisphere's largest granite monolith, Bald Rock, is located near Tenterfield.

Fishing is excellent, with trout in the streams of the tablelands, and cod and yellow-belly in the lower New England rivers to the west. You can also fish, picnic, swim, sail or water-ski at Pindari and Copeton dams.

Other towns in the New England area – Ashford, Delungra, Guyra, Tingha, Walcha, Uralla and Deepwater, and the city of Armidale – also have much to offer.

For further information, contact the Visitors Centre and Coach Station, 82 Marsh St, Armidale; (02) 6772 4655; freecall, 1800 627736. See also: individual text entries in A–Z listing for those towns indicated by bold type. Map reference: 123 M7.

NEW SOUTH WALES

villages of the surrounding Hunter Valley region. **Of interest:** Queens Wharf, on Wharf Rd, centrepoint of foreshore redevelopment, has indoor and outdoor restaurants, 'boutique' brewery, observation tower linked by walkway to the City Mall, a part of Hunter St. Sydney-style terrace houses along nearby city streets. City parks and gardens. Regional art gallery, Laman St. Historic customs house (1877) in Scott St, now a cafe. City Hall, King St. In King Edward Park, Wolfe St: Obelisk (1850) marks site of Newcastle's first windmill; Soldiers Baths (1880s) off Shortland Espl., now a public pool; Bogey Hole, hole cut in rocks by convict labour, now a public pool; band rotunda (1898). Merewether Baths, off Scenic Dr., largest ocean baths in southern hemisphere. Heritage walk, river and harbour cruises; contact Tourist information for details. Maritime and Military Museum at Fort Scratchley, Nobbys Rd. Scenic walks along foreshore. Jan.: National Maritime Regatta. Mar.: Surfest; Beaumont Street Jazz Arts Fair. Aug.: Jazz Festival. **In the area:** Many fine surf beaches. On and around Lake Macquarie, 20 km S, a huge aquatic playground with well-maintained parks lining foreshore: lake cruises on *Macquarie Lady* and *Macquarie Enterprise*, both leave from Toronto Wharf and Belmont Public Wharf; Dobell House, (47 Dobell Dr., Wangi Wangi) home of artist Sir William Dobell, has collection of his work and memorabilia; tours of power station available at Eraring; Aboriginal art and craft at Bahtabah Land Council Visitors Centre, Lakeview Pde. Frazer Park, a coastal recreation area south of Swansea. Shortland Wetlands, 15 km W, a bird habitat, with a canoe trail. About 50 km NW is Australia's famous wine region, the Hunter Valley. Fighter World, museum and high-tech exhibition at Williamtown RAAF base, 20 km N. Yuelarbah Track, part of Great North Walk from Sydney to Newcastle, covers 25 km from Lake Macquarie to Newcastle harbour (details at Tourist information). **Tourist information:** 92 Scott St; (02) 4929 9299. **Accommodation:** 27 hotels, 30 motels, 13 cara./camp. parks.

Nimbin
Pop. 274

MAP REF. 123 Q2, 505 Q12

The Aquarius Softlicks festival in 1973 established Nimbin as the alternative culture capital of Australia. Today Nimbin's peaceful, friendly atmosphere, and the buildings designed and decorated to reflect the community's ideas and beliefs, attract visitors wishing to experience an alternative lifestyle. **Of interest:** In Cullen St: shops, painted in psychedelic colours, featuring homemade products, local art and craft; Triple Blah Theaterette, showing variety of short films; Choices Cafe, offering great views over the valley; Nimbin Museum, dedicated to hippy culture and history of St Aquarius; town-hall mural featuring Aboriginal art; Rainbow Power Company, Alternative Way, alternative power supplier, now exporting (tours available). Country market, 4th Sun. each month at Showgrounds; outlet for local craftspeople. Sept.: Show. **In the area:** Eco-tours of area, inquire at Tourist information. Spectacular volcanic Nimbin Rocks, 3 km S, on Lismore Rd. At The Channon, 15 km SE, 'alternative' craft market in Coronation Park, 2nd Sun. each month; also Music Bowl Live Band Concert, each Nov. World Heritage-listed Nightcap National Park, 10 km NE. Calurla Tea Gardens, 10 km N on Lillian Rock Rd, offers spectacular views, farmhouse cooking and live music. **Tourist information:** Lismore Visitor Information Centre, cnr Ballina and Molesworth sts, Lismore; (02) 6622 0122. **Accommodation:** 2 motels, 1 B&B, 2 hostels, 1 cara./ camp. park.

Nowra
Pop. 21 942

MAP REF. 116 E12, 119 I4, 121 K11

A popular tourist centre, Nowra is the principal town of the Shoalhaven district on the south coast. Bomaderry is on the northern side of the river. **Of interest:** Historic Houses Trust-property Meroogal (1885), cnr Worrigee and West sts (open weekends). Shoalhaven Historical Museum, cnr Plunkett and Kinghorne sts, in old police station. On Shoalhaven River: fishing, water-skiing, canoeing, sailing and cruises on MV *Christine* (leaving from wharf, Riverview Rd, Mon., Wed., Fri., Sun. and daily during school holidays). Hanging Rock, via Junction St, has fine views. Nowra Animal Park, Rockhill Rd. Bens Walk, alongside river; Bomaderry Creek Walk from Bomaderry (contact Tourist information for pamphlets). Market, 3rd Sun. each month at Showground. Oct.: Spring Festival. **In the area:** Many beautiful beaches within 30-km radius of town. Australian Naval Aviation Museum, 7 km SW at HMAS *Albatross*. Cambewarra Lookout, 12 km NW. At Kangaroo Valley, 23 km NW, historic buildings include Friendly Inn (National Trust-classified); Pioneer Settlement Reserve, reconstruction of dairy farm of 1880s; Hampden Bridge (1898), oldest suspension bridge in Australia. Fitzroy Falls in Morton National Park, 38 km NW; also in park (turn off at Kangaroo Valley), Tallowa Dam water catchment area, 42 km NW, ideal for picnicking; just before park, Sharpley Vale Fruit World, a working fruit farm. Historic Bundanon, 21 km W, gifted to the nation by artist Arthur Boyd and his wife Yvonne, guided tours only of National Estate-listed homestead, Bundanon collection and Arthur Boyd's studio (tickets need to be obtained from Tourist information, advance bookings essential). Fresh fish and oyster sales at Greenwell Point, 14 km E. **Tourist information:** Shoalhaven Tourist Centre, 254 Princes Hwy, Bomaderry; (02) 4421 0778. **Accommodation:** 1 hotel, 10 motels, 5 cara./camp. parks. **See also:** The Illawarra Coast.

Nundle
Pop. 261

MAP REF. 123 K12

The history of this small town began in the early gold-rush era during the 1850s. Well known for its fishing, Nundle is situated 60 km SE of Tamworth, at the foot of the Great Dividing Range, in a district that supports sheep, cattle, wheat and timber. **Of interest:** In Jenkins St: Court house; antique shop; historic Peel Inn (1860s). Goldmining display in restored coffin factory, Gill St. Aug.–Sept., Dec.: Camp Drafting and Dog Trials. **In the area:** Hanging Rock and Sheba Dams Reserve, 11 km E, for picnicking, bushwalking and camping. Fossicking at Hanging Rock; gold panning on Peel River. Chaffey Dam, 11 km N. Fossickers Way tour through scenic New England countryside, brochure available from Tourist information. **Tourist information:** cnr Peel and Murray sts, Tamworth; (02) 6766 9422. **Accommodation:** 1 hotel, 1 motel, 1 cara./camp. park.

Nyngan
Pop. 2311

MAP REF. 125 R10

The centre of a sheep, wheat and wool

district, Nyngan is located 603 km NW of Sydney beside the Bogan River. **Of interest:** Historic buildings, especially in Cobar and Pangee sts. Historical Museum at railway station, Pangee St, has local memorabilia (open Mon.–Sat.). Apr.: Anzac Day Race Meeting. May: Agricultural Show. **In the area:** Cairn on private property, 65 km S, marking geographic centre of NSW. Grave of Richard Cunningham, 70 km S, the botanist with explorer Major Mitchell's party, speared by Aborigines in 1835. Bird sanctuary in Macquarie Marshes, 64 km N. **Tourist information:** Burns Video, Pangee St; (02) 6832 1155. **Accommodation:** 2 hotels, 1 hotel/motel, 3 motels, 1 B&B, 2 cara./camp. parks.

Orange
Pop. 29 635

MAP REF. 120 G6

A prosperous city set in rich red volcanic soil and famous for its apples, parks and gardens, Orange is 264 km NW of Sydney on the slopes of Mt Canobolas. An obelisk marks the birthplace of the city's most famous citizen, poet A.B. (Banjo) Paterson; his birthday is celebrated with the Banjo Paterson Festival. **Of interest:** Historic Cook Park, Summer St, has begonia conservatory (flowers Feb.–May), duck ponds, fernery and picnic area. Museum, McNamara St. Civic Centre, Byng St, comprises Regional Art Gallery, City Library, Visitors Centre and exhibition rooms. Feb.–Mar.: Banjo Paterson Festival. **In the area:** Campbell's Corner, 8 km S on Pinnacle Rd, a roadside picnic/barbecue spot Lucknow Village, 10 km SE. Golden Memories Museum, 22 km SE at Millthorpe, has over 5000 exhibits, including grandma's kitchen and blacksmith's shop; also art and craft centre. Gallery of Minerals, 1 km E, mineral and fossil collection. Agriculture Research Centre, 5 km N, field days held Nov. Ophir goldfields, 27 km N, site of first discovery of payable gold in Australia in 1851, features fossicking centre, picnic area, walking trails to historic gold tunnels, tours of working goldmine and Ophir Reserve. Borenore Caves, 17 km W, has picnic/barbecue facilities. Lake Canobolas Park, 8 km SW via Cargo Rd, has recreation and camping area, deer park, children's playground, picnic/barbecue facilities; trout-fishing in lake. Mt Canobolas Park, a 1500-ha bird and animal sanctuary, 14 km SW. Wineries open for tastings and sales (check times with

Town Hall building, Nyngan

Tourist information): Cargo Road Wines, 12 km W, and Canobolas-Smith Wines, 15 km W, both on Cargo Rd; Highland Heritage Estate, 3 km E on Bathurst Rd. **Tourist information:** Civic Gardens, Byng St; (02) 6361 5226. **Accommodation:** 9 hotels, 9 motels, 15 B&B, 2 cara./camp. parks.

Parkes
Pop. 8784

MAP REF. 120 D5

The settlement of Currajong was renamed Parkes following the visit of NSW's first Governor, Sir Henry Parkes (1815–96) who, when a politician, contributed much to Australian Federation. Situated 364 km W of Sydney on the Newell Hwy, Parkes is today the commercial and industrial centre of an important agricultural area. **Of interest:** Tourist drive (90 min.), a self-guide car tour following arrows; self-guide historic walk around north Parkes including one of town's oldest houses, Balmoral, noted for its excellent iron lacework (brochures for both at Tourist information). Motor Museum, cnr Bogan and Dalton sts, displays vintage and veteran vehicles, and local art and craft. Henry Parkes Historical Museum, Clarinda St, has memorabilia and library of 1000 volumes (the personal library of Sir Henry Parkes). In north Parkes: imposing views of town

from Memorial Hill, at eastern end of Bushman St; Pioneer Park Museum (Pioneer St), in historic school and church, has displays of early farm machinery and transport; Kelly Reserve (Newell Hwy), playground and picnic/barbecue facilities in bush setting; Bushmans Hill Reserve (Newell Hwy), at site of old goldmine. Jan.: Elvis Revival. Easter: Sports Festival. June: Central West Jazz Triduum. Oct.: Country Music Spectacular. **In the area:** Australia Telescope Visitors Centre, 23 km N, has excellent educational aids explaining use of giant saucer-shaped telescope. At Peak Hill, 48 km N: open-cut goldmine lookout offering views of goldmine; camel park. **Tourist information:** Kelly Reserve, Newell Hwy; (02) 6862 4365. **Accommodation:** 5 hotels, 11 motels, 4 cara./camp. parks.

Picton
Pop. 2116

MAP REF. 105 J11, 116 E2, 119 I2, 121 K9

Picton, named after Sir Thomas Picton, hero of Waterloo, is 80 km SW of Sydney on Remembrance Dr. (former Hume Hwy). The old buildings and quiet hills of this small town seem to echo the past. **Of interest:** Historic buildings: old railway viaduct (1862) over Stonequarry Creek, seen from Showgrounds off Menangle St; St

NEW SOUTH WALES

Mark's Church (1848), Menangle St; George IV Inn, Argyle St, incorporating Scharer's Little Brewery. Country markets in Menangle Rd, 4th Sat. each month. Jan.: Rodeo. Nov.: Village Fair. **In the area:** Sydney Skydiving Centre, 5 km E. On Remembrance Dr.: Jarvisfield (1865), 2 km N, family home of pioneer landholders, now clubhouse of Antill Park Golf Club; Wool Away! Woolshed, 3 km N, has bush dances Fri. and Sat. nights. Over the Road, 4 km W, tearoom and several hectares of gardens (open Sat., Sun., school holidays , weekdays by appt). At Thirlmere, 5 km SW: Railway Transport Museum; Festival of Steam held 1st Sun. in Mar. Further 3 km, Thirlmere Lakes National Park protects five linked freshwater lakes; scenic drive around lakes. Wirrimbirra Sanctuary, 13 km S, native flora and fauna; overnight cabins available. Dingo Sanctuary, 15 km S (open Sat. and Sun.). **Tourist information:** 62 Menangle St; (02) 4677 1167. **Accommodation:** 2 hotels, 1 motel, 1 cara. park.

Pitt Town   Pop. 632

MAP REF. 105 L6

One of the five Macquarie Towns, Pitt Town was named after William Pitt the elder, and was marked out on a site to the east of the present village in January 1811. The rich alluvial river flats provided early Sydney with almost 50 per cent of its food supply, which was transported by boat down the Hawkesbury River and south along the coast to Sydney Town. July: Fun Run. **In the area:** Old Manse, belonging to oldest Presbyterian (now Uniting) Church in Australia, 8 km N at Ebenezer. **Tourist information:** Ham Common Bicentenary Park, Richmond Rd, Clarendon; (02) 4588 5895. **Accommodation:** None. **See also:** The Hawkesbury.

Port Macquarie   Pop. 26 798

MAP REF. 109 G7, 123 P12

Founded as a convict settlement in 1821, and one of the oldest towns in the State, Port Macquarie is now a major holiday resort, situated at the mouth of the Hastings River, 423 km N of Sydney. **Of interest:** Award-winning Hastings Historical Museum, Clarence St, in 15 rooms of commercial building (built 1835–40), has displays of convict and pioneer relics. St Thomas' (1824), Church St, a convict-built church

designed by convict architect Thomas Owen. In Horton St: historic cemetery dating from 1842; Kooloonbung Creek Nature Reserve, 50 ha of natural bushland with walking trails. Roto House and Macquarie Nature Reserve, Lord St, a koala hospital and study centre. Port Macquarie Observatory, William St. Maritime museum, William St. Fantasy Glades, Pacific Dr., with rainforest gardens and picnic/barbecue facilities. Billabong Koala and Aussie Wildlife Park (Billabong Dr.) and Kingfisher Park (Kingfisher Rd), for close-up look at Australian animals. World of Models, Bay St. Town Beach, has surf at one end, sheltered coves at other. Peppermint Park, has slides, roller-skating. River cruises daily. Walk following coastal headlands from breakwall to lighthouse (8 km). Hydro-golf, Boundary St, a golf course incorporating a large dam. Market in Findlay St, 2nd and 4th Sun. each month. Jan.: Golden Lure Tournament (deep-sea fishing). July: Lifestyle. **In the area:** Scenic drives to Ellenborough Falls, 85 km SW; to Wauchope and Timbertown, 20 km W; 4WD tours into hinterland; bus tours of surrounding area (brochures available at Tourist information). Exceptionally good fishing and all water sports. Charter fishing available; Harley Davidson motor-bike tours, horseriding, abseiling. Skirmish (paintball game), skydiving; contact Tourist information for details. Thrumster Village Pottery, 10 km W. Cassegrain Winery, 13 km W; Discovery Concert held here under the stars each Oct. Sea Acres Rainforest Centre, 4 km S, includes elevated boardwalk and guided tours of rainforest. **Tourist information:** cnr Clarence and Hay sts; (02) 6583 1077; freecall, 1800 025935. **Accommodation:** 1 hotel/motel, 38 motels, 3 B&B, 15 cara./camp. parks.

Queanbeyan   Pop. 19 383

MAP REF. 119 E5, 120 G13, 139 G4, 142 H3

Adjoining Canberra, Queanbeyan has a special relationship with the Australian capital. The town, proclaimed in 1838, is named from a squattage held by an ex-convict innkeeper, Timothy Beard, on the Molonglo River and called 'Quinbean' ('clear waters'). **Of interest:** History Museum, Farrer Pl. Byrne's Mill (1883) now a restaurant, Collett St. Byrne's Mill House, cnr Collett and Morisset sts, now Queanbeyan Books

and Prints. Design Plus Gallery, Monaro St, for pottery and silk. Art Centre, Trinculo Pl. Michelago Steam Train rides, depart station in Henderson St (first Sun. each month). Cottage markets, 2nd Sun. each month. Nov.: Queanbeyan Celebrations; Agricultural Show. Dec.: Country Music Festival. **In the area:** At Bungendore, 26 km NE: historic village square contains colonial-style shops; Woodworks sells local art and crafts. Bywong Mining Town, 31 km NE, a re-creation of an early mining settlement. Googong Dam, 10 km S, for fishing; bushwalking and wildlife refuge on shore. London Bridge Woolshed and Shearers' Quarters, 24 km S; walk 1 km to limestone formation. **Tourist information:** cnr Farrer Pl. and Lowe St; (02) 6298 0241. **Accommodation:** 3 hotels, 18 motels, 1 B&B, 2 cara./camp. parks.

Quirindi   Pop. 2830

MAP REF. 123 J12

Appropriately named after an Aboriginal word meaning 'nest in the hills', this town in the Liverpool Ranges was proclaimed in 1856. It was one of the first towns in Australia to organise the game of polo. **Of interest:** Historical Cottage and Museum, Station St (open Fri. p.m. and Sat. a.m.). Jan.: Wallabadah Cup Meeting (New Year's Day). **In the area:** Who'd-A-Thought-It Lookout, 2 km NE, for views over ranges and plains. **Tourist information:** Sports Centre, 248 George St; (02) 6746 2128. **Accommodation:** 5 hotels, 2 motels, 1 cara./camp. park.

Raymond Terrace   Pop. 11 159

MAP REF. 112 E6, 121 N4

An important wool-shipping centre in the 1840s, several historic buildings remain in this town, set on the banks of the Hunter and William rivers. **Of interest:** Significant buildings: court house (1838) (cnr William St and Pacific Hwy), still in use; Church of England and rectory (Glenelg St), built of hand-hewn sandstone in 1830s; numerous buildings in historic King St, along waterfront. Sketchley Cottage, on Pacific Hwy, a museum of memorabilia. Mar.: Oz Ski (waterskiing races and events). Oct.: Twin Rivers Festival. **In the area:** Hunter Region Botanic Gardens, 2 km S on Pacific Hwy at Motto Farm, has over 2000 native plants and several theme gardens. Fighter

Lindeman's Winery, Pokolbin, is one of the major wineries in the Hunter Valley

Vineyards and Wineries

A vineyard holiday takes you through peaceful, ordered countryside and gives you the chance to learn more about wine and its making at first hand. It also gives you a perfect excuse for wine-tasting and, later, sampling the local wines with a meal in a first-class restaurant in the area. The obvious place to head for in New South Wales is the famous Hunter Valley. It is not far from Sydney (2 hours' drive each way) and, with some 70 wineries, must rate as one of the most important wine-growing districts in Australia. Although it can be a pleasant day trip from Sydney to the Hunter, it is well worth booking into a motel in the area for at least one night, to do it justice. Mid-week with lower tariffs and fewer crowds, is the best time to visit.

The Hunter is Australia's oldest commercial wine-producing area, wine having first been made there in the 1830s. The Hunter's table wines, both red and white, still rank among the best in Australia.

Most of the early colonial vineyards in the region have vanished. Some family concerns have been taken over by the larger companies such as Lindemans and McWilliams.

The high reputation of the district is maintained by such well-known properties as Mount Pleasant, Oakvale, Drayton's, Tyrrell's, Tulloch's Glen Elgin, Wyndham and Rothbury.

Most wineries welcome visitors and are open for inspection and wine-tastings daily. Several have picnic grounds, barbecue facilities and excellent restaurants which make for a pleasant day's outing.

The Cellar at McGuigan Hunter Village, Blaxland's at Pokolbin and the Casuarina at North Pokolbin are among the restaurants in the area.

The McGuigan Hunter Village at Pokolbin has wine tastings, wine sales, a gallery, accommodation at the Vineyard Resort, specialty shops, a cheese factory, a restaurant, kiosk, picnic facilities, an adventure playground for children and an aquagolf driving range.

It is best to go at vintage time – usually around February in the Hunter – if you want to see a vineyard in full swing. However, this is the most hectic time of year for vignerons, so do not expect their undivided attention. For an idea of the range of wineries in the district, try Tyrrell's and Drayton's wineries for a glimpse of the more traditional family approach, and Lindeman or Hunter Estate for the modern 'big company' style.

South of Sydney at **Camden** is Gledswood, birthplace of Australia's wine industry. The first vines were planted here in 1827; the winery was re-established as Gledswood Cellars in 1970. The winery also offers an art gallery, shearing demonstrations and picnic facilities. Hayrides and candle-lit dinners for parties can be arranged.

You could also have an enjoyable wine-tasting holiday in the Riverina towns of **Griffith** and **Leeton**, in the other main winegrowing area of the State. Griffith, Leeton and **Narrandera** are the main towns in the Murrumbidgee Irrigation Area, which grows 80 per cent of the State's wine-producing grapes. Well known wineries such as McWilliam's, de Bortoli and Rosetto & Sons are open to visitors who wish to taste the wines of the Riverina. In Leeton, visitors are welcome to sample the vintages at Toorak Winery and Lillypilly Estate.

Mudgee, 261 kilometres north-west of Sydney, is also in an area where fine wines are produced from some dozen wineries. Other smaller vineyards are scattered throughout the State – some of them quite close to Sydney.

For further information on the Lower Hunter area, contact the Lower Hunter Visitor Information Centre, Turner Park, Aberdare Rd, Cessnock; (02) 4990 4477. For information on the other wine areas, contact the local tourist information centres in the area. **See also:** individual text entries in A–Z listing for those towns indicated by bold type. **Map reference**: 113 (for Lower Hunter).

NEW SOUTH WALES

The Golden Guitar at the Country Collection near Tamworth

World, RAAF Base Williamtown, 16 km E. Morpeth, 31 km SW, a historic township with art, craft and antique shops. **Tourist information:** Council Offices, 116 Pacific Hwy; (02) 4983 1333. **Accommodation:** 5 motels, 2 cara./camp. parks.

Richmond   Pop. 18 766

MAP REF. 105 K6, 121 K7

One of the five Macquarie towns and sister town to Windsor, 5 km E, Richmond was proclaimed a town in 1810. **Of interest:** Historic buildings: Hobartville (privately-owned), Castlereagh Rd; Toxana (1841), Windsor St, now an art gallery (open Sun.); St Peter's Church (1841), also in Windsor St, and adjacent graveyard where several notable pioneers, including William Cox and Australia's convict chronicler Margaret Catchpole, are buried. Sept.: Hawkesbury District Orchid Spring Show. **In the area:** RAAF base, 3 km E on Windsor–Richmond Rd, oldest Air Force establishment in Australia; used for civilian flying from 1915. University of Western Sydney, 3 km S; foundation stone laid in 1895. Vale Lookout, 20 km W, for stunning views over Grose Valley. Panorama Point Lookout at Kurrajong Heights, 13 km NW, for views across to Sydney skyline. Markets each Sat. at Bilpin, 31 km NW. Hawkesbury Lookout, 15 km SW. **Tourist information:** Ham Common Bicentenary Park, Richmond Rd, Clarendon; (02) 4588 5895. **Accommodation:** 1 hotel, 1 hotel/motel, 2 motels. **See also:** The Hawkesbury.

Robertson   Pop. 252

MAP REF. 116 E8, 119 I3, 121 K10

The link between the Southern Highlands and the coast, Robertson sits at the top of the Macquarie Pass. Vantage points in the area offer spectacular views of the coast. It is the centre of the largest potato-growing district in NSW. Mar.: Agricultural Show. **In the area:** Fitzroy and Belmore falls in Morton National Park, 10 km SW; Visitors Centre near Fitzroy Falls. Mannings Lookout over Kangaroo Valley, 16 km SW. Robertson Rainforest, 2 km S. Carrington Falls and State-award-winning Minnamurra Rainforest Centre, with elevated boardwalk, in Budderoo National Park, 10 km SE. **Tourist information:** Southern Highlands Visitor Information Centre, 62–70 Main St, Mittagong; (02) 4871 2888; freecall, 1800 656176. **Accommodation:** 1 hotel, 1 motel, 2 B&B.

Rylstone   Pop. 721

MAP REF. 120 I4

Aboriginal hand-paintings on a sandstone rock overhang are a feature of the region, which is west of the Great Dividing Range on the Cudgegong River, north-east of Bathurst. **Of interest:** Historic buildings, especially in Louee St, including The Half Pie Gallery (formerly bank), and post office. Feb.: Rylstone-Kandos Show. **In the area:** Many camping spots and fishing areas on Capertee, Cudgegong and Turon rivers. Industrial Museum (open weekends) at Kandos, 3 km S. Lake Windamere, 19 km W, for water sports and trout fishing (Fishing Festival held here in Oct.); camping and picnic/barbecue facilities on shore. Fern Tree Gully, 16 km N, tree ferns in subtropical forest. Military Vehicle Museum, 20 km N. Dunn's Swamp, 18 km E, for camping, fishing and bushwalking. Glen Davis, 56 km SE on Capertee River, surrounded by sheer cliff faces. Wollemi National Park, 60 km SE, for wilderness bushwalking and excellent canoeing. **Tourist information:** Newsagency, Louee St; (02) 6379 1126. **Accommodation:** 4 hotels, 1 motel, 1 B&B, 1 cara./camp. park.

Sawtell   Pop. 10 809

MAP REF. 123 P8

This peaceful family holiday town, 8 km S of Coffs Harbour, has safe beaches and tidal creeks for fishing, swimming and surfing. **Of interest:** Playground and picnic/barbecue facilities at Boambee Creek Reserve, Sawtell Rd. **In the area:** Enchanting walks and drives in surrounding bush and mountains, including Sawtell Reserve. White-water rafting on Nymboida, Gwydir and Murray rivers. **Tourist information:** Coffs Harbour Visitors and Convention Centre, cnr Ross Ave and Marcia St, Coffs Harbour; (02) 6652 1522. **Accommodation:** 2 hotels, 2 motels, 1 cara./ camp. park.

Scone   Pop. 3329

MAP REF. 121 K1

This town set in beautiful country on the New England Hwy, 280 km N of Sydney, is the world's second largest thoroughbred and horse-breeding centre. **Of interest:** Historical Society Museum, Kingdon St (open Wed. and Sun.). Hungry Horse Gallery and Restaurant, part of Tourist information opposite Elizabeth Park, Kelly St. Market at Tourist information, last Sun. each month. May: Horse Festival. Nov.: Rodeo. **In the area:** Tours of thoroughbred studs and sheep station can be organised through Tourist information. Lake Glenbawn, 15 km E, for water sports, good picnic/barbecue facilities and camping on shore. Barrington Tops National Park, 80 km E, for scenic drives and walks. Jazz Festival in Oct. at Moonan Flat, 50 km NE. Burning Mountain at Wingen, 20 km N, a deep coal seam that has been smouldering for at least 1000 years. **Tourist information:** cnr Susan and Kelly sts; (02) 6545 1526. **Accommodation:** 3 hotels, 5 motels, 2 B&B 1 hostel, 2 cara./camp. parks.

Shellharbour   Pop. 1754

MAP REF. 116 H8, 121 K10
This attractive holiday resort 7 km S of Lake Illawarra is one of the oldest settlements on the south coast. A thriving port in the 1830s, its importance declined once the south coast railway opened. Apr.: Sunshine Festival. Aug.: Shelcove Aquatic and Outdoor Expo. **In the area:** Bike paths; bike hire available (contact Tourist information). Killalea Recreation Park, 3 km S. Blackbutt Forest Reserve, 2 km W. BMX circuit at Croom Regional Sporting Complex, 8 km W. Bass Point Headland and Marine Reserve, 5 km SE, has picnic area with views; offshore, good scuba diving, snorkelling, fishing and surfing. Fine beach at Warilla, 3 km N. Lake Illawarra, 7 km N; boat hire available. **Tourist information:** Lamberton House, Shellharbour Square, Blackbutt; (02) 4221 6169. **Accommodation:** 1 hotel, 2 motels, 3 cara./camp. parks. **See also:** The Illawarra Coast.

Singleton   Pop. 11 861

MAP REF. 121 L3
Set beside the Hunter River in rich grazing land, Singleton is the geographical heart of the Hunter Valley. New wealth in the form of huge open-cut coal mines has joined the traditional rural industry and transformed Singleton into one of the most progressive country centres in the State. **Of interest:**

Monolithic sundial on riverbank in James Cook Park, Ryan Ave, largest in southern hemisphere; built as Bicentennial project. Sales of herbs at Dullwide Herbs, Falbrook Rd. Oct.: Festival of Wine and Roses. **In the area:** Royal Australian Infantry Corps Museum of Small Arms, 5 km S, traces development of the infantry corp from 15th century. Village Fair held in Sept. at Broke, 26 km S. Broke-Fordwich winery area of Hunter Valley; contact Tourist information for details. Yengo National Park, 15 km S, features extensive Aboriginal carvings and paintings (tours available, contact Tourist information). Wollemi National Park, 15 km SW, a large wilderness park. Bayswater Power Station, 26 km NW on New England Hwy, biggest thermal power station in southern hemisphere; Lake St Clair, 30 km N, has extensive recreational and waterway facilities; camping on shore; nearby, magnificent views of Mt Royal Range. **Tourist information:** Shire Offices, Queen St; (02) 6572 7267. **Accommodation:** 8 hotels, 2 hotel/motels, 5 motels, 2 B&B, 2 cara./camp. parks.

Stroud   Pop. 556

MAP REF. 121 N3
There are many historic buildings in this delightful, small country town, 75 km N of Newcastle. The convict-built Anglican Church of St John, built in 1833 of local clay bricks, with its beautiful stained glass windows and cedar furnishings, is one of the finest. **Of interest:** Rectory of St John's (1836), Stroud House (1832), Parish House (1837), court house, post office and Quambi House – all in Cowper St. Underground silo (one of 8 built in 1841) at Silo Hill Reserve, off Broadway St. July: International Brick and Rolling-pin Throwing. Sept.-Oct.: Rodeo. Nov.: Branch Picnic Races. **Tourist information:** Great Lakes Tourist Board, Little St, Forster; (02) 6554 8799. **Accommodation:** 1 hotel, 1 hostel, 1 camp. park.

Tamworth   Pop. 31 716

MAP REF. 123 J11
This prosperous city at the junction of the New England and Oxley hwys is the country music capital of Australia, as well as being the heart of many other cultural and musical activities. Thousands of fans flock here for the 10-day Australasian country music festival, held each Jan.

since 1973. Tamworth, with its attractive public buildings and parks and gardens, is also the commercial capital of northern NSW. **Of interest:** Country Music Hands of Fame cornerstone at Hands of Fame Park, Kable Ave, has hand imprints of country music stars, including Tex Morton, Slim Dusty and Smoky Dawson. Country Music Roll of Renown at Radio Centre, on New England Hwy at Calala, dedicated to country-music artists who have contributed to Australia's heritage. National Trust-classified Calala Cottage, Denison St, home of Tamworth's first mayor. City Gallery, Marius St, exhibits works by Turner, Hans Heysen and Will Ashton; also home of National Fibre Collection. Weswal Gallery, Brisbane St. Tininburra Gallery, Moore Creek Rd, Oxley Park Wildlife Sanctuary, north off Brisbane St. Oxley Lookout for views of city and rich Peel Valley, at top of White St; lookout is starting point for Kamilaroi walking track (6.2 km), brochure available at Tourist information. Powerstation Museum, cnr Peel and Darling sts, traces Tamworth's history as first city in southern hemisphere to have electric street lighting. Market, 2nd Sun. each month at Showground Pavilion. Jan.: Australasian Country Music Festival. May: Gold Cup Race Meeting. **In the area:** Country Collection, 6 km S on New England Hwy, fascinating gemstone collection and location of 12-metre Golden Guitar, Gallery of Stars Wax Museum, Great Australian Ice-creamery and famous Longyard Hotel. Lake Keepit State Recreation Area, 57 km NW, for water sports; good visitor facilities. Fossickers Way tour through scenic New England countryside commences at historic goldmining town of Nundle, 63 km SE; brochures available at Tourist information. Chaffey Dam, 45 km SE, for sailing; Dulegal Arboretum on foreshore. Warrabah National Park, 75 km N. **Tourist information:** cnr Murray and Peel sts; (02) 6766 9422. **Accommodation:** 7 hotels, 2 hotel/motels, 31 motels, 2 B&B, 4 cara./camp. parks.

Taree   Pop. 16 303

MAP REF. 109 C13, 121 P1, 123 N13
Taree on the Pacific Hwy, 310 km N of Sydney, serves as the manufacturing and commercial centre of the Manning River district. **Of interest:** Manning River cruises depart from wharf at end

NEW SOUTH WALES

of Pulteney St. Houseboats available for hire. Dinghy hire available at Crescent Ave. Jan.: Aquatic Festival. Apr.-May: Taree and District Eisteddfod. **In the area:** Joyflights over Manning Valley depart from airport, southern outskirts of town on Lansdowne Rd. 4WD tours, mountain-bike tours through nearby State forest, forest drives and walking trails in Manning Valley (details at Tourist information). Good surfing beaches on coast 16 km E. Manning River, a 150-km navigable waterway, with beaches, good fishing and holiday spots. Easy car access to top of Ellenborough Falls (160-m drop) on Bulga Plateau, 50 km NW. The Big Buzz Funpark, 15 km S on Lakes Way, Rainbow Flat. Crowdy Bay National Park, 40 km NE, offers wildflowers in spring, fishing, swimming, bushwalking and camping. Scenic Coopernook Forest Dr., starts at Forest Headquarters north of Coopernook, 20 km NE; one highlight is Big Nellie (a large volcanic plug), rising 560 m above sea level. Railway Crossing Family Fun Park at Harrington, 30 km N. High Adventure Fun Park, 38 km N on Pacific Hwy, a light airsports (including both paragliding and hang-gliding) training and recreational centre. Middle Brother State Forest, 50 km N. **Tourist information:** Manning Valley Tourist Information Centre, Pacific Hwy, Taree North; (02) 6552 1900; freecall, 1800 80 1522. **Accommodation:** 6 hotels, 21 motels, 3 B&B, 3 cara./camp. parks.

Tathra
Pop. 1571

MAP REF. 117 G8, 119 G10, 243 R6

Tathra is a relaxed seaside town, centrally located on the south coast of NSW, 18 km SE of Bega and midway between Merimbula and Bermagui. Tathra is ideal for a family holiday, with its patrolled 3-km long surf beach, safe swimming for small children at Mogareeka Inlet (the sandy mouth of the Bega River), and good fishing spots. Diving and deep-sea fishing charters at Kianinny Bay. **Of interest:** National Trust-classified historic wharf (1860s), Wharf Rd. Above wharf, Maritime Museum displays variety of memorabilia of visiting ships. Oct.: Amateur Fishing Competition. **In the area:** Fishing and water sports on Lake Wallagoot, 9.5 km S. Bournda National Park, 11 km S of town, for camping, swimming and bushwalking. Mimosa Rocks National Park,

17 km N, a picturesque coastal park. **Tourist information:** Tathra Wharf, Wharf Rd; (02) 6494 4062. **Accommodation:** 1 motel, 1 hotel/motel, 1 B&B, 4 cara./ camp. parks.

Temora
Pop. 4279

MAP REF. 119 A2, 120 C10, 127 R8

Temora is the commercial centre for the rich wheat district of the northern and western Riverina, which also supports oats, barley, fat lambs, pigs and cattle. **Of interest:** Temora Rural Museum, Wagga Rd, has working displays, and rock and mineral collection (open p.m.). Feb.: Golden Gift (foot race). **In the area:** Lake Centenary, 3 km N, for boating, swimming and picnics. Paragon Gold Mine at Gidginbung, 15 km N (open by appt). **Tourist information:** Temora Community Centre, Hoskins St; (02) 6978 0500. **Accommodation:** 3 motels, 1 cara./camp. park.

Tenterfield
Pop. 3310

MAP REF. 123 M4, 505 N13

The countryside around Tenterfield, at the northern end of the New England highlands in northern NSW, offers a contrast of rugged mountains and serene rural landscapes. Primarily a sheep- and cattle-grazing area, other industries include logging and sawmilling, and tourism. Autumn in Tenterfield is spectacular. **Of interest:** Centenary Cottage (1871), Logan St, has local history collection. Early residential buildings in Logan St. Self-guide Historic Town Walk, leaflet available from Tourist information. Sir Henry Parkes Library and Museum in School of Arts (1876), Rouse St, features relics relating to Sir Henry Parkes, who made his famous Federation speech there in 1889. Hand-made saddles at Tenterfield Saddler (1860s), High St. Apr.: Oracles of the Bush (Australian culture and bush poetry festival). Oct.: Federation Festival; Spring Wine Festival; Highland Gathering. Nov.: Australian Line-dancing Exhibition. **In the area:** Mt McKenzie Granite Drive, 30-km circular route beginning and ending at Molesworth St (in town) includes Ghost Gully. Bluff Rock, 10 km S on New England Hwy, unusual granite outcrop. Thunderbolt's Hideout, 11 km NE. Gold mine at Drake, 31 km NE. Boonoo Boonoo Falls (210-m drop), within Boonoo Boonoo National Park,

32 km NE. Good views from summit of Bald Rock, largest granite monolith in Australia, 35 km N in Bald Rock National Park. Girraween National Park (in Qld) renowned for its wildflowers and granite outcrops. Aboriginal cultural tours to Boonoo Boonoo and Bald Rock national parks; contact Tourist information. **Tourist information:** 157 Rouse St; (02) 6736 1082. **Accommodation:** 4 hotels, 2 hotel/ motels, 6 motels, 3 B&B, 4 cara. parks. **See also:** New England.

Terrigal
Pop. 7453

MAP REF. 105 Q4, 108 H5, 121 M6

Excellent surfing is one of the main attractions of this popular holiday town on the Central Coast. **In the area:** The Skillion, 3 km SE, a headland offering coastal views. Several good surfing beaches: Wamberal Beach (3 km N); Shelly Beach (13 km N); Avoca Beach (7.5 km S). Central Park Family Fun Centre, 6 km N at Forresters Beach, has waterslide, fun cars and barbecues. Secluded beaches and pockets of rainforest at Bouddi National Park, 17 km S. **Tourist information:** Rotary Park, Terrigal Dr.; (02) 4385 4430. **Accommodation:** 4 resorts, 1 hotel, 5 motels, 1 B&B, 1 hostel, 1 cara./camp. park.

The Entrance
Pop. 37 831

MAP REF. 105 Q3, 108 H2, 121 M6

Blessed with clean beaches, this beautiful lakeside and ocean town between Sydney and Newcastle is the family holiday playground of these two cities. **Of interest:** Daily pelican feeding at 3.30 p.m. in the Amphitheatre, Memorial Park in Marine Pde. Art and craft market, each Sun. in Bayview Ave. Jan.: Australia Day Family Concert and Fireworks. Nov.: Celtic Festival. Dec.: Tuggerah Lakes Mardi Gras Festival. **In the area:** Fishing on lakes – Tuggerah, Budgewoi and Munmorah – and ocean beach. During summer months, prawning on lakes. Water sports on Lake Tuggerah. Extensive collection of shells at Shell Museum, 1 km N at Dunleith Caravan Park. Bushwalking trails in Wyrrabalong National Park, 6 km N. Crackneck Point Lookout, 6 km S, for coastal views. **Tourist information:** Memorial Park, Marine Pde; (02) 4334 4213. **Accommodation:** 3 hotels, 10 motels, 12 cara. parks.

Thredbo   Pop. 200

MAP REF. 118 D13, 119 C10

This popular mountain village lies in the heart of Kosciusko National Park between Jindabyne and Khancoban. Its short history began in 1962 with a lease granted by the State government for resort development. In summer Thredbo attracts anglers, mountain-bikers and bushwalkers; a chairlift ride from the village places visitors within walking distance of Australia's highest summit, Mt Kosciusko (2228m). Winter snows transform Thredbo into one of the State's premier ski resorts; the ski season runs from the June long weekend to the

October long weekend. **Of interest:** A range of chairlifts (including quad lifts) access a variety of marked downhill ski trails from beginners to advanced; also cross-country skiing, ski school and ski hire. In summer and early autumn: inline skate hire for use at the resort; Alpine Slide rides; canoe hire for use in the resort ponds; walks around the village, including Meadows Nature Walk through ti-tree and Thredbo Village Walk for the diversity of alpine architecture; mountain-bike riding on the Village Bike Track and various other tracks around Thredbo (bike hire available); Australian Institute of Sport Alpine Training Centre, used by athletes

for high-altitude training, has a range of quality sporting facilities. Jan.: Blues Festival. May: Jazz Festival. **In the area:** Skiers can access Perisher and Mt Blue Cow ski fields via the Skitube from Bullocks Flat Terminal, 15 km NE. Crackenback chairlift operates year-round from the resort to Eagles Nest Mountain Hut; from here, in summer, a 12 km-return walk amongst wildflowers along an alpine walkway leads to Mt Kosciusko via Kosciusko Lookout. Alternatively return from Eagles Nest to Thredbo on Merritts Nature Walk. Guided alpine walks also available, contact Tourist information for details. Trout fishing on Thredbo River and at

Caves and Caverns

Magical underground limestone caves are one of the wonders of New South Wales. Glittering limestone stalactites and stalagmites, caused by the ceaseless dripping of limestone-impregnated water over tens of thousands of years, glow eerily in cathedral-like caves. These delicate formations of ribbed columns, frozen cascades, 'tapestries' and 'shawls' look like part of a subterranean fairyland.

The most famous are the **Jenolan Caves**. Since being first explored in 1838, several million people have visited them. Situated on a spur of the Great Dividing Range, on the south-west edge of the Blue Mountains, they are open daily for guided tours. The caves are surrounded by a 2416-hectare flora and fauna reserve with walking trails, kiosk, cafe and picnic/barbecue facilities. Accommodation includes the charming Tudor-style guest house, Jenolan Caves House; and Binda Bush Cabins, 8 kilometres from the caves precinct, on the road into the reserve.

The **Wombeyan Caves** are set in a pleasant valley in the Southern Highlands, 193 kilometres south-west of Sydney. They can be reached from the Wombeyan turn-off, 60 kilometres north-west of Mittagong. From here a well-surfaced but narrow road winds through spectacular mountain scenery. The alternative route (recommended for caravanners) is via Goulburn and Taralga. Five of the caves are easily accessible by graded paths. They are fully developed for visitors, with steps and handrails, and are open daily or on demand for self-guide, historical and adventure caving tours. There is a Visitors Centre and facilities exist for camping, as well as family or group accommodation. Walking tracks lead to waterfalls, mountain

Jenolan Caves House provides accommodation for visitors to the Jenolan Caves

lookouts and a spectacular limestone canyon (excellent swimming area).

The **Abercrombie Caves** are on the edge of the Great Dividing Range, 65 kilometres south of Bathurst; they can also be accessed from Oberon or Goulburn. Regular guided and self-guide tours of the caves are available. The caves are set in a 2200-hectare reserve which features the largest natural bridge in the southern hemisphere; swimming, fishing and fossicking in Grove Creek; scenic bushwalks; rich variety of flora and fauna; a kiosk; and camping facilities.

The **Yarrangobilly Caves**, 6.5 kilometres off the Snowy Mountains Highway, 109 kilometres north-west of Cooma, are open daily, except Christmas

Day (but subject to winter road conditions) for self-guide or guided tours. On weekends, school and public holidays, additional tours are available. Four caves in the area have been developed and are open for inspection (one with wheelchair access). During summer and Easter school holidays, tours include a torchlit Castle Cave Walk. An added attraction in the area is a thermal pool with naturally heated water at 27°C all year round. The caves are a feature of Kosciusko National Park and are surrounded by spectacular limestone gorges and densely forested mountains. Bring your own food and drink; there is no kiosk in the area. Sweets are sold at the office and there are soft drink and coffee machines, and gas barbecues.

The **Wellington Caves** form part of the Wellington Caves complex which consists of two show caves (the Cathedral Cave with its huge stalagmite and the beautiful Gaden Cave), an aviary, picnic and barbecue facilities, kiosk and a caravan park with self-contained lodges. Guided cave tours are available daily (except Christmas Day). Wellington Caves are located 8 kilometres south of Wellington, 1 kilometre from the Mitchell Highway.

For further information: on Jenolan Caves, contact Jenolan Caves Reserve Trust, (02) 6359 3311; on Wombeyan Caves, (02) 4843 5976; on Abercrombie Caves, (02) 6368 8603; on Yarrangobilly Caves, (02) 6454 9597; on Wellington Caves, contact Wellington Shire Offices, (02) 6845 1733. **Map references:** for Jenolan Caves, 104 F8, 120 I7; for Wombeyan Caves, 120 I9; for Abercrombie Caves, 119 F1, 120 G8; for Yarrangobilly Caves, 118 D1, 119 C7; and for Wellington Caves, 120 F3.

Bawley Beach, near Ulladulla

Lake Jindabyne, 34 km NE. Horseriding and station accommodation at historic Tom Groggin, 24 km SW on the Alpine Way. **Tourist information:** Friday Dr.; (02) 6459 4198, or Snowy Region Visitor Centre, Kosciusko Rd, Jindabyne; (02) 6456 2444. **Accommodation:** 1 hotel, 1 hostel, 61 apartments and lodges. **See also:** The Snowy Mountains.

Tibooburra   Pop. 150

MAP REF. 124 D3

The name of this former gold town, 337 km N of Broken Hill, comes from an Aboriginal word meaning 'heaps of rocks'. The town is surrounded by granite outcrops and was previously known as The Granites. **Of interest:** In Briscoe St: buildings of local stone, including court house (1888), Family Hotel (1888) and Tibooburra Hotel (1890); School of the Air (tours during term time). June (or July): Tibooburra Festival. Oct.: Gymkhana and Rodeo (long weekend). **In the area:** Nearby goldfields. Self-guide historic Gold-mining Walk and Granite Scenic Walk (contact Tourist information for brochures) in Sturt National Park, adjacent to town; the park has four camping grounds and is a semi-desert area noted for its wildlife and geological features; Explorers Tree, at western end of park, tree faintly blazed by explorer Charles Sturt; pastoralists display at Mt Wood (27 km E). Check road conditions before travelling in this area; read section on Outback Motoring. Cameron Corner,

140 km NW, where three States meet. At former gold township of Milparinka, 42 km S: restored court house, remains of old police station, bank, general store and post office, but Albert Hotel is town's only active concern. Depot Glen billabong, 14 km NW of Milparinka, where Sturt stayed marooned for 6 months in 1845; 1 km further east, grave of James Poole, a member of Sturt's 1845 expedition. Further 7 km N of Depot Glen is Mt Poole, where cairn commemorates Charles Sturt's expedition. **Tourist information:** National Parks and Wildlife Service, Briscoe St; (08) 8091 3308. **Accommodation:** 2 hotels, 1 motel/ cara./camp. park.

Tingha   Pop. 831

MAP REF. 123 K7

This small tin-mining town is 28 km SE of Inverell. **Of interest:** Campbells Honey Farm, Swimming Pool Rd. **In the area:** Fossicking for gems (quartz, sapphires and topaz); fossicking lessons provided by owner of caravan park to guests only. Smith's Mining and Natural History Museum at Green Valley Farm, 10 km S, displays several artifacts, antiques, minerals and gemstones; cabin accommodation available. Good water-skiing, boating and excellent fishing on Copeton Dam, 15 km W. **Tourist information:** Tingha Gems Caravan Park, Swimming Pool Rd; (02) 6723 3234. **Accommodation:** 1 hotel, 1 cara. park. **See also:** New England.

Tocumwal   Pop. 1587

MAP REF. 127 M12, 240 I2

This peaceful Murray River town on the Newell Hwy is ideal for boating, fishing, swimming and water-skiing. **Of interest:** Huge fibreglass codfish in town square. Old Railway Store, Deniliquin St, has scale models of Australian trains. Picnic area with lawns and sandy river beach, 200 m from town square. Numerous walks, contact Tourist information for walking guides. A 36-hole golf course, Barooga–Corowa Rd on eastern outskirts of town. Market at Foreshore Park, Anzac Ave, 1st Sat. each month. Mar.: Pioneer Skills Day. Easter: Easter Eggs-Travaganza. June: Country Craft Fiesta. **In the area:** River Murray Heritage Centre, 3 km N. Nallama, 15 km W on Tuppal Rd, a historic farm settlement with grave site and giant lemon-scented gum (check opening times). Ulupna Island flora and fauna reserve, Murray River. Binghi Boomerang Factory at Barooga, 19 km SE. Aerodrome, 5 km NE, largest RAAF base in Australia during World War II, now houses world-renowned Sportavia Soaring Centre (gliding joy flights and tuition packages available). The Rocks and Blowhole, 11 km NE on Rocks Rd, have an association with an Aboriginal legend (explained on nearby board); once a stone quarry. **Tourist information:** Tocumwal River foreshore; (03) 5874 2131. **Accommodation:** 4 hotels, 1 hotel/ motel, 10 motels, 2 B&B, 6 cara./camp. parks.

Toukley   Pop. 6520

MAP REF. 105 Q2, 121 M6

Situated on the peninsula between Tuggerah and Budgewoi lakes, this coastal hamlet offers pollution-free beaches and breathtaking scenery. **Of interest:** Local art on display at Tourist information, Wallarah Rd. Open-air markets, each Sun. at Shopping Centre carpark, Yarralla Rd. Sept.: Azalea festival. Oct.: Cycle Classic. **In the area:** Lakes, venue for all water sports. During summer months, prawning from lake foreshores. Rock pool at Cabbage Tree Bay, 5 km E. Norah Head Lighthouse, 5 km E. Many bushwalking trails in magnificent Munmorah State Recreation Area, 10 km N, and in Red Gum Forest in Wyrrabalong National Park, 4 km S. **Tourist information:** Wallarah Point Park, Wallarah Rd,

Gorokan; (02) 4392 4666. **Accommodation:** 1 hotel, 6 motels, 4 cara./camp. parks.

Tumbarumba — Pop. 1548

MAP REF. 119 B7

A former goldmining town in the western foothills of the Snowy Mountains, 504 km SW of Sydney, Tumbarumba has much to offer the visitor who prefers to get off the beaten track. It is an ideal base for day trips to the Snowy Mountains. **Of interest:** Bicentennial Botanic Gardens, Prince St. Wool and Craft Centre, Bridge St (also Tourist information, open Tues.–Sun., also Mon. in school holidays), includes Historical Society Museum, which features a working model of water-powered timber mill. Jan.: New Year's Day Rodeo. Nov.: Heritage Week. **In the area:** White-water rafting, fly fishing, paragliding, trail rides (contact Tourist information for details). Site of old Union Jack Mine, 3 km N. Pioneer Women's Hut, 8 km NW on Wagga Rd, a domestic, rural history museum (open Wed., Sat. and Sun.). Paddy's River Falls, 16 km S, cascades drop 60 m; nearby, walking track and picnic area. Henry Angel Trackhead, 7 km SE on Tooma Rd, starting point for a section of Hume and Hovell Walking Track, and has facilities for campers and picnickers. At Tooma, 34 km SE: historic hotel, tearooms and store. Mt Selwyn Ski Resort, 70 km SE. Murray 1 Power Station, 10 km SE of Khancoban on Alpine Way (guided tours daily). **Tourist information:** Wool and Craft Centre, 10 Bridge St; (02) 6948 2805. **Accommodation:** 2 hotels, 1 motel, 2 B&B, 2 cara./camp. parks.

Tumut — Pop. 5955

MAP REF. 119 C5, 120 D12, 142 A2

Situated on the Snowy Mountains Hwy, 424 km SW of Sydney, Tumut attracts visitors all year. Close to ski resorts and the great dams of the Snowy Mountains Hydro-electric Scheme, it is also well known for spectacular mountain scenery. **Of interest:** CSR Woodpanels and Softwood, Adelong Rd (open by appt, contact Tourist information). Millet broom factory, Snowy Mountains Hwy. Bakehouse Gallery, Winyard St. Pleasant river walk along Tumut River, from Elm Dr. Tours to power stations: Tumut 3 (45 km S) and Tumut 2

(115 km S); contact Tourist information. Apr.-May: Festival of the Falling Leaf. **In the area:** Excellent fishing in Tumut and Goobraganda rivers. White-water rafting, canoeing, horseriding, abseiling, hang gliding and scenic flights, contact Tourist information for details. Two access points for Hume and Hovell Walking Track (track extends from Gunning to Albury but various access points allow for shorter walks). Fishing at Triton Trout Farm, 19 km E (open Wed.–Mon.). Largest African violet farm in Australia, 7 km S on Tumut Plains Rd (open Tues.–Sun.). Blowering Reservoir, 10 km S, major centre for water sports, fishing for rainbow trout, brown trout and perch; lookout over dam wall. Blowering Cliffs walk (5 km) in Kosciusko National Park, 19 km S; set of outstanding granite cliffs overlooking reservoir. Talbingo Dam and Reservoir, 40 km S and set in steep wooded country, is second tallest rock-filled dam in Australia. Kiandra, 95 km S, an old gold-mining town. **Tourist information:** Fitzroy St (Snowy Mountains Hwy); (02) 6947 1849. **Accommodation:** 4 hotels, 2 hotel/motels, 8 motels, 5 B&B, 2 cara./camp. parks.

Tweed Heads — Pop. 5360

MAP REF. 123 Q1, 499 I11, 505 Q11

Tweed Heads, the State's most northern town, and its twin town Coolangatta, across the border, are popular holiday destinations at the southern end of the Gold Coast. **Of interest:** World's first laser-beam lighthouse sits atop Point Danger, one half in NSW and the other in Qld; nearby, cliff-edge walk (dolphins may be seen offshore) and picnic spots. Tweed Endeavour cruise boats, operating from River Tce, visit locations along Tweed River. Fishing and diving charters available, and houseboats for hire (details at Tourist information). Feb.: Tweed Valley Triathlon. Aug.: Bowls Tournament. **In the area:** Idyllic beaches, reserves and coastal towns on Tweed Coast, particularly Kingscliff, 14 km S, and other villages south including Bogangar and Pottsville. Minjungbal Aboriginal Cultural Centre, just over Boyds Bay Bridge, features Aboriginal ceremonial bora ring, museum and nature walk through sections of mangroves and rainforest. Melaleuca Station, 9 km S on Pacific Hwy at Chinderah, a re-created 1930's railway

station set in tea-tree plantation and has train rides, tea-tree oil distillation plant and animal nursery. Tropical Fruitworld, 15 km S on Pacific Hwy (guided tours of plantation available). Pioneer Plantation, Pottsville Rd, Mooball, a working banana plantation featuring a six-wheel-drive trip to top of Banana Mountain. **Tourist information:** Wharf St; (07) 5536 4244. **Accommodation:** 2 hotels, 22 motels, 6 cara./camp. parks.

Ulladulla — Pop. 7381

MAP REF. 119 I6, 121 J13, 143 P4

Ulladulla, a fishing town, is the main centre along this section of the South Coast, a stretch of beautiful coast, coastal lakes and lagoons with white sandy beaches. **Of interest:** Town's oldest building (c. 1868) houses Millard's Cottage Restaurant, Princes Hwy. Funland, Princes Hwy, large indoor family fun park. At Warden Head, lighthouse, views and walking tracks. Coomie Nulunga Cultural Trail (30 min.), starts Deering St, opposite Lighthouse Oval carpark. Native plants, birdlife and walks at South Pacific Heathland Reserve, Dowling St. Ulladulla Wildflower Reserve, cnr Green and Warden sts. Coastal Patrol Markets, 2nd Sun. each month at harbour wharf. Easter: Blessing of the Fleet. **In the area:** Historic Milton, 7 km NW on Princes Hwy; Settlement Markets on hwy, 1st Sat. each month; Settlers Fair held in Oct. Pointer Gap Lookout, 20 km NW, for coastal views. Mollymook, 2 km N, for surfing and excellent fishing. Narrawallee Beach, 4 km N. Nearby Narrawallee Inlet has calm, shallow water ideal for children. Bendalong, 36 km N. Sussex Inlet, 47 km N, holds fishing carnival in May. Lakes Conjola (23 km NW) and Burrill (5 km SW), ideal for swimming, fishing and water-skiing. Views from summit of Pigeon House Mountain in Morton National Park, 25 km NW. **Tourist information:** Princes Hwy; (02) 4455 1269. **Accommodation:** 3 hotels, 20 motels, 5 B&B, 1 hostel, 4 cara./camp. parks. **See also:** The Illawarra Coast.

Uralla — Pop. 2324

MAP REF. 123 L9

'Gentleman' bushranger Thunderbolt was shot dead by a local policeman in 1870, at Kentucky Creek, south-east of

Cotton crop near Wee Waa

NEW SOUTH WALES

this charming New England town. Rich gold discoveries were made in the vicinity in the 1850s. **Of interest:** Self-guide Heritage Walking Tour, contact Tourist information for brochure. In Bridge St: Hassett's Military Museum, displays local and national military history and memorabilia; Statue of Thunderbolt (his grave is in old Uralla Cemetery, John St); also variety of craft, antique and bric-a-brac shops. McCrossin's Mill (1870), Salisbury St, now a museum with goldfields history displays, a re-created joss house honouring the many Chinese who came to the diggings, Thunderbolt exhibits and collection of Thunderbolt paintings. Old Uralla court house, Hill St, now library. Brass and Iron Lace Foundry, operating since 1872 (open Mon.–Fri.). Market, 2nd Sun. each month (Sept.–May). **In the area:** Dangars Lagoon, 2 km E on Walcha Rd, a bird sanctuary with bird hide. Mt Yarrowyck Aboriginal rock-art site, 23 km NW off Bundarra Rd. Fossicking at Old Rocky River diggings, 5 km W; nearby, pleasant picnic spot. Thunderbolt's Rock, 6 km S, used by the bushranger as a lookout; can be climbed with care. Gostwyck, 11 km SE, one of oldest properties in area, not open to

public. **Tourist information:** Bridge St; (02) 6778 4496. **Accommodation:** 1 hotel, 1 hotel/motel, 3 motels, 1 B&B, 2 cara./camp. parks. **See also:** New England.

Urunga   Pop. 2666

MAP REF. 123 P9

Located at the junction of the Bellinger and Kalang rivers, and alongside a broad lagoon, Urunga is one of the best fishing spots on the north coast. The town is 32 km S of Coffs Harbour. **Of interest:** Water sports and fishing. In Morgo St, safe river swimming pool for children, with picnic reserve. July: Bowling Club Carnival. **In the area:** Beautiful beach for surfing and swimming at Hungry Head, 3 km S. At Raleigh, 4 km N: winery, horseriding and go-kart complex. **Tourist information:** The Honey Place, Pacific Hwy; (02) 6655 6160. **Accommodation:** 1 hotel, 5 motels, 1 B&B, 4 cara./camp. parks.

Wagga Wagga   Pop. 40 875

MAP REF. 120 B12, 127 R10

This prosperous city – the largest inland city in NSW – is 478 km SW of Sydney just off the Hume Hwy. Wagga Wagga is a major centre for industry, commerce, education, agriculture and the home of two important military bases. The town is renowned for its cultural pursuits and performing arts. **Of interest:** Botanic Gardens (excellent) and Zoo on Willans Hill; a miniature railway runs through gardens. Historical Museum, adjacent to gardens, has indoor and outdoor exhibits. City Art Gallery, Gurwood St, features National Art Glass collection. Riverina Galleries, The Esplanade. Mar.: Australian Veterans Games. Sept.: National Festival of the Voice. Nov.: Festival of Wagga Wagga. **In the area:** Lake Albert, 7 km S, for water sports. RAAF Museum, 10 km E. Wagga Wagga Winery, 15 km NE; tasting area and restaurant have early Australiana theme. On road to winery, Eunonyhareenyha Cottage offers teas in delightful riverside setting (usually open weekends). Charles Sturt Winery at Charles Sturt University (Riverina Campus), 6 km NW. Aurora Clydesdale Stud and Pioneer Farm, 9 km W of Collingullie on Sturt Hwy. Tours of military base at Kapooka, 9 km SW. The Rock, 32 km SW, a small town noted for its unusual scenery; walking trails through a flora and fauna reserve lead to summit of The Rock (365 m approx).

Tourist information: Tourism Wagga Wagga, Tarcutta St; (02) 6923 5402. **Accommodation:** 12 hotels, 24 motels, 6 B&B, 6 cara./camp. parks.

Walcha   Pop. 1782

MAP REF. 123 L10

This town on the eastern slopes of the Great Dividing Range was first settled in 1832. **Of interest:** Pioneer Cottage and Museum, Derby St, features first Tiger Moth plane used for crop-dusting in Australia, and a replica of blacksmith's shop. Court house (1878), cnr Derby and Apsley sts. In South St: Anglican Church (1862); St Patricks Church (1881). Fenwicke House, 19th-century terrace in Fitzroy St, now art gallery. Jan.: Australia Day Breakfast in the Park. Feb.: Agricultural Show. **In the area:** Trout fishing. Ohio Homestead (1842), 4 km E (open by appt). Oxley Wild Rivers National Park, 20 km E, encompasses a high plateau, deep gorges and numerous waterfalls including Wollomombi (220 m) considered the highest in Australia; Apsley, where seven platforms together form a bridge over the Apsley River and provide access to both sides of the gorge and waterfall; and Tia Section of park developed for visitors centres around the major waterfalls, other areas left as wilderness. **Tourist information:** 106E Fitzroy St; (02) 6777 1075. **Accommodation:** 2 hotels, 2 hotel/motels, 1 motel, 1 B&B, 1 cara./camp. park. **See also:** New England.

Walgett   Pop. 2091

MAP REF. 122 C7

Walgett is situated at the junction of the Barwon and Namoi rivers, 300 km NW of Dubbo. With its airport and railhead, it is also the gateway to the opal fields around Lightning Ridge. **Of interest:** First European settler's grave on banks of Namoi River, northern end of town. Oct.: Weekend Extravaganza (raft races and go-karts). **In the area:** Good fishing all year. Grawin, Glengarry and Sheepyard opal fields, 70 km W. (Motorists are warned water is scarce; adequate supply should be carried.) One of largest inland lakes in Australia, Narran Lake, 96 km W via Cumborah Rd, is a wildlife sanctuary; no facilities for private visits, but light aircraft tours can be arranged through Walgett Aero Club; (02) 6828 1344. **Tourist information:** Shire Offices, 77 Fox St; (02) 6828 1399.

Accommodation: 2 hotel/motels, 3 motels, 1 cara./camp. park.

Warialda   Pop. 1285

MAP REF. 122 I5

The first administrative centre in the north-west of the State, this town on Gwydir Hwy, 63 km NW of Inverell, is in a stud farm and wheat-growing district. **Of interest:** Historic buildings, especially on Stephen and Hope sts. Self-guide historic walk around town; Koorilgur Nature Walks (contact Tourist information). Historic Carinda House, Stephen St, now a craft outlet. Historic graves (from 1850s) in bushland setting at Pioneer Cemetery, Queen and Stephen sts. Well's Family Gem and Mineral Collection in Heritage Centre, Hope St; also has Aboriginal artifacts and bottle display. May: Agricultural Show. **In the area:** Good picnic spots, camping, fossicking, wildflowers (in spring) and prolific wildlife at Cranky Rock Nature Reserve, 8 km E. **Tourist information:** Shire Offices, Hope St; (02) 6729 1016. **Accommodation:** 1 hotel, 1 motel, 1 cara./camp. park.

Warren   Pop. 2036

MAP REF. 122 B13

The centre for the surrounding wool and cotton district, Warren is on the Oxley Hwy, 126 km NW of Dubbo. Located beside the Macquarie River, it is a popular spot for anglers. **Of interest:** In Burton St: Macquarie Park, on banks of river; The Craft Shop for local craft. Tiger Bay Wildlife Reserve, a wetlands reserve at northern outskirts of town on Oxley Hwy. May: Golden Fleece Race Day. Nov.: Cotton Cup Racing Carnival. **In the area:** Excellent racecourse (known as 'Randwick of the West') 3 km W, location for Cotton Cup Racing Carnival. Warren Weir, 5 km SE. **Tourist information:** The Craft Shop, Burton St; (02) 6847 3181. **Accommodation:** 2 hotels, 2 motels, 2 cara./camp. parks.

Wauchope   Pop. 4297

MAP REF. 109 E8, 123 O12

A major re-creation of a typical timber town of the 1880s at nearby Timbertown has put Wauchope on the tourist map. The town is the centre of a timber-getting, dairying, beef-cattle and mixed-farming area on the Oxley Hwy, 19 km W of Port Macquarie. **Of interest:** Train Meadows, King Creek Rd, has model-train display. Mar.: Lasiandra Festival. Oct.: Colonial Carnival. **In the area:** Timbertown, re-created village with shops, including craft gallery and leather goods outlet, and school, 3 km W on edge of Broken Bago State Forest, features working bullock team, horse-drawn wagons, smithy, woodturner, steam-powered train and sleeper-cutting demonstrations. Adjacent small weatherboard church houses Historical Society Museum. Broken Bago Winery, 8 km SW. Old Bottlebutt, 6 km S, largest known bloodwood tree in State. The Big Bull, 2 km E off Oxley Hwy, has dairy-farming display, hay rides and animal nursery. Billabong Animal Park, 10 km E. **Tourist information:** cnr Hay and Clarence sts, Port Macquarie; (02) 6583 1077; freecall, 1800 025935. **Accommodation:** 2 hotels, 2 motels, 1 hostel, 1 cara./camp. park.

Wee Waa   Pop. 2030

MAP REF. 122 F8

This small town near the Namoi River is the centre of a cotton-growing district producing the highest cotton yield in Australia. **Of interest:** Guided tours (Apr.–Aug.) from Namoi Cotton Co-op, Short St, to Merah North Cotton Gin (9 km) and cotton farms. Apr.: Agricultural Show. **In the area:** Cuttabri Wine Shanty, 25 km SW, an original Cobb & Co. coaching-stop between Wee Waa and Pilliga. Yarrie Lake, 24 km S, for boating and birdwatching. **Tourist information:** Newell Hwy, Narrabri; (02) 6792 3583. **Accommodation:** 1 hotel, 2 motels, 2 cara. parks.

Wellington   Pop. 5433

MAP REF. 120 F3

Limestone caves are one of the interesting features of this town at the junction of the Macquarie and Bell rivers, 362 km NW of Sydney. **Of interest:** Town walking tour and driving tours of surrounding countryside, contact Tourist information. Historical Museum in old bank (1883), cnr Percy and Warne sts. Cameron Park, attractive area on western side of main street (Mitchell Hwy). Mar.: The Wellington Boot (horseraces); Vintage Fair. Aug.: Eisteddfod. **In the area:** Wellington Caves, 9 km S, features Cathedral Cave and smaller Gaden Cave with its rare cave coral and phosphate mine (guided tours available). Nearby, aviary, opal shop, craft shop, picnic/barbecue facilities and kiosk. Markeita Cellars, 16 km S in village of Neurea. Rabbit Farm, 20 km S, has shearing demonstrations of angora rabbits; also alpacas. At Burrendong State Recreation Area, 32 km E: Lake Burrendong, for watersports and fishing; panoramic views of lake from spillway; Burrendong Arboretum, a native flora reserve; bird-watching, walking tracks; camping facilities and cabin accommodation. Glenfinlass Wines, 8 km SW on Parkes Rd. Nangara Gallery, 26 km SW, Australia-wide collection of Aboriginal artifacts. From Mt Arthur Reserve, 3 km W of town, walking trails to lookout at summit of Mt Binjang; maps from Tourist information. **Tourist information:** Cameron Park, Nanima Cr.; (02) 6845 1733. **Accommodation:** 7 hotels, 4 motels, 1 B&B, 4 cara./camp. parks.

Wentworth   Pop. 1447

MAP REF. 126 C6, 238 F2

This historic town at the junction of the Murray and Darling rivers was once a busy riverboat and customs port; today it is a quiet holiday town. **Of interest:** In Beverly St: Rotary Folk Museum; Old Wentworth Gaol (1881). Court house (1870s), Darling St. Historic convent, Cadell St. Historic PS *Ruby*, in Fotherby Park, Wentworth St. River cruises on MV *Loyalty*, depart from end Darling St. Lock 10, weir and park for picnics. Nov.: Wentworth Cup (held on Melbourne Cup Day). **In the area:** Houseboat hire available. Perry's sand hills, 5 km NW. Model aircraft display at Yelta, 12 km E. At Buronga, 26 km E: Oasis Botanical Gardens, River Rd; Orange World and Stanley Wine Co. both on Silver City Hwy. Mungo National Park, 157 km NE, a World Heritage Area. **Tourist information:** 180-190 Deakin Ave, Mildura; (03) 5021 4424. **Accommodation:** 2 hotels, 6 motels, 2 B&B, 2 cara. parks.

West Wyalong   Pop. 3458

MAP REF. 120 B8, 127 Q6

This former goldmining town, at the junction of the Mid Western and Newell hwys, celebrated its centenary in 1994. It is the business centre of a prosperous wheat, wool and mixed-farming

Opal fields, White Cliffs

NEW SOUTH WALES

area, and the gateway to the Riverina and central-west regions of the State. **Of interest:** On Newell Hwy: Aboriginal Artifacts Gallery (open Mon.–Fri.); Bland District Historical Museum, with historical displays and scale model of a goldmine. Sept.: Agricultural Show. Oct.: Highways Festival (biennial, odd-numbered years). **In the area:** Bird sanctuary and fishing at Lake Cowal, 48 km NE via Clear Ridge, largest natural lake in NSW. Weethalle Whistlestop, 65 km W on Hay Rd, for Devonshire teas, art and craft. At Barmedman, 32 km SE, Mineral Water Pool, believed to provide relief from arthritis and rheumatism. **Tourist information:** McCann Park, Newell Hwy; (02) 6972 3645. **Accommodation:** 6 hotels, 12 motels, 2 cara./camp. parks.

White Cliffs   Pop. 219

MAP REF. 124 F8

White Cliffs, 97 km NW of Wilcannia, is a town where pioneering is a way of life. The opal fields were the first commercial fields in NSW; the first lease was granted in 1890, and in the boom years at the turn-of-the-century, the fields were supporting 4500 people. Precious opal is still mined today. Jewelled opal 'pineapples' are found only in this area. Road access to the town is via a graded gravel road (sealed in parts), suitable for conventional cars and caravans when driven with care in dry weather. **Of interest:** Tour (3 hours) of town, includ-

ing local historical features, and opportunity to fossick for opal in surrounding opal fields; details at Tourist information. In town centre: historic buildings including old police station (1897), public school (1900) and post office (1900); camping, barbecue facilities and swimming-pool in Reserve; pioneer children's cemetery; Joe's Stubby Opal Shop, built with glass stubbies; Country Crafts at the post office. Just south: solar power station (tours available), rugged outback golf course. On the southern outskirts around Smith's Hill: Top Level Opals; Outback Treasures (opal jewellery and Aboriginal art); Underground Dugout Motel. On the eastern outskirts around Turley's Hill: Eagles Gallery, underground complex with variety of local arts and crafts (open on request); Jock's Place, dugout home and museum; P.J.'s Underground B&B. On the northern outskirts: Wellington's Underground Art Gallery; Brian Moore's Opal Showroom. May: Gymkhana and Rodeo. July: Royal Flying Doctor Ball. **In the area:** Mootwingee National Park, 90 km SW, guided tours of Aboriginal rock-art sites in cooler months (extremely hot in summer). **Tourist information:** General Store; (02) 8091 6611. **Accommodation:** 1 hotel, 1 motel, 1 B&B, 1 cara./camp. park.

Whitton   Pop. 340

MAP REF. 127 O8

Whitton, 24 km W of Leeton, is the oldest town in the Murrumbidgee Irrigation Area and has rice and grain storage facilities. **Of interest:** Court house and gaol museum, Gogeldrie St. **In the area:** Gogeldrie Weir, 14 km SE. **Tourist information:** Yanco Ave, Leeton; (02) 6953 2832. **Accommodation:** 1 hotel.

Wilcannia   Pop. 942

MAP REF. 124 G10

Once the 'queen city of the west', this quaint township, 196 km NE of Broken Hill, still has many impressive sandstone buildings. It was proclaimed a town in 1864 and was a key inland port in the days of paddlesteamers. Declining in the early 1920s with the advent of the car, today it is the service centre for a far-flung rural population. **Of interest:** Self-guide historic town tour (brochure available from Tourist information)

introduces several fine stone buildings, including in Reid St: post office (1877), prison and court house (1880), and Athenaeum Chambers (1890). Opening bridge (1895) across Darling River; paddlesteamer wharf upstream. **In the area:** Opal fields at White Cliffs, 97 km NW. At Tilpa, 140 km NE, hotel (continuous licence since 1894) on banks of Darling River. **Tourist information:** Shire Offices, Reid St; (08) 8091 5909. **Accommodation:** 2 hotels, 2 motels, 1 cara./camp. park.

Windsor   Pop. 1869

MAP REF. 105 K6, 121 K7

A town for lovers of history and early architecture, Windsor is one of the oldest towns in Australia, situated 56 km NW of Sydney. **Of interest:** St Matthew's Church, Moses St, oldest Anglican Church in Australia, designed by Francis Greenway and convict-built in 1817. Nearby graveyard is even older. Court house, Court St, is another Greenway building. In Thompson Sq.: The Doctor's House (1844), privately-owned; Hawkesbury Museum, formerly Daniel O'Connell Inn (1843). Many other fine buildings in historic George St and Thompson Sq. Self-guide tourist walk/drive in town, brochures at Tourist information. Craft market, each Sun. in Windsor Mall. May: Bridge to Bridge Power Boat Classic. Oct.: Bridge to Bridge Canoe Classic. Nov.: Bridge to Bridge Water Ski Classic. **In the area:** Self-guide tourist drives in surrounding area, including historic tour of Hawkesbury River lowlands; contact Tourist information for brochures. Cattai National Park, 14 km NE, has historic homestead, friendship farm, horse and pony rides for children, canoe hire, picnic/barbecue facilities and camping area. Australian Pioneer Village, 6 km N, features Rose Cottage, considered oldest timber dwelling in Australia; wagon and buggy collection; good picnic/barbecue facilities and lake with paddle-boats. At Ebenezer, 14 km N: Tizzana Winery; Uniting Church (1809), claimed to be oldest church in Australia still holding regular services; nearby, old cemetery and schoolhouse (1817). **Tourist information:** Ham Common Bicentenary Park, Clarendon; (02) 4588 5895. **Accommodation:** 3 motels, 1 B&B. **See also:** The Hawkesbury.

Wingham   Pop. 4407

MAP REF. 109 B13, 121 O1, 123 N13

The oldest town along the Manning River, 13 km NW of Taree, Wingham was established in 1836. The area was important as a source of timber and remains so today, together with beef cattle and dairy farming. **Of interest:** Manning Valley Historical Society Museum, part of attractive village square with several prominent historic buildings, bounded by Isabella, Bent, Farquhar and Wynter sts. Historic walk through town, brochure from Tourist information. Jan.: Rodeo. Mar.: Agricultural Show. May: Manning Valley Beef Week. Nov.: Rodeo. **In the area:** Fine bush scenery. The Wingham Brush, Isabella St, close to town centre, is one of the few remaining subtropical flood-plain rainforests in NSW; with orchids, ferns, Moreton Bay fig trees, grey-headed flying foxes and 100 species of birds. Bulga Forest Dr. through timbered country north-west of town, past Ellenborough Falls, 40 km N, one of the highest single drop falls in southern hemisphere; contact Tourist information for brochure. **Tourist information:** Pacific Hwy, Taree North; (02) 6552 1900; freecall, 1800 801522. **Accommodation:** 2 hotels, 2 motels, 1 B&B.

Wisemans Ferry   Pop. 400

MAP REF. 105 M3, 121 K6

Situated beside the Hawkesbury River, 66 km NW of Sydney, Wisemans Ferry is an important recreational area for those interested in water sports. Two vehicular ferries provide transport across the river. **Of interest:** Wisemans Ferry Inn, Old Northern Rd, was named after founder of original ferry service and innkeeper, and is said to be haunted by his wife, whom he allegedly pushed down the front steps of the inn to her death. **In the area:** Dharug National Park, on northern side of river, features include a wealth of Aboriginal rock engravings; convict-built Old Great North Rd, one of great engineering feats of early colony and containing fine examples of convict-built stonework dating back to 1828; walk or cycle along lower section (closed to vehicles) from ferry. **Tourist information:** Ham Common Bicentenary Park, Richmond Rd, Clarendon; (02) 4588 5895. **Accommodation:** 1 hotel, 1 motel, 6 cara./camp. parks. **See also:** The Hawkesbury.

Wollongong   Pop. 211 417

MAP REF. 114, 116 H6, 121 K10

The area surrounding Wollongong, the third largest city in NSW, contains some of the South Coast's most spectacular scenery. **Of interest:** Illawarra Historical Society Museum, Market St, includes a handicraft room and a Victorian parlour. Wollongong City Gallery, cnr Burelli and Kembla sts. Spectacular mall in Crown St with soaring steel arches and water displays. Botanic Gardens in Northfields Ave. Rhododendron Park, Parish Ave, Mt Pleasant. Nan Tien Temple, huge Buddhist temple in Berkeley Rd, Berkeley (closed Mon.). Surfing beaches and rock pools, to north and south. Foreshore parks for picnicking. Wollongong Harbour, home to fishing fleet. On Endeavour Dr.: fish market; historic lighthouse (1872). On the foreshore of Port Kembla Harbour, at the southern end of the city, is the highly automated steel mill operated by BHP, an export coal loader and the largest grain-handling facility in NSW. Market, each Thurs. and Sat. at Steeles Stadium No. 2, off Harbour Rd. Aug.: South Coast Youth Arts and Skills Festival. Dec.: Junior Surf Lifesaving Championships. **In the area:** Lake Illawarra, 5 km S, stretching from South Pacific Ocean to foothills of Illawarra Range, has good prawning, fishing and sailing; boat hire available. Seaside village of Shellharbour, 22 km S; walking trails in nearby Blackbutt Reserve. Illawarra Escarpment, forming western backdrop to city, provides vantage points for lookouts at Stanwell Tops, Sublime Point, Mount Keira and Mount Kembla. Bulli Lookout, at top of escarpment near Bulli Pass, a steep, scenic drive down (or up) the escarpment with stunning coastal views. Lawrence Hargraves Memorial and Lookout at Bald Hill, 36 km N, site of aviator Lawrence Hargrave's first attempt at flight in early 1900s; now favourite spot for hang-gliding. Symbio Koala Gardens, 44 km N at Helensburgh. Mt Kembla Village, 15 km W, scene of tragic mining disaster in 1902, features monument in church; original miners' huts; several historic buildings, including former post office now Historical Museum, pioneer kitchen and blacksmith's shop; also reconstruction of Mt Kembla disaster. **Tourist information:** 93 Crown St; (02) 4228 0300. **Accommodation:** 4 hotels, 8 motels, 1 B&B, 1 hostel. **See also:** The Illawarra Coast.

Woolgoolga   Pop. 3660

MAP REF. 123 P7

This charming seaside town on the Pacific Hwy, 25 km N of Coffs Harbour, is popular with anglers as there is excellent beach and offshore fishing in the area. The banana industry became established in the district in the 1930s attracting a sizeable population of Indian migrants to the town. **Of interest:** Guru Nanak Sikh Temple, River St, place of worship for town's Indian population. Art Gallery, Turon Pde, exhibits paintings and pottery. **In the area:** Clean, sandy beaches, a feature of this coast. Yuraygir National Park, 10 km N, for bushwalking, canoeing, fishing, surfing, swimming, picnicking and camping on this beautiful stretch of unspoiled coastline. Wedding Bells State Forest, 14 km NW. **Tourist information:** Visitors and Convention Bureau, Pacific Hwy, Coffs Harbour; (02) 6652 1522. **Accommodation:** 7 motels, 3 cara./camp. parks.

Woy Woy   Pop. 12 206

MAP REF. 105 P4, 108 F8, 121 L6

Woy Woy, situated 90 km N of Sydney and 6 km S of Gosford, is the commercial centre for the surrounding holiday villages and national parks abutting the magnificent Brisbane Water and Broken Bay. May: Motor Show. Nov.: Oyster and Wine Festival. **In the area:** Boating, fishing and swimming on Brisbane Water, Broken Bay and Hawkesbury River. Mt Ettalong Lookout, 6 km S, for spectacular coastal views. Pearl Beach (12 km S), ideal for a stroll at sunset. Brisbane Water National Park, 3 km SW, noted for spring wildflowers, bushwalks and birdlife; within the park, features include Staples Lookout (7 km W), for magnificent coastal views; Bulgandry Aboriginal engravings (9 km W); Warrah Lookout, for views and spring wildflowers. Bouddi National Park, 12 km E, has good fishing, bushwalks and swimming areas; wreck of PS *Maitland* at Maitland Bay, a beautiful unspoiled coastal environment. Near entrance to park, Marie Byles Lookout offers good views of Sydney. Wreck of WWI ship *Parramatta*, Hawkesbury River near Milson Island; accessible only by boat. **Tourist information:** 200 Mann St,

NEW SOUTH WALES

Gosford; freecall, 1800 806258. **Accommodation:** On peninsula: 3 hotels, 2 motels, 1 B&B, 3 cara./camp. parks.

Wyong   Pop. 3902

MAP REF. 105 P2, 109 F1, 121 M6

Wyong is situated on the Pacific Hwy between Tuggerah Lakes and the State Forests of Watagan, Olney and Ourimbah. The town developed as a result of the construction of the Sydney to Newcastle railway, completed in 1889. **Of interest:** District Museum, Cape Rd, has historical displays relating to early ferry services across lakes, and forest logging. Country Fair, 3rd Sun. each month, at racecourse on Racecourse Rd. Mar.: Festival of Arts. Oct.: Cycle Classic. **In the area:** Hinterland popular for bushwalking and camping. Burbank Nursery, 3 km S at Tuggerah, features 20 ha of azaleas (flowering time Sept.). Fowlers Lookout over forest, 10 km SW. Macadamia Nut Plantation, 18 km W in beautiful Yarramalong Valley. The Durren Pottery, 20 km NW, uses local clay (open by appt, contact Tourist information). Frazer Park, 28 km NE, a recreational park in a natural bush setting. Within the State forests to the north: Mandalong Lookout, Muirs Lookout and picnic area in Onley State Forest; Wishing Well, destination for Watagan Mountains Walking Trail in Watagan State Forest; Flat Rock Lookout and picnic area in Corrabare State Forest. **Tourist information:** Wallarah Point Park, Wallarah Rd, Gorokan; (02) 4392 4666. **Accommodation:** 2 hotels, 1 motel, 2 cara./camp. parks.

Yamba   Pop. 3707

MAP REF. 123 Q5

This prawning and fishing town at the mouth of the Clarence River offers sea, lake and river fishing. It is the largest coastal resort in the Clarence Valley. **Of interest:** Story House Museum, River St, displays historical records of early Yamba. Views from base of lighthouse, reached via steep Pilot St. Off Yamba Rd, departure point for daily passenger ferry services to Iluka, and river cruises (Wed. and Fri.). Nearby, boat hire available. Market, 4th Sun. each month, at oval on River St. Sept.-Oct.: Family Fishing Festival. **In the area:** Houseboat hire at Brushgrove, 35 km SW. Lake Wooloweyah, 4 km S, for fishing and prawning. Yuraygir National

Park, 5 km S, for swimming, fishing and bushwalking in area dominated by sand ridges and banksia heath. The Blue Pool, 5 km S at Angourie, a freshwater pool, only 50 m from ocean, of unknown depth and origin; popular swimming and picnic spot. **Tourist information:** Lower Clarence Visitors Centre, Ferry Park, Pacific Hwy, Maclean; (02) 6645 4121. **Accommodation:** 1 hotel, 9 motels, 3 cara. parks.

Yanco   Pop. 651

MAP REF. 127 O8

Located 8 km S of Leeton, this town is where Sir Samuel McCaughey developed his own irrigation scheme, which led to the establishment of the Murrumbidgee Irrigation Area. **Of interest:** In Binya St: Powerhouse Museum (open by appt); Aquatic Park. May: Murrumbidgee Farm Fair. **In the area:** McCaughey's mansion, 3 km S, now an agricultural high school; nearby Yanco Agricultural Institute, open to public. Extensive red gum forests along the Murrumbidgee River. Well-marked forest drives lead to sandy beaches and many pleasant fishing spots. **Tourist information:** Yanco Ave, Leeton; (02) 6953 2832. **Accommodation:** 1 hotel.

Yass   Pop. 4828

MAP REF. 119 D4, 120 F11

Near the junction of two major highways (the Hume and the Barton), this interesting old town is on the Yass River, surrounded by beautiful, rich, rolling country, 280 km SW of Sydney and 55 km from Canberra. **Of interest:** Grave of Hamilton Hume who discovered Yass Plains in 1824, in Yass Cemetery (signposted from Ross St). National Trust-classified Cooma Cottage (1830), 3 km E, where Hume lived for 40 years, (open 10 a.m.–4 p.m., closed Tues.). Hamilton Hume Museum, Comur St. Self-guide heritage walk and tourist drive, contact Tourist information. Marked walk (2 km) along Yass River, begins Riverbank Park, Comur St. Market, 2nd Sat. each month. Mar.: Agricultural Show. Nov.: Rodeo. **In the area:** Crisp Art Glass and Crisp-Grow Lavender Nursery, 19 km NW on Hume Hwy. Lake Claredon Trout Farm at Bookham, 49 km NW. At Wee Jasper, 53 km SW: Goodradigbee River for trout fishing; Micalong Creek; Carey's Cave, with superb limestone

formations (guided tours, contact Tourist information); access point for Hume and Hovell Walking Track. Burrinjuck State Recreation Area (surrounds Burrinjuck Dam), 54 km SW off Hume Hwy, for bushwalking, water sports and fishing. Numerous wineries in Murrumbateman area, 19 km S, on Barton Hwy (contact Tourist information for details). Quamba Emu Farm 10 km NE on Wargeila Rd. **Tourist information:** Coronation Park, Comur St; (02) 6226 2557. **Accommodation:** 4 hotels, 7 motels, 2 B&B, 1 cara./camp. park.

Young   Pop. 6666

MAP REF. 119 C2, 120 D9

Attractive former goldmining town in the western foothills of the Great Dividing Range, 395 km SW of Sydney. Today, cherries and prunes are the area's best-known exports, as well as flour and fabricated steel. **Of interest:** Lambing Flat Folk Museum, Campbell St, for reminders of town's colourful history, including 'roll-up' flag carried by miners during infamous anti-Chinese Lambing Flat riots of 1861. Burrangong Art Gallery, Olympic Way. Blackguard Gully with historic pug-mill, on Boorowa Rd, a reconstruction showing early goldmining methods. Nov.–Dec.: National Cherry Festival. **In the area:** J. D.'s Jam Factory, at north-western outskirts of town on Grenfell Rd, open for tours, tastings and devonshire teas. Chinaman's Dam recreation area, 4 km SE, with picnic/barbecue facilities, children's playground and scenic walks. Nearby, Pat's Doll and Memorabilia Museum. At Murringo Village, 21 km E: several historic buildings; home of glass blower and engraver Helmut Hiebl. Wineries open for tastings and sales: Woodonga Hill Winery (8 km N); Demondrille Vineyard (15 km SE), open weekends or by appt. **Tourist information:** Olympic Way; (02) 6382 5433. **Accommodation:** 6 hotels, 6 motels, 1 hotel/motel, 8 B&B, 1 cara./camp. park.

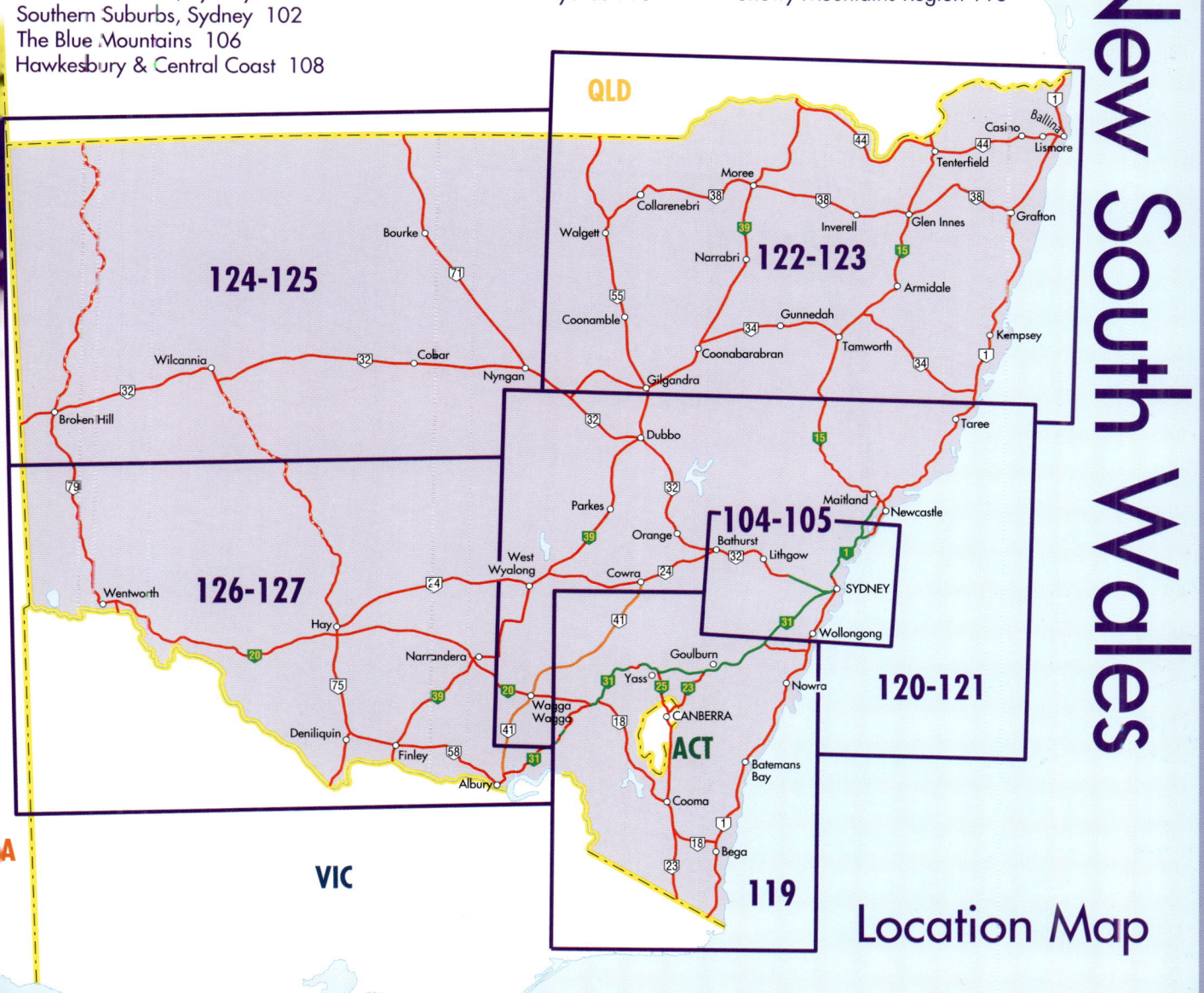

New South Wales

Location Map

PORT JACKSON

Walsh Bay

DARLING HARBOUR

Millers Point

The Rocks

Sydney Cove

Circular Quay

Government House

ROYAL BOTANIC GARDENS

Farm Cove

Mrs Macquarie's Point

Mrs Macquarie's Chair

The Andrew (Boy) Charlton Swimming Pool

Wooloomooloo Bay

SYDNEY

East Sydney

Cockle Bay

Darling Harbour

Tumbalong Park

Chinese Garden

Ultimo

Haymarket

Chinatown

Accommodation ■
ANA Hotel 1 D4
Hilton 2 E8
Hotel Intercontinental 3 F5
Park Hyatt 4 D2
Quay West 5 D4
Regent 6 D4
Renaissance Sydney Hotel 7 E5
Ritz Carlton 8 F4
Russell Hotel 9 D4
The York 10 C6
YWCA 11 F10

General Information ■
AAT Kings/Australian Pacific Coach 12 E3
Ansett Australia 13 G11
Captain Cook Cruises 14 E4
Central Railway Station 15 E13
General Post Office 16 D7
Interstate Coach Terminal 17 E13
Motoring Organisation (NRMA) 18 C7
Police Headquarters 19 G10
Qantas Travel Centre 20 E9, 21 E6
Rocks Visitors Centre 22 D3
Tourist Information 23 D6

Places of Interest ■
Aquarium 24 B8
Art Gallery of NSW 25 H7
Australian Museum 26 G9
Cadman's Cottage 27 D3
Cenotaph 28 D7
Centrepoint 29 E8
Chinese Garden 30 C11
Dixon Street (Chinatown) 31 D11
Explorer Bus 32 E4
Government House 33 F3
Holy Trinity (Garrison) Church 34 C3
Hyde Park Barracks 35 F7
The Mint Museum 36 F7
Mrs Macquarie's Chair 37 I3
Museum of Contemporary Art 38 D4
Museum of Sydney 39 E5
National Maritime Museum 40 A8
Opera House 41 F2
Parliament House 42 F6
Powerhouse Museum 43 B12
Queen Victoria Building 44 D9
State Library of NSW 45 F6
Sydney Harbour Bridge Pylon Lookout 46 D1
Sydney Harbour Casino 47 A6
Sydney Tower at Centrepoint 29 E8
Town Hall 48 D9

Accommodation Only a sample range is listed; inclusion is not necessarily a recommendation.

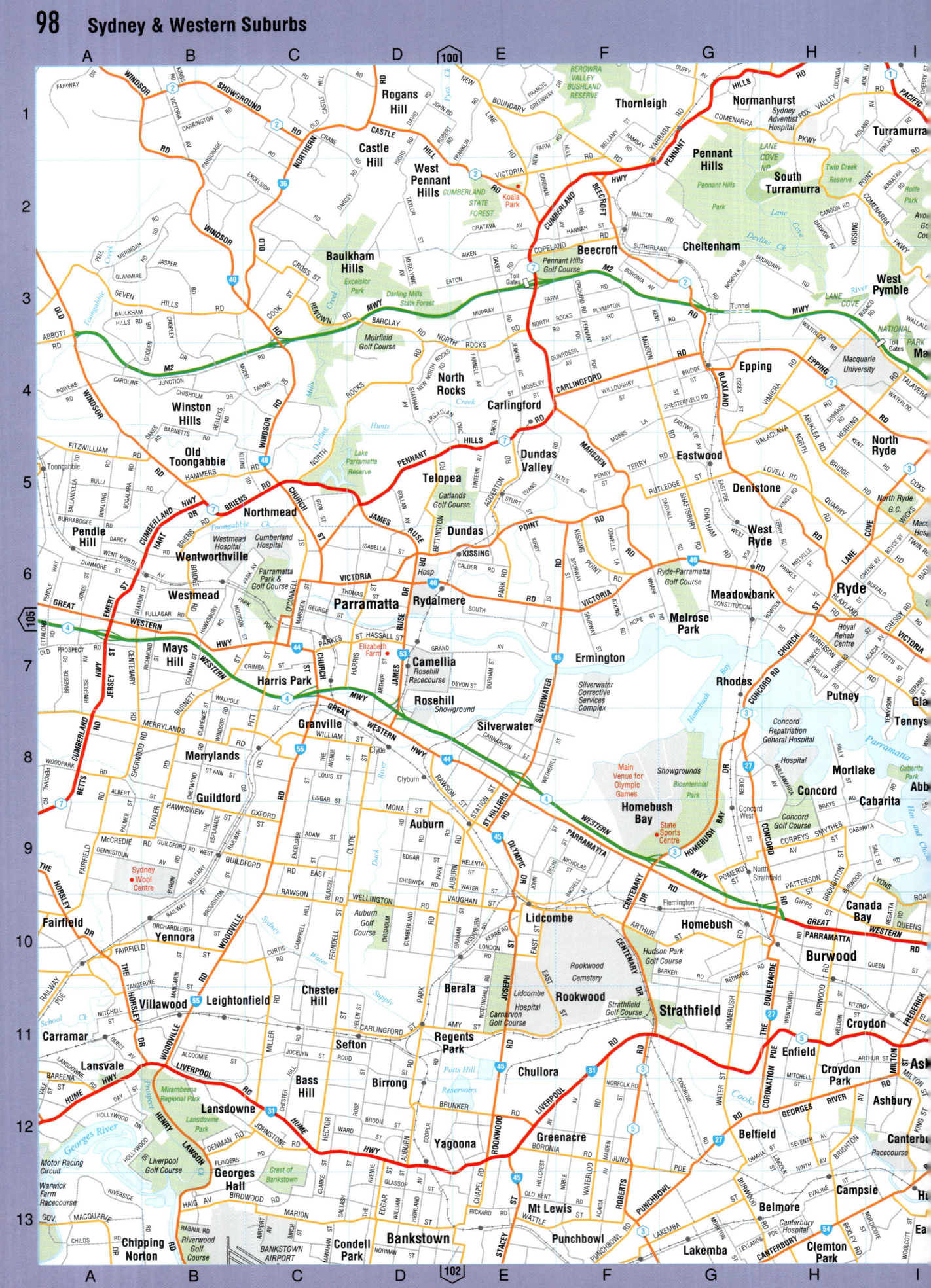

0 1 2 3 4 5 km

J K L M N O P Q R

Broken Bay

108

Porto Bay
Gunyah Point
Juno Point
Ferry
West Head
KU-RING-GAI CHASE NP
Barrenjoey Head
Lookout
Shark Rock
★ Barrenjoey Lighthouse

VIZE SPUR
CENT SPUR
Challenger Head
Hungry Beach
Great Mackerel Beach
Palm
Barrenjoey Beach
Palm Beach Golf Course
Sandy Beach
Falm Beach

Jerusalem Bay
Cowan Water
Hallets Beach
Refuge Bay
Little Pittwater Bay
PACIFIC
BARRENJOEY
Whale
RYNIA
CYNCHEA
Whale Beach
Little Head

KU-RING-GAI CHASE
FOLLY SPUR
WATA RIDGE
Creek
Cowan Point
Cowan
Creek
KU-RING-GAI CHASE NATIONAL PARK
Longnose Point
Careel Bay
GEORGE ST
PATRICK
Careel Bay
Bangalley Head

NATIONAL PARK
Cottage Point
COTTAGE
Yeomans Bay
Yeomans Creek
HEAD
Towlers Bay
RIVERVIEW
RIVIERA AV
CENTRAL
PDE
Avalon
RC
14
TASMAN
Avalon
St Michael's Cave
Hole in the Wall

Cowan
Coal and Candle Creek
Smiths Creek
POINT
LIBERATOR
GENERAL SAN MARTIN
Scotland Island
Refuge Cove
Taylors Point
AVALON PDE
Clareville
Avalon Golf Course
Avalon Beach
Bilgola Head

KU-RING-GAI CHASE
LIBERATOR
GENERAL SAN MARTIN DR
DR
Scotland Island
Church Point
HUDSON
PLATEAU
Bilgola
BARRENJOEY RD

NATIONAL PARK
Smiths Creek
CREEK
PITTWATER
MINKARA
NARLA
LENTARA RD
RD
Newport
IRRUBEL RD
Newport Beach
Newport Beach
GLADSTONE ST
MYOLA RD
Bungan Head

Duffys Forest
Terrey Hills Country Club (Golf Course)
BOODALIE
McCARRS
McCarrs Creek
CABBAGE
TREE RD
CICADA GLEN RD
WALTER RD
Bayview
Bayview GC
MONA
DARLEY
BASSETT ST
CRESCENT
Bungan Beach
BARRENJOEY

ratah Park
NAMBA RD
THIDUNGRA
TOORONGA RD
COOYONG
RD
MYOORA RD
3
MONA VALE
Baha'i Temple
CHILTERN
LANE COVE RD
SAMUEL ST
MAXWELL ST
EMMA ST
Ingleside
VINEYARD
PARK ST
Mona Vale
MONA
RD
Mona Vale Golf Course
Mona Vale Hospital

Terrey Hills
MONA VALE
POWDER
Monash Golf Course
INGLESIDE RD
MACPHERSON
GARDEN
WARRIEWOOD RD
Warriewood
WORKS
JACKSONS
14
North Narrabeen Reserve
Turimetta Head

GARIGAL NATIONAL PARK
Deep Creek
Muller Creek
Elanora Golf Course
ANANA
RICKARD RD
PITTWATER RD
Narrabeen Head

Ring-Gai
dflower arden
3
FOREST
MONA VALE
Elanora Heights
22
OCEAN ST
Narrabeen Beach

SOUTH

St Ives Showground
Middle Harbour Creek
WAKEHURST PKWY
Narrabeen Lakes
Pipeclay Point Reserve
Collaroy Beach

PACIFIC

GARIGAL NATIONAL PARK
WAY
MORGAN
RALSTON AV
22
NSW Academy of Sport
Cromer Golf Course
ROSE AV
EDGECLIFFE
Collaroy Plateau
PITTWATER BLVD

Belrose
ELM
OXFORD FALLS RD
PKWY
Wheeler Heights
SOUTH
TORONTO AV
HILL
VETERANS
Collaroy
BEACH RD
Long Reef Golf Course
Long Reef Poin

OCEAN

Davidson
KAMBORA
BLACKBUTTS
WAY
Middle Creek
Oxford Falls
CARAWA RD
CREEK
FISHER RD NTH
ANZAC AV
WESTMORLAND RD
Long Reef Beach

NATIONAL
PRAHRAN
GRACE AV
WAKEHURST
22
IRIS ST
Beacon Hill
McINTOSH
PRESCOTT
14
Dee Why Lagoon
Dee Why Beach

PARK
Frenchs Forest
DEAKIN ST
BROWN
MAXWELL PDE
WARRINGAH RD
FRENCHS FOREST RD
Narraweena
29
ALFRED
VICTOR RD
Dee Why
FISHER
Dee Why Head
Harbord Lagoon

KOOLA
SAIALA
CHURCHILL
WARRINGAH
CURRIE
COOK ST
29
Allambie Heights
Allenby Park
BEACON HILL RD
PACIFIC
PITTWATER
HEADLAND
PDE
12

Roseville Golf Course
TRYON
WELLINGTON
MELWOOD
STANLEY ST
WAKEHURST PKWY
GARIGAL NATIONAL PARK
Manly-Warringah War Memorial Park (Manly Dam Reserve)
Brookvale
ABBOTT
PITT
GRIFFIN
Wingala
Curl Curl

99
Warringah Golf Course
WYADRA AV
Dee Why Head

J K L M N O P Q R

A B C D E F G H I

1

St Johns Park
Canley Heights
Carramar
Villawood
Leightonfield
Chester Hill
Berala
Regents Park
Rookwood
Strathfi
Canley Vale
Cabramatta
Lansvale
Woodville
Liverpool
Sefton
Bass Hill
Birrong
Chullora

2

Mount Pritchard
Cabramatta Golf Course
Cabramatta Sports Ground
Hollywood
Lansdowne
Johnstone
Yagoona
Greenacre
Motor Racing Circuit
Warwick Farm Racecourse
Liverpool Golf Course
Georges Hall
Crest of Bankstown

3

Ashcroft
Hargrave Park
Warwick Farm
Liverpool Hospital
Chipping Norton
Georges Hall
Birdwood
Condell Park
Bankstown
Mt Lewis
Punchbowl
Wiley Park
Lake

4

Liverpool
Lurnea
Moorebank
Newbridge
Milperra
Bankstown Airport
Bankstown Golf Course
Bankstown Hospital
Canterbury
Roselands

5

Casula
Chatham Village
Anzac Village
South Western Mwy
New Brighton Golf Course
Riverlands Golf Course
Toll Gates
Lt Cantello Reserve
Deepwater Park
Kelso Park
Milperra
Western
South
Panania
Revesby
Riverwood
Narwee
Beve Hill

6

Wattle Grove
Hammondville
Sewage Treatment Works
Holsworthy
East Hills
Picnic Point
Padstow
Peakhurst
Mort
Pe

7

Holsworthy Village
Holsworthy Barracks
Pleasure Point
Sandy Point
Picnic Point
Georges River National Park
Georges River NP
Lugarno
Hurstville Golf Course
Oatley Park

8

Military
Alfords Point
Georges River NP

9

Reserve
Illawong
Bangor
Menai
Como
Oyster Bay
Bonnet Bay
Woronora
Jannali

10

Woronora Heights
Sutherland
Kirraw

11

Lucas Heights
Australian Nuclear Science and Technology Organisation
Illawarra
Loftus
Tramway Museum

12

Yarrawarrah
Princes
Farnell
Royal

13

Engadine
Heathcote
Heathcote National Park
National Park

A B C D E F G H I

0 1 2 3 4 5 km

J K L M N O P Q R

99

1
Croydon · Haberfield · Leichhardt · Annandale · Ultimo · Surry Hills · Paddington · Edgecliff · Bellevue Hill · Woollahra
Croydon Park · Ashfield · Summer Hill · Petersham · Camperdown · University of Sydney · Sydney University Hospital · CITY · Cleveland · Redfern · Victoria Barracks · Sydney Cricket Ground · Bonci · Woollahra · Centennial Park · Bondi Junction · Waverley

2
Ashbury · Canterbury · Lewisham · Stanmore · Enmore · Newtown · Erskineville · Alexandria · Zetland · Kensington · Moore Park · Randwick Racecourse · Randwick · Clovelly · Bronte

3
Camsie · Hurlstone Park · Dulwich Hill · Marrickville · Sydenham · St Peters · Beaconsfield · Rosebery · The Australian Golf Course · University of NSW · Kingsford · Coogee · Coogee Bay

4
Clemton Park · Earlwood · Undercliffe · Turrella · Tempe · Mascot · International Terminal · Domestic Terminal · Eastlakes · Daceyville · The Lakes Golf Course · Commonwealth Property

5
Bexley North · Bardwell Park · Arncliffe · Banksia · SYDNEY AIRPORT DR · Tunnel · Botany · Bankstown · Pagewood · Maroubra Junction · Maroubra · Malabar

6
Kingsgrove · Bexley · Forest · Rockdale · Kyeemagh · Banksmeadow · Hillsdale · Matraville · Chifley · Malabar

7
Hurstville · Carlton · Kogarah · Brighton-le-Sands · BOTANY · BAY · Container Terminal · Phillip Bay · Prince Henry Hospital · Little Bay · Randwick Golf Course

8
Allawah · Connells Point · Beverley Park · Ramsgate · Monterey · Sans Souci · Dolls Point · La Perouse · Bare Island · Botany Bay National Park

9
Blakehurst · Sylvania · Sandringham · Georges River Bridge · Captain Cook Bridge · Towra Point Nature Reserve · Captain Cook's Landing Place · Kurnell · Cape Solander

10
Sylvania Waters · Sylvania Heights · Taren Point · Woolooware Bay · Cook · SOUTH

11
Miranda · Caringbah · Woolooware · Potter Point · PACIFIC

12
Yowie Bay · Dolans Bay · Cronulla · BATE BAY · OCEAN

13
Lilli Pilli · Port Hacking · Burraneer · Maianbar · Port Hacking Point

J K L M N O P Q R

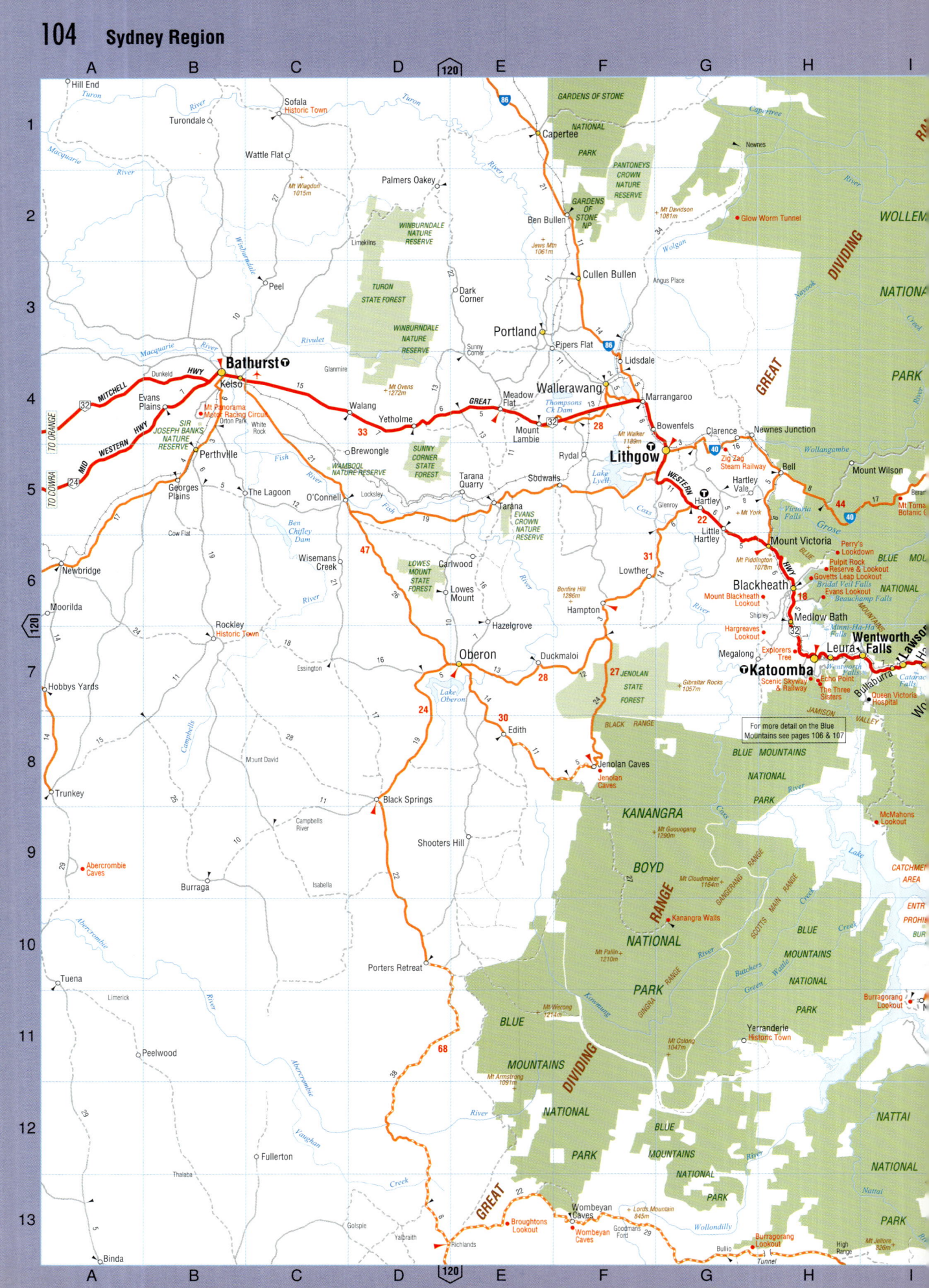

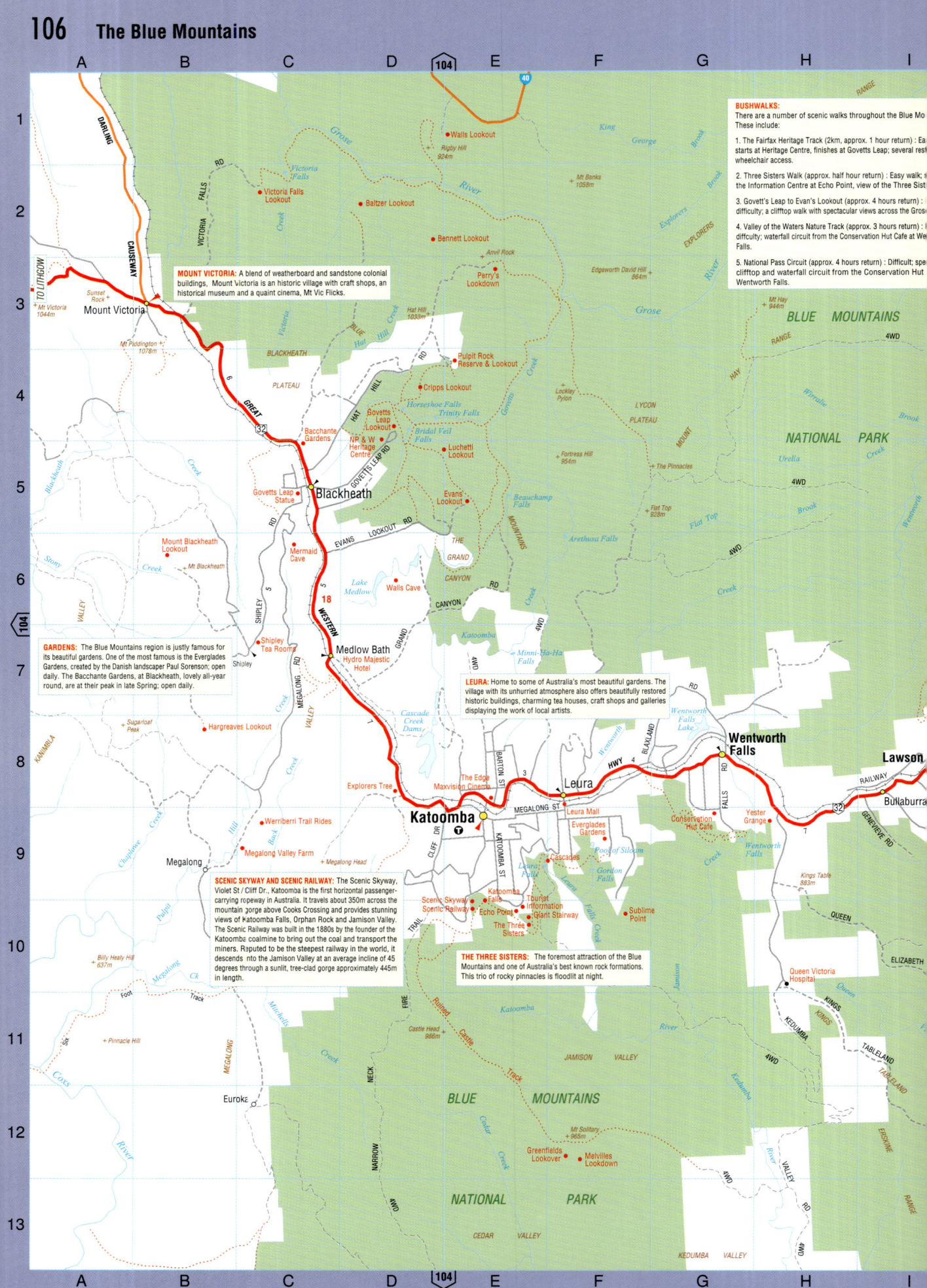

104

BUSHWALKS:
There are a number of scenic walks throughout the Blue Mo
These include:

1. The Fairfax Heritage Track (2km, approx. 1 hour return) : Ea
starts at Heritage Centre, finishes at Govetts Leap; several rest
wheelchair access.

2. Three Sisters Walk (approx. half hour return) : Easy walk;
the Information Centre at Echo Point, view of the Three Sist

3. Govett's Leap to Evan's Lookout (approx. 4 hours return) :
difficulty; a clifftop walk with spectacular views across the Gros

4. Valley of the Waters Nature Track (approx. 3 hours return) : I
difficulty; waterfall circuit from the Conservation Hut Cafe at Wer
Falls.

5. National Pass Circuit (approx. 4 hours return) : Difficult; spe
clifftop and waterfall circuit from the Conservation Hut
Wentworth Falls.

MOUNT VICTORIA: A blend of weatherboard and sandstone colonial buildings, Mount Victoria is an historic village with craft shops, an historical museum and a quaint cinema, Mt Vic Flicks.

GARDENS: The Blue Mountains region is justly famous for its beautiful gardens. One of the most famous is the Everglades Gardens, created by the Danish landscaper Paul Sorenson; open daily. The Bacchante Gardens, at Blackheath, lovely all-year round, are at their peak in late Spring; open daily.

LEURA: Home to some of Australia's most beautiful gardens. The village with its unhurried atmosphere also offers beautifully restored historic buildings, charming tea houses, craft shops and galleries displaying the work of local artists.

SCENIC SKYWAY AND SCENIC RAILWAY: The Scenic Skyway, Violet St / Cliff Dr., Katoomba is the first horizontal passenger-carrying ropeway in Australia. It travels about 350m across the mountain gorge above Cooks Crossing and provides stunning views of Katoomba Falls, Orphan Rock and Jamison Valley. The Scenic Railway was built in the 1880s by the founder of the Katoomba coalmine to bring out the coal and transport the miners. Reputed to be the steepest railway in the world, it descends into the Jamison Valley at an average incline of 45 degrees through a sunlit, tree-clad gorge approximately 445m in length.

THE THREE SISTERS: The foremost attraction of the Blue Mountains and one of Australia's best known rock formations. This trio of rocky pinnacles is floodlit at night.

0 1 2 3 4 5 km

J K L M N 105 O P Q R

WHY ARE THE BLUE MOUNTAINS SO BLUE ?
The whole area is heavily timbered with eucalypts which constantly disperse fine droplets of oil into the atmosphere. These droplets cause the blue light-rays of the sun to be scattered more effectively, thus intensifying the usual light refraction phenomenon which causes distant objects to appear blue.

N

BLUE MOUNTAINS

NATIONAL PARK

Grose River

Hawkesbury Heights

Hawkesbury Lookout

AGNES BANKS NAT RES

Yellow Rock Lookout

Winmalee

Norman Lindsay Gallery & Museum

SINGLES

RIDGE RD

Springwood

Valley Heights

Faulconbridge

Corridor of Oaks

Sir Henry Parkes' Grave

Clarinda Falls

Lawsons Lookout

Fitzgerald Creek

RICKARD RD

Warrimoo

32

Blue Mtn 725m

GLOSSOP

Lake Woodford

Kings Cave

Caleys Repulse Cairn

Linden

Numantia Falls

Sassafras Creek

Magdala Falls

Martins Falls

Martins Lookout

12

RAILWAY PDE

RUSDEN RD

BATHURST RD

Hazelbrook

31

Woodford

Glenbrook Creek

Lost World Lookout

Bunyan Lookout

Blaxland

Wascoe Siding Miniature Railway

MITCHELLS

Lennox Bridge

Elizabeth Lookout

Lapstone Zg Zag Walking Track

PASS

Marges Lookout

John Whitton Monument

WESTERN MWY

44

4

Lapstone

TO SYDNEY

Cataract Falls

RLY WAY

BEDFORD RD

THE OAKS

WESTERN RIDGE

St Helens Gully

Glenbrook

Tourist Info mation

BRUCE

EXPLORERS RD

Leslie Falls

Goondrai Rill

Brook

Jellybean Pool

Portal Lookout

Tunnel View Lookout

North Hill 656m

Mt Bedford 639m

Scorpion Hill 563m

4WD

HELICOPTER SPUR

Tobys Creek

Kamka Creek

RED HANDS

THE OAKS FIRE TRAIL

Campfire

Euroka Clearing

Red Hands Cave

West Hill 666m

TOURIST INFORMATION:
Glenbrook (Gt Western Hwy)
Katoomba (Echo Point)

BLUE MOUNTAINS

RIDGE

NOTTS

Glen

Erskine

NATIONAL PARK

Mt Gibson 605m

Erskine Creek

The Oaks Picnic Ground

NEPEAN LOOKOUT

Attic Cave

Erskine Lookout

Nepean Lookout

Word Cave

JACK EVANS TRACK

BREAKFAST CREEK FIRE TRAIL

PARK

FAIRLIGHT RD

RIVER CLOSE

Nepean River

MULGOA RD

Wallacia

SAFE BUSHWALKING:
Plan your trip well in advance.
Check local weather conditions before departure.
Take note of fire bans in the area.
Always allow for extra clothing and food.
Ensure you have a good supply of drinking water.
Allow for adequate rest periods when walking.
When bushwalking in a group, always stay together.
Always inform a friend, relative or local police about your trip in case of an emergency.

CASTLEREAGH RD

73

105

J K L M N 105 O P Q R

1 2 3 4 5 6 7 8 9 10 11 12 13

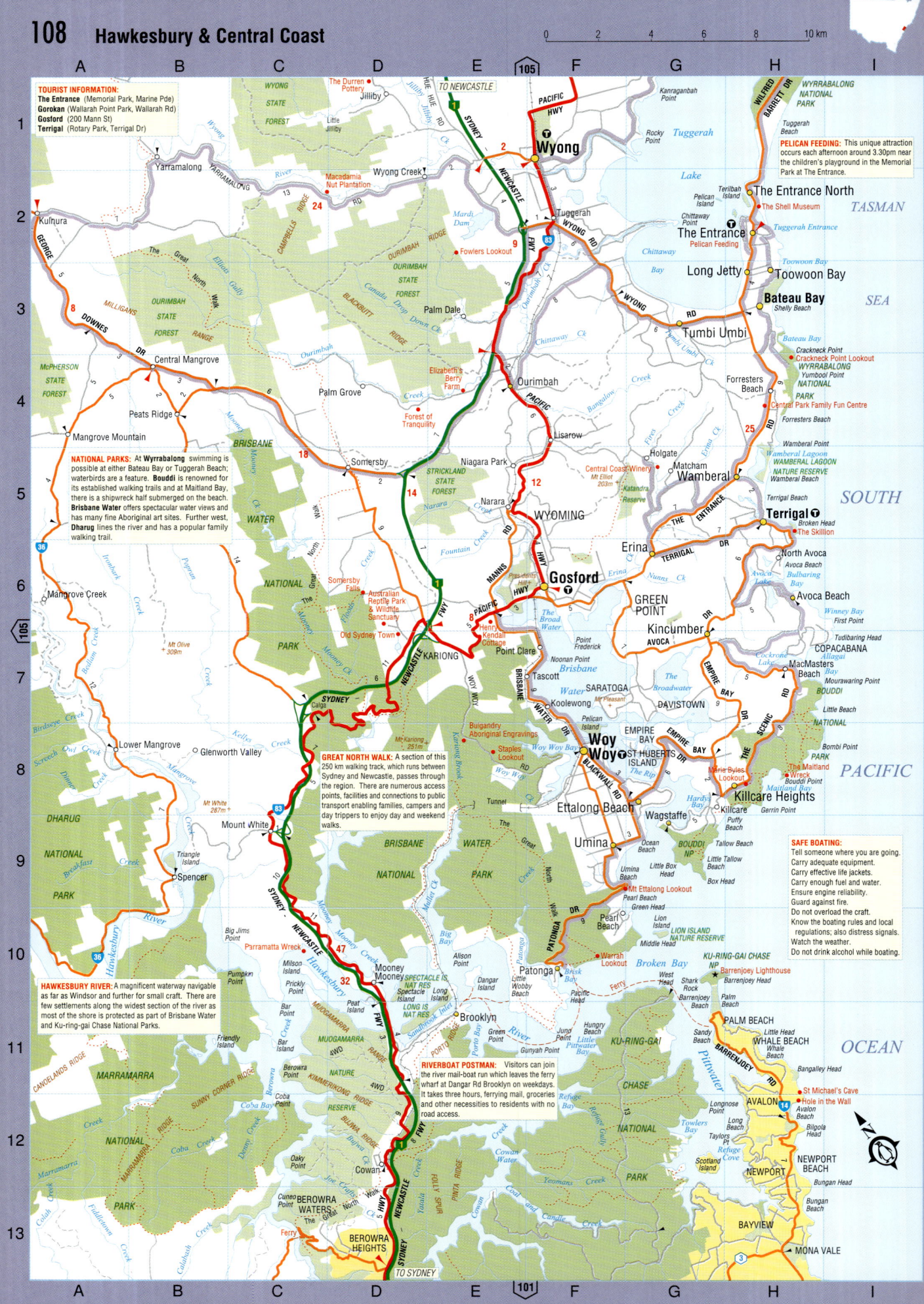

TOURIST INFORMATION:
The Entrance (Memorial Park, Marine Pde)
Gorokan (Wallarah Point Park, Wallarah Rd)
Gosford (200 Mann St)
Terrigal (Rotary Park, Terrigal Dr)

PELICAN FEEDING: This unique attraction occurs each afternoon around 3.30pm near the children's playground in the Memorial Park at The Entrance.

NATIONAL PARKS: At **Wyrrabalong** swimming is possible at either Bateau Bay or Tuggerah Beach; waterbirds are a feature. **Bouddi** is renowned for its established walking trails and at Maitland Bay, there is a shipwreck half submerged on the beach. **Brisbane Water** offers spectacular water views and has many fine Aboriginal art sites. Further west, **Dharug** lines the river and has a popular family walking trail.

GREAT NORTH WALK: A section of this 250 km walking track, which runs between Sydney and Newcastle, passes through the region. There are numerous access points, facilities and connections to public transport enabling families, campers and day trippers to enjoy day and weekend walks.

SAFE BOATING:
Tell someone where you are going.
Carry adequate equipment.
Carry effective life jackets.
Carry enough fuel and water.
Ensure engine reliability.
Guard against fire.
Do not overload the craft.
Know the boating rules and local regulations; also distress signals.
Watch the weather.
Do not drink alcohol while boating.

HAWKESBURY RIVER: A magnificent waterway navigable as far as Windsor and further for small craft. There are few settlements along the widest section of the river as most of the shore is protected as part of Brisbane Water and Ku-ring-gai Chase National Parks.

RIVERBOAT POSTMAN: Visitors can join the river mail-boat run which leaves the ferry wharf at Dangar Rd Brooklyn on weekdays. It takes three hours, ferrying mail, groceries and other necessities to residents with no road access.

TOURIST INFORMATION:
Kempsey (Pacific Hwy, South Kempsey)
Port Macquarie (Cnr Clarence & Hay Sts)
Taree (Pacific Hwy, Taree North)

FOREST DRIVES: There are abundant scenic drives through spectacular stands of eucalypts, and lush rainforest in this timber growing district. Follow parts of the trail of Surveyor General John Oxley where in 1818 he made his way across the Great Dividing Range to the mouth of the Hastings River at Port Macquarie.

HASTINGS RIVER: Starting from the slope of eastern streams of the Great Divide and fed by the Ellenborough and Forbes Rivers, this beautiful waterway of deep pools and sandy banks stretches over 100 km.
In the wet season the Hastings River swells with rapid torrents excellent for white water rafting and exhilarating canoe adventures.

TIMBERTOWN: Only three kilometres west of Wauchope, this re-created sawmillers village is a tribute to the hardy timber pioneers of 1880. Ride the restored steam-train or Cobb & Co coach to bush camps for demonstrations of sleeper-cutting, shingle-splitting and bullock-yolking. The authentic late 1880s hotel serves damper and roast meats with Australian bushsongs for entertainment.

CAMDEN HAVEN RIVER: This river runs through a cluster of picturesque towns surrounded by forests, national parks, unspoilt coast and cool, clean waterways. Magnificent views from North Brother mountain. Sailing, fishing and hang-gliding are popular in the area.

ELLENBOROUGH FALLS: One of the highest single-drop falls in the State, with a 160-metre sheer descent. A relaxing drive through scenic dairy country and the state forest leads to the falls. The spectacular Ellenborough Falls is on the edge of the New England Tableland.

CROWDY BAY NATIONAL PARK: Numerous walking tracks are found within the park linking sand dunes and plains rich in wildflowers to swamp wonderlands — home to the spoonbill, ibis and gracious jabiru. Diamond Head is named for the quartz crystals found in the region's rocks. Crowdy Bay is well-known for the 101 bird species that inhabit the area.

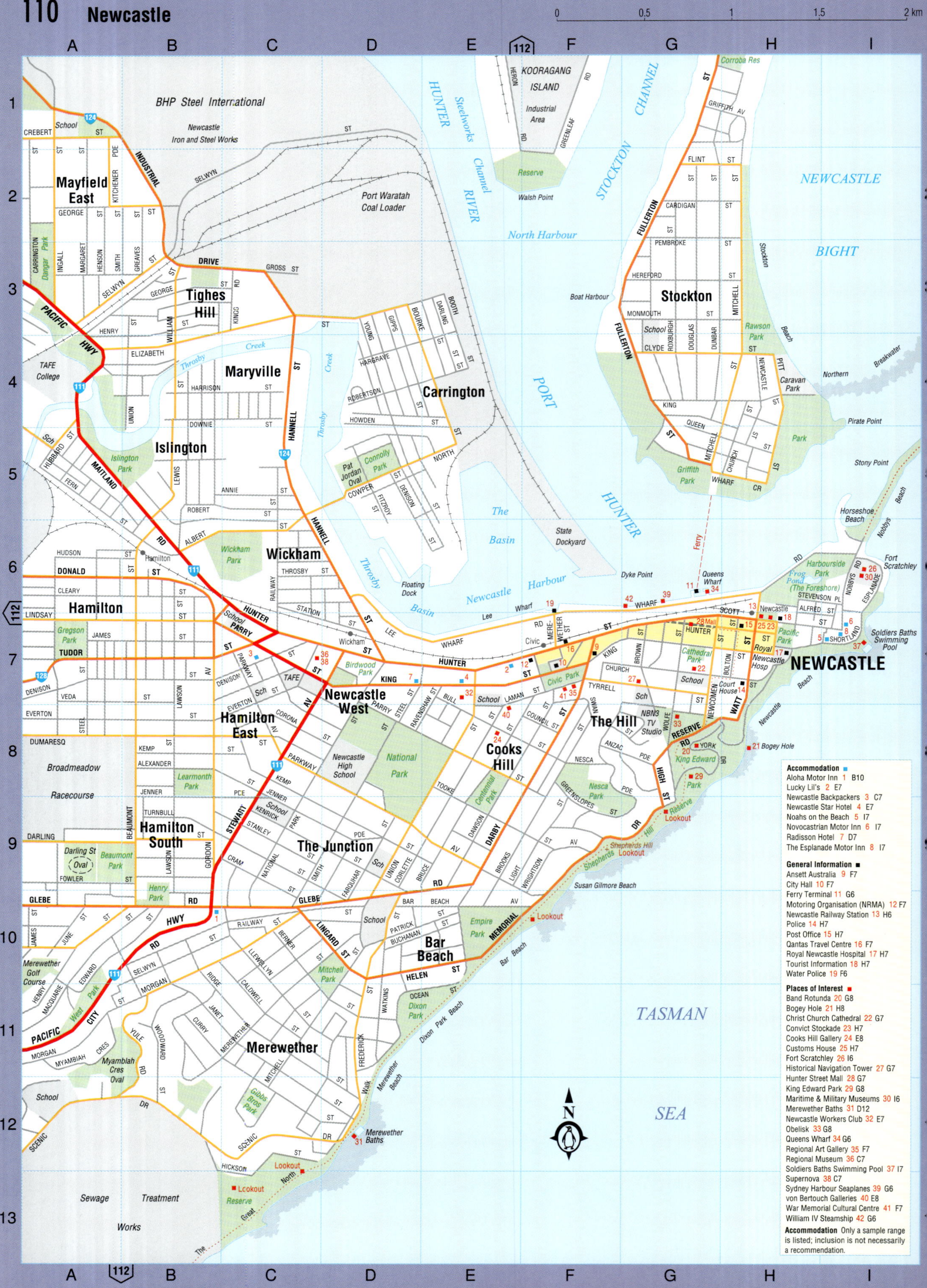

0   0.5   1   1.5   2 km

A B C D E 112 F G H I

Map labels

BHP Steel International

Newcastle Iron and Steel Works

KOORAGANG ISLAND
Industrial Area

Port Waratah Coal Loader

Mayfield East

Tighes Hill

Maryville

Islington

Carrington

Wickham

Hamilton

Hamilton East

Newcastle West

Cooks Hill

The Hill

NEWCASTLE

Stockton

Broadmeadow Racecourse

Hamilton South

The Junction

Bar Beach

Merewether

TASMAN SEA

HUNTER RIVER
PORT HUNTER
STOCKTON CHANNEL
NEWCASTLE BIGHT

N

Accommodation ■
Aloha Motor Inn 1 B10
Lucky Lil's 2 E7
Newcastle Backpackers 3 C7
Newcastle Star Hotel 4 E7
Noahs on the Beach 5 I7
Novocastrian Motor Inn 6 I7
Radisson Hotel 7 D7
The Esplanade Motor Inn 8 I7

General Information ■
Ansett Australia 9 F7
City Hall 10 F7
Ferry Terminal 11 G6
Motoring Organisation (NRMA) 12 F7
Newcastle Railway Station 13 H6
Police 14 H7
Post Office 15 H7
Qantas Travel Centre 16 F7
Royal Newcastle Hospital 17 H7
Tourist Information 18 H7
Water Police 19 F6

Places of Interest ■
Band Rotunda 20 G8
Bogey Hole 21 H8
Christ Church Cathedral 22 G7
Convict Stockade 23 H7
Cooks Hill Gallery 24 E8
Customs House 25 H7
Fort Scratchley 26 I6
Historical Navigation Tower 27 G7
Hunter Street Mall 28 G7
King Edward Park 29 G8
Maritime & Military Museums 30 I6
Merewether Baths 31 D12
Newcastle Workers Club 32 E7
Obelisk 33 G8
Queens Wharf 34 G6
Regional Art Gallery 35 F7
Regional Museum 36 C7
Soldiers Baths Swimming Pool 37 I7
Supernova 38 C7
Sydney Harbour Seaplanes 39 G6
von Bertouch Galleries 40 E8
War Memorial Cultural Centre 41 F7
William IV Steamship 42 G6

Accommodation Only a sample range is listed; inclusion is not necessarily a recommendation.

Thick roads represent recommended approach and bypass routes.

0 5 10 15 20 km

PORT STEPHENS: Stretching 24-km inland with a cluster of idyllic fishing villages inside the port and exhilarating game fishing on the ocean side of the peninsula. Several dolphin-watching cruises operate out of Nelson Bay.

TOURIST INFORMATION:
Cessnock (Turner Park, Aberdare Rd)
Maitland (Cnr New England Hwy and High St)
Nelson Bay (Victoria Pde)
Newcastle (92 Scott St)

For more detail on Newcastle see page 110

THE GREAT NORTH WALK: Take a day or weekend walk along this spectacular 250-km trail linking Sydney and Newcastle. Numerous lookouts provide a chance to rest and view this magnificent region.

For more detail on Lower Hunter Vineyards see page 113

WATAGAN MOUNTAINS: These timber-rich mountains were the source of quality blackbutt, she-oak, tallow wood and red cedar in the 1830s. They mark the western boundary of the Lake Macquarie Basin.

SOUTH

PACIFIC

OCEAN

TASMAN

SEA

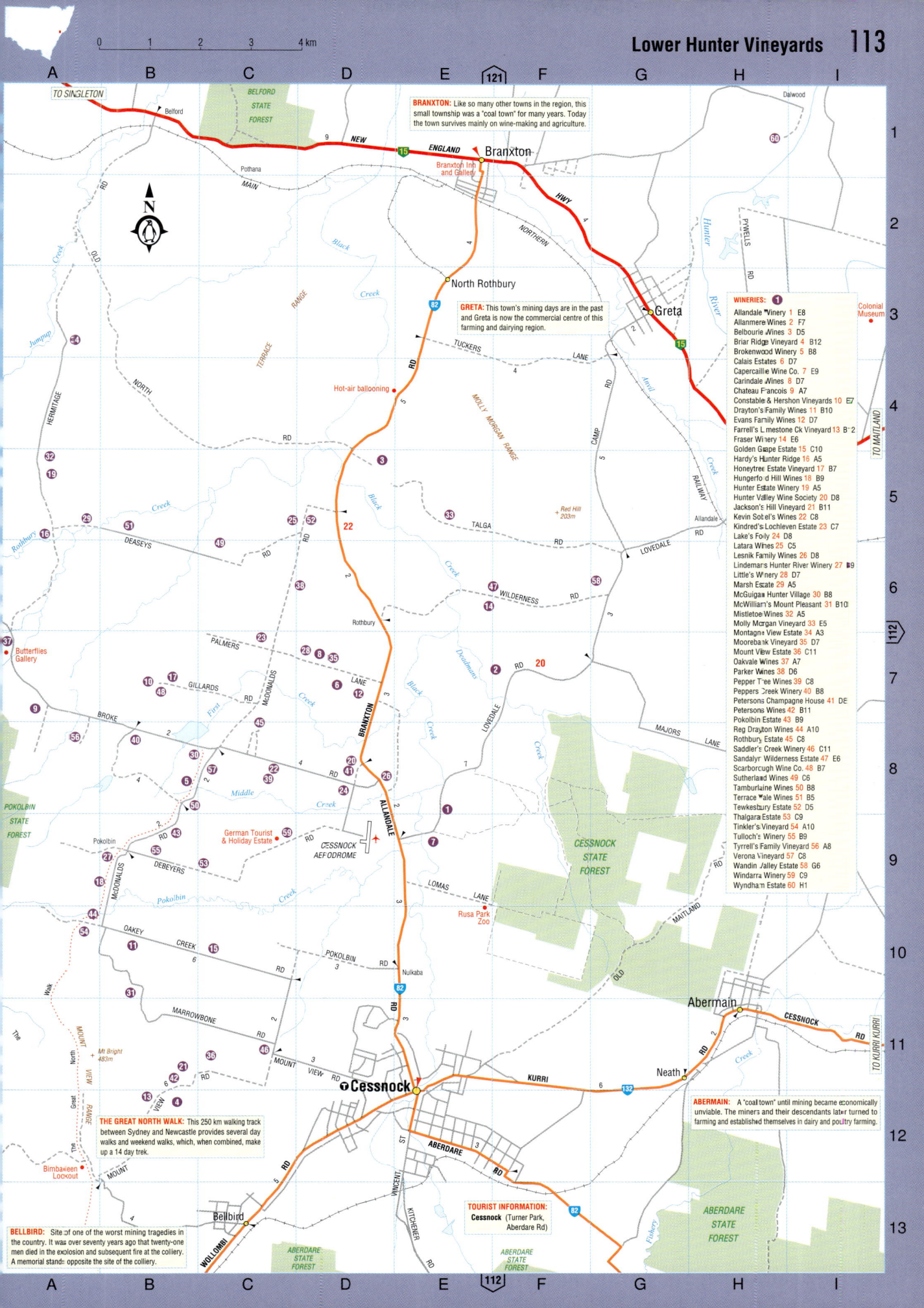

TO SINGLETON

BELFORD STATE FOREST

BRANXTON: Like so many other towns in the region, this small township was a "coal town" for many years. Today the town survives mainly on wine-making and agriculture.

Branxton
Branxton Inn and Gallery

NEW ENGLAND HWY

NORTHERN HWY

North Rothbury

GRETA: This town's mining days are in the past and Greta is now the commercial centre of this farming and dairying region.

Greta

Hot-air ballooning

TUCKERS LANE

MOLLY MORGAN RANGE

Red Hill 203m

TALGA RD

WILDERNESS RD

LOVEDALE RD

CAMP RD

RAILWAY RD

Allandale

HERMITAGE RD

NORTH RD

TERRACE RD

DEASEYS RD

PALMERS RD

GILLARDS RD

McDONALDS RD

BROKE RD

Rothbury

BRANXTON RD

LANE

ALLANDALE RD

Butterflies Gallery

German Tourist & Holiday Estate

CESSNOCK AERODROME

Rusa Park Zoo

LOMAS LANE

MAJORS LANE

CESSNOCK STATE FOREST

Pokolbin

DEBEYERS RD

McDONALDS RD

OAKEY CREEK RD

POKOLBIN RD

Nulkaba

MARROWBONE RD

Mt Bright 483m

MOUNT VIEW RD

MOUNT VIEW RANGE

Bimbadeen Lookout

Cessnock

KURRI

Abermain

Neath

THE GREAT NORTH WALK: This 250 km walking track between Sydney and Newcastle provides several day walks and weekend walks, which, when combined, make up a 14 day trek.

ABERDARE RD

VINCENT ST

KITCHENER RD

Bellbird

WOLLOMBI RD

ABERDARE STATE FOREST

TOURIST INFORMATION:
Cessnock (Turner Park, Aberdare Rd)

ABERMAIN: A "coal town" until mining became economically unviable. The miners and their descendants later turned to farming and established themselves in dairy and poultry farming.

ABERDARE STATE FOREST

Fishery Creek

BELLBIRD: Site of one of the worst mining tragedies in the country. It was over seventy years ago that twenty-one men died in the explosion and subsequent fire at the colliery. A memorial stands opposite the site of the colliery.

TO MAITLAND

Dalwood

PWELLS RD

Hunter River

Colonial Museum

TO KURRI KURRI

CESSNOCK RD

WINERIES:
Allandale Winery 1 E8
Allanmere Wines 2 F7
Belbourie Wines 3 D5
Briar Ridge Vineyard 4 B12
Brokenwood Winery 5 B8
Calais Estates 6 D7
Capercaillie Wine Co. 7 E9
Carindale Wines 8 D7
Chateau Francois 9 A7
Constable & Hershon Vineyards 10 E7
Drayton's Family Wines 11 B10
Evans Family Wines 12 D7
Farrell's Limestone Ck Vineyard 13 B12
Fraser Winery 14 E6
Golden Grape Estate 15 C10
Hardy's Hunter Ridge 16 A5
Honeytree Estate Vineyard 17 B7
Hungerford Hill Wines 18 B9
Hunter Estate Winery 19 A5
Hunter Valley Wine Society 20 D8
Jackson's Hill Vineyard 21 B11
Kevin Sobels Wines 22 C8
Kindred's Lochleven Estate 23 C7
Lake's Folly 24 D8
Latara Wines 25 C5
Lesnik Family Wines 26 D8
Lindemans Hunter River Winery 27 B9
Little's Winery 28 D7
Marsh Estate 29 A5
McGuigan Hunter Village 30 B8
McWilliam's Mount Pleasant 31 B10
Mistletoe Wines 32 A5
Molly Morgan Vineyard 33 E5
Montagna View Estate 34 A3
Moorebank Vineyard 35 D7
Mount View Estate 36 C11
Oakvale Wines 37 A7
Parker Wines 38 D6
Pepper Tree Wines 39 C8
Peppers Creek Winery 40 B8
Petersons Champagne House 41 D8
Petersons Wines 42 B11
Pokolbin Estate 43 B9
Reg Drayton Wines 44 A10
Rothbury Estate 45 C8
Saddler's Creek Winery 46 C11
Sandalyn Wilderness Estate 47 E6
Scarborough Wine Co. 48 B7
Sutherland Estate 49 C6
Tamburlaine Wines 50 B8
Terrace Vale Wines 51 B5
Tewkesbury Estate 52 D5
Thalgara Estate 53 C9
Tinkler's Vineyard 54 A10
Tulloch's Winery 55 B9
Tyrrell's Family Vineyard 56 A8
Verona Vineyard 57 C8
Wandin Valley Estate 58 G6
Windarra Winery 59 C9
Wyndham Estate 60 H1

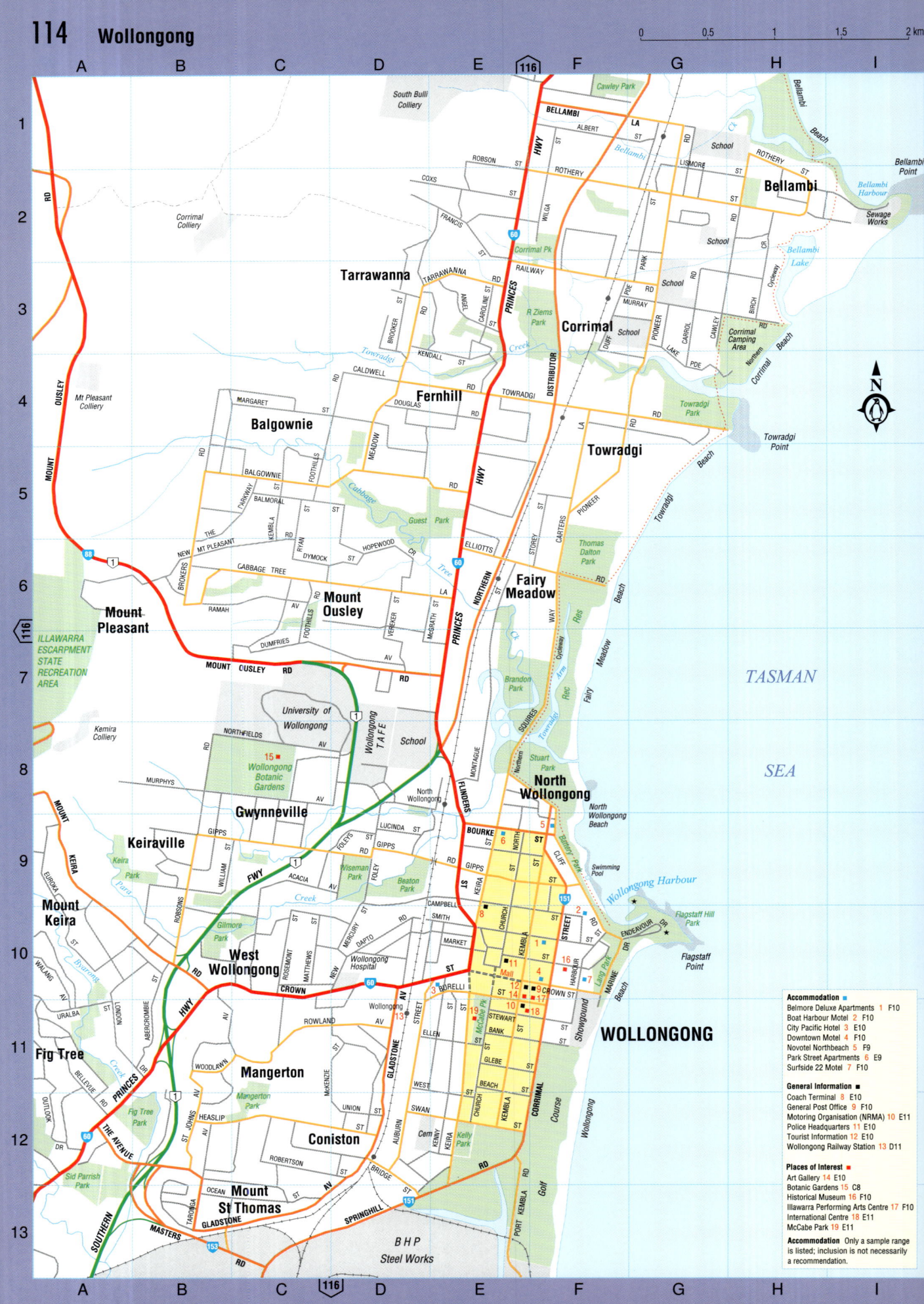

Accommodation

Belmore Deluxe Apartments	1 F10
Boat Harbour Motel	2 F10
City Pacific Hotel	3 E10
Downtown Motel	4 F10
Novotel Northbeach	5 F9
Park Street Apartments	6 E9
Surfside 22 Motel	7 F10

General Information

Coach Terminal	8 E10
General Post Office	9 F10
Motoring Organisation (NRMA)	10 E11
Police Headquarters	11 F10
Tourist Information	12 E10
Wollongong Railway Station	13 D11

Places of Interest

Art Gallery	14 E10
Botanic Gardens	15 C8
Historical Museum	16 F10
Illawarra Performing Arts Centre	17 F10
International Centre	18 E11
McCabe Park	19 E11

Accommodation Only a sample range is listed; inclusion is not necessarily a recommendation.

0 1 2 km

TO SYDNEY

Thirroul

Bulli Pass

The Elbow

Bulli

Woonona
Heights

Woonona

Russell
Vale

Bellambi

Corrimal

Tarrawanna

Fernhill

Towradgi

Balgownie

Reidtown

Fairy Meadow

Mount
Ousley

North
Wollongong

Mount
Pleasant

University of
Wollongong

Wollongong
Botanic Gardens

Gwynneville

Keiraville

Mount
Keira

WOLLONGONG

West
Wollongong

McArthur

Mangerton

Figtree

Coniston

Mount
St Thomas

Mount
Kembla

B H P Steel Works

TO DAPTO   TO KIAMA

Thick roads represent recommended approach and bypass routes.

TASMAN

SEA

0 5 10 15 20 km

TOURIST INFORMATION:
Bomaderry (254 Princes Hwy)
Camden (Camden Valley Way)
Kiama (Blowhole Point Rd)
Mittagong (62-70 Main St)
Wollongong (93 Crown St)

DAMS: The dams in this region are open to the public during the day. Picnic areas and barbecue facilities are available.

MACQUARIE PASS NATIONAL PARK: This small park preserves a section of the Illawarra escarpment and offers bushwalking through open eucalypt forest. Picnic facilities available.

MINNAMURRA RAINFOREST CENTRE: Visitors have the opportunity to walk through and experience the forest habitat unique to this region. A raised wooden pathway takes visitors along the creek and into the rainforest to view the flora and fauna.

CATHEDRAL ROCKS: Distinctive rock formation which may be viewed from Cliff Drive or at a closer range by approaching from the north.

GLOW WORM GLEN: Glow worms are larvae of the fungus gnat. The blue glow they emit lures their prey (insects) into their web nest. The hungrier the glow worm, the brighter it glows. The glen is a 25 minute walk from the end of William St, Bundanoon. Glow worms are visible only at night and are very sensitive to noise.

BUDDEROO NATIONAL PARK: A small but delightful national park noted for its fine views and excellent walking tracks. The spectacular Carrington Falls lie within its boundaries.

KANGAROO VALLEY: This picturesque valley is surrounded by towering sandstone cliffs. There are many delightful picnic spots along the banks of the river which is popular for fishing, swimming and canoeing.

WILD COUNTRY PARK: This wildlife refuge provides a natural rainforest setting for the animals and birds. Visitors can enjoy the quiet and fascinating environment, as well as various attractions offered including a sub-tropical rainforest walk, slab hut museum and free-ranging native wildlife.

ORCHARDS: There are many orchards in the region particularly in the Penrose region, 10km from Bundanoon, and Yerrinbool district, north of Mittagong. The best time to visit and buy freshly picked fruit and vegetables is from January to June.

KINGSFORD SMITH MEMORIAL AND LOOKOUT: Commemorates this famous aviator's historic flight to New Zealand in 1933. The lookout offers panoramic views of Seven Mile Beach National Park.

BARREN GROUNDS BIRD OBSERVATORY: An established bird watcher's mecca. The observatory is the habitat of several endangered bird species. Located on top of Jamberoo Mountain it has numerous established walking trails through its windswept heathland. Wildlife-watching programs also run throughout the year.

MORTON NATIONAL PARK: Sandstone cliffs, hundreds of metres high in places, tower over the wooded valley through which flows the Shoalhaven River and its many tributaries. Erosion of the sandstone has formed impressive gorges and cascading waterfalls drop to the valley floor including the renowned Fitzroy Falls at the Moss Vale end of the park.

GREENWELL POINT: Visitors to this major fishing village can view the fishing fleet and buy fresh fish and locally grown oysters.

For more detail on Wollongong see page 114

CENTRAL TILBA: Founded in 1895, this town was classified by the National Trust in 1974 to preserve it for posterity. Visitors can enjoy the craft shops, a deer park, winery and tea rooms.

THE TRIANGLE: So called because on a map the road pattern linking the three towns, Central Tilba, Bermagui, and Cobargo, is distinctly triangular. The surrounding area offers the visitor scenic places, superb fishing facilities and an insight into the country's heritage.

CANDELO: Little has changed in this village since the Nineteenth Century giving it an old-world charm.

TOURIST INFORMATION:
Bega (Gipps St)
Bermagui (BP Service Station, 8 Coluga St)
Cooma (119 Sharp St)
Eden (Princes Hwy)
Merimbula (Beach St)
Narooma (Princes Hwy)
Tathra (Tathra Wharf, Wharf Rd)

PAMBULA: Historic village renowned for its quaint buildings now housing craft shops and restaurants. Sunday markets held second Sunday of each month. Nearby Pambula beach, a patrolled surfing beach, has excellent picnic spots on its foreshore where kangaroos and wallabies may be seen feeding in the early mornings and late afternoons.

FISHING: Every year thousands of anglers come to this section of the Coast to enjoy their favourite sport. Fisheries, however, are limited, and restrictions have been placed in order that they be protected. Contact NSW Fisheries for information regarding protected species, quantities of fish taken in any one day, minimum sizes and method of capture.

BEN BOYD NATIONAL PARK: Over 9000 hectares of rocky but beautiful coastline flanking Twofold Bay. Flowering heaths and colourful banksias add to the area's attraction. Prominent features in the park include Boyds Tower, constructed in the 1840s, and The Pinnacles, a formation that dates back about 65 million years. The Pinnacles walking track is popular with visitors.

WONBOYN LAKE: Reputed to be the finest fishing spot in this section of the coast, note that the road leading to the lake is unsealed.

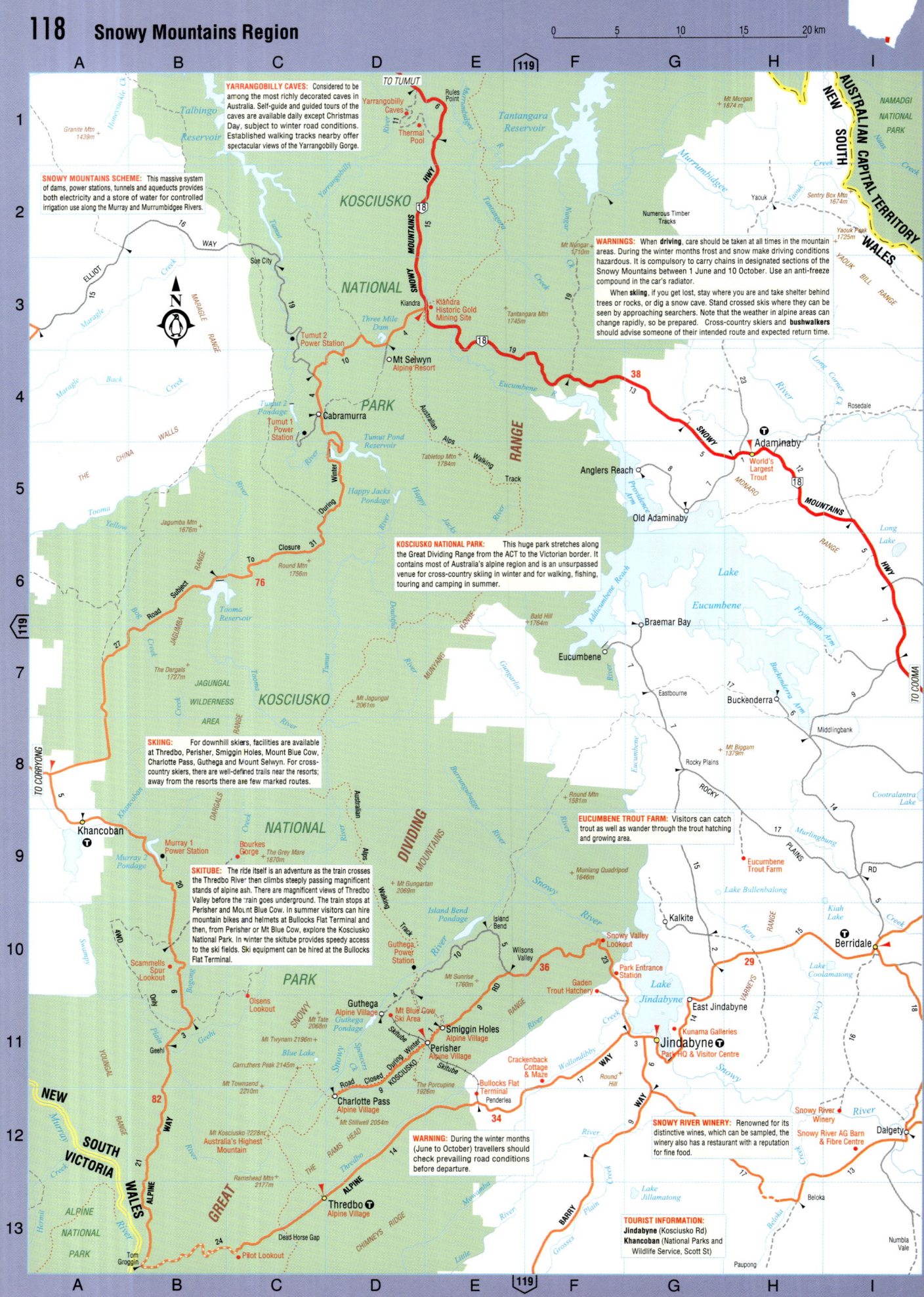

YARRANGOBILLY CAVES: Considered to be among the most richly decorated caves in Australia. Self-guide and guided tours of the caves are available daily except Christmas Day, subject to winter road conditions. Established walking tracks nearby offer spectacular views of the Yarrangobilly Gorge.

SNOWY MOUNTAINS SCHEME: This massive system of dams, power stations, tunnels and aqueducts provides both electricity and a store of water for controlled irrigation use along the Murray and Murrumbidgee Rivers.

WARNINGS: When **driving**, care should be taken at all times in the mountain areas. During the winter months frost and snow make driving conditions hazardous. It is compulsory to carry chains in designated sections of the Snowy Mountains between 1 June and 10 October. Use an anti-freeze compound in the car's radiator.

When **skiing**, if you get lost, stay where you are and take shelter behind trees or rocks, or dig a snow cave. Stand crossed skis where they can be seen by approaching searchers. Note that the weather in alpine areas can change rapidly, so be prepared. Cross-country skiers and **bushwalkers** should advise someone of their intended route and expected return time.

KOSCIUSKO NATIONAL PARK: This huge park stretches along the Great Dividing Range from the ACT to the Victorian border. It contains most of Australia's alpine region and is an unsurpassed venue for cross-country skiing in winter and for walking, fishing, touring and camping in summer.

SKIING: For downhill skiers, facilities are available at Thredbo, Perisher, Smiggin Holes, Mount Blue Cow, Charlotte Pass, Guthega and Mount Selwyn. For cross-country skiers, there are well-defined trails near the resorts; away from the resorts there are few marked routes.

SKITUBE: The ride itself is an adventure as the train crosses the Thredbo River then climbs steeply passing magnificent stands of alpine ash. There are magnificent views of Thredbo Valley before the train goes underground. The train stops at Perisher and Mount Blue Cow. In summer visitors can hire mountain bikes and helmets at Bullocks Flat Terminal and then, from Perisher or Mt Blue Cow, explore the Kosciusko National Park. In winter the skitube provides speedy access to the ski fields. Ski equipment can be hired at the Bullocks Flat Terminal.

EUCUMBENE TROUT FARM: Visitors can catch trout as well as wander through the trout hatching and growing area.

WARNING: During the winter months (June to October) travellers should check prevailing road conditions before departure.

SNOWY RIVER WINERY: Renowned for its distinctive wines, which can be sampled, the winery also has a restaurant with a reputation for fine food.

TOURIST INFORMATION:
Jindabyne (Kosciusko Rd)
Khancoban (National Parks and Wildlife Service, Scott St)

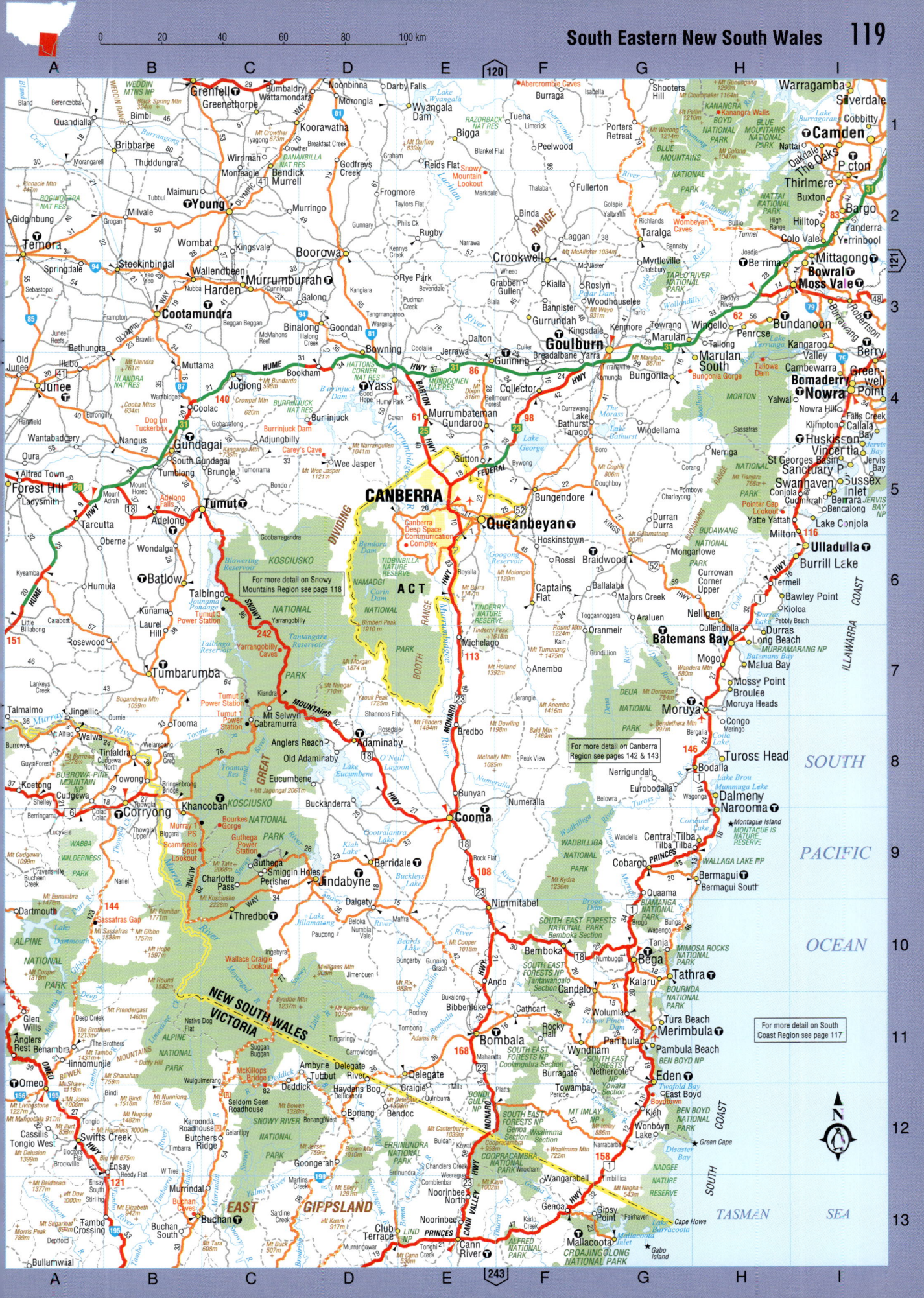

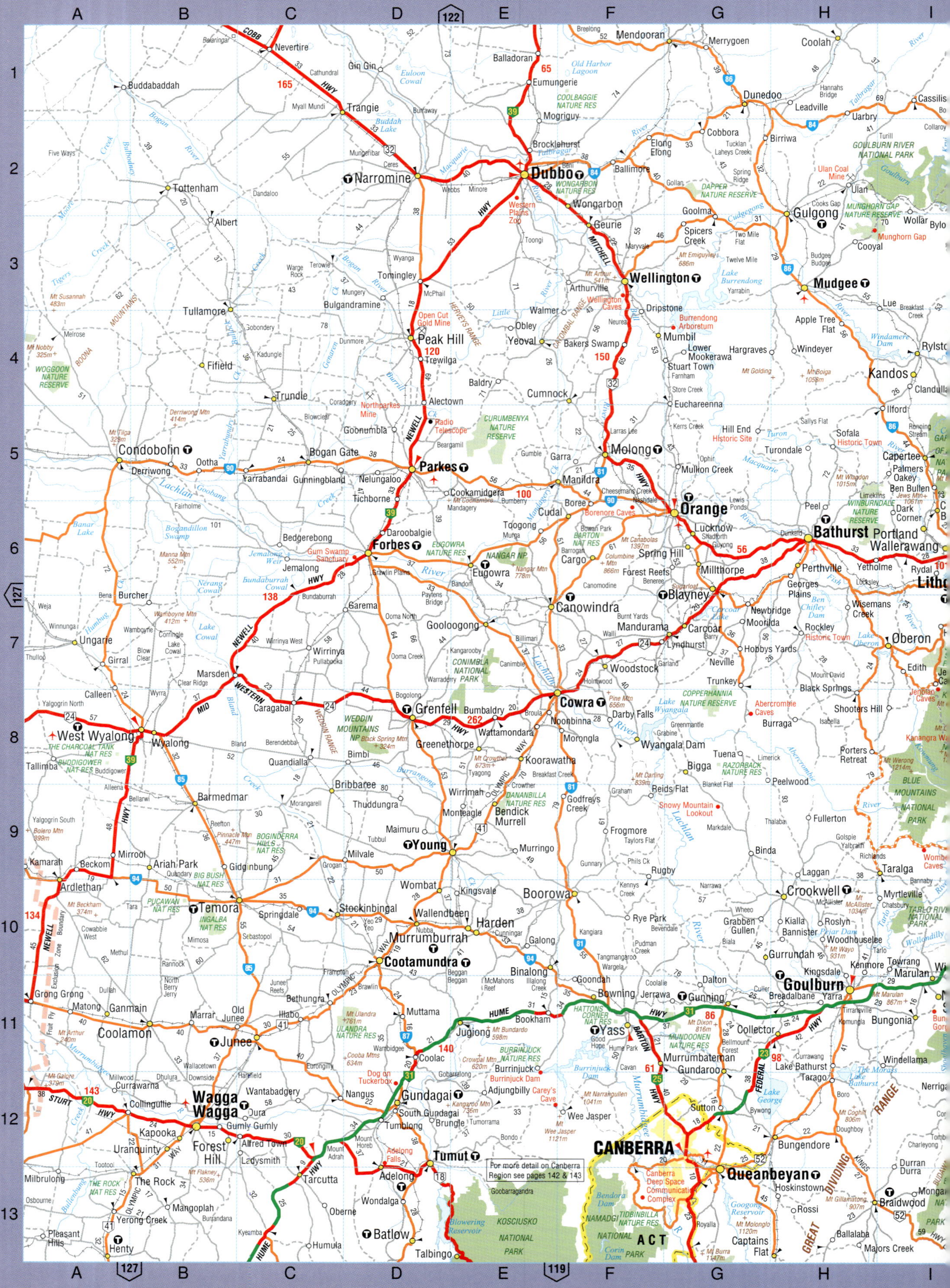
A
B
C
D
E
F
G
H
I
1
2
3
4
5
6
7
8
9
10
11
12
13
122
127
119
Nevertire
Buddabaddah
Trangie
Gin Gin
Balladoran
Eumungerie
Mogriguy
Mendooran
Merrygoen
Coolah
Dunedoo
Leadville
Uarbry
Cassilis
Cobbora
Birriwa
Elong Elong
Ballimore
Brocklehurst
Dubbo
Narromine
Tottenham
Albert
Wongarbon
Geurie
Gulgong
Goolma
Spicers Creek
Mudgee
Wellington
Tomingley
Bulgandramine
Tullamore
Dripstone
Arthurville
Peak Hill
Trewilga
Obley
Yeoval
Bakers Swamp
Mumbil
Stuart Town
Hargraves
Windeyer
Kandos
Rylstone
Fifield
Trundle
Alectown
Baldry
Cumnock
Eurimbula
Ilford
Condobolin
Ootha
Derriwong
Yarrabandai
Gunningbland
Bogan Gate
Nelungaloo
Parkes
Goonumbla
Molong
Mullion Creek
Orange
Cookamidgera
Manildra
Cudal
Borenore Caves
Tichborne
Daroobalgie
Forbes
Eugowra
Toogong
Cargo
Lucknow
Spring Hill
Millthorpe
Bathurst
Portland
Wallerawang
Lithgow
Capertee
Bedgerebong
Jemalong
Bandon
Canowindra
Blayney
Carcoar
Mandurama
Lyndhurst
Perthville
Oberon
Burcher
Garema
Gooloogong
Newbridge
Ungarie
Girral
Marsden
Woodstock
Neville
Trunkey
Calleen
Caragabal
Grenfell
Bumbaldry
Cowra
Darby Falls
Black Springs
West Wyalong
Wyalong
Wattamondara
Noonbinna
Morongla
Wyangala Dam
Greenethorpe
Koorawatha
Bimbi
Quandialla
Tuena
Bigga
Barmedman
Bribbaree
Thuddungra
Monteagle
Bendick Murrell
Reids Flat
Godfreys Creek
Frogmore
Young
Maimuru
Murringo
Fullerton
Mirrool
Ariah Park
Gidginbung
Milvale
Binda
Ardlethan
Beckom
Kamarah
Temora
Springdale
Stockinbingal
Wombat
Kingsvale
Boorowa
Rugby
Laggan
Crookwell
Taralga
Wallendbeen
Harden
Murrumburrah
Rye Park
Kialla
Bannister
Cootamundra
Galong
Binalong
Bowning
Jerrawa
Gunning
Dalton
Goulburn
Marulan
Grong Grong
Matong
Ganmain
Coolamon
Marrar
Old Junee
Junee
Bethungra
Illabo
Muttama
Jugiong
Bookham
Yass
Collector
Bungonia
Coolac
Murrumbateman
Gundaroo
Lake Bathurst
Tarago
Windellama
Wagga Wagga
Collingullie
Currawarna
Wantabadgery
Nangus
Gundagai
South Gundagai
Tumblong
Brungle
Adjungbilly
Wee Jasper
Sutton
Bungendore
Kapooka
Uranquinty
Forest Hill
Gumly Gumly
Alfred Town
Ladysmith
Tarcutta
Tumut
Adelong
CANBERRA
Queanbeyan
Hoskinstown
Braidwood
The Rock
Mangoplah
Yerong Creek
Henty
Oberne
Wondalga
Batlow
Humula
Talbingo
Captains Flat
Majors Creek
Rossi
For more detail on Canberra Region see pages 142 & 143
KOSCIUSZKO NATIONAL PARK
BLUE MOUNTAINS NATIONAL PARK
GOULBURN RIVER NATIONAL PARK
ACT
NEWELL HWY
MID WESTERN HWY
OLYMPIC WAY
HUME HWY
STURT HWY
MITCHELL HWY
FEDERAL HWY
BARTON HWY
COBB HWY

A B 504 C D CARNARVON E F G 505 H I

1
Nindigully
BARWON
Bungunya
Toobeah
GORE HWY
BENDIDEE NATIONAL PARK
Commoron
39 85
55
16
Talwood
200
69
HWY
Goondiwindi
39
CUNNINGHAM
118
Gradule
22
50

2
Dirrbandi
Noondoo
20
44
Daymar
78
Weir
River
35
Boomi
37
Boggabilla
39
49
Kurumbul
Yallaroi
BRUN
162
73
Thallon
23
Macintyre
153
HWY
62

3
Hebel
CASTLEREAGH
19
Mungindi
26
Caloona
18
River
Barwon
42
118
127
North Sta
39
Croppa Creek
NEWELL
Crooble
Mosquito Creek

QUEENSLAND
NEW SOUTH WALES
504

4
Goodooga
47
New Angledool
20
31
99
49
Gundabloui
Neeworra
Weemelah
30
Garah
42
Moppin
50
Ashley
26
18
18
CAREUNGA NATURE RESERVE
Camurra
Milguy
Crooble

5
134
Angledool Lake
21
107
57
Mogil Mogil
50
134
Bullarah
38
Gwydir
67
GWYDIR
67
Moree
39
Pallamallawa
Wariale
Lightning Ridge
Opal Mines
55
Collarenebri
Pokataroo
Merrywinbone
HWY
River
29
Biniguy
50
Gravesend
Warialde
Rai

6
Grawin Opal Mines
106
NARRAN LAKE NATURE RESERVE
Cumborah
CASTLEREAGH
75
GWYDIR
Rowena
89
Doreen
Nowley
Millie
97
53
Tycannah
Gurley
64
Terry Hie Hie
36
Bellata
SAMILAROI NATURE RESERVE
Binga

7
Barwon
70
River
Walgett
Waminda
Cryon
Bugilbone
184
92
Namoi
Goangra
Burren Junction
Cubbaroo
50
Merah North
42
Edgeroi
44
Courada
Grattai Mtn 1310m
103
MOUNT
Upper Horton
Cobba

8
50
Carinda
55
Coombogolong
Gidginbilla Dam
Teridgerie
Come-by-Chance
99
Milchomi
Pilliga
57
Cuttabri
Yarrie Lake
CSIRO Observatory
Narrabri West
Narrabri
KAPUTAR
Mt Kaputar 1508m
Derian Mtn 855m
RANGE
Barr

9
75
HWY
Wingadee
85
Gwabegar
Merebene
Barradine
Kenebri
SCRUB
Salt Caves
PILLIGA
39
118
Turrawan
56
37
Baan Baa
42
Boggabri
99
40
Kelvin
Lake Keepit
Upper

10
208
MACQUARIE MARSHES NATURE RESERVE
Quambone
58
Macquarie Marshes
Gilgooma
71
Baradine
Wittenbra
PILLIGA NATURE RESERVE
Rocky Glen
Black Mtn 502m
OXLEY
Gunnedah
30
Carroll
Curlewis
Piallwa

11
Coonamble
56
Tooloon
17
Combara
55
WARRUMBUNGLE
Bugaldie
RANGE
Yearinan
39
Garrawilla
108
Mullaley
Cox
Spring Ridge
37
Breeza

12
27
Gradery
43
31
21
Combara
28
24
Tenandra
42
Bulaway Mtn 1003m+
Siding Springs Observatory
Bullaroble 1014m
Skywatch Observatory
Coonabarabran
Ulamambri
Purlewaugh
Tambar Springs
Premer
Caroona
Lake Goran
Quip

13
MITCHELL
Miowera
59
Belaringar
Gin Gin
Nevertire
HWY
34
164
OXLEY
49
Collie
36
Curban
Kamber
39
Gilgandra
FLORA RESERVE
52
Mendooran
Merrygoen
Coolah
Pine Ride

Warren
Inglegar
Reedy Corner
77
Armatree
28
Gular
Gulargambone
34
Tooraweenah
94
Warkton
WARRUMBUNGLE NATIONAL PARK
Mt Exmouth 1205m
The Breadknife
Mt Spire 1071m
34
Windurong
55
Murrawal
BINNAWAY NATURE RESERVE
Binnaway
Deringulla
Bomera
Tamarang
Colly Blue
Connemarra

Mullengudgery
Cathundral
Balladoran
65
Eumungerie
120
Old Harbor Lagoon
Euloon Cowal
Breelong
Neilrex
New Mollyann
Weetaliba
WEETALIBAH NATURE RESERVE
Ulinda
Oakey Creek
46
Bundella
Yarraman
Blackville
44
CEDAR NATURE RE
LIVERPOOL
RANGE
86
39

QUEENSLAND
NEW SOUTH WALES

NEW SOUTH WALES
SOUTH AUSTRALIA

STURT NATIONAL PARK

Corner Store
CAMERON CORNER
Explorers Tree
Binerah Downs
Waka
Frome
Twelve Mile Creek
Creek
Tilcha
Hewart Downs
Yandama
Yandama
Winnathee
Hawker Gate House
Mt Shannon 332m
MT BROWN RANGE
Smithville House
Lake Wallace
Lake Want
Big Salt Lake
Pimpara Lake
Starvation Lake
Turleys Gate
Packsaddle
Sanpah
Pine Ridge
Pine View
Westwood Downs
Boughams Gate
Teilta
Floods Creek
Morphetts Creek
Wilangee
BARRIER RANGE
Purnamoota
MUNDI MUNDI PLAIN
Umberumberka Reservoir
Silverton Historic Town
Stephens Creek
Stephens Creek Reservoir
SILVER CITY HWY
Cockburn
BARRIER HWY
Mutooroo
Burta
Ascot Vale
Pine Point

Warri Warri Gate
Onepah
Adelaide Gate
Teurika
Tibooburra
Pindera Downs
Poole's Cairn
Depot Glen Bilabong
Poole's Grave
Milparinka
Yantara
Yantara Lake
Salt Lake
Lake Bullea
Cobham
Dalmuir
Pulgamurtie
Kooninberry Mtn
Packsaddle Roadhouse
Nundora
Lake Bancannia
Noonthorangee Range
The Selection
Koonawarra
Wertago
Mootwingee National Park
Aboriginal Historic Site
Bynguano Range
Bengoro Range
Jones Lake
Coogee Lake
Comarto
Glenora
Hazel Vale
Little Topar Roadhouse
Purnamoota
Stephens Creek
Scopes Range
Fruit Fly Exclusion Zone Boundary
Kinalung
Horse Lake
Box Tank
Pamamaroo Lake
Tandure Lake
Menindee Lake
Kinchega National Park
Cawndilla Lake
Menindee

Whyjonta
Clifton Downs
Lake Altiboulka
Gumpopla
Turkey Creek
McCallum Park
Pulchra
Allandy
Morden Creek
Nuntherungie
Oak Vale
Cootawundi
Tarella
Coona Coona
Coturaundee Nature Reserve
Mt Daubeny
Churinga
Glen Lyon
Cawkers Well
Four Mile Lake
Malta Lake
Seven Mile Creek
Amphitheatre Lake
Dead Horse Lake
Wallace Lake
Big Ampi
Darling River

Lake Callamulcha
Hamilton Gate
Waverley Gate
Moombidary
Berrawinnia Downs
Owen Downs
Ourimbah
Barrajong
Koridina
Wana
Colane
Baronna Downs
Bundarra
Petita
The Range
Nantilla
Questa Park
Glendara
Purnanga
Cawnalmurtee
McGurty Hill
Goodwood
Caradoc
Peery
Mandalay
White Cliffs
Opal Mines
Momba
Nine Mile Lakes
Ulalie
Lake Dick
Oulilla Lake
Mt Murchison 203m
Hamilton (ruin)
Mena Murtee
Wilcannia
Lake Woytchugga
Poopelloe Lake
Lake Gunyulka
Talyawalka
Cowary
Teryawynia
Nyngynderry
Glen Albyn
Dry Lake
Teryawynya Lake
Glen Ora
Albemarle
Victoria Lake
MANARA HILLS
MACCULLOCHS RANGE
COBB HWY
BARRIER HWY
Tonga Lake
Mullawoolka Basin
Lake Yantabangee
Poloka Lake
Gilpoko Lake
Peri Lake
Talalara
Wild Duck
Nocoleche

32 514 515 126 305 75 178 196 49 339 55 272

SILVER CITY HWY

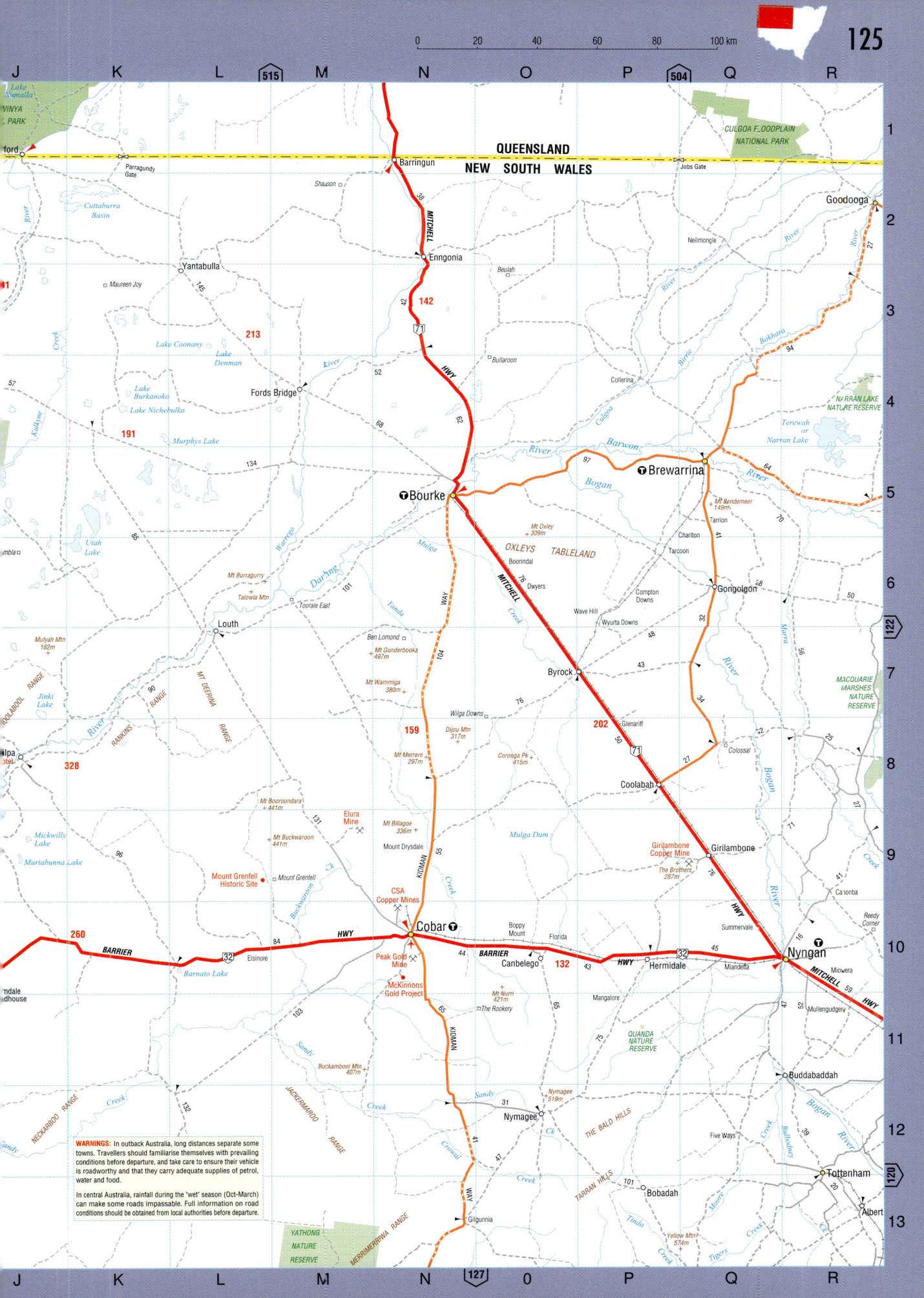

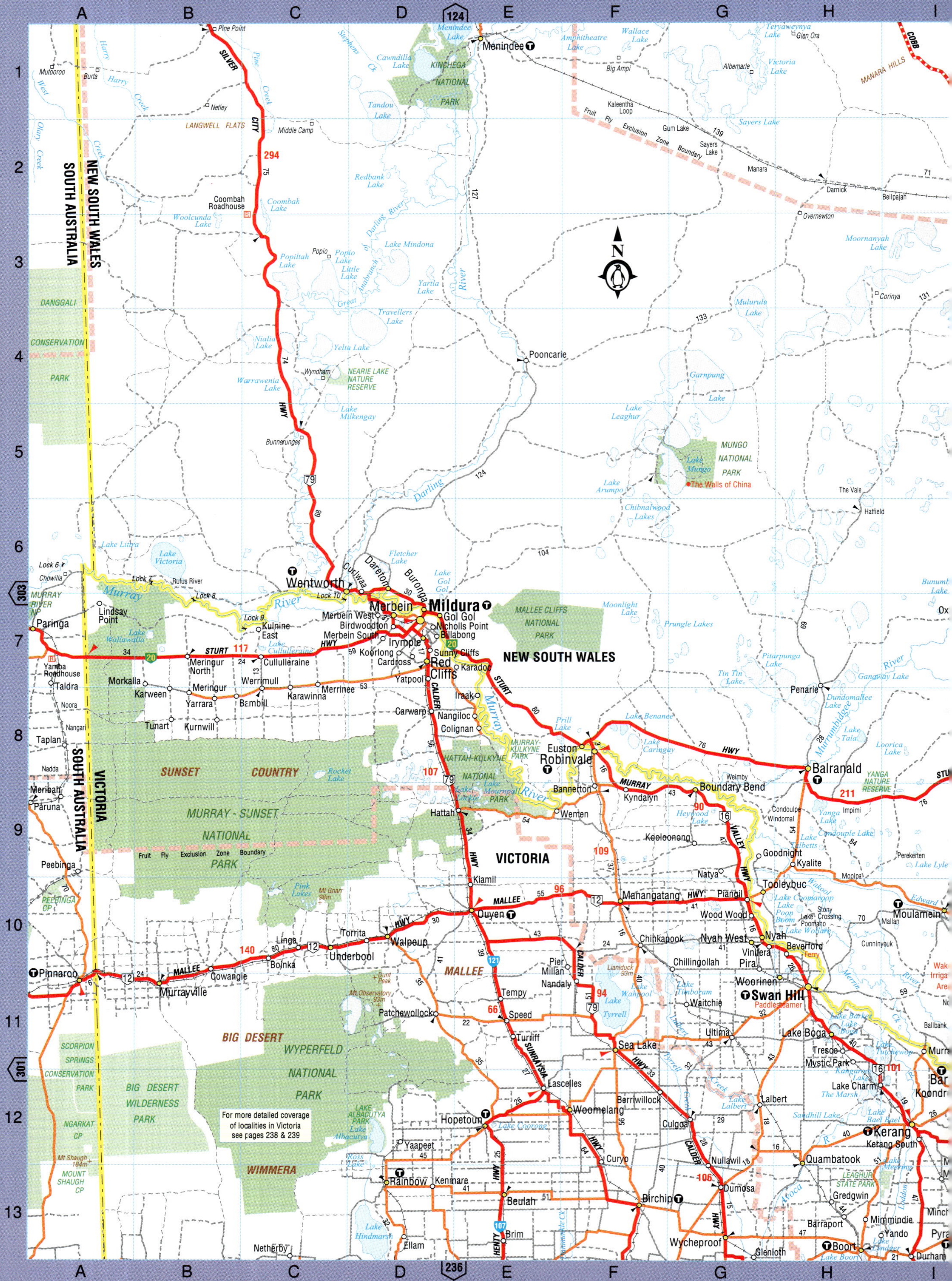

Grid reference letters (top and bottom): A B C D E F G H I
Grid reference numbers (left and right): 1 2 3 4 5 6 7 8 9 10 11 12 13

NEW SOUTH WALES
SOUTH AUSTRALIA
VICTORIA

Towns and localities:
Mutooroo, Burta, Harry, Pine Point, Netley, Middle Camp, Menindee, Big Ampi, Kaleentha Loop, Manara Hills, Glen Ora

Coombah Roadhouse, Redbank Lake, Coombah Lake, Tandou Lake, Cawndilla Lake, Stephens Ck, KINCHEGA NATIONAL PARK, Amphitheatre Lake, Wallace Lake, Victoria Lake, Albemarle, Sayers Lake, Darnick, Beilpajah

LANGWELL FLATS, Woolcunda Lake, Popiltah Lake, Popio Lake, Little Lake, Lake Mindona, Yartla Lake, Travellers Lake, Pooncarie, Garnpung Lake, Mulurulu Lake, Corinya, Overnewton, Moornanyah Lake

DANGGALI CONSERVATION PARK, Nialia Lake, Yelta Lake, Great Anabranch, Darling River, Warrawenia Lake, NEARIE LAKE NATURE RESERVE, Lake Milkengay, Bunnarungee, Lake Leaghur, Garnpung, Lake Tandou, Hatfield, The Vale

MUNGO NATIONAL PARK, Lake Mungo, The Walls of China, Chibnalwood Lakes, Lake Arumpo

Lock 6, Chowilla, Lock 7, Lock 8, Lock 9, Lake Victoria, Rufus River, Murray River NP, Paringa, Lindsay Point, Kulnine East, Wentworth, Curlwaa, Dareton, Burongo, Fletcher Lake, Lake Gol Gol, MALLEE CLIFFS NATIONAL PARK, Moonlight Lake, Prungle Lakes, Bunumburt Lake, Ox

Yamba Roadhouse, Taldra, Morkalla, Karween, Meringur North, Meringur, Yarrara, Bembil, Werrimull, Cullulleraine, Merbein West, Birdwoodton, Merbein South, Irymple, Koorlong, Cardross, Red Cliffs, Merbein, Mildura, Gol Gol, Nicholls Point, Billabong, Sunny Cliffs, Karadoc, NEW SOUTH WALES, Pitarpunga Lake, Tin Tin Lake, Penarie, Gangway Lake, Dundomalee Lake

Noora, Nangari, Tunart, Kurnwill, Karawinna, Merrinee, Yatpool, Iraak, Carwarp, Nangiloc, Colignan, MURRAY-KULKYNE PARK, Euston, Robinvale, Lake Benanee, Loorica Lake, Lake Tala

Meribah, Paruna, Taplan, Nadda, SUNSET COUNTRY, Rocket Lake, HATTAH-KULKYNE NATIONAL PARK, Bannerton, Kyndalyn, Boundary Bend, Weimby, Condoulpe, Windomal, Balranald, YANGA NATURE RESERVE, Impimi, Yanga Lake

Peebinga, MURRAY-SUNSET NATIONAL PARK, Hattah, Wemen, MOURNPALL River, Koraleigh, Goodnight, Kyalite, Moolpa, Perekerten, Lake Lyle

PEEBINGA CP, Pink Lakes, Mt Gnarr 98m, Kiamil, Natya, Pianiil, Tooleybuc, Wakool, Edward River, Moulamein

Pinnaroo, Linga, Torrita, Walpeup, Underbool, Tempy, Ouyen, Mahangatang, Wood Wood, Woorinen, Pira, Viniera, Nyah West, Nyah, Beverford, Cunninyeuk

Murrayville, Cowangie, Boinka, MALLEE HWY, Patchewollock, Speed, Turriff, Pier Millan, Nandaly, Chinkapook, Chillingollah, Swan Hill, Lake Boga, Tresco, Mystic Park, Kangaroo Lake

BIG DESERT, WYPERFELD NATIONAL PARK, SCORPION SPRINGS CONSERVATION PARK, BIG DESERT WILDERNESS PARK, NGARKAT CP, Mt Shaugh 184m, MOUNT SHAUGH CP, Lake Albacutya, Lake Hindmarsh, Ultima, Lalbert, Lake Lalbert, Culgoa, Berriwillock, Woomelang, Sea Lake, SUNRAYSIA, Lascelles, Waitchie, Lake Tyrrell, Lake Wahpool, Lianiduck, Kerang, Ketang South, Quambatook, The Marsh, Sandhill Lake, Lake Bael Bael, LEAGHUR STATE PARK

WIMMERA, Hopetoun, Yaapeet, Rainbow, Kenmara, Beulah, Brim, Ellam, Netherby, Lake Corrong, Lake Albacutya, Ross Lakes, Birchip, Curyo, Nullawil, Dumosa, Wycheproof, Glenloth, Boort, Mitiamo, Durham, Yando, Barraport, Mimmindie, Pyramid, Gredgwin, Lake Meran, Lake Boort

Highways and route numbers:
SILVER CITY HWY, STURT HWY, CALDER HWY, MALLEE HWY, HENTY HWY, SUNRAYSIA HWY, MURRAY VALLEY HWY

Route markers: 124, 294, 303, 20, 117, 79, 121, 140, 96, 109, 94, 66, 101, 105, 211, 236, 301, 107

COBB HWY

For more detailed coverage of localities in Victoria see pages 238 & 239

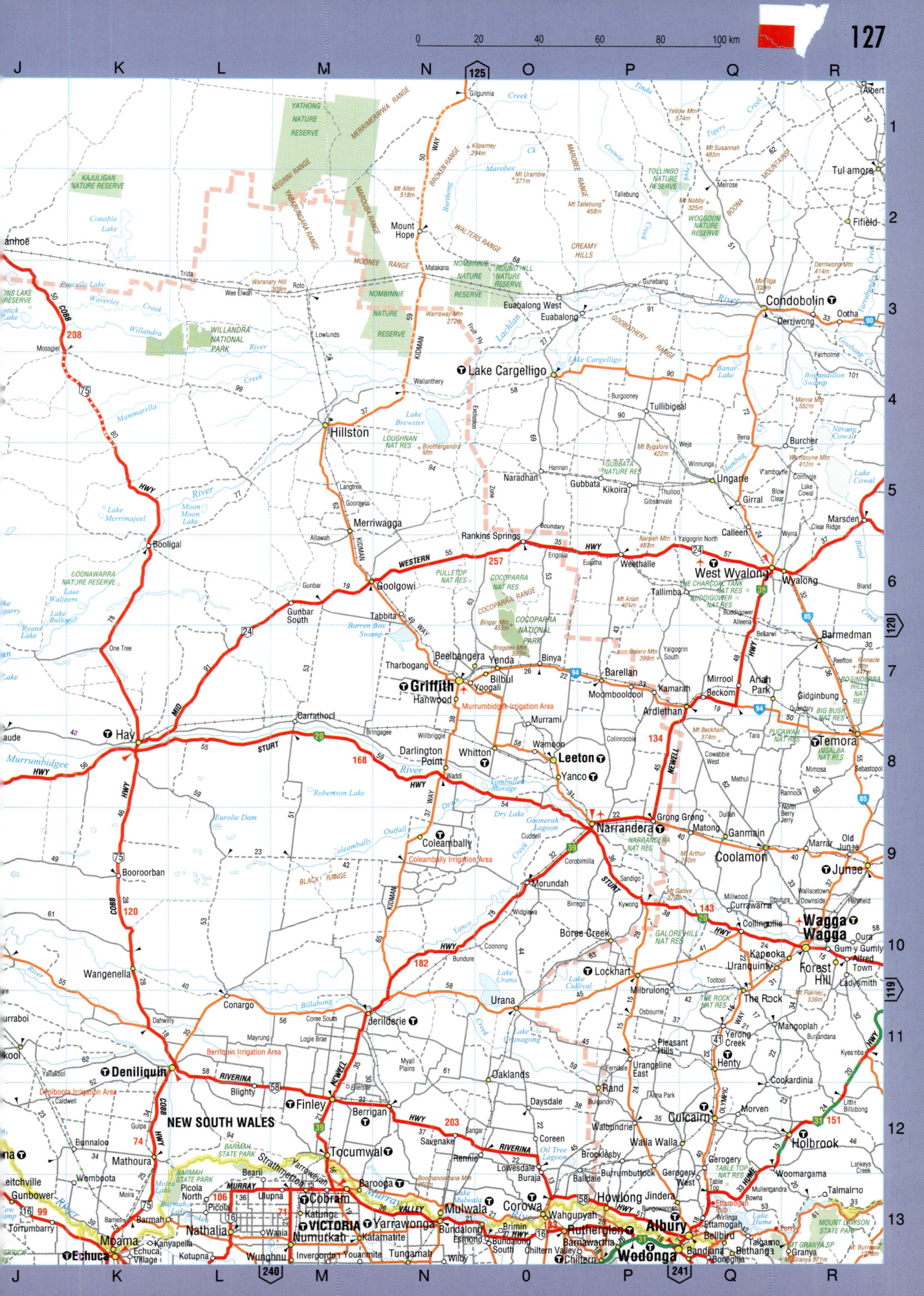

Australian Capital Territory

The Nation's Capital

A.C.T.

The nation's capital is a 2400 square-kilometre area with an air of spaciousness and grace, typical of eastern rural Australia and enhanced by the beautiful valley of the Molonglo River and the surrounding hills, mountains and pastureland.

The Australian Capital Territory is surrounded by New South Wales and lies roughly halfway between Sydney and Melbourne. It was created by the Commonwealth Constitution Act of 1901 when the Commonwealth of Australia was inaugurated: a nation was formed from the six colonies.

One of the provisions of the Act was that the seat of government should be on land vested in the Commonwealth. Nine years of prolonged wrangling followed, as two Royal Commissions and parliamentary committees considered the various claims of established towns and cities to be the federal capital, before the location of the new territory and the site for the new city was decided. In addition, the area of Jervis Bay on the south coast of New South Wales was ceded to the Commonwealth to provide a seaport for the nation's capital.

Melbourne was the provisional seat of government until 1927 when a temporary building was erected in Canberra. This building was used until 1988 when the new House of Parliament was completed.

Canberra, Australia's modern capital city, was built on an undulating plain in an amphitheatre of the Australian Alps. The Molonglo River, a tributary of the Murrumbidgee River, runs through the city and was dammed in 1964 to create Lake Burley Griffin, around which Canberra has been developed.

It is one of the world's best-known fully-planned cities and is a source of pride for Australians and interest for overseas visitors. Its public buildings, its areas of parkland and bush reserves, its leafy suburbs and broad tree-lined streets have resulted from brilliant planning by its architect, Walter Burley Griffin, and from care taken in its development over the years. Its architecture and its atmosphere are unique and stimulating considering there is little over 50 years old. Although the city has an air of being contrived, it contains so much that educates, absorbs and stimulates the visitor; Canberra's somewhat sterile quality is soon forgotten.

The land on which the city is sited was discovered in 1820 by Charles Throsby Smith and his party of explorers. The area became known as Limestone Plains and was destined for settlement as grazing property. The first European settler, Joshua Moore, took up a thousand acres (2500 hectares) of land on the Murrumbidgee River in 1824 and named his property Canberry, which is an Aboriginal word meaning 'meeting place'. A year later Robert Campbell, a wealthy Sydney merchant, took up 4000 acres (10 000 hectares) of land, which formed the first part of the Duntroon estate.

When the land for the new city was acquired by the Commonwealth Government in 1911 it contained only

NOT TO BE MISSED
in the Australian Capital Territory Map Ref.

- **Australian National Botanic Gardens** – large collection of Australian native plants 140 F9
- **Australian War Memorial** – one of the world's outstanding war museums 138 H4
- **Cockington Green** – feel like a giant in a miniature English village 139 E2
- **Lanyon** – an historic homestead refurbished to reflect country life in the 1800s 139 E7
- **Namadgi National Park** – famous for its rugged beauty and mountain scenery 139 C9
- **National Film and Sound Archive** – radio, film, television and sound recording memorabilia 138 B4
- **National Gallery of Australia** – has an excellent collection of Aboriginal art 138 F9
- **Parliament House** – impressive architecture; designed to preserve the contour of Capital Hill 138 C11
- **Questacon** – for hands-on interactive displays from microbes to earthquakes 138 D8
- **Sportex** – an interactive sports exhibition at the nation's premier training facility 140 F7
- **Tidbinbilla Nature Reserve** – home to koalas, kangaroos and other native fauna 139 C6

Anzac Day, Memorial Ave, Canberra

Spring in Canberra

CLIMATE GUIDE

AUSTRALIAN CAPITAL TERRITORY

	J	F	M	A	M	J	J	A	S	O	N	D
Maximum °C	28	27	24	20	15	12	11	13	16	19	23	26
Minimum °C	13	13	11	7	3	1	0	1	3	6	9	11
Rainfall mm	58	56	53	49	49	37	40	48	52	68	62	53
Raindays	8	7	7	8	9	9	10	11	10	11	10	8

Telstra Tower on Black Mountain has public viewing galleries

two small villages. Construction of the first public buildings started in 1913, and in 1914 a rail service was opened between Sydney and the new capital. The Depression and World War II slowed construction, but the rate of development has been spectacular since the mid-1950s and the population is now over 300 000.

There are four distinct seasons in the ACT: a warm spring, a hot dry summer, a brilliant cool autumn, and a cold winter with occasional snow. Perhaps the best time to visit is in the autumn, when there is a magnificent display of golden foliage. Almost two million Australian and overseas visitors come to the ACT each year.

A.C.T.

CALENDAR OF EVENTS

Note: The information given here was accurate at the time of printing. However, as the timing of events held annually is subject to change and some events may extend into the following month, it is best to check with the local tourism authority or event organisers to confirm the details.

JANUARY
Public holidays: New Year's Day; Australia Day.
Canberra: Australia Day Celebrations; Canberra World Cup Showjumping; Street Machine Summernats (national hot-rod exhibition and races).

FEBRUARY
Canberra: Royal Canberra Show; Multicultural Festival; St Valentine's Jazz Festival.

MARCH
Public holiday: Canberra Day.
Canberra: Black Opal Stakes; Canberra Festival; Canberra Vintage Festival (sometimes April); Autumn Fest; PGA Seniors Golf; National Folk Festival (sometimes April).

EASTER
Public holidays: Good Friday; Easter Monday.

APRIL
Public holiday: Anzac Day.
Canberra: Anzac Day Parade and Service at Australian War Memorial; ACT Heritage Festival; Australian Science Festival.

JUNE
Public holiday: Queen's Birthday. **Canberra:** National Capital Dancesport Championships.

SEPTEMBER
Canberra: Floriade.

OCTOBER
Public holiday: Labour Day.

Canberra: Canberra Cup; Floriade (contd); Oktoberfest; Festival of Contemporary Arts; Cycle Classic.

NOVEMBER
Canberra: Rally of Canberra.

DECEMBER
Public holidays: Christmas Day; Boxing Day.

CANBERRA

Australia's Capital City

The impressive Anzac Parade stretches from the War Memorial to Lake Burley Griffin

As well as being Australia's capital, Canberra is a model city. Its unique concentric circular streets, planted with more than 12 million trees and shrubs, are set graciously on the shores of the constructed Lake Burley Griffin. Driving in Canberra can be challenging; it is wise to study a map before beginning to tour.

The old Parliament House, completed in 1927, and a number of government department buildings and hostels for public servants were among the first buildings in the national capital. They are now dwarfed by the grand buildings of later development, which have turned Canberra into a showpiece.

A number of lookouts on the surrounding hills give superb views of the city. The 195-metre **Telstra Tower** on Black Mountain is the highest. **Mount Ainslie** offers fine views of central Canberra and Lake Burley Griffin. **Red Hill** overlooks Parliament House, South Canberra and the Woden Valley. **Mount Pleasant** has memorials to the Royal Regiment of Australian Artillery and the Royal Australian Armoured Corps at its summit.

The city took on a new character in 1964 when Lake Burley Griffin was created. The shoreline totals 35 kilometres and the lake is popular for swimming, sailboarding, rowing, sailing and fishing, while ferries operating from Acton Jetty offer day and dinner cruises.

In recent years Canberra has spread outwards across the plains, with satellite towns at Belconnen, Woden, Tuggeranong, Weston Creek and Gungahlin, but the focus is still the city centre and the modern architectural development around Lake Burley Griffin.

Black Mountain, close to the city centre and the lakeshore, is topped by a telecommunications tower with public viewing galleries and a revolving restaurant. On the lower slopes of Black Mountain are the **Australian National Botanic Gardens**. They follow Walter Burley Griffin's original plan for an Australian native garden. The superb gardens have arrowed walks, which allow for varying degrees of stamina, and take visitors through areas of foliage indigenous to various Australian regions. In the rainforest area a misting system simulates rainforest conditions. The **Australian Institute of Sport** is on the edge of Black Mountain Reserve in Bruce. One of the newest features at the Institute is the interactive sports exhibition **Sportex** which provides hands-on opportunities and displays of sporting equipment and technology. Tours of Sportex, the training facilities and stadiums are conducted daily by resident athletes.

Most of Canberra's major buildings lie within a triangle that is formed by Kings, Commonwealth and Constitution avenues, with **Capital Hill** at the apex and the central business district on the northern corner. On Capital Hill is the **new Parliament House**, topped by its massive flagpole. A grassed walkway forms the roof of Parliament House and provides visitors with splendid views of Canberra. In front is the **old Parliament House**, open to the public.

On the southern foreshore of Lake Burley Griffin is the **National Gallery of Australia**, which houses an outstanding collection of both modern and

Statue of Simpson and his donkey at the Australian War Memorial

A.C.T.

CANBERRA ON FOOT

The following are some of the walks around Canberra.

- **National Trust self-guide walks: 1.** A 3-kilometre circuit through the heritage suburb of Reid. **2.** Around Lake Burley Griffin.

- **Umbrella Walking Tours:** depart twice daily from the Foundation Stone and twice daily from the flagpoles at Parliament House, for a guided 90-minute walking tour around the heart of Canberra; bookings essential.

Brochures are available for the self-guide walks; for these and for further information, contact Canberra Visitor Centre, Northbourne Ave, Dickson; (02) 6205 0044.

post-modern art, including a wide representation of Australian painters. In the grounds, works by Australian and international sculptors are placed in a landscape setting. In this Sculpture Garden the gallery's restaurant is in a 'misty oasis', an artificial fog sculpture created by the Japanese artist Fujiko Nakaya. A footbridge connects the National Gallery and the **High Court of Australia**, the nation's final court of appeal. The court's lofty public gallery is encircled by open ramps that lead off to the courts, and it features Jan Senbergs' murals reflecting the history, functions and operations of the High Court.

Further along the foreshore is the **National Library of Australia**, which contains more than 5 million books, as well as newspapers, periodicals, films, historical documents and photographs. The foyer features three magnificent tapestries woven from Australian wool in Aubusson, France, and superb stained-glass windows, the work of the Australian artist Leonard French.

Also on the foreshore of the lake between the National Library and the High Court is **Questacon – The National Science and Technology Centre** in King Edward Terrace. The Centre features hands-on science displays where simple do-it-yourself experiments and explanations make the understanding of everyday scientific principles easy. Adults and children alike are enthralled for hours by the hundreds of exhibits in the five galleries (Waves, Microcosm, Forces, Visions, and 0011-OTC). Further south of the lake is the **Canberra Railway Museum**, which has Australia's oldest working steam locomotive (built in 1878), as well as four other engines and 40 carriages.

Lake Burley Griffin is the centrepiece of Canberra. On the lake are three places of interest: the **Carillon** on Aspen Island, a three-column belltower that was a gift from the British Government to mark Canberra's Jubilee; the **Captain Cook Memorial**, a 150-metre water jet and terrestrial globe on the foreshore; and the **National Capital Exhibition** at Regatta Point, which has a pavilion with exhibits showing Canberra's development.

The lake is surrounded by parklands, most with picnic facilities. One of the largest is **Commonwealth Park** on the northern foreshore, with its wading pools and cherry-tree grove. Another lakeside park is **Weston Park**, which

Australian Institute of Sport, first-class facilities for the nation's elite athletes

features superb conifer trees, a maze, a miniature train and a playground for able and disabled children. Cycling is popular in Canberra; there are more than 280 kilometres of cycle paths, and it is possible to cycle around the lake. Bikes can be hired near the ferry terminal. Sightseeing cruises of the lake are available. Paddle-boats, windsurfers and sailing boats also can be hired. Hot-air ballooning is popular throughout the year, and during the **Canberra Festival** in March a fleet of balloons takes off each morning.

Although the **National Museum of Australia** (which will include the Gallery of Aboriginal Australia) is still in the planning stage, its Yarramundi Visitor Centre off Lady Denman Drive on the shores of the lake features objects from the museum's extensive collections, a viewing platform and a theatrette. The old Parliament House also features museum items. The **National Aquarium and Australian Wildlife Sanctuary**, further along Lady Denman Drive near Scrivener Dam, has over 60 display tanks containing marine and freshwater fish. It also has koalas, kangaroos, dingos and little (fairy) penguins.

Anzac Parade stretches from the northern side of the lake to the **Australian War Memorial** and is one of Australia's most frequently visited attractions. The War Memorial houses a huge collection of relics, models and paintings from all theatres of war. Its cloisters, pool of reflection, hall of memory and many galleries of war relics provide an unforgettable experience. It is also the site of the Tomb of the Unknown Soldier.

An interesting walk to the summit of **Mount Ainslie** starts from the picnic grounds behind the War Memorial.

Another distinctive landmark in Canberra is the **Academy of Science**, in Gordon Street, Acton. Its copper-covered dome rests on arches set in a circular pool. Nearby, the **National Film and Sound Archive** in McCoy Circuit displays movie memorabilia and has public screenings from its collection of historic films, radio and television programs. Also at Acton is the **Australian National University**, set in 145 hectares of landscaped gardens.

Diplomatic missions bring an international flavour to the city's architecture. It is well worth driving around the suburb of Yarralumla to see

Cockington Green, a popular attraction just out of Canberra

the many high-commission and embassy buildings. The official residence of Australia's Governor-General is on Dunrossil Drive at Yarralumla. In Deakin, on the corner of Adelaide Avenue and National Circuit, is the **Prime Minister's Lodge**, the official residence of the Australian Prime Minister. The **Royal Australian Mint** in Denison Street, Deakin, has plate-glass windows in its visitors' gallery, allowing excellent views of the coin-making process.

Despite the gleaming modern style of the city of Canberra, there are still interesting vestiges of the old Limestone Plains settlement. In Campbell the sandstone homestead of the **Duntroon estate**, now the Officer's Mess at Duntroon Royal Military College, is the finest old house in the ACT. The single-storey part of the house was built in 1833 and the two-storey extension was completed in 1856. Guided tours of the **Australian**

Defence Force Academy and the **Royal Military College** are available. Nearby is the **Australian-American Memorial** which celebrates America's contribution to Australia's defence during World War II.

The **Church of St John the Baptist** off Anzac Park dates back to 1841 and its tombstones and other memorials provide a record of much of the area's early history. The adjacent schoolhouse containing relics of this history is regularly open to visitors. Many of the stained-glass windows of St John's Church commemorate members of the pioneer families, including Robert Campbell, the founder of Duntroon estate. **Blundell's farmhouse** on the northern shore of the lake was built in 1858 by Campbell for his ploughman, and has been furnished by the Canberra and District Historical Society with pieces contemporary to the district's early history. **Calthorpes House**, in

Mugga Way, Red Hill, is a 1920s family home that has survived almost unchanged providing a fascinating glimpse of the life-style of those times.

The **central business district** of Canberra surrounds London Circuit at the end of Commonwealth Avenue. **Civic Centre** is the major retail area. At the head of the **Civic Square** is the **Canberra Theatre Centre** and nearby in Petrie Plaza is the old St Kilda merry-go-round, a favourite with children. The **Canberra Casino** is off Binara Street in Glebe Park. For touring the city's attractions, the **Canberra Explorer** bus service runs every hour, 7 days a week, around a 25-kilometre route with 19 stops. Leave the bus any time and reboard, or take the full-hour tour.

Each Saturday and Sunday at the Gorman House Arts Centre, just 5 minutes walk from the city centre in Ainslie Avenue, Braddon, talented young artists and actors present exhibitions and performances, and craftspeople display their wares. The showground at Hall, a small village on the outskirts of Canberra, is covered with over 300 stalls on the first Sunday of the month, selling home produce and folk art. An old bus depot at Kingston provides an undercover market selling quality hand-crafted items each Sunday. **Exhibition Park**, on the corner of the Federal Highway and Flemington Road at Mitchell, is the venue for many of Canberra's major events.

Around Canberra too there are many attractions. **Cockington Green** on the Barton Highway, 9 kilometres north of the city, is a miniature English village (named after Cockington in Devon, UK). Adjacent is the historic village of **Ginninderra**, featuring craft studios, an art gallery, shops and a restaurant. **Federation Square**, a shopping area nearby, features a number of craft and specialty shops, and children's play areas. Directly opposite Ginninderra on the Barton Highway is the 300-exhibit **National Dinosaur Museum**, between Gold Creek Road and Northbourne Avenue.

The **Bywong Mining Town** at Geary's Gap NSW (off the Gundaroo Road), is a re-creation of the mining settlement that prospered in the late 1800s. Tourists can see working machinery and enjoy panning for gold. Bywong is open daily. Special programs as well as guided tours are available.

A.C.T.

Blundell's farmhouse, an historic building in the heart of Canberra

At the **Tidbinbilla Nature Reserve**, a 40-minute drive south-west of the city, an area of more than 5500 hectares has been developed to enable visitors to see kangaroos and koalas in a bushland setting. There are good picnic and barbecue facilities at the reserve. Nearby is the **Corin Forest Recreation Area**, with a 1-kilometre alpine slide,

bushwalking and skiing in winter. Another favourite spot is the **Cotter Dam** and Reserve, 22 km west of the city, where there are pleasant picnic and camping areas, a restaurant, river swimming and a children's playground. Nearby is the **Mount Stromlo Observatory**, its large silver domes and buildings housing the huge telescope of

the Department of Astronomy of the Australian National University. Located further south at Tidbinbilla is the **Canberra Deep Space Communications Complex**, a deep-space tracking station, featuring spacecraft models and audiovisual presentations. It is operated by the Department of Science for the US National Aeronautics and Space Administration.

The historic homestead **Lanyon**, 30 kilometres south of the city, enjoys the National Trust's highest classification. Set in landscaped gardens and picturesque parklands on the banks of the Murrumbidgee River, Lanyon serves as a reminder of nineteenth-century rural living. There is a collection of Sidney Nolan paintings housed in the Nolan Gallery on the property. Further south and also on the Murrumbidgee River is the historic **Cuppacumbalong** homestead with its cottages, outbuildings, private cemetery, craft centre, restaurant, picnic areas and river swimming.

For further information on Canberra and the ACT, contact the Canberra Visitor Centre, Northbourne Ave, Dickson; (02) 6205 0044; freecall, 1800 026156.

Wining and Dining

Canberra is the Australian base for diplomatic missions from all over the world, and this has resulted in a wide variety of restaurants. Eating out can be a cosmopolitan 'feast' in the national capital. The city has approximately 300 restaurants specialising in modern Australian cuisine and a host of traditional ethnic styles including Asian, Mediterranean, Turkish and Russian.

Good wine is the natural accompaniment to a good meal – the Canberra district has 16 wineries producing a range of fine cool-climate wines.

Wines were first produced in the area in the 1860s, but the burgeoning of boutique wineries in the region has only occurred in recent decades. The wineries are clustered around the townships of Hall and Murrumbateman to the north of Canberra, and Bungendore to the east. The wineries are almost exclusively small,

Fine, cool climate wines are produced at local wineries

family-owned enterprises, where you can chat to the winemaker when you make your purchase at the cellar door; check first for

opening times. For further information contact Canberra Visitor Centre, Northbourne Ave, Dickson; (02) 6205 0044; freecall, 1800 026166.

TOURS from Canberra

More than 50 per cent of the city of Canberra is national park and nature reserve. Canberra is unique in that bushland is an easy drive from the city centre. A longer leisurely drive takes the visitor to the heart of the Snowy Mountains in the south or to the picturesque coastal resorts in the east.

Bungendore and Braidwood

35 km and 90 km from Canberra via the Kings Highway

This popular route passes Lake George, which mysteriously empties periodically. At Bungendore, the Village Square features an historic re-creation from the 1850s telling the story of a local bushranger. The entire township of Braidwood has been classified by the National Trust. Antique and art and craft shops, museums and restaurants are found in many of the town's lovely old sandstone buildings.

Batemans Bay

150 km from Canberra via the Kings Highway

This popular resort is at the mouth of the Clyde River. Of particular interest are the penguins and other birds at Tollgate Island Wildlife Reserve. In the area are many picturesque coastal resorts and the old gold mining towns of Mogo and Araluen.

The Snowy Mountains

228 km from Canberra via the Monaro and Snowy Mountains highways

The Snowy Mountains, centre of the world-famous hydro-electric scheme, is an all-year-round resort and tourist area. Thredbo is the centre of activity during the ski season. Lake Eucumbene is very popular for water sports and trout fishing.

Jervis Bay

285 km from Canberra via the Kings and Princes highways

This fine natural port was the site of the Royal Australian Navy Training College, established in 1915. In that year its jurisdiction was transferred from New South Wales to the ACT, to give the federal capital sea access. Popular Aboriginal-owned Jervis Bay National Park is jointly managed by the Wreck Bay Aboriginal Community Council and the Australian Nature Conservation Agency. The area has several holiday towns ideal for swimming, fishing, boating and bushwalking.

Namadgi National Park

30 km from central Canberra via the Tuggeranong Parkway and Tharwa Drive to Tharwa

Namadgi National Park, the most northerly alpine environment in Australia, covers some 40 per cent of the ACT. The special qualities of remoteness and rugged beauty that make up a wilderness are evident in the area surrounding the park's highest point, Bimberi Peak (1911 m). The Visitor Centre on Naas Rd (2 km s of Tharwa) provides excellent information on the park and has hands-on displays and audiovisuals. Public access roads in the park pass through majestic mountain scenery. Picnic areas, some with barbecues and toilets, are sited along most roads. The pleasant bushland settings at Mt Clear and Orroral are ideal for low-key camping. Many of Namadgi's attractions lie beyond its main roads and picnic areas. There are over 150 kilometres of marked walking tracks. Bushwalkers who venture into Namadgi's more remote parts reap some of the park's greatest rewards. Namadgi's streams attract trout anglers. Horseriding is permitted in certain areas and cross-country skiing is possible when snow conditions permit.

Batemans Bay, popular with the land-locked residents of Canberra

A. C. T.

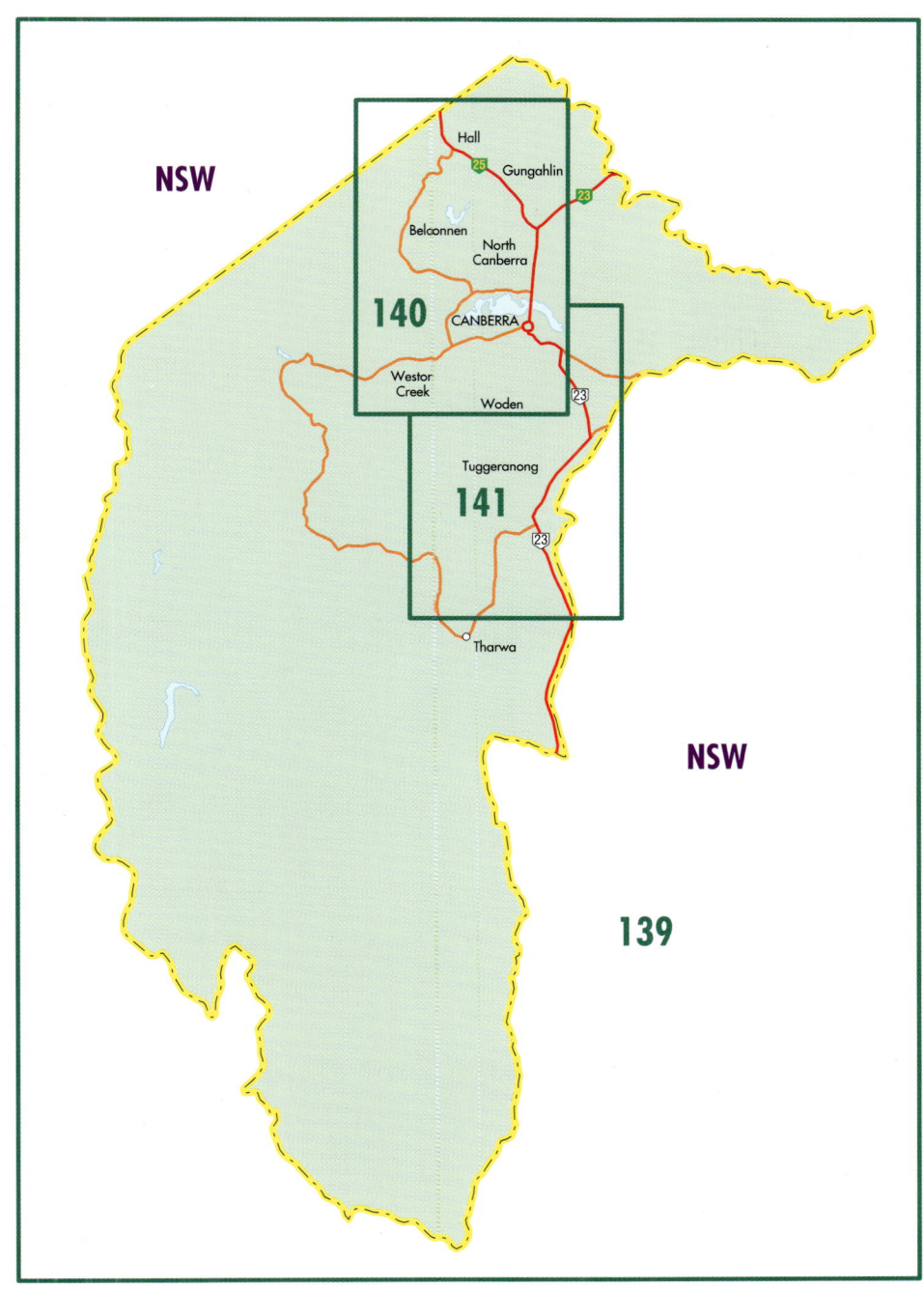

Australian Capital Territory

NSW

Hall

Gungahlin

Belconnen

North
Canberra

140

CANBERRA

Weston
Creek

Woden

141

Tuggeranong

Tharwa

NSW

139

Other Map Coverage

Central Canberra 138
Canberra Region 142

Location Map

0   0.25   0.5   0.75   1 km

Accommodation ■
Best Western Motel Monaro 1 G13
Capital Parkroyal 2 E4
Hotel Kurrajong 3 E10
Hyatt Hotel 4 C8
James Court Apartment Hotel 5 D2
Macquarie Hotel 6 E12
Rydges Canberra 7 C5
Rydges Capital Hill 8 D12

General Information ■
Ansett Australia 9 D3
Canberra Railway Station 10 H13
Coach/Bus Terminal 11 D3
General Post Office 12 D3
Motoring Organisation(NRMA) 13 D2
Qantas Travel Centre 14 D3

Accommodation Only a sample range is listed; inclusion is not necessarily a recommendation.

Places of Interest ■
Australian National University 15 B5
Australian War Memorial 16 H4
Blundell's Farmhouse 17 F7
Canberra Theatre Centre 18 D4
Captain Cook Memorial Water Jet 19 D7
Carillon 20 F8
Casino Canberra 21 E4
High Court of Australia 22 E8
Jewish Memorial Centre 23 D12
The Lodge 24 A11
National Capital Exhibition, Regatta Point 25 D6
National Film and Sound Archive 26 B4
National Gallery of Australia 27 F9
National Library of Australia 28 D8
Old Parliament House 29 D9
Parliament House 30 C11
Questacon 31 D8
Royal Canberra Yacht Club 32 B8

TO GOULBURN, YASS

Mt Ainslie Lookout

Braddon

Ainslie Public School

Ainslie Hostel

Canberra Nature Park

Acton

Fellows Oval

South Oval

CSIRO Head Office

Campbell High School

Remembrance Nature Park

Australian War Memorial 16

Reid

Reid Park

Australian National University

CANBERRA

City Hill

Casino Canberra

Glebe Park

Fairbairn AV

St Thomas More Convent

Campbell

Campbell Public School

PARKES

Footbridge

Footbridge

WAY

Commonwealth Park

Parkes WAY

West Basin

LAKE

Ferry Terminal and Boat Hire

Nerang Pool

Footbridge

Gallipoli Reach

Captain Cook Memorial Water Jet 19

Regatta Point

Springbank Island

Hospital Point

Acton Peninsula

Central Basin

BURLEY

GRIFFIN

Attunga Point

Lennox Gardens

Lotus Bay

National Library of Australia 28

High Court of Australia 22

National Gallery of Australia 27

Carillon 20 Aspen Island Footbridge

Russell

Australian American Memorial

Canberra Nature Park

Northcott

Stirling Park

Parkes

Old Parliament House 29

Kings Avenue Bridge

Bowen Place

Grevillea Park

East Basin

Molonglo River

TO CANBERRA AIRPORT

MORSHEAD DR

Yarralumla

Capital Hill

Parliament House 30

Barton

Bowen Park

Jerrabomberra

Jerrabomberra Wetlands

Adelaide AV

The Lodge 24

Forrest

Forrest Public School

Telopea Park High School

Kingston

Deakin

La Trobe Park

Manuka Oval

Collins Park

Canberra Railway Museum

Canberra

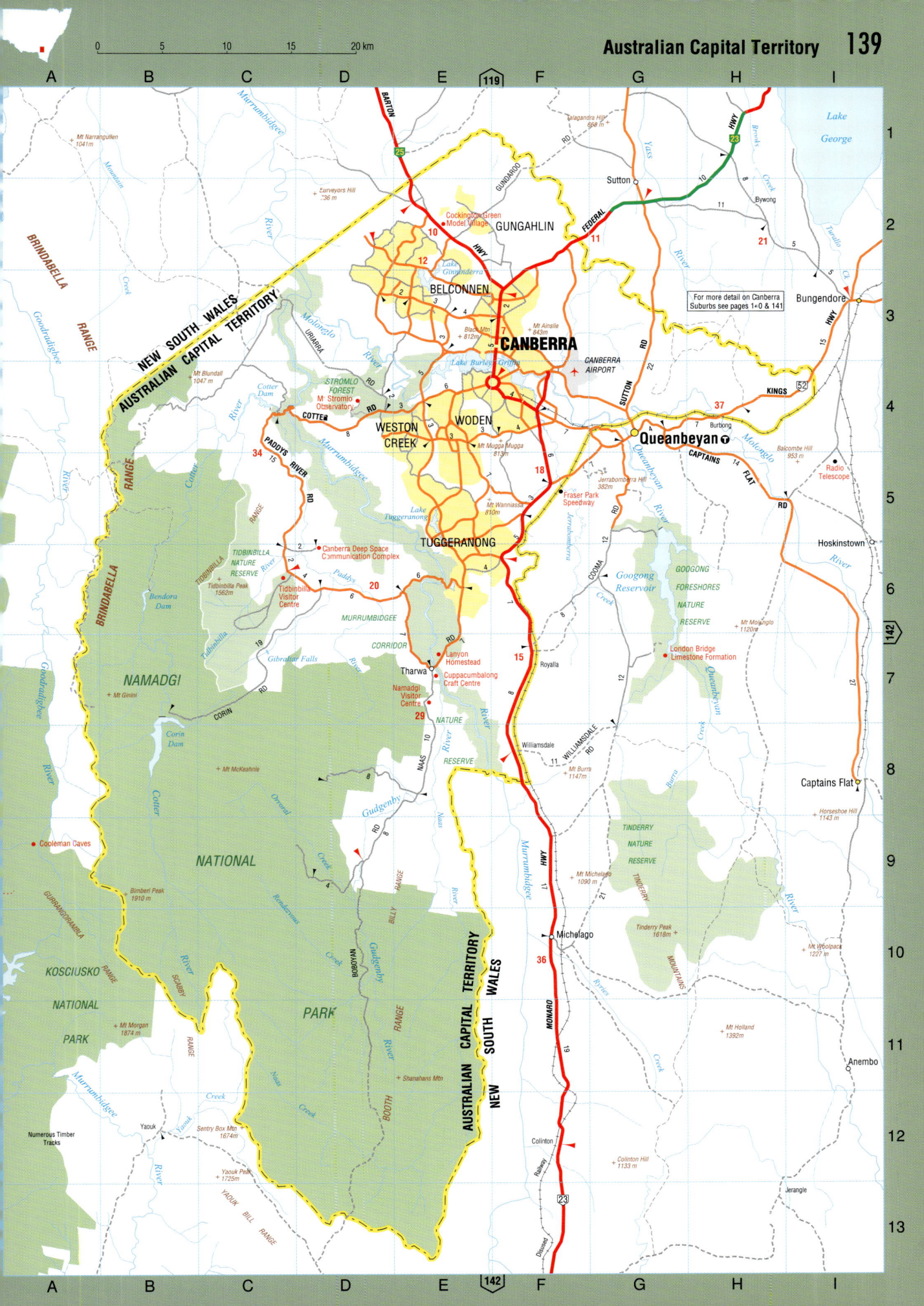

A B C D E F G H I

1
2
3
4
5
6
7
8
9
10
11
12
13

0   5   10   15   20 km

NEW SOUTH WALES

AUSTRALIAN CAPITAL TERRITORY

BARTON HWY

Mt Narrangullen 1041 m

Mt Blundall 1047 m

BRINDABELLA RANGE

Goodradigbee River

Murrumbidgee River

Molonglo River

Surveyors Hill 836 m

Cockington Green Model Village

GUNGAHLIN

GUNDAROO

Lake Ginninderra

BELCONNEN

Black Mtn 812 m

CANBERRA

Lake Burley Griffin

CANBERRA AIRPORT

Mt Ainslie 843 m

Stromlo Forest
Mt Stromlo Observatory

URIARRA

Cotter Dam

COTTER RD

PADDYS RIVER

WESTON CREEK

WODEN

Mt Mugga Mugga 813 m

Lake Tuggeranong

Mt Wanniassa 810 m

TUGGERANONG

Fraser Park Speedway

Jerrabomberra Hill 382 m

SUTTON RD

Queanbeyan

Molonglo River

CAPTAINS FLAT RD

KINGS HWY

Burbong

Balcombe Hill 953 m

Radio Telescope

Hoskinstown

Bungendore

Lake George

Sutton

FEDERAL HWY

YASS RIVER

Talagandra Hill 654 m

Bywong

Tidbinbilla Peak 1562 m

TIDBINBILLA NATURE RESERVE

Tidbinbilla Visitor Centre

Canberra Deep Space Communication Complex

Gibraltar Falls

NAMADGI

Mt Ginini

CORIN RD

Corin Dam

Mt McKeahnie

Bendora Dam

Cooleman Caves

BRINDABELLA RANGE

Goodradigbee River

MURRUMBIDGEE CORRIDOR

Lanyon Homestead

Tharwa

Cuppacumbalong Craft Centre

Namadgi Visitor Centre

NATURE RESERVE

Gudgenby

NAAS RD

Williamsdale

WILLIAMSDALE RD

Royalla

Googong Reservoir

GOOGONG FORESHORES NATURE RESERVE

London Bridge Limestone Formation

Mt Molonglo 1120 m

Queanbeyan River

Captains Flat

Horseshoe Hill 1143 m

NATIONAL

Bimberi Peak 1910 m

KOSCIUSKO RANGE

NATIONAL

PARK

Mt Morgan 1874 m

Numerous Timber Tracks

Yaouk

Yaouk Peak 1725 m

Sentry Box Mtn 1674 m

YAOUK BILL RANGE

Murrumbidgee River

Naas Creek

Shanahans Mtn

BOBOYAN RD

BOBOYAN RANGE

Gudgenby River

BILLY RANGE

BOOTH RANGE

AUSTRALIAN CAPITAL TERRITORY

NEW SOUTH WALES

Mt Burra 1147 m

MONARO HWY

Murrumbidgee River

Ryries Creek

Michelago

Mt Michelago 1090 m

TINDERRY NATURE RESERVE

Tinderry Peak 1618 m

TINDERRY MOUNTAINS

Mt Holland 1392 m

Mt Woolpack 1227 m

Anembo

Mt Colinton 1133 m

Colinton

Colinton Hill 1133 m

Railway

Jerangle

For more detail on Canberra Suburbs see pages 140 & 141

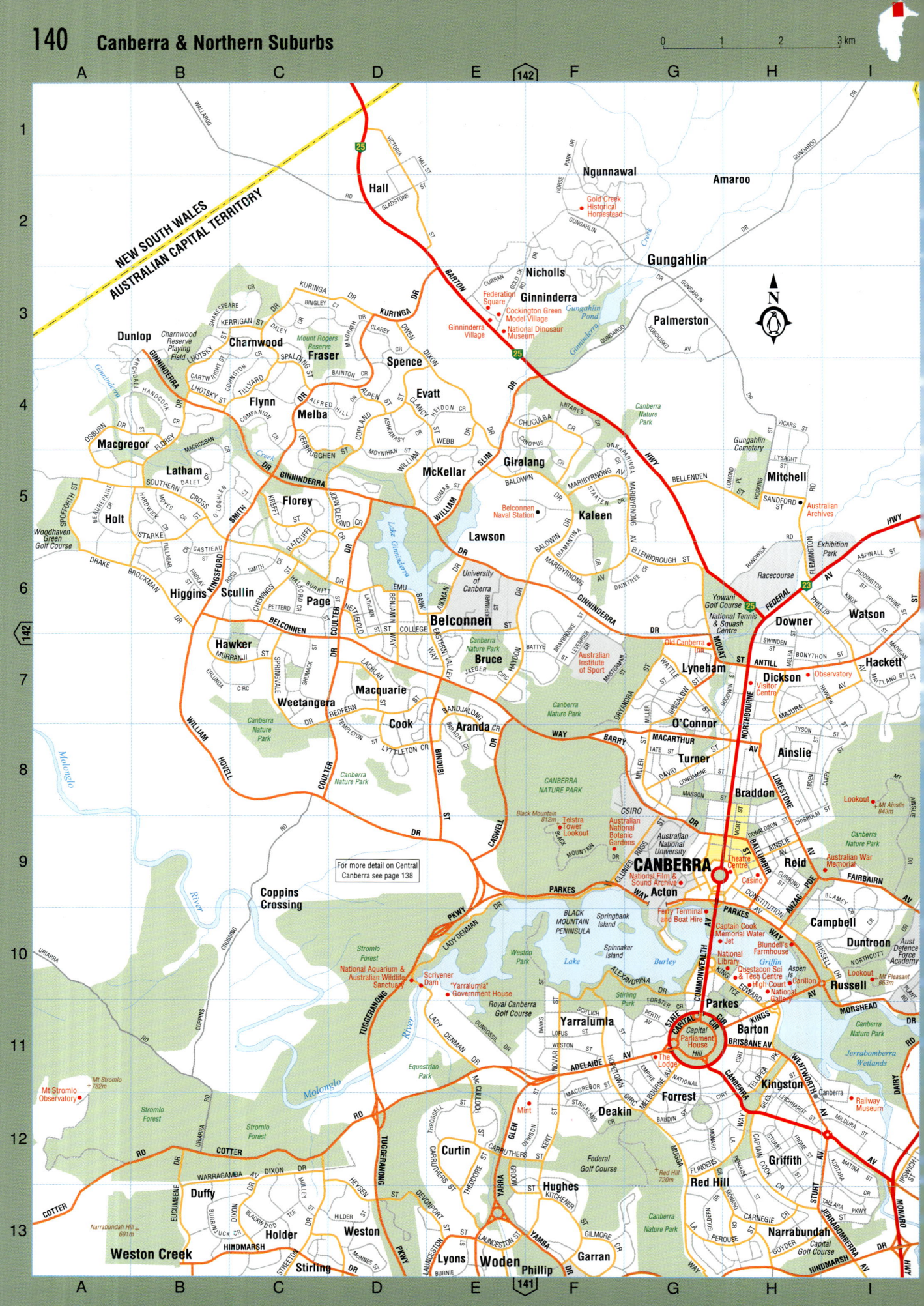

For more detail on Central
Canberra see page 138

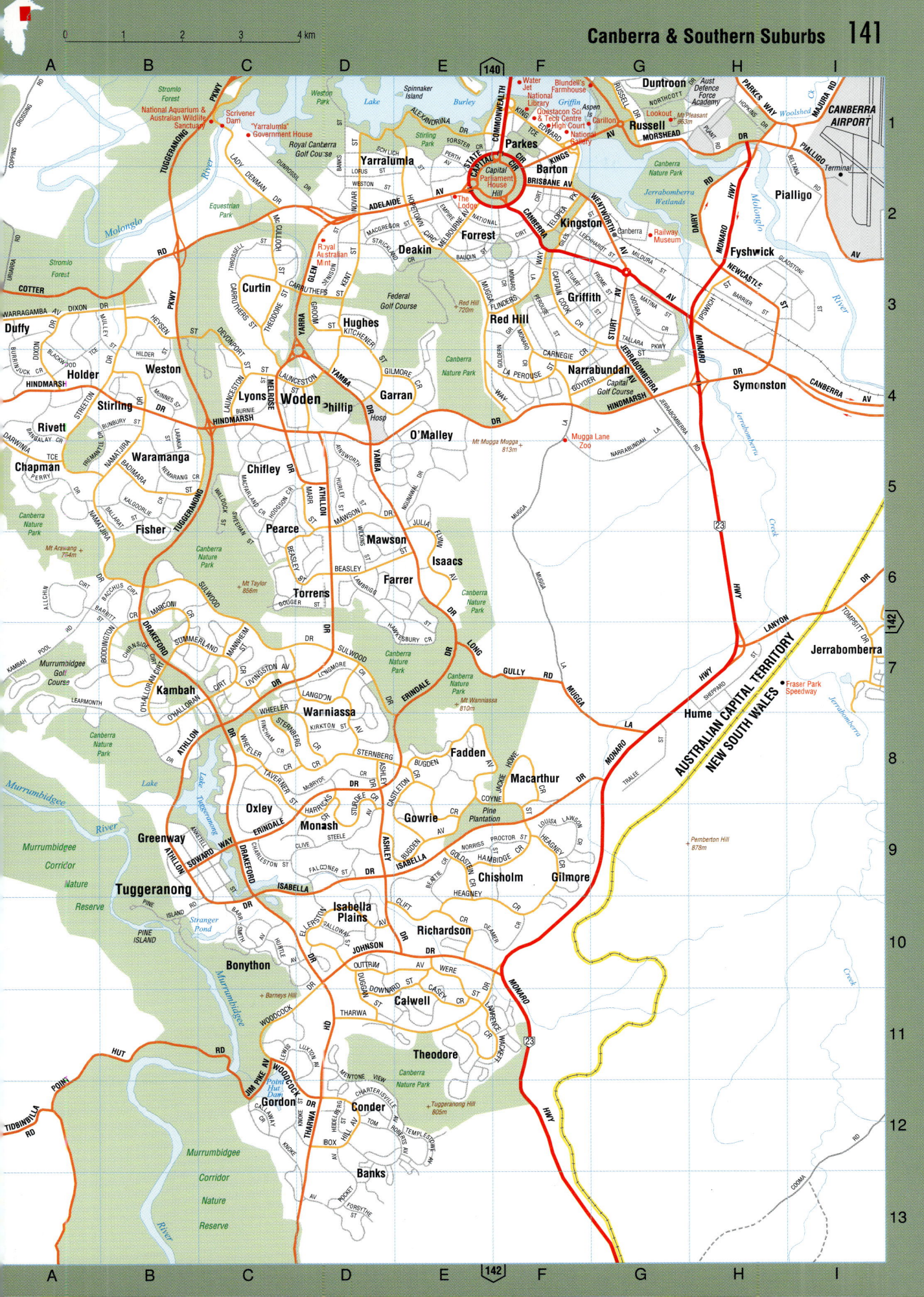

NEW SOUTH WALES

AUSTRALIAN CAPITAL TERRITORY

CANBERRA

GUNGAHLIN

BELCONNEN

WESTON CREEK

WODEN

TUGGERANONG

CANBERRA AIRPORT

Queanbeyan

Sutton

TO YASS

TO GOUL

For more detail on Australian Capital Territory see page 139

For more detail on Snowy Mountains Region see page 118

KOSCIUSKO NATIONAL PARK

NAMADGI NATIONAL PARK

BRINDABELLA RANGE

SNOWY MOUNTAINS

GREAT DIVIDING MOUNTAINS

GUBRANDERAMELA RANGE

FIERY RANGE

Brungle
Gocup
Tumorramma
Bondo
Carey's Cave
Mt Wee Jasper 1121m
Wee Jasper

Gadara
Tumut
Lacmalac
Argelong
Gilmore
Windowie
Wereboldera

Batlow
Blowering Dam Lookout
Blowering Reservoir

Pilot Hill
Talbingo
Jounama Pondage
Tumut 3 Power Station

Goobarragandra

Goobarragandra River

Yarrangobilly
Yarrangobilly Caves
Rules Point

Tantangara Reservoir

Mt Morgan 1874m

Bimberi Peak 1910m

Mt Stromlo Observatory
Cotter Dam

Tidbinbilla Peak 1562m
Tidbinbilla Visitor Centre
Canberra Deep Space Communication Complex
TIDBINBILLA NATURE RESERVE

Bendora Dam

Corin Dam

Tharwa
Namadgi Visitor Centre
Cuppacumbalong Craft Centre
Royalla
Williamsdale

Mt Burra 1147m

London Bridge Limestone Formation

GOOGONG FORESHORES NATURE RESERVE
Googong Reservoir
Mt Malonglo 1120m

Captains

TINDERRY NATURE RESERVE
Tinderry Peak 1618m

Michelago

Mt Holland 1392m

Sue City
Kiandra
Mt Selwyn Alpine Resort
Cabramurra
Tumut 2 Power Station
Tumut 1 Power Station
Tumut Pond Reservoir
Tabletop Mtn 1784m

Mt Nungar 1710m

Yaouk

Yaouk Peak 1725m

Shannons Flat

Mt Flinders 1484m

Colinton

Bredbo

Mt Dowling 1198m

Jerangle

Peak View

Round Mtn 1756m
Tooma Reservoir
Jagumba Mtn 1676m

Doubtful River

Bald Hill 1764m

Anglers Reach
Old Adaminaby
World's Largest Trout
Adaminaby

Rosedale

Long Lake
O'Neill Lagoon
Muddah Lake

Bunyan

Numeralla
Countegany

McInally Mtn 1085m

Bililingra Siding
Chakola

Mt Jagungal 2061m

Eucumbene
Braemar Bay

Buckenderra
Middlingbank
Rocky Plains
Mt Biggam 1379m

Kalkite

Cootralantra Lake
Killmacoola Lake

Cooma Llama Farm
Cooma
Mt Glorious Lookout

Arable Lake

Numeralla

Murray 1 Power Station
Scammells Spur Lookout
Olsens Lookout
Mt Tate 2068m
Guthega Power Station
Guthega Alpine Village
Smiggin Holes Alpine Village
Perisher Alpine Village
Charlotte Pass Alpine Village
Mt Kosciusko 2228m Australia's Highest Mountain
Mt Townsend 2210m
Mt Twynam 2196m

Muniang Quadripod 1646m
Mt Gungartan 2069m
Island Bend Pondage
Island Bend

Snowy Valley Lookout
Gaden Trout Hatchery

Eucumbene Trout Farm

Berridale

Rock Flat

East Jindabyne
Lake Jindabyne
Jindabyne
Lake Coolamatong
Kiah Lake

Ramshead Mtn 2177m
Thredbo Alpine Village
Dead Horse Gap

Moonbah

Snowy River Winery

Dalgety

Coonerang

TO ALBURY
TO CORRYONG
TO BEGA

WARNING: During the winter months (June to October), travellers should check prevailing conditions before departure.

MONARO HWY
SNOWY MOUNTAINS HWY
SNOWY MOUNTAINS RANGE
ALPINE WAY

TO NOWRA

Klimpton
Callala Bay
Huskisson
Tomerong
Vincentia
Wandandian
St Georges Basin
Hyams Beach
SANCTUARY POINT
JERVIS BAY TERRITORY
Jervis Bay
Sassafras
Nerriga
MORTON
NATIONAL PARK
Mt Sassafras 823m
Swan Lake
Sussex Inlet
St Georges Basin
Green Patch
Conjola
Cudmirrah
Berrara
Swanhaven
JERVIS BAY NATIONAL PARK
Bendalong
Manyana
Cunjurong Point
Lake Conjola
Narrawallee
Pointer Gap Lookout
Yatte Yattah
Mt Tianjara 768m
Mt Corang 863m
Pigeon House Mtn 719m
Milton
Mollymook
ULLADULLA
Burrill Lake
Mt Coghill 806m
Boro
Mt Fairy
Lower Boro
Corang
Charleyong
Tomboye
Nerrigan
Burrill Lake
Tabourie Lake
Termeil
ILLAWARRA
Bawley Point
MURRAMARANG ABORIGINAL RESERVE
Kioloa
Durras Lake
Pebbly Beach
East Lynne
Benandarah
Depot Beach
Durras
Long Beach
Cullendulla
Batemans Bay
Shell Museum
Batehaven
MURRAMARANG NATIONAL PARK
Surf Beach
Malua Bay
Mogo
Rosedale
Bimbimbie
Tomakin
Mossy Point
Broulee
Mogendoura
Yarragee
Gundary
Mullenderee
Moruya
Moruya Heads
Kiora
The Anchorage
Congo
DEUA NATIONAL PARK
Mt Donovan 784m
Bergalia
Meringo
Bendethera Mtn 997m
Turlinjah
Coila Lake
Tuross Head
Lake Tuross
Bodalla
Nerrigundah
Potato Point
Lake Brou
Eurobodalla
Wagonga
Mummuga Lake
Dalmeny
Kianga
BODALLA STATE FOREST
Narooma
Tilba Valley Vineyard Deer Park
Corunna Lake
Montague Island
MONTAGUE IS NATURE RESERVE
Corunna
Central Tilba Historic Village
Mt Dromedary
Tilba Tilba
Peak Alone 954m
GOURA NAT RES
Wandella
Yowrie
EUROBODALLA NATIONAL PARK
WALLAGA LAKE NP
Wallaga Lake
Cobargo
Bermagui
Bermagui South
BERMAGUEE NATURE RESERVE
TO BEGA
Quaama

GREAT DIVIDING RANGE
KINGS HWY
Butmaroo
Doughboy
Braidwood Historic Town
Mongarlowe
BUDAWANG NATIONAL PARK
Currockbilly Mtn 828m
Mt Mogood 391m
Durran Durra
Ballalaba
Majors Creek
Reidsdale
Monga
Currowan Corner Upper
Shallow Crossing
Araluen North
Araluen
Nelligen
Runnyford
Oranmeir
Kain
The Big Hole and Marble Arch
Gundillion
Togannoggera
Mt Gillamatong 907m
Mt Coghill 806m
Belowra
Wadbilliga

SOUTH PACIFIC OCEAN
SOUTH COAST

N

0 5 10 15 20 km

Victoria

Garden State

VICTORIA

Victoria is an ideal State for the motoring tourist. In one day's drive, you can explore mountain country, pastoral landscape and spectacular coastline, yet still arrive at your destination in time to watch the sunset.

Victoria's earliest explorers, of course, were from a pre-motor age. What they saw did little to arouse their enthusiasm. After an unsuccessful attempt at settlement in the Port Phillip area in 1803, it was not until 1834 that expeditions from Van Diemen's Land, searching for more arable land, settled along the south-west coast of Victoria. Their glowing reports prompted John Batman and John Fawkner to investigate the Port Phillip area and then purchase land on opposite sides of the Yarra from the local Aborigines. The Colonial Office in London expressed disapproval of these transactions, but in those times possession was nine-tenths of the law.

A squatting colony grew rapidly in the district and the new town was named Melbourne after the British Prime Minister of the day. Nervous of inheriting the penal system of settlement, Victoria sought separation from New South Wales; it was granted in 1851. At about that time, gold was discovered near Ballarat and the State's population more than doubled within a year. Apart from a serious but short-lived setback caused by land speculation in the early 1890s, Victoria has gone from strength to strength ever since.

Today Victoria is the most closely settled and industrialised part of the nation, and is responsible for about one-third of the gross national product. Melbourne has been traditionally regarded as the financial capital of the country.

Melbourne's inner areas are graced by spacious parks and street upon street of elegant and well-preserved Victorian and Edwardian architecture, contrasting strongly with modern tower blocks. It is renowned also for its retail shopping, theatres, restaurants, cultural festivals, major events and Australian Rules Football.

Beyond the city, the Dandenong Ranges, fifty kilometres to the east, are noted for their forests of eucalyptus and graceful tree ferns, their many established gardens and an increasing number of restaurants, wineries and galleries that are popular with visitors. Phillip Island, less than two hours' drive from Melbourne, is famed for its unique little (fairy) penguin parade as well as for its good surfing. To the south and south-west, the Mornington and Bellarine peninsulas provide Melbourne with its seaside playgrounds, which are extremely popular during the summer months.

The weather can be unpredictable in Victoria, particularly along the coastal regions. Despite its rather volatile weather, the State enjoys a generally temperate climate. Spring, late summer and autumn provide the most settled and pleasant touring weather. The road system is good and penetrates most areas; as a result much of the State can be reached easily in a day's driving.

Each of Victoria's five main geographical regions has its own special attraction. The central and western districts, due north and west of

NOT TO BE MISSED
in Victoria

	Map Ref.
● **Gippsland Lakes** – one of the State's most outstanding holiday areas	233 Q5
● **Great Ocean Road** – 250 kilometres of breathtaking coastal scenery	235 K11
● **Lake Eildon** – sheltered waters ideal for all water sports – and houseboats	219 P1
● **Paddlesteamer ride on the Murray River** – experience this magnificent waterway	239 O11
● **Penguin Parade at Phillip Island** – a delightful spectacle each evening at sunset	221 M13
● **Sovereign Hill** – fascinating re-creation of a goldmining township	229 N11
● **Spa towns of Daylesford and Hepburn Springs** – mineral springs, great scenery	218 E2
● **The Grampians** – beautiful scenery and wildflowers, particularly in spring	234 H2
● **Wilsons Promontory** – an impressive coastal national park	233 J11
● **Yarra Valley** – good scenery and excellent wineries	222

The Twelve Apostles, rock formations in Port Campbell National Park

Wilsons Promontory, one of the State's most spectacular national parks

properties. No exploration of this region would be complete without a drive along the aptly named Great Ocean Road, which runs for 400 kilometres along the dramatic south-west coast. The rock formations in Port Campbell National Park are without doubt its most imposing sight, but along its length there are excellent beaches and pleasant small holiday towns.

The north-east high-country region has equally magnificent scenery, historic towns including Beechworth and Chiltern, and is dotted with winter ski resorts. While also popular in spring and summer, this region would hardly ever be described as crowded, and the wildflowers, sweeping views and clear air can be enjoyed with a fair degree of solitude. Fishing, bushwalking and climbing are well provided for. Down in the foothills, the Eildon Reservoir and Fraser National Park area are good for water sports.

Gippsland stretches to the southeast; it contains some of the State's most beautiful and varied country. Rolling pastures lead to densely

Melbourne, offer highlights including the historic goldfield areas, with well-preserved, attractive towns such as Bendigo, Castlemaine and Ballarat, the popular spa towns of Daylesford and Hepburn Springs, and the Grampians, a beautiful national park, particularly noted for its spring wildflowers and native fauna. Travelling south from these impressive ranges brings you into the western district, where rich grazing land is dotted with many splendid old

CALENDAR OF EVENTS

Note: The information given here was accurate at the time of printing. However, as the timing of events held annually is subject to change and some events may extend into the following month, it is best to check with the local tourism authority or event organisers to confirm the details. The calendar is not exhaustive. Most towns and regions hold sporting competitions, arts and craft exhibitions, agricultural and flower shows, music festivals and other such events annually. Details of these events are available from tourism outlets.

JANUARY
Public holidays: New Year's Day; Australia Day.
Melbourne: Australian Open (grand slam tennis championships); Summer Live (at the Arts Centre); Marvellous Melbourne Jazz Festival. **Apollo Bay:** Beach Horse Races. **Ballarat:** Triathlon. **Blackwood:** Shindig Festival. **Cobram:** Peaches and Cream Festival (biennial, odd-numbered years).

Daylesford: Daylesford Gift (horse race). **Geelong:** Summer Festival. **Hanging Rock:** Picnic Race Meeting. **Heyfield:** Dairy Carnival. **Hoddles Creek:** Upper Yarra Draught Horse Festival. **Jeparit:** Beach Carnival. **Lakes Entrance:** Larger than Lakes Festival. **Lorne:** Pier to Pub Swim; Surf to Mountain Foot Race. **Maryborough:** Highland Gathering. **Metung:** Regatta. **Mornington Peninsula:** Wine and Food Festival. **Orbost:** Australian Wood Design Exhibition. **Portland:** Foreshore Carnival. **Portsea:** Swim Classic. **Terang:** New Year's Day Family Picnic; Australian Stockhorse Weekend. **Yarrawonga:**) Sailing Regatta.

FEBRUARY
Melbourne: Australian Masters (golf tournament); Formula 500 (motor racing); Autumn Racing Carnival; Chinese New Year Festival. **Ballarat:** Great Southern Swap Meet. **Beechworth:** Drive Back in Time (car rally). **Broadford:** Country Music Festival. **Buninyong:** Gold King Festival.

Camperdown: Leura Festival. **Cohuna:** Aquatic Festival. **Colac:** Otway Harvest Festival. **Donald:** Dead Centre Motorbike Rally. **Edenhope:** Henley-on-Lake Wallace. **Echuca:** Southern 80 Ski Race; Riverboats, Food, Jazz and Wine Festival. **Foster:** Agricultural Show. **Geelong:** Pako Multicultural Festa. **Halls Gap:** Grampians Jazz Festival. **Hamilton:** Beef Expo. **Hanging Rock:** Vintage Car Rally. **Healesville:** Coldstream Country and Western Festival; Sounds by the Water Concert (at the Maroondah Reservoir). **Korumburra:** Coal Creek Twilight Music and Theatre Festival. **Leongatha:** Cycling Carnival. **Maldon:** Camp Draft. **Portland:** Fishing Competition. **Seymour:** Alternative Farming Expo. **Shepparton:** Bush Market Day. **Traralgon:** Music in the Park. **Warrnambool:** Wunta Fiesta.

MARCH
Public holiday: Labour Day. **Melbourne:** Australian Formula One Grand Prix; Moomba Festival, including International Dragon Boat Festival; Grape Grazing (at wineries in Yarra Valley). **Apollo Bay:** Music Festival. **Ararat:** Jailhouse Rock Festival. **Bairnsdale:** Riviera Festival. **Ballan:** Arcadian Festival. **Ballarat:** Begonia Festival; Antique Fair. **Bendigo:** Madison 10 000 Cycling Race. **Casterton:** Vintage Car Rally. **Charlton:** Country Music Festival. **Colac:** Food and Wine Festival. **Corryong:** High Country Festival. **Eaglehawk:** Dahlia and Arts Festival. **Erica:** King of the Mountain Woodchop. **Geelong:** Highland Gathering. **Harrietville:** Bushman's Classic. **Healesville:** Australian Car Rally Championship; Grape Grazing. **Horsham:** Wimmera Machinery Field Days; Apex Fishing Competition. **Inverloch:** Jazz Festival. **Korumburra:** Karmai (giant worm) Festival. **Kyabram:** Rodeo. **Kyneton:** Country Music Festival. **Maffra:** Harvest Festival. **Mansfield:** Harvest Festival. **Marlay Point** (near Sale): Yacht race to Paynesville. **Merrijig:** Rodeo. **Mildura:** Great Mildura Paddleboat Race (biennial, odd numbered

years). **Moe:** Jazz Festival; Blue Rock Classic. **Mount Beauty:** Conquestathon Fun Climb. **Myrtleford:** Tobacco, Hops and Timber Festival. **Nagambie:** Goulburn Valley Vintage Festival. **Numurkah:** Art Show. **Omeo:** Picnic Races. **Port Fairy:** Folk Festival. **Portland:** Dahlia Festival. **Rutherglen:** Tastes of Rutherglen. **Sale:** Sale Cup. **Seymour:** Rafting Festival. **Sorrento:** Street Festival. **Swan Hill:** Red Gum Festival. **Thorpdale:** Potato Festival. **Warragul:** Gippsland Field Days. **Yea:** Autumn Fest.

EASTER
Public holidays: Good Friday; Easter Monday; **State-wide:** Easterbike (various locations). **Alexandra:** Art Show. **Beechworth:** Golden Horseshoes Festival. **Bendigo:** Fair (features Chinese dragon). **Buchan:** Rodeo. **Echuca:** Working Horse Fair. **Kyabram:** Antique Aeroplane Fly-in. **Lake Bolac:** Yachting Regatta. **Maffra:** Farming Festival. **Maldon:** Fair. **Mallacoota:** Festival. **Omeo:** Rodeo and Market. **Paynesville:** Gold Cup

Speedboat Championships. **Patchewollock:** Easter Sports. **Quambatook:** Australian Tractor Pull Championship. **Stawell:** Easter Gift; Grampians Highland and National Dancing Club Championships. **Torquay:** Bells Beach Surfing Classic. **Warracknabeal:** Vintage Machinery and Vehicle Rally. **Wonthaggi:** Coal Skip Fill. **Wunghnu:** Tractor Pull Festival. **Yarram:** Tarra Festival.

APRIL
Public holiday: Anzac Day. **State-wide:** Heritage Week. **Melbourne:** Comedy Festival. **Bairnsdale:** East Gippsland Agricultural Field Days. **Ballarat:** Eureka Jazz Festival. **Bendigo:** Chrysanthemum and Garden Expo; Bendigo by Bike. **Bright:** Autumn Festival. **Colac:** Country Music Festival. **Echuca:** Barmah Muster. **Emerald:** Great Train Race. **Geelong:** Heritage and Vintage Rally; Alternative Farmvision. **Inglewood:** Blue Eucalyptus Festival (biennial, even-numbered years). **Mansfield:** Balloon Festival. **Tallangatta:** Dairy Festival.

wooded hill country, still relatively unpopulated and peaceful. National parks such as Tarra-Bulga and Wilsons Promontory are all well worth visiting. The coastal region includes the Ninety Mile Beach which borders the Gippsland Lakes system – Australia's largest inland waterway – and the beautiful Croajingolong National Park, a wilderness area.

Following the course of the Murray can be an interesting way of exploring Victoria's north. The river begins as a narrow, rapidly-flowing alpine stream near Mt Kosciusko, and changes to a broad expanse near the aquatic playgrounds of Lakes Hume and Mulwala; there are many waterbird and wildlife reserves, national parks, flourishing citrus and wine-growing areas, sandy river beaches, and fascinating glimpses of life in the riverboat era at cities such as Echuca, Swan Hill and Mildura.

A good network of sealed roads means Victoria's unique diversity of attractions, both natural and constructed, are easily accessible to the motoring tourist.

CLIMATE GUIDE

MELBOURNE

	J	F	M	A	M	J	J	A	S	O	N	D
Maximum °C	26	26	24	20	17	14	13	15	17	20	22	24
Minimum °C	14	14	13	11	8	7	6	7	8	9	11	13
Rainfall mm	48	47	52	57	58	49	49	50	59	67	60	59
Raindays	8	7	9	12	14	14	15	16	15	14	12	11

LAKES ENTRANCE REGION

	J	F	M	A	M	J	J	A	S	O	N	D
Maximum °C	24	24	22	20	17	15	15	16	17	19	20	22
Minimum °C	14	15	13	11	8	6	5	6	7	9	11	13
Rainfall mm	57	35	55	61	79	65	55	57	57	61	73	74
Raindays	8	7	10	10	12	13	12	14	13	13	13	11

BENDIGO REGION

	J	F	M	A	M	J	J	A	S	O	N	D
Maximum °C	29	29	25	21	16	13	12	14	16	20	24	26
Minimum °C	14	15	13	9	7	4	3	5	6	8	11	13
Rainfall mm	34	32	36	41	55	60	56	58	54	53	38	33
Raindays	5	4	5	7	10	12	13	13	11	10	7	6

ALPINE REGION

	J	F	M	A	M	J	J	A	S	O	N	D
Maximum °C	18	19	15	10	6	3	1	3	5	9	13	15
Minimum °C	8	9	7	4	1	-2	-4	-2	-1	1	4	5
Rainfall mm	88	59	121	154	195	175	266	256	210	179	168	172
Raindays	10	7	12	12	15	16	19	19	17	15	15	14

MAY

Melbourne: Next Wave Festival (biennial, even-numbered years). **Bairnsdale:** Go-Kart Street Grand Prix. **Beechworth:** Harvest Festival. **Bendigo:** View Street Jazz Festival. **Casterton:** Polocrosse Championships. **Chiltern:** Antique Fair. **Cobram:** Rotary Art Show. **Daylesford:** Hepburn Swiss-Italian Festival. **Halls Gap:** Grampians Gourmet Weekend. **Kalorama:** Chestnut Festival. **Lake Goldsmith** (near Beaufort): Steam Rally. **Warrnambool:** Southern right whales due at Logans Beach; Racing Carnival.

JUNE

Public holiday: Queen's birthday. **Melbourne:** Melbourne International Film Festival. **Ballarat:** Open Fire Festival. **Cobram:** Antique Fair. **Donald:** Scottish Dancing Weekend. **Echuca:** Steam, Horse and Vintage Car Rally. **Geelong:** Wool Week; Celtic Festival. **Mornington:** Queen's Birthday Wine Weekend. **Murtoa:** Murtoa Cup. **Omeo:** Back to Back. **Rutherglen:** Winery Walkabout Weekend.

JULY

Melbourne: Le Boite Festival (choral singing). **Bright:** Winter Wonderland Festival. **Camperdown:** One Act Play Festival. **Daylesford:** Mid-winter Festival. **Hamilton:** Eisteddfod. **Omeo:** Winter Classic. **Swan Hill:** Italian Festa. **Warburton:** Winterfest.

AUGUST

Ballarat: Royal South Street Eisteddfod opens. **Casterton:** Woodturning Demonstration Exhibition. **Falls Creek:** International Ski Marathon Kangaroo Hoppet. **Hamilton:** Sheepvention. **Harrietville:** International Ski Marathon Kangaroo Hoppet. **Mount Beauty:** Kangaroo Hoppet Festival. **Olinda:** Rhododendron Festival. **Speed:** Mallee Machinery Field Days. **Wodonga:** Wine and Food Festival.

SEPTEMBER

State-wide: Opening of Australia's Open Garden Scheme. **Melbourne:** Australian Football League and Association Finals; Royal Melbourne Show; Tesselaar's Tulip Festival

(at Silvan). **Anglesea:** Angair Wildflower Festival. **Bacchus Marsh:** Pioneer Day Festival. **Chiltern:** Art Show. **Cowes:** Motor Racing. **Halls Gap:** Wildflower Exhibition. **Horsham:** Agricultural Show. **Kyneton:** Daffodil and Arts Festival. **Leongatha:** Daffodil and Floral Festival. **Maryborough:** Golden Wattle Festival. **Nhill:** Wildflower Exhibition (at Little Desert Lodge). **Wedderburn:** Wool Expo; Historic Engine Exhibition. **Yarrawonga:** Ice Breaker Yacht Regatta.

OCTOBER

Melbourne: Oktoberfest; Spring Racing Carnival, including Caulfield Cup; International Festival of the Arts; Fringe Arts Festival; Lygon Street Festival. **Ararat:** Golden Gateway Festival. **Avoca:** Wool and Wine Festival, includes Avoca Cup (horse race). **Ballarat:** Royal South Street Eisteddfod ends. **Bendigo:** Orchid Club Spring Show. **Bright:** Alpine Spring Festival. **Buchan:** Art and Craft Festival. **Charlton:** Art Show. **Cobram:** Sun Country Dolls, Bears and Collectables Show.

Colac: Garden Expo. **Cowes:** Grand Prix Motorcycle Race; Superbike Championships. **Creswick:** Brackenbury Classic Fun Run. **Dimboola:** Agricultural Show. **Euroa:** Wool Week; Agricultural Show. **Geelong:** Show; Racing Carnival. **Heathcote:** Golden Grape Festival. **Hopetoun:** Agricultural Show. **Horsham:** Spring Garden Festival. **Little Desert:** Wildflower Exhibition (near Nhill). **Maldon:** Vintage Car Hill Climb. **Mallacoota:** Round Robin Cup. **Metung:** Garden and Small Farm Fair. **Moe:** Moe Cup. **Myrtleford:** International Festival (biennial, even-numbered years). **Port Fairy:** Spring Music Festival. **Pyramid Hill:** Pioneer Machinery Display. **Rainbow:** Iris Festival. **Tallangatta:** Arts Festival. **Wangaratta:** Agricultural Show. **Warrnambool:** Melbourne –Warrnambool Cycling Classic. **Woodend:** Macedon Ranges 'Budburst' Wine Festival (at nearby wineries).

NOVEMBER

Public holiday: Melbourne Cup Day (Vic metro. only).

Melbourne: Spring Racing Carnival, including Melbourne Cup and Oaks Day. **Ballarat:** Springfest Extravaganza; Ballarat Cup. **Beechworth:** Celtic Festival. **Benalla:** Rose Festival; Agricultural Show. **Bendigo:** National Swap Meet; Racing Carnival. **Casterton:** Street-car Drag Racing. **Castlemaine:** Spring Garden Festival (biennial, odd-numbered years); State Festival (biennial, even-numbered years); **Clunes:** Agricultural Show. **Daylesford:** Agricultural Show. **Dimboola:** Rowing Regatta. **Dunkeld:** Dunkeld Cup. **Harrow:** National Bush Billycart Championship. **Healesville:** Gateway Festival. **Kyneton:** Kyneton Cup. **Lakes Entrance:** Recfish Fishing Expo. **Maldon:** Folk Festival. **Mansfield:** Mountain Country Festival. **Maryborough:** Energy Breakthrough. **Marysville:** Wirreanda Festival. **Mornington:** Tea Tree Festival. **Mornington Peninsula:** Peninsula Wine and Music Gala. **Nagambie:** Shiraz Challenge. **Ouyen:** Farmers Festival. **Port Albert:** Regatta.

Portland: Antique Fair; Pioneer Week. **Sale:** Agricultural Show. **Shepparton:** Strawberry Festival. **Skipton:** Art Show. **Wandin:** Cherry Festival. **Wangaratta:** Festival of Jazz and Blues. **Wodonga:** World Cup Show Jumping. **Yarragon:** Dairy Fest. **Yarram:** Seabank Fishing Contest.

DECEMBER

Public holidays: Christmas Day; Boxing Day. **Melbourne:** Finish of Great Victorian Bike Ride. **Apollo Bay:** Aquathon. **Bendigo:** Tram Spectacula. **Broadford:** Hells Angels Concert. **Corryong:** Folk Music Festival (in Nariel Valley). **Daylesford:** Highland Gathering. **Dunkeld:** Festival. **Eildon:** Christmas Eve Gala Night. **Gisborne:** Festival. **Horsham:** Kannamaroo Festival. **Lakes Entrance:** New Year's Eve fireworks. **Lancefield:** Horse Festival. **Nagambie:** Rowing Regatta. **Port Fairy:** Moyneyana Festival. **Nariel Valley:** Folk Music Festival. **Portland:** Surfboat Marathon. **Woodend:** Five Mile Creek Festival.

MELBOURNE

Most Livable City

The banks of the Yarra River, a peaceful retreat for city dwellers

At first glance, Melbourne may look like any other modern city with its skyline crammed with concrete and glass. However, if you look a little closer you'll find the real Melbourne: clanging trams, swanky boutiques, friendly taxi drivers, Australian Rules football, fickle weather and BYOs (restaurants to which you bring your own liquor) by the hundred. Add to this Melbourne's traditional virtues of tree-lined boulevards, magnificent public gardens, elegant buildings and imposing Victorian churches and banks – and the Melbourne Cricket Ground – and you'll have some idea of the city.

In recent years, Melbourne has become a polyglot society with a huge influx of migrants from many countries, particularly from Asia and Greece; it has one of the largest Greek-speaking populations in the world. This cosmopolitan influence is reflected in Melbourne's bustling markets, delicatessens and restaurants. Eating out has become one of the great Melbourne pastimes, and the numerous city and suburban restaurants provide an opportunity to sample a tempting variety of food cultures.

Situated at the head of Port Phillip and centred on the north bank of the Yarra River, Melbourne has a population of over three million. Suburbs stretch in all directions, particularly around the east coast of the bay and out to the Dandenongs, a picturesque mountain range east of Melbourne.

Both John Batman and John Pascoe Fawkner were associated in the founding of Melbourne in 1835, and Melbourne soon entered a boom period with the discovery of gold in the State in 1851. The goldfields of Bendigo, Ballarat and Castlemaine attracted fortune-hunters from all over the world, and by 1861 Melbourne had become Australia's largest city. By the end of the century it was firmly established as the business and cultural centre of the colony.

Today Melbourne's position as a financial and cultural centre of the nation is shared with Sydney, but it has an elegance and style all its own. Melbourne has been the only Australian capital to retain its network of electric trams. The once familiar clang of the old green thunderers is heard less often, although some of these have been given a new lease of life; most have been replaced by new trams and the light rail. The World Health Organisation has rated Melbourne as one of the least polluted cities of its size in the world; Melbourne has also been acclaimed the world's most livable city by the internationally renowned Population Crises Centre, based in Washington D.C., USA.

Melbourne has a huge range of retail stores, and one of its highlights is the shopping in the city area, at **Southgate** across the Yarra, and in such suburbs as fashionable **South Yarra**. Several other

VICTORIA

NOT TO BE MISSED

in Melbourne

	Map Ref.
● **Colonial Tramcar restaurant** – dine and see the sights at the same time	212 F11
● **Healesville Sanctuary** – excellent collection of native fauna	219 N5
● **National Gallery** – known for its excellent Australian collection	212 F10
● **Puffing Billy** – see the beautiful Dandenongs by taking a steam-train ride	216 F13
● **Queen Victoria Market** – always bustling and noisy – and fun	212 B4
● **Rialto Towers Observation Deck** – for stunning 360° views of the city	212 B9
● **Royal Botanic Gardens** – considered among the best in the world	212 H13
● **Scienceworks** – award-winning science and technology museum	214 I9
● **Southgate** – wine, dine or shop beside the Yarra River	212 E9
● **Williamstown** – take a ferry to this fascinating former maritime village	214 I11

suburbs such as **Carlton, Camberwell, Prahran, Armadale** and **Toorak** rival the city centre with their up-market retail stores and restaurants.

Melburnians are also great sports lovers and this is reflected in the huge crowds that attend cricket and Australian Rules football matches. A peculiarly Melbourne phenomenon is the football fever that grips the city each year, with enthusiasm building up to mass hysteria on Grand Final day in late September.

The **Melbourne Cricket Ground** is the venue for many sporting and entertainment fixtures. Located just outside the Members' entrance, the **Australian Gallery of Sport** celebrates Australian sporting history. The **Olympic Museum**, located in the Gallery of Sport, houses memorabilia dating back to the first modern Olympics, held in Olympia in 1896. The **Melbourne Cricket Club Museum**, featuring members' exhibits, is located in the Members Pavilion.

Horseracing is another popular Melbourne spectator sport and the **Melbourne Cup** at **Flemington Racecourse** brings Australia to a halt for three minutes on the first Tuesday of each November. Melbourne's other main racecourses are at Caulfield, Moonee Valley and Sandown Park; the **Victorian Racing Museum** is at Caulfield Racecourse. The city's 3½ week **Spring Racing Carnival** runs from early October to early November. **Moomba** in March, the **Comedy Festival** in April and the **Melbourne International Festival of the Arts** in October are other outstanding events on the Melbourne calendar.

The **Melbourne Park Tennis Centre** hosts the **Australian Open**, one of the world's four grand slam events, in January each year. The Centre Court with its unique retractable roof can accommodate 16 000 people, and is used also as a venue for a variety of entertainment extravaganzas.

The new **Crown Entertainment Complex** alongside the Yarra River near the Spencer Street Bridge houses the Crown Casino and Hotel. Across Spencer Street is the **Exhibition Centre** which is the venue for major trade exhibitions. Nearby, the *Polly Woodside*, a square-rigged commercial sailing ship built in 1885, is moored (off Lorimer St) and is the focal point of the **Melbourne Maritime Museum**. Across the river is the **World Congress Centre**, on the

The Southgate riverside development

corner of Flinders and Spencer streets. Next door are the **Centra on the Yarra** hotel and the **World Trade Centre** which hosts international trade displays.

Further along Flinders Street past the Banana Alley Vaults is the **Flinders Street Station** complex, the main terminus for the suburban rail system. The **Underground Rail Loop** located on the edge of the central business district has three stations. Above ground, the distinctive burgundy-and-cream **City Circle tram**, which is free, offers a daily 10-minute service (between 10 a.m. and 6 p.m.) around the central city area. The circuit, along Flinders, Spring and Nicholson streets, Victoria Parade and La Trobe and Spencer streets, takes 30

minutes. The **City Explorer** tourist bus departs from outside the Victorian Visitors Information Centre, corner of Little Collins and Swanston streets, regularly between 9.30 a.m. and 4 p.m., and stops at the major attractions.

To get a different view of Melbourne, take a river cruise on the Yarra; cruise boats depart from the **Princes Walk Terminal**, near Princes Bridge. The Yarra Yarra Water Taxi service is available from Southgate, on the opposite bank of the river (bookings required). The exciting Southgate development includes several restaurants, wine bars, a licensed food court, outdoor eating areas, shops and the **Sheraton Towers Southgate** hotel.

ACCOMMODATION

HOTELS

Grand Hyatt
123 Collins St, Melbourne
(03) 9657 1234

Le Meridien at Rialto
495 Collins St, Melbourne
(03) 9620 9111

Novotel on Collins
270 Collins St, Melbourne
(03) 9650 5800

Rockman's Regency
Cnr Exhibition and Lonsdale sts,
Melbourne
(03) 9662 3900

Sheraton Towers Southgate
1 Brown St, Southbank
(03) 9696 3100

The Hotel Como
630 Chapel St, South Yarra
(03) 9824 0400

Hotel Sofitel
25 Collins St, Melbourne
(03) 9653 0000

The Windsor
103 Spring St, Melbourne
(03) 9633 6000

FAMILY AND BUDGET

City Limits Motel
20 Little Bourke St, Melbourne
(03) 9662 2544

Lygon Lodge
220 Lygon St, Carlton
(03) 9663 6633

The Hotel Y
489 Elizabeth St, Melbourne
(03) 9329 5188

The Victoria Vista Hotel
215 Little Collins St, Melbourne
(03) 9653 0441

MOTEL GROUPS: BOOKINGS

Best Western 1800 22 2166

Flag 13 2400

Travelodge 1300 363300

This list is for information only; inclusion is not necessarily a recommendation.

Parks and Gardens

The beautiful Queen Victoria Gardens, located on the banks of the Yarra River

Melbourne is a city that has grown to become a place of dignity and beauty, designed as it was with wide, tree-shaded streets and magnificent public gardens. The feeling for greenery and open space has been maintained by individual residents, many of whom take great pride in their gardens, whether they be planted with exotic species or with Australian native trees and shrubs.

The jewel of Victoria is the **Royal Botanic Gardens**, situated beside the Yarra River. There are 36 hectares of plantations, flower-beds, lawns and ornamental lakes, so superbly laid out and cared for that they are considered to be among the best in the world.

The site was selected in 1845 but the main work on their development was carried out by Baron Ferdinand von Mueller, who was appointed Government Botanist in 1852. He was succeeded

by W. R. Guilfoyle, a landscape artist, who further remodelled and expanded the gardens. The gardens are now a favourite place for people on Sundays. Families flock to picnic, feed the waterbirds on the lakes, or take a pleasant stroll.

Adjoining the gardens and flanking St Kilda Road is another large area of parkland, the **Kings Domain**, comprising 43 hectares of tree-shaded lawns and containing the Shrine of Remembrance, La Trobe's Cottage, which was the first Government House, and the Sidney Myer Music Bowl, an unconventional aluminium and steel structure that creates a perfect amphitheatre for outdoor concerts in the summer months, and is converted into an ice-skating rink during winter. This vast garden area is completed by the adjoining **Alexandra** and **Queen Victoria gardens**, a further 52 hectares of parkland.

The city's first public gardens were the **Flagstaff Gardens** at William Street, West Melbourne. A monument in the gardens bears a plaque describing how the site was used as a signalling station to inform settlers of the arrival and departure of ships at Williamstown. On the other side of the city in East Melbourne are the **Treasury** and **Fitzroy gardens** near the State government offices. In the Fitzroy Gardens is the explorer Captain Cook's cottage, which was transported in 1934 from the village of Great Ayton, Yorkshire, where Cook was born, and which was re-erected to commemorate Melbourne's centenary. Also in these gardens is a model Tudor village, laid out near an ancient tree trunk carved with tiny figures by the late Ola Cohn and known as the fairy tree. Another garden close to the city is the **Carlton Gardens**, in which the domed

Exhibition Building is situated. It was erected for the Great Exhibition of 1880, and was for 27 years the meeting-place of the Victorian Parliament; Federal Parliament met in the State Parliament buildings while awaiting the building of the nation's capital at Canberra.

Melbourne also has large recreational areas around the city and throughout the urban region.

Albert Park Lake, located in the suburb of Albert Park, is a constructed lake comprising the remnants of an original swamp. Today the lake is used for sailing and rowing. The surrounding parkland and buildings, on 218 hectares, cater for a variety of outdoor and indoor sports, and is the venue for the annual Australian Formula One Grand Prix, a choice which led to protests over its impact on the parkland. The park is open to visitors outside restrictions for Grand Prix preparations and activities.

Fawkner Park, between St Kilda Road and Punt Road just south-east of the city, offers a refuge within cultured nature in the nineteenth-century tradition, with orderly avenues, playing ovals and lawns. It is extremely popular for social sports, with many games taking place on Sundays between families and friends.

Brimbank Park (and Horseshoe Bend Children's Farm) at Keilor is a showcase of native grasslands, plains and redgums on the Maribyrnong River. There are walks, and activities include birdwatching, kiteflying and picnicking. It is also significant for its geological and archaeological history. Horseshoe Bend Children's Farm is open every third Sunday of the month.

The Museum of Modern Art at Heide, in Templestowe Road, Bulleen, is a special combination of art and garden. Heide was the home of John and Sunday Reed, who in the 1930s and 1940s were patrons of Sidney Nolan, Arthur Boyd, Charles Blackman, Albert Tucker, Joy Hester and other important Australian painters. The 5.8 hectare property was bought by the State Government in the 1980s and developed into a public park and art gallery. It features both exotic species, including a beautiful kitchen garden still planted and tended, and natives, all in a setting on a bend in the Yarra River. There are also sculptures spread throughout the park and the original gallery, which was built in 1968 by the Reeds as a gallery-home.

Jells Park at Wheelers Hill is one of the most popular parks in Melbourne attracting more than a million visitors a year. At 127 hectares there is an 11.5 hectare lake with waterbirds feeding and nesting, and open areas and tracks for walking, jogging, rollerblading or bikeriding. Birdwatching is popular at the park and there are facilities for picnics and barbecues.

Yarra Bend Park, which incorporates Studley Park boathouse at Fairfield, is the last refuge of bushland in inner-city Melbourne and on the Yarra River. Yarra Bend Park is a large, scattered nature reserve which takes in the Studley Park boathouse, the junction of Merri Creek and the Yarra River, which was an important meeting site for indigenous clans, and Dights Falls. There is a multi-purpose recreation area, two golf courses – the Yarra Bend Golf Course, regarded as the State's best public golf course, and the nine-hole Studley Park Golf Course – and picnic facilities.

For more detailed information on Melbourne's parks and gardens, and on various garden festivals and displays, contact the Victorian Visitor Information Centre, Melbourne Town Hall, cnr Little Collins and Swanston sts, Melbourne; (03) 9658 9949. **See also:** National Parks.

Studley Park boathouse in Yarra Bend Park

The city centre is compact, its wide streets laid out in a grid system. Take a tram to the top of **Collins Street** and wander back down – the street somehow epitomises Melbourne.

Looking down on Collins Street, in Spring Street, is the elegant **Old Treasury Building**, built in 1853, now refurbished and open as a museum featuring the **Melbourne Exhibition** which explores Melbourne's fine architecture and colourful social history. Just down from Spring Street is the august **Melbourne Club**, mecca to Melbourne's Establishment. On the opposite side of the street on the Exhibition Street corner is **Collins Place**, an impressive multi-storey complex that houses the **Hotel Sofitel** in one of its high towers. Described as 'the city within the city', this complex has many shops and boutiques open all weekend.

Continuing down the hill you will see fashionable boutiques and two old churches, the **Uniting Church** and **Scots Church**. Across the road the **Grand Hyatt** hotel complex has an interesting food hall and shopping plaza at street level. Just down the hill is the graceful porticoed **Baptist Church**, built in 1845, and further down are Melbourne's imposing **Town Hall**, used for receptions and concerts, and Melbourne's

grandest Gothic Cathedral, **St Paul's** Cathedral in Swanston Walk. The **City Square,** located on the corner of Collins Street and Swanston Walk, is being constructed. The historic, refurbished **Regent Theatre** is situated nearby in Collins Street.

Further down Collins Street are two large shopping complexes, **Australia-on-Collins** and **Sportsgirl.** Nearby is the elegant **Block Arcade** with its mosaic floor, glass and iron-lace roof and stylish shops. The small lane at the back of this arcade (Block Place) leads through to Little Collins Street and to another gracious old arcade. This is the **Royal Arcade** where, every hour, the huge statues of mythical figures, Gog and Magog, strike the hour. This arcade leads through to the **Bourke Street Mall,** between Elizabeth and Swanston streets. Several department stores and fashion chains, including **Myer,** Australia's largest department store, and **David Jones,** front on to the mall. David Jones has another store on the opposite side and its food hall is worth a visit to see the beautifully presented displays. Nearby, the shopping complex **Centrepoint** is a handy place to browse under shelter or to stop for a snack in one of its many coffee bars. You can sit and watch city buskers from the seats that are

provided in the mall, but when crossing the mall be aware of the trams – the only traffic, apart from delivery and emergency vehicles, allowed in this block. The **Half-Tix** booth in the mall offers the opportunity to purchase theatre tickets for the day's performances at reduced prices. There is also a **tourist information booth** in the mall; half-day, guided, shopping and sightseeing tram tours, which utilise the regular tram service, depart from here; bookings are essential.

A combination of bookshops and bistros occupies the uppermost block of **Bourke Street.** The coffee bar at **Pellegrini's** is a great favourite. On the Spring Street corner is one of the last of Melbourne's grand old hotels, the elegant **Windsor** (1883), which looks over the peaceful **Treasury Gardens.** Proudly surveying the city from its location on Spring Street is the classical-style **State Parliament House.** The Corinthian style of the Legislative Council Chamber is a legacy of Melbourne's golden era. **St Patrick's Cathedral** with its massive blocks of bluestone can be seen from the elegant gardens that surround Parliament House. Melbourne's gracious and beautifully restored **Princess Theatre**, is also in Spring Street.

Gordon Place, at the top of Little Bourke Street, is a unique building designed by the colonial architect William Pitt in 1883. The building is now an attractive tourist apartment complex.

If you like Chinese food, do not miss Melbourne's **Chinatown** in Little Bourke Street, between Spring and Swanston streets. Dozens of fascinating restaurants, grocery shops and mixed stores date back to Melbourne's post-gold-rush days, when it became the city's Chinese quarter. The standard of the restaurants is good, and prices vary from fairly cheap to very expensive. Among the outstanding eating-houses are the Bamboo House, the Flower Drum and the Mask of China. Located in the heart of Chinatown at Cohen Place, the **Museum of Chinese Australian History** is worth a visit.

Just half a block away in Lonsdale Street is the huge retail complex **Melbourne Central** which features a 20-storey, glass cone enclosing a historic shot tower. Melbourne Central and the department store **Daimaru** together occupy most of the block bounded by Lonsdale, Swanston, La Trobe and Elizabeth streets and are well serviced by

---

MELBOURNE ON FOOT

The following is a selection of walking tours available.

- **Art & About:** Guided walks highlighting cultural side of city; bookings essential; charge applies.

- **Booklovers Walk:** Guided walk includes the State Library and various bookshops; bookings essential; charge applies.

- **Chinatown Heritage Walk:** Guided walk includes Museum of Chinese Australian History.

- **Chocolate Indulgence:** Guided walk around major chocolate outlets; bookings essential; charge applies.

- **Melbourne Heritage Walks:** 6 self-guide walks providing an insight into the city's history and architecture.

- **Murder and Mystery Tour:** Guided night tour examining some of the murders and unsolved mysteries around Melbourne; bookings essential; charge applies.

- **Queen Victoria Market Foodies Tour:** Guided tour of this famous market; bookings essential; charge applies.

- **Royal Botanic Gardens:** Guided walk, free of charge.

- **Walking Melbourne:** Various self-guide walks prepared by the National Trust; booklet available.

For further information, contact the Victorian Visitor Information Centre, Melbourne Town Hall, cnr Little Collins and Swanston sts, Melbourne; (03) 9658 9949.

VICTORIA

Museum station on the underground rail loop. There is a direct walk-through access between Melbourne Central and the Myer department store. Further east along Lonsdale Street, Greek music cafés and flaky pastry shops make Melbourne a mini-Athens.

The **Museum of Victoria** located in Swanston Street has many interesting exhibits, including a large collection of Australiana, natural history, the legendary racehorse Phar Lap and the **Children's Museum**, a first in Australia. This imposing old building also houses the **Planetarium** (where slides are projected on the ceiling); the magnificent domed **State Library** and the **La Trobe Library**. Further east along La Trobe Street is the **National Philatelic Centre**.

A block away, in Russell Street, is the grim **Old Melbourne Gaol** and **Penal Museum** with its chillingly macabre exhibits, including the gallows where folk-hero and bushranger Ned Kelly swung. The gaol's atmosphere becomes even more dramatic and enthralling during the after-dark tours which incorporate live theatre.

More cheerful sights such as clothing, souvenirs, plants, cheeses, sausages and decoratively arranged vegetables can be seen at Melbourne's bustling **Queen Victoria Market**, bounded by Peel, Victoria and Elizabeth streets, and open Tuesdays, Thursdays, Fridays, Saturdays and Sundays. Guided tours of the market are available. Alongside in Victoria Street are cafes and covered outdoor-eating areas. From here it is only a short stroll to the beautiful **Flagstaff Gardens**, once used as a pioneer graveyard and later as a signalling station. Today this is a pleasant place for the whole family to relax, with shady old trees, a children's playground, tennis courts and barbecues. Facing the park in King Street you can see **St James' Old Cathedral**, built in 1839.

The lower part of the city is the sedate legal and financial sector. Back towards the city centre along William Street are the former **Royal Mint** and the **Supreme Court** and **Law Courts**, which were built between 1877 and 1884. At the bottom end of Collins Street is the luxury hotel **Le Meridien at Rialto**. The elaborate Rialto building and its neighbours, erected between 1889 and 1893, have been retained as a facade to this towering hotel and office complex, the tallest building in the

The dome at Melbourne Central, built to protect the shot tower

southern hemisphere. An **observation deck** on level 55 provides 360-degree views of Melbourne from internal and external viewing areas. As well, RialtoVision, a 20-minute film of major Melbourne and Victorian tourist attractions, screens here every half-hour.

In contrast, two of Melbourne's finest city parks, the old **Treasury Gardens** and the beautiful **Fitzroy Gardens**, lie on the eastern boundary of the central city grid. The John F. Kennedy Memorial is located beside the lake in the Treasury Gardens. The Fitzroy Gardens have superb avenues of huge English elms planted along gently contoured lawns, giving them a serene beauty all year round. Attractions within the gardens include **Captain Cook's Cottage**, the intricately carved **Fairy Tree**, a model Tudor village, a restaurant and kiosk, and a children's playground.

The **Carlton Gardens**, located north-east of the city, flank the **Exhibition Building** – a grandiose domed hall originally built for the Great Exhibition in 1880 and still used for trade fairs. The southern side of the gardens has an ornamental pond and ornate fountain while the northern section has an adventure playground and a mini-traffic circuit that is popular with junior cyclists. This area is currently being redeveloped for the new Museum of Victoria, due for completion in the year 2000.

The **Victorian Arts Centre** is just over Princes Bridge on St Kilda Road,

south of the central business area, and comprises the **National Gallery of Victoria**, the **Melbourne Concert Hall**, three theatres, other performance spaces, several gallery areas, and a variety of restaurants and bars. The National Gallery features a fine collection of Australian and overseas masterpieces. The intricate stained-glass ceiling of the Great Hall was designed by Australian artist Leonard French. The Concert Hall is used for classical music and large concerts. It also contains the **Performing Arts Museum**, which offers a programme of regularly changing exhibitions covering the whole spectrum of the performing arts. The theatres include the **State Theatre** for opera, ballet and large musicals, the **Playhouse** for drama and the **George Fairfax Studio** for experimental theatre. Not far away at the **Malthouse**, 117 Sturt Street, South Melbourne, the Playbox Theatre Company has two theatres.

The **Kings Domain**, across St Kilda Road, is a huge stretch of shady parkland where you will see: the **Myer Music Bowl**, used in the summer months as the venue for outdoor concerts and in the winter months as an ice-skating rink; the tower of **Government House** (open to the public on the third Sunday in October); the majestic, pyramid-style **Shrine of Remembrance**, which dominates St Kilda Road; the **Old Observatory** in Birdwood Avenue and, just past this, **La Trobe's Cottage**, Victoria's first

Rippon Lea, a National Trust property at Elsternwick

VICTORIA

Government House. This quaint cottage with many original furnishings – a reminder of Melbourne's humble beginnings – was brought out from England by the first Governor (La Trobe) in prefabricated sections. It is now a National Trust property, furnished in the original style with many of La Trobe's personal belongings. The main entrance to the **Royal Botanic Gardens** is nearby. With lush, landscaped gardens and gently sloping lawns, attractively grouped trees and shrubs, shady ferneries and ornamental lakes, the gardens are a peaceful retreat for city dwellers. Many of the majestic old oaks in the western end of the garden are over 100 years old. The tearooms, open daily, offer morning and afternoon teas, and lunch. Guided walks operate at 11 a.m. and 2 p.m. daily (not Mondays and Saturdays) departing from the Visitor Centre; there is no charge.

If you walk through the gardens you will come to shady **Alexandra Avenue**, which runs beside the Yarra River. Barbecues are dotted along the Yarra's grassy banks and are good for a family picnic. At weekends, you can hire bicycles and ride the scenic **Yarra River Cycle Path**.

Nearby **Albert Park**, just south of St Kilda Road, is another good place for families – and sports enthusiasts. There are barbecues on the edge of the lake and boats are available for hire. You can jog or cycle around the lake, play golf on the adjoining public golf course or swim at the **Melbourne Sports and Aquatic Centre**, the nation's largest integrated sport and leisure facility. This park is the venue for the annual Australian Formula One Grand Prix car race.

Albert Park and its neighbouring suburbs, **South Melbourne** and **Port Melbourne**, are popular places with their trendy restaurants, bookshops, pubs and markets leading down to Melbourne's bayside beaches. The beachfront is ideal for a bayside stroll; the more energetic can hire a bike, a sailboard or a pair of rollerblades and join the local crowd. In Coventry Street, South Melbourne are three portable houses, assembled in the 1850s, of the kind popular in Victoria during the goldrush era. The **Chinese Temple of See Yup Society**, a nineteenth-century Chinese temple, still a place of worship, is in Clarendon Street.

In cosmopolitan **St Kilda** are **Luna Park** and the enormous **Palais Theatre**, relics of the days when St Kilda was Melbourne's leading seaside playground. In **Fitzroy Street** the grand old hotels in the street have been restored and their ground floors opened as stylish cafes, bistros, art cinemas and restaurants. St Kilda is worth a visit, particularly on Sundays, when a collection of art and craft stalls appears on the **Esplanade**, and **Acland Street** offers bookshops, restaurants and luscious continental cakes. For a delightful fish meal, visit The Pavilion restaurant or take-away on Jacka Boulevard. The Stokehouse restaurant on the foreshore and the kiosk at the end of St Kilda Pier, are also popular eating places. The **Jewish Museum** is in nearby Alma Road.

Located just outside St Kilda at 192 Hotham Street, Elsternwick, is **Rippon Lea**, a National Trust property, that is open daily. This huge Romanesque mansion is well-known for its beautiful English-style landscaped gardens and strutting peacocks.

Two of Melbourne's wealthiest suburbs are **South Yarra** and **Toorak**. **Como**, another magnificent National Trust mansion, is in Como Avenue, off Toorak Road. Set in pleasant gardens, which once spread down to the river, Como, with its charming balconies, is a perfect example of nineteenth-century colonial grandeur.

Although many of Toorak's and South Yarra's grand old estates have been subdivided, there is no shortage of imposing gates and high walls screening huge mansions. You could easily spend the best part of a day strolling down **Toorak Road**. With its boutiques, expensive restaurants and gourmet food shops – this is a place to see and be seen.

Another of Melbourne's great shopping streets, **Chapel Street**, crosses Toorak Road in South Yarra. Here yet more fashion boutiques, and antique and jewellery shops abound, but the air is not quite so rarefied, nor are the price tags quite as high. The **Jam Factory**, a huge refurbished redbrick factory has shops and a multi-screen cinema complex. Further on towards Malvern Road, Chapel Street becomes more cosmopolitan and the emphasis shifts from fashion to food. The **Prahran Market** is around the corner in Commercial Road. This market springs to life on Tuesdays, Thursdays, Fridays and Saturdays. Catch a tram down nearby **High**

Street to Armadale and you will come to Melbourne's antique area. As well as antique shops, art and craft galleries, and designer-clothes shops stretch along High Street for several blocks.

Melbourne's city centre has been revitalised by Sunday trading and the popularity of the various shopping complexes. Once-depressed inner suburbs north of the Yarra have also been recharged with life. Theatres, theatre restaurants, antique shops, trendy fashion boutiques and dozens of cafes and restaurants have bloomed in the suburbs of **Carlton**, **North Fitzroy** and **Richmond**. Most of the elegant iron-lace terrace houses in the more fashionable inner suburbs have been lovingly restored, but these areas still have a lively mixture of migrants and Australian old-timers. Carlton has one of the largest concentrations of beautiful Victorian houses in Melbourne. Its shady wide streets and squares of restored terraces can make you forget you are within walking distance of a modern city.

Lygon Street, known locally as 'little Italy', is lined with Italian restaurants, delicatessens, bookshops, boutiques and 'arty' shops. Have lunch and take in the Carlton scene at Jimmy Watson's, Melbourne's oldest wine bar, at 333 Lygon Street.

Carlton is also the site of **Melbourne University**; located in the University grounds – a mixture of original ivy-clad buildings and modern blocks – are the **Grainger Museum** and the **University Gallery**. Nearby is **Parkville**, another little pocket of gracious Victorian terraces and shady streets. And at the **Melbourne Zoo**, just across nearby **Royal Park**, you can see a magnificent collection of butterflies in the walk-through Butterfly House, families of lions at play from the safety of a 'people cage', an enclosed bridge that takes you right through the lions' large, natural-looking enclosure and other interesting animal enclosures. These innovations are typical of the zoo's policy of making enclosures for animals as large and as natural as possible, with a minimum of bars. There is also an amusement park, bistro and kiosk.

Melbourne's old metropolitan meat market at 42 Courtney Street, North Melbourne has been converted to a large craft gallery and workshop complex. The **Meat Market Craft Centre** features changing exhibitions, as well as demonstrations and sales of a range of high-quality crafts including woodwork. For more information on craft shops and galleries, contact Craft Victoria on (03) 9417 3111.

Another old inner suburb worth exploring is **Fitzroy**, which is similar in character to Carlton. Raffish **Brunswick Street**, Fitzroy, has an interesting mixture of cafes, bookshops, clothes boutiques, nurseries, pubs and first-class BYOs. The **Mary MacKillop Centre** is at 11 Brunswick Street, and features various exhibits relating to her life. In the suburb of **Fairfield**, a few kilometres east of Fitzroy, are the **Fairfield Park Boathouse and Tea Gardens**, with rowing skiffs and canoes for hire.

East Melbourne, another notable area with beautiful terrace houses, has such 'grand old ladies' as **Clarendon Terrace** (in Clarendon Street) with its graceful, colonnaded central portico, and **Tasma Terrace** in Parliament Place, which now houses the National Trust Preservation Bookshop. The **Fire Services Museum of Victoria** is at 48 Gisborne Street, East Melbourne.

Swan Street, Richmond has one of the best selections of Greek restaurants in Melbourne. Most are quite cheap and unpretentious with excellent food enhanced by a lively atmosphere. **Victoria Street**, the Vietnamese heartland of the city, is crammed with restaurants, grocery shops and mixed stores. Restored Victorian shops in **Bridge Road** house both boutiques and bargain 'seconds' outlets. As well as Bridge Road, factory outlets and seconds shops can be found in Swan Street and Church Street, making Richmond the bargain shopping district of Melbourne.

It is possible in Melbourne to dine and see the sights at the same time. The **Colonial Tramcar restaurant** is a restaurant aboard a 1927 tram, thus allowing patrons to enjoy a meal in elegant style while travelling through Melbourne and some of its suburbs. This has proved so popular that three old-style trams are now in use. Another novel way to wine and dine is aboard **The Showboat**, a cruising restaurant, which leaves from North Wharf, West Melbourne.

South-west of the city is Melbourne's oldest suburb **Williamstown**, founded in the 1830s. This fascinating former maritime village has many quaint old seafront pubs, churches, cottages and relics of its days as an important seaport. Because it was shielded from modern development until the completion of the West Gate Bridge to the city centre, Williamstown retains a strong seafaring character. At weekends you can see over HMAS *Castlemaine* – a World War II minesweeper restored by the Maritime Trust – and picnic along the grassy foreshore. You can also see model ships, early costumes and relics at the Williamstown **Historical Museum** located in Electra Street and look over a superb exhibition of old steam locomotives at the **Railway Museum** in Champion Road, North Williamstown. Bay cruises are available, stopping at the bayside suburbs of Williamstown and St Kilda. The historic steam-tug *Wattle* cruises around the bay and river, except in January, when it conducts seal-colony viewing cruises from Rye pier to the Mornington Peninsula; it does not operate from June to September.

The award-winning science and technology museum, **Scienceworks**, is located alongside a former pumping station in the suburb of **Spotswood**, close to Williamstown and only a ten-minute drive from the city. Australia's first plane and car are exhibited here along with a variety of other exhibits.

Closer to the city is the **Living Museum of the West**, Australia's first eco-museum, at Pipemakers Park, Van Ness Avenue, in the suburb of **Maribyrnong**. It presents the environment and heritage of the total community, the focus being on the people of the region. Cruises on the Maribyrnong River visit some of the attractions to the west and north-west of Melbourne. At the **Craigieburn** note-printing branch of the Reserve Bank of Australia, visitors can observe the printing of Australian currency notes; ring (03) 9303 0444 for an appointment.

For more information on Melbourne there are a number of guidebooks available. The Victorian Visitor Information Centre at the Melbourne Town Hall, cnr Little Collins and Swanston sts, (03) 9658 9949, provides maps, brochures and other information. **The Met**, Melbourne's public transport system, offers an Explorers Pack consisting of three adult Met passes, a map, and a booklet of tourist attractions in and around Melbourne, and suggested day trips on public transport. Contact 131 638 or visit the Met shop in the city at 103 Elizabeth Street.

TOURS from Melbourne

The bridge at San Remo links the mainland with Phillip Island

VICTORIA

Some of Australia's most beautiful and interesting tours start from Melbourne and include historic towns and stunning scenery. Many require an overnight stop to do them justice and in such cases booking ahead is strongly recommended.

Ballarat and Sovereign Hill

110 km from Melbourne via the Western Freeway

A must for the tourist if only to visit Sovereign Hill, arguably the most authentic reconstruction of a nineteenth-century goldmining township in the world. **See:** Ballarat entry in A–Z listing; and the Golden Age.

Werribee Park

35 km from Melbourne via the Princes Highway

Just outside Werribee, an outer suburb of Melbourne, is Werribee Park, a large estate with a magnificent Italianate mansion of some sixty rooms, built in the 1870s for the Chirnside brothers, who had established a pastoral empire in the western district. Now owned by the Victorian Government, Werribee Park is open daily. There are extensive formal gardens, a restaurant and kiosk. Nearby are the Victorian State Rose Garden, an open range zoo, an equestrian centre, picnic and barbecue facilities and a golf course. Nearby Point Cook RAAF Museum (open Sun.–Fri.) has adjacent picnic and barbecue facilities; the new National Air and Space Museum is being constructed here. There is nude bathing nearby at Campbell's Cove.

Geelong, Queenscliff and Point Lonsdale

107 km from Melbourne via the Princes Highway and Bellarine Highway

Allow two days for this tour. Spend some time in Geelong, especially around the historic waterfront and at the National Wool Museum, before continuing to Queenscliff and Point Lonsdale. Stay overnight at a classic nineteenth-century hotel; try the Vue Grand, Ozone or the Queenscliff, each located in Queenscliff. **See:** Individual town entries for Geelong and Queenscliff in A–Z listing.

The Great Ocean Road and the Otway Range

140 km from Melbourne along the south-west coast
See: The Great Ocean Road.

Yarra Valley wineries

40–60 km from Melbourne via the Maroondah and Melba highways, or via Heidelberg, Greensborough and the Diamond Valley

Throughout the Yarra Valley, there are numerous vineyards and wineries, from Cottlesbridge in the north to Warburton in the south (centred on Coldstream/Yarra Glen), that produce premium reds and whites that are acclaimed world-wide. Of these, over 30 have cellar-door facilities and many are open daily. Some offer picnic facilities and several – such as Fergusson, De Bortoli, Kellybrook and Yarra Burn – have restaurants on the premises. **See also:** Wine Regions.

Healesville Sanctuary

60 km from Melbourne via the Maroondah Highway

To see all of Australia's distinctive fauna in one huge natural enclosure, take a one-day tour to Healesville Sanctuary. Many of the animals roam freely; there are 'walk-through' aviaries, excellent nocturnal displays and viewing of the extraordinary platypus at the World of the Platypus exhibit. The highlight, however, is the 'Where Eagles Fly' exhibit, for which rangers and birds of prey combine in an awe-inspiring display. The sanctuary is open daily and has a kiosk, self-service restaurant, and picnic and barbecue facilities. **See also:** Healesville entry in A–Z listing.

Warburton and the Upper Yarra Reservoir

96 km via the Maroondah and Warburton highways

This tour through some of Victoria's high country offers excellent scenic driving. Some of the Warburton-Upper Yarra Dam area may be snow-covered in mid-winter. Visit wineries in the Yarra Valley region on the way. If you visit in the warmer months, go trout fishing at Tommy Finn's Trout Farm near Warburton and picnic by the Upper Yarra Reservoir; the road on to Lake Mountain offers superb views. For a longer tour, you can return via the Acheron Way to Warburton, Yarra Junction, cross the range to Noojee, and return via Warragul and the Princes Highway. Further extend your trip and discover the local produce of the Gippsland region; Gippsland produces some of the world's great cheeses. **See also:** Warburton and Warragul entries in A–Z listing; and Yarra Valley wineries tour, above.

Healesville Sanctuary displays native fauna in a bushland setting

The Dandenong Ranges

50 km from Melbourne via the Burwood Highway

See: The Dandenongs; and Emerald and Olinda entries in A–Z listing.

Phillip Island

140 km from Melbourne via the South Eastern Freeway and the South Gippsland and Bass highways

See: Phillip Island; and Cowes entry in A–Z listing.

South Gippsland and Wilsons Promontory

230 km from Melbourne via the South Gippsland Highway

Leaving Melbourne behind, you drive through Cranbourne, Korumburra and Leongatha, and the lush, rolling hills and the spectacular countryside of South Gippsland to Foster, where you turn right towards the southernmost point on the Australian mainland at Wilsons Promontory National Park. See kangaroos and koalas, and take some short (or long) bushwalks to tiny coves and sandy beaches. This tour deserves at least two days. Return along the coast road through Inverloch, a popular seaside town and Wonthaggi, South Gippsland's largest town. **See also:** Individual town entries in A–Z listing; and entry for Wilsons Promontory National Park in National Parks.

Mornington Peninsula

100 km from Melbourne via the Nepean Highway

See: The Mornington Peninsula; and Flinders, Mornington and Sorrento entries in A–Z listing.

The Mornington Peninsula

Cliff-top walking track at Cape Schanck, the most southerly point on the peninsula

VICTORIA

This boot-shaped promontory separating Port Phillip and Western Port, is a mixture of holiday towns, varying in size and tourist development, and inland rural countryside.

The main holiday towns on the Port Phillip side of the peninsula include **Mornington**, Dromana, Rosebud, Rye, Blairgowrie, **Sorrento** and Portsea. As well as safe bayside beaches, there are excellent surf beaches, particularly along the stretch of rugged coast between Portsea and Cape Schanck at the end of the peninsula. The Mornington Peninsula National Park includes the key beaches in this area – Portsea, Sorrento, Diamond Bay, Koonya and Gunnamatta. A number of cliff-top walking tracks have been established linking Cape Schanck to Point Nepean. Swimming is considered safe only in those areas controlled by the Surf Lifesaving Association.

The Western Port side of the peninsula is less developed, much of its foreshore having remained relatively unspoiled and being still devoted to farming and grazing land. The holiday towns of Hastings, Somers, Shoreham and **Flinders** are located on this side. French Island, which is set in the centre of this bay, was a Victorian penal settlement for forty years and is now administered by the Victorian government as a State park. The island is notable for its fauna.

The Mornington and Bellarine peninsulas are linked for vehicle access by the Peninsula Searoad car and passenger ferry, which operates daily between Sorrento and Queenscliff. A passenger ferry links Sorrento, Portsea and Queenscliff in the summer season as well.

Frankston, now mainly a residential area for Melbourne commuters, could also be considered the gateway to the peninsula. It is within easy reach of good beaches on Port Phillip Bay including Daveys Bay, Canadian Bay and Mount Eliza.

The peninsula itself is well developed for tourists, with good sporting facilities and many art galleries, craft shops and restaurants. It is a burgeoning wine-producing area and many vineyards are open for tastings and cellar-door sales. On the long weekend in June, the wine producers on the peninsula organise 'all wineries under one roof' at the Regional Gallery, Dunns Road, Mornington. Other peninsula festivals include the Wine and Food Festival in January, and the Peninsula Wine and Music Gala in November. Because of the area's popularity it is advisable to book accommodation well ahead during the summer and Easter seasons. The Port Phillip Bay foreshore from Dromana to Blairgowrie is almost entirely devoted to campers and caravans during these peak seasons.

For further information on the area contact Peninsula Tourism, Nepean Hwy, Dromana; (03) 5987 3078; freecall, 1800 804009. **See also:** text entries for Flinders, Mornington and Sorrento in A–Z listing. **Map references:** 220-21.

The Dandenongs

These ranges, 50 kilometres from the centre of Melbourne, are a tourist attraction renowned for their beauty. Heavy rainfall and rich volcanic soil have created a lush vegetation with spectacular hills and gullies crowded with creepers, tree ferns and soaring mountain ash. The area is fairly closely settled and there are a number of pretty townships dotted about the hills.

It has long been a traditional summer retreat for people from Melbourne and many of the gracious old homes have now been converted into guest houses and restaurants.

The entire area is famous for its beautiful gardens and for its great variety of European trees, particularly attractive in spring and autumn. Many excellent restaurants, art and craft galleries, antique shops and well-stocked plant nurseries add to the charm of these hills, ideally placed for a relaxed day's outing from Melbourne. At 633 metres, Mount Dandenong is the highest point of the ranges, and at its summit there are excellent views, picnic facilities and a restaurant from which a magnificent night-time view of Melbourne can be seen.

Ferntree Gully National Park, Doongalla and Sherbrooke Forest are part of the 1920-hectare **Dandenong Ranges National Park,** where you can see lush trees and ferns, and a wide variety of flora and fauna. The lyrebird and eastern whipbird can be heard here. Sherbrooke Forest, on the road from Belgrave to Kallista, is unspoiled bushland with a large population of lyrebirds. A tourist road runs through the park area from Ferntree Gully to Montrose. William Ricketts Sanctuary, on Mount Dandenong Tourist Road, is a natural forest area in which Ricketts, a musician and naturalist who died in 1993, sculpted a number of Aboriginal figures and symbolic scenes in clay. Near Sherbrooke, the Alfred Nicholas Memorial Gardens, 13 hectares of a formerly private garden, are open to the public.

The Puffing Billy narrow-gauge steam train, one of the Dandenongs' most famous attractions, leaves from Belgrave and travels 14 kilometres to Emerald Lake. The Puffing Billy Steam Museum at Menzies Creek, open Saturday, Sunday and public holidays, displays some restored locomotives and rolling-stock. This small train runs several times

daily except on Christmas Day and fire-ban days. A timetable is available from the RACV, 230 Collins St, Melbourne, (03) 9650 1522; or telephone (03) 9870 8411 for recorded information. Each April, the Great Train Race is held: runners attempt to race Puffing Billy from Belgrave to Emerald Lake Park.

Emerald was the first settlement in the area and is situated on a high ridge. It has a number of interesting galleries and in the surrounding countryside there are lavender farms and attractive picnic spots. **Olinda**, a pretty township, is the location of the National Rhododendron Gardens which is even more beautiful in spring, when the annual show is held. Another spring flower festival is Tesselaar's Tulip Festival held at Tesselaar's Farm near Silvan.

For further information on the Dandenongs, contact Dandenong Ranges Tourism, 64 Monbulk Rd, Belgrave; (03) 9752 6554. **See also:** National Parks and text entries for Emerald and Olinda in A–Z listing. **Map references:** 216, 219 M7, 222 A11, 232 E4.

Alfred Nicholas Memorial Gardens, near Sherbrooke

VICTORIA from A to Z

The Great Ocean Road, near Anglesea

Alexandra
Pop. 1965

MAP REF. 219 O1, 241 J11

Alexandra is a farming and holiday centre, 24 km W of Lake Eildon. The nearby Goulburn River is one of the most important freshwater fisheries, particularly for fly-fishers, close to Melbourne. **Of interest:** Timber and Tramway Museum in former railway station, Station St. Historic buildings: National Trust-classified post office and adjacent law courts, Downey St. Also in Downey St, Alexandra Potters (closed Sun.). Nielson Glass, Bayley St (Mon.–Fri.). Rotary Park, Grant St. Monthly community market, Sept.–May; contact Tourist information for date. Easter: Art Show. Oct.: Open Gardens Weekend. **In the area:** Excellent walks at Fraser National Park, 16 km E. Bonnie Doon, 37 km NE near Lake Eildon, a good base for trail-riding, bushwalking, water sports and scenic drives. McKenzie Nature Reserve, southern edge of town, virgin bushland with abundance of winter and spring orchids. Pioneer Education Centre at Taggerty, 18 km S in the Acheron Valley; good trout fishing in nearby rivers. Cathedral Range State Park, 3 km S of Taggerty, for camping, bushwalking, rock climbing and trout fishing. **Tourist information:** 45a Grant St; (03) 5772 1100; freecall, 1800 652 298. **Accommodation:** 4 hotels, 2 motels, 8 B&B, 2 cara./camp. parks.

Anglesea
Pop. 1965

MAP REF. 218 E12, 225 C11, 235 Q9

This attractive seaside town on the Great Ocean Rd offers excellent swimming and surfing. The golf course is renowned for its tame kangaroos that graze there. **Of interest:** Melaleuca Gallery, Great Ocean Rd. Coogoorah Park, on Anglesea River, a bushland reserve with waterways, islands, boardwalks, bridges and picnic areas. Viewing platform, behind town in Coalmine Rd, overlooks open-cut, brown-coal mine and power station. Sept.: Angair Wildflower Festival. **In the area:** J.E. Loveridge Lookout, 1 km W. Point Roadknight beach, 2 km SW. Angahook-Lorne State Park, access from Anglesea or Aireys Inlet (10 km SW on Great Ocean Rd). At Aireys Inlet, lighthouse, Eagle Rock Pde. Further south, Memorial Arch, commemorating construction of Great Ocean Rd. 35-km Surf Coast Walk, from Jan Juc (south of Torquay) to Moggs Creek (south of Aireys Inlet); brochure from Tourist information. Ironbark Basin, north off Point Addis Rd, for walks, birdlife and cliff-top views of coastline. Point Addis Koori Cultural Walk, contact Tourist information for brochure. **Tourist information:** From caravan, Anglesea riverbank (Christmas–Easter, daily; winter, Fri.–Mon.). **Accommodation**: 3 motels, 1 B&B, 3 cara./camp. parks. **See also:** The Great Ocean Road.

Apollo Bay
Pop. 894

MAP REF. 223 G12, 235 N12

The Great Ocean Rd leads to this attractive coastal town, the centre of a rich dairying and fishing area, and the base for a huge fish-freezing plant. The wooded mountainous hinterland offers memorable scenery and there is excellent sea and river fishing in the area. The rugged and beautiful coastline has been the scene of many shipwrecks in the past. **Of interest:** Bass Strait Shell Museum, Noel St. Old Cable Station Museum, Great Ocean Rd. Self-guide walks, leaflet from Tourist information. Market on foreshore each Sat. Jan.: Beach Horse Races. Mar.: Music Festival. Dec.: Aquathon (swimming and running race). **In the area:** Carisbrook Falls, 14 km NE on Great Ocean Rd; nearby walking tracks to spectacular views. Grey River Scenic Reserve, 24 km NE. Marriners Lookout, 1.6 km NW, for views across Skenes Creek and Apollo Bay. Crows Nest Lookout, 5 km NW, on Tuxion Rd. Paradise Scenic Reserve in beautiful Barham River Valley, 10 km NW. Beauchamp Falls, 20 km NW; scenic walk from picnic area to falls. In Otway National Park, 13 km SW, excellent bushwalking through park to sea; scenic Elliot River and adjacent Shelly Beach; Maits Rest rainforest boardwalk; 300-yr-old National Trust-registered native beech tree. Lavers Hill, once a booming timber centre, 53 km W. Melba Gully State Park, 3 km W of Lavers Hill, features fern gullies, myrtle beech trees, also glow-worm habitat; self-guide rainforest walk available. Scenic touring roads: Turton's Track, 25 km N; and Wild Dog Rd, 3 km E. **Tourist information:** 155 Great Ocean Rd; (03) 5237 6529. **Accommodation:** 2 hotels, 20 motels, 15 B&B, 2 hostels, 6 cara./camp. parks. **See also:** The Great Ocean Road.

Ararat
Pop. 7633

MAP REF. 228 D8, 235 K2, 237 K13

The Ararat area gold boom came in 1857. It was short-lived and sheep farming became the basis of the town's economy. Today the town is the commercial centre of a prosperous farming and winegrowing region. The area also produces fine merino wool. The first vines in the district were planted by French settlers in 1863 and the town of Great Western, 16 km NW of Ararat, gave its name to some of Australia's most famous wines. **Of interest:** Beautiful bluestone buildings in Barkly St: post office, town hall, civic square and war memorial. Also in Barkly St, Ararat Art Gallery, a regional gallery specialising in wool and fibre pieces by leading artists. Chinese Gold Discovery Memorial, Lambert St. Langi Morgala Folk Museum, Queen St, displays Aboriginal weapons and artifacts. Alexandra Park and Botanical Gardens, Vincent St, features orchid glasshouse display, walk-in fernery and herb garden. J-Ward, Old Ararat Gaol, off Lowe St, (open Sun.; guided tours available), Mar.: Jailhouse Rock Festival. Oct.: Golden Gateway Festival. **In the area:** Green Hill Lake, a constructed lake 4 km E off Western Hwy, ideal for fishing and water sports. Langi Ghiran State Park, 14 km E off Western Hwy, has scenic walks and children's playground. At Buangor, 23 km SE: century-old Buangor Hotel and old Cobb & Co. changing station (c. 1860); 18 km further on, Mt Buangor State Park includes Fern Tree Waterfalls. One Tree Hill Lookout, 5 km NW, for 360° views Wineries, most open for tastings and cellar-door sales, *north-west of town*: Garden Gully Vineyard (15 km), Seppelt Great Western Winery (17 km) established in 1865 and specialising in dry red and sparkling wines (its underground cellars classified by National Trust) and Best's wines (19 km); *east of town*: Mt Langi Ghiran Wines (20 km); *south of town*: Montara Winery (3 km); *west of town*: Cathcart Ridge Winery (6 km). Cathcart, 6 km W, and, further 20 km W, Mafeking, once a bustling settlement with 10 000 people; when walking in these areas, remember to watch for deep mine shafts. **Tourist information:** Barkly St; (03) 5352 2096; freecall, 1800 657158. **Accommodation:** 5 hotels, 6 motels, 4 B&B, 2 cara./camp. parks. **See also:** Wine Regions.

Avoca   Pop. 1004

MAP REF. 228 I5, 237 M12

In the Central Highlands region, Avoca was established with the discovery of gold in the area in 1852. Located at the junction of the Sunraysia and Pyrenees hwys, the surrounding Pyrenees Range foothills offer attractive bushwalking and possible sighting of kangaroos, wallabies and koalas. **Of interest:** Early National Trust-classified bluestone buildings: old gaol, Davy St; powder magazine, Camp St; court house and one of State's earliest pharmacies still operating on original site, Lalor's (1854), in High St. Self-guide walk (or drive) available, contact Tourist information. Also in High St.: antique shops, Albion House and Somewhere in Time; and Rock and Gem Museum. Market in grounds of historic state school (1878), Barnett St; 2nd Sat. each month (not Jan.). Oct.: Wool and Wine Festival, includes Avoca Cup (horse race). **In the area:** Cemetery, northern outskirts of town, has early Chinese burial sites. At Elmhurst, 26 km SW, Oasis Crystal Gallery for local art and craft. Fishing: Avoca River, near town; Wimmera River 42 km W. Several wineries including Mt Avoca vineyard, 7 km W; Blue Pyrenees, 8 km W; Redbank Winery, Redbank, 20 km NW; Summerfield Winery, Moonambel Village, 20 km NW; Mountain Creek Vineyard and Warrenmang Vineyard, NE of Moonambel; Taltarni Wines and Dalwhinnie Wines, 5 km W of Moonambel. **Tourist information:** High St; (03) 5465 3767. **Accommodation:** 2 hotels, 2 motels, 1 B&B, 1 cara./camp. park. **See also:** Wine Regions.

Bacchus Marsh   Pop. 13 000

MAP REF. 218 G5, 229 R13, 232 A3, 235 R4

The trees of the Avenue of Honour provide an impressive entrance from the east to Bacchus Marsh, which is 49 km from Melbourne. This long-established town is in a fertile valley, once marshland, between the Werribee and Lerderderg Rivers. **Of interest:** Manor House, Manor St, home of town's founder, Captain Bacchus; privately owned. In Main St: original blacksmith's shop and cottage; court house, lockup and National Bank (all National Trust-classified); Border Inn (1850), thought to have been State's first service stop for Cobb & Co. coaches travelling to goldfields. In Gisborne Rd: Holy Trinity Anglican Church (1877); Express Building Art Gallery. Ra Ceramics and Crafts, Station St. Big Apple Tourist Orchard, Avenue of Honour. Sept.: Pioneer Day Festival. **In the area:** Lerderderg Gorge, 10 km N, for picnics, bushwalking and swimming. Long Forest Flora Reserve, 2 km NE, features bull mallee, some specimens centuries old. Merrimu Reservoir and Wombat State Forest, both about 10 km NE. Willows Historic Homestead, 14 km E at Melton. Maddingley open-cut coal mine, 3 km S. At Brisbane Ranges National Park, 16 km SW steep-sided Anakie Gorge, walking tracks and wildflowers in spring. Werribee Gorge, 10 km W. At Blackwood, 26 km NW: Mineral Springs Reserve; Garden of St Erth cemetery dating back to 1855; Shindig Festival on Australia Day Sat. (Jan.). Wineries and vineyards: St Anne's Vineyard on Western Fwy, 6 km W, has a bluestone cellar built from remains of old Ballarat gaol; Craiglee Winery and Goonawarra Vineyard, Sunbury 47 km NE; Wildwood Vineyard, Bulla, 9 km SE. **Tourist information:** Shire Offices, Main St; (03) 5367 2111. **Accommodation:** 4 hotels, 1 motel, 1 cara./camp. park. **See also:** The Golden Age.

Bairnsdale   Pop. 10 770

MAP REF. 233 P4, 242 F13

Located on the river flats of the Mitchell River, this East Gippsland trade centre and holiday town is at the junction of the Princes Hwy, the Omeo Hwy and the road east to Lakes Entrance. Its position makes Bairnsdale an excellent base for touring the region. **Of interest:** Historical Museum (1891), Macarthur St, contains items of local historical interest. St Mary's Church, Main St, features wall and ceiling murals by Italian artist Francesco Floreani. Krowathunkooloong, Aboriginal Keeping Place and Museum, Dalmahoy St, houses history, heritage and culture of East Gippsland Koories; canoe tree in Howitt Park, Princes Hwy, 4-m-long scar made around 170 years ago when bark stripped from tree to make a canoe — both included in Bataluk Cultural Trail, brochure available from Tourist information. Adjacent to post office, Port of Bairnsdale site and river walk. Self-guide heritage walks, contact Tourist information. Market at Howitt Park, Princes Hwy, 4th Sun. each month. Mar.: Riviera Festival. Apr.: East Gippsland Agricultural Field Days. May: Go-Kart Street Grand Prix. **In the area:** Mitchell River empties into Lake King at Eagle Point, where it forms the famous silt jetties which stretch 8 km into lake; view from Eagle Point Bluff. Boardwalk (closed during duck season) across part of McLeod Morass, a bird wetland habitat; southern outskirts of town, access from Macarthur St. Jolly Jumbuk Country Craft Centre, 5 km E on Princes Hwy, has woollen products

The elegant statuary pavilion in the Botanic Gardens, Ballarat

for sale. Metung, 30 km E, a picturesque fishing village on shores of Lake King. Mitchell River National Park, near Lindenow, 15 km W, features excellent bushwalking tracks and Den of Nargun, Aboriginal cultural site in gorge and part of Bataluk Cultural Trail. Scenic drive north along Omeo Hwy through Tambo River valley; stunning in spring when wattles bloom. Nicholson River Winery, 15 km E, and Golvinda Winery, 15 km W at Lindenow. **Tourist information:** 240 Main St; (03) 5152 3444. **Accommodation:** 2 hotels, 11 motels, 1 B&B, 1 hostel, 3 cara./camp. parks. **See also:** Gippsland Lakes.

Ballan   Pop. 1053

MAP REF. 218 F4, 229 Q12, 235 Q4, 240 C13
A small town on the Werribee River, noted for its mineral springs. **Of interest:** Caledonian Park, eastern edge of town, offers picnic areas and swimming. Mar.: Arcadian Festival. **In the area:** Good trout fishing in Pikes Creek Reservoir, 12 km E. **Tourist information:** Shire Offices, cnr Stead and Steiglitz sts; (03) 5366 7100. **Accommodation:** 2 hotels, 2 cara./camp. parks.

Ballarat   Pop. 64 980

MAP REF. 218 C4, 227, 229 M11, 235 O3, 240 A13
Ballarat is Victoria's largest inland city, situated in the Central Highlands. Its inner areas retain much of the charm of its gold-boom era, with many splendid original buildings still standing. Ballarat was just a small rural township in 1851, when its rich alluvial goldfields were discovered. Within two years it had a population of nearly 40 000. Australia's only civil battle occurred here in 1854, when miners refused to pay Government licence fees and fought with police and troops at the Eureka Stockade. Today Ballarat is a bustling city featuring many galleries, museums, and antique and craft shops. It has excellent recreational facilities and beautiful garden areas and parks, making it most attractive to visitors. The begonia is the city's floral emblem. **Of interest:** In Lydiard St: Fine Art Gallery, Australia's largest and oldest regional gallery, has comprehensive collection of Australian art, including works by Lindsay family; Her Majesty's Theatre (1875), oldest, intact, purpose-built theatre in Australia; Craig's Royal Hotel and George Hotel for dining and accommodation in old-world surroundings. Lake Wendouree, used for water sports, and paddle-steamer tours with commentary on history of city. At Botanic Gardens adjoining the lake area: Robert Clarke Horticultural Centre, showcase for famous begonias; Adam Lindsay Gordon Cottage; Tramway Museum, featuring vintage trams; Prime Ministers' Avenue, displaying busts of Australian prime ministers; elegant statuary pavilion nearby. Vintage Tramway, via Wendouree Pde (rides available weekends, public and school holidays). In Eureka St: award-winning Montrose Cottage (1856), first masonry cottage built on the goldfields; Eureka Museum. Eureka Exhibition, cnr Stawell and Eureka sts, has historical information on Eureka Rebellion. The Old Curiosity Shop, Queen St, for pioneer relics. In Stawell St South: Eureka Stockade Park, with life-size replica of the famous battle; self-guide Eureka Trail. Ballarat Wildlife and Reptile Park, cnr York and Fussell sts, features native animals in natural habitat. Sovereign Hill, in Main St, is a major tourist attraction; it is a world-class reconstruction of a goldmining settlement, with orientation centre and working displays, and features Blood on the Southern Cross, a night sight-and-sound spectacular re-creating the Eureka rebellion; Proctor's Wheelwright Factory, a working replica of wooden carriage-wheel production; panning for gold; re-created shops and businesses; guided lamplight tours during Begonia Festival in Mar.; barbecue facilities, kiosk, restaurant and licensed hotel; accommodation. Adjoining Sovereign Hill, Gold Museum features exhibits of gold history, large collection of gold coins and display of the uses of gold 'today and tomorrow'. Each Sun.: Sunnyside Mill Market, Mill St; Trash and Treasure Market at Showgrounds, Creswick Rd. Pleasant Street Market, 4th Sun. each month. Jan.: Triathlon. Feb.: Great Southern Swap Meet. Mar.: Begonia Festival; Antique Fair. Apr.: Eureka Jazz Festival. June: Open Fire Festival (music and visual arts). Aug.–Oct.: Royal South Street Eisteddfod. Nov.: Springfest Extravaganza; Ballarat Cup. **In the area:** On western edge of city, Avenue of Honour (22 km) and Arch of Victory, honouring those who fought in World War I. Great Southern Woolshed, 8 km E, an authentic working woolshed with demonstrations by shearers, classers and working sheep dogs. Nearby, Kryal Castle, reconstruction of a medieval castle offering family entertainment. White Swan Reservoir, 8 km NE off Daylesford Rd, attractive picnic spot with water views. Lake Burrumbeet, 22 km NW, for water sports and excellent trout fishing; scenic picnic spots on shore. At Yendon, 15 km SW, Yuulong Lavender Estate (check opening times). Well-known Yellowglen Winery, 24 km SW at Smythesdale. Berringa Mines Historic Reserve, 8 km SE of Smythesdale. At Buninyong, 13 km S: Flora and Bird Park, with raised walkway and 60 parrot aviaries; Buninyong Antiques; The Corner Store Antiques and Old Wares; Andrew Scott Furniture, handcrafted furniture made on premises; Australian Bush Inspired Paintings and Pottery; market on 1st Sun. each month; in Feb.,

Gold King Festival, celebrates early history of town. Enfield State Park, near Enfield, 16 km S of Ballarat, features 61 species of orchid and some remains of goldworkings. Mt Buninyong Lookout, 13 km SE. Lal Lal Falls (30 m) on Moorabool River, 18 km SE of city. Nearby, Lal Lal Blast Furnace, beautiful archaeological remains from 19th century. **Tourist information:** cnr Sturt and Albert sts; (03) 5332 2694. **Accommodation:** 11 hotels, 27 motels, 34 B&B, 1 hostel, 8 cara./camp. parks. **See also:** The Golden Age; Wine Regions.

Beaufort   Pop. 1171

MAP REF. 228 H9, 235 M3

This small town on the Western Hwy, midway between Ballarat and Ararat, has a gold-rush history, like so many of the other towns in this area. The discovery of gold at Fiery Creek swelled its population in the late 1850s to nearly 100 000. Today Beaufort is primarily a centre for the surrounding pastoral and agricultural district. **Of interest:** Historic court house (key available from Tourist information), Livingstone St. Turn-of-century band rotunda, Neill St. **In the area:** Mt Cole State Forest, 16 km NW via Raglan, for bushwalks, native flora and fauna, picnic and camping facilities. Lake Goldsmith, 14 km S; Steam Rally held in May. **Tourist information:** Shire Offices, 5 Lawrence St; (03) 5349 2000, cr The Cooperative Crafts, Neill St. **Accommodation:** 3 hotels, 1 motel, 1 cara./camp. park.

Beechworth   Pop. 3136

MAP REF. 241 O6, 242 A3

Once the centre of the great Ovens gold-mining region, Beechworth lies 24 km off the Ovens Hwy, between Wangaratta and Wodonga on 'The Kelly Way'. This is one of Victoria's best-preserved and most beautiful gold towns, magnificently sited in the foothills of the Alps. Its public buildings are of architectural merit and the whole town has been classified as historically important by the National Trust. The rich alluvial goldfield at Woolshed Creek was discovered by a local shepherd during the 1850s. A total of 4 121 918 ounces of gold was mined in 14 years. A story is told of Daniel Cameron, campaigning to represent the Ovens Valley community: he rode through the town at the head of a procession of miners from Woolshed, on a horse shod with golden

shoes. Sceptics claim they were merely gilded, but the tale is an indication of what Beechworth was like during the boom, when its population was 42 000 and it boasted 61 hotels and a theatre at which international celebrities performed. **Of interest:** Use of local honey-coloured granite in fine 1850s government buildings (especially in Camp and Ford sts), and in powder magazine (1860) in Gorge Rd on northern outskirts of town. Daily historic town tour from Tourist information; bookings essential. In Albert Rd: Harness and Carriage Museum, run by National Trust; Tanswell's Hotel, privately restored lacework building; Ned Kelly's cell, under Shire Offices; Beechworth Gaol (1859), still used as a prison. Former Bank of Victoria building, now Rock Cavern with gemstone collection; cnr Camp and Ford sts. In Ford St: historic former Bank of Australasia, now offering fine dining in elegant surroundings; Country Rustica and Buckland Gallery. In Camp St: Beechworth Galleries; Beechworth Bakery. In Loch St: Robert O'Hara Burke Memorial Museum, displays relics of gold rush and features 16 mini-shops depicting town's main street as it was more than 100 years ago. Bicycle hire, horseriding and maps for walking tours and gem/gold fossicking available from Tourist information. Market at Town Hall gardens, Ford St, on Easter Sat., Sat. on Queen's birthday weekend, 3rd Sat. in Sept., and 3rd Sat. in Nov. Feb.: Drive Back in Time (rally of vintage, veteran and classic vehicles). Easter: Golden Horseshoes Festival. May: Harvest Festival. Nov.: Celtic Festival. **In the area:** On northern outskirts of town: cemetery; Chinese burning towers; Chinese cemetery. Beechworth Historic Park (surrounds town): Woolshed Falls historic walk through former alluvial goldmining sites; Gorge Scenic Drive (5 km) starts north of town; gold fossicking in limited areas. Fletcher Dam, Beechworth Forest Drive, 3 km SE towards historic village of Stanley. Kelly's lookout, Woolshed Creek, about 4 km N. **Tourist information:** Rock Cavern, cnr Ford and Camp sts; (03) 5728 1374. **Accommodation:** 2 hotels, 5 motels, 11 B&B, 2 cara./camp. parks.

Benalla   Pop. 8334

MAP REF. 230 A2, 241 K7

This small city, just off the Hume Fwy, is 40 km SW of Wangaratta. During the late 1870s Benalla experienced the activities

of the notorious Kelly Gang, who were eventually captured at nearby Glenrowan in 1880. It is also the birthplace of Sir Edward ('Weary') Dunlop, and Michael J. Savage, NZ Prime Minister in the 1940s. **Of interest:** Lake Benalla, created in the Broken River, has on-shore recreation and picnic facilities, and is a haven for birds; self-guide walk around lake, contact Tourist information for brochure. In Bridge St: Botanical Gardens, with splendid rose gardens; Art Gallery, on shores of lake, features important Ledger Collection of Australian paintings. In Mair St: a 3-dimensional ceramic mural; Pots 'n' More, for paintings, pottery and craft; Costume and Pioneer Museum, has Ned Kelly's cummerbund on display. At aerodrome on northern outskirts of town: centre for Gliding Club of Victoria; hot-air ballooning and glider flights available. Market, Faukner Dr., 4th Sat. each month. Nov.: Rose Festival; Agricultural Show. **In the area:** Reef Hills Regional Park, 4 km S on Midland Hwy: 2040 ha of forest with wide variety of native flora and fauna. At Swanpool, 23 km S, 1950s-style cinema showing classic films. Pleasant day trip south-east to King Valley and spectacular Paradise Falls. Winton Motor Raceway, 10 km NE. **Tourist information:** Pots 'n' More, 14 Mair St; (03) 5762 1749. **Accommodation:** 5 hotels, 8 motels, 3 B&B, 1 cara./camp. park.

Bendigo   Pop. 57 427

MAP REF. 226, 229 Q2, 237 Q9, 240 C3

This is one of Victoria's most famous goldmining cities. Sited at the junction of five highways, it is central for trips to many other gold towns nearby. The gold rush began here in 1851 and gold production continued for 100 years. The affluence of the period can still be seen today in many splendid public and commercial buildings. **Of interest:** Shamrock Hotel (1897), cnr Pall Mall and Williamson St, Bendigo's famous landmark. Sacred Heart Cathedral, largest outside Melbourne, Wattle St. Alexandra Fountain at Charing Cross. Renaissance-style post office (1887) and law courts (1896), Pall Mall. Self-guide heritage walk, brochure available from Tourist information. In View St: Bendigo Art Gallery (1890); National Trust-classified Dudley House (1859), has historical display. Central Deborah Gold Mine, Violet St, in working order,

Shamrock Hotel, Bendigo

a vivid reminder of Bendigo's history. Vintage Talking Trams (taped commentary), run from mine on 8-km city trip (includes stop at Tram Depot Museum displaying 30 vintage trams). Golden Dragon Museum, Bridge St, features Chinese history of goldfields, largest display of Chinese processional regalia in the world (including world's oldest imperial dragon 'Loong' and longest imperial dragon 'Sun Loong', more than 100 m long) and classical Chinese gardens adjacent to museum. Lookout tower in Rosalind Park. Discovery Science and Technology Centre, Railway Pl., has more than 100 hands-on displays; Bendigo Woollen Mills, Lansell St West, tours available. Bus tours, in red London-style buses, of major attractions; contact Tourist information. Sun. market at Showgrounds, Holmes Rd. Mar.: Madison 10 000 Cycling Race. Easter: Fair (first held 1871, features Chinese dragon). Apr.: Chrysanthemum and Garden Expo; Bendigo by Bike. May: View Street Jazz Festival. Oct.: Orchid Club Spring Show. Nov.: National Swap Meet (Australia's largest meet for vintage car and bike enthusiasts);

Racing Carnival. Dec.: Tram Spectacular. **In the area:** Excellent art and antiques. Fortuna Villa mansion (1871), Chum St, 2 km S (open Sun.) One Tree Hill observation tower, 4 km S, panoramic views. At Mandurang, 8 km SE, historic Chateau Dore winery (open daily); Orchid Nursery; Tannery Lane Pottery. Camel Farm, 20 km SE at Sedgwick, offers rides and treks (check opening times). Arakoon Resort, 18 km SE, aquatic fun park (check opening times). Lake Eppalock, 26 km SE, camping, fishing and water sports; nearby (9 km N of Redesdale), Eppalock Ridge winery (open by appt). Bendigo Cactus Gardens, (established 1937) classified by National Trust, 3 km NE at White Hills. At Epsom, 6 km NE: Bendigo Pottery, Australia's oldest working pottery (tours and sales, open daily); Bendigo Car Museum, part of Pottery complex; Sun. market. National Trust-classified Chinese Joss House, built by Chinese miners; 1 km N at Emu Point (open daily). At Whipstick State Park, 21 km N: wildlife, old goldmining areas, bushwalking, cycling; goldpanning in gullies after rains; nearby, Hartland's Eucalyptus Factory and Historic Farm (tours on Sun.), built 1890 to process eucalyptus oil obtained from surrounding scrub. At Eaglehawk, site of goldrush in 1852, 6.5 km NW: reminders of mining days; fine examples of 19th-century architecture, many classified by National Trust; self-guide heritage tour, contact Tourist information; Dahlia and Arts Festival held each Mar. Balgownie Estate winery, 10 km NW (open Mon.–Sat.). Chateau Leaman winery, 10 km SW (open Wed.–Mon.). Bendigo Mohair Farm, Lockwood, 11 km SW (guided tours Mon.–Fri., admission free). **Tourist information:** Old Post Office, 51–67 Pall Mall; (03) 5444 4433. **Accommodation:** 5 hotels, 26 motels, 20 B&B, 13 cara./camp. parks. **See also:** The Golden Age; Wine Regions.

Birchip   Pop. 827

MAP REF. 126 F13, 237 K4

On the main rail link between Melbourne and Mildura, Birchip gets its water supply from the Wimmera-Mallee stock and domestic channel system. **Of interest:** In Cumming Ave: Big Red (Mallee bull); Historical Society Museum, in old court house (open by appt). **In the area:** Sites of historic interest within Shire are indicated by

markers; leaflet from Tourist information. Junction of two major irrigation channels constructed in early 1900s, 1 km N. Sections of original Dog Fence, a vermin-proof barrier constructed in 1883 between Murray River near Swan Hill and South Australian border, 20 km N. Tchum Lake, 8 km E, facilities onshore for motor boats, caravans and camping. **Tourist information:** Shire Offices, 22 Cumming Ave; (03) 5492 2200. **Accommodation:** 2 hotels, 1 motel, 1 cara./camp. park.

Boort   Pop. 801

MAP REF. 126 H13, 237 O5

A pleasant rural and holiday town on the shores of Lake Boort. The lake is popular for water sports, has good picnic facilities and beaches, and offers redfin fishing. There is prolific native birdlife in the area. **Tourist information:** Boort Lake Caravan Park, Durham Ox Rd; (03) 5455 2064. **Accommodation:** 1 motel, 1 cara./camp. park.

Bright   Pop. 1881

MAP REF. 231 L5, 241 P8, 242 C6

In the heart of the beautiful Ovens Valley and at the foothills of the Victorian Alps, Bright is an attractive tourist centre. The town offers easy access to the ski resorts of Mt Hotham, Mt Buffalo and Falls Creek, and a number of ski-hire shops in the town stay open late during the winter season. The discovery of gold was responsible for the town's beginnings; remains of alluvial goldfields can still be seen. The area is excellent for bushwalking, horseriding, mountain-bike riding and trout fishing, and is very photogenic, particularly in autumn. **Of interest:** Avenues of deciduous trees, planted in 1930s, particularly beautiful in spring and autumn. In Gavan St: Gallery 90; Country Collectables; Centennial Park with its deep weir (ideal for swimming in summer), children's playground and picnic facilities. Bright Art Gallery and Cultural Centre, Mountbatten Ave. Historical Museum, old railway station, Station Ave. Lotsafun Amusement Park, entrance Mill Rd. Ovens River flows through town; picnic and camping spots alongside. Variety of safe, well-marked walking tracks in Bright area, in particular, Canyon Walk along Ovens River retraces 1850s goldseekers' path; leaflets available at Tourist information. Hang-gliding, paragliding and 4WD tours available, inquire at

VICTORIA

The Golden Age

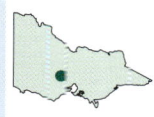

The cities and towns of the goldfields region of Victoria came to a peak of style and affluence in the 1880s, an affluence built on the first gold discoveries in the 1850s. The towns display all the frivolity and grandeur of Victorian architecture, having grown up during a period when it was believed that gold and wealth would be a permanent benefit in Victoria.

The two major cities of the region are Ballarat and Bendigo, but there are many other towns, in the area. They all have historic houses and public buildings, and many have other trappings of the past – statues, public gardens (some with lakes), ornamental bandstands and grand avenues of English trees. Spring and autumn are the best seasons to visit this region, because then there are not the extremes of summer and winter temperatures, and the flowers and foliage are at their best.

It is a quiet region now. The remaining small towns serve the surrounding rich pastoral district, and secondary industries and services centre on the two cities. It was once, however, an area of frantic activity. Gold was found at Clunes in 1851 and within three months 8000 people were on the diggings in the area between Buninyong and Ballarat. Nine months later 30 000 people were on the goldfields and four years later 100 000. The population of the city of Melbourne dwindled and immigrants rushed to the diggings from Great Britain, America and many other countries. Ships' crews, and sometimes even their captains, abandoned their vessels and trekked to the diggings to try their luck. Tent cities sprang up on the plains as men dug and panned for gold. There were remarkable finds of huge nuggets in the early days, but finally the amount of gold obtained by panning in the rivers and by digging grew less and less. The communities

were remarkable: there were shanty towns, the streets crowded day and night with hawkers and traders; there were pubs and dancing-rooms, and continuous sounds of music and revelry.

As time went on, the surface gold was worked out and expensive company-backed operations followed: mining in deep shafts, then the ore was stamped and crushed in steam-powered plants on the surface. The success of these methods heralded a new era, that of the company mines, outside investors and stock-exchange speculation. It led to a much more stable workforce and to the well-established communities that slowly evolved into the towns of the region today. As the pastoral and industrial potential began to be realised and fully exploited, it was the perfect scene for expansion and optimism.

The years between 1870 and 1890 saw the towns embellished with fine civic buildings, mansions,

Main Street at Sovereign Hill, Ballarat's famous tourist attraction

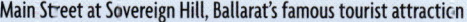

solid town houses, churches, hotels and all the trappings of affluence. Thus Ballarat, Bendigo, Castlemaine and to a lesser extent Clunes, Creswick, Daylesford and Maldon became extraordinary *nouveau riche* visions of the current British taste.

The Western Freeway between Melbourne and Ballarat is at its most scenic as it rises into the Pentland Hills. Just off the freeway is **Bacchus Marsh**, which is approached by a magnificent avenue of North American elms commemorating soldiers who died in the Great War. Bacchus Marsh is adjacent to the Lerderderg and Werribee rivers, which enter dramatic gorges close to the town. Just south of the freeway are the small rural towns of Myrniong and **Ballan**, Gordon, Bungaree and Dunnstown which is dominated by its bluestone distillery and the bulk of Mount Warrenheip, where an excellent view of the district can be had from the summit.

A turnoff to the south near Ballarat leads to Buninyong, the scene of one of the first gold strikes in Victoria. Gold was discovered here at Hiscock's Gully in 1851. The impressive township of Buninyong with its grand tree-lined main street has a number of striking buildings: the Crown Hotel and white-walled Uniting Church are of the 1860s, while the combined council chambers and court house of 1886 are in rich Italianate design, unified by a central clock tower.

The city of **Ballarat** was laid out to the west of the diggings within twelve months of the first discovery of gold. The design included a magnificent chief thoroughfare, Sturt Street, wide enough for future plantations and monuments. The primitive buildings of early settlement were gradually replaced by boom-style architecture in the 1880s; many superb buildings survive to this day.

Gold was discovered in Ballarat in 1851, and a visit to the Red Hill Gully Diggings at Sovereign Hill will show you something of the life of those early days. Without doubt, Sovereign Hill is the major attraction in Ballarat. This re-created goldmining township is a fascinating place for a day's outing to interest all the family.

North of Ballarat, on the Midland Highway is **Creswick**, a picturesque valley town with a wonderfully ornate town hall. The bluestone tower of St John's Church dominates the town's western hill and on the hilltop across the valley is a Tudor-style hospital building which is now a school of forestry.

Turn off the highway to **Clunes** where gold was discovered in July 1851. It proved difficult to get supplies to this remote township, so the rush was limited and the later discoveries at Buninyong and Ballarat quickly diverted attention from this area.

Flora statue in the Botanic Gardens, Ballarat

On the Western Highway, 133 kilometres northwest of Ballarat, past **Ararat** (where a gold rush began in 1857), is **Stawell**. Gold was discovered at the present site of Stawell in 1853; by 1857 there was a population of 30 000, and the township was proclaimed in 1858. Goldmining continued until 1920.

North-east of Ballarat up the Midland Highway is **Daylesford**, another former goldmining town set in wooded hills around Wombat Hill Gardens and Lake Daylesford. On the hill are groves of rhododendrons, exotic trees and a lookout tower that provides a view of Mount Franklin (a perfectly preserved volcanic crater) and Mount Tarrengower. Several kilometres north of Daylesford are natural springs containing lime, iron, magnesia and other minerals. This is the famed Hepburn Spa, which attracted visitors in the nineteenth century for its medicinal properties and is still popular with tourists. Bottling mineral water is the town's main industry.

Further north on the road to Bendigo is **Castlemaine**, a larger town and one of the most picturesque in the region. The streetscape in the centre of the town has remained virtually unaltered since the early days, for the prosperity of the 1860s diminished and the town settled down to a quieter rural life.

Nearby **Maldon** was declared a notable town by the National Trust in 1962. The winding streets are flanked by low buildings, with deep verandahs shading the bluestone pavements laid in 1866.

The city of **Bendigo** is the jewel of the region and is Victoria's most outstanding example of a boom town. Gothic- and classical-style buildings have been designed in vast proportions, richly ornamented and combined with the materials of the age, cast iron and cast cement.

The goldfields region can be enjoyed in three days or three weeks, according to time and taste. Bendigo Goldseeker Tours organise gold-fossicking excursions and include instruction in the use of metal detectors. A great way to see the region is via the 'Goldfields Tourist Route', a 450-kilometre triangle road route linking Ballarat, Ararat, Stawell, **Avoca, Maryborough,** Bendigo, Castlemaine and Daylesford. Free maps marking the route are available at the Victorian Visitor Information Centre, Melbourne Town Hall, cnr Little Collins and Swanston sts, Melbourne, all RACV offices and various tourist information centres throughout the goldfields region.

More detailed information can be obtained from the Bendigo Tourist Information Centre, Old Post Office, 51–67 Pall Mall; (03) 5444 4433. **See also:** individual text entries in A–Z listing for those towns indicated by bold type. **Map references:** 226–29.

VICTORIA

Tourist information. Market, Burke St, 3rd Sun. each month. Apr.: Autumn Festival. July: Winter Wonderland Festival. Oct.: Alpine Spring Festival. **In the area:** Wandiligong, National Trust-classified hamlet in scenic valley, 6 km SE; linked to Bright by road, and walking and cycle track. Scenic drives in the area to: Tower Hill Lookout, 4 km NW; Huggins Lookout, 2 km S; Clearspot (stunning views), 13 km S; from Alpine Road south-east to Mt Hotham, superb views of Mt Feathertop, the Razor Back and Mt Bogong. At Porepunkah, 6 km NW at junction of Ovens and Buckland rivers, Boyntons of Bright winery; further 10 km, Snowline Deer and Emu Farm in Hughes Lane, Eurobin. Mount Buffalo Chalet, 33 km W. **Tourist information:** Gavan St; (03) 5755 2275; freecall, 1800 622936. **Accommodation:** 2 hotel/motels, 11 motels, 6 B&B, 2 hostels, 7 cara./camp. parks.

Broadford   Pop. 2215

MAP REF. 219 K1, 240 G11

A small town off the Hume Fwy near Mt Piper. **Of interest:** In historic precinct, High St: display of old printing equipment in *Broadford Courier* building (check opening times); replica of drop-slab pioneer cottage; school room. Picnic/barbecue facilities and rotunda in park in town centre. Feb.: Country Music Festival. Dec.: Hells Angels Concert. **In the area:** Reg Hunt motorcycle complex, 5 km E on Strath Creek Rd, has regular motorcycle events. Continue to Strath Creek for beautiful scenic drive through Valley of a Thousand Hills. At Kilmore, 14 km SW: fine old buildings, including Whitburgh Cottage (1857); cable tram rides in Hudson Park. **Tourist information:** Newsagency, 67 High St; (03) 5784 1487. **Accommodation:** 2 hotels, 1 motel, 1 B&B.

Buchan   Pop. 220

MAP REF. 119 B13, 242 I11

This small town, set in the heart of Gippsland mountain country north-east of Bairnsdale, is famous for its remarkable series of limestone caves. **Of interest:** Tours of Royal and Fairy Caves, conducted daily (adventure tours also available); park and spring-fed swimming pool located at Caves Reserve. Easter: Rodeo. Oct.: Art and Craft Festival. **In the area:** Schoolhouse (1865), at Suggan Buggan, 64 km N.

Uniting Church at Bright, in the beautiful Ovens Valley

South of Suggan Buggan, Eagle Loft Gallery, for local art and craft. Snowy River National Park, for spectacular mountain scenery, 10 km NW of Suggan Buggan. Outstanding views from lookout over Little River Gorge, 70 km N on road to McKillops Bridge; Little River Falls near Gorge. Stonehenge Rockhounds Museum, 7 km SW at Buchan South. **Tourist information:** General Store, Main St; (03) 5155 9202. **Accommodation:** 2 motels, 1 hostel, 2 cara./camp. parks.

Camperdown   Pop. 3315

MAP REF. 223 C5, 235 L8

This south-western town on the Princes Hwy has the English-style charm of gracious buildings and avenues of elms. More than 50 buildings are of historical significance and can be seen by following the Heritage Trail; brochure from Tourist information. The centre for a rich pastoral district, Camperdown is also noted for fishing – in the volcanic crater lakes in the area. **Of interest:** Clock tower (1896), cnr Manifold and Pike sts. Also in Manifold St: Historical Society Museum; court house; post office. Old Mill, Curdie St, has gallery, plant nursery, restored buggies and tea-rooms in 120-yr-old restored building. Craft market at Finlay Ave or Theatre Royal, 1st Sun. each month. Feb.: Leura Festival (parades and festivities). July: One Act Play Festival. **In the area:** At Mt Noorat, near Noorat, 21 km NW: Alan Marshall Memorial Walking Track, off Glenormiston Rd, 3-km summit and return (1 hr) or crater-rim 1.5-km circuit (30 min.); excellent views over Western District. Mt Leura, 1 km W, extinct volcano next to the perfect cone shape of Mt Sugarloaf; lookout offers views over numerous crater lakes and volcanoes, north across plains to the Grampians. Cobden, peaceful dairying town, 13 km

s. Further 27 km s, at Timboon: Timboon Farmhouse, cheese tastings and sales; Old Timboon Railway Line Walk (10 km). Picturesque road leads from Timboon to tiny seaside village of Port Campbell, 18 km s. Lake Corangamite, 13 km e, Victoria's largest salt lake. Excellent fishing lakes including Bullen Merri, 3 km w; and Purrumbete, 4 km se, well stocked with Quinnat salmon, also has excellent water-sports facilities, picnic spots and caravan park. **Tourist information:** Fragrant Cottage, Old court-house building, Manifold St; (03) 5593 2288. **Accommodation:** 3 hotels, 3 motels, 3 B&B, 1 cara./camp. park.

Cann River   Pop. 336

MAP REF. 119 E13, 243 N11

A popular stop for Sydney-Melbourne motorists using the Princes Hwy. Excellent fishing and bushwalking in the rugged hinterland. **In the area:** Coopracamba National Park, 15 km n near NSW border. Croajingolong National Park, main access 27 km s, stretches from Sydenham Inlet to NSW border; incorporates Captain James Cook Lighthouse Reserve at Point Hicks, and Tamboon, Wingan and Mallacoota inlets. **Tourist information:** Natural Resources and Environment Information Centre, Princes Hwy; (03) 5158 6351. **Accommodation:** 1 hotel, 3 motels, 1 cara./camp. park.

Casterton   Pop. 1808

MAP REF. 234 C4

Given the Roman name meaning 'walled city' because of lush hills surrounding the valley, Casterton is on the Glenelg Hwy, 42 km e of the South Australian border. The Glenelg River flows through the town. Overlooking the town is a large illuminated scout emblem carved into a hillside. **Of interest:** Historical museum, Old Railway Buildings, cnr Jackson and Clarke sts (open by appt). David Geschke Fine Porcelain Gallery, Racecourse Rd. In Henty St: Bryan Park; Alma and Judith Zaadstra Fine Art Gallery. Tourist information centre displays local art and craft. Canoes for hire; contact Tourist information. Mar.: Vintage Car Rally. May: Polocrosse Championships. Aug.: Woodturning Demonstration Exhibition. Nov.: Street-car Drag Racing. **In the area:** Mainly grazing land with rolling hills and areas of natural forest;

excellent bushwalks, variety of fauna and flora. Bilston's Tree, 30 km n on Glenmia Rd, 50 m high and arguably world's largest red gum tree in terms of timber mass. Baileys Rocks, 50 km n in Dergholm State Park, unique green coloured giant granite boulders. Other interesting geological formations: The Hummocks, 12 km ne; The Bluff, 20 km sw, exposed geological formations dating back 150 million years surrounded by excellent scenery; nearby slab cottage (1870), school (1875) and picnic facilities (open Sun. and public holidays). Killara Camels, 70 km sw, for camel treks along Glenelg River; contact Tourist information for details. Long Lead Swamp 11 km w on Penola Rd has waterbirds, kangaroos and emus, and trail-bike track. Angling Club Reserve, Roseneath, 24 km nw. National Trust-classified Warrock Homestead (1843), 26 km ne, unique collection of 33 buildings erected by founder, George Robertson; (open working day on Easter Sun.). **Tourist information:** Shiels Tce; (03) 5581 2070. **Accommodation:** 2 hotel/motels, 1 motel, 1 B&B, 1 cara./camp. park.

Castlemaine   Pop. 6812

MAP REF. 229 P5, 237 Q11, 240 C10

Along with Kyneton and Maldon, Castlemaine epitomises the goldmining towns of north-western Victoria. An attractive and interesting town, it is built on low hills at the foot of Mt Alexander, at the intersection of the Pyrenees and Midland hwys, 119 km from Melbourne. In the 1850s and 1860s enormous quantities of gold were found in its surface fields. This gold boom saw Castlemaine grow rapidly and many of its fine old buildings were built during this period. **Of interest:** National Trust-operated Market Museum (1862), Moystyn St, Palladian-style building, with local arts and crafts, and historic displays. Midland Hotel, Templeton St, and Imperial Hotel, Lyttleton St, have splendid iron lacework verandahs. Also in Lyttleton St: court house; town hall and library; regional art gallery and museum. Theatre Royal, Hargraves St. Buda Historic Home and Garden, Urquhart St, home from late 1850s of silversmith and jeweller Ernest Leviny and his family, with preserved home and gardens of the era. Botanic Gardens, Parker St, designed by Baron von Mueller who also designed the

Melbourne Botanic Gardens. Old gaol, now restaurant and hostel, Bowden St (guided tours daily). Nov.: Spring Garden Festival (odd-numbered years); State Festival (even-numbered years). **In the area:** Excellent restaurants and antique shops. Burnett Gallery and Garden, Burnett Rd, North Castlemaine (open weekends). At Harcourt, 10 km ne: Skydancers, a walk-through orchid and butterfly nursery; good fishing; scenic picnic spots; Harcourt Valley Vineyard; Blackjack Vineyards; Mt Alexander wineries. On Mt Alexander, 19 km ne, koala reserve. Historic Forest Creek Gold Mine, on road to Chewton (4 km se), tours and gold panning available (contact Tourist information). At Chewton, 4 km se: Wattle Gully goldmine; Dingo Farm (puppy time July–Aug.); market each Sat. At Fryerstown, 10 km se: ruins of Duke of Cornwall mine; Herons Reef Cultural Heritage Gold Diggings (tours available, contact Tourist information for details). Chinese cemetery and mineral springs at Vaughan, 12 km s. Big Tree, a giant red gum over 500 years old, 11 km sw at Guildford. At Newstead, 16 km sw: winery; pottery. **Tourist information:** Duke St; (03) 5470 6200. **Accommodation:** 5 hotels, 3 motels, 23 B&B, 2 cara./camp. parks. **See also:** The Golden Age.

Charlton   Pop. 1182

MAP REF. 237 M6

A supply centre for a rich wheat district, Charlton is set on the banks of the Avoca River, at the intersection of the Calder and Borung hwys in north-central Victoria. **Of interest:** Fishing in Avoca River. Walking track along river, from town to weir (about 2 km one-way). Mar.: Country Music Festival. Oct.: Art Show. **In the area:** Wooroonook Lake, 12 km w, for swimming and boating. Bish Deer Farm, further 18 km w. At Wycheproof, 30 km nw: Mt Wycheproof, a mere 43 m high and smallest mountain in world; Centenary Park and Willandra Historical Museum, on Broadway; local art and craft at Polls Gallery, Charles St. Wychitella State Forest, 27 km e, for a variety of interesting native flora and fauna, including the lowan (mallee fowl). **Tourist information:** Shire Offices, 1 High St; (03) 5491 1755. **Accommodation:** 2 hotels, 2 motels, 1 cara./camp. park.

VICTORIA

Chiltern   Pop. 1157

MAP REF. 127 P13, 241 N4, 242 A2

Halfway between Wangaratta and
Wodonga, Chiltern is 1 km off the
Hume Fwy. It was once a goldmining
boom town with 14 suburbs. Many of its
attractive buildings have been classified
by the National Trust. **Of interest:**
In Conness St: Athenaeum Museum
(1866), features Goldfields Library collection; The Pharmacy (1868), National
Trust-owned chemist shop with its original features; Stephen's Motor Museum,
for motoring memorabilia. Self-guide
historic walk, leaflet available from
Tourist information. Famous Grapevine,
cnr Conness and Main sts, formerly
Grape Vine Hotel, boasts the largest
grapevine in Australia (in Guinness Book
of Records, planted 1867). National
Trust-classified Federal Standard newspaper office, Main St, dates from
goldmining era (1860–61) (open by appt
for groups). Picnic spots with barbecues
at Lake Anderson, via Main St. Walking
track from lake-shore over bridge to
National Trust-classified 'Lake View',
Victoria St, home of author Henry Han-
del Richardson (open weekends, public
and school holidays). May: Antique Fair.
Sept.: Art Show. **In the area:** Chiltern
Regional Park, surrounding town, for
bushwalking, nature observation, picnicking; tourist drives and guided
walking tours available (contact Tourist
information). Magenta open-cut mine, 2
km E. Pioneer Cemetery, 2 km N. Black
Dog Creek Pottery, 3 km NW on
Chiltern Valley Rd. Alpaca Farm, 1 km
W on Rutherglen Rd (open Thurs.–
Tues.) Mt Pilot Pottery, 10 km S on
Beechworth Rd. **Tourist information:**
Famous Grapevine, Main St; (03) 5726
1395. **Accommodation:** 1 hotel, 1
motel, 2 B&B, 1 cara./camp. park.

Clunes   Pop. 846

MAP REF. 218 C2, 229 L7, 231 O2, 237 O13,
240 A11

The first reported gold find in the State
was made at Clunes on 7 July 1851 when
James Esmond announced his discovery
of 'pay dirt'. The town, some 35 km N of
Ballarat, has several bluestone buildings
classified by the National Trust, and the
verandahed elegance of Fraser St is worth
noting. Surrounding the town are a number of rounded hills (extinct volcanoes)
and a good view of them can be obtained

Historic colonial home 'Lake View', Chiltern

about 3 km S, on the road to Ballarat. **Of
interest:** Old post office (1873), now second-hand bookshop, cnr Bailey and
Service sts (open weekends). In Bailey St:
town hall and court house (1870); Bottle
Museum, in former South Clunes State
School; Queens Park, established over
100 years ago on banks of Creswick
Creek. Butter Factory Gallery, Cameron
St, sculpture and art gallery. In Fraser St:
the Weavery, handwoven fabrics;
Museum, open weekends, public and
school holidays. Nov.: Agricultural Show.
In the area: Clunes Homestead Furniture, 1 km NW on Talbot Rd. At Talbot,
historic town 18 km NW: many 1860–70
buildings, particularly in Camp St and
Scandinavian Cres.; Arts and Historical
Museum, Camp St, in former Primitive
Methodist Church (1870); Bull and
Mouth restaurant, old bluestone building
(1860s) formerly hotel. At Mt Beckworth,
8 km W, a scenic reserve with variety of
native flora and fauna. **Tourist information:** Clunes Museum, Fraser St; (03)
5345 3592. **Accommodation:** 1 hotel, 1
motel, 1 cara./camp. park. **See also:** The
Golden Age.

Cobram   Pop. 3797

MAP REF. 127 M13, 241 J3

Magnificent wide sandy beaches are a feature of the stretch of the Murray River at
Cobram, so picnicking, fishing and water
sports are popular here. This is also fruit-
growing country; the clingstone variety of

peach was developed here. **Of interest:**
Log Cabin, opposite Tourist information
in Punt Rd, historic cottage built in Yarrawonga in 1875 and moved piece by piece.
Rotary dairy, 200 cows, on outskirts of
town; open at milking time, 4–5 p.m.
daily. Market in Punt Rd, 2nd Sat. each
month. Jan.: Peaches and Cream Festival
(odd-numbered years). May: Rotary Art
Show. June: Antique Fair. Oct.: Sun
Country Dolls, Bears and Collectables
Show. **In the area:** Matata Deer Farm on
Tocumwal road, 5 km NW. Sportavia
Soaring Centre at Tocumwal airport, 20
km NW. Heritage Farm Wines, 5 km W
on Murray Valley Hwy, with 116-m
woodcarving depicting scenes of early
Murray River life. At Strathmerton, 16 km
W: Cactus Country, a cactus farm; Coonanga Homestead. Monichino winery, 15
km S towards Numurkah. Just east of
town, Quinn Island on Murray River;
self-guide nature walk available (contact
Tourist information). Strathkellar Wines,
8 km E on Murray Valley Hwy. Binghi
Boomerang Factory at Barooga, 4 km NE.
Tourist information: The Old Grain
Store, cnr Station St and Punt Rd; (03)
5872 2132. **Accommodation:** 3 hotels, 4
motels, 3 cara./camp. parks. **See also:**
The Mighty Murray.

Cohuna   Pop. 2071

MAP REF. 127 J12, 237 Q3, 240 C2

Between Kerang and Echuca on the
Murray Valley Hwy, Cohuna is

surrounded by dairy farms. The town is located beside Gunbower Island, formed by the Murray River on the far side and Gunbower Creek just across the highway from the town. This island is covered in red gum and box forest, which provides a home for abundant waterfowl and other birdlife as well as kangaroos and emus. The forest is subject to flooding and a large part of the island has breeding rookeries during the flood periods. Feb.: Aquatic Festival. Mar.: Show. **In the area:** Two-hour cruises in the *Wetlander* along Gunbower Creek, inquire at Tourist information. On Gunbower Island: birdlife, picnic/barbecue facilities and forest tracks for walking (map available at local shops). Major Mitchell Trail, 1700-km signposted trail that retraces this famous explorer's footsteps from Mildura to Wodonga via Portland; at Cohuna, signposted trail along Gunbower Creek, down to Mt Hope. Kow Swamp, 23 km S, a bird sanctuary; picnic spots and good fishing at Box Bridge. Mt Hope (110 m), about 28 km S, for easy rock climbing; good views from summit and beautiful wildflowers in spring. Cohuna Grove Cottage, 4 km SE on Murray Valley Hwy, local art and craft. Kraft factory, shop (open a.m. Mon.–Fri.), 16 km SE at Leitchville. Torrumbarry Weir, 40 km SE, during winter, entire weir structure is removed from the river; in summer, water-skiing above the weir. Mathers Waterwheel Museum, Brays Rd, 9 km W, memorabilia. **Tourist information:** Golden River Tourism, 25 Murray St, Barham; (03) 5453 3100. **Accommodation:** 1 hotel/motel, 1 motel, 1 cara./camp. park.

Colac   Pop. 10 241

MAP REF. 218 B11, 223 G7, 235 N9

Colac is situated on the eastern edge of the volcanic plain that covers much of the Western District of Victoria. It is the centre of a prosperous, closely settled agricultural area and is sited on the shores of Lake Colac, which has good fishing and a variety of water sports. **Of interest:** Historical Centre, Gellibrand St (open Thurs., Fri., Sun. p.m.). Botanic Gardens, Queen St. Barongarook Creek, has prolific birdlife and walking track alongside leading to Sculpture Park on Princes Hwy, with its permanent and special exhibitions. Self-guide town walk leaflet and information on full-day mountain scenic drive are available,

contact Tourist information for details. Feb.: Otway Harvest Festival. Mar.: Food and Wine Festival. Apr.: Country Music Festival. Oct.: Garden Expo. **In the area:** Irrewarra Homestead, 15 km N. Red Rock Lookout, 22 km N near Alvie, 30 volcanic lakes can be seen from here, including Lake Corangamite, Victoria's largest saltwater lake. Floating Island Reserve, 17 km W, a lagoon with islands that change position. Gellibrand Pottery, 10 km S. Burtons Lookout, 13 km S, views of Otway hinterland. Red Rock Winery, 15 km S (check opening times). Otway Ranges, about 30 km S, features beautiful winding roads and lush mountain scenery. Tarndwarncoort Homestead, 15 km E. At Birregurra, 20 km E, interesting old buildings. **Tourist information:** cnr Murray and Queen sts; (03) 5231 3730. **Accommodation:** 1 hotel/motel, 4 motels, 3 cara./camp. parks.

Coleraine   Pop. 1089

MAP REF. 234 E4

Situated 35 km NW of Hamilton, the Coleraine area was first settled by the Henty and Whyte brothers in 1838 for pastoral grazing. Today the primary products are fine-wool sheep and beef cattle. **Of interest:** Historic railway station, Pilleau St, now Tourist information centre. In Whyte St: Matthew Cooke's Blacksmiths Shop (1888), open Sun. or by appt; Karam, an antique & bric-a-brac shop, formerly shop where Helena Rubenstein first made cosmetics. **In the area:** At Point's Arboretum, southern outskirts of town on Coleraine–Portland Rd: largest number of eucalyptus species in southern hemisphere, also other native plants, prolific birdlife, lookout and picnic area. Historic homesteads: National Trust-classified Warrock Homestead (1843), 20 km W towards Casterton; Glendinning Homestead with wildlife sanctuary, near Balmoral, 49 km N. Gardens of Glendinning Homestead and Mistydown Perennials (also at Balmoral); contact Tourist information for brochure and opening times. Rocklands Reservoir, 12 km E of Balmoral, for fishing and boating; caravan/camping park nearby. Black Range State Park, on northern shores of reservoir, has walking tracks. Wannon Falls, 14 km SE, and Nigretta Falls, 24 km SE. **Tourist information:** Old Railway Station, Pilleau St; (03) 5575 2733. **Accommodation:** 2 hotels, 1 cara./ camp. park.

Corryong   Pop. 1226

MAP REF. 119 B8, 242 G2

Situated in alpine country, Corryong is at the gateway to the Snowy Mountains. The district offers superb mountain scenery and excellent trout fishing. The Murray River near Corryong is a brisk and gurgling stream running through forested hills. **Of interest:** Jack Riley, reputedly 'The Man from Snowy River', came from these parts and his grave is in Corryong cemetery. The Man from Snowy River Folk Museum, Hanson St, features scale model of Riley's original shack and a period costume collection. Large wooden galleon, Murray River Hwy. Mar.: High Country Festival. **In the area:** Scenic drive west from Corryong. Scenic views: Players Hill Lookout, 1 km SE; Mt Mittamatite and Emberys Lookout, 10 km N; lookout with views over Kosciusko National Park at Towong, 12 km NE; Sassafras Gap, 66 km S. Trout fishing at Tintaldra, 23 km N. Canoeing and mountain-bike excursions from Walwa, 47 km NW. Emu Farm, 4 km W on Murray Valley Hwy. At Burrowa-Pine Mountain National Park, 27 km W: Cudgewa Bluff Falls, excellent scenery and bushwalking tracks. At Berringama, 30 km W, Beetoomba Bison Ranch with American bison, souvenir shop in a Tee Pee and bison burgers. In Nariel Valley, 12 km SW: trout fishing in Nariel Creek; Folk Music Festival in Dec. Upper Murray Fish Farm, 38 km S. **Tourist information:** Mt Mittamatite Caravan Park, Tallangatta Rd; (02) 6076 1152. **Accommodation:** 2 hotel/ motels, 2 motels, 2 cara./camp. parks.

Cowes   Pop. 2658

MAP REF. 219 L12, 221 O11, 232 E9

This is the main town on Phillip Island, a popular resort area in Western Port linked to the mainland by a bridge at San Remo. Cowes is on the northern side of the island and is the centre for hotel and motel accommodation. It has pleasant beaches, safe for children, and the jetty is popular for fishing and swimming. The town has a number of art and craft shops, and a variety of restaurants. Sept.: Motor Racing. Oct.: Grand Prix Motorcycle Race; Superbike Championships. **In the area:** Summerland Beach, on southern shore, about 13 km SW, famous for its nightly penguin parade. Colonies of fur seals can be seen year-round on Seal Rocks, and off southern shores; also

VICTORIA

Phillip Island

Penguin parade at Summerland Beach, one of the State's most popular tourist attractions

Phillip Island (10 300 hectares) is situated at the entrance to Western Port, 120 kilometres south-east of Melbourne. Once over the bridge between San Remo and Newhaven, the greatest attraction for visitors is the fascinating little (fairy) penguin parade on Summerland Beach. The penguins spend the day out at sea catching whitebait for their young. Each evening at sunset they return in small groups and waddle up the beach to their sand-dune burrows. Visitors watch the parade under subdued floodlights from elevated stands and walkways. No flashlight photography is permitted. The Phillip Island Penguin Reserve is open daily. (Inquiries (03) 5956 8300; bookings for parade (03) 5956 8691.)

Seal Rocks at the south-west tip of the island is home to colonies of fur seals. At the peak of the breeding season, about 9000 seals can be seen there. A ferry service from Cowes allows close-up views of the seals sunbathing on the rocks. Coin-operated telescopes give landlubbers a view of the seals from The Nobbies kiosk. Nearby, The Nobbies,

a big rock outcrop, can only be reached at low tide. The Blow Hole here is best seen at high tide.

Take the road down to the surf beach at Cape Woolamai, a rugged granite headland. A two-hour walk leads to the highest point on the island, from where there are breathtaking views of the coastline. The sand dunes all along the Cape are the home of many short-tailed shearwaters (muttonbirds). Arriving from Siberia on their annual migration, the birds nest in the rookeries here in spring and summer. Koalas can be seen at the Koala Conservation Centre, which features an elevated boardwalk in the treetops.

Visit nearby historic Churchill Island, reached by bridge near Newhaven. A pamphlet available at Tourist information outlines the Homestead Walk (the homestead was built in 1872). There are several walking trails on the island.

Everyone will enjoy hand-feeding the tame emus, kangaroos and wallabies at the Phillip Island Wildlife Park, which is set in 32 hectares of bushland. Other fauna to be seen there include wombats, venomous and non-venomous snakes,

eagles and pelicans. Nearly 7 hectares is wetlands, consisting of ponds and waterways that are breeding grounds for rare and endangered birds.

Some unusual bird species make their homes in the Rhyll swamp and bird sanctuary on the northern side of the island. Pelicans, ibis, royal spoonbills, swans and gulls inhabit the swamplands there.

The Phillip Island Nature Park has been created to develop and integrate the island's significant wildlife attractions by upgrading facilities while conserving natural features.

Also on the north coast is **Cowes**, the most popular summer resort on Phillip Island. Its unspoilt beaches are sheltered for safe swimming, yachting and other water sports.

For further information on attractions, ticket sales for the penguin parade, and information and maps for self-guide walks and nature tours, contact Information Bass Coast, Phillip Island Rd, Newhaven; (03) 5956 7447. **See also:** text entry for Cowes in A–Z listing. **Map references: 221 N12, 232 E9.**

short-tailed shearwaters (muttonbirds) Oct.–Apr. Phillip Island Vineyard and Winery, Berrys Beach Rd, for tastings, sales and casual dining. On Phillip Island Rd: Wildlife Park has native fauna in natural environment, 3 km S; A Maze 'N Things, 7 km SW; Koala Conservation Centre, features elevated boardwalk. Racing circuit, 6 km S, venue for Grand Prix Motorcycle Race. Australian Dairy Centre at Newhaven, 16 km SE, museum and cheese factory. At Churchill Island, 2 km from Newhaven, historic homestead and walking tracks. Feed pelicans, 11a.m. on foreshore opposite San Remo Fishing Co-op. Wildlife Wonderland, including the Giant Worm and Wombat World, 9 km E of San Remo. Rhyll swamp and bird sanctuary, 8 km E. **Tourist information:** Phillip Island Rd, Newhaven; (03) 5956 7447 (tickets for Phillip Island attractions available here). **Accommodation:** 17 hotel/motels, 9 B&B, 1 hostel, 13 cara./camp. parks. **See also:** Phillip Island.

Creswick   Pop. 2387

MAP REF. 218 C3, 229 M9, 235 O2, 237 O13, 240 A12

This picturesque town, situated 18 km N of Ballarat on the Midland Hwy, nestles at the foot of the Creswick State Forest. One of the richest alluvial goldfields in the world was discovered here. **Of interest:** Mullock heaps on Lawrence Rd. Creswick Historical Museum, Albert St. Gold Battery, Battery Cres. Cemetery, Clunes Rd, with early miners' graves and Chinese section. In Melbourne Rd: Koala Park; St Georges Lake. Oct.: Brackenbury Classic Fun Run. **In the area:** Surrounding volcanic bushland and forest areas attract field naturalists and bushwalking enthusiasts. Creswick Forest Nursery, 1 km E. World of Dinosaurs, 1.5 km E off Midland Hwy, life-size models in bushland setting. Gold panning, in Creswick Creek, 4 km E. Tangled Maze Nursery, a maze formed by climbing plants, 5 km E. At Smeaton, 16 km N: Smeaton House (1850s); Anderson's Mill (1860s); Tuki Trout Farm. Tumblers Green Nursery, 1 km W. **Tourist information:** Vincent St, Daylesford; (03) 5348 1339. **Accommodation:** 1 motel, 2 B&B, 1 cara./camp. park. **See also:** The Golden Age.

Daylesford   Pop. 3347

MAP REF. 218 E2, 229 P8, 235 Q2, 237 Q13, 240 B12

Daylesford and Hepburn Springs, 4 km

N, together constitute a spa town, with 65 documented mineral springs, many with hand pumps. Daylesford rambles up the side of Wombat Hill, at the top of which are the Botanical Gardens. **Of interest:** Hepburn Springs Spa Complex, in the Mineral Springs Reserve, Forest Ave, offers public and private baths, flotation tanks, massage and a sauna. Convent Gallery with beautiful gardens, in former girls' school, Daly St. Nearby, Wombat Hill Botanical Gardens and lookout tower. In Vincent St: Alpha Hall Galleria, in former silent movie house (closed Tues.-Wed.); historical museum in former School of Mines (open weekends). Central Springs Spa Reserve and Lake Daylesford, Central Springs Rd; Tipperary Walking Track runs from here to Mineral Springs Reserve (leaflet available, contact Tourist information). Lyonville spring, 15 km SE. Loddon Falls, 10 km NE. Glenlyon Reserve, 11km NE. Market near railway station, Sun. a.m.; during market, Central Highlands Tourist Railway runs hourly rail-motor services between Daylesford and Musk (1st and 3rd Sun. each month), and ganger's trolleys operate to Wombat Forest alternate Sun. Jan.: Daylesford Gift (horse race). May: Hepburn Swiss-Italian Festival. July: Mid-winter Festival. Nov.: Agricultural Show. Dec.: Highland Gathering. **In the area:** Breakneck Gorge, 5 km N. Mt Franklin, an extinct volcano, 13 km N. At Trentham, 23 km SE: interesting buildings; waterfalls to the north. Yandoit, a settlement of Swiss-Italian heritage, 18 km NW. Sailors Falls, 5 km S. **Tourist information:** Vincent St; (03) 5348 1339. **Accommodation:** 4 hotels, 7 motels, 40 B&B, 3 cara./camp. parks. **See also:** The Golden Age.

Derrinallum   Pop. 280

MAP REF. 223 C2, 235 L6

A small rural town servicing the local pastoral farming community and surrounded by volcanic plains. **In the area:** Significant dry-stone walls, immediately west of town. Mt Elephant, 2 km SW, a scoria cone of volcanic origin rising high above surrounding plains. At Darlington, 15 km SW: Elephant Bridge Hotel, a 2-storey bluestone building, classified by National Trust. For fishing and water sports: Lake Tooliorook, 6 km SE; Deep Lake, 5 km NW. **Tourist information:** Fragrant Cottage, Old Court House

building, Manifold St, Camperdown; (03) 5593 2288. **Accommodation:** 1 hotel/motel.

Dimboola   Pop. 1581

MAP REF. 236 F7

This is a peaceful town on the tree-lined Wimmera River, 35 km NW of Horsham. **Of interest:** Walking track along Wimmera River. Oct.: Agricultural Show. Nov.: Rowing Regatta. **In the area:** At Little Desert National Park, 6 km SW, self-guide walks, including Pomponderoo Hill Nature Walk (1 km) from Horseshoe Bend picnic and camping area at river's edge. At Wail, 11 km SE, well-stocked Natural Resource League forest nursery. Ebenezer Mission Station (founded 1859), near Antwerp on Jeparit Rd, 15 km N. Pink Lake, coloured salt lake, 9 km NW. At Kiata, 26 km W, mallee fowl can be seen in Lowan Sanctuary all year. **Tourist information:** Mog's Menagerie, 119 Lloyd St; (03) 5389 1290. **Accommodation:** 2 hotels, 1 motel, 1 cara./camp. park.

Donald   Pop. 1505

MAP REF. 237 K7

At the junction of the Sunraysia and Borung hwys, Donald is situated on the Richardson River. **Of interest:** Historic police station (1874), Wood St. Railway steam engine, Steam Loco Park, cnr Hammill and Walker sts. Agricultural museum, Hammill St. Historic water pump by lake in caravan park. Bullocks Head Lookout, Byrne St. Large, unusual growth on box tree beside Richardson River. Kooka's Country Cookies, Sunraysia Hwy, has tours and sales. Market in Byrne St, 3rd Sat. each month. Feb.: Dead Centre Motorbike Rally. June: Scottish Dancing Weekend. **In the area:** Angora Goat Farm, 1 km E on Racecourse Rd. Deer farm, 10 km E on Charlton Rd. Glengar River Sanctuary, 2 km NE on Borung Hwy, contains grave of first woman settler in district. Mt Jeffcott, 20 km NE, for flora, fauna and views of Lake Buloke. Good fishing in Richardson River. River flows into Lake Buloke, 10 km N, a wetlands area. Watchem Lake, 30 km N, good fishing and water sports. Wimmera Mallee Emu Farm, 10 km W on Stawell Rd. **Tourist information:** Caravan Park, Hammill St; (03) 5497 1764. **Accommodation:** 3 hotels, 2 motels, 2 B&B, 1 cara./camp. park.

VICTORIA

Drysdale

Pop. 1166

MAP REF. 218 H9, 225 H7, 232 B6

This is primarily a service centre for the local farming community on the Bellarine Peninsula. **Of interest:** In High St: Old Court House Museum, home of the Bellarine Historical Society; Drysdale Community Crafts. Community Market, every 3rd Sun. (Sept.–Apr.) at Recreation Reserve, Duke St. **In the area:** Lake Lorne picnic area, 1 km SW. Nearby Bellarine Peninsula Railway offers steam-train rides between Drysdale and Queenscliff, weekends and summer holidays; locomotives and carriages dating back to 1870s on display. Adjoining township of Clifton Springs had a brief burst of fame in the 1870s when the therapeutic value of its mineral-spring water was discovered. Soho Nursery and Fine Arts Gallery, 6 km E. Local wineries include Scotchmans Hill Winery, 8 km NE on Scotchmans Road. Historic Spray Farm Winery, Portarlington Rd (open weekends and public holidays). At Portarlington, a popular seaside resort, 8 km NE, historic flourmill (1857), Turner Crt, restored by National Trust and now a venue for historical displays; Lavender Cottage Gallery, Fenwick St; Public Reserve, Sprout St; safe bay for children to swim. At St Leonards, a small beach resort, 13 km W: Edwards Point Wildlife Reserve, Beach Rd; memorial on The Esplanade commemorates landing by Matthew Flinders in 1802, and John Batman and his party in 1835. **Tourist information:** A Maze'N Things, 1570 Bellarine Hwy, cnr Grubb Rd, Wallington; (03) 5250 2669. **Accommodation:** 1 hotel, 3 B&B.

Dunkeld

Pop. 440

MAP REF. 234 H4

On the Glenelg Hwy, 32 km NE of Hamilton, Dunkeld is the southern gateway to the Grampians and is convenient for trips to the Chimney Pots, a landmark in the Grampians National Park, 25 km N. **Of interest:** Historical museum, in old church in Templeton St, features history of area's Aborigines, local wool industry and explorer Major Mitchell's journeys. Self-guide walk or drive of historic places of interest, leaflet available from Tourist information. Nov.: Dunkeld Cup (horse race) Dec.: Festival. **In the area:** Walking tracks to

Paddlesteamers on the Murray River at Echuca

top of Mt Sturgeon (3 km N) and Mt Abrupt (8 km N); both climbs steep, but good views. Easier walk to Mt Piccaninny, 4½ km S. Freshwater Lake Reserve, 8 km N. **Tourist information:** Glenelg Hwy; (03) 5577 2558. **Accommodation:** 1 hotel/motel, 1 B&B, 2 cara./camp. parks.

Dunolly

Pop. 686

MAP REF. 229 L3, 237 O10

A small town in north-central Victoria, in the heart of the gold country and on the Goldfields Tourist Route. 'Welcome Stranger', considered to be the largest nugget ever discovered, was found 15 km NW at Moliagul. The district has produced more nuggets than any other goldfield in Australia; 126 were unearthed in the town itself. Ninety per cent of alluvial gold mined world-wide comes from this area. **Of interest:** Restored Dunolly Court House, Market St, has display relating to historic gold discoveries in area (open Sat., Sun., public and school holidays). Next door, original lockup (1859) and stables. In Broadway: handsome original buildings; Goldfields Historical and Arts Society collection, includes replicas of some of town's most spectacular nuggets (open weekends or by appt). Self-guide bike rides of region, leaflet available at Tourist information. **In the area:** Countryside abounds with colourful spring wildflowers and native fauna. Gold panning in local creeks. Laanecoorie Reservoir, 16 km E. Tarnagulla, 16 km NE, a small mining town with splendid Victorian

architecture; mine (not open to public) and flora reserve nearby. At Moliagul, 15 km NW: monuments mark spot where 'Welcome Stranger' nugget found in 1869 and birthplace of Rev. John Flynn, founder of Royal Flying Doctor Service; Welcome Stranger Discovery Walk, leaflet available at Tourist information. **Tourist information:** Court House, Market St; (03) 5468 1205. **Accommodation:** 2 hotels, 1 motel, 6 B&B, 1 cara./camp. park.

Echuca

Pop. 9438

MAP REF. 127 K13, 240 E4

Echuca and its twin town Moama, across the river in NSW, are at the junction of the Murray, Campaspe and Goulburn rivers. Echuca, now a city and once Australia's largest inland port, took its name from an Aboriginal word meaning 'meeting of the waters', while Moama means 'place of the dead'. An iron bridge joins the two. **Of interest:** Port of Echuca, restored to the period of its heyday with its massive red gum wharf; paddlesteamer *Pevensey* (renamed *Philadelphia* for TV mini-series *All the Rivers Run*); D26 logging barge, PS *Alexander Arbuthnot*; PS *Adelaide*; all available for cruises (cruise times displayed at wharf entrance). Also part of the Port's attractions, all in Murray Esplanade: Star Hotel, underground bar with escape tunnel; Bridge Hotel, built by Henry Hopwood, founder of Echuca, who ran original punt service; Red Gum Works has woodturning demonstrations; award-winning Sharp's Magic Movie

Puffing Billy runs between Belgrave and Emerald

VICTORIA

House and Penny Arcade; Echuca Wharf Pottery; Tisdall Wines, tastings and cellar-door sales; Coach House and Carriage collection; port tour available. In High St: Echuca Historical Society Museum (1867) in former police station; Gumnutland, model village; World in Wax museum. National Holden Museum, Warren St. Cruises available on paddlewheelers *Canberra* and *Pride of the Murray*; accommodation and cruises on paddlesteamer *Emmylou*; MV *Mary Ann* cruising restaurant. Houseboat hire available, inquire at Tourist information for details. Feb.: Southern 80 Ski Race from Torrumbarry Weir to Echuca; Riverboats, Food, Jazz and Wine Festival. Easter: Working Horse Fair. Apr.: Barmah Muster. June: Steam, Horse and Vintage Car Rally. **In the area:** Camping, fishing, water sports and bushwalking. In Moama: Silverstone Go-Kart Track; Horseshoe Lagoon reserve; Aqua Farms Yabbie Farm; Market, 2nd Sun. p.m. each month. At Barmah State Forest 39 km NE: Dharnya Aboriginal Interpretative Centre, has excellent historical display of culture of local Yorta Yorta people; wetlands cruises, fishing, swimming at Barmah Lake. Near Mathoura, 40 km NE: Moira Forest Walkway and Bird Observatory;

Picnic Point recreational area. **Tourist information:** Old Pumphouse, cnr Heygarth St and Cobb Hwy; (03) 5480 7555. **Accommodation:** 42 motels, hotels, holiday units and homesteads, 5 B&B, 11 cara. parks. **See also:** The Mighty Murray; Wine Regions.

Edenhope   Pop. 821

MAP REF. 236 C11

On the Wimmera Hwy, just 30 km from the border with South Australia, Edenhope is situated on the shores of Lake Wallace, a haven for waterbirds. When full, the lake is popular for water sports and fishing. **Of interest:** Cairn, beside lake in Lake St, commemorating visit of first all-Aboriginal cricket team to England; team was coached by T.W. Willis, who was also the founder of Australian Rules football. Feb.: Henley-on-Lake Wallace. **In the area:** At Harrow, one of Victoria's oldest inland towns, 32 km SE: historic buildings including Hermitage Hotel (1851) and log gaol (1862); cemetery contains grave of first Aboriginal cricketer, Johnny Mullagh; National Bush Billycart Championship in Nov. Rocklands Reservoir, part of Wimmera-Mallee irrigation system, for fishing and boating; 65 km E. About 50 km W, over

SA border, Naracoorte Caves Conservation Park. **Tourist information:** Shire Offices, 49 Elizabeth St; (03) 5585 9900. **Accommodation:** 1 hotel, 1 motel, 1 B&B, 1 cara./camp. park.

Eildon   Pop. 740

MAP REF. 219 P2, 230 A12, 241 K11

Built to irrigate a vast stretch of northern Victoria and to provide hydro-electric power, Lake Eildon is the State's largest constructed lake and is a popular resort area, surrounded by the beautiful foothills of the Alps within Eildon State Park. Various self-guide walks and drives, and horseriding available, contact Tourist information. There are excellent recreational facilities around the foreshores, two major boat harbours, launching ramps, picnic grounds and many lookout points. Power boat and houseboat hire available at boat harbours. Dec.: Christmas Eve Gala Night. **In the area:** Signposted Lake Eildon Wall lookout, 1 km N. Lake cruises from Eildon Boat Harbour. Eildon Pondage and Goulburn River, for excellent fishing. There is no closed season for trout in Lake Eildon, which is also stocked with Murray cod; redfin abound naturally. Inland fishing licence required for anglers over 16 years old. Eildon State Park surrounding town, has walking tracks, and camping and picnicking at Jerusalem Inlet. Mt Pinninger (503 m), 3 km E, for panoramic views of Mt Buller, the Alps and lake. Snobs Creek Fish Hatchery, 6 km SW, where millions of trout bred and used to stock lakes and rivers. Just past the hatchery, Snobs Creek Falls. Eildon Deer Park nearby, on Goulburn Valley Hwy. Rubicon Falls, 18 km SW, via Thornton. Jamieson, 57 km SE, an old mining town at junction of Goulburn and Jamieson rivers surrounded by dense, bush-clad mountain countryside. Mt Skene, 48 km SE of Jamieson, has colourful wildflowers Dec.–Feb. (road closed in winter). Scenic drive to Fraser National Park, 16 km NW: popular Candlebark Gully Nature Walk; other scenic walks in area; camping. **Tourist information:** Main St; (03) 5774 2909. **Accommodation:** 4 motels, 2 B&B, 3 cara./camp. parks.

Emerald   Pop. 4693

MAP REF. 219 M7, 222 C13, 232 F5

The Puffing Billy steam railway runs between Belgrave and this pretty town, the first European settlement in the

Dandenong Ranges. **Of interest:** Many galleries and craft shops. Restored Victorian 'red rattler' train, Monbulk Rd, now restaurant with gallery and model railway. Emerald Lake Park, once part of famous Nobelius Nursery, Emerald Lake Rd. Environmental Centre, with walking tracks and barbecues. Emerald Lake and surrounds, one of the area's most attractive and best-equipped picnic and swimming sites (includes waterslides, paddleboats, model railway, kiosk and tearooms). Lake sited on Dandenongs Walk Track, 40-km trail from Cockatoo and Gembrook to Sassafras. Apr.: Great Train Race (runners attempt to race Puffing Billy from Belgrave to Emerald Lake Park). **In the area:** At Menzies Creek, 5 km NW: Cotswold House, fine food and views; Lake Aura Vale, for sailing and picnics. Sherbrooke Art Gallery, Monbulk Rd, Belgrave (11 km NW). Monbulk Animal Kingdom, Swales Rd, Monbulk (11 km NW). Australian Rainbow Trout Farm, Macclesfield (8 km N). Bimbimbie Wildlife Park, Paternoster Rd, Mount Burnett (12 km SE). Trail rides available at Sherbrooke Equestrian Park, 3 km W on Wellington Rd. Further 2 km along, Cardinia Reservoir Park, for good views, picnic spots and native fauna including kangaroos which roam freely in the park. **Tourist information:** Possum's Cottage, 348 Main Rd; (03) 5968 6110. **Accommodation:** 1 hostel. **See also:** The Dandenongs.

Euroa   Pop. 2772

MAP REF. 240 I8

A small town 151 km NE of Melbourne, just off the Hume Fwy, Euroa is a good base for exploring the Strathbogie Ranges and tablelands. The town name originated from the Aboriginal *yerao*, meaning 'joyful'. The district was traversed by the explorers Hume and Hovell in 1824 and Major Mitchell in 1836, and in 1879 was proclaimed a municipality. The Kelly gang staged a daring robbery here, rounding up some 50 hostages at the nearby Faithfull Creek station and then making off with £2200. **Of interest:** Several historic buildings, including National Bank and post office in Binney St. In Kirkland Ave: Seven Creeks Park; Farmers Arms historical museum (open Sun. p.m.). Miniature steam-train rides, Turnbull St (last Sun. each month). Parachuting School, Drysdale Rd (open weekends). Wildflower walks in spring, leaflet available at Tourist information. Oct.: Agricultural Show; Wool Week. **In the area:** Forlonge Memorial, off Euroa–Strathbogie road, 10 km SE, commemorates Eliza Forlonge, who with her sister imported first merino sheep into Victoria. Scenic drive to Gooram Falls (20 km SE) and around Strathbogie Ranges. Mt Wombat lookout, 25 km SW, spectacular views of surrounding country and Alps. Balloon Flights Victoria, 10 km SW. At Longwood, 14 km SW: historic buildings especially White Heart Hotel; horse-drawn carriage rides available. Faithfull Creek Waterfall, 9 km NE. **Tourist information:** Mon.–Fri., Community Centre, Binney St; (03) 5795 2777. Weekends and public holidays: Tourist Information Centre, Kirkland Ave (adjacent to Seven Creeks Park); (03) 5795 1263. **Accommodation:** 3 motels, 1 cara./camp. park.

Flinders   Pop. 451

MAP REF. 219 J12, 221 J11, 232 D9

Flinders is the most southerly town on the Mornington Peninsula. In clear weather there are spectacular clifftop views across the bay to The Nobbies and Seal Rocks on Phillip Island. **Of interest:** Several historic buildings, including Birrbi (1870s), the earliest remaining dwelling in Flinders; and Wilga (1880s), finely detailed Victorian-era home with large hedge; both in King St. Flinders Golf Links, Wood St, is spectacularly located on West Head with views across Bass Strait. **In the area:** Ace Hi horseriding and wildlife park, 11 km W. Cape Schanck lighthouse (1859), 15 km W. At Main Ridge, 15 km NW: Drum Drum Wildflower Farm, working flower and blueberry farm; Pots That Smile, both in Davos St; Sunny Ridge Strawberry Farm, Mornington–Flinders Rd, pick-your-own berries in season; Pig and Whistle, an authentic English pub on Purves Rd. At Red Hill 17 km N: community market, first Sat. each month (Sep.–May); variety of galleries on Mornington–Flinders Rd, including Marion Rosetzky Gallery, hand-painted tiles; Noel's, cottage-style gallery; White Hill Gallery, hand-painted silk; and the Post Office Gallery. Also in the Red Hill area, several wineries with cellar-door sales, including Darling Park Vineyards, Port Phillip Estate, Craig Avon Vineyard, Hanns Creek Estate and Red Hill Estate. At Shoreham, 6 km NE, Ashcombe Maze and Water Gardens, Red Hill Rd, hedge mazes surrounded by gardens (closed Aug.) The Barn Art and Craft Centre, at Merricks, 13 km NE on Bittern–Dromana Rd, has more than 40 different local craft displays (open Wed.–Mon.) At Balnarring 21 km NE: Emu Plains Market, third Sat. each month (Nov.–May); Coolart Homestead, with historic displays, gardens, wetlands bird observation area (open 11–5 daily); several wineries with cellar-door sales including Balnarring, Kings Creek and Willow Creek vineyards. Good surfing at Point Leo, 5 km E of Shoreham. **Visitor information:** Peninsula Tourism, Point Nepean Rd, Dromana; (03) 5987 3078; freecall, 1800 804 009. **Accommodation:** 1 hotel, 1 motel, 2 B&B, 1 cara./camp. park. **See also:** The Mornington Peninsula; Wine Regions.

Foster   Pop. 1078

MAP REF. 233 J10

A picturesque small town within easy reach of Corner Inlet, Waratah Bay and Wilsons Promontory on the south-east coast of Victoria, and about 170 km from Melbourne. **Of interest:** In Main St: Historical Museum, in old post office; Stockyard Gallery. Feb.: Agricultural Show. **In the area:** Foster North Lookout, 6 km NW. Scenic drive to Fish Creek, 11 km SW; in town, Fish Creek Potters. Pleasant beach resorts: Waratah Bay, 34 km SW; Walkerville, 36 km SW; Port Franklin, 12 km SE. Cape Liptrap, 46 km SW, excellent views of rugged coastline and Bass Strait. Good surf beach at Sandy Point, 22 km S; surrounding protected waters of Shallow Inlet popular for fishing, windsurfing and swimming. Toora, 12 km E. Turtons Creek, 18 km N, old gold-rich area; lyrebirds sometimes seen in tree-fern gullies nearby. Near Turtons Creek, horse-drawn wagons and trail riding. **Tourist information:** Stockyard Gallery, Main St; (03) 5682 1125. **Accommodation:** 2 motels, 10 B&B, 1 cara./camp. park.

Geelong   Pop. 126 306

MAP REF. 218 F9, 224, 225 E7, 232 A6, 235 R7

Geelong, on Corio Bay, is the largest provincial city in Victoria. It is a major manufacturing and processing centre, and has a strong tradition in wool selling and storage. The Corio Bay area was first settled in the 1830s and, apart from

National Parks

Although it is Australia's smallest mainland State, Victoria houses over 100 national, state, wilderness and regional parks. Victoria's parks protect representative samples of a wide range of the State's land and vegetation types: from alps, open grasslands and mallee to rainforests, tall forests, coasts, volcanic plains and heathlands. Spring and summer are the best seasons to visit the many parks noted for their wildflowers. In summer, sun lovers can head for parks along the coast to swim, surf, canoe, boat or fish. Autumn, with its mild weather, beckons the bushwalker, and winter means skiing at alpine parks.

Around Melbourne

At **Organ Pipes National Park,** only 20 kilometres north-west of Melbourne, there are fascinating rock formations: a series of hexagonal basalt columns rising more than 20 metres above Jacksons Creek. These 'organ pipes' were formed when lava cooled in an ancient river bed. While this is the best-known feature of the small 85-hectare park, it is also excellent for picnics, walks and bird-observing. Nearby is the 650-hectare **Woodlands Historic Park** which features the charming Woodlands Homestead that was brought from Britain as a wooden 'kit' home and erected here in 1843. A favourite haunt of bushwalkers, 50 kilometres north-east of

Unusual basalt columns, Organ Pipes National Park

Melbourne, is **Kinglake National Park,** where wooded valleys, fern gullies and timbered ridges provide a perfect setting for two beautiful waterfalls, Masons and Wombelano falls. From a lookout, visitors can enjoy a panoramic view of the Yarra Valley, Port Phillip Bay and the You Yangs Range.

Just 35 kilometres east of Melbourne is the green wonderland of the 1920-hectare **Dandenong Ranges National Park**. This park includes tree-fern gullies in which huge fronds of ferns form a canopy overhead, screening the sun and creating a cool, moist environment in which mosses, delicate ferns and flowers, including over 30 orchid species,

all thrive. There are more than 20 species of native animals in the park, including echidnas, platypuses, ringtail possums and sugar gliders; kookaburras, rosellas and cockatoos often visit picnic areas. The spectacular rufous fantail can be seen in the summer months. There are over 100 bird species, but make sure you identify them by sight and not by sound only, because the lyrebird can mimic many of their calls.

Mornington Peninsula National Park is probably the most interesting park close to Melbourne, mainly because for more than 100 years the Point Nepean area was out of bounds to most people. It has associations with early settlement, quarantine, shipping and defence. As one of Victoria's major Bicentennial projects, an information centre, walking tracks, displays and other facilities were provided during 1988-9. Today

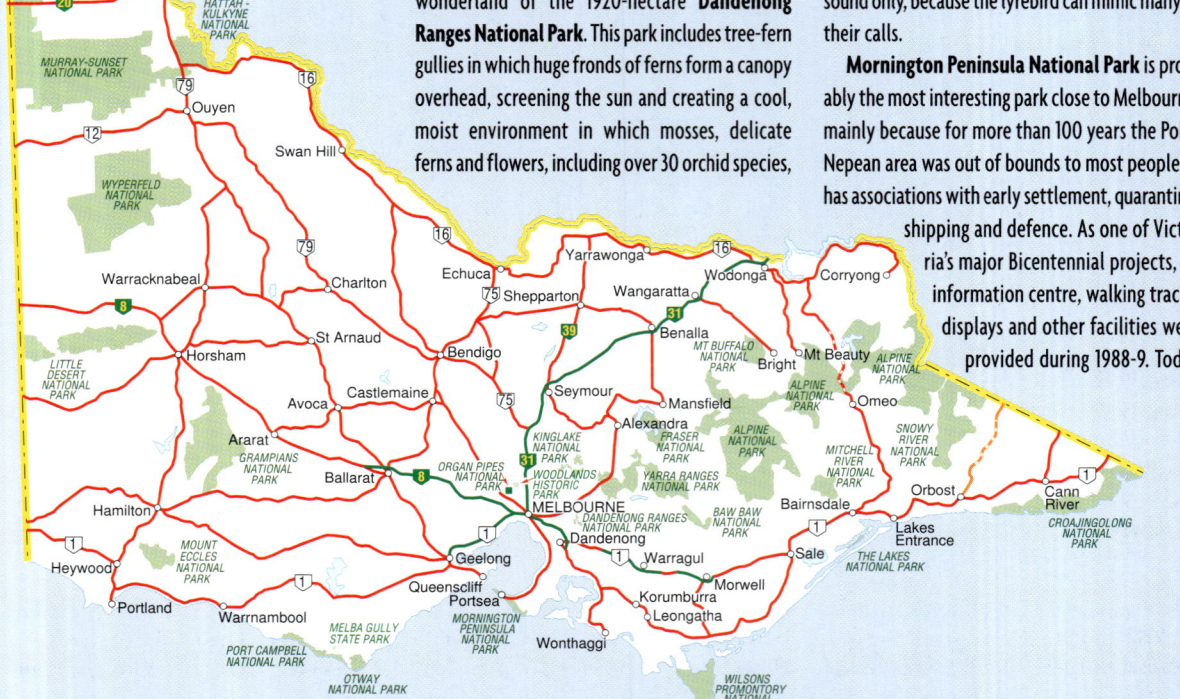

Tidal River in Wilsons Promontory National Park, one of the State's most popular national parks

the park has a total area of 2680 hectares and stretches from Point Nepean to Cape Schanck. To prevent overcrowding and damage to the environment, no more than 600 people are permitted in the Point Nepean section at any one time; so bookings for day visits (with a park-use fee) are required. Vehicles are not permitted to the tip of Point Nepean, so walking, cycling or taking the transporter are the ways to get around. Highlights of the point are Fort Nepean, the cemetery with burials dating from the 1850s and the fascinating Cheviot Hill and Pisterman's Track walks.

Yarra Ranges National Park, the most recent national park proclaimed in Victoria, is located just north-east of Melbourne. The majestic eucalypts and lush tree-fern glades of the Black Spur on the Marcondah Highway form a dramatic gateway to Marysville, Lake Mountain, Alexandra and Lake Eildon. Further south, along the Yarra Valley via Warburton, is Mt Donna Buang. The park includes some of Melbourne's water catchment areas which are generally closed to public access. The moist forests of the Yarra Ranges are considered to be of national botanical significance, and they provide vital habitats for many unique animals. In particular, the forests of mountain ash — the world's tallest flowering plant — provide the habitat for Leadbeater's possum, an endangered species that is hollow-dependent. Thought to be extinct for many years, Leadbeater's possum was rediscovered in these forests in 1961.

Coastal Parks

Wilsons Promontory National Park in Gippsland is the best known coastal park and one of the most popular in Victoria. The Prom, as it is known, really does have something for everyone. There is a concentration of amenities and accommodation, including camping and caravan sites, and cabins at Tidal River, as well as the visitor information centre and park office. Leaflets for 80 kilometres of walking tracks are available here, and visitors should also inquire about the long but rewarding lighthouse walk. Other natural attractions include secluded bays and magnificent stretches of beaches, granite outcrops, and spectacular wildflowers that begin blooming in late winter and continue through spring. Wilsons Promontory is very popular, particularly in summer. Campsites are available only by ballot for the Christmas and Easter holiday periods.

The unusual rock structures found at **Port Campbell National Park** — The Twelve Apostles, The Arch and Loch Ard Gorge — are majestic formations sculpted out of soft limestone cliffs by the relentless sea. While it is the spectacular coastal scenery that makes this park so popular, it is also an interesting park for birds, with around 100 species being recorded. The park was a popular place with Aboriginal people too, if the number of shell middens along the coast is an indication. And it is especially notorious for being part of the 'Shipwreck Coast'.

Closer to Melbourne are the beautiful lush tree-fern gullies and towering mountain-ash forests of the **Otway National Park**. The special **Melba Gully State Park** is situated to the north-west of Otway National Park near Lavers Hill. Because of the treacherous nature of the waters of Bass Strait, a lighthouse was the first piece of 'civilisation' at Cape Otway; it was opened in 1848 after two years in the building. Cottages adjacent to the lighthouse can be booked for accommodation. Activities to be enjoyed include sightseeing all year (even in winter storms), while camping, surfing, fishing and walking are most enjoyable in spring and summer. There are guided walks in summer to see the glow-worms at Melba Gully.

Eastern Victoria, with its mild and fairly wet climate, has vast areas of dense forest. These are attractive to bushwalkers and campers, who will find here a wide range of trees — mainly eucalypts, but also native pines, banksias and paperbarks.

Some of the most attractive coastal scenery close to any major regional centre can be found in and around **The Lakes National Park.** The park is surrounded by the waters of the extensive Gippsland Lakes system, ideal for sailing, boating and fishing. The 2390-hectare park harbours a large population of kangaroos and more than 140 bird species. Camping, picnicking and an excellent network of walking tracks provide distractions for those who are land-based.

Croajingolong National Park has 87 500 hectares of coastline and hinterland stretching from Sydenham Inlet to the New South Wales border. The area contains remote rainforest, woodland, ocean beaches, rocky promontories, inlets and coves. Several rare species of wildlife can be found here, such as the smoky mouse and the ground parrot, and in spring the visitor will see an array of wildflowers. There is a wide range of activities for visitors at Croajingolong, with a holiday centre at Mallacoota and other towns along the Princes Highway offering accommodation and fine food.

In the north-east of the State

The **Alpine National Park,** created in December 1989 and currently covering approximately 642 000 hectares, is the State's largest national park. Stretching along the Great Dividing Range, the park links with Kosciusko National Park in New South Wales and its neighbour Namadgi National Park in the Australian Capital Territory in a grouping of national parks that encompasses almost all of south-east Australia's alpine areas. The park protects the habitats of a variety of flora and fauna,

Snow gums, Baw Baw National Park

including the rare mountain pygmy possum (the world's only exclusively sub-alpine marsupial). The Alps are renowned for their sublime landscapes, features characterised by Mount Bogong and Mount Feathertop (Victoria's highest mountains) and the unique Bogong High Plains. During spring and summer the high plains are carpeted with wildflowers; more than 1100 native plant species are found in the park, including 12 found nowhere else in the world. The park is ideal for bushwalking, horseriding and cross-country skiing. Both Falls Creek and Mount Hotham ski resorts are surrounded by the Alpine National Park. In the summer months most roads provide easy access for vehicles, allowing a range of scenic drives with short walks to lookouts and other points of interest. Some huts in the park, popular places for walkers to visit, are being restored for their historic value.

Mount Buffalo National Park, north-west of Bright, encompasses Mount Buffalo plateau with its granite tors and rounded boulders. In milder weather, the park, with its bubbling streams and cascading waterfalls, offers visitors over 80 kilometres of marked walking tracks. The wildflowers on the high plains are at their best between November and March. Wombats, wallabies, lyrebirds, rosellas and gang-gang cockatoos may be seen. In winter, skiers can enjoy excellent cross-country and beginners' downhill skiing.

Canoeists will find excitement shooting the rapids or exploring the gorges of **Snowy River National Park** or **Mitchell River National Park,** both in East Gippsland, while bushwalkers can hike through beautiful forest scenery.

Baw Baw National Park covers the granite Baw Baw plateau at the southern end of Victoria's high country, and sections of the Thomson and Aberfeldy river valleys. It offers good cross-country skiing in winter: Baw Baw Alpine Village abuts the park. Numerous walking tracks are popular in summer, including a 20-kilometre section of the Australian Alps Walking Track, which extends from Walhalla to Cowombat Flat on the New South Wales border. In summer, visitors can take short walks to the track and to the plateau, or follow cross-country ski trails. Colourful wildflowers bloom on the plateau in summer. The park is home to Leadbeater's possum and the Baw Baw frog (both endangered species), as well as wombats, wallabies, echidnas, platypuses, gliders and several types of snakes and lizards. Crimson rosellas, yellow-tailed black cockatoos, gang-gangs and lyrebirds are common.

Fraser National Park centres on Lake Eildon, and offers boating, sailing, water skiing, fishing and swimming, and a number of walking tracks, including a nature trail near Devil Cove. The park's western boundary, along the Puzzle Range, provides scenic views over nearby peaks and Coller Bay. There are many kangaroos and wallabies in the park. Crimson rosellas, cockatoos, galahs and kookaburras visit the camping grounds, and around the lake there are cormorants, pelicans, ducks, swans, herons and ibis.

In the west of the State

The 167 200-hectare **Grampians National Park** offers marvellous scenery, wildlife and tourist facilities. The park is famous for its rugged sandstone ranges, waterfalls, wildflowers, wide variety of birds and mammals, as well as its Aboriginal rock-art sites. The peaks rise to heights of over 1000 metres and form the western edge of the Great Dividing Range. The Grampians are no doubt best seen on foot and there are many walking tracks, such as the well-marked Wonderland Track, through to the more challenging walks across the Major Mitchell Plateau.

Mount Eccles in south-west Victoria, is one of several parks that contain rock formations of great geological interest. An extinct volcano, a lava canal, lava cave and the formation called the Stony Rises are exceptional features, while the crater contains the tranquil Lake Surprise.

The surprise for most visitors to **Little Desert National Park** is to discover that it is neither little (at 132 000 hectares) nor a desert. It is best known for its amazing displays of wildflowers in spring; more than 600 flowering-plant species are found here, including more than 40 ground orchids. Another special feature of the Little Desert is that mallee fowl are found here. These birds build mounds for eggs and the mounds can be as much as 5 metres in diameter and 1.5 metres high.

Wyperfeld National Park in the north-west also contains hundreds of species of plants and birdlife, and is also a great park to visit in the spring, autumn and winter. In good rainfall years there are colourful spring wildflower displays, and in the autumn and winter the visitor will enjoy crisp, clear days — perfect for bushwalking and birdwatching.

The vast **Murray-Sunset National Park** contains a diversity of semi-arid environments from riverine floodplains to heathlands, salt lakes and woodlands, which support a tremendous variety of wildlife, particularly birdlife. It is the second largest national park in the State covering 633 000 hectares. This park is best visited in the cooler months of the year.

Another park in the north-west of the State is **Hattah-Kulkyne National Park.** Typically, summers here are long, hot and dry; rainfall is usually less than 300 millimetres per year. The animals of this area have evolved strategies for avoiding or tolerating heat and dryness: some burrow, others just rest during the heat of the day; some birds catch thermals to cooler air. After rainfall and flooding from the Murray River, the serenely beautiful Hattah Lakes system transforms the park into a bird haven and a wonderful wildflower landscape.

For more information on Victoria's national parks, contact the Outdoors Information Centre of the Department of Natural Resources and Environment at 240 Victoria Pde, East Melbourne; (03) 9412 4795. Web site address http://www.nre.vic.gov.au

VICTORIA

a rush to the diggings during the gold boom, Geelong has grown and prospered steadily. It is a pleasant and well-laid-out city with lovely views across the bay. **Of interest:** National Wool Museum, in historic bluestone woolstore cnr Mooraboo and Brougham sts, features sound and audio-visual displays, re-created shearers' quarters and millworker's cottage; Tourist information centre in foyer. Interesting buildings (more than 100 with National Trust classifications) include: Merchiston Hall (1856), Garden St, East Geelong; Osborne House (1858), bluestone mansion housing Maritime Museum, Swinburne St, North Geelong; beautiful Corio Villa (1856), prefabricated cast-iron house, at Eastern Beach. The following are open to the public: The Heights (1855), 14-roomed prefabricated timber mansion surrounded by delightful gardens, Aphrasia St, Newtown; Barwon Grange (1855), Fernleigh St, Newtown. Christ Church, Moorabool St, oldest Anglican church in Victoria still in continuous use. Customs House, Brougham St. Geelong Art Gallery, State's largest regional gallery; Performing Arts Centre; both in Little Malop St. Wintergarden, 51 McKillop St, historic building housing gallery, nursery, antiques and gift shop. Pottage Crafts, 189 Moorabool St. Eastern Beach and Park, swimming in fully restored 1930s seabathing complex. Beachfront Scenic Drive. Botanic Gardens, Garden St, in Eastern Park, overlooking Corio Bay. Johnstone Park, cnr Mercer and Gheringhap sts. Queens Park, Queens Park Rd, Newtown, has walks to Buckleys Falls. Balyang Bird Sanctuary, Shannon Ave, Newtown. Extensive walking tracks and bike paths alongside Barwon River. Boat ramps on Corio Bay beaches. Good river and bay fishing. Steampacket Gardens Market on foreshore at Eastern Beach, 1st Sun. each month. Jan.: Summer Festival. Feb.: Pako Multicultural Festa. Mar.: Highland Gathering. Apr.: Heritage and Vintage Rally; Alternative Farmvision. June: Wool Week; Celtic Festival. Oct.: Show; Racing Carnival. **In the area:** In Greater Geelong: 14 wineries (details from Tourist information); Norlane Water World, 7 km N. Lara, 19 km N, swept by bushfires in 1969 but some historic buildings remain. Nearby, You Yangs, a range of distinctive granite hills in You Yangs Regional Park, has walking tracks, picnic grounds and information centre. Between Lara and You Yangs,

Serendip Sanctuary, once purely a wildlife research station, now open to public, has nature trails, bird hides and visitors' centre. Anakie, a township at foot of Brisbane Ranges, 31 km N. Brisbane Ranges National Park, 34 km N, has many species of ferns and flowering plants, and native fauna; Discovery Walk leads to Anakie Gorge (leaflet available). Nearby Fairy Park, with miniature houses and scenes from fairytales. Mt Anakie Winery; Staughton Vale winery; both north of Anakie on Staughton Vale Rd. Steiglitz, 10 km NW of Anakie, once a gold town, now almost deserted, has restored court house (1875) (open Sun.). Batesford, 10 km NW of Geelong, a picturesque market garden township with a history of winemaking; Sandstone Travellers Rest Inn (1849) across Moorabool River from present hotel. Meredith, 46 km NW, one of the oldest towns in Victoria, once a stopping-place for diggers on their way to the goldfields. Fyansford, 5 km W on outskirts of city, one of oldest settlements in region: historic buildings including Swan Inn, Balmoral Hotel (1854) and Fyansford Hotel; Information Centre at Common Reserve has interpretative material on history, flora and fauna of region; Monash Bridge across Moorabool River thought to be one of first reinforced-concrete bridges in Victoria. Brownhill Observation Tower, 10 km SW, at Ceres, excellent view of surrounding areas. Deakin University's Institute of the Arts, 13 km SW, at Waurn Ponds. At Moriac, 20 km SW, horse-drawn caravan hire. The Bellarine Peninsula begins about 16 km E (see text entries for Drysdale, Portarlington, Queenscliff and Ocean Grove). Great Ocean Rd from Torquay provides spectacular coastal scenery. **Tourist information:** National Wool Museum, 26–32 Moorabool St; (03) 5222 2900; freecall, 1800 620888. **Accommodation:** 7 hotels, 27 motels, 17 B&B, 14 cara./camp. parks. **See also:** The Great Ocean Road.

Gisborne   Pop. 2819

MAP REF. 216 H3, 232 B2, 240 E13

Once a stopping-place for coaches and foot travellers on their way to the Castlemaine and Bendigo goldfields, Gisborne is an attractive township (now bypassed by the Calder Hwy) on the way to Woodend and Kyneton. Market, Brantome St, 1st. Sun. each month. Dec.: Festival. **In the area:** Mount

Macedon, 15 km N, memorial cross at summit. Mt Aitken Estates Winery, 6 km S. **Tourist information:** Ampol Road Pantry; (03) 5428 2541. **Accommodation:** 2 hotels, 1 motel, 1 cara./camp. park (at Macedon). **See also:** Wine Regions.

Glenrowan   Pop. 345

MAP REF. 230 D1, 241 M6

Glenrowan, 220 km NE of Melbourne, is the famous site of the defeat of Ned Kelly and his gang by the police in 1880. **Of interest:** On Old Hume Hwy: Ned Kelly Memorial Museum and Homestead; Kate's Cottage, gifts and souvenirs behind huge 6-m high statue of Ned Kelly; engrossing computer-animated show of the capture of Ned Kelly. **In the area:** Nearby wineries: Baileys of Glenrowan, Taminick Gap Rd (just NW of town); Auldstone Cellars, and Booths Taminick Cellars, both on Booths Rd, Taminick, 10 km NW; HJT Vineyards, Keenan Rd (near Lake Mokoan). **Tourist information:** Kate's Cottage, Old Hume Hwy; (03) 5766 2448. **Accommodation:** 1 motel, 1 cara. park. **See also:** Wine Regions.

Halls Gap   Pop. 334

MAP REF. 234 I1, 236 I12

Beautifully sited in the heart of the Grampians, this little village is adjacent to Lake Bellfield and surrounded by the Grampians National Park and a network of scenic roads. Feb.: Grampians Jazz Festival. May: Grampians Gourmet Weekend. Sept.–Oct.: Wildflower Exhibition. **In the area:** The area is noted for its wildflowers. Bushwalking, camping, rock climbing and abseiling in national park, one of largest in State; Visitors Centre, 2 km from town. Brambuk Aboriginal Living Cultural Centre, 2 km S. Boroka Vineyards, 2 km E. Lake Fyans, 17 km E, for swimming, fishing, yachting and water-skiing. At Roses Gap Recreation Park, Roses Gap Rd, 21 km N, in Northern Grampians section of park, scenic walks, fitness track, accommodation and camping. Reids Lookout and The Balconies, 12 km NW. Mackenzie Falls, 17 km NW. Wartook Pottery and Restaurant, 20 km NW. **Tourist information:** Grampians Rd; (03) 5356 4247. **Accommodation:** 8 motels, 2 hostels, 4 cara./camp. parks. **See also:** The Grampians; National Parks.

Hamilton
Pop. 10 200

MAP REF. 234 F5

Known as the 'Wool Capital of the World', Hamilton is a prosperous and pleasant city less than an hour's drive from the coastal centres of Portland, Port Fairy and Warrnambool to the south and the Grampian Ranges to the north. **Of interest:** Big Woolbales Complex, designed in shape of five huge woolbales on Henty Hwy, focuses on wool industry, and has woolshed memorabilia and craft centre. Hamilton Country Spun Woollen Mill and Factory, Peck St, has sales and tours (Mon.–Fri.). HIRL (Hamilton Institute of Rural Learning), North Boundary Rd, has nature trail and breeding area for eastern barred bandicoots (open Mon.–Fri.). Land-care tours available, bookings essential (contact Tourist information). Hamilton Art Gallery, Brown St, contains Herbert Shaw Collection. Lake Hamilton, Ballarat Rd, for water sports and trout fishing; sandy beach, jogging and cycling tracks, and picnic facilities on shore. On banks of lake, Sir Reginald Ansett Transport Museum, Glenelg Hwy, has historical collection and memorabilia of transport industry; Ansett Airlines began in Hamilton in 1931. Botanical Gardens (established 1870), French St, has native animal enclosure, free-flight aviary and historic band rotunda. Hamilton Pastoral Museum, in former St Luke's Lutheran Church, on Glenelg Hwy (open weekends or by appt). Hamilton History Centre, Gray St, features histories of early western Victorian families. Hamilton is the starting point for Mary MacKillop Pilgrims Drive; grave of Mary's father in cemetery (Henty Hwy). Feb.: Beef Expo. July: Eisteddfod. Aug.: Sheepvention (features sheep and wool inventions on show and farmdog championships). **In the area:** Summit Park, Nigretta Rd, 15 km NW, specialises in the raising of Saxon-Merino sheep for superfine wool production. Nigretta Falls, 15 km NW, has viewing platform nearby. Wannon Falls, 19 km W. Mt Eccles National Park, 35 km S, near MacArthur, features Mt Eccles, crater Lake Surprise (one of 3 extinct volcanoes) and lava caves. Grampians Tour (good day trip from Hamilton) to Dunkeld, Grampians National Park, Halls Gap, Ararat and back via Glenthompson. At Cavendish, 25 km N, three beautiful private gardens, contact Tourist information for brochure. **Tourist information:** Lonsdale St; (03) 5572 3746; freecall, 1800 807056. **Accommodation:** 3 hotel/motels, 7 motels, 1 hostel, 2 cara./camp. parks.

Harrietville
Pop. 250

MAP REF. 231 M8, 241 Q9, 242 C7

Tucked into the foothills of Mt Hotham and Mt Feathertop, Harrietville is a convenient accommodation centre for skiers at Mt Hotham or holidaymakers in north-east Victoria. Gold was discovered here in 1862, and the gold-rush village was proclaimed a township in 1879. **Of interest:** Pioneer Park, Alpine Rd, an open-air museum and picnic area. Audrey's Dolls and Crafts, Cobungra Court, hand-made porcelain dolls. Bushmarket, 3rd Sun. in Jan. and Easter Sun. Mar.: Bushman's Classic (mountain cattlemen's race). Aug.: International Ski Marathon Kangaroo Hoppet. **In the area:** Lavender Farm, at northern edge of town on Alpine Rd (closed during winter). Bushwalking in high mountain country of Alpine National Park, which surrounds town (weather conditions can be harsh and change suddenly); walking tracks to Mt Feathertop (1922 m), 20 km return; Mt Hotham (1859 m), 65 km return. Mt Hotham Alpine Village, 32 km SE, during summer, bushwalking (Australian Alps Walking Track passes through village) in Bogong High Plains and Dargo High Plains; during winter, excellent downhill and cross-country skiing. Dinner Plain Alpine Village, 44 km SE, during summer, bushwalking and horseriding; during winter, good cross-country skiing. Crystal Waters Trout Farm and, nearby, Mountain Fresh Trout Farm, 5 km N, offer fishing and educational displays. **Tourist information:** Old General Store, Alpine Rd; (03) 5759 2553. **Accommodation:** 1 hotel/motel, 1 chalet, 1 lodge, 1 cara./camp. park.

Healesville
Pop. 6264

MAP REF. 219 N5, 222 E6, 232 F3

Surrounded by mountain forest country, Healesville is about a one and a half hour's drive from Melbourne along the Maroondah Hwy. It has been a popular resort town since the turn of the century, as the climate is cool and pleasant in summer and the area offers excellent bushwalks and beautiful scenic drives. **Of interest:** Trolley rides, Healesville railway station to Yarra Glen (Sun. only). Yarra Valley Winery Tours, inquire at Tourist information. Market, River St, 1st Sun. each month. Feb.: Coldstream Country and Western Festival. Mar.: Australian Car Rally Championship; Grape Grazing. Nov.: Gateway Festival. **In the area:** World-famous Healesville Sanctuary, 4 km S on Badger Creek Rd: 32-ha reserve housing a variety of native birds and animals in largely natural bushland setting, yet displays enable animals to be seen in close proximity; picnic/barbecue facilities, kiosk and self-service restaurant available. On way to Healesville Sanctuary, HCP Antique Emporium, a large, undercover antique market; Hedgend Maze, Albert Rd; pottery, lapidary and art gallery at Nigel Court; Corranderrk Aboriginal Cemetery, 3 km S. Opposite sanctuary, Galina Beek Living Cultural Centre has authentic Aboriginal arts and crafts. Mallesons Lookout, 8 km S, views of Yarra Valley through to Melbourne. Yarra Ranges National Park, just east of town: majestic mountain ash forests and fern gullies; within park, superb drive through forest over Black Spur, picnic facilities at top; Badger Weir Park, 7 km SE, majestic park in natural setting; Tuscany Gallery, 5 km E; Donnelly's Weir Park, 4 km N, start of 5000-km Bicentennial National Trail to Cooktown (Qld) for horseriders and walkers; Mt St Leonard, 14 km N, fine views from summit. Maroondah Reservoir Park, 3 km NE: magnificent park in sylvan setting, walking tracks and lookout nearby, Sounds by the Water concert held each Feb. At Toolangi, 17 km NW: Forest Discovery Centre, displays of timber industry and its history; Singing Garden of C.J. Dennis, a beautiful, formal garden; Sculpture Studio, sculpture from recycled timbers. At Yarra Glen, 14 km W: historic Grand Hotel; Yarra Valley Racing Centre, 5 km E; Gulf Station (1854), historic homestead, 2 km N. Sugarloaf Reservoir Park, 10 km W of Yarra Glen, for fishing, sailing and walking. At Yering, south of Yarra Glen, Yarra Valley Dairy offers cheese tastings Thurs.–Mon. There are around 30 wineries in the area open for cellar-door sales and tastings; contact Tourist information for details. **Tourist information:** Yarra Valley Healesville Visitor Information Centre, 127 Maroondah Hwy; (03) 5962 2600. **Accommodation:** 4 motels, 20 B&B, 3 cara./camp. parks. **See also:** Wine Regions.

VICTORIA

Heathcote   Pop. 1507

MAP REF. 240 E9

In attractive countryside on the McIvor Hwy, Heathcote is set along the McIvor Creek, 47 km SE of Bendigo. **Of interest:** McIvor Cottage, in old court house, High St: historical display, art and craft, and tourist information. Pink Cliffs, Pink Cliffs Rd, off Hospital Rd, brilliant mineral staining created by eroded spoil from gold sluices. Old Heathcote Hospital (1859), Hospital Rd. McIvor Range Reserve, off Barrack St. Heathcote Winery, High St. Oct.: Golden Grape Festival. Nov.: Show. **In the area:** Lake Eppalock, 10 km W, one of the State's largest lakes. Alpaca farm and children's farm 7 km S. Mount Ida Lookout, 4 km N, excellent views. Wineries nearby: Zuber Estate (5 km S); Wild Duck Creek Estate (10 km S); Jasper Hill and Huntleigh Vineyards (6 km N), McIvor Creek Wines (10 km SW) and Eppalock Ridge Vineyards (22 km SW). **Tourist information:** McIvor Cottage, High St; (03) 5433 3677. **Accommodation:** 1 hotel, 1 hotel/motel, 1 motel, 1 B&B, 1 cara./camp. park.

Hopetoun   Pop. 704

MAP REF. 126 E12, 236 H3, 238 H13

This small Mallee town, south-east of Wyperfeld National Park, was named after the seventh Earl of Hopetoun, first Governor-General of Australia. Hopetoun was a frequent visitor to the home of Edward Lascelles, who was largely responsible for opening up the Mallee area. **Of interest:** In Evelyn St, two National Trust-classified homes: Hopetoun House (1891) built for Lascelles; Corrong Homestead (1846), home of first European settler in area, Peter McGinnis. Mallee Mural and leadlight window in Shire Offices, Lascelles St, depict history of the Mallee. Lake Lascelles, end Austin St, for boating, swimming and picnics. Oct.: Agricultural Show. **In the area:** Wyperfeld National Park, 50 km W; information centre in park. Swamp Tank Museum at Turriff, 45 km NE. Nearby at Speed, Mallee Machinery Field Days held in Aug. **Tourist information:** Shire Offices, 75 Lascelles St; (03) 5083 3001. **Accommodation:** 1 hotel, 1 hotel/motel, 1 cara./camp. park.

Horsham   Pop. 12 552

MAP REF. 236 G9

Situated at the junction of the Western,

Wimmera and Henty hwys, Horsham is generally regarded as the capital of the Wimmera region. It is a popular base for tours of the region, particularly to the Little Desert National Park, 40 km NW, to the Grampians, some 50 km SE and to Mt Arapiles, 32 km W. **Of interest:** Botanic Gardens, cnr Baker and Firebrace sts. Horsham Art Gallery, Wilson St, features Mack Jost collection of Australian art. Cottage Delights, Dooen Rd, for plants and crafts. May Park, Dimboola Rd. Apex Adventure Island, a children's playground in Barnes Rd. Golf Course Rd: Horsham Rocks and Gems and Country Crafts; Wool Factory, producing top quality, extra-fine wool from Saxon-Merino sheep (tours daily). Attractive picnic spots and viewing places for spectacular sunsets alongside Wimmera River. Market, 2nd Sat. each month at showgrounds, McPherson St. Mar.: Wimmera Machinery Field Days; Apex Fishing Competition. Sept.: Agricultural Show. Oct.: Spring Garden Festival. Dec.: Kannamaroo Festival. **In the area:** Water sports and good fishing for redfin, trout and Murray cod in lakes in area, including: Green Lake (13 km SE), Pine Lake (16 km SE), Taylors Lake (18 km SE), Toolondo Reservoir (44 km SW), home of the fighting brown trout and Rocklands Reservoir (90 km S) on Glenelg River, built to supplement Wimmera-Mallee irrigation scheme. Mt Arapiles, 32 km W, popular climbing rock with 360-degree views from lookout. Black Range Cashmere and Thryptomene Farm, 40 km S (4WD tours available, bookings essential, through Tourist information). Grampians National Park, 50 km SE, famous for its rugged sandstone ranges, wildflowers, waterfalls, wildlife and Aboriginal rock-art sites. At Jung, 10 km NE, market last Sat. each month. Little Desert National Park, 40 km NW. **Tourist information:** 20 O'Callaghan's Pde; (03) 5382 1832; freecall, 1800 633218. **Accommodation:** 6 hotels, 15 motels, 2 B&B, 2 hostels, 2 cara./camp. parks.

Inglewood   Pop. 740

MAP REF. 237 O8, 240 A7

North along the Calder Hwy from Bendigo are the 'Golden Triangle' towns of Inglewood and Bridgewater on Loddon. Sizeable gold nuggets have been found in this area: the largest 'Welcome Stranger' found at Moliagul, weighed 65 kg; two other large nuggets were found

at Kingower in the last decade. **Of interest:** Old eucalyptus oil distillery, Calder Hwy (northern end of town). Old court house, Southey St, now displays historical memorabilia of region (open by appt). Inglewood Gipsy Tours (wagons drawn by Clydesdales) Grant St. Blanche Barkley Winery, Kingower–Rheola Rd. Apr.: Blue Eucalyptus Festival (even-numbered years). **In the area:** Passing Clouds winery, 11 km W at Kingower. Kooyoora State Park, 16 km W, features well-known Melville Caves, once haunt of notorious bushranger Captain Melville. Kangderaar Vineyard, 15 km SW at Rheola. At Bridgewater on Loddon, 8 km SE: fishing, water-skiing, parachute jumping (at weekends) and Water Wheel Vineyards. **Tourist information:** The Motor Company, Brook St; (03) 5438 3558. **Accommodation:** 1 hotel, 1 motel, 1 cara./camp. park. **See also:** Wine Regions.

Inverleigh   Pop. 282

MAP REF. 218 E9, 225 B6, 235 P7

On the Leigh River, this little town 29 km W of Geelong has a number of historic buildings. **Of interest:** On Hamilton Hwy: former Horseshoe Inn; two-storey hotel; Church of England; Presbyterian Church; State school. **In the area:** Fishing in Leigh and Barwon rivers. Inverleigh Common, 2 km N, a bushland and fauna reserve. Barunah Plains Homestead (open by appt), 17 km W. **Tourist information:** Geelong Otway Tourist Information Centre, National Wool Museum, 26–32 Moorabool St, Geelong; (03) 5222 2900. **Accommodation:** None.

Inverloch   Pop. 2195

MAP REF. 232 G10

This is a small seaside resort on Anderson Inlet, east of Wonthaggi. It has long stretches of excellent beach with good surf, and is very popular during the summer months. **Of interest:** Environment Centre, selling books and natural products, and Shell Museum, The Esplanade. Mar.: Jazz Festival. **In the area:** Adjacent to town, Anderson Inlet, most southerly habitat of mangroves; nearby, Townsend Bluff and Maher's Landing for bird-watching. Inverloch–Cape Paterson scenic road to the south-west through Bunurong Cliff Coastal Reserve, offers views equal to those on Great Ocean Rd. At Cape Paterson, spear fishing and

Wildlife-Watching

Victoria has some marvellous wildlife-watching opportunities. Besides the ever-popular penguins at Phillip Island there are many interesting encounters to be had, including picnicking amongst kangaroos, peaking at a malleefowl as it tends its nesting mound, and watching thousands of shearwaters fly home to their roosts at dusk.

In Melbourne

Thanks to Melbourne's wonderful gardens and reserves, native animals can still be seen in the city. The lake in the **Botanic Gardens** in the inner-suburb of South Yarra is a habitat for black swans, cormorants, ducks, moorhens and coots.

Melbourne's possums have adapted well to their urban environment. There are two varieties: the smaller ringtail with its white-tipped tail, and the larger brushtail possum. Brushtails are the more brash of the two, and can often be seen rummaging after dark on the lawns in the **Fitzroy and Alexandra gardens**.

Westgate Park is an unlikely bird sanctuary in an industrial area under the busy eastern approach to the Westgate Bridge. This does not discourage seabirds and waterbirds from using this valuable wetland: ducks, coots, pelicans and swans share the sanctuary, and ibis breed on one of the park's islands between July and October. **Jells Park** in Wheelers Hill is another prime suburban birdwatching site, particularly in September when migratory Japanese snipe arrive at the lake. A bird hide allows the snipe to be viewed undisturbed.

Melbourne is on the shores of **Port Phillip**, which is home to schools of bottlenose dolphins and seals. Dolphin- and seal-viewing boat tours operate from the bayside towns of Sorrento and Queenscliff. Cruises also leave for Pope's Eye Nature Reserve within the bay to view Australasian gannets. Pope's Eye and other nearby navigation structures are the only fabricated structures in the world where gannets nest.

Also within the bay is a colony of little (fairy) penguins. Cruises leave in daylight hours from Southbank and St Kilda pier to view the penguins feeding on whitebait, and at night to see them coming ashore at St Kilda. For more information on Melbourne parks contact Parks Victoria, Vault 11, Banana Alley, Flinders St, Melbourne; (03) 9287 7140.

Around Melbourne

The most famous penguin-watching spot is a couple of hours south of Melbourne at **Phillip Island**. At Summerland Beach the little (fairy) penguins come ashore each evening to their burrows in the sand-dunes. At the visitors centre nesting penguins can be spied on through peepholes in their specially designed nesting boxes. From May to July these birds can be seen nest-building, and from August to January eggs are laid and chicks raised. February to April are good months to see the penguins moulting.

Koalas can also be seen in their natural habitat from raised walkways at the Koala Conservation Centre on the island. Ferry trips leave from Cowes to Seal Rocks on the south-western tip of the island, allowing close-up views of a large colony of fur seals. At San Remo, pelicans get a fish meal daily on the waterfront.

South-west of Melbourne near Lara is **Serendip Wildlife Reserve**. This grassland and wetland habitat has viewing hides, and is a good location to see native birds. Visitors can see waterbirds such as spoonbills, grebes and ducks, as well as several birds-of-prey species.

On the South-West Coast

Just off the coast near Port Campbell is **Mutton Bird Island**, a bird colony free from introduced predators. Thousands of migratory short-tailed shearwaters

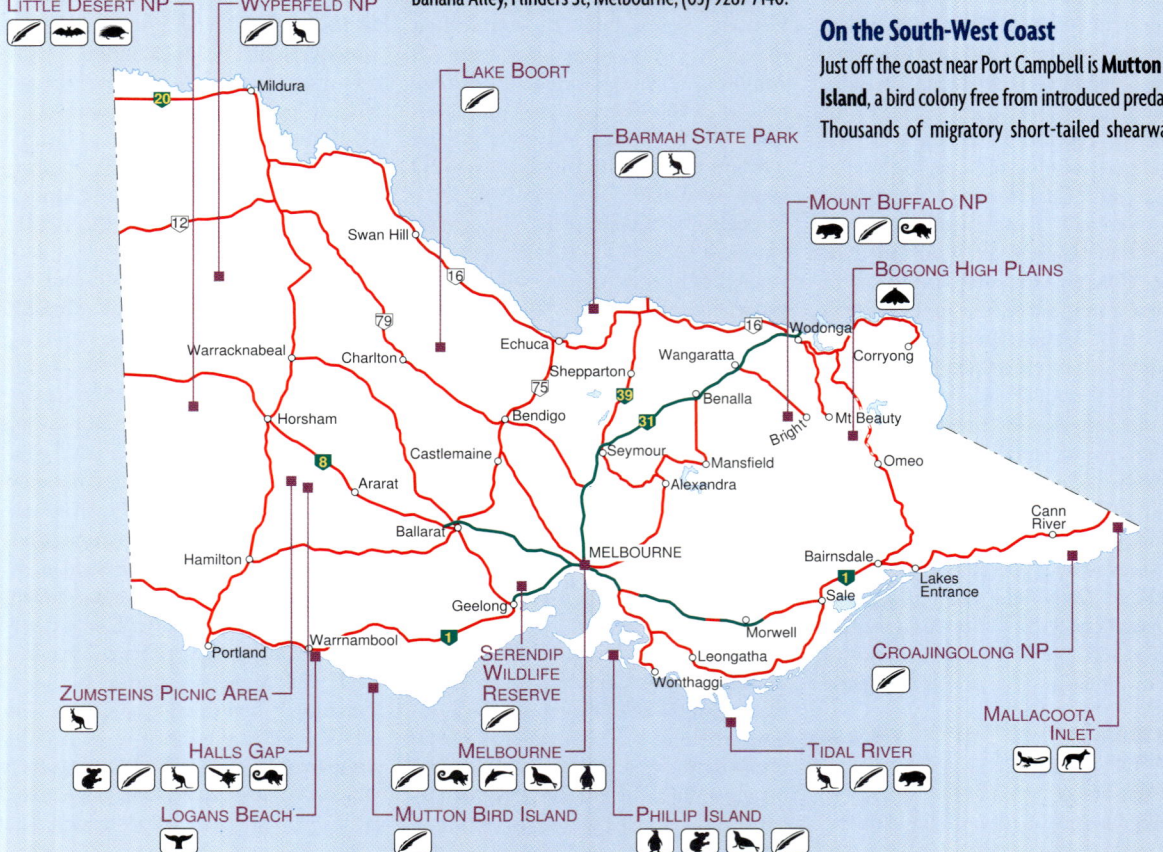

(muttonbirds) arrive from the north Pacific and nest on the island between September and April.

The most famous visitors to the south-west coast are southern right whales. After spending the summer months in the plankton-rich sub-Antarctic waters, they return to breeding grounds at **Logans Beach** near Warrnambool between May and October. Southern rights are slowly increasing in numbers after being decimated by commercial whaling earlier in the century. While there is no guarantee of spotting a whale, these months offer the best chance of seeing one of these huge but graceful mammals close to shore.

In the Grampians

The rugged sandstone ranges of the Grampians offer some of the best opportunities for wildlife-watching in south-western Victoria. Koalas can be seen around **Halls Gap**, and boisterous flocks of sulphur-crested cockatoos and corellas arrive each evening to roost in the eucalypts opposite the town's shops. Eastern grey kangaroos are common in grassland around the town, particularly at dawn and dusk. For a closer look at our national symbol, visit **Zumsteins picnic area** in the Grampians National Park. Kangaroos graze there freely throughout the day. During school holidays national park rangers conduct night wildlife-watching walks from the visitors centre at Halls Gap. On these informative walks several species are likely to be seen by torchlight, including gliders, owls, kangaroos, ringtail and brushtail possums, and wallabies.

In the Mallee

North of the Grampians is **Wyperfeld National Park**. Follow the Lake Brambruk Nature Walk to see emus, kangaroos, soaring wedge-tailed eagles, and the endangered regent parrot. Wyperfeld's best-known bird is the threatened malleefowl. The male builds a large nesting mound comprising a core of organic material covered by a layer of sand. With a little patience there is a good chance of seeing a malleefowl scratching around its mound, particularly from October to March. **Little Desert National Park** also has malleefowl, along with small insectivorous bats which can be seen flying on summer evenings, and a healthy population of short-beaked echidnas.

Around the Murray and in the North-Central Region

Barmah State Park in north-central Victoria provides a unique bird habitat. Floods are common between July and October; a good time for boat tours to look for water birds. Eastern grey kangaroos

Koalas can be seen in their natural habitat at the Koala Conservation Centre, Phillip Island

WILDLIFE-WATCHING ETHICS

- Do not disturb wildlife or wildlife habitats. Keep the impact of your presence to a minimum. Use available cover or hides wherever possible.
- Do not feed wildlife, even in urban areas. (Note: supervised feeding is allowed at some locations)
- Be careful not to introduce exotic plants and animals – definitely no pets.
- Stay on defined trails.

can be readily seen throughout the forest, though you will need a torch and some patience to glimpse the less-common nocturnal marsupials.

Lake Boort is a haven for birdlife in the north-central region, and is a significant breeding ground. In spring several species raise their young in the logs and rushes around the lake.

In the North-Eastern Highlands

One of Victoria's most popular native species is the common wombat, and a good place to see this burrowing marsupial is in **Mount Buffalo National Park**. They tend to venture out at dusk to graze on snow grass flats. The chalet within the park attracts a good population of the colourful crimson rosellas. An equally colourful but much smaller park resident

is the flame robin, the male having a bright red breast. Lake Catani within the park is a good location to see the retiring lyrebird. Bring a torch to the lake and search for ringtail possums after dark in the surrounding eucalypts.

The Bogong moth played an important part in the lives of local Aborigines prior to European settlement. Each summer Aboriginal groups trekked to the high country to feast on the insects. Thousands of the moths still inhabit the **Bogong High Plains** in summer, and the best places to find them are in rock crevices.

On the Eastern Coast

The Mallacoota region offers wildlife-watchers a good chance to see large tree goannas, particularly along the picnic sites at **Mallacoota Inlet**. The elusive dingo can occasionally be spotted along beaches in the area, and their tracks can be seen in the sand. There is a large bird population in **Croajingolong National Park** – over 300 species in fact. Glossy-black cockatoos are attracted to the native casuarina trees along the walking track to Genoa Peak within the park. King parrots and lyrebirds can also be seen.

At Wilsons Prom

Wilsons Promontory National Park has no shortage of wildlife. Eastern grey kangaroos and emus graze on grassland at **Tidal River**, and blond-coloured wombats emerge at dusk at Norman Beach. This is also a good area for short-tailed shearwaters (muttonbirds). Kookaburras and flame robins are easily seen, while Easter is prime-time for flocks of rainbow lorikeets as they arrive to feed on flowering coastal banksias.

For a good introduction to Victorian wildlife visit Healesville Sanctuary, just east of Melbourne. A range of native wildlife is on display in natural surroundings. The platypus display offers an intimate view of this unique animal, and the birds of prey enclosure has daily feeding demonstrations. The Department of Natural Resources and Environment publishes a booklet, *Wildlife Watching in Victoria*, which is an invaluable guide to over 90 viewing sites. For more information on wildlife watching in national parks contact the Department of Natural Resources and Environment at 240 Victoria Pde, East Melbourne; (03) 9412 4795. For more information on bird-watching contact the Bird Observers Club of Australia, 183 Springvale Rd, Nunawading 3131; (03) 9877 5342. **See also:** National Parks; Phillip Island; The Prom; The Grampians.

Picturesque Lake Boga, north-west of Kerang

surfing. Tarwin River, 20 km SE, offers good fishing. Beaches, natural bushland and wildlife at Venus Bay nearby. **Tourist information:** Community Centre, A'Beckett St; (03) 5674 2706. **Accommodation:** 2 motels, 2 B&B, 4 cara./camp. parks.

Jeparit   Pop. 440

MAP REF. 236 F6
This little town in the Wimmera, 37 km N of Dimboola, is 5 km SE of Lake Hindmarsh, the largest natural freshwater lake in Victoria. The late Sir Robert Menzies was born here in 1894. **Of interest:** Sir Robert Menzies Spire, Sands Ave. Menzies Square, cnr Charles and Roy sts, site of dwelling where Menzies was born. Wimmera-Mallee Pioneer Museum, Charles St, at southern entrance to town: 4-ha complex of colonial buildings furnished in period, and displays of restored farm machinery. Jan.: Beach Carnival. Oct.: Agricultural Show. **In the area:** Safe beaches, fishing and camping at Lake Hindmarsh, 5 km NW. Wildflowers, native fauna and walking tracks at Wyperfeld National Park, 44 km N and Little Desert National Park, 40 km SW. **Tourist information:** Wimmera-Mallee

Pioneer Museum, Charles St; (03) 5397 2101. **Accommodation:** 1 hotel, 1 hotel/motel, 1 cara./camp. park.

Kaniva   Pop. 762

MAP REF. 236 C7
Kaniva in the west Wimmera, 43 km from Bordertown, SA, is just north of Little Desert National Park, which is noted for its wildflowers in spring. **Of interest:** Historical museum, Commercial St, has large collection of items of local history (open by appt). Mayfair Cement Works, Progress St, has garden pots and fountains for sale. **In the area:** Billy-Ho Bush Walk, a 3-km self-guide walk in Little Desert National Park, begins some 10 km S; numbered pegs allow identification of various species of desert flora (brochure available at Tourist information). Mooree Reserve, 20 km SW of town. National Trust-classified railway station (1889) at Serviceton, 23 km W (key available from Serviceton General Store). Waterbird farm, 20 km NW, breeds black swans and other species (open by appt). **Tourist information:** 41 Commercial St; (03) 5392 2418. **Accommodation:** 2 hotels, 2 motels, 1 cara./camp. park.

Kerang   Pop. 4024

MAP REF. 126 I12, 237 P3, 239 P13, 240 A2
Some 30 km from the Murray River and 60 km from Swan Hill, Kerang is the centre of a productive rural area and lies at the southern end of a chain of lakes and marshes. Some of the world's largest breeding-grounds for ibis and other waterfowl are found in these marshes. The ibis is closely protected because of its value in controlling locusts and other pests. **Of interest:** Old water tower, cnr Murray Valley Hwy and Shadforth St. Museum, Riverwood Drive, features cars and farm machinery. **In the area:** Apex Park recreation area near the first of the three Reedy Lakes (8 km NW); the second has a large ibis rookery. Lakes Meran, Reedy, Kangaroo and Charm are suitable for water sports and other excellent fishing. Gunbower State Forest, 25 km N, significant red-gum habitat, flora and fauna. At Murrabit, 29 km N on the Murray and surrounded by picturesque river forests: historic building and sawmill; country market, 1st Sat. each month. Lake Boga, 44 km NW, has good sandy beaches. At Easter, Australian Tractor Pull Championship at Quambatook, 42 km SW. **Tourist information:** Golden Rivers Tourism, 25 Murray St, Barham (NSW); (03) 5453 3100. **Accommodation:** 4 hotels, 1 hotel/motel, 3 motels, 2 cara./camp. parks. **See also:** The Mighty Murray.

Koo-wee-rup   Pop. 1106

MAP REF. 219 M10, 232 F7
Well known for its Potato Festival held each March, this town near Western Port is in the middle of Australia's largest asparagus-growing district. **Of interest:** Historical Society Museum, Rossiter Rd (open Sun.). **In the area:** Bayles Flora and Fauna Park, 8 km NE. At Tynong, 20 km NE: Victoria's Farm Shed; Gumbaya Park, in landscaped native bushland. At Pakenham, 21 km N: Military Vehicle Museum, Army Rd; Berwick-Pakenham Historical Society Museum, John St. Royal Botanic Gardens, 28 km NW at Cranbourne, all native species. At Cardinia, 6 km W, Australian Pioneer Farm offers opportunities to shear sheep and milk cows. Fishing and boating at Tooradin, 10 km W, on Sawtell's Inlet. On South Gippsland Hwy towards Tooradin: Harewood House (1850s), has original furnishings (open weekends);

VICTORIA

Swamp Observation Tower, offers views of surrounding swamp and Western Port. **Tourist information:** Newsagency, 277 Rossiter Rd; (03) 5997 1456. **Accommodation:** 1 motel.

Korumburra   Pop. 2906

MAP REF. 219 O12, 232 H8

The giant Gippsland earthworm, sought by anglers and geologists alike, is found near this town, situated on the South Gippsland Hwy, 116 km SE of Melbourne. The area surrounding the town is given to dairying and agriculture, and the countryside is hilly. **Of interest:** Coal Creek Historical Village, cnr South Gippsland Hwy and Silkstone Rd, a recreation of 19th-century coal-mining village on original site of Coal Creek mine (commenced in 1890s) (orientation centre in Mechanics' Institute near entrance). Feb.: Coal Creek Twilight Music and Theatre Festival. Mar.: Karmai (giant worm) Festival. **In the area:** South Gippsland Railway tourist train offers rides through 40 km of countryside linking Leongatha, Korumburra, Loch and Nyora (Sun. and public holidays). Gooseneck Pottery, 4 km SE at Ruby. Old School Tea Room in 1916 primary-school building; 6 km SE, off South Gippsland Hwy. Leongatha, 14 km SE. Top Paddock Cheeses, tastings and sales of traditional, curd and soft cheeses, 4 km NW at Bena. At Loch, 16 km NW: antiques, art and craft. At Poowong, 18 km NW: Poowong Pioneer Chapel, fine example of German architecture; Mudlark Pottery. **Tourist information:** cnr South Gippsland Hwy and Silkstone Rd; (03) 5655 2233. **Accommodation:** 2 hotels, 1 motel, 2 B&B, 1 cara./camp. park.

Kyabram   Pop. 5540

MAP REF. 240 G5

A prosperous town in the Murray-Goulburn area, just 40 km NW of Shepparton, Kyabram is located in a rich dairying and fruit-growing district. **Of interest:** Community-owned waterfowl and fauna park on Lake Rd has five ponds with waterbirds and 15-ha of open-range parklands with native fauna. The Stables, adjacent to fauna park, for pottery and crafts. Mr Ilzyn's Cottages, Breen Ave: mansions, hotels and farmhouses from around the world, all in miniature. Mar.: Rodeo. Easter: Antique Aeroplane Fly-in. **Tourist information:**

Faura park, 75 Lake Rd; (03) 5852 2883. **Accommodation:** 3 hotels, 2 motels, 2 cara./camp. parks. **See also:** The Mighty Murray.

Kyneton   Pop. 3940

MAP REF. 218 G1, 235 R1, 237 R12, 240 D11

Little more than an hour's drive from Melbourne, along the Calder Hwy, Kyneton is a well-preserved, attractive town with several interesting bluestone buildings. Farms around the town prospered during the gold rushes, supplying large quantities of fresh food to the Ballarat and Bendigo diggings. **Of interest:** In Piper St: Kyneton Museum in former bank (c.1865), drop-log cottage in grounds; Steam Mill, restored to operational condition (open weekends); Meskills Woolstore, has wool spinning mill, and yarn and garments for sale. Botanic Gardens, Clowes St, an 8-ha area above river with 500 specimen trees. Historic buildings: town's churches; mechanics institute, Mollison St; old police depot, Jenning St. Self-guide walks, see Tourist information. Mar.: Country Music Festival. Sept.: Daffodil and Arts Festival. Nov.: Kyneton Cup. **In the area:** Two-storey bluestone mills on either side of town; both on Calder Hwy. Upper Coliban, Lauriston and Malmsbury reservoirs, all nearby. At Malmsbury, 10 km NW: historic bluestone railway viaduct; Bleak House (1850s) with rose garden; The Mill (1861), National Trust-classified, has gallery, restaurant and accommodation. At Trentham, 22 km SW: historic foundry; Jargon Crafts; Minifie's Berry Farm, pick-your-own in season. At Blackwood, further 14 km S, Garden of St Erth. Carlsruhe Gallery and Campaspe Art Gallery at Carlsruhe, 5 km SE. Trentham Falls, 20 km SE. Burke and Wills Camel farm, 15 km SE on Calder Hwy at Woodend. Turpins Falls and Cascade Falls with picnic area and walk, 22 km N near Metcalfe. **Tourist information:** Jean Haynes Playground, High St; (03) 5422 6110 (closed Tues. and Thurs.). **Accommodation:** 1 hotel, 2 motels, 4 B&B, 1 cara./camp. park.

Lake Bolac   Pop. 266

MAP REF. 222 C13, 229 J5

In the Western District plains area, this small town on the Glenelg Hwy is by a 1460-ha freshwater lake that has sandy beaches around a 20-km shoreline and

is good for fishing (eels, trout, perch and yellow-belly), boating and swimming. There are several boat-launching ramps. Easter: Yachting Regatta. **Tourist information:** Lake Bolac Motel, Glenelg Hwy; (03) 5350 2218. **Accommodation:** 1 motel, 1 B&B, 1 cara./camp. park.

Lakes Entrance   Pop. 4622

MAP REF. 233 R5, 242 H13

This extremely popular holiday town is at the eastern end of the Gippsland Lakes, which form the largest inland network of waterways in Australia. They cover an area of more than 400 sq. km. and are separated from the ocean by a thin sliver of sand dunes forming a large part of the Ninety Mile Beach, which stretches south to Seaspray. A bridge across the Cunningham Arm gives access to the surf beach from Lakes Entrance. The town is well suited for the holiday maker, catering for both seaside recreation and exploration of the mountain country to the north. It is the home port for a large fishing fleet and many pleasure craft. Large cruise vessels conduct regular sightseeing tours of the lakes throughout the year. Fishing, both ocean and beach, is popular, as are swimming and surfing on a variety of good beaches. **Of interest:** Fisherman's Co-operative, Bullock Island, has viewing platform and fish for sale. Seashell Museum, The Esplanade. Potteries and galleries. Contact Tourist information for details on: Sightseeing cruises of lakes; boat hire; fishing charters; joy flights; and guide for Bataluk Cultural Trail which covers Aboriginal heritage in the East Gippsland area. Market each Sun., The Esplanade. Jan.: Larger than Lakes Festival. Nov.: Recfish Fishing Expo. Dec.: New Year's Eve Fireworks. **In the area:** Carriage tours available from East Gippsland Carriage Co., just east of town. Lake Bunga, 3 km E, has nature trail on foreshore. Kinkuna Country Family Fun Park, 3.5 km E on Princes Hwy. Lake Tyers (6–23 km NE, depending on access point): sheltered waters ideal for fishing, swimming and boating; cruises depart from Fishermans Landing; Lake Tyers Forest Park, for walking, wildlife, picnicking and camping. Braeburne Park Orchards, 6 km N. Woodsedge, 8 km N on Baades Rd: gallery, furniture workshop and glass-blowing demonstrations. Wyanga Park Vineyard and Winery, 10 km N; also reached by boat trip from town. Buchan

Alpine Country

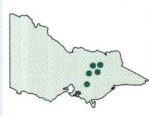

To the east and north-east of Melbourne, the gently rounded peaks of the Victorian Alps stretch, seemingly endlessly, under clear skies. They are much lower than alpine ranges in other parts of the world, lacking sheer escarpments and jagged peaks, but they still stand majestic, especially when covered in snow. These blue ranges are not high enough to have a permanent cover of snow, but the expanses of the rolling mountains are ideal in winter for cross-country and downhill skiing.

The skiing season officially opens on the Queen's Birthday long weekend each June and closes in October, but it often actually extends beyond these dates. Each year, thousands of people flock to the snow for the enjoyment of skiing, for snowboarding or just to enjoy the beauty of nature.

There is bountiful fishing in the lakes and trout streams. Tennis, rock climbing, sailing, swimming, canoeing and water-skiing are popular sports in the summer. Many riding schools in the valleys provide for those who want to explore the countryside on horseback. For the more energetic, bushwalking in this beautiful rugged country is a must. Despite their summer beauty, however, the alps can still claim the life of an ill-prepared bushwalker. Make sure you have the necessary equipment and knowledge and always tell someone where you are going and when you expect to be back.

Victoria's ski resorts are all located within easy reach of Melbourne.

Mount Donna Buang, 95 km from Melbourne, via Warburton. Sightseeing and novice skiing.

Lake Mountain, 120 km from Melbourne, via Healesville. Sightseeing and cross-country skiing.

Mount Baw Baw, 177 km from Melbourne, via Drouin. Beginners, novices and cross-country skiing. **Mount St Gwinear** nearby, is popular for cross-country skiing.

Mount Buller, 221 km from Melbourne, via Mansfield. For beginners to advanced skiers. Ski hire and instruction.

Mount Stirling, 250 km from Melbourne, near Mount Buller. Cross-country skiing. Most trails start at Telephone Box Junction. Visitor centre with public shelter, ski hire and trail maps.

Mount Buffalo, 331 km from Melbourne, via Myrtleford. Includes Dingo Dell (6 km) and Cresta (10 km). Beginners, families and cross-country skiing. Ski hire and instruction.

Falls Creek, 356 km from Melbourne, via the Snow Road through Oxley. Protected ski runs for novices, intermediate and advanced skiers; good cross-country skiing. Ski hire and instruction.

Mount Hotham, 367 km from Melbourne, via the Snow Road through Oxley. Known as the 'powder snow capital' of Australia. For experienced downhill skiers. Also cross-country skiing. Ski hire and instruction.

Dinner Plain, a 10-minute ski-shuttle ride from Mount Hotham. Offers ski hire, cross-country skiing and horseriding.

For further information on all resorts, contact the Alpine Resorts Commission, 36 Rutland Rd, Box Hill; (03) 9895 6900, or the Falls Creek Information Centre, Bogong High Plains Tourist Rd, Falls Creek; (03) 5758 3224. **See also:** Safe Skiing. **Map references:** 228-29; for Lake Mountain, 232 H2; for Mount Donna Buang, 232 G3; and for Mount Baw Baw, 233 J4.

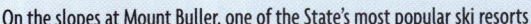

On the slopes at Mount Buller, one of the State's most popular ski resorts

VICTORIA

Royal Cave at Buchan Caves, north of Lakes Entrance

Caves, 55 km N, well worth a visit; cave tours and adventure-caving. Day trips to old mining areas around Omeo, 126 km NW. Good views: Jemmy's Point, 1 km W, and Nyerimilang Heritage Park, 10 km NW; Heritage Park includes 1920s homestead, farm buildings and East Gippsland Botanic Gardens; Rose Pruning Day here in July features demonstrations (clippings given to the public). At Swan Reach, 14 km NW, Rosewood Pottery; Malcolm Cameron Studio Gallery (open weekends). At Metung, 15 km W: Chainsaw Sculpture Gallery has chainsaw sculpture and display of Annemieke Mein's embroidery art; boat hire; regatta in Jan. each year. Nicholson River (24 km W) and Golvinda wineries (50 km NW), via Bairnsdale. **Tourist information:** cnr Esplanade and Marine Pde; (03) 5155 1966; freecall, 1800 637060. **Accommodation:** 2 hotel/motels, 20 motels, 1 hostel, 20 cara./camp. parks. **See also:** Gippsland Lakes; Wine Regions.

Lancefield   Pop. 1063

MAP REF. 218 I2, 240 E11

This historic township with its wide streets and Victorian buildings is located 67 km NW of Melbourne. **Of interest:** Old Macedonia House (1889), Main Rd, now Antique Centre of Victoria. Mechanics Hall (1868), High St. Dec.: Horse Festival. **In the area:** Cleveland, an historic home and winery, 2 km E on Shannons Rd. A number of wineries and nurseries; horseriding; inquire at Tourist information. Monument Creek Herb Farm, Monument Rd, 5 km W. At

Romsey, 7 km S: excellent Victorian architecture; Sydney Seymour Cottage, Palmer St; nearby, Cope-Williams Romsey Vineyard, Glenfern Rd. At Monegeetta, 15 km S, Mintaro Homestead (1882) replica (but smaller) of Melbourne's Government House (not open to public). **Tourist information:** Centre Vic Motor Inn, Main Rd; (03) 5429 1777. **Accommodation:** 1 motel, 1 cara./camp. park.

Leongatha   Pop. 3968

MAP REF. 219 P13, 232 H9

Located near the foothills of the Strzelecki Ranges, Leongatha is a large dairying area and a good base for trips to Wilsons Promontory, the seaside and fishing resorts on the coast. **Of interest:** Historic Society Museum (check opening times) and Art and Craft Gallery, McCartin St. Mushroom Crafts and Pottery, Bair St. Cash's Weaving Factory, Holt St. Feb.: Cycling Carnival. Sept.: Daffodil and Floral Festival. **In the area:** South Gippsland Railway tourist train, from Leongatha to Korumburra, Loch and Nyora (Sun. and public holidays). Firelight Museum, 9 km N, features antique lamps and firearms. About 21 km N, excellent scenic driving along Grand Ridge Rd to Tarra-Bulga National Park (120 km E). At Meeniyan, 17 km SE, excellent craft shop. Mossvale Park, 16 km NE: impressive plantation of exotic trees, good picnic/barbecue facilities; venue for Victorian State Orchestra performance each Feb. At Mirboo North, 23 km NE: Grand Ridge Brewing Company, viewing of beer-brewing process and sales; Colonial Bank Antiques. Brackenhurst Rotary

Dairy, 5 km E on Christoffersens Rd, has 350 cows, also museum (open from 3.30 p.m. daily). Gooseneck Pottery, 9 km NW at Ruby. Korumburra, 14 km NW along South Gippsland Hwy. **Tourist information:** CAB, Michael Place Complex; (03) 5662 2111. **Accommodation:** 2 motels, 1 B&B, 1 cara./ camp. park.

Lorne   Pop. 1143

MAP REF. 218 D13, 225 A13, 235 P10

The approaches to Lorne along the Great Ocean Rd, whether from east or west, are quite spectacular. The town is one of Victoria's most attractive coastal resorts. It has a year-round mild climate and the superb mountain scenery of the Otways nearby. Captain Loutit gave the district the name of Loutitt Bay. The village of Lorne was established in 1871, became popular with pastoralists from inland areas, and developed rather in the style of an English seaside resort. When the Great Ocean Rd opened in 1932 Lorne grew more popular; however, the town itself has remained relatively unspoiled, with good beaches, surfing, and excellent bushwalking in the hills. **Of interest:** Teddy's Lookout, at edge of George St behind town, has excellent bay views. Foreshore reserve. Shipwreck Walk along beach. Paddle boats available for hire. Qdos Contemporary Art Gallery, Mountjoy Pde. Lorne Fisheries on pier; daily supplies from local fleet. Shell Shop and Museum, William St. Jan.: Pier to Pub Swim; Surf to Mountain Foot Race. **In the area:** Surrounding town: Angahook-Lorne State Park, features Erskine Falls (5 km NW of town) and many walking tracks, including one to Kalimna and Phantom waterfalls from Sheoak Picnic area (about 4 km from town). Scenic drives: west in the Otway Ranges; south-west or north-east along Great Ocean Rd. Allenvale, 2 km W. Cumberland River Valley, 4 km SW, has walking tracks and camping ground. Mt Defiance, 10 km SW. Wye River, 17 km SW, for fishing and surfing. Gentle Annie Berry Gardens, 26 km NW via Deans Marsh. **Tourist information:** 144 Mountjoy Pde; (03) 5289 1036. **Accommodation:** 2 hotel/motels, 6 motels, 3 B&B, 1 hostel, 5 cara./camp. parks. **See also:** The Great Ocean Road.

Maffra   Pop. 3879

MAP REF. 233 M5

The area around Maffra supports

Railway station at Maldon, a National Trust-classified town

intensive farming due to the Macalister Irrigation Scheme. **Of interest:** Maffra Sugar Beet Museum, River St. Mineral and gemstone display in court house, Johnson St. All Seasons Herb Gardens, Foster St. Mar.: Harvest Festival. Easter: Farming Festival (Sat.). **In the area:** At Heyfield 10 km W, Dairy Carnival in Jan. Lake Glenmaggie, 11 km N of Heyfield, popular water-sports venue. Spectacular scenic drives along forest road north (closed in winter), which follows Macalister Valley to Licola (54 km from Heyfield), and to Mt Tamboritha (20 km NE of Licola) in the Alpine National Park; or to Jamieson (147 km) and access to snowfields or Lake Eildon. Road north from Maffra, via Briagolong, leads to historic town of Dargo (86 km N) and over Dargo High Plains (check road conditions in winter). Lake Tali Karng, located in Alpine National Park, 60 km NE of Licola, is a major focus for bushwalking in season. Trail-riding and horseback tours from Valencia Creek, 17 km N of Maffra, and from Licola. At Briagolong, 22 km NE: historic hotel, and art and craft shops. Australian Wildlife Art Gallery and Sculpture, 25 km E. **Tourist information:** The Court House, 8 Johnson St; (03) 5141 1811. **Accommodation:** 3 hotels, 1 motel, 1 B&B, 1 cara./camp. park.

Maldon   Pop. 1174

MAP REF. 229 O4, 237 P11, 240 B10
The National Trust has declared Maldon the 'First Notable Town' in Australia, on the basis that no other town has such an interesting collection of 19th-century

buildings, nor such a collection of European trees. Situated 20 km NW of Castlemaine in central Victoria, Maldon is very popular with tourists, especially during the Maldon Easter Fair, and in spring when the wildflowers are in bloom. The deep reef goldmines in the area were among Victoria's richest, and at one stage 20 000 men worked on the nearby Tarrangower diggings. Enthusiasts still search for gold in the area. **Of interest:** Anzac Hill, southern end of High St, for good view of town. Many notable buildings, mostly constructed of local stone: Maldon Hospital (1860), cnr Adair and Chapel sts; post office (1870), High St; old council offices, High St (now folk museum); Dabb's General Store, with faithfully restored old storefront, Main St. National Trust properties: former Denominational (Penny) School, Camp St; Welsh Congregational Church, cnr Camp and Church sts; Cumquat Tea Rooms, High St. The Beehive Chimney (1862), south end of Church St. Castlemaine and Maldon Preservation Society runs steam trains from railway station, Hornsby St (Sun. and public holidays). Town walking tour, leaflet available from Tourist information. Feb.: Camp Draft. Easter: Fair. Oct.: Vintage Car Hill Climb. Nov.: Folk Festival. **In the area:** Bushwalks and intriguing rock formations. Panoramic views from Mt Tarrangower Lookout Tower, 2 km W. Carmen's Tunnel, 2 km SW, a vivid reminder of hardships of goldmining days. Cairn Curran Reservoir, 10 km SW, for water sports and fishing; picnic facilities on shore and sailing club near spillway.

North-east, goldmining dredge beside road to Bendigo. 'Porcupine Township', 3 km NE, a reconstructed goldmining town. Nuggetty Ranges and Mt Moorol, 2 km N. **Tourist information:** High St; (03) 5475 2569. **Accommodation:** 3 motels, 10 B&B, 2 cara./camp. parks. **See also:** The Golden Age.

Mallacoota   Pop. 961

MAP REF. 119 G13, 243 Q11
On the Gippsland coast, at the mouth of a deep inlet of the same name, Mallacoota is a seaside and fishing township, and a popular holiday centre. The Croajingolong National Park surrounds the town. Bushwalking and birdwatching are popular activities in the area. Contact Tourist information for details on: lake and river cruises, and scenic drives and walks. Easter: Festival. Oct.: Round Robin Cup (popular soccer tournament). **In the area:** Gipsy Point, 16 km NW, a quiet holiday retreat set in attractive countryside. Genoa, 24 km NW on Princes Hwy, last town before entering NSW; nearby Genoa Falls; Genoa Peak, for magnificent views. Bastion Point (2 km SE) and Betka (5 km S) are good surfing beaches. **Tourist information:** 57 Maurice Ave; (03) 5158 0788. **Accommodation:** 3 motels, 4 cara./ camp. parks. **See also:** National Parks.

Mansfield   Pop. 2178

MAP REF. 230 C10, 241 L10
A popular inland resort at the junction of the Midland and Maroondah hwys, Mansfield is 3 km E of the northern arm of Lake Eildon. It is the nearest sizeable town to Mt Buller Alpine Village and Mt Stirling Alpine Resort. **Of interest:** Self-guide historic walk available, contact Tourist information for brochure. Troopers' Monument, junction of High St and Midland Hwy, monument to three police officers shot by Ned Kelly at Stringybark Creek, near Tolmie in 1878; graves in Mansfield cemetery. Nearby, National Trust-classified courthouse. Highton Manor (1896), Highton Lane. Hot-air balloon flights, camel treks and horse trail-riding available, contact Tourist information for details. Bush market, 4 times a year, check Tourist information for dates. Mar.: Harvest Festival. Apr.: Balloon Festival. Nov.: Mountain Country Festival. **In the area:** Road north-east over mountains to Whitfield in the King River Valley

(62 km) passes through spectacular scenery. Powers Lookout, 44 km NE, for views over King River Valley (former vantage point for bushranger Harry Power). Lake William Hovell, 85 km NE, for boating, canoeing and fishing. Scenic drives, picnics, camping and bushwalking at Mt Samaria State Park, 14 km N. At Lake Nillahcootie, 20 km NW: boating, fishing, canoeing and sailing. Houseboat hire at Lake Eildon, 15 km S. South, Howqua, Jamieson and Goulburn rivers offer trout fishing and gold fossicking. Historic buildings at old goldmining town of Jamieson, 37 km S, on Jamieson River. Delatite Winery, on Stoneys Rd, 7 km SE. At Merrijig, 18 km SE, rodeo in Mar. each year. Craig's Hut, 50 km E, used for filming *The Man from Snowy River*; no vehicle access to Craig's Hut in winter. Alpine National Park, 60 km E, for bushwalking and 4-wheel driving. **Tourist information:** In railway station, Maroondah Hwy; (03) 5775 1464. **Accommodation:** 3 hotels, 1 hotel/motel, 2 motels, 6 B&B, 1 hostel, 1 cara./camp. park. **See also:** Wine Regions.

Maryborough   Pop. 7623

MAP REF. 229 L5, 237 O11

First sheep farming, then the gold rush, and now secondary industry have contributed to the development of this small city on the northern slopes of the Great Dividing Range, 70 km N of Ballarat. Maryborough is in the centre of an agricultural and forest area. **Of interest:** Pioneer Memorial Tower, Bristol Hill. Worsley Cottage (1894), Palmerston St, a historical museum (open Sun.) Old railway station (1892), Railway St, now a complex housing Tourist information,

antique gallery and woodwork shop. Central Goldfields Art Gallery, in old fire station, Neill St. Phillips Gardens, Alma St. Imposing Civic Square buildings, Clarendon St. On northern outskirts of town, Animal Haven, Griffith St, fauna park also offering trout and yabbie fishing. Jan.: Highland Gathering, New Year's Day. Sept.: Golden Wattle Festival (includes Gumleaf Playing Championship). Nov.: Energy Breakthrough (energy expo). **In the area:** Aboriginal wells, 4 km S. Once-thriving gold towns of Bowenvale and Timor; both 8 km NW from town. **Tourist information:** Railway station complex, Railway St; (03) 5460 4511. **Accommodation:** 1 hotel/motel, 6 motels, 8 B&B, 1 cara./camp. park.

Marysville   Pop. 662

MAP REF. 219 O4, 222 I3, 232 G2, 241 J13

The peaceful sub-alpine town of Marysville owes its existence first to gold, as it was on the route to the Woods Point goldfields, and later to timber milling. It is 37 km NE of Healesville, off the Maroondah Hwy. The town is surrounded by attractive forest-clad mountain country and is a popular resort all year round. **Of interest:** In Murchison St: Country Touch, pottery; Hidden Talents, local art and crafts. Bruno's Art and Sculpture Garden, Falls Rd. Sawyer's Marysville Museum, Darwin St, features vintage cars and accessories. Nicholl's Lookout, Cumberland Rd, for excellent views of surrounding area. Market, 2nd Sun. each month. Nov.: Wirreanda Festival (Festival of Tall Trees) **In the area:** Numerous bushwalking tracks lead to a variety of beauty spots: 3 min. walk to Steavenson Falls

from Falls Rd (walk and falls illuminated at night); 4-km loop walk in Cumberland Memorial Scenic Reserve, 16 km E; 2-hr walk to Keppel's Lookout; 30-min. walk to Mt Gordon (begins 2 km W of town). Lady Talbot Drive Forest Drive through surrounding area, contact Tourist information for details Lake Mountain, 19 km E: accessible walking and cross-country skiing trails and tobogganing. Big River State Forest, 30 km E: camping, good fishing and gold fossicking. Lake Eildon, 46 km NE, and Fraser National Park, 59 km NE, within easy driving distance. Fraser National Park offers boating, sailing, water skiing, fishing and swimming, and a number of walking tracks. At Buxton, 10 km NW: zoo; trout farm; Australian Bush Pioneer's Farm, at foot of Mt Cathedral; nearby, Cathedral Range State Park. **Tourist information:** Murchison St; (03) 5963 4567. **Accommodation:** 1 hotel/motel, 3 motels, 12 B&B, 1 cara./camp. park.

Milawa   Pop. 120

MAP REF. 230 G1, 241 N6

Milawa is 16 km SE of Wangaratta on what is known as the Snow Road, which links Oxley, Milawa and Markwood with Wangaratta to the west and the Ovens Hwy to the east. Brown Brothers Vineyard has operated here since 1889, producing quality wines. **Of interest:** Milawa Mustards, off Snow Rd, has wide range of mustards and attractive cottage garden. Milawa Cheese Company, Factory Rd, for specialist cheeses. At Oxley, 4 km W: bicycle tours available from Bogong Jack Adventures; John Gehrig Wines; Reads Winery. Other wineries in area: Markwood Estate Winery, 6 km E; Avalon Vineyard, 4 km

Craig's Hut near Mansfield, used for filming *The Man from Snowy River*

N of Whitfield; Darling Estate Wines, near Cheshunt. **Tourist information:** Wangaratta and Region Visitors Information Centre, cnr Handley St and Tone Rd, Wangaratta; (03) 5721 5711. **Accommodation:** 1 motel, 1 B&B, 1 cara./camp. park. **See also:** Wine Regions.

Mildura   Pop. 23 176

MAP REF. 126 D7, 238 G3

Sunny mild winters and picturesque locations on the banks of the Murray River make Mildura and neighbouring towns popular tourist areas. Mildura, on the Sunraysia Hwy, 557 km N of Melbourne, is a pleasant city that developed along with the expansion of irrigation of the area. Alfred Deakin, statesman and advocate of irrigation, persuaded the Chaffey brothers, Canadian-born irrigation experts, to visit this region. They recognised its potential and selected Mildura as the first site for development. The early days of the project were fraught with setbacks, but by 1900 the citrus-growing industry was well established and, with the locking of the Murray completed in 1928, Mildura soon became a city. **Of interest:** Statue of W.B. Chaffey, Mildura's first mayor, Deakin Ave. Mildura Arts Centre complex, Cureton Ave, includes Rio Vista, original Chaffey home, now museum displaying colonial household items. Paddlesteamers leave from Mildura Wharf, end of Madden Ave, for trips on Murray and Darling rivers: PS *Melbourne*, 2-hr round trips; PS *Avoca*, luncheon and dinner cruises; PS *Coonawarra*, 5- and 6-day cruises; PV *Rothbury*, day cruise to Trentham Winery (each Thurs.). Humpty Dumpty Tourist Farm, Cureton Ave. Snakes and Ladders, 17th St, fun park featuring dunny collection which includes Marilyn Munroe's toilet. Mildura Lock Island and Weir. Aquacoaster waterslide, cnr Seventh St and Orange Ave. Dolls on the Avenue, Benetook Ave. Pioneer Cottage, Hunter St. The Citrus Shop, Deakin Ave, for local citrus products. Mar.: Great Mildura Paddleboat Race (odd-numbered years). **In the area:** Many vineyards, including Lindemans Karadoc Winery (20 km S), largest winery in southern hemisphere; Allambie Wine Co. (south off Murray Valley Hwy); Trentham Estate (south off Sturt Hwy); Mildara Wines (9 km W). River Road Pottery, 10 km W. Woodsie's Gem Shop, 6 km SW. At Irymple, 6 km S, Sunbeam

Dried Fruits, tours available. Red Cliffs, 15 km S, important area for citrus and dried fruit industries; 'Big Lizzie' steam traction engine in town. Bushwalking in Hattah-Kulkyne National Park, 70 km S. In NSW: Yabbies at Gol Gol Fisheries, 2 km N; Orange World, 6 km N, offers tours of citrus-growing areas. Golden River Zoo, 3 km NW, has both native and exotic species located in natural surroundings. **Tourist information:** 180 Deakin Ave; (03) 5021 4424. **Accommodation:** 3 hotels, 44 motels, 25 cara./ camp. parks. **See also:** The Mighty Murray; Wine Regions.

Moe   Pop. 17 000

MAP REF. 219 R10, 233 J7

Situated on the Princes Hwy, 134 km SE of Melbourne, Moe is a rapidly-growing residential city in the La Trobe Valley and a gateway to the alpine region. **Of interest:** Old Gippstown pioneer township, Lloyd St, re-creation of 19th-century community with over 30 restored buildings brought from surrounding areas and fine collection of fully restored horse-drawn vehicles. Cinderella Dolls, Andrew St. Picturesque race track, Waterloo Rd. Mar.: Jazz Festival; Blue Rock Classic (cross-country horse race). Oct.: Moe Cup (horse race). **In the area:** Mair's Coalville Vineyard, Moe South Rd (open by appt). Edward Hunter Heritage Bush Reserve, 3 km S via Coalville St. Blue Rock Dam, 20 km NW, for fishing, swimming and sailing. Scenic road north-east, leads to picturesque old mining township of Walhalla, Thomson Reservoir nearby, and through mountains to Jamieson, 147 km further north (check road conditions in winter). North of Willow Grove: Baw Baw plateau, excellent for bushwalking and abundant wildflowers in summer; Mt Baw Baw and Mt Saint Gwinear, for cross-country and downhill skiing. **Tourist information:** Old Gippstown, Lloyd St; (03) 5127 3082. **Accommodation:** 3 motels, 1 B&B, 1 hostel, 2 cara./camp. parks.

Mornington   Pop. 16 103

MAP REF. 219 K10, 221 J4, 232 B8

Mornington retains its small-town character while being easily accessible from Melbourne. It offers an excellent base from which to explore the Mornington Peninsula. **Of interest**: Historic Mornington pier, first built in 1850s. Studio City Pop and Media

Museum, Nepean Hwy, has film, television, radio and pop-music memorabilia. Self-guide town walk includes gaol and court house on The Esplanade; brochures available from Tourist information. Mornington Peninsula Regional Gallery, Dunns Rd, has print and drawing collections, including works by Dobell, Drysdale and Nolan (open Tues.–Sat.). Motorised trolley rides, operate from Bungower Road level crossing each Sun. (12 noon – 5 p.m.). National Antique Centre, 65 Tyabb Rd, has a wide range of antiques and bric-a-brac. Local historic display, housed in old post office, cnr Main St and The Esplanade. Street market on Main St each Wed., and Mornington Racecourse craft market on 2nd Sun. each month. June: Queen's Birthday Wine Weekend. Nov.: Tea Tree Festival. **In the area:** Ballam Park (1845), 14 km NE on Cranbourne Rd at Frankston, French farmhouse-style homestead (open Sun.). At Baxter, 14 km NE: Mulberry Hill, Golf Links Rd, former home of artist Sir Daryl Lindsay and Joan Lindsay, author of *Picnic at Hanging Rock* (open Sun. p.m.). At Tyabb, 16 km E, Tyabb Packing House, Mornington–Tyabb Rd, for antiques and collectables. Several wineries, between Tyabb and Hastings, with cellar-door sales, including Barak Estate, Ermes Estate, Stumpy Gully Vineyard and Moorooduc Estate. Several festivals celebrate Peninsula produce, including the Wine and Food Festival in Jan. and the Peninsula Wine and Music Gala in Nov. At Hastings, 21 km SE on Western Port: fauna park; wetlands area and 2-km coastal wetlands walk through most southerly-located mangroves in world. Coastline between Mornington and Mount Martha (7 km S), features sheltered sandy bays separated by rocky bluffs and backed by steep-wooded slopes; along this stretch is Fossil Beach, one of only two exposed fossil plains in world. At Mount Martha, The Briars historic property (1866), incorporates established gardens, buildings housing a significant collection of Napoleonic artifacts and furniture, wetland areas, bird hides and bushland walks. At Dromana, 16 km S, is Arthurs Seat, a mountain named after a similar Scottish mountain by Lieutenant John Murray in 1802; a 20-minute chairlift ride up the mountain to Arthurs Seat State Park offers spectacular views over the bay (chairlift operates at weekends and during school and public holidays from June–Aug., and daily from then to end May); picnic facilities at top of chairlift, as well as several walks, including short walk to Flinders Lookout, Two Bays walk from Latrobe Parade, Eaton's Cutting walk and Kings Falls circuit walk; on Purves Rd: historic Seawinds Park, has gardens, sculptures, short walks and sweeping views; Pine Ridge Car and Folk Museum; riding school for horse-rides. **Tourist information:** Peninsula Tourism, Point Nepean Rd, Dromana; (03) 5987 3078; freecall, 1800 804009. **Accommodation:** 4 hotels, 1 motel, 4 B&B, 1 cara./camp. park. **See also:** The Mornington Peninsula; Wine Regions.

Morwell   Pop. 15 423

MAP REF. 233 J7

Morwell, 150 km SE of Melbourne, is situated in the heart of the La Trobe Valley. This valley contains one of the world's largest deposits of brown coal. Morwell is an industrial town with a number of secondary industries. **Of interest:** PowerWorks, off Princes Hwy, dynamic displays on electrical industry. In Commercial Rd: La Trobe Regional Gallery; Rose Garden. **In the area:** Scenic day tours, brochure available from Tourist information. Lake Narracan and Hazelwood Pondage, 5 km S, has warm water hence ideal for year-round water sports. Tarra-Bulga National Park, 47 km SE, renowned for fern glades, waterfalls, rosellas, lyrebirds and koalas. Morwell National Park, 12 km S, has good walking tracks. At Yinnar, 12 km SW, Arts Resource Collective in old butter factory. Views of Moe, Yallourn North and valley between Strzelecki Ranges and Baw Baw mountains at Narracan Falls, about 27 km W. To the north, 66 km through dense mountain country, old mining township of Walhalla. Further on, Thomson Reservoir and the beautiful Tanjil and Thomson River valleys. **Tourist information:** PowerWorks Visitors Centre, Commercial Rd; (03) 5135 3415. **Accommodation:** 2 hotels, 9 motels, 2 cara./camp. parks.

Mount Beauty   Pop. 1837

MAP REF. 231 N5, 241 Q8, 242 D6

Situated in the Upper Kiewa Valley, 344 km NE of Melbourne, Mount Beauty was originally an accommodation town for workers on the Kiewa Hydro-electric Scheme in the 1940s. An ideal holiday centre, the town lies at the foot of Mount

The Great Ocean Road

Very few roads can offer a continuous stretch of more than 250 kilometres of breathtaking scenery, but the Great Ocean Road, along Victoria's south-west coast, does exactly that. Built to honour the servicemen of World War I and completed in 1932, the road has dramatic stretches of precipitous cliffs, idyllic coves and wide beaches.

The Great Ocean Road begins at **Torquay**, not far from Geelong. This is a popular surfing spot and the road leads past a collection of famous surfing and safe swimming beaches and resorts. **Lorne** is one of the most charming of these. Despite offering modern holiday amenities and plenty of seaside entertainment for families, its gracious old hotels and guest houses remain as a reminder of days gone by. Behind the town, the Otway Ranges, which stretch from **Anglesea** to Cape Otway, offer beautiful hills, waterfalls and excellent walking tracks.

After **Apollo Bay,** the road leaves the coast and winds through the ferny slopes of Cape Otway. This is rainforest country, silent and untouched, and well worth exploring. Many of the roads are unsealed but quite adequate for standard cars. Try to visit the Melba Gully State Park to the west of the tiny town of Lavers Hill. Shipwreck Trail signs begin on the eastern side of Lavers Hill. This point marks the beginning of the 'Shipwreck Coast', which stretches through **Port Campbell** and **Warrnambool** to **Port Fairy.** Photographers can be seen risking life and

A section of the Great Ocean Road near Lorne

limb to take advantage of the dramatic coastal scenery; it is advisable, however, for drivers to keep their eyes firmly on the road. The coastline takes on tortured, twisted shapes, with amazing rock formations like The Twelve Apostles — huge stone pillars looming out of the surf, carved over time by the incessant action of the sea.

At Princetown, the Great Ocean Road returns to hug the coastline along the entire length of **Port Campbell National Park** and follows the coast to the Bay of Islands, 8 kilometres east of the small seaside town of Peterborough, where four shipwrecks are located along the coast. Here the Curdies River enters the sea in a wide, sandy inlet beloved of anglers.

For further information, contact the Great Ocean Road Visitor Information Centre, Great Ocean Rd, Apollo Bay; (03) 5237 6529. **See also:** National Parks and individual text entries in A–Z listing for those parks and towns indicated by bold type. **Map references:** 223 A10, 223 F12.

Bogong, Victoria's highest mountain (1986 m). A multitude of ski hire outlets services skiers on their way to Falls Creek in winter. In summer, the area is one of Australia's premier mountain-bike locations; also the town services bushwalkers heading for the high plains. **Of interest:** Leaflets outlining walks, excursions and other activities, and information on mountain-bike hire, horseriding and hang-gliding from Tourist information. Heritage Museum, at Tourist information centre. Mar.: Conquestathon Fun Climb of Mt Bogong. Aug.: Kangaroo Hoppet

Festival (cross-country ski race). **In the area:** Scenic drive to Falls Creek (30 km SE) and the Bogong High Plains (not accessible in winter); skiing at Falls Creek. Bogong Village, 16 km SE and walks around nearby Lake Guy. Good water sports and fishing at Mount Beauty Pondage, Falls Creek Rd, 26 km SE. Tawonga Gap, 13 km NW, features scenic lookout over two valleys. **Tourist information:** Australian High Country Visitors Centre, Kiewa Valley Hwy; (03) 5754 3172. **Accommodation:** 6 motels, 2 cara./camp. parks.

Murtoa   Pop. 878

MAP REF. 236 I9

Murtoa is situated around picturesque Lake Marma, 30 km E of Horsham on the Wimmera Hwy. It is in the centre of Victoria's wheat belt. **Of interest:** Huge wheat-storage silos and facilities. Many buildings c. 1880. Original shopping centre c. 1900, McDonald St. Four-storey railway water-tower (1886), Soldiers Ave, now a museum with James Hill's taxidermy collection of some 500 birds and animals, prepared between 1885 and 1930, (open Sun. p.m.). Lake

The Prom

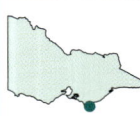

Wilsons Promontory, at the southernmost tip of the mainland, is one of Victoria's largest and most spectacular national parks. 'The Prom', as it is affectionately known to Victorians, has an impressive range of landscapes, including tall forested ranges, luxuriant tree fern valleys, open heaths, salt marshes and long drifts of sand dunes. Its wide, white sandy beaches are truly magnificent, some dominated by spectacular granite tors and washed by a rolling surf. There are also safe swimming beaches, particularly at Norman Bay near the main camping area at Tidal River. At the aptly named Squeaky Beach, the sand squeaks underfoot.

Two lookouts in particular offer magnificent views across Bass Strait and offshore islands: Sparkes Lookout, off the main road to Tidal River, and the lookout at the Mt Oberon carpark.

Birds and other wildlife abound on the Prom: lorikeets, rosellas and flame robins; kookaburras and blue wrens are in evidence, even in the main general store area at Tidal River village; and for the more dedicated and patient birdwatcher, sightings of treecreepers and herons can be the reward.

Emus feed unperturbed on the open grassland by the side of the main road at the park entry area at Yanakie Isthmus, and kangaroos and wallabies seem unimpressed by their human observers. At night, wombat-spotting by torchlight is a favourite pastime with children staying in the Tidal River area.

There are more than 150 kilometres of walking tracks in the Wilsons Promontory National Park. Some cover short walks, such as the nature trail in Lilly Pilly Gully, where the vegetation varies from

Refuge Cove, a beautiful cove on the eastern side of the Prom

bushland inhabited by koalas, to rainforest with ancient tree ferns and trickling streams. Other longer walks can be taken to such places as Sealers Cove or to the tip of the Prom, where there is a lighthouse dating from 1859. Cottages adjacent to the lighthouse can be booked for accommodation. Hikers should consider tide times to make creek crossing easier.

At the visitor information centre and park office at Tidal River, leaflets are available detailing walking tracks and the flora and fauna of the park.

During summer and Easter, park rangers give talks and spotlight tours as well as leading children's nature activities. Permits are required for all overnight hikes.

For further information contact the Wilsons Promontory National Park, Park Office, Tidal River; (03) 5680 9555, or for accommodation bookings (03) 5680 9500. **Map reference:** 233 K12.

Marma, around which is a walking track, offers birdwatching and spectacular sunsets. Stick Shed (1941) built from 640 unmilled tree trunks, Wimmera Hwy on eastern side of town. Jan.: Race Meeting, New Years Day. June: Murtoa Cup **In the area:** Barrabool Forest Reserve, 7 km S, has wildflowers in spring (difficult access in winter). **Tourist information:** Marma Gully Antiques, 50 Marma St; (03) 5385 2422. **Accommodation:** 2 hotels, 1 cara./camp. park.

Myrtleford   Pop. 2862

MAP REF. 231 J2, 241 O7, 242 B5
On the Ovens Hwy, 45 km SE of Wangaratta, the town of Myrtleford is surrounded by an area that produces hops, timber, vegetables, chestnuts and wine. It also has some of the largest walnut groves in the southern hemisphere. The Ovens Valley was opened up by graziers. Later gold was discovered, and creeks there are still popular for gold panning and gem fossicking. **Of interest:** The Phoenix Tree, sculptured butt of a red gum, crafted by Hans Knorr, on highway at town entrance. The Big Tree, Smith St, a huge old red gum. Town's original school, Albert St, now restored (open Thurs., Sun. or by appt). Myrtleford Mart, Myrtle St, for bric-a-brac. Swing bridge over Myrtle Creek, Standish St. Reform Hill Lookout, end of Halls Rd; scenic walking track from Elgin St leads to lookout. Rotary Park, Myrtle St, and Apex Park, Standish St, both delightful picnic spots and rest areas. Mar.: Tobacco, Hops and Timber Festival. Oct.: International Festival (even-numbered years). **In the area:** Rosewhite Vineyards, 8 km SE, just off Ovens Hwy (open Wed., Fri.–Mon.). Near Eurobin, 16 km SE, Red Deer and Emu Farm; C.J & L. Leita Berry Farm, for home-made jams and berries in season (Dec.–Mar.). Nug Nug Quarter Horse Stud and Dingo Breeding, 16 km S (open by appt). Good fishing at Lake Buffalo (25 km S), Ovens River and Buffalo River. Mt Buffalo National Park and historic towns of Beechworth, Yackandandah and Bright, within easy driving distance. **Tourist information:** Ponderosa Cabin, 29–31 Clyde St; (03) 5752 1727. **Accommodation:** 1 hotel, 1 hotel/motel, 2 motels, 1 hostel, 2 cara./camp. parks.

Nagambie   Pop. 1215

MAP REF. 240 G8
Between Seymour and Shepparton on the Goulburn Valley Hwy, Nagambie is on the shores of Lake Nagambie, which was created by the construction of the Goulburn Weir in 1891. Rowing and yachting regattas, speedboat and water-ski tournaments are held here throughout the year. **Of interest:** Several National Trust-classified buildings. Historical Society display of colonial Victoriana and early horsedrawn vehicles, in old Shire Offices, High St. Pottery, art and craft shops. The Nut House, High St, for Australian nuts and Australian-made products. Mar.: Goulburn Valley Vintage Festival. Nov.: Shiraz Challenge (competition for the best shiraz). Dec.: Rowing Regatta, Boxing Day. **In the area:** National Trust-classified buildings at Chateau Tahbilk Winery, 6 km SW. Mitchelton Winery, 10 km SW off Goulburn Valley Hwy, also has 60-m observation tower and scenic river cruises on the Goulburn River (check times). Osicka's Vineyard, Graytown, 24 km W. David Traeger Wines, on Goulburn Valley Hwy, southern side of town. Longleat Winery, 23 km N, near Murchison. At Murchison: Italian War Memorial and chapel; Meteorite Park, site of 1969 meteorite fall. Days Mill, flour mill with buildings dating from 1865, 5 km S of Murchison. **Tourist information:** 145 High St; (03) 5794 2647. **Accommodation:** 5 motels, 2 B&B, 3 cara./camp. parks. **See also:** Wine Regions.

Natimuk   Pop. 464

MAP REF. 236 F9
This Wimmera town, 27 km W of Horsham, is at the southern end of the Little Desert. It is close to the striking Mt Arapiles, a 356-m sandstone monolith that has been described as 'Victoria's Ayers Rock' and is located in the Mount Arapiles-Tooan State Park. A drive to the summit reveals a scenic lookout and a telecommunications relay station. The mountain was first climbed by Major Mitchell in 1836 and today is popular with rock-climbing enthusiasts. **Of interest:** In Main St: Arapiles Historical Society Museum in old court house (open by appt); Arapiles Craft Shop for local craft. **In the area:** Lake Natimuk, 2 km N, for water sports. Duffholme Museum, 21 km W. Mount Arapiles-Tooan State Park, 12 km SW. Toolondo Reservoir, 30 km S, for excellent trout fishing. **Tourist information:** Natimuk Hotel, Main St; (03) 5387 1300.

Accommodation: 1 hotel/motel, 1 B&B, 1 hostel, 1 cara./camp. park.

Nhill   Pop. 1891

MAP REF. 236 D7
The name of this town is possibly derived from the Aboriginal word *nyell*, meaning 'white mist on water'. A small wheat town on the Western Hwy, exactly half-way between Melbourne and Adelaide, it claims to have the largest single-bin silo in the southern hemisphere (in Davis Ave). The town is the starting point for tours of the Little Desert. **Of interest:** Historical Society Museum, McPherson St (open by appt). In Victoria St: cottage of John Shaw Neilson, lyric poet, (in Jaypex Park); Draught Horse Memorial to famous Clydesdales, indispensable in opening up Wimmera region, (in Goldsworthy Park); Lowana Craft Shop, for local craft. Post office (1888), Nelson St, National Trust-classified. **In the area:** Little Desert National Park, via Kiata, 23 km S. Nearby, Little Desert Lodge operates day tours of Little Desert; Little Desert Wildflower Exhibition held here in Oct. Mallee Dam, 20 km W, is important location for native birdwatching and has birdhide for visitors. Prolific birdlife also seen on Hermans Hill Tourist Walk through mallee and heathland to hill overlooking Big Desert Wilderness Park; inquire at Tourist information. Big Desert Wilderness Park, via Yanac 32 km NW, on track north to Murrayville; exploration of this remote area by walking tracks only. **Tourist information:** Victoria St; (03) 5391 3086. **Accommodation:** 3 hotels, 4 motels, 1 cara./camp. park.

Numurkah   Pop. 3128

MAP REF. 127 M13, 240 I4
Numurkah, 35 km N of Shepparton on the Goulburn Valley Hwy, is only half an hour from some sandy beaches and excellent fishing spots on the Murray River. The town is in an irrigation area concentrating on dairying, and was originally developed through the Murray Valley Soldier Settlement Scheme. **Of interest:** In Melville St: Steam and Vintage Machinery Display; historical museum (open Sun. p.m.); Court House Crafts; Street market for bric-a-brac. Marie's House of Dolls, Meiklejohn St. Mar.: Art Show. **In the area:** Potts Herbs nursery, 5 km N. The Palmyard, specialist palm

tree nursery, 6 km N. Glenarron, 8 km N, a tourist dairy farm. Monichino's Winery, Katunga, 11 km N. At Strathmerton: Kraft cheese factory; Cactus Country cactus and succulent garden (2 ha); Coonanga Historic Homestead, features blacksmith shop. Ulupna Island flora and fauna reserve, 21 km N, near Strathmerton, has large koala population; Red Gum Wildlife Tours of Ulupna Island. Barmah State Park, 40 km NW, largest red gum forest in southern hemisphere; safari tours available. Morgan's Beach Caravan Park, at edge of forest on bank of Murray River, offers bushwalking and horseriding (horses for hire and facilities for visitors' horses). Waaia Wildlife Park, 10 km NW. Historic buildings set on banks of Broken Creek at Nathalia, 20 km W. At Wunghnu 5 km S: Institute Tavern in restored Mechanics Institute (c. 1880); Tractor Pull Festival at Easter. Brookfield Historic Holiday Farm and Museum, 6 km SE. **Tourist information:** Cactus Country, Murray Valley Hwy, Strathmerton; (03) 5874 5271. **Accommodation:** 2 hotels, 2 motels, 1 cara./camp. park.

Ocean Grove   Pop. 10 069

MAP REF. 218 G10, 225 G9, 232 A7, 235 R8
At the mouth of the Barwon River, Ocean Grove offers fishing and surfing, while nearby Barwon Heads offers safe family relaxation along the shores of its protected river. Both holiday towns are linked by a bridge over the Barwon River estuary, and are popular in the summer months as they are the closest ocean beaches to Geelong, 22 km to the NW. **Of interest:** Ocean Grove Nature Reserve, Grubb Rd. **In the area:** Jirrahlinga Koala and Wildlife Sanctuary, Taits Rd, Barwon Heads. Mangrove swamps in Lake Connewarre State Game Reserve, 7 km N. At Wallington, 8 km N: A Maze'N Things; Koombahla Park Equestrian Centre; Country Connection Adventure Park. **Tourist information:** A Maze'N Things, 1570 Bellarine Hwy (at Grubb Rd), Wallington; (03) 5250 2669. **Accommodation:** Ocean Grove: 3 motels, 1 hotel/motel, 2 B&B, 5 cara./camp. parks. Barwon Heads: 1 hotel, 1 motel, 2 cara./camp. parks.

Olinda   Pop. 981

MAP REF. 216 F11, 219 M7, 222 B11, 232 E4
This picturesque town in the centre of the Dandenong Ranges is well-known for its gardens and galleries. Devonshire teas are a tradition in the Dandenongs, and there are a number of tea rooms and cafes in Olinda and the surrounding area. **Of interest:** Several galleries, including Touchstone Gallery, Monash Ave; Olinda Art Gallery, Parsons La. Aug.: Rhododendron Festival. **In the area:** On Olinda–Monbulk Rd: National Rhododendron Gardens, superb displays of rhododendrons and azaleas in season; R.J. Hamer Arboretum, walking tracks amongst 100 ha of rare and exotic trees. At Silvan, 12 km NE: tulip farms; Silvan Reservoir, surrounding area has walking tracks and picnic facilities; Silvan Winery, open for tastings on weekends and public holidays; Tesselaar's Tulip Festival held each Sept. Several walks and picnic areas amongst mountain-ash forest in Dandenong Ranges National Park; lyrebirds occasionally seen along walking tracks. At Sherbrooke, 4 km S, Alfred Nicholas Gardens, featuring quaint ornamental lake and boathouse; George Tindale Memorial Garden, flowering plants under mountain ash trees. William Ricketts Sanctuary, 1 km N, sculptures by the famous Australian artist and conservationist set in native bushland. Mount Dandenong lookout, 2 km N, spectacular views over Melbourne. Kawarra Australian Plant Garden, 1.5 km N at Kalorama, extensive native plant collection. **Tourist information:** 64 Monbulk Rd, Belgrave; (03) 9752 6554. **Accommodation:** 1 motel, 20 B&B, 1 cara./camp. park. **See also:** The Dandenongs; National Parks.

Omeo   Pop. 274

MAP REF. 119 A12, 242 F8
The high plains around Omeo were opened up in 1835 when overlanders from the Monaro region moved their stock south to these lush summer pastures. Its name is an Aboriginal word meaning 'mountains', and the township is set in the heart of the Victorian Alps at an altitude of 643 m. It is used as a base for winter traffic approaching Mt Hotham from Bairnsdale, 120 km S, and for bushwalking expeditions to the Bogong High Plains during summer and autumn. Omeo has suffered several natural disasters. It was damaged by earthquakes in 1885 and 1892, and was half destroyed by the Black Friday bushfires of 1939. Nevertheless, several old buildings remain. **Of interest:** In the A.M. Pearson Historical Park, Day Ave: old court house (1861) now museum; present court house (1892); log gaol (1858); stables; blacksmiths. Also in Day Ave: post office (1891); Commercial Bank (1890); Colonial Bank (1889) now bookshop; school (1866); 19th century timber buildings including D.C.N.R. office, C.W.A. Hall and Petersens Gallery. Mar.: Picnic Races. Easter: Rodeo and Market. Nov.: Agricultural and Pastoral Show (includes Wool Awards). **In the area:** High-country horseback and 4WD tours, bushwalking, trout fishing, skiing and white-water rafting (in spring); scenic drive to Bairnsdale, the Wineries and Riverside Drive — inquire at Tourist information. Omeo has a gold-rush history; high cliffs left after sluicing for gold, stone walls and tunnel openings can be seen at the Oriental Claims, 1.5 km W on Alpine Rd; gold panning popular along Livingstone Creek. Remains of State's first hydro-electric plant (power for Cassilis goldfield), 25 km W off Victoria Falls Rd. Mt Markey Winery, Cassilis Rd, Cassilis, 15 km S. Blue Duck Inn (1890s) is a base for fishing at Anglers Rest, 29 km NW. Benambra, 20 km NE. Taylors Crossing suspension bridge, part of Australian Alps Walking Track, 44 km NE, off Tablelands Rd. Scenic drives: Tambo River valley between Swifts Creek and Bruthen (97 km S), especially beautiful in autumn; to Benambra then Corryong, 148 km NE; Omeo Hwy through Mitta Mitta to Tallangatta (172 km NW); from Omeo through Dinner Plain to Mt Hotham. Note: all scenic drives listed cross state forests (be alert for timber trucks) or alpine areas (check road conditions in winter). **Tourist information:** Octagon Bookshop, Day Ave; (03) 5159 1411. **Accommodation:** 1 hotel, 1 hotel/motel, 1 motel, 4 B&B, 1 cara./ camp. park.

Orbost   Pop. 2515

MAP REF. 243 J12
Situated on the banks of the Snowy River, this Gippsland timber town is on the Princes Hwy, surrounded by spectacular coastal and mountain territory. **Of interest:** Old Pump House, behind Slab Hut (Tourist information centre, cnr Nicholson and Clarke sts); hut (1872) relocated from its original site 40 km away. Orbost Rainforest Centre, Lochiel St, audiovisual display explaining complex nature of rainforest ecology.

VICTORIA

Gippsland Lakes

Many people regard the Gippsland Lakes as the most outstanding holiday area in Victoria. Dominated as it is by Australia's largest system of inland waterways, it certainly does live up to all the superlatives accorded it. With the foothills of the high country just to the north and the amazing stretch of the Ninety Mile Beach separating the lakes from the ocean, the region offers a variety of natural beauty and recreational activities. Here the choice really is yours — lake, river or ocean fishing, boating, cruising, surfing, swimming, birdwatching or just sitting by the water.

Within easy reach of the Lakes area the high country begins, so it is possible to vary a waterside trip with days exploring the alpine reaches (some minor roads may be closed in winter) and some of the fascinating little old townships such as **Omeo**, **Briagolong** and Dargo. The road across the Dargo High Plains and the Alpine Road leading to Hotham Heights passes through some stunning country. Check your car thoroughly before you set off — service stations are scarce along the way.

Wellington, King, Victoria, Reeve and Coleman — these five lakes cover more than 400 square kilometres and stretch parallel to the Ninety Mile Beach for almost its entire length. **Sale**, at the western edge of the region, is the local base for the development of the Bass Strait oil and gas fields. Both Sale and **Bairnsdale**, further east on the banks of the Mitchell River, make excellent bases for holidays on the lakes or for alpine trips. The main resort towns are **Lakes Entrance**, at the mouth of the Lakes; **Paynesville**, a mecca for boating and

The township of Lakes Entrance at the mouth of the Gippsland Lakes

fishing enthusiasts; Metung, a departure point for cruising holidays on the lakes; and Loch Sport, nestled between Ninety Mile Beach, Lake Victoria and the national park.

The Lakes National Park, the **Mitchell River National Park**, and the hills and valleys of the alpine foothills to the north, all provide plenty of opportunities for bushwalking, for enjoying nature or for simply enjoying the peace.

For further information on the Gippsland Lakes area, contact local tourist information centres: at Lakes Entrance (cnr Esplanade and Marine Pde, (03) 5155 1966); at Bairnsdale (240 Main St, (03) 5152 3444); at Sale (Princes Hwy, (03) 5144 1108). **See also:** National Parks and individual text entries in A–Z listing for those parks and towns indicated by bold type. **Map reference:** 233 P6.

Port Fairy, a charming coastal fishing village

In Nicholson St: Historical Museum; Croajingolong Mohair Farm, has garments, yarns, fleeces, fabrics and leathergoods; Snowy River Country Craft; Lorna's doll display. Netherbyre Gemstone and Art Gallery, cnr Browning and Carlyle sts. Market, Nicholson St, 2nd Sun. each month. Jan.: Australian Wood Display. **In the area:** Beautiful Bonang Hwy, unsealed in parts, leads north-east through mountains to Delegate in NSW. At Bonang, 97 km NE: Aurora Mine, a working goldmine (bookings essential). Walking in Snowy River National Park (25 km NW) and Errinundra National Park (54 km NE); latter has rainforest boardwalk. Tranquil Valley Tavern, on banks of Delegate River near NSW border, about 18 km N of Bonang. Spectacular drive to Buchan, 58 km NW, leads to Little River Falls and McKillop's Bridge on the Snowy River. Scenic coastal drive to Marlo and Cape Conran (30 km E) starts just west of Orbost, returns to Princes Hwy near Cabbage Tree Creek. Cabbage Tree Palms Flora Reserve, 27 km E. Bemm River, on Sydenham Inlet, 57 km E, popular centre for bream anglers. Baldwin Spencer Trail, a 262-km scenic driving circuit following route of explorer; incorporates Snowy River estuary and Errinundra National Park. **Tourist information:** The Slab Hut, cnr Nicholson and Clarke sts; (03) 5154 2424. **Accommodation:** 2 hotels, 4 motels, 4 B&B, 1 cara./camp. park.

Ouyen   Pop. 1337

MAP REF. 126 E10, 238 H9

At the junction of the Calder and Mallee hwys, Ouyen is about 100 km S of Mildura, north-east of the Big Desert area. Nov.: Farmers Festival. **In the area:** Tag-along (own vehicle tagging along behind 4WD tour) and 4WD tours available; contact Tourist information. Hattah-Kulkyne National Park, 34 km N, with abundant wildlife, bird-watching, bushwalking, canoeing and wildflowers in spring. Pink lakes are outstanding subjects for photography in Murray-Sunset National Park, 60 km W. At Patchewollock, 41 km SW, Easter Sports (with camel-racing). At Speed, 39 km S, Mallee Machinery Field Days in Aug. **Tourist information:** Oke St; (03) 5092 1000. **Accommodation:** 1 hotel, 3 motels, 1 cara./camp. park.

Paynesville   Pop. 2444

MAP REF. 233 Q5

A popular tourist resort 18 km from Bairnsdale on the McMillan Straits, Paynesville is a mecca for fishing and boating enthusiasts, and is noted for yachting and speedboat racing as well as water-skiing. **Of interest:** In the Esplanade: St Peter-by-the-Lake (1961) church, incorporating seafaring symbols; Community Craft Centre. Market at Gilsenan Reserve, 2nd Sun. each month. Mar.: Marlay Point–Paynesville Yacht Race. Easter: Gold Cup Speedboat Championships. **In the area:** Rotomah Island Bird Observatory, 8 km S by boat. Ninety Mile Beach, 10 km S by boat; ferry crosses Straits to Raymond Island. On Raymond Island: Koala Reserve; Riviera Meadows, a miniature animal farm. The Lakes National Park, to the east, 5 km by boat to Sperm Whale Head; otherwise via Loch Sport. Cruises on MV *Lakes Odyssey*. Organised scenic tours of lakes. Boat charter and hire. Dolphins in bay. **Tourist information:** Paynesville Marine Service, Esplanade; (03) 5156 6554. **Accommodation:** 1 motel, 2 B&B, 3 cara./camp. parks. **See also:** Gippsland Lakes.

Port Albert   Pop. 307

MAP REF. 233 L10

This tiny historic town on the south-east coast, 120 km SE from Morwell, was the first established port in Victoria. Sailing boats from Europe and America once docked at the large timber jetty here. Boats from China brought thousands of Chinese to the Gippsland goldfields. Originally established for trade with Tasmania, Port Albert was the supply port for Gippsland pioneers until the railway from Melbourne to Sale was completed (1878). The timber jetty is still crowded today, as Port Albert is a commercial fishing port and its sheltered waters are popular with anglers and boat owners. Some of the original stone buildings are still in use and have been classified by the National Trust. **Of interest:** Historic buildings in Tarraville Rd: original government offices and stores; Bank of Victoria (1861), now Maritime Museum with photographs and relics of the area. Warren Curry Art Gallery, also in Tarraville Rd, features Australian country-town streetscapes. Port Albert Hotel, Wharf St, first licensed in 1842 and possibly the oldest hotel still operating in State. **In the area:** At Tarraville, 5 km NE, Christ Church (1856),

VICTORIA

first church in Gippsland. Swimming at Mann's Beach, 10 km NE. Surfing at Woodside on Ninety Mile Beach, 34 km NE. Wildlife sanctuary on St Margaret Island, 12 km E. Alberton, 8 km NW, once the administrative centre of Central Gippsland. Tarra-Bulga National Park, 41 km NW. **Tourist information:** cnr South Gippsland Hwy and Silkstone Rd, Korumburra; (03) 5655 2233. **Accommodation:** 1 hotel/motel, 2 cara./camp. parks.

Port Campbell
Pop. 234

MAP REF. 223 A10, 235 K11

This small crayfishing village and seaside resort is situated in the centre of Port Campbell National Park and on a spectacular stretch of the Great Ocean Rd. **Of interest:** Historical Museum, Lord St (open school holidays). Loch Ard Shipwreck Museum, Lord St, has relics from the *Loch Ard* wrecked in 1878 at Loch Ard Gorge (7 km SE). Self-guide Discovery Walk (2.5 km), leaflet from Tourist information. Good fishing from rocks and pier; boat charters for fishing and diving available. Market, Cairns St, each Sun. in summer. **In the area:** Port Campbell National Park surrounds town, its coastal features include world-famous Twelve Apostles (12 km SE), Loch Ard Gorge (7 km SE), London Bridge, now fallen down, (5 km W) and The Arch (6 km W). Walking tracks, scenic drives and historic shipwreck sites; Historic Shipwreck Trail links sites along 'Shipwreck Coast', from Moonlight Head to Port Fairy. Glenample, first homestead in area; survivors of *Loch Ard* recuperated there, 12 km E on Great Ocean Rd, (check opening times). Gibson Steps, 13 km SE, cut into limestone cliff face. Otway Deer and Wildlife Park, 20 km E. Picturesque road leads north to pretty timbered township of Timboon, centre of dairy area. Nearby, pick-your-own berries (in season) at Berry World. Just south of Timboon, Timboon Farmhouse has cheese tastings and sales. **Tourist information:** National Parks Office, Morris St; (03) 5598 6382. **Accommodation:** 1 hotel, 4 motels, 1 hostel. 1 cara./camp. park. **See also:** The Great Ocean Road.

Port Fairy
Pop. 2467

MAP REF. 234 G9

The home port for a large fishing fleet and an attractive, rambling holiday resort. Port Fairy is 29 km W of Warrnambool with both ocean and river as its borders. The town's history goes back to whaling days. At one time it was one of the largest ports in Australia. Over 50 of its small cottages and bluestone buildings have been classified by the National Trust. This charming old-world fishing village is popular with heritage lovers and holidaymakers. **Of interest:** Self-guide historic walks of town, contact Tourist information for details. History Centre, Gipps St, in old court house. Battery Hill, end Griffith St, old fort and signal station at mouth of river. National Trust-classified buildings: splendid timber home of Captain Mills, Gipps St; Mott's Cottage, 5 Sackville St. Other attractive buildings: Old Caledonian Inn, Bank St; Seacombe House and ANZ Bank building, Cox St; St John's Church of England (1856), Regent St; *Gazette* Office (1849), Sackville St. Ornamental Shoe and Boot (displays), Princes Hwy. Hot Glass Studio, Regent St. Mar.: Award-winning Folk Festival. Oct.: Spring Music Festival. Dec.: Moyneyana Festival (includes eel and ferret races, and busking competitions). **In the area:** Historic Shipwreck Trail, linking sites along 'Shipwreck Coast' between Port Fairy and Moonlight Head; Mahogany Walk to Warrnambool, taking 6–7 hr one-way (return by bus); brochures available at Tourist information. Griffiths Island, connected to east of town by causeway, has lighthouse and short-tailed shearwater rookeries; spectacular nightly return of the short-tailed shearwaters (muttonbirds) to island from Sept.–Apr. Australia's only mainland colony of short-tailed shearwaters at Pea Soup Beach and South Beach, on southern edge of town. Lady Julia Percy Island, 10 km off coast, home for fur seals; only accessible by experienced boat operators in calm weather. Yambuk and Lake Yambuk, 17 km W. Mt Eccles National Park, 56 km NW. Tower Hill, 14 km E, fascinating area with an extinct volcano and crater lake with islands. **Tourist information:** 22 Bank St; (03) 5568 2682. **Accommodation:** 7 motels, 16 B&B, 8 cara./camp. parks. **See also:** The Great Ocean Road.

Portland
Pop. 10 115

MAP REF. 234 D9

Portland, situated about 75 km E of the South Australian border, is the most western of Victoria's major coastal towns and is the only deep-water port between Melbourne and Adelaide. It was the first permanent settlement in Victoria, founded by the Henty family in 1834. Today it is an important industrial and commercial centre, and a popular summer resort with beaches, surfing, fishing and outstanding coastal and forest scenery. **Of interest:** Number of self-guide and guided walks in and around Portland including the Walk in the Footsteps of Mary MacKillop around sites significant during Mary's time in Portland (guided tours also available), details at Tourist information. Botanical Gardens (1857), Cliff St. More than 200 early buildings, some National Trust-classified: customs house and court house in Cliff St; Steam Packet Inn (1842) and Mac's Hotel in Bentinck St. History House, Charles St, a historical museum and family research centre in old town hall (1863). Fawthrop Lagoon, Glenelg St, has prolific birdlife. Powerhouse Car Museum, Percy St. Good views from Watertower Lookout, Clifton Crt, requires climbing 133 steps (displays of memorabilia on the way) to 360° view, excellent position for whale watching; also from Portland Battery, Battery Hill. Portland Aluminium Smelter (guided tours available, check times). Kingsley Winery (tastings and sales outlet), Bancroft St. Jan.: Foreshore Carnival. Feb.: Fishing Competition. Mar.: Dahlia Festival. Nov.: Antique Fair; Pioneer Week. Dec.: Surfboat Marathon. **In the area:** Alcoa reclamation and revegetation projects. Edward Henty's homestead Burswood, Cape Nelson Rd. Cape Nelson State Park, 11 km SW, offers spectacular coastal scenery and National Trust-classified lighthouse, (check opening times). Safe swimming and surfing at Cape Bridgewater, 21 km SW; also nearby, petrified forest (formed by sand engulfing an ancient forest), blowholes, freshwater springs and the Watering Place; 2-hour walk to see Australian fur seals from viewing platform; and walks to Cape Duquesne and Discovery Bay, both further west. For the more energetic, the 250-km Great South West Walk, a scenic circular track from Tourist information centre through a number of national parks and State forests to Discovery Bay and Cape Nelson (can be covered in easy stages), inquire at Tourist information for details. Barrett's Gorae West Wines, 20 km W. Mt Richmond National Park, 25 km NW. Lower Glenelg National Park,

44 km NW via Kentbruck, has spectacular gorges, colourful wildflowers, native birds and excellent fishing. Along coastal road is charming hamlet of Nelson, 70 km NW; here, launch trips to Glenelg River mouth at Discovery Bay available, also good water-ski area. Nearby Princess Margaret Rose Caves, tours available. Narrawong State Forest, 18 km NE. Historical displays at Caledonian Inn, Henty Hwy, 8 km N. At Heywood, 22 km N: Cave Hill Gardens; Bower Birds Nest Museum. **Tourist information:** Cliff St; (03) 5523 2671; freecall, 1800 035567. **Accommodation:** 10 motels, 6 B&B, 3 hostels, 7 cara./camp. parks.

Pyramid Hill   Pop. 546

MAP REF. 126 I13, 237 Q5, 240 B4

A small country town some 40 km SW of Cohuna and 100 km N of Bendigo, Pyramid Hill was named for its unusually shaped hill, 187 m high. **Of interest:** Historical museum, McKay St (open Sun.). A climb to the top of Pyramid Hill provides scenic views of the surrounding irrigation and wheat district (there is also a Braille walking trail for visually impaired people). Oct.: Pioneer Machinery Display. **In the area:** Terrick Terrick State Park, 11 km SE, large Murray Pine forest reserve with numerous granite outcrops (southernmost outcrop called Mitiamo Rock), walks, variety of birdlife and other fauna. Mt Hope, 10 km NE, named by explorer Major Mitchell. **Tourist information:** Newsagency, 12–14 Kelly St; (03) 5455 7036. **Accommodation:** 1 hotel, 1 cara./camp. park.

Queenscliff   Pop. 3681

MAP REF. 218 H10, 220 B5, 225 I9, 232 B7

Queenscliff, 31 km E of Geelong on the Bellarine Peninsula, was established as a commercial fishing centre in the 1850s and still has a large fishing fleet based in its harbour. The town looks out across the famous and treacherous Rip at the entrance to Port Phillip. **Of interest:** Queenscliff Maritime Centre, Weeroona Pde, explores town's long association with sea and days of sailing ships. Adjacent Marine Studies Centre, offers summer holiday programme for visitors. Fort Queenscliff (1882), King St, built during the Crimean War, includes Black Lighthouse (1861), White Lighthouse (1862). Other historic buildings include: Vue Grand Hotel, Hesse St; Ozone and

Queenscliff hotels, Gellibrand St. Historical tours leave from pier. In Hesse St: Queenscliffe Arcade, for local art and craft; Seaview Gallery in Seaview House. In Hobson St: Hobson's Choice Gallery; The Grand Ballroom Gallery. Bellarine Peninsula Railway operates steam train between Queenscliff (station in Symonds St) and Drysdale (8 km NW) on weekends and summer holidays; also display of historic locomotives and carriages at station. Regular passenger ferry service operates between Queenscliff and Portsea across bay in summer and school holidays. Daily vehicle and passenger ferry service between Queenscliff and Sorrento (about 45 min.). 'Snorkelling with the seals', inquire at Tourist information. Point Lonsdale (6 km SW) extensively developed as holiday and tourist resort. Queenscliff market at Symonds St, last Sun. of month (Aug.–Apr.). Market at Princes Park (Gellibrand St), last Sun. of month (Sept.–May). Pt Lonsdale market at Bowen Rd, 2nd Sun. each month. **In the area:** Marine life viewing at Harold Holt Marine Reserve, which includes Mud Island and coastal reserves. Lake Victoria, 1 km W of Point Lonsdale. At Wallington, 13 km NW: A Maze'N Things; horseriding at Australian Equestrian Academy; Country Connection Adventure Park; pick-your-own fruit and vegetable farms. **Tourist information:** A Maze'N Things, 1570 Bellarine Hwy, Wallington; (03) 5250 2669. **Accommodation:** Queenscliff: 4 hotels, 4 cara./camp. parks. Point Lonsdale: 2 motels, 2 cara./camp. parks.

Rainbow   Pop. 587

MAP REF. 126 D13, 236 F4

This Wimmera township, 70 km N of Dimboola, is near Lake Hindmarsh, popular for fishing, boating and water-skiing. **Of interest:** Pasco's Cash Store (1928), Federal St, an original country general store. National Trust-classified Yurunga Homestead (1910) in Gray St, on northern edge of town, has large selection of antiques and original fittings. Oct.: Iris Festival. **In the area:** Lutheran church (1901), 10 km W, at Pella, has old pipe organ, only one other of its kind in State. Lake Albacutya Park, 12 km N, lake only fills when Lake Hindmarsh overflows. Wyperfeld National Park, 30 km N via sealed road north from Yaapeet. **Tourist information:** Pasco's Cash Store, Federal St; (03) 5395 1020. **Accommodation:** 2 hotels, 1 motel, 1 cara./camp. park.

Robinvale   Pop. 1795

MAP REF. 126 F8, 239 J6

This small, well-laid-out town on the NSW border, 83 km SE of Mildura, is almost entirely surrounded by bends in the Murray River. The surrounding area is ideal for the production of citrus, dried fruit and wine grapes. It is a picturesque town, and water sports and fishing are popular along the river. **Of interest:** In Moore St: McWilliams Wines; Lexia Room features historical exhibits. Rural Life Museum, Bromley Rd (open by appt). **In the area:** Euston weir and lock on Murray, 3 km downstream. Robinvale Wines, Greek-style winery, 5 km S on Sea Lake Rd. Kyndalyn Park almond farm, 23 km SE. Hattah-Kulkyne National Park, 66 km SW. **Tourist information:** Bromley Rd; (03) 5026 1388. **Accommodation:** 1 hotel, 3 motels, 2 cara./camp. parks. **See also:** Wine Regions.

Rochester   Pop. 2527

MAP REF. 240 E6

On the Campaspe River, 28 km S of Echuca, Rochester is the centre for a rich dairying and tomato-growing area. A small, busy town, it has some attractive older buildings and boasts the largest dairy factory in Australia. **Of interest:** In Moore St: 'The Oppy Museum' (open Mon.–Fri.); opposite, statue of Sir Hubert Opperman, champion cyclist; Pinpandoor Gallery, for local crafts. Historical Plaque Trail, brochure available at Tourist information. **In the area:** Random House Homestead, amid 4 ha of gardens beside river in Bridge Rd, on eastern edge of town. Campaspe Siphon, 3 km N, an engineering achievement, where the Waranga-Mallee irrigation channel runs under the Campaspe River. District channels are popular with anglers as plentiful redfin and carp. Pleasant lakes in district, popular for fishing and water sports, including Greens Lake and Lake Cooper (14 km SE). **Tourist information:** Railway Station, Moore St; (03) 5484 1860. **Accommodation:** 3 hotels, 1 motel, 1 cara./camp. park.

Rushworth   Pop. 1012

MAP REF. 240 G7

Rushworth, 20 km W of Murchison, off the Goulburn Valley Hwy, still shows

VICTORIA

Wine Regions

Vineyard in the Yarra Valley region

Viticulture developed in Victoria following the 1850s gold rush. Unsuccessful diggers began planting vines as a source of income. Later, Edward Henty and William Rye brought cuttings to the new colony and by 1868 more than 1200 hectares of vines had been established. The light, dry wines produced in these vineyards won wide acclaim, but the event of phylloxera saw a promising industry decline until the early 1960s, when it started to re-emerge and develop into what it is today.

One of the oldest regions is in the north-east of the State, 270 kilometres from Melbourne. **Rutherglen** and the other nearby wine-making towns of Wahgunyah, **Glenrowan** and Milawa produce wine unique to each of the region's environmental subcultures. Many of the wineries are still managed by the descendants of the founders. The region is famed for its rich flavoursome reds, and for the exotic range of fortified wines such as Rutherglen muscat, Rutherglen tokay and its famous port-style wine. On the June long weekend, a winery walkabout is organised so that wine-lovers can visit the vineyards and sample some of the fine wines of the north-east. It is advisable to book accommodation in advance if planning a visit at this time.

West along the Murray, the towns of **Echuca**, **Swan Hill** and **Mildura** are part of the Murray Valley and north-west region known for the production of wines for everyday drinking.

About 200 kilometres west of Melbourne, between Stawell and Ararat, is the little town of Great Western, where the Seppelt and Best wineries developed in the 1860s. Since then they have consistently produced fine wines, including the renowned champagne-style Great Western Special Reserve from the Seppelt winery. The vineyards of Great Western are also noted for their rich red and full-flavoured white table wines.

At **Ararat**, Trevor Mast's Mt Langi Ghiran Wines and the Montara Winery, both produce excellent wine with their own individual character.

To the north-east of Great Western is the region of the Pyrenees with the towns of **Avoca**, Redbank and Moonambel. Here are the Taltarni, Mt Avoca, Redbank, Blue Pyrenees, Summerfield, Dalwhinnie and Warrenmang wineries.

Stretching from **Shepparton** along to **Nagambie**, **Seymour** and **Mansfield** is the picturesque region of the Goulburn Valley with a contrast in wineries from the historic, classified buildings of Chateau Tahbilk to the modern wineries of Delatite and Mitchelton. One grape variety from the region to win acclaim is the Marsanne, a distinct and rather unusual white wine.

One of the two oldest regions near Melbourne is the Yarra Valley region, which is centred round Cottles Bridge and St Andrews (at the northern end), Yarra Glen, Lilydale, Coldstream and **Healesville** (in the central part of the region), and Seville and **Warburton** (to the south). This region's premium wine has had a rebirth after starting in the early 1850s and petering out as late as the 1920s. There is a wide range of wines produced in the area, from sparkling wine to quality reds and white table wines. Wineries of particular interest include Domaine Chandon for its sparkling wines and splendid tasting room, and Fergusson, Kellybrook, Yarra Burn and De Bortoli for an enjoyable restaurant lunch in the Valley. There are many other wineries worth visiting, including Bianchet for the merlot and verduzzo wines, and St Huberts, one of the first wineries in the re-birth of the district. Grape Grazing, a food and wine festival, is held every March.

Another wine-producing region close to Melbourne is the Mornington Peninsula area. A cool-climate winegrowing district, its vineyards nestle between farming and coastal hamlets. The main spread covers the area from Dromana, through Red Hill and across the Peninsula to Merricks and Balnarring, with Mornington, Main Ridge and Mt Martha offering isolated vineyards. Most vineyards are open, usually on weekends and public holidays, for cellar-door tastings and sales; some open for sales and visits by appointment only. The wine producers in this area organise the Queen's Birthday Wine Weekend at the Regional Gallery in Mornington, during the long weekend in June.

North of Melbourne's Tullamarine Airport, wineries dot the landscape with pockets of vines stretching into the Macedon Ranges; some were established in the 1860s, others more recently. They include Knight's Granite Hills, Wildwood, Hanging Rock, Virgin Hills, Craiglee, Goonawarra, Cleveland, Cope-Williams, Flynn and Williams — each with its own distinct quality and character.

The Heathcote-Bendigo region is, like so many of Victoria's wine regions, goldmining country that gave up much hidden wealth in the period from 1850–1900. Today there are many wineries scattered throughout the region, around the townships of **Heathcote**, Kingower, **Bendigo** and Bridgewater on Loddon. Wineries include Passing Clouds, Jasper Hill, Osicka's, Zuber Estate, Water Wheel, Chateau Leamon and Mildara's Balgownie.

In the last 30 years Victoria's wine industry has changed from an industry in decline, with about 25 commercial vineyards, to a flourishing concern with more than 300 commercial vineyards and 100 smaller ones. Most larger wineries are open daily for tastings and sales; some of the small wineries have restricted opening times, so check with the winery before visiting.

Tourism Victoria publish an excellent guide, *Wine Regions of Victoria* describing more than 200 wineries; a copy of the guide as well as further information on Victoria's wine regions can be obtained from the Victorian Visitor Information Centre, Melbourne Town Hall, cnr Little Collins and Swanston sts, Melbourne, (03) 9650 1522. **See also:** individual text entries in A–Z listing for those towns indicated by bold type. **Map reference:** 222, for Yarra Valley region.

Museum in the Historical Precinct, Shepparton

traces of its gold-rush days. Many of the town's attractive original buildings still stand, witnesses to the days when Rushworth was the commercial centre for the surrounding mining district. **Of interest:** Nearly all the buildings in High St are National Trust-classified: St Pauls Church of England; band rotunda; former Imperial Hotel (now a private residence); Glasgow Buildings; the Whistle Stop. Also in High St, History Museum in Mechanics Institute (1913) (open by appt). **In the area:** Rushworth State Forest, 3 km s, largest natural ironbark forest in world. At Whroo Historic Area, 7 km s: Balaclava Hill open-cut goldmine, Whroo cemetery and Aboriginal waterhole (all with visitor access). Twelve Acres Winery and Akora Wildlife Sanctuary for sick and injured fauna, both 20 km s. Further south, remnants of deserted goldmining towns Angustown, Bailieston and Graytown. At Murchison, 21 km E: Meteorite Park, site of meteorite fall 1969; nearby, Longleat Winery and Campbell's Bend picnic reserve. At Waranga Basin, 6 km NE: water sports, fishing, camping and excellent picnic facilities. **Tourist information:** Guided Tours of Victoria, 31 High St; (03) 5856 1612. **Accommodation:** 1 hotel, 1 hotel/motel, 2 cara./camp. parks.

Rutherglen
Pop. 1876

MAP REF. 127 O13, 241 N4

Rutherglen is the centre of one of the most important winegrowing areas in Victoria. There is a cluster of vineyards surrounding the town, with winegrowing country stretching south to the Milawa area. Most wineries reflect their history; of particular interest is the National Trust-classified winery building at All Saints, 10 km NW. Other wineries include Anderson, Bullers, Campbells, Chambers, Cofield, Fairfield, Gehrig Estate, Jones, Morris, Mount Prior, Pfeiffer, Stanton and Killeen, Sutherland Smith and Warabilla; contact Tourist information for opening times. Mar.: Tastes of Rutherglen. June: Winery Walkabout Weekend. **Of interest:** Main St, a fully preserved example of late 19th-century, small-town architecture. Historic walk/drive/cycle of town, contact Tourist information for maps and details. Common School Museum, just behind Main St, for local memorabilia in fully restored 1800s schoolroom. Walkabout Cellars, Main St. Market in Main St, 4th Sun. each month. **In the area:** Scenic day trips to Albury-Wodonga, Yarrawonga, Lake Mulwala, Corowa, Beechworth, Bright or Mt Buffalo. Old Customs House at Wahgunyah, 10 km NW, relic of days when duty was payable on goods

coming from NSW. Lake Moodemere, 8 km W, with canoe trees around lake; lake is good for water sports; fauna reserve nearby. **Tourist information:** cnr Drummond and Main sts; (02) 6032 9166. **Accommodation:** 2 hotels, 6 motels, 7 B&B, 1 cara./camp. park. **See also:** The Mighty Murray; Wine Regions.

St Arnaud
Pop. 2741

MAP REF. 237 L9

This old goldmining town is on the Sunraysia Hwy between Donald and Avoca, and is surrounded by forest and hill country. Many of the town's historic iron-lacework decorated buildings are National Trust-classified and together form a nationally-recognised historic streetscape. **Of interest:** Queen Mary Gardens, Napier St. Worm Farm, Millet St. Oct.: Agricultural Show. **In the area:** Good fishing in Avoca River and at Teddington Reservoir, 28 km s. St Peter's Church (1869), made of pebbles, at Carapooee, 11 km SE. Melville Caves, 38 km E, famous as haunt of bushranger Captain Melville. At Lake Batyo Catyo, 35 km NW: fishing, water sports and camping. **Tourist information:** The Old Post Office, 2 Napier St; (03) 5495 2313. **Accommodation:** 3 hotels, 3 motels, 1 B&B, 1 cara./camp. park.

Sale
Pop. 13 858

MAP REF. 233 N6

Sale is the main administrative city in Gippsland. In nearby Bass Strait, there is a concentration of offshore oil development. Just over 200 km E of Melbourne on the Princes Hwy, Sale is convenient for exploration of the whole Gippsland Lakes area, which extends from Wilsons Promontory to Lakes Entrance, and is bordered to the north by the foothills and mountains of the Great Divide and, most of the way along the coast, by the famous Ninety Mile Beach. **Of interest:** Port of Sale, thriving during the days of the paddlesteamers. In Foster St: Lake Guthridge, with fauna park and adventure playground; historical museum; Regional Arts Centre; bronze of Mary MacKillop in St Mary's Church. Also in Foster St, Ramahyuck Aboriginal Corporation, for locally-produced art and craft; Wetlands Information Centre, cnr Foster and York sts — both part of Bataluk Cultural Trail which begins in Sale (details and brochure available at Tourist information). Attractive

VICTORIA

buildings: Our Lady of Sion Convent; clock tower; Victoria Hall; Criterion Hotel, with its beautiful lacework verandahs. RAAF base, Raglan St, home of the famous Roulettes aerobatic team. Pedestrian Mall, cnr Cunningham and Raymond sts has local art including Annemieke Mein bronzes. Sale Common and State Game Refuge, protected wetlands area with boardwalk, on southeast edge of town. Mar.: Sale Cup (horse race). Nov.: Agricultural Show. **In the area**: Maffra and Heyfield (18 km), both north-west of town in intensively cultivated country. Australian Wildlife Art Gallery, 25 km NE at Munroe, has wildlife paintings and sculpture. Holey Plains State Park, 14 km SW. Seaspray, 32 km S, on Ninety Mile Beach, offers excellent surfing and fishing; as do Golden and Paradise beaches, 35 km from Sale, and Loch Sport, a further 30 km; nearby, The Lakes National Park and Rotamah Island Bird Observatory, 15 km from Loch Sport. Marlay Point, 25 km E on shores of Lake Wellington, has extensive boat launching facilities; yacht club here sponsors overnight yacht race to Paynesville each Mar. Popular rivers for fishing include the Avon, close to Marlay Point, and the Macalister, Thomson and La Trobe, especially at Swing Bridge (1883), 5 km S of Sale. **Tourist information**: Central Gippsland Tourism, Princes Hwy; (03) 5144 1108 **Accommodation**: 9 motels, 4 B&B, 2 cara./camp. parks. **See also**: Gippsland Lakes.

Seymour   Pop. 6558

MAP REF. 240 G10

Seymour is a commercial, industrial and agricultural town on the Goulburn River, 98 km N of Melbourne. The area was recommended by Lord Kitchener during his visit in 1909 as being suitable for a military base. Nearby Puckapunyal was an important training place for troops during World War II and is still a major army base. **Of interest**: In Emily St: Royal Hotel, featured in Russell Drysdale's famous 1941 painting 'Moody's Pub'; old court house (1864), for local art and Tourist information; Old Goulburn Bridge (1891), preserved as historic relic; walking track alongside Goulburn River. Goulburn Park, cnr Progress and Guild sts, has picnic and swimming areas. Steam Train Preservation Society, has restored steam engine and carriages for viewing (by appt. only).

Feb.: Alternative Farming Expo. Mar.: Rafting Festival. **In the area**: Mitchelton and Chateau Tahbilk vineyards, near Nagambie, 23 km N. Other wineries nearby: Somerset Crossing Vineyards, 2 km S; Hankin's Wines, 5 km NW on Northwood Rd; Hayward's Winery, 12 km SE near Trawool. Army Tank and Transport Museums at Puckapunyal army base, 10 km W. Trawool Valley Angora Stud, 11 km SE. Spotted Jumbuk, 5 km E on Highland Rd, features spotted sheep. Capalba Park Alpacas, 11 km E on Kobyboyne Rd. **Tourist information**: The old court house, Emily St; (03) 5799 0233. **Accommodation**: 5 motels, 3 cara./camp. parks. **See also**: Wine Regions.

Shepparton   Pop. 30 511

MAP REF. 240 I6

The 'capital' of the rich Goulburn Valley, this thriving, well-developed city, 175 km N of Melbourne, has 4000 ha of orchards within a 10-km radius and 4000 ha of market gardens along the river flats nearby. The area is irrigated by the Goulburn Irrigation Scheme. The central shopping area is surrounded by parkland. **Of interest**: Solar display at Visitors Centre, Wyndham St. Art gallery in Civic Centre, Welsford St, features Australian paintings and ceramics. Parkside Gardens and Aboriginal Keeping Place, Parkside Dr., a tourist, educational and cultural centre. Historical Museum, in Historical Precinct, High St (open even-dated Sun. p.m.). Redbyrne Pottery, Old Dookie Rd, has variety of local pottery. Victoria Park Lake, Tom Collins Dr., for water sports. In Andrew Fairley Ave, SPC, a huge cannery; guided tours during fruit season (Jan.–Apr.). Lemnos-Campbells soup cannery and Ardmona fruit cannery at Mooroopna, 5 km W. (All three have direct sales.) Reedy Swamp Walk, at end of Wanganui Rd, for prolific birdlife in wetland area. Fruit Connection, at rest stop on causeway, has arts and crafts, wine tastings and sales. Trash and treasure market, Melbourne Rd, each Sun. Feb.: Bush Market Day. Nov.: Strawberry Festival. **In the area**: Mud Factory Pottery, 6 km S on Goulburn Valley Hwy. Several vineyards, including Longleat at Murchison, 34 km S. Also at Murchison, craft and collectables market, 4th Sat. each month. At Kialla, 5 km SE: Boxwood Pottery; Elm Vale Nursery. Historic Brookfield Homestead, 20 km

N on Goulburn Valley Hwy, features old farm machinery and shearing sheds (open by appt). Craft market at Mooroopna, 5 km W, 1st Sun. each month. Victoria's Irrigation Research Institute, east of Tatura, 16 km W of Shepparton. **Tourist information**: 534 Wyndham St; (03) 5831 4400; freecall, 1800 808839. **Accommodation**: 4 hotels, 18 motels, 3 B&B, 6 cara./camp. parks. **See also**: Wine Regions.

Skipton   Pop. 462

MAP REF. 228 H13, 235 M4

This small township on the Glenelg Hwy, south-west of Ballarat, is situated in an important pastoral and agricultural district. The town was a major centre for merino sheep sales in the 1850s. **Of interest**: Eel factory, Cleveland St, snap freezes eels netted in region and exports them mainly to Germany. Adjacent to eel factory, Gibson's Doll Display. Bluestone Presbyterian Church, National Trust-classified, Montgomery St. Nov.: Art Show. **In the area**: Mooromong, 11 km NW, notable historic homestead (open by appt). Mt Widderin Cave, 6 km S, volcanic cave with large underground chamber (tours by appt). Kaolin Mine, 10 km E (open by appt). **Tourist information**: Roadhouse, Glenelg Hwy; (03) 5340 2131. **Accommodation**: 1 hotel.

Sorrento   Pop. 1501

MAP REF. 218 I11, 220 D7, 225 I10, 232 B8

Situated on a thin strip of land between Port Phillip and Bass Strait, Sorrento was the site of Victoria's first official settlement in 1803. Lack of water initially forced its abandonment, though the area has been a popular seaside holiday destination since the 1870s. The township is close to historic Point Nepean and to major surf and bayside beaches. **Of interest**: Collins Settlement Historic Site on Sullivan Bay, marking the State's first settlement, includes early settlers' graves. Several self-guide walks around the township, passing jetties, boat sheds and sandstone cliffs; contact Tourist information for brochures. Sorrento Hotel, Hotham Rd; Continental Hotel, Ocean Beach Rd; and Koonya Hotel, The Esplanade; all fine examples of early Victorian architecture. Nepean Historical Society Museum and Heritage Gallery, Melbourne Rd, houses collection of artifacts and memorabilia in the

National Trust-classified Mechanics Institute (1877). Adjacent is Watt's Cottage (1869), constructed of wattle and daub, and the Pioneer Memorial Garden. Peninsula Galleries, 138 Ocean Beach Rd, features paintings, silks and furniture. A vehicular and passenger ferry operates between Sorrento and resort town of Queenscliff across the bay; ferries depart adjacent to Sorrento pier and return daily. Craft market, last Sat. each month at Sorrento Primary school, cnr Kerferd and Coppin rds. Mar.: Street Festival. **In the area:** Cruises to Pope's Eye Nature Reserve, only fabricated structure in the world where gannets nest; dolphin and seal cruises available; contact Tourist information for details. Portsea, 4 km NW, opulent holiday township with safe swimming on its bayside beach and good jetty-fishing. Portsea Swim Classic held here in Jan. Mornington Peninsula

National Park, including Sorrento, Rye and Portsea back beaches, features wild coastline and excellent surfing; London Bridge, at Portsea back beach, a unique rock formation; Point Nepean; Fort Nepean, the fort's guns fired the first allied shots in both world wars (access to the point and the fort by daily transportation service departing Portsea, except on Bike and Hike Day, 4th weekend of each month, when the 10-km return trip is made on foot or by bicycle); former Quarantine Station (1859) on Point Nepean, built following deaths from smallpox on a vessel anchored in nearby Weroona Bay (tour includes quarantine and army health services museums each Sun. and public holidays). McCrae Homestead (1844), 18 km E, drop-slab constructed National Trust property (open daily 12 noon –4.30 p.m.); nearby, McCrae Gallery, 38 Burrell St, McCrae, for local pottery

and folk art. At the bayside resort town of Rosebud, 16 km E: Gordon Studio Glassblowers, 1591 Nepean Hwy; summer fishing launches which depart from Rosebud pier; safe family beaches. Cruises depart from Rye pier, just south of Rosebud, to seal colonies in Port Phillip. **Tourist information:** Peninsula Tourism, Point Nepean Rd, Dromana; (03) 5987 3078; freecall, 1800 804009. **Accommodation:** 3 hotels, 3 motels, 2 B&B, 1 cara./camp. park. **See also:** The Mornington Peninsula; Wine Regions.

Stawell
Pop. 6339

MAP REF. 222 C5, 231 J12

North-east of Halls Gap and 123 km NW of Ballarat on the Western Hwy, Stawell is well sited for tours to the northern Grampians. It is the home of the Stawell Easter Gift, Australia's most famous

The Grampians

The massive sandstone ranges of the Grampians in western Victoria provide some of the State's most spectacular scenery. Rising in peaks to heights of over 1000 metres, they form the western extremity of the Great Dividing Range. The explorer Major Mitchell climbed and named the highest peak Mt William in July 1836 and gave the name 'The Grampians' to the ranges because they reminded him of the Grampians in his native Scotland.

On 1 July 1984, these rugged mountain ranges became a national park. The park offers good scenery, wildlife and tourist facilities. It is a superb area for scenic drives on good roads; bushwalking and rock climbing are also popular. The western and northern Grampians have Aboriginal rock-art sites. Lake Bellfield provides for sailing and rowing, and there is trout fishing in the lake and in Fyans Creek.

There is plenty of wildlife to be seen: koalas and kangaroos are numerous, and echidnas, possums and platypuses can be found, while more than 100 bird species have been identified.

Apart from their scenic grandeur, the Grampians are best known for the beauty and variety of their wildflowers. There are more than 1000 species of ferns and flowering plants native to the region and they are at their most colourful from August to November. The Halls Gap Wildflower Exhibition is held annually in September.

The Grampians, rugged sandstone ranges in western Victoria

Halls Gap, which takes its name from a pioneer pastoralist who settled in the eastern Grampians in the early 1840s, is the focal point of the area and offers a wide variety of accommodation.

For further information, contact the Stawell and Grampians Tourism Information Centre, 54 Western Hwy, West Stawell; (03) 5358 2314; freecall, 1800 246880, or the Halls Gap Tourist Information Centre, Grampians Rd, Halls Gap; (03) 5356 4247, or the Grampians National Park Visitors Centre, Grampians Rd, Halls Gap; (03) 5356 4381. **See also:** Grampians National Park entry in National Parks; and text entry for Halls Gap in A–Z listing. **Map references:** 228 A7, 234 H1, 236 H12.

VICTORIA

professional foot race. **Of interest:** Follow the Arrows, a self-guide city tour (maps available at Tourist information). Stawell Gift Hall of Fame Museum, in Athletic Club, Central Park, cnr Seaby and Napier sts. Big Hill, local landmark and goldmining site; at summit, Pioneers Lookout indicates positions of famous mines. Old cyanide vats, Leviathans Rd, last used in 1935 to extract gold from tailings. Casper's World in Miniature Tourist Park, London Rd, has scale working models of famous world features such as Eiffel Tower, dioramas and commentaries. In Main St: Fraser Park, has various items of mining equipment on display; Doll and Toy Museum, private collection (open Wed.–Sun. p.m.). Pleasant Creek Court House Museum, Western Hwy. Market, Sloane St, 1st Sun. each month. Easter: Easter Gift (professional foot race); Grampians Highland and National Dancing Club Championships. **In the area:** Joyflights and balloon flights. Bunjil's Shelter, 11 km S off Pomonal Rd, Aboriginal rock paintings in ochre. The Sisters Rocks, 3 km SE, huge granite tors beside Western Hwy. Wineries at Great Western, Ararat and Halls Gap. At Great Western, picturesque wine village, 14 km SE: The Diggings pottery; Country Textures Craft. Goldmining at Stawell Gold Mine, 2.5 km E; viewing areas off Reefs Rd. Overdale Station, Landsborough Rd, 10 km E, offers guided tours during school holidays. National Trust property, Tottington Woolshed, rare example of 19th-century woolshed, 55 km NE on road to St Arnaud. Deep Lead Flora and Fauna Reserve, 6 km W, off Western Hwy. Excellent lakes for all water sports: Lake Fyans, 17 km SW; Lake Wartook, in Grampians National Park, 60 km W; Lake Lonsdale, 12 km NW. **Tourist information:** 54 Western Hwy; (03) 5358 2314; freecall, 1800 246880. **Accommodation:** 1 hotel, 8 motels, 3 B&B, 2 cara./camp. parks. **See also:** The Grampians; The Golden Age; Wine Regions.

Swan Hill
Pop. 9357

MAP REF. 126 H1, 239 N11

In 1836 when the explorer Thomas Mitchell camped on the banks of the Murray, he named the spot Swan Hill because the black swans had kept him awake all night. The township became a busy 19th-century river port and today it is a pleasant city and major holiday centre on the Murray Valley Hwy, 350 km NW of Melbourne. The climate is mild and sunny, and the river offers good fishing, boating and water sports. **Of interest:** Australia's first heritage museum, the Pioneer Settlement, at end of Gray St on Little Murray River, features local Aboriginal culture and life in the last century, staff in period costume, old-fashioned transport and Sound and Light tour (bookings essential); riverboats: PS *Pyap* (daily Murray cruises). Regional Gallery of Contemporary Art, opposite Pioneer Settlement. Burke and Wills Fig Tree, Curlewis St, considered largest in Australia, commemorates explorers' visit. Market, Curlewis St, 3rd Sun. each month. Mar.: Red Gum Festival. July: Italian Festa. **In the area:** Lakeside Nursery and Gardens, 10 km NW, with over 300 roses on view. Buller's winery at Beverford, 11 km NW. Historic Tyntynder Homestead (c. 1846), National Trust-classified, 20 km NW on Murray Valley Hwy. Farmers market at Nyah, 23 km NW on hwy, 2nd Sat. each month. Pheasant farm and aviaries at Nowie North, 20 km NW. At Tooleybuc, 46 km NW (in NSW): village atmosphere in this tranquil riverside town; fishing, picnicking and riverside walks; River Retreat craft shop, Lea St. Piambie State Forest, 70 km N. Murray Downs Homestead, 2 km NE over bridge into NSW on Moulamein Rd, historic sheep, cattle and irrigation property, also animal park and children's playground; daily river cruises from Murray Downs River Cruises wharf on MV *Kookaburra*. At Lake Boga, 15 km SE: Imperial Egg Gallery, collection of egg artwork; lake nearby ideal for water sports. Best's St Andrew's Vineyard near Lake Boga. Amboc Mohair Farm, Mystic Park, 29 km SE. **Tourist information:** 306 Campbell St; (03) 5032 3033; freecall, 1800 625373. **Accommodation:** 2 hotels, 16 motels, 4 B&B, 6 cara./camp. parks. **See also:** The Mighty Murray; Wine Regions.

Tallangatta
Pop. 1021

MAP REF. 241 Q5, 242 D2

When the old town of Tallangatta was submerged in 1956 for the construction of the Hume Weir, many of its buildings were moved to a location above the shoreline. Today, situated 42 km SE from Wodonga on the Murray Valley Hwy, the town has the benefit of this large lake and boasts an attractive inland beach. It is the easternmost main Murray River town and is directly north of the beautiful alpine region of Victoria. **Of interest:** The Hub, Towong St, for art and craft; The Hub also houses Lord's hut, the only remaining slab hut in the district. Self-guide walks and drives; leaflets from Tourist information. Apr.: Dairy Festival. Oct.: Arts Festival. **In the area:** Laurel Hill Trout Farm at Eskdale, 33 km S; buy or catch-your-own (picnic/barbecue facilities). Scenic drives include: to Cravensville; from Mitta Mitta along Omeo Hwy; to Tawonga. At Mitta Mitta, 60 km S, remnants of large open-cut gold mine; Baratralia Emu Farm. Australian Alps Walking Track passes over Mt Wills, 48 km S of Mitta Mitta. Lake Dartmouth, 58 km SE, for good trout fishing and boating. Traron Alpacas, 15 km E, at Bullioh, has alpacas and other animals, yarns and garments for sale, and Paulownia trees (Chinese trees grown for shade or fodder). Gold panning tours to Granya, 28 km NE; contact Tourist information. **Tourist information:** The Hub, 35–37 Towong St; (02) 6071 2611. **Accommodation:** 2 hotels, 1 motel, 1 cara./camp. park.

Terang
Pop. 1937

MAP REF. 223 A6, 235 K8

Terang, located on the Princes Hwy in a predominantly dairy-farming area, is a well-laid-out town with grand avenues of deciduous trees, recognised by the National Trust. The town is well-known for its horseracing facilities and events. **Of interest:** Early 20th-century commercial architecture. In High St: Gothic-style sandstone Presbyterian church; cottage crafts shop in old court house. Historical museum, Princes Hwy, features replica of early dairy. Self-guide historic town walk, leaflet available at Tourist information. Walking track (4.8 km) beside lake beds and National Trust-classified trees (entrance behind Civic Centre, High St). Jan.: New Year's Day Family Picnic (at Racing Club); Australian Stockhorse Weekend. **In the area:** Intricately constructed dry stone walls, built 1860s, are a common sight in district. Noorat, 6 km N, birthplace of Alan Marshall, author of *I Can Jump Puddles*; Alan Marshall Walking Track, a gentle climb to summit of extinct volcano with excellent views of crater, surrounding district and across to Grampians. Glenormiston Agricultural College, 4 km further N, tastefully developed around an historic mansion. Model

Airworld Aviation Museum near Wangaratta

Barn Australia, 5 km E, good collection of model cars. Ralph Illidge Wildlife Sanctuary, 17 km S. **Tourist information:** Clarke Saddlery, 105 High St; (03) 5592 1164. **Accommodation:** 4 hotels, 2 motels, 1 B&B, 1 cara./camp. park.

Torquay   Pop. 4887

MAP REF. 218 F11, 225 E10, 235 Q9

The popularity of this resort, 22 km S of Geelong, is well-known. Close to the town are the excellent surfing beaches, Bells and Jan Juc, which attract surfers from all over the world. The Torquay Surf Lifesaving Club is the largest in the State. Torquay also marks the eastern end of the Great Ocean Rd, a spectacular drive south-west to Anglesea and beyond. **Of interest:** In Geelong Rd: Mary Elliott Pottery; The Gallery. Surfworld Plaza, cnr Geelong and Beach rds; surfing products and national surfing museum. Craft Cottage, Anderson St. Barbara Peake's Studio, Sarabande Cr. Large sundial, Fishermans Beach foreshore. Torqair Vintage Aeroplane Flights, Blackgate Rd, offers joyflights. Easter: Bells Beach Surfing Classic. **In the area:** Bicycle track along Surfcoast Hwy, Grovedale to Anglesea; various walks and scenic drives; contact Tourist information. Experimental wind-power generator at Breamlea, 10 km NE. Rebenberg Winery (open weekends) and Downunda Weaving Studio at Mt Duneed, 11 km N. Horserides at Sea Mist, 22 km NW on Wensleydale Station Rd, Moriac. Museum of early Australian

horse-drawn carriages near Bellbrae, 6 km W. At Bellbrae: Pottery Studios, Moores Rd; Atelier Design Centre, Bones Rd; in Portreath Rd Fast 'n' Fun, radio-controlled models; Spring Creek Trail Rides. **Tourist information:** Surfworld Museum, cnr Geelong and Beach rds; (03) 5261 4606. **Accommodation:** 3 motels, 4 cara./ camp. parks. **See also:** The Great Ocean Road.

Traralgon   Pop. 19 699

MAP REF. 233 K7

Situated on the Princes Hwy, 164 km SE of Melbourne, Traralgon is one of the La Trobe Valley's main cities, the others being Moe and Morwell. **Of interest:** Walking tours, heritage drive; contact Tourist information. Old post office and court house, cnr Franklin and Kay sts. On Princes Hwy: Band rotunda and miniature railway at Victory Park. Gippsland Shop, exhibition and sales of local crafts. Feb.–Mar.: Music in the Park. **In the area:** Loy Yang power station, 5 km S (tours available Sun. p.m., bookings essential). PowerWorks, dynamic displays on electrical industry, off Princes Hwy near Morwell. Giant mountain ash trees and ferns, walks and scenic drives at Tarra-Bulga National Park, about 40 km S. Tarra-Bulga Visitor Centre at Balook, Grand Ridge Rd, has interpretive displays. **Tourist information:** Shop 1, Southside Central, Princes Hwy; (03) 5174 3199. **Accommodation:** 9 motels, 5 cara./ camp. parks.

Walhalla   Pop. 17

MAP REF. 233 K5

The tiny goldmining town of Walhalla is tucked away in dense mountain country in Gippsland. The drive, 46 km N from Moe, passes through some spectacular scenery. Walhalla is set in a narrow, steep valley, with sides so sheer that its cemetery has graves that have been dug lengthways into the hillside. It is the only Victorian town not connected to electricity; generators must be used. **Of interest:** Historic buildings and relics of gold-boom days. Excellent local walks. Long Tunnel Extended Goldmine, one of the most successful in the State (guided tours, check times). Rotunda (1896). Spett's Cottage (1871), furnished in the period. Old Fire Station (1901), hand-operated fire engine and fire memorabilia. Post office (1886). Old bakery (1865), oldest surviving building in town, near rebuilt hotel. Museum, gold-era memorabilia. Windsor House (1890). Cricket ground, perched on top of 200-m hill. Walhalla Goldfield Railway, runs Sat., Sun. and public holidays. Gold panning in Stringers Creek which runs through town, contact Tourist information for tuition. **In the area:** Deloraine Gardens, terraced gardens just north of town. Australian Alps Walking Track (655 km) commences at Walhalla. Cross-country skiing and walking in Baw Baw National Park, which edges western side of town. Rawson, 8 km SW, built for construction of nearby Thomson Dam. At Erica, 12 km SW: timber industry display at Erica Hotel; Elderberry Cottage, gardens and nursery; Erica Craftworks features resident wood turner; Mountain Saddle Safaris; King of the Mountain Woodchop, held each Mar. Thomson River, 4 km S for excellent fishing, canoeing and white-water rafting. Moondarra State Park, 30 km S. Traralgon, major city in the La Trobe Valley, 35 km S. Scenic road between Walhalla and Jamieson (140 km N); check weather conditions. **Tourist information:** Museum and General Store, Main St; (03) 5165 6250. **Accommodation:** 2 B&B. **See also:** Gippsland Lakes.

Wangaratta   Pop. 15 984

MAP REF. 241 M6

The Ovens Hwy to Bright and the Victorian Alps, through the Ovens Valley, branches off the Hume Fwy just near

VICTORIA

The Mighty Murray

P S *Cumberoona* cruises the river near Albury

As a present-day explorer, a trip following the course of the Murray River is an opportunity to discover a rich cross-section of Australian country and its history, as well as the infinite variety of natural beauty and wildlife the river itself supports.

The source

The Murray has its source on the slopes of Mount Pilot, high in the Alps. Here it is just a gurgling mountain stream, rushing through some breathtaking mountain scenery. This is the area of the Snowy Mountains Hydro-Electric Scheme and the great Australian snowfields.

The upper Murray

The upper reaches of the river flows through the scenic area around Jingellic and Walwa, and on to the beautiful Lake Hume near **Albury** and **Wodonga** before continuing past **Corowa**, the birthplace of Federation, and into Lake Mulwala.

Lakes, beaches and red gums

As it flows from the aquatic playgrounds of Lakes Hume and Mulwala, the Murray becomes a wide and splendid river. Lined with magnificent red gums in the region around **Cobram**, the riverbanks are transformed into wide sandy beaches. This is ideal holiday country with pleasant resort towns: **Yarrawonga**, Mulwala, **Barooga** and **Tocumwal.**

Wine country

Victoria's main winegrowing area is centred around **Rutherglen** and extends to the wineries of Cobram and the Ovens and Goulburn valleys. The wineries welcome visitors and many offer conducted tours.

The heyday of the riverboats

Famous river towns like **Echuca, Swan Hill** and **Wentworth** have carefully preserved much of the history of the colourful riverboat era. The Port of Echuca, the Swan Hill Pioneer Settlement and the historic Murray Downs Homestead are a must if you are in the area. Children especially will delight in the 'living museum' aspect of these river towns, with their original buildings, paddlesteamers and old wharves faithfully restored.

Wildlife

The Murray's abundant bird and animal life is protected by national parks and in a number of sanctuaries and reserves stretching from the banks of the river. Spoonbills, herons, eagles, harriers and kites abound. The **Hattah-Kulkyne** and Murray-Kulkyne national parks include a section of the river frontage and the Hattah Lakes system. More than 220 species of birds have been recorded here and red kangaroos can be regularly seen; a rare experience in Victoria. The other major park near the river, **Murray-Sunset National Park,** includes a section of the riverine plains of the Murray and supports a varied array of native fauna including the mallee fowl. Near Picnic Point in the Moira State Forest, near Mathoura, waterbirds and wildlife abound and can be seen from the observatory in this beautiful red gum forest. At **Kerang**, which lies at the beginning of a chain of lakes and marshes, you can see huge breeding grounds for the splendid ibis. **Kyabram** has a famous community-owned fauna and waterfowl park which is open daily, and almost all of Gunbower Island is a protected sanctuary for wildlife.

Sunraysia

The beautiful climate of **Mildura** supports flourishing citrus and winegrowing industries as well as attracting countless holidaymakers to the Sunraysia area. Upstream is Red Cliffs, a town founded after World War I by returned soldiers, who turned it into a model irrigation town, and the surrounding areas into prosperous winelands. At the junction of the Murray and the Darling lies **Wentworth,** one of the oldest of the river towns, with an historic gaol and the beautifully preserved paddlesteamer *Ruby*. From Wentworth, holidaymakers can cruise along the Darling River in MV *Loyalty*.

Riverland

The Murray crosses into South Australia and at **Renmark** begins its splendid flow down to its mouth at Lake Alexandrina. The banks are lined with such historic river towns as **Renmark, Morgan** and **Murray Bridge. Goolwa** at its mouth has a strong tradition of shipbuilding, originating from the busy riverboat days. Renmark, like Mildura, is famous for its year-round sunshine. This South Australian stretch of the Murray offers splendid river scenery and birdlife, excellent fishing and water sports, and the chance to enjoy the many wineries in the area.

Further information is available from the tourist information centres in the various towns along the river, including Swan Hill, (03) 5032 3033; Mildura, (03) 5021 4424; Cobram, (03) 5872 2132; Echuca, (03) 5480 7555; or Yarrawonga, (03) 5744 1989. **See also:** National Parks and individual text entries in A–Z listing for those parks and towns indicated by bold type.

Flagstaff Hill Maritime Museum, Warrnambool

Wangaratta, north-east of Melbourne. The surrounding fertile area produces wool, wheat, tobacco, kiwifruit, walnuts, chestnuts, hops and table-wine grapes. **Of interest:** In cemetery, Tone Rd, grave of Daniel 'Mad Dog' Morgan, the bushranger; his headless body was buried here, the head having been sent to Melbourne for examination. Kooringa Native Plants, Warby Range Rd. At Tourist information centre, cnr Tone Rd and Handley St: Mrs Stell's House in Miniature; history of Kelly Gang. Paddys market each Sun. a.m. at Co-Store car park. Oct.: Agricultural Show. Nov.: Festival of Jazz and Blues. **In the area:** Airworld Aviation Museum, 7 km s, has world's largest collection of flying antique civil aircraft. Road 27 km s to Moyhu leads to beautiful King Valley and Paradise Falls. Network of minor roads allows exploration of unspoiled area and tiny townships of Whitfield (54 km s), Cheshunt and Carboor. King Valley scenic drive runs beside King River to Whitfield and Powers Lookout (74 km s). Newton's Prickle Berry Farm at Whitfield. Many vineyards around towns of Glenrowan (sw), Milawa (se) and Rutherglen (ne). Glenrowan, 16 km

sw, famed for its Ned Kelly history. At Warby Range State Park, 12 km w: good vantage points, picnic spots and variety of bird and plant life. Interesting old gold township Eldorado, 20 km ne, has largest gold dredge in the southern hemisphere, built in 1936; historical museum; general store; potteries. Nearby, Reids Creek, popular with anglers, gem-fossickers and gold-panners. Wombi Toys, Whorouly, 25 km se. **Tourist information:** cnr Tone Rd and Handley St; (03) 5721 5711. **Accommodation:** 2 hotels, 1 hotel/motel, 13 motels, 3 B&B, 3 cara./camp. parks. **See also:** Wine Regions.

Warburton   Pop. 2504

MAP REF. 219 O6, 222 H9, 232 G3
Warburton was established with the gold finds of the 1880s; however, by the turn of the century it had found its niche as a popular tourist town with fine guest houses. It is surrounded by the foothills of the Great Dividing Range and is only a 90-minute drive from Melbourne. **Of interest:** Several art and craft, and old wares shops. July: Winterfest (wood festival). **In the area:** Bushwalking, riding

and birdwatching. Tommy Finn's Trout Farm, 2 km w. Yarra Junction Historical Museum, 10 km w. Cherry Festival in Nov. at Wandin, 27 km w. Mt Donna Buang, 7 km nw, popular day-trip destination from Melbourne, often snow-covered in winter. The Acheron Way begins 2 km e of Warburton, giving access to views of Mt Donna Buang, Mt Victoria and Ben Cairn, on the scenic 37-km drive north to St Fillans. Upper Yarra Dam, 23 km ne. South of town along Warburton Hwy, an attractive area of vineyards: Yarra Burn, Lillydale and Oak Ridge Estate. Walk from Powelltown, 27 km se, to East Warburton (leaflet from Tourist information); this is one branch of the Centenary Trail (the other branch leads from Warburton to Baw Baw National Park). Between Powelltown and Noojee, rainforest gully walk to Ada Tree, a giant mountain ash. Upper Yarra Draught Horse Festival in Jan. at Hoddles Creek, 15 km sw. Yellingbo State Fauna Reserve, 25 km sw. **Tourist information:** Yarra Valley-Healesville Visitor Information Centre, 127 Maroondah Hwy, Healesville; (03) 5962 2600. **Accommodation:** 1 hotel, 2 motels, 1 cara./camp. park.

Warracknabeal   Pop. 2687

MAP REF. 236 H6
Situated at the intersection of the Borung and Henty hwys, 350 km nw of Melbourne, Warracknabeal is in the centre of a rich grain-growing area. The Aboriginal name means 'the place of the big red gums shading the watercourse'. **Of interest:** Historical Centre, 81 Scott St, includes pharmaceutical collection, a wide variety of clocks and antique child's nursery (open p.m.). Black Arrow Tour of historic buildings (self-guide drive or walk) and other walks including the Yarriambiack Creek Walk; leaflets available from Tourist information. National Trust-classified buildings: in Scott St, post office (1907); Warracknabeal Hotel (1872), with its beautiful iron lacework; original log lockup (1872), Devereaux St, built when town acquired its first permanent policeman. Lions Park, on Yarriambiack Creek, has picnic spots, and flora and fauna park. Easter: Vintage Machinery and Vehicle Rally. **In the area:** North Western Agricultural Machinery Museum, 3 km s on Henty Hwy, displays of farm machinery from last 100 yrs. Angip Lane Antiques, in old church, 18 km nw on road to

VICTORIA

Jeparit. Green Gables Game, 16 km SW on Borung Hwy, a guinea fowl, pheasant and partridge farm. **Tourist information:** 119 Scott St; (03) 5398 1632. **Accommodation:** 4 hotels, 3 motels, 1 B&B, 1 cara./camp. park.

Warragul   Pop. 8910

MAP REF. 219 P10, 232 H6

Most of Melbourne's milk comes from this prosperous dairy-farming area 103 km SE of Melbourne. It is also an important commercial centre. **Of interest:** West Gippsland Arts Centre, Civic Place. Lillico Garden Railway, Copelands Rd. Mar.: Gippsland Field Days. **In the area:** Wild Dog Winery, 5 km S on Warragul–Korumburra Rd (open daily by appt). At Drouin West, 9 km W; Oakbank Angoras and Alpacas; Fruit and Berry Farm. Victoria's Farm Shed, off Princes Fwy at Tynong (32 km W), has farm animal and agricultural displays, including shearing, sheep-dog workouts and milking. Further 3 km W, Gumbaya Park, a family fun park. Wildflower sanctuary at Labertouche, 16 km NW. At Neerim South, 17 km N: Tarago River Cheese Company; picnic/barbecue facilities at nearby Tarago Reservoir. Further 7 km N, at Nayook: Fruit and Berry Farm; Country Farm Perennials Nursery and Gardens. At Noojee, 10 km NE of Nayook Alpine Trout Farm; trestle bridge. Scenic drives through mountain country near Neerim South, 19 km N. Gourmet Deli Trail, brochure available, guides visitors on a food trip around this scenic region via various farms, cheese producers, wineries, nurseries, restaurants and food outlets. Darnum Musical Village, 8 km E. Township of Yarragon, 13 km SE, has good shopping for antiques, crafts, gourmet food and boutique wines; Dairy Fest held in Nov. Trafalgar Lookout, Narracan Falls and Henderson's Gully near Trafalgar, 21 km SE. At Thorpdale (known for its potatoes), 33 km SE: potato bread from bakery; Potato Festival in Mar. Grand Ridge Rd, spectacular 140-km drive starting at Mirboo North (50 km SE) and traversing top of Strzelecki Ranges. At Childers, 31 km SE: Sunny Creek Fruit and Berry Farm Windrush Cottage. Mt Worth State Park, 19 km SE. Nature reserves and picnic spots: Glen Cromie (Drouin West), Glen Nayook (south of Nayook) and Toorongo Falls (just north of Noojee). **Tourist information:** Shop 1,

Southside Central, Princes Hwy, Traralgon; (03) 5174 3199. **Accommodation:** 3 motels, 1 B&B, 1 cara./camp. park.

Warrnambool   Pop. 25 500

MAP REF. 234 I9

A beautiful seaside city, Warrnambool is located 263 km SW of Melbourne on Lady Bay, where the Princes Hwy meets the Great Ocean Rd. First-class sporting, cultural and entertainment facilities and beautifully developed and maintained parks and gardens have resulted in Warrnambool being awarded Victoria's Premier Town title a record 3 times. **Of interest:** Flagstaff Hill Maritime Museum, Merri St, a reconstructed 19th-century Maritime Village with Entrance Gallery Orientation Centre introducing visitors to Maritime Village experience, featuring Flagstaff Hill tapestry, with themes of Aboriginal history, sealing, whaling, exploration, immigration and settlement. Over 100 ships were wrecked on the coast near Warrnambool; famous earthenware Loch Ard Peacock, recovered from *Loch Ard* wreck in 1878, is on permanent display at Flagstaff Hill Maritime Museum. Annual visit of rare southern right whales, usually May–Oct. (viewing platform east of town at Logans Beach). The Kid's Country Treasure Map (available at Tourist information) provides informative way for the whole family to enjoy Warrnambool. In Timor St: Performing Arts Centre; Art Gallery. In Gilles St: Customs House Gallery; History House, with local memorabilia (open by appt). Botanic Gardens (designed by Guilfoyle in 1879), Botanic Rd. Fletcher Jones Gardens, Raglan Pde. Lake Pertobe Adventure Playground, Pertobe Rd. Portugese Padrao, Cannon Hill, monument to Portugese explorers. The Potter's Wheel, Liebig St. Thunder Point Reserve, end Macdonald St. Middle Island, off Pickering Point, colony of little (fairy) penguins. Wollaston Bridge (over 100 years old) unusual design, on northern outskirts of town. Heritage trail walk and arrow tour of city start at Tourist information centre (self-guide leaflets available from Tourist information). Feb.: Wunta Fiesta. May: Racing Carnival. Oct.: Melbourne– Warrnambool Cycling Classic. **In the area:** Tower Hill State Game Reserve, 14 km W, features one of Victoria's largest and most recently active volcanoes; nature walk starts at the Natural History Centre

within reserve. Port Campbell National Park, 54 km SE, 32-km spectacular stretch of scenic and historic coastline. Robert Ulmann Studio, 4 km E, paintings of Australian flora and fauna. Allansford Cheese World, 10 km E, for cheese tasting, sales and viewing of cheese production. Ralph Illidge Sanctuary, 32 km E, wildlife and nature walks. Historic Shipwreck Trail links sites of wrecks along the 'Shipwreck Coast' from Port Fairy (29 km W) to Moonlight Head (112 km E). Mahogany Walk from Warrnambool–Port Fairy (22 km), along beach dunes. Helicopter and joy flights along coast, contact Tourist information. In late spring, early summer at Hopkins Falls, 13 km NE, hundreds of baby eels can be seen migrating up the falls. At Koroit, 18 km NW: historic buildings, in commercial and church precincts, classified by National Trust; botanic gardens. **Tourist information:** 600 Raglan Pde; (03) 5564 7837. **Accommodation:** 10 hotels, 23 motels, 6 B&B, 8 cara./camp. parks. **See also:** The Great Ocean Road.

Wedderburn   Pop. 764

MAP REF. 237 N7

Once one of Victoria's richest goldmining towns in the 'Golden Triangle', Wedderburn is on the Calder Hwy, 73 km NW of Bendigo. Gold is still found around the town. **Of interest:** At northern edge of town: Hard Hill area, former gold diggings and Government Battery, Wilson St; Kuku-Yalanji, Wallaby Dr., an Aboriginal art and craft gallery. In High St: Museum and General Store (1910), restored building that is furnished and stocked as it was at turn of century; coach-building factory; old bakery, converted into a pottery. Sept.: Wool Expo; Historic Engine Exhibition. **In the area:** Christmas Reef Mine, 3 km E, a working tourist mine. Mount Korong, 16 km SE, for rock scrambling and bushwalking. Wychitella Forest Reserve, 16 km N, a wildlife sanctuary in mallee forest. **Tourist information:** Shire Offices, High St; (03) 5494 3200. **Accommodation:** 1 hotel, 1 motel, 2 B&B, 1 cara./camp. park.

Welshpool   Pop. 241

MAP REF. 233 K10

Welshpool is a small dairying town and nearby Port Welshpool is a deep-sea port servicing fishing and oil industries.

Barry Beach Marine Terminal, 8 km S of the South Gippsland Hwy, services the offshore oil rigs in Bass Strait. **In the area:** Excellent fishing and boating. At Port Welshpool, Maritime Museum. Agnes Falls, 19 km NW, highest falls in State. Scenic drive west with panoramic views from Mt Fatigue, off South Gippsland Hwy. Near Toora, 11 km W, Franklin River Reserve has nature walk. **Tourist information:** cnr South Gippsland Hwy and Silkstone Rd, Korumburra; (03) 5655 2233. **Accommodation:** 1 motel, 1 B&B, 2 cara./camp. parks.

Winchelsea   Pop. 969

MAP REF. 218 D10, 225 A8, 235 P8

This town is on the Barwon River, 37 km W of Geelong. It originated as a watering-place and shelter for travellers on the road to Colac from Geelong. **Of interest:** On Princes Hwy: Barwon

Bridge, with its graceful stone arches, opened 1867 to handle increasing westward traffic; Alexandra's Antiques and Art Gallery; Barwon Hotel (1842), housing museum of Australiana; old Shire Hall, restored turn of the century bluestone building. **In the area:** National Trust property, Barwon Park Homestead, 3 km N on Inverleigh Rd (open Sun. and Wed.). Country Dahlias, gardens open Feb.–Apr.; 5 km S on Mathieson Rd. Killarney Park Lavender Farm, 6 km S (open Sept.–May). **Tourist information:** Newsagency, Willis St; (03) 5267 2026. **Accommodation:** 1 hotel, 1 motel, 1 cara./camp. park.

Wodonga   Pop. 39 975

MAP REF. 127 Q13, 241 P4, 242 B2

Wodonga is the Victorian city – Albury, the NSW city – in a twin-city complex astride the Murray in north-east Victoria. Albury-Wodonga, with the

attractions of the Murray and nearby Lake Hume, makes a good base for a holiday. **Of interest:** On Lincoln Causeway: Gateway complex includes working craft shops, tourist information and restaurant; Harveys Fish Farm, view or catch Australian native fish. Sumsion Gardens, Church St, a beautiful lakeside park. In Melrose Dr., largest outdoor tennis centre in Australia. Day tours around Wodonga, contact Tourist information for brochures. Border Country Fair, 2nd Sun. each month. Feb.: Sports Festival. Apr.: Wodonga Show. Aug.: Wine and Food Festival. Nov.: World Cup Show Jumping. **In the area:** Military Museum, 4 km SE, at Bandiana. Hume Weir, 15 km E; Hume Weir Trout Farm. Mt Granya State Park, 56 km E, offers spectacular views of alps. Nearby touring areas include: Upper Murray, mountain valleys of north-east Victoria; Murray Valley; Riverina district. Short drive 36 km S leads to

The Great Southern Touring Route

The Great Southern Touring Route takes in the highlights of south-western Victoria including three major regional cities – Geelong, Ballarat and Warrnambool – as well as some of the nation's finest natural and constructed attractions.

The route takes you through **Geelong** – take the time to visit the National Wool Museum there and learn about Australia's wool industry using interactive displays – to **Torquay** where you can visit the famous surfing museum, Surfworld and nearby Bells Beach, venue for the international Surfing Classic held at Easter. From Torquay, you travel along the Great Ocean Road, one of the world's most spectacular coastal drives, and through the beautiful Otway Ranges with its tree ferns and sparkling waterfalls. Visit Flagstaff Hill at **Warrnambool**; here centuries of colourful maritime history is faithfully recorded.

Heading north the landscape changes dramatically as you approach the Grampians, a famous wilderness retreat renowned for its spring wildflowers and the Brambuk Living Cultural Centre at Halls Gap, which provides an insight into the ancient culture of the local Aboriginal communities. South-east lies **Ballarat**, a grand Victorian city built on gold discoveries in the 1850s,

The beautiful Otway Ranges with its treeferns and sparkling waterfalls

and nearby is Sovereign Hill where goldfields' history comes to life.

For further information, contact the tourist information centres at Ballarat, cnr Sturt and Albert sts, (03) 5332 2694; at Geelong, 29–32 Moorabool St, (03) 5222 2900; at Warrnambool,

600 Raglan Pde, (03) 5564 7837; or the Grampians Tourist Information Centre, 54 Western Hwy, West Stawell, (03) 5358 2314; freecall, 1800 246880. **See also:** The Great Ocean Road; The Grampians; The Grampians National Park entry in National Parks; and individual text entries in A–Z listing for those towns indicated by bold type.

VICTORIA

picturesque township of Yackandandah. Nearby towns worth visiting: Beechworth (47 km), Wangaratta (68 km), both south-west; and Rutherglen, 42 km NW. **Tourist information:** Gateway Tourist Information Centre, Lincoln Causeway; (02) 6041 3875. **Accommodation:** 4 hotels, 11 motels, 2 cara./camp. parks. **See also:** The Mighty Murray.

Wonthaggi
Pop. 5751

MAP REF. 232 G10

Once the main supplier of coal to the Victorian Railways, Wonthaggi, situated 8 km from Cape Paterson in Gippsland, is South Gippsland's largest town. It began as a tent town in 1909 when the coal mines were opened up by the State government following industrial unrest in the coalfields in NSW. The mines operated until 1968. Easter: Coal Skip Fill. **In the area:** State Coal Mine, 1.5 km S on Cape Paterson Rd, features tours of re-opened Eastern Area Mine, with experienced former coalminer as guide, and museum of mining activities. Cape Paterson, 8 km S in Bunurong Marine Park, for surfing, swimming, snorkelling and scuba diving. Scenic drives: to beaches at Inverloch, 13 km SE; to Tarwin Lower, 35 km SE. George Bass Coastal Walk from Kilcunda, 11 km NW; brochures available for this and other walks in the area at Tourist information. Market, 4th Sun. each month at Grantville, north on Bass Hwy. **Tourist information:** Watts St; (03) 5672 2484. **Accommodation:** 1 hotel, 2 motels, 1 hostel, 2 cara./camp. parks.

Woodend
Pop. 2743

MAP REF. 218 G2, 232 A1, 235 R2, 240 D12

The township of Woodend is situated on the Calder Hwy, an hour's drive north of Melbourne. It acquired its name from its position at the end of the Black Forest. During the gold rushes (1850s), travellers sought refuge from mud, bogs and bushrangers at the 'wood's end' around Five Mile Creek. Later the town developed, as shops and services were established for the passing trade. The main danger for today's travellers is 'black ice' in winter; hazard warning lights are installed on the Calder Hwy. **Of interest:** On Calder Hwy: Bluestone bridge (1862) crossing Five Mile Creek, on northern outskirts of town; St Mary's Anglican Church (1864); clock tower,

Yackandandah, an historic town classified by the National Trust

built as WWI memorial. Court house (1870), Forest St; check at Tourist information for opening times. Walks, cycling and horseriding nearby; inquire at Tourist information. Craft market, 3rd Sun. each month (Oct.–May). Dec.: Five Mile Creek Festival. **In the area:** Black gum trees (*E. aggregata*), Woodend region is only place in State where these trees are found. Hanging Rock, 8 km NE, a massive rock formation made famous by Joan Lindsay's story and subsequent film *Picnic at Hanging Rock*; picnic races held nearby in Jan. (New Year's Day) and Australia Day; vintage car rally held in Feb. Mt Macedon (1013 m), 10 km E, has WWI memorial cross at summit; area around renowned for its beautiful gardens, many open autumn and spring. Scenic drives and bushwalks in Macedon Regional Park. At Macedon, 8 km SE, Church of the Resurrection has stained-glass windows designed by Leonard French. Over 15 wineries in region (maps available at Tourist information), close to town is Hanging Rock Winery, at Newham (8 km NE); Macedon Ranges 'Budburst' wine festival held last weekend in Oct. At Gisborne, 18 km SE: Gisborne Steam Park; craft outlets. Barringo Wildlife Reserve at New Gisborne, 21 km SE. Potato-growing area and old goldmining town of Trentham, 25 km SW; nearby, Trentham Falls. Firth Park in Wombat Forest, East Trentham. Art and craft gallery at Tylden, 13 km W. At Lancefield, 28 km NE: Antique Centre; wineries in surrounding area including Mount Williams, Cope-Williams and Glen Erin Grange. At

Carlsruhe, 18 km NW: galleries, crafts and antiques. **Tourist information:** High St, beside Five Mile Creek; (03) 5427 2033. **Accommodation:** 1 hotel, 1 B&B.

Yackandandah
Pop. 601

MAP REF. 241 P5, 242 B3

Located about 27 km S of Wodonga, this exceptionally attractive town with avenues of English trees and traditional verandahed buildings, has been classified by the National Trust. Yackandandah is in the heart of the north-east goldfields (gold was discovered here in 1852), but today it is better known for its historic buildings. **Of interest:** Number of original buildings in High St: post office; several banks and general stores; Bank of Victoria (1865), now historical museum (open Sun. and school holidays). Self-guide walking tour; brochure from Tourist information. Ray Riddington's Premier Store and Gallery, High St. Art and craft from: Yackandandah Workshop, cnr Kars and Hammond sts; Wildon Thyme, High St. Numerous antique shops, including Finders Bric-a-Brac and Old Wares, Frankly Speaking (both in High St); Vintage Sounds Restorations, Wyndham St (old and antique gramophones, telephones and radios). Yackandandah Trail Rides, contact Tourist information. Yack Track Tours offer tours of Kars Reef Goldmine; 4WD tours for wine tasting, goldpanning and bushwalking; bookings essential. Market in Welsford St, 2nd Sat. each month. **In the area:** Creeks

The Regent Theatre in Commercial Road, Yarram

and old diggings in Yackandandah area still yield specimens of alluvial gold to amateur prospectors. Lavender Patch Plant Farm, 4 km W on Beechworth Rd. Picturesque Indigo Valley, 6 km NW; scenic drive leads through rolling hills along valley floor to Barnawatha. Near Barnawatha, Koendidda Historic Homestead and gardens, Pooleys Rd. At Allans Flat, 10 km NE: The Vienna Patisserie, for quality Austrian cakes (closed Tues.); Schmidt's Strawberry Winery. At Leneva, 16 km NE, Wombat Valley Tramways small-gauge railway operates at Easter or by appt for groups. At Dederang, 25 km SE, art and craft. **Tourist information:** Finders Bric-a-Brac and Old Wares, 28 High St; (02) 6027 1222. **Accommodation:** 2 hotels, 3 B&B, 1 cara./camp. park.

Yarram   Pop. 2006

MAP REF. 233 L9

This old-established South Gippsland town, 225 km by road from Melbourne, has some interesting original buildings and a pleasant golf course inhabited by relatively tame kangaroos. It is situated between the Strzelecki Ranges and Bass Strait. **Of interest:** Tarra Spinning Wheels, Alberton Rd, has spinning wheels, boat wheels, beds and general wood turning. Regent Theatre (1930), Commercial Rd; cinema operates on weekends and in school holidays. Easter: Tarra Festival. Nov.: Seabank Fishing Contest. **In the area:** Historic towns: Alberton (6 km S), early settlers' graves in cemetery; Tarraville (11 km SE), Christ Church (1856) and maritime museum in old bank building; Port Albert (14 km S), site of first European settlement in Gippsland. Ninety Mile Beach, popular with surfers and anglers, begins just north of Port Albert. Beaches patrolled in summer: Woodside Beach, 29 km E; Seaspray, 68 km NE. Fishing beaches: Manns, 16 km SE; McLoughlins, 29 km E. Native animal zoo, 19 km E at Woodside. To the north, Australian Omega Navigation Facility with 432-m-high steel tower. In the Strzelecki Ranges, 27 km NW: Tarra-Bulga National Park, hilly and densely forested with mountain ash, myrtle and sassafras, spectacular fern glades, splendid river and mountain views, the occasional koala as well as rosellas and lyrebirds, wagon rides through ranges available, contact Tourist information. In the Tarra Valley, north-west of town: Eilean Donan Gardens and Riverbank Nursery; splendid gardens; two caravan parks; horseriding nearby. At Hiawatha, 46-km circuit drive from Yarram: Minnie Ha Ha Falls on Albert River; nearby, picnic facilities; horses for hire. Won Wron Forest, 16 km N on Hyland Hwy, has wildflowers in spring. **Tourist information:** The Court House, Rodger St; (03) 5182 6553. **Accommodation:** 2 hotels, 3 motels, 2 cara./camp. parks.

Yarrawonga   Pop. 3603

MAP REF. 127 N13, 241 K3

A pleasant stretch of the Murray and the attractive Lake Mulwala have made this border town and Mulwala (in NSW) extremely popular holiday resorts. The 6000-ha lake was created in 1939 during the building of the Yarrawonga Weir, which controls the irrigation waters in the Murray Valley. **Of interest:** Around the lake and along the river: sandy beaches and still waters, ideal for water sports; abundant birdlife. The Yarrawonga and Mulwala foreshore areas: shady willows, giant water-slides, barbecues and boat ramps. At Tourist information: Old Yarra Mine Shaft houses a large collection of gems, minerals and fossils. Canning A.R.T.S. Gallery, Belmore St. Tudor House Clock Museum, Lynch St. Daily cruises on *Paradise Queen* or *Lady Murray*, depart Bank St. Canoe and boat hire, horse-riding available, contact Tourist information. Bush market, 2nd and 4th Sun. each month at railway station, Sharp St. Market at Irvine St, 3rd Sun. each month. Jan.: Sailing Regatta. Sept.: Ice Breaker Yacht Regatta. **In the area:** At Mulwala: Pioneer Museum, Melbourne St (open Wed.–Sun.); Linley Park Animal Farm and Fauna Park, Corowa Rd. Fishing in Murray River (no licence required). Fyffefield Winery, 19 km W on Murray Valley Hwy. Matata Deer Farm, Cobram, 42 km W. Historical Museum, 35 km SW at Katamatite. **Tourist information:** Irvine Pde; (03) 5744 1989. **Accommodation:** 4 hotels, 2 hotel/motels, 9 motels, 5 cara./camp. parks. **See also:** The Mighty Murray.

Yea   Pop. 995

MAP REF. 219 M1, 240 I11

This town, 58 km N of Yarra Glen, stands beside the Yea River, a tributary of the Goulburn River. Set in pastoral and dairyfarming land, it is well situated for touring around Mansfield, Eildon and the mountains, and to the gorge country between Yea and Tallarook, as well as south-east to Marysville. There are some beautiful gorges and fern gullies close to the Yea–Tallarook road. **Of interest:** In High St: Beaufort Manor (1870s); General Store (1887). Mar.: Autumn Fest. **In the area:** Many scenic drives in area, contact Tourist information. Pick-your-own fruit at Berry King Farm, Two Hills Rd, 28 km S at Glenburn. Kinglake National Park, 30 km S, for beautiful waterfalls, tall eucalypts, fern gullies and impressive views. Spectacular Wilhelmina Falls, 32 km S via Melba Hwy. In Murrindindi Reserve, 11 km SE: Murrindindi Cascades and wildlife including wombats, platypuses, lyrebirds. Flowerdale Winery, 23 km SW on Whittlesea–Yea Rd. Ibis rookery at Kerrisdale, 17 km W. Grotto, a beautiful old church, in the hills 27 km N at Caveat. Mineral springs at Dropmore, 47 km N off back road to Euroa. Several good campsites along Goulburn River. **Tourist information:** Shire Offices, The Semi-Circle; (03) 5797 2209; Legendary Country Tourism, 11 High St, Mansfield; (03) 5775 1464. **Accommodation:** 2 hotels, 2 motels, 1 cara./camp. park.

VICTORIA

Location Map

Victoria

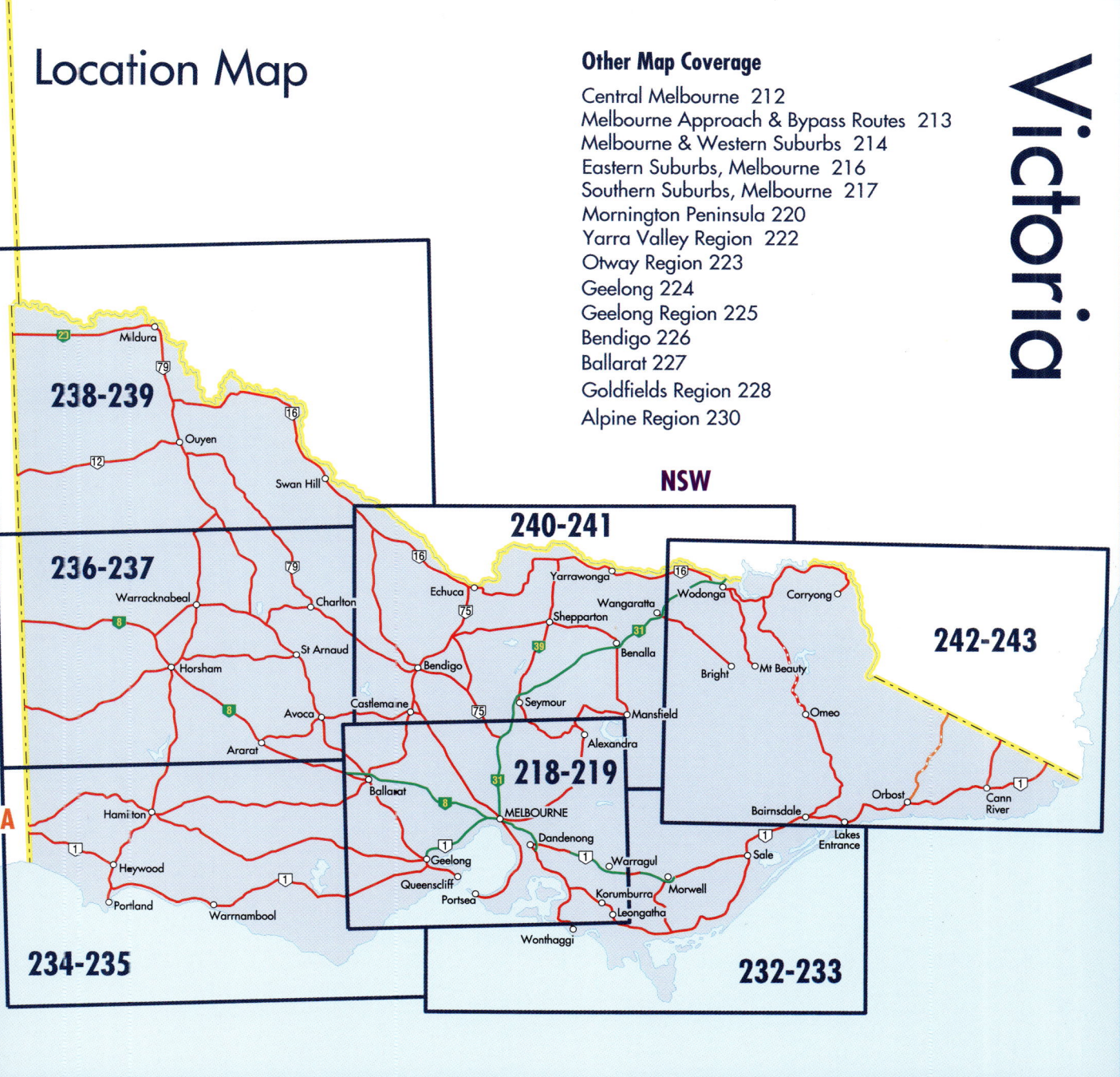

NSW

238-239 — Mildura, Ouyen, Swan Hill
236-237 — Warracknabeal, Charlton, Horsham, St Arnaud, Avoca, Ararat, Castlemaine
240-241 — Echuca, Yarrawonga, Wangaratta, Shepparton, Benalla, Bendigo, Seymour, Mansfield, Alexandra
242-243 — Wodonga, Corryong, Bright, Mt Beauty, Omeo, Orbost, Cann River, Bairnsdale, Lakes Entrance
218-219 — Ballarat, MELBOURNE, Dandenong, Geelong, Queenscliff, Portsea, Warragul, Sale
234-235 — Hamilton, Heywood, Portland, Warrnambool
232-233 — Korumburra, Leongatha, Morwell, Wonthaggi

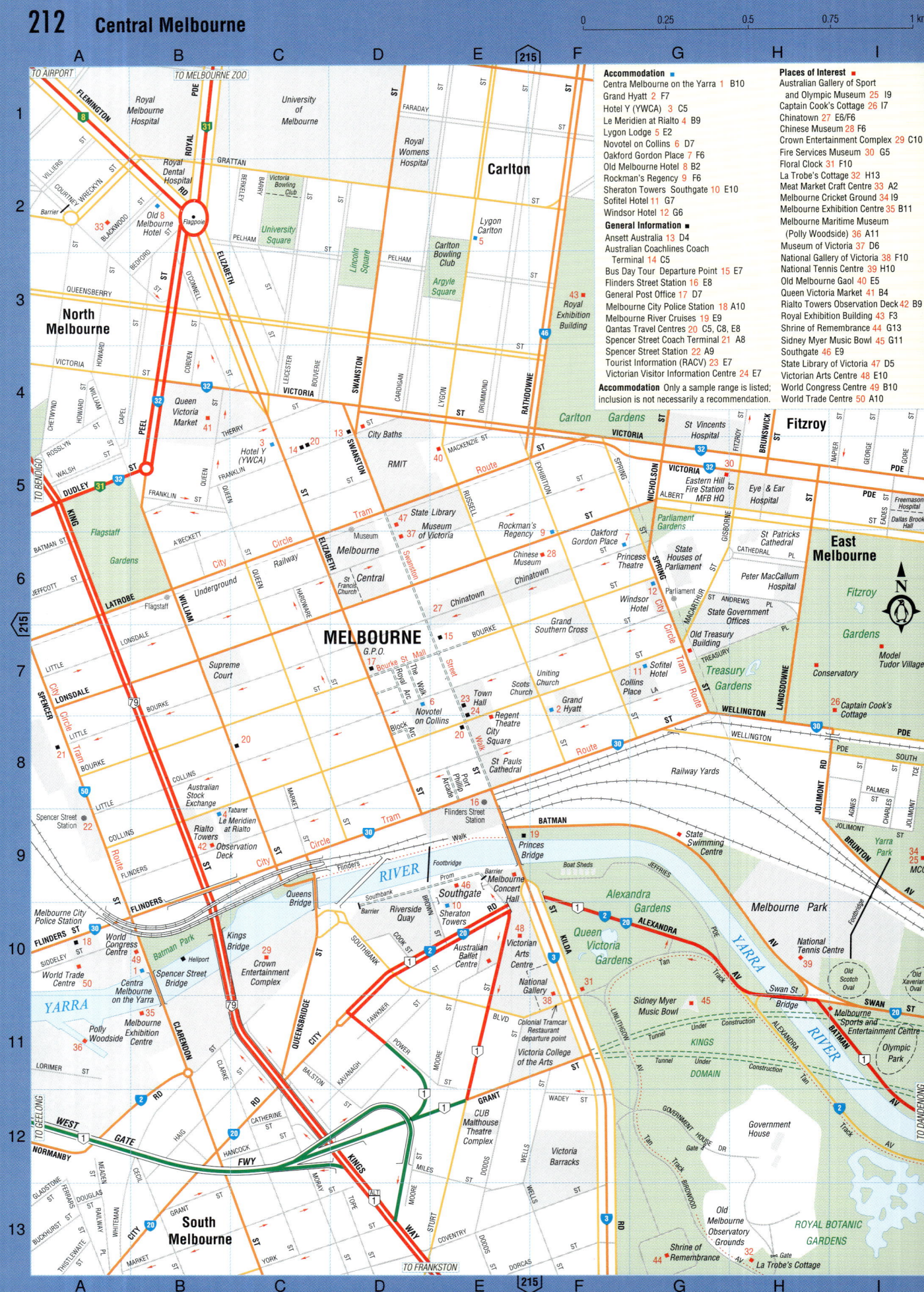

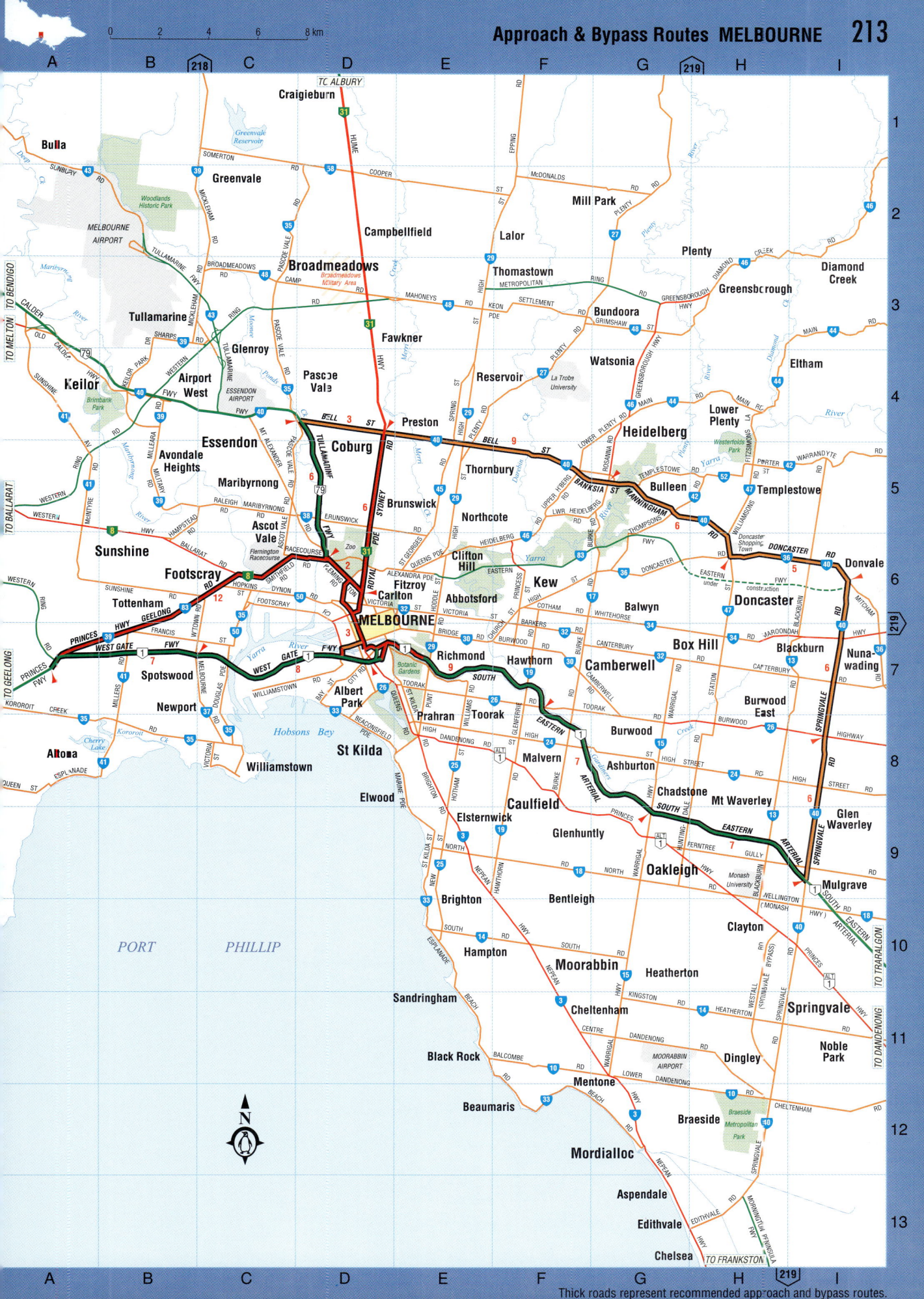

Thick roads represent recommended approach and bypass routes.

A B C D 218 E F G H I

1 2 3 4 5 6 7 8 9 10 11 12 13

MELBOURNE AIRPORT

SUNBURY 43
Greenvale Centre
WOODLANDS HISTORIC PARK
Victoria Police
Westme
Attwood
Broa Shoppi
BROADMEADOWS
ORGAN PIPES NATIONAL PARK
CALDER
Calder Park Thunderdome
Keilor Public Golf Course
Tullamarine Country Club
Domestic & International Terminals
TULLAMARINE FWY
Tullamarine 43
MICKLEHAM RD
MELROSE
CARRICK 80
G
MELTON 54
HWY
Sydenham
Taylors Lakes
OLD CALDER FWY
SHARPS
Keilor Park
Westfield Shopping Town
Oa
ESSE AIR
Str
WESTERN
BALLARAT
Rockbank 8
Department of Defence
Department of Communications Radio 3RN 3LO
Keilor Downs
TAYLORS
GREEN GULLY RD
Keilor 41
Kealba
KEILOR PARK DR
Keilor Cem.
FULLARTON
Airport West
MATTHEWS
Keilor East
KEILOR
Niddrie
Essend
WESTERN FWY
KINGS RD
St Albans
Deer Park Central Shopping Centre
Commonwealth of Australia Office of Defence Production
Deer Park
MAIN RD
ST ALBANS RD
Ginifer
FURLONG
WESTERN RING RD 80
Brimbank Park
MILLERA DR
DINAH PDE
ROSEHILL
HOFFMANS
COOPER
Buckley Park
Avondale Heights
MILITARY RD
Maribyrnong
M
Commonwealth of Australia Department of Defence
RALEIGH RD
MAR
ROSAMOND
Highpoint Shopping Centre
Maidstone
Footscr
BALLARAT
Braybrook
Medway Golf Course
HAMPSTEAD
MITCHELL
Royal M Show
8 37
STATION RD
WESTERN HWY
BALLARAT RD
Albion
Selwyn Park
ANDERSON RD
DEVONSHIRE RD
DUKE ST
Sunshine
SOUTH RD
Skinner Reserve 38
Dobson Reserve
RAAF Depot
BARKLY
Western Hospital
GORDON
Footscray West
Commonwealth of Australia Office of Defence Production
Deer Park
TILBURN RD
FORREST RD
Glengala
Ardeer
Sunshine Golf Course
Hill Reserve
WRIGHT ST 41
MARKET RD
SUNSHINE RD
Tottenham
Hansen Reserve
Middle Footscray
Seddon
50
MT DERRIMUT RD
FITZGERALD RD
Derrimut Grasslands
BOUNDARY RD
32
SOMERVILLE RD
Brooklyn
FAIRBAIRN RD
GEELONG RD
Footscray Cemetery
Yarravil
ROBINSONS RD
PIPE RD
DOHERTYS RD
PRINCES HWY 83
WEST GATE 1 FWY
FRANCIS ST 41
Mc Ivor Reserve
Westgate Golf Course
Tarneit
HOPKINS RD
Truganina
Crematorium and Lawn Cemetery
Altona Gate Shopping Centre
BLACKSHAWS RD
MASON ST
MILLS ST
Newport Lakes Parkland
Spotswood
Scienceworks
West G Bri
Newpo Powe Statio
37
THE ST
SAYERS RD
FITZGERALD RD
PRINCES FWY
KORORIT CREEK RD
GRIEVE PDE
MILLERS RD
Altona Lakes Public Golf Course
Newport
Cemetery
Railway Museum 35
North Williamstown
DERRIMUT RD
HOGANS RD
Hogans Road Reserve
Laverton Lake Recreation Reserve
FORSYTH RD
PALMERS RD
Laverton RAAF Base
Victorian Baseball & Softball Park
Laverton
AB Shaw Reserve
MAIDSTONE ST
Grant Reserve
Westona
Cherry Lake
Altona
Seaholme
Altona Sports Park
VICTORIA ST
ESPLANADE
Hoppers Crossing
Werribee Plaza Shopping Centre
HEATHS RD
Mossfiel Reserve
MORRIS RD
OLD GEELONG RD
1
Aircraft
CENTRAL AV
MERTON ST
VICTORIA ST
QUEEN ST 41
Kooringal Golf Course
BLYTH ST
PDE
Altona Meadows
Galvin Park
TARNEIT RD
MARKET RD
SHAWS RD
Hoppers Crossing
Department of Agriculture
State Research Farm
SNEYDES RD
POINT COOK RD
Point Cook
BALLAN RD
Werribee Racecourse
Werribee
DUNCANS RD
HOPPERS LA
PRINCES
MALTBY
BYPASS
Zoological Park State Equestrian Centre
Werribee Park
AVIATION RD
Point Cook RAAF Base
Point Cook Metropolitan Park
Werribee Mansion
PORT PHILLIP
Spirit of Tasmania Station B
N

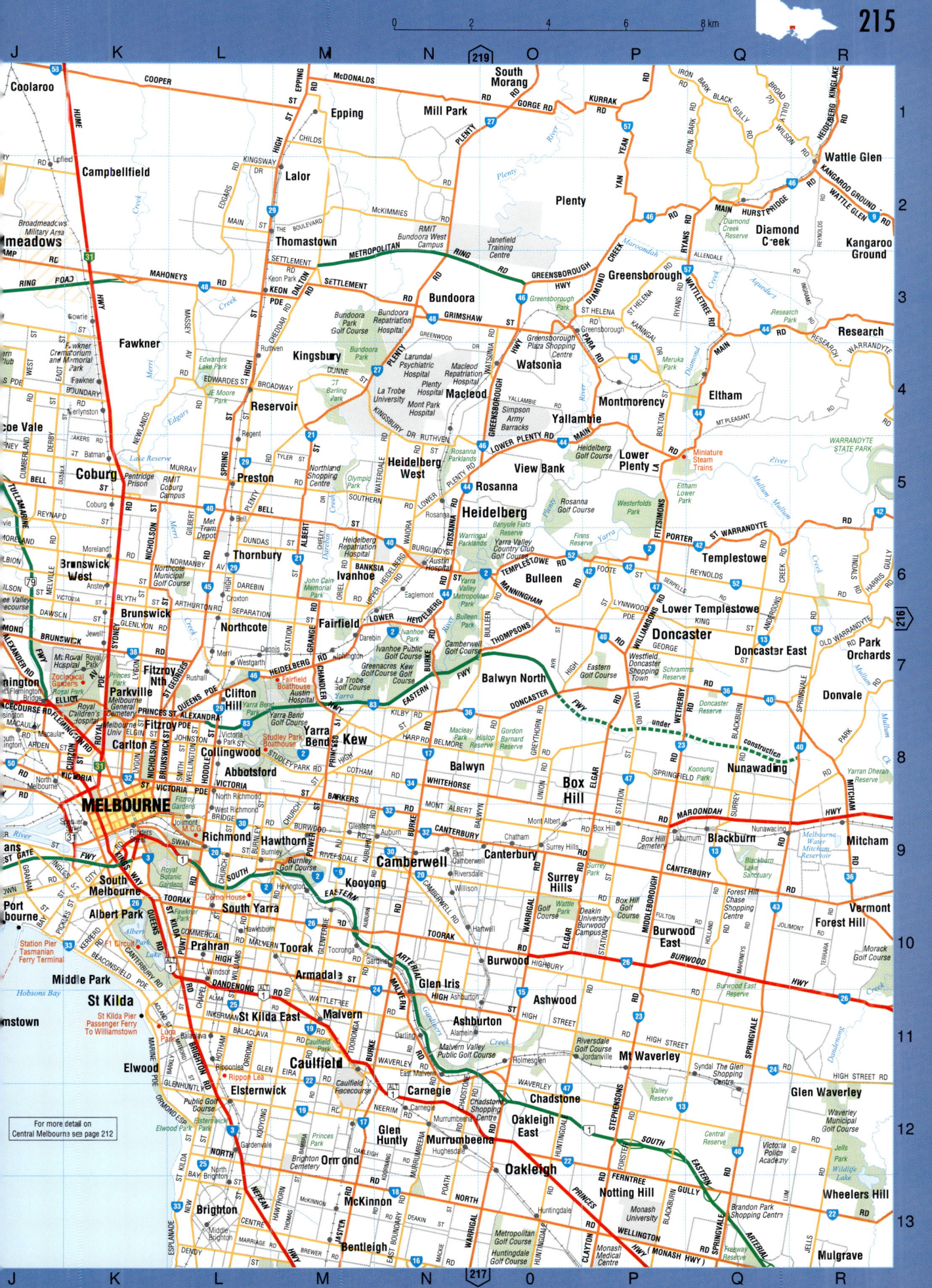

For more detail on Central Melbourne see page 212

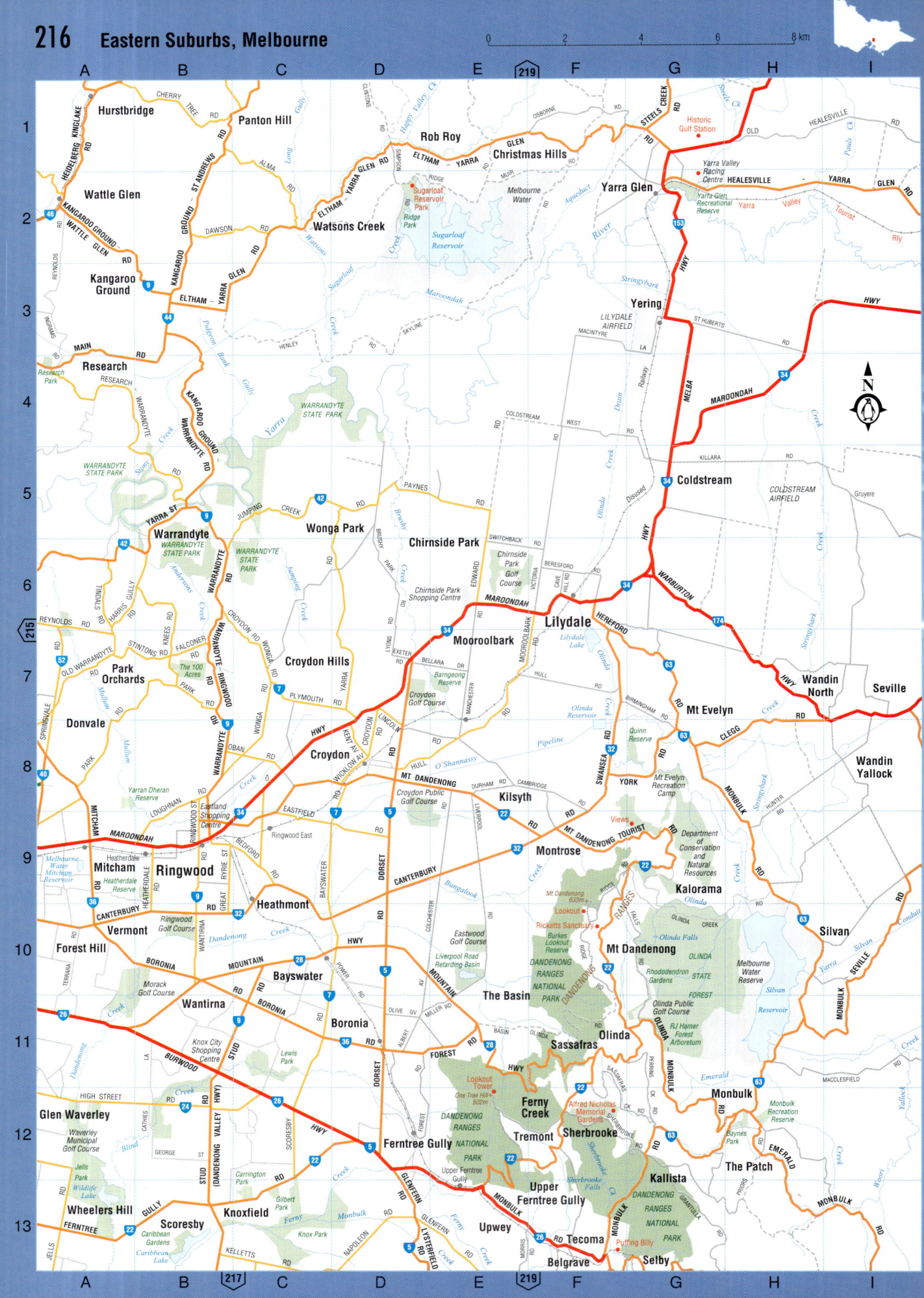

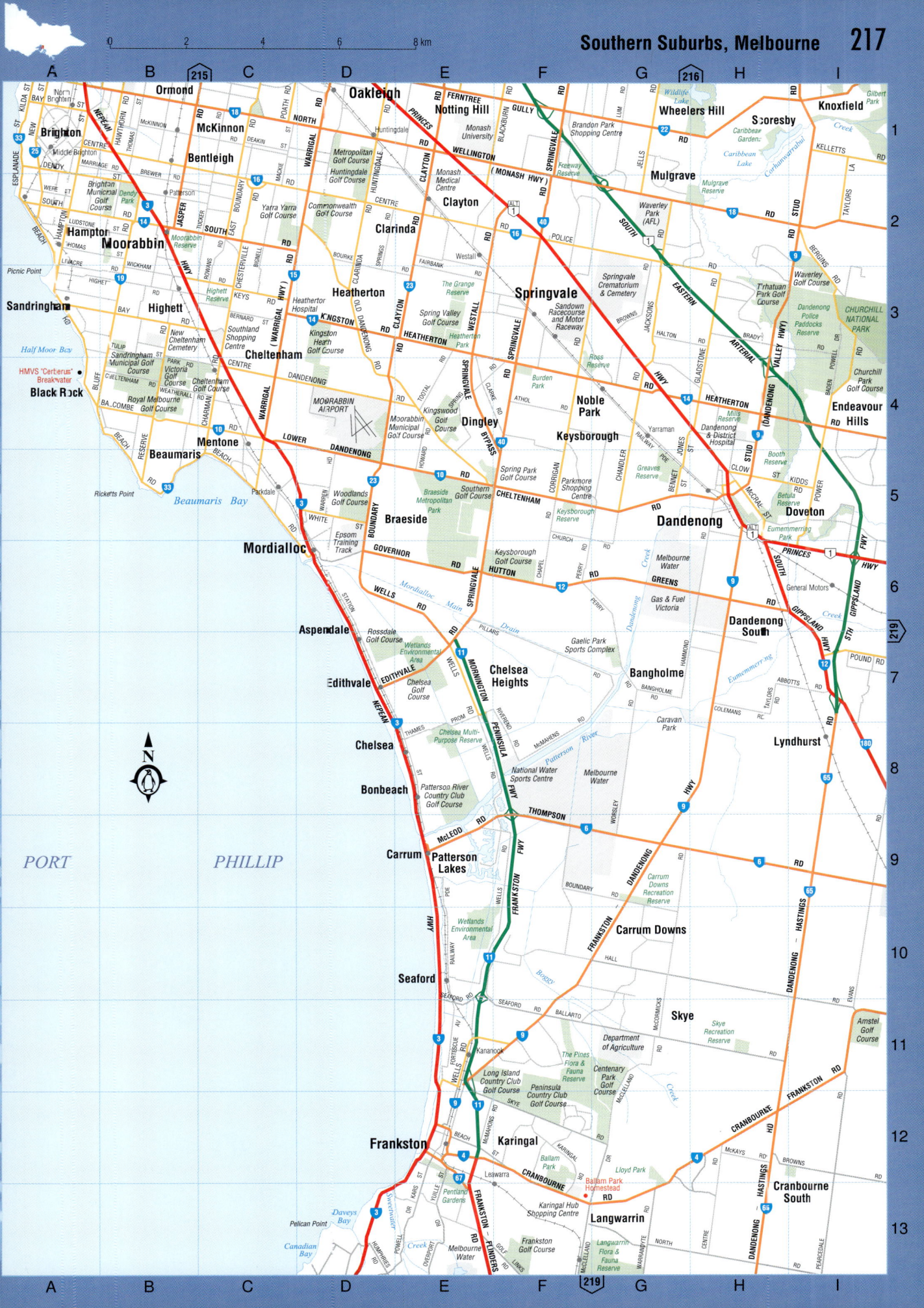

BASS STRAIT

BALLARAT · GEELONG · COLAC · Melton · Werribee · Hoppers Crossing · Bacchus Marsh · Woodend · Kyneton · Malmsbury · Macedon · Gisborne · Sunbury · Diggers Rest · Keilor · Footscray

Lamplough · Majorca · Talbot · Amherst · Lexton · Evansford · Waubra · Learmonth · Creswick · Clunes · Smeaton · Campbelltown · Daylesford · Hepburn Springs · Trentham · Blackwood · Greendale · Myrniong · Ballan · Gordon · Bungaree · Dunnstown · Mount Helen · Buninyong · Sebastopol · Mt Clear · Wendouree · Nerrina

Trawalla · Burrumbeet · Cardigan Village · Miners Rest · Haddon · Snake Valley · Smythesdale · Scarsdale · Linton · Newtown · Happy Valley · Piggoreet · Mannibadar · Illabarook · Rokewood Junction · Corindhap · Rokewood · Dereel · Enfield · Grenville · Mount Mercer · Cargerie · Elaine · Meredith · Steiglitz · Sheoaks · Anakie · Lethbridge · Maude · Bannockburn · Teesdale · Shelford · Cressy · Berrybank · Duverney · Wingeel · Inverleigh · Gheringhap · Batesford · Fyansford · Ceres

GEELONG · Lara · Little River · Werribee · Hoppers Crossing · Avalon Airfield · Point Wilson · Corio Bay · Portarlington · Clifton Springs · Drysdale · St Leonards · Queenscliff · Point Lonsdale · Portsea · Sorrento · Ocean Grove · Barwon Heads · Breamlea · Torquay · Bellbrae · Anglesea · Aireys Inlet · Fairhaven · Lorne · Eastern View

Colac · Elliminyt · Irrewillipe · Beeac · Warrion · Alvie · Coragulac · Cororooke · Warncoort · Birregurra · Deans Marsh · Winchelsea · Moriac · Mount Moriac · Freshwater Creek · Bambra · Yeodene · Forrest · Gellibrand · Carlisle River

Mount Macedon · Riddells Creek · Romsey · Lancefield · New Gisborne · Carlsruhe · Tylden · Woodend · Trentham

GREAT DIVIDING RANGE · WESTERN HWY · MIDLAND HWY · GLENELG HWY · HAMILTON HWY · PRINCES HWY · SURFCOAST HWY · BELLARINE HWY · CALDER FWY · GREAT OCEAN ROAD

Lake Corangamite · Lake Colac · Lake Beeac · Lake Gnarpurt · Lake Martin · Lake Weering · Lake Modewarre · Lake Connewarre · Corio Bay

BASS STRAIT

N

BELLARINE

PENINSULA

MURRADOC RD

Bellarine
Spray Farm
Winery

Scotchmans
Hill Winery

Mannerim

225

Tourist

BELLARINE L. HWY

Railway

Indented Head
Indented Head

St Leonards
South Red Bluff

The Bluff

EDWARDS
POINT
WILDLIFE
RESERVE

Edwards Point

Swan
Bay

Duck Island

Queenscliff
Golf
Course

Swan
Island

Bellarine
Peninsula
Railway

Queenscliff

White
Lighthouse

Black
Lighthouse

Fort
Queenscliff

Point Lonsdale

Pt Lonsdale

The Rip

Point Nepean

Fort
Nepean

Nepean
Bay

MORNINGTON
PENINSULA NP

Cheviot Beach

COMMONWEALTH
LAND

MORNINGTON

London Bridge

PENINSULA

Portsea Golf
Course

Portsea
Surf Beach

NATIONAL PARK

Observatory Point
Ticonderoga
Bay

Weeroona
Bay

Portsea

Portsea
Golf
Course

Collins
Bay

Point King

Sorrento
Golf Course

Sorrento

The Sisters

Collins Settlement
Historic Site

Sorrento
Back Beach

Jubilee Point

Diamond Bay

Koonya Beach

Spray Point

Koreen Point

Pearces Beach

The Divide

The Sisters

Blairgowrie

White
Cliffs

Rye

Tootgarook

MELBOURNE RD

MORNINGTON

PENINSULA

NATIONAL

PARK

POINT

CANTERBURY RD

JETTY RD

DUNDAS ST

Observation
Hills

BROWNS RD

TRUEMANS RD

BROWNS RD

The Dunes
Golf Links

Eagle Ridge
Golf Course

SANDY RD

Rye
Ocean Beach

Capri
Beach

Boags Rocks
Gunnamatta
Surf Beach

MORNINGTON

PENINSULA

NATIONAL

PARK

National
Golf Course

Cape
Schanck
Golf Course

MEAKINS RD

Cape Schanck Lighthouse

Bushranger
Bay

Cape
Schanck

Picnic
Point

The
Arch

PORT

PHILLIP

N

Mud
Islands

Spirit of Tasmania Ferry
Station Pier to Devonport

Car & Passenger

Ferry

Ferry

Capel   Sound

Dromana

McCrae

McCrae Homestead

Eastern Lighthouse

Rosebud

Rosebud
West

Rosebud
Golf
Course

NEPEAN
RD

MORNINGTON PENINSULA

Arthurs Seat
Chairlift
Arthurs Seat
309m

ARTHURS
SEAT
STATE PARK

ARTHURS SEAT RD

6

67

Rosebud
Country
Club

JETTY RD

PURVES RD

MAIN CREEK RD

BALDRYS RD

Boneo

MORNINGTON

PENINSULA

BONEO RD

ROSEBUD

67

Main

Stockport Ck

FLINDERS

School Hill
184m

MORNINGTON

Safety B

Martha Poi

Drom
Ba
Safe

Baln

Bale

Bound

Arthu

SH.

Main
Ridges

6

Tea Tree Ck

Cairns
Ck

Simmons
Bay

16

25

BASS   STRAIT

HISTORICAL HOMES: The Mornington Peninsula
array of magnificently preserved historical home
Visit Coolart at Somers, a century-old mansion
in landscaped gardens, or the simple 1844 drop slab
McCrae Homestead. The Briars, an 1860s homestead a
Martha, houses a significant collection of Napoleonic
and furniture.

ARTHURS SEAT STATE PARK: Originally named after a similar
mountain near Edinburgh, Scotland during the first exploration
of Port Phillip Bay. Take a ride on the 72-seat chairlift for
spectacular views of the Peninsula and Bay. Enjoy a short
walk to scenic Flinders Lookout and to Seawinds Gardens.

MORNINGTON PENINSULA NATIONAL PARK: This
magnificent park extends from the tip of Point Nepean
to Cape Schanck. An unusual transporter service operates,
taking visitors to Cheviot Beach, Observatory Point and the
historical Fort Nepean. Numerous walking tracks provide
easy access to London Bridge, Cape Schanck Lighthouse
and endless spectacular coastal scenery.

TOURIST INFORMATION:
Phillip Island (Phillip Island Rd, Newhaven)
Flinders, Mornington & Sorrento
(Point Nepean Rd, Dromana)

Please refer to Mornington Peninsula feature
on page 158 for more information on this region.

WINERIES: ①
Balnarring Vineyard 1   L7
Barak Estate 2   L4
Craig Avon Vineyard 3   K7
Darling Park Vineyards 4   K8
Dromana Estate Vineyards 5   J7
Dunstan's Poplar Bend 6   I9
Elan Vineyard 7   L7
Ermes Estate 8   L5
Hanns Creek Estate 9   K8
Hickinbotham 10   J6
Karina Vineyard 11   J7
Kings Creek Vineyard 12   L7
Main Ridge Estate 13   I8
Maritime Estate 14   J9
Merricks Estate 15   K9
Miceli Vineyard 16   I8
Moorooduc Estate 17   L5
Mornington Vineyards
   Estate 18   K6
Paringa Estate 19   J9
Port Phillip Estate 20   K8
Red Hill Estate 21   J9
Stonier's Winery 22   K9
Stumpy Gully Vineyard 23   L4
Tanglewood Downs Estate 24   K6
T'Gallant 25   K8
Tucks Ridge 26   J9
Tuerong Estate 27   I9
Vintina Estate 28   K3
Willow Creek Vineyard 29   L7
Wyldcroft Estates Winery 30   K8

0 2 4 6 8 10 km

J K L M N O P Q R

FRANKSTON

TO MELBOURNE

CRANBOURNE RD

4

LANGWARRIN

Daveys Bay

Pelican Point

Canadian Bay

Ballam Park Homestead

Langwarrin Flora & Fauna Reserve

219

Mt Eliza

Sunnyside Beach

Schnapper Point

Mornington Golf Course

Frankston Reservoir

Baxter Park

5

Baxter

BAXTER – TOORADIN

Pearcedale

BROWNS RD

TO DANDENONG

Five Ways

CLYDE FIVEWAYS RD

Devon Meadows

MANKS SOUTH

180

Cannons Creek

Cannons

Warneet

Tooradin

TO KORUMBURRA

BAXTER TOORADIN RD

Mornington

Fishermans Beach

Fossil Beach

Balcombe

The Briars Homestead

Martha Course

Studio City Pop & Media Museum

Mornington Racecourse

Civic Reserve

Sunday Craft Market

TYABB

Somerville

EROMOSA ROAD WEST

EROMOSA ROAD EAST

Bungower

Mooroduc

MORNINGTON

Tyabb

TYABB RD

Western Port Airfield

BHP Steel Western Port Works

BAYVIEW RD

GRAYDENS

HODGINS

Devilbend Golf Course & Rec Res

Devilbend Reservoir

Bittern Reservoir

WESTERN PORT

Scrub Point

FRENCH ISLAND: Named in 1802 by Captain Bauclin, leader of a French scientific expedition, this naturally protected island of state parkland provides the perfect habitat for rare white–breasted sea eagles, potoroos and koalas.

Quail Island

Watson Inlet

Bembridge 9 Hole Golf Course

Hastings

Long Point

Long Island

Hastings Bight

Sandstone Island

FRENCH ISLAND STATE PARK

Mt Wellington 98m

Fairhaven

The Pinnacles 66m

FRENCH

ISLAND

BITTERN – DROMANA

Red Hill

Bittern

MYERS

Balnarring Racecourse

Emu Plains Market

Bittern

WOOLLEYS

Crib Point

DROMANA RD

Balnarring

SANDY POINT RD

Coolart Reserve

Coolart Homestead

Balnarring Beach

Point Summer

Somers

Somers Beach

South Beach

Crib Point

Stony Point

Passenger Ferry

Tankerton Jetty

Tankerton

HMAS Cerberus

Hanns Inlet

(PROHIBITED AREA)

Western Park Beach

Sandy Point

Tortoise Head

Loag Point

Red Hill South

Merricks

Merricks Beach

Merricks North

STALEYS

POINT LEO

Reeds Waterholes

Ashcombe Maze

Point Leo

Shoreham

Shoreham Beach

ASHCOMBE MAZE: Wander through the large green hedge maze with one kilometre of pathways, or wind your way through the beautiful rose maze of over 1200 colourful and fragrant roses. The tea room and extensive gardens provide perfect places for relaxation.

Passenger Ferry

Rocks

Penguin Rock

Seal

Cowes

CHURCH ST

Cowes Golf Course

Observation Point

McHaffie Point

VENTNOR RD

COWES

RHYLL

Bird Sanctuary

Rhyll Inlet

Rhyll

Fishermans Point

WESTERN PORT

Flinders

Kennon Cove

West Head

Ferry

Ventnor

VENTNOR RD

BEACH

PHILLIP ISLAND NATURE PARK

PHILLIP

Wildlife Park

Koala Res

Koala Conservation Centre

A Maze 'n Things

NEWHAVEN RD

PHILLIP ISLAND: This year-round tourist destination with diverse coastline is an excellent weekend getaway. Visit the rugged terrain of the Nobbies and view the seal colony at Seal Rocks. Wander through various sections of Phillip Island Nature Park. Every evening the little (fairy) penguins parade up Summerland Beach providing a delightful natural wildlife spectacular.

Cat Bay

Swan Lake

BACK BEACH

THE GAP RD

Phillip Island Winery

ISLAND

Racing Circuit

RHILL

PHILLIP ISLAND NATURE PARK

Cunningham Bay

Swan Bay

Australian Dairy Centre

Churchill Island

Newhaven

Woody Point

Point Grant

Penguin Parade

The Nobbies

Seal Rocks

Phillip Is Penguin Reserve

Berrys Beach

Storm Bay

Pyramid Rock

Phillip Is Airport

186

The Narrows

San Remo

0 2 4 6 8 10 km

A B C D E F G H I

Wineries: 1

Allinda 1 C5
Blanchet Winery 2 A7
Brahams Creek Winery 3 H8
Broussard's Chum Creek
  Winery 4 D5
Coldstream Hills 5 D8
De Bortoli Winery and
  Restaurant 6 C5
Domaine Chandon Australia 7 C6
Eyton on Yarra 8 D7
Fergusson Winery and
  Restaurant 9 C5
Kellybrook Winery and
  Restaurant 10 A7
Lillydale Vineyards 11 D9
Lirralira Estate 12 A8
Long Gully Estate 13 D5
Lovey's Estate -
  Mount Hope Wines 14 C5
Monbulk Winery 15 C11
Oakridge Estate 16 C10
Paternoster 17 D13
St Huberts Vineyard 18 C7
Shantell Vineyard 19 C4
Tarrawarra Vineyard 20 D6
Warramate Vineyard 21 D7
Watsons Wines 22 D10
Yarra Burn Winery and
  Restaurant 23 F9
Yarra Edge Vineyard 24 A7
Yarra Ridge Vineyard 25 B6
Yarra Yering Vineyard 26 D7
Yering Station Vineyard 27 B6

KINGLAKE NATIONAL PARK: Home to numerous lyrebirds and wombats, the Kinglake National Park areas were established to protect the wet eucalypt forests on the Great Dividing Range. Tranquil walks through fern gullies and forested spurs take you to the Wombelano and Mason's Falls.

TOOLANGI-BLACK RANGES: Toolangi (once) home of C.J. Dennis, author of 'The Sentimental Bloke' is a mountainous berry producing area nestled in the Black Ranges State Forest. Picturesque roadways provide easy access to the spectacular Wilhelmina Falls and Murrindindi Cascades. There are excellent riding tours available in the area, taking you along rugged mountain tracks and tranquil river paths. Trout and Blackfish can be caught in the Murrindindi River.

GULF STATION: Now owned by the National Trust, Gulf Station at Yarra Glen is one of Victoria's oldest pastoral properties dating back to the 1850s. Visitors can step back in time, explore the original timber buildings, cottage gardens and participate in farm activities.

HEALESVILLE SANCTUARY: Home to over 200 of Australia's unique birds, animals and reptiles, including some endangered species. Healesville Sanctuary, open every day of the year, is recognised as Australia's top wildlife park. Spend the day venturing among friendly kangaroos, emus and wombats in naturally designed enclosures.

SILVAN RESERVOIR: Located on the edge of beautiful Olinda State Forest, Stonyford picnic ground at the magnificent Silvan Reservoir provides excellent BBQ facilities. Stop along the Monbulk Road for breathtaking views of the region.

PUFFING BILLY: This superbly restored vintage steam train ambles its way from the ferny stands of Belgrave through the cool rainforest to Emerald Lake.

TOURIST INFORMATION:
Healesville (127 Maroondah Hwy)
Marysville (Murchison St)

TO YEA
TO ALEXANDRA
Glenburn
Buxton
Buxton Trout Farm
Marysville
Narbethong
Black Spur
Healesville
Yarra Glen
Yering
Steels Creek
Dixons Creek
Toolangi
Coldstream
Lilydale
MT Evelyn
Wandin North
Seville
Wandin Yallock
Woori Yallock
Yarra Junction
Launching Place
Wesburn
Millgrove
Warburton
Big Pats Creek
Don Valley
Yellingbo
Gladysdale
Hoddles Creek
Three Bridges
Powelltown
Kalorama
Silvan
Olinda
Monbulk
Macclesfield
Menzies Creek
Avonsleigh
Clematis
Emerald
Cockatoo
Gembrook
Belgrave
Selby
The Patch
Upper Ferntree Gully

GREAT DIVIDING RANGE
KINGLAKE NATIONAL PARK
YARRA RANGES NATIONAL PARK
DANDENONG RANGES NATIONAL PARK

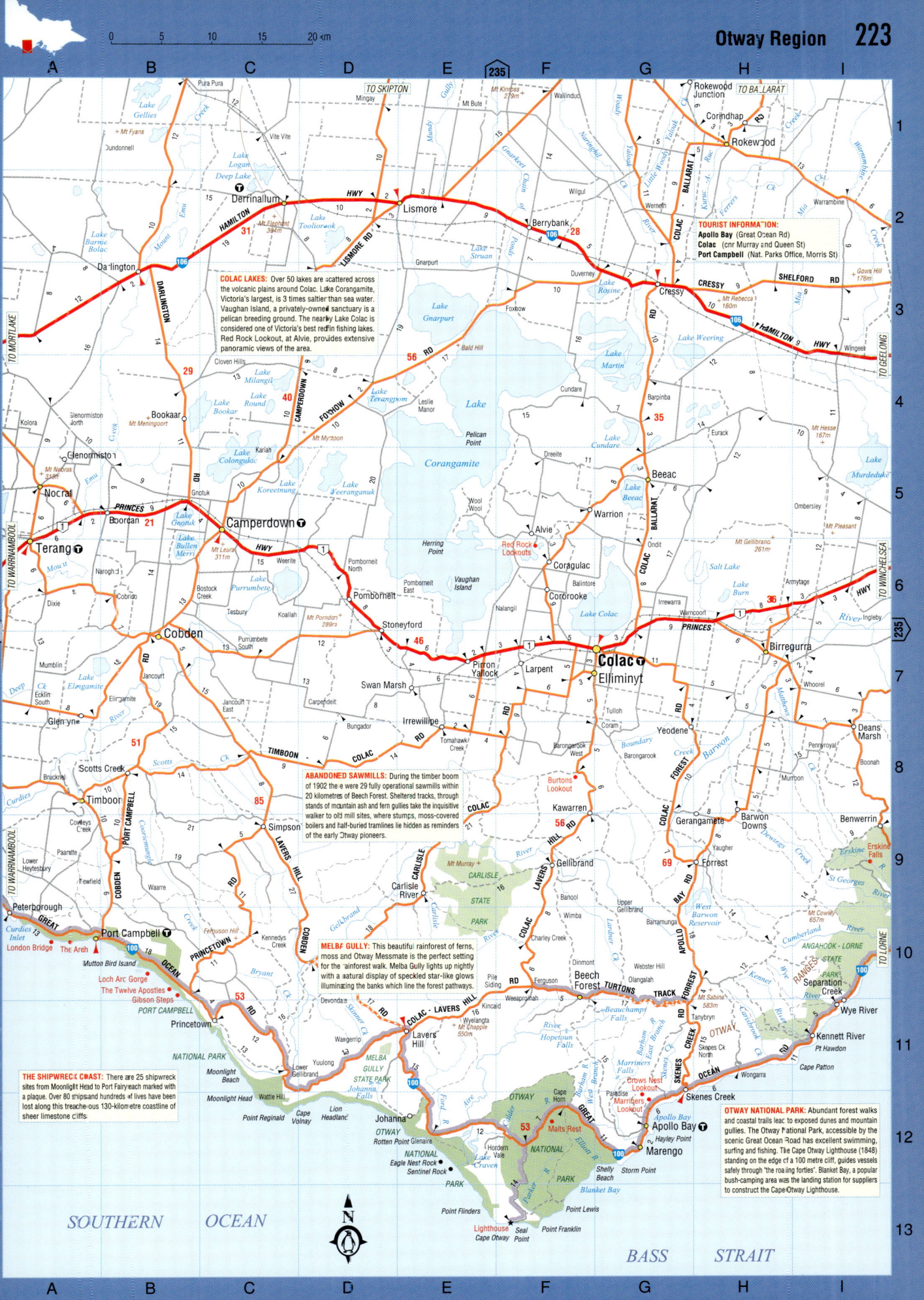

COLAC LAKES: Over 50 lakes are scattered across the volcanic plains around Colac. Lake Corangamite, Victoria's largest, is 3 times saltier than sea water. Vaughan Island, a privately-owned sanctuary is a pelican breeding ground. The nearby Lake Colac is considered one of Victoria's best redfin fishing lakes. Red Rock Lookout, at Alvie, provides extensive panoramic views of the area.

TOURIST INFORMATION:
Apollo Bay (Great Ocean Rd)
Colac (cnr Murray and Queen St)
Port Campbell (Nat. Parks Office, Morris St)

ABANDONED SAWMILLS: During the timber boom of 1902 there were 29 fully operational sawmills within 20 kilometres of Beech Forest. Sheltered tracks, through stands of mountain ash and fern gullies take the inquisitive walker to old mill sites, where stumps, moss-covered boilers and half-buried tramlines lie hidden as reminders of the early Otway pioneers.

MELBA GULLY: This beautiful rainforest of ferns, moss and Otway Messmate is the perfect setting for the rainforest walk. Melba Gully lights up nightly with a natural display of speckled star-like glows illuminating the banks which line the forest pathways.

THE SHIPWRECK COAST: There are 25 shipwreck sites from Moonlight Head to Port Fairy each marked with a plaque. Over 80 ships and hundreds of lives have been lost along this treacherous 130-kilometre coastline of sheer limestone cliffs.

OTWAY NATIONAL PARK: Abundant forest walks and coastal trails lead to exposed dunes and mountain gullies. The Otway National Park, accessible by the scenic Great Ocean Road has excellent swimming, surfing and fishing. The Cape Otway Lighthouse (1848) standing on the edge of a 100 metre cliff, guides vessels safely through 'the roaring forties'. Blanket Bay, a popular bush-camping area was the landing station for suppliers to construct the Cape Otway Lighthouse.

SOUTHERN OCEAN

BASS STRAIT

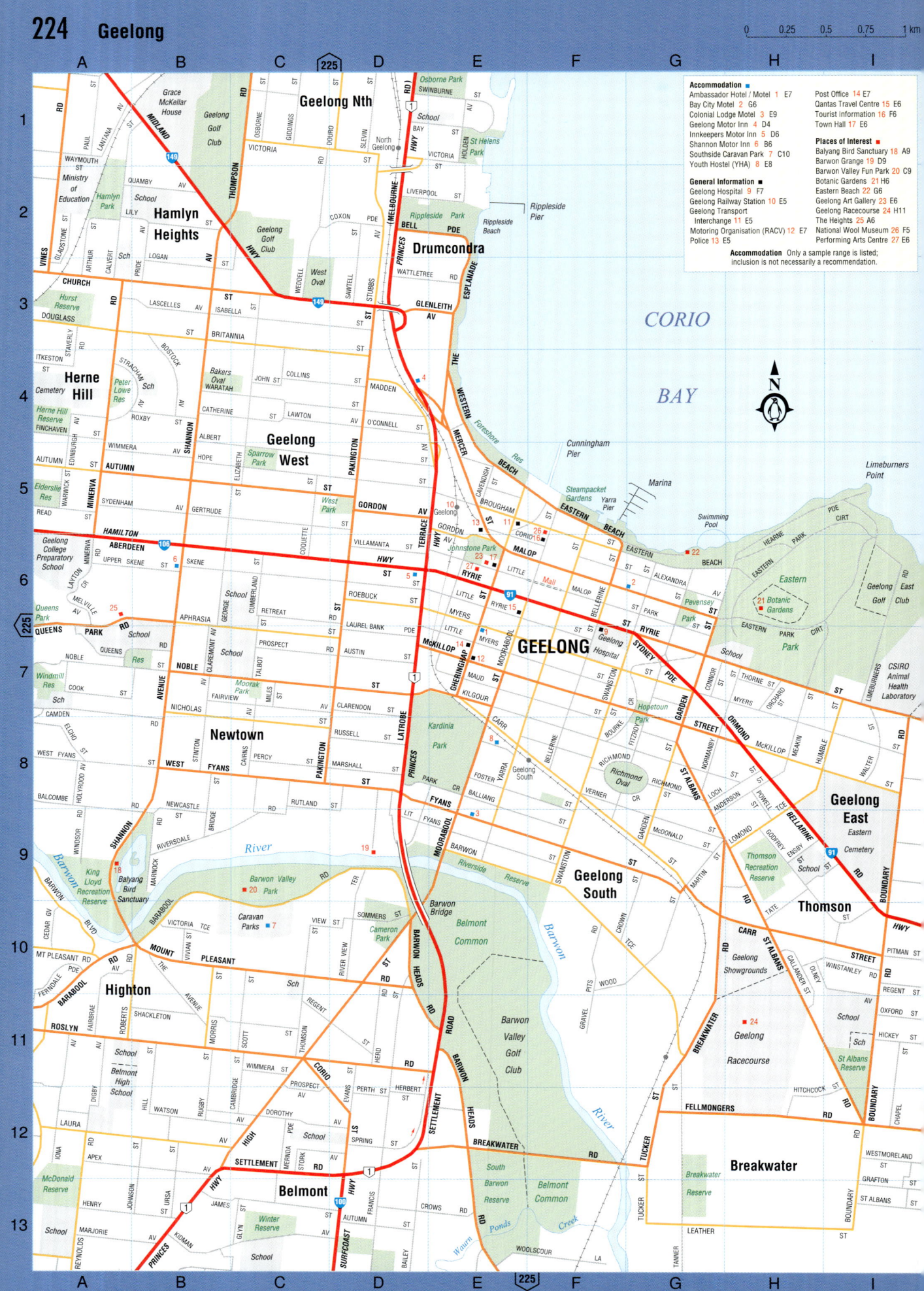

0   0.25   0.5   0.75   1 km

Geelong Nth

Geelong Golf Club

Grace McKellar House

Hamlyn Heights

Drumcondra

CORIO

BAY

Accommodation
Ambassador Hotel / Motel 1 E7
Bay City Motel 2 G6
Colonial Lodge Motel 3 E9
Geelong Motor Inn 4 D4
Innkeepers Motor Inn 5 D6
Shannon Motor Inn 6 B6
Southside Caravan Park 7 C10
Youth Hostel (YHA) 8 E8

General Information
Geelong Hospital 9 F7
Geelong Railway Station 10 E5
Geelong Transport Interchange 11 E5
Motoring Organisation (RACV) 12 E7
Police 13 E5

Post Office 14 E7
Qantas Travel Centre 15 E7
Tourist Information 16 F6
Town Hall 17 E6

Places of Interest
Balyang Bird Sanctuary 18 A9
Barwon Grange 19 D9
Barwon Valley Fun Park 20 C9
Botanic Gardens 21 H6
Eastern Beach 22 G6
Geelong Art Gallery 23 E6
Geelong Racecourse 24 H11
National Wool Museum 26 F5
The Heights 25 A6
Performing Arts Centre 27 E6

Accommodation Only a sample range is listed; inclusion is not necessarily a recommendation.

Herne Hill

Geelong West

Eastern Beach

Marina

Limeburners Point

Cunningham Pier

Steampacket Gardens

Yarra Pier

Swimming Pool

Eastern Beach

Eastern Park

Botanic Gardens

Geelong Golf Club

Geelong East Club

CSIRO Animal Health Laboratory

Newtown

GEELONG

Geelong Hospital

Richmond Oval

Geelong South

Kardinia Park

Hopetoun Park

Geelong East

Eastern Cemetery

Thomson

Barwon Valley Park

King Lloyd Recreation Reserve

Balyang Bird Sanctuary

Barwon Bridge

Belmont Common

Barwon Valley Golf Club

Thomson Recreation Reserve

Geelong Showgrounds

Geelong Racecourse

St Albans Reserve

Highton

Roslyn

Belmont High School

Caravan Parks

Cameron Park

Barwon Common

Breakwater

Belmont

Winter Reserve

McDonald Reserve

South Barwon Reserve

Belmont Common

Breakwater Reserve

Ponds Creek

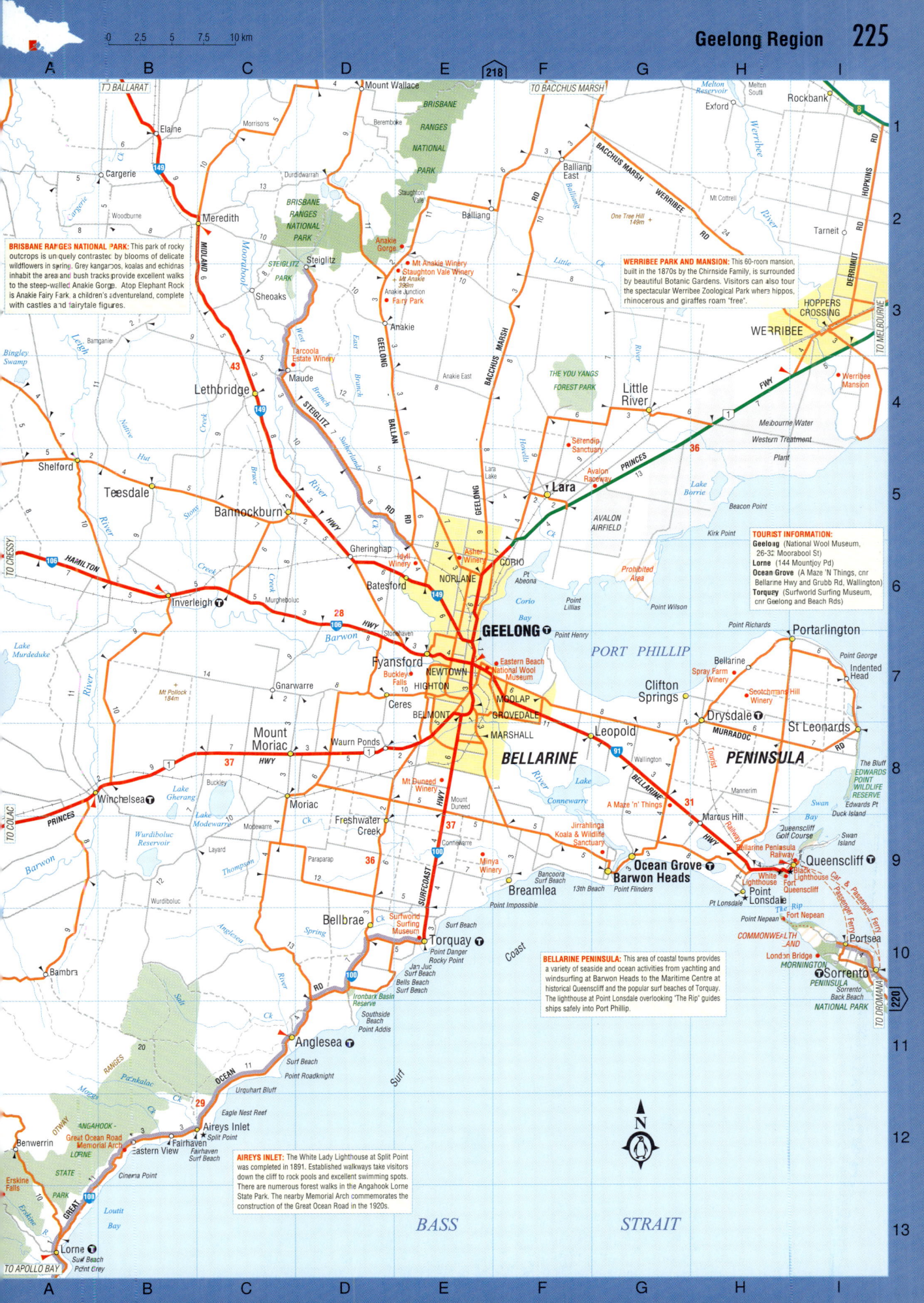

0   200   400   600 m

A   B   C   D   E   F   G   H   I

North
Bendigo

N

229

Showgrounds
Playground

Kindergarten

St Peters
Primary School

Atkins
Street
Reserve

Oval

Bowling
Club

Recreation
Complex

Uniting
Church

Post
Office

Cambrian
Hotel

St Johns
Anglican Church

Bendigo
North
Primary
School

Tyson's Reef
Hotel

Lake
Weeroona

Weeroona
Potteries

Lakeview
Motor Inn

Tea House
Motor Inn

Julie Anna
Inn

Bendigo
and North District
Base Hospital

Ambulance
Station

Bendigo
Tennis Complex

Rising Sun
Hotel

Anne Caudle
Centre

Garden
Gully
Oval

Waterloo
Hotel

Bendigo
Sports
Centre

St Killans
Primary School

Tram
Museum

Bendigo
Woollen Mills

Lansell
West

Saleyards

Tennis Courts
Bowling Green
Croquet

H.M. Prison
Bendigo

Bendigo
Aquatic Centre

Queen
Elizabeth
Oval

Bendigo
Senior
Secondary
College

Camp Hill
Primary
School

Oval Motel

Bendigo Central
Motor Lodge

Albert
Hotel

Bendigo TAFE

Fire Station

Rosalind   Park

BENDIGO

Fernery

Footbridge

Brian Boru
Hotel

McIvor
Motor Inn

McIvor
Highway
Hotel

Footbridge

Visitor
Information
Centre

Dispensary

Shamrock
Hotel

Town
Hall

Library

Cumberland
Hotel

Y.M.C.A.

City Centre
Motel

Alexandra
Fountain

Allans
Walk

Killians Wk
Bank
Arcade

Market

St Andrews

Sacred Heart
Cathedral

Bendigo
Antique
Market

Arc

Myers

St Pauls
Cathedral

Hopetoun
Hotel

Ewing
Park

Central
Deborah
Mine

Discovery
Science and
Technology
Centre

Bendigo
Railway
Station

Brougham
Arms
Hotel

Croquet
Club

Bowling Club
PALMERSTON

229

A   B   C   D   E   F   G   H   I

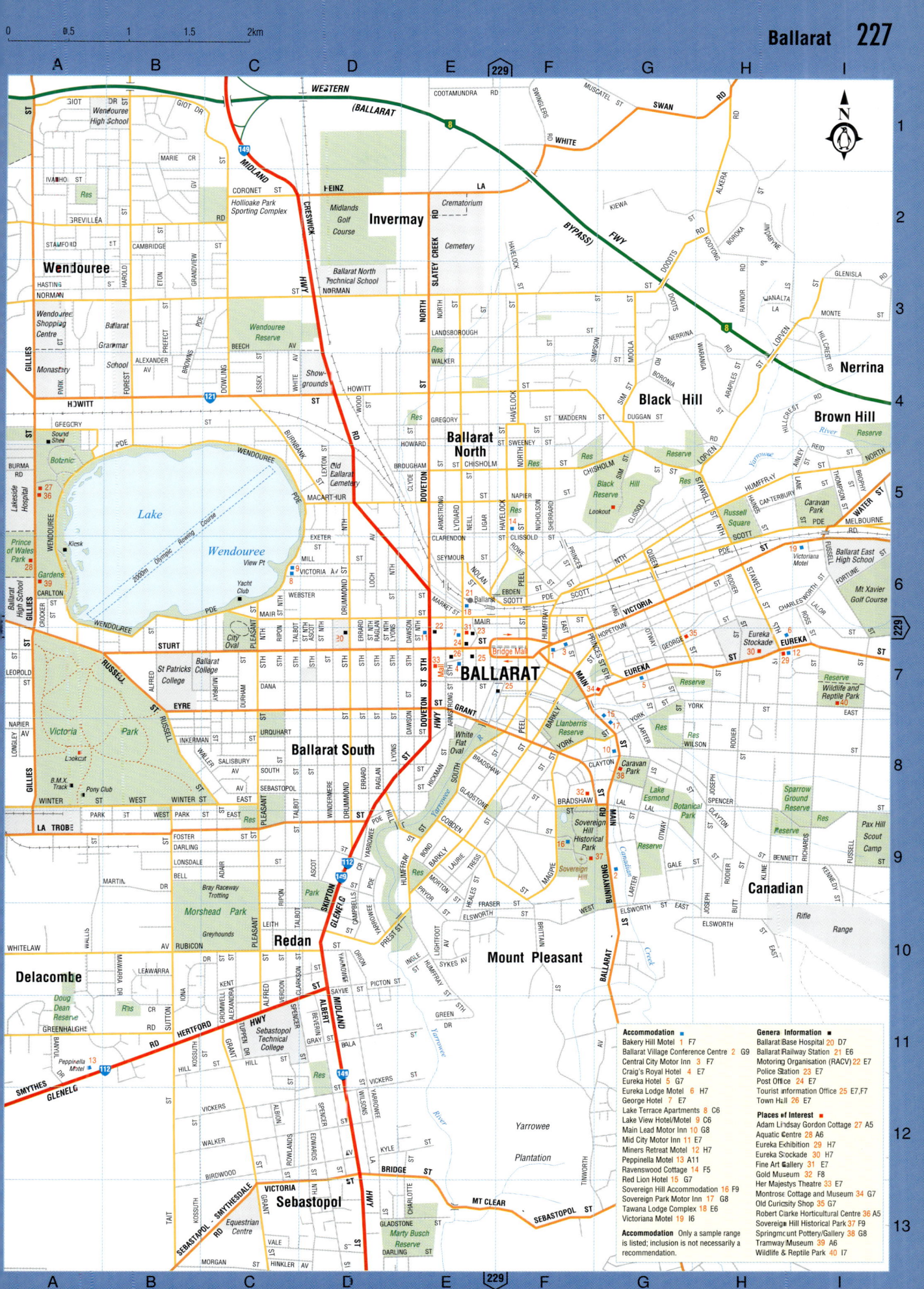

Accommodation ■
Bakery Hill Motel 1 F7
Ballarat Village Conference Centre 2 G9
Central City Motor Inn 3 F7
Craig's Royal Hotel 4 E7
Eureka Hotel 5 G7
Eureka Lodge Motel 6 H7
George Hotel 7 E7
Lake Terrace Apartments 8 C6
Lake View Hotel/Motel 9 C6
Main Lead Motor Inn 10 G8
Mid City Motor Inn 11 E7
Miners Retreat Motel 12 H7
Peppinella Motel 13 A11
Ravenswood Cottage 14 F5
Red Lion Hotel 15 G7
Sovereign Hill Accommodation 16 F9
Sovereign Park Motor Inn 17 G8
Tawana Lodge Complex 18 E6
Victoriana Motel 19 I6

Accommodation Only a sample range
is listed; inclusion is not necessarily a
recommendation.

General Information ■
Ballarat Base Hospital 20 D7
Ballarat Railway Station 21 E6
Motoring Organisation (RACV) 22 E7
Police Station 23 E7
Post Office 24 E7
Tourist Information Office 25 E7,F7
Town Hall 26 E7

Places of Interest ■
Adam Lindsay Gordon Cottage 27 A5
Aquatic Centre 28 A6
Eureka Exhibition 29 H7
Eureka Stockade 30 H7
Fine Art Gallery 31 E7
Gold Museum 32 F8
Her Majestys Theatre 33 E7
Montrose Cottage and Museum 34 G7
Old Curiosity Shop 35 G7
Robert Clarke Horticultural Centre 36 A5
Sovereign Hill Historical Park 37 F9
Springmount Pottery/Gallery 38 G8
Tramway Museum 39 A6
Wildlife & Reptile Park 40 I7

GREAT WESTERN: The vineyards of this area are famous for producing high quality champagne-style wine, as well as red and dry white table wines. Wineries where tastings and sales are available include: Best's Concongella Winery, Seppelt Great Western Winery and Garden Gully Vineyard.

GRAMPIANS NATIONAL PARK: The park is famous for its waterfalls, wildflowers, wide variety of birds and mammals, as well as its aboriginal rock art sites. The massive sandstone ranges of the Grampians provide some of the state's most spectacular scenery. Popular activities in the park include rock-climbing, bushwalking, and scenic drives; Lake Bellfield is good for sailing and rowing, and there is excellent trout-fishing in the lake and in Fyans Creek.

TOURIST INFORMATION:
Ararat (Barkly St)
Avoca (High St)
Ballan (Shire Offices, cnr Stead & Steiglitz Sts)
Ballarat (Cnr Sturt & Albert Sts)
Beaufort (Shire Offices, 5 Lawrence St)
Bendigo (51-67 Pall Mall)
Castlemaine (Duke St)
Clunes (Museum, Fraser St)
Dunolly (Market St)
Maldon (High St)
Maryborough (Railway St)
Stawell (54 Western Hwy)

TO HORSHAM
TO ST ARNAUD
TO DUNKELD

GRAMPIANS
NATIONAL
PARK

GREAT DIVIDING RANGE

Lubeck, Wal Wal, Glenorchy, Deep Lead, Stawell, Illawarra, Mokepilly, Bellellen, Great Western, Pomonal, Armstrong, Moyston, Ararat, Cathcart, Barton, Maroona, Rossbridge, Willaura, Stavely, Wickliffe, Lake Bolac, Mininera, Streatham, Westmere, Tatyoon

Wallaloo, Wallaloo East, Kanya, Callawadda, Riachella, Campbells Bridge, Morri Morri, Greens Creek, Joel Joel, Joel South, Shays Flat, Navarre, Tulkara, Landsborough, Crowlands, Dunnewarthy, Ben Nevis, Eversley, Warra Yadin, Warrak, Langi-Ghiran, Bayindeen, Dobie, Langi Logan, Ballyrogan, Shirley, Yalla Y Poora, Carranballac

Tottington, Paradise, Rostron, Winjallok, Stuart Mill, Redbank, Barkly, Frenchmans, Moonambel, Tanwood, Warrenmang, Percydale, Avoca, Glenlofty, Glenshee, Glenpatrick, Amphitheatre, Elmhurst, Mt Cole, Mt Buangor, Buangor, Middle Creek, Eurambeen, Beaufort, Raglan, Chute, Main Lead, Nerring, Skipton, Manmba, Mena Hill, Lake Goldsmith, Stockyard Hill, Mt Emu, Lake Wongan, Lake Goldsmith

KARA KARA STATE PARK
Teddington Reservoir
PYRENEE
THE RANGE
LANGI-GHIRAN STATE PARK
MT BUANGOR STATE PARK
Lake Lonsdale
Lake Fyans
Lake Bellfield
Mt William
Reservoir
Kalymna Falls
Mt William Swamp
Lake Muirhead
Lake Buninjon
Lake Bolac
Lake McLaren
Lake Wongan
Lake Goldsmith
Slater Lake

Mt Drummond, Mt Cassel 689m, Mt William 1167m, Mt Ararat 616m, Mt Moorambool 522m, Mt Challicum, Mt Stavely 326m, Mt Langi-Ghiran 922m, Ben Nevis 877m, Mt Buangor 968m, Mt Cole 899m, Mt Avoca 750m, Ben More, Mt Lonarch 610m, Ben Major 610m, Mt Bolangum 373m, Bald Hill 340m, Widderin 360m

Bunjil's Shelter
One Tree Hill Lookout
Lookout Hill 969m
Rhymney Reef
Norval
Denicull Creek

Wimmera River, Richardson River, Concongella River, Seven Mile Creek, Avon River, Sundi Creek, Campbells Ck, Mt Emu Creek, Glenelg River, Hopkins River, Mortlake, Fiery Creek, Georges Ck, Bill Ck, Good Morning Ck, Nekeya Ck, Nokoa Ck

WESTERN HWY, GOLDFIELDS TOURIST ROUTE, AVOCA RD, SUNRAYSIA HWY, PYRENEES HWY, GLENELG HWY, SKIPTON RD, MORTLAKE RD, ARARAT RD

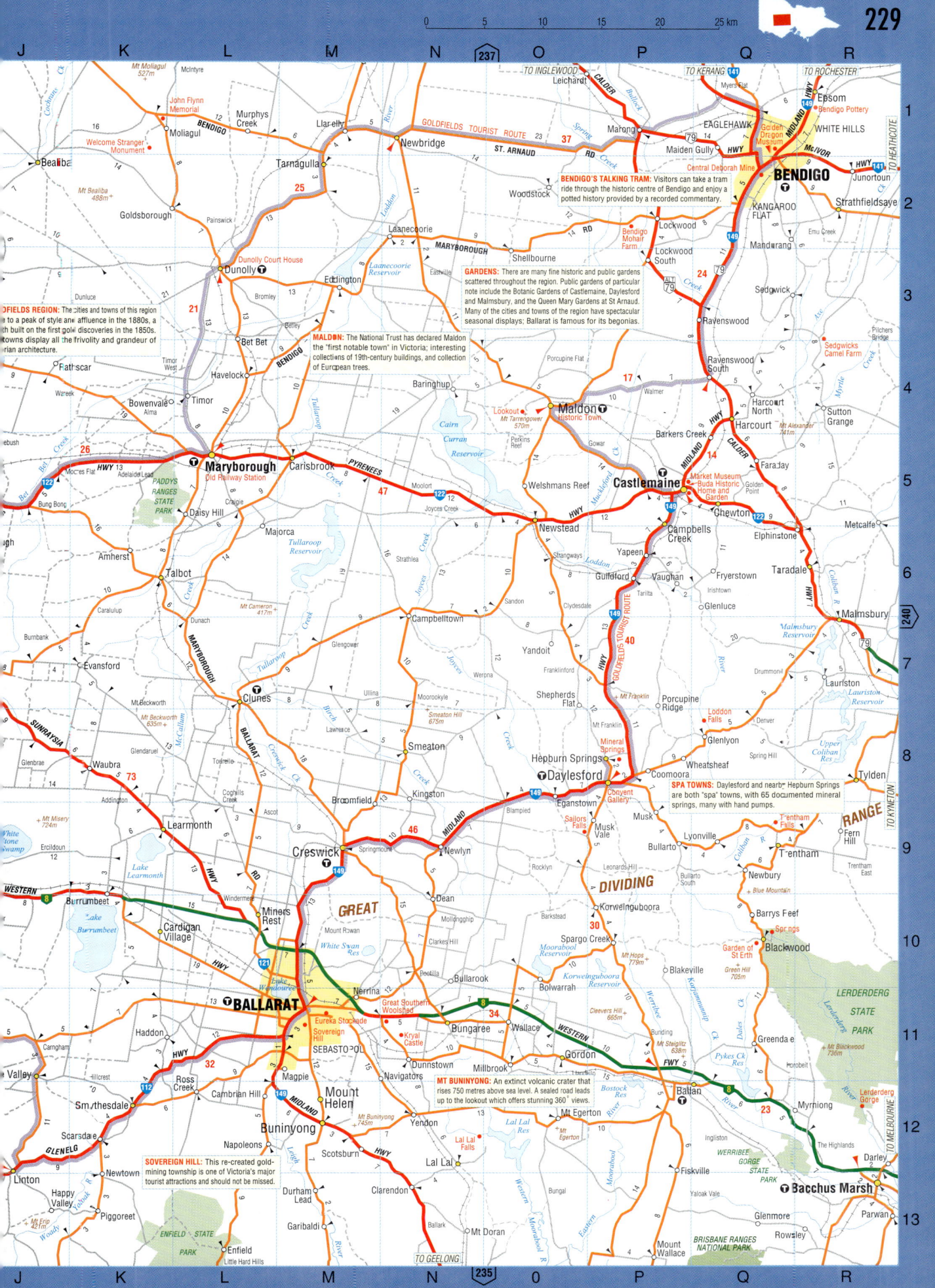

J K L M N O P Q R

1 2 3 4 5 6 7 8 9 10 11 12 13

TO INGLEWOOD
TO KERANG
TO ROCHESTER
TO HEATHCOTE

Leichardt
Myers Flat
Epsom
CALDER
Bendigo Pottery
Bullock
EAGLEHAWK
WHITE HILLS
Mt Moliagul 527m
John Flynn Memorial
McIntyre
Murphys Creek
Llanelly
GOLDFIELDS TOURIST ROUTE
23
37
Marong
Golden Dragon Museum
Moliagul
BENDIGO
Welcome Stranger Monument
Newbridge
ST. ARNAUD
Maiden Gully
HWY
Junortoun
Strathfieldsaye
Bealiba
Mt Bealiba 488m
Goldsborough
Tarnagulla
25
Woodstock
Central Deborah Mine
KANGAROO FLAT
Painswick
Laanecoorie
MARYBOROUGH
RD
Lockwood
Mandurang
Dunolly Court House
Shellbourne
Bendigo Mohair Farm
Lockwood South
24
79
Sedgwick
Fatt scar
21
Dunolly
Eddington
Bromley
Bet Bet
Ravenswood
Sedgwicks Camel Farm
Wareek
Timor West
BENDIGO
Ravenswood South
Harcourt North
Sutton Grange
Bowenvale
Timor
Havelock
Baringhup
17
Walmer
Harcourt
Mt Alexander 741m
Faraday
26
HWY 13
Maryborough Old Railway Station
Carisbrook
PYRENEES
Maldon Historic Town
Barkers Creek
MIDLAND
CALDER
122
Moores Flat
Bung Bong
PADDYS RANGES STATE PARK
Daisy Hill
Craigie
Moolort
122
12
Castlemaine
Market Museum Buda Historic Home and Garden
Golden Point
Metcalfe
Amherst
Majorca
Newstead
Chewton
122
Elphinstone
Talbot
Dunach
Campbelltown
Yandoit
Campbells Creek
Yapeen
Taradale
Burnbank
Evansford
Clunes
Smeaton
Shepherds Flat
Hepburn Springs
Mineral Springs
Glenlyon
Tylden
Waubra
73
Learmonth
Creswick
46
MIDLAND
Daylesford
Musk Vale
Trentham
RANGE
Burrumbeet
Miners Rest
Dean
DIVIDING
Spargo Creek
30
Blackwood
BALLARAT
Bungaree
34
WESTERN
Gordon
Ballan
23
Bacchus Marsh

241 TO WANGARATTA

GLENROWAN — MYRTLEFORD

TO WANGARATTA

Winton North

Ned Kelly Memorial Museum

Glenrowan

Lake Mokoan

Oxley

Milawa

Markwood

Everton

Ovens

Bowman

OVENS

25

John Gehrig Wines

Brown Brothers Vineyard

Skehan

Markwood Estate Vineyard

Whorouly

Winton Motor Raceway

Winton

Glenrowan West

Docker

Bobinawarrah

Whorouly South

Whorouly East

Merrian

MIDLAND HWY

Broken

149

Benalla

HUME 31

Greta West

Greta

Byrne

Moyhu

Meadow Creek

Carboor

Merriang South

Cropper Creek

WANGARATTA

King River

Hurdle Creek

Meadow Creek

Claremont

Carboor Upper

Buffalo River

TO EUROA

REEF HILLS PARK

Exclusion Zone

Fruit Fly

Holland

Lurg

Lurg Upper

Hansonville

Angleside

Dwyer

Edi

WHITFIELD

Edi Upper

Karn

Kelfeera

Greta South

Fifteen Mile School

Ryans Creek

King Valley

Black Range

MIDLAND HWY

Mallum

Molyullah

Ryans Creek

Middle Creek

Myrrhee

Whitfield

BLACK RANGE

Dandongadale

TOURIST INFORMATION:
Bright (Gavan St)
Mansfield (Maroondah Hwy)
Mount Beauty (Kiewa Valley Hwy)
Myrtleford (29-31 Clyde St)

Swanpool

Lima

Moorngag

153

64

Samaria

Wrightley

Cheshunt

Whitlands

Powers Lookout

Paradise Falls

Typo

Lima East

Mt View

Mt Warrick 944m

ALPINE

WARNINGS: When driving, care should be taken at all times in the Mountain areas. During the winter months frost and snow can make driving conditions hazardous. It is compulsory to carry chains in designated sections of the Victorian Alps between 1 June and 10 October. Use an anti-freeze compound in the car's radiator.
When skiing, if you get lost, stay where you are and take shelter behind trees or rocks, or dig a snow cave. Stand crossed skis where they can be seen by approaching searchers. Note that the weather in alpine areas can change rapidly, so be prepared. Cross-country skiers and bushwalkers should advise someone of intended route and expected return time.

Tallangatook

MOUNT SAMARIA STATE PARK

Mt Samaria 950m

Lima South

Lake Nillahcootie

WHITFIELD RD

Lake William Hovell

NATIONAL

Mt Typo

Bennies

153

Mt Strathbogie 1007m

Barjarg

Bridge Creek

Toombullup

Tolmie

Mahaikah

MANSFIELD

Table Top

Mt Cobbler 1628m

Lake Co

PARK

SNOWY

Barjarg

MIDLAND HWY LINK

153

Nillahcootie

ALT 153

HWY

Barwite

Bobs Creek

NATIONAL

TO YEA

153

MAROONDAH HWY

Maindample

ALT 153

Ford

Mansfield

Delatite Winery

164

Merrijig

Sawmill Settlement

Mirimbah

The Pinnacle

Mt Stirling 1745m

Ski Area

Lake Eildon

FRASER NP

EILDON STATE PARK

BLUE RANGE

MANSFIELD

Piries

Boorolite

MT BULLER

164 RD

47

Mt Timbertop

Mt Buller 1804m

Mt Buller Alpine Village

Mt Koonika

Mt Buggery

Mt Thorn

Mt Enterprise

Goughs Bay

WOODS POINT RD

37

Macs Cove

Howqua

Mt Lovick

Track

TO ALEXANDRA

Eildon

Snobs Creek

LAKE EILDON: The lake's sheltered waters are ideal for fishing, boating and water skiing. Houseboat holidays are popular, and regular and chartered cruises are available. The surrounding State Park has established walking tracks, some offering panoramic views of the Victorian Alps.

Howqua

Jamieson

Mt Darling

The Bluff

The Governor

Australian Alps

Mt McDonald 1625m

Jamieson River

241

TO WANGARATTA

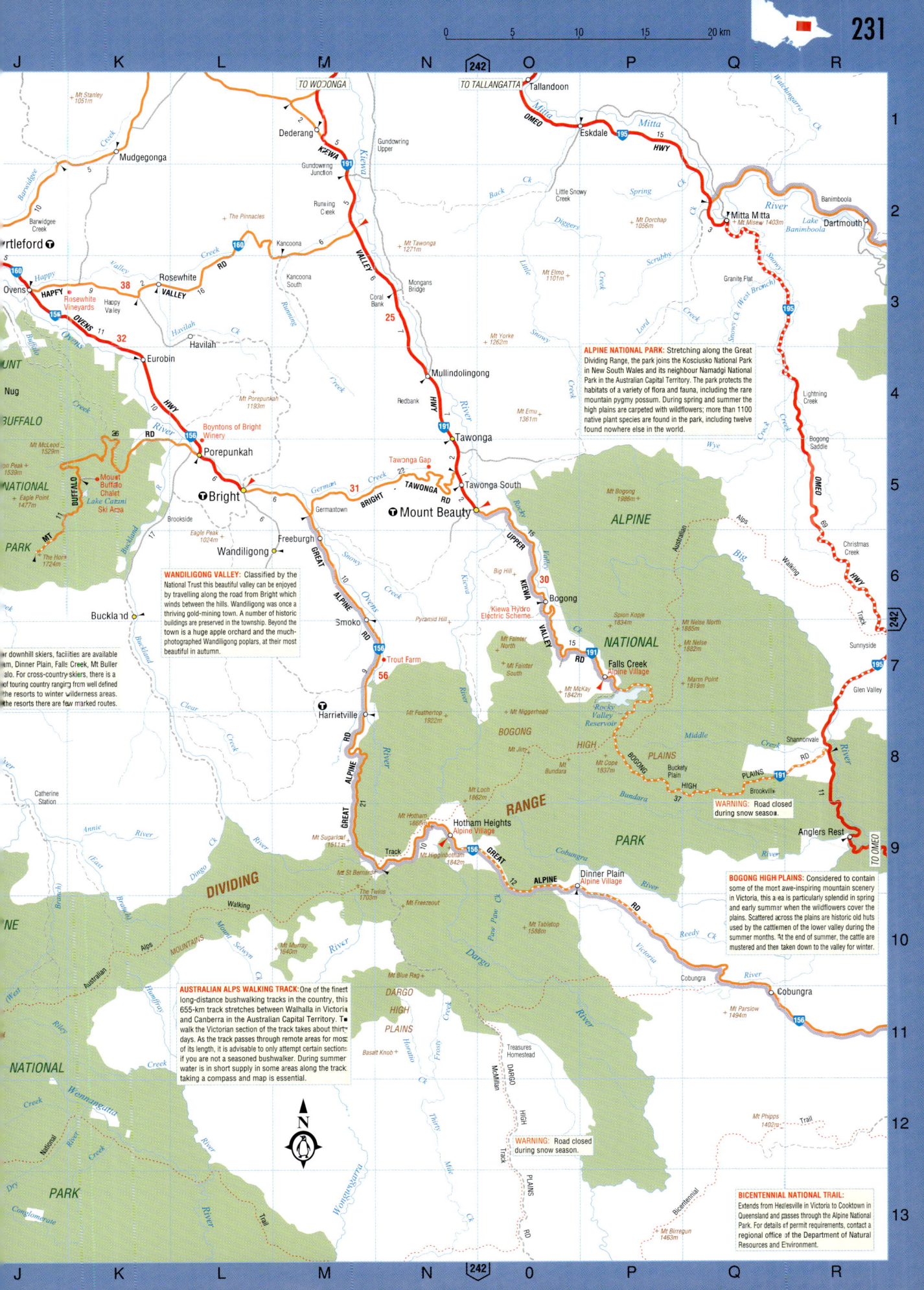

ALPINE NATIONAL PARK: Stretching along the Great Dividing Range, the park joins the Kosciusko National Park in New South Wales and its neighbour Namadgi National Park in the Australian Capital Territory. The park protects the habitats of a variety of flora and fauna, including the rare mountain pygmy possum. During spring and summer the high plains are carpeted with wildflowers; more than 1100 native plant species are found in the park, including twelve found nowhere else in the world.

WANDILIGONG VALLEY: Classified by the National Trust this beautiful valley can be enjoyed by travelling along the road from Bright which winds between the hills. Wandiligong was once a thriving gold-mining town. A number of historic buildings are preserved in the township. Beyond the town is a huge apple orchard and the much-photographed Wandiligong poplars, at their most beautiful in autumn.

WARNING: Road closed during snow season.

BOGONG HIGH PLAINS: Considered to contain some of the most awe-inspiring mountain scenery in Victoria, this area is particularly splendid in spring and early summer when the wildflowers cover the plains. Scattered across the plains are historic old huts used by the cattlemen of the lower valley during the summer months. At the end of summer, the cattle are mustered and then taken down to the valley for winter.

AUSTRALIAN ALPS WALKING TRACK: One of the finest long-distance bushwalking tracks in the country, this 655-km track stretches between Walhalla in Victoria and Canberra in the Australian Capital Territory. To walk the Victorian section of the track takes about thirty days. As the track passes through remote areas for most of its length, it is advisable to only attempt certain sections if you are not a seasoned bushwalker. During summer water is in short supply in some areas along the track; taking a compass and map is essential.

WARNING: Road closed during snow season.

BICENTENNIAL NATIONAL TRAIL: Extends from Healesville in Victoria to Cooktown in Queensland and passes through the Alpine National Park. For details of permit requirements, contact a regional office of the Department of Natural Resources and Environment.

Map grid columns: A B C D E F G H I
Map grid rows: 1–13

Tylden, Newham, Hanging Rock, Rochford, Romsey, Bylands, Wandong, Heathcote Junction, Flowerdale, Mt Caroline 515m, Break O Day, Murrindindi, Taggerty, Rubicon, EILDON STATE PARK, Jam

Woodend, Mt Macedon 1013m, Mount Macedon, Darraweit Guim, Upper Plenty, Hazeldene, Mt Mitchell 957m, Glenburn, MAROONDAH HWY, Buxton, TORBRECK RANGE, ROYSTON STATE PARK, BLUE RANGE

Macedon, New Gisborne, Riddells Creek, Clarkefield, Monegeetta, Wallan, Mt Disappointment 793m, Kinglake West, Pheasant Creek, KINGLAKE NATIONAL PARK, Glenburn, Mt Klondyke 869m, Toolangi, St Fillans, Narbethong, Mt Juliet 1105m, Marysville, Lake Mountain 1470m Ski Area, Mt Duffy 1028m

Bullengarook East, Gisborne, LERDERDERG STATE PARK, Rosslynne Res, Toolern Vale, Bulla, Yuroke, Craigieburn, Yan Yean, Mernda, Cottles Bridge, Smiths Gully, St Andrews, Steels Creek, Dixons Creek, Black Spur, YARRA RANGES NATIONAL PARK, Mt Strickland 1219m, Upper Yarra Reservoir, DIVI

Lerderderg Gorge, Bacchus Marsh, Diggers Rest, Melton, Rockbank, Organ Pipes NP, Woodlands Historic Park, Thomastown, Warrandyte State Park, Lilydale, Coldstream, Woori Yallock, Millgrove, Warburton, McMahons Creek, GREAT, For more detail on Yarra Valley Region see page 222, Mt Horn 1134m

Balliang East, Parwan, Exford, Footscray, Melbourne, Ringwood, Wandin North, Seville, Yallock, Silvan, Launching Place, Yarra Junction, Gladysdale, Three Bridges, Powelltown, La Trobe, Icy Creek

Rowsley, Tarneit, Altona, Oakleigh, Brighton, Dandenong, Olinda, Monbulk, Macclesfield, DANDENONG RANGES, NP, Nangana, Avonsleigh, Hoddles Creek, Noojee

Little River, Werribee, Point Cook, For more detail on Melbourne Region see pages 218 & 219, Churchill NP, Lysterfield Lake Park, Belgrave, Emerald, Cockatoo, Gembrook, BUNYIP STATE PARK, BLACK SNAKE RANGE, GEMBROOK PARK, Mt Towt 353m, Labertouche, Tarago Reservoir, Neerim, Neerim South

Lara, Port Phillip, Dandenong, Cardinia Reservoir, Upper Beaconsfield, Berwick, Beaconsfield, Nar Nar Goon, Pakenham, PRINCES FWY, Tynong, Garfield, Bunyip, Longwarry, Drouin, Warragul, Buln Buln, Shady Creek, Willi

Geelong, Portarlington, Bellarine, Indented Head, St Leonards, Frankston, Baxter, Pearcedale, Cranbourne, Cardinia, Cora Lynn, Bayles, Modella, Ripplebrook, Drouin South, Darnum, Nilma, Yarrag, Trafa

Clifton Springs, Drysdale, Marshall, Leopold, Ocean Grove, Marcus Hill, Queenscliff, Mornington, Mount Martha, Somerville, Warneet, Tooradin, Koo-wee-rup, Lang Lang, Heath Hill, Athlone, Mt Worth 518m, Ellinbank, Mt Worth State Park, Allambee, Chilcern

Breamlea, Barwon Heads, Pt Lonsdale, Point Nepean, Portsea, Sorrento, Dromana, Red Hill, Bittern, Tyabb, Hastings, Western Port, FRENCH ISLAND STATE PARK, FRENCH ISLAND, Crib Point, Stony Point, Tankerton, Grantville, Nyora, Poowong, Strzelecki, Mt Eccles, Hallston

Rye, Safety Beach, Balnarring, Somers, Shoreham, Flinders, Ventnor, Cowes, Rhyll, Corinella, Kernot, Glen Forbes, Korumburra, Jumbunna, Ruby, Coal Creek Historical Village, SOUTH GIPPSLAND, Wooreen, Mornington Peninsula, MORNINGTON PENINSULA NATIONAL PARK

For more detail on Mornington Peninsula see pages 220 & 221, Cape Schanck, The Nobbies, Penguin Parade, Newhaven, Churchill Island, Bass, Woolamai, Archies Creek, Kongwak, Leongatha, Leongatha South, Outtrim, Koonwarra, Meeniyan, PHILLIP ISLAND, Cape Woolamai, San Remo, Kilcunda, Dalyston, Dudley, BASS, Pound Creek, Tarwin, Stony Creek, Buffalo, Fish Creek

Wonthaggi, State Coal Mine, Inverloch, Cape Paterson, Cape Paterson, BUNURONG MARINE PARK, Venus Bay, Venus Bay, Tarwin Lower, Tarwin Meadows, Waratah North, Mt Liptrap 171m, Walkerville, Waratah Bay, Walkerville South, Cape Liptrap

BASS STRAIT

Calder Fwy, Western Fwy, Hume Fwy, Princes Fwy, Nepean Hwy, South Gippsland Hwy, Bass Hwy

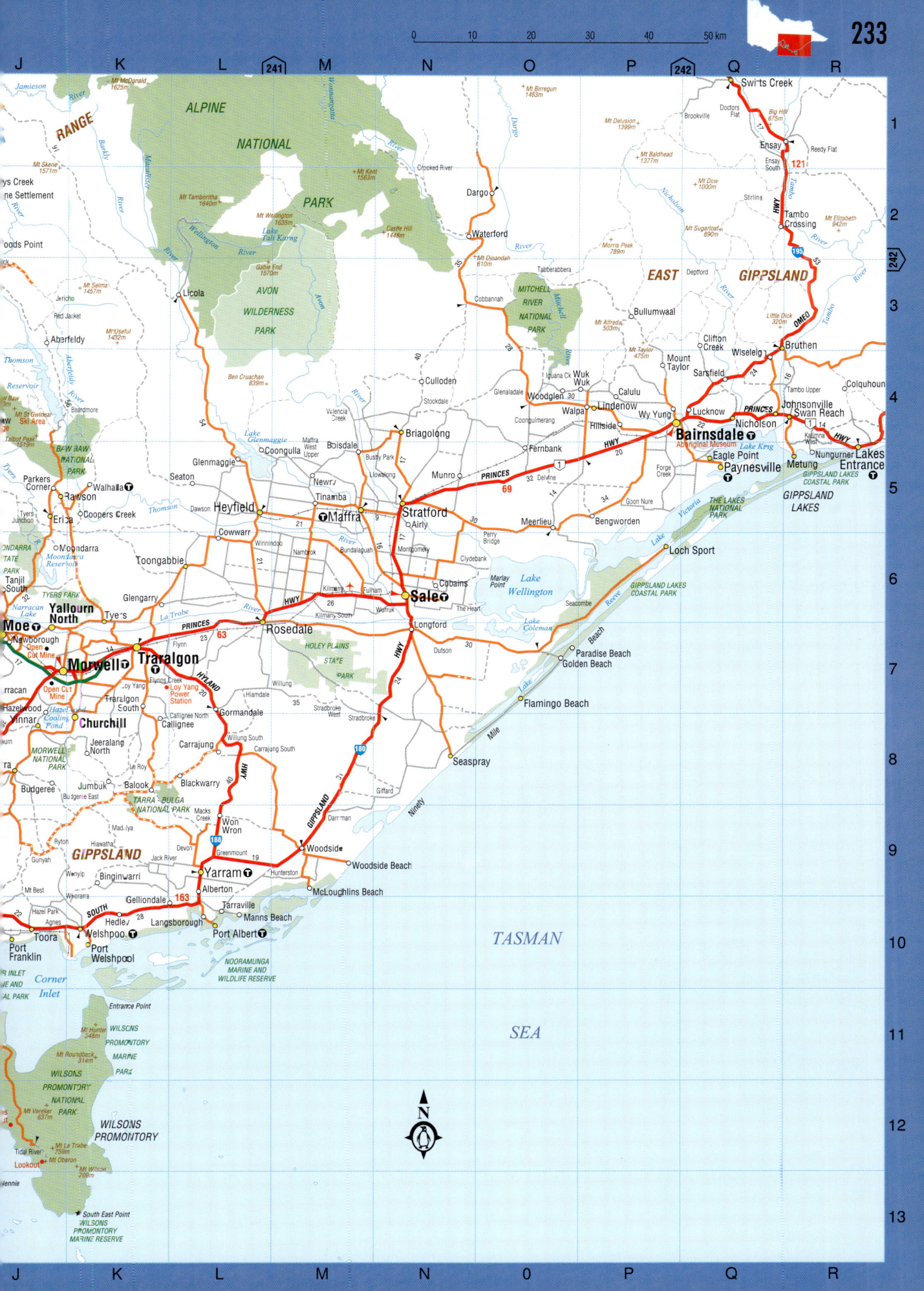

Joanna
Langkoop
White Lake
Lake Kanagulk
River
BLACK RANGE STATE PARK
Zumsteins
MacKenzie Falls
Mt Difficult Lookout
Wartook Res
Wrattonbully
Kadnook
Connewirricoo
21
Harrow
Moree
107
Glenisla
Aboriginal Paintings
Halls Gap
Pomona
Mt Wil
Comaum
Poolaijelo
Powers Creek
Culla
29
Balmoral
65
GRAMPIANS
Lake Bellfield
Mt W
116
DERGHOLM
Chetwynd
STATE
Pigeon Ponds
Englefield
Glendinning
Woohlpooer
Rocklands Reservoir
Caddens Flat
Moora Moora Reservoir
NATIONAL
THE
Cherrypool River
Tarrayoukyan
Coojar
Vasey
Gatum
Mooralla
VICTORIA RANGE
GRAMPIANS
PARK
Penola
Dorodong
Dergholm
PARK
37
Nareen
Gringegalgona
Karabeal
SERRA
Mirranatwa
Rose neath
Brimboal
Konong Wootong North
Brit Brit
Mt Dundas 466m
Mt Machersey 352m
Mt Abrupt 826m
Victoria Valley
Mt Nelson 838m
Warrock Homestead
33
Wando Bridge
Wando Vale
Konong Wootong
Cavendish
Bryan Swamp
Victoria Point
30
Dunkeld
Glenthompson
GL
Lake Mundi
Dunrobin
Carapook
Wootong Vale
Gritjurk
Melville Forest
Bulart
Kyup
Moutajup
18
Casterton
29
Wannon
Kanawalla
Strathkellar
Warrayure
Lake Linlithgow
Lake Repose
Heathfield
Sandford
Paschendale
Hilgay
Henty
32
Tahara Bridge
Tarrenlea
34
Wannon
Bochara
Hamilton
112
Lake Bullrush
Strathdownie
GLENELG 112
Merino
Tahara
DISTRICT
Grassdale
Yulecart
Tarrington
Lake Kennedy
Croxton East
37
Mil Lel
Lindsay
24
River
WESTERN
Digby
25
Yatchaw
Tabor
HAMILTON
Penshurst
Mt Rouse 370m
Glenburnie
Ardno
Myaring
River
107
86
Buckleys Swamp
Gazette
88
106
Yahl
Caroline
PRINCES
32
Purnim
Marp
Stokes
38
Branxholme
Mt Napier 439m
Mt Napier STATE PARK
Warrabrook
27
Caramut
Donovans Landing
Glenelg
Wanwin
Drik Drik
Crawford
Hotspur
Wallacedale
Byaduk North
Byaduk
Minhamite
Princess Margaret Rose Caves
LOWER GLENELG NATIONAL PARK
Dartmoor
Winnap
Greenwald
Condah
Knebsworth
MacArthur
Hawkesdale
Nelson
Mumbannar
River
26
Lyons
100
41
Myamyn
26
River
River
Oxbow Lake
Fitzroy
Mt Van Dyke 183m
Milltown
MOUNT ECCLES NP
Lake Condah
Woolsthorpe
DISCOVERY BAY
19
Surrey
Drumborg
HENTY HWY
17
Homerton
Bessiebelle
32
Broadwater
Dunmore
49
Winslow
COASTAL PARK
Lake Bung Bung
Kentbruck
Mt Kincaid 197m
107
Heywood
Orford
Warrong
Willatook
40
Southern Cross
Grassme
Discovery Bay
Mt Richmond
53
Mt Richmond 229m
Gorae West
Gorae
Heathmere
Tyrendarra
St Helens
Kirkstall
Koroit
Mailor's Flat
MT RICHMOND NATIONAL PARK
27
Narrawong
PRINCES
Crossley
Tower Hill
Illowa
Wang
Tarragal
Cashmore
Bolwarra
25
Tyrendarra East
Codrington
1
Yambuk
Toolong
Rosebrook
28
Killarney
Tower Hill
Bushfield
Dennington
Petrified Forest & Blowholes
Cape Duquesne
Trewalla
Mt Chaucer 140m
Portland
96
16
Shaw River
Aringa
21
Rosebrook
Port Fairy
Warrnambool
PRINCES
Al
Cape Bridgewater
Cape Bridgewater
Danger Point
Cape Sir William Grant
Portland Bay
Lady Julia Percy Island
Moyne River
Cape Nelson
CAPE NELSON STATE PARK
N

SOUTHERN   OCEAN

BASS STRAIT

Grid columns: J K L M N O P Q R
Grid rows: 1–13

Major towns and features:

Great Western, Armstrong, Ararat, Buangor, Beaufort, Crowlands, Elmhurst, Amphitheatre, Lexton, Lamplough, Amherst, Talbot, Daisy Hill, Majorca, Campbelltown, Clunes, Creswick, Smeaton, Hepburn Springs, Daylesford, Trentham, Newbury, Woodend, Kyneton, Malmsbury, Taradale, Langley, Carlsruhe, Tylden

BALLARAT, Miners Rest, Cardigan Village, Burrumbeet, Learmonth, Waubra, Broomfield, Kingston, Newlyn, Dean, Bullarto, Spargo Creek, Blackwood, Bullengarook East, Greendale, Myrniong, Bacchus Marsh, Parwan

Skipton, Smythesdale, Scarsdale, Linton, Happy Valley, Newtown, Buninyong, Napoleons, Scotsburn, Mt Helen, Dunnstown, Bungaree, Wallace, Gordon, Ballan, Millbrook, Navigators, Bolwarrah

Streatham, Westmere, Lake Bolac, Derrinallum, Lismore, Mannibadar, Cape Clear, Piggoreet, Illabarook, Dereel, Grenville, Elaine, Meredith, Steiglitz, Sheoaks, Maude, Anakie, Lethbridge, Little River, Lara

Berrybank, Cressy, Shelford, Teesdale, Bannockbank, Inverleigh, Bannockburn, Batesford, Fyansford, GEELONG, Leopold, Ocean Grove

Darlington, Camperdown, Terang, Cobden, Noorat, Boorcan, Pomborneit, Beeac, Warrion, Alvie, Coragulac, Colac, Elliminyt, Birregurra, Winchelsea, Moriac, Mount Moriac, Freshwater Creek, Bellbrae, Torquay, Breamlea, Barwon Heads, Marshall

Swan Marsh, Stoneyford, Larpent, Yeodene, Barwon Downs, Gerangamete, Forrest, Deans Marsh, Bambra, Benwerrin, Eastern View, Aireys Inlet, Fairhaven, Anglesea

Timboon, Simpson, Gellibrand, Carlisle River, Beech Forest, Weeaproinah, Lorne, Separation Creek, Wye River, Kennett River

Peterborough, Port Campbell, London Bridge, The Arch, Loch Ard Gorge, The Twelve Apostles, Gibson Steps, Princetown, Lavers Hill, Johanna, Apollo Bay, Marengo, Skenes Creek, Cape Patton, Cape Otway

National Parks: LANGI-GHIRAN STATE PARK, MT BUANGOR STATE PARK, ENFIELD STATE PARK, BRISBANE RANGES NATIONAL PARK, WERRIBEE GORGE STATE PARK, LERDERDERG STATE PARK, ANGAHOOK LORNE STATE PARK, OTWAY NATIONAL PARK, PORT CAMPBELL NATIONAL PARK, CARLISLE STATE PARK, MELBA GULLY STATE PARK, STEIGLITZ PARK

Lakes: Lake Burrumbeet, Lake Goldsmith, Lake Wongan, Lake Bolac, Lake McLaren, Lake Learmonth, Lake Corangamite, Lake Colongulac, Lake Gnarpurt, Lake Martin, Lake Murdeduke, Lake Weering, Lake Connewarre

Highways/routes: WESTERN HWY, PYRENEES HWY, SUNRAYSIA HWY, MIDLAND HWY, GLENELG HWY, HAMILTON HWY, PRINCES HWY, GREAT OCEAN RD, CALDER HWY, PRINCES FWY

For more detail on Goldfields Region see pages 228 & 229
For more detail on Ballarat see page 227
For more detail on Geelong Region see page 225
For more detail on Otway Region see page 223

Scale: 0 10 20 30 40 50 km

A B C D E F G H I

1 2 3 4 5 6 7 8 9 10 11 12 13

BIG DESERT

WYPERFELD

NATIONAL

PARK

WIMMERA

SCORPION SPRINGS PARK

BIG DESERT WILDERNESS PARK

NGARKAT CP

Mt Shaugh 184m

MOUNT SHAUGH CP

LAKE ALBACUTYA PARK

Lake Albacutya

Ross Lake

Kurnbrunin

Albacutya

Peila

Yaapeet

Baring

Willa

Yarto

Nypo

Hopetoun West

Burroin

Dattuck

Wathe

Gama

Speed

Turriff

Turriff West

Turriff East

Lascelles

SUNRAYSIA

Hopetoun

Lake Coorong

Goyura

Nyallo

Roseberry

Hopevale

Rainbow

Kenmare

Brentwood

Werrap

Beulah West

Beulah East

Galaquil

Galaqui East

Perenna

Lake Hindmarsh

Lake Hindmarsh

Ellam

Dalmalee

Willenabrina

Brim

Lah

Baker

Netherby

Lorquon West

Detpa

Angip

Yellangip

Crymelon

Batchica

HWY

Yanac

Lorquon

Ni Ni

Woorak West

Balrootan North

Jeparit

Peppers Plains

Tarranyurk

Aubrey

Cannum

Warracknabeal

Challum

Mellis

Broughton

Yanac South

Propodollah

Woorak

Allanby

Glenlee

Gerang Gerung

Antwerp

Katyil

Wallup

Ailsa

Sheep Hills

Nulla

Telopea Downs

Yearinga

Sandsmere

Yarrock

Bleak House

Boyeo

Nhill

Tarranginnie

Salisbury

Kiata

Arkona

Dart Dart

Murra Warra

Kellalac

Minyip

Dinyarrak

Diapur

WESTERN

Kaniva

Miram

Lawloit

Winiam

BORUNG

Blackheath

Byrneville

Kewell

Coromby

Wolseley

Serviceton

Lillimur

Yanipy

Winiam East

Dimboola

Wail

HENTY

Murtoa

Ru

Custon

Lillimur South

Miram South

Kinimakatka

Pimpinio

Dahlen

Jung

Bangham

BANGHAM CP

LITTLE

DESERT

NATIONAL

PARK

Polkammet

Dooen

Longerenong

Ashe

Lemon Springs

Grass Flat

Lake Wyn Wyn

Quantong

Vectis

Drung Drung

Marma

Frances

Minimay

Peronne

Mortat

Goroke

Gymbowen

Duffholme

Mitre

Mitre Lake

Arapiles

Natimuk

Horsham

Drung Drung South

Neuarpurr

Morea

Dopewora

MT ARAPILES TOOAN STATE PARK

Mt Arapiles 370m

Todan

Lower Norton

Haven

McKenzie Creek

Green Lake

Pine Lake

Taylors Lake

Booroopki

Kangawall

Noradjuha

WESTERN

Wimmera

Kybybolite

Tallageira

Bringalbert

Ozenkadnook

Karnak

Wonwondah North

Wonwondah East

Flat Rock Caves

Dadswells Bridge

DIFFICULT RANGE

Patyah

Awonga

Ullswater

Clear Lake

Jallumba

Nurrabiel

Lah-Arum

Mt Difficult 810m

Mt Dif Looko

Hynam

Koppamurra

Apsley

Lake Wallace

WIMMERA

Charam

Miga Lake

Wombelano

North Lake

Toolondo

Connangorach

Mockinya

Heathvale

Zumsteins

MacKenzie Falls

Wartook Reservoir

Mt Zero

Langkoop

Edenhope

Douglas

White Lake

Lake Kanagulk

Toolondo Reservoir

Mt Talbot 320m

THE BLACK RANGE

Aboriginal Paintings

Halls Gap

GRAMPIANS

Wrattonbully

Kadnook

Harrow

Moree

BLACK RANGE STATE PARK

Glenisla

Cave of Fishes

Lake Bellfield

Moora Moora Reservoir

Joanna

Powers Creek

Connewirricoo

Culla

Pigeon Ponds

Balmoral

Cave of Hands

NATIONAL

Comaum

Poolaijelo

DERGHOLM STATE PARK

Chetwynd

Moree

Tarrayoukyan

Coojar

Englefield

Glendinning

Caddens Flat

Rocklands Reservoir

Woohlpooer

VICTORIA RANGE

PARK

Coonawarra

Glenelg

Chetwynd River

Glenelg River

River

SOUTH AUSTRALIA

VICTORIA

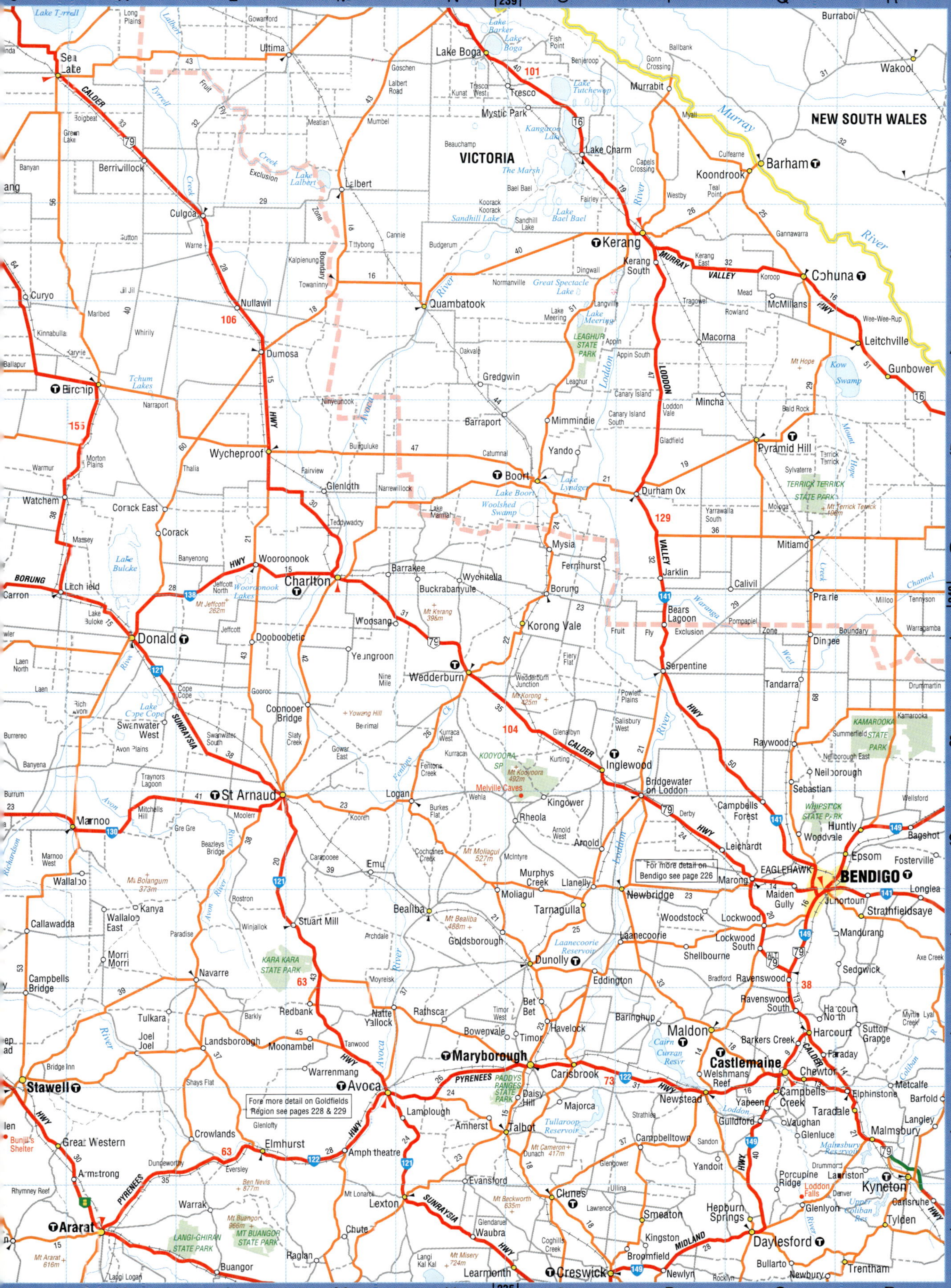

NEW SOUTH WALES

VICTORIA

0 10 20 30 40 50 km

Major towns and places:

Sea Lake, Ultima, Lake Boga, Lake Barker, Lake Boga, Fish Point, Burraboi, Wakool, Barham, Koondrook, Cohuna, Leitchville, Gunbower, Pyramid Hill, Kerang, Boort, Durham Ox, Mitiamo, Terrick Terrick State Park, Quambatook, Dumosa, Nullawil, Birchip, Wycheproof, Charlton, Donald, Wooroonook, Korong Vale, Wedderburn, Serpentine, Bears Lagoon, Dingee, Prairie, Tandarra, Raywood, Huntly, Epsom, Bagshot, Bendigo, Eaglehawk, Inglewood, Bridgewater on Loddon, Newbridge, Marong, Maiden Gully, Strathfieldsaye, Longlea, St Arnaud, Marnoo, Stawell, Navarre, Landsborough, Avoca, Redbank, Maryborough, Dunolly, Tarnagulla, Laanecoorie, Lockwood, Ravenswood, Harcourt, Maldon, Castlemaine, Chewton, Carisbrook, Newstead, Guildford, Taradale, Malmsbury, Kyneton, Ararat, Great Western, Elmhurst, Lexton, Clunes, Smeaton, Hepburn Springs, Daylesford, Trentham, Creswick, Learmonth, Kingston, Newbury

Kara Kara State Park, Langi-Ghiran State Park, Mt Buangor State Park, Kamarooka State Park, Whipstick State Park, Paddys Ranges State Park

Murray River, Loddon River, Avon River, Richardson River

Calder Hwy, Borung Hwy, Sunraysia Hwy, Pyrenees Hwy, Midland Hwy, Loddon Valley Hwy, Murray Valley Hwy

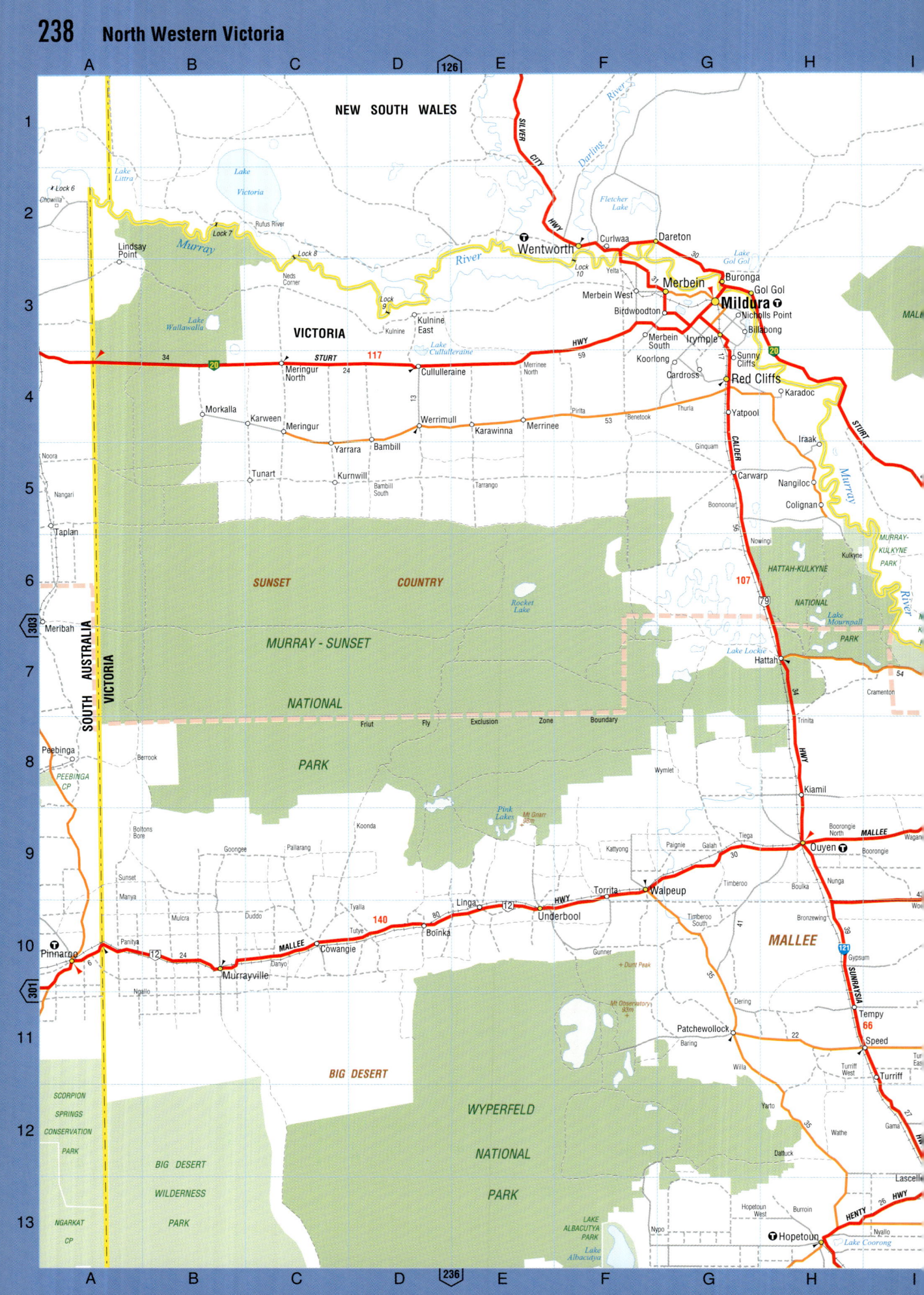

NEW SOUTH WALES

VICTORIA

Lindsay
Point

Lock 6
Chowilla

Lake
Littra

Lake
Victoria

Murray

Lock 7

Lock 8

Neds
Corner

Rufus River

Lock 9

Kulnine
East

Kulnine

Lake
Wallawalla

Lake
Cullulleraine

Wentworth

Curlwaa

Dareton

Lake
Gol Gol

Fletcher
Lake

SILVER CITY HWY

Darling River

Yelta

Lock 10

Merbein

Merbein West

Birdwoodton

Merbein
South

Buronga

Gol Gol

Mildura

Nicholls Point

Billabong

Irymple

HWY

STURT 117

Meringur
North

24

Cullulleraine

Merbein North

59

Koorlong

Cardross

Sunny
Cliffs

Red Cliffs

Karadoc

Morkalla

Karween

Meringur

Werrimull

Karawinna

Merrinee

Pirlta

Benetook

Thurla

Yatpool

Iraak

Murray

Yarrara

Bambill

13

53

Ginquam

Tunart

Kurnwill

Bambill
South

Tarrango

Boonoonar

Carwarp

Nangiloc

Colignan

SUNSET COUNTRY

Rocket
Lake

56

Nowingi

107

HATTAH-KULKYNE

Kulkyne

MURRAY-
KULKYNE
PARK

Meribah

303

MURRAY - SUNSET

NATIONAL

Lake
Mournpall

79

NATIONAL

PARK

Lake Lockie

Hattah

54

Cramenton

Friut Fly Exclusion Zone Boundary

Trinita

Peebinga

Berrook

Peebinga
CP

PARK

Pink
Lakes

Mt Gnarr
38m

Wymlet

HWY

Kiamil

Taplan

Boltons
Bore

Goongee

Pallarang

Koonda

Kattyong

Paignie

Galah

Tiega

Boorongie
North

Ouyen

Boorongie

MALLEE

Wagant

Sunset

Manya

Mulcra

Duddo

Tyalla

Linga

HWY 12

Underbool

Torrita

Walpeup

Timberoo

Boulka

Nunga

Woo

Murrayville

Ngallo

Panitya

12 24

Danyo

Cowangie

MALLEE

Boinka

80

Tutye

140

Gunner

Dunt Peak

Timberoo
South

41

Bronzewing

MALLEE

Dering

39

121

SUNRAYSIA

Gypsum

Tempy

66

Pinnaroo

301

6

35

Mt Observatory
93m

Patchewollock

Baring

Willa

22

Speed

Turriff
West

Turriff

BIG DESERT

WYPERFELD

NATIONAL

PARK

Yarto

Wathe

35

Dattuck

Gama

27

SCORPION

SPRINGS

CONSERVATION

PARK

BIG DESERT

WILDERNESS

PARK

Hopetoun
West

Burroin

HENTY HWY

NGARKAT
CP

Lake
Albacutya
Park

Lake
Albacutya

Nypo

Hopetoun

Lake Coorong

Nyallo

Lascell

26

SOUTH AUSTRALIA

VICTORIA

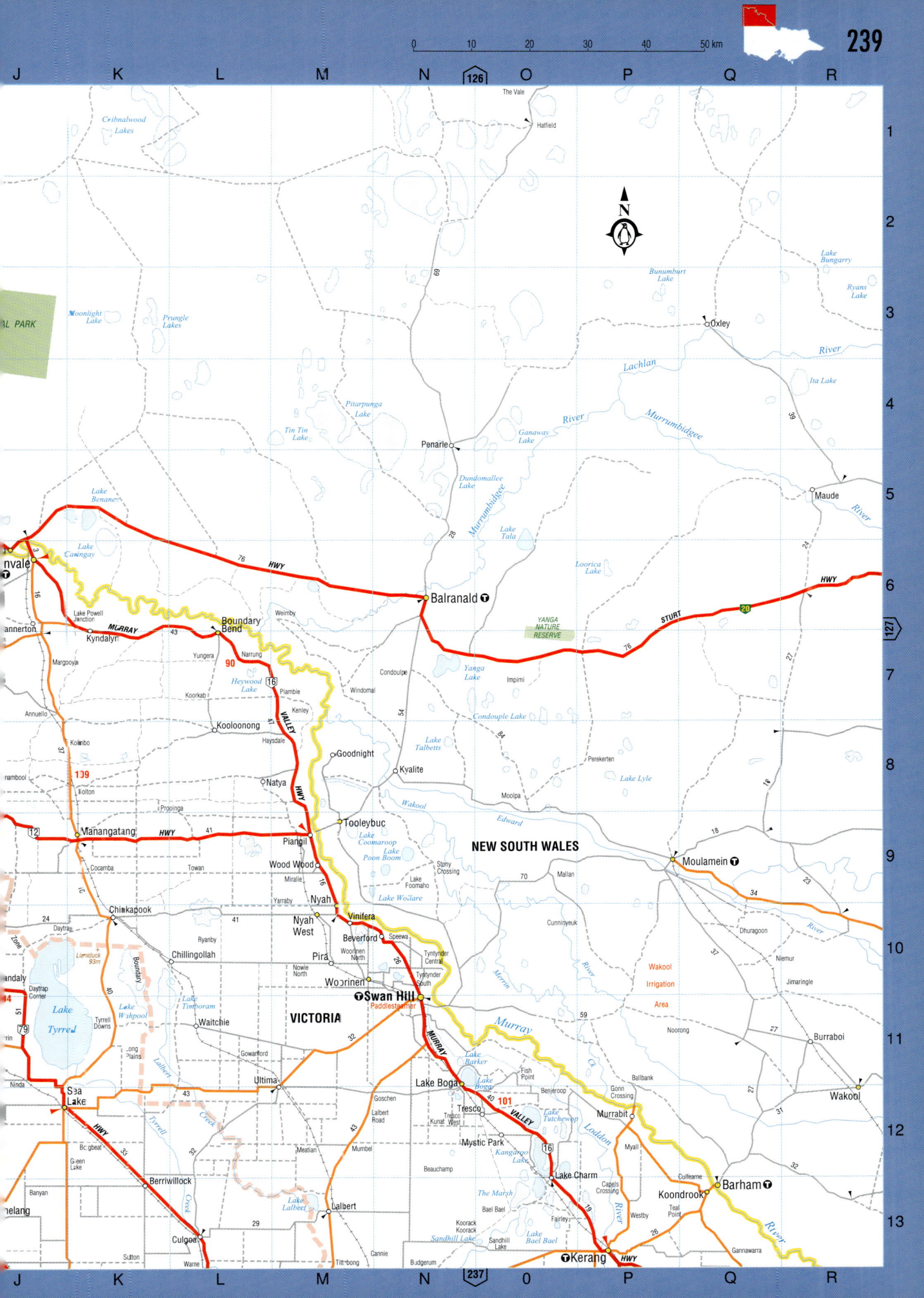

NEW SOUTH WALES

VICTORIA

BARMAH STATE PARK

Lake Charm
Fairley
Kerang
Kerang South
Koondrook
Barham
Culfearne
Caldwell
Deniboota Irrigation Area
Blighty
RIVERINA
Tocum

Cohuna
McMillans
Koroop
Wee-Wee-Rup
Leitchville
Gunbower
Bunnaloo
Womboota
Mathoura
Gulpa
Picola North
Picola
Yalca North
Ulpna
Strathmerton
Bearii
Katur

Murray River
Macorna
Mincha
Pyramid Hill
Torrumbarry
Patho
Wharparilla North
Barnes
Barmah
Narioka
Kanyapella
Nathalia
Waaia
Numurk
Wunghnu
Invergordon
Marun

Yando
Durham Ox
Mologa
Mitiamo
Roslynmead
Wharparilla
Echuca
Echuca Village
Kotupna
Koyuga
Kaarimba
Mundoona

Fernihurst
Jarklin
Calivil
Prairie
Lockington
Bamawm
Ballendella
Nanneella
Simmie
Strathallan
Wyuna
St Germains
Tongala
Undera North
Bunbartha
Zeerust
Undera
Lancaster
Tallygaroop

Bears Lagoon
Serpentine
Dingee
Warragamba
Rochester
Diggora
Fairy Dell
Girgarre
Merrigum
Mooroopna
Sheppa

Fiery Flat
Tandarra
Drummartin
Hunter
Elmore
Corop
Stanhope
Byrneside
Tatura
Kialla West
Honeysuckle

Inglewood
Raywood
Neilborough
Sebastian
Wellsford
Goornong
Barnadown
Colbinabbin
Rushworth
Waranga
Murchison
Murchison East

Bridgewater on Loddon
Campbells Forest
Huntly
Bagshot
Muskerry East
Colbinabbin West
Wanalta
Mathiesons
Moorilim
Arcadia

Arnold
Leichardt
Woodvale
Epsom
Fosterville
Runnymede
Creek View
Cornella
Graytown
Angustown
Goulburn Weir
Waring

Llanelly
Marong
EAGLEHAWK
BENDIGO
Longlea
Toolleen
Mt Camel
Redcastle
Bailieston
Lake Nagambie
Nagambie
Longwood

Newbridge
Tarnagulla
Woodstock
Maiden Gully
Junortoun
Axedale
Knowsley
Myola
Mt Carmel
Moormbool
Northwood
Tabilk
Locksley
Longwood East

Arnold West
Lockwood
Lockwood South
Mandurang
Eppalock
Derrinal
Ladys Pass
Mt Ida
Costerfield
Avenel

Eddington
Shellbourne
Strathfieldsaye
Axe Creek
Heathcote
Argyle
Mangalore
Mt Bernard
Dropmore

Baringhup
Ravenswood
Harcourt North
Sutton Grange
Mia Mia
Redesdale
Majors Creek
Puckapunyal
Army Base
Seymour
Whiteheads Creek
Kobyboyn
Ruffy
Tarcombe

Carisbrook
Maldon
Harcourt
Faraday
Metcalfe
Tooborac
Northwood
Tallarook
Highlands
STRATHBOGIE

Majorca
Newstead
Castlemaine
Chewton
Elphinstone
Barfold
Glenhope
Pyalong
High Camp
Broadford
Trawool
Yea

Clunes
Campbelltown
Yapeen
Guildford
Vaughan
Taradale
Malmsbury
Langley
Willowmavin
Kilmore
Tyaback
Reedy Creek
Strath Creek
Flowerdale

Creswick
Smeaton
Kingston
Hepburn Springs
Daylesford
Porcupine Ridge
Lauriston
Kyneton
Tylden
Lancefield
Romsey
Bylands
Wandong
Heathcote Junction
Hazeldene
Glenburn

Newlyn
Broomfield
Bullarto
Trentham
Newbury
Drummond
Glenlyon
Carlsruhe
Newham
Rochford
Darraweit Guim
Wallan
Upper Plenty
Beveridge
Kinglake West
Glenvale

BALLARAT
Bungaree
Wallace
Gordon
Blackwood
Macedon
Mount Macedon
New Gisborne
Riddells Creek
Gisborne
Monegeetta
Kalkallo
Whittlesea
Donnybrook
Woodstock
Kinglake
Steels Creek

Dunnstown
Millbrook
Ballan
Myrniong
Lerderderg Gorge
Bullengarook East
Toolern Vale
Sunbury
Yuroke
Craigieburn
Mernda
Cottles Bridge
Smiths Gully

J K L M N O P Q R

0 10 20 30 40 50 km

1 2 3 4 5 6 7 8 9 10 11 12 13

NEW SOUTH WALES

VICTORIA

Berrigan
Daysdale
Rand
Bulgandry
Alma Park
Culcairn
Morven
Holbrook

Savenake
Sangar
Coreen
Walbundrie
Walla Walla
Gerogery
Woomargama

Riverina
Rennie
Lowesdale
Brocklesby
Burrumbuttock
Gerogery West
Table Top
Mullengandra

Barooga
Mulwala
Corowa
Howlong
Jindera
Ettamogah Pub
Lake Hume
Wymah

Yarrawonga
Wahgunyah
Rutherglen
Browns Plains
Barnawartha North
Albury
Bellbird
Bethanga
Granya

Katamatite
Esmond
Bundalong South
Chiltern Valley
Barnawartha
Wodonga
Bandiana
Bonegilla
Ebden
Old Tallangatta

Tungamah
Peechelba
Springhurst
Chiltern
Middle Indigo
Barnawartha
Baranduda
Barandua
Lake Hume
Tallangatta

Dookie
St James
Lake Rowan
Boomanoomana
Indigo Upper
Leneva
Kiewa
Tangambalanga
The Cascade

Devenish
Thoona
Wangaratta
Tarrawingee
Beechworth
Silver Creek
Yackandandah
Allans Flat
Osbornes Flat
Kergunyah
Gundowring North
Noorongong
Yabba

Benalla
Glenrowan
Oxley
Markwood
Everton
Stanley
Mt Big Ben
Kergunyah South
Gundowring
Tallandoon
Eskdale

Winton
Greta West
Greta
Whorouly
Gapsted
Barwidgee Creek
Mudgegonga
Dederang
Mitta Mitta

Baddaginnie
Moyhu
Meadow Creek
Whorouly South
Merriang
Myrtleford
Rosewhite
Kancoona
Mt Tawonga
Little Snowy Creek

Warrenbayne
Tatong
Carboor
Ovens
Havilah
Eurobin
Mullindolingong
Tawonga

Swanpool
Lima
Edi
King Valley
Nug Nug
Buffalo
Porepunkah
Tawonga South
Alpine

Strathbogie
Edi Upper
Myrrhee
Whitfield
Mount Buffalo National Park
Bright
Freeburgh
Mount Beauty
Bogong

Barjarg
Tolmie
Cheshunt
Buckland
Wandiligong
Smoko
Falls Creek
Rocky Valley Reservoir

Merton
Bonnie Doon
Maindample
Mansfield
Powers Lookout
Harrietville
Hotham Heights
Dinner Plain
High

Alexandra
Eildon
Merrijig
Mirimbah
Ski Area Mt Stirling
Mt Buller
Abbeyard
Mt Hotham
Dargo High Plains
Cobungra

Thornton
Rubicon
Goughs Bay
Macs Cove
Howqua
Mt Howitt
Mt Murray
Mt Tabletop

Jamieson
Kevington
Mt McDonald
Snowy Dividing Range
Howitt Plains
Mt Phipps

Marysville
Buxton
Gaffneys Creek
Alpine National Park
Mt Skene
Dargo

Woods Point
Waterford

For more detail on Alpine Region see pages 230 - 231

Howlong · Jindera · Ettamogah · Bowna · Talmalmo · Jingellic · Ournie · Tooma

RIVERINA · Murray River · Great Northern · Murray Valley Hwy · Hume Fwy · Hume Hwy

Albury · Wodonga · VICTORIA · Bandiana · Baranduda · Bonegilla · Ebden · Bellbird · Bethanga · Granya · Koetong · Walwa · Mt Alfred · Mt Burrowa · Tintaldra

Chiltern · Indigo · Barnawartha · Chiltern State Park · Leneva · Huon · Tallangatta · Old Tallangatta · Murray Valley · Bullioh · Darbyshire · Shelley · Cudgewa · Corryong · Thowgla · Khancoban · Murray Power Stn

Beechworth · Woolshed · Wooragee · Yackandandah · Allans Flat · Osbornes Flat · Kiewa · Kergunyah · Gundowring · Berringama · Colac Colac · Scammells Spur Lookout

Everton · Markwood · Whorouly · Gapsted · Mudgegonga · Dederang · Tallandoon · Eskdale · Mitta Mitta · Dartmouth · Lake Dartmouth · WABBA WILDERNESS PARK

Myrtleford · Ovens · Rosewhite · Havilah · Mullindolingong · Tawonga · Tawonga South · Tawonga Gap · OMEO HWY · ALPINE NATIONAL PARK

Eurobin · Nug Nug · Porepunkah · Bright · Freeburgh · Wandiligong · Mount Beauty · Bogong · Falls Creek Alpine Village · Kiewa Hydro Electric Scheme · Sunnyside · Glen Wills · Mt Bogong · Deep Creek

MOUNT BUFFALO NATIONAL PARK · Mount Buffalo Chalet · The Horn · Buckland · Smoko · Harrietville · BOGONG HIGH PLAINS · Hotham Heights · Dinner Plain · Shannonvale · Anglers Rest · Benambra · Hinnomunjie · BOWEN MOUNTAINS · ALPINE NATIONAL PARK

ALPINE NATIONAL PARK · Mt Cobbler · Mt Stirling Ski Area · Mt Howitt · GREAT DIVIDING RANGE · GREAT ALPINE RD · Cobungra · Omeo · Cassilis · Tongio West · Tongio · Swifts Creek · Karoon

HOWITT PLAINS · SNOWY RANGE NATIONAL PARK · AVON WILDERNESS PARK · Licola · Dargo · Waterford · Brookville · Doctors Flat · Ensay · Ensay South · Reedy Flat · Murrindal · Buchan

DARGO HIGH PLAINS · MITCHELL RIVER NATIONAL PARK · Cobbannah · Bullumwaal · Tabberabbera · Deptford · Tambo Crossing · Buchan South · Buchan Caves · EAST

Culloden · Stockdale · Briagolong · Glenaladale · Woodglen · Lindenow · Calulu · Wuk Wuk · Wy Yung · Clifton Creek · Mount Taylor · Sarsfield · Wiseleigh · Bruthen · Nowa Nowa · Wairewa · Tostaree

Fernbank · Valencia Creek · Lake Glenmaggie · Coongulmerang · Hillside · Walpa · Lucknow · BAIRNSDALE · Nicholson · Johnsonville · Swan Reach · Metung · Nungurner · Lakes Entrance · Lake Tyers · Colquhoun

PRINCES HWY · Lake King

0 10 20 30 40 50 km

J K L M N O P Q R

NSW / Victoria South Coast region map

SNOWY MOUNTAINS RANGE

Cabramurra
Tumut Pond Reservoir
Anglers Reach
Adaminaby
Rosedale
Old Adaminaby
Bredbo
Mt Finders 1484m
Mt Dowling 1198m
Bald Mtn 1489m
Bendethera Caves
Bendethera Mtn 997m
Bergalia

KOSCIUSKO NATIONAL PARK
Mt Jagungal 2061m
Encumbene
Buckenderra
O'Neill Lagoon
Bunyan
Peak View
Numeralla
Tuross Falls
DEUA NATIONAL PARK
Bodalla
146
Lake Brou
Nerrigundah
Eurobodalla
Wagonga
Dalmeny
Narooma

Eucumbene
Lake Eucumbene
Murrumbidgee River
MONARO HWY
Railway
McInally Mtn 1085m
Numerella
WADBILLIGA
Tuross River
Belowra
Wandella
Central Tilba
Tilba Tilba

Cooma
Cootralantra Lake
Kiah Lake
Lake Jindabyne
Berridale
108
Rock Flat
Mt Kydra 1236m
NATIONAL PARK
Cobargo
Wallaga Lake NP
Quaama
Bermagui
Bermagui South

Thredbo Alpine Village
Smiggin Holes
Perisher Alpine Village
Dead Horse Pass
Jindabyne
ALPINE WAY
Snowy River
Dalgety
Maffra
Beloka
Nimmitabel
Brogo Dam
BEMBOKA NATIONAL PARK
Mt Mewin
Brogo
BIAMANGA NATIONAL PARK
Murrah River
Wapengo
Bunga

Lake Jillamatong
Paupong
Numbla Vale
Beards Lake
Bungarby
SNOWY MOUNTAINS HWY
Bemboka
Numbugga
Morgans Crossing
Tanja
MIMOSA ROCKS NATIONAL PARK
Bega
Tathra
Kalaru

Craigie Lookout
Ingebyra
Jimenbuen
Mt Cooper 1018m
Gunning Grach
Ando
Bibbenluke
TANTAWANGALO NATIONAL PARK
Bimbaya
Kameruka
Candelo
Wolumla
Yellow Pinch Dam
SOUTH
Tura Beach
Merimbula
BOURNDA NATIONAL PARK

Mt Rix 988m
Rodney
Bukalong
Black Lake
Cathcart
Rocky Hall
COOLANGUBRA NATIONAL PARK
Wyndham
Pambula
Pambula Beach
PACIFIC
BEN BOYD NATIONAL PARK

NEW SOUTH WALES
VICTORIA
Byadbo Mtn 1217m
Mt Alexander 1075m
Tombong
Tingaringy
Carrowidgin
Bombala
168
Maharatta
Burragate
YOWAKA NATIONAL PARK
Nethercote
Towamba
Eden
East Boyd
OCEAN

SNOWY RIVER NATIONAL PARK
Deddick
McKillops Bridge
Tubbut
Ambyne
Delegate River
Delegate
Graigie
Mila
White Rock Mtn 1093m
Platts
GENOA NATIONAL PARK
Rockton
Pericoe
Boydtown
Twofold Bay
Kiah

Mt Bowen 1320m
Bonang West
Bonang
Haydens Bog
Dellicknora
Bendoc
Quinburra
BONDI GULF NATIONAL PARK
Buldah
Mt Canterbury 1039m
Howal
Wonboyn Lake
Wonboyn
BEN BOYD NATIONAL PARK
Narrabarba
Green Cape

ERRINUNDRA NATIONAL PARK
Mt Jersey 759m
Brown Mtn 1010m
Martins Creek
Goongerah
Mt Ellery 1291m
Errinundra
Combienbar
Chandlers Creek
Weeragua
Mt Kaye 1002m
COOPRACAMBRA NATIONAL PARK
Cooracambra 958m
Wroxham
Wangarabell
MADGEE NATURE RESERVE
158
SOUTH
Timbillica
Mt Nagha 543m

GIPPSLAND
199
Sardine Creek
Mt Kuark 917m
Club Terrace
LIND NP
Noorinbee North
Noorinbee
Wangarabell
Genoa
Gipsy Point
Lake Barracoota
Cape Howe

Mt Buck 507m
Brodribb River
Cabbage Tree Creek
Bellbird Creek
170
PRINCES HWY
Tonghi Creek
Cann River
CANN VALLEY HWY
ALFRED NATIONAL PARK
Karlo Creek
Mallacoota
Mallacoota Inlet
Gabo Island

Orbost
Tabbara
Mt Cann 530m
Bemm River
CROAJINGOLONG NATIONAL PARK
Tamboon
Mt Everard 371m
Wingan Inlet
Little Rame Head

Marlo
Lake Corringle
Cape Conran
Pearl Point
Point Ricardo
Sydenham Inlet
Tamboon Inlet
Point Hicks (Cape Everard)
Rame Head

TASMAN SEA

N

For more detail on South Coast see page 117

South Australia

Festival State

The festivals of South Australia provide an excellent chance for people to discover a community at its liveliest. Given the number and variety of festivals – the Adelaide Festival of Arts, the Barossa Valley Vintage Festival, Schutzenfest, the Greek Glendi Festival and the Cornish Kernewek Lowender – it seems South Australians enjoy making the most of life.

This energetic spirit also seems to indicate that South Australians have triumphed over what might seem to be a rather depressing statistic: it is the driest State in the driest continent, two-thirds is near-desert and eighty-three per cent receives an annual rainfall of less than 250 millimetres. But these facts are easily forgotten when you visit the lush green Barossa Valley or explore the beauty of the Flinders Ranges.

South Australia's initial settlement began as the result of one man's idea for creating a model colony. Edward Gibbon Wakefield believed that the difficulties of other Australian colonies were caused by the ease with which anyone could obtain land. He claimed that if land was sold at two pounds an acre, only men of capital could buy; those who could not would provide a supply of labour, and the money generated would encourage investment and the development of resources. In 1834 he decided to test his ideas in the Gulf St Vincent area. Lieutenant-Colonel Light was dispatched as Surveyor-General to select a site. Despite financial difficulties in its early days, South Australia went on to lead Australia (and sometimes the world) in many social reforms.

In the 1990s South Australia's economy remains traditionally agrarian yet secondary industry provides nine out of ten jobs. Olympic Dam is one of the world's biggest copper mines and probably the biggest uranium mine. Leigh Creek coalfields supply the fuel for the State's power needs. South Australia also mines most of the world's opals. Coober Pedy, the main opal-mining town, produces eighty-five per cent of Australia's opals.

The gulf lands of South Australia enjoy a Mediterranean climate while the further north you go, the hotter and more inhospitable the temperatures become. Adelaide, the capital, with its average annual rainfall of 585 millimetres, enjoys a mid-summer average maximum temperature of about 28°C and a mid-winter average maximum of 15°C. Seventy-two per cent of the population lives here, making South Australia the most urbanised of all the States. Adelaide inherited its orderly and pleasant layout from its first Surveyor-General, Colonel Light, and many of its attractive original stone buildings have survived. The rolling hills of the Mount Lofty Ranges make a picturesque backdrop.

The Stuart Highway is completely sealed, making it possible to drive from Port Augusta to central Australia on an all-weather road. Before negotiating other roads in the north and west of the State – the desert regions – certain precautions should be taken (see: Outback Motoring). If you feel intrepid, the opal towns of Coober Pedy and Andamooka are fascinating. Temperatures climb to more than 40°C in Coober Pedy during summer (hence much of the town was built underground), so ensure you choose a cool period for your trip.

NOT TO BE MISSED
in South Australia

	Map Ref.
• **Adelaide Hills** – historic towns, wineries, galleries and beautiful scenery	296 D10
• **Barossa wine region** – Australia's most famous wine-producing area	296 E4
• **Coorong National Park** – one of the best natural bird sanctuaries in Australia	301 E5
• **'Copper Triangle' towns (Kadina, Moonta, Wallaroo)** – rich mining history	302 I6
• **Innes National Park** – impressive coastal scenery and wildflowers in spring	302 G10
• **Kangaroo Island** – unique scenery, pristine vegetation and native fauna	302 F11
• **Mount Gambier** – caves and crater lakes, particularly the beautiful Blue Lake	301 H12
• **Victor Harbor** – coastal resort town; take horse-drawn tram to Granite Island	303 I11
• **Whalers Way (Port Lincoln)** – stunning cliff-top drive near Port Lincoln	302 D8
• **Wilpena Pound** – extraordinary geological formation in the Flinders Ranges	299 E8

The colours of spring in the Flinders Ranges

Richly coloured hills in the Painted Desert, near Coober Pedy in central South Australia

The spectacular Flinders Ranges have passable roads, although some are unsealed. Wilpena Pound and Arkaroola are the main resort bases. The Heysen Trail (commemorating the South Australian painter Sir Hans Heysen) is a well-defined hiking trail that reaches from Cape Jervis almost to Quorn, with extensions into the Flinders Ranges.

Both the Yorke and Eyre peninsulas have attractive, unspoilt coastlines. Port Lincoln, on the Eyre Peninsula, is a popular base for game fishing and on the Yorke Peninsula the towns of Wallaroo, Moonta and Kadina – known collectively as Little Cornwall – are well worth a visit.

South of Adelaide is Victor Harbor, the south coast's largest town. A little

further on is Coorong National Park, renowned for its prolific birdlife, near the mouth of the Murray River at Lake Alexandrina. Here the river completes its 2600-kilometre course. A trip along the Riverland section of the Murray reveals historic towns, bountiful citrus orchards and extensive vegetable crops – all maintained by irrigation from the Murray. The

SOUTH AUSTRALIA

CALENDAR OF EVENTS

Note: The information given here was accurate at the time of printing. However, as the timing of events held annually is subject to change and some events may extend into the following month, it is best to check with the local tourism authority or event organisers to confirm the details. The calendar is not exhaustive. Most towns and regions hold sporting competitions, arts and craft exhibitions, agricultural and flower shows, music festivals and other such events annually. Details of these events are available from local tourism outlets.

JANUARY
Public holidays: New Year's Day; Australia Day. **Adelaide:** Sheffield Shield (cricket); Schutzenfest; Blessing of the Waters (at Glenelg). **Ardrossan:** Ardrossan Alive (biennial, odd-numbered years). **Hahndorf:** Founders Day. **Kingston S.E.:** Yachting Regatta; Lobster Fest. **Loxton:** Apex Fisherama. **Minlaton:** Yacht Race. **Murray Bridge:** State Championship Swimming. **Penola:** Vignerons Cup. **Port Germein:** Festival of the Crab. **Port Lincoln:** Tunarama Festival. **Port MacDonnell:** Oz Rock Music Festival.

Port Pirie: Australia Day Celebrations. **Robe:** Beer Can Regatta. **Streaky Bay:** Perlubie Beach Sports and Race Day; Family Fish Day Contest. **Tanunda:** Oompah Fest. **Tumby Bay:** Fishing Competition. **Victor Harbor:** Granite Island Regatta. **Wallaroo:** New Year's Day Regatta. **Whyalla:** Australian Amateur Snapper Fishing Championship. **Wilmington:** Rodeo.

FEBRUARY
Adelaide: Womadelaide. **Aldinga Beach:** Historic Bike Race; Multicultural Festival. **Berri:** Rodeo; Speedboat Spectacular. **Coonalpyn:** Trash Farming Field Day (biennial,

even-numbered years). **Goolwa:** Milang to Goolwa Freshwater Classic Yacht Race. **Kingscote:** Racing Carnival. **Loxton:** Mardi Gras. **Mount Compass:** Compass Cup Cow Race. **Peterborough:** Rodeo. **Port Lincoln:** Lincoln Week Regatta. **Tailem Bend:** Gumi Racing Festival. **Waikerie:** International Food Fair.

MARCH
Adelaide: Adelaide Festival of Arts (biennial, even-numbered years); Fringe Festival (runs parallel to Adelaide Festival); The Australian Festival for Young People (biennial, odd-numbered years);

Glendi Greek Festival. **Goolwa:** Wooden Boat Festival (biennial, odd-numbered years). **Kapunda:** Celtic Music Festival (weekend before Easter). **Kingscote:** Racing Carnival. **Mintaro:** Paddys Market. **Mount Barker:** Power of the Past. **Streaky Bay:** Race Meeting. **Tanunda:** Essenfest. **William Creek:** Race Meeting and Gymkhana (weekend before Easter).

EASTER
Public holidays: Good Friday; Easter Monday. **Andamooka:** Easter Family Fun Day and White Dam Walk. **Barmera:** Lake Bonney Yachting Regatta.

Barossa Valley: Vintage Festival (biennial, odd-numbered years). **Berri:** Carnival. **Ceduna:** Horseracing Carnival. **Clare:** Easter Races. **Cobdogla:** Art and Craft Fair. **Coober Pedy:** Opal Festival. **Jamestown:** Bilby Hunt. **Kadina:** Bowling Carnival. **Oakbank:** Easter Racing Carnival. **Waikerie:** Horse and Pony Club Gymkhana.

APRIL
Public holiday: Anzac Day. **Laura:** Folk Fair. **Maitland:** Agricultural Show. **Port Pirie:** SA Longtrack Speedway Championships.

MAY
Public holiday: Adelaide

lakes and lagoons at the river's mouth abound with birdlife and offer excellent fishing as well as seasonal duck-shooting. Mount Gambier, near the southern Victorian border, is the commercial centre of the south-east; it has Australia's largest pine forest and the beautiful Blue Lake.

The fame of South Australia's wine regions extends well beyond Australian shores. The Barossa, McLaren, Riverland, Clare Valley, Langhorne Creek, Adelaide Hills and Coonawarra wine regions – all have distinct specialities determined by soil and climate. In the famous Barossa Valley region, there are more than forty wineries. The valley was originally settled by German Lutherans who planted orchards, olive groves and vineyards, and built charming towns and wineries very much in Germanic style. To explore this area, particularly around the time of the Vintage Festival (held every odd-numbered year), is to discover a region and lifestyle unique in Australia.

South Australia offers a quality of grandeur and individuality quite different from that of other States.

CLIMATE GUIDE

ADELAIDE

	J	F	M	A	M	J	J	A	S	O	N	D
Maximum °C	29	29	26	22	19	16	15	16	18	21	24	27
Minimum °C	17	17	15	13	10	9	8	8	9	11	13	15
Rainfall mm	20	21	24	44	68	72	67	62	51	44	31	26
Raindays	4	4	5	9	13	15	16	16	13	11	8	6

VICTOR HARBOR REGION

	J	F	M	A	M	J	J	A	S	O	N	D
Maximum °C	24	24	23	21	19	16	15	16	18	20	22	23
Minimum °C	16	16	15	12	10	8	8	8	9	11	12	14
Rainfall mm	22	20	23	43	62	71	74	67	55	46	28	23
Raindays	4	4	6	10	14	15	16	16	14	11	8	6

BAROSSA VALLEY

	J	F	M	A	M	J	J	A	S	O	N	D
Maximum °C	29	29	26	22	17	14	13	14	17	20	24	27
Minimum °C	14	14	12	9	7	5	4	5	6	8	10	12
Rainfall mm	18	19	24	42	61	52	66	63	58	50	28	22
Raindays	5	3	5	9	13	12	16	16	13	11	8	6

WILPENA REGION

	J	F	M	A	M	J	J	A	S	O	N	D
Maximum °C	31	31	27	24	17	14	13	15	20	24	27	29
Minimum °C	16	16	13	9	6	4	3	3	5	9	11	14
Rainfall mm	34	25	20	19	51	57	67	50	33	35	14	25
Raindays	3	3	2	3	8	8	9	7	5	6	4	4

Cup Day. **Adelaide:** Adelaide Cup Racing Carnival. **Aldgate:** Autumn Leaves Festival. **Burra:** Antique and Decorating Fair. **Clare:** Gourmet Weekend. **Hawker:** Horseracing Carnival. **McLaren Vale:** From the Sea and the Vines Festival. **Mannum:** Houseboat Hirers' Open Days. **Naracoorte:** Swap Meeting; Young Riders Equestrian Event. **Oodnadatta:** Race Meeting and Gymkhana. **Seppeltsfield:** Hot Air Balloon Regatta. **Stansbury:** Sheepdog Trials. **Waikerie:** Riverland Rock 'n' Roll Festival. **Yorke Peninsula:** (Kadina/Moonta/ Wallaroo): Kernewek

Lowender (Biennial, odd-numbered years).

JUNE
Public holiday: Queen's Birthday. **Barmera:** South Australian Country Music Festival and Awards. **Gawler:** Three-day Equestrian Event. **Penola:** Festival.

JULY
Willunga: Apple Blossom Festival. **Woomera:** 4th of July Celebrations.

AUGUST
Barossa Valley: Classic Gourmet Weekend. **Cleve:** Eyre Peninsula Field Days (biennial, even-numbered years). **Crystal Brook:** Agricultural Show. **Gawler:** Agricultural

Show. **Kadina:** Agricultural Show. **Strathalbyn:** Collectors, Hobbies and Antique Fair. **Yacka:** Sheepdog Trials.

SEPTEMBER
Adelaide: Royal Adelaide Show; Bay to Birdwood Run (vintage car rally; biennial, even-numbered years). **Balaklava:** Agricultural Show. **Beltana:** Picnic Race Meeting and Gymkhana. **Ceduna:** Agricultural Show. **Hawker:** Art Exhibition. **Keith:** Market Day. **Kimba:** Agricultural Show. **Moonta:** Agricultural Show. **Paskeville:** Yorke Peninsula Field Days (biennial, odd-numbered years).

Port Pirie: Blessing of the Fleet. **Robe:** Blessing of the Fleet. **Stirling:** Food and Wine Affair.

OCTOBER
Public holiday: Labour Day. **Adelaide:** SA Football League Finals. **Andamooka:** Opal Festival. **Barmera:** Agricultural Show. **Barossa Valley:** Music Festival. **Bordertown:** Clayton Farm Vintage Field Day. **Ceduna:** Oyster-Fest. **Clare:** Agricultural Show. **Coober Pedy:** Horse Races. **Edithburgh:** State Windsurfing Speed Trials; Gala Day. **Jamestown:** Agricultural Show. **Kingscote:** Agricultural Show. **Loxton:** Agricultural Show. **McLaren Vale:** One

Continuous Picnic; Wine Bushing Festival. **Marree:** Outback Ball (biennial, even-numbered years). **Naracoorte:** Agricultural Show. **Port Pirie:** Festival of Country Music. **Renmark:** Rose Festival. **Robe:** Art/Craft Festival. **Strathalbyn:** Glenbarr Scottish Festival; **Victor Harbor:** Folk and Music Festival. **Yorketown:** Picnic Races and Gymkhana.

NOVEMBER
Adelaide: Christmas Pageant. **Berri:** Art, Craft and Fine Food Fair. **Clare:** Spring Festival. **Gawler:** Country Music Festival; Sutch is Light. **Hahndorf:** Blumenfest. **Kapunda:** Antique and Craft Fair;

Agricultural Show. **Loxton:** Loxton Lights Up. **Mount Gambier:** Blue Lake Festival. **Murray Bridge:** Big River Challenge Festival. **Port MacDonnell:** Bayside Festival. **Port Pirie:** Cycling and Athletics Carnival.

DECEMBER
Public holidays: Christmas Day; Boxing Day; Proclamation Day. **Adelaide:** Proclamation Day Celebrations at Glenelg). **Barmera:** Christmas Pageant and Fireworks. **Jamestown:** Christmas Pageant. **Naracoorte:** Street-Traders Party; Carols by Candlelight. **Renmark:** Christmas Pageant; Rowing Regatta. **Streaky Bay:** Carols by the Sea.

ADELAIDE

The Elegant City

The Rotunda in Elder Park with St Peter's Cathedral in the background

SOUTH AUSTRALIA

NOT TO BE MISSED

in Adelaide

	Map Ref.
• **Adelaide Festival Centre** – hub of the famous Adelaide Festival of Arts	290 E7
• **Botanic Gardens** – take a free, guided tour of these beautiful formal gardens	290 G7
• **Central Market** – fresh produce market in the centre of the city	290 D10
• **Cleland Wildlife Park** – well-displayed native fauna in a bushland setting	293 N9
• **Explorer Tram** – efficient and fun way to tour the attractions of the city	290 E8
• **Glenelg** – take the tram to this historic, seaside resort town	292 C11
• **Jam Factory Craft and Design Centre** – see artists creating and their creations	290 D8
• **Light's Vision lookout** – views of city's broad streets and spacious parks	290 D6
• **St Peter's Cathedral** – one of Australia's finest cathedrals	290 E6
• **South Australian Museum** – unique collection of Aboriginal artifacts	290 F8

Adelaide, a gracious, well-planned city, is set on a narrow coastal plain between the rolling hills of the Mount Lofty Ranges and the blue waters of Gulf St Vincent. Surrounded by parkland, Adelaide combines the vitality of a large modern city (population around one million) with an easy-going Australian lifestyle.

Thanks to the excellent planning and foresight of Colonel Light, the first Surveyor-General, Adelaide is laid out on a grid pattern, its wide streets allowing easy access for locals and visitors alike. Adelaide is the only major world city completely surrounded by parklands. These parklands feature children's playgrounds, sports fields, barbecues, and tables and chairs under shady trees. The beautiful, formal **Botanic Gardens** on the north-east side of the city have 16 hectares of Australian and imported plants, and artificial lakes where children can feed ducks and swans; free guided tours are available. While there, do not miss the **Palm House**, an extensive glasshouse brought out from Germany in 1871. In the north-east corner is the **Bicentennial Conservatory,** housing exotic tropical plants from all over the world. Two serpentine viewing paths on upper and lower levels have wheelchair access. At **Rymill Park** on the east side there is a children's boating lake with rowing boats for hire. Near the eastern end of South Terrace are the **Himeji Gardens**, a blend of traditional Japanese lake, mountain and dry gardens. The gate is modelled on that of a temple, and a water bowl is provided for visitors to purify themselves by washing their hands and mouths. At **Veale Gardens** to the south of the city there are fountains, rockeries and formal rose gardens. A restaurant is set in parkland and overlooks the waters of the River Torrens near the weir, north of North Terrace.

Adelaide Arcade, one of the city's historic buildings

Near the tree-lined boulevard of **North Terrace** on the edge of the city centre there are some fine colonial buildings. These include **Holy Trinity Church**, the oldest church in South Australia. The foundation stone was laid by Governor Hindmarsh in 1838, and the clock was made by Vulliamy, clockmaker to the English King William IV. Near this western end of North Terrace is the **Adelaide Gaol**, last used in 1988, and now open for inspection each Sunday. Also on North Terrace are the grand **Newmarket Hotel**, built 1884, and the **Lion Arts Centre**, home to the Mercury Cinema and the Jam Factory Craft and Design Centre where free, guided tours to see the artists at work are available.

The historic Adelaide Railway Station building, also in North Terrace, has been magnificently restored and now houses the elegant **Adelaide Casino**. The casino is part of the Adelaide Plaza, which includes the **Adelaide Convention Centre** and **Exhibition Hall**, and the luxurious **Hyatt Regency Adelaide Hotel**.

On the corner of King William Road is the present **Parliament House**. Nearby is **Government House**, the oldest building in Adelaide.

The **State Library**, on the corner of Kintore Avenue, holds many major collections. In the Mortlock Wing, volumes on South Australia share space with Donald Bradman's trophies in a beautifully restored Victorian building. Behind the Library is the **Migration Museum**, the first museum to tell the stories of Australia's migrants. Close by,

in the former armoury, is the **Police Museum**. Back on North Terrace, the **South Australian Museum** and the **Art Gallery of South Australia** rub shoulders. The museum holds the world's largest collection of Aboriginal artifacts and features this in a range of exhibits. The collections of the Art Gallery give one of the best overviews of Australian art available. It also houses important collections of sculptures, paintings and decorative arts from around the world.

The **University of Adelaide** is also on North Terrace. Walk through the attractively landscaped grounds to see the blend of classic and contemporary architecture, and the **Museum of Classical Archaeology** where you can view some 500 objects, many dating back to the third millennium BC. **Elder Hall**, with its spectacular pipe organ, is a fine concert venue.

Ayers House, headquarters for the National Trust of South Australia, is at the eastern end of North Terrace. Sir Henry Ayers bought the property in 1855 and it became one of the major venues for social functions during Ayers' seven terms as Premier of the State. A charming nineteenth-century residence with slate roof and shuttered bay windows, Ayers House today has an elegant formal restaurant as well as an informal bistro which extends into a courtyard, enabling visitors to enjoy the historic surroundings while dining. The National Aboriginal Cultural Institute **Tandanya** is on the corner of Grenfell Street and East Terrace.

Back in the heart of the city on King William Street is **Edmund Wright House**, another important reminder of Adelaide's heritage. Built in 1878, the building has an elaborate Renaissance facade. Other historic buildings in the city include the **Adelaide Town Hall** in King

William Street, with its formal portico entrance and graceful tower, Adelaide Arcade, off Rundall Mall, the **General Post Office** and the **Treasury Buildings** on the corner of Victoria Square.

In North Adelaide there are many fine old colonial buildings, from delightful stone cottages to stately homes and grand old hotels with lacework balconies and verandahs. **St Peter's Cathedral** in King William Road is one of Australia's finest cathedrals and is a fitting backdrop to the beautiful **Pennington Gardens**. There is an excellent view from **Light's Vision** on Montefiore Hill. A bronze statue of Colonel Light overlooks the city with its broad streets and spacious parks.

The **River Torrens** flows through many of Adelaide's parks. The banks are landscaped, lined with gums and willows, and perfect for a lazy picnic lunch. Walking and cycling trails wind through some of the city's scenic parklands and along the riverbanks. A delightful way of travelling to the **Adelaide Zoological Gardens** is provided by a fleet of *Popeye* motor launches which cruise the river. The zoo has a large collection of animals and reptiles, and is noted for its variety of Australian birdlife. There is a walk-through aviary sheltering many species of unusual land and water birds, and a nocturnal house designed to display those animals and birds that are most active at night. The zoo is located in a beautiful setting featuring magnificent trees (including exotic species), rock beds and rose gardens.

Also situated on the curving banks of the Torrens is the world-renowned **Adelaide Festival Centre**, hub of the biennial Adelaide Festival of Arts, held every even-numbered year. This streamlined, modern building contains a

ACCOMMODATION

HOTELS

Hilton
233 Victoria Sq., Adelaide
(08) 8217 2000

Country Comfort Inn
226 South Tce, Adelaide
(08) 8223 4355

Hindley Parkroyal
65 Hindley St, Adelaide
(08) 8231 5552, 1800 82 2633

Hyatt Regency
North Tce, Adelaide
(08) 8231 1234

Stamford Plaza
150 North Tce, Adelaide
(08) 8461 1111

FAMILY AND BUDGET

Grosvenor Vista Hotel
North Terrace, Adelaide
(08) 8407 8888

Motel Adjacent Casino
25 Bank St, Adelaide
(08) 8231 8881

Paringa Motel
15 Hindley St, Adelaide
(08) 8231 1000, 1800 08 8202

YMCA
76 Flinders St, Adelaide
(08) 8223 1611

MOTEL GROUPS: BOOKINGS

Best Western 131779

Flag 13 2400

Travelodge 1300 363300

This list is for information only; inclusion is not necessarily a recommendation.

The famous Glenelg tram

SOUTH AUSTRALIA

2000-seat lyric theatre, drama and experimental theatres, and an imposing amphitheatre which is ideal for outdoor entertainment. The building has been acclaimed as one of the finest performing venues in the world. The Southern Plaza incorporates a spectacular environmental sculpture by German artist O. H. Hajek. There are also some fine contemporary tapestries and paintings hung inside the building. Group tours can be arranged, and restaurant and bar facilities are available. The Festival Centre has walkways linking it to King William Road, Parliament House, Adelaide Railway Station, the Casino and the Hyatt Regency hotel. Nearby is an attractive old band rotunda located in **Elder Park**.

Adelaide has a bustling shopping complex centred around **Rundle Mall**. With more than 820 shops, Rundle Mall is the largest pedestrian shopping mall in the southern hemisphere. The tree-lined paved area has a fountain, modern sculpture, an information booth, fruit and flower stalls, and seats where you can sit and watch the passing parade. Buskers and outdoor cafes add to the cosmopolitan atmosphere. In the surrounding arcades and streets are shops ranging from major department stores to tiny specialist boutiques. **King William Street** is lined with impressive bank and insurance buildings, while

Hindley Street has clusters of restaurants, cafes, continental food shops, nightclubs and Aussie pubs. A bonus for shoppers are the free Bee-line bus service and the free City Loop service which operate in the inner-city area.

Make a trip to **Melbourne Street** in North Adelaide for some of the city's most exclusive shops; **Unley Road** for exclusive boutiques; **Magill Road** for antiques and second-hand treasures; the **Parade** at Norwood for all of the above plus great delis, coffee shops, home design stores and bookshops. **King William Road** at Hyde Park has many stylish specialty shops, cafes and boutiques. Shops in **Glen Osmond Road** at Eastwood offer a wide variety of top-label fashions at reduced prices.

A fascinating shopping experience is a visit to the **Central Market** behind the Hilton hotel, with its stalls stacked high with fresh produce (open Tuesday, and Thursday to Saturday; tours available). Nearby arcades sell clothing, wine and spirits; this area is also home to Adelaide's **Chinatown** with its many food stalls, restaurants and colourful shopping complex. The east end of the city around **Rundle Street** has experienced a rebirth, with busy coffee houses, pubs, restaurants and a host of absorbing craft shops and boutiques. The **East End Markets** have become Rundle Street's focus on Friday, Saturday and Sunday, selling everything from fresh fish, meat and vegetables to clothing and jewellery, and local arts and crafts.

In Norwood the **Orange Lane Market** (open Saturday and Sunday) features second-hand goods, homemade produce, local crafts and stalls. The **Brickworks Market and Leisure Complex** at Thebarton (open Friday to Sunday) sells produce and bric-a-brac, and is part of a 6-hectare complex featuring an amusement park. Another popular market featuring fresh produce and a variety of other goods is the **Junction Markets** on Prospect Road, Kilburn (open Saturday and Sunday). At Port Adelaide the **Fisherman's Wharf**, located at the end of Commercial Road, sells produce and quality bric-a-brac; and at the **North Arm Fish Market**, on Moorhouse Road, fresh fish can be bought direct from the boats; both are open Sundays. Some of these markets are also open on public holidays and during school holidays; check opening times with the South Australian Travel Centre, (08) 8212 1505.

Adelaide is renowned for its restaurants. The city is credited with being the birthplace of modern Australian cuisine. Some of the best restaurants are tiny and crowded, with fast service and super-cheap prices. Others are set in historic buildings, serving international-class cuisine in gracious surroundings. **Hindley Street** offers a wide range of cosmopolitan eating. **Gouger Street**, near the Central Market, is known as $10 street – if you can't get a good meal for less than $10, you're in the wrong street – it is particularly noted for its excellent seafood cafes, and South Australian seafood is definitely worth sampling. **Rundle Street** has a wide variety of cafes and restaurants, while **O'Connell Street** and **Melbourne Street**, North Adelaide have an array of friendly cafes.

Adelaide also has some fine old pubs. Some are friendly 'locals', others incorporate restaurants, wine bars and dance floors. The **Stag Hotel** in Rundle Street is located in a beautifully restored heritage building with a first-class restaurant and bar. It is typical of the boutique-style hotel; there are a number of these hotels within the inner-city area.

Take a leisurely tour around the city's attractions in a replica of a road-registered tram. The tram has on-board commentary. Board or alight the **Explorer Tram** as many times as you wish at any of the stopping points; the tram returns to any given point approximately every 2½ hours.

The longest guided busway system in the world, **TransAdelaide's O-Bahn**, runs north-east from the city centre. It travels beside the River Torrens in its own landscaped park from Adelaide to a major shopping centre at **Tea Tree Plaza**, and there are stations at **Klemzig** and **Paradise**. Walking paths and cycling tracks follow the busway track to Tea Tree Plaza, and along the way offer views over reservoirs, foothills and the city.

Not to be missed in Adelaide are the marvellous beaches, stretching right along the coastline, with wide sandy shores and clear blue waters. Most are only a short drive from the city centre. **Glenelg**, the best known, can be reached by taking the famous 1929 **Glenelg tram** from Victoria Square to the foreshore in Glenelg. Spoil yourself by dining at the **Stamford Plaza**, or stroll down Jetty Road window-shopping. The **Magic Mountain Waterslide and Amusement Centre** provides entertainment. Restaurants abound, and Greek food here is a specialty. Grand old homes and guest houses along the foreshore are a reminder of Glenelg's days as a seaside resort for the wealthy. The first settlers came ashore here in 1836 and proclaimed the colony of South Australia under a gum tree. The **Old Gum Tree** remains, with a commemorative plaque, in McFarlane Street. HMS *Buffalo* played a significant part in South Australia's early settlement and the replica of the vessel at Glenelg is, appropriately, a setting for a maritime museum and restaurant.

Other beaches include **Brighton**, **West Beach**, **Henley**, **Grange** and **Semaphore**. Many beaches have sailboards and catamarans for hire, while the jetties are used for promenading, swimming and fishing. **Fort Glanville** at Semaphore is the oldest fortress in South Australia. The **Semaphore to Fort Glanville Tourist Railway** runs south along the seafront for more than 2 kilometres, from the Semaphore Jetty to Fort Glanville and the nearby caravan park; it operates daily during school holidays, and on all public holidays and Sundays during the summer months. Further south, near Hallett Cove, is the **Hallett Cove Conservation Park**, established to preserve the remnants of glacial features that probably occurred 270 million years ago.

Adelaide's suburbs have much to offer the visitor. A short drive west towards the suburb of **Grange** is **Sturt's Cottage** built in 1840, and home of Captain Charles Sturt, the famous pioneer and explorer. Managed by the Charles Sturt Memorial Museum Trust, the cottage with its period furniture and many of Sturt's belongings recalls the early days of South Australia.

In **Wayville**, just south-west of the city, the **Investigator Science and Technology Centre** with its hands-on 'gizmos' provides fun for the family; it is located in the International Pavilion, Wayville Showgrounds (enter from Rose Terrace). Also at the showgrounds in early September, the **Royal Adelaide Show** brings the country to the city.

Port Adelaide has many imposing colonial buildings, a reminder of the port's heyday in the 1880s. Noteworthy are the police station and court house, town hall, shipping and transport building, and Ferguson's bond store. Visitors to the **Port Dock Station Railway Museum** in Lipson Street can ride miniature steam trains. The museum has a large collection of locomotives, rolling stock, platform displays, a theatrette and an operating HO-gauge model railway. Also located in Lipson Street is the **South Australian Maritime Museum**, complete with lighthouses and ships. A few blocks away is the **South Australian Historical Aviation Museum** in Mundy Street which houses the Woomera rocket collection. Commercial Road is the location for the **South Australian Military Vehicle Museum**. There are a variety of cruises and fishing trips available from Port Adelaide.

At **St Kilda**, further north, is the **Australian Electric Transport Museum** where you can take trips on restored trams. A guided walk along the 1.7 km boardwalk of the **St Kilda Mangrove Trail** is an experience not to be missed.

Near the suburb of **Rostrevor**, east of the city, the **Morialta Conservation Park** has a ruggedly beautiful gorge and many walking tracks. **Brownhill Creek Recreation Park** with its giant pine and gum trees in a quiet valley setting is ideal for barbecues and picnics. **Belair National Park** has picnic grounds, bushland, a children's playground and the former summer residence of the Governor. The renowned **Cleland Wildlife Park** displays kangaroos, koalas, wombats and other native fauna in their natural surroundings.

Cowell Jade, at Unley, sells jewellery and carvings made from local jade. The **South Australian Society of Model and Experimental Engineers** headquarters, in the nearby suburb of **Millswood**, has field days (open to visitors) twice a month. For magnificent views of Adelaide, take a trip to **Windy Point Lookout** or to the summit of **Mount Lofty**. At night, the lights of the city are particularly impressive.

For the sports enthusiast, Adelaide offers horseracing at **Victoria Park**, **Morphettville** and **Cheltenham**; greyhound-racing at **Angle Park**; tennis, squash, swimming and golf. Pools, water-slides, fountains, river rapids, waterfalls, and gym, spa and sauna facilities are a feature of the **Adelaide Aquatic Centre** in North Adelaide. The **City Golf Links** in North Adelaide command splendid views of the city. **Adelaide Oval**, on King William Road, is a venue for interstate and international cricket matches, while the **Memorial Drive Tennis Courts** have played host to international players since 1929. The **Ice Arena** in Thebarton has skating and the world's first indoor artificial ski slope. For kart-racing enthusiasts, **Kart-Mania** has safe, supervised race tracks at Richmond and Gepps Cross.

As well as the diversions the city itself offers, Adelaide is an excellent base for tours of the surrounding hills and nearby wine regions.

For further information on Adelaide, contact the South Australian Travel Centre, 1 King William St, Adelaide; (08) 8212 1505; freecall, 1800 882092; fax (08) 8303 2231.

ADELAIDE ON FOOT

The following is a selection of walking tours available.

- **Botanic Gardens: 1.** Guided walk; free of charge. **2.** Self-guide walk concentrating on water features within gardens.

- **Historic properties:** Self-guide walk with supplied audio-cassette prepared by National Trust (also includes places of interest); charge applies.

- **Linear Park:** Walking and cycling track from the hills, through city parklands to the sea.

- **North Adelaide:** Self-guide heritage walk.

- **North Terrace:** Self-guide walk highlighting indoor and outdoor works of art.

- **Port Adelaide:** Self-guide heritage walk.

- **St Kilda:** Various guided walks through mangrove area near town; bookings essential; charge applies.

Pamphlets are available for the self-guide walks. For further information, contact the South Australian Travel Centre, 1 King William St, Adelaide; (08) 8212 1505.

TOURS from Adelaide

Vineyards at Seppeltsfield, in the Barossa Valley

One of Adelaide's greatest assets is its proximity to a number of fascinating regions. Vineyards and wineries, rolling hills and quaint villages, seaside resorts and beautiful wildlife reserves are all within an easy drive of South Australia's capital.

Barossa Valley

50 km from Adelaide via the Sturt Highway

A must for visitors to Adelaide is the Barossa, Australia's premier wine-producing region. Located north-east of Adelaide, the Barossa boasts more than forty wineries and a multitude of historic buildings, galleries, cafes and restaurants. Visit Gawler, Lyndoch, Tanunda, Seppeltsfield, Nuriootpa and Angaston, detouring at will to smaller villages and visiting the tasting facilities at the wineries; make sure the driver is happy to forgo this pleasure! Alternatively, extend your visit and stay overnight at one of the many accommodation outlets in the area. The major festival here is the Barossa Valley Vintage Festival which starts on Easter Monday each odd-numbered year. In August the Barossa Classic Gourmet Weekend offers visitors the opportunity to sample and enjoy fine wines and gourmet food. The award-winning Barossa Music Festival is held in October. **See also:** Festival Fun; Vineyards and Wineries, and individual town entries in A–Z listing.

Clare Valley

135 km from Adelaide via the Sturt Highway and Highway 32 (Highway 83 optional north of Tarlee)

The Clare Valley produces superb wines and the region is known internationally for its riesling. Driving north through Kapunda, Australia's first mining town, you will pass some of the State's richest pastoral country, noted for its stud sheep. The wine towns begin at Auburn and continue to Watervale, Sevenhill and Clare. The area is noted for its prize-winning table wines. Sevenhill Cellars winery was started by two Jesuit priests in 1851 and still operates today. Slightly further afield, there are several fine colonial buildings, such as the magnificent Martindale Hall at Mintaro, which was used in the film *Picnic at Hanging Rock*. The area also has many charming parks and picturesque picnic spots. **See also:** Vineyards and Wineries, and individual town entries in A–Z listing.

McLaren region

42 km from Adelaide via the South Road

Another trip for wine-lovers is to the vineyards of the McLaren region. There are more than 50 wineries in the area, often in picturesque bush settings. All are well signposted and most have winetastings and cellar-door sales.

Hardy's Reynella, Chapel Hill, Seaview and Wirra Wirra are some of the names to recognise. Your return trip could include a visit to the nearby beaches of Moana, Port Noarlunga and Christies. **See also:** Vineyards and Wineries; The Fleurieu Peninsula and individual town entries in A–Z listing.

Adelaide Hills and Hahndorf

28 km from Adelaide via the South Eastern Freeway

See: The Adelaide Hills.

Fleurieu Peninsula

112 km from Adelaide to its furthest point via the South Road

See: The Fleurieu Peninsula. On the return trip do not miss historic Strathalbyn first settled in 1839, on the banks of the River Angas. Milang, 20 km to the south-east, is on the shores of Lake Alexandrina. Take your camera – the birdlife is fascinating. **See also:** individual town entries in A–Z listing.

National Motor Museum

Birdwood, 43 km from Adelaide via the North-East Road

The National Motor Museum (open daily) houses the most important motor-vehicle collection in Australia. Veteran, vintage and classic cars, and motorcycles number more than 300 and the grounds are a perfect venue for a picnic. At Gumeracha, west of Birdwood, is the Toy Factory, where you can climb the largest wooden rocking horse in the world. Drive back to Adelaide through Mount Torrens to the small town of Lobethal, which was founded in the 1840s. The Archives and Historical Museum houses a remarkable exhibit: the old Lobethal College, complete with shingled roof, which was built in 1845 (open Sunday afternoons). Fairyland Village at Lobethal has fourteen chalets, each depicting a fairytale or a nursery rhyme (open daily). There is a scenic route through Basket Range and Norton Summit back to Adelaide.

SOUTH AUSTRALIA

The Adelaide Hills are scenically delightful, particularly in spring and autumn

The Adelaide Hills

The Adelaide Hills, only half an hour's drive from the city, are a scenic blend of gently rolling hills, market gardens, vineyards and orchards with historic towns and farm buildings nestled in valleys. Cleland Wildlife Park in the **Cleland Conservation Park** on the slopes of Mount Lofty displays native birds and animals in a bush setting. The Gorge Wildlife Park at Cudlee Creek houses a large, privately-owned wildlife collection.

Just off the main highway are the townships of Stirling, with its beautiful trees and historic homes; Aldgate, nestled in a picturesque valley; and Bridgewater with its historic water wheel (1860), now part of the restored mill that houses the winemaking and maturation plant for Petaluma's premium sparkling wines. The lookout at the summit of Mount Lofty (726 m) offers spectacular views of Adelaide. Festivals in this section of the hills include the Autumn Leaves Festival held in May at Aldgate and at Stirling, the Food and Wine Affair held in September.

Hahndorf is probably the best-known town in the area. Settled by Silesian and Prussian refugees in 1839, its main street is lined with old elms and chestnut trees. Some of the buildings have been restored and the town has an old-world feel about it. The Hahndorf Academy and Art Gallery has a good general collection of paintings. A local German heritage museum is part of the gallery. The bakeries here sell delicious *apfelstrudel*, cheesecake and Black Forest cake, and small shops offer interesting local handicrafts and home-made preserves. Other attractions include a model train village, a clock museum and a strawberry farm. The heritage of the town is celebrated with several festivals: Founders Day, in January, and Blumenfest, the festival of flowers held in November.

On the outskirts of Hahndorf on the road to Oakbank is The Cedars, the home and studio of Sir Hans Heysen whose paintings depicted the area's beauty so well. Guided tours are available Sunday to Friday. Two of South Australia's oldest townships, Nairne and Mount Barker, lie to the east and south-east of Hahndorf. Mount Barker showgrounds is the venue each March for Power of the Past (vintage cars, engines and motorcycles).

In the town of Oakbank the Easter Racing Carnival, Australia's biggest picnic race meeting, is held with great fanfare every Easter. North of Oakbank, the townships of Forest Range, Lenswood and Basket Range are surrounded by apple orchards. There is an interesting archive and historical museum at nearby Lobethal. At Woodside, Melba's Chocolate Factory and Heritage Park is a popular attraction. From Hahndorf, the back road passes through winding hills and farmland to the old goldmining town of Echunga. The Warrawong Sanctuary at Mylor is a leader in the preservation of rare and endangered animals and is open to the public. At **Belair National Park** there are walks, a wildlife park, Old Government House and a native plant nursery.

For more information, contact the Adelaide Hills Tourist Information Centre, 41 Main St, Hahndorf; (08) 8388 1185. **See also:** Vineyards and Wineries, Festival Fun, and National Parks (for those parks indicated by bold type). **Map reference:** 296 D10.

Festival Fun

Because good food and wine go hand in hand with festivities, it seems appropriate that South Australia is both the nation's wine capital and home to some of Australia's major festivals. During the year, a wide variety of festivals is held throughout South Australia, ranging from the cultural extravaganza of the Adelaide Festival to carnivals in several country towns.

Each even-numbered year in March, Adelaide becomes the cultural centre of Australia as it hosts the **Adelaide Festival of Arts.**

Since it started in 1960, the Adelaide Festival has grown from a modest 51 performances to over 300, with as many as 30 competing for attention in one day. The Festival includes concerts, carnivals and street-theatre. The focal point of the festival is the Adelaide Festival Centre, which stands on 1.5 hectares on the banks of the River Torrens, just 2 minutes' walk from the commercial heart of the city.

The **Fringe Festival** runs parallel to the Adelaide Festival. What started as a rejected performers' way of being on show during the Festival is now an integral part of its colour and excitement, and attracts large numbers in its own right. The Fringe offers a treasure trove of cheaper (often free) performances, some experimental, as well as well-known acts.

Each odd-numbered year in March, the Festival Centre organises a youth arts festival, **The Australian Festival for Young People,** which focuses its attention on the arts for children and young people.

Also each odd-numbered year the popular music festival **Womadelaide** is held in the Botanic Gardens during the last weekend in February.

The **Barossa Valley Vintage Festival,** in Australia's premier wine-producing district just one hour's drive from Adelaide, is also held in odd-numbered years. Traditionally a thanksgiving celebration for a successful harvest, the seven-day festival starts on Easter Monday. There is music and dancing, good food, wine-tasting, a vintage fair, float processions and traditional dinners like the *weingarten* – a big feast featuring German folk songs. The grand finale takes the form of a spectacular fair held at the oval in Tanunda Park, where dancers in colourful national costumes dance around an 18-metre-high maypole, while food and

The Barossa Classic Gourmet Weekend combines the pleasures of wine, food and music

wine are served in the marquees surrounding the oval. The **Barossa Classic Gourmet Weekend** in August combines the pleasures of wine, food and good music over two days. Another major festival in the region is the award-winning **Barossa Music Festival,** held in October.

During the long weekend in May the Clare Valley wineries host the **Gourmet Weekend,** which includes tastings and a progressive Sunday luncheon around the wineries.

Each May, the McLaren region hosts the From the Sea and the Vines Festival, a celebration of seafood and wine. McLaren Vale is the venue for **One Continuous Picnic,** held on the October long weekend; wineries and restaurants provide opportunities to sample the vintages of the McLaren region. The **McLaren Vale Wine Bushing Festival** follows at the end of October, a time of fun and festivity with craft exhibitions, parades, picnics and formal balls to celebrate the new vintage.

South Australia is a State of many cultures, which accounts for the many ethnic festivals held every year. The largest of these is **Schutzenfest,** held in Adelaide each January. Traditionally a shooting festival to raise funds for various charities, it has grown into the biggest German-style beer festival held outside Germany.

In March, the Greek community organises the **Glendi Festival** to coincide with the Greek National Day. In May, every odd-numbered year, the colourful **Kernewek Lowender** (Cornish family festival) is held, centred around Kadina, Moonta and Wallaroo on the scenic Yorke Peninsula. There

is music, Cornish dancing, a pasty-making competition and a wheelbarrow race.

For two weeks in June, Barmera is the country music capital of the State, when visitors from all over Australia attend the **Country Music Festival.**

Other South Australian festivals include the **Tunarama Festival** at the fishing port and resort of Port Lincoln, held every Australia Day holiday in January. Australia's only festival dedicated to a fish, it features competitions, displays, a street procession, sports, a fireworks spectacular and the famous tuna-tossing event. In April the people of Laura, a small town in the lower Flinders Ranges, organise a **Folk Fair** that attracts thousands of visitors.

Each Easter Monday, the Great Eastern Steeplechase, part of the **Oakbank Easter Racing Carnival** is raced at Oakbank racecourse. This carnival is billed as the largest picnic meeting in the southern hemisphere and leads up to the running of the famous **Adelaide Cup** in May at Morphettville racecourse.

One special event for children and adults is the November **Christmas Pageant** in the city streets of Adelaide. Floats depicting well-known nursery rhymes and fairytale characters thrill all those who line the streets to welcome Father Christmas to South Australia.

Information on South Australia's festivals can be obtained from the South Australian Travel Centre, 1 King William St, Adelaide; (08) 8212 1505. **See also:** individual town entries in A–Z listing.

SOUTH AUSTRALIA

SOUTH AUSTRALIA from A to Z

Aldinga Beach
Pop. 3541

MAP REF. 297 E5, 298 A11, 301 B3, 303 K10

A small holiday town 49 km s of Adelaide, near the Fleurieu Peninsula renowned for its good fishing, surfing, and diving. **Of interest:** Gnome Caves, Aldinga Beach Rd, a children's attraction. Feb.: Historic Bike Race; Multicultural Festival. **In the area:** At Aldinga, 4 km NE, St Ann's Anglican Church (1866); Uniting Church (1863). McLaren Vale, 16 km NE, centre of winegrowing region with more than 50 wineries. Maslin Beach, 10 km N, Australia's first nude bathing beach. At Port Willunga Beach, 3 km NW, ruins of *Star of Greece* (1888) visible at low tide. Bush trails through Aldinga Scrub Conservation Park, 16 km sw, leaflets available at Tourist information. Off-shore, Aldinga Aquatic Reserve has a rare reef formation and good diving. Lookout, 6 km sw, views of Gulf St Vincent. Lookout, 23 km sw, views of Myponga Reservoir. At Myponga, 16 km s, historic buildings; Myponga Reservoir. Begonia Farm, 28 km s; open Oct.–Apr. **Tourist information:** Aldinga Bay Holiday Village, Esplanade; (08) 8556 5019. **Accommodation:** 2 B&B, 1 cara./camp. park. **See also:** The Fleurieu Peninsula; Vineyards and Wineries.

Andamooka
Pop. 471

MAP REF. 304 G4

Andamooka is surrounded by opal fields and is located about 600 km N of Adelaide, to the west of the salt pan Lake Torrens. The road to Andamooka from the turnoff at Roxby Downs is now sealed. The town is off the beaten track, conditions are harsh in summer, the weather is severe and water is precious. Many people live in dugouts to protect themselves from the extreme heat. Visitors need to obtain a precious-stone prospecting permit from the Mines Department in Adelaide before staking out a claim and trying their luck. Looking for opals on mullock dumps left by miners requires permission from the owners of the claim. There are tours of the area, including underground mine tours and showrooms with opals for sale. **Of interest:** In Main St: Duke's Bottle

Collingrove Homestead (1850), a National Trust property near Angaston

House, made of empty beer bottles; Andamooka Press, working printing museum in underground house (open daily); Andamooka Gems and Trains, mineral specimens and model railway; quaint 1930s miners' cottages, next to creek bed. Art and craft market, 1st Sun. each month. Easter: Family Fun Day and White Dam Walk. Oct.: Opal Festival. **In the area:** Roxby Downs, 30 km w, service town for nearby Olympic Dam where copper, gold, silver and uranium are mined; tours of mining operations available. At Woomera, 120 km sw, Heritage Centre and Missile Park, with displays of rockets and aircraft. **Tourist information:** Main St; (08) 8672 7062. **Accommodation:** 1 hotel, 1 motel, 1 B&B, 1 cara./camp. park.

Angaston
Pop. 1819

MAP REF. 296 G4, 300 I5, 303 M8

Angaston is in the highest part of the Barossa Valley; within 79 km of the coast, it is 361 m above sea level. The town is named after prominent 1830s Barossa Valley settler, George Fife Angas. **Of interest:** Angas Park Fruit Co., Murray St, produces dried fruit and nuts (open daily). For local art and craft: Angaston abbey, Murray St; Bethany Arts and Crafts, Washington St. Easter: Barossa Valley Vintage

Festival (odd-numbered years). Aug.: Barossa Classic Gourmet Weekend. Oct.: Barossa Music Festival. **In the area:** Good view of Barossa Valley from Mengler's Hill Lookout, 8 km sw. Yalumba Winery, 2 km s. Collingrove Homestead (1850), 7 km se, National Trust property once owned by Angas pioneering family; viewing and accommodation available (meals only by prior arrangement). Henschke Cellars, 10 km se. Mountadam Winery at Eden Valley, 19 km se. At Springton, 27 km se: Grand Cru Estate; Herbig Tree; Herbig Homestead Heritage Centre (open by appt); Merindah Mohair Farm (open daily). Yookamurra Sanctuary, 54 km NE, for local wildlife and plant species (check opening times); guided walks and tours and accommodation available (bookings essential). **Tourist information:** Barossa Wine and Visitor Centre, 66 Murray St, Tanunda; (08) 8563 0600; freecall, 1800 812662. **Accommodation:** 2 hotels, 1 motel, 7 B&B. **See also:** Vineyards and Wineries.

Ardrossan
Pop. 1008

MAP REF. 303 J7

Ardrossan, 148 km NW of Adelaide, is the largest port on the east coast of Yorke Peninsula. An important outlet for wheat, barley and dolomite, it is an attractive town with excellent crabbing and fishing from the jetty. **Of interest**: Ardrossan and District Historical Museum, Fifth St. The stump jump plough was invented here in the late 1800s; restored plough on display on cliffs at end of First St in East Tce. Jan.: Ardrossan Alive, outdoor music festival (odd-numbered years). **In the area:** Salt and dolomite mines. BHP Lookout, 2 km S. For keen divers, *Zanoni* wreck off coast, 20 km SE (permission required to dive). Clinton Conservation Park, 40 km N. **Tourist information:** Ardrossan Caravan Park, Park Tce; (08) 8837 3262. **Accommodation:** 2 hotel/motels, 2 cara./camp. parks.

Arkaroola   Pop. 10

MAP REF. 299 G3, 305 M3

Arkaroola is a remote village settlement, founded in 1968, in the northern Flinders Ranges, about 660 km N of Adelaide. This privately-owned property of 61 000 ha has been opened as the Arkaroola-Mt Painter Resort and Wilderness Sanctuary. The area's rugged outback country is crossed by incredible quartzite ridges, deep gorges and rich mineral deposits, and is a haven for birdlife and rare marsupials. **Of interest:** Astronomical Observatory (check viewing times). Mineral and Fossil Museum. Outdoor Pastoral and Mining Museum. Pioneer cottage. **In the area:** At nearby Gammon Ranges National Park, extensive wilderness areas; ruins of Cornish-style smelters (1861). Scenic waterholes Bolla Bollana, and Nooldoonooldoona, 12 km NW. Famous Mt Painter, 10 km N; further 20 km N, breathtaking views from Freeling Heights, overlooking Yudnamutana Gorge. Siller's Lookout overlooking Lake Frome (a salt lake), 16 km N. Weetootla Gorge, permanent springs, 31 km SW. Italowie Gap, 42 km SW; 4WD vehicles required; recommended for experienced bushwalkers only. Big Moro Gorge, with rock pools, 59 km S (Aboriginal Land Permit required for entry, contact Nepabunna Community Council, (08) 8648 3764); note access to gorge may require 4WD. Mt Chambers Gorge, with Aboriginal rock carvings, 98 km S. Marked walking trails, self-guide pamphlets available from Tourist information. Ridgetop Tour, spectacular 42-km 4WD trip across Australia's most rugged mountains; 'tagalong' 4WD tours (take your own

4WD, but join an organised convoy); scenic flights and guided tours available; contact Tourist information for details. **Tourist information:** Visitors Information Centre; (08) 8648 4848. **Accommodation:** 3 motels, 1 hostel, 1 cara./camp. park. **See also:** The Flinders Ranges; National Parks.

Balaklava   Pop. 1439

MAP REF. 303 K6

Balaklava, in a picturesque setting on the banks of the River Wakefield, 91 km N of Adelaide, was named after a famous battle in the Crimean War. **Of interest:** National Trust Museum, May Tce, has relics of district's early days of European settlement (check opening times). Country Crafters for local craft, 30 George St. Court House Gallery and Shop, Edith Tce, community art gallery. Urlwin Park Agricultural Museum, Short Tce. Lions Club Walking Trail along Wakefield River and through town (brochure available at Tourist information). Racecourse, Racecourse Rd, a major country racecourse. Weekend glider joy-flights, contact Tourist information. Sept.: Agricultural Show. **In the area:** Devils Gardens, 7 km NE on Auburn Rd; The Rocks Reserve, 10 km E; both with picnic facilities. Beachside town of Port Wakefield, 26 km W at head of Gulf St Vincent. **Tourist information:** Country Crafters, 30 George St; (08) 8862 2070. **Accommodation:** 2 hotels, 1 cara./camp. park.

Barmera   Pop. 1859

MAP REF. 303 P7

The sloping shores of Lake Bonney make a delightful setting for the Riverland town of Barmera, 214 km NE of Adelaide. Lake Bonney is ideal for swimming, water-skiing, sailing, boating and fishing. The surrounding irrigated land is given over mainly to vineyards, but there are also apricot and peach orchards, and citrus groves. Soldier settlement after World War I marked the beginning of today's community-oriented town. **Of interest:** Donald Campbell Obelisk, Queen Elizabeth Dr., commemorates Campbell's attempt on world water-speed record in 1964. Rocky's Country Hall of Fame, Barwell Ave. Bonneyview Wines, Sturt Hwy, has gallery, restaurant and picnic facilities (open daily). Easter: Lake Bonney Yachting Regatta. June: SA Country

Music Festival and Awards. Oct.: Agricultural Show. Dec.: Christmas Pageant and Fireworks. **In the area:** At North Lake, 10 km NW, ruins of Napper's Old Accommodation House (1850) preserved by National Trust. Loch Luna Game Reserve, 16 km NW; wetlands cruise available by appt, contact Tourist information. At Overland Corner, 19 km NW on Morgan Rd: hotel (1859), now also National Trust museum; self-guide historical walking trail. Near Monash, 8 km NE, Wein Valley Estate Winery. Highway Fern Haven, 5 km E on Sturt Hwy, rare ferns in tropical setting (open daily). At Cobdogla, 5 km W: Irrigation Museum, with the only working Humphrey Pump in the world, photos and memorabilia of Loveday Internment Camp (brochure available for self-guide drive to remains of camp site, 3 km SW), as well as steam rides, historic displays and picnic areas; Cobdogla Coloured Wool, featuring spinning demonstrations, lamb-feeding and coloured fleeces; Chambers Creek, for canoeing and prolific birdlife; Art and Craft Fair at Easter. Moorook Game Reserve, 16 km SW, includes Wachtels Lagoon with birdlife and walking trail. Nearby, Yatco Lagoon abounds with a variety of birdlife. **Tourist information:** Barmera Travel Centre, Barwell Ave; (08) 8588 2289. **Accommodation:** 2 motels, 1 hotel/motel, 3 cara./camp. parks.

Beachport   Pop. 443

MAP REF. 301 F10

First settled as a whaling station in the 1830s, Beachport is a quiet little town 51 km S of Robe. Rivoli Bay nearby provides safe swimming beaches as well as shelter for lobster boats. One of the State's longest jetties stretches out into the waters of Rivoli Bay and is very popular with anglers. **Of interest:** Old Wool and Grain Store, Railway Tce, now National Trust Museum with whaling, shipping and local history exhibits. Artifacts Museum, McCourt St, Aboriginal heritage displays. Centenary Park in town centre has barbecues, tennis, playgrounds and skateboard track. Heritage walk, maps available from National Trust Museum; other walking trails, maps available from District Council. **In the area:** At Lake George, 4 km N, waterbirds, windsurfing and fishing. Beachport Conservation Park, between Lake George and the Southern

Brachina Gorge, near Blinman, one of the scenic attractions in the Flinders Ranges

Ocean, features Aboriginal shell middens and walking trails (self-guide leaflets available from Tourist information) Bowman Scenic Drive from base of lighthouse to Woolleys Rock (5 km N) for spectacular views of Southern Ocean; on the way, visitors can swim in Pool of Siloam, a lake with high salt content and reputed therapeutic benefits. Woakwine Cutting, 10 km N on Robe Rd, extraordinary drainage project, with observation platform and machinery exhibit. **Tourist information:** District Council, McCourt St; (08) 8735 8029. **Accommodation:** 1 hotel, 1 motel, 1 hostel, 2 cara./camp. parks.

Berri   Pop. 3733

MAP REF. 303 Q7

The commercial centre of the Riverland region, Berri is 227 km NE of Adelaide. Once a wood-refuelling stop for paddle-steamers and barges which plied the Murray River, the town was first proclaimed in 1911. This is fruit- and vine-growing country, dotted with peaceful picnic and fishing areas. **Of interest:** Earth Works, Sturt Hwy, for local arts and crafts. Berri Art Gallery, Wilson St. Water Tower Lookout (17 m), Fiedler St, for panoramic views of river and town. River crossings on Riverland's only twin ferries crossing Murray River

(vehicular, 24-hr service, free of charge). Nearby, sculpture and cave memorial to Jimmy James, Aboriginal tracker. Houseboats and canoes for hire, contact Tourist information. Feb.: Rodeo; Speedboat Spectacular (subject to river condition). Easter: Carnival. Nov.: Art, Craft and Fine Food Fair. **In the area:** On Sturt Hwy: large range of dried fruit and confectionery at Angas Park Kiosk, 3 km W; Berri Estates winery and distillery, largest winemaking facility in southern hemisphere, 13 km W. Murray River National Park, 10 km SW, features Kia Kia Nature Trail for bushwalkers. Martin's Bend, 2 km E, popular for water-skiing and picnicking. Berrivale Orchards, 4 km N on Sturt Hwy, has educational audiovisual on Riverland's history and various stages in processing of fruit (open Mon.–Fri., Sat. a.m.). Wilabalangaloo flora and fauna reserve, 5 km N, off Sturt Hwy, features walking trails, spectacular scenery, museum and paddlewheeler (check opening times). Rollerama roller-skating centre nearby. At Monash, 12 km NW on Morgan Rd, Monash Adventure Park, features maze, flying fox and rope bridge. Nearby, Wein Valley Estate Winery. **Tourist information:** 24 Vaughan Tce; (08) 8582 1655. **Accommodation:** 1 hotel/motel, 3 motels, 1 hostel, 1 cara./camp. park.

Blinman   Pop. 30

MAP REF. 299 E6, 305 K6

Blinman, 478 km N of Adelaide and 30 km from the magnificent Flinders Ranges National Park, was a thriving copper-mining centre from 1860 to 1890. **Of interest:** Several historic buildings in Mine Rd including hotel (1869), post office (1862) and police station (1874). **In the area:** Great Wall of China, ironstone-capped ridge, 10 km S on Wilpena Rd. Further south, beautiful Aroona Valley and ruins of old Aroona Homestead; nearby Mt Hayward and Brachina Gorge. Scenic Glass Gorge, beautiful wildflowers in spring, and Parachilna Gorge, between Blinman and Parachilna; nearby, the Blinman Pools, fed by a permanent spring. Scenic drive east through Eregunda Valley then northeast to Mt Chambers Gorge with its rock pools and Aboriginal carvings, then north-west to view spectacular Big Moro Gorge off Arkaroola Rd (Aboriginal Land Permit required, contact Nepabunna Land Council, (08) 8648 3764; note access to gorge may require 4WD). **Tourist information:** Post office, Mine Rd; (08) 8648 4874. **Accommodation:** 1 hotel/motel, 1 cara./camp. park.

Bordertown   Pop. 2235

MAP REF. 301 H6

Bordertown is a quiet town on the Dukes Hwy, 274 km SE of Adelaide. Growth was stimulated after 1852 when it became an important supply centre for the goldfields of western Victoria. Today the area is noted for wool, cereals, meat and vegetable production. **Of interest:** Robert J.L. Hawke, former Australian Prime Minister, was born here and his childhood home, in Farquhar St, has been renovated and includes memorabilia (open Mon.–Fri.). Apex park, Woolshed St. **In the area:** Bordertown Wildlife Park, Dukes Hwy, has native birds and animals, including pure white kangaroos. Historic Clayton Farm, 3 km S, features vintage farm machinery and thatched buildings (open p.m. Sun.–Fri.). Clayton Farm Vintage Field Day, held Oct. long weekend. At Mundulla, 10 km SW, Mundulla Hotel (1884), a National Trust building with restaurant, tearooms and craft shop. At Padthaway, 42 km SW, an 1882 homestead housing Padthaway Estate winery (meals and accommodation available). Nearby, picnic areas located among magnificent red gums and stringybarks at Padthaway Conservation Park. Bangham Conservation Park, 30 km SE, near the town of Frances. **Tourist information:** Council Chambers, 43 Woolshed St; (08) 8752 1044. **Accommodation:** 1 hotel, 1 hotel/motel, 3 motels, 1 cara./ camp. park.

Burra
Pop. 1191

MAP REF. 303 L5

Nestled in Bald Hills Range, 154 km N of Adelaide, Burra, a former copper-mining centre, is one of the country's best-preserved mining towns. Copper was discovered in 1845 and extracted to the value of almost $10 million before the mine closed in 1877. The district of Burra Burra (Hindi for 'great great') is now famous for stud merino sheep, and Burra is the market town for surrounding farms. *Breaker Morant* was filmed here. **Of interest:** Passport key-hire system allows visitors to walk or drive around 11 km of heritage buildings, museums, mine shafts and lookout points (details from Tourist information). Daily 2-hr bus tours of town and its mining history (bookings essential, contact Tourist information). Burra Creek miners' dugouts, alongside Blyth St, where over 1500 people lived during the boom; 2 dugouts preserved. Cemetery, off Spring St. Heritage and cemetery walks, details from Tourist information. Burra Mine Open Air Museum, off Market St, 'Enginehouse Museum' built in 1858 and reconstructed in 1986 near archaeological excavation of 30-m entry tunnel to Morphett's Shaft; also features ore dressing tower, powder magazine and offers spectacular views of open-cut mine and town. Market Square Museum, opposite Tourist information office. Malowen Lowarth Museum, Kingston St, in old miner's cottage. In Bridge Tce: underground cellars of old Unicorn Brewery; Paxton Square Cottages (1850), 33 two-, three- and four-roomed cottages built for Cornish miners, now restored as visitor accommodation. In Burra North: police lockup and stables (1849), Tregony St; Redruth Gaol (1857), off Tregony St; Bon Accord Mine buildings (1846), Railway Tce, now a museum complex. Picturesque spots alongside Burra Creek for swimming, canoeing and picnicking.

May: Antique and Decorating Fair. **In the area:** Chatswood Farm Gallery, 14 km S at Hanson. Wineries in the Clare Valley, about 40 km SW (inquire at Tourist information). Scenic 90-km Dares Hill Drive, begins 30 km N near Hallett (maps available from Tourist information). Barracas Park Alpacas, eastern outskirts of town (off Paradise St). Burra trail rides, 4 km E. Mongolata gold mine, 27 km E, tours available by appt. Burra Gorge, 27 km SE. **Tourist information:** 2 Market Sq.; (08) 8892 2154. **Accommodation:** 4 hotels, 1 motel, 15 B&B, 1 cara./camp. park.

Ceduna
Pop. 2753

MAP REF. 311 N9

Near the junction of the Flinders and Eyre hwys, Ceduna is the last major town before you cross the Nullarbor from east to west. It is the ideal place to check your car and stock up with food and water before the long drive. Ceduna is set on Murat Bay with its sandy coves, sheltered bays and offshore islands. It is an ideal base for a beach holiday, offering swimming, diving, fishing, water-skiing, windsurfing and boating. The port at Thevenard, 3 km SW, handles bulk grain, gypsum and salt. The fishing fleet is noted for its large whiting hauls. Snapper, salmon, tommy ruff and crab are other catches. There was a whaling station on St Peter Island in the 1850s. According to map references in Swift's *Gulliver's Travels*, the tiny people of Lilliput might well have lived on St Peter Is. (visible from Thevenard) or the Isles of St Francis. **Of interest:** Old Schoolhouse National Trust Museum, Park Tce, features pioneering items and artifacts from atomic testing at Maralinga (open Mon.–Sat.). Easter: Horseracing Carnival. Sept.: Agricultural Show. Oct.: Oyster-Fest. **In the area:** Oestmann's Fish Factory at Thevenard Boat Haven, tours available (best to go prior to 9 a.m.). At Denial Bay, 13 km W: McKenzie Ruins, site of original settlement; Clear Water oyster farm, tours available. Picnicking, surfing and safe fishing at Denial Bay and Davenport Creek with its pure white sandhills (west of town), and to the south-east, at Decres Bay, Laura Bay and Smoky Bay (boat charter for diving and fishing available at Ceduna). Southern right whales can be seen June–Oct. along coast west of Ceduna

particularly at head of Bight, 300 km W (tours available). At Penong, 73 km W: more than 40 windmills which draw town's water from underground; Penong Woolshed museum with local crafts (open 10 a.m.–4 p.m. daily); Goanywea camel day-rides and safaris (May–Oct.). Amazing sand dunes and excellent surf at Cactus Beach, 94 km W. Caves, western side of Nullarbor (guided tours only, book at Tourist information). Spectacular coastline includes prominent headland at Point Brown, 56 km SE, renowned for its surf beaches, salmon fishing and coastal walks. **Tourist information:** 58 Poynton St; (08) 8625 2780. **Accommodation:** 1 hotel/motel, 3 motels, 1 hostel, 5 cara./camp. parks. **See also:** The Eyre Peninsula.

Clare
Pop. 2575

MAP REF. 303 L5

Set in rich agricultural and pastoral country, this charming town was first settled by Europeans in 1842; it was named after County Clare in Ireland. The area is famed for its prize-winning table wines. Wheat, barley, honey, stud sheep and wool are other important regional industries. The first vines were planted by Jesuit priests at Sevenhill in 1848; today Sevenhill Cellars still produces table and sacramental wines. **Of interest:** National Trust museum housed in old police station (1850), cnr Victoria Rd and Neagles Rock Rd (open Sat., Sun. and holidays). Clarevale Museum, Lennon St, has winemaking memorabilia, housed in 1878 building. Stately Wolta Wolta Homestead (1846), West Tce, built by pastoralist John Hope and still owned by Hope family; homestead rebuilt after Ash Wednesday fires (open Sun. 10 a.m.–1 p.m.). Lookouts at Billy Goat Hill, from Wright St; Neagles Rock, Neagles Rock Rd. Maynard Memorial Park, Pioneer Ave. Historic town walk, self-guide leaflets available from Tourist information. Easter: Easter Races. May: Gourmet Weekend. Nov.: Spring Festival. **In the area:** More than 20 wineries in the area (most open for inspection and cellar-door sales, check opening times); *around Clare:* Tim Adams' Wines, Jim Barry Wines, Tim Knappstein Wines, Eldredge Wines, Leasingham Wines, Wendouree Cellars and Duncan Estate Winery; *in Polish Hill River district* (12 km SE): Pike's

SOUTH AUSTRALIA

Polish Hill River Estate, Paulett Wines and The Wilson Vineyard; *at Mintaro* (19 km SE): Mintaro Cellars and Reilly's Cottage; *at Sevenhill* (7 km S): Sevenhill Cellars established 1851 and featuring monastery buildings, including historic St Aloysius Church, Stringy Brae Wines, Waninga Wines, Skillogalee Wines, Jeanneret Wines and Mitchell Winery; *around Penwortham* (10 km S): Penwortham Wines and Pearson Wines; *around Watervale* (12 km S): Clos Clare, Crabtree of Watervale, Stephen John Wines, Quelltaler Estate which also has a wine museum, Rosenberg Cellars and Horrocks Winery; *around Auburn* (26 km S): Taylors Wines and Grosset Wines. Also at Mintaro (19 km SE): historic Martindale Hall (featured in the film *Picnic at Hanging Rock*), offers accommodation and dining (closed Christmas Day and Good Friday); slate quarry, operational since 1856 (not open for tours). Also at Auburn (26 km S): birthplace of poet C.J. Dennis in 1876; many historic buildings (accommodation available in some), maintained by National Trust (self-guide walking-tour leaflets available); Kollektakan Museum, featuring Coca-Cola memorabilia. At Blyth, 13 km W: flora and fauna in Padmainda Reserve; Medika Gallery, originally a Lutheran church (1886), specialising in Australian bird and flower paintings. Scenic drive 12 km S to Spring Gully Conservation Park (not well signposted) featuring rare red stringybarks. Springfarm Galleries, Springfarm Rd, 4 km SE. Bungaree Station Homestead (1841), historic merino sheep station 12 km N; station store sells knitting yarns, original patterns and hand-knitted Bungaree jumpers (tours and accommodation available). Geralka Rural Farm, a working farm 25 km N of Clare (tours available). **Tourist information:** Town hall, 229 Main North Rd; (08) 8842 2131. **Accommodation:** 1 hotel, 2 hotel/motels, 3 motels, 3 B&B, 1 cara./camp. park. **See also:** Festival Fun; Vineyards and Wineries.

Cleve   Pop. 738

MAP REF. 302 F5

Surrounded by rich farming country, this inland town on the Eyre Peninsula was first settled by Europeans in 1853. **Of interest:** Old Council Chambers Museum, Third St (contact Tourist information for appt). Aug.: Eyre Peninsula Field Days (even-numbered years). Oct.: Agricultural Show. **In the area:** Yeldulknie Conservation Park, 5 km N. Hincks and Bascombe Well conservation parks (located 35 and 90 km W respectively). Enjoy scenic drive along escarpment of Cleve-Cowell Hills. Arno Bay, 24 km SE, and Cowell, 42 km E, both have excellent swimming beaches and jetties that are popular with anglers. **Tourist information:** District Council, 13 Main St; (08) 8628 2004. **Accommodation:** 1 hotel/motel, limited cara./camp. facilities.

Coffin Bay   Pop. 343

MAP REF. 302 C8

A picturesque holiday town and fishing village located on the shores of a beautiful estuary 51 km NW of Port Lincoln; sailing, water-skiing, swimming and fishing are popular here. The coastal scenery in this area is magnificent. Oysters cultivated in Coffin Bay are among the best in the country. The bay's unusual name was bestowed by Matthew Flinders in 1802 to honour his friend Sir Isaac Coffin. **Of interest:** Oyster Farm, also renowned for its lobster, The Esplanade. Oyster Walk, a 6-km foreshore walkway from the caravan park to beyond Crinolin Point; leaflet available from Tourist information. Charter boats and boat hire available. **In the area:** Coffin Bay National Park and Kellidie Bay Conservation Park surround township; beautiful wildflowers abundant in both parks in spring. Farm Beach 50 km N; further 5 km N, Gallipoli Beach, location for film *Gallipoli*. Yangie Trail drive, 10 km S via Yangie Bay lookout (magnificent coastal views to Point Avoid). Further 50 km N, scenic stretch of Flinders Hwy between Mount Hope and Sheringa. At Koppio, 45 km NW: Blacksmith's museum; Kurrabi Lodge tea gardens. **Tourist information:** Beachcomber Agencies, The Esplanade; (08) 8685 4057. **Accommodation:** 1 motel, 1 cara./camp. park. **See also:** The Eyre Peninsula.

Coober Pedy   Pop. 2491

MAP REF. 309 R11

In the heart of South Australia's outback, 845 km N of Adelaide on the Stuart Hwy, is the opal-mining town of Coober Pedy. This is the last stop for petrol between Cadney Homestead (151 km N) and Glendambo (252 km S) on the Stuart Hwy. The name Coober Pedy is Aboriginal for 'white man's hole in the ground' – many of the town's inhabitants live in dugouts (at a constant 24°C underground) for protection from the severe summer temperatures, often reaching 45°C, and the cold winter nights. There is also a complete lack of timber for building. The countryside is desolate and harsh, and the town has reticulated water provided from a bore 23 km N. Opals were discovered here in 1915; today there are thousands of mines in the area. **Of interest:** Demonstrations of opals being cut and polished; jewellery and polished stones for sale. On eastern edge of town: Big Winch Lookout, Italian Club Rd; Old Timers Mine, Crowders Gully Rd, a mine museum and

The unique landscape of The Breakaways, near Coober Pedy

interpretive centre with self-guide walks. In Hutchison St: Umoona underground mine and museum, has interpretive section and underground mine tours; underground churches, including St Peter and St Pauls; Desert Cave, an international underground hotel complete with shopping complex. Underground Catacomb Church, Catacomb Rd. Guided tours of mines and town available, contact Tourist information. Easter: Opal Festival. Oct.: Coober Pedy Races. **In the area:** *Opal fields pocked with diggings; beware of unprotected mine shafts. Avoid entering any field area unless escorted by someone who knows the area.* For safety reasons, visitors to the mines are advised to join a tour. Trespassers on claims can be fined a minimum of $1000. Underground Pottery, 2 km W, features local pottery. The Breakaways, 30 km N, 40-sq. km reserve featuring unique landscape and good views; it has been used as a backdrop in many films and commercials; return via road passing part of the dog fence, a 9600-km fence stretching across Australia built to protect sheep properties in the south from wild dogs. Arckaringa Hills, 234 km N, richly coloured hills in an area known as the Painted Desert; also renowned for its flora and fauna. At William Creek, 170 km E: hotel; Race Meeting and Gymkhana held weekend before Easter. **Tourist information:** Council Offices, Hutchison St; (08) 8672 5298; freecall, 1800 637076. **Accommodation:** 1 hotel, 1 hotel/ motel, 8 motels, 1 B&B, 3 hostels, 4 cara./camp. parks. **See also:** The Outback.

Coonalpyn
Pop. 266

MAP REF. 301 F4, 303 O12

This tiny town on the Dukes Hwy is 180 km SE of Adelaide. It is a good base to explore the Mt Boothby (30 km SW) and Carcuma (20 km NE) conservation parks, and to see grey kangaroos, echidnas, emus and malleefowl. In summer, access to both parks is discouraged because of heat and fire danger. If planning to visit just before or just after summer, it is advisable to check bushfire danger and fire restrictions before entering parks; for Mt Boothby Conservation Park information, phone (08) 8575 1200; for Carcuma Conservation Park information, phone (08) 8757 2261. **Of interest:** Mural depicting town's history in pedestrian subway under trainline.

Adjacent to mural, dog exercise park. Daisy Patch Nursery, Richards Tce, for native plants. Feb.: Trash Farming Field Day (even-numbered years). **In the area:** Scenic 26-km loop drive, maps available at Tourist information.At Tintinara, 28 km SE, Apex Park; historic buildings at Tintinara Homestead, 9 km W. **Tourist information:** 33 Poyntz Tce; (08) 8571 1020. **Accommodation:** 1 hotel, 1 cara./camp. park.

Coonawarra
Pop. 40

MAP REF. 234 A2, 236 A13, 301 H10

The European settlement of Coonawarra goes back to 1890 when John Riddoch subdivided 2000 acres (800 ha) of his vast landholding for the development of orchards and vineyards. Although the vines flourished and excellent wines were made, demand was not high until a resurgence of interest in the 1950s and 1960s, and the region became recognised as an important winegrowing area. The terra rossa soil and dedicated viticulturalists and winemakers combine to produce award-winning white and red table wines. **Of interest:** Art gallery at Chardonnay Lodge, Penola Rd. **In the area:** Wineries, most open for tastings and cellar-door sales, including (from N to S): The Ridge Wines, Redman Wines, Brands Laira Wines, Wynns Coonawarra Estate, Rouge Homme, Zema Estate, Mildara Wines, St Mary's Vineyard (15 km E), Katnook Estate, Highbank Wines, Leconfield Coonawarra, Bowen Estate, Balnaves of Coonawarra, Hazelgrove Winery, Hollick Wines, Wetherall Wines, Punters Corner, Penfolds and Ladbroke Grove Wines. **Tourist information:** 27 Arthur St, Penola; (08) 8737 2855. **Accommodation:** 1 motel. **See also:** Vineyards and Wineries.

Cowell
Pop. 695

MAP REF. 302 G5

A small, pleasant township 108 km S of Whyalla, Cowell is on the almost landlocked Franklin Harbour. One of the world's major jade deposits is in the district. The sandy beach at Cowell is safe for swimming; fishing is excellent. Oyster farming is a local industry and fresh oysters can be purchased year-round from various outlets. **Of interest:** Old post office and attached residence (1888), Main St, now Franklin Harbour

National Trust Historical Museum. On Lincoln Hwy: open-air agricultural museum; Cowell Jade Motel, has displays of local jade jewellery and sales. Boats available for hire. **In the area:** Franklin Harbour Conservation Park, south of town, has good fishing spots. Swimming and excellent fishing locations abound, including around Gibbon Point, 15 km S. Arno Bay, 48 km S, a popular holiday town with sandy beaches and jetty for fishing. **Tourist information:** Council Offices, Main St; (08) 8629 2019. **Accommodation:** 2 hotels, 1 motel, 1 B&B, 2 cara./camp. parks. **See also:** The Eyre Peninsula.

Crystal Brook
Pop. 1282

MAP REF. 303 J3

Once part of a vast sheep station, this town, 25 km SE of Port Pirie, is now a major centre for the sheep, beef and cereal industries of the region. **Of interest:** National Trust Museum, Brandis St, has local history collection in first two-storeyed building in town, original butcher's shop and bakery; underground bakehouse behind building. Crystal Crafts, Bowman St, for local craft. Picnicking in creekside parks. Aug.: Agricultural Show. **In the area:** Bowman Park, 5 km E, surrounds ruins of Bowman family property Crystal Brook Run (1847), and has excellent native fauna. Heysen Walking Trail runs through Bowman Park. At Gladstone, 21 km NE, set in rich rural country in Rocky River Valley: tours of Gladstone gaol (1881); Trend Drinks Factory, home of Old Style Ginger Beer (tours available). At Laura, boyhood town of C.J. Dennis, author of *The Songs of a Sentimental Bloke*, 32 km N: cottage crafts; art galleries; historic buildings; self-guide walking-tour, leaflet available at Biles Art Gallery, Herbert St (open Sat., Sun. and public holidays); Folk Fair at Beetaloo Valley and Reservoir (west of Laura) in Apr. Near Wirrabara, 50 km N, scenic walks through pine forests. At Redhill, 25 km S: riverside walk; museum; craft shop; antique shop. Koolunga, 10 km E of Redhill, has cottage industry (potters and painters) outlets and picnic areas. Salt lakes around Snowtown, 50 km S. Nearby on Lochiel–Ninnes Rd, lookout with superb views of inland lakes and countryside. Yacka, 40 km SE, has sheepdog trials in Aug. **Tourist information:** District Council Offices, Bowman St;

(08) 8636 2150. **Accommodation:** Crystal Brook, 2 hotels, 1 cara./camp. park. Bowman Park, 1 hostel.

Edithburgh
Pop. 453

MAP REF. 302 I10

Located on the foreshore at the south-eastern tip of Yorke Peninsula, Edithburgh overlooks Gulf St Vincent and Troubridge Island. **Of interest:** Native Flora Park (17 1/2 ha), Ansty Tce. Edithburgh Museum, Edith St, has historical maritime collection (check opening times). Bakehouse Arts and Crafts, Blanche St, for local crafts. Town jetty, end of Edith St, built in 1873. Natural tidal pool, excellent for swimming. Offshore skindiving. Nature walks, south to Sultana Point and north to Coobowie, brochures available from Tourist information. Oct.: State Windsurfing Speed Trials; Gala Day. **In the area:** Nearby Sultana Point, 2 km S, for boating, fishing and swimming. Scenic drive south-west along coast to Innes National Park. Coobowie, 5 km N, a popular coastal town. Tours to Troubridge Island Conservation Park (1/2 hour by boat). **Tourist information:** Newsagency and Deli, Blanche St; (08) 8852 6230. **Accommodation:** 1 hotel/motel, 3 motels, 2 B&B, 1 cara./camp. park. **See also:** The Yorke Peninsula.

Elliston
Pop. 242

MAP REF. 302 B5

Nestled in a small range of hills on the shore of Waterloo Bay, Elliston is a pleasant coastal town and the centre for a cereal-growing, mixed-farming and fishing community. Known for its rugged and scenic coastline, excellent fishing and safe swimming beaches, Elliston is a popular holiday destination. **Of interest:** Town hall mural, Main St, an art history of town and district. **In the area:** Just north of town: clifftop walk at Waterloo Bay; good surfing near Anxious Bay. Walkers Rocks, 15 km N, has good beaches, rock fishing and a camping area. Talia Caves, 40 km N. Camel Beach, 50 km N, good salmon fishing. Lock's Well Beach and Sheringa Beach to south, for surf fishing. Scenic drives north and south of town offer superb views of magnificent coastline; good views also from Cummings Monument Lookout, just off hwy near Kiana, 52 km S. Flinders Is., 35 km offshore (limited accommodation). **Tourist information:** District Council, Beach Tce; (08) 8687 9177. **Accommodation:** 1 hotel/motel, 1 motel, 2 cara./camp. parks. **See also:** The Eyre Peninsula.

Gawler
Pop. 13 835

MAP REF. 296 D5, 303 L8

Settled by Europeans in 1839, Gawler, 40 km NE of Adelaide, is an historic town and the centre for a thriving agricultural district. It is also the gateway to the famous Barossa Valley. **Of interest:** Historic buildings: Gawler Mill, Bridge St; old telegraph station, Murray St (open Sun. or obtain key from Tourist information). Old Eagle Foundry, King St, now a B&B (also open to tourists). Para Para (1862), Penrith Ave, historic residence (open Sat., Sun. and public holidays). Anglican Church, has interesting pipe organ (open Sun. or by appt, contact Tourist information). Walking tour of Church Hill district (adjacent to Murray St), a State Heritage Area. Self-guide walking and driving tours, leaflets from Tourist information. Dead Man's Pass Reserve, end Murray St, has picnic facilities and walking trails. June: Three-day Equestrian Event. Aug.: Agricultural Show. Nov.: Country Music Festival; Sutch is Light (lighting of Australia's tallest Christmas tree in late Nov.) **In the area:** Restored Willaston post office, 2 km N. Roseworthy Agricultural Museum, 15 km N on Roseworthy campus of University of Adelaide, is a dryland farming museum featuring vintage farm implements, engines and

The Yorke Peninsula

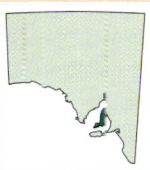

Yorke Peninsula was put on the map by the discovery of rich copper-ore deposits in 1861 and the influx of thousands of miners, including so many from Cornwall that the **Wallaroo–Moonta–Kadina** area became known as Little Cornwall. Today, it is one of the world's richest wheat and barley regions.

The drive down the highway on the east coast is mainly within sight of the sea. Many of the east-coast towns have excellent fishing from long jetties once used for loading grain ships. Beach, surf and rock fishing are excellent, as is crabbing.

The west coast of Yorke Peninsula is lined with safe swimming beaches and excellent coastal scenery. **Port Victoria,** the last of the windjammer ports, was once the main port of call for sailing ships transporting grain. Further north, Moonta's old stone buildings give it a sense of history and the Moonta mines tell of its mining heyday.

Innes National Park with its diverse hinterland, birdlife and impressive coastal scenery is on the southern tip of the Peninsula. Visit the site of a once-flourishing township, Inneston. Pondalowie Bay is a must for surfers. Rocky cliff tops and windswept headlands provide vantage points for views across Investigator Strait.

For further information, contact the Yorke Peninsula Visitor Information Centre, 51 Taylor St, Kadina; (08) 8821 2093. **See also:** Innes National Park entry in National Parks, and individual text entries in A–Z listing for those towns indicated by bold type. **Map reference:** 302 H8.

Historic miner's cottage, Moonta

working tractors (open Wed. and 3rd Sun. each month, tours by appt). Astronomical Society of SA's observatory at Stockport, 30 km N, has public viewing nights (check at Tourist information for details). Scholz Park Museum, 54 km N, at Riverton. Wellington Hotel at Waterloo, 76 km N (near Manoora), once Cobb & Co. staging point. **Tourist information:** 2 Lyndoch Rd; (08) 8522 6814. **Accommodation:** 1 hotel, 1 motel, 4 B&B, 2 cara./camp. parks.

Goolwa
Pop. 3018

MAP REF. 297 I7, 301 C3, 303 L11

Goolwa is a rapidly-growing holiday town on the last big bend of the Murray River, 12 km from its mouth near Lake Alexandrina. Once a key port in the golden days of the riverboats, the area has a strong tradition of shipbuilding, trade and fishing. Today, the area is ideal for boating, fishing and aquatic sports, and popular with birdwatchers and photographers. Southern right whales visit the bay July–Sept. **Of interest:** Historic buildings in B.F. Laurie Lane, off Cadell St: distinctive railway superintendent's house (1852), known as 'the round-roofed house'; RSL Club, in former stables of Goolwa Railway (1853). In Cadell St, display of first horse-drawn railway carriage used in SA between Goolwa and Port Elliott from 1854. Cockle Train, steam-train rides between Goolwa and Victor Harbor (check times at Tourist information). National Trust Museum, Porter St, housed in former blacksmith's shop dating from 1870s. Next door, in original but rebuilt cottage, Goolwa Print Room. Both hotels, the Goolwa in Cadell St and the Corio in Railway Pl., date from 1850s. Signal Point River Murray Interpretive Centre, The Wharf, computerised display of river and district before European settlement, and the impact of local development. South Coast Regional Arts Centre, wharf precinct, in restored original police station. Clydesdale wagon rides (Sat., Sun. and school holidays); day and overnight boat trips to the Coorong via Murray River (Oct.–June) – depart from wharf. Armfield Slip, Admiral Tce, has working exhibition of boat building. Expresso Junction emu farm, Airport Rd, for tours of working emu farm. Feb.: Milang to Goolwa Freshwater Classic Yacht Race. Mar.: Wooden Boat Festival (odd-numbered years). **In the area:** Excellent fishing. Bird sanctuary east of Goolwa, has swans, pelicans and other waterfowl, also bird hide. Nearby, the

The Eyre Peninsula

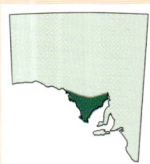

The western side of Eyre Peninsula is exposed to the full force of the Southern Ocean

The Eyre Peninsula is a vast region stretching from Whyalla in the east to the Western Australian border in the west, and, in a north-south direction, from the Gawler Ranges to Port Lincoln. Spencer Gulf borders the eastern edge of the peninsula, along which are located a number of small coastal towns featuring sheltered waters, safe swimming, white sandy beaches and excellent fishing from either shore or boat. The peaceful resort towns of **Cowell,** Arno Bay and Port Neill are charming. Cowell has the added attraction of being one of the world's major sources of black and green jade.

Whyalla is the second largest city in South Australia and acts as an important gateway to Eyre Peninsula. Located near the top of Spencer Gulf, this bustling, industrially-based city also offers a wide range of attractions for the visitor.

The southern Eyre Peninsula includes the tourist resort towns of **Tumby Bay,** famous for its fishing and the beautiful Sir Joseph Banks Group of islands nearby; the jewel in the crown, the city of **Port Lincoln,** nestled on blue Boston Bay; and **Coffin Bay,** with its magnificent sheltered waters.

In stark contrast to the sheltered waters of Spencer Gulf, the west coast is exposed to the full force of the Southern Ocean and offers some of the most spectacular coastal scenery to be found in Australia. This coast is punctuated by a number of bays and inlets and, not surprisingly, several resort towns have flourished where shelter can be found from precipitous cliffs and pounding surf. **Elliston,** Venus Bay, Port Kenny, **Streaky Bay,** Smoky Bay and **Ceduna** – all offer the visitor a diverse range of coastal scenery, good fishing and other water-related activities. The only known mainland breeding colony of sea lions (at Point Labatt), and Murphy's Haystacks, windworn granite inselbergs over 1500 million years old, are both south of Streaky Bay.

Ceduna provides a vital service and accommodation facility for traffic across Australia, and acts as a gateway information centre for visitors approaching the region from the west.

The hinterland of Eyre Peninsula encompasses the picturesque Koppio Hills in the south, the vast grain-growing tracts of the central region and the eternal beauty of the Gawler Ranges in the north.

The Nullarbor, the western corridor into the region, is a vast treeless plain, bordered in the south by towering limestone cliffs that drop sheer to the pounding Southern Ocean. Here schools of southern right whales can be seen along the coastline between June and October on their annual breeding migration. Sightings of these beautiful creatures occur regularly and are on the increase.

For more information on the area, contact the Eyre Peninsula Tourism Association, Jobomi House, Liverpool St, Port Lincoln; (08) 8682 4688. **See also:** individual text entries in A–Z listing for those towns indicated by bold type. **Map reference:** 302 C6.

SOUTH AUSTRALIA

Barrages, desalination points that prevent salt water from reaching the Murray River. MV *Aroona*, PS *Mundoo* and MV *Coorong Pirate* cruise to mouth of the Murray, the Coorong, the Barrages and the Lower Murray. On Hindmarsh Is. (via ferry), Captain Sturt lookout and monument, location of first European sighting of mouth of Murray River. Scenic flights available; airport 5 km N. At Currency Creek, 8 km N: Canoe Tree; Tonkin's Currency Creek Winery (with restaurant and fauna park); creekside park and walking trail. Tooperang Trout Farm, 20 km NW. **Tourist information:** Old Library, cnr Cadell St and Goolwa Tce; (08) 8555 1144. **Accommodation:** 3 motels, 4 B&B, 3 cara./camp. parks. **See also:** The Fleurieu Peninsula.

Hawker   Pop. 345

MAP REF. 299 D10, 305 J9

This outback town in the centre of the northern Flinders Ranges is 369 km N of Adelaide. Once a railway town, it is now the centre of a unique area that attracts visitors from both Australia and overseas to marvel at the colouring and grandeur of the many ranges that make up the Flinders. **Of interest:** Museum at Hawker Motors, cnr Wilpena and Cradock rds. Historic buildings: post office (1882), Hawker Hotel (1882), both in Elder Tce; old railway-station complex (1885), Leigh Creek Rd. Heritage walks through town, scenic flights and 4WD tours available, contact Tourist information. May: Horseracing Carnival. Sept.: Art Exhibition. **In the area:** Moralana Scenic Drive, 42 km N, joins roads to Wilpena and Leigh Creek. At Merna Mora Station, 46 km N, station holidays available. Walking trail and scenic lookout at Jarvis Hill, 5 km SW. Rock paintings at Yourambulla Caves, 11 km S. Historic Kanyaka ruins, 32 km S off main road to Quorn. Ruins at Wilson, Hookina, Wonoka and Willow Waters; check directions at Hawker before departure. **Tourist information:** Hawker Motors, cnr Wilpena and Cradock rds; (08) 8648 4014. **Accommodation:** 1 hotel/motel, 1 motel, 2 cara./camp. parks. **See also:** The Flinders Ranges; National Parks.

Innamincka   Pop. 9

MAP REF. 307 Q7, 514 H10

This tiny settlement, 1027 km NE of Adelaide, is built around a hotel and trading post on the Strzelecki Track, and is on the banks of the Cooper Creek. *Motorists intending to travel along the track should ensure road conditions are suitable by phoning the Northern Roads Condition Hotline on (08) 11633 before departing; also read the section on Outback Motoring. There are no supplies or petrol between Lyndhurst and Innamincka.* **Of interest:** Rebuilt Australian Inland Mission hostel, now houses National Parks office. Boat and canoe hire available. **In the area:** Picturesque Cullyamurra Waterhole on Cooper Creek, 16 km NE, has Aboriginal rock carvings and excellent fishing. Various memorials to explorers Burke and Wills near Innamincka; famous 'Dig Tree' is best known, 40 km across border in Qld. Coongie Lakes, a haven for wildlife, 103 km NW (road conditions can vary considerably, 4WD recommended). **Tourist information:** Trading Post, Main St; (08) 8675 9900. **Accommodation:** 1 hotel/motel. **See also:** The Outback.

Jamestown   Pop. 1359

MAP REF. 303 L3, 305 K13

Jamestown is a well-planned country town 205 km N of Adelaide. The surrounding country produces stud sheep and cattle, cereals, dairy produce and timber. **Of interest:** Heritage murals, Ayr St. Railway Station Museum, Irvine St (open Sun. and by appt). Parks along banks of Belalie Creek (ideal for picnicking); banks floodlit at night. Easter: Bilby Hunt. Oct.: Agricultural Show. Dec.: Christmas Pageant. **In the area:** Scenic drive through Bundaleer Forest Reserve, 9 km S, towards New Campbell Hill for panoramic views of plains towards Mt Remarkable and The Bluff. Near Spalding, 34 km S: series of open waterways with picnic areas and trout fishing opportunities; Geralka Rural Farm, 49 km S, working commercial farm (tours available). Appila Springs, scenic picnic spot 8 km from Appila, 24 km NW. **Tourist information:** Country Retreat Caravan Park, 103 Ayr St; (08) 8664 0077. **Accommodation:** 3 hotels, 1 hotel/motel, 1 cara./camp. park.

Kadina   Pop. 3536

MAP REF. 302 I6

The largest town on Yorke Peninsula, Kadina is the chief commercial centre for the region. The town's history includes the boom copper-mining era during the 1800s and early 1900s, when thousands of Cornish miners flocked to the area; the community is still proud of its ancestry. **Of interest:** Historic hotels: the Wombat, the Kadina, both in Taylor St; Royal Exchange, Digby St, with its iron lace balconies and shady verandahs. National Trust Kadina Heritage Museum complex, includes Matta House (1863), home of manager of Matta Matta Copper Mine, agricultural machinery, blacksmith's shop, printing museum, old Matta mine, and the Kadina Story, a display depicting the history of Kadina and Wallaroo. Banking and Currency Museum, 3 Graves St, a unique private museum (check opening times). Wallaroo Mines site, open for signposted self-guide walking tour. Creative Activities Network, personalised learning experiences of hiking, gardening, historical walks, sailing, etc. with local residents (available throughout region, contact Tourist information). Easter: Bowling Carnival. May: Prize-winning Kernewek Lowender, a Cornish festival, held in conjunction with Wallaroo and Moonta (odd-numbered years). Aug.: Agricultural Show. **In the area:** Moonta, 18 km SW. Wallaroo, 10 km W. Yorke Peninsula Field Days at Paskeville, 19 km SE, in Sept. (odd-numbered years). **Tourist information:** 51 Taylor St; (08) 8821 2093. **Accommodation:** 3 hotels, 2 motels, 1 B&B, 1 cara./camp. park. **See also:** Festival Fun; The Yorke Peninsula.

Kapunda   Pop. 1979

MAP REF. 296 E3, 303 L7

Kapunda is situated 80 km N of Adelaide on the edge of the Barossa Valley. Copper was discovered here in 1842 and Kapunda became Australia's first mining town. At one stage the population rose to 5000 and there were 16 hotels in town. A million pounds' ($2m) worth of copper was dug out before the mines closed in 1878. **Of interest:** Historic Ford House, an 1860s general store with unusual vaulted iron roof now a B&B. In Hill St: Kapunda Museum (1870s); Bagot's Fortune, mine interpretation centre with mining history displays. Kapunda Gallery, cnr Main and Hill sts, a significant regional gallery. High School's main building on West Tce, off Clare Rd, formerly residence of famous cattle king Sir Sidney Kidman. 'Map Kernow' (Son of Cornwall), 8-m tall

'Larry Lobster', Kingston S.E.

bronze statue at southern entrance to town, end of Main St. Heritage trail and historic mine walking trail, maps available from Tourist information. Mar.: Celtic Music Festival (weekend before Easter). Nov.: Agricultural Show; Antique and Craft Fair. **In the area:** Pines Reserve, 6 km NW, nature reserve and wildlife. Historic local stone buildings at Tarlee, 16 km NW. Scholz Park Museum (open by appt) and heritage-listed railway station (not open) at Riverton, 30 km NW. Scenic drive 26 km NE through sheep, wheat and dairy country to Eudunda. **Tourist information:** 5 Hill St; (08) 8566 2902. **Accommodation:** 1 hotel, 1 B&B, 1 cara./camp. park.

Keith   Pop. 1176

MAP REF. 301 G6, 303 P13

Keith is a farming town on the Dukes Hwy, 241 km SE of Adelaide, in the centre of the former Ninety Mile Desert, now called Coonalpyn Downs. The area has been transformed from infertile pasture to productive farming by the use of plant nutrition and modern farming methods. **Of interest:** National Trust-classified buildings in Heritage St: former Congregational Church (1910), with 11 locally-made leadlight windows depicting the town's life and pioneering history; The Old Manse. Sept.: Market Day, local arts and crafts. **In the area:** Mount Rescue Conservation Park, 16 km N, a vast expanse of sandplain with heath, pink

gums, Aboriginal campsites and burial grounds and an abundance of native wildlife. Old Settlers Cottage (1894), 2 km NE on Emu Flat Rd. Ngarkat Conservation Park, 25 km NE, has variety of flora and fauna. Mt Monster Conservation Park, 10 km S, for scenic views and diverse wildlife. **Tourist information:** Council Chambers, 43 Woolshed St, Bordertown; (08) 8752 1044. **Accommodation:** 1 hotel/motel, 1 motel, 1 cara./camp. park.

Kimba   Pop. 682

MAP REF. 302 F3, 304 E13

A small town on the Eyre Hwy, Kimba is at the edge of the outback. This is sheep- and wheat-growing country. **Of interest:** On Eyre Hwy: historical museum featuring Pioneer House (1908), school and blacksmith's shop; the Big Galah, locally mined and crafted jade, including rare black jade, at adjacent Gem Shop. Pug 'n' Pine Gallery, High St, for locally-made craft. Sept.: Agricultural Show. **In the area:** Sturt Desert Pea nursery on Eyre Hwy, 1 km W. Walking trail 1 km NE of town, goes ½ km through bushland to White's Knob lookout (360° views). Lake Gilles Conservation Park, 20 km NE, habitat for malleefowl. Caralue Bluff, 20 km SW, for rock climbing, good flora and fauna. Pinkawillinie Conservation Park, 45 km W. Gawler Ranges, north-west, vast wilderness area; check road conditions and read section on Outback Motoring. **Tourist information:** Kimba Halfway Across Australia Gem Shop, Eyre Hwy; (08) 8627 2112. **Accommodation:** 1 hotel/motel, 1 motel, 1 cara./camp. park.

Kingscote   Pop. 1443

MAP REF. 302 I12

The largest town on Kangaroo Island, 120 km SW of Adelaide, Kingscote was the first official European settlement in the State (1836). There are numerous ways to get to the island from the mainland: vehicular ferries from Cape Jervis (1 hour), passenger ferries from Glenelg (2½ hours) and from Cape Jervis (½ hour); and there is an air service from Adelaide (½ hour). **Of interest:** Cairn on foreshore marks State's first post office. Hope Cottage, Centenary Ave, National Trust Folk Museum. St Alban's Church, Osmond St has stained-glass windows and pioneer memorials. Town's cemetery, Seaview Rd, is oldest in State.

Rock pool, for swimming. Fishing from jetty for squid, tommy ruff, trevally, garfish and snook. Christo's Wagon Rides, Clydesdale-drawn wagon rides from The Esplanade (in summer). Feb.: Racing Carnival. Oct.: Agricultural Show. **In the area:** Jumbuck shearing demonstrations, 17 km S on Birchmore Rd. Eucalyptus oil distillery, 20 km S on Willsons Rd, off South Coast Rd. Clifford's Honey Farm, 25 km S. Mt Thisby Lookout, 50 km S, for spectacular views. American River, a fishing village about 50 km E. At Penneshaw, on the north-east coast of Dudley Peninsula, where vehicular ferry arrives from Cape Jervis: Folk Museum in former old Penneshaw School; penguin tours, depart from Penguin Interpretive Centre; Dudley, Cape Hart and Pelican Lagoon conservation parks on peninsula. Antechamber Bay, about 20 km SE of Penneshaw, excellent for bushwalking, fishing and swimming. Island Pure, 12 km W at Cygnet River, a sheep-milk dairy. Gum Creek Marron Farm, 24 km W. At Stokes Bay, 62 km W, natural rock tunnel leads to rock pool (ideal for swimming). On western end of island: Flinders Chase National Park, sanctuary for some of Australia's rarest wildlife; Cape Borda Lighthouse, north-west; Remarkable Rocks and Admirals Arch, south-west (boardwalk for viewing New Zealand fur seals at Admirals Arch). Guided tours available for Seal Bay, Kelly Hill Caves, Cape Borda and Cape Willoughby lighthouses. **Tourist information:** Kangaroo Island Visitor Information Centre, Howard Dr., Penneshaw; (08) 8553 1185. **Accommodation:** 2 hotels, 4 motels, 1 hostel, 1 B&B, 2 cara./camp. parks. **See also:** Kangaroo Island.

Kingston S.E.   Pop. 1425

MAP REF. 301 F8

Located at the southern end of the Coorong National Park on Lacepede Bay, Kingston S.E. is a farming and fishing town, and seaside resort. The multitude of shallow lakes and lagoons in the area are a haven for bird-life and a delight for naturalists and photographers. **Of interest:** Unusual analemmatic sundial, adjacent to Apex Park, in East Tce. Historic post office (1867), Holland St. National Trust Pioneer Museum (1872), Cooke St. Cape Jaffa Lighthouse (built 1860s, dismantled and re-erected in 1970s),

Vineyards and Wineries

South Australia produces more than 50 per cent of the wines and 65 per cent of the brandy made in Australia. Kilometres of vineyards stretch over valleys, plains and hillsides throughout several key winegrowing regions: the Barossa, McLaren Vale, Clare Valley, Murray Valley, Adelaide Hills, Coonawarra, Langhorne Creek and around Padthaway. New areas emerging include the Southern Eyre Peninsula, Kangaroo Island, Coppamurra, Mount Benson, Adelaide Plains and Mount Gambier.

The **Barossa,** encompassing Barossa Valley and Eden Valley, Australia's most famous wine-producing area, is located about 55 kilometres north-east of Adelaide. It is a warm and intimate place of charming old towns, with vineyards spreading across undulating hills in well-tended, precise rows. Visitors can appreciate the beauty of the region from a hot-air balloon and afterwards enjoy a champagne breakfast.

The Barossa Valley was named in 1837 by Colonel Light in memory of Barrosa in Spain, where he fought a decisive battle in 1811. The recorded spelling 'Barossa' was an error that was never rectified. The district was settled in 1839 by English and Germanic settlers. Today the Barossa has a distinctive culture and atmosphere that derives from this Germanic concentration in the mid-nineteenth century and is evidenced in the vineyards, the stone buildings, the restaurants, the bakeries and the Lutheran churches that dot the region.

The Barossa produces a wide variety of grapes, in particular shiraz grapes used in some classic red wines. Some of the most famous wineries of the Barossa are Yalumba, Orlando, Penfolds, Seppelts, Wolf Blass and Peter Lehmann. Some wineries are still run by members of the same families that established them last century. Others have been taken over by big international companies, but the distinctive qualities of the region's wine remain. There are many medium-size wineries making excellent wines, such as Grant Burge, Bethany, Basedow, Krondorf, Henschke and many boutique wineries specialising in producing quality wines, including Barossa Settlers, Elderton, Rockford, Turkey Flat, Gnadenfreil Estate, Charles Cimicky and St Hallett.

The **McLaren** region just south of Adelaide is noted for its intensely-flavoured reds and whites.

Grape picking, in the McLaren region on the Fleurieu Peninsula

Nestled in the gentle folds of the Mount Lofty Ranges with a westerly view to the sea lies the township of McLaren Vale, the centre of this winegrowing area. There are more than fifty wineries located in the region, among them Chapel Hill, Hardy's Reynella, Haselgrove, Seaview and Wirra Wirra, and they range from very large to very small. In most of the wineries, the person at the cellar door is the person who makes the wine — meet your maker at McLaren!

The vineyards of the **Clare Valley** are about 130 kilometres north of Adelaide and produce fine table wines, including much of Australia's quality reisling. Winemaking in the valley dates back to 1852, and most of the current wineries are small family-owned operations. Four of the better-known wineries are Taylors, Leasingham, Sevenhill and Jim Barry.

Near the Victorian border is the **Murray Valley** region, famous for a wide range of products from top-quality table wines to ouzo and brandy. The well-known wineries include Kingston Estate at Kingston-on-Murray and Angove's near Renmark.

Winemaking is rapidly expanding throughout the **Adelaide Hills.** It is a particularly beautiful region to tour especially in autumn. Wineries include Karl Seppelts Grand Cru Estate, Gumeracha Cellars, Hillstowe and Petaluma. This area is noted especially for its complex chardonnays. Closer to Adelaide are Petaluma and Stonyfell Wineries.

The **Coonawarra** in the far south-east is best known for its award-winning red and white table wines from a small area of unique, rich, volcanic soil. The Coonawarra boasts Australia's most expensive viticultural real estate and produces most of the country's great cabernet sauvignon. The established wineries of the area are Wynns, Mildara, Redmans and Rouge Homme. Newer wineries include Haselgrove, Rymill, Balnaves and Hollicks.

The **Langhorne Creek** region is around 70 kilometres south of Adelaide, resting between the foothills of the Mount Lofty Ranges and Lake Alexandrina. It is a rapidly-expanding wine region and produces mostly red wines with soft tannins, with Bleasdale Vineyards being the best-known winery.

Sixteen vineyards in the **Padthaway** region produce grapes for both red and white wines, particularly chardonnay, and Padthaway Estate has cellar-door sales. The **Southern Peninsula** region is one of the State's newest. Located around Port Lincoln and North Shields are the two major wineries in this area: Boston Bay Wineries and Delacolline Estate. **Kangaroo Island** established its first vineyard in 1987 and produces grapes for red wine. There is no winery on the island.

Most of the South Australian wineries are open for inspection, tastings and cellar-door sales.

For further information about hours of inspection and winery tours, contact the South Australian Travel Centre, 1 King William Street, Adelaide; (08) 8212 1505. For more specialist information on South Australian wineries, contact the South Australian Wine and Brandy Industry Association, 555 The Parade, Magill; (08) 8331 0042. **Map references:** 298, for McLaren region; 300, for Barossa region.

Marine Pde. Fresh lobsters in season (Oct.–Apr.). Giant 'Larry Lobster' at entrance to town, Princes Hwy. Jan.: Lobster Fest; Yachting Regatta. **In the area:** Butchers Gap Conservation Park, 6 km SW, has walking trails. Scenic drive south-west to Cape Jaffa, a small fishing village. The Granites, 18 km N, unique rock formations. Mt Scott Conservation Park, 20 km E. Jip Jip Conservation Park, 50 km NE. **Tourist information:** The Big Lobster, Princes Hwy; (08) 8767 2555. **Accommodation:** 2 hotels, 3 motels, 1 hostel, 1 cara./camp. park. **See also:** The Coorong.

Leigh Creek   Pop. 1378

MAP REF. 299 D4, 305 J4

Located in the Flinders Ranges, Leigh Creek is the second-largest town north of Port Augusta. The economy is based on the large open-cut coalfield. The open-cut eventually consumed the original township, about 13 km N, and in 1982 residents moved to the new township. The extensive development and tree-planting scheme that followed transformed the new site into an attractive oasis. **In the area:** Viewing area for coal workings, 3 km from turnoff to coalfields, north on Hawker–Marree Hwy (free tours on Sat., Mar.–Oct., and school holidays). Copley Hotel, 6 km N. Lyndhurst (39 km N) and Marree (119 km N), respective end points of Strzelecki and Birdsville tracks. At Lyndhurst, unique gallery of sculptures by well-known talc-stone artist 'Talc Alf'. A further 5 km N of Lyndhurst, are the Ochre Pits, where Aborigines used to dig for ochre. Aroona Dam, 4 km W, in steep-sided valley with richly coloured walls; scenic picnic area near gorge. Gammon Ranges National Park, 64 km E, wilderness area. 'Almost ghost' town of Beltana 25 km S, declared an historic reserve; Picnic Race Meeting and Gymkhana held here in Sept. Sliding Rock Mine ruins, 60 km S; access track rough in places. Lakes Eyre, Frome and Torrens, all dry salt pans which occasionally fill with water; Desert Parks Pass required for Lake Eyre National Park (see National Parks for contact numbers and addresses). *As with all outback driving, care must be taken; check road conditions with Northern Roads Condition Hotline on (08) 11633 before departure.* **Tourist information:** (08) 8675 4316. **Accommodation:** 1 motel, 1 cara./camp. park. **See also:** The Flinders Ranges; National Parks.

Loxton   Pop. 3322

MAP REF. 303 Q7

Known as the Garden City of the Riverland region, Loxton is 251 km NE of Adelaide. The surrounding irrigated land supports thriving citrus, wine, dried-fruit, wool and wheat industries. The area was first named Loxtons Hut, after a boundary rider from the Bookpurnong Station built a primitive pine and pug hut here. The largest war-service settlement scheme in the State was carried out here. **Of interest:** Art galleries and craft shops, for local paintings and handcrafts. Loxton District Historical Village, on riverfront, with over 30 re-created buildings, and machinery and implements from late 1880s to mid-1900s. Nearby, pepper tree planted by Loxton over 110 years ago. Nature trail along riverfront, details at Tourist information. Canoes available for hire. Jan.: Apex Fisherama. Feb.: Mardi Gras. Oct.: Agricultural Show. Nov.: Loxton Lights Up (Christmas Lights). **In the area:** Excellent wines at Australian Vintage, Bookpurnong Rd (to Berri) in Loxton North. Picnic on banks of river at Habels Bend, 3 km NW. Lock 4, 14 km N, on Murray River. Moore's Woodlot, 10 km SE, 60 000 trees watered and fertilised by factory and town waste. **Tourist information:** Bookpurnong Tce; (08) 8584 7919. **Accommodation:** 1 hotel/motel, 1 B&B, 1 cara./camp. park.

Lyndoch   Pop. 956

MAP REF. 296 E6, 300 C9, 303 L8

At the southern end of the Barossa Valley and a 40-min drive from Adelaide, Lyndoch is one of the oldest towns in the State. Early industry was farm-oriented, and four flour mills operated in the area. The Para River was used to operate a water mill in 1853. Vineyards were established early, but the first winery was not set up until 1896. **Of interest:** SA Museum of Mechanical Music, Barossa Valley Way. **In the area:** Wineries, most open for tastings and cellar-door sales, include *to the north of town:* Kies Estate Cellars, Burge Family Winemakers, Charles Cimicky Wines and Chateau Yaldara Estate; *east of town:* Kellermeister Wines and Barossa Settlers; *south of town:* Twin Valley Estate; *west of town:* Wards Gateway

Cellar. *At Rowland Flat,* 5 km NE: Jenke Vineyards, Rovalley Estate, Orlando Wines and LiebichWein. Local art at Old School Gallery, 9 km W. Goldfields Walk, 10 km W, brochure available at Tourist information. Barossa Reservoir and Whispering Wall, 8 km SW, an acoustic phenomenon allowing messages whispered at one end to carry audibly to the other end, 140 m away. At Kersbrook, 22 km S: historic buildings; trout farm. **Tourist information:** Barossa Wine and Visitor Centre, 66 Murray St, Tanunda; (08) 8563 0600; freecall, 1800 812662. **Accommodation:** 1 motel, 5 B&B, 1 cara./camp. park. **See also:** Vineyards and Wineries.

McLaren Vale   Pop. 1469

MAP REF. 296 A13, 297 F4, 298 D8, 301 B2, 303 K10

Centre of the McLaren winegrowing region, in which about 50 wineries flourish, McLaren Vale is 42 km S of Adelaide. Winemaking really began in 1853 when Thomas Hardy bought Tintara Vineyards. Today, Hardy's Tintara is the largest winery operating in the area. **Of interest:** Historic buildings: Hotel McLaren, Main Rd; Congregational Church and Salopian Inn, both in Willunga Rd. Almond Train, Main Rd, variety of local almond produce housed in restored railway carriage. May: From the Sea and the Vines Festival. Oct.: One Continuous Picnic; Wine Bushing Festival. **In the area:** Scenic drive through wine region; starts ½ km W on Main Rd. Many historic buildings are now restaurants, wineries, tearooms and galleries. Most wineries open for tastings and cellar-door sales. At Hardy's Tintara Wines, on the north-western outskirts of town, huge Moreton Bay fig tree in grounds and Fleurieu Peninsula Fine Arts housed in old cellar. McLaren Vale Olive Grove, 3 km N, has olive growing, crushing and bottling, and sales (tours available). Old Noarlunga, historic village 8 km NW. **Tourist information:** The Cottage, Main Rd; (08) 8323 8537. **Accommodation:** 2 motels, 10 B&B, 1 cara./camp. park. **See also:** Festival Fun; Vineyards and Wineries.

Maitland   Pop. 1066

MAP REF. 302 I7

Maitland is a modern, well-planned town in the heart of Yorke Peninsula, and the centre for this rich agricultural area. Wheat, barley, wool and beef cattle are the main primary industries. Parks surround the town centre and provide both locals and visitors with many pleasant picnic spots. **Of interest:** St John's Anglican Church (1876), cnr Alice and Caroline sts, with stained-glass depicting Biblical stories in Australian settings. Lions Bicycle Adventure Park, off Elizabeth St. Maitland National Trust Museum, located in former school, cnr Gardiner and Kilkerran tces, has displays on local history (check opening times). The Artist's Window, Robert St, has local art and craft for sale. Self-guide nature and history trail, information and leaflets available from District Council, Elizabeth St. Apr.: Agricultural Show. **In the area:** The 'copper triangle' towns of Moonta, Kadina and Wallaroo, 35 km N. Coastal town of Balgowan, 15 km W, has safe, sandy beaches and is popular with anglers. **Tourist information:** Yorke Peninsula Visitor Information Centre, 51 Taylor St, Kadina; (08) 8821 2093. **Accommodation:** 2 hotels. **See also:** The Yorke Peninsula.

Mannum   Pop. 2025

MAP REF. 296 I9, 301 D1, 303 M9

Mannum, 82 km E of Adelaide, is one of the oldest towns on the Murray River. Picturesque terraced banks overlook the river. Wool, beef and cereals are produced in the region, and the town is the starting point for the Adelaide water-supply pipeline. The *Mary Ann*, the first paddle-steamer on the Murray, left Mannum in 1853 and the first steam car was built in town in 1894 by David Shearer. **Of interest:** Mary-Ann Reserve, a popular recreation reserve on banks of Murray; PS *River Murray Princess* moored here. Historic Leonaville Homestead (1883), River Lane built by town's first private developer, Gottlieb Schuetze. PS *Marion* built in 1897, located in Arnold Park, Randell St. Twin ferries to eastern side of river and scenic upriver drive. Lookout, off Purnong Rd to east. River cruises available weekends in summer. May: Houseboat Hirers' Open Days. **In the area:** Excellent scenic drive from Wongulla to Cambrai; begins 20 km N. Choni Cottage country collectables, 10 km NW on Palmer Rd. Kia Marina, 8 km NE, largest river marina in State (boats and houseboats available for hire).

Water sports at Walker Flat, 26 km NE. Scenic drive north-east along road to Purnong, runs parallel to a bird sanctuary for 15 km. Mannum Waterfalls Reserve, 10 km S, for picnics and scenic walks. **Tourist information:** PS *Marion* in Arnold Park, Randell St; (08) 8569 1303. **Accommodation:** 1 motel, 6 B&B, 2 cara./camp. parks.

Marree   Pop. 85

MAP REF. 304 I1

Marree is a tiny outback town 645 km N of Adelaide at the junction of the legendary Birdsville and Oodnadatta tracks. There are remnants of date palms planted by the Afghan traders who drove their camel trains into the outback in the 1800s and played a significant role in 'opening up' the outback. Desolate saltbush country surrounds the town, now a service centre for the vast properties of the north-east of the State and for travellers. **Of interest:** Replica of early bush mosque. Mosaic sundial. Camel sculpture, made out of railway sleepers. Oct.: Outback Ball (even-numbered years). **In the area:** *For motorists attempting the Birdsville and Oodnadatta tracks, care must be taken, as with all outback driving. These tracks are unsealed with sandy patches. Heavy rain in the area can cut access for several days. Motorists are advised to ring the Northern Roads Condition Hotline on (08) 11633 for information before departing;* read section on Outback Motoring. On the Birdsville Track, fuel available only at Marree, Mungerannie Roadhouse (204 km N) and Birdsville. On the Oodnadatta Track, fuel available only at Marree, William Creek (202 km NW) and Oodnadatta. Lake Eyre National Park, 90 km N, accessible via Muloorina Station; Desert Parks Pass required (see section on National Parks for more information). Ruins of railway sidings from original Ghan line to Alice Springs at Curdimurka Siding and Bore, about 90 km W. Bubbler Mound Springs and Blanche Cup Mound Springs, 130 km W. Further 6 km W, prolific birdlife at Coward Springs, an extensive pond formed by warm water bubbling to the surface; nearby old date palms and remnants of old plantation. **Tourist information:** Outback Roadhouse, Oodnadatta Track; (08) 8675 8360. **Accommodation:** 1 hotel, 2 cara./camp. parks. **See also:** The Outback.

Melrose   Pop. 205

MAP REF. 303 J2, 305 J12

Melrose is the oldest town in the Flinders Ranges, a quiet settlement at the foot of Mt Remarkable, 268 km N of Adelaide. **Of interest:** Historic buildings: old police station and court house (1862), Stuart St, now a National Trust Museum featuring colonial antiques, bric-a-brac and farm implements; ruins of Jacka's Brewery (former flour mill, 1877), Lambert St; North Star Hotel (1854), Nott St; Mt Remarkable Hotel (1857), Stuart St. Melrose Inn (1857), Nott St, a National Trust-property but not open to the public. Serendipity Gallery, Stuart St. Historic walk available, contact Tourist information for brochure. Pleasant walks and picnic spots along creek. Scenic views from War Memorial and Lookout Hill, Joe's Rd. Further on, Cathedral Rock. **In the area:** Walking trail with superb views (allow 5 hrs return) from town to top of Mt Remarkable (956 m); map at Tourist information. Mt Remarkable National Park, 2 km W. Near Murray Town, 14 km S: scenic lookouts at Box Hill, Magnus Hill and Baroota Nob; scenic drive west through Port Germein Gorge; 3 km SW is Murratana sheep property specialising in breeding sheep with coloured wool (visitors welcome). Booleroo Steam Traction Preservation Society's Museum, Booleroo Centre, 15 km SE (open by appt). **Tourist information:** Caravan Park, Joes Rd; (08) 8666 2060. **Accommodation:** 1 hotel, 1 cara./ camp. park.

Meningie   Pop. 818

MAP REF. 301 D4, 303 M12

Meningie is set on the edge of the freshwater Lake Albert and the northern tip of the vast salt pans of the Coorong National Park, 159 km from Adelaide. It is a farming area, and approximately 40 professional net anglers are employed on the lakes and the Coorong; fishing is a major industry in the town. The area abounds with a variety of birdlife including ibis, pelicans, cormorants, ducks and swans. Sailing, boating, water-skiing and swimming are popular. **In the area:** Camp Coorong, 12 km S, Aboriginal museum and cultural centre; Aboriginal food tours available, inquire at Tourist information. At The Coorong, south

National Parks

Nowhere else in Australia can wildlife be seen in such close proximity and in such profusion as in the parks of South Australia. To protect its valuable native animals and plants, and to conserve the natural features of the landscape, this State has set aside over 20 per cent of its total area as national, conservation and recreation parks, and regional and game reserves.

In addition to 17 national parks, the South Australian Department of Environment and Natural Resources also manages 211 conservation parks, 13 recreation parks, 10 game reserves and 7 regional reserves. The main criteria for each category, as stated in the National Parks and Wildlife Act of 1972, are as follows:

National parks. Areas with wildlife or natural features of national significance.

Conservation parks. Areas for the preservation and conservation of native flora and fauna representative of South Australia's natural heritage, although historical features may also be included in these parks.

Recreation parks. Areas for outdoor recreation in a natural setting.

Game reserves. Areas suitable for the management and conservation of native game species, usually duck and quail. Hunting of some species during restricted open seasons.

Regional reserves. A category established in 1988 which protects, at present, seven areas within South Australia considered to contain important wildlife and natural features, but where natural resources, such as minerals, may be needed in the future.

The range of climatic zones in South Australia enables visitors to enjoy these parks throughout the year; coastal parks are cool in summer and autumn, while mountain areas are ideal to visit in winter and spring. In summer, however, many of the State's parks are very hot and have a high fire danger. If planning to visit during the peak fire season, it is advisable to check bushfire danger and fire restrictions. Contact the Department of Environment and Natural Resources, (08) 8204 1910 for more details.

In the south-east of the State

A unique, successful experiment of familiarising people with native fauna is evidenced at Cleland Wildlife Park in the centre of the larger **Cleland Conservation Park,** located on the slopes of

The Cazneaux Tree, near Wilpena in the Flinders Ranges National Park

Mount Lofty overlooking Adelaide. Here visitors are able to walk freely among the animals, which are housed in a natural bush setting in conditions similar to their native habitat.

Within Adelaide's southern suburbs is **Belair National Park,** which offers self-guide walks, forested hills, spectacular views, parrots, wildflowers, an adventure playground, tennis courts, picnic facilities and the opportunity to tour Old Government House.

The Coorong, one of the State's finest national parks and of international importance, is 185 kilometres from Adelaide, south of the mouth of the mighty Murray River. From the Aboriginal word *karangh,* meaning 'narrow neck', the Coorong is a series of saltwater lagoons fed by the Murray and separated from the sea by Younghusband Peninsula. In the park are six island bird sanctuaries, prohibited to the public, but which can be viewed through binoculars. These islands house rookeries of pelicans, crested terns and silver gulls. More than 280 species of birds have been recorded in the Coorong. The ocean beach is a favourite haunt of anglers. You can take the pleasant drive along the coast road beside the waterway, stopping to camp or picnic. At dusk, kangaroos and

wombats can be seen feeding on the grassed open areas in the park.

Bool Lagoon Game Reserve is on the southern flat plains of South Australia, near Naracoorte. The lagoon's natural cycle of flooding and drying out is perfect for breeding of waterbirds. In spring, when the water is deepest, the thousands of black swans that crowd the lagoon are spectacular. In summer and autumn, when the water is shallow, waterfowl and waders flock to feed on the rich plant life. Bool Lagoon is also the largest permanent ibis rookery in Australia. Dense thickets of paperbark and banks of reeds in the reserve's central reaches provide a safe breeding ground. A network of boardwalks provides access to wildlife without disturbing the natural environment.

The **Naracoorte Caves** are preserved in a small conservation park, now a World Heritage Area, in the south-east of the State. These impressive caves enclose a wonderland of stalagmites, stalactites, shawls, straws and other calcite formations. Four of the limestone caves, including Blanche Cave, the first to be discovered (1845), are open for inspection through guided or adventure tours. A tour through the museum that is set up in Victoria Fossil Cave gives visitors the chance to see skeletons of such extinct animals as giant browsing kangaroos, a hippopotamus-sized wombat and a marsupial lion.

In the north of the State

The Flinders Ranges, extending for 430 kilometres, contain three national parks. **Mount Remarkable National Park** lies in a rugged and densely vegetated area of the southern Flinders Ranges. Mount Remarkable itself rises to 995 metres, and provides spectacular views over the surrounding country. The rock is red quartzite and glows a beautiful red at sunset. Two creeks flow through the park, providing water for river red gums, white cypress pines and brilliant wildflowers in spring. Alligator Gorge, the weathered red cliffs of which are a photographer's delight, and Mambray Creek, have a number of well-marked walking tracks.

The **Flinders Ranges National Park,** with its total area of 94 908 hectares, is one of the major national parks in Australia. The Wilpena section, in the south of the park, comprises the famed Wilpena Pound and the Wilpena Pound Range, covering an area of 10 000 hectares. The Pound is one of the most extraordinary geological formations in Australia. Developed in the Cambrian period, it is a vast oval rock bowl, ringed with sheer cliffs and jagged rocks, and with a flat floor covered with trees and grass. A homestead dating back to 1889 still stands. Native rock paintings at Arkaroo Rock indicate that this was a significant area in Aboriginal mythology. Twenty-five kilometres north of Wilpena is the Oraparinna section of the park. The 68 500 hectares of this section were a sheep station last century, at one time maintaining more than 20 000 sheep.

Further north the **Gammon Ranges National Park,** an arid, isolated region of rugged ranges and deep gorges, provides visitors with the experience of an extensive wilderness area. The mountains sparkle with exposed formations of quartz, fluorspar, hematites and ochres, making the region a gem-hunter's paradise (fossicking not permitted in geological sites). The Gammon Ranges are a sanctuary for many species of native fauna, including the western grey kangaroo, the big red kangaroo, the grey euro or hill kangaroo and the yellow-footed rock wallaby. Nearby, the remote settlement of Arkaroola offers motel accommodation and a serviced camping ground.

Further north, in the State's arid lands, over 8 million hectares have been set aside to protect the unique desert environment. Some of the parks and reserves in this vast desert area require a Desert Parks Pass from the Department of Environment and Natural Resources. These parks include Lake Eyre National Park, Witjira National Park, Innamincka Regional Reserve and Simpson Desert Conservation Park. Passes can be obtained from either the Adelaide Information Centre (77 Grenfell St, Adelaide, 5000; (08) 8204 1910) or from 60 Elder Tce, Hawker, 5434; (086) 48 4244. The pass is valid from the date of purchase; it allows twelve months' bush camping in Lake Eyre National Park, Witjira National Park, Innamincka Regional Reserve and Simpson Desert Conservation Park and Regional Reserve. The Desert Parks Pass also entitles you to free camping in Flinders Ranges and Gammon Ranges National Parks. The pass is part of the *Desert Parks South Australia Handbook* which also includes detailed information and maps on each park and reserve, and is available from the Department's offices in Adelaide and at Hawker as described above.

Lake Eyre, the central feature of the park of the same name, is one of the world's greatest salinas or salt lakes, and is 16 metres below sea level at its lowest point. Contrarily, it is the hub of a huge internal drainage system while being located in the driest part of the Australian continent. In this area vegetation is sparse, but after heavy rains when the area floods, the ground is carpeted with colourful wildflowers, and the animal and bird populations attracted by the plant rejuvenation, rise accordingly. Care needs to be taken when visiting this area; 4WD vehicles are preferred for access to the park and campers must be fully self-sufficient.

Witjira National Park, 170 kilometres north of Oodnadatta, is an area of vast desert landscapes, gibber plains, sand dunes, salt pans and mound springs, upwellings of the Great Artesian Basin. Visitors may explore this extremely arid environment from the park's oasis, Dalhousie Springs.

The **Innamincka Regional Reserve** covers much of the flood prone country around the Cooper and Strzelecki creeks up to the Queensland border. These arid wetlands, which comprise a series of semi-permanent overflow lakes, hold many surprises for bird-watchers.

The **Simpson Desert Conservation Park,** which is for the more adventurous park visitor, consists of spectacular red sand dunes, which in places can run parallel for hundreds of kilometres, as well as salt lakes, flood-out plains, hummock

The Great Australian Bight forms the southern boundary of the Nullarbor National Park

grasslands, gibber desert, gidgee woodland, tablelands and mesas.

In the south-west of the State

On the south-west tip of Yorke Peninsula is the 10 000-hectare **Innes National Park,** where the ground is blanketed with wildflowers in spring and birdwatching is a favourite pastime. As well as native bushland and magnificent coastal scenery, there is good fishing at the beaches. Walking trails lead to the coast and to the historic ruins of Inneston (1913). This small settlement once housed miners who dug for gypsum, used for plaster and chalk; for many years nearly every schoolchild in Australia was taught with the aid of blackboard chalk mined here and shipped from Stenhouse Bay. Camping and accommodation are available.

Flinders Chase National Park, encompassing most of the western end of Kangaroo Island, protects pristine natural vegetation including mallee, forests and stunted coastal plants. Bushwalkers can enjoy trails along creeks to secluded beaches, or follow the rugged coastline to observe the full force of the Southern Ocean. Lighthouses and keepers' cottages provide cultural interest; visitors may see kangaroos, koalas, fur seals, echidnas and platypuses, as well as a wide variety of bird and plant life. **Seal Bay Conservation Park,** also on Kangaroo Island, allows visitors the opportunity to

see Australian sea lion-breeding colonies. The adjoining **Cape Gantheaume Conservation Park** is a wilderness area attracting experienced bushwalkers. More information is available from the Department of Environment and Natural Resources office at 37 Dauncy St, Kingscote (PO Box 39, Kingscote 5223); (08) 8553 2381.

The Eyre Peninsula, bordered to the north by the Eyre Highway, contains a number of parks. Coffin Bay National Park and Lincoln National Park feature wilderness areas and spectacular coastal scenery. Both these national parks provide excellent opportunities for bush camping, birdwatching and bushwalking. **Coffin Bay National Park** is 50 kilometres west of Port Lincoln and takes in all of Coffin Bay Peninsula. The western coastline faces the Great Australian Bight while the eastern part has sheltered sandy beaches and islands. Inquire locally about safe swimming.

Lincoln National Park, a 15-kilometre drive south of Port Lincoln, occupies a large part of Jussieu Peninsula and is surrounded by small islands. At its northern tip, on Stamford Hill, the Flinders Monument commemorates exploration by Matthew Flinders in 1802. From this hill visitors can enjoy spectacular views of the surrounding area.

Diverse bird habitats are provided at **Lake Gilles Conservation Park,** also on Eyre Peninsula,

by the salt lakes and the dry mallee and western myall vegetation.

In the west of the State

Situated along the Eyre Highway in the far west corner of the State, the **Nullarbor National Park** offers spectacular views of the Great Australian Bight. The park itself is entirely desert, with patches of mallee scrub and some ground cover of bluebush and saltbush; it is renowned for its unique desolate, eerie beauty. The Nullarbor Plain's substratum of limestone has been eroded to form one of the largest underwater cave systems in the world, popular with experienced potholers and cave divers. Access to the caves is only available through arrangement with the Far West office of the Department of Environment and Natural Resources (11 McKenzie St, Ceduna; (08) 8625 3144). The caves provide almost the only shelter for animals. Most species, including a large population of hairy-nosed wombats, are nocturnal.

Many of South Australia's national parks charge camping and entrance fees. For further information on camping restrictions, entry permits and fees, and general advice on visiting the State's national parks, contact the South Australian Department of Environment and Natural Resources Information Centre, 77 Grenfell St, Adelaide 5000 (GPO Box 1047, Adelaide 5001); (08) 8204 1910.

and west: inland waterways, islands, ocean beach and wildlife. Scenic drive west following Lake Albert, adjacent to Lake Alexandrina, the largest permanent freshwater lake in the country (50 000 ha). Poltalloch Homestead, 30 km NW, one of the oldest in the region (accommodation and tours available, contact Tourist information). Further west, channel between lakes is crossed by free ferry service at Narrung. **Tourist information:** Melaleuca Centre, 76 Princes Hwy; (08) 8575 1259. **Accommodation:** 1 hotel, 2 motels, 3 B&B, 1 cara./camp. park. **See also:** The Coorong.

Millicent
Pop. 5118

MAP REF. 301 G11

A thriving commercial and industrial town 50 km from Mt Gambier, Millicent is in the middle of a huge tract of land reclaimed in the 1870s. Today rural and fishing industries contribute to the area's prosperity, with pine forests supporting a paper mill and a sawmill. **Of interest:** On northern edge of town, gum trees surround a fine swimming lake and picnic area. Award-winning National Trust Museum and Admella Gallery, housed in original primary school (1873); Mt Gambier Rd. Shell Garden, Williams Rd, unusual display surrounded by fuchsias, ferns and begonias (open Dec.–Apr.). **In the area:** Nangula Country Market, 7 km SE, held 2nd Sun. each month (not Jan.). Tantanoola, 21 km SE, home of famous 'Tantanoola Tiger' (a Syrian wolf shot in the 1890s; 'tiger' now stuffed and displayed in the Tantanoola Tiger Hotel. Underground caves, 20 km SE in Tantanoola Caves Conservation Park, fascinating limestone formations; also at Caves, Trevor Peters' 4-ha terraced cottage garden and restored National Trust cottage (open Sept.–Apr., check opening times). National Trust Woolshed (1863) at Glencoe, 29 km E (tours available, contact Tourist information for details). Scenic pine-forest drive to Mount Burr, 10 km NE. Fresh farm flowers, 20 km N at Furner. Massive sand dune system and fascinating flora and fauna in Canunda National Park, 27 km W (accessed from Millicent and Southend); scenic self-guide walks (leaflets available). **Tourist information:** 1 Mt Gambier Rd; (08) 8733 3205. **Accommodation:** 1 hotel/ motel, 2 motels, 2 B&B, 2 cara./camp. parks.

Minlaton
Pop. 796

MAP REF. 302 I9

Minlaton is a prosperous town serving the nearby coastal towns on Yorke Peninsula. The town, 209 km W of Adelaide, was originally called Gum Flat because of the giant eucalypts in the area. Pioneer aviator Harry Butler, pilot of the Red Devil, a 1916 Bristol monoplane, was born here. **Of interest:** In Main St: Harry Butler Memorial; fauna park; National Trust Museum, check opening times; Harvest Corner, for local crafts. **In the area:** Gum Flat Homestead Gallery, 1 km E, pioneer homestead with local artists' work. At Port Vincent, 25 km E: good swimming, yachting and water-skiing; Yacht Race in Jan. Gipsy Waggon holidays at Brentwood, 14 km SW. Scenic Port Rickaby and Bluff Beach, 16 km NW. **Tourist information:** Harvest Corner, Main St; (08) 8853 2600. **Accommodation:** 1 hotel/motel, 1 B&B, 1 cara./camp. park.

Mintaro
Pop. 80

MAP REF. 303 L5

The township nestles among rolling hills and rich agricultural land, 19 km SE of Clare. Classified as a Heritage Town, Mintaro is a timepiece of early colonial architecture. Many of the buildings display the fine slate for which the district is world-renowned; the quarry opened in 1854. **Of interest:** Early colonial buildings, 18 with heritage listings. Heritage walk, brochure at Tourist information. Two historic cemeteries. Mar.: Paddys Market, food and bric-a-brac. **In the area:** Magnificent classical architecture of Martindale Hall (1880), 3 km SE; location for film *Picnic at Hanging Rock* (check opening times); overnight accommodation and dining available. Clare, 19 km NW; more than 20 wineries nearby. **Tourist information:** Town Hall, 229 Main North Rd, Clare; (08) 8842 2131. **Accommodation:** 1 hotel.

Moonta
Pop. 2723

MAP REF. 302 I6

The towns of Moonta, Kadina and Wallaroo form the corners of the area known as the 'Copper Triangle' or 'Australia's Little Cornwall'. Moonta is a popular seaside town 163 km NW of Adelaide, with pleasant beaches and good fishing at Moonta Bay. A rich copper-ore deposit was discovered here in 1861 and soon thousands of miners, including many from Cornwall, flocked to the area. The mines were abandoned in the 1920s with the slump in copper prices and rising labour costs. **Of interest:** Stone buildings, charming Queen Square and picturesque town hall opposite the Square in George St. All Saints Church (1873), cnr Blanche and Milne tces. Galleries, including the Pug 'n' Dabble, George St. Prize-winning Cornish festival, Kernewek Lowender is held in conjunction with nearby towns of Kadina and Wallaroo in May (odd-numbered years). Sept.: Agricultural Show. **In the area:** Moonta Mines, a State Heritage Area about 2 km SE, on Arthurton Rd: Moonta Mines National Trust Museum (old primary school), Cornish miner's cottage (1870) furnished in period style, pump house, shafts, tailings heaps and ruins of mines offices. On weekends and public and school holidays, Moonta Mines Railway takes visitors from Moonta Mines National Trust Museum through mines area. **Tourist information:** Town Hall, George St; (08) 8825 2622. **Accommodation:** 2 hotels, 1 motel, 4 B&B, 2 cara./camp. parks. **See also:** Festival Fun; The Yorke Peninsula.

Morgan
Pop. 446

MAP REF. 303 N6

Once one of the busiest river ports in the State, Morgan is a quiet little township on the Murray River, 154 km NE of Adelaide. **Of interest:** Self-guide heritage trail covers historic sites: the impressive wharves (1877), standing 12 m high, constructed for the riverboat industry; customs house and court house near railway station, reminders of town's thriving past. Picnic/barbecue facilities, with children's play area, near customs house. Dockyards, on Oval Rd (tours by appt). Port of Morgan Historic Museum in old railway buildings on riverfront, off High St (open by appt). PS *Mayflower* (1884), still operating; details from museum's caretaker. Houseboats available for hire. **In the area:** Morgan Conservation Park, across river. Fossicking for fossils near township. White Dam Conservation Park, 9 km NW. On Renmark Ave: Engineering and Water Supply Pumping Station, 2 km E (tours by

Wildlife-Watching

Pelicans are a familiar sight along the south-eastern coast

South Australia's wildlife is varied and interesting, and it is worth taking the time to spot some of the State's wildlife: look underground at migratory bats in Naracoorte Caves, up into the rocky Flinders Ranges for a view of sure-footed euros, or out into the Southern Ocean for a glimpse of southern right whales.

Around Adelaide

Victor Harbor, just south of Adelaide, should be the first stop for would-be whale-watchers. Over 25 whale and dolphin species swim off the South Australian coast, and the South Australian Whale Centre at Victor Harbor has a whale and dolphin interpretive display explaining the life-cycles of these popular mammals. The centre's Whale Information Network tracks the movements of migratory whales and offers up-to-date statewide information on the best whale-watching localities.

Southern right whales enjoy the State's shallow coastal waters, offering a wonderful spectacle as they tail-wave and body-roll just offshore. The centre's free map shows the most likely viewing sites around town when they arrive between May and October. Connected by causeway to Victor Harbor is Granite Island, a haven for little (fairy) penguins. There is a penguin interpretive centre on the island as well as nightly penguin-viewing walks.

Kangaroo Island also has a healthy population of little (fairy) penguins. Guided tours operate at Seal Bay to view the resident colony of Australian sea lions, while Admirals Arch in Flinders Chase National Park is the spot to encounter New Zealand fur seals. A coastal boardwalk enables visitors to gain a good view of the seals as they drag themselves ashore from their fishing excursions to rest.

In the South-East of the State

This corner of the State is rich in wildlife. Bent wing bats migrate each spring from south-eastern Australia to the Bat Cave in **Naracoorte Caves Conservation Park**, where they join the cave's resident bat population. The Bat Cave Video Centre above this famous cave provides a unique view of the bats' daily activities. Four infra-red cameras in the caves are connected to monitors in the centre, allowing visitors to view the tiny mammals without disturbing them. The video images give a sense of actually moving through the bat's underground environment. Each evening between November and February thousands of bats fly from the cave to feed on insects, a wonderful bat-watching opportunity.

Bool Lagoon Game Reserve lies halfway between Adelaide and Melbourne. The lagoon is a vital habitat and essential drought refuge for many rare and endangered bird species. Its cycle of flooding and drying-out is perfect for the breeding patterns of waterbirds. In spring thousands of black swans crowd the lagoon. This is also a good season to take the daily guided tour into the heart of the lagoon along the Tea-tree Boardwalk, where ibis and spoonbills nest in the foliage. In summer and autumn migratory birds, such as sharp-tailed sandpipers, green shanks and godwits, can be found rummaging about the exposed shallows of the lagoon.

Also in the south-east is the **Coorong National Park**, which curves 145 kilometres along the coast; here, 238 species of native birds live amongst the narrow saltwater lagoon, sand dunes, saltpans, claypans and forest. Take binoculars to view rookeries of pelicans, crested terns and silver gulls. Pied oystercatchers rummage along the beaches — their unusual flattened bills allow them to dig up and open cockles. Special visitors to the Coorong lagoon are flocks of tiny red-necked stints, which migrate to the Coorong from Siberia via Japan each year.

In the Southern-Central Region of the State

Migrating southern right whales arrive at the rugged coastline of **Lincoln National Park** each winter, and Sleaford Bay is a good locality to see one of these giant mammals. For those visitors out-of-season or out-of-luck, several bird species are readily seen. White-breasted sea eagles and ospreys breed on the park's offshore islands, and glide effortlessly along the coastal cliffs in search of fish. The best place to see these birds-of-prey is in Memory Cove wilderness area. Other readily-seen birds include rock parrots, honeyeaters and thornbills.

In the North-East of the State

Mount Remarkable National Park lies on the southern edge of the Flinders Ranges. Just outside the park there are red kangaroos in the open plains surrounding Mambray Creek. Adelaide rosellas, little corellas and kookaburras are also residents, their riotous calls frequently breaking the peace of the plains. Within the park, sugar gums and native pines in Mambray Creek Gorge offer shelter for rock-climbing kangaroos such as the commonly-seen euros. From a distance these may be confused with grey kangaroos, though euros are stockier than other kangaroos, and have darker paws, hindfeet and tail-tips. Keep an eye out in this area for the yellow-footed rock wallaby, one of the Flinders Ranges' rarer marsupials.

Cleland Wildlife Park at Mount Lofty, just outside Adelaide, provides a good overview of South Australian wildlife. Visitors can view dingoes, kangaroos and wallabies, or join a guided night walk to spot nocturnal natives. Koalas are the park's most popular attraction. For more information on wildlife-watching in national parks, contact the South Australian Department of Environment and Natural Resources Information Centre, 77 Grenfell St, Adelaide 5000 (GPO Box 1047, Adelaide 5001); (08) 8204 1910. For more information on bird-watching contact the Bird Observers Club of Australia, 183 Springvale Rd, Nunawading, Victoria 3131; (03) 9877 5342. **See also:** Kangaroo Island, National Parks, The Coorong, The Flinders Ranges.

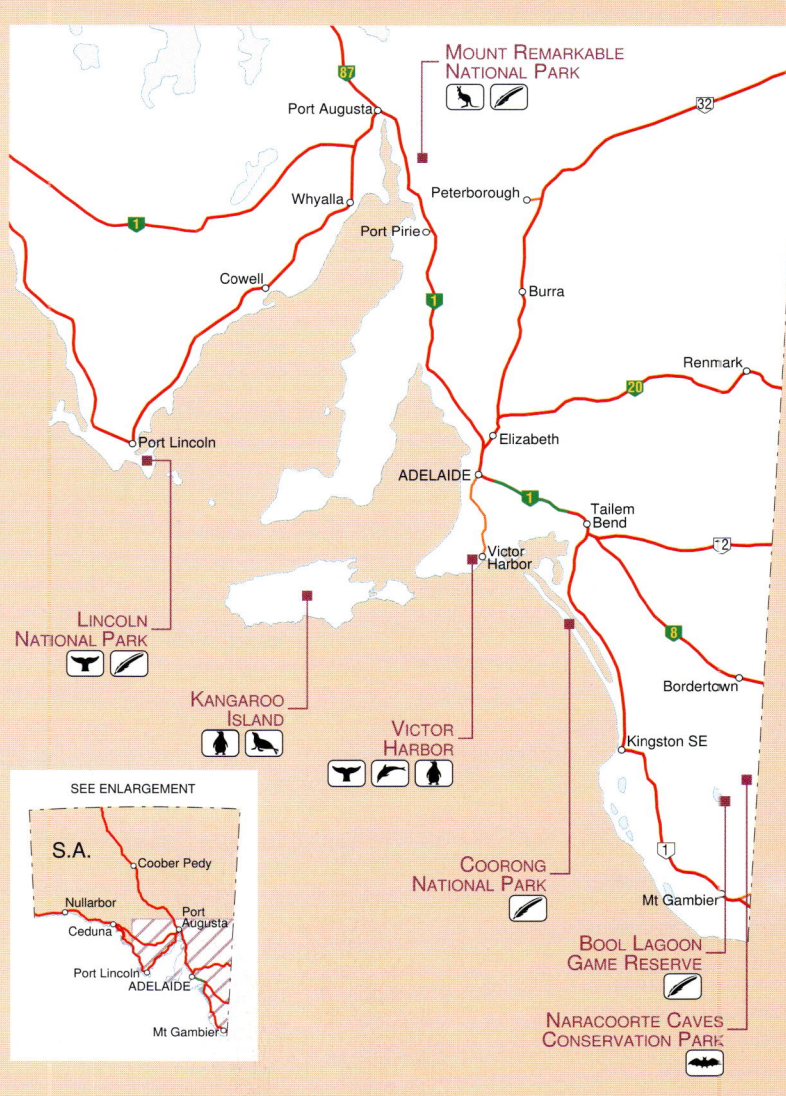

Naracoorte Caves, a World Heritage area, south-east of Naracoorte

SOUTH AUSTRALIA

appt); Nor-West Bend private museum, 8 km E (open by appt); overnight horse trail rides, book at Nor-West Bend; Riverland Camel Farm and Trail Ride, 13 km E (day and overnight trips available). Free ferry across river, on road to Waikerie (operates 24 hours). **Tourist information:** Morgan Road-house, Fourth St; (08) 8540 2205. **Accommodation:** 1 hotel, 1 hotel/motel, 1 motel, 1 cara./camp. park.

Mount Gambier   Pop. 21 153

MAP REF. 301 H12

In 1800 Lieutenant James Grant, sighted an extinct volcano and named it Mount Gambier. The city is on the slopes of the volcano, in the centre of the largest softwood pine plantation in the country. Surrounded by rich farm-ing, horticulture, viticulture and dairy country, Mount Gambier is 460 km SE of Adelaide. The Hentys built the first dwelling in the area in 1841 and by 1850 there was a weekly postal service to Adelaide. The white Mount Gambier stone used in most of the buildings, together with many fine parks and gar-dens, make an attractive environment. **Of interest:** Historic buildings: town hall (1862), Commercial St; post office (1865), Bay Rd; many old hotels. Heritage walks, leaflets from Tourist information. Open caves: Cave Garden, Bay Rd; Umpherston Sinkhole, Jubilee Hwy East; Engelbrecht Cave, Jubilee Hwy. Old Court House Law and Heritage Centre, Bay Rd, a National Trust museum. Lewis' Museum, Pick Ave. In Jubilee Hwy East: the Lady Nelson Visitor and Discovery Centre, has full-scale replica of *Lady Nelson* as part of centre's structure; Dimjalla Park, fun park. Riddoch Art Gallery, in complex of 19th century buildings, Commercial St East. Nov.: Blue Lake Festival. **In the area:** On the outskirts of town: crater lakes, particularly Blue Lake (197 m at its deepest) which changes from dull grey to brilliant blue each Nov. then reverts at end of summer; nearby scenic 5-km drive offers lookouts, wildlife reserve, picnic areas and boardwalks; Pumping Station at Blue Lake, daily tours down through pumping station to lake level; tours of timber mills, inspec-tion of treatment process including pines being felled, trimmed and sawn ready for loading; contact Tourist infor-mation for details. Animal and Reptile Park, 10 km N off Penola Rd, animal nursery with native gardens. Tarpeena Fairy Tale Park, 22 km N on Penola Rd. Glencoe Woolshed (1863), 23 km NW, National Trust building (open Sun. p.m. or by appt). Splendid Tantanoola Caves, 30 km W, tours available. Chant's Place

flora and fauna park at Kongorong, 25 km SW. Haig's Vineyard, 4 km S. Winter's Vineyard, 9 km S. Mount Schank, 12 km S, excellent views of surrounding district from summit. Glenelg River cruises from Nelson (Vic.), 36 km SE; tours of spectacular Princess Margaret Rose Caves. **Tourist information:** Lady Nelson Visitor and Discovery Centre, Jubilee Hwy East; (08) 8724 1730. **Accommodation:** 9 hotels, 1 hotel/motel, 21 motels, 5 B&B, 6 cara./camp. parks.

Murray Bridge   Pop. 12 725

MAP REF. 296 I12, 301 D2, 303 M10

Murray Bridge is South Australia's largest river town. The South Eastern Fwy provides access to Adelaide, 80 km away. First settled in the 1850s, it was a centre for the bustling riverboat traders. Murray Bridge overlooks a broad sweep of the Murray River. Water sports, river cruises and excellent accommodation make Murray Bridge a perfect holiday spot. **Of interest:** Captain's Cottage Museum, Thomas St. In Jervois Rd: Butterfly House; Puzzle Park, a funpark for adults as well as children. Heritage and Cultural Community Mural, 3rd St. Cottage Box chocolate factory, Wharf Rd. Riverside reserves: Sturt Reserve, offering fishing, swimming, picnic and playground facilities; Hume Reserve, Hume Rd; Long Island Reserve, Long Island Rd. Sims Park, Lookout Dr., for views of town. Charter and regular cruises on MV *Barrangul* and PS *Captain Proud*; charter cruises on PS *Proud Mary*; town and riverside walk; details at Tourist information. Jan.: State Championship Swimming. Nov.: Big River Challenge Festival, includes speedboat racing, water-skiing events and land-based sporting challenges. **In the area:** Monarto Zoological Park, 10 km W off Old Princes Hwy, an open-range zoo with many endangered species (open Sun. and public and school holidays). Willow Glen Wines, 10 km S on Jervois Rd. Riverglen Marina, 11 km S, has houseboats avail-able for hire. At Tailem Bend, 25 km SE: excellent views across Murray River; Old Tailem Town Pioneer Village, 5 km N; scenic drive via free 24-hour ferry across river to Jervois, then south-west to Wellington where river meets lake; restored court house (1864) complex at Wellington. Talyala Emu Farm, 6 km N on Mannum Rd. Mypolonga, 14 km N, centre for surrounding beautiful citrus and stone-fruit orchard area and rich dairying country. Australia's largest clock, 8 km NW on Palmer Rd. At Avoca Dell, 5 km upstream: boating, water-skiing, mini-golf and good picnic facilities. Thiele Reserve, east of river, good for water-skiing. Other riverside reserves located at Swanport, 5 km SE; White Sands, 10 km SE. Lookouts: White Hill, west on Princes Hwy; east at Swanport Bridge. **Tourist information:** 3 South Tce; (08) 8532 6660. **Accommodation:** 2 hotels, 4 motels, 3 B&B, 1 hostel, 5 cara./camp. parks.

Naracoorte   Pop. 4711

MAP REF. 301 H9

Situated 330 km SE of Adelaide, Naracoorte dates from the 1840s. The area is world-renowned for its limestone caves. Beef cattle, sheep, grains and grapes are the main local primary industries. **Of interest:** Sheep's Back wool museum, art gallery and tourist information centre in former flour mill (1870), MacDonnell St. Naracoorte Museum and Snake Pit, Jenkins Tce, museum collection and live snakes (closed mid-July to end Aug.). Mini Jumbuk Factory, Smith St, for woollen products. Restored locomotive on display in Pioneer Park. Regional Art Gallery, Smith St. Jubilee Park, a nature park with walks and swimming lake, off Park Tce. May: Swap Meeting; Young Riders Equestrian Event. Oct.: Agricultural Show. Dec.: Street-traders Party; Carols by Candlelight. **In the area:** At World Heritage-listed Naracoorte Caves, in Conservation Park, 12 km SE: Victoria Fossil Cave has unique fossilised specimens of Ice Age animals including giant kangaroos and giant wombats; Blanche Cave and Alexandra Cave have spectacular stalagmites and stalactites; bat viewing in new interpretive centre; guided cave tours, self-guide cave tours and adventure tours available. Tiny Train Park, 3 km S, trains and mini-golf. Bool Lagoon Wetlands, 17 km S, a wetland area of international significance and haven for ibis and numerous water-bird species; also guided boardwalks and bird-hide. Coonawarra wine region, located 40 km S. Padthaway and Keppoch wine districts, about 40 km NW. **Tourist information:** The Sheep's Back, MacDonnell St; (08) 8762 1518. **Accommodation:** 2 hotels, 1 hotel/motel, 4 motels, 5 B&B, 2 cara./camp. parks. **See also:** National Parks.

Nuriootpa   Pop. 3321

MAP REF. 296 F4, 300 G4, 303 M7

The Para River runs through the town of Nuriootpa, its course marked by fine parks and picnic spots. The town is the commercial centre of the Barossa Valley. **Of interest:** Coulthard Reserve, off Penrice Rd. Pioneer settler's home, Coulthard House, Murray St (not open). Luhrs Pioneer German Cottage, Light Pass Rd. St Petri Church, First St. Easter: Barossa Valley Vintage Festival (odd-numbered years). Aug.: Barossa Classic Gourmet Weekend. Oct.: Barossa Music Festival. **In the area:** Wineries, *south of town*: Elderton Wines, Tarac Distillers, Penfolds Wines, Kaesler Wines; *west of town*: Heritage Wines, Gnadenfrei Estate, Seppelt Wines, Greenock Creek Cellars; *north-east of town*: The Willows Vineyard, Wolf Blass Wines, Stockwell Wines; *south-east of town*: Barossa Cottage Wines; also other wineries in Barossa Valley; most wineries are open for tastings and cellar-door sales. Hot Air Balloon Regatta in May at Seppeltsfield, 6 km W. **Tourist information:** Barossa Valley Visitor Centre, 66 Murray St, Tanunda; (08) 8563 0600; freecall, 1800 812662. **Accommodation:** 1 hotel, 2 motels, 3 B&B, 1 cara./camp. park. **See also:** Vineyards and Wineries.

Old Noarlunga   Pop. 2000

MAP REF. 296 A12, 297 F3, 298 C7, 301 B2, 303 K10

A small, historic village in the McLaren winegrowing region, Old Noarlunga is 32 km S of Adelaide on the Fleurieu Peninsula. **Of interest:** Church of St Philip and St James (1850), Church Hill Rd. Uniting Church, Malpas St. Old Jolly Miller Hotel (1850), now Noarlunga Hotel, Patapinda Rd. Market Square, site of first public market 1841. Leaflet for self-guide walking tour available. **In the area:** Good swimming and fishing at Port Noarlunga; Christies Beach (10 km NW); Moana Beach (3 km); Maslin Beach (6 km S). About 8 km N of Port Noarlunga, Hallett Cove has tracks left by glaciers millions of years ago. Lakeside Leisure Park at Hackham, 4 km N. At McLaren Vale, 5 km SE, some 50 vineyards and wineries. **Tourist information:** Noarlunga Hotel, Patapinda Rd; (08) 8336 2061. **Accommodation:** None.

Oodnadatta   Pop. 180

MAP REF. 306 B6

A tiny but famous outback town 1050 km NW of Adelaide, Oodnadatta is an old railway town with a well-preserved sandstone station (1890), now a museum. It is believed that the name Oodnadatta originated from an Aboriginal term meaning 'yellow blossom of the mulga'. Fuel and supplies available. May: Race Meeting and Gymkhana. **In the area:** Witjira National Park, gateway to Simpson Desert, 180 km N; hot thermal ponds at Dalhousie Springs; nearby, Dalhousie ruins (of early pastoral station); camping and accommodation at Mt Dare Homestead and at Dalhousie Springs; Desert Parks Pass required (see National Parks section for information). The Oodnadatta Track runs from Marree through Oodnadatta and joins Stuart Hwy at Marla, 200 km W. Scenic drive to Painted Desert, 100 km SW. **Tourist information:** Pink Roadhouse, Ikaturka Tce; (08) 8670 7822; freecall, 1800 802074. **Accommodation:** 1 hotel, 1 cara./camp. park.

Penola   Pop. 1147

MAP REF. 234 A3, 301 I10

The oldest town in the south-east of the State, Penola, 50 km N of Mount Gambier, has fine examples of slab and hewn-timber cottages erected in the 1850s. Several famous names are associated with Penola. Poets Adam Lindsay Gordon, John Shaw Neilson and Will Ogilvie left a legacy of poetry inspired by their stay here. The first school in Australia catering for children regardless of income or social class was established here in 1866 by Mother Mary MacKillop, recently beatified. The stone classroom in which she taught is on the corner of Portland St and Petticoat Lane. **Of interest:** In Petticoat Lane: heritage buildings, and art and craft shops. At Tourist information: details of self-guide heritage walk; John Riddoch Interpretive Centre featuring local history displays; Hydrocarbon Centre featuring hands-on and static displays of oil process. Jan.: Vignerons Cup. June: Penola Festival. **In the area:** Yallum Park Homestead (1880), 8 km W, historic homestead built by John Riddoch, founder of Coonawarra wine industry. Signposted walk at Penola Conservation Park, 10 km W. Coonawarra region, 10 km N, with more than 20 wineries; most open for tastings and cellar-door sales. **Tourist information:** Arthur St; (08) 8737 2855. **Accommodation:** 1 hotel, 1 hotel/motel, 1 motel, 2 hostels, 1 cara./camp. park.

Peterborough   Pop. 2138

MAP REF. 303 L2, 305 K12

Peterborough is an old railway town 250 km N of Adelaide, surrounded by grain-growing and pastoral country. It is the principal town on the Port Pirie to Broken Hill railway line. **Of interest:** Historic narrow-gauge steam-train journeys to Orroroo or Eurelia; check times. Rann's Museum, 144 Moscow St, exhibits historic railway equipment and farm implements. The Gold Battery, end Tripney Ave, an ore-crushing machine (open by appt). Saint Cecilia, Callary St, gracious home (with splendid stained glass) once a bishop's residence, offering accommodation, dining and murder-mystery nights. In Queen St: Ley's Museum, exhibition of antiques; Victoria Park. Feb.: Rodeo. **In the area:** Terowie, 24 km SE, old railway town with several historic buildings. Dare's Hill Circuit Tour, between Terowie and Hallet (31 km S). At Orroroo, 37 km NW: historic buildings; Yesteryear Costume Gallery with display of fashion from 1850s; nearby, scenic walk among Aboriginal carvings along Pekina Creek; panoramic views from Black Rock Peak, east. At Magnetic Hill, 8 km W of Black Rock, a vehicle with the engine turned off can roll uphill! **Tourist information:** Main St; (08) 8651 2708. **Accommodation:** 3 hotels, 1 hotel/ motel, 1 motel, 1 hostel, 1 cara./camp. park.

Pinnaroo   Pop. 645

MAP REF. 126 A11, 238 A10, 301 I3, 303 R10

This little township on the Mallee Hwy is located only 6 km from the Victorian border. **Of interest:** Australia's largest cereal collection (1300 varieties), Pinnaroo Institute, Railway Tce Sth; weekdays only, obtain key from Tourist information. Historical Museum in railway station, Railway Tce Sth. Working printing museum, South Tce (open by appt only, contact Tourist information).

Nearby, animal park and aviary with native birds. Farm-machinery museum at showgrounds, Homburg Tce. **In the area:** Walking trail in Karte Conservation Park, 30 km NW on Karte Rd. Gum Family Collection of farm machinery, 25 km N at Kombali Homestead. Peebinga Conservation Park, 42 km N on Loxton Rd. In Scorpion Springs Conservation Park, 28 km S, walking trail at Pine Hut Soak. Ngarkat Conservation Park, 48 km S, popular with birdwatchers. Pertendi walking trail, 49 km S. Near Lameroo, 39 km W, Byrne Homestead (1898) built of pug and pine; (3 km SE along Yappara Rd, contact Tourist information to gain entry); Baan Hill Reserve, 20 km SW, a natural soakage area surrounded by sandhills and scrub; Billiatt Conservation Park, 37 km N. **Tourist information:** Council Offices, Day St; (08) 8577 8002. **Accommodation:** 2 hotels, 1 motel, 1 B&B, 1 cara./camp. park.

Port Augusta   Pop. 14 595

MAP REF. 299 A12, 304 I11

A thriving industrial city at the head of Spencer Gulf and in the shadow of the Flinders Ranges, Port Augusta is the most northerly port in South Australia. It is 308 km from Adelaide and is a vital supply centre for the outback areas of the State and the large sheep stations of the district. Port Augusta is an important link on the Indian–Pacific railway and a stopover for the famous Ghan train to Alice Springs, which departs from Adelaide. The city has played an intrinsic role in the State's development since the State Electricity Trust built a series of major power stations here. Fuelled by coal from the huge open-cut mines at Leigh Creek, the stations generate more than a third of the State's electricity. **Of interest:** Multi-award-winning Wadlata Outback Centre, Flinders Tce, provides introduction to the sights and sounds of the outback. Homestead Park Pioneer Museum, Elsie St, has large photographic collection, picnic areas, blacksmith's shop, old steam train and crane, and rebuilt 130-year-old pine-log Yudnappinna Homestead. Royal Flying Doctor Service Base, Vincent St, open weekdays. School of the Air, Power Cres., tours during school-term time. Curdnatta Art and Pottery Gallery in town's original railway station, Commercial Rd

(check opening times). Self-guide heritage walk, includes town hall (1887), Commercial Rd; court house (1884) with cells built of Kapunda marble, cnr Jervios St and Beauchamp's Lane; St Augustine's Church (1882), Church St, with its magnificent stained glass (brochure available from Tourist information). Scenic views and picnic facilities in parks adjacent to: McLellan Lookout, Whiting Pde, site of Matthew Flinders landing in 1802; Water Tower Lookout (1882), Mitchell Tce. Matthew Flinders Lookout, end of McSporran Cres., provides excellent view of Gulf and Flinders Ranges. Trash and Treasure market at Homestead Park, Elsie St, 3rd Sun. each month. **In the area:** Australian Arid Lands Botanic Gardens, Stuart Hwy, northern outskirts of town. Northern Power Station, northern outskirts (tours Mon.–Fri.). Scenic drive north-east to splendid Pichi Richi Pass, historic Quorn, and Warren Gorge; or see the same sights by train on the Pichi Richi Railway, a 33-km round trip operating from Quorn (Easter–Nov.). Winninowie Conservation Park, 30 km SE. Hancocks Lookout, 38 km SE towards Wilmington, provides excellent views of surrounding country including Port Augusta and Whyalla; turnoff road dangerous when wet. Mt Remarkable National Park, 63 km SE, features rugged mountain terrain, magnificent gorges and abundant wildlife. Historic Melrose, 65 km SE, oldest town in Flinders Ranges. **Tourist information:** Wadlata Outback Centre, Flinders Tce; (08) 8641 0793. **Accommodation:** 7 hotels, 9 motels, 1 hostel, 3 cara./ camp. parks.

Port Broughton   Pop. 681

MAP REF. 303 J4

A small port on the extreme northwest coast of Yorke Peninsula, Port Broughton is 169 km from Adelaide. On a protected inlet, the town is a major port for fishing boats and is renowned for its deep-sea prawns. **Of interest:** Safe swimming beach along foreshore. Historical Museum (old school building), Harvey St, and Cottage Museum, Kadina Rd, contain much of town's history. In Harvey St, Shandelé porcelain dolls made and on display. Historic walking trail, contact Tourist information. **In the area:** Fisherman's Bay, 10 km N, a popular fishing, boating and

Kangaroo Island

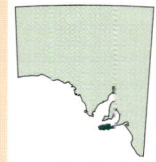

Only 120 kilometres south-west of Adelaide, Kangaroo Island, the third largest Australian island, shows nature in its wildest and purest form. A walk through bush or along coastal cliffs may provide glimpses of wallabies, koalas, echidnas or, of course, kangaroos; there are also many species of birds and wildflowers.

Visitors may fly to the island from Adelaide (Emu Airways, Albatross Airlines and Kendell Airlines) or go by ferry. The ferry *Super Flyte* takes passengers from Glenelg to Kingscote (September to April). The vehicular ferries *Philanderer III* and *The Navigator* and the passenger ferry *Valerie Jane* operate from Cape Jervis to Penneshaw. Tours are available and hire vehicles include cars, mopeds and bicycles. A bus service operates between Kingscote and the airport. A shuttle bus operates twice daily between Penneshaw and Kingscote. Kangaroo Island's waters offer excellent fishing; game-fishing charters are available and fishing equipment can be hired.

At the four main towns, **Kingscote,** American River, Parndana and Penneshaw, there is a range of accommodation from hotels and motels, through flats and cottages, to camping, cabins and bed-and-breakfasts. Many farms also provide bed and breakfast accommodation.

American River, nestled in a pine-fringed bay, is ideal for fishing, scuba diving and canoeing. Pelican Lagoon is a sanctuary for birds and fish. Penneshaw overlooks the passage separating the island from the mainland. Little (fairy) penguins promenade on the rocks here at night. Penguin-watching tours leave from the Penguin Interpretive Centre.

The coastline of the island varies from the several kilometres of safe swimming beach at Emu Bay in the north to the rugged cliffs and roaring surf of the south. However, in the south, D'Estrees Bay's wide deserted beach is ideal for fishing, collecting shells and exploring. **Cape Gantheaume** and **Seal Bay conservation parks** are located on this exposed southern coast. Seal Bay has a permanent colony of Australian sea lions. New Zealand fur seal colonies are found near Admirals Arch on Cape du Couedic. Also on the south coast are limestone formations in the caves at Kelly Hill Conservation Park. At Cape Borda, on the north-west tip of the island, is one of the most picturesque of Australia's old lighthouses; there are guided tours daily, arranged through the Department of Environment and Natural Resources at Cape Borda. Other attractive spots along the northern coast include the rugged rocks at Harveys Return; Western River Cove with its idyllic white beach; a superb protected bay at Snelling Beach; and Stokes Bay, where a secret tunnel leads to the beach. On the western

Australian sea lions, Seal Bay

end of the island, which is dominated by the soaring eucalypt forests of the **Flinders Chase National Park,** are two of the island's natural wonders: Admirals Arch, a huge arch where on sunny afternoons stalactites can be seen in silhouette against a background of the deep blue Southern Ocean, and the Remarkable Rocks, huge, unusually shaped granite boulders.

For further information contact the Kangaroo Island Tourist Information Centre, Howard Drive, Penneshaw; (08) 8553 1185. **See also:** National Parks for those parks indicated by bold type and the text entry for Kingscote in A–Z listing. **Map references:** 297 A11, 302 F11.

SOUTH AUSTRALIA

holiday spot. Heritage copper-mining towns of Moonta, Wallaroo and Kadina, 47 km s. **Tourist information:** Yorke Peninsula Visitor Information Centre, 51 Taylor St, Kadina; (08) 8821 2093. **Accommodation:** 1 hotel, 1 hotel/ motel, 2 cara./camp. parks.

Port Elliot   Pop. 1203

MAP REF. 297 H8, 301 C3, 303 L11

Only 5 km NE of Victor Harbor, Port Elliot is a charming, historic coastal town with the main focus on scenic Horseshoe Bay, the town's beach. The town was established in 1854, the same year Australia's first public horse-drawn railway operated between Goolwa and Port Elliot. **Of interest:** Along The Strand: National Trust historical display at railway station (1911); council chamber (1879); police station (1853); St Jude's Church (1854); spectacular views from Freeman's Knob at end of The Strand. Port Elliot Art Pottery, Main Rd. Guided walks of town available, contact Tourist information. **In the area:** Crows Nest Lookout, 6 km N, breathtaking views of coast. North-east between town and Middleton, Basham Beach Regional Park has coastal trails with interpretive signage. At Middleton, 6 km NE, Heritage Bakery; old flour mill, largest building in town; further 5 km, Middleton Winery. **Tourist information:** Dodd & Page Land Agents, 51 The Strand; (08) 8554 2029. **Accommodation:** 2 hotels, 1 motel, 1 cara./camp. park.

Port Lincoln   Pop. 11 345

MAP REF. 302 D8

Port Lincoln, originally considered as a possible site for the State's capital, is attractively sited on the clear waters of Boston Bay, which is three times the size of Sydney Harbour. The port, 250 km due west of Adelaide across St Vincent and Spencer gulfs, was reached by Matthew Flinders in 1802 and settled by Europeans in 1839. With its sheltered waters, Mediterranean climate, scenic coastal roads and attractive farming hinterland, Port Lincoln is a popular holiday destination. It is also the base for Australia's largest tuna fleet and tuna-farming industry, and an important export centre for wheat, wool, fat lambs, live sheep, frozen fish, lobster, prawns, abalone and tuna. The coastline is deeply indented, offering magnificent scenery, sheltered coves, steep cliff faces and impressive surf beaches. **Of interest:** Boston Bay for swimming, water-skiing, yachting and excellent fishing. Mill Cottage Museum (1867) and Settler's Cottage Museum, both in picturesque Flinders Park. Old Mill lookout, Dorset Place, offers views of town and bay. Lincoln Hotel (1840), Tasman Tce, oldest hotel on Eyre Peninsula. Axel Stenross Maritime Museum, Lincoln Hwy, north end of town; nearby, First Landing site. Rose-Wal Memorial Shell Museum in grounds of Eyre Peninsula Old Folks Home, Flinders Hwy. Arteyrea Gallery, Washington St, community art centre. M.B. Kotz Collection of Stationary Engines, Baltimore St. Parnkalla Walking Trail, winds around edge of harbour (brochure available at Tourist information). Lincoln Cove, off St Andrews Tce, includes marina, leisure centre with waterslide, holiday charter boats and base for commercial fishing fleet. Boat charter available for game fishing, diving, day fishing and island cruises; yacht charter available. Regular launch cruises of Boston Bay and Boston Island. *Dangerous Reef Explorer* available for group charter to Dangerous Reef, off Boston Island, home for large sea-lion colony, an underwater marine viewing platform and a commercial tuna farm. Apex Wheelhouse, original wheelhouse from tuna boat *Boston Bay*, adjacent to Kirton Point Caravan Park, Hindmarsh St. Jan.: Tunarama Festival, (Australia Day holiday) celebrates opening of tuna season. Feb.: Lincoln Week Regatta. **In the area:** Several pleasant parks close to town. Vast natural reserves abounding in wildlife, within a day's outing. Winter Hill Lookout, 5 km NW on Flinders Hwy. Greenpatch Farm, 15 km NW, has native animals and bird-feeding (open Fri.–Sun. or by appt). Wildflowers in spring, 30 km NW near Wanilla. Boston Bay Winery, 6 km N on Lincoln Hwy; Delacolline Estate Winery, Whillas Rd (both offer sales on weekends or by appt). At Poonindie, 20 km N, church (1850) with two chimneys. At Koppio, 38 km N: Koppio Smithy Museum (open Tues.–Sun. and school holidays) also houses barbed wire and fencing equipment museum; Woodlands Lodge, local crafts (open Tues.–Sun.); Tod Reservoir museum with heritage display and nearby picnic area. Award-winning Quandong Farm, 45 km N, has orchids, quandong seedlings and trees (open Tues. for tours or by appt). Tumby Bay, 48 km N, small beach resort. At Lincoln National Park, 20 km S: wildlife, extensive network of walking trails including access to Flinders Monument on Stamford Hill for panoramic views, cliff-top walk to impressive coastal scenery and Flinders Tablet in Memory Cove, a plaque in memory of crew members lost in seas nearby during Flinders' 1802 epic voyage (gate key and entry pass required; contact National Parks office at Port Lincoln). Whalers Way, a privately-owned, scenic, clifftop tourist drive on southernmost tip of Eyre Peninsula: stunning coastal scenery from Flinders Lookout (permit required, contact Tourist information). On road to Whalers Way: Constantia Designer Craftsmen, world-class furniture factory and showroom (guided tours available); historic Mikkira sheep station, open during winter. Offshore islands for boating enthusiasts: Boston, Spilsby and Thistle islands have accommodation; Thistle and Wedge islands (both privately-owned), popular with bluewater sailors and anglers. **Tourist information:** Civic Centre, Tasman Tce; (08) 8682 4577. **Accommodation:** 3 hotels, 7 motels, 2 cara./camp. parks. **See also:** Festival Fun; The Eyre Peninsula.

Port MacDonnell   Pop. 677

MAP REF. 301 H13

Port MacDonnell is 28 km s of Mount Gambier. It is a quiet fishing town that was once a thriving port. The rock-lobster fishing fleet here is the largest in the State. **Of interest:** Maritime Museum, Meylin St, features salvaged artifacts from shipwrecks and photographic history of town. Jan.: Oz Rock Music Festival. Nov.: Bayside Festival. **In the area:** 'Dingley Dell' (1862, but restored), 2 km W, home of poet Adam Lindsay Gordon, now a museum. Opposite, start of Germein Reserve boardwalk, an 8-km return walk through wetlands. Cape Northumberland Lighthouse, on coastline west of town. Devonshire teas at Ye Olde Post Office Tea Rooms at Allendale East, 6 km N. Walking track to summit of Mt Schank, 10 km N, crater of extinct volcano. Nearby Mt Schank Fish Farm has fresh fish and yabbies for sale. Heading east, good surf fishing at Orwell Rocks. Sinkholes for experienced cave divers at

Commercial fishing fleet moored at Lincoln Cove, Port Lincoln

Ewens Ponds, 7 km E, and Picaninnie Ponds Conservation Parks, 20 km E. **Tourist information:** *Lady Nelson* Visitor and Discovery Centre, Jubilee Hwy East, Mount Gambier; (08) 8724 1730. **Accommodation:** 1 hotel, 1 motel, 2 cara./ camp. parks.

Port Pirie
Pop. 14 110

MAP REF. 303 J3, 304 I13

Huge grain silos and smelters' chimneys dominate the skyline of Port Pirie, 227 km N of Adelaide on Spencer Gulf. Situated on the tidal Port Pirie River, the city is a major industrial and commercial centre. The first European settlers came in 1845; wheat farms and market gardens were established around the sheep industry in the region. Broken Hill Associated Smelters began smelting lead in 1889 and today the largest lead smelters in the world treat thousands of tonnes of concentrates annually from the silver, lead and zinc deposits at Broken Hill, NSW. Wheat and barley from the mid-north of the State are exported from here and there is a thriving fishing industry. Port Pirie is also a vital link in the road and rail routes to Alice Springs, Darwin, Port Augusta and Perth. Wheat farms, rolling hills and the ocean are all close by. Swimming, water-skiing, fishing and yachting are popular sports on the river. **Of interest:** Regional Tourism and Arts Centre, Mary Elie St, features local and touring exhibitions, and craft shop. National Trust Museum Buildings, Ellen St, includes Victorian pavilion-style railway station. Historic residence 'Carn Brae', Florence St, features antique exhibits and a collection of over 2500 dolls. Town walks (brochure available at Tourist information): National Trust walking tours; Journey Landscape walk, a nature walk commencing behind Tourist information centre. On waterfront: loading and discharging of Australian and overseas vessels. Tours of Pasminco Metals BHAS smelting works, details from Tourist information. Northern Festival Centre in Memorial Park, venue for local and national performances; Gertrude St. Jan.: Australia Day celebrations. Apr.: SA Longtrack Speedway Championships. Sept.: Blessing of the Fleet and associated festivals, celebrate role of Italians at turn of century in establishing local fishing industry. Oct.: Festival of Country Music. Nov.: Cycling and Athletics Carnival. **In the area:** Weeroona Island, a good fishing, holiday area accessible by car, 13 km N. Port Germein, a beachside town 24 km N, with wooden jetty said to be longest in southern hemisphere; Festival of the Crab held here in Jan. Southern reaches of Flinders Ranges within 50 km. **Tourist information:** Regional Tourism and Arts Centre, Mary Elie St; (08) 8633 0439. **Accommodation:** 2 hotels, 1 hotel/motel, 4 motels, 3 cara./ camp. parks.

Port Victoria
Pop. 313

MAP REF. 302 H7

A tiny township on the west coast of Yorke Peninsula, Port Victoria was once the main port for sailing ships carrying grain from the area. **Of interest:** Geology trail, booklet available from Tourist information. Swimming and jetty fishing, from original 1888 jetty at end of Main St. National Trust Maritime Museum, on jetty (check opening times). **In the area:** Conservation Islands are breeding areas for several bird species. Wardang Island, Aboriginal reserve, 10 km off coast; permission required from Point Pearce Community Council. Underwater Maritime Heritage Trail for scuba divers in waters around Wardang Island, includes visits to 8 wrecks (self-guide leaflet available). **Tourist information:** Yorke Peninsula Visitor Information Centre, 51 Taylor St, Kadina; (08) 8821 2093. **Accommodation:** 1 hotel/motel, 2 cara./camp. parks. **See also:** The Yorke Peninsula.

Quorn
Pop. 1056

MAP REF. 299 B12, 304 I10

Nestled in a valley in the Flinders Ranges, 331 km N of Adelaide, Quorn was established as a railway town on the Great Northern Railway in 1878. Built by Chinese and British workers, the line was closed in 1957; part of the line through Pichi Richi Pass has been restored as a tourist railway taking passengers on the scenic 33-km round trip. **Of interest:** Historic buildings; historic walk leaflet available from Tourist information. In Railway Tce.: Quorn Mill (1878), originally a flour mill, now motel and restaurant; Quornucopia Galley; railway station, departure point for Pichi Richi Railway (operates Easter–end Nov.). Nairana Craft Centre, First St. **In the area:** Colourful rocky outcrops of Dutchman's Stern, 6 km W; walking trails in area. Junction Gallery, 16 km N on Yarrah Vale Rd. Warren Gorge, 22 km N, popular with climbers. Buckaringa scenic drive, 32 km N, through the ranges north of town (signposted). Proby's Grave, 35 km N; Hugh Proby was the first settler at Kanyaka sheep station. Kanyaka Homestead, 42 km NE, ruins of historic sheep station. Nearby, Kanyaka Death Rock, overlooks permanent waterhole, once an Aboriginal ceremonial ground. Towns of Bruce and Hammond, 22 km and 38 km SE respectively, feature 1870s architecture; at Hammond, unusual museum and restaurant in original bank building. Scenic drive 10 km S to Devil's

Peak, Pichi Richi Pass, Mt Brown Conservation Park and picturesque Waukarie Creek, 16 km away; walking trails in area. **Tourist information:** 3 Seventh St; (08) 8648 6419. **Accommodation:** 2 hotels, 2 hotel/motels, 1 motel, 2 B&B, 1 cara./camp. park.

Renmark
Pop. 4256

MAP REF. 303 Q6

Renmark is at the heart of the oldest irrigation area in Australia, 260 km NE of Adelaide on the Sturt Hwy. In 1887 the Chaffey brothers from Canada were granted 250 000 acres (100 000 ha) to test their irrigation scheme. Today lush orchards and vineyards thrive with the water piped from the Murray River. There are canneries, wineries and fruit-juice factories. Wheat, sheep and dairy cattle are other local industries. **Of interest:** Historic Renmark Hotel, Murray Ave, community-owned and run. National Trust Museum 'Olivewood', former Chaffey homestead, cnr Renmark Ave (Sturt Hwy) and 21st St. Display of old hand-operated wine-press, Renmark Ave. One of the Chaffeys' original wood-burning irrigation pumps on display outside Renmark Irrigation Trust Office, original Chaffey Bros. office, in Murray Ave. PS *Industry* (1911), now floating museum moored behind Tourist information. Riverland Fruit Co-op packing shed, Renmark Ave, near 19th St, sales of local products (group tours available). Zenith Art Gallery, Murtho St; Ozone Art Gallery, Ral Ral Ave. Houseboats for hire. Oct.: Rose Festival. Dec.: Christmas Pageant; Rowing Regatta. **In the area:** On Sturt Hwy: Renmano Winery, 5 km SW; unique collection of fauna, particularly reptiles, at Bredl's Wonder World of Wildlife, 7 km SW. Ruston's Roses, 4000 varieties, 7 km SW off Sturt Hwy (open Oct.–May). Angove's winery and distillery, Bookmark Ave, 5 km SW. On Loch 5 Rd: SA Water Corporation Loch 5 and Weir, 2 km SE; Margaret Dowling National Trust Park, 3 km SE, an area of natural bushland. At Paringa, 4 km E: suspension bridge (1927); Bert Dix Memorial Park; the Black Stump, root system of river red gum estimated to be about 500 years old; houseboats available for hire. Dunlop Big Tyre spans Sturt Hwy at Yamba Roadhouse, 16 km SE; also fruit fly inspection point (no fruit allowed into SA). Scenic drive 40 km E into Vic. to see spring blossoms

at Lindsay Point Almond Park. Headings Lookout tower, 16 km NE, for excellent views of surrounding irrigated farmland and river cliffs. Murtho Forest Reserve, 19 km NE. Danggali Conservation Park, 60 km N, vast area of mallee scrub, bluebush and black oak woodland, and wildlife. **Tourist information:** Tourist and Heritage Centre, Murray Ave; (08) 8586 6704. **Accommodation:** 1 hotel/motel, 4 motels, 1 B&B, 1 hostel, 3 cara./camp. parks. **See also:** Festival Fun.

Robe
Pop. 730

MAP REF. 301 F9

A small, historic town on Guichen Bay, 336 km S of Adelaide, Robe is a fishing port and holiday centre. The rugged, windswept coast has many beautiful and secluded beaches. Lagoons and salt lakes surround the area and wildlife abounds; penguins appear on the beach in the evening in summer. In the 1850s, Robe was a major wool port. During the gold rush, 16 500 Chinese disembarked there and travelled overland to the goldfields to avoid the Victorian Poll Tax. **Of interest:** National Trust buildings, and art and craft galleries, especially in Smillie and Victoria sts. Historic Interpretation Centre in Library building, Victoria St, has displays and tourist information including leaflets on self-guide heritage walks and drives. Old Customs House Museum (1863), Royal Circus (check opening times). Karatta House, summer residence of Governor Sir James Fergusson in 1860s, off Christine Dr. (not open). Caledonian Inn (1858), Victoria St, accommodation and meals. Crayfish fleet anchors in Lake Butler (Robe's harbour); fresh crays and fish Oct.–Apr. Jan.: Beer Can Regatta. Sept.: Blessing of the Fleet. Oct.: Art/Craft Festival. **In the area:** Long Beach (17 km long), 2 km N. Historic home Lakeside (1884), now offers accommodation and caravan park, 2 km SE on Main Rd. Waterskiing on adjacent Lake Fellmongery. Narraburra Woolshed, 14 km SE. Beacon Hill, 2 km S, panoramic views. Little Dip Conservation Park, 13 km S, features a complex moving sand-dune system, salt lakes, freshwater lakes and abundant wildlife. The Obelisk at Cape Dombey, 3 km W. **Tourist information:** Robe Library, Victoria St; (08) 8768 2465. **Accommodation:** 2 hotels, 6 motels, 5 B&B, 4 cara./camp. parks.

Roxby Downs
Pop. 1999

MAP REF. 304 F4

A modern township built to accommodate the employees of the Olympic Dam mining project, Roxby Downs is 85 km N of Pimba, which is just off Stuart Hwy, 555 km N of Adelaide. A road from Roxby Downs joins the Oodnadatta Track just south of Lake Eyre South, 125 km N of Roxby. **In the area:** Olympic Dam Mining Complex, 15 km N, daily tours of mining operations available mid Mar.–mid Nov. Heritage Centre and Missile Park, 90 km S at Woomera. **Tourist information:** Council Offices, Richardson Pl.; (08) 8671 0010. **Accommodation:** 1 motel, 1 cara./camp. park.

Stansbury
Pop. 513

MAP REF. 302 I9

Situated on the lower east coast of Yorke Peninsula, Stansbury was originally known as Oyster Bay because the bay was once one of the best oyster beds in the State. In days gone by, ketches shipped grain across the gulf from Stansbury to Port Adelaide. A popular holiday destination, the town has scenic views of Gulf St Vincent. The bay is excellent for water sports, including diving and water-skiing. May: Sheepdog Trials. **Of interest:** School House Museum, in first Stansbury school (1878), North Tce. Jetty fishing. **In the area:** Lake Sundown, 15 km NW, one of many salt lakes in area; photographer's delight at sunset. **Tourist information:** Yorke Peninsula Visitor Information Centre, 51 Taylor St, Kadina; (08) 8821 2093. **Accommodation:** 1 hotel, 2 motels, 2 cara./camp. parks.

Strathalbyn
Pop. 2623

MAP REF. 297 I4, 301 C3, 303 L10

An inland town with a Scottish heritage, on the Angas River, Strathalbyn is 58 km S of Adelaide and a designated heritage township. The picturesque Soldiers Memorial Gardens follow the river through the town, offering shaded picnic grounds. **Of interest:** National Trust Museum, in old police station and court house; Rankine St. St Andrew's Church (1848), Alfred Pl. Old Provincial Gas Company (1868), South Tce. Antique and craft shops. Aug.: Collectors, Hobbies and Antique Fair. Oct.: Glenbarr Scottish Festival;

The Flinders Ranges

Moralana Scenic Drive, south of Wilpena Pound, one of many scenic drives in the ranges

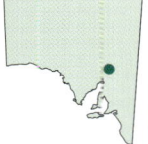

The Flinders Ranges are part of a mountain chain which extends for 430 kilometres from its southern end (between Crystal Brook and Peterborough) to a point 160 kilometres east of Marree. The most spectacular peaks and valleys are in three areas: the first in the **Melrose–Wilmington** area; the second, north-east of **Port Augusta;** and the third, east of **Leigh Creek.** The Flinders, while similar in scale to many of Australia's mountain ranges, are totally different in both colouration and atmosphere. There is a unique quality in the contrast of the dry, stony land and richly-lined rock faces – the characteristics of a desert range – with the rich vegetation of the river red gums, casuarinas, native pines and wattles that clothe the valleys and cling to hillsides and rock crevices. In spring, after rain, the display of wildflowers is sometimes breathtaking, carpeting the whole region with masses of reds, pinks, yellows, purples and white. The wildflowers, together with the natural beauty of the rock shapes, pools, caves and twisted trees, make the Flinders Ranges a favourite haunt of photographers and artists. Many paintings by Sir Hans Heysen embody the shape and spirit of the ranges.

The Flinders is served by good roads. A pleasant trip, which will take in the best of the scenery, is the drive north-east from Port Augusta through the Pichi Richi Pass to **Quorn** and **Hawker,** and from there on the loop road to Parachilna, circling the Wilpena Pound area. But to explore the unique quality of the Flinders, it is better to spend more time; stay at one of the locations offering accommodation and explore this fascinating region, preferably on foot or by vehicle. There are kilometres of signposted tracks in the ranges but, as it is still only too easy to lose your way, it is important to be equipped with a good map and to follow a planned route. Drivers should avoid using the secondary roads after rain; they can be treacherous when wet.

The best-known feature of the Flinders Ranges is Wilpena Pound, an elevated basin covering about 50 square kilometres and encircled by sheer cliffs, which are set in a foundation of purple shale and rise through red stone to white-topped peaks. The only entrance is a narrow gorge, through which a creek sometimes flows. The external cliffs rise to more than 1000 metres, but inside is a gentle slope to the floor of the plain. The highest point in the Pound is St Mary's Peak, at 1165 metres, which dominates the northern wall and provides a magnificent view over the mountains. Within the Pound are low, rounded hills and folded ridges, grasslands and pine-clad slopes that descend to the gums along Wilpena Creek. It is a wonderland of birdlife: rosellas, galahs, red-capped robins, budgerigars and wedgetailed eagles are common here. Bushland possums and endangered yellow-footed wallabies can also be seen.

There is a resort at **Wilpena,** catering for levels of accommodation from camping to a modern motel. In this central section of the ranges are Warren Gorge, Brachina Gorge, Yourambulla Cave with its Aboriginal drawings, the Hills of Arkaba, considered the most beautiful spur in this region, Bunyeroo and Aroona valleys and the **Flinders Ranges National Park.**

Other features in the Flinders that are spectacular include, in the central section, Stokes Hill Lookout and the Great Wall of China, a long rocky escarpment; and in the northern section, Mount Chambers and Chambers Gorge which can be reached by vehicle or on foot.

The far northern region of the ranges also invites exploration. The 61 000-hectare privately-run property **Arkaroola** is a sanctuary situated in rugged outback country featuring quartzite razorback ridges over elongated valleys, once the sea bed of a great continental shelf, the legacy that remains is rippled rock with embedded marine fossils. There is a profusion of wildlife: emus, ducks, parrots, cockatoos, galahs, marsupial mice, possums and yellow-footed rock wallabies – all abound in large numbers. Accommodation and camping is available at Arkaroola. Nearby is **Gammon Ranges National Park.**

From the heavily-timbered slopes in the southern ranges, through picturescue gorges and rolling plains to the arid ranges of the north, the Flinders offer a variety of experiences. In addition to its unique flora and fauna, and its rugged beauty, the region contains an important Aboriginal heritage and traces of early pioneering days.

For further information on the area, contact Flinders Ranges and Outback South Australia Tourism, PO Box 666, Adelaide 5001, (08) 8373 3430. **See also:** National Parks and individual text entries in A–Z listing for those parks and towns indicated by bold type. **Map reference:** 299.

Agricultural Show. **In the area:** Lookout, 7 km SW, for views over town and district. Lakeside holiday town of Milang, 20 km SE, an old riverboat town; Port Milang Historical Railway Station, a local history museum. Langhorne Creek, 15 km E: centre for winegrowing district; museum in town. Pottery at Paris Creek, near Meadows, 15 km NW. Iris gardens, 2 km W of Meadows (open Oct.–Mar.). Old gold diggings at Jupiter Creek Goldfields, 35 km NW. **Tourist information:** Old Railway Station, South Tce; (08) 8536 3212. **Accommodation:** 1 hotel, 1 hotel/motel, 3 B&B, 1 cara./camp. park.

Streaky Bay   Pop. 957

MAP REF. 311 P12

Streaky Bay, 727 km NW of Adelaide, is a holiday town, fishing port and agricultural centre for the cereal-growing hinterland. Matthew Flinders, the explorer, named the bay for the streaking effect caused by seaweed in its waters. The town is almost surrounded by small bays and coves, pleasant sandy beaches and spectacular towering cliffs. Crayfish and many species of fish abound, and fishing from boat or jetty is good. **Of interest:** At Tourist information: fishing information and interesting shark replica. Restored Engine Centre, Alfred Tce, has exterior historic murals. Old School House Museum, Montgomery Tce. Hospital Cottage (1864), first building in Streaky Bay. St Canutes Catholic Church, Poochera Rd. Jan.: Family Fish Day Contest; Perlubie Beach Sports and Race Day. Mar.: Race Meeting. Dec.: Carols by the Sea. **In the area:** Magnificent coastal scenery and rugged cliffs. Scenic drive via Cape Bauer and the Blowhole, 20 km NW, offers spectacular cliff-top views across the bight. Half-day tourist drive south east to diving and snorkelling areas, Point Labatt Conservation Park and Murphy's Haystacks (2 sculptural groups of ancient pink granite rocks). Point Labatt Conservation Park, 55 km SE, has only permanent colony of sea lions on Australian mainland. Port Kenny, 62 km SE on Venus Bay, offers excellent fishing. Further 12 km S, fishing village of Venus Bay; nearby, breathtaking views from Needle Eye Lookout. Spectacular limestone caves at Talia, 88 km SE. Bairds Grave Monument, 25 km S. Felchillo Oasis, 9 km NE, includes quandong park (where fruit is grown) and wildlife sanctuary. **Tourist information:** Streaky Bay Motel, 13–15 Alfred Tce; (08) 8626 1126. **Accommodation:** 1 hotel/motel, 1 motel, 1 B&B, 1 hostel, 1 cara./camp. park. **See also:** The Eyre Peninsula.

The Coorong

The Coorong National Park curves along the southern coast of South Australia for 145 kilometres, extending from the mouth of the Murray River in the north almost to the township of Kingston S.E. in the south. A unique area, it has an eerie isolation, a silence broken only by the sounds of any of the 238 species of native birds wheeling low over the scrub and dunes, and the pounding of waves from the Southern Ocean.

The Coorong proper is a shallow lagoon, a complex system of low-lying salt pans and clay pans. Never more than 3 kilometres wide, the lagoon is divided from the sea by the towering white sandhills of Younghusband Peninsula, known locally as the Hummocks. One of the best natural bird sanctuaries in Australia, the Coorong is home for giant pelicans, cormorants, ibis, swans and terns.

Access to the park is gained by leaving the Princes Highway at Salt Creek and following the old road along the shore. Noonameena, Mark Point and Long Point in the northern section can be accessed from the turnoff at Meningie. Explore the unspoiled stretches of beach where the rolling surf washes up gnarled driftwood and beautiful shells. Year-round access to the beach is from a point further south known as 'the 42 mile'; the final 1.3

Coorong National Park protects a unique landscape and bird sanctuary

kilometres is suitable for 4WD or walking. The coastal scenery is magnificent.

For those who wish to explore in comfort, **Meningie** in the north and the fishing port of **Kingston S.E.** in the south have a range of accommodation and can be used as touring bases. Camping is permitted in the Coorong National Park; however, in the Younghusband Peninsula section, it is allowed in designated areas only. Permits may be obtained from local commercial outlets (look for the pelican logo), from self-registration points in the park or from the Coorong Shop in Meningie. The area is rich in history as well as being a naturalists' haven; pick up the *Coorong Tattler* for details. Fishing, boating and walking are popular.

For further information, contact the Department of Environment and Natural Resources office, Meningie; (08) 8575 1200. **See also:** Coorong National Park entry in National Parks and text entries for Kingston S.E. and Meningie in A–Z listing. **Map references:** 301 E5, 303 N13.

Swan Reach   Pop. 230

MAP REF. 303 N8

Swan Reach is a quiet little township on the Murray River, about 100 km E of Gawler. Picturesque river scenery and excellent fishing make it an increasingly popular holiday destination. **In the area:** Swan Reach (11 km W) and Ridley (5 km S) conservation parks. Punyelroo, 7 km S, offers fishing, boating and water-skiing. Yookamurra Sanctuary, 21 km NW, a conservation project, including eradication of feral animals and restocking with native animals (guided walks and overnight accommodation offered, bookings essential). The Murray Plains Museum, 45 km NW (open by appt). Nildottie, nearby junction of Marne and Murray rivers, 14 km S. Water sports at Walker Flat, 26 km S. **Tourist information:** Swan Reach Supermarket, Anzac Ave; (08) 8570 2036. **Accommodation:** 1 hotel, 1 cara./camp. park.

Tanunda   Pop. 3087

MAP REF. 296 F5, 300 F6, 303 L8

The town of Tanunda is the heart of the Barossa wine region. It was the focal point for early German settlement, growing out of the village of Langmeil, established in 1843, part of which can be seen in the western areas of town. **Of interest:** Fine examples of Lutheran churches. Historical museum in former post and telegraph office (1865), Murray St features collections specialising in German heritage. Barossa Wine and Visitor Centre, incorporates the Wine Interpretation Centre, 66 Murray St. Award-winning Kev Rohrlach Collection, Barossa Valley Way, Tanunda Nth, displays range from pioneering heritage to satellites. Story Book Cottage and Whacky Wood (for children), Oak St. Barossa Kiddypark, Menge St, family funpark with rides. Jan.: Oompah Fest. Mar.: Essenfest. Easter: Barossa Valley Vintage Festival. Aug.: Barossa Classic Gourmet Weekend. Oct.: Barossa Music Festival. **In the area:** Local wineries, *to the north*: Basedow Wines, Old Barn Wines, Veritas Winery, Richmond Grove Barossa Winery, Stanley Bros, Peter Lehmann Wines, Chateau Dorrien Wines and Tolley Pedare Winery; *to the south*: Turkey Flat Vineyard, Lanzerac Estate Wines, St Hallet Wines, Grant Burge Wines,

St Canutes Catholic Church, an historic church in Streaky Bay

Rockford Wines, Charles Melton Wines and Krondorf Wines. Bethany, first German settlement in Barossa, 4 km S, a pretty village with creekside picnic area, pioneer cemetery, attractive streetscapes, a winery (Bethany Wines) and a walking trail along Rifle Range Rd. Norm's Coolie Sheep Dogs, south off Barossa Valley Way, 3 performances weekly (Mon., Wed. and Sat.). The Keg Factory, makers of kegs, barrel furniture and wine racks, St Hallet Rd. At Kersbrook, 40 km S: historic buildings; trout farm. The Barossa section of the famous Heysen Trail, details at Tourist information. **Tourist information:** Barossa Wine and Visitor Centre, 66 Murray St; (08) 8563 0600; freecall, 1800 812662. **Accommodation:** 1 hotel, 1 hotel/motel, 2 motels, 18 B&B, 1 cara./camp. park. **See also:** Festival Fun; Vineyards and Wineries.

Tumby Bay   Pop. 1147

MAP REF. 302 E7

Tumby Bay is a pretty coastal town 49 km N of Port Lincoln on the east coast of the Eyre Peninsula. The town is well-known for its long crescent beach and white sand. Lawns and picnic/barbecue facilities are found along the foreshore. **Of interest:** C. L. Alexander National Trust Museum, in old wooden schoolroom on West Tce (open Fri. and Sat. p.m.). Police station (1871), Tumby Tce. For local art and craft: Rotunda Art Gallery, Tumby Tce; Briar Craft Shop, Wibberly Tce; Tumby Cottage Crafts, North Tce. Interpretive mangrove boardwalk, Berryman St, a 70-m walk (signs explain ecology of mangroves). Combined tour of Norm's worm farm, herb garden and bonsai display, Yaringa Ave. Two jetties, one more than 100 years old. Jan.: Fishing Competition. **In the area:** Rock and surf fishing. At Lipson Cove, 10 km NE, visitors can walk across to Lipson Island at low tide. Rugged, beautiful scenery and fishing at Poonta and Cowley's beaches, 15 km NE; catches include snapper, whiting and bream. At Port Neill, 42 km NE: grassed foreshore for picnics; safe swimming beach; Vic and Jill Fauser's Museum; Port Neill Lookout, 1 km N, for spectacular views. Fishing, sea lions, dolphins and birdlife at Sir Joseph Banks Group of islands, south-east off coast; charter tours available. Trinity Haven Scenic Drive leads south along coast. Island Lookout for spectacular views, 3 km S. Excellent fishing at Thuruna, 10 km S. **Tourist information:** Hales Minimart, 1 Bratten Way; (08) 8688 2584. **Accommodation:** 2 hotels, 1 motel, 1 cara./camp. park. **See also:** The Eyre Peninsula.

Victor Harbor   Pop. 5930

MAP REF. 297 G8, 301 B4, 303 L11

A popular coastal town and regional 'capital' of the Fleurieu Peninsula,

Victor Harbor is 84 km S of Adelaide. Established in the early days of whaling and sealing (1830s), the town overlooks historic Encounter Bay, protected by Granite Island. **Of interest:** Historic buildings: original Congregational Church (1869), Victoria St; Mount Breckan (1879), Renown Ave; Adare House (1852), The Drive; Old Customs House (1867), now a National Trust Museum, Flinders Pde; St Augustine's Church (1869), Burke St; Telegraph Station Art Gallery, in former telegraph station (1866); Coral St old goods shed (1890), Railway Tce. Whale-watching, from May–Sept. SA Whale Centre, Railway Tce, has educative displays to aid conservation of the 25 species of whale and dolphin in southern Australian waters. Jan.: Granite Island Regatta. Oct.: Folk and Music Festival. **In the area:** On Granite Island, joined to mainland by 630 m causeway (walk or take horse-drawn tram built in 1894): chairlift (operates school holidays and weekends) offering magnificent views of land and sea; little (fairy) penguin rookeries, Fairy Penguin Interpretive Centre. The Bluff (Rosetta Head), facing Encounter Bay; worth 100-m climb for views. Waitpinga Beach, 17 km SW. Deep Creek Conservation Park, 50 km SW, features spectacular flora and fauna, rugged cliffs and section of Heysen Trail for walking. Located alongside, Talisker Conservation Park, site of historic silver-lead mine has old mine buildings and diggings. At tip of Fleurieu Peninsula, Cape Jervis, 70 km SW, offers panoramic views to Kangaroo Island. Hindmarsh Falls, 15 km NW, has pleasant walks and spectacular waterfalls. Spring Mount Conservation Park, 14 km NW. Glacier Rock at Inman Valley, 19 km NW, shows effect of glacial erosion (said to be the first recorded discovery of glaciation in Australia). Hindmarsh and Inman rivers, north and west of town respectively, good fishing and peaceful picnic spots on-shore. Greenhills Adventure Park, 3.5 km N on banks of Hindmarsh River. Urimbirra Wildlife Park, 5 km N. Next door, Wild Rose miniature village. Opposite, Nangawooka Flora Reserve with more than 1200 species of Australian plants. At Mt Compass, 24 km N: pottery; Cow Race held here each Feb. Nearby, strawberry and blueberry farms, begonia farm and nursery, and Tooperang Trout Farm. The Steam Ranger, a restored, tourist railway service, operates between Victor Harbor and Goolwa, via Port Elliot. **Tourist information:** 10 Railway Tce; (08) 8552 5738. **Accommodation:** 2 hotels, 9 motels, 8 B&B, 1 hostel, 4 cara./camp. parks. **See also:** The Fleurieu Peninsula.

Waikerie   Pop. 1748

MAP REF. 303 O6

Waikerie, the citrus centre of Australia, is surrounded by an oasis of irrigated vegetable gardens, lush orchards and

The Fleurieu Peninsula

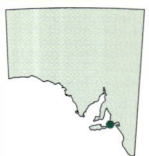

Starting 22 kilometres south of Adelaide, the Fleurieu Peninsula region stretches from O'Halloran Hill for about 90 kilometres to Cape Jervis on the west coast, and east around the vast fresh waters of Lake Alexandrina, where the Murray River meets the sea.

The ocean scenery varies from magnificent cliff faces and roaring surf to wide, sandy beaches and sheltered bays and coves. Maslin Beach is renowned as Australia's first nude bathing beach. Cape Jervis, located at the tip of the Peninsula, commands a clear view across Backstairs Passage to Kangaroo Island.

McLaren Vale, the centre of the McLaren wine-producing region, has more than 50 wineries. Some are in historic buildings with attached restaurants; most are open for tastings and cellar-door sales.

Inland there are historic buildings, particularly at **Willunga**, where public buildings vie with small cottages for the visitor's attention. The almond orchards around here are a marvellous sight, especially when they bloom at the end of winter. The Almond Blossom Festival is held in late July to early August. Ideal for keen walkers as well as those looking for a quiet picnic spot are a number

Rapid Bay, on the west coast of the Peninsula

of conservation parks. There is a scenic drive around Myponga Conservation Park.

Victor Harbor is one of South Australia's most popular beach resorts. Either walk or take the historic horse-drawn tram along the causeway to Granite Island to see the colony of little (fairy) penguins. Spend time in **Port Elliot** to take in its history and perhaps take a ride to Goolwa on the Cockle Train, a steam train restored from the original line opened in 1854; for operating times inquire at Tourist information.

There is superb fishing at **Goolwa.** Once a busy port, it is now the starting point for paddle-steamer cruises up the Murray, and cruises to Hindmarsh Island and the Barrages.

For further information on the area, contact the Victor Harbor Tourist Information Centre, 10 Railway Tce, Victor Harbor; (08) 8552 5821 or (08) 8552 5738. **See also:** individual text entries in A–Z listing for those towns indicated by bold type. **Map references:** 297 E7, 301 B4.

SOUTH AUSTRALIA

vineyards in mallee-scrub country in the Riverland. Situated 170 km NE of Adelaide, the town has beautiful views of river gums and sandstone cliffs along the Murray River. The river and lagoons in the area teem with birdlife, and the mallee scrub is a haven for parrots and other native birds. **Of interest:** Waikerie Citrus-packing House, Sturt Hwy, one of the largest in Australia. Rain Moth Gallery, Peake Tce. Lions Park, on riverfront. Harts Lagoon, Ramco Rd, a wetland area for birds with bird hide for viewing. Houseboat hire available. Feb.: International Food Fair. Easter: Horse and Pony Club Gymkhana. May: Riverland Rock 'n' Roll Festival. **In the area:** On Sturt Hwy: clifftop lookout and walk, northern outskirts of town; The Orange Tree, 2 km E, fruit products and river-viewing platform. Area internationally acclaimed as a glider's paradise; joy rides and courses available at Gliding Club, 4 km E off Sturt Hwy. Devlin's Pound, 11 km E, part of river where Devlin's ghost sighted. Holder Bend Reserve and Maize Island Conservation Park, 6 km NE. Crystallised gypsum fossils are found in abundance at Broken Cliffs on northern side of river near Lock 2, close to Taylorville. Brookfield Conservation Park, 11 km W, home of southern hairy-nosed wombat. At Blanchetown, 42 km W: first of Murray River's 6 SA locks; lookout at Blanchetown Bridge; floating restaurant. **Tourist information:** The Orange Tree, Sturt Hwy; (08) 8541 2332. **Accommodation:** 1 motel, 1 hotel/ motel, 1 cara./camp. park.

Wallaroo Pop. 2465

MAP REF. 302 I6

Situated 154 km NW of Adelaide, Wallaroo is a key shipping port for Yorke Peninsula, exporting barley and wheat. Processing of rock phosphate is another major industry here. The safe beaches and excellent fishing in this historical area make it a popular tourist destination. In 1859 vast copper-ore deposits were discovered. A smelter was built, thousands of Cornish miners arrived and Wallaroo and surrounding areas boomed until the 1920s, when copper prices dropped and the industry slowly died out. The nearby towns of Moonta and Kadina form part of the trio known as Australia's 'Little Cornwall', and the area still has many reminders of its colourful past. **Of**

Horse-drawn tram, a popular attraction at Victor Harbor

interest: Several charming old Cornish-style cottages in district. At cemetery, Moonta Rd, grave of Caroline Carleton, author of 'Song of Australia'. National Trust Wallaroo Heritage and Nautical Museum, Jetty Rd, maritime exhibits in town's original post office (1865). Historical walks, brochure available at museum or town hall (guided tours on Sun.). Historic buildings: old railway station, Owen Tce; and in Jetty Rd, customs house (1862); Hughes chimney stack (1865), which contains over 300 000 bricks and is more than 7 m square at its base. Wallaroo–Kadina Tourist Train operates from Wallaroo railway station, John Tce (2nd Sun. each month and during school holidays). Jan.: New Year's Day Regatta. May: Prize-winning Kernewek Lowender, Cornish festival held in conjunction with Moonta and Kadina (odd-numbered years). **In the area:** Fascinating towns of Moonta and Kadina. Bird Island, 10 km S, renowned for its good crabbing. **Tourist information:** Yorke Peninsula Visitor Information Centre, 51 Taylor St, Kadina; (08) 8821 2093. **Accommodation:** 1 hotel, 1 hotel/motel, 2 motels, 3 cara./camp. parks. **See also:** Festival Fun; The Yorke Peninsula.

Whyalla Pop. 25 526

MAP REF. 302 I2, 304 H13

Whyalla, northern gateway to Eyre Peninsula, has grown from a small settlement known as Hummock Hill in 1901 to the largest provincial city in the State and an important industrial centre based on steel. It is famous for its heavy industry, particularly the enormous iron and steel works, and ore mining in the Middleback Ranges. A shipyard operated

from 1939–78, and the largest ship ever built in Australia was launched here in 1972. Whyalla is a modern city with safe beaches, good fishing and boating, and excellent recreational facilities. The area enjoys a sunny Mediterranean-type climate. **Of interest:** Whyalla Maritime Museum, Lincoln Hwy, features the largest permanently land-locked ship in Australia, the former 650-tonne corvette *Whyalla* (entry includes guided tour on ship), and a collection of models, including one of the biggest 'OO' gauge model railways in Australia. Next door, Tanderra Craft Village (open last weekend each month). Mount Laura Homestead Museum (National Trust), Ekblom St; check opening times. Whyalla Art Gallery, Darling Tce. Foreshore area, includes safe beach, jetty for recreational fishing, landscaped picnic and barbecue area, and marina with boat-launching facilities. Hummock Hill lookout, Queen Elizabeth Dr. Flinders Lookout, Farrel St. Ada Ryan Gardens, Cudmore Tce, mini-zoo and picnic facilities under shady trees. Guided tours of steel works Mon., Wed. and Sat.; bookings at Tourist information (for safety reasons, visitors must wear long-sleeve top, trousers and closed footwear). Large, arid-lands wildlife and reptile sanctuary, south-east on Lincoln Hwy, near airport (open daily, bookings essential). Tourist drive, brochure from Tourist information. Jan.: Australian Amateur Snapper Fishing Championship. **In the area:** Port Bonython, 34 km E. At Point Lowly, 36 km E: lighthouse (1882), oldest building in area (not open); scenic coastal drive along Fitzgerald Bay to Point Douglas. Whyalla Conservation Park, 10 km N off Lincoln Hwy,

One of Willunga's many historic buildings

includes 30-minute walking trail over Wild Dog Hill. At Iron Knob, 53 km NW: iron-ore quarries (tours available Mon.–Fri.); Mining Museum; Iron Knob Mineral and Shell Display. **Tourist information:** Lincoln Hwy; (08) 8645 7900; freecall, 1800 088589. **Accommodation:** 4 hotels, 2 hotel/motels, 4 motels, 1 B&B, 2 cara./camp. parks. **See also:** The Eyre Peninsula.

Willunga
Pop. 1164

MAP REF. 296 B13, 297 F4, 301 B3, 303 K10
An historic town that was surveyed in 1839, Willunga was named from the Aboriginal word *willa-unga*, meaning 'the place of green trees'. The town is at the southern edge of the McLaren winegrowing region and is also a major almond-growing centre. **Of interest**: Historic pug cottages and fine examples of colonial architecture. National Trust police station and court house (1855), High St. Anglican church, with Elizabethan bronze bell, St Andrews Tce. Quarry (1842), Delabole Rd, operated for 60 years, now National Trust site. July: Almond Blossom Festival. **In the area:** Cowshed Gallery at Yundi, 9 km E. Mt Magnificent Conservation Park, 12 km SE, offers western grey kangaroos in bushland, scenic walks, picnic areas and good views from the summit. Begonia Farm, 16 km S. Strawberry farm,

4 km N. Kyeema Conservation Park, 14 km NE, for birdlife, good hiking and camping. **Tourist information:** Bakery, 16 High St; (08) 8556 2323. **Accommodation:** 1 hotel, 4 B&B.

Wilmington
Pop. 250

MAP REF. 299 C13, 303 J1, 305 J11
A tiny settlement formerly known as Beautiful Valley, Wilmington is located 290 km N of Adelaide in the Flinders Ranges. **Of interest:** In Main St: police station (1880), now a private residence; old coaching stables (1880) at rear of Wilmington Hotel; early 20th-century billiard rooms (open by appt). Butter Factory (1898), adjacent to school, off Main St. Beautiful Valley Aussie Relics Museum, Main North Rd (open by appt). Jan.: Rodeo. **In the area:** Many scenic drives in surrounding region. Views of Spencer Gulf at Hancock's Lookout, 8 km W, at beginning of Horrocks Pass off road to Port Augusta. Mount Remarkable National Park, 13 km S, features crystal-clear mountain pools, dense vegetation and abundant wildlife; Mambray Creek and spectacular Alligator Gorge in park. Historic Melrose, 24 km S, oldest town in Flinders Ranges. Booleroo Steam and Traction Preservation Society's Museum (open by appt), Booleroo Centre, 48 km SE. Hammond, historic railway town;

26 km NE. At Carrieton, 56 km NE: historic buildings; Aboriginal carvings, 5 km along Belton Rd; scenic drive to deserted Johnberg. **Tourist information:** Wilmington Hotel, Main St; (08) 8667 5154. **Accommodation:** 1 hotel, 2 cara./camp. parks.

Wilpena
Pop. 20

MAP REF. 299 E8, 305 K7
Wilpena, 429 km N of Adelaide, consists of a motel and caravan park outside Wilpena Pound. The Pound, part of the Flinders Ranges National Park, is a vast natural amphitheatre surrounded by colossal peaks that change colour depending on the light. The only entrance is through a narrow gorge and across Sliding Rock. In 1900 a wheat farmer built a homestead inside the Pound, but a flood destroyed the log road and the farm was abandoned. **In the area:** Organised tours, self-guide drives, 4WD tours, scenic flights, bushwalking and mountain climbing in surrounding countryside; brochures available at Tourist information. Numerous walking trails in Wilpena Pound, including one to St Mary's Peak, the highest point (1165 m) in the Pound. Aboriginal rock carvings and paintings at Arkaroo Rock on slopes of Rawnsley Bluff, 20 km S, and at Sacred Canyon, 16 km E. At Rawnsley Park station, 20 km S on Hawker Rd, demonstrations of sheep-drafting and shearing (Sept.–Oct.). Appealinna Homestead (1851), 16 km N off Blinman Rd, ruins of house built of flat rock from creek bed. Scenic drives: Stokes Hill Lookout, 2 km NE; Bunyeroo and Brachina gorges, Aroona Valley, 5 km NW; Moralana Scenic Drive, 25 km S; Wangarra Lookout, 10 km SW. **Tourist information:** Wilpena Pound Motel; (08) 8648 0004. **Accommodation:** 1 motel, 2 cara./ camp. parks. **See also:** The Flinders Ranges.

Woomera
Pop. 1600

MAP REF. 304 F6
Established in 1947 as a site for launching British experimental rockets, Woomera was, until 1982, a prohibited area to visitors. The town, 490 km NW of Adelaide, is still administered by the Defence Department. **Of interest:** Missile Park and Heritage Centre, cnr Dewrang and Banool sts, displays of rockets, aircraft and weapons. Old

SOUTH AUSTRALIA

The Outback

Motorists contemplating travel in the outback should prepare their vehicles and familiarise themselves with expected conditions in advance.

The outback of South Australia covers a vast area and is one of the most remote areas of the world; conditions are harsh, the climate extreme and distances are daunting.

The countryside is usually dry, barren and dusty, but freak rains and heavy floods can transform the land. The enormous, salt Lake Eyre, dry creek beds and waterholes fill, wildflowers bloom and birdlife flocks to the area.

The main road to the Northern Territory, the Stuart Highway, is a sealed road. From **Port Augusta** to **Alice Springs** the road covers a distance of 1227 kilometres. Turn off the highway to visit **Woomera**, the mining town of **Roxby Downs,** Olympic Dam and the opal-mining town of **Andamooka.**

Petrol, food and supplies are available at Port Augusta, Pimba, Glendambo, Coober Pedy, Cadney Homestead, Marla and Kulgera just over the Northern Territory border.

The notorious Birdsville Track starts at **Marree,** once a supply outpost for Afghan camel traders, and follows the route originally used to drove cattle from south-west Queensland to the railhead at Marree. The track lies between the Simpson Desert, with its giant sand dunes, and the desolate Sturt's Stony Desert. Artesian bores line the route, pouring out 64 million litres of salty boiling water every day. The road is well maintained; however, care should be taken during and after heavy rains. *Petrol and supplies are available at Marree and Mungerannie, and at Birdsville over the Queensland border.*

The Oodnadatta Track runs from Marree to **Oodnadatta** and continues on to join the Stuart Highway at Marla, 200 kilometres west. *Fuel is available only at Marree, William Creek and Oodnadatta.*

The Strzelecki Track begins at Lyndhurst; a harsh, dusty road, it stretches 459 kilometres to the almost deserted outpost of **Innamincka,** with *no stops for petrol or supplies.*

Motorists intending to travel in the outback should be prepared and well equipped (read the section on Outback Motoring). Many of the roads in the outback are unsealed with sandy patches. Heavy rain can cut access for several days. Motorists are advised to ring the Northern Roads Condition Hotline on (08) 11633 for information before departure.

For further information on the area, contact Flinders Ranges and Outback South Australia Tourism, PO Box 666, Adelaide 5001, (08) 8373 3430. **See also:** individual text entries in A–Z listing for those towns indicated by bold type. **Map references:** 304–309.

Remote outback scene in northern South Australia

Innes National Park, south-west of Yorketown

SOUTH AUSTRALIA

Guard Gate, Old Pimba Rd, opal sales. Breen Park picnic area, Girrahween Ave. July: 4th of July Celebrations. **In the area:** Roxby Downs, 78 km N, service centre for Olympic Dam mining operations (tours of mining operations available). Andamooka opal field, 107 km NE (tours available). **Tourist information:** Eldo Hotel, Kotara Cres.; (08) 8673 7867. **Accommodation:** 1 hotel, 1 cara./camp. park.

Wudinna   Pop. 573

MAP REF. 302 C3, 304 B13

Wudinna is a small settlement on the Eyre Hwy, 571 km NW of Adelaide. The township is the gateway to the timeless Gawler Ranges and has become an important service point for the Eyre Peninsula. Wilderness safaris available. **In the area:** Mt Wudinna, second largest granite outcrop in southern hemisphere, 10 km NE; at summit (261 m) scenic views, at base, recreation area. Nearby, Turtle Rock, turtle-shaped ancient granite rock. Signposted tourist drives to all major rock formations in the area. Prolific wildlife and wildflowers in spring. At Minnipa, 37 km NW: Dryland Farming Research centre; Pildappa Rock (wave rock); Tcharkuldu Rock; Poondanna (Brazil) Rock. Darkes Memorial, 50 km

W, memorial to early explorer speared to death. **Tourist information:** Council Offices, Burton Tce; (08) 8680 2002. **Accommodation:** 1 hotel/motel, 1 motel, 1 cara./camp. park.

Yankalilla   Pop. 408

MAP REF. 297 D7, 301 B3, 303 K11

A growing settlement just inland from the west coast of Fleurieu Peninsula, Yankalilla is 35 km W of Victor Harbor. **Of interest:** In Main St: Uniting Church (1878); Bungala House, for gifts and pottery; Enchanted Collections, also sell gifts and pottery; Yankalilla Hotel, offers country-style counter meals; historical museum. **In the area:** Seaside town of Normanville, 4 km W. Bay Tree Farm, 14 km SW on Cape Jervis Rd, has herbs, flowers, afternoon teas in farm setting. Cape Jervis, 35 km S, departure point for vehicular ferries to Kangaroo Island. Glacier Rock, a 500 million-year-old Cambrian quartzite, 22 km E. Steep hillsides and gullies, and western grey kangaroos at Myponga Conservation Park, 9 km NE. At Myponga, 14 km NE: begonia farm (open Oct.–Apr.); Myponga Reservoir surrounds, ideal for barbecues or picnics. **Tourist information:** Council Offices, Main St; (08)

8558 2048. **Accommodation:** Yankalilla, 1 hotel. Normanville, 1 motel, 2 cara./camp. parks.

Yorketown   Pop. 738

MAP REF. 302 I9

The principal town at the southern end of Yorke Peninsula, Yorketown's shopping centre services the surrounding cereal-growing district. Yorketown is surrounded by extensive inland salt lakes (some are pink), which are still worked. Oct.: Picnic Races and Gymkhana. **In the area:** At Innes National Park, 77 km SW: rugged coastal scenery and peaceful hinterland; Inneston, historic mining town in park, managed as historic site by the Department of Environment and Natural Resources. Many shipwrecks along this section of coast including *The Ethel* (remains of wreck located near Inneston). Surfing at Daly Head, 50 km W. South of Daly Head, Blowhole. At Corny Point, on north-western tip of Peninsula, 55 km NW: lighthouse; lookout; camping; fishing. Toy Factory, 5 km NE, locally-crafted wooden toys. **Tourist information:** Yorketown Caravan Park, Memorial Dr.; (08) 8852 1563. **Accommodation:** 1 hotel, 1 hotel/motel, 1 cara./camp. park. **See also:** The Yorke Peninsula.

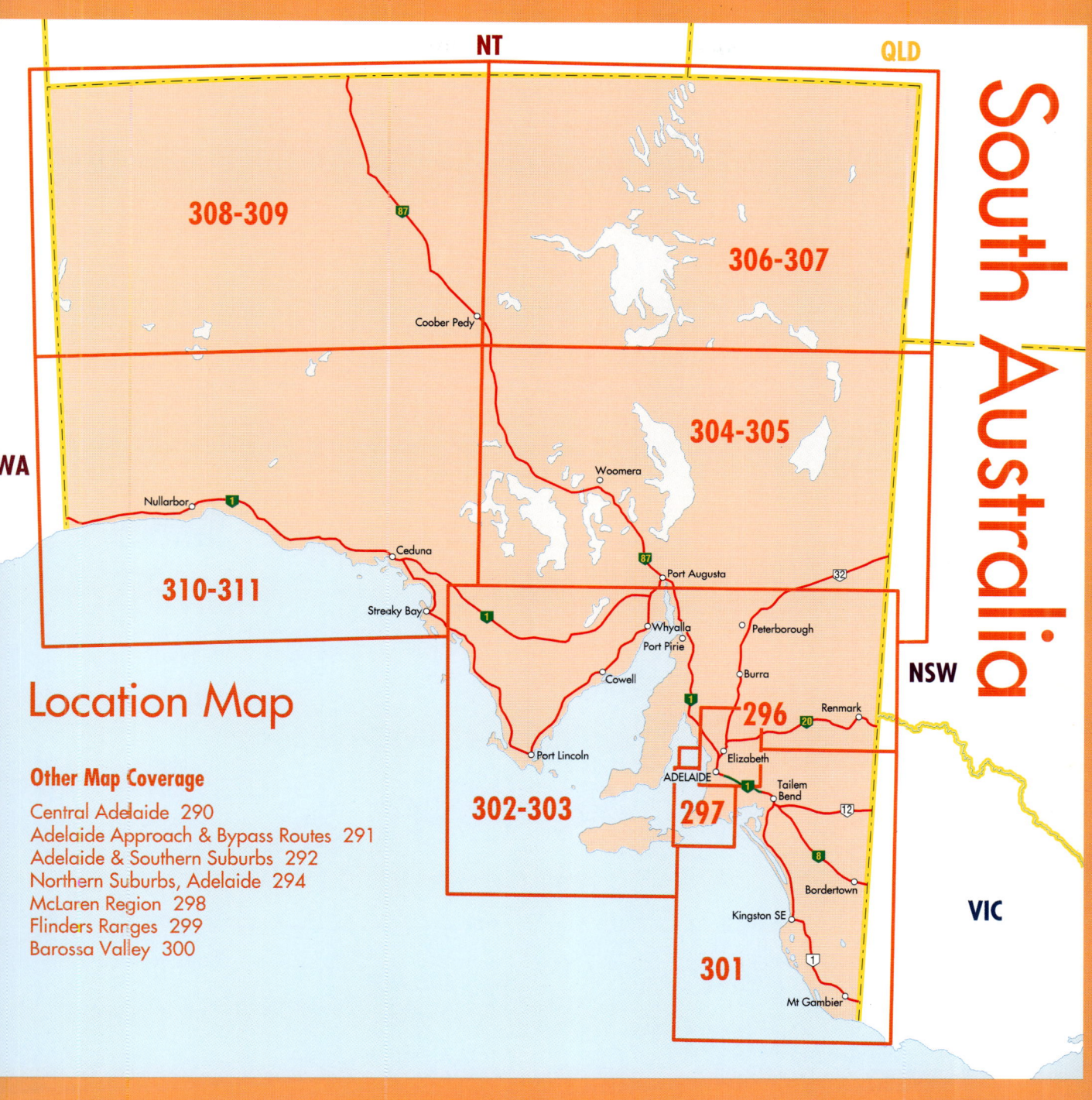

South Australia

NT **QLD**

308-309

306-307

WA

304-305

310-311

Coober Pedy

Woomera

Nullarbor

Ceduna

Streaky Bay

Location Map

Other Map Coverage

Central Adelaide 290
Adelaide Approach & Bypass Routes 291
Adelaide & Southern Suburbs 292
Northern Suburbs, Adelaide 294
McLaren Region 298
Flinders Ranges 299
Barossa Valley 300

302-303

Cowell

Port Lincoln

Port Augusta

Whyalla
Port Pirie

Peterborough

Burra

296

Renmark

NSW

Elizabeth

ADELAIDE

297

Tailem
Bend

Bordertown

VIC

Kingston SE

301

Mt Gambier

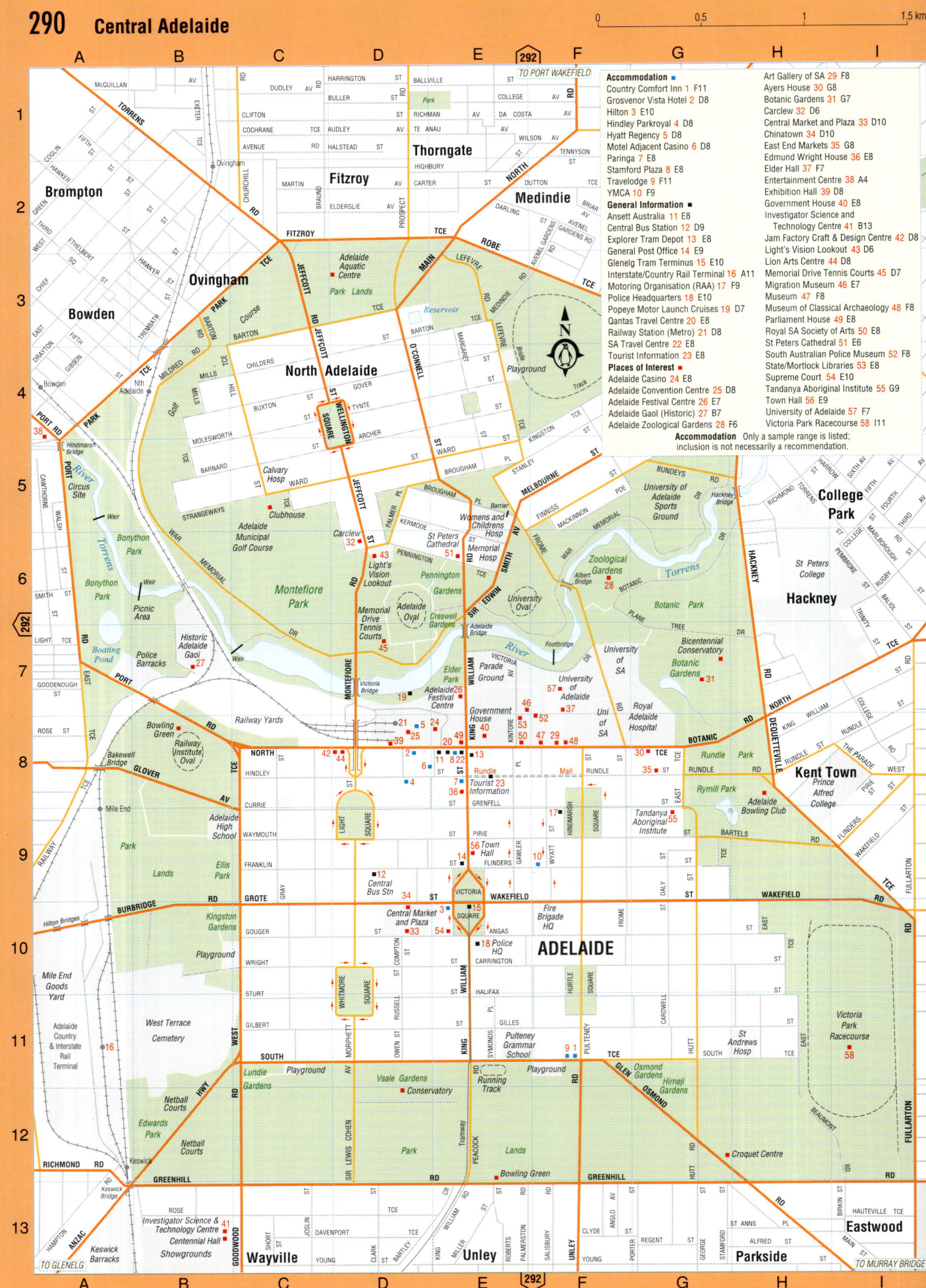

0   0.5   1   1.5 km

Accommodation ■
Country Comfort Inn **1** F11
Grosvenor Vista Hotel **2** D8
Hilton **3** E10
Hindley Parkroyal **4** D8
Hyatt Regency **5** D8
Motel Adjacent Casino **6** D8
Paringa **7** E8
Stamford Plaza **8** E8
Travelodge **9** F11
YMCA **10** F9

General Information ■
Ansett Australia **11** E8
Central Bus Station **12** D9
Explorer Tram Depot **13** E8
General Post Office **14** E9
Glenelg Tram Terminus **15** E10
Interstate/Country Rail Terminal **16** A11
Motoring Organisation (RAA) **17** F9
Police Headquarters **18** E10
Popeye Motor Launch Cruises **19** D7
Qantas Travel Centre **20** E8
Railway Station (Metro) **21** D8
SA Travel Centre **22** E8
Tourist Information **23** E8

Places of Interest ■
Adelaide Casino **24** E8
Adelaide Convention Centre **25** D8
Adelaide Festival Centre **26** E7
Adelaide Gaol (Historic) **27** B7
Adelaide Zoological Gardens **28** F6

Art Gallery of SA **29** F8
Ayers House **30** G8
Botanic Gardens **31** G7
Carclew **32** D6
Central Market and Plaza **33** D10
Chinatown **34** D10
East End Markets **35** G8
Edmund Wright House **36** E8
Elder Hall **37** F7
Entertainment Centre **38** A4
Exhibition Hall **39** E8
Government House **40** E8
Investigator Science and
  Technology Centre **41** B13
Jam Factory Craft & Design Centre **42** D8
Light's Vision Lookout **43** D6
Lion Arts Centre **44** D8
Memorial Drive Tennis Courts **45** D7
Migration Museum **46** E7
Museum **47** F8
Museum of Classical Archaeology **48** F8
Parliament House **49** E8
Royal SA Society of Arts **50** E8
St Peters Cathedral **51** E6
South Australian Police Museum **52** F8
State/Mortlock Libraries **53** E8
Supreme Court **54** E10
Tandanya Aboriginal Institute **55** G9
Town Hall **56** E9
University of Adelaide **57** F7
Victoria Park Racecourse **58** I11

Accommodation Only a sample range is listed;
inclusion is not necessarily a recommendation.

Thick roads represent recommended approach and bypass routes.

Grid columns: A B C D E F G H I
Grid rows: 1–13

Semaphore Park
West Lakes Shore
West Lakes
Tennyson
Royal Park
Hendon
Albert Park
Alberton
Queenstown
Cheltenham
Pennington
Mansfield Park
Greyhound Racing Club
Regency Park
Kilburn
Blair Athol
Woodville North
Woodville Gardens
Ferryden Park
Regency Golf Course
Dudley Park
Prospect
Woodville
Cheltenham Racecourse
Kilkenny
Croydon Park
West Croydon
Croydon
Devon Park
Renown Park
Fitzroy
Ridleyton
Brompton
Bowden
Woodville West
Beverley
Allenby Gardens
Hindmarsh
Entertainment Centre
North Adelaide
Riverside Golf Course
Delfin Island
Seaton
Seaton Park
Royal Adelaide Golf Course
Findon
Flinders Park
Brickworks Markets
Kings Res
West Thebarton
Thebarton
Grange
East Grange
Grange Jetty
Charles Sturt Memorial Museum
Kidman Park
Henley Beach
South Grange
Fulham Gardens
Underdale
Torrensville
Torrens River
ADELAIDE
Mile End
Lockleys
Brooklyn Park
Henley Jetty
Fulham
Kooyonga Golf Course
Cowandilla
Hilton
Mile End Goods
Keswick
Burbridge
West Beach
Kart-Mania
Richmond
Keswick Barracks
Wayville
HMAS Australia
Marleston
Ashford
Goodwood
Millswood
West Beach
ADELAIDE AIRPORT
Domestic Terminal
International Terminal
Sir Richard Williams
Netley
Kurralta Park
Patawalonga Golf Course
Plympton
Black Forest
Clarence Park
Westbourne Park
Glenelg North
James Golf Course
Melrose
Camden Park
Glandore
Cross
Cumberland Park
Glenelg
HMS Buffalo
Magic Mountain
Glenelg Jetty
Novar Gardens
Morphettville Racecourse
Plympton Park
Melrose Park
Colonel Light Gardens
Glengowrie
Morphettville
Ascot Park
Park Holme
Daw Park
Glenelg South
Somerton Park
Oaklands
Warradale Military Camp
Oaklands Park
St Marys
Cemetery
Pasadena
Warradale
Marion
Mitchell Park
North Brighton
Hove
Clovelly Park
Brighton
Brighton Jetty
Flinders University
Eden Hills
Shepherds Hill Recreation Park

GULF ST VINCENT
Holdfast Bay
Glenelg – Kingscote Passenger Ferry

For more detail on Central Adelaide see page 290

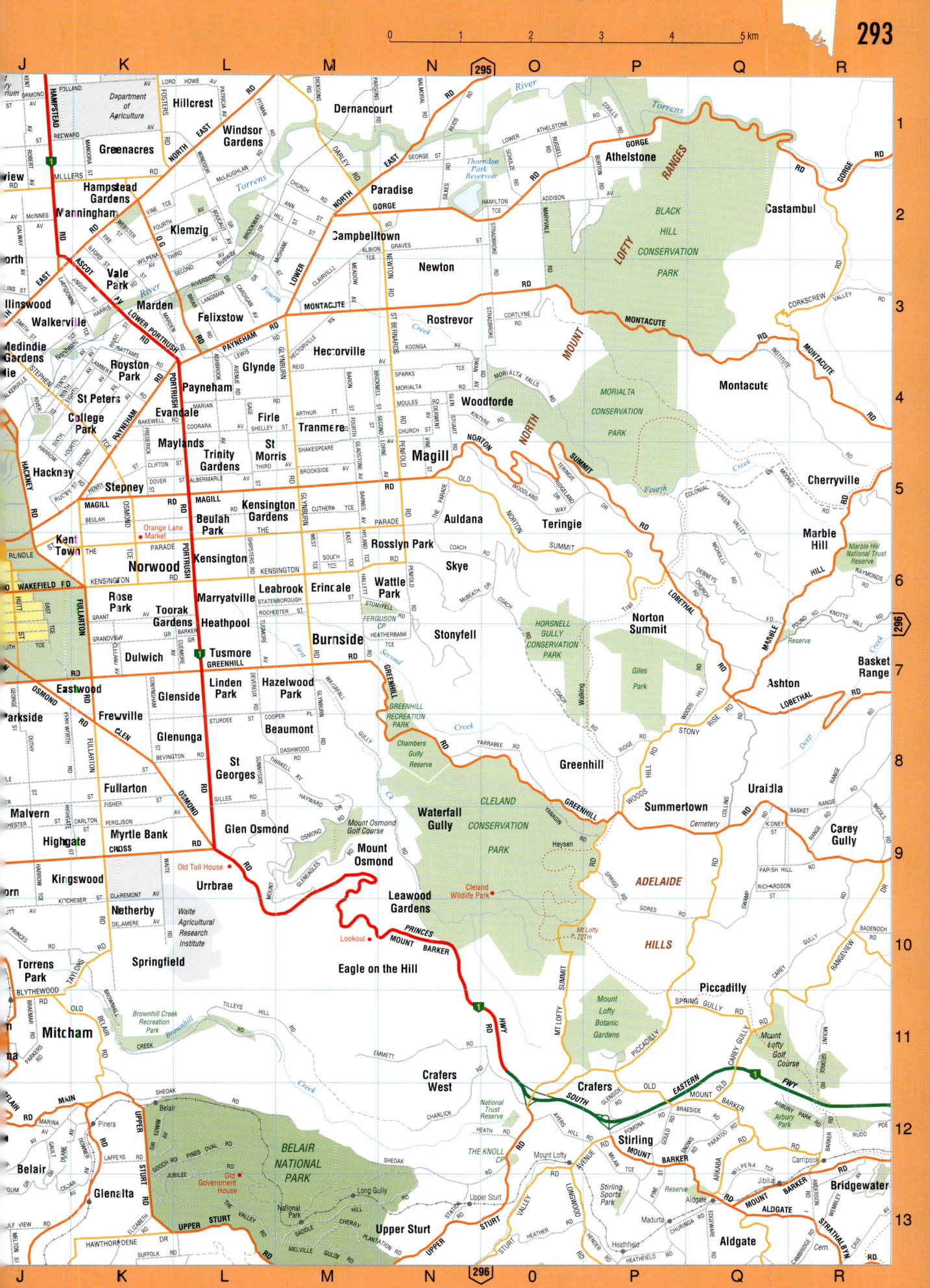

A B C D E F 296 G H I

1
2
3
N

4
5
6
7
8
9
10
11
12
13

A B C 292 D E F G H I

GULF ST VINCENT

Outer Harbor

LEFEVRE PENINSULA

Outer Harbor

Overseas Passenger Terminal
Outer Harbor North Haven Golf Course
North Haven
Osborne
Midlunga
Gedville
SA Police Academy
STRATHFIELD TCE
Draper
Taperoo
Largs North
Largs Bay
Largs
Peterhead
Semaphore
Birkenhead
Exeter
Semaphore South
Glanville
Fort Glanville
Ethelton
Semaphore Park
West Lakes Shore
Delfin Island
West Lakes
Royal Park
Riverside Golf Course
Lochside

Largs Bay

Salt Crystallization Pans

BARKER

Light
Passage
Torrens Reach

TORRENS ISLAND CONSERVATION PARK

Mutton Cove
Quarantine Station
Australian Submarine Corporation

TORRENS ISLAND

Power Station
Garden Island

North Arm Fish Market
North Arm
MOORHOUSE RD

Angas Inlet

BARKER INLET AQUATIC RESERVE

INLET

EASTERN PASSAGE

Salt Crystallization Pans

Winston Park SA Equestrian Centre

Australian Electric Transport Museum

Salt Crystallization Pans

Bolivar Sewage Treatment Works

Bolivar

Waterloo Corner

PRINCES HWY
WAKEFIELD
Speed Kartway

Globe Derby Park Trotting Tracks

Para River
Little

Salt Crystallization Pans

SOUTH ROAD CONNECTOR

Dry Creek
SALISBURY HWY

Gillman
Wingfield
Ottoway
Port Adelaide
S.A. Maritime Museum
Port Dock Railway Museum
Fishermans Wharf Markets

Athol Park
Angle Park
Pennington
Mansfield Park
Rosewater
Alberton
Queenstown
Cheltenham
Woodville North
Woodville Gardens
Woodville
Albert Park
Cheltenham Racecourse
Greyhound Racing Club
Regency Park
Regency Golf Course
Ferryden Park
Kilburn
Junction Market
Tube Mills
CHURCHILL
CAVAN
GRAND
SOUTH RD

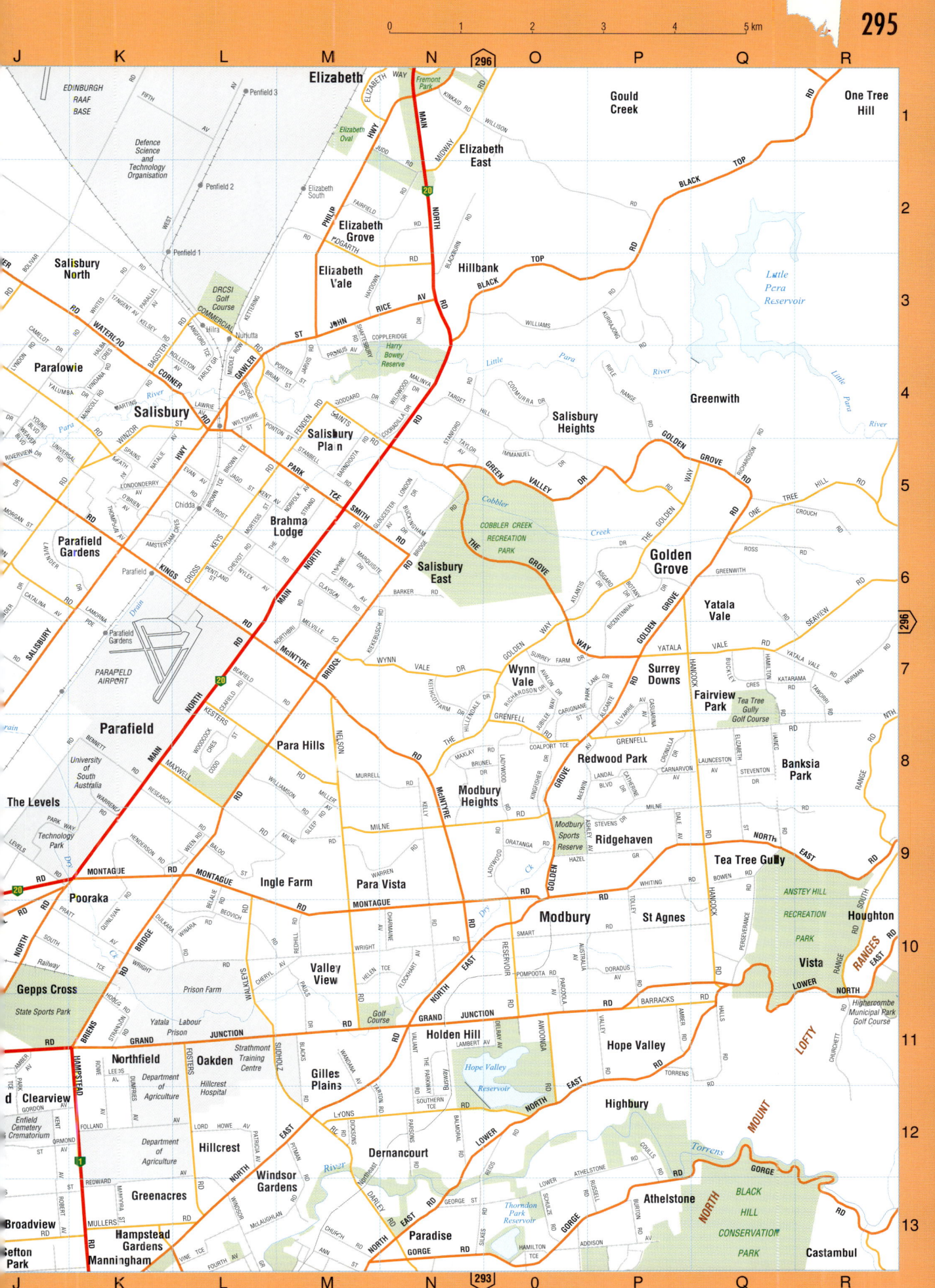

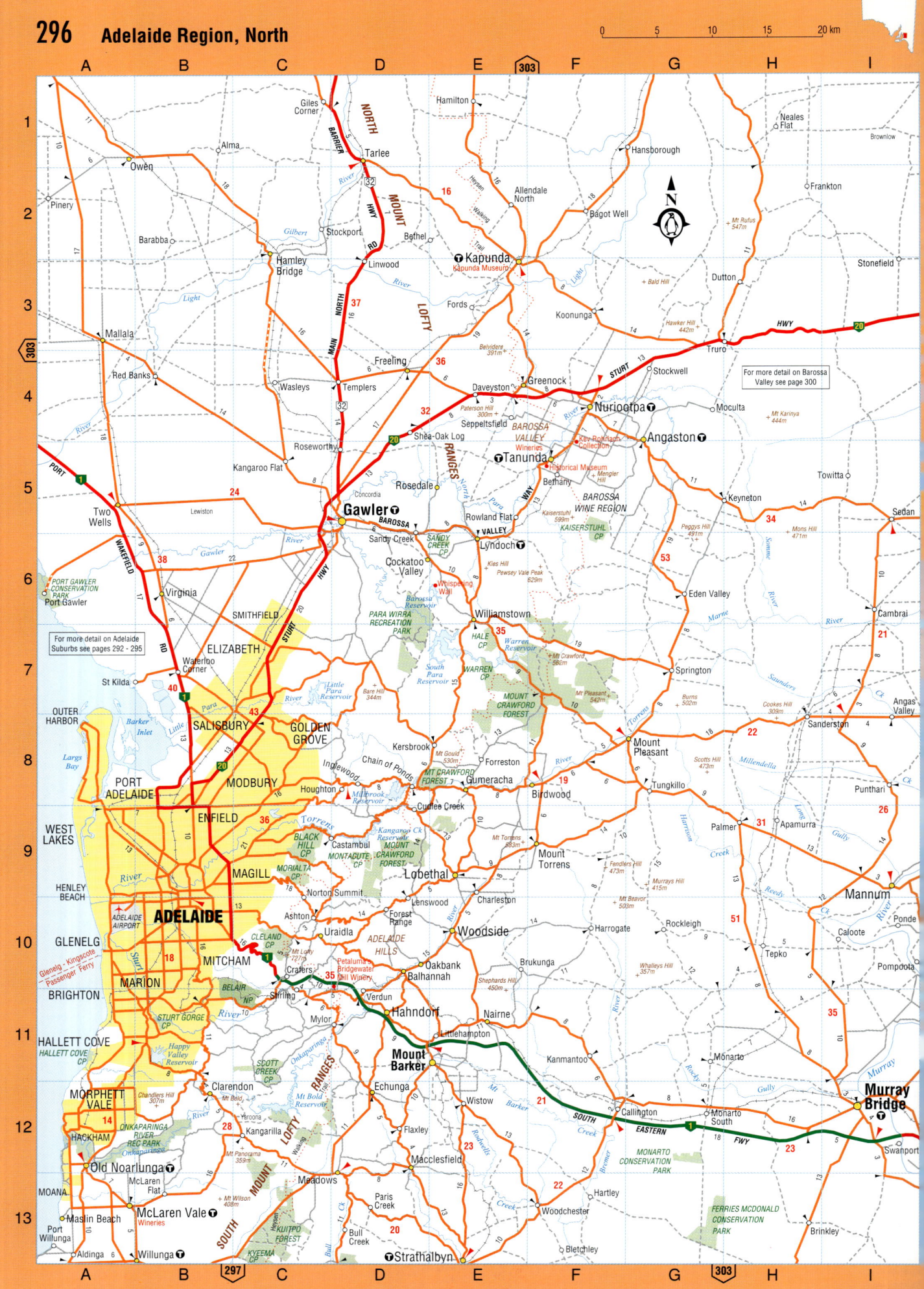

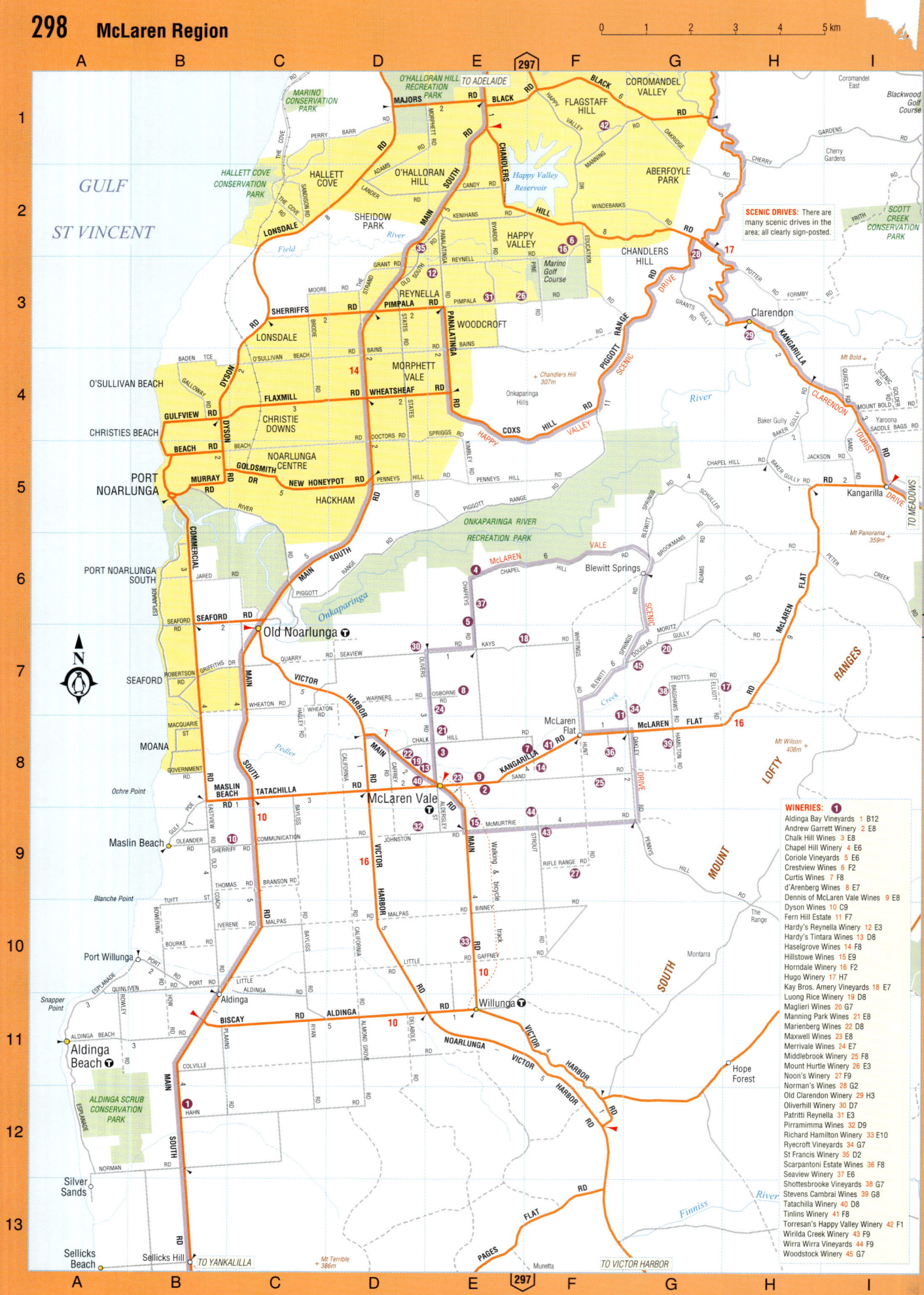

0 1 2 3 4 5 km

GULF
ST VINCENT

SCENIC DRIVES: There are
many scenic drives in the
area; all clearly sign-posted.

WINERIES: ❶

Aldinga Bay Vineyards 1 B12
Andrew Garrett Winery 2 E8
Chalk Hill Wines 3 E8
Chapel Hill Winery 4 E6
Coriole Vineyards 5 E6
Crestview Wines 6 F2
Curtis Wines 7 F8
d'Arenberg Wines 8 E7
Dennis of McLaren Vale Wines 9 E8
Dyson Wines 10 C9
Fern Hill Estate 11 F7
Hardy's Reynella Winery 12 E3
Hardy's Tintara Wines 13 D8
Haselgrove Wines 14 F8
Hillstowe Wines 15 E9
Horndale Winery 16 F2
Hugo Winery 17 H7
Kay Bros. Amery Vineyards 18 E7
Luong Rice Winery 19 D8
Maglieri Wines 20 G7
Manning Park Wines 21 E8
Marienberg Wines 22 D8
Maxwell Wines 23 E8
Merrivale Wines 24 E7
Middlebrook Winery 25 F8
Mount Hurtle Winery 26 E3
Noon's Winery 27 F9
Norman's Wines 28 G2
Old Clarendon Winery 29 H3
Oliverhill Winery 30 D7
Patritti Reynella 31 E3
Pirramimma Wines 32 D9
Richard Hamilton Winery 33 E10
Ryecroft Vineyards 34 G7
St Francis Winery 35 D2
Scarpantoni Estate Wines 36 F8
Seaview Winery 37 E6
Shottesbrooke Vineyards 38 G7
Stevens Cambrai Wines 39 G8
Tatachilla Winery 40 D8
Tinlins Winery 41 F8
Torresan's Happy Valley Winery 42 F1
Wirilda Creek Winery 43 F9
Wirra Wirra Vineyards 44 F9
Woodstock Winery 45 G7

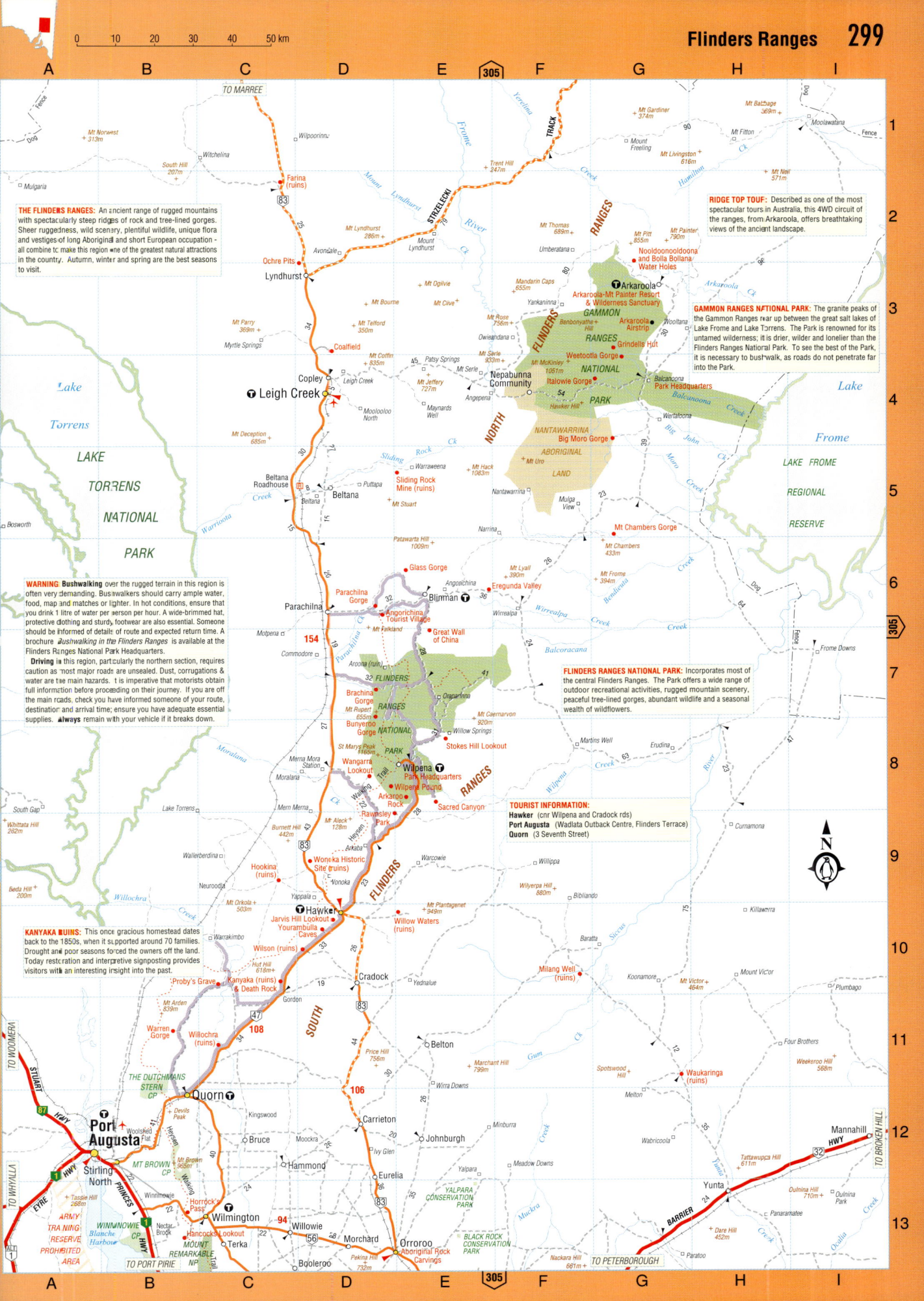

THE FLINDERS RANGES: An ancient range of rugged mountains with spectacularly steep ridges of rock and tree-lined gorges. Sheer ruggedness, wild scenery, plentiful wildlife, unique flora and vestiges of long Aboriginal and short European occupation - all combine to make this region one of the greatest natural attractions in the country. Autumn, winter and spring are the best seasons to visit.

RIDGE TOP TOUR: Described as one of the most spectacular tours in Australia, this 4WD circuit of the ranges, from Arkaroola, offers breathtaking views of the ancient landscape.

GAMMON RANGES NATIONAL PARK: The granite peaks of the Gammon Ranges rear up between the great salt lakes of Lake Frome and Lake Torrens. The Park is renowned for its untamed wilderness; it is drier, wilder and lonelier than the Flinders Ranges National Park. To see the best of the Park, it is necessary to bush-walk, as roads do not penetrate far into the Park.

WARNING: Bushwalking over the rugged terrain in this region is often very demanding. Bushwalkers should carry ample water, food, map and matches or lighter. In hot conditions, ensure that you drink 1 litre of water per person per hour. A wide-brimmed hat, protective clothing and sturdy footwear are also essential. Someone should be informed of details of route and expected return time. A brochure *Bushwalking in the Flinders Ranges* is available at the Flinders Ranges National Park Headquarters.

Driving in this region, particularly the northern section, requires caution as most major roads are unsealed. Dust, corrugations & water are the main hazards. It is imperative that motorists obtain full information before proceeding on their journey. If you are off the main roads, check you have informed someone of your route, destination and arrival time; ensure you have adequate essential supplies. **Always** remain with your vehicle if it breaks down.

FLINDERS RANGES NATIONAL PARK: Incorporates most of the central Flinders Ranges. The Park offers a wide range of outdoor recreational activities, rugged mountain scenery, peaceful tree-lined gorges, abundant wildlife and a seasonal wealth of wildflowers.

TOURIST INFORMATION:
Hawker (cnr Wilpena and Cradock rds)
Port Augusta (Wadlata Outback Centre, Flinders Terrace)
Quorn (3 Seventh Street)

KANYAKA RUINS: This once gracious homestead dates back to the 1850s, when it supported around 70 families. Drought and poor seasons forced the owners off the land. Today restoration and interpretive signposting provides visitors with an interesting insight into the past.

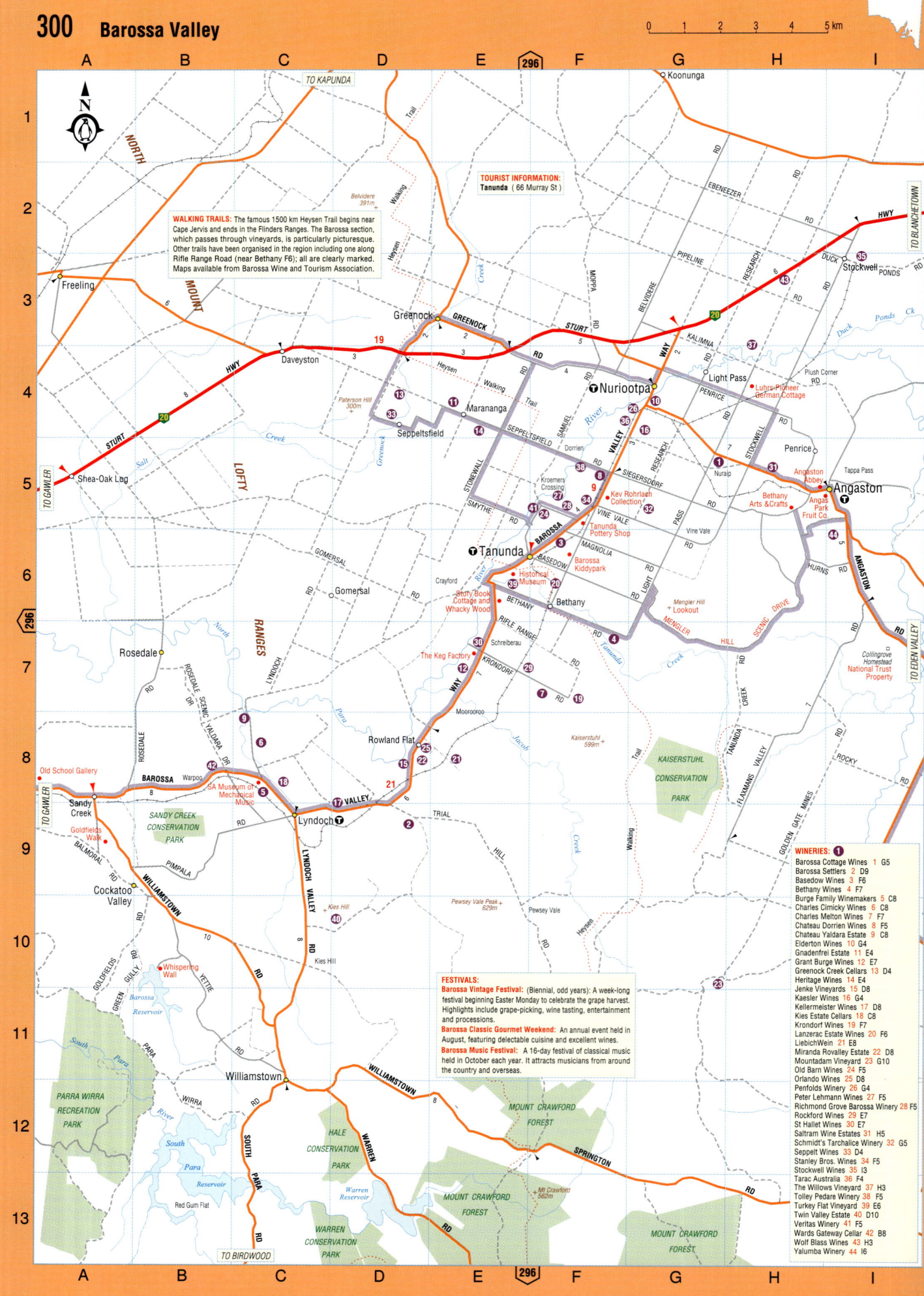

0 1 2 3 4 5 km

TOURIST INFORMATION:
Tanunda (66 Murray St)

WALKING TRAILS: The famous 1500 km Heysen Trail begins near Cape Jervis and ends in the Flinders Ranges. The Barossa section, which passes through vineyards, is particularly picturesque. Other trails have been organised in the region including one along Rifle Range Road (near Bethany F6); all are clearly marked. Maps available from Barossa Wine and Tourism Association.

FESTIVALS:
Barossa Vintage Festival: (Biennial, odd years): A week-long festival beginning Easter Monday to celebrate the grape harvest. Highlights include grape-picking, wine tasting, entertainment and processions.
Barossa Classic Gourmet Weekend: An annual event held in August, featuring delectable cuisine and excellent wines.
Barossa Music Festival: A 16-day festival of classical music held in October each year. It attracts musicians from around the country and overseas.

WINERIES: 1
Barossa Cottage Wines 1 G5
Barossa Settlers 2 D9
Basedow Wines 3 F6
Bethany Wines 4 F7
Burge Family Winemakers 5 C8
Charles Cimicky Wines 6 C8
Charles Melton Wines 7 F7
Chateau Dorrien Wines 8 F5
Chateau Yaldara Estate 9 C8
Elderton Wines 10 G4
Gnadenfrei Estate 11 E4
Grant Burge Wines 12 E7
Greenock Creek Cellars 13 D4
Heritage Wines 14 E4
Jenke Vineyards 15 D8
Kaesler Wines 16 G4
Kellermeister Wines 17 D8
Kies Estate Cellars 18 C8
Krondorf Wines 19 F7
Lanzerac Estate Wines 20 F6
LiebichWein 21 E8
Miranda Rovalley Estate 22 D8
Mountadam Vineyard 23 G10
Old Barn Wines 24 F5
Orlando Wines 25 D8
Penfolds Winery 26 G4
Peter Lehmann Wines 27 F5
Richmond Grove Barossa Winery 28 F5
Rockford Wines 29 E7
St Hallet Wines 30 E7
Saltram Wine Estates 31 H5
Schmidt's Tarchalice Winery 32 G5
Seppelt Wines 33 D4
Stanley Bros. Wines 34 F5
Stockwell Wines 35 I3
Tarac Australia 36 F4
The Willows Vineyard 37 H3
Tolley Pedare Winery 38 F5
Turkey Flat Vineyard 39 E6
Twin Valley Estate 40 D10
Veritas Winery 41 F5
Wards Gateway Cellar 42 B8
Wolf Blass Wines 43 H3
Yalumba Winery 44 I6

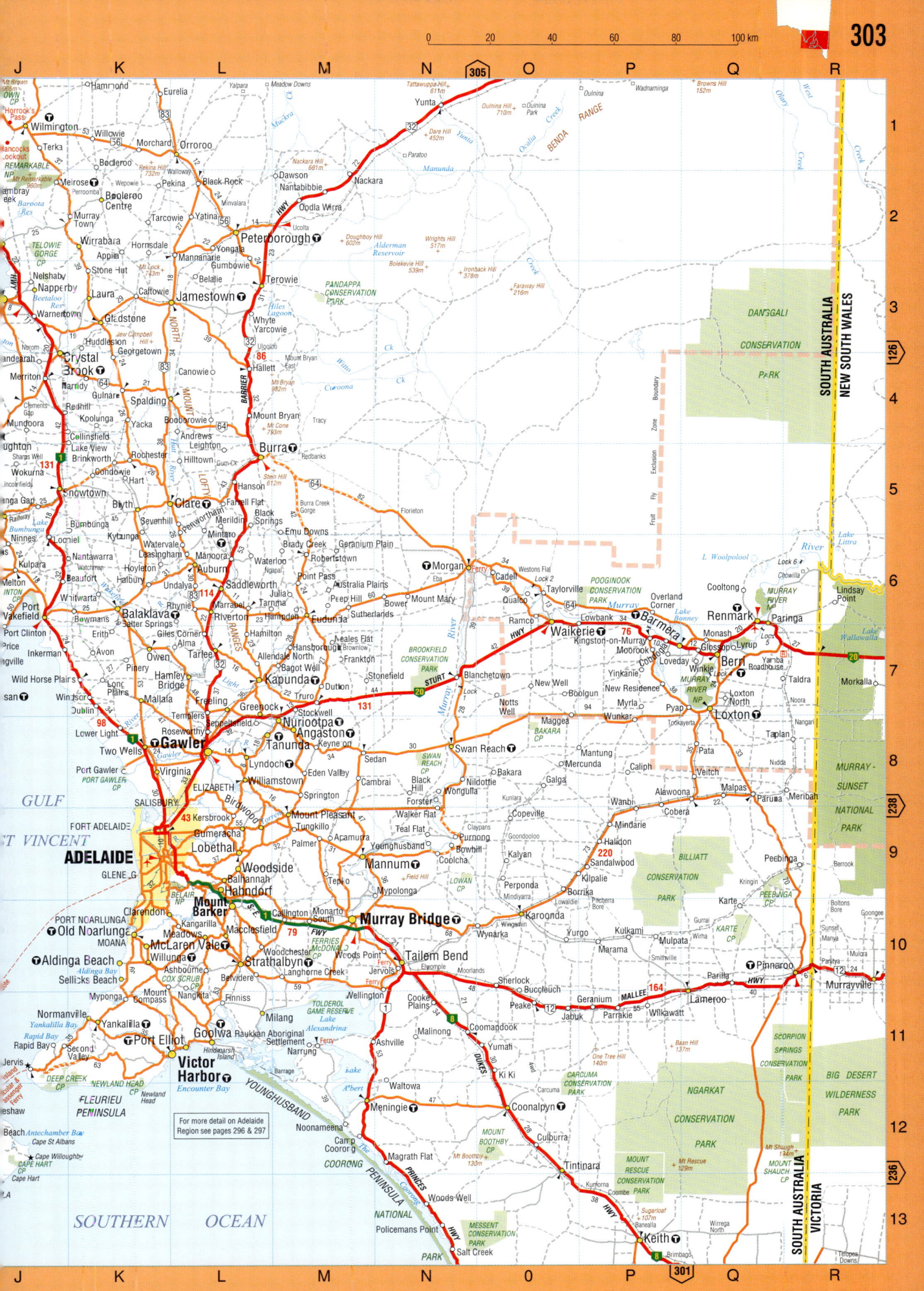

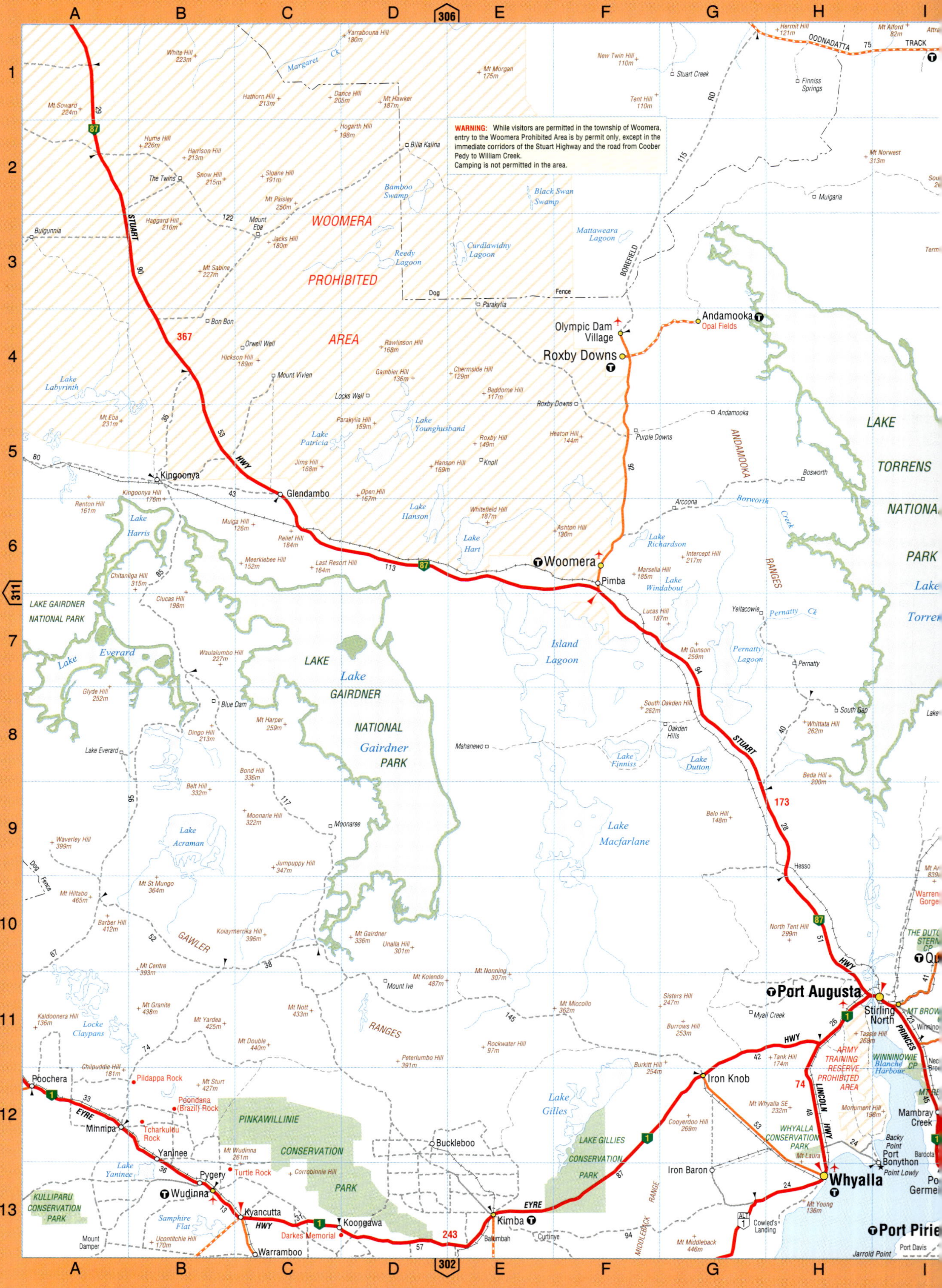

WARNING: While visitors are permitted in the township of Woomera, entry to the Woomera Prohibited Area is by permit only, except in the immediate corridors of the Stuart Highway and the road from Coober Pedy to William Creek. Camping is not permitted in the area.

WOOMERA PROHIBITED AREA

LAKE TORRENS NATIONAL PARK

LAKE GAIRDNER NATIONAL PARK

LAKE GAIRDNER NATIONAL PARK

GAWLER RANGES

PINKAWILLINIE CONSERVATION PARK

KULLIPARU CONSERVATION PARK

LAKE GILLIES CONSERVATION PARK

WHYALLA CONSERVATION PARK

ARMY TRAINING RESERVE PROHIBITED AREA

Places: Oodnadatta Track, Mt Alford 82m, Attra, Hermit Hill 121m, Stuart Creek, Finniss Springs, Mulgaria, Mt Norwest 313m, Soul, New Twin Hill 110m, Tent Hill 110m, Black Swan Swamp, Mattaweara Lagoon, Borefield, Andamooka, Opal Fields, Olympic Dam Village, Roxby Downs, Andamooka, Purple Downs, Bosworth, Bosworth, Arcoona, Lake Richardson, Intercept Hill 217m, Pernatty, Lake Macfarlane, Hesso, Port Augusta, Stirling North, Iron Knob, Iron Baron, Whyalla, Port Pirie, Port Germe, Minnipa, Yaninee, Pygery, Wudinna, Kyancutta, Koongawa, Warramboo, Kimba, Poochera, Mt Soward 224m, Mt Eba, Kingoonya, Glendambo, Woomera, Pimba

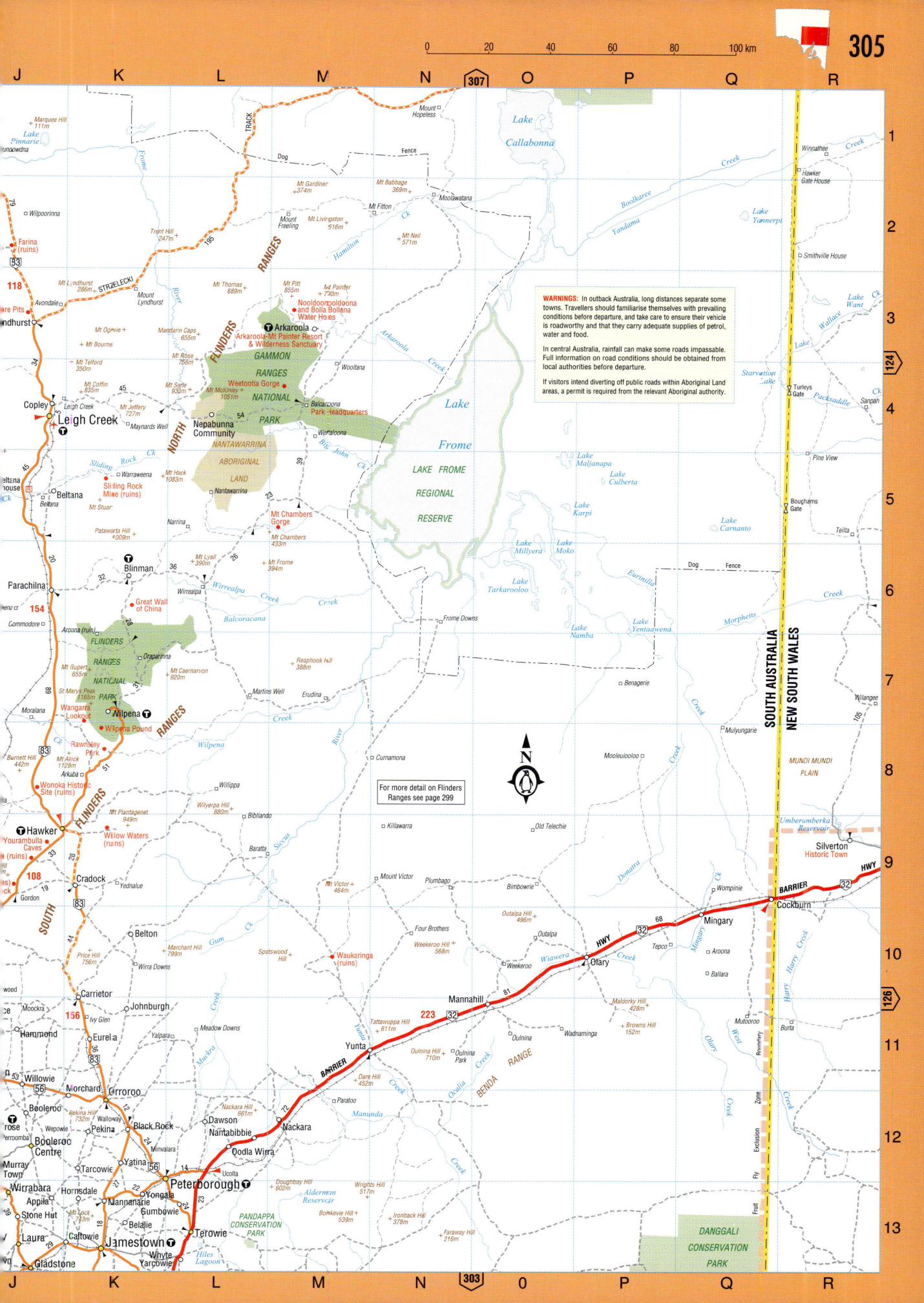

A B C D 423 E F G H I

NORTHERN TERRITORY

SOUTH AUSTRALIA

Poeppel C

+ Mt Wilyunpa
227m

Mount Dare

+ Mt Apperda
245m

+ Mt Allnerta
222m

Mirranponga
Pongunna
Lake

Larrys Hill
63m

+ Pilan
80m

SIMPSON DESERT

1

+ Mt Weeahlekiminne
292m

WITJIRA

SIMPSON DESERT

CONSERVATION

PARK

Blood Creek
Bore

+ Mt Hammersley
229m

SIMPSON DESERT

Poolowanna
Lake

Beale Hill
53m

2

+ Mt Crispe
279m

Dalhousie
Springs

NATIONAL

REGIONAL

Perra Perra
Poolanna Lake

+ Mt Emery
289m

Dalhousie (ruins)

+ Mt Dillon
234m

RESERVE

SIMPSON DESERT

Ephemeral
Lakes

3

PARK

WARNING: Visitors planning to enter Desert Parks are required to contact
the National Parks and Wildlife Service. A Desert Pass is necessary.

Lake
Griselda

Umarc
Lake

Hamilton

+ Mt Yangalee
244m

SIMPSON

REGIONAL

4

Mount Sarah

DESERT

Willawilaninna
Lake

+ Mt Sarah
260m

Creek

RESERVE

+ Mt Alexander
285m

Macumba

5

Macumba

River

Pialpotingoona
Lake

Pantoowarinna
Lake

War

Lake
Noolyeana

Peeramudlayeppa
Lake

6

+ Mt Carulina
211m

Oodnadatta

+ Mt Areebinna
245m

Millyeewilpa
Lake

Pompapillinna
Lake

309

+ Hanns Hill
238m

+ Stewart Hill
180m

Warburton

7

Mt Dutton +
176m

OODNADATTA

Koolkootinnie
Lake

Ka

Arckaringa

Peake

Creek

+ Mt Kingston North
209m

Neales

8

Creek

Creek

+ Mt Denison
238m

Creek

River

LAKE EYRE

Mount Barry

Peake

Lambing

Umbum

Lake

NATIONAL

195

+ Ricketts Hill

Eyre

Lake

9

Aimee

Lake
Conway

Hawker

Creek

Creek

North

PARK

+ Mt Margaret
412m

Four Hills
105m

LAKE EYRE

TRACK
203

Nilpinna

Davenport

Creek

NATIONAL

10

WARNING: While visitors are permitted in the township of Woomera,
entry to the Woomera Prohibited Area is by permit only, except in the
immediate corridors of the Stuart Highway and the road from Coober
Pedy to William Creek.
Camping is not permitted in the area.

+ Mt Anna
265m

Douglas

PARK

ELLIOT PRICE
CONSERVATION
PARK

405

Ruby Hill
+ 111m

11

Lake
Cadibarrawirracanna

166

Anna Creek

William Creek

OODNADATTA

Lake
Frances

Creek

Creek

WOOMERA

Creek

Warriner

Lake
Ellen

12

STUART

Dog

Engenina

PROHIBITED

Beresford Hill
71m

127

LAKE EYRE

Lake Eyre
South

Fence

600

Francos

Balta

Campeera Hill
158m

AREA

Bidna Beudna Hill
162m

Coward
Springs

Creek

NATIONAL

PARK

Welcome

87

+ Mt Pearhyn
216m

+ Mt Woods
170m

+ Mt Sandy
223m

Brumby

Margaret

+ Mt Purvis
201m

+ Mt Riddoch
182m

Fence

New Peter Hill
163m

Hamilton Hill
40m

Blanche Cup
Mound Springs

Curdimurka
(ruins)

Hermit Hill
121m

+ Mt Alton
82m

13

HWY

+ Yarrabouna Hill
180m

Creek

TRACK

75

A B C 304 D E F G H I

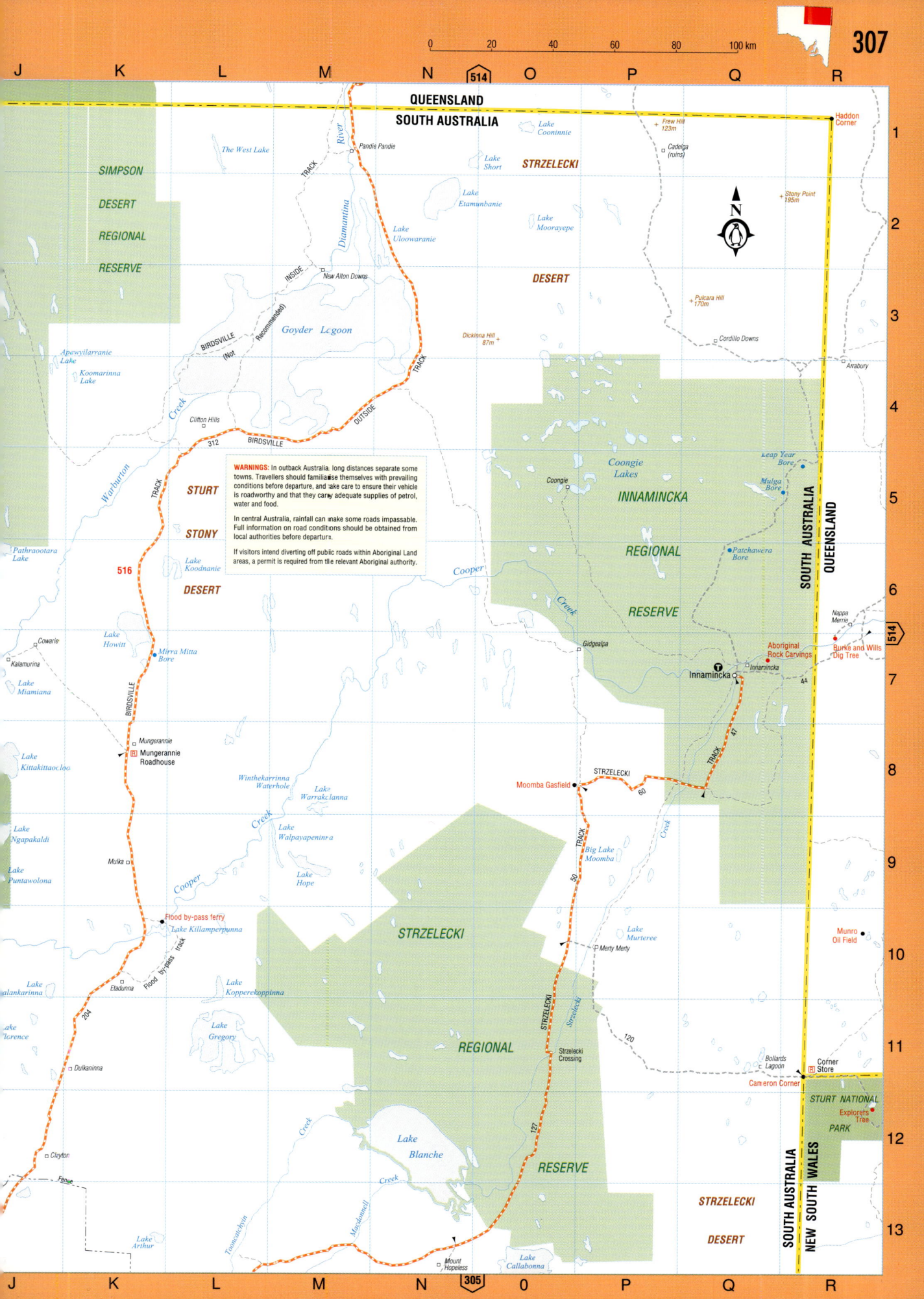

J K L M N 514 O P Q R

0 20 40 60 80 100 km

QUEENSLAND
SOUTH AUSTRALIA

SIMPSON

DESERT

REGIONAL

RESERVE

The West Lake

Pandie Pandie

River

Diamantina

TRACK

INSIDE

New Alton Downs

Recommended

BIRDSVILLE

(Not

Goyder Lagoon

OUTSIDE

BIRDSVILLE

TRACK

Lake Coominnie

Lake Short

STRZELECKI

Lake Etamunbanie

Lake Uloowaranie

Lake Moorayepe

DESERT

Frew Hill 123m

Cadelga (ruins)

Stony Point 195m

Pulcara Hill 170m

Dickinna Hill 87m

Cordillo Downs

Arrabury

Haddon Corner

N

Apewyilarranie Lake

Koomarinna Lake

Creek

Warburton

Clifton Hills

312

TRACK

STURT

STONY

Lake Koodnanie

516

DESERT

Pathraootara Lake

Cowarie

Kalamurina

Lake Miamiana

Lake Howitt

Mirra Mitta Bore

BIRDSVILLE

Coongie

Coongie Lakes

INNAMINCKA

REGIONAL

RESERVE

Cooper

Creek

Gidgealpa

Leap Year Bore

Mulga Bore

Patchawera Bore

Nappa Merrie

Aboriginal Rock Carvings

Burke and Wills Dig Tree

Innamincka

SOUTH AUSTRALIA

QUEENSLAND

514

WARNINGS: In outback Australia, long distances separate some towns. Travellers should familiarise themselves with prevailing conditions before departure, and take care to ensure their vehicle is roadworthy and that they carry adequate supplies of petrol, water and food.

In central Australia, rainfall can make some roads impassable. Full information on road conditions should be obtained from local authorities before departure.

If visitors intend diverting off public roads within Aboriginal Land areas, a permit is required from the relevant Aboriginal authority.

Lake Kittakittaooloo

Mungerannie

Mungerannie Roadhouse

Winthekarrinna Waterhole

Lake Warrakclanna

STRZELECKI

TRACK

47

44

TRACK

Moomba Gasfield

60

STRZELECKI

Big Lake Moomba

Lake Ngapakaldi

Lake Puntawolona

Mulka

Cooper

Creek

Lake Walpayapeninra

Lake Hope

50

Lake Murteree

Merty Merty

Munro Oil Field

Flood by-pass ferry

Lake Killamperpunna

Flood by-pass track

Etadunna

204

Lake Kopperekoppinna

Lake Gregory

STRZELECKI

REGIONAL

STRZELECKI

Strzelecki

120

Bollards Lagoon

Corner Store

Dulkaninna

Strzelecki Crossing

127

Cameron Corner

STURT NATIONAL

Explorers Tree

PARK

Lake Arthur

Clayton

Fanue

Creek

Toonodook

Macdonnell

Lake Blanche

Creek

RESERVE

Lake Callabonna

Mount Hopeless

STRZELECKI

DESERT

SOUTH AUSTRALIA

NEW SOUTH WALES

J K L M N 305 O P Q R

1 2 3 4 5 6 7 8 9 10 11 12 13

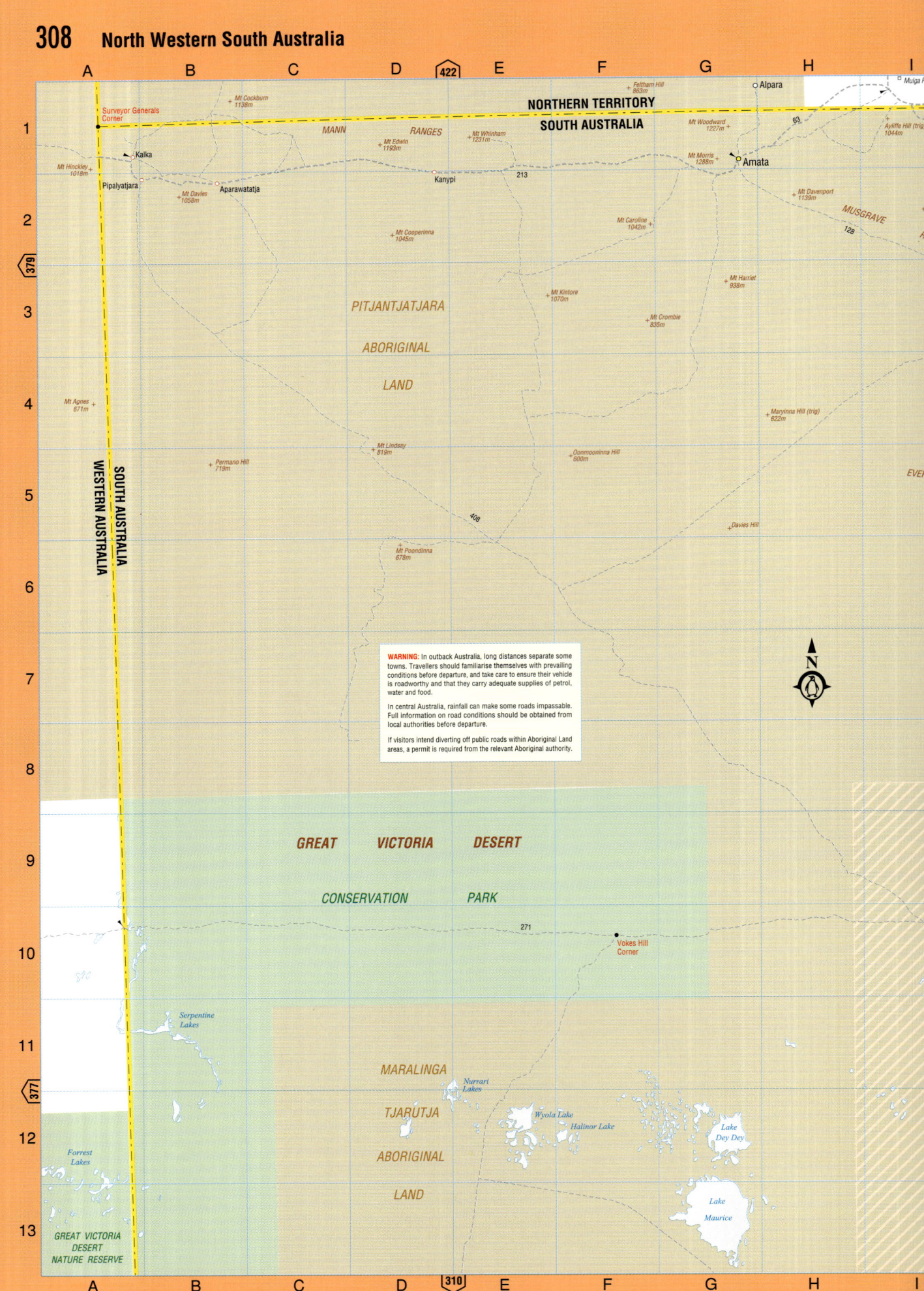

A B C D E F G H I

422

NORTHERN TERRITORY
SOUTH AUSTRALIA

Surveyor Generals Corner

MANN RANGES

+ Mt Cockburn 1138m

+ Mt Edwin 1193m

+ Mt Whinham 1231m

+ Feltham Hill 863m

○ Alpara

+ Mt Woodward 1227m

63

+ Ayliffe Hill (trig) 1044m

□ Mulga P

Mt Hinckley 1018m

● Kalka

Pipalyatjara

+ Mt Davies 1058m

● Aparawatatja

Kanypi

213

Mt Morris 1288m

◗ Amata ○

+ Mt Davenport 1139m

MUSGRAVE

+ Mt Cooperinna 1045m

Mt Caroline 1042m

128

PITJANTJATJARA

+ Mt Kintore 1070m

+ Mt Harriet 938m

ABORIGINAL

+ Mt Crombie 835m

LAND

Mt Agnes 671m +

+ Maryinna Hill (trig) 822m

+ Mt Lindsay 819m

+ Oonmooninna Hill 600m

EVER

Permano Hill 719m +

408

+ Davies Hill

+ Mt Poondinna 678m

WARNING: In outback Australia, long distances separate some towns. Travellers should familiarise themselves with prevailing conditions before departure, and take care to ensure their vehicle is roadworthy and that they carry adequate supplies of petrol, water and food.

In central Australia, rainfall can make some roads impassable. Full information on road conditions should be obtained from local authorities before departure.

If visitors intend diverting off public roads within Aboriginal Land areas, a permit is required from the relevant Aboriginal authority.

N

GREAT VICTORIA DESERT

CONSERVATION PARK

271

● Vokes Hill Corner

Serpentine Lakes

MARALINGA

Nurrari Lakes

TJARUTJA

Wyola Lake

Halinor Lake

Lake Dey Dey

Forrest Lakes

ABORIGINAL

LAND

Lake Maurice

GREAT VICTORIA DESERT NATURE RESERVE

SOUTH AUSTRALIA
WESTERN AUSTRALIA

379

377

310

A B C D E F G H I

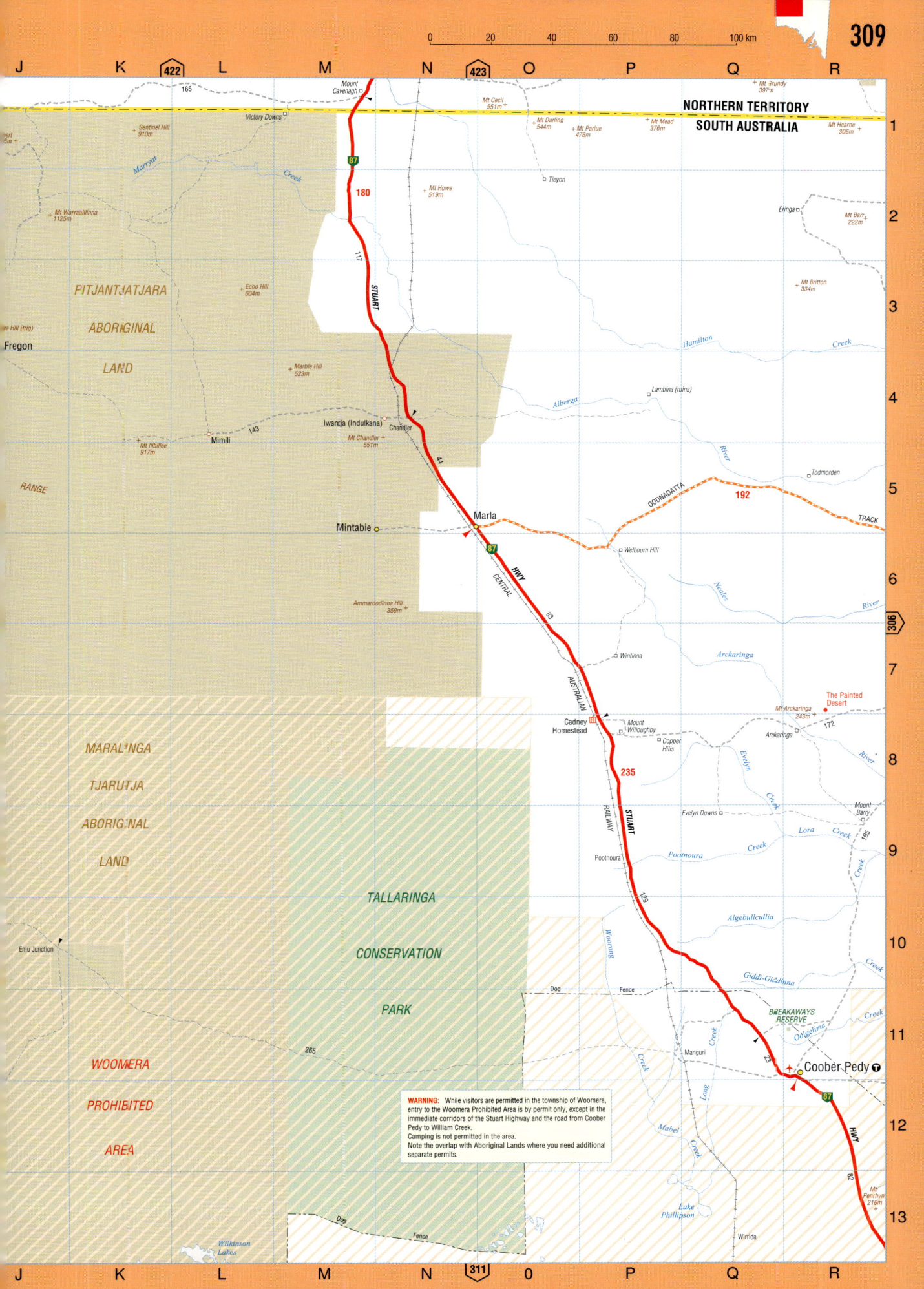

NORTHERN TERRITORY

SOUTH AUSTRALIA

J K L M N O P Q R

0 20 40 60 80 100 km

Mount
Cavenagh

Victory Downs

165

87

180

117

+ Mt Warrawillinna
1125m

Sentinel Hill
910m

PITJANTJATJARA

ABORIGINAL

LAND

Fregon

Maryat

Creek

STUART

Mt Cecil
551m

Tieyon

+ Mt Darling
544m

+ Mt Parlue
478m

+ Mt Mead
376m

+ Mt Grundy
397m

Eringa

+ Mt Barr
222m

+ Mt Hearne
306m

Mt Howe
519m

Echo Hill
604m

Marble Hill
523m

Hamilton

Creek

Alberga

River

Lambina (ruins)

Todmorden

RANGE

+ Mt Ilbillee
917m

Mimili

143

Iwantja (Indulkana)

Mt Chandler
551m

Chandler

44

Marla

Mintabie

OODNADATTA

192

TRACK

87

HWY

CENTRAL

83

Welbourn Hill

Neales

River

Ammaroodinna Hill
359m

306

AUSTRALIAN

Wintinna

Arckaringa

The Painted
Desert

Mt Arckaringa
243m

172

MARALINGA

TJARUTJA

ABORIGINAL

LAND

Emu Junction

Cadney
Homestead

235

Mount
Willoughby

Copper
Hills

Arckaringa

RAILWAY

STUART

Evelyn Downs

Evelyn

Creek

Lora

Creek

Mount
Barry

198

TALLARINGA

CONSERVATION

PARK

265

Pootnoura

129

Pootnoura

Creek

Algebullcullia

Giddi-Giddinna

Creek

WOOMERA

PROHIBITED

AREA

Dog

Fence

Woorong

Creek

BREAKAWAYS
RESERVE

Manguri

23

Oolgelima

Creek

Coober Pedy

Long

Creek

87

HWY

Mabel

Creek

83

Mt Penrhyn
216m

Lake
Phillipson

Wilkinson
Lakes

Dog

Fence

Wirrida

WARNING: While visitors are permitted in the township of Woomera,
entry to the Woomera Prohibited Area is by permit only, except in the
immediate corridors of the Stuart Highway and the road from Coober
Pedy to William Creek.
Camping is not permitted in the area.
Note the overlap with Aboriginal Lands where you need additional
separate permits.

422

423

306

311

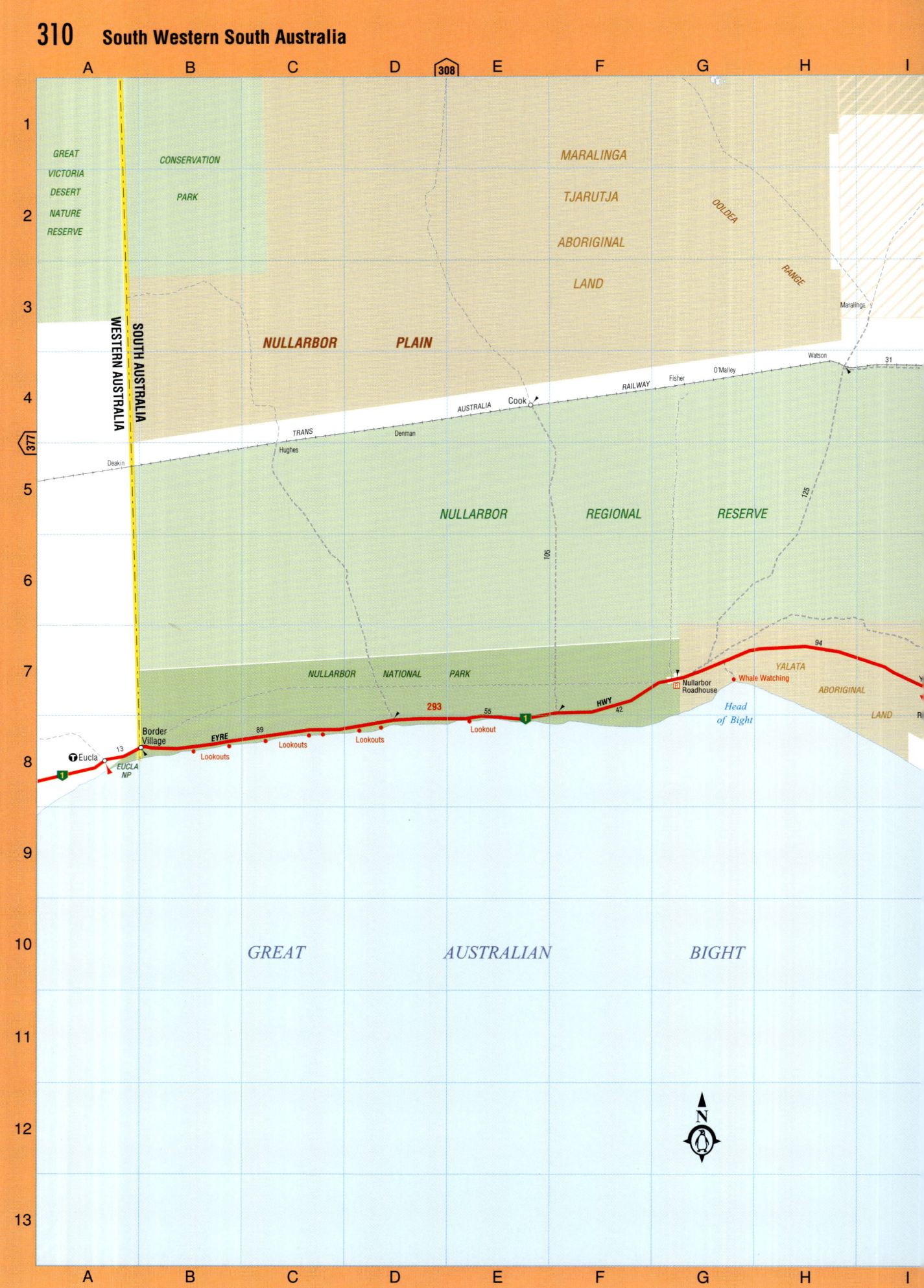

GREAT
VICTORIA
DESERT
NATURE
RESERVE

CONSERVATION

PARK

MARALINGA

TJARUTJA

ABORIGINAL

LAND

OOLDEA

RANGE

WESTERN AUSTRALIA

SOUTH AUSTRALIA

NULLARBOR   PLAIN

Maralinga

308

377

Watson

31

RAILWAY   Fisher   O'Malley

AUSTRALIA   Cook

TRANS   Denman

Deakin   Hughes

125

NULLARBOR   REGIONAL   RESERVE

105

NULLARBOR   NATIONAL   PARK

94

YALATA

ABORIGINAL

LAND

Nullarbor
Roadhouse

Whale Watching

Head
of Bight

293

55

HWY   42

Lookout

EYRE   89

Lookouts   Lookouts

Lookouts

Border
Village

13

Eucla

EUCLA
NP

1

GREAT   AUSTRALIAN   BIGHT

N

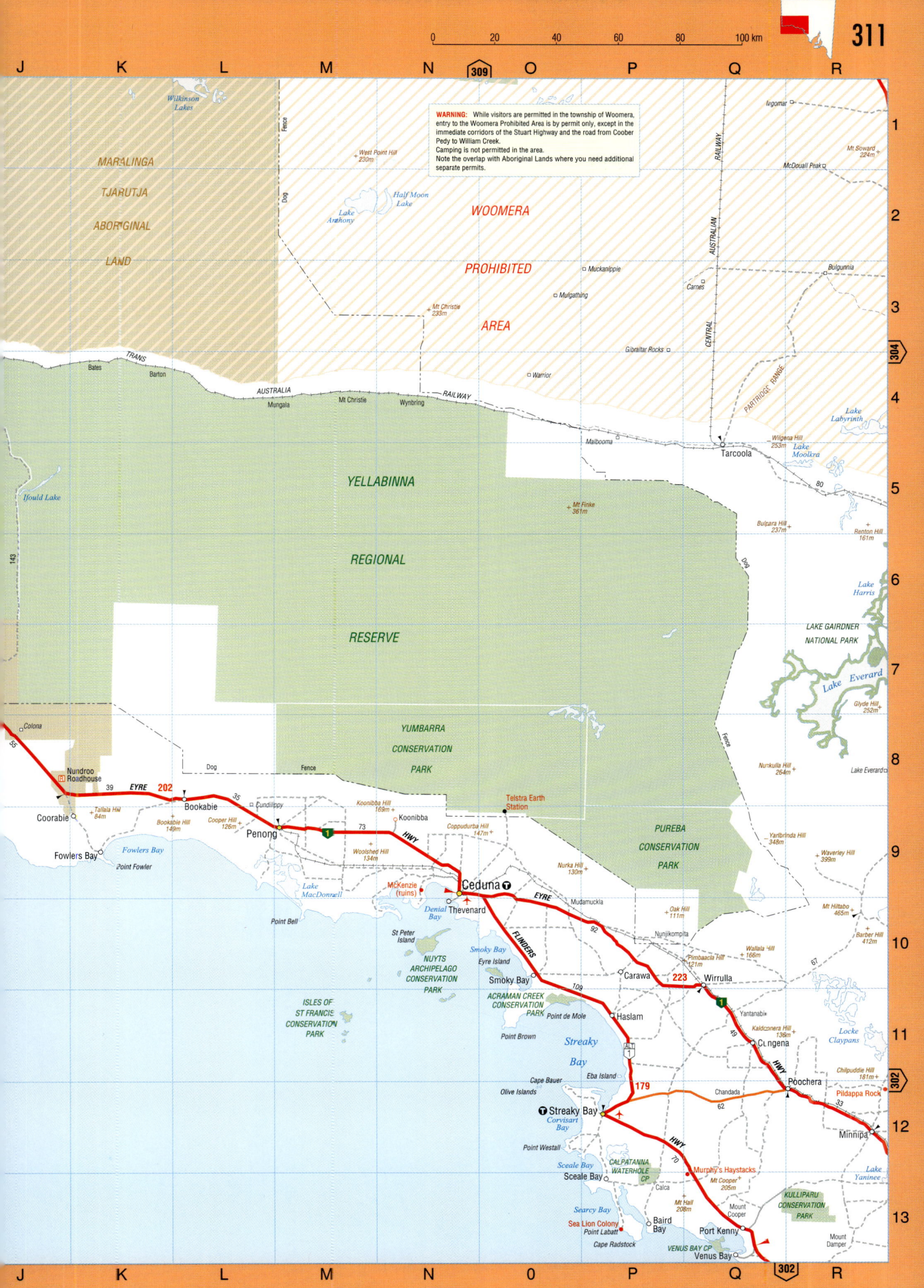

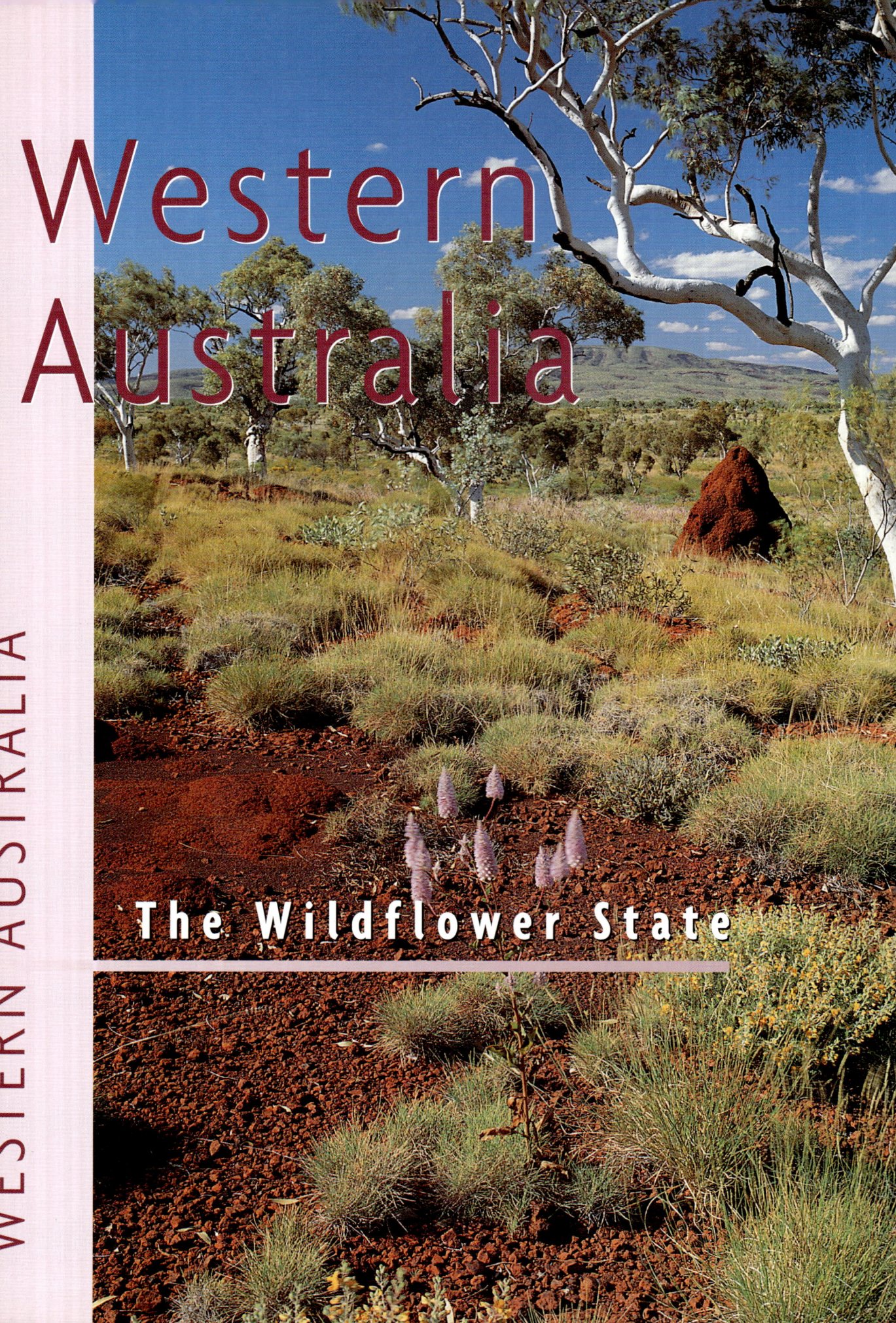

Western Australia

Australia

The Wildflower State

Western Australia, the largest of the Australian States and Territories, covering roughly one-third of the Australian continent, has less than one-tenth of the nation's population. For the traveller, the contrast in scenery is just as great.

Even a casual glance at a map of Australia will quickly reveal that a motor-touring holiday in Western Australia requires a great deal of thought and advance planning. For one thing, just getting there from the eastern States involves travelling huge distances, so fly/drive or MotoRail facilities are well worth investigation; and, given that it is almost one-third the size of the whole of Australia, unless you have unlimited time and energy, touring by road will only get you to certain sections. The south-west region is relatively easily and pleasantly covered by car, but to travel the unique north and north-east requires more time and careful planning. Once you have settled your method of travel, you will find an amazing State waiting to be explored.

Despite the fact that the Dutch had mapped the western coastline of Australia as early as the sixteenth century, it was not until 1826 that a British party from Sydney landed at King George Sound (Albany) and then only for fear of possible French colonisation. Three years later Perth, the first non-convict settlement in the country, was founded by Captain James Stirling. Due mainly to the ruggedness and sheer size of the land, the West remained pretty much as it had always been until 1892, when gold was discovered at Coolgardie and the first economic boom for the region began. Today it is an immensely rich mineral State, its thriving economy still growing.

The beautiful city of Perth has the best climate of any Australian capital with a midwinter average maximum temperature of 18°C, a year-round average maximum of 21°C and an average of almost eight hours of sunshine a day. The climate in the north of the State is tropical, and as you travel south the climate becomes sub-tropical and then temperate.

It is easy to assume from a map that Perth is a coastal city; in fact, it is 19 kilometres inland, up the broad and beautiful Swan River, home of the black swan. A city of over one million people, Perth is large enough to offer excitement and variety, yet compact enough to be seen quite easily. King's Park, 404 hectares of natural bushland, is only a short drive from the city centre, and nearby ocean beaches offer the visitor year-round swimming and surfing.

Nearby Rottnest Island is small and sandy and only 20 kilometres off the coast of Fremantle. Regular air and ferry services from Perth will take you to this popular holiday island, where even the surrounding sea has been declared a sanctuary. Reefs and shipwrecks attract skin-divers to this area.

The southern corner of this State is aptly described as the garden of Western Australia. Hardwood forests of massive karri and jarrah trees soar

NOT TO BE MISSED

in Western Australia

Map Ref.

- **Broome** – once the world's leading pearling centre, now a beautiful holiday destination and gateway to the spectacular West Kimberleys — 380 G9
- **Dales Gorge** – breathtaking gorge in Karijini National Park — 378 C4
- **Hotham Valley Tourist Railway** – for sightseeing combined with the romance and nostalgia of train travel — 366 C11
- **John Forrest National Park** – stunning wildflower displays in spring — 366 D4
- **Kalgoorlie** – for its flamboyant architecture from the gold-boom days — 376 I6
- **Margaret River** – for magnificent coastal and river scenery, caves and craft outlets – and excellent wine — 369 C7
- **Nambung National Park** – a moonscape of coloured quartz studded with limestone pillars, some 4 metres high — 376 B6
- **Shark Bay** – where wild dolphins swim into the shallows at Monkey Mia — 375 B10
- **Valley of the Giants** – a beautiful drive; allow time to take the Tree Top Walk through the giant stands of karri and tingle trees — 370 H12
- **Wildflowers** – a brilliant display across the State each spring

Ghost gums in the spectacular Karijini National Park

WESTERN AUSTRALIA

The scenic Great Ocean Drive, near Esperance

above the hundreds of different species of wildflowers that bloom from September to November. Great surfing beaches and coastal panoramic views add to the attractions of the south-west region, with such popular locations as Margaret River, Busselton, Yallingup and Albany. Further east is Esperance renowned

for its stunning beaches as is nearby Cape Le Grand National Park which also features wildflowers in season and scenic walks. The Margaret River region is a must, whether or not you are interested in wine. The region is fertile and beautiful, and the vineyards flourish on the rich loam that is perfect for grape-growing. At the end of

a day's drive you can sample some notable results of these conditions.

North-east of this well-vegetated corner, and 596 kilometres from Perth, is the one-time gold-boom area around Kalgoorlie-Boulder, surrounded by small historic mining towns such as Coolgardie and Broad Arrow. South of Kalgoorlie-Boulder the modern town of Kambalda owes its prosperity to nickel. Further east you reach the Nullarbor Plain; further north are the Great Victoria and Gibson deserts.

Along the Brand Highway, 424 kilometres north of Perth, is Geraldton, situated on the coast where you can sample freshly caught crays. Between August and October, the roadsides between Perth and Geraldton are ablaze with wildflowers. Further north you can see a splendid range of flora and fauna in Kalbarri National Park and explore the spectacular coastal gorges and cliffs. Magnificent beaches, excellent fishing and coral reefs are the main attractions along the coast north of Geraldton. At Monkey Mia on Shark Bay, wild dolphins come close to the shore to be fed. Carnarvon, renowned

CALENDAR OF EVENTS

Note: The information given here was accurate at the time of printing. However, as the timing of events held annually is subject to change and some events may extend into the following month, it is best to check with the local tourism authority or event organisers to confirm the details. The calendar is not exhaustive. Most towns and regions hold sporting competitions, regattas and rodeos, art, craft and trade exhibitions, agricultural and flower shows, music festivals and other events annually. Details of these events are available from local tourism outlets.

JANUARY
Public holidays: New Year's Day; Australia Day. **Perth:** Hopman Cup (tennis, contd); Perth Cup (horseracing); Vines Golf Classic. **Busselton:** Performing Arts Beach Festival; Australia Day Yacht Regatta; Kidz Film Festival. **Denmark:** Pantomime. **Esperance:** Sailboard Classic; Turf Racing (contd). **Fremantle:** Sardine Festival. **Geraldton:** Windsurfing Classic. **Harvey:** Australia Day Breakfast. **Hopetoun:** Summer Festival. **Mandurah:** Festival. **Mount Barker:** Wine Festival. **Narrogin:** State Gliding Championships.

FEBRUARY
Perth: Chinese New Year Festival; Festival of Perth.

Boyup Brook: Country Music Awards. **Dwellingup:** Log Chop Day. **Esperance:** Offshore Angling Classic. **Katanning:** Triathlon. **Margaret River:** Leeuwin Estate Concert; Wine and Food Festival.

MARCH
Public holiday: Labour Day. **Perth:** Festival of Perth (contd). **Augusta:** Dragon Boat Racing. **Brookton:** Old Time Motor Show (biennial, even-numbered years). **Bunbury:** Aqua Spectacular; Show. **Busselton:** Blue-water Classic; National Old Machinery Rally. **Dwellingup:** Log Chop Day. **Kalbarri:** Sport Fishing Classic. **Mount Barker:** Machinery Field Day. **Nannup:** Music Festival. **Pemberton:** King

Karri Karnival. **Wagin:** Woolorama.

EASTER
Public holidays: Good Friday; Easter Monday. **Albany:** Great Southern Wine Festival. **Dongara:** Horse Races. **Donnybrook:** Apple Festival. **Lancelin:** Beach Buggy Championships.

APRIL
Public holiday: Anzac Day. **Perth:** National Trust Heritage Week. **Albany:** Festival of Albany. **Beverley:** Art Exhibition. **Broome:** Rotary Dragon Boat Classic. **Busselton:** Heritage Week. **Exmouth:** Billfish Bonanza. **Kununurra:** Dam to Dam Regatta. **Mundaring:** Mundaring Hills Festival.

MAY
Boyup Brook: Autumn Art

Affair. **Carnarvon:** Fremantle–Carnarvon Yacht Race (biennial, even-numbered years). **Eucla:** Golf Day. **Fremantle:** Fremantle–Carnarvon Yacht Race (even-numbered years); Rhythm and Blues Festival. **Gingin:** British Car Day. **Kununurra:** Ord River Festival. **Narrogin:** Music Eisteddfod. **Toodyay:** Moondyne Festival.

JUNE
Public holiday: Foundation Day. **Perth:** Western Australia Week. **Carnarvon:** Seafood Festival (biennial, even-numbered years). **Cossack:** Fair and Yachting Regatta. **Geraldton:** Batavia Celebrations; Foodfest. **Kambalda:** Sky Diving Gathering. **Karratha:**

Pilbara Pursuit Jetboat Classic. **Kununurra:** Ord River Festival (contd). **Manjimup:** 15 000 Motocross. **Wagin:** Foundation Day.

JULY
Perth: Perth Marathon. **Carnarvon:** Festival. **Cossack:** Cossack–Wickham Fun Run. **Derby:** Boab Festival; Country Music Festival. **Exmouth:** Exmo Week; Arts and Crafts Show. **Fitzroy Crossing:** Rodeo. **Halls Creek:** Agricultural Show. **Kununurra:** Ord River Festival (contd). **Marble Bar:** Cup Race Weekend. **Onslow:** Arts and Crafts Festival. **Wickham:** Cossack–Wickham Fun Run.

AUGUST
Perth: City to Surf Fun

for its succulent prawns, is an industrial fishing port at the mouth of the Gascoyne River. Ningaloo Marine Park protects the 260-kilometre coral reef near Coral Bay. Nearby, the town of Exmouth is world famous for its year-round fishing, particularly game-fishing, and its beaches.

The Pilbara region has some of the country's most spectacular gorges in Karijini (Hamersley Range) National Park. This is where Western Australia's second economic boom began, with the exploitation of the dramatic Hamersley Range, which is literally a mountain of iron. The Range stretches for 320 kilometres, yet from the air seems dwarfed by endless stretches of red sand.

At the State's very top is the Kimberley region, with the spectacular King Leopold Range in the west and Purnululu (Bungle Bungle) National Park in the east. The region's economy is based on diamond mining, as well as the more traditional cattle industry. A visit to this remote, dramatic region with its gorges and rivers is a unique experience – in keeping with many areas of Australia's largest State.

CLIMATE GUIDE

PERTH

	J	F	M	A	M	J	J	A	S	O	N	D
Maximum °C	30	31	29	25	21	19	18	18	20	22	25	27
Minimum °C	18	19	17	14	12	10	9	9	10	12	14	17
Rainfall mm	8	12	19	45	123	184	173	136	80	54	21	14
Raindays	3	3	4	8	14	17	18	17	14	11	6	4

ALBANY REGION

	J	F	M	A	M	J	J	A	S	O	N	D
Maximum °C	25	25	24	22	19	17	16	16	17	19	21	24
Minimum °C	14	14	13	12	10	8	8	7	8	9	11	12
Rainfall mm	27	24	28	63	102	103	124	106	82	78	48	25
Raindays	8	9	11	14	18	19	21	21	18	15	13	10

KALGOORLIE VALLEY

	J	F	M	A	M	J	J	A	S	O	N	D
Maximum °C	34	32	30	25	20	18	17	18	22	26	29	32
Minimum °C	18	18	16	12	8	6	5	5	8	11	14	17
Rainfall mm	22	28	19	19	28	31	26	20	15	16	18	15
Raindays	3	4	4	5	7	8	9	7	5	4	4	3

DERBY REGION

	J	F	M	A	M	J	J	A	S	O	N	D
Maximum °C	36	35	35	35	33	31	30	32	35	36	37	37
Minimum °C	26	26	25	22	19	16	14	16	20	23	25	26
Rainfall mm	182	155	110	32	22	10	6	1	0	2	17	84
Raindays	12	10	8	2	1	1	1	0	0	0	2	6

Run. **Avon Valley National Park** (near Toodyay): Avon Descent. **Beverley:** Agricultural Show. **Broome:** Shinju Matsuri; Opera Under the Stars. **Carnarvon:** Arts Festival. **Dampier:** Game-fishing Classic. **Dowerin:** Field Days. **Halls Creek:** Races. **Harvey:** Daffodil Day. **Karratha:** FeNaCLNG Festival. **Katanning:** Prophet Mohammad's Birthday. **Mullewa:** Wildflower Show. **Nannup:** Daffodil Weekend. **Newman:** Fortescue Festival. **Northam:** Avon River Festival. **Pingelly:** Art and Tulip Festival. **Port Hedland:** Spinifex Spree. **Roebourne:** Royal Show; Roebourne Cup and Ball. **Tom Price:** Nameless Festival. **Walyunga National Park** (near Mundaring): Avon

Descent. **Wyndham:** Top of the West Festival.

SEPTEMBER
Public holiday: Queen's Birthday. **Perth:** Football League Finals; Kings Park Wildflower Festival; Perth Royal Show; Rally Australia. **Augusta:** Spring Flower Show. **Beverley:** Duck Race. **Boyup Brook:** Country Music Weekend. **Brookton:** Wildflower Show (biennial, odd-numbered years). **Broome:** Shinju Matsuri (contd). **Carnamah:** Agricultural Show. **Coolgardie:** Camel Races; Coolgardie Day. **Corrigin:** Agricultural Show. **Cossack:** Art Awards; Art Ball. **Cranbrook:** Wildflower Show. **Kalgoorlie:** Kalgoorlie Cup; Spring Festival.

Kojonup Wildflower and Country Festival. **Kukerin:** Tracmach Vintage Fair. **Mingenew:** Lions Expo. **Mullewa:** Wildflower Show (contd); Agricultural Show. **Narrogin:** Orchid Show. **Perenjori:** Agricultural Show. **Ravensthorpe:** Wildflower Show; Wool Day. **Southern Cross:** Agricultural Show. **Toodyay:** Highland Games.

OCTOBER
Perth: Spring in the (Swan) Valley Festival; Kings Park Wildflower Festival (contd). **Augusta:** Spring Flower Show (contd). **Boyup Brook:** Blackwood River Marathon Relay to Bridgetown; Spring Garden Expo. **Bridgetown:** Blackwood

Classic; Blackwood River Marathon Relay. **Busselton:** West Coast Golf Open. **Esperance:** Agricultural Show. **Eucla:** Eucla Shoot. **Fremantle:** Blessing of the Fleet. **Geraldton:** Festival of Geraldton. **Harvey:** Agricultural Show. **Jilakan Rock** (near Kulin): Picnic Race Day. **Kukerin:** Tracmach Vintage Fair (contd). **Leonora:** Art Prize. **Merredin:** Vintage Car Festival (biennial, odd-numbered years). **Morawa:** Music Spectacular. **Narrogin:** Spring Festival; Texpo. **Northam:** Rodeo; Avon Valley Country Life and Leisure Festival. **Northcliffe:** Mountain Bike Championship. **Walpole:** Wildflower Week. **Yallingup:** October Festival.

York: Jazz Festival.

NOVEMBER
Albany: Perth–Albany Ocean Yacht Race. **Bridgetown:** Blues at Bridgetown. **Brookton:** Wildflower Show (biennial, odd-numbered years). **Broome:** Mango Festival. **Bunbury:** Bunbury Fest. **Cranbrook:** Art Show. **Dongara:** Blessing of the Fleet. **Dunsborough:** Down South Dive Classic. **Exmouth:** Gamex. **Fitzroy Crossing:** Barra Splash. **Fremantle:** Festival Fremantle. **Jurien:** Expo and Blessing of the Fleet. **Kalbarri:** Blessing of the Fleet. **Kalgoorlie:** Goldfields Mining Expo. **Northam:** Avon Valley Country Music Festival. **Rockingham:** Spring Festival. **Wickepin:** Art and Craft

Show (biennial, even-numbered years). **Wyndham:** Hang Gliding Competition. **York:** Rose Festival.

DECEMBER
Public holidays: Christmas Day; Boxing Day. **Perth:** Australian Derby; Christmas Pageant; Hopman Cup. **Cervantes:** Slalom Carnival. **Derby:** Boxing Day Sports. **Esperance:** Turf Racing. **Katanning:** Caboodle. **Kwinana:** Christmas Carnivale. **Lancelin:** Ledge Point Ocean Race. **Mount Barker:** Mardi Gras. **Rockingham:** Christmas Regatta; Cockburn Sound Yachting Regatta. **Yallingup:** Malibu Competition.

PERTH

A Friendly City

The beautiful Kings Park overlooks the city

WESTERN AUSTRALIA

With a Mediterranean-type climate and a river setting, Perth is made for an outdoor lifestyle. Within easy reach of the city lie clean surf beaches, rolling hills, tranquil forests and well-kept parklands. The Swan River winds through Perth and suburbs, widening to lake size at Perth and Melville Waters; and the Canning River provides another attractive waterway through the southern suburbs.

The city centre, 19 kilometres upstream from the port of Fremantle, is on the Swan River and surrounded by a series of gardens, parks and reserves, including the magnificent 404-hectare Kings Park. The green slopes of Mount Eliza in Kings Park contrast dramatically with Perth's skyline, and the serene blue hills of the Darling Range can be seen in the distance.

Perth was founded by Captain James Stirling in 1829, but the progress of the isolated Swan River Settlement, made up entirely of free settlers, was slow; it was not until the first shipment of convicts arrived in 1850 that the colony found its feet. The convicts were soon set to work building roads, bridges and fine public buildings, and in 1856 Perth was proclaimed a city. Gold discoveries in the State in the 1880s gave Perth another boost, and more recently, the huge diamond finds in the Kimberley and the reopening of goldmines in the Kalgoorlie-Boulder region have stimulated new growth.

The capital has a population of just over 1.2 million, many of whom live in the suburbs that stretch north and south. Perth is cosmopolitan, home to people born in Britain, New Zealand, Italy, the Netherlands, Malaysia, Vietnam, the Philippines, Greece and South Africa. In addition, of a total Aboriginal population of 42 000 in the State, almost 12 000 live in the capital.

The city centre is compact, and easy to explore. Travel by bus or train within the city's **Free Transit Zone** (FTZ), day or night, seven days a week. A free regular bus service, the **CATS** (Central Area Transit System) operates around central Perth; CATS bus shelters are a high-tech experience: you can check the electronic monitor to establish the estimated time of arrival of the next bus. Other services connect the city with East and West Perth, and Northbridge. A fun way to discover the city is on the **Perth Tram**, a wooden replica of the city's first trams. You can break your journey at any point and rejoin later.

Most of Perth's shops and arcades are in the blocks bounded by St Georges Terrace and William, Wellington and Barrack streets, centring around **Hay Street Mall**, **Raine Square Shopping Plaza**, and **Murray Street Mall** and

NOT TO BE MISSED in Perth	Map Ref.
• **Ferry trip** – along the Swan River to the fascinating port town of Fremantle	360 D8
• **Kings Park** – a huge bushland reserve offering magnificent views of the city and splendid wildflower displays in spring	360 A6
• **Lake Monger** – to see black swans and other species of water bird	361 D6
• **London Court** – to watch knights on horseback joust above one entrance while St George and the dragon do battle over the other	360 D6
• **Market** – at weekends in Fremantle, has a unique atmosphere created by the ornate gold-rush-era architecture	368 F8
• **Northbridge** – for its cosmopolitan restaurants and art galleries	360 D4
• **Perth Mint** – the closest most people get to a fortune	360 F7
• **Perth Tram** – a fun way to discover the city and its attractions	360 E6
• **Scitech Discovery Centre** – absorbing hands-on science and technology displays	360 A3
• **Underwater World** – to meet sharks and other marine creatures face to face	364 A5

Forrest Place Mall. Perth's shopping and business area is linked by pedestrian malls, overpasses and underground walkways, enabling access, unhampered by motor vehicles. Perth's unique **London Court**, an Elizabethan-style arcade, runs from Hay Street Mall to St Georges Terrace. At the Hay Street entrance, four knights on horseback joust above a replica of Big Ben every 15 minutes, while St George and the Dragon do battle above the clock over the St Georges Terrace entrance. Perth's decorative **Town Hall** on the corner of Hay and Barrack streets was built by convicts between 1869 and 1879.

Stately **St Georges Terrace**, Perth's financial and professional heart, is worth strolling down. Start at the western end, where you will see **Parliament House**; when Parliament is not sitting, there are guided tours Monday to Friday. Nearby is the mellow brickwork of **Barracks Arch** (all that remains of the Tudor-style Pensioner Barracks built in 1863).

Continuing along St Georges Terrace you come to the charming **Cloisters** (1858), a former boys' school that has been integrated with the modern complex behind. The ecclesiastical-looking building nearby is the Old Perth Boys' School, now the National Trust giftshop and cafe. The **Palace Hotel**, a grand old Victorian iron-lace bal-conied hotel, has been modified as a banking chamber and forms an impressive exterior facade for Perth's second largest building, the Bankwest Tower. Located further along the terrace is an ornate Victorian church – **Trinity Church Chapel** – and the arched entrance to London Court. The impressive **Treasury Building** on the corner of Barrack Street overlooks **Stirling Gardens**, part of the **Supreme Court Gardens**. The **Orchestral Shell**, within the gardens, is the venue for various concerts and Carols by Candlelight. **St George's Cathedral** and the **Deanery** are two other interesting old buildings at this end of St Georges Terrace. On the opposite side is one of Perth's oldest buildings, the **Old Court House** (1836), and the turrets of the Gothic-style **Government House** in its lush private gardens.

Further along is the modern **Perth Concert Hall**, which seats 1900 and is used for everything from hard rock to opera. Inside, a restaurant, a tavern and a cocktail bar cater for music lovers. At the eastern end of Hay Street is the

Decoration above entrance to London Court

Perth Mint, where a spectacular viewing gallery provides views of pure gold bars being poured and moulded.

Just north of the city centre in Northbridge is the attractive **Perth Cultural Centre** complex. Nationally and internationally renowned artworks are on display in the **Art Gallery of Western Australia**. Nearby is the **Alexander Library**, and the original Perth Gaol (1856) within the modern complex of the **Western Australian Museum**. A blue whale skeleton, Aboriginal artifacts and a stuffed native bird display are among the exhibits.

A visit to the Cultural Centre could be combined with a meal at one of the many reasonably-priced restaurants in this area, as cosmopolitan **Northbridge** is also the centre of the city's nightlife. Numerous hotels, nightclubs and piano bars offer a variety of live entertainment.

At the City West shopping complex in West Perth are the **Omni Theatre**

and the award-winning **Scitech Discovery Centre**. The specially constructed theatre presents visitors with real adventure experiences, and the centre has a hands-on science and technology display. **It's a Small World**, in Parliament Place, West Perth, has a fascinating collection of miniatures ranging from historic miniature railways to push-button animation.

Just west of the city centre, in Havelock Street, is the **Old Observatory**, now the headquarters for the National Trust; four of its rooms are open to the public. The new **Perth Observatory**, at Bickley, has a substantial display centre and night tours are available, bookings essential. **Kings Park** is one of Perth's major attractions. Within this huge natural bushland reserve there are landscaped gardens and walkways, lakes, children's playgrounds, lookouts and the **Botanic Gardens** on **Mount Eliza Bluff**, where a blaze of Western Australian wildflowers is to be seen in spring. You can drive by car through the park or hire a bicycle, stopping at the many scenic lookouts over the city and river; or you can wander on foot along the many walking trails right to the top of Mount Eliza. Within the park the magnificently-sited **War Memorial** also offers splendid views of the city.

Other city parks include **Hyde Park**, with its waterbirds, ornamental lake and English trees, and the beautiful **Queens Gardens**, with a replica of London's Peter Pan statue. Just north-west of the city centre is **Lake Monger**, a favourite picnic spot that is also the home of black swans, ducks and other varieties of birds. **Matilda Bay**, on the Swan River, offers grassed areas and ample shade, with stunning views of the Swan River and Perth city skyline. The **Swan River Estuary Marine Park** includes three

WESTERN AUSTRALIA

areas: Alfred Cove, Pelican Point and Milyu. South-west of the city centre is **Wireless Hill Park**, a natural bushland area with a grassed picnic and play ground area with beautiful wildflowers in spring; a **Telecommunications Museum**, housed in the original Wireless Station; and three viewing towers.

The **Swan River foreshores**, on both the city side and South Perth, provide pleasant walking and cycling trails. Bicycles can be hired just off Riverside Drive near the Causeway.

A pleasant way to visit **Perth's Zoo**, with its magnificent garden environment and nocturnal house, is to catch a ferry from the Barrack Street Jetty. The trip can be combined with a visit to the **Old Mill**, on the South Perth foreshore. This picturesque whitewashed windmill, built in 1838, now houses an interesting collection of early colonial relics.

Further north along the coast at Sorrento is **Hillarys Boat Harbour**. A day can easily be spent here, enjoying the atmosphere and variety of **Sorrento Quay** or experiencing the thrill of **Underwater World**, where you are transported through a submerged acrylic tunnel on moving walkways to see the enormous variety of under-water life. From September to November, charter boats at the harbour offer visits to see whales basking between Perth and Rottnest Island.

Swimming and surfing are part of the joy of Perth and several beautiful Indian Ocean beaches – including **Cottesloe**, **Swanbourne** (a nude bathing beach), **City**, **Scarborough**,

Trigg and **Port** – are within easy reach of the city.

There are many other places of interest around Perth, including the historic port of **Fremantle**, which underwent a complete facelift in preparation for the America's Cup challenge in 1987. In Fremantle you can relive the past by strolling along the streets of terraced houses, or visiting the city's magnificent historic buildings. Relax at one of the many alfresco cafes in **South Terrace**, home also for the National Trust-classified **Fremantle Markets**, open every weekend and well worth a visit. The **Fremantle Tram** offers various hourly tours around the city's attractions.

The **University of Western Australia**, with its Mediterranean-style buildings and landscaped gardens in the riverside suburb of Crawley, is also worth seeing. The university's **Fortune Theatre** has been built as a replica of Shakespeare's Fortune Theatre in Elizabethan London.

At nearby **Subiaco**, a popular shopping and market area an easy train ride from the city, you will find the Aboriginal art gallery **Indiginart** in Hay Street; there is another, the **Creative Native Gallery**, in King Street in the city and in High Street, Fremantle. **Adventure World** in the southern suburb of Bibra Lake offers among its attractions a wildlife park, animal circus, rides and Australia's largest swimming-pool, and is open from October to April. **Cables Water Ski Park** at Spearwood features cable tows for water skiing, a water slide and mini golf.

Perth's sporting facilities are excellent, with two major racecourses, **Ascot** and **Belmont Park**; night pacing at **Gloucester Park** (the famous WACA cricket ground is near here); greyhound racing at **Cannington**; and speedcar and motorcycle racing at the **Claremont Showgrounds**. Major athletics meetings, rugby and soccer matches are held at **Perry Lakes Stadium**, and Australian Rules football finals at **Subiaco Oval**. Hockey is played at the **Commonwealth Hockey Stadium**, the first Astroturf stadium in Australia. The **Superdrome** hosts several international sporting events.

Perth offers the visitor a wide range of entertainment. The modern **Perth Entertainment Centre** (home of the Perth Wildcats basketball team), in Wellington Street, seats 8000. At the **Burswood Casino**, across the river at Rivervale, you can try your luck at the tables, or enjoy the five-star splendour of the hotel. Another resort complex is **Raddison Observation City Resort Hotel** on the coast at Scarborough. Perth also offers an excellent range of accommodation to suit all requirements.

During February and March, the **Festival of Perth** combines the visual arts, theatre, music and film. A festive occasion occurs every weekend on the Art Gallery and Museum Concourse where handcrafted items can be purchased at the **Galleria Art and Craft Market** and at the **Station Street Markets** at Subiaco with its range of bric-a-brac, live entertainment and a garden courtyard providing a colourful atmosphere. Other weekend markets include the **Scarborough Fair Markets**, with specialty stalls and a food hall; **Stock Road Markets** at Spearwood, undercover markets with a circus theme; **Gosnells Railway Markets**, with its old-world charm; **Canning Vale Sunday Markets**, one of the biggest undercover markets; **Subiaco Pavilion Markets**, held in a stylishly restored warehouse; and, at Midland, the **Military Markets** include a wildlife sanctuary, and the **Sunday Markets** are held in an open carpark.

PERTH ON FOOT

There are many walking tours around Perth and its suburbs. The W.A. Heritage Committee, as part of Australia's 1988 Bicentenary, established a state-wide network of heritage trails; the Perth Heritage Trails listed below are part of this network.

- **Guntrips Walking Tours:** 2-hour guided walks including the Cultural Walk around the city and the Western Walk which takes in Kings Park; bookings essential.

- **Heritage Walk:** 2-hour guided walk of central business district; bookings essential.

- **Perth Heritage Trails:** self-guide heritage trails around central Perth; East Perth; Northbridge; West Perth; Subiaco; Jolimont; Shenton Park; and foreshore.

- **Perth Walking Tours:** guided 2-hour walks concentrating on architecture, history and heritage; bookings essential.

- **Subiaco Guided Walks:** Historic homes, Rokeby Road and City Square; bookings essential.

For brochures for the self-guide walks and for further information, contact the Western Australian Tourist Centre, cnr Forrest Place and Wellington St, Perth; (08) 9483 1111.

For further information on Perth and Western Australia, contact the Western Australian Tourist Centre, Albert Facey House, cnr Forrest Place and Wellington St, Perth; (08) 9483 1111 or 1800 812 808.

TOURS from Perth

With the Indian Ocean surf beaches beckoning from the west, the peaceful Darling Range on the east and the Swan River meandering through Perth from Fremantle to the Swan Valley vineyards, there are many enjoyable trips within easy reach of Perth.

Vineyards at Houghtons Winery in the Swan Valley

Ferry Cruises

From the Barrack Street Jetty, ferries leave regularly to Fremantle, Rottnest Island and Swan Valley. Other cruises will take you to the historic riverside home Tranby. From Wednesday to Saturday nights, in season, you can have dinner aboard a vessel that leaves the Barrack Street Jetty in the early evening and returns at midnight. Daily ferry services to Rottnest Island, Perth's popular hideaway and once the site of the infamous Rottnest Native Prison, also leave from Hillarys Boat Harbour and from Fremantle. **See:** Rottnest Island.

Fremantle

19 km from Perth via the Stirling or Canning highways

A visit to this fascinating old port can make an interesting round trip by car if you return via the opposite side of the river. Fremantle is also easily accessible by bus, train and boat. Just 10 minutes from Fremantle is Adventure World, a fun park featuring a wide variety of entertainment. Adventure World is open most weekends, and daily except Christmas Day and Good Friday, between October and April. **See:** Entry for Fremantle in A–Z listing.

Serpentine Dam

54 km from Perth via the South Western Highway

Picnic beside the Serpentine Dam, which is set among peaceful hills and beautiful landscaped gardens of wildflowers.

Pioneer Village, Armadale

29 km from Perth via the Albany Highway

Pioneer Village is a reconstruction of the days of the gold rush and features gold panning and live theatre. Nearby is Araluen Botanic Park, with its beautiful gardens and waterfalls. Close to Armadale, Tumbulgum Farm features a farm show, an Aboriginal cultural show and Showcase WA, which offers WA-made products for purchase. At nearby Gosnells, the Cohunu Koala Park renowned for its koalas also has a wide range of other Australian fauna.

York

97 km from Perth via the Great Southern Highway

See: Entry for York in A–Z listing.

Historic Guildford in the Swan Valley

18 km from Perth via Guildford Road or the Great Eastern Highway

On the way, visit the Craft Centre at Mount Lawley, and the rail museum in Bassendean. At Guildford, the old court house and gaol in Meadow Street houses a folk museum (open Sundays), next door is the Village Potters gallery. A 40-kilometre heritage trail starts at the Success Hill Reserve and retraces the steps of Captain Stirling on his 1827 search for a site for the new settlement. Just north-east of Guildford in Ford Street, West Midland, is Woodbridge, a gracious mansion overlooking the river, beautifully restored and furnished by the National Trust. Whiteman Park, 7 km north of Guildford, has train and tram rides, and the Trade Village, where trades people ply traditional skills. There are numerous wineries in the area, including the historic Houghtons Wines. Craft shops, galleries and antique shops also abound.

John Forrest National Park

28 km from Perth on the Great Eastern Highway

This huge bushland park in the Darling Range features walking trails, streams, waterfalls and a safe swimming pool for children. Three kilometres east of the park is the old Mahogany Inn (1837), now the oldest residential inn in Western Australia. At weekends enjoy a Devonshire tea.

Mundaring Weir

42 km from Perth via the Great Eastern Highway

This water catchment area, which provides water for the goldfields over 500 kilometres away, is surrounded by picnic areas. The O'Connor Museum explains the construction and operation of this complex water scheme. Kalamunda History Village is nearby.

Walyunga National Park

35 km from Perth via Guildford Road and the Great Northern Highway

The Avon River flows through this beautiful bushland park, renowned for its wildflower display in spring. It is a popular picnic spot and there are signposted walking trails. Each year in August, the Avon Descent, a major white-water canoeing event is held here.

Yanchep National Park

50 km from Perth via the Mitchell Freeway and Wanneroo Road

See: Entry for Yanchep in A–Z listing and Yanchep National Park entry in National Parks.

Rottnest Island

The island's resident marsupial, the quokka

Commodore Willem de Vlamingh referred to Rottnest Island as a 'terrestrial paradise' when he landed there in 1696, and holidaymakers still flock to the island to enjoy its peace, beauty and unique natural and historic features. A low, sandy island, just 20 kilometres west of Fremantle, Rottnest is a public reserve. Only 11 kilometres long and about 5 kilometres wide, it has an attractive coastline, with many small bays and coves, sparkling white beaches and turquoise waters. Vlamingh named it Rottnest, or Rat's Nest, for the island's marsupial resident, the quokka, which he believed to be a type of rat.

The Rottnest Hotel, completed in 1864, was originally the summer residence of the governors of Western Australia. Now commonly known as the Quokka Arms, it is a good place to stay, or just to enjoy a relaxing drink in the beer garden. Rottnest Lodge Resort has modern convention facilities in an informal setting. Other accommodation includes units, cabins, hostels and a camping area.

There is no lack of things to do on Rottnest Island. Cars are not permitted (which contributes to the wonderful sense of peace), but you can hire a bicycle and explore the island. You may even catch a glimpse of peacocks and pheasants, which were introduced at the turn of the century. Special 2-hour coach tours of the island are conducted twice daily. There are free, guided walks covering the history of the early settlement departing daily, as well as self-guide walks for which there are brochures at the Visitor Centre. A train operates several times daily on a 7-kilometre route from the historic settlement area to the Oliver Hill Battery. Oliver Hill Lookout, located next to the battery, offers views across the salt lakes to the mainland. Other lookouts on the island include Vlamingh Lookout, near the hotel and the highest point of the circular 1-km trail known as the Vlamingh Memorial Heritage Trail; and Jeannies Lookout, popular with photographers.

There are tennis courts, a 9-hole golf course and bowling facilities. You can hire a boat, dinghy or canoe, take a joy flight over the island, play mini-golf or go trampolining; or you can just laze on the beach in the sunshine. If you enjoy snorkelling, there is an underwater snorkelling trail on Pocillopora Reef off the south of the island. Scuba diving is available; contact the Dive, Surf and Ski Shop.

The *Underwater Explorer*, a glass-bottomed pleasure cruiser, leaves regularly from Main Jetty, giving glimpses of shipwrecks, reefs and a startling array of fish. Ferries operate daily services to Rottnest from Barrack Street Jetty in Perth and also from Fremantle and Hillarys Boat Harbour. There are daily flights from Perth. As all wildlife on Rottnest is protected, no pets and no guns of any description, including spear guns, are allowed on the island. In the interests of their health and survival, please do not feed the quokkas.

For further information, contact the Rottnest Visitor Centre, Henderson Ave; (08) 9372 9752.

WESTERN AUSTRALIA

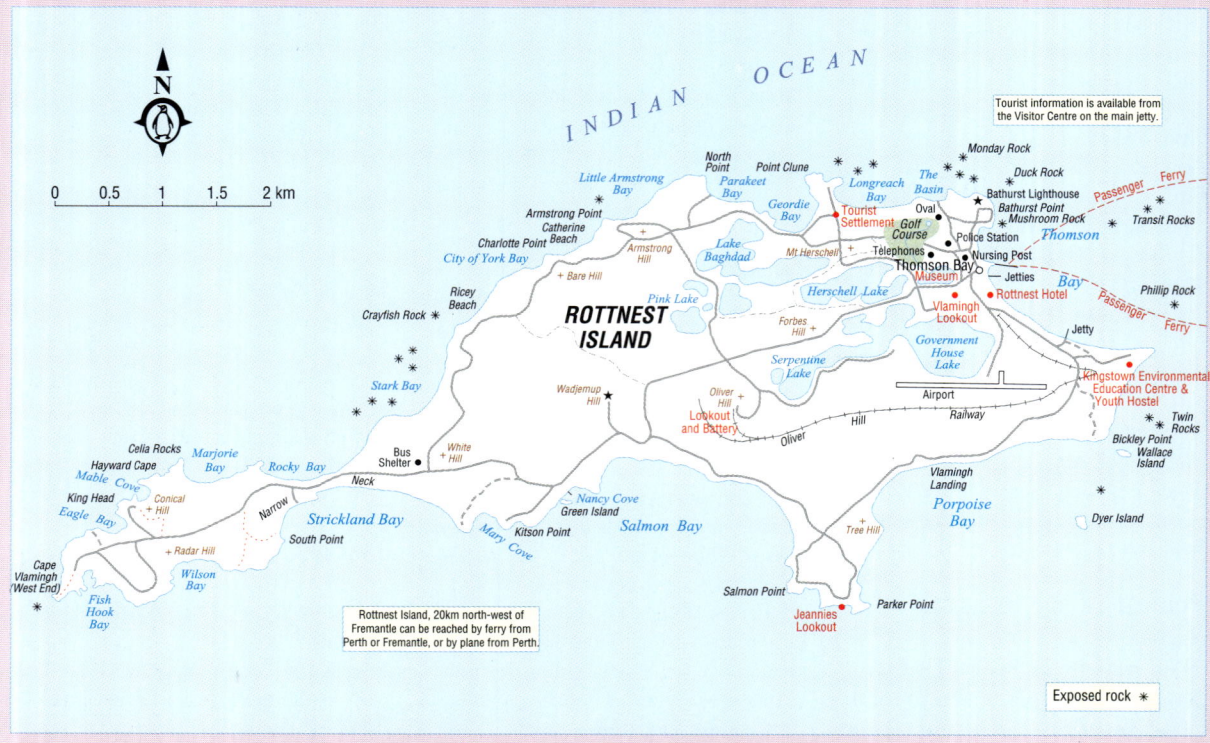

WESTERN AUSTRALIA
from A to Z

Albany
Pop. 18 826

MAP REF. 371 N12, 374 H13, 376 F12

Picturesque Albany is the State's oldest town. On the edge of King George Sound and the magnificent Princess Royal Harbour, the town is 406 km S of Perth. Albany dates back to 1826, when a military post was established to give the English a foothold in the West. Whaling was important in the 1840s; in the 1850s Albany became a coaling station for steamers bound from England. As WA's most important holiday centre, it offers visitors a wealth of history and a variety of coastal, rural and mountain scenery. Its harbours, weirs and estuaries provide excellent fishing. **Of interest:** Colonial Buildings Historic Walk, self-guide brochure from Tourist information. Old Post Office-Intercolonial Communications Museum, cnr Stirling Tce and Spencer St. Victorian shopfronts in Stirling Tce. Outlet for Alkoomi Wines, Lower Stirling Tce. In Residency Rd: Residency Museum (1850s), originally home of Resident Magistrates, now houses historical and environmental exhibits; Old Gaol and Museum (1851) has two gaols in one. Vancouver Arts Centre, Vancouver St. House of Gems, Frenchman Bay Rd. Outlet for Galafrey Wines, Proudlove Pde. Old Farm (1836), Middleton Rd, Strawberry Hill, site of first Government farm in WA. Faithfully restored Patrick Taylor Cottage (1832), Duke St, has extensive collection of period costume and household goods. Extravaganza Plaza, next to Esplanade Hotel, Middleton Beach, features art and craft. Princess Royal Fortress (commissioned 1893) on Mt Adelaide, Albany's first federal fortress. Mt Adelaide Forts Heritage Trails, starting cnr Apex Dr. and Forts Rd; self-guide leaflets from Tourist information. On Princess Royal Dr.: the *Amity*, a full-scale replica of brig that brought Major Lockyer and convicts to establish Albany in 1826; Amity Crafts, for local art and craft. Anzac Light Horse Memorial statue, near top of Mt

Historic Old Farm at Strawberry Hill, Albany

Clarence, off Marine Dr.; spectacular view from here and from John Barnesby Memorial Lookout at Mt Melville. Southern right whale-watching cruises, operate daily from town jetty (July–mid Oct.). Easter: Great Southern Wine Festival. Apr.: Festival of Albany. Nov.: Perth–Albany Ocean Yacht Race. **In the area:** Fishing at: Jimmy Newhill's Harbour, 20 km S; Frenchman Bay, 25 km S; Emu Point, 8 km NE; Oyster Harbour, 15 km NE. *To the north*: Deer-O-Dome deer farm (6 km); Porongurup National Park (37 km) featuring huge granite peaks and easy walking tracks to peaks providing splendid views; Stirling Range National Park (80 km) for climbing and bushwalking, breathtaking scenery, brilliant wildflowers in spring, some unique to area. *To the west towards Denmark*: West Cape Howe National Park (30 km) one of south coast's most popular parks for walking, fishing, swimming and hang-gliding, and has one of best lookouts on coast; Torbay Head in park is southernmost point in WA. Care should be taken when exploring the coast; king waves can be dangerous and have been known to rush in unexpectedly, with fatal consequences. *To the*

south: Shell Museum (10 km), open Sun.–Fri.; Torndirrup National Park (17 km) for spectacular coastal views; The Gap and Natural Bridge (18 km); the Blow Holes (19 km). *To the south-east*: Camp Quaranup (20 km), site of old quarantine station, historical walk south on Geake Point; Albany Whaleworld at Cheyne's Beach Whaling Station (25 km) which ceased operation in 1978; in its heyday, the Station's chasers took up to 850 whales per season. *To the east*: Willowie Game Park (30 km); Nanarup (20 km) and Little Beach (40 km) have sheltered waters; Two Peoples Bay Marron Farm (20 km); Two Peoples Bay Nature Reserve (40 km). **Tourist information:** Old Railway Station, Proudlove Pde; (08) 9841 1088. **Accommodation:** 5 hotels, 9 motels, 15 B&B, 2 hostels, 10 cara./camp. parks. **See also:** The Southern Region.

Augusta
Pop. 838

MAP REF. 367 C13, 369 D12, 374 B11, 376 B11

Set on the slopes of the Hardy Inlet, the town of Augusta overlooks the mouth of the Blackwood River, the waters of Flinders Bay and rolling, heavily wooded countryside. Augusta is one of the oldest settlements in WA and a popular holiday town. Jarrah, karri and pine forests supply the district's 100-year-old timber industry. **Of interest:** In Blackwood Ave: Historical Museum; Lumen Christi Catholic Church. Crafters Croft, Ellis St, for art and craft. Mar.: Dragon Boat Racing. Sept.-Oct.: Spring Flower Show. **In the area:** Picturesque coastline. Excellent swimming and surfing. Good fishing in river and ocean; marron (freshwater lobster) caught in season (marron fishing licence required, available from post office, Blackwood Ave). Augusta–Busselton Heritage Trail, details from Tourist information. Cruises on Blackwood River and Hardy Inlet available. Panoramic views from Hillview Lookout and golf course, 6 km NW. Jewel Cave, famous for its colourful limestone formations, and Moondyne Cave, for guided adventure tours; both 8 km NW. Alexandra Bridge, 10 km N, a charming picnic spot with towering jarrah trees and beautiful wildflowers in spring. Boranup Maze, 18 km N. Boranup Lookout, 19 km N, fine views of Leeuwin-Naturaliste National Park, also pleasant picnic spot. Lake Cave and Mammoth Cave, both 30 km N. The Landing Place, 3 km S, where first European settlers landed in area. Whale Rescue Memorial, 4 km S, to people who helped save a large pod of pilot whales beached here in 1986. Matthew Flinders Memorial, 5 km S. Cape Leeuwin, 8 km SW, most southwesterly point of Australia and where Indian and Southern oceans meet; at Cape, lighthouse (1895) and old water wheel. **Tourist information:** Leeuwin Souvenirs, Blackwood Ave; (08) 9758 1695. **Accommodation:** 1 hotel/motel, 1 motel, 1 hostel, 4 cara./camp. parks.

Australind   Pop. 4407

MAP REF. 367 G4, 374 C8, 376 C10
The popular holiday town of Australind is located 11 km NE of Bunbury on the Leschenault Estuary. Fishing, crabbing, swimming and boating on the estuary and the Collie River are the main attractions. **Of interest:** In Paris Rd: Henton Cottage (1841); restored Church of St Nicholas (1842), thought to be smallest church in WA. On Old Coast Rd: Rock and Gem Museum (check opening times with Tourist information); Pioneer Memorial. Scenic 2-km drive along Cathedral Ave, a shaded avenue of paperbark trees. **In the area:** Cemetery, 2 km N, has pioneer graves and beautiful wildflowers in season. Kemerton Industrial Park (SCM Chemicals), 15 km N, has guided tours; contact Tourist information. Pleasant beach towns to the north: Binningup (26 km) and Myalup (30 km). **Tourist information:** Harvey Tourist and Interpretative Centre, South Western Hwy, Harvey; (08) 9729 1122. **Accommodation:** 3 B&B, 2 cara./camp. parks.

Balladonia   Pop. 10

MAP REF. 377 L8
Balladonia is on the Eyre Hwy, 191 km E of Norseman. At this point, the road crosses gently undulating dryland forest through the Fraser Range. Visitors can see claypans typical of the region and old stone fences built by pioneer farmers in the 1800s. In July 1979, debris from the US Skylab fell to earth near the town. **In the area:** Wildflowers in spring. Balladonia Station Homestead (1886), 22 km E behind old telegraph station, has a gallery of paintings depicting local history (open by appt). Newmans Rocks, 50 km W on Eyre Hwy. **Tourist information:** Balladonia Hotel/Motel; (08) 9039 3453. **Accommodation:** 1 hotel/motel, 1 cara./camp. park (limited facilities). **See also:** Crossing the Nullarbor.

Beverley   Pop. 818

MAP REF. 374 F4, 376 D8
On the Avon River, 130 km E of Perth, is the town of Beverley. **Of interest:** Delightful picnic spots beside Avon River. Aeronautical Museum, Vincent St, shows development of aviation in WA and includes biplane built in 1929 by local aircraft designer Selby Ford. In Hunt Rd: Dead Finish (1872), one of oldest buildings in town and once hotel in town centre, but with the coming of the railway in 1886 the town centre moved nearer the station (open Sun. or by arrangement with Tourist information); Barry Ferguson's Garage, has display of old hand-operated machinery (open normal trading hours). Apr.: Art Exhibition. Aug.: Agricultural Show. Sept.: Duck Race (with plastic ducks). **In the area:** The Avon Ascent, a self-guide drive tour of the Avon Valley; leaflet from Tourist information. Magnificent view from top of Seaton Ross Hill, Top Beverley Rd, on northern outskirts of town. Restored St Paul's Church (consecrated 1862), opposite original town site, 5 km NW. Avondale Discovery Farm, 6 km W, has range of farm implements, a museum and Clydesdale horses. Restored church, St John's in the Wilderness (consecrated 1895), 27 km SW. **Tourist information:** Aeronautical Museum, Vincent St; (08) 9646 1555. **Accommodation:** 2 hotels, 1 cara./camp. park.

Boyup Brook   Pop. 584

MAP REF. 370 E2, 374 E9, 376 D11
A small town near the junction of Boyup Creek and the Blackwood River, Boyup Brook is a centre for the district's sheep, dairy-farming and timber industries. Blackboys, huge granite boulders, shaded pools, charming cottages and farms are scenic features. **Of interest:** Pioneers Museum, Jayes Rd. Sandy Chambers Art Studio, Gibbs St, for artworks; outside are aviaries and camels. Stagline Woollen Clothing, Henderson St. Flax Mill, on Blackwood River off Barron St. Haddleton Flora Reserve, Arthur River Rd. Pioneer Garden, Kojonup Rd. Carnaby Collection of beetles and butterflies at Tourist information. Bicentennial Walk Trail, details at Tourist information. Feb.: Country Music Awards. May: Autumn Art Affair. Sept.: Country Music Weekend. Oct.: Blackwood River Marathon Relay (running, canoeing, horseriding, cycling, swimming to Bridgetown); Spring Garden Expo. **In the area:** Visits to farms (wheat, sheep, pig, goat, deer and angora); Boyup Brook Flora Drive; details for both at Tourist information. Glacial rock formations at Glacier Hill, 18 km S. Wineries: Scotts Brook, 18 km SE (open by appt only); Blackwood Crest at Kulikup, 40 km E. Harvey Dickson Country Music Centre, 5 km NE (open by appt only). Gregory Tree blazed by explorer Captain Gregory in 1845, 15 km NE. School and teacher's house (1900) at Dinninup, 21 km NE. At Wilga, 22 km NW, vintage engines and old timber-mill. Stormboy Jumpers, 20 km W on Jayes Rd, for locally-produced woollen goods (make appt at Tourist information). **Tourist information:** cnr Bridge and Able sts; (08) 9765 1444. **Accommodation:** 1 hotel, 1 B&B, 1 hostel, 1 cara./camp. park. **See also:** The Southern Region.

Camel riding on Cable Beach, near Broome

Bremer Bay — Pop. 250

MAP REF. 376 G11

Bremer Bay, a popular holiday destination 181 km NE of Albany, was named in 1849 by Surveyor-General John Septimus Roe in honour of the captain of HMS *Tamar*, Sir Gordon Bremer. The town was built around the Old Telegraph Station at the mouth of Wellstead Estuary (named after John Wellstead, who settled in the area in the 1850s). **Of interest:** Fishing, boating, scuba diving and water-skiing. Rammed-earth buildings, including hotel/motel, Franton Way; church in John St, overlooking estuary. **In the area:** Abundant wildflowers July–Oct. Fitzgerald River National Park, 17 km N. At Point Ann, 45 km NE whale-watching (June–Nov.). Military museum at Jerramungup, 90 km NW. At Fisheries Beach, 6 km W, good boat-launching facilities. **Tourist information:** Roadhouse, Gnombup Tce; (08) 9837 4093. **Accommodation:** 1 hotel/motel, 1 B&B, 1 cara./camp. park. **See also:** The Southern Region.

Bridgetown — Pop. 2017

MAP REF. 370 C3, 374 D10, 376 D11

Bridgetown is a quiet spot in undulating country in the south-west corner of WA. Here the Blackwood River, well stocked with marron and trout, curves through some of the prettiest country in the State. The first European settlers arrived in 1857 and the first apple trees

were planted soon after. **Of interest:** In Hampton St: Bridgetown Pottery; Brierley Jigsaw Gallery (at Tourist information); Gentle Era craft shop; St Paul's Church (1911), with paintings by local artists; Memorial Park, a peaceful picnic location. Bridgedale (1862), on South Western Hwy near bridge and overlooking river, constructed of local clay and timber by first European settler John Blechynden; restored by National Trust (check opening times). Also on South Western Hwy, Blackwood River Park for picnics and walks along river. Market, 2nd Sun. each month at Blackwood River Park. Oct.: Blackwood Classic, a 250-km power-boat event; Blackwood River Marathon Relay (running, canoeing, swimming, horseriding and cycling the 58.3 km course between Bridgetown and Boyup Brook). Nov.: Blues at Bridgetown. **In the area:** Wildflowers and apple blossom in spring. Geegelup Heritage Trail (52 km) retraces history of agriculture, mining and timber (details from Tourist information). Scenic drives through rolling green hills, orchards and valleys into noted karri and jarrah timber country (contact Tourist information). Fine views: Sutton's Lookout, off Phillip St; Hester's Hill, 5 km N. Greenbushes Historical Park, 18 km N, has displays of tin-mining industry. Art and craft outlets at Ballingup, 28 km N, including Old Cheese Factory Art and Craft Centre. Bush walking and picnicking at Bridgetown Jarrah Park, 15 km W and also at Karri Gully, a further 5 km W. **Tourist information:** Hampton St;

(08) 9761 1740. **Accommodation:** 2 hotels, 1 motel, 6 B&B, 1 cara./camp. park. **See also:** The Southern Region.

Brookton — Pop. 576

MAP REF. 374 F5, 376 D8

An attractive town 137 km SE of Perth, near the Avon River in the heart of fertile farming country, Brookton was founded in 1884 when the Great Southern Railway line was opened. **Of interest:** In Robinson Rd: Old Police Station Museum (key available at Tourist information); St Mark's Anglican Church (1895); Old Railway Station, houses Tourist information, and art and craft shop. Lions Picnic Park, off Corrigin Rd, at eastern entrance to town. Mar.: Old Time Motor Show (even-numbered years). Sept.: Wildflower Show (odd-numbered years). **In the area:** Nine Acre Rock, 12 km E on Brookton–Kweda Rd, one of the largest natural granite outcrops in the area; nearby remnants of pioneer Jack Hansen's home. County Peak, 10 km E, offers bushwalking, picnic area and spectacular views from summit. Christmas Tree Well Picnic Area, 60 km E. Yenyening Lakes Nature Reserve, 35 km NE, for picnics and water-skiing (if adequate water). Boyagin Rock, 18 km SW, a reserve with picnic ground. **Tourist information:** Old Railway Station, Robinson Rd; (08) 9642 1316. **Accommodation:** 2 hotels, 1 cara./camp. park.

Broome — Pop. 8906

MAP REF. 380 G9

Situated on the coast at the southern tip of the Kimberley, Broome enjoys wide beaches, turquoise water and a warm climate with plenty of sunshine. Closer to Bali than to Perth, and with an international airport, the town is lively and cosmopolitan. The discovery of pearling grounds off the coast in the 1880s led to the foundation of Broome township in 1883. By 1910 Broome was the world's leading pearling centre. However, the industry began to suffer when world markets collapsed in 1914. With increasing tourism, Broome is again rapidly expanding. **Of interest:** Self-guide heritage trail (2 km) introduces buildings and places of interest; contact Tourist information for brochure. Chinatown, including Pearl Emporiums, reminder of Broome's early

WESTERN AUSTRALIA

multicultural mix. Historical Society Museum, in Old Customs House, Saville St. Library, Haas St. Captain Gregory's House, Carnarvon St (not open to public). Several art galleries. In Hamersley St: Bedford Park, relics of Broome's history; Court house (former Cable House). Crocodile Park, Cable Beach Rd. Shell House, Guy St, contains one of largest shell collections in Australia. Sun Pictures, Carnarvon St, opened 1916 and believed to be oldest operating outdoor theatre in world. On Port Dr.: Chinese Cemetery; Japanese Cemetery (graves of early Japanese pearl divers). Pioneer Cemetery in Apex Park. Market, each Sat. at court house. Apr.: Rotary Dragon Boat Classic. Aug.: Opera Under the Stars. Aug.–Sept.: Shinju Matsuri (Festival of the Pearl) recalls Broome's heyday. Nov.: Mango Festival. **In the area:** Beaches, ideal swimming spots and prized by collectors for beautiful shells. Good fishing all year. Staircase to the Moon: natural phenomenon, visible at most full moons during dry season (Apr.–Oct.); caused by moonlight reflecting off exposed mudflats at extreme low tides; best seen from southern end of Dampier Tce (dates and times from Tourist information); markets often held on town beach, Robinson St, to coincide with the phenomenon. Hovercraft *Spirit of Broome* visits local beaches. Safaris, cruises, scenic flights, short tours. Charter boats: 6- to 10-day Kimberley expeditions to coral reefs, Rowley Shoals, Prince Regent River and waterfalls at Kings Cascades. Day tours to: former Lombadina Mission, 200 km NE; Cape Leveque, 220 km NE. Cable Beach, 3 km NW, is 22 km long, named after underwater cable that links Broome to Java. At Gantheaume Point, 5 km SW, giant dinosaur tracks believed to be 130 million years old; can be seen 30 m from base of cliff when tide is out. Broome Bird Observatory, 18 km E at Roebuck Bay. Willie Creek Pearl Farm, 35 km N, tours available. **Tourist information:** cnr Bagot St and Great Northern Hwy; (08) 9192 2222. **Accommodation:** 5 hotels, 1 hotel/ motel, 4 hostels, 1 B&B, 6 cara./camp. parks. **See also:** The Kimberley.

Bunbury   Pop. 24 003

MAP REF. 367 F4, 374 C8, 376 C10
Bunbury, 'Harbour City', is the second largest urban area in WA and serves as the major port, commercial and regional centre for the south-west. Situated 185 km S of Perth on the Leschenault Estuary, at the junction of the Preston and Collie rivers, it is one of the State's most popular tourist areas, with a warm temperate climate, beautiful beaches and the Darling Range in the distance. Originally called Port Leschenault, Bunbury was settled by Europeans in 1838, and the whalers who anchored in Koombana Bay provided a market for the pioneer farmers. Today the port is the main outlet for the thriving timber industry, mineral sands and the produce of the fertile hinterland. **Of interest:** Heritage trails, contact Tourist information. King Cottage (1880), Forrest Ave, an historical museum with displays depicting domestic life at turn of century (open p.m). Tree-lined pathways lead to Boulter's Lookout, Haig Cres., for views of city, suburbs, hills and farmland. Lighthouse, Ocean Dr., a notable landmark, painted in black and white checks, has lookout at base. Marlston Hill Lookout, Apex Dr., was original site of lighthouse and was used by early whaling fleet as a whale-spotting vantage point. The Lighthouse Beach pathway follows the coastline from the lighthouse to the original harbour breakwater. Art Gallery, cnr Victoria and Carey sts. Centenary Gardens, cnr Wittenoom and Prinsep sts in city centre, a peaceful picnic spot. Grassed foreshore of estuary has picnic/barbecue facilities, playground and boat ramp. Miniature railway, Forrest Park, Blair St. Excellent beaches; surf club at Ocean Beach. Drive along breakwater to Koombana Bay, with its modern harbour facilities and popular for water-skiing and boating; in Koombana Dr., Dolphin Discovery Centre, offers chance to wade or swim with dolphins under ranger guidance; opposite, beginning of mangrove boardwalk (with interpretive signage) through the southern-most mangrove colony in WA. Good fishing for bream, flounder, tailor and whiting in bay, and deep-sea fishing. Succulent blue manna crabs in season in estuary. Great variety of birdlife in bush near waters of inlet. Big Swamp Wildlife Park, Prince Phillip Dr., displays more than 100 species of native birds, mammals and reptiles. Historic wooden jetty in outer harbour, popular for fishing and crabbing. Mar.: Show; Aqua Spectacular. Nov.: Bunbury Fest. **In the area:** Gelorup Museum, 12 km S. St Mark's (1842), 5 km SE at Picton, oldest church in WA, restored, retains some of original timber structure. Boyanup Transport Museum, 20 km SE. Church of St Nicholas (1842), 11 km N, at Australind, thought to be smallest church in WA. Off Old Coast Road: Spring Hill Homestead (1855), 26 km N (not open to public); scenic drive, with good crabbing and picnic spots on way (contact Tourist information for details). **Tourist information:** Old Railway Station, Carmody Pl.; (08) 9721 7922. **Accommodation:** 9 hotels, 8 motels, 3 B&B, 2 hostels, 5 cara./camp. parks. **See also:** The Southern Region.

Busselton   Pop. 8936

MAP REF. 367 D7, 369 F3, 374 B9, 376 C10
First settled by Europeans in the 1830s, and one of the oldest towns in WA, Busselton is a pleasant seaside town at the centre of a large rural district. Situated 228 km S of Perth, on the shores of Geographe Bay and the picturesque Vasse River, the town is a popular holiday destination. Inland are jarrah forests for the local timber industry, dairy and beef cattle farms, and vineyards. Fishing is important, particularly crayfish and salmon in season. **Of interest:** Prospect Villa (1855), Pries Ave, a two-storey colonial building (now motel). Opposite, Ballarat Engine, first steam locomotive in WA. St Mary's (1844), Peel Tce, oldest stone church in State. Villa Carlotta (1897), Adelaide St, boarding school for 50 years, now guest house. Jetty, on beachfront near Queen St, longest timber jetty (2 km) in Australia; partially destroyed by Cyclone Alby in 1978, still popular with anglers. Near jetty on beachfront: Oceanarium; Nautical Lady Entertainment Centre with its Jetty Point tower, nautical museum and small train which runs along the jetty. Old Court House Arts Centre, Queen St. In Peel St: Old Butter Factory Museum, on riverbank, displays old butter- and cheese-making equipment; Vasse River Parkland, with barbecue/picnic facilities. In Layman Rd: Wonnerup House (1859), a National Trust Museum and fine example of colonial Australian architecture furnished in period style; restored old school and teacher's house, built of local timber. Archery Park and Minigolf, Bussell Hwy. Bay has good sheltered beaches for swimming. Western coast ideal for

Western Wildflowers

Kangaroo paw, the floral emblem of Western Australia

The sandplains, swamps, flats, scrub and wood ands of south-western Australia light up with colour in spring as the 'wildflower State' puts on its brilliant display. The plains can become carpeted, almost overnight, with the gold of everlastings or feather flowers, or the red and pinks of boronia and leschenaultia. The banksia bushes throw up their red and yellow cylinders along the coast and in the woodlands, grevilleas spill their flowers down to the ground and orchids proliferate. Flowering gums on the south coast become a mass of red and the felty kangaroo paws invade the plains. Lilies, banksias, parrot bush, flame peas, feather flowers and native foxgloves – all are displayed in a magnificent abundance.

There are over 9000 named species and 2000 unnamed species of wildflowers in Western Australia, giving the State one of the richest floras in the world. Around 75 per cent of them are unique to the region, although they may have family connections with other plants of northern or eastern Australia. Isolation by the barrier of plain and desert that separates the west from the eastern States has caused plants on both sides to pursue their own evolution; some families of plants are unique to the west.

On even a short trip to Perth, visitors can see a wide variety of Western Australian wildflowers. At King's Park close to the city, wildflower species give a brilliant display between August and October. Visitors in any part of the south-west at that time will see wildflowers all around them. Often, however, it is in the State's national parks that the full beauty of massed wildflowers is best seen. Only 25 kilometres east of Perth on the Great Eastern Highway is **John Forrest National Park**, on the edge of the Darling Range escarpment. On these undulating hills and valleys the undergrowth of the jarrah forest is rich in flowering plants; red and green kangaroo paw, swamp river myrtle, blue leschenaultia and pink calytrix are the most common. Fifty kilometres north of Perth is **Yanchep National Park**, a place of coastal limestone and sandy plains, covered with wildflowers. There are many places further north that are worth visiting; one such is **Kalbarri National Park**, 670 kilometres north of Perth, at the mouth of the Murchison River. The park contains magnificent flowering trees and shrubs of banksia, grevillea and melaleuca, while the ground beneath is covered with many species, such as leschenaultia, twine rushes and sedges.

Prolific displays of wildflowers can also be found throughout the wheat belt, forests and sandplains of the south-west. Dryandra Woodland, a few kilometres from Narrogin in the south-west, has magnificent woodlands of wandoo and powderbark, with brown mallet and bush thickets. An important sanctuary for the mallee fowl and numbat, this forest contains a number of species of dryandra.

Another interesting area of Western Australia is **Stirling Range National Park**, 450 kilometres south of Perth and near the Porongurup Range. The Stirlings are very jagged peaks that rise above flat farmlands. The scenery is magnificent and wildflowers abound, many unique to the region. There are banksias here, as well as dryandra, cone bushes, cats paws and a number of mountain bells, which have red or pink flower heads. The bare granite domes and the boulders of the Porongurup Range tower over slopes of flowering trees such as *Banksia grandis* and creepers such as the native clematis.

There are many coastal parks around Albany. **Torndirrup National Park** is an area of coastal hills and cliffs, and such scenic features as the Gap, the Blowhole and the Natural Bridge. In the stunted, windswept coastal vegetation there are many wildflowers, including the endemic giant-coned *Banksia praemorsa* and the Western Australian Christmas tree with its brilliant orange flowers.

Twenty-five kilometres east of Albany is the peaceful and beautiful Two Peoples Bay Nature Reserve, which has thickets of mallee, banksia and peppermint, together with many flowering shrubs and plants. Along the coast west of Albany is **Walpole-Nornalup National Park**, where dense karri forest mingles with red tingle, jarrah, marri, casuarina and banksia trees, and many wildflowers including the kangaroo paw, the potato orchid and the babe-in-cradle orchid.

Although most wildflowers occur in the south-west of the State, northern areas also have displays peculiar to climatic changes and times of rainfall. While enjoying Western Australia's brilliant native flora, visitors should remember that wildflowers are protected under the State's *Native Flora Protection Act*.

For further information on national parks and wildflower display areas, contact the Western Australian Tourist Centre or the Department of Conservation and Land Management, 50 Hayman Rd (GPO Box 104), Como WA 6152; (08) 9334 0333. **See also:** National Parks for those parks indicated by bold type.

Coastline near Carnarvon

surfing. Jan.: Australia Day Yacht Regatta; Kidz Film Festival; Performing Arts Beach Festival. Mar.: Blue-water Classic (fishing); National Old Machinery Rally. Apr.: Heritage Week (at Woonerup House). Oct.: West Coast Golf Open. **In the area:** Woodcrafts; locally produced gourmet items; several protea nurseries. Scenic drive west for excellent views of rugged coast at Eagle Bay, 30 km; Sugar Loaf Rock, 35 km; Cape Naturaliste, 39 km. At Cape Naturaliste lighthouse, whale-watching platform (best time Oct.–Dec.) and information boards. Wildflower, scenic, canoe and 4WD tours; whale-watching cruises and flights (Oct.–Dec.); Augusta–Busselton Heritage Trail; details for all from Tourist information. Orchid farm at Vasse, 9 km W. Wildwood Pottery, 16 km W. Quindalup Fauna Park, 20 km W, has birds, fish, tropical butterflies and native mammals on display. Bannamah Wildlife Park; Country Life Farm with hayrides, boat rides and children's farm; both 26 km W. Over 30 wineries in Willyabrup Valley, 30 km SW, and around town of Margaret River, 47 km SW; most open for tastings and cellar-door sales, contact Tourist information. Whistle Stop, a miniature railway, on Vasse Hwy, 11 km SE. Bunyip Craft Centre, 7 km E. **Tourist information**: Civic Centre Complex, Southern Dr.; (08) 9752 1288. **Accommodation:** 4 hotels, 7 motels, 13 B&B, 1 hostel, 12 cara./camp. parks. **See also:** The Southern Region.

Caiguna   Pop. 12

MAP REF. 377 N8

Caiguna is the first stop for petrol and food after the long drive from Balladonia, 182 km W. This section of the Eyre Hwy is one of the longest straight stretches of sealed road in Australia. **In the area:** South of town, Nuytsland Nature Reserve, scenic area bounded by sheer cliffs fronting the Southern Ocean. **Tourist information:** John Eyre Motel; (08) 9039 3459. **Accommodation:** 1 motel, 1 cara./camp. park. **See also:** Crossing the Nullarbor.

Carnamah   Pop. 367

MAP REF. 376 C5

Carnamah is a small, typically Australian country town, 290 km N of Perth. Wheat and sheep are the local industries. **Of interest:** Historical Society Museum, McPherson St, displays old farm machinery reflecting agricultural heritage. Sept.: Agricultural Show. **In the area:** Several old goldmining and ghost towns 40–50 km E; area rich in minerals and popular with gemstone enthusiasts. MacPherson Homestead (1880), 1 km E, grounds open to the public, house open by appt. Water colour at Yarra Yarra Lakes, 2 km W, ranges in colour from red to green to blue; many varieties of migratory birds collect here; colourful wildflowers

in surrounding area in season. Lake Indoon, 61 km SW, for water-skiing. Tathra National Park, 50 km SW, renowned for variety of wildflowers in spring. **Tourist information:** Shire Offices, McPherson St; (08) 9951 1055. **Accommodation:** 1 hotel/motel, 1 cara./camp. park.

Carnarvon   Pop. 6901

MAP REF. 375 B8

Carnarvon, at the mouth of the Gascoyne River, 904 km N of Perth, is the commercial centre of the Gascoyne region. The district was seen in 1616 by Dirk Hartog. Another explorer, Willem de Vlamingh, landed at Shark Bay in 1697. Pioneers arrived in 1876; by the 1880s there were a number of European settlers in the region. Today, sheep, beef cattle and fishing are important industries, and the Gascoyne River has been tapped for irrigation for the extensive tropical fruit and vegetable plantations. The Overseas Telecommunications Commission earth station (no longer operating) is at nearby Browns Range. The USA National Aeronautics and Space Administration (NASA) operated here from 1964–74. Carnarvon has warm winters and takes on a tropical appearance when the bougainvilleas and hibiscus bloom. **Of interest:** The main street (c.1880s) was 40 m wide, built to enable camel trains to turn; it is now divided by a row of trees with centre parking and gardens. Jubilee Hall (1887), Francis St. Pioneer Park, Olivia Tce. Tropical Bird Park, Angelo St. Rotary Park, North West Coastal Hwy. Courtyard markets at civic centre, Robinson St, 1st Sat. each month. June: Seafood Festival. July: Carnarvon Festival; Fremantle–Carnarvon Yacht Race (even-numbered years). Aug.: Arts Festival. **In the area:** Excellent fishing for snapper or groper, game-fishing for marlin or sailfish; charter boats available. On Babbage Island, 5 km off Carnarvon, museum at lighthouse keeper's cottage. Prawning factory, 6 km off Binning Rd; tours in season, usually mid-Apr.–late Oct. (contact Tourist information). One Mile Jetty, 5 km NW, almost 1500 m long (partially closed to public). Pelican Point, 8 km NW, for picnics and swimming. Westoby Plantation, 4 km E, tours available. Mammoth 157-m diameter reflector ('the Big Dish'), 8 km E, offers

The Southern Region

Two Peoples Bay, east of Albany

The southern corner of Western Australia is a lush green land. Its gently rolling hills are crossed by rivers winding through deep-sided valleys. The soils are fertile and the farms prosperous. Along the coast there are beautiful bays, rugged coastline and the roaring Southern Ocean, and inland, majestic towering karri and jarrah forests. The countryside is dotted with orchards and many wildflowers in season; Western Australia is one of the richest areas of flora in the world.

Pinjarra, 84 kilometres south of Perth, is one of the State's oldest districts. It has interesting historic buildings and makes a good base for touring the surrounding area.

Near **Harvey** there is fine agricultural land and the undulating farms stretch to the foothills of the Darling Range. North-west of Harvey is Yalgorup National Park (one of only three sites in Western Australia with stromatolites), where the lakes attract a wide variety of birdlife.

The coast of the south-west is fascinating: an unusual mixture of craggy outcrops and promontories, sheltered bays with calm waters and beaches pounded by rolling surf. The length of the coast, together with the many rivers and estuaries, makes the south-west an angler's paradise. The Murray, Harvey and Brunswick rivers and their tributaries are only some of the streams annually stocked with trout.

The main port for the south-west, **Bunbury** rests on Geographe Bay looking out over the Indian Ocean. It is a perfect holiday town. One of the oldest towns in the State, **Busselton**, sited on the Vasse River, has a wealth of pioneer houses, many restored and open to the public.

Margaret River on the river of the same name, offers beaches, caves, magnificent scenery and world-class wineries. The **Leeuwin-Naturaliste National Park** combines a scenic rugged coast with magnificent wildflowers and the tall timbers of karri and jarrah forests. **Yallingup** is known for its excellent surf and spectacular limestone caves.

Bridgetown, **Donnybrook** and Greenbushes are small townships tucked away in green, hilly country and pretty apple orchards. Goldmining flourished briefly here at the turn of the century. **Manjimup** and **Pemberton** are world famous for the source of their timber, the karri and jarrah trees. Here some of the world's tallest trees reach straight up, often to 80 and 90 metres. The Pemberton, Scott, Warren and Brockman national parks are nearby, and were introduced to protect the unique environment.

The southern region has an important historical heritage. **Albany** was the first town in Western Australia, established two and a half years before the Swan River colony. Major Edmund Lockyer landed here in 1826 to claim the western half of the continent as British territory.

Albany is the unofficial capital of the area, and retains a charming English atmosphere from the colonial days. The town looks out over the magnificent blue waters of Princess Royal Harbour in King George Sound. There are numerous scenic drives around the coast to the Gap, the Natural Bridge and the Blowholes. There are also stretches of golden sand and secluded bays. The fishing is superb. **Denmark**, a holiday destination, lies on the banks of the tranquil Denmark River, and the little village of Nornalup nestles near the Frankland River. Near Nornalup is the awe-inspiring Valley of the Giants, best seen from the Treetop Walk which is 40 metres above the ground.

The vineyards around **Mount Barker** produce award-winning wines. Mount Barker itself is the gateway to the Stirling and Porongurup mountain ranges, both within the confines of national parks. The Porongurup Range has granite peaks dominating giant hardwood trees, and a maze of wildflowers and creepers. There are many easy climbs, rewarded by splendid views.

The high, jagged peaks of the Stirling Range (the highest is Bluff Knoll at 1073 metres) tower over virgin bushland. The peaks can sometimes be seen shrouded in mist, and on occasions even tipped with snow. There are more than 100 bird species in the **Stirling Range National Park** and native animals are plentiful. Look also for the beautiful wild orchids, Stirling banksia and mountain bells.

Small towns, including Tambellup with its colonial buildings, and thriving towns such as **Katanning**, **Kojonup**, Gnowangerup and Jerramungup are all surrounded by peaceful rural farmland.

For further information contact the tourist information centres listed for those towns indicated by bold type. **See also:** National Parks and A–Z listing for those national parks and towns indicated by bold type. **Map references:** for Margaret River, 369; for Albany region, 370.

Limestone caves at Yallingup

WESTERN AUSTRALIA

views of area from platform of dish. Rocky Pool, 55 km E along Gascoyne Rd, deep billabong ideal for swimming, also onshore picnic facilities. Munro's Banana Plantation, 10 km N via hwy and South River Rd, has fresh-picked fruit and vegetables for sale in season (tours available Sun.–Fri.). Department of Agriculture Research Station, 3 km from South River Rd turnoff (book at Tourist information). Bibbawarra artesian bore, 16 km N, where hot water surfaces at 70°C; picnic area nearby. Miaboolya Beach, 22 km N, has good fishing, crabbing and swimming. Blowholes, 70 km N, where water forced 20 m into air; about 1 km S, a superb sheltered beach with oysters on rocks, but beware of king waves and tides. Just north of blowholes, cairn commemorating loss of HMAS *Sydney* in 1942. A further 30 km N, excellent fishing at Cape Cuvier. **Tourist information:** Robinson St; (08) 9941 1146. **Accommodation:** 6 hotel/motels, 2 hostels, 1 B&B, 7 cara./camp. parks.

Cocklebiddy   Pop. 11

MAP REF. 377 O8

This tiny settlement is on the Eyre Hwy, between Madura and Caiguna, 310 km from the SA border. **In the area:** Cocklebiddy Cave, just north-west, for experienced speleologists only (directions at Wedgetail Inn). To the south, a dirt track leads to the Escarpment, for magnificent views of Southern Ocean; from here 4WD necessary to reach both Eyre Bird Observatory and Post Office Historical Society Museum in old telegraph station building (guided tours available, 24-hr notice required, contact Tourist information). **Tourist information:** Wedgetail Inn; (08) 9039 3462. **Accommodation:** 1 hotel/motel, 1 cara./camp. park (limited facilities). **See also:** Crossing the Nullarbor.

Collie   Pop. 7684

MAP REF. 374 D8, 376 C10

Collie, the centre of the State's only coal-producing region, plays an integral part in WA's development. Set in dense jarrah forest, 202 km S of Perth near the winding Collie River, the town has an abundance of attractive parks and gardens. There are fine views on the drive into Collie from the South Western Hwy. **Of interest:** In Throssell St: tourist coal mine, guided tours daily; Historical and Mining Museum, in old Roads Board buildings, displays history of area and of coal industry; Steam Locomotive Museum; old police station (1926); post office (1898); art gallery, at Shire Office, has collection of local art. Old court house, cnr Wittenoon and Pendleton sts. Impressive All Saints' Anglican Church, Venn St, built in Norman style. Soldiers Park, Steer St, on banks of Collie River, has shady trees and lawns, ideal for picnics. Suspension bridge over river, River Ave. Minninup Pool, off Mungalup Rd, set in bushland; wildflowers in season. Market at Westrail Reserve, Forrest St, 1st Sun. each month. **In the area:** Scenic drive to Collie River, 5 km W. Wellington Dam and Honeymoon Pool, 15 km W, in heart of Collie River Irrigation Scheme, popular attractions offering fishing, and bushwalking and grassy picnic spots on shore. Beautiful picnic area surrounds Harris Dam, 14 km N. Muja Power Station, 24 km SE (tours available, contact Tourist information). View Muja open-cut mines from viewing platform, 28 km SE. (*Muja* is Aboriginal word for bright yellow Christmas tree that grows in area.) **Tourist information:** Throssell St; (08) 9734 2051. **Accommodation:** 5 hotels, 1 hotel/motel, 2 motels, 1 B&B, 1 cara./camp. park.

Coolgardie   Pop. 1063

MAP REF. 376 I6

The old goldmining town of Coolgardie is 550 km east of Perth and 39 km SW of Kalgoorlie-Boulder. After Arthur Bayley and William Ford found alluvial gold at Fly Flat in 1892, Coolgardie grew to a boom town of 15 000 people, 23 hotels, 6 banks and 2 stock exchanges in just 10 years. The main street was wide enough for camel trains to turn, splendid public buildings were erected and ambitious plans were made. Sadly, the gold soon petered out. By 1985 there were only 700 people in the town; however, with an increase in tourism, the population of this pleasant town is increasing. **Of interest:** Series of historic markers placed around town, documenting historic points of interest; index to all markers located in Bayley St, next to Tourist information. Historic buildings in Bayley St include Goldfields Exhibition building (1898), most comprehensive prospecting museum in WA; post office (1898); old gaol; Denver City Hotel (1898), with handsome verandahs; Ben Prior's Open-air Museum, displays include wagons, horse- and camel-drawn vehicles. Railway Station (1896), Woodward St, now a museum with transport exhibition and display of famous Varischetti mine rescue. Warden Finnerty's house (1895), McKenzie St, striking example of early Australian architecture and furnishings. Adjacent, C.Y. O'Connor Dedication, a fountain and water course in memory of O'Connor who masterminded the Coolgardie Water Scheme. St Anthony's Convent, Lindsay St, now boarding school. Gaol Tree, Hunt St, used for restraining prisoners in early gold-rush days. Lions Bicentennial Lookout, near southern end of Hunt St. Lindsay's Pit Lookout, over open-cut gold mine; Ford St. Sept.: Coolgardie Day; Camel Races. **In the area:** Eastern Goldfields Heritage Trail, details from Tourist information. Cemetery, 1 km W, evokes harsh early days of gold rush. Camel farm, 4 km W. Kurrawang Emu Farm, 20 km E. **Tourist information:** Bayley St; (08) 9026 6090. **Accommodation:** 1 hotel, 3 motels, 2 cara./camp. parks. **See also:** The Goldfields.

Coral Bay   Pop. 726

MAP REF. 375 B5

The Ningaloo Coral Reef system approaches the shore at Coral Bay, 150 km S of Exmouth. Unspoilt expanses of white beaches offer good swimming, snorkelling, boating and fishing. **In the area:** Ningaloo Marine Park, just off beach. Good views of reef from glass-bottomed boats. Diving equipment hire available. Numerous shipwreck sites at Pt Cloates, 8 km N; also ruins of Norwegian Bay whaling station (1915). **Tourist information:** Bayview Holiday Village, Robinson St; (08) 9942 5932. **Accommodation:** 1 hotel/motel, 2 cara./camp. parks.

Corrigin   Pop. 725

MAP REF. 374 H5, 376 E8

Rich farming country surrounds Corrigin, 230 km SE of Perth. **Of interest:** In Kunjin St: pioneer museum; miniature railway, inquire at Tourist information. RSL monument, Gayfer St, is a Turkish mountain gun from Gallipoli. Art and craft shop, Walton St. Sept.: Agricultural Show. **In the area:** Good views from observation tower, 3 km W, on Wildflower Scenic Drive, (well signposted). Dog cemetery, 5 km W. Kunjin emu and

The Nullarbor cliffs, south of Cocklebiddy

alpaca farm, 18 km W. Yealering Lake and picnic ground, 40 km SW. Gorge Rock, 20 km SE, ideal for picnics. **Tourist information:** Shire Offices, Lynch St; (08) 9063 2203. **Accommodation:** 1 hotel, 1 motel, 1 cara./camp. park.

Cossack   Pop. 1, 1 dog & 1 galah

MAP REF. 375 G1, 378 A1

Cossack, once called Tien Tsin, has had a chequered history. Located at the mouth of the Harding River, it was the first port in the north-west and serviced the nearby town of Roebourne, as well as being the centre of a gold rush and the location for a turtle-product factory. Pearling in WA began at Cossack before moving to Broome in the 1890s. Cossack was also a centre for the Pilbara's developing pastoral and mining industries. Today it is a ghost town, but almost completely restored. **Of interest:** Historic buildings (all open Apr.–Christmas): in Pearl St, court house (now museum), bond store (now tea-room), and post and telegraph office; in Perseverance St, police quarters (budget accommodation all year). Cemetery, off Perseverance St, has headstones reflecting town's colourful past. Fishing, crabbing and swimming; boat hire available. June: Fair and Yachting Regatta. Sept.: Art Awards; Art Ball. **Tourist information:** Roebourne Tourist Bureau, Queen St, Roebourne; (08) 9182 1060. **Accommodation:** 1 hostel. **See also:** The Hamersley Range.

Cranbrook   Pop. 306

MAP REF. 371 L6, 374 H11, 376 E11

In the 1800s sandalwood was exported from Cranbrook to China, where it was used as incense. Today this attractive town near the foothills of the Stirling Range, 320 km SE of Perth, is a sheep and wheat centre. Sept.: Wildflower Show. Nov.: Art Show. **In the area:** Frankland Heritage Trail, details from Tourist information. Gateway to Stirling Arch, Salt River Rd, a picnic area with native garden. Sukey Hill Lookout, 5 km E off Salt River Rd. Stirling Range National Park, 15 km SE. High-quality table wines produced in Frankland district, 50 km W. Lake Poorrarecup, 55 km SW, for swimming and water skiing; good picnic facilities, playground and camping on foreshore. **Tourist information:** Shire Offices, Gathorne St; (08) 9826 1008. **Accommodation:** 1 hotel, 1 B&B, 1 cara./camp. park.

Cue   Pop. 394

MAP REF. 375 H13, 376 E1, 378 B13

Cue, 650 km NE of Perth on the Great Northern Hwy, grew up as a boom town, an important centre for the Murchison goldfields. Today its well-kept stone buildings are a testimony to those frenzied days. **Of interest:** National Trust-classified buildings in Austin St: bandstand built over well, water from which was said to have started a typhoid epidemic; impressive government offices. Former Masonic Lodge (1899), Dowley St, built largely of corrugated iron. **In the area:** Gemstone fossicking; heritage trail; a number of Aboriginal art sites – contact Tourist information for details. Day Dawn, 5 km W, original town site on gold reef; town disappeared when reef died out in 1930s, mine manager's house is last remaining building; the new operating open-cut mine can be viewed from here. Big Bell, 30 km W, large mine opened in 1989 (access restricted). Walga Rock, 50 km W, a monolith 1.5 km long and 5 km around base (second largest in Australia) with largest gallery of Aboriginal rock paintings in WA (details from Tourist information). Wilgie Mia Red Ochre Mine, 64 km NW, mined by Aborigines 30 000 years ago. **Tourist information:** Apr.–Oct.: Robinson St, (08) 9963 1216; Nov.–May: Shell Garage, Northern Hwy, (099) 63 1051. **Accommodation:** 2 hotels, 1 cara./ camp. park.

Dampier   Pop. 1810

MAP REF. 375 G1

A model town with modern facilities, Dampier lies on King Bay, facing the unique islands of the Dampier Archipelago. Hamersley Iron Pty Ltd established the town as a port for ore mined from two of the world's richest iron-ore deposits, Tom Price and Paraburdoo. The town's deepwater port with its export facilities loads over 50 million tonnes of ore yearly. Salt is harvested from ponds near the port. **Of interest:** Jurat Reserve, Haig Close. Tours of the Hamersley Iron port facility available Mon.–Fri. (bookings (08) 9144 4600). Boating, sailing, fishing, diving, windsurfing and swimming. Game-fishing, charter boat hire; contact Tourist information for details. Aug.: Game-fishing Classic. **In the area:** North West Shelf Gas Project on Burrup Peninsula 8 km NW, has Visitors Centre (open weekdays, except public holidays). Aboriginal rock carvings on Burrup Peninsula, details from Tourist information. Hearsons Cove, 6 km S, popular tidal swimming beach and picnic area. Pilbara Railway Historical Society Museum, 10 km SE, home of *Pendennis Castle* steam locomotive (open Sun.). **Tourist information:** 4548 Karratha Rd, Karratha; (08) 9144 4600. **Accommodation:** 2 motels, 1 cara./camp. park. **See also:** The Hamersley Range.

National Parks

Thistle Cove, one of many magnificent bays protected by Cape Le Grand National Park

The national parks of Western Australia are tourist attractions in themselves: their spectacular displays of wildflowers create a paradise for photographers and a wonderland for bushwalkers and campers. Western Australia has more than 9000 named species and 2000 unnamed species of wildflowers, growing undisturbed in their natural surroundings. One quarter of these species cannot be found anywhere else and they lure admirers from all over the world. The best months to see them are from August to October. This is also the best time for camping trips and bushwalking.

Around Perth

There are many national parks around Perth well worth a visit. At **Nambung National Park**, 230 kilometres north of Perth on the coast, unusual rock formations are to be found. Here a moonscape of coloured quartz is studded with fantastic limestone pillars ranging in size from stony 'twigs' to 4 metre high columns. This is the unique Pinnacle Desert, a favourite subject for photographers. **Yanchep National Park**, about 50 kilometres north of Perth on a belt of coastal limestone, has forests of massive tuart trees. Islands on Loch McNess, within the park, are waterfowl sanctuaries. Yanchep is also famed for its underground limestone caves and spring wildflowers.

Some 80 kilometres north-east of Perth is **Avon Valley National Park**; its most popular attractions are upland forests and river valleys, as well as beautiful wildflowers in season. The highest point in the park is Bald Hill, which provides panoramic views of the Avon River. After winter rains, a tributary of the Avon, Emu Spring Brook, spills 30 metres down in a spectacular waterfall.

A cluster of national parks to the east of Perth includes **John Forrest National Park**, which was Western Australia's first proclaimed national park. With the Darling Escarpment within its boundaries, the park features granite outcrops, dams and waterfalls, creeks and rock pools. Other nearby national parks are **Kalamunda**, **Greenmount**, **Gooseberry Hill** and **Lesmurdie Falls**, all within 20–25 kilometres of Perth. The Bibbulmun Track, a walk trail that links Forest, east of Perth, to the area once occupied by the Bibbulmun people of the south coast, begins its 650-kilometre route in Kalamunda National Park.

Proclaimed as the State's first flora and fauna reserve in 1894, **Serpentine National Park** is about 60 kilometres south of Perth and a firm favourite of day trippers who picnic at the falls area in the park. Jarrah and marri forests, and wildflowers in spring, are some of the park's attractions.

In the south of the State

Leeuwin-Naturaliste National Park extends along the rugged south-west coast. There are over 100 limestone caves in the area, some containing fossils of marsupials, no longer found on the mainland. The park is home to rare ospreys and rufous bristlebirds, as well as the more common sea birds. Whales can occasionally be seen offshore.

Along the lower south-west coast of the State is **Walpole-Nornalup National Park**, 15 861 hectares of wilderness in which creeks gurgle under tall eucalypts, rivers meander between forested hills and inlets rich in fish create a haven for anglers and boating enthusiasts. A network of roads and walking tracks, through forests of karri and tingle, attracts bushwalkers and birdwatchers.

About 100 kilometres east is **West Cape Howe National Park**, the spectacular coastline of which includes the gabbro cliffs of West Cape Howe and the granite of Torbay Heads, fronting the cold waters of the Southern Ocean. Extensive coastal heath, swamps, lakes and karri forest cover the inland area, and the park is popular with anglers, bushwalkers, rock climbers and hang-gliders.

The South Western Highway bisects **Shannon National Park**, 358 kilometres south of Perth. Within the park is the former timber-milling town site of Shannon. The remainder of the park consists of towering karri and jarrah forests, surrounding the Shannon River.

Stirling Range National Park, 450 kilometres south-east of Perth, is one of Australia's outstanding reserves. Surrounded by a flat, sandy plain, the Stirling Range rises abruptly to over 1000 metres, its jagged peaks veiled in swirling mists. The cool, humid environment created by these low clouds contributes to the survival of 1000 flowering plant

Purnululu National Park in the north of the State

species, some of which, like the mountain bells, are found nowhere else in the world.

Brilliant displays of wildflowers are also a feature of the nearby **Porongurup National Park**, where the granite domes of the Porongurup Ranges are clothed in a forest of karri trees.

Spectacular coastal scenery is the main attraction of the **Torndirrup National Park** on the Flinders Peninsula, 460 kilometres south of Perth. Also on the south coast are other outstanding parks, including **Cape Le Grand National Park**, with its magnificent bays and beaches, protected by granite headlands, located 40 kilometres east of Esperance.

Two other parks are near Esperance, both to the west of the town. **Stokes National Park** hugs the coastline around Stokes Inlet and features long sandy beaches and rocky headlands backed by sand dunes and low hills. Stokes Inlet and its associated lakes support a rich variety of wildlife. Inland from Stokes lies **Peak Charles National Park**. A walk to the ridge of this ancient granite peak allows sweeping views of its companion, Peak Eleanora, and over the dry sandplain heaths and salt-lake systems of the surrounding country.

One of the loveliest sections of the south coast of Western Australia is **Fitzgerald River National Park**, through which the rugged Barren Range (named by Matthew Flinders) stretches from west to east. The park's 330 000 hectares comprise gently undulating sandplains, river valleys, precipitous cliff edges, narrow gorges, and beaches for swimming and rock fishing. The park contains many rare species of flora and fauna.

In the north of the State

North of Geraldton, the visitor will discover the wild beauty of ancient landscapes, unsurpassed at **Kalbarri National Park**. Its 183 000 hectares encompass the lower reaches of the Murchison River, which winds its way through spectacular gorges to the Indian Ocean. Sea cliffs in layers of multi-coloured sandstone loom over the crashing white foam at Red Bluff.

Cape Range National Park, near Exmouth, is cut by deep gorges but arid for most of the year, Yardie Creek being the only permanent water. Vegetation is sparse, except around the creek and after cyclonic storms have flooded the area. Kangaroos are common and fairly tame, and there are over 80 species of reptiles in the park.

In the Pilbara, 1400 kilometres north of Perth, is **Karijini National Park**, in the Hamersley Range and part of a massive block of weathered rock over 450

kilometres long. Within this huge, spectacular park are many well-known gorges, including Dales Gorge, its strata in horizontal stripes of blue, mauve, red and brown dating back almost 2000 million years. A trail in the park winds up to Mt Bruce, the State's second highest point. Interpretive displays along the trail provide an insight into the Aboriginal heritage, as well as the flora and fauna, of the area. Further north, still in the Pilbara, **Millstream-Chichester National Park** encompasses almost 200 000 hectares of clay tablelands and sediment-capped basalt ranges. At Millstream, on the Fortescue River, natural freshwater springs have created an oasis in arid country. In contrast, there are the Chichester Ranges: rolling hills, hummocks of spinifex, white-barked snappy gums on the uplands, and pale coolibahs along the usually dry watercourses.

In the far north of Western Australia are the national parks of the Kimberley region. The largest of these parks, **Geikie Gorge**, has an area of 3136 hectares and is 20 kilometres north-east of Fitzroy Crossing. The multi-coloured cliffs are reflected in the placid waters of the Fitzroy River, which flows through the gorge. The area is too rugged for extensive walking, but organised boat trips go up the river through the gorge, enabling visitors to see one of Australia's most beautiful waterways.

Other nearby national parks are **Windjana Gorge** and **Tunnel Creek**, both north-west of Geikie Gorge. Tunnel Creek is a permanent watercourse that

flows underground for 750 metres. It is possible to walk through the high, wide tunnel to a small river beach beyond; some deep wading may be necessary, and carry a torch.

South of Lake Argyle is the spectacular **Purnululu National Park**, with its tiger-striped, beehive-shaped domes, deep gullies and unique palms. Because of the fragility of internal roads in wet conditions, this park is closed from approximately 1 January to 1 April.

Mirima National Park, only 2.5 kilometres east of Kununurra, has features typical of the Kimberley: banded sandstone outcrops similar to those of the Bungle Bungle massif, boab trees, red soil dotted with eucalypts, and black kites circling overhead. Aboriginal rock paintings are also a feature of the park.

For further information on Western Australia's national parks, contact the Department of Conservation and Land Management, 50 Hayman Rd (GPO Box 104), Como, WA 6152; (08) 9334 0333. Web site address http://www.calm.wa.gov.au

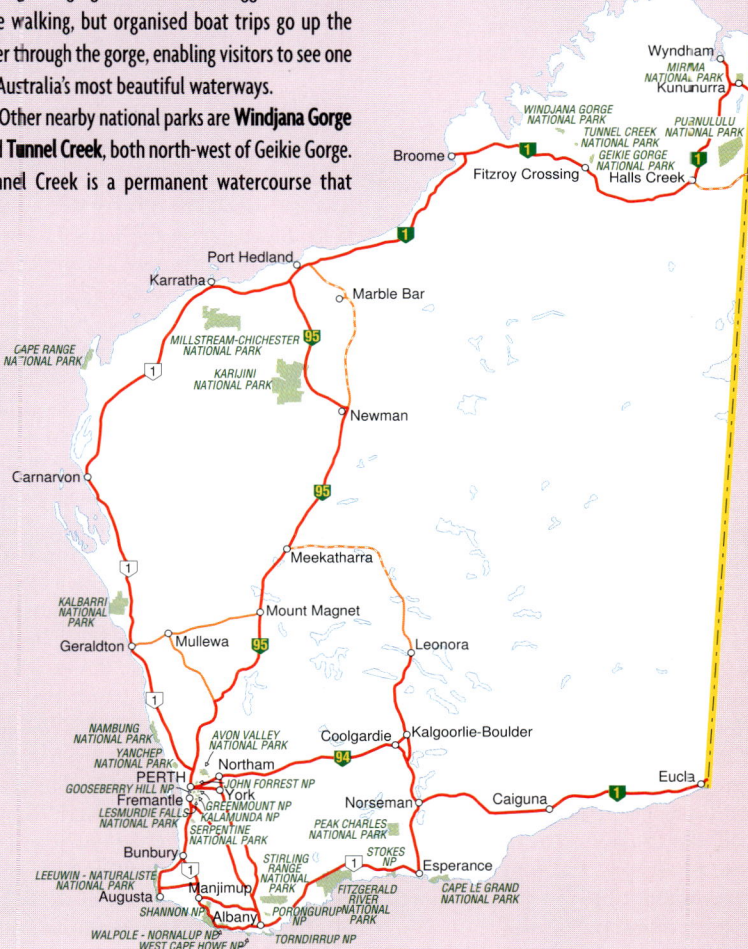

WESTERN AUSTRALIA

Denham
Pop. 943

MAP REF. 375 B10

Two peninsulas form the geographical feature of Shark Bay, 833 km from Perth. Denham is the most westerly town in Australia and the main centre for the Shark Bay region. Dirk Hartog, the Dutch navigator, landed on an island at the entrance to Shark Bay in 1616. Pearling developed as the main industry and the population was a mixture of Malays, Chinese and Europeans. Until recently, Shark Bay was known only for its excellent fishing, but today it is renowned for the wild dolphins, which come inshore to be fed at nearby Monkey Mia. **Of interest:** Shark Bay Fisheries, Dampier Rd (check opening times at Tourist information). Pioneer Park, Hughes St. **In the area:** Monkey Mia, 26 km NE, where wild dolphins come inshore to be fed; local rangers and information centre provide information on these wonderful animals. On Monkey Mia Rd, Aquaria aquatic wildlife park. Shark Bay Heritage Trail, contact Tourist information. Town Bluff, an interesting guided walk south along beaches. Catamarans MV *Hartog Explorer* and *Sea Eagle* offer variety of cruises. Safaris and coach tours available. Boat trips (weekends), also charter flights, to historic Dirk Hartog Island (homestead and backpackers' accommodation available on island). Francois Peron National Park, 7 km N, includes Peron Homestead with its famous 'hot tub' containing hot artesian water. Eagle Bluff, 20 km S, habitat of sea eagle. Nanga Bay Resort, 50 km S, huge sheep station with motel units, restaurant, tourist facilities, sailboards, dinghy hire on beach and charter fishing. Shell Beach, 50 km S, 110-km stretch of unique Australian coastline comprising countless tiny shells. Striking scenery at Zuytdorp Cliffs, 160 km S and extending further south to Kalbarri (4WD access only). On shores of Hamelin Pool, 100 km SE: historic displays in Flint Cliff Telegraph Station and Post Office Museum (1894); stromatolites ('living rocks') in nature reserve. Spectacular coastal scenery at Steep Point, westernmost point on mainland (260 km W by road, 4WD only). **Tourist information:** 83 Knight Tce; (08) 9948 1253. **Accommodation:** 2 resorts, 1 hotel/motel, 4 cara./camp. parks.

Denmark
Pop. 1586

MAP REF. 371 K12, 374 G13, 376 E12

The attractive 100-year-old coastal town of Denmark, 54 km W of Albany, is at the foot of Mt Shadforth, overlooking the tranquil Denmark River. The town offers good fishing, sandy white beaches and scenic drives through farming country and karri forests. The dense hardwood forests supply timber for local mills. **Of interest:** Kurrabup Aboriginal Art Gallery, McLeod Rd. Michael Cartwright Art Studio, McNabb Rd. In Mitchell St: Historical Museum; Cottage Industries Shop. Denmark Gallery, Strickland St. Alpaca stud and tourist farm, Scotsdale Rd. Jassi Skincraft, Glenrowan Rd, off Mt Shadforth Scenic Drive. In Holling Rd, Berridge and Thornton parks, both along riverbank, offer shaded picnic areas. Craft and antique gallery at Old Butter Factory, North St. Mt Shadforth Lookout, top of Mohr Dr., for magnificent views. Market days, popular craft market with entertainment held on the banks of the river in Jan., Easter and Dec. (contact Tourist information for dates). Jan.: Pantomime. **In the area:** Scotsdale Rd–McLeod Rd Tourist Drive; Mokare and Wilson Inlet Heritage Trail; details from Tourist information. Twelve wineries in Denmark-Mount Barker-Albany region, 15 km E. Meelia Strawberry Farm; Eden Gate Blueberry Farm; both 25 km E. Jonathan Hook Ceramics, Lantzke Rd, 5 km NW. Mt Romance Emu Farm, 40 km NW, has showroom for emu-oil products. Wildflower Farm, 6 km W. Tinglewood Wines, 8 km W. Wynella Living Museum, 15 km W. Bartholomew's Meadery, 20 km W. Spiral Studio Pottery, 25 km W. Parry's Beach, 25 km W, for fishing (salmon in season). Majestic Merino Wool Craft Shop, 38 km W. Misty Creek Marron Farm, 40 km W. Valley of the Giants, 53 km W, massive karri and tingle trees best seen from Tree Top Walk. Boating, fishing, bushwalking and scenic drives around Nornalup, 50 km W, and Walpole, 66 km W, adjacent to Walpole-Nornalup National Park. Lookout from top of Monkey Rock, 10 km SW. Sheltered swimming at Greens Pool and William Bay at William Bay National Park, 17 km SW. Ocean Beach, 8 km S, for good surfing. **Tourist information:** Strickland St; (08) 9848 2055. **Accommodation:** 2 hotel/motels, 1 motel, 2 B&B, 4 cara./camp. parks. **See also:** The Southern Region.

Derby
Pop. 3022

MAP REF. 372 B9, 381 J7

Derby is an administrative centre for several Aboriginal communities and a hinterland rich in pastoral and mineral wealth. Located near King Sound, 223 km NE of Broome, the town is an ideal base for exploring the outback regions of the Kimberley. Roads have been greatly improved, including the Gibb River Rd, spanning the 647 km from Derby to the junction of the Great Northern Hwy between Wyndham and Kununurra. However, as rain usually closes this road and many others in the area between Nov.-Mar., check local conditions before setting out on any excursion. **Of interest:** In Loch St: Botanic Gardens; Old Derby Gaol; Wharfinger House museum, with photographic display. In Clarendon St: Kimberley School of the Air; Royal Flying Doctor Service. Ngunga Craft Shop, Stanley St. Derby Wharf, good place to see the large difference in water level between high and low tides. Market, Clarendon St, each Sat., May–Sept. July: Country Music Festival; Boab Festival (rodeo, mardi gras, mud football). Dec.: Boxing Day Sports. **In the area:** Charter boats to various locations including Buccaneer Archipelago and Walcott Inlet. Charter flights over Kimberley coast and Cockatoo and Koolan islands. Pigeon Heritage Trail, from Derby to Windjana Gorge and Tunnel Creek National Park (details from Tourist information). Prison Tree, 7 km S, boab (or baobab) tree reputedly used as prison in early days. Located close by, Myall's Bore, a 120-m-long cattle trough. Fitzroy River empties into King Sound, 48 km S. Tours available to: spectacular Windjana Gorge, 145 km E in Windjana Gorge National Park; remarkable Tunnel Creek in Tunnel Creek National Park, 184 km E, where colonies of flying foxes can be seen if you wade through tunnel with torch; also Pigeon's Cave, hideout of Aboriginal outlaw active in 1890s. King Leopold Ranges, 200 km E. Sir John Gorge, 350 km E (4WD access only). Lennard Gorge, 190 km NE (4WD recommended). Barnett River Gorge, 340 km NE (4WD recommended). Mitchell Plateau, 580 km NE

William Bay, south-west of Denmark

via Gibb River Rd and Kalumburu Rd, features spectacular Mitchell Falls, King Edward River and Surveyor's Pool; in this remote region, visitors must be entirely self-sufficient (read section on Outback Motoring before departure). **Tourist information:** 1 Clarendon St; (08) 9191 1426. **Accommodation:** 3 hotels, 1 hostel, 1 cara./camp. park. **See also:** The Kimberley.

Dongara   Pop. 1677

MAP REF. 376 B4

Dongara and the nearby town of Port Denison are quiet towns on the coast 359 km N of Perth. Dongara has beaches, reef-enclosed bays and an abundance of delicious rock lobster. There is good fishing in the waters around Port Denison. **Of interest:** Several historic buildings in Waldeck St: Anglican rectory (1882) and church (1884); old police station (1870); Royal Steam Flour Mill (1894). Russ Cottage (1870), Point Leander Dr. Main street, Moreton Tce, shaded by huge 90-year-old Moreton Bay fig trees. In cemetery, Dodd St, headstones date from 1874. Heritage Trail from Old Mill to historic Priory Lodge, brochure from Tourist information. Easter: Horse Races; Market at old police station, Easter Sat. Nov.: Blessing of the Fleet. **In the area:** Fisherman's Lookout, near Leander Point, Port Denison, for panoramic views of harbour. At Eneabba, 81 km SE, mineral sand mining with large concentrations of rutile.

Holiday towns south-west of Eneabba: Leeman, 38 km, and Green Head, 50 km. Western Flora Caravan Park, 60 km S, noted for its spring wildflowers in bushland and river setting. **Tourist information:** Old Police Station Building, 5 Waldeck St; (08) 9927 1404. **Accommodation:** 1 hotel/motel, 1 motel, 1 hostel, 5 cara./camp. parks.

Donnybrook   Pop. 1570

MAP REF. 367 H6, 374 C8, 376 C10

The township of Donnybrook, the home of the Granny Smith apple, is at the heart of the oldest apple-growing area in WA, 210 km S of Perth. Gold was found here in 1897, but mined for only four years. Donnybrook stone has been used in construction State-wide. **Of interest:** On South Western Hwy, Anchor and Hope Inn (1865), once staging post for mail coaches. Rotary Lookout, Trigwell St East. Arboretum, junction Irishtown Rd and South Western Hwy. Trigwell Place, near river at southern end of town on South Western Hwy, has picnic/barbecue facilities and playground. Easter: Apple Festival. **In the area:** Scenic drives, details from Tourist information. Glen Mervyn Dam, 30 km NE, onshore picnic/barbecue facilities. Rosedeane Tourist Farm, 12 km SE at Lowden. At Balingup, 30 km SE: Old Cheese Factory, now art and craft centre; Tinderbox, sells herbs and herbal remedies; Birdwood Park Fruit Winery; further 2 km, Golden Valley Tree Park. **Tourist**

information: 'Old' Railway Station, South Western Hwy; (08) 9731 1720. **Accommodation:** 2 hotels, 1 motel, 2 B&B, 2 hostels, 1 cara./camp. park. **See also:** The Southern Region.

Dumbleyung   Pop. 292

MAP REF. 374 H8, 376 E10

Dumbleyung lies in the central south of WA, 217 km E of Bunbury and 224 km N of Albany. **Of interest:** Craft and Tourist Shop, Absolon St. **In the area:** Historic Schools heritage trails and scenic drives, details from Tourist information. Lake Dumbleyung, 10 km W via Rollands–Lake King Hwy, here Donald Campbell established new world water-speed record in 1964; lake area is ideal for swimming, boating and birdwatching. At Kukerin, 39 km E: Wheatbelt Wildflower Drive, includes Tarin Rock Nature Reserve; Tracmach Vintage Fair held in Sept.-Oct. **Tourist information:** Shire Offices, Harvey St; (08) 9863 4012. **Accommodation:** 1 hotel, 1 cara./camp. park.

Dunsborough   Pop. 656

MAP REF. 367 C7, 369 C2, 374 B9, 376 B10

Dunsborough is a quiet town on Geographe Bay, west of Busselton, popular because of its beaches. **Of interest:** Hutchings Antique Museum, Newbury Rd. For local art: Dunsborough Gallery, Naturaliste Tce; Cyrillean Gallery, Dunn Bay Rd. Bush Cottage Crafts, Commonage Rd. In Wildwood Rd: Moonshine Brewery; Rivendell Gardens. Market at Dunsborough Hall, cnr Gibney St and Gifford Rd, 2nd Sat. each month. Nov.: Down South Dive Classic. **In the area:** Good beaches: Meelup, 5 km N; Eagle Bay, 8 km N; Bunker Bay, 12 km NW. Whale-watching boat charters, Sept.–Dec.; scuba diving, snorkelling and canoeing; 4WD, wildflower, winery, craft and Pemberton tours available; details from Tourist information. Bannamah Wildlife Park, 2 km W. Torpedo Rock, 10 km W. Several wineries situated in the south-west; contact Tourist information for details. Sugarloaf Rock, 12 km NW. Cape Naturaliste Lighthouse and Museum, 13 km NW (closed Mon.); several walking tracks in area. **Tourist information:** Shop 3, Naturaliste Tce; (08) 9755 3299. **Accommodation:** 1 hotel, 3 B&B, 1 hostel, 2 cara./camp. parks.

Round House, Fremantle, Western Australia's oldest building

WESTERN AUSTRALIA

Dwellingup
Pop. 383

MAP REF. 366 D11, 374 D6, 376 C9

This small town, 24 km SE of Pinjarra and 109 km from Perth, was rebuilt after being destroyed in the 1961 bushfire. The road into town offers panoramic views of the Indian Ocean and Peel Inlet. The impressive jarrah forests nearby supply the local timber mill. Bauxite is mined in the area. **Of interest:** In Marrinup St: country-style meals in Community Hotel; photographic exhibition at Tourist information. Forest Heritage Centre, Acacia Rd, has fascinating timber-related exhibits, tree-tops walk, forest trails and fine wood products. Forest Ranger Tour, a steam-train ride operated by Hotham Valley Tourist Railway between Perth and Dwellingup, and return (operates May–Oct.) Etmilyn Forest Tramway, old-style steam train from railway station into jarrah forest; check times. Feb.: Log Chop Day. **In the area:** Scarp Lookout, 7 km S; further 3 km, Scarp Pool, a popular recreational area. Lane Pool Reserve, 10 km S, large recreational area in jarrah forest. Loop walk, starts 3 km SW and passes scenic Marrinup Falls. Oakly Dam and Falls, located 7 km SW. **Tourist information:** Marrinup St; (08) 9538 1108. **Accommodation:** 1 hotel, 1 B&B.

Esperance
Pop. 7066

MAP REF. 377 J10

Wide sandy beaches, scenic coastline and the offshore islands of the Recherche Archipelago are all attractions near Esperance, on the south coast of WA. The town, 720 km from Perth via Wagin, is the port and service centre for the productive agricultural and pastoral hinterland. In 1863, the first permanent European settlers came to this area. The town boomed during the 1890s as a port for the goldfields. From the 1950s, when scientists realised that the heath plains could become fertile pasture and farming country, the town's development began in earnest. **Of interest:** Municipal Museum, James St, displays old machinery, furniture and farm equipment; also display of Skylab, which fell to earth over Esperance in 1979. Public Library, Windich St, has collection of books on history of Esperance. Art and craft centre at Old Cannery, Norseman Rd. Mermaid Marine Leather, Wood St, produces and sells fine fashion leathers from discarded fish skins. Charter boats and dive instruction at Esperance Diving Academy, 56 The Esplanade. Fishing and seal watching from Tanker Jetty. Five-km waterfront walk and cycle pathway. Beach-fishing excursions, motorcycle tours and horseriding available. Jan.: Sailboard Classic. Feb.: Offshore Angling Classic. Oct.: Agricultural Show. Dec.-Jan.: Turf Racing. **In the area:** Great Ocean Dr., 39-km loop road along spectacular coastline; passes Windfarms, supplier of 17 per cent of town's electricity, Salmon Beach (5 km W), Twilight Cove (12 km W) and Ten Mile Lagoon (16 km W); map available from Tourist information. Whale watching (June–Nov.) as Southern Right whales visit coastal bays and protected waters in area to calve. Rotary Lookout, or Wireless Hill, 2 km W, for panoramic views of bay, town and Recherche Archipelago. Pink Lake, 5 km W, a pink saltwater lake. Twilight Cove, 12 km W, a sheltered swimming beach. Views of bay and islands from Observatory Point and Lookout, 17 km W. Monjingup Lake Reserve, 20 km W. Dalyup River Wines 42 km W (open weekends and public holidays). Recherche Archipelago (Bay of Isles), 105 small unspoiled islands provide haven for seals and sea lions. Launch cruises (3½ hours) around Gull, Button, Charlie, Woody and other islands (available daily); landing permitted only on Woody Island. Full-day cruises to Woody Island, island developed as tourist attraction (overnight camping facilities). Cape Le Grand National Park, 56 km E, features spectacular coastline, attractive beaches (Lucky Bay, Hellfire Bay and Thistle Cove), scenic walks and beautiful wildflowers in spring for which the region is famous; also features Whistling Rock, a rock shaped by the elements that 'whistles' when certain winds blow, and magnificent view from Frenchmans Peak. Cape Arid National Park, 120 km E, for fishing and camping; 4WD routes. Helms Arboretum, 15 km N. Telegraph Farm, 21 km N on South Coast Hwy, has proteas, deer, buffalo and native animals (farm tours available). Speddingup Wildflower Sanctuary, 35 km N, offers guided walks through magnificent wildflowers in season. **Tourist information:** Museum Village, Dempster St; (08) 9071 2330. **Accommodation:** 3 hotels, 11 motels, 2 B&B, 2 hostels, 7 cara./camp. parks. **See also:** Crossing the Nullarbor.

Eucla
Pop. 30

MAP REF. 310 A8, 377 R7

Eucla is just 12 km from the WA-SA border, on the Eyre Hwy. There is a quarantine checkpoint for westbound travellers at the border; visitors should ensure they are not carrying fruit, vegetables, honey, used fruit and produce containers, plants or seeds. **Of interest:** Local history museum at motel. May: Golf Day. Oct.: Eucla Shoot. **In the area:** Bureau of Meteorology Weather Station, 1 km S. Cross on escarpment overlooking ocean and sand-covered ruins of old telegraph station and former town site, 5 km S, dedicated to all Eyre Hwy travellers; cross is illuminated at night. Highway westward from Eucla descends to coastal plain via Eucla Pass. Midway down Pass (about 200 m), track to left leads to old town site and ruins among sand dunes. Nine-hole golf course, 7 km N. Weebubby Cave, 12 km NW; for experienced cavers only. **Tourist information:** Motor Hotel; (08) 9039 3468 **Accommodation:** 1 hotel/motel, 1 motel, 1 cara./camp. park. **See also:** Crossing the Nullarbor.

Exmouth   Pop. 3128

MAP REF. 375 C3

Exmouth is one of the newest towns in Australia and was founded in 1967 as a support town for the US Naval Communications station, which is the main source of employment in the area. Excellent year-round fishing and nearby beaches have made Exmouth a major tourist destination. The town is situated on the north-eastern side of North West Cape, which is the nearest point in Australia to the continental shelf, so there is an abundance of fish and other marine life in the surrounding waters. **Of interest:** Ocean Exhibits Museum, Pellew St. Ningaloo Impressions Gallery and Studio, Eurayle St. Apr.: Billfish Bonanza. July: Exmo week; Arts and Crafts Show. Nov.: Gamex (world-class game-fishing). **In the area:** Turtle-nesting, Nov.–Jan.; coral-spawning during Mar.; boat cruises and air flights available Mar.–June to view whale sharks; humpback whales can be seen Sept.–Nov. from lighthouse, 17 km N, also regular whale-watching boat tours; snorkellers can swim with manta rays if rays located by cruise boats. Swimming, snorkelling and fishing; coral-viewing boat cruises; safari tours of Cape; dive courses and dive trips; Lightfoot heritage trail – details on all from Tourist information. In Cape Range National Park, south of town: Shothole Canyon, a spectacular gorge easily accessed via Shothole Canyon Rd and linked by walking trail to Charles Knife Canyon; Yardie Creek Gorge, with its deep blue water and multi-coloured rock; Milyering Visitor Centre, 52 km SW; abundant wildlife, picnic spots, scenic lookouts and walking trails. Prawn fishery, 23 km S, tours available in season (May–Oct.). Ningaloo Marine Park, 14 km W of Cape, largest fringing coral reef

in Australia; 500 fish species identified and 220 reef-building coral species. Charter fishing at Bundegi Beach jetty, 14 km N. Panoramic views from Vlaming Head Lighthouse, 17 km N; guided tours of lighthouse available. Wreck of SS *Mildura*, 100 m off-shore. **Tourist information:** Payne St; (08) 9949 1176. **Accommodation:** 2 hotels, 1 motel, 2 hostels, 4 cara./camp. parks.

Fitzroy Crossing   Pop. 1119

MAP REF. 372 G11, 381 L9

In the Kimberley, where the road north crosses the Fitzroy River, is the settlement of Fitzroy Crossing, 254 km inland from Derby. Once a sleepy little hamlet, the last few years have seen unprecedented growth of the town as a result of Aboriginal settlement, mining by Western Metals at Cadjebut, 80 km SE, and an increase in the number of visitors to the nearby Geikie Gorge National Park. July: Rodeo. Nov.: Barra Splash (barramundi fishing competition). **In the area:** Between Dec. and Mar., check road conditions before setting out on any excursions, as area is prone to flooding. Picturesque waterholes surrounding town support abundance of fish and other wildlife. Magnificent Geikie Gorge, 20 km NE in Geikie Gorge National Park, has rich variety of wildlife, including plentiful sawfish, barramundi, stingrays (adapted to fresh water) and freshwater crocodiles; best seen by boat (daily boat trips available May–Nov.). Flights available to Diamond Gorge and Sir John Gorge (on Fitzroy River above Geikie Gorge); contact Tourist information for details. Fitzroy River Lodge tourist complex, on Great Northern Hwy. Tunnel Creek National Park, 110 km NW, features creek tunnel through mountain range; Aboriginal guided tours available. Windjana Gorge National Park, 145 km NW, has rock pools supporting variety of fish and birdlife, and walking trails; Aboriginal guided tours available. Mimbi Caves, 95 km SE, only open for tours with Aboriginal guide. **Tourist information:** Flynn Dr.; (08) 9191 5355. **Accommodation:** 1 hotel, 2 motels, 1 hostel, 2 cara./camp. parks.

Fremantle   Pop. 27 000

MAP REF. 362 B11, 366 B5, 368, 374 C4

The largest port in the State and western gateway to Australia, Fremantle is a

bustling city 19 km S of Perth. It is a city of contrasts, with galleries and museums, beautiful sandy white beaches and many historic buildings, a reminder of the city's heritage. Captain Charles Fremantle arrived in May 1829 to 'take possession' of 'the whole of the west coast of New Holland', and was followed one month later by Captain James Stirling, who brought a small group to found the first Australian colony made up entirely of European free settlers. The engineer C.Y. O'Connor, who began the Goldfields Water Scheme, was responsible for building the harbour that turned Fremantle into an important port. The city has become home to many more recent immigrants. With its old-world charm and cosmopolitan culture, Fremantle is one of the most fascinating port cities in Australia. **Of interest:** Fremantle tram, departs from Town Hall, cnr William and Adelaide sts; various tours available including linking with ferry to Perth then trip on Perth tram to Burswood Casino and return. Many coffee shops and restaurants in South Terrace's 'Cappuccino Strip'. Pavement cafes and excellent restaurants. *Near the waterfront:* Round House (1830), end of High St, oldest building in WA, a 12-sided structure constructed as gaol; Whalers Tunnel (1837), connects High St to original shipping beach; Joan Campbell's Bathers Beach Gallery, near The Round House, in converted boatshed. In Cliff St: Maritime Museum (1860s), fine example of colonial Gothic architecture; Port Authority Building, Fremantle's tallest building offering panoramic views from roof; Boat Museum, on Victoria Quay not far from Maritime Museum, features STS *Leeuwin*, traditional square rigger (weekend, day and half-day tours available Sept.–Dec.); The Docks complex of souvenir shops and cafe/gallery, Victoria Quay. In Beach St: Wildflower Factory; Nature's Gem House. Adjacent to Marine Tce and the Esplanade Reserve: modern Challenger Harbour marina facilities developed for first Australian defence of the America's Cup; Fremantle's largest fishing fleet, which works Australia's most valuable fishing grounds (mainly lobster), and its considerable Italian community, give city a Mediterranean flavour; nearby, Success Yacht Harbour, headquarters of 100-year-old Fremantle Sailing Club; Kailis' Fish Market and cafe, and Fremantle Crocodile Park, both at Fishing Boat Harbour. Georgian style Old Customs

WESTERN AUSTRALIA

House (1853), cnr of Clifton and Phillimore sts. In Phillimore St: Chamber of Commerce (1912) and Old Fremantle Fire Station (1908). *In the central business district:* Spare Parts Puppet Theatre, Short St, has permanent puppet display and regular performances. The Bannister Street Craftworks in old warehouse, Bannister St. Henry St Station, Henry St, a huge model railway. Quaint old building, 5 Mouat St, originally housed German Consulate and shipping offices. Film and Television Institute, Adelaide St. In Henderson St, Warders' Quarters, two-storey cottages occupied until recently by prison staff. St John's Church and Square (1882); Town Hall (1887) in Kings Sq., cnr William and Adelaide sts. In South Tce: Fremantle Markets with seafoods, crafts, antiques, clothing, souvenirs (open Fri.–Sun.); Sail & Anchor Hotel, Australia's first pub brewery, serves specialty beers. *On the outskirts of the city centre:* Former Fremantle Gaol (1851–9), The Tce via Fairbairn St, a forbidding building of local stone (open to visitors); adjacent Fremantle Prison Museum; War Memorial Park, commanding excellent views. Magnificent Samson House (1900), cnr Ellen and Ord sts, has guided tours. Shell Museum, Beach St. Fremantle Museum and Arts Centre, Finnerty St, has musical performances in courtyard during summer. History of WA's electricity and gas at World of Energy Museum, Parry St. East Fremantle Heritage Trail, contact Tourist information for brochure. Art and craft market at Pioneer Park, Phillimore St, each Sun. Jan.: Sardine Festival. May: Fremantle–Carnarvon yacht race (even-numbered years); Rhythm and Blues Festival. Oct.: Blessing of the Fleet. Nov.: Festival Fremantle. **In the area:** Swimming at Port, Leighton and South beaches. Ferries to Rottnest Island, 20 km W, from wharf daily; also charter boats to Rottnest. Whale-watching boat tours, in spring and summer. Attractions nearby: Adventure World, 8 km SE; Pioneer Village, 29 km SE; Cohunu Koala Park, 19 km SE. **Tourist information:** Town Hall, Kings Square, cnr William and Adelaide sts; (09) 9431 7878. **Accommodation:** 10 hotels, 2 hotel/ motels, 1 motel, 11 B&B, 3 hostels.

Gascoyne Junction   Pop. 38

MAP REF. 375 D8

Located 170 km E of Carnarvon, at the junction of the Gascoyne and Lyons rivers, this town is the administration centre for the surrounding region. The old-fashioned pub is a good rest stop before the many scenic attractions of the Kennedy Range National Park, 60 km N. Mt Augustus National Park, 294 km NE, features several walks and drives. **Tourist information:** Junction Hotel; (08) 9943 0504. **Accommodation:** 1 hotel.

Geraldton   Pop. 24 361

MAP REF. 376 A3

The key port and administration centre for the mid-west region, Geraldton is 424 km N of Perth on Champion Bay. A year-round sunny climate and a mild winter make it one of the State's most popular holiday destinations. The flourishing city has interesting museums, excellent accommodation, white, sandy beaches and good fishing. Rich agricultural land surrounds Geraldton and the district is noted for beautiful spring wildflowers and picturesque countryside. The Houtman Abrolhos Islands, so named in the 16th century, lie 64 km off the coast and are used mainly as a base for rock-lobster fishing. **Of interest:** Heritage trail, contact Tourist information. In Cathedral Ave: Queens Park Theatre, surrounded by gardens; St Francis Xavier Cathedral, designed by Mons. John C. Hawes, architect of some fine buildings in and around Geraldton. On Marine Tce: Sir John Forrest Memorial; Geraldton Museum (includes maritime display building and old railway building), features relics from shipwrecks off coast. Art Gallery, cnr Durlacher St and Chapman Rd. Old Gaol Craft Centre, Bill Sewell Complex, Chapman Rd. Tourist lookout and wishing well on Waverley Heights, Brede St. Point Moore Lighthouse (1878), Willcock Dr. Excellent fishing from town's breakwater. At Fisherman's Wharf in season, Nov.–June, watch huge hauls of lobster being unloaded. Lobster factory tours, inquire at Tourist information. Jan.: Windsurfing Classic. June: Batavia Celebrations; Foodfest. Oct.: Festival of Geraldton. **In the area:** For good fishing: Sunset Beach, 6 km N; Drummond Cove, 10 km N; mouth of Greenough River, 10 km S. Banks of Greenough River, favourite place for picnics; market held here 3rd Sun. each month; Greenough River Walk, starts at river mouth; safe swimming for children in river. Greenough hamlet, 24 km S, a National Trust-restored village preserved to look as it did in 1880s (guided tours available). Ellendale Bluffs and Pool, 45 km SE, a permanent waterhole at base of steep rock face. Mill's Park Lookout, 15 km NE on Waggrakine Cutting, offers views over Moresby Range and coastal plain towards Geraldton. Chapman Valley, 35 km NE, a farming district noted for its spectacular wildflowers in spring. Kalbarri, 164 km N, surrounded by beautiful Kalbarri National Park. **Tourist information:** Bill Sewell Complex, cnr Bayley St and Chapman Rd; (08) 9921 3999. **Accommodation:** 14 hotel/motels, 2 B&B, 1 hostel, 7 cara./camp. parks.

Gingin   Pop. 473

MAP REF. 374 C2, 376 C7

Situated 83 km N of Perth and 30 km from the coast, Gingin is mainly a centre for mixed farming, horticulture, and cattle and sheep breeding. An interesting day trip from Perth, it offers alternative return trips touring coastal centres or inland via the scenic Chittering Valley. The town is built around a loop of Gingin Brook, which rises from nearby springs and flows strongly all year. **Of interest:** Town has village-like atmosphere. Fine examples of traditional Australian architecture, in Weld St: St Luke's Anglican Church (1860s), Granville (1871), Uniting Church (1868), and Dewar's House (1886); in Brockman St: Philbey's Cottage (1906). Uniforms of the World Museum, Brook St (closed Mon.). Granville Scenic Park, Weld St. Adjacent to park, Jim Gordon V.C. Trail, a delightful 1/2-hour walk along Gingin Brook. May: British Car Day. **In the area:** Gingin cemetery, northern outskirts of town on Dewar Rd, renowned for its prolific display of Kangaroo paws in spring. At Bullsbrook, 30 km S: The Maze; Bullsbrook Antiques and Cottage Crafts. Golden Grove Citrus Orchard, at Lower Chittering, 30 km SE. At Bindoon, 24 km E: Neroni Wines; Chittering Valley Estate; Kay Road Art and Craft Gallery. Sewell Leisure Park, 44 km NE, offers golf, rides, flora, fauna and picnic/barbecue facilities. **Tourist information:** Shire Offices, 7 Brockman St; (08) 9575 2211. **Accommodation:** 1 hotel/motel, 1 cara./camp. park.

Guilderton
Pop. 385

MAP REF. 374 B2, 376 C7

Located at the mouth of the Moore River, 94 km from Perth, Guilderton is both a popular day trip from Perth and a holiday destination. There is excellent fishing in both river and sea, and safe swimming for children. Dutch relics have been found here, possibly from the wreck of the *Vergulde Draeck* (the Gilt Dragon) in 1656. **Of interest:** Cruises on Moore River, depart Edward St; contact Tourist information for details. **In the area:** Seabird, 20 km N, a small but growing fishing village with safe beach. **Tourist information:** Caravan park, 2 Dewar St; (08) 9577 1021. **Accommodation:** 1 cara./camp. park.

Halls Creek
Pop. 1305

MAP REF. 373 N11, 361 P9

In the heart of the Kimberley, 2832 km from Perth, at the edge of the Great Sandy Desert, is Halls Creek, site of WA's first gold find in 1885. Between 1885–7, 10 000 men came to the Kimberley fields in search of gold then gradually drifted away, leaving 2000 on the diggings. Today mineral exploration is still carried out and the pastoral industry is supported by steady beef prices. **Of interest:** Russian Jack Memorial, Thomas St, honours early European settlers. July Agricultural Show. Aug.: Races. **In the area:** Aerial tours and 4WD safaris, contact Tourist information. China Wall, 6 km SE, a natural quartz formation. Fishing, swimming and picnicking at Sawpit Gorge, 40 km SE. Prospecting at Old Halls Creek, 16 km E, also mud-brick ruins of original settlement. Caroline Pool, near old town site off Duncan Rd, for swimming (best Oct.–May). Purnululu National Park, 160 km NE with its spectacular Bungle Bungle rock formations. Wolfe Creek Meteorite Crater, 148 km S, almost 1 km wide, 49 m deep and second largest meteorite crater in world. **Tourist information:** Great Northern Hwy; (08) 9168 6262. **Accommodation:** 1 hotel, 1 motel, 1 cara./camp. park. **See also:** The Kimberley.

Harvey
Pop. 2597

MAP REF. 367 H2, 374 C7, 376 C10

The thriving town of Harvey is set in some of the best agricultural country in Australia, 139 km S of Perth. Bordered by the Darling Range and the Indian Ocean, the fertile plains make perfect dairying country. The town's irrigation storage dams, with their recreation areas, have become popular tourist attractions. **Of interest:** Historical Society Museum, in old railway station (1914), Harvey St (open p.m. 1st, 3rd, 5th Sun. each month). Tourist information, South Western Hwy, has dairy industry displays, Moo Shoppe and local craft sales. Stirling Cottage, behind Tourist information, replica of 1880s home of May Gibbs (author of *Snugglepot and Cuddlepie*). Internment Camp Memorial Shrine, South Western Hwy, built by prisoners of war in 1940s; obtain key from Tourist information. Jan.: Australia Day Breakfast. Aug.: Daffodil Day. Oct.: Agricultural Show. **In the area:** Weir, 3 km E, off Weir Rd; Weir Walk, a 1-km trail alongside Harvey River. Scenic drive around north-west side of Stirling Dam (venue for world canoe championships), 17 km E, leads to Harvey Falls and Trout Ladder. Section of Bibbulmun Track, 17 km E (walking track extends from Perth to Walpole). Hoffmans Mill, 25 km NE, has picnic and camping facilities. Logue Brook Dam, 15 km NE, for swimming, water-skiing and trout fishing. At Yarloop, 15 km N: historic steam-age Workshops Museum (closed Tues.); heritage trail, details from museum; local craft at Blue Gum Studio. Yalgorup National Park, 35 km NW. Myalup and Binningup beaches, 25 km W off Old Coast Rd, are wide and sandy, ideal for swimming, fishing and boating. Kemerton Industrial Park (SCM Chemicals), 20 km S; group tours available, contact Tourist information. **Tourist information:** South Western Hwy; (08) 9729 1122. **Accommodation:** 1 hotel, 1 motel, 1 cara./camp. park. **See also:** The Southern Region.

Hopetoun
Pop. 206

MAP REF. 376 H11

Hopetoun is a peaceful holiday town overlooking the Southern Ocean. The town is 49 km S of Ravensthorpe and offers rugged and beautiful coastal scenery, and year-round wildflowers. Once called Mary Anne Harbour, the town has a colourful history. **Of interest:** White-sand beaches, sheltered bays, excellent fishing. Chatterbox Craft, Veal St, for local art and craft. Jan.: Summer Festival. **In the area:** Self-drive scenic drives, brochures at Tourist information. Lookout at Table Hill, 1 km N, offers 360° views over town and ocean, and has cairn to explorer John Eyre. Dunn's Swamp, 5 km N, for picnics, bushwalking and birdwatching. Lookout at No Tree Hill, 27 km NW, offers views across to Eyre Range. Fitzgerald River National Park, 10 km W, includes the Barrens, a series of rugged mountains, undulating sandplains and steep narrow gorges; East Mt Barren Footpath, a 10-km walk to summit; Hamersley Inlet, a scenic picnic and camping spot. Take care fishing from rocks – king waves can roll in unexpectedly and take lives. **Tourist information:** Going Bush Information Stop, Morgans St, Ravensthorpe; (08) 9838 1277. **Accommodation:** 1 hotel, 1 motel, 1 cara./camp. park.

Hyden
Pop. 150

MAP REF. 376 F8

Hyden is 351 km east of Perth, in the semi-arid eastern wheat area of WA. **In the area:** Fascinating rock formations, especially Wave Rock, 4 km E, a 2700 million-year-old granite outcrop rising 15 m, like a giant wave about to break; at Wave Rock: wildlife park; coffee shop; caravan park with chalets; Pioneer Town, with good collection of Australiana; lace collection (from 1600) at Visitors Centre. Other rock formations within walking distance of Wave Rock: Hippo's Yawn; The Falls; The Breakers. Aboriginal rock paintings at Mulka's Cave, 18 km N of Wave Rock. Nearby, The Humps, another unusual granite formation. **Tourist information:** Wave Rock Visitors Centre, Wave Rock Rd, 4 km E of town; (08) 9880 5182. **Accommodation:** 1 hotel/motel, 1 cara./camp. park.

Jurien
Pop. 603

MAP REF. 376 B6

Located 266 km N of Perth on the shores of a sheltered bay, Jurien is a lobster-fishing centre. The town is also a growing holiday destination because of its magnificent safe swimming beaches, excellent climate and reputation as an angler's paradise. Jurien boat harbour, a 17-ha inland marina, has excellent facilities for boating enthusiasts. **Of interest:** Tours of rock-lobster processing factory, Roberts Rd, in fishing

Wildlife-Watching

Besides the wonderful variety of birds and marsupials, much of Western Australia's wildlife can be found swimming in the State's clear coastal waters. There are some exciting encounters to be had: try a beachside meeting with Monkey Mia's dolphins, or a boat trip to see Ningaloo Reef's mysterious whale sharks. The adventurous can even don snorkel and mask to swim with tropical fish or manta rays.

In Perth

Swan Estuary Marine Park is a welcome sight for migratory birds each spring. Several important sections of Perth's picturesque waterway have been set aside, including Alfred Cove, Pelican Point and Milyu. Between August and November the birds touch down on the warm mudflats of the estuary and stay on until late March. Some of the smallest seasonal visitors are red-necked stints. Weighing in at a tiny 30–40 grams, they arrive each year from their breeding grounds in Arctic Siberia.

Perth also has some rather unusual wildlife-watching locations. Golfers at **Joondalup public golf course** in the city's northern outskirts look out for resident western grey kangaroos when teeing off. Kangaroos are quite common on local courses.

Around Perth

Rottnest Island is a short ferry ride from the port of Fremantle, and is a 'must-see' for wildlife-watchers. The island gained its name after its marsupial quokkas were originally mistaken for rats by the early Dutch explorer Vlamingh. Dusk and dawn are the best times to glimpse these animals, though sharp-eyed tour-bus drivers can often locate them through the day. Good quokka-spotting locations are around the bakery at Thomson Bay and at Watsons Glade near the road to Jeannies Lookout (eastern arm).

The stunning turquoise waters surrounding the island will provide some memorable experiences. At Pocillopora Reef off the south of the island is an underwater snorkelling trail which should not be missed. The reef is named after its beautiful pink coral, and is alive with marine-life. Snorkellers can fin through coral landscapes, following a series of illustrated underwater plaques which explain the reef's plants and animals. Each stopping point has handles for snorkellers to hold

Dolphins at Monkey Mia, near Denham

while they read — fortunately there is one breath's worth of information per plaque.

Perth-based travellers have several good mainland parks and reserves within a short drive for wildlife-watching. **Avon Valley National Park** has a healthy population of echidnas; their long trench-like diggings can be seen throughout the park. Late afternoon is a good time to view western greys in the park as they move into open areas after having spent their day in thick bushland. Euros are also present, although these sure-footed kangaroos prefer the steeper rocky country.

John Forrest National Park just south of Perth is good for bird-watching. Unusually named and brilliantly coloured 'twenty eight' parrots can be seen throughout the woodlands, along with less common red-capped parrots. Rufous and golden whistlers are noisy park residents, and New Holland honeyeaters enjoy the wildflower season each spring. Also keep an eye out for racehorse goannas on the park's roads and tracks.

In the North of the State

One of the State's classic wildlife experiences is the chance to interact with the dolphins at **Shark Bay**, north of Perth. Bottlenose dolphins often swim into the sandy shallows at Monkey Mia to contact humans and receive small offerings of fish.

The best time to meet these marine mammals is between 8 a.m. and 1 p.m. when they are fed under the supervision of park rangers. As with all wild animals, the dolphins may feel more sociable on some days than others. Part of the attraction of Monkey Mia is that the dolphins set the day's agenda, and visitors respond to their moods rather than forcing the animals to perform on cue.

Shark Bay supports a myriad of marine-life besides dolphins; sea turtles, school sharks, manta rays and dugongs flourish in the area. At Eagle Bluff, twenty kilometres south of Denham, school sharks and turtles can sometimes be seen in the clear green waters below. Boat tours leave from Monkey Mia to view the dugongs or 'sea cows' which graze amongst the seagrass beds. Dugongs feature unusual flattened snouts which are designed to shovel through the sand in search of the choicest plants. A catamaran also leaves from Denham to spot a variety of marine-life, including the giant yet harmless manta rays.

Further north again near Exmouth is Ningaloo Reef, Western Australia's largest coral reef and one of its most spectacular features. The diversity of marine-life is incredible and is protected by **Ningaloo Marine Park**. April to May are the best months to view its most famous visitors, the whale sharks. These are huge but docile fish with beautifully mottled backs and flattened heads.

They swim with their mouths open to filter the tiny marine organisms on which they feed. While the complete life-cycle of the world's largest fish is a mystery, it is now believed that their arrival corresponds with the recently discovered phenomenon of mass coral-spawning at Ningaloo. The spawning results in an abundance of food for the sharks. Fortunately for whale shark-watchers, when the fish arrive they cruise slowly just under the surface and can be seen from boat cruises and air flights from Exmouth.

September to November is a good time for humpback whale-watching cruises at Ningaloo, as the whales travel to their Antarctic feeding grounds and north-west shelf breeding area. Humpbacks are the show-ponies of the whale world. It is hard to believe just how active these huge mammals are, until you see 30 tonnes of whale launching itself from the water or splashing its mighty tail – humpbacks are anything but shy and retiring. Cruises leave regularly from Exmouth during the whale season.

Another good reason to visit during these months is the arrival of large schools of manta rays at the reef. They are more elusive than humpbacks, though once a school is located, snorkellers on tour boats out of Exmouth have a chance to swim amongst these harmless plankton-feeders. There is also a small year-round population of mantas in Coral Bay.

Extending to the shores of Ningaloo Marine Park is **Cape Range National Park**, and within this park is a rich tidal inlet called Mangrove Bay. The bay is home to some of the park's 125 bird species, particularly waders such as ibis and heron which emerge onto the exposed flats at low tide. A birdhide provides a good discreet viewpoint, and a stroll along the boardwalk gives a fascinating perspective on life in the inlet. There is also a fauna hide at Mangrove Bay, built alongside a waterhole which is a magnet for surrounding wildlife. Keep an eye out here for emus, euros and flocks of galahs. Also in the park is Yardie Creek Gorge where regular cruises operate. Bring a pair of binoculars to spot ospreys and herons nesting on the cliff-faces, as well as numerous black-footed rock wallabies.

On the South-West Coast

Southern right whales spend time off the southern coast around **Albany** each year from July to mid-October. Albany's association with whales has not always been a friendly one, with commercial whaling ceasing only in 1978. Whale numbers are now on the increase, and Whaleworld near Albany provides a good introduction to the behaviour and life-cycles of these magnificent aquatic mammals.

Whale-watching cruises depart daily from Albany's wharf in season. For land-based spotters there is no better location than the platform constructed at Point Ann in Fitzgerald River National Park. If whales are about, Point Ann offers the best chance to see one. With a bit of extra luck you may see a mother whale with her calf.

For more information on wildlife-watching in national parks and reserves contact the Department of Conservation and Land Management, 50 Hayman Rd (GPO Box 104), Como, WA 6152; (08) 9334 0333. For more information on bird-watching contact the Bird Observers Club of Australia, 183 Springvale Rd, Nunawading, Victoria 3131; (03) 9877 5342. **See also:** National Parks and Rottnest Island.

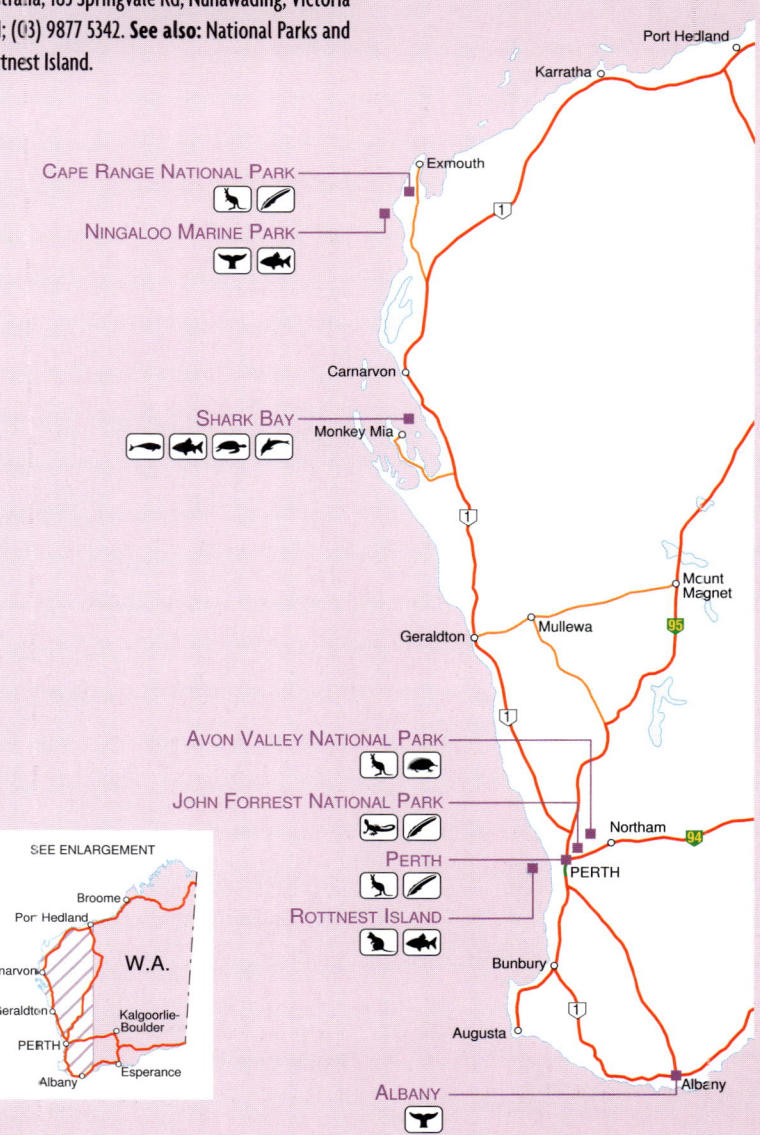

WESTERN AUSTRALIA

Early Australian architecture in Hannan St, Kalgoorlie

season. Nov.: Expo and Blessing of the Fleet. **In the area:** Spectacular sand dunes along coast. Cockleshell Gully, 31 km N, has great diversity of flora and fauna. Stockyard Gully National Park, 50 km N (4WD access only), has walk through 300-m Stockyard Gully Tunnel along winding underground creek (torch necessary, guided tours available). Lesueur National Park, 25 km E, noted for its variety of wildflowers in spring. At Cervantes, 55 km S, Slalom Carnival (windsurfing) held in Dec. Nearby, Nambung National Park, featuring The Pinnacles, thousands of spectacular calcified spires, 1–4 m high and around 30 000 years old, scattered over 400 ha of multi-coloured sand (guided coach tours daily); check road conditions before leaving Jurien if taking coastal track (main signposted route further inland recommended). Waddi Farms, Koonah Rd, off Brand Hwy, Badgingarra, 60 km SE, has wildflowers, emu farm, native gardens, shop and restaurant. **Tourist information:** Shire Offices, Bashford St; (08) 9652 1020. **Accommodation:** 1 hotel/motel, 1 cara./camp. park.

Kalbarri   Pop. 1521

MAP REF. 375 C13, 376 A2
This popular holiday town is between

Geraldton and Carnarvon, 661 km N of Perth. The town's picturesque setting on the Murchison River estuary, its year-round sunny climate and the spectacular gorges of the river running through the Kalbarri National Park attract a growing number of tourists. Kalbarri is also noted for excellent fishing and the brilliance of more than 500 wildflower species. **Of interest:** In Grey St: Recollections, a doll and marine museum; Fantasy Land; Gemstone Mine. In Porter St: Kalbarri Entertainment Centre; bicycle hire available. Pelican feeding, on foreshore (8.45 a.m.). Mar.: Sport Fishing Classic. Nov.: Blessing of the Fleet. **In the area:** Majestic coastal gorges and precipitous red cliffs dropping to Indian Ocean. *River Queen* ferry cruises, camel safaris, coach, 4WD, motorbike and abseiling adventure tours, canoe safaris and joy flights available; contact Tourist information. Kalbarri National Park, a large area of magnificent virgin bushland surrounding town, includes spectacular Murchison River gorges, 11 km E; Meanarra Lookout, 7 km E; spectacular coastal views from Hawks Head Lookout and Ross Graham Lookout, both 39 km E; abundance of wildlife and native flora; no camping. Red Bluff, 3 km S, for swimming, fishing and rock climbing. Rainbow Jungle

and Tropical Bird Park, 3.5 km S; Cairn at Wittecarra Creek, 4 km S, marking site of first permanent landing of Europeans in Australia (two Dutchmen sent ashore for their part in *Batavia* mutiny in 1629). Kalbarri Big River Ranch, 3 km E, for horseriding. The Loop and Z Bend lookouts, 30 km NE. **Tourist information:** Allen Community Centre, Grey St; (08) 9937 1104. **Accommodation:** 1 hotel/motel, 2 motels, 1 hostel, 4 cara./camp. parks.

Kalgoorlie-Boulder   Pop. 25 016

MAP REF. 376 I6
At the heart of WA's largest goldmining area is the city of Kalgoorlie-Boulder, 597 km E of Perth and centred on the famous Golden Mile, reputed to be the richest square mile in the world. Over 1300 tonnes of gold have been mined from this small area. Paddy Hannan found gold in 1893; by 1902 the population was 30 000, with 93 hotels operating. Fortunes were made overnight; the impressive stone buildings and magnificent wide streets recall the town's boom past. Miners set up their tents on the Golden Mile near the Great Boulder Mine, and this camp became the town of Boulder. One of the greatest difficulties facing the miners in this semi-desert area was lack of water. Determination and the brilliant scheme of engineer C.Y. O'Connor saved the day. A pipeline was completed in 1903, carrying water an incredible 563 km from a reservoir near Perth. Goldmining continues with renewed vigour now that gold prices have risen. The Kalgoorlie-Boulder region is also an important pastoral district for high-quality wool. **Of interest:** Heritage walk along Hannan St, booklet available from Tourist information. Fine examples of early Australian architecture, in Hannan St: Exchange, Palace and Australia hotels; Government buildings; Kalgoorlie Post Office; distinctive Kalgoorlie Town Hall (1908), featuring impressive staircase and paintings by local artists. Also in Hannan St: Museum of the Goldfields and British Arms Hotel (1899), with display recalling heyday of gold-rush boom; statue of Paddy Hannan; Goldfields Aboriginal Art Gallery. Paddy Hannan's Tree, Outridge Tce, marks site of first gold find in Kalgoorlie. School of Mines Museum, Egan St, includes world-class display of most minerals found in WA.

At Hannans North Historical Mining Complex, Broad Arrow Rd, underground and surface tours, and gold-pouring demonstrations available. Super Pit Lookout, off Eastern Bypass Rd. In Burt St: Boulder Town Hall (1908), has regular art exhibits; Eastern Goldfields Historical Museum, in Boulder railway station. Picturesque Cornwall Hotel (1898), Chesapeake St. Royal Flying Doctor Base, at airport (off Gatacre St), serves one of largest areas in Australia; tours available weekdays. Hammond Park, Lyall St, a wildlife sanctuary with small lake and scale model of Bavarian castle. Mt Charlotte Reservoir and Lookout, off Sutherland St; reservoir is storage for Kalgoorlie's vital fresh-water supply. The Loop Line, a tourist railway line around the Golden Mile; timetable at Tourist information. Sept.: Kalgoorlie Cup; Spring Festival. Nov.: Goldfields Mining Expo. **In the area:** City is an ideal base for visiting old goldmining towns in district (all within a day's drive and all active again): Coolgardie, 37 km SW; Broad Arrow, 38 km N; Ora Banda, 54 km NW; Kookynie, 200 km N; Leonora-Gwalia, 235 km N. WA's only two-up school, 7 km N of Kalgoorlie, on eastern side of road to Menzies. Rowle's Lagoon, 34 km NW, excellent for water sports. Kurrawang Emu Farm, 18 km W, also features Aboriginal artifacts (closed Sun., tours available). **Tourist information:** 250 Hannan St; (08) 9021 1966. **Accommodation:** 17 hotels, 19 motels, 6 cara./camp. parks. **See also:** The Goldfields.

Kambalda
Pop. 4259

MAP REF. 377 J7

Kambalda's goldmining history lasted from 1897 to 1906, during which time 30 000 ounces of gold were produced. When the gold petered out, so did the town. In 1966, however, rich nickel deposits were discovered and the town has since boomed. Today Kambalda, 634 km E of Perth, consists of two well-planned centres (Kambalda and Kambalda West), 6 km apart, and is noted for its environmental protection policy. **Of interest:** Several pleasant picnic areas in centre of town. Red Hill lookout, off Gordon Adams Rd, offers excellent views of area, including vast Lake Lefroy (510 sq. km.). June: Sky Diving Gathering. **In the area:** Land yachting on salt bed of lake. Defiance Open Cut Gold Mine Lookout, 20 km

S; obtain entry permit from town's Western Mining office. **Tourist information:** Emu Rocks Rd, Kambalda West; (08) 9027 1446. **Accommodation:** 1 hotel, 1 cara./ camp. park. **See also:** The Goldfields.

Karratha
Pop. 11 325

MAP REF. 375 G1

This clean, modern town was established on Nickol Bay in 1968 as a result of the continuing development of the Hamersley Iron Project. There was a lack of suitable land for expansion at Dampier and a need for a new regional centre. The town grew even faster when Woodside Petroleum developed the immense offshore gas reserve on the North West Shelf, and Karratha now has the best facilities in the north-west. Karratha's warm winter temperatures make it a good place to escape the southern cold. **Of interest:** Largest shopping centre outside Perth, Welcome Rd. Excellent views from TV Hill lookout, Millstream Rd. June: Pilbara Pursuit Jetboat Classic. Aug.: FeNaCLNG Festival. **In the area:** Scenic flights, day tours and safari tours of Pilbara outback; contact Tourist information for details. Jaburara Heritage Trail, 3.5 km W on Main Rd, includes Aboriginal rock carvings. Chichester Range Camel Trail and Millstream-Chichester National Park, 124 km S. **Tourist information:** 4548 Karratha Rd; (08) 9144 4600. **Accommodation:** 2 motels, 1 hostel, 3 cara./camp. parks. **See also:** The Hamersley Range.

Katanning
Pop. 4139

MAP REF. 371 L1, 374 H9, 376 E10

A thriving town 186 km N of Albany, Katanning's well-planned streets have some impressive Federation buildings. The countryside is given over to grain-growing and pastoral activities, and is noted for its fine merino sheep. **Of interest:** Old Mill Museum (1889), cnr Clive St and Austral Tce, features outstanding display of vintage roller flour-milling process. Majestic Kobeelya mansion (1902), Brownie St, a country retreat now owned by Baptist Church (open by appt). All Ages Playground, Clive St, has miniature steam railway. Old Winery ruins, Andrews Rd, being restored. In Dore St, largest country-based sheep-selling facility in WA;

regular sales on Wed. throughout year, ram sale in Aug. Metro Meats meatworks, Wagin Rd (guided tours by appt, contact Metro Meats or Tourist information). Feb.: Triathlon. Aug.: Prophet Mohammad's Birthday. Dec.: Caboodle. **In the area:** Katanning–Piesse Heritage Trail, details from Tourist information. Lakes surrounding town are excellent for swimming, boating and water-skiing. Stirling Range National Park, 80 km S. Work of local wood-carver John Davis whose subjects include native birds, 60 km SE at Gnowangerup. **Tourist information:** Flour Mill, cnr Austral Tce and Clive St; (08) 9821 2634. **Accommodation:** 3 hotels, 2 motels, 1 hostel, 2 cara./camp. parks. **See also:** The Southern Region.

Kojonup
Pop. 1023

MAP REF. 371 J2, 374 G9, 376 E11

Situated on the Albany Hwy, 154 km NW of Albany, Kojonup takes its name from the Aboriginal word 'kodja', meaning 'stone axe'. In 1837, when surveying the road from Albany to the newly established Swan River settlement, Alfred Hillman was guided to the Kojonup Spring by local Aborigines. Later a military outpost was set up on the site, and this marked the beginning of the town. **Of interest:** In Spring St: Kojonup Spring and picnic area; Military Barracks Museum (1845), Barracks Pl. (open Sun. p.m.). Elverd's Cottage (1851), Soldier Rd, has display of pioneers' tools and implements. On Albany Hwy: Sundial in Hillman Park; Kojonup Brook Walk, a walk alongside stream and featuring swing bridge. Walsh's Cattle Complex, Broomehill Rd, has regular cattle sales S.A. Pederick's Harness Display, Newstead Rd. Farrar Reserve, Blackwood Rd, noted for its wildflower display in Spring. Sept.: Wildflower and Country Festival. **In the area:** Variety of flora (includes more than 60 orchid species) and fauna (especially birds). Outlets for locally made jarrah furniture, hand-turned blackboy articles, woollen jumpers. Yeedabirrup Rock, 10 km E, one of many granite monoliths in area. Proandra Flowers, 20 km W, a protea farm. Orchid Valley Gallery and Jarrah Furniture, 30 km W. Lake Towerrining, 40 km NW, ideal for boating, onshore camping. Tours and farmstay at Kalpara Farm, details from Tourist information. **Tourist information:** Benn Pde;

(08) 9831 1686. **Accommodation:** 1 hotel, 1 hotel/motel, 1 motel, 1 B&B, 1 cara./camp. park. **See also:** The Southern Region.

Kondinin   Pop. 312

MAP REF. 374 I5, 376 F4

The settlement of Kondinin is 278 km SE of Perth. There are sheep stud-farms in the surrounding area. **Of interest:** Craft Shop, Gordon St, for local craft. **In the area:** Kondinin Cottage, eastern outskirts of town on Kondinin–Hyden Rd, a mudbrick settler's cottage with antiques, collectables and rural craftwork. Kondinin Lake, 8 km W, for water-skiing and yachting after a rainy winter. **Tourist information:** Craft Shop, Gordon St; (08) 9889 1130. **Accommodation:** 1 hotel, 1 motel, 1 cara./camp. park.

Kulin   Pop. 321

MAP REF. 374 I6, 376 F9

A centre for the sheep and grain farms of the district, Kulin lies 283 km SE of Perth. The eucalypt species *Eucalyptus macrocarpa* is a spectacular feature of local flora. **In the area:** Several species of native orchids. Jilakin Rock and Lake, 18 km E, a salt lake with salt plants and wildflowers in spring; Jilakin Rock Picnic Race Day, 15 km E, held in Oct. Buckley's Breakaway (pit with coloured hollows caused by granite decomposing to kaolin), 58 km E; also unusual coloured rock formations and wildflowers in area. Hopkins Nature Reserve, 20 km NE, an important flora conservation area. **Tourist information:** Kulin Woolshed, Johnston St; (08) 9880 1275. **Accommodation:** 1 hotel/ motel, 1 cara./camp. park.

Kununurra   Pop. 4061

MAP REF. 373 P2, 381 Q5

Kununurra is situated alongside Lake Kununurra on the Ord River. Adjoining is the magnificent Mirima (Hidden Valley) National Park. The town supports several industries, including agriculture and mining, and is the major centre for the Argyle Diamond Mine (the largest diamond mine in the world) and the Ord River Irrigation Area. **Of interest:** Sales of pink diamonds from the Argyle Diamond Mine, and other gems, at various outlets. Apr.: Dam to Dam Regatta. May–July: Ord River

Festival (float parade, mardi gras, art and craft exhibitions, famous Ord Tiki Race and street party). **In the area:** Kununurra is major starting point for flights and ground tours to: remarkably coloured and shaped Bungle Bungles in the south; Argyle Diamond Mine in the south-west (access only via tour); Mitchell Plateau and Kalumburu in the north-west Kimberley. Minibus tours of local attractions, charter flights and bushcamping; details at Tourist information. Good fishing, barramundi being a prized catch. Mirima (Hidden Valley) National Park, 2 km E (no camping). Warringarri Aboriginal Arts; Kelly's Knob Lookout, for views of surrounding irrigated land; both 2 km N. Melon Farm, Ivanhoe Rd, 8 km N and Banana Farm, 9 km N on River Farm Rd, for tasting and sales (daily May–Oct.). Top Rockz Gallery, 10 km N, exhibits gemstones and precious metals (open May–Sept.). Ivanhoe Crossing, 13 km N, for fishing. Middle Springs, 30 km N; Black Rock Falls, 32 km N, flows only in wet season. Cruises on Lake Kununurra and upstream into the Everglades and rugged gorges; teeming birdlife to be seen. El Questro Station, 100 km SW, features Aboriginal rock art, rugged scenery, hot springs, fishing and boating (camping and accommodation available). Sleeping Buddha (Elephant Rock), 10 km S. Pandanus Wildlife Park; Zebra Rock Gallery; both 16 km S. Scenic Lake Argyle, 72 km S in Carr Boyd Range, largest constructed lake in southern hemisphere, was created by Ord River Dam which transformed mountain peaks into rugged islands. **Tourist information:** Coolibah Dr.; (08) 9168 1177. **Accommodation:** 2 hotels, 2 motels, 2 hostels, 5 cara./ camp. parks. **See also:** The Kimberley.

Kwinana   Pop. 13 517

MAP REF. 366 B7, 374 C4, 376 C8

Kwinana, 20 km S of the port of Fremantle, is a major industrial centre, containing the BP Oil Refinery and Alcoa's Alumina Works surrounded by pristine wetlands. Kwinana Industrial Complex, built on Cockburn Sound, one of the world's finest natural harbours, was begun in 1951. The town is surrounded by pockets of bush and wetland, providing numerous opportunities for recreation. **Of interest:** Group tours of local industries, contact

Tourist information. At Kwinana Beach: hull of the wrecked SS *Kwinana*; jet skiing (jet ski hire available). Dec.: Christmas Carnivale. **In the area:** Spectacles Wetlands, 5 km NE, on McLachlan Rd, include boardwalk and bird hide (leaflet available at Tourist information). At seaside resort city of Rockingham, 10 km S, cruises to offshore islands, Point Peron (7 km W) and Penguin Island (10 km SW). Sloan's Cottage (1911), 2 km SW at Leda, a restored pioneer cottage (open Mon.–Fri.). Lookout over coast and town on Chalk Hill, western outskirts of town. **Tourist information:** Shire Offices, cnr Gilmore Ave and Sulphur Rd; (08) 9419 2222. **Accommodation:** 1 hotel/motel.

Lake Grace   Pop. 596

MAP REF. 376 F9

A pleasant country town with first-class service facilities. Situated 252 km N of Albany in the peaceful rural countryside of the central south wheat belt, Lake Grace derives its name from the shallow lake just west of the settlement. **Of interest:** In Stubbs St: restored Inland Mission hospital, last in WA; old railway buildings under restoration. **In the area:** Emu farm, South Rd on southern outskirts of town. Roe Heritage Trail, retraces part of J.S. Roe's explorations in 1848; details available from Tourist information. Lookout, 5 km W. **Tourist information:** Lake Grace Newsagency, Stubbs St; (08) 9865 1029. **Accommodation:** 1 hotel/motel, 2 motels, 1 cara./camp. park.

Lake King   Pop. 29

MAP REF. 376 G10

A crossroads centre with a tavern and store, Lake King is a stopping-place for visitors travelling across arid country and through Frank Hann National Park to Norseman. **Of interest:** Interdenominational community church. **In the area:** Colourful wildflowers in season, 5 km W. Lake King, 5 km W, a saltwater lake. At Pallarup, 15 km S, pioneer well; Lake Pallarup. Mt Madden cairn and lookout, 25 km SE, also picnic area. Frank Hann National Park, 32 km E, cross-section of heath flora of inland sandplain. Park is traversed by Lake King–Norseman Rd, a formed gravel all-weather road; check road conditions before departure. No visitor facilities or

WESTERN AUSTRALIA

Crossing the Nullarbor

The trip from Adelaide to Perth along the Eyre Highway is one of Australia's great touring experiences. It is far from monotonous, with breathtaking views of the Great Australian Bight from the road in many places. There is nothing quite like a long straight road stretching as far as the eye can see.

If you are planning a return journey, it is well worth considering driving one way and putting the car on the train for the return. Train bookings need to be made well in advance, even at off-peak times. (**See:** Planning Ahead.)

The Eyre Highway is bitumen for its entire length. The highway is well signposted, with indications of the distance to the next town with petrol and other services.

If the journey is undertaken at a sensible pace, it can be surprisingly relaxing, especially during the quieter times of year. The standard of accommodation along the way is good and reasonably priced with a friendly atmosphere in the bars and dining rooms of the large motel/roadhouses that are strategically situated along the highway. Many friendships have been made during the trip across the Eyre Highway as the same carloads of travellers meet at stopping-places each night.

The highway has certain hazards, including breakaways on the shoulders in places, requiring caution when drivers are overtaking; and kangaroos especially at dusk or after rain. Overtaking also can be hazardous in damp conditions when the spray from the vehicle in front completely cuts visibility ahead. On the other hand, the semitrailer drivers are usually courteous and signal when it is safe to overtake.

The setting sun can make driving somewhat unpleasant for drivers travelling in a westerly direction. Also, do not forget the time changes you will encounter on the way! (**See also:** Time Zones.)

Above all, it is most important to have a safe, reliable car. The settlements along the highway are mainly motels and roadhouses; you could have a long wait for mechanical or medical help.

The journey proper begins at **Port Augusta**, 330 kilometres north-east of Adelaide, at the head of Spencer Gulf. Port Augusta is a provincial city that services a vast area of semi-arid grazing and wheat-growing country to the north and west. As you head out of the city on the Eyre Highway, you see

The Eyre Highway links Port Augusta in South Australia and Norseman in Western Australia

the red peaks of the Flinders Ranges soaring above the sombre bluebush plains; these are the last hills of any size for 2500 kilometres. Through the little towns of **Kimba** and Kyancutta the scenery can vary from mallee scrub to wide paddocks of wheat. This area was once called Heartbreak Plains, a reminder of the time when farmers walked off their land in despair, leaving behind crumbling stone homesteads that today dot the plains.

The highway meets the sea at **Ceduna**, a small town of white stone buildings and limestone streets set against a background of blue-green sea. The waters of the Great Australian Bight here are shallow and unpredictable, but they yield Australia's best catches of its most commercially prized fish, whiting. On the outskirts of Ceduna is a warning sign about the last reliable water. This marks the beginning of the deserted, almost treeless land that creeps towards the Nullarbor Plain. The highway stays close to the coast, and alongside there is always a little scrub and other vegetation.

The name 'Nullarbor' is a corruption of the Latin words meaning 'no trees' and the name is apt. Geologists believe that the completely flat plain was once the bed of a prehistoric sea, which was raised by a great upheaval of the earth.

West of Ceduna the traveller will find **Penong**, a town of 100 windmills, and the breathtaking coastal beauty around Point Sinclair and Cactus Beach. Then on to Nundroo and south to the abandoned settlement of Fowlers Bay, once an exploration depot for Edward John Eyre and now a charming ghost town best-known for its fishing. At the Yalata Roadhouse, run by the Yalata Aboriginal Community, there are genuine artifacts for sale at reasonable prices. Between Nullarbor and Border Village are five of Australia's most spectacular coastal lookouts, over giant ocean swells

pounding the towering limestone cliffs that make up this part of the Great Australian Bight. From June to October there is the chance of spotting the majestic southern right whale on its annual migration along the southern part of the continent. Fuel, refreshments and accommodation are all available at Penong, Nundroo, Nullarbor and Border Village.

The stone ruins of an Aboriginal mission remain at **Cocklebiddy**. The road continues until it reaches the first real town in over 1200 kilometres, **Norseman**, an ideal stopping-place.

From here you turn north to **Kalgoorlie-Boulder** or south to **Esperance** on the coast. At Kalgoorlie-Boulder you will see one of the longest-established and most prosperous goldmining centres in Western Australia. Set in vast dryland eucalypt forest, the town is picturesque in frontier style. Esperance, on the other hand, offers coastal scenery including long, empty beaches. Nearby, wildflowers spread across the countryside in spring.

As you travel west from Kalgoorlie-Boulder, the undulating forest and wildflower scrub continue for a further 250 kilometres until the road reaches the wheat- and wool-growing lands surrounding the towns of **Southern Cross** and **Merredin**. The farmland becomes increasingly rich as it rises into the Darling Range, the beautiful, wooded mountain country that overlooks Perth. At the end of this long journey Perth glitters like a jewel on the Indian Ocean – a place of civilisation and style, of beaches, waterways and greenery.

See also: text entries in the South Australian A–Z listing or in the Western Australian A–Z listing for those towns indicated by bold type.

supplies available between Lake King and Norseman. **Tourist information:** Post office, 13 Ravensthorpe Rd; (08) 9874 4015. **Accommodation:** 1 hotel/motel, 1 cara. park.

Lancelin   Pop. 531

MAP REF. 374 B1, 376 B7

This quiet little fishing town on the shores of Lancelin Bay is 127 km N of Perth. A natural breakwater extends from Edward Island to Lancelin Island, providing a safe harbour and a perfect breeding ground for fish. There are rock lobsters to be caught on the offshore reefs outside the bay. Long stretches of white sandy beach provide an ideal swimming area for children. Lancelin is becoming known as the sailboard mecca of WA and affords a colourful spectacle each Dec. with large numbers of international and interstate windsurfers taking part in the Ledge Point Ocean Race. Easter: Beach Buggy Championships. **In the area:** Large off-road area for dune buggies at northern end of town. Whale-watching, Oct.–Mar. Ledge Point, 15 km S, a community built around fishing industry; good beach fishing. Track (4WD only) leads 55 km N to Nambung National Park; check road conditions before s etting out. **Tourist information:** 102 Gingin Rd; (08) 9655 1100. **Accommodation:** 1 motel, 2 cara./camp. parks.

Laverton   Pop. 1197

MAP REF. 377 J3

Laverton, situated 360 km NE of Kalgoorlie, is a modern satellite town surrounded by numerous old mine workings. Nickel mining in the area has recently ceased but goldmining is booming. With an annual rainfall of around 200 mm, summers are hot and dry; Apr.–Oct. is the recommended time to travel. **Of interest:** Old court house, gaol and railway station, Craigie St. **In the area:** Windarra Heritage Trail, 28 km NW on Windarra Minesite Rd, covers abandoned mine and has interpretive plaques along route. Empress Springs, 305 km NE near Tjukayirla Roadhouse (4WD access only). From Laverton to Ayers Rock (1200 km), all roads are unsealed, and the following points should be noted:

• Permit required to divert from the Laverton–Yulara Rd; obtained from

Aboriginal Planning Authority in Perth or Alice Springs.
• Water is scarce.
• Supplies at Laverton. Fuel, supplies and accommodation at Warburton and Warakurra Roadhouse. Petrol, supplies and accommodation at Tjukayirla Roadhouse, 305 km NE of Laverton.
• Check on road conditions before departure at the Laverton Police Station or at Shire Offices. Roads can be hazardous when wet.
Tourist information: Desert Pea Caravan Park, Weld Dr.; (090) 311 072. **Accommodation:** 1 hotel, 1 motel, 1 cara./camp. park. **See also:** The Goldfields.

Leonora   Pop. 1194

MAP REF. 376 I3

A busy mining centre 243 km N of Kalgoorlie, Leonora has a typical Australian country-town appearance, with wide streets and verandahed shopfronts. The town is the centrepoint of, and railhead for, the north-eastern goldfields, with mining of gold, copper and nickel at Laverton, 120 km NE, and Leinster, 134 km NW. Most of the surrounding country is flat mulga scrub, but there are brilliant wildflowers in Aug. and early Sept. after good rains. Oct.: Art Prize. **In the area:** Three major gold producers, including famous Sons of Gwalia. At Gwalia, 2 km S: museum capturing miners' lifestyle; 1-km heritage trail. Small goldmining town of Menzies, 110 km S, has historical cemetery. Kookynie, 92 km SE, a ghost town with old mine workings; Grand Hotel offers warm welcome. Malcolm, 20 km E; good picnic spot alongside Malcolm Dam. **Tourist information:** Shire Offices, Tower St; (08) 9037 6044. **Accommodation:** 2 hotels, 1 motel, 1 cara./camp. park. **See also:** The Goldfields.

Madura   Pop. 15

MAP REF. 377 P8

The Hampton Tablelands form a backdrop to Madura, 195 km from the WA-SA border, on the Eyre Hwy. The settlement dates back to 1876 when horses for the Indian Army were bred here. Now it is surrounded by private sheep stations. **In the area:** Blowholes at The Pass, 1.5 km N. **Tourist information:** Madura Pass Oasis Motel; (08) 9039 3464. **Accommodation:** 1 motel, 1 cara./camp. park. **See also:** Crossing the Nullarbor.

Mandurah   Pop. 23 343

MAP REF. 366 B9, 374 C5, 376 C9

The popular holiday destination of Mandurah is on the coast, 74 km S of Perth. The Murray, Serpentine and Harvey rivers meet here, forming the vast inland waterway of Peel Inlet and the Harvey Estuary. The river waters and the Indian Ocean offer excellent conditions for yachting, boating, swimming, water-skiing and fishing, and the town becomes a mecca for tourists in holiday periods. **Of interest:** Hall's Cottage, Leighton Rd, a small whitewashed cottage built in 1845 by two of the colony's earliest European settlers (open Sun. p.m.). Christ Church (1870), cnr Pinjarra Rd and Sholl St, features hand-carved furniture. Community Museum, in old school building (1898), Pinjarra Rd (open Tues. and Sun.). Kerryelle's Collectors Museum, Gordon Rd. Parrots of Bellawood Park, 64 Furnissdale Rd. Boat hire and cruises on inlet and river. Dolphins sometimes seen in estuary. Waters attract abundance of birdlife. King Carnival Amusement Park, in Hall Park. Jan.: Festival. **In the area:** Pleasant picnic areas near numerous storage dams in nearby Darling Range; boating and swimming at Waroona and Logue Brook dams. Good beaches at Halls Head, just over old traffic bridge. Bavarian Castle Fun Park, Old Coast Rd, 2 km S. Further south, Dawesville Channel between inland waterways and ocean; good fishing from bridge. Handcrafted sculptures depicting Australian folklore and characters at Bouvard Gallery, 15 km SW on Henry Rd, Melros. Lakes Clifton and Preston, 45 km S, two long, narrow lakes running parallel to coast. Houseboat hire at South Yunderup, 12 km SE. Wineries at Cape Bouvard, Mt John Rd (22 km S); Peel Estate, Fletcher Rd, Baldivis (20 km N). Hamel Forestry Department Nursery, 42 km SE. Western Rosella Bird Park, 5 km E, has native birds in natural settings. Also 5 km E, local art and craft market, Sat., Sun. and public holidays. Durango Gallery, 14 km N in Amarillo Dr., Karnup. **Tourist information:** 5 Pinjarra Rd; (08) 9535 1155. **Accommodation:** 2 hotels, 5 motels, 7 B&B, 11 cara./camp. parks.

Manjimup   Pop. 4353

MAP REF. 370 D6, 374 D10, 376 D11

Fertile   agricultural   country   and

WESTERN AUSTRALIA

Boranup Beach, south of Margaret River

magnificent karri forests surround Manjimup, 307 km S of Perth. This is the commercial centre of the State's south-west, and one of its most diversified horticultural regions: there is a flourishing timber industry, quality fresh fruit (it is WA's largest apple-growing area) and vegetables are grown for the State and Asian markets, and wine, wool and dairying also contribute to the local economy. **Of interest:** Manjimup Regional Timber Park, cnr Edward and Rose sts, a major tourist attraction, includes Visitors Centre, Blacksmith's Shop, Timber Museum with display on development of timber industry in WA, original sawmill steam loco, Age of Steam Museum, Historical Hamlet, Fire Tower Lookout, gallery and tearooms, and picnic/barbecue facilities (timber tours available). WA Chip and Pulp (Paper Wood Co.) mill, Eastbourne Rd (guided tours available). Yallambee Gem Museum, Chopping St. June: 15 000 Motocross. **In the area:** Abseiling, rock-climbing, bushcraft, horse-drawn picnic excursions, forest discovery tours and safari tours available; contact Tourist information. Diamond Tree Fire Tower, 9 km S, a 51-m karri tree in use 1941–74(can be climbed by visitors); nearby, children's adventure trail and picnic/barbecue area. Swimming at Fontys Pool, 10 km S, originally dammed in 1925 for irrigation; picnicking in landscaped surrounds. Collect

your own walnuts and chestnuts in season (Apr.–May) at Fontanini's Nut Farm, located next to Fonty's Pool. Pianc Gully Wines, 10 km S. Bunnings Diamond Woodchip Mill, 12 km S (guided tours available). Black George's Winery and Alpaca Centre, 12 km S on South Western Hwy, features historic cottage, alpaca stud and wine tastings. Nyamup, 20 km SE, an old mill town redeveloped as a tourist village. Southern Wildflowers farm, 33 km SE at Quinninup. King Jarrah, 4 km E, a 47-m-high tree estimated to be 600 years old; heritage trail begins here, contact Tourist information. Pioneer cairn, 9 km NE. Pioneer cemetery, 10 km NE. The 19-km round trip to Dingup, north-east of Manjimup, passes through farmland and forest; at Dingup, church (1896); historic house (1870). Curragundi Wildlife Park, 2 km N (closed Tues.). Constable Wines, Graphite Rd, 8 km W. One Tree Bridge, 22 km W, a single karri tree felled in 1904 to cross Donnelly River; pleasant walk along river edge to the Four Aces (four magnificent karri trees, 300–400 years old). Donnelly River Holiday Village, 28 km W, features abundant wildlife and horseriding. Warren National Park, 40 km SW, good for bushwalking and picnics. **Tourist information:** cnr Rose and Edward sts; (08) 9771 1831. **Accommodation:** 2 hotels, 4 motels, 3 cara./ camp. parks. **See also:** The Southern Region.

Marble Bar   Pop. 383

MAP REF. 378 D2

Widely-known as the hottest town in Australia because of its consistently high temperatures, Marble Bar lies 200 km SE of Port Hedland (last 90 km is unsealed). The town takes its name from the unique bar of red jasper that crosses the Coongan River, 4 km W of town. Alluvial gold was discovered at Marble Bar in 1891, and in 1931 at Comet Mine. Today the major industries are goldmining and pastoral production. Marble Bar is a typical WA outback town. **Of interest:** Government buildings (1895), General St, built using locally-quarried stone. State Battery site (1910), Newman–Tabba Rd (not open to public). July: Cup Race Weekend. **In the area:** Beautiful scenery, especially in winter and after rain when spinifex is transformed into flowering plants; rugged ranges, rolling plains, steep gorges, deep rock pools and many scenic attractions. Jasper deposit at Marble Bar Pool, 4 km W. Nearby, Chinaman's Pool, an ideal picnic spot. Flying Fox Lookout, 6 km SW, spectacular when river is running. Corunna World War II RAAF Base, 40 km SE (worth a visit but open only by appt). Old goldmines at Nullagine, 111 km SE. Good swimming at Coppin's Gap, 68 km NE and Kitty's Gap, further 6 km. **Tourist information:** BP Garage, 1 Francis St; (08) 9176 1041. **Accommodation:** 1 hotel/motel, 1 motel, 1 cara./camp. park. **See also:** The Hamersley Range.

Margaret River   Pop. 1725

MAP REF. 367 C10, 369 C7, 374 A10, 376 B11

Margaret River is a pretty township, nestled on the side of the Margaret River near the coast, 280 km from Perth. The area is noted for its world-class wines, magnificent coastal scenery, excellent surfing beaches and spectacular cave formations. **Of interest:** Historic steam train in Rotary Park, Bussell Hwy; starting point for heritage walks, details from Tourist information. On Bussell Hwy: Old Settlement Craft Village; Margaret River Gallery; Margaret River Pottery. Melting Pot Glass Studio, Boodjidup Rd. 1885 Inn and restaurant, Farrelly St, formerly 1885 homestead. Feb.: Award-winning Leeuwin Estate Concert; Wine and Food Festival. **In the area:** Wineries in the Margaret River region including

The Goldfields

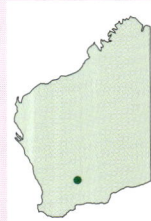

The land that boasted the first goldmining boom in Western Australia is almost as forbidding as that of the far north-west. This is the vast region to the east of Perth that contains the famous towns of Kalgoorlie-Boulder, Coolgardie, Norseman, Kambalda, Leonora, Gwalia and Laverton with Kalgoorlie-Boulder the main centre.

The western gold rush began in 1892 with strikes around **Coolgardie**. The town sprang up from nowhere and enjoyed a boisterous but short life. In 1900 there were 15 000 people, today Coolgardie has a population of 1063. The grand old court house is used now as a museum and has a record of life on the fields as it once was.

In 1893 Irishman Paddy Hannan made a bigger strike of gold at Kalgoorlie. The area became known as the Golden Mile, reputedly the richest square mile in the world.

The modern **Kalgoorlie-Boulder** is a prosperous goldmining centre, producing 70 per cent of the gold mined in Australia. At Hannans North Historical Mining Complex visitors can don a hard hat and cap lamp, and go below the surface, where guides explain the hardships endured by the miners in their search for gold. To the south is **Kambalda**, a new boom town, founded on rich nickel deposits.

Most of the towns north of Kalgoorlie are alive again as a result of the current goldmining operations. Deep underground mines are being replaced by massive open-cuts, which create their own adjacent table top mountains of overburden. The little town of Menzies is a shadow of its former self. The renovated, stately old Gwalia Hotel just outside **Leonora** is one of the few buildings left in what was once one of the State's most prosperous goldmining centres.

Kanowna once boasted a population of 12,000. Now all that remains is old and new mine workings, and historic markers describing what used to be. Siberia, Broad Arrow, Niagara and Bulong are the exotic names of some of the towns that flourished and died in a few short years. Nevertheless, mining is once again active in most of these areas.

See also: individual text entries in A–Z listing for those towns indicated by bold type.

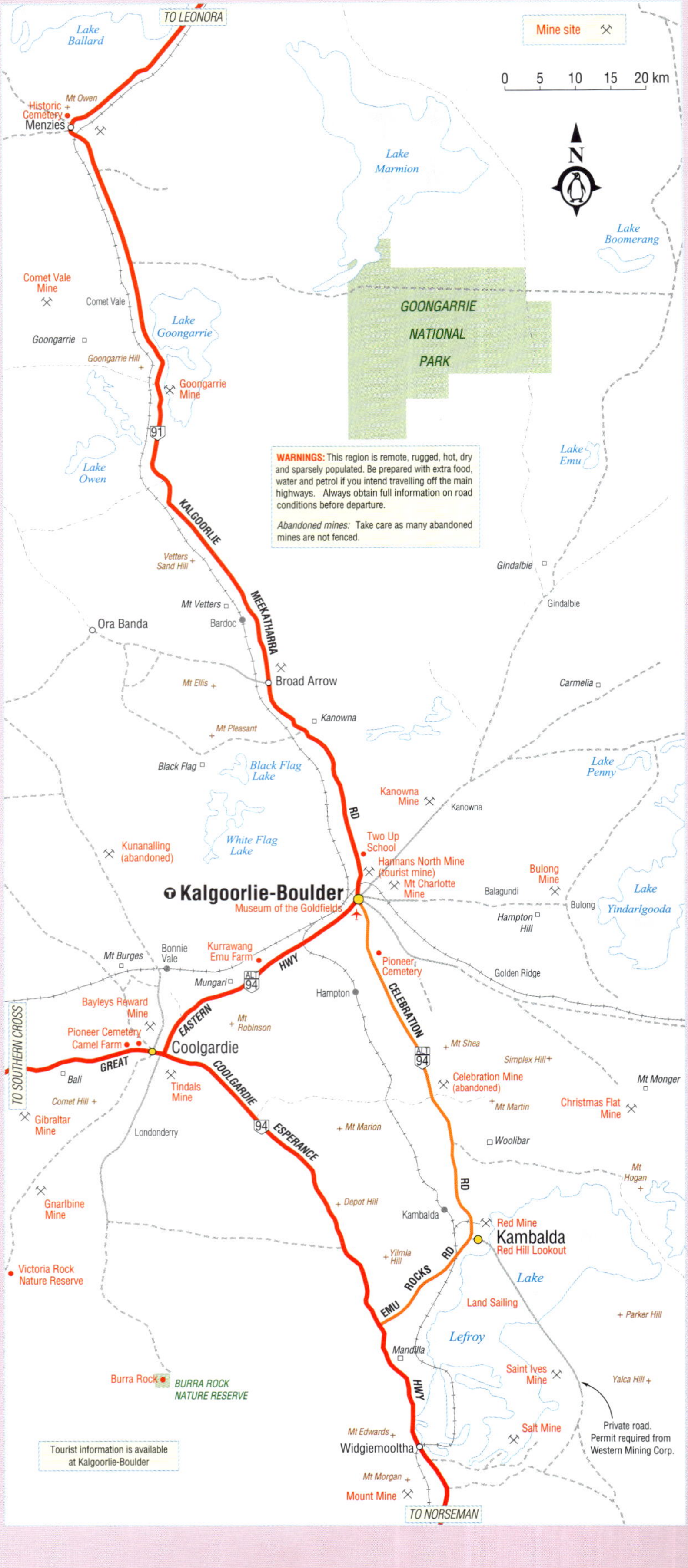

WESTERN AUSTRALIA

Map

Mine site

0 5 10 15 20 km

N

TO LEONORA

Lake Ballard

Mt Owen

Historic Cemetery
Menzies

Lake Marmion

Lake Boomerang

Comet Vale Mine

Comet Vale

Lake Goongarrie

GOONGARRIE NATIONAL PARK

Goongarrie

Goongarrie Hill

Goongarrie Mine

Lake Owen

91

Lake Emu

WARNINGS: This region is remote, rugged, hot, dry and sparsely populated. Be prepared with extra food, water and petrol if you intend travelling off the main highways.   Always obtain full information on road conditions before departure.

Abandoned mines: Take care as many abandoned mines are not fenced.

Vetters Sand Hill

KALGOORLIE

Gindalbie

Gindalbie

Mt Vetters

Bardoc

MEEKATHARRA

Ora Banda

Mt Ellis

Broad Arrow

Carmelia

Kanowna

Mt Pleasant

Lake Penny

Black Flag

Black Flag Lake

Kanowna Mine

Kanowna

RD

Kunanalling (abandoned)

White Flag Lake

Two Up School

Hannans North Mine (tourist mine)

Mt Charlotte Mine

Bulong Mine

Balagundi

Bulong

Lake Yindarlgooda

Kalgoorlie-Boulder
Museum of the Goldfields

Hampton Hill

Mt Burges

Bonnie Vale

Kurrawang Emu Farm

HWY

Pioneer Cemetery

Golden Ridge

Mungari

94

Hampton

CELEBRATION

TO SOUTHERN CROSS

Bayleys Reward Mine

EASTERN

Mt Robinson

Mt Shea

Simplex Hill

Mt Monger

Pioneer Cemetery
Camel Farm

Coolgardie

94

Celebration Mine (abandoned)

Bali

Comet Hill

Tindals Mine

COOLGARDIE

Mt Martin

Christmas Flat Mine

Gibraltar Mine

Londonderry

94

ESPERANCE

Mt Marion

Woolibar

Mt Hogan

Gnarlbine Mine

Depot Hill

RD

Kambalda

Red Mine

Kambalda
Red Hill Lookout

Victoria Rock Nature Reserve

EMU

Yilmia Hill

ROCKS

RD

Lake

Land Sailing

Parker Hill

Lefroy

Saint Ives Mine

Yalca Hill

Private road. Permit required from Western Mining Corp.

Burra Rock

BURRA ROCK NATURE RESERVE

HWY

Mandilla

Salt Mine

Tourist information is available at Kalgoorlie-Boulder

Mt Edwards

Widgiemooltha

Mt Morgan

Mount Mine

TO NORSEMAN

Cowaramup (10 km N) and Willyabrup (20 km N) Leeuwin Estate Winery, 8 km S, has restaurant with contemporary Australian paintings and picnic/barbecue facilities. Eagles Heritage, 5 km S, has large collection of birds of prey. Bellview Shell Museum, 6 km S at Witchcliffe. Boranup Gallery, 20 km S on Caves Rd, Boranup. Trout fishing and marron delicacies at Margaret River Marron Farm, 9 km SE. Pioneer Settlers Memorial, 14 km SE. The Berry Farm and Winery, 15 km SE. Canoe hire available, 22 km SE. Cheese outlets on Bussell Hwy: Fonti's and Margaret River Cheese Factory, 4 km N; Adinfern Farm, 7 km N, also offers demonstrations of a working farm, contact Tourist information for details. At Cowaramup, 10 km N: Antique-a-Brac; Excentrix; Cowaramup Pottery; Silverthread Gallery. Ellensbrook Homestead (1853–5), National Trust property, 15 km NW. Prevelly, on coast 8 km W; Greek Chapel at Prevelly Park. Mammoth Cave, 21 km SW, features fossil remains of prehistoric animals; 4 km on is Lake Cave. Other coastal areas worth visiting include Gracetown, 15 km NW; Redgate, 10 km S; Hamelin Bay, 34 km S. Augusta–Busselton, Margaret River and Hamelin Bay heritage trails, details from Tourist information. **Tourist information:** cnr Tunbridge Rd and Bussell Hwy; (08) 9757 2911. **Accommodation:** 1 hotel, 4 motels, 10 B&B, 2 hostels, 4 cara./camp. parks.

Meekatharra Pop. 1414

MAP REF. 375 I11, 378 C12

Meekatharra lies 768 km NE of Perth on the Great Northern Hwy. Gold, copper and other minerals are mined, and there are huge sheep and cattle stations in the area. Meekatharra was once important as the railhead for cattle that had travelled over and from the Northern Territory or the East Kimberley. **Of interest:** In Main St: State Battery relics; Royal Flying Doctor Service base (open 11 a.m.–1 p.m., Mon.–Fri.). School of the Air, High St, open to public during school term. Old court house, Darlot St. **In the area:** Old goldmining towns, relics of mining equipment, mine shafts; several mines, including Peak Hill (no access), have reopened. Peace Gorge (The Granites), 5 km N. Bilyuin Pool, 88 km NW, for swimming (no water in summer). Mt Gould, 156 km NW; nearby, restored police station. Mt Augusta

National Park, 360 km NW, incorporates Mt Augustus, a sandstone and quartz massif which rises out of arid shrubland, and several good walks and drives. **Tourist information:** Shire Offices, Main St; (08) 9981 1002. **Accommodation:** 2 hotels, 2 motels, 1 cara./camp. park.

Merredin Pop. 3068

MAP REF. 374 I2, 376 F7

A main junction on the important Kalgoorlie–Perth railway line, this important wheat centre is situated 259 km E of Perth. During the late 1800s, Merredin grew up as a shanty town as miners stopped on their way to the goldfields. The town has excellent parks and recreation facilities. **Of interest:** Cummins Theatre (1926), Bates St, oldest theatre outside Perth. Military Museum, East Barrack St, has World War II collection; also departure point for Merredin Peak Heritage Trail (self-guide drive or walk) featuring wildflowers in season, and a number of sites of historical and geological interest (details from Tourist information). Old Railway Station Museum, Great Eastern Hwy. CBH wheat storage and transfer depot, Gamenya Ave, is largest horizontal storage depot in southern hemisphere, with a capacity of 220 000 tonnes. Oct.: Vintage Car Festival (odd-numbered years). **In the area:** Pumping Station No. 4 (1902), 3 km W, designed by C.Y. O'Connor, a fine example of early industrial architecture; station closed 1960 to make way for electrically driven stations. Lookout over Edna May Goldmine, 40 km W. At Kellerberrin, 55 km W: folk museum; scenic lookout at top of Kellerberrin Hill. Durakoppin Wildlife Sanctuary, 27 km N of Kellerberrin, and Gardner Flora Reserve, 35 km SW. Totadgin Dam Reserve, 16 km SW; Totadgin Rock has wave formation similar to Wave Rock. At Bruce Rock, 50 km SW: museum, craft centre and Australia's smallest bank. Good views from summit of Kokerbin Rock, 90 km SW. Picnics and bushwalking near Hunts Dam, 5 km N. Lake Chandler, 45 km N. Mangowine Homestead, 40 km NW at Nungarin, a National Trust-property. Museum, 140 km NW at Koorda; several wildlife reserves in vicinity. **Tourist information:** Barrack St; (08) 9041 1666. **Accommodation:** 2 hotels, 3 motels, 1 cara./camp. park. **See also:** Crossing the Nullarbor.

Mingenew Pop. 357

MAP REF. 376 B4

The little town of Mingenew is in the wheat district of the mid-west, 378 km N of Perth. **Of interest:** Museum, Victoria St, in small, original school building, displays pioneer relics (open Thurs. p.m., or inquire at Tourist information). Views of surrounding wheat-growing area from Mingenew Hill lookout and Pioneer Memorial, off Mingenew– Mullewa Rd. Sept.: Lions Expo (includes wildflower display). **In the area:** Picnic spots at Depot Hill, 15 km W. Dongara, 53 km W, has superb beaches and excellent fishing. At Coalseam Conservation Park, 32 km NE, the State's first coal shafts; Irwin Gorge, riverbed rocks for rock-hunters and wildflowers in spring. **Tourist information:** Post office building, Midland St; (08) 9928 1081. **Accommodation:** 1 hotel, 1 cara./camp. park.

Morawa Pop. 624

MAP REF. 376 C4

Renowned for its grain harvests, Morawa is in the mid-west, 394 km N of Perth. The surrounding area is renowned for its wildflowers in spring. **Of interest:** In Prater St: Historical Museum (open by appt); St David's Anglican Church. Holy Cross Catholic Church, Davis St. Oct.: Music Spectacular. **In the area:** Koolanooka Springs Reserve, 24 km E, ideal for picnics. Bilya Rock Reserve, 4 km W, with 20-min. walk around rock. **Tourist information:** Winfield St; (08) 9971 1421. **Accommodation:** 1 hotel/motel, 1 cara./camp. park.

Mount Barker Pop. 1520

MAP REF. 371 M9, 374 H12, 376 E12

Mount Barker is a quiet, friendly town in the Great Southern district of WA. It is 360 km from Perth, with the Stirling Ranges to the north and the Porongurups to the east. Mt Barker was discovered by Europeans in 1829 and settlers arrived in the 1830s. Vineyards in the area, though relatively new, are producing some top-quality wines. **Of interest:** On Albany Hwy: historic police station and gaol (1868), now museum (open Sat., Sun. and school holidays); Old Station House Craft Shop. Plantagenet Cottage Craft, Mt Barker Rd. Banksia Farm, western end of town (cnr Pearce and Marmion sts). Heritage trail, 30-km drive through town and surrounds; contact Tourist information for map. Jan.: Wine Festival. Mar.: Machinery Field Day. Dec.: Mardi Gras. **In the area:** Wineries, contact Tourist information for details. Lookout on summit of Mt Barker, 5 km SW, pinpointed by 168-m-high television tower, has excellent views of Stirling Ranges across to Albany, worth the drive. St Werburgh's Chapel (1872), 12 km SW, a small mud-walled chapel, privately-owned, overlooking Hay River Valley. Craft at Narrikup Country Store, 16 km S. Porongurup National Park, 24 km E, features granite peaks, karri forests and brilliant seasonal wildflowers. Tall peaks, picturesque plains and over 1000 species of native flora at Stirling Range National Park, 80 km NE. Historic town of Kendenup, 16 km N, location of WA's first gold find. Lake Poorrarecup, 50 km NW; area also noted for orchids and brown and red boronia, which bloom Sept.–Nov. **Tourist information:** 57 Lowood Rd; (08) 9851 1163. **Accommodation:** 1 hotel, 1 hotel/motel, 1 motel, 2 B&B, 1 cara./camp. park. **See also:** The Southern Region.

Mount Magnet   Pop. 1076

MAP REF. 376 E2

The goldmining town of Mount Magnet, a popular stopping-place for motorists driving north to Port Hedland, is 562 km from Perth on the Great Northern Hwy. The surrounding land is used for pastoral farming. There are spectacular wildflowers in the area in spring. **In the area:** Tourist drive (37 km) includes working open-cut gold mine, The Granites and various ghost towns; obtain map from Tourist information. Fossicking for gemstones, but take care as there are dangerous old mine shafts in the area. The Granites, 7 km N, has Aboriginal rock art and picnic spot nearby. Ghost town, Lennonville, 11 km N. Near Sandstone, 166 km E: The Brewery, an historic constructed cave formerly used for beer storage; London Bridge, a rock formation. **Tourist information:** Hepburn St; (08) 9963 4172. **Accommodation:** 2 hotel/motels, 1 hostel, 1 cara./camp. park.

Mullewa   Pop. 739

MAP REF. 376 B3

Gateway to the Murchison goldfields, Mullewa is 99 km from Geraldton. **Of interest:** Kembla Zoo, Stock Rd. In

Maitland Rd: Our Lady of Mount Carmel Church; Monsignor John C. Hawes Priesthouse Museum. Water Supply Reserve, Lovers Lane, features native plants. Mons. Hawes Heritage Trail, details from Tourist information. Aug.–Sept.: Wildflower Show. Sept.: Agricultural Show. **In the area:** Scenic drive, contact Tourist information. Waterfalls after heavy rain, 5 km N near airport. Tallering Peak and Gorge, 58 km N, has spectacular wildflowers in spring. Bindoo Hill Glacier Bed, 40 km NW. Tenindewa Pioneer Well (1900s), a stone-lined well, 18 km W. Butterabby grave site, 18 km S, burial-place of Aborigines hanged there after clash with European settlers. St Mary's Agricultural School, 40 km SE near Tardun. Tallering Station, 40 km NE, has gallery, sheepskin and wool products, and accommodation and camping (open Apr.–Oct.). **Tourist information:** Jose St (May–Nov.) or Shire Offices, cnr Padbury and Thomas sts; (08) 9961 1007. **Accommodation:** 1 hotel, 1 hotel/motel, 1 cara./camp.park.

Mundaring   Pop. 1542

MAP REF. 366 E4, 376 C8

Mundaring is situated on the Great Eastern Hwy, 34 km E of Perth. The picturesque Mundaring Weir, 8 km S of town, is the source of water for the eastern goldfields. The original dam was opened in 1903, and the original pumping station was used until 1955. The attractive hilly bush setting makes the weir a popular picnic spot in summer. **Of interest:** Eastern Hills Showcase, Hartung St, collection of WA arts and crafts in magnificent 1890s home. Fred Jacoby Park, Mundaring Weir Rd, has picnic/barbecue facilities. Sculpture Park, Jacoby St, with sculptures by WA artists. Apr.: Mundaring Hills Festival. **In the area:** Several heritage trails, including Farming Heritage Trail and John Forrest Heritage Trail; contact Tourist information. Lake Leschenaultia, 12 km NW, for swimming and canoeing; walks, camping and picnic/barbecue facilities, and miniature scenic railway on shore. Walyunga National Park, 30 km NW, a beautiful bushland park and location for Avon Descent, a major white-water canoeing event held in Aug. Old Mahogany Inn (1842), 3 km W, WA's oldest residential inn. Mount Olive Stained Glass Studio, 6 km W. John Forrest National Park, 6 km W, on high

point of Darling Range, picnic spot beside natural pool at Rocky Pool. Quatre Sessions Heritage Rose Garden, 9 km W, one of State's largest private collections. At Darlington, 10 km W: Darling Estate Winery, Nelson Rd (open Thurs.–Sun.); Brook Studio, open Fri.–Sun. Bibbulman Track, 20 km SW, a long distance walking trail from Kalamunda (near Perth) to Walpole. Mundaring Weir, 8 km S, water catchment area for goldfields (500 km E); at weir, the C.Y. O'Connor Museum (1880s), housed in former pumphouse building, features models of Eastern Goldfields water supply. Nearby, at Hills Forest, Sights and Sounds which offers night-time outdoor learning experiences including Aboriginal dance groups and bush bands (details at Tourist information). Further 15 km along road, near Kalamunda: Kalamunda National Park; History Village, a collection of historic buildings (open Sat.–Thurs.). Carosa Vineyard, 7 km E at Mt Helena (open Sat. and Sun.). **Tourist information:** Shire Offices, 7000 Great Eastern Hwy; (08) 9290 6666. **Accommodation:** 1 hotel/ motel, 1 hostel, 1 cara. park.

Mundrabilla   Pop. 11

MAP REF. 377 Q8

A tiny settlement on the Eyre Hwy where travellers can break the journey across the continent. There is a bird and animal sanctuary behind the motel. **Tourist information:** Roadhouse; (08) 9039 3465. **Accommodation:** 1 motel, 1 cara./camp. park.

Nannup   Pop. 472

MAP REF. 367 G10, 370 A4, 374 C10, 376 C11

Nannup is a quiet, friendly town in the Blackwood Valley, 290 km S of Perth. The surrounding countryside is lush, gently rolling pasture alongside jarrah and pine forests. **Of interest:** In Brockman St: old police station (1922); Arboretum. In Warren Rd: art and craft centre; Bunnings Timber Mill, largest jarrah sawmill in State (guided tours available Mon., Wed. and Fri.); Nannup Temptations and Crafty Creations, for local art and craft including jarrah goods; Country Mayde, for local craft; Old Templemore Antique Shop; Gemstone Museum, closed Wed. Market in Warren Rd, 2nd Sat. each month. Mar.: Music Festival. Aug.: Daffodil Weekend. **In the area:** Self-guide wildflower (in

The Hamersley Range

Stretching over 300 kilometres through the heart of the mineral-rich Pilbara, the Hamersley Range forms a wild and magnificent panorama. The mountains slope gently up from the south to the flat-topped outcrops and Western Australia's highest peak, Mt Meharry. In the north they rise majestically from golden spinifex plains.

The iron-ore boom in the area has created employment opportunities in this land of sand spinifex, mulga scrub and massive red mountains. Model mining-company towns have sprung up. Gardens, swimming pools, golf courses and communal activities help compensate for the isolation and harsh climate.

Dampier, on King Bay, is a modern iron-ore company town, with a major salt industry nearby. Offshore is the Woodside North West Shelf Gas Project, which is the largest single resource development undertaken in Australia; it includes a 1500-kilometre pipeline. Another side to the town is the Dampier Archipelago, comprising 42 islands of which 25 are incorporated into flora and fauna reserves. Fishing, diving, swimming, boating, camping and bushwalking are allowed around and on several of these outcrops.

Roebourne, the oldest town in the north-west, has been a centre for the pastoral, copper and pearling industries. The old pearling port of **Cossack** is nearby. To the south, the fishing village of **Onslow** and its offshore islands is the perfect holiday retreat. **Karratha** is a modern town and regional centre as is **Wickham**. Wickham's port at Cape Lambert has the tallest and second-longest jetty in Australia, standing 18.5 metres above water and 3 kilometres long. At **Port Hedland**, streamlined port facilities cope with more tonnage than any other port in the country. Ore mined inland at Tom Price, Newman, Paraburdoo and other centres is railed on giant trains to the ports for export.

Fishing in the Port Hedland area is good, with many world records being set. Swimming in the sea can be dangerous, because sharks, sea snakes and poisonous stone fish frequent the waters; always make local enquiries before you swim. **Marble Bar**, considered to be the hottest place in Australia and keeping alive the tradition of the great Australian outback, is 193 kilometres south-east of Port Hedland.

Iron ore mined at Tom Price being railed to the coast for export

Although the main activity in the area is centred on the mining towns of **Tom Price**, Paraburdoo, **Newman** and others, visitors will find many other areas of interest. Spectacular gorges have been carved by watercourses, some with wide, crystal-clear pools. Lush green vegetation thrives and the gorges are cool oases in the harsh climate.

Tom Price is a good base from which to explore the beauty of the Hamersley Range in particular, **Karijini** (Hamersley Range) **National Park**. The breathtaking Dales Gorge, approached through Yampire Gorge, is 45 kilometres long. The splendid Fortescue Falls and Hamersley Gorge with its folded bands of coloured rock, are found here.

One particularly enchanting oasis in the Hamersley Range area is **Millstream-Chichester National Park**, on the Fortescue River, inland from Roebourne. Thousands of birds flock to this delightful spot, where ferns, lilies, palms and rushes grow in abundance. There are two long, deep, natural pools. The springs produce over 36 million litres of water a day from an underground basin, which is piped to Roebourne, Dampier, Karratha, Wickham and Cape Lambert. In contrast to Karijini National Park, the scenery in Millstream-Chichester National Park varies from magnificent views over the coastal plain to the deep permanent river pools of tropical Millstream. This attractive spot offers excellent swimming conditions and pleasant camping areas.

The Hamersley Range is rugged, exciting country, and is enticing and often beautiful. Keep in mind, however, that you are travelling in remote areas. Read the section on Outback Motoring before departure. Old roads are being improved and new ones constructed in an effort to open up one of the oldest areas in the world.

For further information contact Tom Price Tourist Bureau, Central Rd, Tom Price; (08) 9183 1112. **See also:** National Parks and individual text entries for those parks and towns indicated by bold type. **Map references:** 375 G3, 378 A4.

Iron stone rocks and spinifex in the Hamersley Range

spring) and waterfall (in winter) walks, other walking trails, scenic drives of jarrah forest and pine plantations, and Nannup Heritage Trail; details from Tourist information. Blackwood River for canoeing and trout fishing. Hillbrook tulip farm, 1 km S (open July–Sept.). Barrabup Pool, 10 km W. Tathra Wines, 14 km NE. **Tourist information:** 4 Brockman St; (08) 9756 1211. **Accommodation:** 1 hotel/motel, 4 B&B, 1 hostel, 2 cara./camp. parks.

Narrogin   Pop. 4638

MAP REF. 374 G6, 376 E9

The centre of prosperous agricultural country, Narrogin is 192 km SE of Perth on the Great Southern Hwy. Sheep, pigs and cereal farms are the main primary industries. Its name is derived from an Aboriginal word *Gnarojin* meaning waterhole. **Of interest:** Court House Museum (1894), Egerton St, originally a school, later district court house (open Tues., Sat. or by appt). Foxes Lair, Williams Rd, has 5 ha of natural bushland. Lions Lookout, Kipling St, for panoramic views. Restoration Group Museum, Federal St, displays cars, stationary engines and other machinery (open 3rd Sun. each month, or by appt). Centenary Park has pathway marked with 100 commemorative tiles designed by local artists relating to local history. Jan.: State Gliding Championships. May: Music Eisteddfod. Sept.: Orchid Show. Oct.: Spring Festival; Texpo (modern farming displays). **In the area:** Memorabilia at Old Butter Factory, southern outskirts of town on Great Southern Hwy. Heritage trail, brochure at Tourist information. Yilliminning and Birdwhistle rocks, 11 km E, unusual rock formations. Albert Facey's homestead, 40 km E, has a mini-zoo and local craft displays. Dryandra Woodland, 30 km NW, features walking trails and fauna including numbats and mallee fowl. **Tourist information:** 23 Egerton St; (08) 9881 2064. **Accommodation:** 3 hotels, 2 motels, 1 cara./camp. park.

New Norcia   Pop. 73

MAP REF. 374 D1, 376 C6

In 1846 Spanish Benedictine monks established a mission at New Norcia, 132 km N of Perth in an attempt to help the local Aboriginal population. The handsome Spanish-inspired buildings come as a surprise, surrounded by paddocks and distant bushland. The settlement is in the secluded Moore Valley, and wheat, wool and other farm products are produced. New Norcia is owned by the Benedictine Community and is still operating as a monastery. **Of interest:** Heritage trail (2 km) includes inspection of oldest operating flour mill in WA (1879) (mill also has interpretive display), abbey church, cemetery, hotel (1927), Bishops Well, Rosendo Salvado Statue; brochure from Tourist information. Benedictine community's Museum and art gallery, Great Northern Hwy, has priceless collection of religious art, both Australian and European, and Roman, Egyptian and Spanish artifacts (many gifted by Queen Isabella of Spain); museum displays history of monks' involvement with local indigenous population; shop sells local food products and souvenirs. Group accommodation for up to 250 in old convent and college buildings (advance bookings required). Walking tours of monastery buildings available, details from Tourist information. **In the area:** At Mogumber, 24 km SW, one of the State's highest timber and concrete bridges. Historic hotel at Bolgart, 49 km SE. Former Wyening Mission, 50 km SE, an historic site (open by appt. only, inquire at Tourist information for access details). Piawaning, 31 km NE, has magnificent stand of eucalypts just north of town. **Tourist information:** Museum and art gallery, Great Northern Hwy; (08) 9654 8056. **Accommodation:** 1 hotel, 1 guest house (attached to monastery, bookings essential).

Newman   Pop. 5627

MAP REF. 378 D6

This town was built by Mt Newman Mining Co. for employees involved in the extraction of iron ore. Mt Newman ships its ore from Port Hedland, and the two towns are connected by a 426-km railroad. In 1981 responsibility for the town was handed over to the local shire. With the upgrading of the highway and improved tourist facilities in the town, Newman has become a popular stopping-place. **Of interest:** Tours (Mon.–Sat.) of Mt Whaleback mine, largest iron ore open-cut mine in world, depart from Tourist information. BHP Iron Ore Silver Jubilee Museum and Gallery; mining and pastoral museum; both at Tourist information. Radio Hill Lookout, off Newman Dr., for good views over town; walking trail and climb from museum to lookout. Aug.: Fortescue Festival. **In the area:** Opthalmia Dam, 15 km N, for swimming; picnic/barbecue facilities on shore. Good views from Mt Newman, 20 km N. Kalgans Pool, 51 km NW (day trip, 4WD access only). Eagle Rock Falls, 69 km NW, has permanent pools and picnic spots nearby (road to falls requires 4WD). Aboriginal rock carvings, rock pools and waterholes at Wanna Munna, 70 km W, and Punda (4WD only), 75 km NW. **Tourist information:** cnr Fortescue Ave and Newman Dr.; (08) 9175 2888. **Accommodation:** 2 motels, 2 cara./ camp. parks. **See also:** The Hamersley Range.

Norseman   Pop. 1398

MAP REF. 377 J8

Norseman, 195 km S of Kalgoorlie, is the last large town on the Eyre Hwy for travellers heading east towards SA. Gold put Norseman on the map in the early 1890s, and the richest quartz reef in Australia is still being mined today. The town is steeped in goldmining history, with colossal tailings dumps a reminder. The area is popular with amateur prospectors and gemstone collectors; gemstone fossicking permits are available from Tourist information. **Of interest:** Historical Collection, Battery Rd, includes mining tools and household items. Post Office (1896), cnr Prinsep and Ra sts. Heritage trail (33 km), follows original Cobb & Co. route, including descent into a 'decline'; details from Tourist information. In Roberts St: statue, commemorating horse called Norseman, who allegedly pawed the ground and unearthed a nugget of gold, thus starting a gold rush in area; Norseman Tourist Reception Centre, with visitor facilities, day parking and picnic area. Beacon Hill, Mines Rd, offers good views of surrounding salt lakes (spectacular at sunrise and sunset). **In the area:** Dundas Rocks, 22 km S, are 550 million years old; excellent picnic area and old Dundas town site nearby. Bromus Dam, 32 km S, freshwater dam with picnic area nearby. Peak Charles, 50 km S then 40 km off hwy; energetic climbers are rewarded with magnificent views. Gemstone leases on Eyre Hwy and off Kalgoorlie Hwy, details from Tourist information. Five km east of town: Old mines; Jimberlana Dyke, reputedly one of oldest geological areas in world;

Karri forest near Northcliffe

Mt Jimberlana, with walking trail to summit and views. Buldania Rocks, 28 km E, has picnic area and beautiful wildflowers in spring. To south-west, Frank Hahn National Park, 50 km E of Lake King township, traversed by Lake King–Norseman Rd; if travelling this road, check road conditions before departure and note that there are no visitor facilities or supplies available between Norseman and Lake King. **Tourist information:** 68 Roberts St; (08) 9039 1071. **Accommodation:** 2 hotels, 2 motels, 1 hostel, 1 cara./camp. park. **See also:** Crossing the Nullarbor; The Goldfields.

Northam   Pop. 6560

MAP REF. 366 H2, 374 E3, 376 D7
The regional centre of the fertile Avon Valley at the junction of the Avon and Mortlock rivers, Northam is an attractive town. On the Great Eastern Hwy, 99 km E of Perth, it is an important supply point for the farms of the eastern wheat belt. Northam is also a major railway centre. **Of interest:** In Wellington St: Old police station (1866); court house (1896); town hall (1897); Avon Valley Arts Society art and craft shop. Flour Mill (1371), Newcastle St. In Fitzgerald St: Old Railway Station Museum;

Shamrock Hotel (1886), fully renovated. Large swinging bridge over Avon River adjacent to Tourist information. Weir across river, near Peel Tce bridge, forms lake that has a colony of white swans and many other species of native birdlife. Morby Cottage (1836), Old York Rd, built by the Morrells, a pioneer family. National Trust-classified Sir James Mitchell House (1905), cnr Duke and Hawes sts. Historic town walk, Northam–Katrine Heritage Trail; Farming Heritage Trail; details from Tourist information. Aug.: Avon River Festival. Oct.: Northam Rodeo; Avon Valley Country Life and Leisure Festival. Nov.: Avon Valley Country Music Festival. **In the area:** Hot-air ballooning (in cooler months), horseriding and canoeing. Blue Gum Camel Farm, 19 km SW, near Spencer Brook Rd at Clackline, offers camel- and trail-riding in picturesque bushland surroundings. Muresk University of Technology, 10 km S, former early farming property. At Dowerin, 58 km NE: museum; craft centre; Hagbooms Lake; Field Days held here in Aug. In spring, wildflowers abound near Wubin, 190 km N. **Tourist information:** Heaton Ave; (096) 222 100. **Accommodation:** 8 hotels, 1 motel, 6 B&B, 2 cara./camp. parks.

Northampton   Pop. 786

MAP REF. 376 A3
Northampton is an historic town which nestles among gentle hills in the valley of Nokarena Brook, 48 km N of Geraldton. Inland there is picturesque country with vivid wildflowers in spring. The drive west leads to the coast, with beaches for swimming and fishing. **Of interest:** In Hampton Rd: Chiverton House Museum (open Thurs.–Mon.); Bowerbird Collection, a private collection of memorabilia (open Tues.–Sun.); St Mary's Convent and Church, designed by Mons. Hawes. Gwalla church site and cemetery, Gwalla St. Miners' cottages (1860s), Brook St. **In the area:** Wildflower tours in spring, contact Tourist information. Alma Schoolhouse, 12 km N. Near coast at Port Gregory, 47 km NW: Lynton Station, including ruins of labour-hiring depot for convicts (in use 1853–6); Lynton House, (not open), a squat building with slits for windows, probably erected as protection from hostile Aborigines; Sanford House. Hutt Lagoon, near Port Gregory, appears pink in light of midday sun. At Horrocks Beach, 20 km W, pleasant bays, sandy beaches, and good fishing and surfing. **Tourist information:** Hampton Rd; (08) 9934 1488. **Accommodation:** 2 hotels, 1 hotel/motel, 1 hostel, 1 cara./camp. park.

Northcliffe   Pop. 190

MAP REF. 370 C9, 374 D12, 376 D12
Magnificent virgin karri forests surround the little township of Northcliffe, 31 km S of Pemberton in the extreme south-west corner of the State. Unique flora and fauna is to be found in this area. **Of interest:** In Wheatley Coast Rd: Pioneer Museum, has historical relics and photographs; at Tourist information, rock and mineral collection, Aboriginal Interpretation Room and photographic folio of native flora and birds; Northcliffe Art and Craft. South West Timber Trekking Company, off Wheatley Coast Rd, offers horseriding along forest tracks. Mountain bike hire available, contact Tourist information. Oct.: Mountain Bike Championship. **In the area:** Adjacent to town, Forest Park, has Hollow Butt Karri and Twin Karri walking trails, and picnic areas. Fishing, Warren River. Sandy beaches. Petrene Estate Vineyard, 2 km E, has cellar-door sales. Mt Chudalup, 20 km S, a giant

granite outcrop with walking trail to summit for views. Point D'Entre-casteaux, 27 km s; cliffs popular with climbers. Windy Harbour and Salmon Beach, 29 km s. Bibbulmun Track links the three national parks: D'Entrecasteaux (5 km s), Warren (20 km NW) and Shannon (30 km E). Great Forest Tree Drive through Shannon National Park, east of town; picnic spots and signposted walks in park (brochure at Tourist information. Boorara Tree (once used as fire lookout) and Lane-Poole Falls, 18 km SE. **Tourist information:** adjacent to Pioneer Museum, Wheatley Coast Rd; (08) 9776 7203. **Accommodation:** 1 hotel, 1 B&B, 1 cara./camp. park.

Onslow   Pop. 881

MAP REF. 375 D3

Onslow, on the north-west coast of the State, is important as the base for the gas and oil fields off the coast. The town was originally at the mouth of the Ashburton River, but was moved to Beadon Bay in 1925 after constant cyclones caused the river to silt up. The remains of the old town site can still be seen. Onslow was a bustling pearling centre and in the 1890s gold was discovered. During World War II, US, British and Dutch submarines refuelled here, and the town was bombed twice. In 1952 it was the mainland base for Britain's nuclear experiments at Monte Bello Islands. **Of interest:** Heritage trail, contact Tourist information for brochure. July: Arts and Crafts Festival. **In the area:** Excellent fishing. Native fauna, including emus, red kangaroos, sand goannas, and a variety of birdlife. The Sturt desert pea and Ashburton pea are among the many wildflowers that bloom in spring in the area. Termite mounds, 10 km s on Onslow Access Rd; interpretive display explains the mounds. **Tourist information:** Shire Offices, Second Ave; (08) 9184 6001. **Accommodation:** 1 hotel/ motel, 1 hostel, 2 cara./camp. parks.

Pemberton   Pop. 934

MAP REF. 370 C7, 374 D11, 376 C11

The town of Pemberton, 335 km s of Perth, is nestled in a quiet valley, surrounded by towering karri forests. This lush forest area has some of the tallest hardwood trees in the world, and, in spring, brilliant flowering bush plants. Pemberton is known as a centre for

high-quality woodcraft. **Of interest:** Craft outlets include Pemberton Arts and Craft, Broadway Ave; Warren River Arts and Craft, and Peter Kovacsy Studio in Jamieson St; Fine Woodcraft Gallery, Dickinson St. In Brockman St: Karri Visitors Centre, includes museum, with collection of historic photographs and authentic forestry equipment, and Karri Forest Discovery Centre; Pemberton Sawmill, guided tours available Mon.–Fri. Pemberton Tramway, tramcars based on 1907 Fremantle trams operate daily through tall-forest country between Pemberton and Northcliffe; depart from railway station, Railway Cres. On Pump Hill Rd: Forest Park and Pool, offers walking trails and picnic spots; Trout and Marron Hatchery, supplies WA rivers and dams (daily tours available). Mar.: King Karri Karnival. **In the area:** Forest Industry tours into logging and regrowth areas; walking trails; scenic bus tours; 4WD adventure tours, 2 hours to overnight; horseriding; fishing in local rivers (inland fishing licence required for trout and marron); self-guide forest drives; contact Tourist information for details. Wineries: Warren Vineyard, Conte Rd; Gloucester Ridge, Burma Rd; Mountford Wines, Bamess Rd; Salitage, Vasse Hwy; winery tours available, contact Tourist information. Gloucester Tree, signposted off Brockman St, tallest fire lookout in world (over 60 m high with 150 rungs spiralling upwards), open for climbing during daylight hours. Moon's Crossing, 18 km SE, for picnics (4WD access in winter). The Cascades, 8 km s, for picnics, bushwalking and fishing. Brockman Saw Pit, 13 km s, restored to show how timber was sawn in 1860s. King Trout Farm, 8 km SW. Warren National Park, 9 km SW, includes some of best accessible virgin karri forest, also Marianne North Tree (tree was subject of painting by artist) and Dave Evans Bicentennial Tree, both fine lookout trees with picnic facilities and walking tracks nearby. Swamp Willow Farm on Hawke Rd near park, 12 km SW, for local wood-craft. Deep Forest Arabian Stud Farm, 13 km W on Green Rd off Vasse Hwy. Eagle Springs marron farm, 18 km W. Nearby, Beedelup National Park, features falls, suspension bridge, magnificent wildflowers in spring and a giant karri tree with a hole cut through it. Donnelly River Wines, 35 km NW. Marron and dairy farm, 1 km N. Big Brook Dam and Arboretum, 7 km N. Founders Forest, 10 km N on Smiths Rd,

has karri trees over 120 years old. Piano Gully Vineyard, 24 km NE, off South Western Hwy. **Tourist information:** Karri Visitors Centre, Brockman St; (08) 9776 1133. **Accommodation:** 1 hotel/motel, 3 motels, 4 B&B, 1 hostel, 1 cara./camp. park. **See also:** The Southern Region.

Perenjori   Pop. 250

MAP REF. 376 C4

Located on the Wubin–Mullewa Hwy (known as 'Wildflower Way'), 352 km NE of Perth, Perenjori lies on the fringes of the Murchison goldfields and the great sheep stations of the west. **Of interest:** Historical Museum behind Tourist information, Fowler St (open June–Oct., closed Sun.). Arts and Crafts Centre, Russell St. Sept.: Agricultural Show. **In the area:** Wildflowers in season, July–Sept. Many scenic drives, brochures at Tourist information. Salt lakes with variety of waterbirds to be seen, including Mongers Lake (lookout near lake), 50 km NE; Yarra Yarra Lakes, 58 km SW near Three Springs. Perenjori–Rothsay Heritage Trail (180 km), recalls early goldmining days (details from Tourist information). Many gemstones in this mineral-rich region for fossickers. Many gold mines in surrounding area; care should be taken, as unfenced pits make the area dangerous. Aboriginal Stones at Damperwah Soak, 40 km NE (4WD access only). **Tourist information:** Fowler St; (08) 9973 1105. **Accommodation:** 1 hotel, 1 cara./camp. park.

Pingelly   Pop. 763

MAP REF. 374 F5, 376 D9

On the Great Southern Hwy, 154 km SE of Perth, Pingelly is part of the central southern farming district. The cutting of sandalwood was once a local industry, but today the land is given over to sheep and wheat. **Of interest:** In Parade St: Community Craft Centre; Court House Museum. Apex Lookout, Stone St, for fine views of town and country. Aug.: Art and Tulip Festival. **In the area:** Moorumbine Heritage Trail, details from Tourist information. Historic St Patrick's Church (1873), 10 km E at Moorumbine. Tuttanning Flora and Fauna Reserve, 21 km E. County Peak Lookout, 30 m N. Dryandra Reserve, 40 km SW, an ecological oasis with unique flora and fauna including the numbat, WA's fauna emblem; timber also produced. **Tourist information:** Shire Offices, 17 Queen St; (08) 9887 1066. **Accommodation:** 1 hotel, 1 motel, 1 cara./camp. park.

Pinjarra   Pop. 1779

MAP REF. 366 C10, 374 C6, 376 C9

Pinjarra is a pleasant drive 84 km s of Perth, along the shaded South Western Hwy. The town has a picturesque setting on the banks of the Murray River in one of the earliest established districts in WA. The Alcoa Refinery, north-east of town on the South Western Hwy, is the largest alumina refinery in Australia. Pinjarra is a good base for exploring the area. **Of interest:** In Henry St: St John's Church (1862); Heritage Rose Garden, including memorial to WWI and WWII soldiers; Liveringa (1874); Old School (1896); Teacher's House. Edenvale (1888), George St. Suspension bridge across the Murray River, picnic facilities on either side. **In the area:** Heritage trail horseriding; details from Tourist information. Alcoa Scarp Lookout, 14 km E, for good views of coastal plain, surrounding farming area and Alcoa Refinery. Athlone Angora Stud and Goat Farm, 16 km E. Alcoa Refinery, 4 km NE (bus tours on Wed.). At North Dandalup, 10 km NE, Whittakers Mill, for bushwalking, camping and barbecues. Award-winning Tumbulgum Farm, 38 km N at Mundijong, features native and farm animals, Aboriginal culture, farm shows and WA products sales Yalgorup National Park on coast. Old Blythewood (1860s), 4 km s, a former post office, coaching inn and family home (check opening times). Lake Navarino Forest Resort and Waroona Dam, 33 km s, for watersports, fishing, walking and horseriding. **Tourist information:** Pinjarra Tourist Centre (in Edenvale stately home), George St; (08) 9531 1438. **Accommodation:** 4 hotels, 1 motel, 7 cara./camp. parks. **See also:** The Southern Region.

Point Samson   Pop. 180

MAP REF. 375 G1, 378 A1

Point Samson was named in honour of Michael Samson, who accompanied the district's first settler, Walter Padbury, on his 1863 journey. The town was established in 1910 as the major port for the Roebourne district, replacing Cossack, where the harbour had silted up after a cyclone. The port was very active for many years, but today the town supports a small fishing industry and its extremely attractive setting has made it a popular beach destination. **Of interest:** Beach is protected by a coral reef; good swimming, fishing and skindiving. Honeymoon Cove, Johns Creek Rd, for swimming and picnicking. Nearby at John's Harbour, jetty, where fishing trawlers are moored, and boat ramp. Trawlers Tavern, Point Samson Rd, for local seafood. **In the area:** Excellent fishing in tidal rivers and offshore; coast renowned for its game-fishing. Emma Withnell Heritage Trail, details from Tourist information. **Tourist information:** Point Samson Fisheries, Point Samson Rd; (08) 9187 1414. **Accommodation:** 1 cara./camp. park.

Port Hedland   Pop. 11 344

MAP REF. 378 C1, 380 B13

Port Hedland's remarkable growth has been due to the iron-ore boom, which started in the early 1960s. The town was named after Captain Peter Hedland, who reached the harbour in 1863. Today Port Hedland handles the largest export tonnage of any Australian port. Iron ore from some of the world's biggest mines is loaded on to the world's biggest ore carriers. The 2.6-km-long trains operated by BHP Iron Ore arrive seven times daily. Salt production is another major industry, with about 2 million tonnes exported per annum. **Of interest:** Observation Tower, at Tourist information, Wedge St. Lions Park, Hunt St, has pioneer relics. Royal Flying Doctor Base, Richardson St (open 10 a.m. Mon.–Fri.); BHP industrial tours (daily Mar.–Sept., six times a week Oct.–Feb.); book at Tourist information. Don Rhodes Mining Museum, Wilson St. At Two Mile Ridge, opp. fire brigade in Wilson St, Aboriginal carvings in limestone ridge (open Mon.–Fri.). Historic St Matthew's Church (1917), Edgar St, now art gallery and exhibition centre. Old Port Hedland cemetery, Stevens St, has graves of early gold prospectors, and Japanese pearl divers. Aug.: Spinifex Spree. **In the area:** Stairway to the Moon, a natural wonder created when full moon rises over shoreline at low tide; best seen alongside caravan park at Cooke Point (details from Tourist information). Picnic, fish and swim at Pretty Pool, next to Cooke Point caravan park.

(Poisonous stone fish frequent coast, especially Nov.–Mar.; make local inquiries before swimming in sea.) At Cargill Salt, 8 km s, giant cone-shaped mounds of salt awaiting export. Whale-watching trips, June–Oct. Excellent fishing; charter boat hire. Birdlife is abundant in district; watch for bustards, eagles, cockatoos, galahs, ibises, pelicans and parrots. **Tourist information:** 13 Wedge St; (08) 9173 1711. **Accommodation:** 6 hotel/motels, 1 hostel, 3 cara./ camp. parks. **See also:** The Hamersley Range.

Ravensthorpe   Pop. 392

MAP REF. 376 H10

Ravensthorpe, situated 533 km SE of Perth, is the centre of the old Phillips River goldfield. Copper mining was also important here, reaching a peak in the late 1960s; the last copper mine shut in 1972. Many old mine shafts can be seen around the district. Wheat and sheep are the local industries. **Of interest:** Historic buildings: Anglican Church, Dunn St; 'the Big House', old mine manager's house, Carlisle St; in Morgans St, Dance Cottage (museum), Palace Hotel and restored Commercial Hotel (now Community Centre). Also in Morgans St, Rangeview Park features local plant species. Sept.: Wildflower Show, features over 700 local species; Wool Day. **In the area:** Catlin Creek Heritage Trail and self-drive scenic drives, details from Tourist information. Rock-collecting, check locally to avoid trespass. Ravensthorpe Range, 3 km N, and Mt Desmond, 10 km SE, for views. WA Time Meridian at first rest bay west of town. Eremia Camel Farm, 2 km s, offers rides and 'bush tucker'. Fitzgerald River National Park, 46 km s, now Biosphere Reserve for UNESCO. Old copper smelter, 2 km E. **Tourist information:** Going Bush Information Stop, Morgans St; (08) 9838 1277. **Accommodation:** 1 hotel/motel, 1 motel, 1 cara./camp. park.

Rockingham   Pop. 36 675

MAP REF. 366 B7, 374 C4, 376 C8

At the southern end of Cockburn Sound, 45 km s of Perth, Rockingham is a coastal city and seaside destination. Begun in 1872 as a timber port, the harbour fell into disuse with the opening of the Fremantle inner harbour in 1897. Today its magnificent golden beaches

The Kimberley

A group of boab trees, near Kununurra

Until relatively recently the Kimberley region in the far north of Western Australia was only for hardened pioneers and prospectors. Now the National Highway puts it on Australia's travel map and it can offer both excitement and adventure. In addition, the 40 tonne, 18 metre ketch-rigged motor yacht *Opal Shell* cruises along the Kimberley coast out of Derby.

There are two seasons in the Kimberley. The long dry period in winter brings delightful weather, while the green season brings higher temperatures, with monsoonal rains usually falling between December and March.

On the west side, the gateway to the Kimberley is the old pearling town of **Broome**. In the boisterous days of the early 1900s the pearling fleet numbered some 400 luggers with 3000 crewmen. Today cosmopolitan Broome is rapidly expanding into one of Western Australia's most popular tourist destinations. There are many points of interest, including a set of dinosaur tracks believed to have been embedded in limestone 130 million years ago, and Buccaneer Rock, said to be the place where Dampier was wrecked in 1699.

Further north-east is **Derby**, on King Sound near the mouth of the Fitzroy River, a centre for the beef cattle industry of the Fitzroy Valley and the King Leopold Ranges. Just 7 kilometres south of the town is a centuries-old boab tree. Shaped like an inverted wineglass and 14 metres in diameter, it is hollow and is reputed to have been used as a cell for prisoners.

Derby is a useful base for excursions to Windjana Gorge and Tunnel Creek in the Napier Range, and Geikie Gorge near the town of **Fitzroy Crossing**. Fitzroy Crossing is a centre for local Aboriginal communities and also has excellent accommodation and camping facilities. The river gorges here are among the most colourful and spectacular in northern Australia.

The old gold settlement of **Halls Creek**, 16 kilometres from the site of the present town, was the scene of the first gold rush in Western Australia in 1885. Scores of diggers perished of hunger and thirst, and very little gold was found.

Nearby is the meteorite crater at Wolfe Creek, the second largest in the world, with an average depth of 50 metres. The meteorite is believed to have struck the earth about one million years ago. Also near Halls Creek is the China Wall, a natural white quartz outcrop above a placid creek.

The most northerly town and safe port harbour in Western Australia is **Wyndham**, the terminus of the Great Northern Highway and now also the port for the Ord River Irrigation Area as well as for the east Kimberley cattle stations. A 100-kilometre route from Wyndham to **Kununurra** winds through spectacular ancient gorge country.

Kununurra, a lively town with excellent facilities, is the base for Lake Argyle, Hidden Valley National Park and **Purnululu (Bungle Bungle) National Park**. Purnululu is the location of the most unusual geological formations: thousands of beehive shaped mounds striped in black and orange. Ground access is by 4WD between April and end of December only due to fragility of internal roads in wet conditions. South of Lake Argyle is the Argyle Diamond Mine, the world's largest. Kununurra is then linked to Darwin by the National Highway.

For further information contact the Kununurra Tourist Bureau, Coolibah Drive, Kununurra; (08) 9168 1177. **See also:** Entry for Purnululu National Park in National Parks and individual text entries in A–Z listing for those towns indicated by bold type. **Map references:** 372, 373, 381 L6.

The Ord River

The development of the Ord River Scheme was a far-sighted move to develop the tropical north of Western Australia. During the wet season, the rivers of the Kimberley become raging torrents and at times the Ord River empties more than 50 million litres a second into the sea. With the end of the wet season, the rich seasonal pastures die and the land becomes dry again. The Ord River Dam was built to harness this tremendous wealth of water for agriculture.

Lake Argyle is the main storage reservoir. It is the largest constructed lake in Australia. This vast expanse of water is dotted with islands that were once peaks rising above the surrounding valleys. The water of the Ord is now capable of irrigating 72 000 hectares of land.

The area is becoming increasingly attractive to tourists. Surrounding Lake Argyle are rugged red slopes, a haven for native animals, such as the bungarra lizard, the brush-tailed wallaby and the euro. There are lake cruises, bushwalks and a picnic area.

The original Durack Homestead from Argyle Downs Station is also to be found here; once the residence of the cattle-pioneering Durack family, the homestead was moved to its present site to prevent it being covered by the waters of Lake Argyle as it filled. The homestead is a fascinating memorial to the early settlers of the district.

WESTERN AUSTRALIA

and protected waters are Rockingham's main attraction. **Of interest:** Museum, Kent St, features local history exhibits. Lookout and WWII coastal battery at Point Peron, Point Peron Rd. In Civic Blvd.: Art Gallery; Art and Craft Centre. Mersey Point Jetty at Shoalwater, departure point for cruises. Sun. markets at Flinders Lane and Leghorn St. Nov.: Spring Festival. Dec.: Christmas Regatta; Cockburn Yachting Regatta. **In the area:** Old Rockingham and Rockingham–Jarrahdale heritage trails; details from Tourist information. Penguin Island, has a colony of little (fairy) penguins; Penguin Experience Island Discovery Centre (open Oct.–May). Garden Island, home to HMAS *Stirling*, naval base; access by private boat during the day (causeway link to mainland closed to public). Offshore reefs and wrecks, popular with dive enthusiasts; diving excursions and various cruises, including swimming with the dolphins, available, contact Tourist information. Shoalwater Bay Islands Marine Park, extends from just south of Garden Island to Becher Point; cruises of park available, and swim with the seals tours Sept.–June. Near Lake Richmond, 4 km SW, walks, freshwater flora and fauna, and domed stromalites. Marapana Wildlife World, 15 km S, State's first drive-through deer and wildlife park. Wineries: Baldivis Estate, 15 km SE; Peel Estate, 17 km SE. Scenic drive 48 km SE to Serpentine Dam, WA's major water conservation area; noted for its brilliant wildflowers in spring, gardens and bushland; nearby, Serpentine Falls. WA Water Ski Park, 5 km NE, constructed water-ski complex. At nearby Karnup: Pioneer Pottery, Fletcher Rd; self-guide Nature Reserve Environmental Walk; contact Tourist information. On northern outskirts, The Granary, has displays depicting history of grain industry (free guided tours, by appt only). **Tourist information:** 43 Kent St; (08) 9592 3464. **Accommodation:** 2 hotels, 2 motels, 10 B&B, 4 cara./camp. parks.

Roebourne   Pop. 1213

MAP REF. 375 G1, 378 A2

Named after John Septimus Roe, the State's first surveyor-general, Roebourne was established in 1864 and is the oldest town on the north-west coast. It was developed as the capital of the north-west and was at one time the administrative centre for the whole area

north of the Murchison River. As the centre for the early mining and pastoral industries in the Pilbara, it was connected to the pearling port of Cossack, and later to Point Samson, by tramway, for the transport of passengers and goods. Although now overshadowed by the iron-ore and other industries, Roebourne has retained its special character. **Of interest:** Old stone buildings (some National Trust-classified): police station, Queen St; post office (1887), Sholl St; in Hampton St, hospital (1887), and court house; Holy Trinity Church (1894), Withnell St; in Roe St, Union Bank (1889, now Shire library), and Victoria Hotel, last of town's five original pubs. Old Roebourne Gaol (1886), Queen St, now Tourist information centre. Good views from Mt Welcome, Fisher Dr. Aug.: Royal Show; Roebourne Cup and Ball. **In the area:** Emma Withnell Heritage Trail (52 km) passes through Roebourne, Wickham and Cossack, ending at Point Samson. Fishing at Cleaverville, 25 km N. Millstream, 150 km S, former camel watering holes, now offer safe swimming in freshwater springs; walking trails nearby; old homestead now tourist information centre. **Tourist information:** Old Gaol, Queen St; (08) 9182 1060. **Accommodation:** 1 hotel/motel, 1 cara./camp. park. **See also:** The Hamersley Range.

Southern Cross   Pop. 982

MAP REF. 376 G7

A small, flourishing town on the Great Eastern Hwy, 368 km E of Perth, Southern Cross is the centre of a prosperous agricultural and pastoral area, and a significant gold-producing area. The town's wide streets were originally designed to allow camel trains to turn around, and were named after stars and constellations. **Of interest:** First court house in eastern goldfields (1893), Antares St, now a history museum. Other historic buildings: post office (1891), Antares St; Railway Tavern (1890s), Spica St. Restored Palace Hotel, Orion St. Sept.: Agricultural Show. **In the area:** Wildflowers on sandplains in spring. Goldmining activities at Marvel Loch, 35 km S; Bullfinch, 36 km N. Hunt's Soak, 7 km N, a picnic area. Koolyanobbing, 52 km N, built for miners extracting iron ore; mining of the rich iron ore has recommenced recently following closure in 1983. Interesting rock

formations with adjacent areas ideal for picnics at Frog Rock (30 km S), and Baladji Rock (50 km NW). **Tourist information:** Shire Offices, Antares St; (08) 9049 1001. **Accommodation:** 3 hotels, 1 motel, 1 cara./camp. park. **See also:** Crossing the Nullarbor.

Three Springs   Pop. 473

MAP REF. 376 C4

Sir John Forrest named Three Springs, which is 170 km SE of Geraldton. WA's finest talc, exported for use in the ceramics industry, is mined here from an open-cut mine 13 km E. **Of interest:** At southern entrance of town, information bay and small wildflower garden in spring. **In the area:** Wildflower drives (best Aug.–Nov.), details from Tourist information. Cockatoo Canyon, 6 km W. Emu Farm, 14 km W on Eneabba Rd. Eneabba, 58 km SW, a major mineral sands mining centre. Yarra Yarra Lake system, 5 km S, attracts many migratory birds. Pink Lakes, 6 km E. Old copper-mine ruins, 7 km NW. Blue Waters, 18 km NW near Arrino, a picnic area amid river gums. **Tourist information:** Commercial Hotel, Thomas St; (08) 9954 1041. **Accommodation:** 1 hotel/motel.

Tom Price   Pop. 3634

MAP REF. 375 H4, 378 B5

The huge iron ore deposit now known as Mt Tom Price was discovered in 1962, after which the Hamersley Iron Project was established. The construction of a mine, two towns (Dampier and Tom Price) and a railway between the towns followed, all of which was achieved in a remarkably short period of time. Today the town is a green oasis in the dry countryside. The proximity of town to the spectacular Karijini (Hamersley Range) National Park, and a chance to tour an open-cut mining operation, make the town a popular stopping-place. Aug.: Nameless Festival. **In the area:** Hamersley Iron open-cut iron ore mine, tours available departing from Tourist information, Central Rd (contact Tourist information for details). In Karijini National Park, 38 km E: Dales Gorge, with permanent waterfalls; Kalamina Gorge and Pool, the most accessible gorge; Joffre, Hancock, Weano and Red gorges join below Oxer Lookout; Hamersley Gorge, with permanent pools for swimming and

WESTERN AUSTRALIA

coloured folds in rock; trail with interpretive signs on Aboriginal heritage and flora and fauna winds up to Mt Bruce. *To the north-east is Wittenoom, no longer habitable as there is still a significant health risk from microscopic asbestos fibres created by the milling process at the asbestos mine which was closed in 1966. Some mine tailings potentially dangerous especially around old Wittenoom township and Wittenoom Gorge. When entering and exiting national park via Yampire Gorge Road keep car windows closed, observe warning signs and avoid tailings heaps.* Kings Lake, 2 km W, constructed lake; nearby, park with picnic/barbecue facilities. Views of remarkable scenery around Tom Price from Mt Nameless lookout, 6 km W, via walking trail or 4WD track. Aboriginal carvings, 10 km S, details from Tourist information. **Tourist information:** Central Rd; (08) 9188 1112. **Accommodation:** 1 hotel, 1 motel, 1 cara./camp. park. **See also:** The Hamersley Range.

Toodyay   Pop. 604

MAP REF. 366 G1, 374 E2, 376 D7

The historic town of Toodyay, nestled in the Avon Valley, has many charming old buildings recalling its pioneering days. Situated 85 km NE of Perth, the town is surrounded by picturesque farming country and, to the west, virgin bushland. **Of interest:** Classified by the National Trust as an historic town, Toodyay has many buildings of historic significance in or near Stirling Tce, particularly Stirling House (1908), now art gallery, and Toodyay Antiques shop. Connor's Flour Mill (1870s), an imposing structure now housing tourist centre displays a working flour mill and a steam engine in working order. Old Newcastle Gaol Museum (1865), Clinton St, and police stables (1870), opposite, built by convicts with random rubble stone. Duidgee Park, Harper Rd, popular picnic spot on banks of river. Pelham Reserve Lookout, Duke St. Market, Stirling Tce, each Sat. May: Moondyne (colonial and convict) Festival. Sept.: Highland Games. **In the area:** Windmill Hill Cutting, 6 km SE, deepest railway cutting in Australia. Coorinja Winery, 4 km S, begun 1870 (open Mon.–Sat. for tastings and sales). Century-old, 18 span, wooden Ringa Railway Bridge (1888), 6 km S. Hoddywell Archery Park, 8 km S. Emu farm, 15 km SW. White Gum Flower Farm, 9 km SW, just off road to Perth,

with native and exotic flowers under cultivation. Trout farm, 12 km SW, offers fishing and sales. Avon Valley National Park, 25 km SW, for spectacular scenery, seasonal wildflowers and wildlife-watching; Avon Descent, a white-water canoe race, held here in Aug. Cartref Park, 16 km NW, 2 ha of English gardens and landscaped native plants with prolific birdlife. **Tourist information:** Connor's Mill, Stirling Tce; (08) 9574 2435. **Accommodation:** 2 hotels, 1 hotel/motel, 2 cara./camp. parks.

Wagin   Pop. 1293

MAP REF. 374 G8, 376 E10

The prosperous rural countryside that surrounds Wagin supports grain crops and pastures for livestock, especially sheep. Located 177 km E of Bunbury, Wagin's development has been tied to its important location as a railway-junction town. **Of interest:** Wagin Historical Village, Kitchener St, has collection of early pioneer artifacts set in 20 authentic old buildings. Fine Victorian buildings and shopfronts in Tudhoe and Tudor sts. Heritage trail, details from Tourist information. Giant Ram (7 m high), Arthur Rd. Adjacent, park with ponds and waterfalls. Regular trotting meets at Trotting Grounds, Kitchener St. Mar.: Woolorama, attended by sheep farmers from around the nation, attracting crowds of more than 28 000. June: Foundation Day. **In the area:** Corralyn Emu Farm, 4 km N. Mt Latham, 6 km W, for bushwalking and views from summit. Puntapin, 6 km SE, a rock formation used as water-catchment area; wildflowers abound in spring. Lake Norring, 13 km SE, for swimming, sailing and water-skiing. **Tourist information:** Shire Offices, Arthur Rd; (08) 9861 1177; Wagin Historical Village, Showgrounds, Kitchener St; (08) 9861 1232. **Accommodation:** 3 hotels, 2 motels, 1 cara./camp. park. **See also:** The Southern Region.

Walpole   Pop. 290

MAP REF. 370 G12, 374 F13, 376 D12

Walpole is literally where the forest meets the sea. Surrounded by the Walpole-Nornalup National Park where a variety of trees grow, including karri, jarrah and the giant red tingle (*Eucalyptus jacksouii*), unique to the area. The region is known for its wildflowers

in season as well as its wildlife. **Of interest:** Pioneer Cottage in Pioneer Park, South Coast Hwy, opened 1987 to commemorate district pioneers; cottage follows design of early pioneer homes, but not intended as a replica. Daily ferry trips on Nornalup Inlet, depart jetty off Boronia Ave. Houseboats for hire, Boronia St. Bibbulmun Track (530 km), leading south from Kalamunda, 30 km E of Perth, ends at Walpole. Oct.: Wildflower Week. **In the area:** Coalmine Beach Heritage Trail; Knoll Drive, 3 km E; details from Tourist information. At Walpole-Nornalup National Park: Valley of the Giants, 16 km E, famous for its walk amongst old buttressed tingle trees, best seen from Tree Top Walk; also in Valley of the Giants, a boardwalk through a grove of veteran tingle trees known as the Ancient Empire. Tingle trees, off Hilltop Rd, 8 km SE; especially one huge specimen. Circular Pool, on Frankland River, 11 km NE. Mt Frankland National Park, 29 km N. Fernhook Falls, 32 km NW. For bushwalkers, Nuyts Wilderness area, 7 km W, and other walking trails. Ocean, river and inlet for anglers. Peaceful Bay, 28 km SE. **Tourist information:** Pioneer Cottage, Pioneer Park; (08) 9840 1111. **Accommodation:** 1 hotel/motel, 5 B&B, 1 hostel, 3 cara./camp. parks.

Wanneroo   Pop. 6745

MAP REF. 366 B3, 376 C8

Just a short drive from Perth, the district around Wanneroo stretches along 50 km of constantly changing coastline. **Of interest:** Botanic Golf, Burns Beach Rd, tee off in a botanical garden. On West Coast Hwy at Hillarys Boat Harbour: Sorrento Quay, a marine centre and retail complex; Underwater World, with submerged tunnel, touch pool and Microworld display; whale-watch tours (Sept.–Nov.). In Prindiville Dr., Wangara: Gumnut World, a craft outlet, also pioneer village on site; Wanneroo Weekend Markets, huge market in carnival-like atmosphere. In Wanneroo Rd, Conti Estate Wine Cellars and Restaurant. Regular meetings with international competitors at Wanneroo Motor Racing Circuit. **In the area:** Hartridge Vineyards, 10 km NW. **Tourist information:** Gumnut World, 30 Prindiville Dr., Wangara; (08) 9409 6699. **Accommodation:** 1 motel, 1 B&B, 3 cara./camp. parks.

Wickepin
Pop. 245

MAP REF. 374 G6, 376 E9

Wickepin dates back to the 1890s, when the first European settlers came to the district. The town is 214 km SE of Perth in farming country. **Of interest:** Good examples of Edwardian architecture in Wogolin Rd. The town has become well known following the publication of Albert Facey's autobiography *A Fortunate Life.* Nov.: Art and Craft Show (even-numbered years). **In the area:** Wildflowers in spring. Albert Facey Heritage Trail, details from Tourist information. Albert Facey's homestead, 15 km S. Toolibin Lake reserve, 20 km S, has wide variety of waterfowl. Malyalling Rock, 15 km NE. Tiny town of Yealering, and Yealering Lake, 30 km NE. Sewell's Rock Nature Reserve, 44 km NE via Yealering, ideal for picnics and nature walks. **Tourist information:** Wickepin Newsagency and Milkbar, 28 Wogolin Rd; (08) 9888 1070. **Accommodation:** 1 hotel, 1 cara./camp. park.

Wickham
Pop. 1973

MAP REF. 375 G1

Construction of Wickham, 49 km N of Karratha, was begun in 1970 by the Cliff's Robe River Iron Associates. Today the town is still company-owned and operated, now by Robe River Iron Associates. Wickham is the sister town to Pannawonica; iron ore mined at Pannawonica is processed here before being exported from nearby Cape Lambert. **Of interest:** Tours of processing plant and port operations, depart from Robe River Visitors Centre, Wickham Dr. (Mon.–Fri.). Boat Beach, off Walcott Dr. Lookout at Tank Hill, for views of town. July: Cossack–Wickham Fun Run. **In the area:** At Cape Lambert, 10 km NW, tallest and second-longest open-ocean wharf in Australia. **Tourist information:** Roebourne Tourist Bureau, Queen St, Roebourne; (08) 9182 1060. **Accommodation:** Limited budget accommodation. **See also:** The Hamersley Range.

Williams
Pop. 371

MAP REF. 374 F7 376 D9

This historical town enjoys a picturesque setting on the banks of the Williams River, 161 km SE of Perth. **Of interest:** Williams Hotel (1870). **In the**

Connor's Flour Mill (1870s), Stirling Tce, Toodyay

area: Old gravestones in cemetery, on northern outskirts of town. Dryandra State Forest, 25 km N. **Tourist information:** Williams Hotel, Albany Hwy; (08) 9885 1016. **Accommodation:** 1 hotel, 1 motel, 1 cara./ camp. park.

Wyndham
Pop. 860

MAP REF. 373 N1, 381 P4

Wyndham is the most northerly town and safe port harbour in WA. The town consists of two main areas: the original town site of Wyndham Port, situated on Cambridge Gulf, and Wyndham East ('Three Mile'), on the Great Northern Hwy, the residential and shopping area. In 1985 the meatworks, representing Wyndham's main industry, closed. Today Wyndham is a service town for the pastoral industry, mining exploration, tourism and nearby Aboriginal communities. Port now handles live cattle shipment to South-East Asia. **Of interest:** Self-guide cycle tours; heritage walk; contact Tourist information. Historic buildings in Port Town historic precinct, main street (Great Northern Hwy): Port Post Office, now tourist information centre; old Shire Hall, now Boab Art and Craft Gallery; Durack's Wool Store; court house, now historic museum; Anthon's Landing. Warriu Park Aboriginal Monument located in town centre. Port display next to Marine and Harbours offices, near wharf. Crocodile-spotting from wharf. Daily feeding of crocodiles and komodo dragons at Zoological Gardens and Crocodile Park, Varytes Rd, Wyndham Port. Three Mile Caravan Park, off Great Northern Hwy, has huge boab tree, 1500–2000 years old. Aug.: Top of the West Festival. Nov.: Hang Gliding Competition. **In the area:** Self-guide drive, contact Tourist information. To south-west on King River Rd: Aboriginal rock paintings (18 km); prison tree 2000–4000 years old, (22 km); check road conditions before departure. Horse treks from Diggers Rest Station, 33 km W. Alligator Airways Resort, Drysdale River, 80 km NW. Five Rivers Lookout, 5 km N atop Bastion Range, for spectacular views of Kimberley landscape, mountain ranges, Cambridge Gulf, Wyndham Port and rivers. Afghan cemetery, 1 km E. Abundant wildlife at Marlgu Billabong, 7 km E, part of Parry Lagoons, 70 sq. km of wetlands. The Grotto, 36 km E (2 km off road), a rock-edged waterhole, estimated to be 100 m deep, offering a cool, shaded oasis and safe year-round swimming. Sealed road leading to Wyndham passes through splendid gorge country. El Questro Station, 100 km S: vast cattle station, includes Emma Gorge (just over 1 km walking track from parking area to gorge) and Veil Waterfall for swimming; other touring options as well as accommodation available; details from Tourist information. **Tourist information:** Port Post Office, O'Donnell St, Wyndham Port; (08) 9161 1054.

Motor Museum, Avon Tce, York

Accommodation: 1 hotel, 1 hotel/motel, 1 B&B, 1 cara./camp. park. **See also:** The Kimberley.

Yalgoo
Pop. 80

MAP REF. 376 D3

Yalgoo lies 216 km E of Geraldton along an excellent road and is surrounded by typical Australian outback country. Alluvial gold was discovered here in the 1890s. Small traces of gold are still found in the district, which encourages fossicking by locals and visitors. **Of interest:** Court House Museum, Gibbons St. Restored Dominican Convent Chapel, Henty St. **In the area:** Abundant native wildlife in the area and prolific wildflowers in season (July–Sept.). Joker's Tunnel, 12 km SE on Paynes Find Rd, carved through solid rock by early prospectors, named after Joker mining syndicate. **Tourist information:** Shire Offices, 15 Shamrock St; (08) 9962 8042. **Accommodation:** 1 hotel/motel, 1 cara./camp. park.

Yallingup
Pop. 150

MAP REF. 367 B7, 369 C2, 374 A9, 376 B10

Yallingup is known for its excellent surf, with the Australian Surf Championships held in the area. Its limestone caves were a well-known attraction before the turn of the century. **Of interest:** Caves House Hotel, off Caves Rd, built by government as holiday hotel in 1903. Early visitors arrived from Busselton via horse and buggy along dirt road, a journey of 2 hours. Hotel was rebuilt in 1938 after a fire, using locally-milled timber; now has award-winning accommodation and restaurant. Market at Yallingup Hall, Caves Rd, last Sun. each month. Oct.: October Festival. Dec.: Malibu Competition. **In the area:** Ngilgi (Yallingup) Caves, 2 km E. Goanna Gallery and Bush Cottage Market, 8 km SE, for local art and craft. Shearing Shed, Wildwood Rd, 10 km SE, has shearing demonstrations and wool-shop (check opening times). Rivendell Gardens, 10 km SE, pick-your-own strawberries in season. Canal Rocks and Smith's Beach, 5 km SW, offer fishing, surfing and swimming. Gunyulgup Gallery; Yallingup Galleries; both 9 km SW. Wineries in the surrounding region including: Hunts Foxhaven Estate, 3 km S (open by appt only); Wildwood, 5 km S; Cape Clairault Wines, 10 km S; Willyabrup Valley district, 20 km S; Margaret River area, 40 km S; Happ's Vineyard and Pottery, 8 km SE; Abbey Vale Vineyards, 11 km SE, further 8 km, Bootleg Brewery. **Tourist information:** Shop 3, Naturaliste Tce, Dunsborough; (08) 9755 3299. **Accommodation:** 1 hotel, 3 cara./camp. parks. **See also:** The Southern Region.

Yanchep
Pop. 1577

MAP REF. 366 A1, 374 C2, 376 C7

Yanchep is within easy driving distance from Perth, 51 km to the south. **In the area:** Yanchep National Park, 5 km E, covering 2842 ha of natural bushland; in park: Gloucester Lodge Museum has displays of local history including park history in historical building (open Tues., Wed., Sat., Sun. and public holidays); Crystal Cave, startling limestone formations; launch cruises on freshwater Loch McNess (Sun.). Wild Kingdom, 3 km NE, a wildlife park and zoo. Marina at Two Rocks, 6 km NW. Wreck of *Alkimos*, south of Yanchep, said to be guarded by ghost. Picturesque Gnangara Lake, 30 km SE, with picnic facilities onshore. **Tourist information:** Information Office, Yanchep National Park; (08) 9561 1004. **Accommodation:** 1 hotel/motel.

York
Pop. 1562

MAP REF. 366 I4, 374 F3, 376 D8

Founded in 1830, York is set on the banks of the Avon River in the fertile Avon Valley, 97 km from Perth. The town has a wealth of historic buildings, carefully preserved. **Of interest:** Heritage trails, contact Tourist information. In Avon Tce: Old gaol and court house, and police station, built of local stone in 1895; Settlers' House (1850), restored two-storey mud-brick building, now offering old-world accommodation; Castle Hotel and Imperial Inn, fine examples of early coaching inns; Romanesque town hall (1911); Mill Gallery; Loder Antiques; Motor Museum, Australia's best collection of veteran, classic and racing cars (and some bicycles and motorcycles); Talking Points Antique Toy Train Museum, open Sun. and by appt; Sandalwood Yards and Tipperary School, old sandalwood storage area and now site of relocated school (1874); on southern outskirts, historic Balladong Farm, has old buildings and equipment, and domestic animals. Avon Valley Historical Rose Garden, Osnaberg Rd, roses in season. Old railway station (1886), Railway Rd, has railway museum. In Brook St: old hospital, with original shingle roof; Residency Museum (1843), displaying colonial furniture and early photographs. Old-world costumes at The Needle and I, cnr Georgiana and Macarthy sts. Fine churches: Holy Trinity (consecrated 1858), Suburban Rd; St Patrick's (1886), South St; Uniting Church (1888), Grey St. De Ladera Alpaca Farm, North Rd. Archery Park, South St (open Fri.–Sun.); also offers canoe hire. Suspension Bridge (originally 1906) across river in Low St. Picnic/barbecue facilities at Avon Park in Low St. Market in Avon Park, Low St, last Sat. each month. June: Country Music Festival. Oct.: Jazz Festival. Nov.: Rose Festival. **In the area:** Mt Brown lookout, 3 km SE; follow signs from Castle Hotel to Pioneer Dr. and then to Mt Brown. Picnic area overlooking river at Gwanbygine Park, 10 km S. Near Quairading, 64 km E, Toapin Weir and panoramic views from Mt Stirling. **Tourist information:** 105 Avon Tce; (08) 9641 1301. **Accommodation:** 2 hotels, 2 hotel/motels, 1 motel, 8 B&B, 1 cara./camp. park.

WESTERN AUSTRALIA

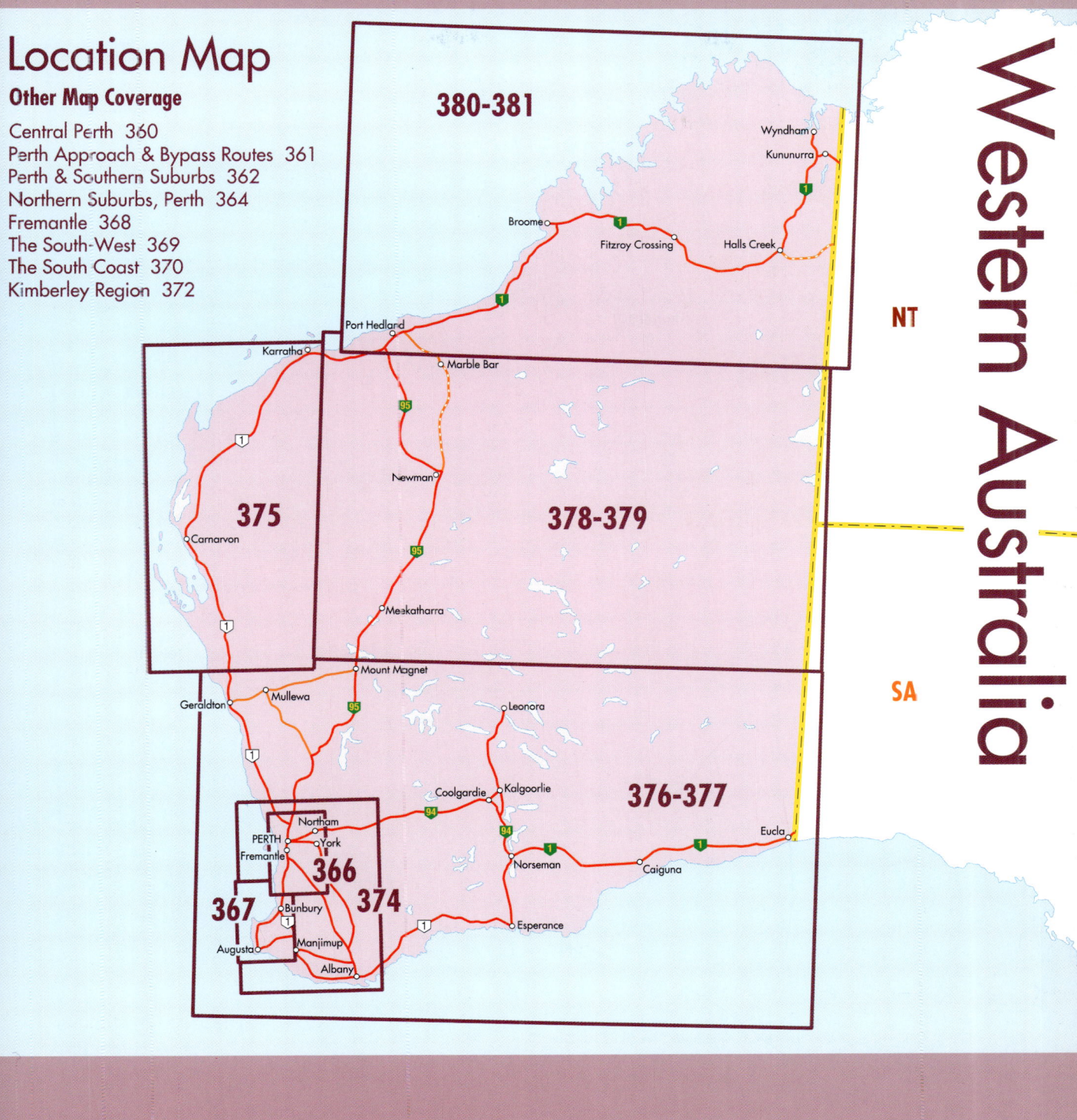

Location Map

Other Map Coverage

Central Perth 360
Perth Approach & Bypass Routes 361
Perth & Southern Suburbs 362
Northern Suburbs, Perth 364
Fremantle 368
The South-West 369
The South Coast 370
Kimberley Region 372

Western Australia

NT

SA

380-381

375

378-379

376-377

366

374

367

Wyndham
Kununurra
Broome
Fitzroy Crossing
Halls Creek
Port Hedland
Karratha
Marble Bar
Newman
Carnarvon
Meekatharra
Mount Magnet
Geraldton
Mullewa
Leonora
Coolgardie
Kalgoorlie
Eucla
PERTH
Northam
Fremantle
York
Norseman
Caiguna
Bunbury
Augusta
Manjimup
Esperance
Albany

0   0.25   0.5   0.75   1 km

Thick roads represent recommended approach and bypass routes.

INDIAN

OCEAN

N

Floreat Beach

City Beach

Swanbourne Beach

North Cottesloe Beach

Cottesloe Beach

Mudurup Rocks

Leighton Beach

Port Beach

North Wharf

Rous Head
North Mole
South Mole
Arthur Head

Challenger Harbour

Fishing Boat Harbour

Success Boat Harbour

South Beach
South Beach

Catherine Pt

Robb Jetty

Empire

Wembley Downs Golf Complex

Churchlands
Edith Cowan University

Herdsman Lake

Glendalough

Lake Monger Reserve

Wildlife Centre

Wembley

Leederville

North Perth

Hyde Park

Highgate

Northbridge

East P

Floreat

Jolimont

West Perth

Kings Park

National Trust Headquarters

Subiaco

Shenton Park

City Beach

Pine Plantation

West Australian Sports Centre

Mt Claremont

Karrakatta Cemetery

Karrakatta

Showground

Claremont

Univ of WA

Pioneer Women's Memorial

Kings Park

The Narrows
The Old Mill

Perth Water

Barrack St Jetty

For more detail on Central Perth see page 360

Perth Zoo

Royal Perth Golf Course

South Perth

Riverside

Adelaide

Swanbourne
Rifle Range

Cottesloe Golf Course

Lake Claremont

Claremont Museum

Crawley

Nedlands

Matilda Bay

Rottnest Island

Swan River

Melville Water

Como Beach

Tom Collins House

Cottesloe

Peppermint Grove
Keanes Pt

Dalkeith

Golf Course

Freshwater Bay

Mosman Bay

Pt Resolution

Pt Currie

Waylen Bay

Pt Heathcote

Coffee Pt

Applecross

Mosman Park

Victoria Street

City of Golf Course

Pt Walter

Pt Dundas

Passenger Ferry

Lucky Bay

Pt Waylen

The Strand

Canning Bridge

Manning

North Fremantle

Blackwall Reach

Rocky Bay

Preston Pt

Chidley Pt

Golf Course

Bicton

Wichman

Attadale

Alfred Cove

Wireless Hill Park

Mt Pleasant

Ardross

Mt Henry Bridge

Stirling Bridge

East Fremantle

Melville

Alfred Cove

Wireless Hill Telecommunications Museum and Lookout

Booragoon

Booragoon Swamp

Brentwood

Canning

Palmyra

Myaree

RAAFA Aviation Museum

Bull Creek

Fremantle

West Australian Maritime Museum
Fremantle Prison Museum
Fremantle Markets
Fremantle Crocodile Park

Royal Fremantle Golf Course

Fremantle Cemetery
Sainsbury

Willagee

Winthrop

Bateman

For more detail on Fremantle see page 368

White Gum Valley

O'Connor

Hilton

Kardinya

Murdoch University

Beaconsfield

South Fremantle

Murdoch

Melville Glades Golf Course

Hamilton Hill

Coolbellup

North Lake

Bibra Lake

Leemir

Jandak

Challenger

Cockburn

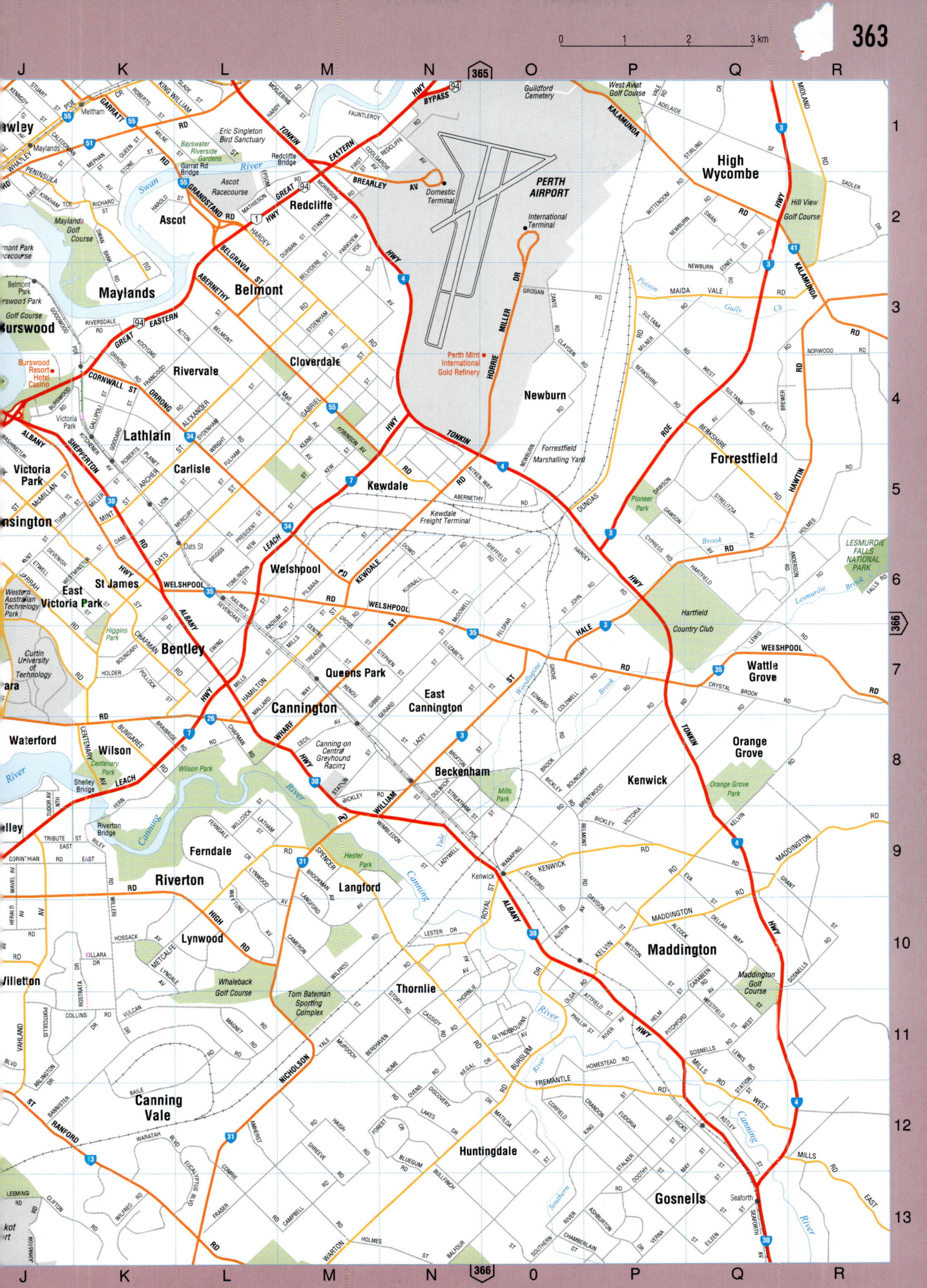

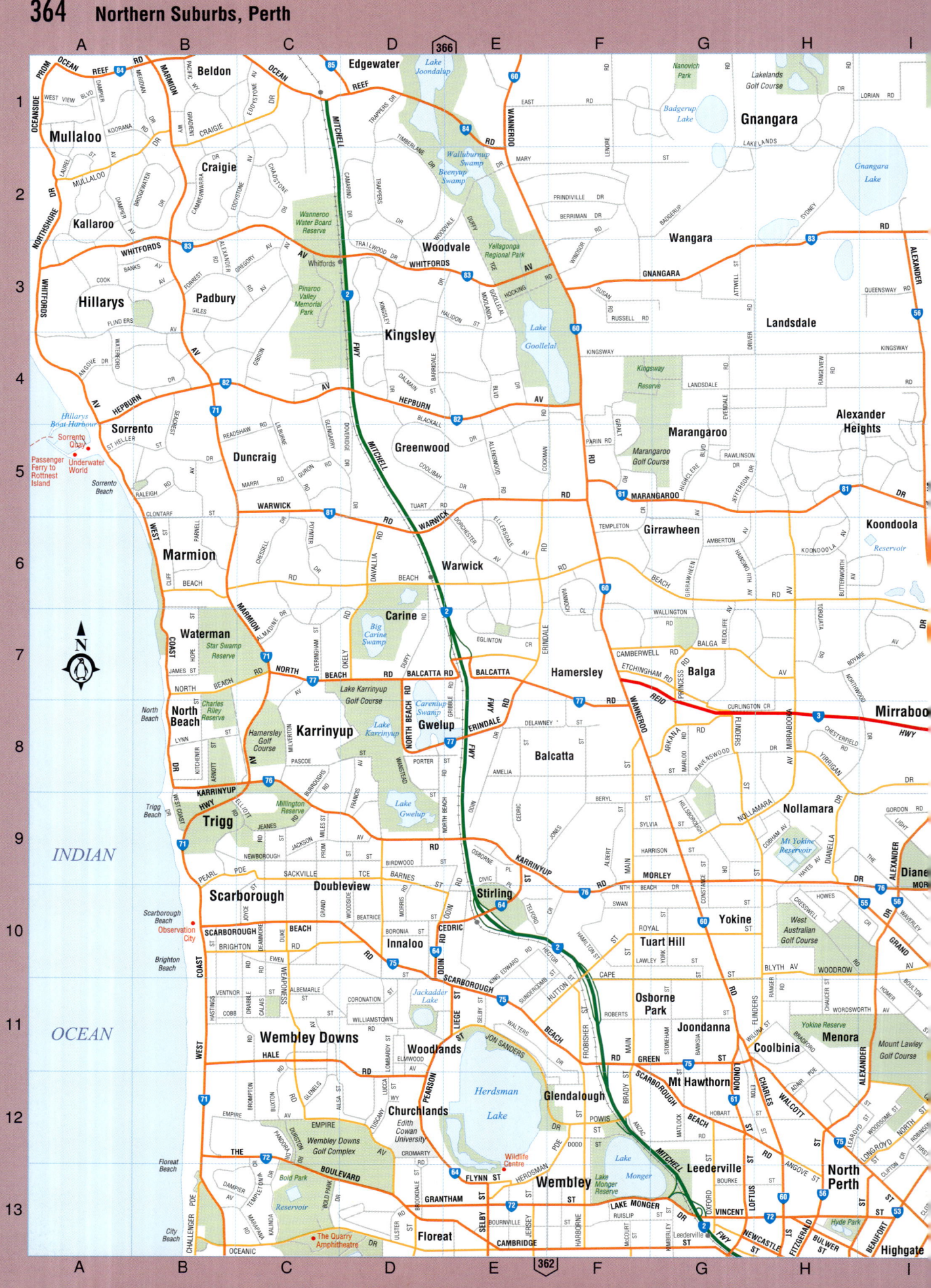

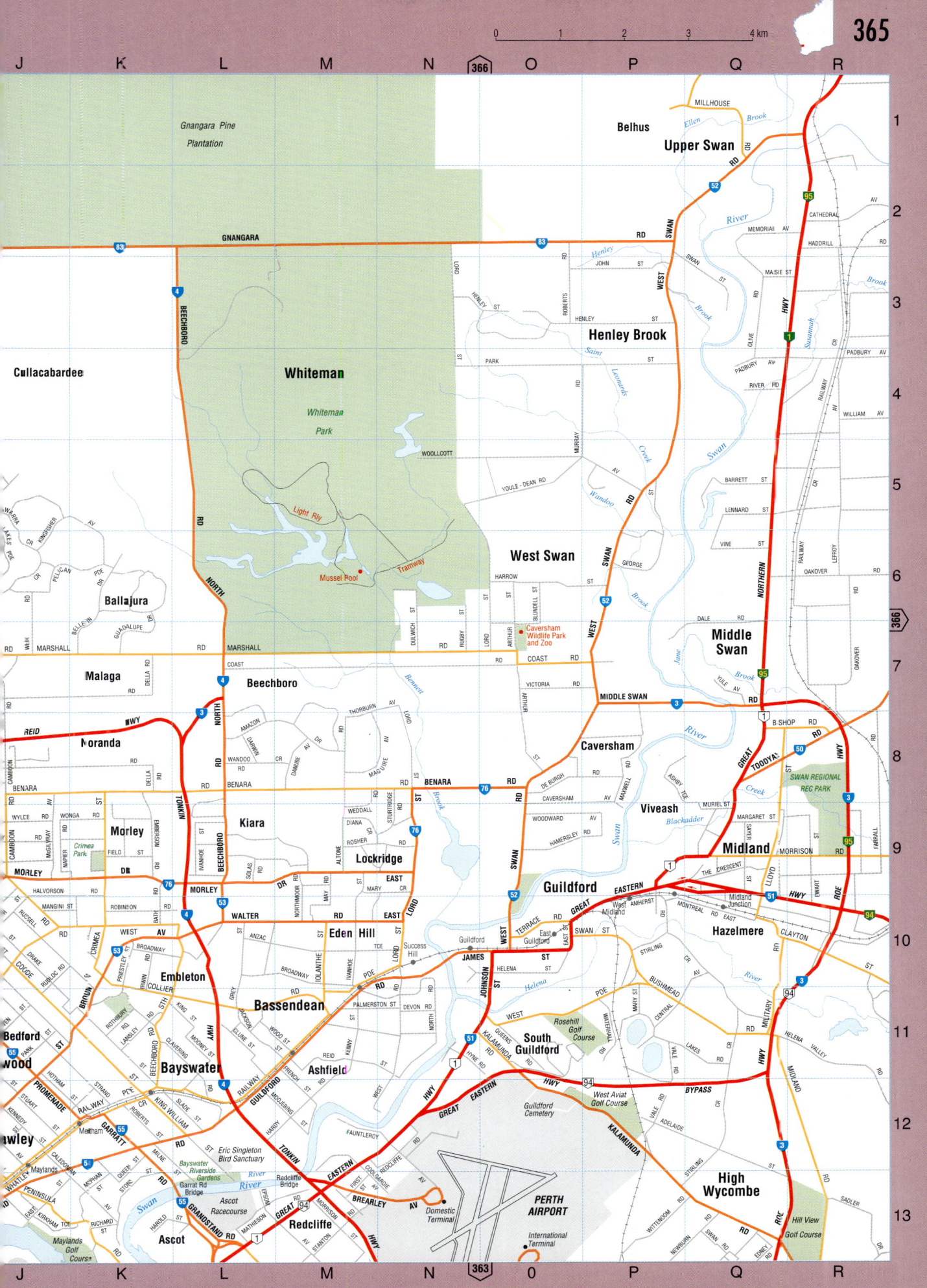

INDIAN OCEAN

0 5 10 15 20 25 km

TO GERALDTON
TO MOUNT MAGNET
BRAND HWY
95
Muchea
Bullsbrook
Pearce RAAF Station
51
NORTHERN HWY
GREAT NORTHERN HWY

Yanchep National Park
Crystal Cave
Yanchep
Yanchep Beach
Eglinton Rock
Quinns Rock
NEERABUP NATIONAL PARK
26
60
Lake Pinjar
Burns
Whitfords Beach
JOONDALUP
WANNEROO
MULLALOO
HILLARYS
Sorrento Quay & Underwater World
SCARBOROUGH
CITY BEACH
MITCHELL FWY
50
83
56
2
WHITEMAN PARK
WHITEMAN
UPPER SWAN
SWAN VALLEY WINE REGION
MIRRABOOKA
GUILDFORD
MIDLAND
PERTH
PERTH AIRPORT
COTTESLOE
CANNINGTON
31
MADDINGTON
30
KELMSCOTT
Cohunu Koala Park
Kelmscott Museum
GREENMOUNT
JANDAKOT
JANDAKOT AIRPORT
Adventure World
ARMADALE
Pioneer Village
FREMANTLE
Passenger Ferry to Rottnest Island
SPEARWOOD
MUNSTER
WATTLEUP
NAVAL BASE
Cockburn Sound
MILITARY AREA
Carnac Island
Garden Island
KWINANA FWY
77
KWINANA
Rockingham
Cape Peron
Safety Bay
Penguin Island
Waikiki
Warnbro Beach
Becher Point
Peelhurst
Singleton
Madora
Halls Head
MANDURAH
Miami
Florida
North Yunderup
South Yunderup
19
Dawesville
Melros
Cape Bouvard
YALGORUP NATIONAL PARK
Lake Clifton
Lake Clifton
71
OLD COAST RD
Preston Beach
YALGORUP NATIONAL PARK
Lake Preston
Peel Inlet
Peel Estuary
Harvey Estuary
Lake Mealup
Lake McLarty
PINJARRA
Hotham Valley Tourist Railway
Coolup
20
SOUTH WESTERN HWY
Hamel
WAROONA
54
21
Wagerup
Yarloop
TO BUNBURY
TO BUNBURY
95 HWY

Byford
Mundijong
20
Tumblegum Farm
Mardella
Serpentine
SERPENTINE NATIONAL PARK
Jarrahdale
Keysbrook
North Dandalup
56
Fairbridge Farm School
Marrinup
Dwellingup
Lane Pool Reserve
Scarp Pool
Nanga
Meelon
Alcoa Scarpe Lookout
Hotham Valley
South Dandalup Dam
Serpentine Dam
Elmilyn
Etmilyn Forest Tramway
Amphion
68
Mt Solus 574m
Mt Keats 474m
Mt Saddleback 75m
Samson Brook Dam
Waroona Dam
Logue Brook Dam

Kyotmunga
AVON VALLEY NATIONAL PARK
Smiths Hill 361m
WALYUNGA NP
MORANGUP NATURE RESERVE
Balup
Gidgegannup
84
Mount Helena
Mundaring
50
35
JOHN FORREST NATIONAL PARK
Darlington
GREENMOUNT NP
Gooseberry NP
O'Connor Museum
KALAMUNDA NP
LESMURDIE FALLS NP
GREAT EASTERN HWY
47
Chidlow
Helena Reservoir
Helena River
Mt Dale 548m
Canning Dam
ALBANY HWY
Canning River
Darling River
Mt Randall 525m
DARLING RANGE
87
Boonering Hill 529m
Bannister
Wandering
Crossman
Boddington
20
Marradong
CAERNARVON HILLS
Dwarda
Crossman River
Hotham River

TOODYAY
Windmill Hill Cutting
Cooringa Winery
Archery Park
Clackline
48
Bakers Hill
Camel Farm
Wundowie
94
GREAT EASTERN HWY
Mokine
115
27
Northam
Neggojerring
Avon River
35
120
24
Historical Balladong Farm
York
York Motor Museum
Dyott Range
Mt Talbot 398m
Talbot River
Talbot Brook
Westdale
Dale River
Ross River
40
94
BROOKTON HWY
30
ALBANY HWY
TO MERREDIN
TO BROOKTON
TO ALBANY

N
Penguin

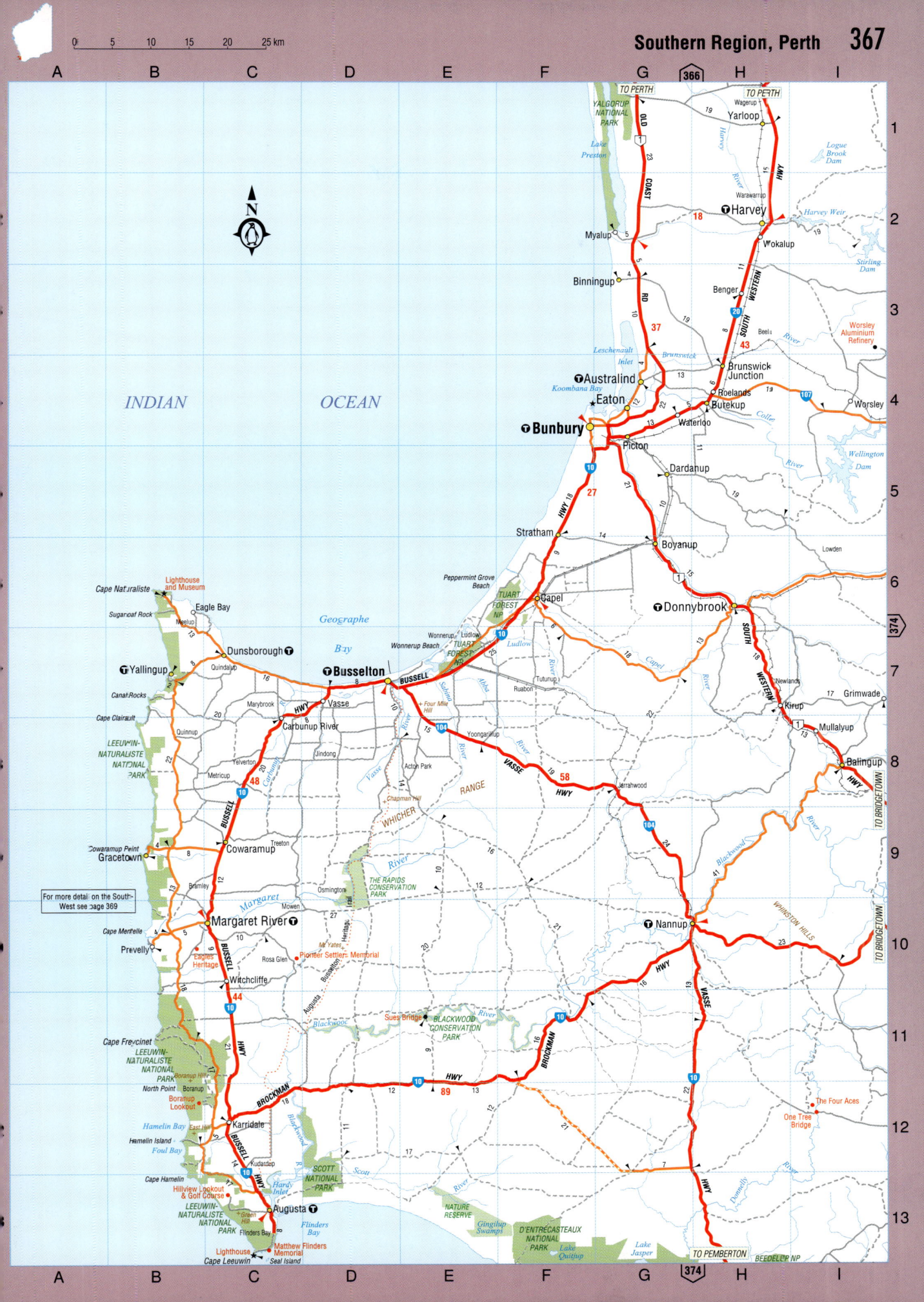

A B C D E F G H I

1

2

3

4

5

6

7

8

9

10

11

12

13

INDIAN OCEAN

N

TO PERTH
TO PERTH
Wagerup
Yarloop
Logue
Brook
Dam

YALGORUP
NATIONAL
PARK
Lake
Preston

Warawarrup
Harvey
Harvey Weir

18
Myalup
Wokalup
Benger
Stirling
Dam

Binningup
20
Brunswick
Junction
Worsley
Aluminium
Refinery

37
43
Roelands
Butekup
Worsley
107

Leschenault
Inlet
Australind
Waterloo
Koombana Bay
Eaton
Bunbury
Picton
Dardanup
Wellington
Dam

27
Stratham
Boyanup
Lowden

Peppermint Grove
Beach
TUART
FOREST
NP
Capel
Donnybrook

Geographe
Bay
Wonnerup Beach
Ludlow
TUART
FOREST
NP
Grimwade
Kirup

Cape Naturaliste
Lighthouse
and Museum
Eagle Bay
Sugarloaf Rock
Meelup
Dunsborough
Quindalup
Busselton
BUSSELL
Vasse
Four Mile
Hill
Yoongarillup
Mullalyup

Yallingup
Canal Rocks
Marybrook
Carbunup River
Jindong
Acton Park
Ruabon
Tutunup
VASSE
HWY
Balingup
TO BRIDGETOWN

Cape Clairault
Quinnup
Yelverton
Metricup
WHICHER
RANGE
Chapman Hill
58
Jarrahwood

LEEUWIN-
NATURALISTE
NATIONAL
PARK
48
104

Cowaramup Point
Gracetown
Treeton
Cowaramup
Bramley
Osmington
THE RAPIDS
CONSERVATION
PARK
Nannup
WINSTON
HILLS

Cape Mentelle
Margaret
River
Mowen
Margaret River
Pioneer Settlers' Memorial
Mt Yates
Bussell Heritage Trail

Prevelly
Eagles
Heritage
Rosa Glen
One Tree
Bridge
The Four Aces

Cape Freycinet
Witchcliffe
44
Sues Bridge
BLACKWOOD
CONSERVATION
PARK
89

LEEUWIN-
NATURALISTE
NATIONAL
PARK
North Point
Boranup
Boranup Hill
Boranup
Lookout
BROCKMAN
HWY

Hamelin Bay
East Hill
Karridale
Kudardup
Hamelin Island
Foul Bay

Cape Hamelin
Hillview Lookout
& Golf Course
LEEUWIN-
NATURALISTE
NATIONAL
PARK
Green
Hill
Augusta
Hardy
Inlet
SCOTT
NATIONAL
PARK
NATURE
RESERVE
Gingilup
Swamps
D'ENTRECASTEAUX
NATIONAL
PARK
Lake Jasper
BEEDELUP NP

Lighthouse
Cape Leeuwin
Matthew Flinders
Memorial
Seal Island
Flinders Bay
TO PEMBERTON
374

For more detail on the South-
West see page 369

0 5 10 15 20 25 km

Accommodation ■
Baillies on the Terrace **1** F9
Esplanade Hotel Fremantle **2** E9
Fremantle Hotel **4** D8
Norfolk Hotel **4** F9
Number 1 High Street **5** D8
Orient Hotel **6** D8
P & O Hotel **7** D8
Sunnys Shining on the
   Swan Hotel **8** H3
Tradewinds Hotel **9** I3

General Information ■
Ferry Terminals **10** A7, C7, H3
Fremantle Sailing Club **11** F12
Police Station **12** F8
Post Office **13** E7, G1
Public Hospital **14** F9
Tourist Information **15** E7
Town Hall **16** E7

Places of Interest ■
Aquatic Centre **17** G5
Boat Museum **18** C7
Crocodile Park **19** D9
Fremantle Markets **20** F8
Fremantle Museum and
   Arts Centre **21** G5
Henry Street Station
   Model Railway **22** D8
Kailis' Fish Market **23** D9
Prison and Museum **24** G8
Round House **25** C8
Samson House Museum **26** G6
WA Maritime Museum **27** D8
War Memorial **28** H7
World of Energy Museum **29** F6

Accommodation Only a sample
range is listed; inclusion is not
necessarily a recommendation.

0   5   10   15   20 km

WINERIES: ●1

- Abbey Vale Vineyard 1 C3
- Amberley Estate 2 C3
- Arlewood Estate 3 C5
- Ashbrook Estate 4 C5
- Brookland Valley Vineyard 5 B5
- Cape Clairault Wines 6 C4
- Cape Mentelle 7 C7
- Carbunup Estate 8 D4
- Chapmans Creek 9 C4
- Chateau Xanadu 10 C7
- Cullen Wines 11 C5
- Driftwood Estate 12 B4
- Evans and Tate 13 C5
- Fermoy Estate 14 C5
- Gralyn Cellars 15 C5
- Green Valley Vineyard 16 C9
- Happ's Vineyard 17 C3
- Hay Shed Hill Winery 18 C5
- Hunt's Foxhaven Estate 19 B3
- Leeuwin Estate 20 C8
- Lenton Brae Estate 21 C5
- Moss Brothers 22 C4
- Pierro 23 C5
- Redgate Wines 24 C8
- Ribbon Vale Estate 25 C5
- Rivendell Vineyard 26 C3
- Rosabrook Estate 27 C7
- Sandalford Wines 28 C5
- Seventy Organic Wines 29 D9
- Treeton Estate 30 D5
- Vasse Felix 31 C5
- Voyager Estate 32 C8
- Wildwood 33 C3
- Willespie 34 C5
- Woodlands 35 C5
- Woody Nook 36 C5
- Wrights Wines 37 C5

INDIAN OCEAN

GEOGRAPHE BAY

SOUTHERN OCEAN

FISHING: The length of the coast, together with the many rivers and estuaries make the region an angler's paradise. Many of the rivers and streams are stocked annually with trout.

TUART FOREST NATIONAL PARK: The park is home to a variety of animals, including the Western Ringtail Possum, an endangered species. The park also protects the State's largest remaining area of Tuart Forest. Tuart, a species of hardwood, only grows on coastal limestone, and hence is unique to the limestone coast of south-western Western Australia.

AUGUSTA-BUSSELTON HERITAGE TRAIL: This trail, which runs from Augusta to Vasse, basically retraces the original track, which, in the 1830s, linked these two towns.

TOURIST INFORMATION:
Busselton (Civic Centre Complex, Southern Dr)
Dunsborough (Shop 3, Naturaliste Tce)
Margaret River (Cnr Tunbridge Rd and Bussell Hwy)

LEEUWIN-NATURALISTE NATIONAL PARK: This narrow strip of protected coastline combines a scenic coast with magnificent wildflowers and the tall timbers of Karri and Jarrah Forests.

CAVES: There are over 350 caves in this region, lying along the Leeuwin-Naturaliste ridge; only some of the caves are open to the public. They include Mammoth Cave, Jewel Cave, Lake Cave and Yallingup Cave - all of which have guided tours daily in summer. Moondyne Cave is an 'adventure' cave open to the public; tour guide provided.

SURFING: The sheltered bays and excellent beaches that dot the coastline of the Yallingup-Margaret River region offer ideal surfing conditions.

CAPE LEEUWIN: From the cape it is possible to see the sun rising over one ocean and setting over another.

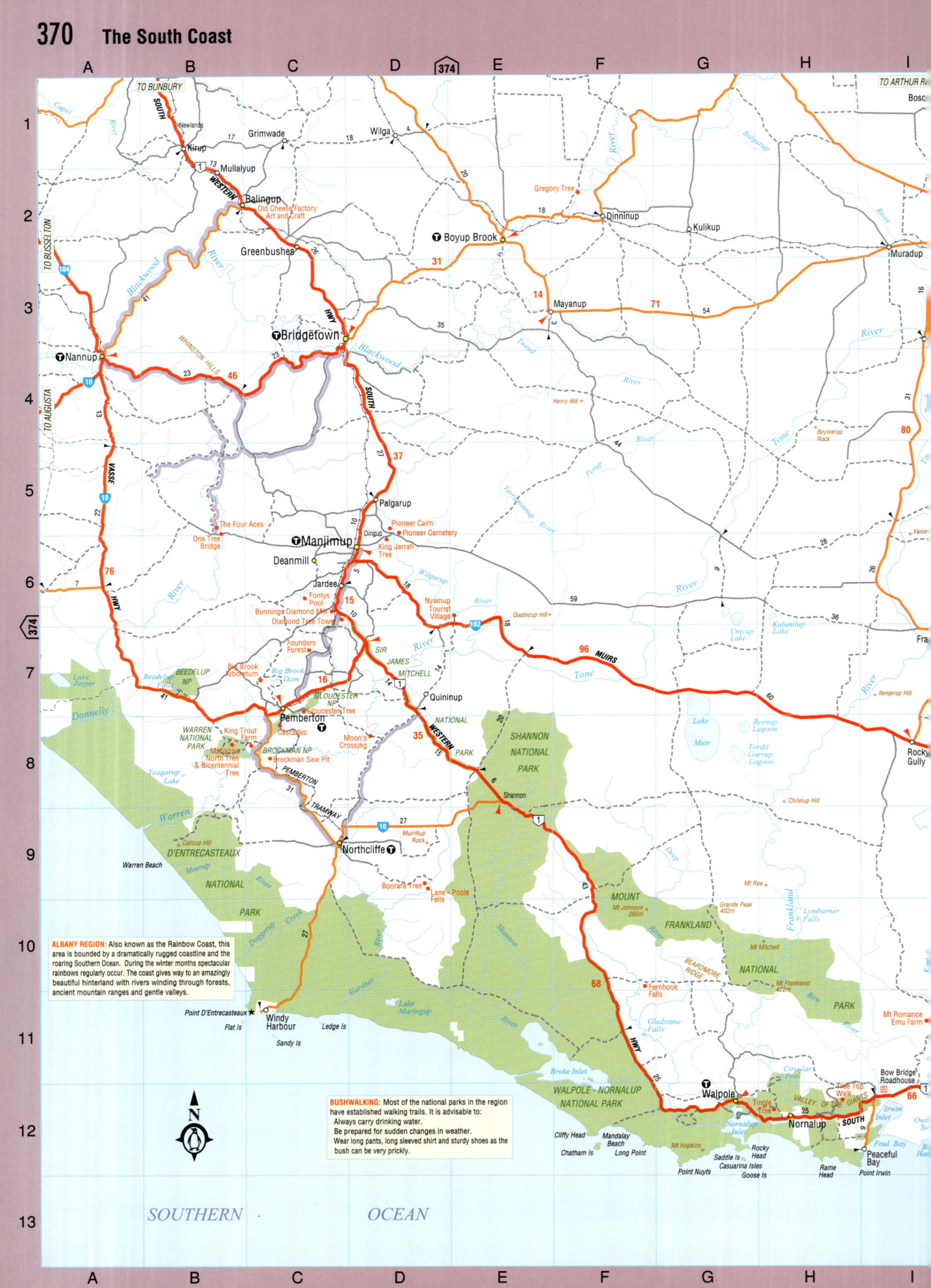

374

A B C D E F G H I

TO BUNBURY

TO ARTHUR RI

Bosc

SOUTH

Capel

River

Newlands

Kirup

17

Grimwade

18

Wilga

4

River

Bulganup

WESTERN

13

Mullalyup

Balingup

Old Cheese Factory
Art and Craft

Gregory Tree

Dinninup

18

Kulikup

River

Greenbushes

26

Boyup Brook

31

14

Mayanup

71

54

Muradup

104

Blackwood

41

River

HWY

Bridgetown

Blackwood

35

3

River

Henry Hill +

Boywerup
Rock

80

Nannup

23

46

SOUTH

23

Whinston Hills

River

27

37

44

Perup

River

Tone

River

31

10

VASSE

22

The Four Aces

One Tree
Bridge

Palgarup

Dingup

Pioneer Cairn
Pioneer Cemetery

Yerriminup River

28

River

Manjimup

King Jarrah
Tree

9

Unicup
Lake

36

Kulunilup
Lake

76

Deanmill

River

HWY

7

Jardee

18

Wilgarup

Nyamup
Tourist
Village

102

18

96

MUIRS

Fra

Fontys
Pool

15

5

River

Quabicup Hill +

59

Tone

River

Bunnings Diamond Mill
Diamond Tree Tower

10

Benjerup Hill +

374

Lake Jasper

Founders
Forest

Beedelup
Falls

BEEDELUP
NP

Big Brook
Arboretum

SIR

JAMES

14

River

60

Lake
Muir

Byenup
Lagoon

Tordit
Gurrup
Lagoon

Rocky
Gully

16

Big Brook
Dam

MITCHELL

1

GLOUCESTER
NP

Gloucester Tree

Pemberton

Quininup

35

WESTERN

NATIONAL

20

SHANNON

NATIONAL

PARK

Chitelup Hill +

Donnelly

WARREN

NATIONAL

PARK

King Trout
Farm

Marianne
North Tree
& Bicentennial
Tree

Cascades

Moon's
Crossing

BROCKMAN NP

Brockman Saw Pit

PEMBERTON

15

PARK

6

Shannon

Deep

Mt Roe +

FRANKLAND

Lymburner
Falls

Yeagarup
Lake

TRAMWAY

27

Muirillup
Rock

18

Northcliffe

River

1

43

MOUNT

Mt Johnson
285m

Granite Peak
402m

Warren

River

D'ENTRECASTEAUX

Calicup Hill +

Meerup

Warren Beach

NATIONAL

River

Boorara Tree

Lane - Poole
Falls

Shannon

River

NATIONAL

Mt Mitchell

BEARDMORE

RIDGE

Mt Frankland
422m

Fernhook
Falls

PARK

Doggerup Creek

27

68

ALBANY REGION: Also known as the Rainbow Coast, this
area is bounded by a dramatically rugged coastline and the
roaring Southern Ocean. During the winter months spectacular
rainbows regularly occur. The coast gives way to an amazingly
beautiful hinterland with rivers winding through forests,
ancient mountain ranges and gentle valleys.

HWY

Mt Frankland

Gardner

River

Lake
Maringup

Mt Romance
Emu Farm

Point D'Entrecasteaux ★

Flat Is

Windy
Harbour

Ledge Is

Sandy Is

25

Broke Inlet

Circular
Pool

Walpole

Tree Top
Walk

VALLEY
OF THE
GIANTS

Bow Bridge
Roadhouse

1

66

BUSHWALKING: Most of the national parks in the region
have established walking trails. It is advisable to:
Always carry drinking water.
Be prepared for sudden changes in weather.
Wear long pants, long sleeved shirt and sturdy shoes as the
bush can be very prickly.

WALPOLE - NORNALUP

NATIONAL PARK

Tingle
Tree

Nornalup
Inlet

Nornalup

25

SOUTH

Irwin
Inlet

N

Cliffy Head

Chatham Is

Mandalay
Beach

Long Point

Mt Hopkins

Rocky
Head

Saddle Is

Casuarina Isles

Goose Is

Rame
Head

Peaceful
Bay

Point Irwin

Foul Bay

Point Nuyts

SOUTHERN · *OCEAN*

A B C D E F G H I

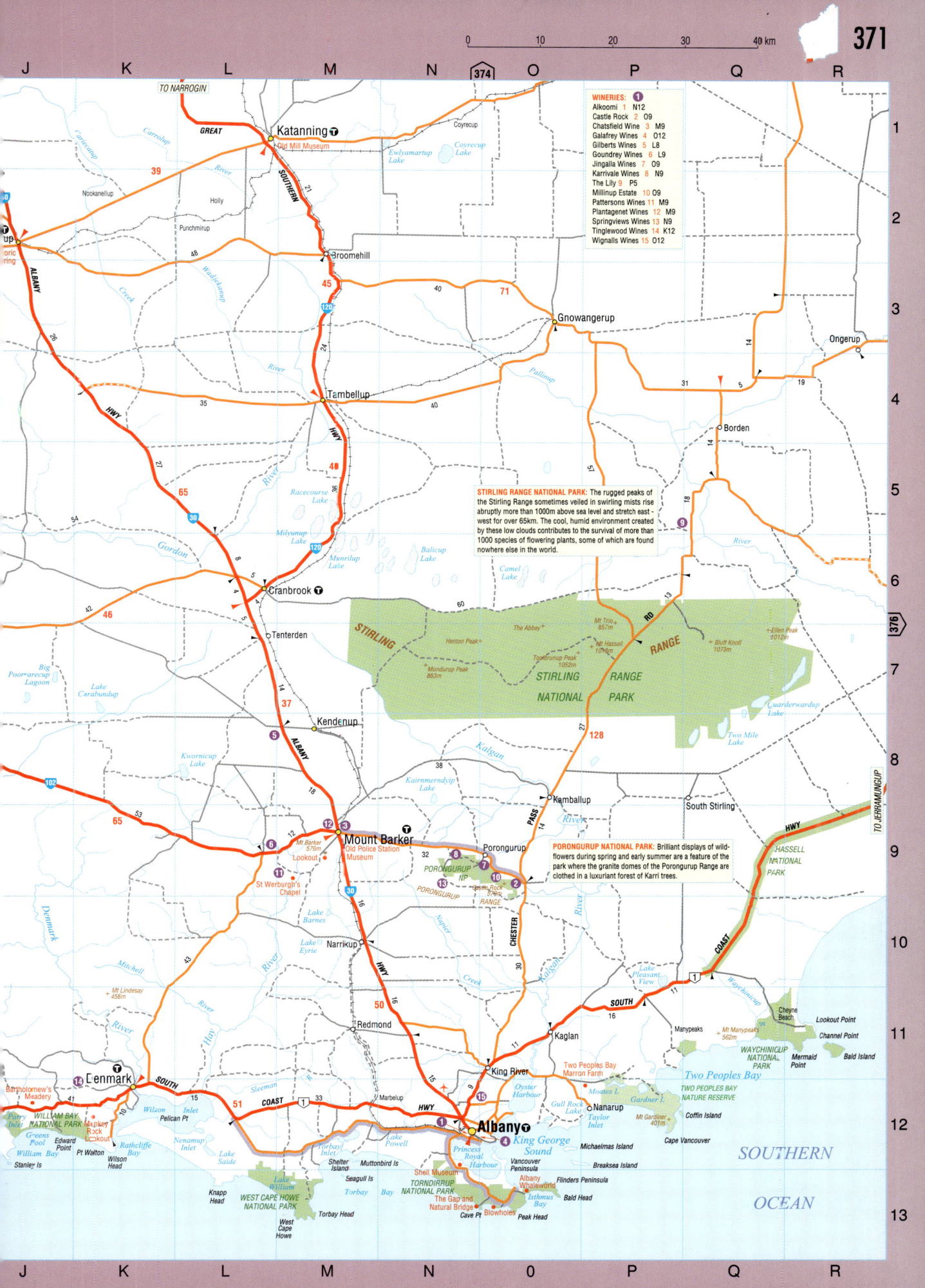

WINERIES: ●

Alkoomi	1 N12
Castle Rock	2 O9
Chatsfield Wine	3 M9
Galafrey Wines	4 O12
Gilberts Wines	5 L8
Goundrey Wines	6 L9
Jingalla Wines	7 O9
Karrivale Wines	8 N9
The Lily	9 P5
Millinup Estate	10 O9
Pattersons Wines	11 M9
Plantagenet Wines	12 M9
Springviews Wines	13 N9
Tinglewood Wines	14 K12
Wignalls Wines	15 O12

TO NARROGIN

GREAT

Katanning
Old Mill Museum

Nookanellup

Holly

Punchmirup

Broomehill

Coyrecup

Ewlyamartup
Lake

Coyrecup
Lake

Gnowangerup

Ongerup

Tambellup

Borden

STIRLING RANGE NATIONAL PARK: The rugged peaks of
the Stirling Range sometimes veiled in swirling mists rise
abruptly more than 1000m above sea level and stretch east -
west for over 65km. The cool, humid environment created
by these low clouds contributes to the survival of more than
1000 species of flowering plants, some of which are found
nowhere else in the world.

Racecourse
Lake

Milyunup
Lake

Menrilup
Lake

Balicup
Lake

Camel
Lake

Cranbrook

Tenterden

STIRLING

Henton Peak

The Abbey

Mt Trio
857m

RANGE

Ellen Peak
1012m

Mondurup Peak
863m

Toolbrunup Peak
1052m

Mt Hassell
1079m

Bluff Knoll
1073m

STIRLING   RANGE

NATIONAL   PARK

Quaarerwardup
Lake

Two Mile
Lake

Kendenup

Kalgan

Kairnmerndyip
Lake

Kamballup

South Stirling

Big
Poorrarecup
Lagoon

Lake
Carabundup

Kwornicup
Lake

Mt Barker
576m
Lookout

Mount Barker
Old Police Station
Museum

PORONGURUP
NP

PORONGURUP

Porongurup

PORONGURUP NATIONAL PARK: Brilliant displays of wildflowers during spring and early summer are a feature of the
park where the granite domes of the Porongurup Range are
clothed in a luxuriant forest of Karri trees.

HASSELL

NATIONAL

PARK

TO JERRAMUNGUP

St Werburgh's
Chapel

Castle Rock
574m

RANGE

Denmark

Lake
Barnes

Lake
Eyrie

Narrikup

CHESTER

Nyinar

Kalgan

River

Lake
Pleasant
View

Cheyne
Beach

Lookout Point

Channel Point

Mitchell

Mt Lindesay
456m

Redmond

Marbelup

King River

Kaglan

SOUTH

Manypeaks

Mt Manypeaks
562m

WAYCHINICUP
NATIONAL
PARK

Mermaid
Point

Bald Island

Denmark
Bartholomew's
Meadery

WILLIAM BAY
NATIONAL PARK

Greens
Pool

Edward
Point

Pt Walton

Wilson
Head

Rathcliffe
Bay

Pelican Pt

Nenamup
Inlet

COAST

Sleeman

Lake
Saide

Lake
William

Shelter
Island

Muttonbird Is

Seagull Is

Torbay
Bay

Marron Farm

Two Peoples Bay

Oyster
Harbour

Nanarup

Taylor Inlet

Gardner I.

Moates L.

Gull Rock
Lake

TWO PEOPLES BAY
NATURE RESERVE

Mt Gardner
401m

Coffin Island

Cape Vancouver

SOUTHERN

Monkey
Rock
Lookout

Stanley Is

Wilson
Inlet

Torbay Inlet

Lake
Powell

Princess
Royal
Harbour

Shell Museum

Vancouver
Peninsula

Albany
Whaleworld

Michaelmas Island

Breaksea Island

King George
Sound

Flinders Peninsula

Bald Head

OCEAN

WEST CAPE HOWE
NATIONAL PARK

Knapp
Head

Torbay Head

West
Cape
Howe

TORNDIRRUP
NATIONAL PARK

The Gap and
Natural Bridge

Cave Pt

Blowholes

Peak Head

Isthmus
Bay

Albany

INDIAN

OCEAN

N

BONAPARTE ARCHIPELAGO

Coronation Island

Brunswick Bay

Heywood Islands

Champagny Island

Augustus Island

Camden Sound

Mt Trafalgar +390m

St George Basin

MACDONALD RANGE

PRINCE REGENT

NATURE

Deception Bay

Kuri Bay Pearl Farm

Hall Point

Mt Lyall 213m

KUNMUNYA

ABORIGINAL

RESERVE

Prince Regent River

Glenelg River

Regent River

Mt Hann 779m

Mt Fyfe 765m

Miners Pe

Drysdale Ri

Mt Bradshaw 455m

King River

Edward River

Morgan River

Roe River

Mitchell River

Mitchell River

Drysdale

ARCHIPELAGO

BUCCANEER

Montgomery Island

Wedge Hill

George Water

Mt Methuen 427m

Mt French

Pantijan

Mt Deborah 399m

Mt Shadforth 510m

Mt Agnes 736m

Mt Jameson 746m

Mt Russ 692m

Mt Hindhaugh

Mt Lochee 310m

EDKINS RANGE

Mt Blythe 436m

Mt Lacy 763m

Doubtful Bay

Sale River

Raft Pt

Eagle Pt

Wood Islands

Cockatoo Island

Koolan Island

Koolan

Yampi Sound

Hidden Island

WOTJALUM ABORIGINAL LAND

Talbot Bay

Secure Bay

Collier Bay

Walcott Inlet

Mt Page 466m

Calder River

Charnley River

KIMBERLEY

Tabletop Mtn 480m

SYNNOT RANGE

Mount Elizabeth

Barnett River Gorge

Mount Barnett

GIBB

Kupingarri Community

BARNETT RIVER

Strickland Bay

Cone Bay

McLARTY RANGE

Mt Nellie 267m

Mt Disaster 266m

KING

AREA

Mt Humbert 474m

Mt Synnot 488m

Mt Glemont 478m

Beverley Springs

PHILLIPS RANGE

Adcock Gorge

Cascade Bay

MILITARY TRAINING

Robinson River

Round Hill

VAN EMMERICK RANGE

Mt Matthew 586m

Mt Hart

LEOPOLD

Mt Hart 667m

Mt Smith 616m

Mt Chalmers 704m

RANGES

Mt House 551m

Mt House

Mt Clifton 537m

Glenroy

Sir John Gor

Long Is

KING

SOUND

Point Torment

Stokes Bay

Meda River

Lennard River

Mt Bell 744m

Lennard Gorge

Mt Herbert 753m

Mt Ord 937m

Mt Estaughs 476m

Adcock River

Mt Leake 697m

Diamond Gorge

Mt Br

Hann River

Mornington

365

RD

TOURIST INFORMATION:
Derby (1 Clarendon St)
Fitzroy Crossing (Flynn Dr)
Halls Creek (Great Northern Hwy)
Kununurra (Coolibah Dr)
Wyndham (O'Donnell St, Wyndham Port)

Napier Downs

WINDJANA GORGE NATIONAL PARK

Windjana Gorge

North Ck

Mt Sherry

Mt Behn 344m

WINDJANA GORGE NATIONAL PARK: Consists of a gorge formed by the Lennard River as it snakes its way through a 350-million year old reef of ancient limestone. The river only flows for short periods but isolated pools support an abundance of fish and birds. A number of interesting walks exist with trail-side signs interpreting features in the gorge.

Derby

Boab Prison Tree

Myall's Bore

43

DERBY HWY

GIBB

Meda River

Kimberley Downs

Mt Marmion 105m

RIVER

Fairfield

Tunnel Ck

TUNNEL CREEK NATIONAL PARK

DEVONIAN REEF NATIONAL PARKS

OSCAR

Millie Windie

Leopold Downs

GIBB RIVER ROAD: Built to carry large road trains of cattle being transported from isolated stations to the ports of Derby and Wyndham. Road conditions vary and it is advisable to check before departure.

TUNNEL CREEK NATIONAL PARK: Provides an opportunity to explore a creek as it tunnels through a mountain range. The tunnel contains permanent pools of water and for those with a torch, prepared to walk through cold water, the walk through is fascinating.

GEIKIE GORGE NATIONAL PARK: Formed by centuries of water eroding through an ancient limestone reef. The gorge contains permanent fresh water and supports a variety of animal life, including freshwater crocodiles. Cruises up the gorge are available.

Mt Clarkson 94m

Yeeda

Willare Bridge Roadhouse

GREAT

NORTHERN

SISTERS PLATEAU

Blina

OSCAR PLATEAU

Ellendale

Calwynyardah

HWY

217

Brooking Spring

GEIKIE GORGE NP

Geikie Gorge

BROOKING GORGE CP

Fossil Downs

Fitzroy River

4WD

only

TO BROOME

1

380

Yakka Munga

Udialla

Fitzroy River

Mt Anderson 306m

Camballin

Liveringa

LOOMA ABORIGINAL RESERVE

Lulugui

Myroodah

Mt Anderson

17 Mile Dam

Mt Wynne 144m

Mt Wynne

Fitzroy Crossing

Gogo

Brooking Spring

38

Mt Pierre 203m

Mt Eli 31

Margaret River

Dampier Downs

Twin Buttes

Babrongan Tower

Mowla Bluff

Greenly Creek

Camelgooda Hill

Mt Jariemai 195m

Mt Fenton 187m

Nerrima

Noonkanbah

NOOGOORA BURR QUARANTINE AREA

Mt Hardman 132m

Mt Abbott

Kalyeeda

Quanbun Downs

Jubilee Downs

Fitzroy River

Dukes Dome 304m

ST GEORGE RANGES

Mt James 175m

Mt Tuckfield 311m

Mt Amy 268m

Mt Thorlan 263m

Mt Piper 337m

Christmas Creek

SPARKE RANGE

Cadjebut Mine

295

Christmas Creek

0 20 40 60 80 100 km

J K L M N O P Q R

DRYSDALE RIVER NATIONAL PARK

OOMBULGURRI ABORIGINAL LAND

Forrest

River

Banjo

Creek

Noogoora Burr Quarantine Area

Mt Connection 163m

Kneebone

Carlton Hill

MIRIMA (HIDDEN VALLEY) NATIONAL PARK: A rugged area of ancient sandstone hills and valleys and of special significance to the Aboriginal people. The park has several pleasant walking trails along the valley and ridges which offer spectacular views of both the park and Kununurra.

Wyndham

BOAB: A symbol of the region, the boab, sometimes called the 'bottle tree', produces furry brown nuts on which local artists carve scenes or animals.

PLATEAU

ONER

RANGE

Ellenbrae Creek

Ellenbrae

165

283

Pimple Peak

Chapman Creek

BLUFF FACE RANGE

DURACK RANGE

Pentecost Downs

Home Valley

4WD only

Prison Tree

Mt Cockburn North 671m

COCKBURN RANGE

El Questro Station tourist resort

Emma Gorge

56

14

42

34

41

45

VICTORIA HWY

Kununurra

Lake Kununurra

MIRIMA (HIDDEN VALLEY) NP

101

HWY

36

KEEP RIVER NATIONAL PARK

Mt Hensman 384m

34

Newry

TO KATHERINE

Lake Argyle Tourist Village

Ord Dam

Mt Brooking 379m

Lake Argyle

The Twins 318m

Rosewood

Mt Quirk 323m

Mt Mary

Waterloo

Dunham Pilot Dam

Dunham River

Ord River

61

56

HWY

Glenhill

CARR BOYD RANGE

151

ARGYLE DIAMOND MINE: The world's largest diamond mine. The pink diamonds from the mine along with other precious gems can be purchased at various outlets in Kununurra.

Argyle Diamond Mine

Lissadell

29

Bow River

Bow Ck

Turkey Ck

34

Spring Creek

80

West Baines River

DUNCAN

253

WARNINGS: In outback Australia, long distances separate some towns. Travellers should familiarise themselves with prevailing conditions before departure, and take care to ensure their vehicle is roadworthy and that they carry adequate supplies of petrol, water and food.

In northern Australia, rainfall during the 'wet' season (October to March) can make some roads impassable. Full information on road conditions should be obtained from local authorities before departure.

If visitors intend diverting off public roads within Aboriginal Land areas, a permit is required from the relevant Aboriginal authority.

Castlereagh Hill

Turkey Creek Roadhouse

Warmun Community

Mt Jarrad 530m

Texas Downs

32

Mt John 526m

OSMOND RANGE

Osmond River

Mt Buchanan 417m

Mt Elder

PURNULULU (BUNGLE BUNGLE) NATIONAL PARK

Mistake Creek

36

Nelson Springs

Mt Panton 340m

Negri River

420

VIOLET HILL

Mabel Downs

ABORIGINAL LAND

Mt Remarkable 748m

Bedford Downs

55

NORTHERN

4WD only

Mt Ranford

DIXON RANGE

Ord River

72

Tableland

Mt King 950m

28

Ord River

Little

Mt Wells 983m

Mt Warton 87m

Tullewa Hill

Fitzroy River

NARRIE RANGE

Mt Laptz 245m

71

Landowne

4WD only

52

74

163

GREAT

Springvale

14

Alice Downs

Panton R

Old Turner

Mt Coghlan 622m

Turner River

Nicholson River

RD

PURNULULU (BUNGLE BUNGLE) NATIONAL PARK: Considered one of Australia's greatest national wonders. The ecology of the park is very delicately balanced as the striped rock formations have a skin of beach lichen and orange silica which if broken, exposes the soft sandstone underneath to erosion. The southern end of the park contains the spectacular beehive formations and awe-inspiring gorges. Vehicle access is limited to 4WD only.

WESTERN AUSTRALIA

NORTHERN TERRITORY

HWY

Nicholson

BUNTINE

Kirkimble

LEOPOLD RANGES

O'Donnell River

Mt Arnhurst 719m

Mt Cummings

34

22

Saunders Creek

Sophie Downs

Mt Dockrell

China Wall

Halls Creek

Moola Bulla

Burks Park

29

Mt Flora 458m

Palm Springs Goldmine

Flora Valley

59

80

Nicholson

Wallamunga

Mt Wittenoom 428m

Mount Amhurst

MUELLER RANGE

Margaret River

Koongie Park

HWY

34

Lamboo

40

TANAMI

Ruby Plains

DUNCAN

55

Canning

Stock Route

Heritage Trail

30

41

DENISON PLAINS

Gordon Downs

GARDNER RANGE

173

Mt Ramsay 421m

NORTHERN

47

Margaret River

11

Louisa Downs

Mary River

Mt Dockrell 500m

Wolfe Creek

RD

GREAT

98

Glidden River

CANNING STOCK ROUTE: Once the longest and loneliest stock route, the 1500-km track enabled the beef cattle from the Kimberley region to be driven to the southern goldfields.

J K L M N O P Q R

381

INDIAN OCEAN

Karratha
Dampier
Wickham
Cape Lambert Point Samson
Karratha Roadhouse
Cossack
Roebourne
Whim Creek

160

293

Montebello Islands
Barrow Island
Cape Preston

MILLSTREAM - CHICHESTER NATIONAL PARK

PILBARA

287

Fortescue Roadhouse

Pannawonica

HAMERSLEY

122

WARNING: Entry to Wittenoom township is not encouraged due to asbestos dust contamination.

Wittenoom

Hamersley Gorge

Nanutarra Roadhouse

Mount Stuart

Wyloo

111

Tom Price

268

Exmouth

220

CAPE RANGE NATIONAL PARK

NINGALOO MARINE PARK

Paraburdoo

217

BARLEE RANGE NATURE RESERVE

KARIJINI (HAMERSLEY RANGE) NATIONAL PARK

Coral Bay

149

Minilya Roadhouse

TROPIC OF CAPRICORN

Burringurrah

KENNEDY RANGE NATIONAL PARK

MT AUGUSTUS NATIONAL PARK

Mt Augustus

H.M.A.S. "Sydney" Memorial Cairn
Blowholes

173

Carnarvon

Gascoyne Junction

111

337

201

FRANCOIS PERON NATIONAL PARK

Monkey Mia
Dolphin sightings

Wooramel Roadhouse

Denham

130

Useless Loop Mine
Eagle Bluff

110 km Shell Beach

Nanga Bay Resort

Overlander Roadhouse

389

Meekatharra

Zuytdorp Cliffs

TOOLONGA NATURE RESERVE

Billabong Roadhouse

278

Murchison

196

ZUYTDORP NATURE RESERVE

Cue

Walga Rock

Kalbarri

KALBARRI NATIONAL PARK

NICHOLSON RANGE

Wilgie Mia Red Ochre Mine

A B C D E F G H I

INDIAN

OCEAN

SOUTHERN

Kalbarri
Northampton
Horrocks
Williguli
Coronation Beach
Geraldton
Walkaway
Greenough
Dongara
Port Denison
Mingenew
Three Springs
Eneabba
Coolimba
Leeman
Green Head
Jurien
Cervantes
Lancelin
Guilderton
Yanchep
Wanneroo
Scarborough
PERTH
Fremantle
Rottnest Island
Kwinana
Rockingham
Singleton
Mandurah
North Dandalup
Pinjarra
Dwellingup
Waroona
Williams
Harvey
Australind
Bunbury
Collie
Capel
Donnybrook
Balingup
Busselton
Dunsborough
Yallingup
Gracetown
Margaret River
Nannup
Bridgetown
Manjimup
Augusta
Cape Leeuwin
Pemberton
Northcliffe
Walpole
Denmark
Albany

Murchison
Cue
Mount Magnet
Yalgoo
Pindar
Mullewa
Nabawa
Nanson
Yuna
Naraling
Morawa
Perenjori
Carnamah
Latham
Coorow
Buntine
Wubin
Dalwallinu
Pithara
Ballidu
Miling
Bindi Bindi
Moora
Dandaragan
New Norcia
Calingiri
Gillingarra
Regans Ford
Bindoon
Toodyay
Gingin
Goomalling
Northam
York
Mundaring
Meckering
Cunderdin
Kellerberrin
Tammin
Armadale
Serpentine
Beverley
Brookton
Pingelly
Cuballing
Narrogin
Wickepin
Wagin
Dumbleyung
Katanning
Broomehill
Gnowangerup
Kojonup
Boyup Brook
Frankland
Cranbrook
Mount Barker

Paynes Find
Mount Magnet
Merredin
Southern Cross
Bruce Rock
Corrigin
Kondinin
Kulin
Lake Grace
Lake King
Ravensthorpe
Hopetoun
Bremer Bay
Jerramungup
Ongerup

Mount Keith
Leinster
Agnew
Sandstone
Leonora
Gwalia
Menzies
Kookynie
Goongarrie
Kalgoorlie-Boulder
Coolgardie
Bullfinch
Westonia

For more detail on South Western
Western Australia see page 374

INDIAN OCEAN

Port Hedland
Cape Thouin
South Hedland
GREAT NORTHERN HWY
380
Goldsworthy
Mt Goldsworthy 131m
Shay Gap
Callawa
Cape Cossigny
Boodarie
Pippingarra
Strelley
Carlindie
Coongan
Muccan
Yarrie
Warrawagine
Depuch Island
32
Cape Lambert
Point Samson
Cossack
Roebourne
160
Whim Creek
Mallina
Indee
Wallareenya
Tabba Tabba
Lalla Rookh
Eginbah
Bamboo Creek
184
ISABELLA RANGE
Mt Negri 176m
Mt Berghaus 86m
Mt Duck 105m
Mt Oscar 145m
Pyramid
Mt Wellard 255m
Mt Constantine 221m
Mt Langenbeck 209m
Kangan
Yandearra
Mt Francisco 313m
Abydos
Marble Bar
Mt Edgar 368m
Mount Edgar
Lake Waukarlycarly
Mt Herbert 366m
Mt Wohler 327m
MILLSTREAM - CHICHESTER NATIONAL PARK
Mt Leal 372m
Mt Richthofen 390m
Mt Bilroth 417m
Coolawanyah
Hooley
White Springs
Woodstock
Hillside
Corunna Downs
Nullagine
138
GREGORY RANGE
THROSSELL RANGE
PATERSON RANGE
KARAKUTIKATI RANGE
Mt Sydney 733m
Telfer Mine
287
HAMERSLEY
Mt Pyrton 845m
Mt Margaret 879m
Mulga Downs
PILBARA
CHICHESTER RANGE NATURE RESERVE
ABORIGINAL LAND
MUNGAROONA RANGE
425
WARNING: Entry to Wittenoom township is not encouraged due to asbestos dust contamination.
Bonney Downs
288
Lake Dora
RUDALL RIVER NATIONAL PARK
BROADHURST RANGE
Mount Brockman
Mt McRae 1027m
Mt Brockman 1129m
Hamersley
Mt Stevenson 1172m
Wittenoom
138
Hamersley Gorge
Munjina Roadhouse
111
Mt Samson 1079m
Mt Vigors 1161m
Dales Gorge
95
Mt Bruce 1235m
Marandoo
Mt Windell 1110m
Noreena Downs
Mt Turner 1014m
Mt Tom Price 1072m
Tom Price
Rocklea
Mt Jope 874m
KARIJINI (HAMERSLEY RANGE) NATIONAL PARK
Mt Barricade 1089m
Mt Trevarton 999m
Juna Downs
Marillana
Roy Hill
Mt Lewin 578m
Balfour Downs
SALTBUSH
Mt Meharry 1251m
ROBERTSON RANGE
Paraburdoo
OPTHALMIA RANGE
Mt Newman 1057m
197
HWY
Newman
Capricorn Roadhouse
Jiggalong Community
Robertson Range
CAPRICORN
ROUTE
Lake Disappointment
Ashburton Downs
TROPIC
Sylvania
375
Mt Elephant 491m
Minier
Turee Creek
Prairie Downs
Savory Creek
STOCK
Mt Boggola 698m
Mt Bresnahan 683m
Bulloo Downs
Weelarrana
95
Pingandy
LITTLE SANDY DESERT
Yannen Lake
Lake Aerodrome
Dooley Downs
Mount Vernon
Mt Vernon 584m
Lake White
Lake
Mt Egerton 994m
Woodlands
Mulgul
Minaritchie Hill 718m
Kumarina Roadhouse
Wonyulgunna Hill 774m
McConkey Hill 543m
Waldburg
COLLIER RANGE NATIONAL PARK
Mt Essendon 906m
Mt Methwin 903m
Mt Salvado 733m
CANNING
Mt Clere 555m
Mingah Springs
Three Rivers
424
CARNARVON RANGES
Mt Deverell 591m
Mt Cecil Rhodes 702m
Glenayle
Mt Moore 548m
Mt Marquis 503m
Coolbilbah Hill 484m
Mt Labouchere 722m
Mt George 621m
Neds Creek
Mt Patterson 610m
Lake Naberu
Granite Peak
Earaheedy
Mt Bates 488m
Bryah
Doolgunna
Mt Fraser 799m
Peak Hill
Mount Padbury
New Springs
Carnegie Homestead
Errabiddy
Mt Gould 710m
Moorarie
Mt Maitland 591m
Karalundi
Mooloogool
Cunyu
127
Mt Hale 732m
Koonmarra
Belele
Peace Gorge (The Granites)
183
Diamond Well
Paroo
Mt Alice West 638m
Jundee
Wongawol
Lorna Glen
Lake Carnegie
Mt Noonie 512m
Nookawarra
Mileura
Munarra
Yandil
Mt Green 618m
Wiluna
Mt Russell 536m
Prenti Downs
Meekatharra
Lake Annean
Murchison Downs
Lake Way
Mt Eureka 499m
Lake Dora
Hochstetler Hill 546m
Wilgie Mia Red Ochre Mine
Annean
Yalgowra Hill
Yagahong Hill 604m
150
Lake Way
Barwidgee
Kalli
Beebyn
Mt Townsend 680m
166
Mt Keith 594m
Wonganoo
Curdawooda Hill 411m
Tuckanarra
Karbar
Yarrabubba
Youno Downs
Gidgee
Mount Keith
Mount Keith
Mt Arthur 617m
196
Coodardy
Taincrow
Yeelirrie
Albion Downs
176
Sanford River
Cue
Cogla Downs
Barrambie
Lake Mason
Booylgoo Springs
Banjawarn
Walga Rock
95
Lakeside
Mt Charles 646m
Austin
Kaluwiri
Bandya

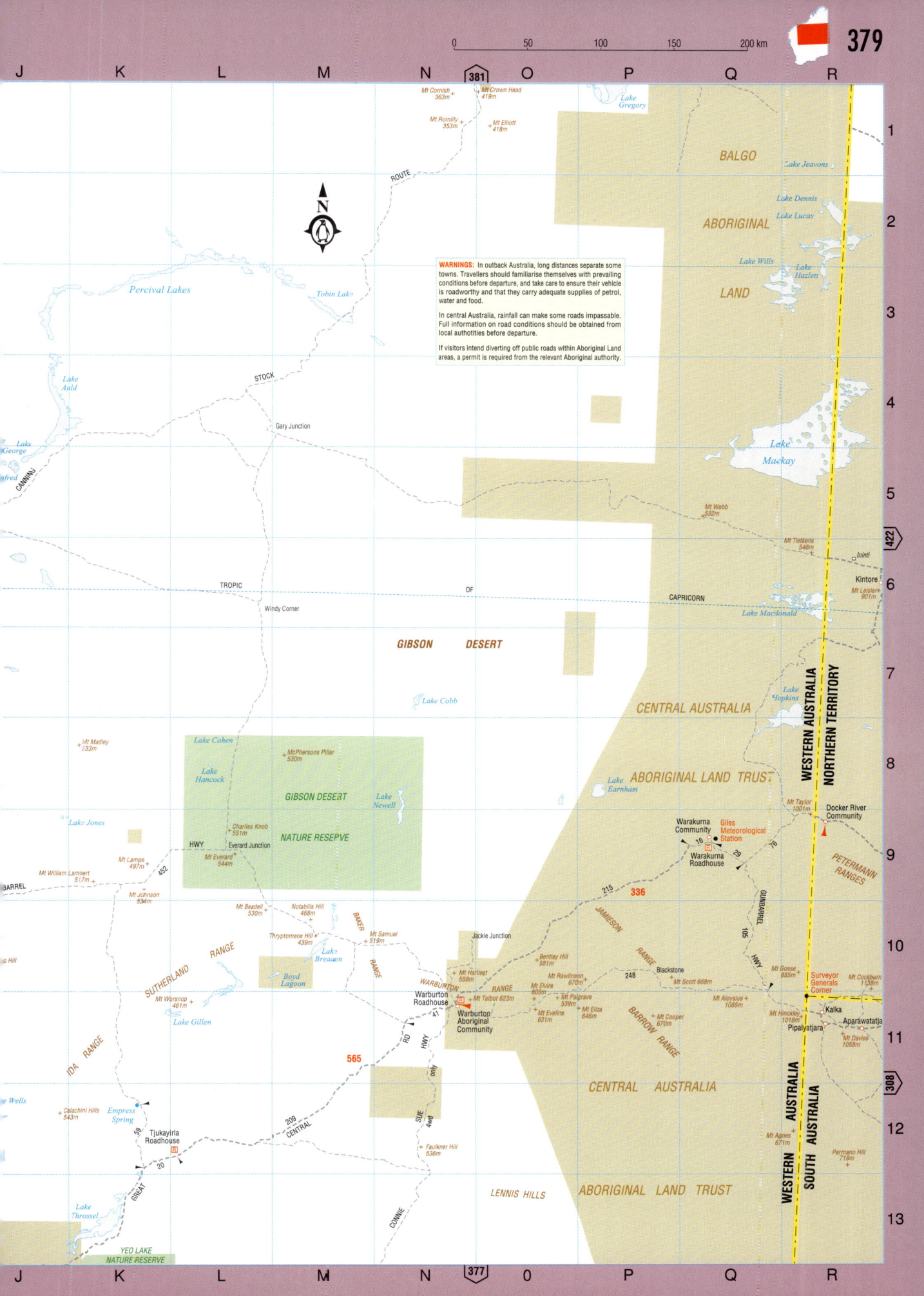

0   50   100   150   200 km

J K L M N O P Q R

381

1
Mt Cornish 363m +   Mt Crown Head 419m
Lake Gregory
BALGO
Lake Jeavons

Mt Romilly 353m +   + Mt Elliott 418m

2
ABORIGINAL
Lake Dennis
Lake Lucas
Lake Hazlett

Percival Lakes
Tobin Lake
LAND
Lake Wills

3
ROUTE
WARNINGS: In outback Australia, long distances separate some towns. Travellers should familiarise themselves with prevailing conditions before departure, and take care to ensure their vehicle is roadworthy and that they carry adequate supplies of petrol, water and food.

In central Australia, rainfall can make some roads impassable. Full information on road conditions should be obtained from local authotities before departure.

If visitors intend diverting off public roads within Aboriginal Land areas, a permit is required from the relevant Aboriginal authority.

Lake Auld
STOCK

4
Lake George
Gary Junction
Lake Mackay

CANNING
Mt Webb 532m +

5
Mt Tietkens 546m +
422

TROPIC
OF
Kintore
Mt Leisler 901m +
Ininti

6
Windy Corner
CAPRICORN
Lake Macdonald

GIBSON   DESERT
7
Lake Cobb
CENTRAL AUSTRALIA
Lake Hopkins

8
Mt Madley 533m +
Lake Cohen
McPhersons Pillar 530m +
ABORIGINAL LAND TRUST
Lake Earnham
Mt Taylor 1001m +
Docker River Community

Lake Hancock
GIBSON DESERT
Lake Newell
Warakurna Community
Giles Meteorological Station

Lake Jones
Charles Knob 581m +
NATURE RESERVE
16
Warakurna Roadhouse
29
PETERMANN RANGES

9
HWY
Everard Junction
Mt Everard 544m +
215
336

BARREL
Mt Lamps 497m +
452
Mt Johnson 534m +
JAMIESON
GUNBARREL HWY
105

Mt William Lambert 517m +
Mt Beadell 530m +
Notabilis Hill 468m
Mt Samuel 519m +
Jackie Junction
Bentley Hill 581m +
RANGE
248
Blackstone
Mt Gosse 885m +
Surveyor Generals Corner
Mt Cockburn 1138m +

10
Thryptomene Hill 439m +
Lake Breaden
BAKER
Mt Elvire 603m +
Mt Rawlinson 670m +
Mt Scott 668m +
Mt Aloysius 1085m +
Kalka
Aparawatatja

Boyd Lagoon
RANGE
WARBURTON
Mt Halfvest 558m +
Mt Paigrave 539m +
Mt Eliza 646m +
Mt Cooper 670m +
Mt Hinckley 1018m +
Pipalyatjara

SUTHERLAND
RANGE
Mt Worsnop 461m +
Lake Gillen
Warburton Roadhouse
Mt Talbot 623m +
Mt Eveline 631m +
BARROW
RANGE
Mt Davies 1058m +

11
Warburton Aboriginal Community
CENTRAL   AUSTRALIA
308

Wells
Calachini Hills 543m +
Empress Spring
IDA
RANGE
RD
HWY
SUE 4wd only
565
CENTRAL
Mt Agnes 671m +

12
Tjukayirla Roadhouse
209
59
20

Faulkner Hill 536m +
Permano Hill 719m +

Lake Throssel
GREAT
CONNIE
LENNIS HILLS
ABORIGINAL   LAND   TRUST

13
YEO LAKE NATURE RESERVE

J K L M N O P Q R

377

WESTERN AUSTRALIA   NORTHERN TERRITORY

WESTERN AUSTRALIA   SOUTH AUSTRALIA

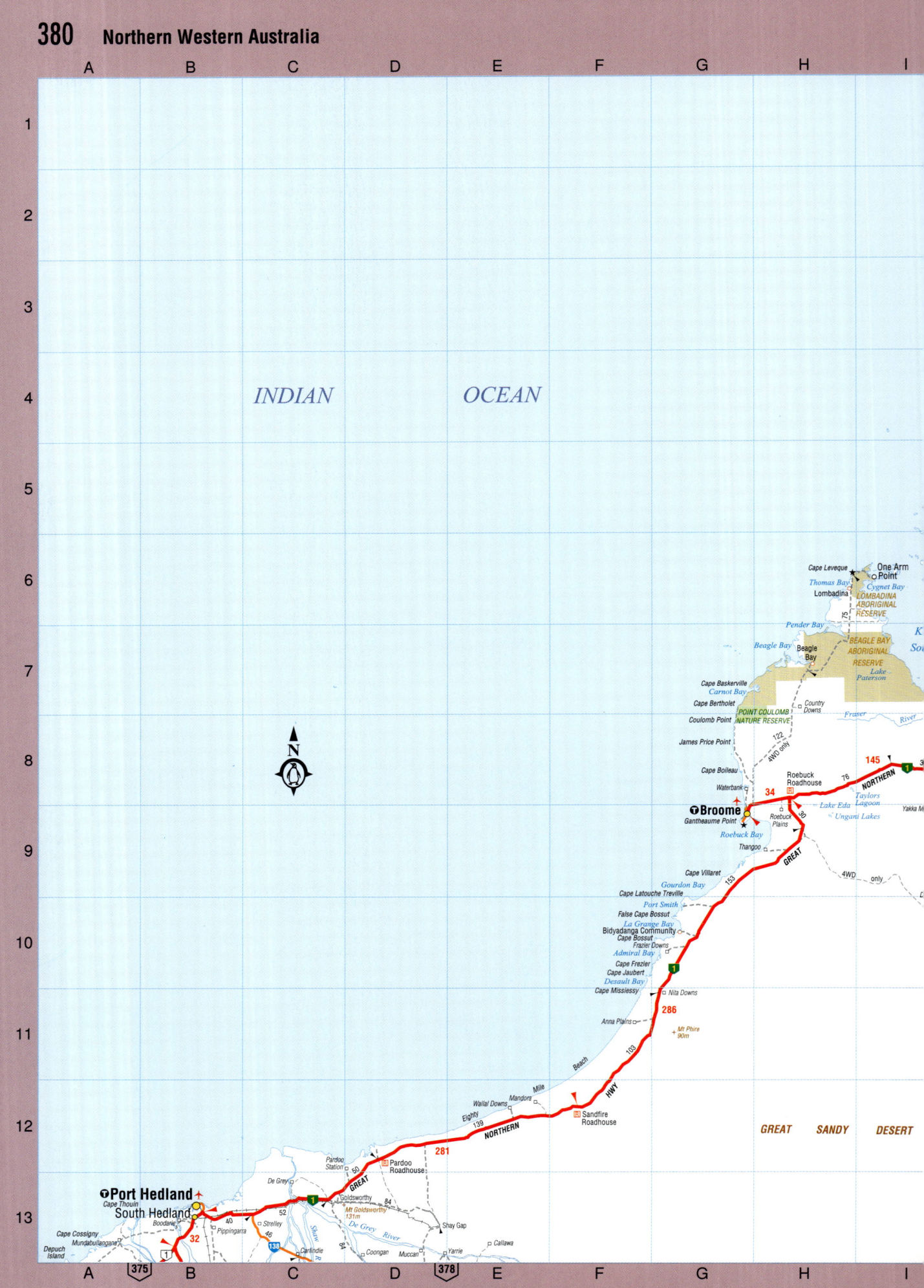

INDIAN OCEAN

GREAT SANDY DESERT

Port Hedland
South Hedland

Broome

Roebuck Roadhouse

NORTHERN HWY

GREAT NORTHERN

Cape Leveque
One Arm Point
Thomas Bay
Cygnet Bay
Lombadina
LOMBADINA ABORIGINAL RESERVE
Pender Bay
Beagle Bay
BEAGLE BAY ABORIGINAL RESERVE
Lake Paterson
Cape Baskerville
Carnot Bay
Cape Bertholet
Country Downs
Coulomb Point
POINT COULOMB NATURE RESERVE
James Price Point
Fraser River
Cape Boileau
Waterbank
Gantheaume Point
Roebuck Bay
Roebuck Plains
Thangoo
Lake Eda
Taylors Lagoon
Ungani Lakes
Yakka M
Cape Villaret
Gourdon Bay
Cape Latouche Treville
Port Smith
False Cape Bossut
La Grange Bay
Bidyadanga Community
Cape Bossut
Frazier Downs
Admiral Bay
Cape Frezier
Cape Jaubert
Desault Bay
Cape Missiessy
Nita Downs
Anna Plains
Mt Phire 90m
Wallal Downs
Mandora
Mile
Eighty
Beach
Sandfire Roadhouse
Pardoo Station
Pardoo Roadhouse
De Grey
Goldsworthy
Mt Goldsworthy 131m
Shay Gap
Cape Thouin
Boodarie
Strelley
Pippingarra
Carlindie
Cape Cossigny
Mundabullangana
Depuch Island
De Grey River
Shaw R
Coongan
Muccan
Yarrie
Callawa

145
34
286
281
32
375
378
138

TIMOR SEA

0   50   100   150   200 km

JOSEPH
BONAPARTE
GULF

Cape Talbot
Cape Londonderry
Cape Rulhieres ★
Cape Bernier

Cape Bougainville
Vansittart Bay
Napier Broome Bay
Cape Whiskey
Cape St Lambert

Admiralty Gulf
KALUMBURU ABORIGINAL LAND
George River
Mt Casuarina 221m+
Lacrosse Island

Montague Sound
Cone Mtn+ 178m
Kalumburu
Carson River
Mt Connor 312m
Mt Leeming 244m
20

Bigge Island
Mt Nicholls 143m
OOMBULGURRI
Cambridge Gulf
ORD RIVER NATURE RESERVE

BONAPARTE ARCHIPELAGO

ADMIRALTY GULF ABORIGINAL RESERVE
Mt Anderson 485m
Theda
DRYSDALE RIVER NATIONAL PARK
King River
Mt Mongona +366m
Adolphus Island
Mt Connection +183m

Mitchell Falls
MITCHELL PLATEAU
Berkeley River
Mt Fraser 366m

York Sound
Mitchell River
Edward River
Morgan River
87
NOOGOORA BURR QUARANTINE AREA
Knebone

Brunswick Bay
42
ABORIGINAL LAND
Wyndham
PARRY'S LAGOON NATURE RESERVE
418

Champagny Island
Mt Trafalgar 390m
PRINCE REGENT NATURE RESERVE
King Edward River
GARDNER PLATEAU
Forrest River
Mt Cockburn North 671m
14
Turtle Point

Deception Bay
Hall Point
Mt Lyall 213m
KUNMUNYA ABORIGINAL RESERVE
Mt Hann 779m+
313
34
Home Valley
56
Kununurra
MIRIMA (HIDDEN VALLEY) NP
KEEP RIVER NATIONAL PARK

Doubtful Bay
Mt Methuen 427m
Mt Deborah 399m+
Miners Pool
Drysdale River
66
El Questro Station tourist resort
41
45
101
34

Mt Lochee 310m
Mt Shadforth 510m
Mt Russ +692m
283
Dunham Pilot Dam
Lake Argyle Tourist Village
Hensman 384m+
Keep River
Newry

Collier Bay
Koolan
Mt Blythe +436m
Mt Lacy 763m+
Gibb River
Chapman River
61
Dunham River
151
Argyle Diamond Mine
The Twins +318m
38

Secure Bay
Mt Pags +466m
Mount Elizabeth
43
27
Durack River
CARR BOYD RANGE
Bow
Rosewood

Mt Nellie 267m+
KING LEOPOLD RANGES
Mt Glemont 478m+
Kupingarri Community
Blackfellow Ck
DURACK RANGE
Lissadell
Mt Quirk +3-3m
Mt Mary 38

TRAINING AREA
Mt Humbert 474m+
Beverley Springs
67
Hann River
Spring Creek
West

Robinson River
Mt Hart
Mt Synnot +488m
Adcock Gorge
Mt House
Turkey Creek Roadhouse
Warmun Community
Mt Jarrad +530m
Texas Downs
Mistake Creek

365
Mt Chalmers 704m+
34
63
Mt Lush 778m+
32
Mt John 526m+
Osmond River
Mt Buchanan +417m
Nelson Springs

Kimberly Downs
Napier Downs
WINDJANA GORGE NATIONAL PARK
Mt Ord 937m+
Glenroy
22
72
Tableland
VIOLET HILL ABORIGINAL LAND
PURNULULU (BUNGLE BUNGLE) NATIONAL PARK
Mt Panton + 340m
116

Mt Herbert 753m+
RANGES
Mt Clifton 537m
Mt King 950m+
163
Kirkimbie

40
46
Mt Percy +188m
Mt Behn 344m+
Mt Broome 931m+
Millie Windie
Mt Brennan 530m+
Mt Warton 437m
Bedford Downs
BUNTINE HWY

50
TUNNEL CREEK NATIONAL PARK
Mt Steith 618m+
Mt Leake 697m+
Mornington
Fitzroy River
Mt Wells 983m+
52
Mt Coghlan +622m
Nicholson
80
HWY

DEVONIAN REEF NATIONAL PARKS
85
Lansdowne
71
Springvale
14
Old Turner
80
Bunda

HWY
217
Blina
Ellendale
54
BROOKING GORGE CP
Leopold Downs
KING LEOPOLD RANGES
Gold River
Mt Barrett 692m+
Saunders Creek
Nicholson River
Kirkimbie

5
30
30
GEIKIE GORGE NP
Fossil Downs
Little Leopold River
22
Moola Bulla
Halls Creek
Flora Valley
80

Mouat Anderson
Cambalilin
Fitzroy Crossing
Mt Pierre 203m+
Margaret River
O'Donnell River
Mt Amhurst 719m+
Mt Flora +458m
Palm Springs Goldmine
Waliamunga

Liveringa
38
Mt Wynne +144m
Mt Harcman +132m
Quanbun Downs
Jubilee Downs
Mt Elma 317m+
Margaret River
Mount Amhurst
Ruby Plains
Mt Coghlan
Sturt Creek
Birrindudu

Myroodah
Luulugui
Noonkanbah
Mt Ball 554m+
Mt Huxley +537m
NORTHERN
34
40
DENISON PLAINS
Mt Wittenoom +28m

80
Mt Harcman +132m
River
Mt Fairbairn 338m+
Mary River
Wolfe River
DUNCAN ROAD
Gordon Downs

Mt James 175m+
Dukes Dome 304m+
Cadjebut Mine
Louisa Downs
Mt Ramsay 421m+
Mt Dockrell +500m
75

Mt Jarlemai 195m+
Mt Fanton 187m+
Mt Tuckfield 311m+
Mt Amy 268m+
Mt Thorian 263m+
Christmas Creek
GREAT
98
295
1
WOLFE CREEK METEORITE CRATER RESERVE

Cherrabun
Mt Piper 337m+
Bohemia Downs
Mt Josephine +419m
Sturt Creek

Lake Merril
Lake Jones
Lake Betty
Lake Mclernon
Billiluna Community
Mt Junction 626m+
Mt Frederick +530m

Tilley Claypan
Lake Lanagan
ROUTE
STOCK
TANAMI ROAD
204

WARNINGS: In outback Australia, long distances separate some towns. Travellers should familiarise themselves with prevailing conditions before departure, and take care to ensure their vehicle is roadworthy and that they carry adequate supplies of petrol, water and food.

In northern Australia, rainfall during the 'wet' season (October to March) can make some roads impassable. Full information on road conditions should be obtained from local authorities before departure.

If visitors intend diverting off public roads within Aboriginal Land areas, a permit is required from the relevant Aboriginal authority.

Beware of man-eating crocodiles in rivers, estuaries and coastal areas.

CANNING
Mt Cornish 363m+
Mt Crown Head 419m+
Balgo Community
Lake Gregory
BALGO ABORIGINAL LAND

Mt Romilly 353m+
Mt Elliott +418m
Lake Jeavons

WESTERN AUSTRALIA
NORTHERN TERRITORY

379

For more detail on the Kimberley Region see pages 362 & 363

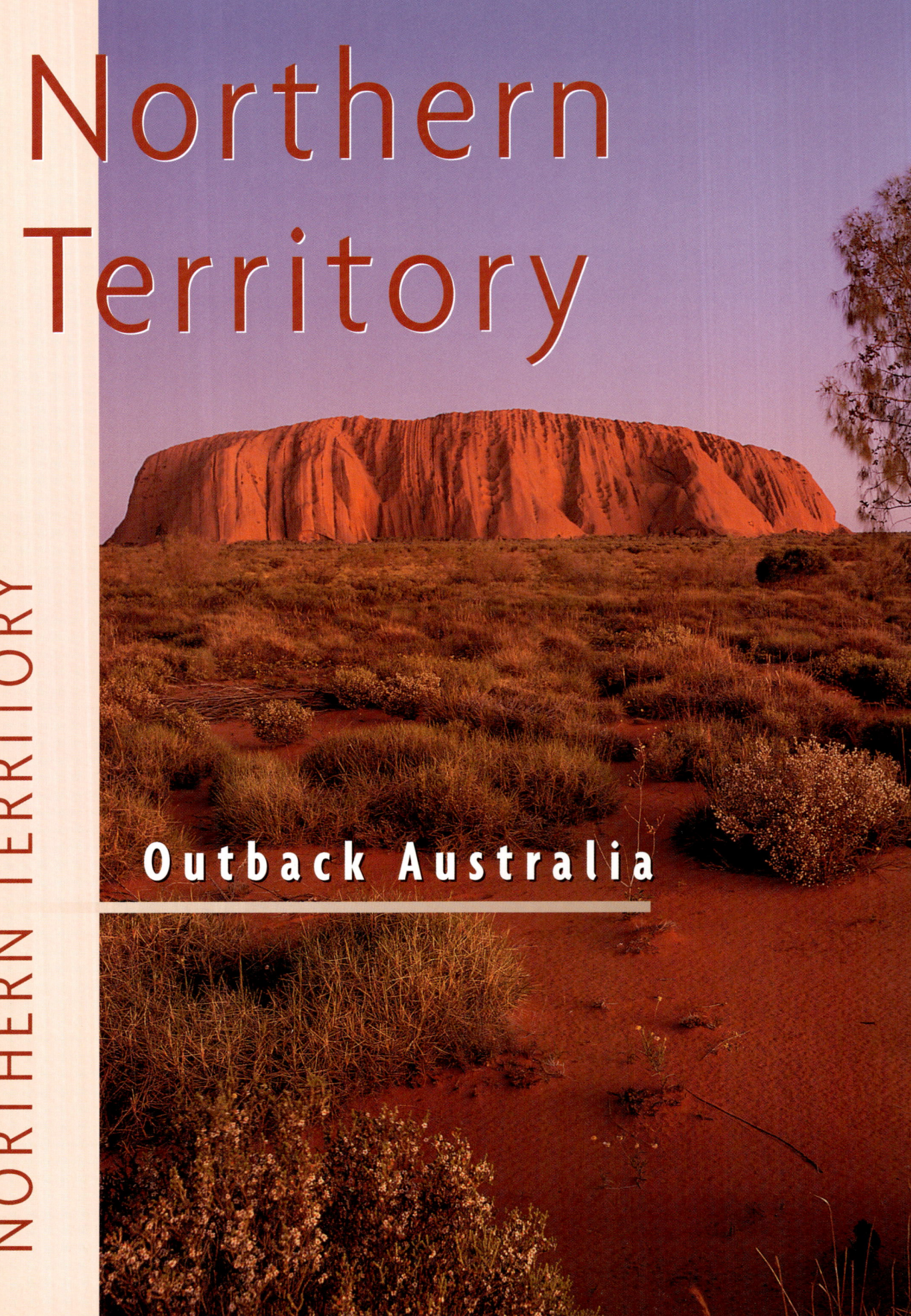

Northern Territory

Outback Australia

There are only three main highways that take motorists into the Northern Territory: the Barkly Highway from Mount Isa in Queensland, the Stuart Highway from South Australia and the Victoria Highway from the extreme north-east of Western Australia.

Given the enormous distances involved, you may well decide to fly, either to Darwin or to Alice Springs, and then hire a car to travel around the area. Alternatively, airlines, coach companies and many tour operators offer day and extended coach tours, coach camping tours, and adventure and safari trek tours, all of which allow you to discover this unique, relatively uninhabited and exciting Territory in experienced hands.

Six times the size of Great Britain, the Northern Territory has a population similar to that of Newcastle in New South Wales. Among numerous places of interest it boasts the famous Red Centre, the world's largest monolith Uluru (Ayers Rock), and many of the best Aboriginal rock-art sites in the continent.

The first, unsuccessful, attempt to settle this huge, forbidding region was not on the mainland at all, but on Melville Island in 1824. It was not until 1869 that a town called Palmerston, later to become Darwin, was established. Originally the Territory was part of New South Wales, when that State's western boundary extended to the 129th east meridian. Later, the Territory was annexed to South Australia and it did not come under Commonwealth control until 1911. In July 1978 the Territory attained self-government.

In terms of monetary value, the Territory's main industry is mining. Gold, bauxite, manganese ore, copper, silver and uranium – all contribute to this industry. The tourist industry ranks second, and beef cattle farming is significant, even though sixteen hectares or more are often required to support one animal.

The dry season, between May and October, is a good time to visit; the average annual rainfall during this period is only 25 millimetres. Between November and April, Darwin has an average annual rainfall of 1500 millimetres, the rain falling mainly in the afternoon and overnight. July is the Northern Territory's coolest month when temperatures in Darwin range between 20° and 30° C. In 'the Alice' (as Alice Springs is affectionately known) the average maximum in August is 22.5° C, cooling at night to around zero.

The Northern Territory's two main centres, Darwin and Alice Springs, are more than 1500 kilometres apart. Darwin, at the 'Top End', with a population of about 78 000, was largely rebuilt after Cyclone Tracy in 1974. It is known for its relaxed lifestyle and beautiful beaches, and makes a perfect jumping-off spot for exploring the Top End region.

If, however, you are going it alone by car, you should research your trip before setting out; read the section on Outback Motoring and bear in mind that the dry season is definitely the most pleasant weather for touring.

NOT TO BE MISSED
in the Northern Territory

Map Ref.

- **Alice Springs Desert Park** – a spectacular showcase of Central Australia's flora and fauna — 417 K3
- **Kings Canyon** – soaring 300-metre sandstone walls and views of valley below — 422 F9
- **Larapinta Trail** – explore the magnificent West MacDonnell Ranges on foot — 417 J3
- **Litchfield National Park** – superb scenery and waterfalls in this beautiful untouched wilderness area — 414 C8
- **Nitmiluk (Katherine Gorge)** – the 13 gorges through which Katherine River flows — 418 G10
- **Ormiston Gorge** – the jewel in the West MacDonnell Ranges — 416 E3
- **Territory Wildlife Park** – drive south-east from Darwin to see excellent displays of native fauna in natural bushland — 414 D4
- **Ubirr** – outstanding rock-art galleries in Kakadu National Park — 413 I3
- **Uluru (Ayers Rock)** – the Centre's most famous landmark — 422 E12
- **Window on the Wetlands Visitor Centre** – for an overview of the conservation value of the wetlands — 414 F4

Uluru (Ayers Rock), the world's greatest monolith

Keep River National Park, south-west of Katherine on the Northern Territory border

NORTHERN TERRITORY

Always make full enquiries about conditions before leaving sealed roads. The Stuart, Arnhem, Kakadu, Victoria and Barkly highways are now all-weather roads, sealed for their entire length. Even so, any driving at night should be undertaken with care because of the danger from wildlife and cattle wandering across the road.

East of Darwin is Kakadu National Park, which is rich in natural and cultural heritage. The section of Arnhem Land east of Kakadu can be explored by extended coach tour or adventure tour. Many Aboriginal lands require entry permission from an Aboriginal Land Council. These lands belong to the Aborigines; their land is sacred to them and should be respected by visitors.

South of Darwin is Katherine with its spectacular gorge, on the southern fringe of Arnhem Land. Freshwater crocodiles are common in the Katherine River, so its beauty is best viewed from either bank. From Katherine, the Stuart Highway continues south to Alice Springs. The major town along the way is Tennant Creek, which is 104 kilometres north of Devil's Marbles. The marbles are a random pile of huge, balancing granite boulders, some of which are almost perfect spheres. An Aboriginal legend says that they are eggs laid by the mythical Rainbow Serpent.

CALENDAR OF EVENTS

Note: The information given here was accurate at the time of printing. However, as the timing of events held annually is subject to change and some events may extend into the following month, it is best to check with the local tourism authority or event organisers to confirm the details. The calendar is not exhaustive. Most towns and regions throughout the Territory hold sporting competitions; regattas; rodeos; art, craft and trade exhibitions; agricultural and flower shows; music festivals and other events annually. Details of these events are available from local tourism outlets.

JANUARY
Public holidays: New Year's Day; Australia Day.
Alice Springs: Lasseter's Indoor Challenge.

EASTER
Public holidays: Good Friday; Easter Monday.
Borroloola: Fishing Classic.

APRIL
Public holiday: Anzac Day.
Alice Springs: Racing Carnival; Country Music Festival.

MAY
Public Holiday: May Day.
Darwin: Arafura Sports Festival (biennial, odd-numbered years); Fred's Pass Rural Show including Litchfield Gift (foot race).
Alice Springs: Bangtail Muster. **Mataranka:** Back to the Never Never Festival; Never Never Art Show.
Tennant Creek: Cup Day; Go-Kart Grand Prix. **Timber Creek:** Rodeo.

JUNE
Public holiday: Queen's Birthday. **Darwin:** Greek Glenti Festival. **Adelaide River:** Bush Race Meeting.
Alice Springs: Finke Desert Race. **Batchelor:** International Skydiving and Parachuting Championships (sometimes held in July).
Katherine: Barunga Sport and Cultural Festival; Katherine Cup; Canoe Marathon.

JULY
Darwin: Agricultural Show (regional public holiday); Darwin Cup Carnival. **Alice Springs:** Camel Cup; Agricultural Show.
Katherine: Agricultural Show (regional public holiday).
Tennant Creek: Agricultural Show (regional public holiday).

AUGUST
Public holiday: Picnic Day.
Darwin: Beer Can Regatta; Festival of Darwin; Darwin Rodeo. **Alice Springs:** Yuendumu Aboriginal Sports Carnival; Rodeo. **Borroloola:** Agricultural Show; Rodeo.
Jabiru: Wind Festival.
Mataranka: Rodeo.

SEPTEMBER
Darwin: National Aboriginal Week. **Daly Waters:** Rodeo.
Katherine: Flying Fox Festival.
Tennant Creek: Desert Harmony Festival. **Timber Creek:** Races.

OCTOBER
Alice Springs: Henley-on-Todd Regatta; Masters Games (mature-age athletic carnival).

NOVEMBER
Alice Springs: Corkwood Festival.

DECEMBER
Public holidays: Christmas Day; Boxing Day.

Many people outside Australia think of Alice Springs as one of the most important towns in Australia. Certainly it has been immortalised on film and in snapshots countless times. No other town, or even tiny settlement, is nearer to the geographic centre of the country. In 1872 Alice Springs was simply a repeater station for the Overland Telegraph Service; today it is not only the centre for the outback cattle industry, but also a lively tourist centre with a permanent population of approximately 20 000.

Uluru (Ayers Rock), 450 kilometres to the south-west in Uluru-Kata Tjuta National Park, is the world's biggest monolith: one huge rock, 9 kilometres in circumference and rising 348 metres above the plain on which it stands. Traditionally the Aborigines made the rock part of their sacred rituals. The mythology of the cave paintings at its base is explained at the Uluru-Kata Tjuta Cultural Centre and on tours conducted by park guides.

The magnificent Kata Tjuta (The Olgas) and, closer to the Alice, the prehistoric palms at Palm Valley, the dramatic Kings Canyon, and Standley Chasm and Ormiston Gorge in the West MacDonnell Ranges – all add their own character to the wonders of the Northern Territory.

CLIMATE GUIDE

DARWIN

	J	F	M	A	M	J	J	A	S	O	N	D
Maximum °C	32	31	32	33	32	31	30	31	32	33	33	33
Minimum °C	25	25	24	24	22	20	19	21	23	25	25	25
Rainfall mm	406	349	311	97	21	1	1	7	19	74	143	232
Raindays	21	20	19	9	2	0	1	1	2	7	12	16

ALICE SPRINGS REGION

	J	F	M	A	M	J	J	A	S	O	N	D
Maximum °C	36	35	32	28	23	20	19	22	27	31	33	35
Minimum °C	21	21	17	13	8	5	4	6	10	15	18	20
Rainfall mm	36	42	37	14	17	15	16	12	9	21	26	37
Raindays	5	5	3	2	3	3	3	2	2	5	6	5

West MacDonnell Ranges

Kata Tjuta (the Olgas)

DARWIN

A Relaxed City

The city of Darwin with State Square in the foreground

NOT TO BE MISSED

in Darwin

Map Ref.

- **Aquascene** – hand-feed fish at high tide **410 A7**
- **Australian Pearling Exhibition** – history of pearling in northern Australia **410 I11**
- **Crocodylus Park** – a safe way to get close to these reptiles **414 D2**
- **Darwin Botanic Gardens** – take the Significant Tree Walk through these splendid tropical gardens **410 C1**
- **Deckchair Cinema** – relax in a deckchair under the stars and see a film (dry season only) **410 I10**
- **East Point Reserve** – excellent recreational area and home to Darwin's Military Museum and a colony of wallabies **411 C2**
- **Indo Pacific Marine** – for an insight into the wonders of the tropical ocean floor **410 I11**
- **Mindil Beach Sunset Markets** – art and craft markets, food stalls and free entertainment (dry season only) **410 A1**
- **Museum and Art Gallery of the Northern Territory** – fine collection of Aboriginal artifacts and fascinating Cyclone Tracy exhibit **411 D7**
- **The Tour Tub** – a fun way to travel around the city's major attractions **410 E9**

The first coastal town established in the Northern Territory was Palmerston in 1864. Located at the mouth of the Adelaide River, it was quickly abandoned after a disastrous wet season in 1865.

Another expedition, led by Surveyor-General George Goyder, established a base at Adam Bay about 50 kilometres east of present-day Darwin. After surveying the area, he recommended that Port Darwin, which had been discovered in 1839 and named after Charles Darwin, would be the best place for a new settlement. The new site was also officially called Palmerston, but the locals referred to it as Port Darwin in order to distinguish it from the original settlement. The name was officially changed to Darwin in 1911 when the Federal Government took control of the Territory.

At first Darwin's development was hampered by its isolation. During World War II, however, the Stuart

Highway was completed, linking Darwin with the railhead at Alice Springs; but even when the town had recovered from the bomb damage of the war, growth was still slow.

The modern Darwin's prosperity is based largely on tourism and the mineral wealth of the Territory. Over the last 20 years the city has developed as a thriving capital that is Australia's gateway to Asia and a strategic defence location for the whole continent.

Life for the early citizens was hard and changed very little until World War II. Graziers and agriculturalists struggled to cope with the violent climatic changes. Gradual development saw the population grow to 45 000 by 1974, when Cyclone Tracy destroyed most of the city. Now the figure has pushed past 78 000, which says something for either the hardiness of its people or the desirability of the rebuilt city as a place to live, or perhaps a bit of both. With Broome, in Western Australia, Darwin is one of Australia's most multicultural settlements, embracing people of 70 racial and cultural backgrounds. Chinese people have always formed a major part of the city's population and, in more recent years, Timorese and South-East Asian refugees have arrived in Darwin and many have stayed. Quite large contingents of armed-forces personnel are also stationed at various bases around Darwin.

In the city there is very little or no rain between May and October, when the average Top End maximum temperature is 32°C. From November to April, maximum Top End temperatures average 33°C with high relative humidity; make sure you take light summer clothing on your holiday! However, Darwin is always good for sailing, swimming, water-skiing or enjoying the sunshine.

The city's business district is much like any other similar-sized city, but with a relaxed and tropical atmosphere all its own. Modern air-conditioned shopping centres serve Darwin's suburbs, which are in two main sections, divided by the international airport.

City sightseeing is conveniently done from air-conditioned motor coaches and mini-buses that make regular tours. The **Tour Tub** is another way to get around the city's attractions. It departs daily from the Smith Street Mall and visitors can hop on or off at their leisure. The city's main attractions are the splendidly tropical 34-hectare **Darwin Botanic Gardens**; the surviving historic buildings, churches, and memorials; the **Reserve Bank**; **State Square** which includes **Parliament House** and the **Supreme Court**; Darwin's busy **harbour** area; and, on the Esplanade overlooking the harbour, the **Beaufort Darwin Centre**, including a world-class hotel and the Entertainment Centre. A lookout on the Esplanade commemorates the fiftieth anniversary of the bombing of Darwin in 1942. Day, half-day and two- and three-hour cruises around the harbour are available, as well as seaplane flights, contact Tourist information.

The elegant colonial architecture of **Government House** is near the southern end of the Esplanade and **Old Admiralty House**, an interesting tropical-style building, is further north.

Christ Church Cathedral was completed and consecrated in March 1975. It incorporates the porch from its predecessor, which was a garrison church during World War II and came under fire from Japanese bombers, but was eventually destroyed by Cyclone Tracy. The new cathedral features a stained glass window in memory of the trawlermen lost at sea during the cyclone. The altar, weighing 2.5 tonnes, was hewn from a jarrah log believed to be more than 400 years old. At the **Civic Centre**, not far from the cathedral, is the 'Tree of Knowledge', an ancient, spreading banyan tree. There are several other interesting places of worship in Darwin, particularly the **Chinese Temple**, where visitors are welcome to inspect the interior.

One of Darwin's most historic hotels, the **Old Victoria** in the Smith Street Mall, is adjacent to a modern shopping complex, at the same time retaining its colonial character with punkahs to cool the Balcony Bar.

For those with cultural interests, the city boasts a theatre group that welcomes visitors' participation in its workshops held in **Brown's Mart**, another historic building. The **Darwin Entertainment Centre** includes a 1000-seat theatre for the performing arts and a gallery. Cinemas are located in Mitchell Street and at Casuarina, and the **Deckchair Cinema** is at the Darwin Wharf Precinct behind Stokes Hill Power Station.

Several art galleries, including some which feature the work of Aboriginal artists, can be visited in the city area. The **Museum and Art Gallery of the Northern Territory** located at Bullocky Point, houses important collections of Aboriginal, Balinese and New Guinean artifacts, works by Australia's most famous painters, the Cyclone Tracy gallery which encapsulates the experience and aftermath of the cyclone and a maritime museum. The annual National Aboriginal Art Award is held here in late August or early September.

At the entrance to the Darwin Wharf Precinct is **Indo Pacific Marine** with its brilliant coral displays particularly the Coral by Night display where artificial light and moonlight highlight the irridescent colours of the coral. Also at the wharf entrance is the **Australian Pearling Exhibition**, which features static, audio-visual and live displays on pearl farming. At the end of the Esplanade, at Doctors Gully off Daly Street, **Aquascene** provides the opportunity to hand-feed the ocean fish, which come in to the jetty each high tide; for feeding times, call (08) 8981 7837. At Burnett Place on the outskirts of the city centre is the

ACCOMMODATION

HOTELS
Beaufort Hotel
The Esplanade, Darwin
(08) 8980 0800

MGM Grand Darwin
Gilruth Ave, Mindil Beach
(08) 8943 8888

Novotel Atrium
100 The Esplanade, Darwin
(08) 8941 0755

The Plaza
32 Mitchell St, Darwin
(08) 8982 0000

FAMILY AND BUDGET
Hotel Darwin
10 Herbert St, Darwin
(08) 8981 9211

Poinciana Inn
84 Mitchell St, Darwin
(08) 8981 8111

Top End Hotel
cnr Daly and Mitchell sts, Darwin
(08) 8981 6511, 1800 626 151 (toll free for reservations)

YWCA, Banyan View Lodge
119 Mitchell St, Darwin
(08) 8981 8644

MOTEL GROUPS: BOOKINGS
Best Western 13 1779
Flag 13 2400
Travelodge 1300 363 300

This list is for information only; inclusion is not necessarily a recommendation.

A spectacular sunset at Fannie Bay

NORTHERN TERRITORY

Myilly Point Heritage Precinct, headquarters for the National Trust. The Trust building houses local art, an information centre and gift shop.

The **MGM Grand Darwin** is a few metres from the shores of **Mindil Beach**. This large complex offers luxury accommodation, restaurants and discos, sporting, gambling and convention facilities and Sunset Jazz every Sunday from May to October. The **Mindil Beach Sunset Markets** operate on the foreshore from May to October; watch the setting sun while browsing through the food, art and craft stalls.

The **East Point Military Museum** at **East Point Reserve** displays artillery, war planes and other militaria close to the gun turrets that were constructed during World War II. The reserve is a popular recreational area with extensive walking and cycling paths, a boardwalk through mangroves, picnic areas, safe, year-round swimming in Lake Alexander and a colony of wallabies. Darwin boasts of its beautiful sunsets and East Point Reserve is one of the best viewing places. Nearby **Fannie Bay** is the site where Ross and Keith Smith landed their Vickers Vimy aircraft in 1919, completing the first flight

from the UK to Australia. One of the most beautiful spots in the world to have had a prison, Fannie Bay also has some fine beaches. The former gaol, now the **Fannie Bay Gaol Museum**, features displays on the history of the gaol between 1883 and 1979 as well as providing an insight into Darwin's main museum.

For 'croc-spotting' in the city, **Crocodylus Park** is located at the end of McMillans Road, near the airport. The park is a research base and public education forum featuring videos, a museum, crocodile feeding and tours. Further north past the airport is **Casuarina Coastal Reserve**, an area which includes a long, white sandy beach, dunes, mangrove and monsoon vine thickets, patches of rainforest, World War II artillery observation posts and a registered Aboriginal Sacred Site, Old Man Rock. Darwin's best-known annual event is probably the Beer Can Regatta, held each August. The competing boats and other floating craft are constructed out of cans, and it is a day with lots of family fun.

Darwin's restaurants offer an excellent choice of cuisine, and there are also wine bars that offer varied menus and pleasant settings for lunch and dinner.

To the north of the city area, Darwin's suburbs have been virtually rebuilt since 1974. The tropical climate has encouraged a lush regrowth and the gardens are a feast of beautiful bougainvilleas, hibiscus and alamanders.

Sporting interests are well served in Darwin. There are four golf courses, a motor sports complex, a racecourse and facilities for tennis, squash, bowls (lawn and tenpin) and football (Aussie Rules, Rugby and Soccer). Swimming pools are located on Ross Smith Avenue, and at Casuarina, Nightcliff and Palmerston. Box jellyfish are common in the waters off Darwin between October and May, so swimming in the sea during this period is not recommended.

Darwin is the natural jumping-off point for touring the Top End. The pressure on luxury hotels and motels is often great and a range of alternative, less luxurious accommodation has developed, offering affordable alternatives. Many caravan parks in Darwin have permanent residents, so it is worth booking ahead.

For further information on Darwin, contact the Darwin Region Tourism Association, Beagle House, cnr Mitchell and Knuckey sts (PO Box 4392, Darwin 0801); (08) 8981 4300.

DARWIN ON FOOT

Darwin is a compact and well-designed city and most areas can be comfortably explored on foot. The following is a selection of walking tours available around Darwin and its suburbs.

- **Darwin Botanic Gardens** – 3 self-guide walks through different environments; pamphlets available from Information Centre at Geranium Street entrance to gardens

- **Historical Stroll** – self-guide walk highlighting historical side of central city; route contained in Visitors Guide *Darwin and the Top End Today*

Darwin tourism authorities have prepared a series of pamphlets *Darwin: discovering our city* for self-guide walks around the city and suburbs. They include:

- **The City** – highlighting history, administrative buildings and major cultural centres

- **East Point** – recreational area with Military Museum and wallaby colony

- **The Esplanade** – stroll through foreshore park with its lookouts, memorial sites and heritage features

- **Northern Suburbs** – featuring recreational, sporting, cultural and scenic attractions

- **The Wharf** – maritime precinct combining working port and tourist attractions

Pamphlets for the self-guide walks are available from the Darwin Region Tourism Association, Beagle House, cnr Knuckey and Mitchell sts, Darwin; (08) 8981 4300.

TOURS from Darwin

Fogg Dam, a wildlife sanctuary 65 kilometres south-east of Darwin

In the 'dry', many tours of places of interest are accessible by bus or conventional vehicle. Safaris by air and 4WD take sporting enthusiasts to less accessible areas for sightseeing, shooting and fishing. The best time to go bush is May to September.

Harbour cruises

Ferries depart daily from the Cullen Bay Marina on the western side of the city to Mandorah on the Cox Peninsula, an ideal place for a relaxed day on the beach, swimming or fishing. Cruises on the harbour provide a delightful way to see the city shores. Various cruises are available as well as seaplane scenic flights; sunset cruises are popular. There is also a wide range of fishing tours available around various locations in Darwin Harbour.

Air tours

Several tours by air from Darwin are available, including day or weekend excursions, and fishing and shooting trips. A three-day air tour into Western Australia, including a jungle cruise at Lake Kununurra, the Hidden Valley, the Carr Boyd Ranges, Lake Argyle and the Ord River, makes a most enjoyable trip if you can spare the time.

Howard Springs Nature Park

31 km from Darwin via the Stuart Highway

There is safe swimming here in a spring-fed pool surrounded by monsoon forest. Avid birdwatchers can spot 50 or more species in a few hours; varieties of reptiles abound. Picnic areas and a kiosk are provided.

Fogg Dam

65 km from Darwin via the Arnhem Highway

Fogg Dam was built in the late 1950s to service the short-lived rice-growing plantations near Humpty Doo. Since then, the area has served as a wildlife sanctuary. A sunrise or sunset tour of this area offers an excellent opportunity to view animals and birds on the move between their feeding grounds and where they sleep. Not only is Fogg Dam a likely spot to see the Top End's birdlife, but you are also likely to see wallabies and water pythons. The nearby swamps are the haunt of the elegant jabiru. Other birds in abundance are the pelican, egret, galah, cockatoo and kitehawk. A signposted trail and boardwalk provide access through patches of monsoon rainforest and paperbark swamp. The tour route then goes on to the Marrakai Plains where many species of birds can also be seen. Millions of dollars were lost in this area when the rice irrigation scheme at Humpty Doo failed. Nearby is Gows Reptile Farm, which has the largest range of snakes in Australia (250 species), as well as many lizards. Further along the highway on the top of Beatrice Hill is the Window on the Wetlands Visitor Centre which provides an excellent overview of the conservation value of the wetlands.

Crocodile Farm, a large commercial crocodile farm, 40 kilometres south-east of Darwin

NORTHERN TERRITORY

Cruises on the Adelaide River

64 km from Darwin via the Arnhem Highway

For a look at nature as you have never seen it, take a river cruise on which you will see jumping crocodiles from the safety of an air-conditioned vessel.

Kakadu National Park

250 km from Darwin via the Arnhem Highway

World Heritage-listed Kakadu is rich in natural and cultural heritage. Apart from abundant wildlife, the scenery here is dramatic and there are many fine examples of ancient Aboriginal rock art at various sites in the park. The drive is fascinating, and can be topped off by a cruise on the East Alligator River or Yellow Water. You would be unlucky not to see crocodiles, as well as wallabies, and the birdlife is prolific; however, sightings of buffalo are becoming rare. The Arnhem Highway is sealed all the way to Jabiru, and you could do the trip in your own car or a hired vehicle. Approximately 100 kilometres south of Jabiru are the Jim Jim Falls, accessible only by 4WD and only in the dry season. There are many good camping spots on Jim Jim Creek and other bill-abongs. The safari guides have local knowledge and can show you far more than if you explore this area on your own. **See also**: Aboriginal Art; The Top End; National Parks.

Crocodile Farm

40 km from Darwin via the Stuart Highway

Australia's first and largest commercial crocodile farm has over 7000 crocodiles, that range in length from just a few centimetres to 4 metres. There are feeding displays and tours daily. Be adventurous and try some farm-raised crocodile delicacies.

Territory Wildlife Park at Berry Springs

56 km from Darwin via the Stuart Highway

A wildlife park of international standard, located in more than 400 hectares of bushland at Berry Springs, the Territory Wildlife Park is designed to display only animals native and feral to the Northern Territory. The exhibits are all connected by a 4-kilometre link road and include open-moated enclosures, with kangaroos, wallabies, dingoes, bustards, buffalo and banteng; a naturally-occurring lagoon where native birds can be viewed from a hide; an aquarium that features an acrylic walk-through tunnel for underwater viewing of large fresh water fish; a series of aviaries that display birds in natural habitats; a walk-through rainforest aviary; and the second largest nocturnal house in the world, artificially moonlit, where visitors can see about 50 species of mammal, bird and reptile. The park is a project of the Parks and Wildlife Commission of the Northern Territory. Adjacent to the Territory Wildlife Park is the Berry Springs Nature Park, which features a spring-fed swimming area. The park is ideal for a picnic.

Litchfield National Park

144 km from Darwin via the Stuart Highway

This popular park covers 143 000 hectares and features the 'Lost City', an area of weathered sandstone pillars; giant magnetic termite mounds; monsoonal rainforest and many waterfalls which are spring-fed and hence flow year-round. Wangi and Florence falls are easily accessible; at Wangi Falls there is a huge natural pool, ideal for swimming. The park also offers short and extended bushwalking tracks, and picnic and barbecue facilities.

NORTHERN TERRITORY
from A to Z

Adelaide River
Pop. 356

MAP REF. 414 E8, 418 E7

A small settlement set in pleasant country 112 km SE of Darwin on Stuart Hwy, Adelaide River was the location for 30 000 Australian soldiers during World War II. **Of interest:** On Stuart Hwy: Motor Cycle Haven, a collection of motor cycles and memorabilia; historic railway station (1888), with displays of local history. At Fresh Food Kiosk, Memorial Dr., resides Charlie the buffalo, 'star' of the films *Crocodile Dundee* 1 and 2. June: Bush Race Meeting. **In the area:** War cemetery, just north of town. Litchfield National Park, 75 km NW, a picturesque wilderness area featuring spectacular waterfalls, bushwalks and prolific wildlife; main entrance via Batchelor on sealed road. Daly River township, 114 km SW, for great fishing, local Aboriginal arts and crafts, native flora and fauna in surrounding area. Organised tours available to Daly River Aboriginal Land Trust area, 100 km west of Daly River. Robin Falls, 10 km S, flow during rainy season. **Tourist information:** Fresh Food Kiosk, Memorial Dr.; (08) 8976 7166. **Accommodation:** 1 hotel/motel, 1 cara./camp. park.

Aileron
Pop. 50

MAP REF. 422 I6

A popular rest stop on Stuart Hwy, Aileron is 132 km N of Alice Springs. **Of interest:** At Roadhouse: Aboriginal art, native wildlife, Sunday roast lunch, playground and picnic/barbecue facilities **In the area:** Ryans Well Historical Reserve, 7 km SE. **Tourist information:** Roadhouse, Stuart Hwy; (08) 8956 9703. **Accommodation:** 1 hotel/motel, 1 hostel.

Alice Springs
Pop. 20 448

MAP REF. 417 K3, 423 J8

Alice Springs is at the heart of the Red Centre, almost 1500 km from the nearest capital city, and is a base for many

The Old Telegraph Station, just north of Alice Springs

tourist attractions including Uluru (Ayers Rock). The area has a strong beef-cattle industry with British Hereford and Shorthorn being the main breeds. Other industries include cut-flowers, camel meat and date-growing. More than 350 000 visitors a year pass through this modern, well-maintained town set in the heart of the MacDonnell Ranges. The Todd River, which runs through the town, is dry except after heavy rains; for the annual Henley-on-Todd Regatta in Oct. the boats are carried or fitted with wheels. Between May and Sept. days are warm and nights can be cold. For the rest of the year daytime temperatures rise into the high 30s but nights are milder. Rains, usually brief, can come at any time of year. The town site was seen by William Whitfield Mills in 1871, when he was surveying a route for the Overland Telegraph Line. He named the Todd River after the SA Superintendent of Telegraphs, Sir Charles Todd, and a nearby waterhole Alice Springs after Lady Todd. The first settlement was at the repeater station, built for transmitting messages across the continent. In 1860 John McDouall

Stuart had passed about 50 km W of the site. He named Central Mt Sturt after Captain Sturt, who had commanded an earlier expedition, however the SA Government renamed the mountain in Stuart's honour. Pastoralist John Ross also helped look for a route for the telegraph line. Until 1880 the repeater station was the only reason for the existence of a handful of people in this remote area, then the Government sent surveys north seeking suitable sites for railheads. The township of Stuart, 3.2 km from the telegraph station, was gazetted in 1880, but the railway remained unbuilt. Regular supply was maintained by the expensive and slow camel train from Port Augusta. Even the discovery of gold at Arltunga, 113 km NE of the settlement, did little to develop Stuart. The Federal Government took control of NT from SA in 1911; from that time the township developed slowly. The Australian Inland Mission stationed Sister Jane Finlayson there in 1916 and the growing needs of the area led to the establishment of Adelaide House nursing hostel in 1926. The railway was completed in 1929. The service became

The Red Centre

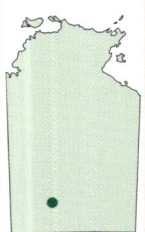

The first priority for most tourists in the Red Centre is Uluru (Ayers Rock). About 450 kilometres south-west of the Alice, the world's greatest monolith rises majestically 348 metres above a wide, sandy floodplain covered in spinifex and desert oak. The rock is 9 kilometres in circumference and, with the movement of the sun during the day, it changes colour through shades of fiery red, delicate mauve, blues, pinks and browns. When rain falls it veils the rock in a torrent of silver.

Yulara, about 20 minutes' drive north of Uluru, is a self-contained township; it has accommodation, a supermarket, and other shops and services. Ayers Rock Resort at Yulara offers a range of accommodation: the top-class Sails in the Desert Hotel, the Outback Pioneer Hotel and Lodge, the Desert Gardens four-star resort, Spinifex Lodge, Emu Walk self-contained serviced apartments, and well-equipped camping grounds. With its prize-winning design, Yulara does not intrude into the landscape but blends into the ochre colours of the desert. If you can, allow for a stay of at least two days, this will give you time to explore Uluru and see a sunrise and a sunset there, and to visit Kata Tjuta (The Olgas) – the two most famous attractions in **Uluru-Kata Tjuta National Park.**

An excellent way to familiarise yourself with the region is to spend an hour or so at the Yulara Visitors Centre. Displays depict the geology, history, flora and fauna of the region, and there is a spectacular collection of photographs. Audiovisual shows are held regularly. Excellent displays of Aboriginal culture and arts are also available at the Uluru-Kata Tjuta Cultural Centre on the road to Uluru. This splendidly-designed building is in the shape of two snakes.

According to Aboriginal legends, Uluru and Kata Tjuta were created and given their distinctive forms during the Tjukurpa or creation period. At the base of Uluru there are cave paintings and carvings made thousands of years ago by members of the Loritja and Pitjanjatjara groups. It is not difficult to appreciate that this is a sacred place of ancient times, particularly for its traditional owners.

Do not attempt the 1.6-kilometre climb of Uluru unless you are fit and well, and have a good head for heights, or if the weather is hot – the track is

Uluru (Ayers Rock), the star attraction in the Red Centre

exposed and steep, and casualties are common. The climb follows a religious track, and the Anangu (the traditional owners) prefer visitors to take some of the other discovery walks in the park and near the rock itself. Taking the 9-kilometre circuit walk around the base of Uluru, you will see rock art, the Mutitjulu (Sound Shell), a cavity as smooth as if formed by the sea, and the Taputji (Kangaroo Tail), a 160-metre strip of stone. Tours include the Mala Walk, the Edible Desert Walk (Aboriginal bush tucker) and the Liru Walk, conducted by Aboriginal guides. Self-guide walks are also an option; maps are available at the Uluru-Kata Tjuta Cultural Centre on the road to Uluru.

Some 50 kilometres to the west are Kata Tjuta (The Olgas), a cluster of rounded, massive rocks equally mysterious. They too are dramatic and vividly coloured. The tallest dome of Kata Tjuta, Mount Olga, is 546 metres above the oasis-like Valley of the Winds that runs through the rock system. Ernest Giles, who first saw Mount Olga named it after the Queen of Spain.

Accommodation, meals and tours from Yulara to the unusual flat-topped Mount Conner are available; bookings at Yulara. Curtin Springs cattle station and roadside inn is on the Lasseter Highway, 82 kilometres east of Yulara.

A good way to see many of the tourist attractions in the Red Centre is to start from **Alice Springs**. You can take advantage of the various tours that operate from there, or take your own vehicle. A few tourist destinations require 4WD; check before you set out. The Mereenie Loop Road route, 4WD recommended, links Alice Springs with Kings Canyon

and Uluru, via the West MacDonnell Ranges, and Glen Helen. It allows most of the attractions to the west and south of Alice Springs to be incorporated in a circular route without major backtracking. As the Loop Road passes through Aboriginal land, a permit is required. Check road conditions with Tourist information before departure.

The Alice Springs Telegraph Station Historical Reserve is only 3 kilometres north of Alice Springs. The original Alice Springs settlement's stone buildings have been restored by the Parks and Wildlife Commission of the Northern Territory and furnished with artifacts from early this century. There is also an historic display. Guided tours are available half-hourly. The 570-hectare reserve offers bushwalking, picnicking and wildlife observation. A small waterhole, the original water source for the settlement, from which Alice Springs obtained its name, is nearby. The telegraph station was built to link Port Augusta to Darwin, the link continuing by submarine cable to Java. Completed in 1872, the line was used until 1932, when operations were transferred to the site at the corner of Parsons Street and Railway Terrace in Alice Springs. The telegraph station site then housed an Aboriginal Mission, The Bungalow, which closed in 1963.

An interesting day tour from Alice Springs is to visit the attractions of the **West MacDonnell National Park**. The beautiful Standley Chasm, 50 kilometres west, is managed by the Angkerle Aboriginal Corporation. This colourful cleft in the West MacDonnells is only 5 metres wide. At midday when the sunlight reaches the floor of the chasm, turning the walls a blazing red, it is a memorable sight. On the way, Simpsons Gap, 18 kilometres west of Alice Springs, can be visited at the same time and has walking access. A sealed bike track links Alice Springs and Simpsons Gap.

Further west, about 133 kilometres from Alice Springs on the Finke River, are Glen Helen and Ormiston gorges. Their colours were captured by the famous Aboriginal artist Albert Namatjira; they also lend themselves to photography, as does the sunrise on Mount Sonder to the west. Glen Helen Homestead, an accommodation base for the West MacDonnells, is currently closed for renovations. Check re-opening date with Tourist information. A day tour to the region is available from Alice Springs.

A 4WD day tour from Alice Springs will also take you to Palm Valley and the Finke River Gorge, 155 kilometres south-west. The Finke River is one of the oldest watercourses in the world and to walk along its bed is an unforgettable experience. Palm Valley, with its rock pools, cycad palms and *Livistona* palms unique to the area, is yet another of the wonders of the Centre. The plant life has such a prehistoric appearance that to enter the valley is like taking a trip back in time. These two attractions can also be visited by taking a two-day tour from Alice Springs. Also well worth a visit is the restored Mission at **Hermannsburg**, birthplace of the artist Albert

Namatjira, 125 kilometres west of Alice Springs, on the way to Palm Valley – arrive for their splendid morning tea, lunch or afternoon tea.

Kings Canyon, 330 kilometres south-west of Alice Springs in **Watarrka National Park**, is one of the most interesting and scenic areas of the Centre. The climb to the rim of the canyon is fairly arduous, but well worth the effort. Even more spectacular views can be obtained by crossing via the small, railed Cotterills Bridge, near the old, nerve-racking tree-trunk bridge. The Lost City and the Garden of Eden are superb sights here. The Kings Canyon Resort and Kings Creek Camping Ground provide accommodation in this area.

East of Alice Springs in the East MacDonnell Ranges are Corroboree Rock, which is of significance to the Eastern Arrernte Aborigines; the scenic Trephina Gorge; N'Dhala Gorge, which has a variety of flora and ancient rock engravings; and Ruby Gap Nature Park, a picturesque area only accessible to high-clearance 4WD.

The Arltunga Historical Reserve, 110 kilometres east of Alice Springs, beyond Trephina Gorge, preserves memorabilia of the goldmining era in the region. Little evidence remains of the shanty town that grew up after 1887 when alluvial gold was found. You can explore the stone ruins, scattered workings, gravestones and go down a mine. At the

Visitors Centre there are historical exhibits, with a gaol and restored police station 2 kilometres away. There is a private camping ground next to the reserve and the hotel offers meals and has antiques on display. Fossicking in the area is good. **Ross River** Homestead, 88 kilometres east of Alice Springs, offers a range of outback experiences and comfortable accommodation.

Thirty-five kilometres south of Alice Springs are the ancient Ewaninga Rock Carvings or petroglyphs. Signs along a short walk explain Aboriginal use of this area.

A turning off the Stuart Highway about 140 kilometres south-west of Alice Springs leads to the Henbury meteorite craters. The Henbury craters are believed to have been formed several thousand years ago when a falling meteor broke into pieces and hit the earth. The largest of the 12 craters is 180 metres wide and 15 metres deep; while the smallest is 6 metres wide and only a few centimetres deep.

For further information about the attractions of the Red Centre, contact the Central Australian Information and Interpretive Centre, Gregory Tce, Alice Springs; (08) 8952 5800. **See also**: National Parks and A–Z listing for those parks and towns indicated by bold type. **Map reference**: 416-17.

The Mereenie Loop Road

The Mereenie Loop Road links Glen Helen to **Kings Canyon** in the far south-west. The road is mainly gravel or dirt and a 4WD vehicle is strongly recommended. As a section of the road passes through Aboriginal Land, a permit is required; these are obtainable in **Alice Springs** (contact Tourist information), Kings Canyon and Yulara. This route links Alice Springs with Kings Canyon and Uluru (Ayers Rock) via the West MacDonnell Ranges, and Glen Helen, without major backtracking.

Heading west from Alice Springs and along Namatjira Drive, this route passes the major attractions of the **West MacDonnell National Park**, including Simpsons Gap, Standley Chasm, Ellery Creek Big Hole and Serpentine and Ormiston gorges, before reaching Glen Helen. An alternative route to access the Mereenie Loop Road from Alice Springs is to continue on Larapinta Drive via **Hermannsburg** and, if travelling by 4WD, it is possible to divert to Palm Valley in **Finke Gorge National Park**.

After Glen Helen, the route leads south-west to Kings Canyon in **Watarrka National Park**. After Glen Helen it is possible to divert to Tnorala (Gosse Bluff), a spectacular crater formed 130 million years ago; a separate permit is

Valley of the Domes, Kings Canyon

required to enter the Tnorala Conservation Reserve which is included in the Mereenie Tour Pass.

From Watarrka visitors can travel via Luritja Road and Lasseter Highway to **Yulara** and **Uluru-Kata Tjuta National Park**. A minimum of two days should be allowed for the journey. Hotel-style accommodation is available at Kings Canyon Resort and Yulara, or inquire

about camping locations at Tourist information. Various informative Aboriginal cultural tours are available at certain landmarks along the way. Contact Tourist information for details. **See also:** National Parks and A–Z listing for those parks and towns indicated by bold type; and Aboriginal-operated Tours. **Map references:** 416 A5, 422 F9.

known as *The Ghan*, after the Afghan camel drivers it had replaced. As the township grew there was too much confusion between Stuart and Alice Springs, only 3 km apart, so the name Stuart was dropped. **Of interest:** In Todd Mall: Flynn Memorial Church, in memory of founder of Royal Flying Doctor Service; Adelaide House, originally hospital now museum housing pedal-radio equipment used by Flynn and other memorabilia; various outlets for Aboriginal art and artifacts. Aboriginal Art and Culture Centre, Todd St. Royal Flying Doctor Service base, Stuart Tce (tours daily). In Hartley St: Panorama 'Guth', a 360° landscape painting of Central Australia; Minerals House, featuring geological and mineral displays (open Mon.–Fri.). Old Stuart Gaol, Parsons St. Strehlow Research Centre, cnr Larapinta and Memorial Dr., has a collection of artifacts of Arrernte people. Technology, Transport and Communications Museum, Memorial Dr. Araluen Arts Centre, Larapinta Dr., focal point for performing and visual arts. *At the northern end of town:* Anzac Hill, West Tce, for excellent views of town; School of the Air, Head St. *Across the river:* Lasseter's Casino, Barrett Dr.; Olive Pink Flora Reserve, cnr Barrett Dr. and The Causeway, Australia's only arid-zone botanic garden. Market at Todd Mall, 2nd Sun. in months Mar.–Dec., and Thurs. evenings in summer. Jan.: Lasseter's Indoor Challenge (several competitions including backgammon, bridge and scrabble). Apr.: Racing Carnival; Country Music Festival. May: Bangtail Muster. June: Finke Desert Race. July: Camel Cup; Agricultural Show. Aug.: Yuendumu Aboriginal Sports Carnival; Rodeo. Oct.: Henley-on-Todd Regatta; Masters Games (mature-age athletic carnival). Nov.: Corkwood Festival (art, craft, music and dance). **In the area:** Great variety of tours of varying duration covering scenic attractions, Aboriginal culture and specialist interests; experience these by bus or coach, limousine, 4WD safari, Harley-Davidson motorcycle, camel, horse, aircraft, helicopter or hot-air balloon (contact Tourist information for details). *To the north:* Old Telegraph Station (3 km), an historic reserve with original stone buildings and equipment. *To the north-east:* At Gemtree (140 km), fossicking for garnet or zircon. Mud Tank zircon field offering prospecting for zircons, guided fossicking tours and

you can have your gems cut at the caravan park. *To the east:* Pitchi Richi Sanctuary (2 km), an open-air museum displaying William Ricketts clay sculptures; Frontier Camel Farm (7 km) features camel rides, reptile house and museum displays highlighting importance of camels and their Afghan masters to the area; nearby, Mecca Date Gardens, Australia's first commercial date farm; Alice Springs Winery, NT's only commercial winery (11 km); Emily Gap (13 km) and Jessie Gap (18 km) nature parks. *To the south:* Old Timers' Museum (5 km) features exhibits of 1890s era; Transport Heritage Centre (10 km S) has re-creation of a 1930s railway siding and unique display showing ingenuity used to overcome hardships in developing the outback; Ghan Preservation Society rail museum at MacDonnell Siding (10 km) features the *Old Ghan* which runs on 23.5 km of private line between MacDonnell Siding and Ewaninga (trip includes meal at siding stop); Ewaninga Rock Carvings Conservation Reserve (39 km), an Aboriginal cultural site with rock engravings; Chambers Pillar Historical Reserve (149 km) includes 50-m high rock pillar which served as a landmark feature for the Centre's early pioneers and explorers. *To the south-west:* Virginia Camel Farm (93 km) offers camel rides and trail rides; Henbury Meteorites Conservation Reserve (147 km). *To the west:* Alice Springs Desert Park, Larapinta Dr. on western outskirts of town, features desert animals and plants, and their traditional use and management by Aboriginal people; Grave site of Rev. John Flynn (5 km); Simpsons Gap (18 km); Standley Chasm (50 km). Ellery Creek Big Hole (93 km); Serpentine Gorge (104 km); Ochre Pits (119 km), natural quarry once mined by Aborigines; Ormiston Gorge (132 km); Glen Helen Gorge (133 km); the nearby Glen Helen Homestead, used as a base by many to explore the area, is closed for renovations (check at Alice Springs Tourist information for re-opening date); Redbank Gorge (170 km, 4WD access only); Hermannsburg (125 km); Tnorala (Gosse Bluff) meteor crater (210 km, 4WD access only, permit required, note permit for Mereenie Loop also allows access to Tnorala); most of these attractions are in the West MacDonnell National Park, so too is the famous Larapinta Trail, a well-marked walking track that winds through the

West MacDonnell Ranges. A sealed bicycle path links Alice Springs to Simpsons Gap. The Mereenie Loop Road route links Alice Springs, Kings Canyon and Uluru (Ayers Rock) via the West MacDonnell Ranges, and Glen Helen; permit required, inquire at Tourist information for details. **Tourist information:** Gregory Tce; (08) 8952 5800. **Accommodation:** 5 resorts, 2 hotels, 16 motels, 1 B&B, 3 hostels, 6 cara./camp. parks. **See also:** Aboriginal Art; The Red Centre.

Barkly Homestead   Pop. 20

MAP REF. 421 N11

Barkly Homestead is a comfortable fuel or accommodation stop at the junction of Barkly and Tablelands hwys, 187 km E from the junction of Stuart and Barkly hwys. **Accommodation:** 1 motel, 1 cara./camp. park.

Barrow Creek   Pop. 30

MAP REF. 423 J4

Located on the Stuart Hwy, 282 km N of Alice Springs, Barrow Creek was originally a telegraph station and a rest stop for cattle-droving on the North–South stock route. **Of interest:** Old Telegraph Station (1872). Barrow Hotel (1932). **Tourist information:** Barrow Creek Hotel; (08) 8956 9753. **Accommodation:** 1 hotel/motel, 1 cara./camp. park.

Batchelor   Pop. 635

MAP REF. 414 D7, 418 E7

Former town for Rum Jungle mine (now closed), Australia's first uranium mine, Batchelor is now the gateway to Litchfield National Park. **Of interest:** Mini-replica of Karlstein Castle of Bohemia. Scenic flights, parachuting and gliding, at airport. June (or July): International Skydiving and Parachuting Championships. **In the area:** Rum Jungle Lake, 10 km W, ideal for swimming. Litchfield National Park, 40 km W, a wilderness area with rivers, spectacular waterfalls (Wangi, Sandy Creek, Florence and Tolmer), bushwalks, fauna, magnetic termite mounds, pockets of scenic rainforest, secluded waterholes and well-equipped camping grounds. **Tourist information:** Rum Jungle Motor Inn, Rum Jungle Rd; (08) 8976 0123. **Accommodation:** 1 motel, 1 cara./camp. park.

The Top End

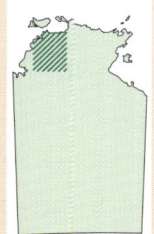

Darwin is a major tourist destination with its warm weather, excellent beaches and abundance of fish, but its real attraction is as a base for exploring the wild and fascinating country at the 'Top End'. Here you see wide billabongs covered with lilies, clouds of magpie geese wheeling above the trees, crocodiles sunning themselves on waterside rocks, plunging waterfalls in the wet season, rows of pillar-like termite mounds, spectacular cliff and rock features, and caves and cliffs bearing the Aboriginal rock art of the past.

A number of parks and conservation reserves protect and manage the features of the region and make them accessible to travellers. The most spectacular of these, in an area fast becoming one of the top natural tourist attractions in Australia, is **Kakadu National Park**, in the vast and wild country along the East and South Alligator rivers.

Kakadu has World Heritage status; it is considered to be of outstanding national and international significance for both its natural features and its cultural heritage. Its western boundary is 140 kilometres from Darwin, and the park encompasses an area of 1 307 300 hectares (almost 20 000 square kilometres). The majority of land within the park is owned by the Aboriginal people, and has been leased to the Australian Nature Conservation Agency (ANCA) under a joint management agreement for all visitors to enjoy.

Kakadu contains a wealth of archaeological and rock-art sites that provide insights into Aboriginal culture. The park's traditional owners are willing to share their knowledge and understanding of their land so that visitors will appreciate the importance of Kakadu and share responsibility for its protection.

Kakadu is unique in that it encompasses an entire river catchment, the South Alligator River system, and within it are found all the major habitat types of the Top End. The park is rich in vegetation, ranging from pockets of rainforest through dwarf shrubland to open forest and swamps. The abundant wildlife includes many animals unique to the area, such as the banded pigeon, the oenpelli python and black wallaroo. Features in the park include Yellow Water (Ngurrungurrudjba), a spectacular wetlands area with prolific birdlife, particularly in the dry season, and Ubirr and Nourlangie Rock, where there is

Ubirr, a major rock-art site in Kakadu National Park

Aboriginal rock art. A spectacular point in the park is the Jim Jim Falls, 215 metres high and with a sheer drop of 152 metres of water pouring (in the wet season) over a rugged escarpment (4WD access only).

North of the Jim Jim Falls is the East Alligator River, a well-known fishing ground where barramundi can be caught and where the river reaches wind through spectacularly beautiful country. Visits to some isolated locations in the park are subject to a permit system to limit visitor numbers, because of the sensitive nature of those areas.

As crocodiles are present in the park, swimming is not recommended and those who fish from the banks of rivers or from boats should take care.

Visit the Bowali Visitor Centre on the Kakadu Hwy just before Jabiru and obtain a copy of the *Visitor Guide,* an excellent publication full of helpful information. Accommodation in the park consists of hotels, caravan parks, a youth hostel, and private and national park camping grounds. Facilities are available for the disabled. Fuel, food and provisions may be obtained at Jabiru township, Border Store, Kakadu Holiday Village and Cooinda. Visitors over sixteen years of age pay a park use fee (valid for fourteen days).

Spectacular **Litchfield National Park** is just a 2-hour drive south from Darwin. It offers stunning sandstone formations, magnetic termite mounds, four major waterfalls and year-round swimming. There are delightful short walks, camping sites within the park and, for the adventurous, a 4WD trail is open during the dry season.

Small parks close to Darwin are Berry Springs, 65 kilometres south, and Howard Springs, 35 kilometres south-east. Berry Springs is noted for its warm water, pleasant and safe swimming, and its birdlife. Adjacent to Berry Springs is the Territory Wildlife Park, where visitors can see animals and birds of the area in a bush setting; shuttle trains assist visitor access. At Howard Springs the pool is surrounded by rainforest; again, the park abounds in birds and other wildlife.

Along the Stuart Highway, 310 kilometres south-east of Darwin, are the town of **Katherine** and the spectacular **Nitmiluk (Katherine Gorge) National Park.** Here the river flows between the brilliantly-coloured walls of the gorge, which reach a height of 60 metres. A boat tour through the gorge is guaranteed to be a highlight of any holiday.

A further 110 kilometres south-east of Katherine is **Elsey National Park**, which includes the Mataranka Pool Reserve, where thermal springs are surrounded by lush tropical forest and the water is permanently at body temperature.

Four-wheel drive wildlife safaris can be arranged in Darwin; an ideal way to see the country and experience something of life in the Top End. There are major roads to all these Top End attractions. However, if you are contemplating an unguided tour of the region, it is vital to recognise that, should you stray into unknown areas, you may experience difficulties, so it is important to plan carefully. **See also:** Outback Motoring.

For further information on Kakadu, contact Park Manager, Kakadu National Park, PO Box 71, Jabiru NT 0886; (08) 8938 1100. A *Visitor Guide* to the park is available from the ANCA: GPO Box 636, Canberra ACT 2601; and GPO Box 1260, Darwin NT 0800; or from Park Headquarters. For further information on the Top End contact the Darwin Region Tourism Association, Beagle House, cnr Mitchell and Knuckey sts (PO Box 4392, Darwin 0801); (08) 8981 4300. **See also:** National Parks and individual text entries in A–Z listing for those parks and towns indicated by bold type. **Map references:** 414-15, 418-19.

NORTHERN TERRITORY

Aboriginal Art

Art is one of the essential elements in Aboriginal culture, often using symbols to communicate ideas that cannot be expressed in any other way. Rich and complex beliefs embodied in the Dreaming are expressed in art with many layers of meaning in a variety of contexts, from the sacred and secret realm of ceremony to the more public domain. Aboriginal art takes many forms from the enduring rock engravings and paintings to the more ephemeral forms including body decoration, and bark and ground paintings.

There is an enormous regional diversity, for example in the desert regions, ground paintings are common, whereas in Arnhem Land bark paintings are made. Rock art is the oldest surviving type of Aboriginal art and is widely distributed throughout the continent. The most extensive and possibly the oldest rock art in the world can be found in the Victoria River District, Arnhem Land plateau in the Top End of the Northern Territory, in the Kimberley in north-western Western Australia and the sandstone country of the Quinkin Reserves around Laura in far north Queensland. Simple engraved lines are found in caves in south-eastern Australia and the Nullarbor Plain, and engravings and petroglyphs ranging from simple designs to cryptic symbols are distributed across the continent from Sydney through southern Australia to the Pilbara in Western Australia.

Aboriginal contemporary artists continue the cultural traditions that are thousands of years old. In recent years there has been a flowering of traditional and contemporary themes applied to ceramics, fabrics, paintings and prints.

The following includes some of the places where rock art can be seen, as well as the major Aboriginal galleries and shops where paintings and artifacts can be viewed or purchased.

'X-ray' art at Nourlangie Rock in Kakadu National Park

At the Top End

Western Arnhem Land, which includes Kakadu National Park, is the major rock-art area in the Top End. Kakadu has representation of all the diverse rock-art styles to be found in western Arnhem Land and the two most accessible sites for visitors are Ubirr and Nourlangie Rock. Some of the sites have been carbon-dated at 60 000 years, and others go back even earlier. The earliest images include hand stencils and grass prints (made by dipping clumps of grass in pigment then throwing them against a rock wall to produce an image). Some of the most spectacular sites in western Arnhem Land can be seen via a number of exclusive safari camps; contact the Darwin Region Tourism Association for details.

Eastern Arnhem Land is one of the traditional strongholds for bark paintings. The Buku Larrnaggay Art Centre at Yirrkala near Nhulunbuy and the Namabara Arts and Crafts Centre, also near Nhulunbuy, have outstanding collections. Traditionally bark painting was transient and the designs were secret or sacred. The designs are complex and identify ancestral beings and their relationship to each other and the landscape against a background of intricate crosshatching. The production of bark paintings for sale involved the use of non-secret designs and techniques that preserved both bark and pigments. Eastern Arnhem Land has numerous art and craft centres in remote communities that can be accessed by special charters; contact the Darwin Region Tourism Association for details.

The Museum and Art Gallery of the Northern Territory at Bullocky Point, Darwin has an extensive collection of Aboriginal art and artifacts. It also hosts the prestigious Aboriginal Art Award in late August or early September each year.

Aboriginal Galleries and Shops

Darwin: Ampiji, Darwin Airport • Framed the Darwin Gallery, cnr Geranium St and Stuart Hwy • Raintree Aboriginal Art Gallery, Shop 1, 18 Knuckey St • Riji Dij, Shop 3, Anthony Plaza • Shades of Ochre Aboriginal Art Gallery, Shop 2, Parap Pl., Parap.
Kakadu National Park: Bowali Visitor Centre, Kakadu Hwy • Warradjan Cultural Centre, Cooinda Rd, Yellow Waters.
Katherine: Creative Native Art Gallery, Shop 2, Lot 4, Katherine Tce • Mimi Aboriginal Arts and Crafts, Shop 9, Southgate Complex, Lindsay St.

In Central Australia

Ground painting was once a widespread practice in Central Australia, and is still practised occasionally today. The paintings are used for storytelling and ceremonial purposes, and the designs, based on significant landscape features and mythological creatures, are painted on prepared earth usually with ochre, and the background filled with dots. Ground painting formed the basis for 'dot painting' which is practised today using western mediums.

Aboriginal Galleries and Shops

Alice Springs: Aboriginal Art and Culture Centre, 86 Todd St • Aboriginal Desert Art Gallery, 87 Todd Mall • Aboriginal Dreamtime Gallery, 71 Todd Mall • Arunta Art Gallery and Book Shop, 70 Todd St • Mbantua Gallery, Gregory Tce • The Original Dreamtime Art Gallery, 63 Todd Mall • Papunya Tula Artists Pty Ltd, 78 Todd St • Warumpi Arts, Shop 7, 105 Gregory Tce.
Tennant Creek: Anyinginyi Arts and Crafts, cnr Irvine and Schmidt sts.
Yulara: Mulgara Gallery, Foyer of Sails in the Desert Hotel, Ayers Rock Resort • Uluru-Kata Tjuta Cultural Centre, within park on road to Uluru.

For further information about Aboriginal art sites and Aboriginal galleries and shops: in the Top End, contact Darwin Region Tourism Association, Beagle House, cnr Mitchell and Knuckey sts; (08) 8981 4300; in Central Australia, contact Central Australian Tourism Industry Association, Gregory Tce, Alice Springs; (08) 8952 5199.

Borroloola   Pop. 594

MAP REF. 419 O13, 421 O3

A small settlement on the banks of the McArthur River and once one of the larger and more colourful frontier towns, Borroloola is now very popular with fishing and 4WD enthusiasts. **Of interest:** Fishing charter available, contact Tourist information. Museum in old police station (1886), Robinson Rd. Self-guide heritage walk. Scenic flights over town and Sir Edward Pellew Islands available. Easter: Fishing Classic. Aug.: Agricultural Show; Rodeo. **In the area:** Cape Crawford, 113 km SW, base for seeing Bukalara Rock Formations (60 km E), mass of chasms winding through ancient sandstone formations (in very remote area, guide recommended); and Lost City, accessible only by helicopter and visitors must be accompanied by a guide. **Tourist information:** McArthur River Caravan Park, Robinson Rd; (08) 8975 8721. **Accommodation:** 1 hotel, 1 motel, 1 cara./camp. park.

Daly Waters   Pop. 298

MAP REF. 420 I3

Situated 4 km N of the junction of Stuart and Carpentaria hwys, Daly Waters became the first international refuelling stop for Qantas in 1935. **Of interest:** Historic hotel (1930), Stuart St. Sept.: Rodeo. **In the area:** Airport museum, 1 km NE, off Stuart Hwy at Old Daly Waters aerodrome. Tree, 1 km N, reputedly marked with the letter S by explorer John McDouall Stuart. **Tourist information:** Daly Waters Hotel, Stuart St; (08) 8975 9927. **Accommodation:** 1 hotel, 1 motel, 1 cara./camp. park.

Dunmarra   Pop. 30

MAP REF. 420 I4

This stopping-place on the Stuart Hwy is 8 km S of the Stuart and Buchanan hwys junction, and 361 km N of Tennant Creek. **Of interest:** Historic photograph collection at Wayside Inn. **Tourist information:** Wayside Inn; (08) 8975 9922. **Accommodation:** 1 motel, 1 cara./camp. park.

Elliott   Pop. 423

MAP REF. 421 J6

Elliott is on the Stuart Hwy, 254 km N of Tennant Creek. **In the area:** At

Finke River Gorge National Park, south of Hermannsburg

Newcastle Waters, an old droving town 24 km N: bronze statue of 'The Drover'; several historic buildings. **Tourist information:** Elliott Hotel, Stuart Hwy; (084) 69 2069. **Accommodation:** 1 hotel/motel, 2 cara./camp. parks.

Hermannsburg   Pop. 422

MAP REF. 416 F5, 422 H9

This isolated Aboriginal community, 132 km W of Alice Springs, occupies the site of a former church mission station. For many years it was the home of the famous painter Albert Namatjira. **Of interest:** Strehlow's House (1897), now tearooms renowned for their apple strudel. Old manse (1888), now a gallery housing watercolour paintings by Aboriginal artists of the Hermannsburg school; guided tours available. Remains of church mission station, including schoolhouse (1896) and tannery (1941). Museum in the Old Colonists House (1885) displays historic items from missionary era. **In the area:** Monument to Albert Namatjira on Larapinta Dr., 8 km E. Cultural tours and camping at Wallace Rockhole Aboriginal community, 50 km SE. Finke River Gorge National Park, 20 km S (4WD access only), features red cabbage palms (*Livistona mariae*), in Palm Valley, and amazing rock formations: 'amphitheatre', 'sphinx' and 'battleship'. Tnorala (Gosse Bluff) meteorite crater, 35 km W (Mereenie Loop Pass required to get there). **Tourist information:** Kata-Anga Tearooms; (08) 8956 7402. **Accommodation:** None.

Jabiru   Pop. 1731

MAP REF. 413 H5, 415 P4, 418 H6

A mining town within the Kakadu National Park, 280 km from Darwin on Arnhem Hwy, Jabiru's services are designed to limit the effect of the town on the surrounding World Heritage National Park. **Of interest:** Gagudju Crocodile Hotel, Flinders St, a 250-m crocodile-shaped building; design was approved by the Gagudju people, to whom the crocodile is a totem. Kakadu Frontier Lodge and Caravan Park, Jabiru Dr., laid out in traditional Aboriginal circular motif. Jabiru Olympic Swimming Pool, Civic Dr., largest in NT; nearby, 9-hole golf course. Fishing and safari tours available. Aug.: Wind Festival. **In the area:** Tourist walk (1.5 km) from town centre through bush to Bowali Centre, an Aboriginal cultural centre. Nourlangie Rock, 25 km SE, has significant Aboriginal rock art featuring prominently around its base. Yellow Water near Cooinda, 45 km SE, a landlocked billabong with prolific flora and fauna, particularly waterbirds; best seen by a cruise in flat-bottomed boat (departs near Gagudju Cooinda Lodge). Nearby, Warradjan Cultural Centre, built in shape of a Warradjan (pig-nosed turtle), offering displays and Aboriginal craft gallery. Further south, Jim Jim Falls and Twin Falls (both 4WD access only), the two largest falls in park after rains (Nov.–Apr.). North of Jabiru is another renowned Aboriginal rock-art site,

The spectacular Katherine Gorge, near Katherine

NORTHERN TERRITORY

Ubirr, in Kakadu National Park, with galleries featuring a range of styles; ranger-guided walks and tours available. Ranger Uranium Mine, 6 km E, daily tours May–Oct. (information from Kakadu Air Services at Jabiru Air Terminal). At airport, scenic flights available over unique Kakadu territory – see virtually inaccessible sandstone formations standing 400 m above vast floodplains, seasonal waterfalls, wetland wilderness, remote beaches and ancient Aboriginal rock art sites. **Tourist information:** 6 Tasman Plaza; (08) 8979 2548. **Accommodation:** 1 hotel, 1 cara./camp. park. **See also:** The Top End.

Katherine   Pop. 7064

MAP REF. 418 G10

Katherine is on the southern side of the Katherine River 320 km SE of Darwin. Katherine River was named after a daughter of one of the sponsors of John McDouall Stuart, who first saw it in 1862. The town's economic mainstays are the Mt Todd goldmine, tourism and the Tindal RAAF airbase, 27 km SE. Sited in some of NT's most promising agricultural and grazing country, it is the centre of scientific experiments designed to improve the beef-cattle industry. **Of interest:** Katherine Museum, Gorge Rd. Railway Station Museum, Railway Tce, has displays covering history of railways in the area; old steam engine adjacent to museum. School of the Air, Giles St; open weekdays a.m. O'Keefe

House, one of oldest houses in town; Riverbank Dr. Self-guide Pioneer Walk around town, heli tours, scenic flights, 4WD safaris, barramundi fishing tours, horse trail-rides available, contact Tourist information. Market, Warburton St, each Sat. (Apr.–Sept.). June: Burunga Sport and Cultural Festival; Katherine Cup; Canoe Marathon. July: Agricultural Show. Sept.: Flying Fox Festival (community festival including theatre and music). **In the area:** Nitmiluk (Katherine) Gorge in Nitmiluk National Park, 29 km NE, has ancient rock walls dotted with caves and Aboriginal paintings thousands of years old decorate both faces of the gorge above the floodline. Numerous reptile and amphibian species are found here, and kangaroos and wallabies in hundreds crowd in to drink in higher reaches of gorge. Self-guide nature walk available, contact Tourist information for brochure. The best way to see the gorge is by flat-bottomed boat; you can hire a canoe and camp in the gorge overnight, or take a guided tour; cruises run daily (book at Tourist information); (no motorboats allowed in gorge May–Oct.). Weather is hot (yet countryside is at its best) Nov.–Mar., but there is little humidity for the remaining months of the year, when it is warm during the day and cool at night. Also in park, Edith Falls, 62 km N; surrounding area ideal for bushwalking, picnicking and camping. Oldest remaining homestead in NT, historic Springvale Homestead (1879) built by Alfred Giles,

8 km W on Shadforth Rd; Aboriginal Corroboree performed here each Mon., Wed. and Sat. (May–Sept.); market at homestead each Sun., Apr.–Sept. Rowlands Dairy, 12 km W on Florina Rd, where 600–1200 cows milked daily; tours weekdays. Cutta Cutta Caves Nature Park, 26 km SE (cave tours daily). Elsey National Park near Mataranka Homestead, 115 km SE, features thermal pool believed to have therapeutic powers. National Trust-classified Old Gallon Licensed Store (1847), 2 km E on Giles St, marks original site of township. Manyallaluk (formerly Eva Valley Station), 100 km NE, combines Aboriginal culture tours with magnificent scenery of wilderness park. **Tourist information:** cnr Lindsay St and Katherine Tce; (08) 8973 8888. **Accommodation:** 2 hotel/motels, 8 motels, 3 hostels, 8 cara./camp. parks. **See also:** Aboriginal Art; The Top End.

Kings Canyon   Pop. 50

MAP REF. 422 F9

Kings Canyon, an enormous natural amphitheatre with 100-m sheer rock faces is the main feature of Watarrka National Park, 325 km SW of Alice Springs. Kings Canyon Resort is situated in the park and provides a convenient base to explore the region. Aboriginal tours and scenic flights available. **In the area:** 6-km circuit walk of Kings Canyon, features boardwalk through prehistoric cycads in lushly vegetated Garden of Eden; unusual rock formations, particularly The Lost City; views across the canyon. Also within park, Carmichael Crag (3 km N) displays majestic colours, particularly at sunset. Mereenie Loop Rd to Glen Helen; permit required. **Tourist information:** Kings Canyon Resort; (08) 8956 7442. **Accommodation:** 1 resort, 1 cara./camp. park.

Larrimah   Pop. 20

MAP REF. 418 I12, 420 I2

Larrimah is located on the Stuart Hwy, 90 km N of Daly Waters. **Of interest:** Historical museum, Mahoney St. Green Park, Stuart Hwy, has crocodiles and buffaloes. **In the area:** ghost town of Birdum, 9 km S. **Tourist information:** Green Park Tourist Complex, Stuart Hwy; (08) 8975 9937. **Accommodation:** 1 hostel, 2 cara./camp. parks.

Aboriginal Lands

In the Northern Territory, Commonwealth and Northern Territory laws do not permit people to enter Aboriginal land unless they have been issued with a permit.

It should be noted that as a general rule, Land Councils have been asked by traditional owners not to issue entry permits for unaccompanied tourist travel. This does not affect visitors travelling on organised tours on to Aboriginal land where tour bookings include the necessary permit.

When making an application for entry to any Aboriginal land, applicants must state the reason for entry, dates and duration of intended stay, names of persons travelling, vehicle details, and itinerary and routes to be used while on these lands. Permits can be issued only after consultation and approval of the traditional owners and relevant Aboriginal communities. Processing permit applications can take two to six weeks hence this is something to bear in mind when planning your trip. It is the right of traditional owners of Aboriginal land to refuse entry permits.

All public roads that cross Aboriginal lands are exempt from the permit requirements; the exemption covers the immediate road corridor only. If travellers are unsure about the status of roads on which they are driving, they should seek advice from the Land Councils before departure. If there is a likelihood of a need to enter Aboriginal land for any reason, including fuel, travellers should seek permits from the relevant Land Councils. Some towns within Aboriginal land are also exempt from the provisions.

A pass is required to travel on the Mereenie Loop Road, which links Glen Helen with Kings Canyon and passes through Aboriginal land. Passes may be obtained from the CATIA office in Alice Springs, or from Hermannsburg or Kings Canyon. Travellers also receive an information brochure.

A number of tourist ventures operate on Aboriginal land; they include tourist camps and outlets for artworks and artifacts. For details contact Northern Territory Tourist Commission, 67 Stuart Hwy, Alice Springs; (08) 8951 8555.

The relevant land councils to whom applications for permits and any inquiries must be directed in writing, are:

Alice Springs and Tennant Creek regions:
Central Land Council Permits
33 Stuart Hwy, PO Box 3321
Alice Springs NT 0871
(08) 8951 6320

Darwin, Nhulunbuy and Katherine regions:
Northern Land Council
9 Rowling St, PO Box 42921
Casuarina NT 0811
(08) 8920 5100

Melville and Bathurst islands:
Tiwi Land Council
PO Box 38545
Winnellie NT 0821
(08) 8981 4898

Tnorala (Gosse Bluff), a spectacular crater on Aboriginal land near Glen Helen

Historic Elsey Cemetery, near Mataranka

NORTHERN TERRITORY

Mataranka — Pop. 180

MAP REF. 418 I11

This small town is 110 km SE of Katherine. **Of interest:** On Stuart Hwy: Stockyard Gallery, for NT artists' works including leather sculpture; Territory Manor, daily feeding of barramundi. May: Back to the Never Never Festival; Never Never Art Show at Stockyard Gallery. Aug.: Rodeo. **In the area:** Elsey National Park, 5 km E, featuring thermal pool, popular for swimming, surrounded by rainforest with walking tracks, camping area, canoe hire and departure point for walking trail to Mataranka Falls at Twelve Mile Yards. Mataranka Homestead Tourist Resort, near thermal pool, offers camping, horse riding, scenic flights, river cruises and barramundi fishing; also replica of Elsey Homestead. Elsey Cemetery, 20 km S, graves of outback pioneers immortalised by Mrs Aeneas Gunn (who lived at Elsey Station Homestead 1902–3) in *We of the Never Never;* nearby, stone cairn marking site of original Elsey Station Homestead. **Tourist information:** Stockyard Gallery, Stuart Hwy; (08) 8975 4530. **Accommodation:** 1 hotel, 3 motels, 1 hostel, 5 cara./camp. parks. **See also:** The Top End.

Nhulunbuy — Pop. 3 934

MAP REF. 419 P5

Nhulunbuy is on the north-eastern tip of Arnhem Land, on the Gove Peninsula. The whole of the peninsula is held as freehold by the traditional owners. Originally built as a service town for the bauxite-mining industry, Nhulunbuy is now also the administrative centre for the Arnhem Land region. Access is by a year-round daily air service from Darwin or Cairns. During the northern dry season there is 4WD access, requiring a permit from Northern Land Council (see Aboriginal Lands). **In the area:** Bark paintings and intricately-woven baskets at Buku Larrnaggay Art Centre and Museum at Yirrkala, a former mission 19 km SE, and at Namabara Arts and Crafts, 10 km N (didgeridoo and basket-weaving demonstrations available by arrangement). Stunning beaches with tropical-blue water, accessible with readily-obtainable recreational permit (inquire at Tourist information for details). Guided 4WD tours, and boat charters for game and barramundi fishing, reef and wreck diving, and crocodile spotting; contact Tourist information. **Tourist information:** Walkabout Arnhem Land Resort Hotel, Westal St; (08) 8987 1777. **Accommodation:** 1 hotel/motel, 1 motel.

Noonamah — Pop. 8

MAP REF. 414 E4, 418 E6

Noonamah is on the Stuart Hwy, 38 km S of Darwin. **In the area:** Over 7000 crocodiles at Crocodile Farm, just south of town; feeding displays and tours available. Howard Springs Nature Park, 22 km NW, for safe swimming, bird watching and picnicking. On Cox Peninsula Rd: Berry Springs Nature Park (14 km SW), safe swimming in spring-fed pool surrounded by monsoon forest; alongside, Territory Wildlife Park, exhibiting native fauna in 400-ha bushland setting viewed via walking trails or motorised, open train. Tumbling Waters Deer Park, 23 km SW. Majestic Orchids, orchid-growing area, 25 km SW. Manton Dam, 20 km S, ideal for water sports and picnicking on foreshore. **Tourist information:** Hotel; (08) 8988 1054. **Accommodation:** None.

Pine Creek — Pop. 437

MAP REF. 413 A13, 414 I13, 418 F8

On the Stuart Hwy, 90 km NW of Katherine, Pine Creek experienced a brief gold rush in the 1870s; today the town is experiencing a resurgence following the reopening of goldmining operations. **Of interest:** Numerous historic buildings. Heritage trail through town, brochure available at Tourist information. Miners Park, Main Tce, displays historic mining machinery. Railway Station museum, off Main Tce (check opening times). Museum and Library, Railway Tce. Mine Lookout, off Moule St. Restored steam ore crusher at Gun Alley Gold Mining, Gun Alley; gold-panning tours available. **In the area:** Gold fossicking (licence required). Copperfield recreation Dam, 6 km SW, foreshore ideal for picnics. Umbrawarra Gorge, 22 km SW, good for swimming, rock climbing and walking. Edith Falls, 50 km SW in north-western end of Nitmiluk National Park, for swimming and bushwalking in surrounding area. Bonrook Lodge and Station, 6 km SE , a sanctuary for wild horses. The Rock Hole, 65 km NE via Kakadu Hwy, a secluded waterhole (4WD access only). Gunlom (Waterfall Creek), 110 km NE via Kakadu Hwy, beautiful falls and permanent waterhole in Kakadu National Park. Butterfly Gorge Nature Park (4WD access only), 108 km NW named for large numbers of butterflies which settle in its rock crevices. **Tourist information:** Diggers Rest Motel, 32 Main Tce; (08) 8976 1442. **Accommodation:** 1 hotel/motel, 2 cara./camp. parks.

Aboriginal-operated Tours

For over 60 000 years the Aboriginal people have developed a unique understanding of the relationship between the physical and spiritual world. Today a number of Aborigines work professionally to share their knowledge with visitors. There is a wide range of Aboriginal-operated tours available throughout the Northern Territory, each offering the Aboriginal perspective of their particular area. For further information on Aboriginal-operated tours in the Northern Territory contact the Northern Territory Holiday Information HELPLINE; 1800 62 1336.

Location	Tour name	Features
AT THE TOP END		
KAKADU NATIONAL PARK	Guluyambi Aboriginal Cultural Cruise	• 1½ hour cruise along East Alligator River • spectacular contrasting scenery • landscape interpreted by Aboriginal guide
	Magela Cultural and Heritage Tours	• journeys through the more remote and restricted areas of the park as guests of Bunidji people • small groups only
EASTERN ARNHEM LAND	Davidson's Safaris	• award-winning wilderness experience • operates all seasons • includes airboat or cruise boat over wetlands to extensive rock-art galleries
	Dreamtime Safari	• exclusive, luxury camp • Talabon people demonstrate traditional dance, arts and crafts, and storytelling
	The Arnhemlander Aboriginal Cultural Tour	• visit rock-art sites, Mikinj Valley • learn bush skills, food gathering and preparation • visit Injalak Arts and Crafts centre at Oenpelli • most tours accompanied by an Aboriginal guide
	Umorrduk Safaris	• exclusive safari camp • rock-art galleries • interpretation of land, history and mythology of Aboriginal culture
BATHURST AND MELVILLE ISLANDS (100 km offshore of Darwin)	Tiwi Tours	• one day cultural tour with Tiwi guides • also 2–3 day tours exploring islands' features.
KATHERINE Springvale Station Homestead (8 km W)	Aboriginal Corroboree	• traditional Aboriginal dance performance • historic homestead
Manyallaluk Community (100 km NE)	Manyallaluk Aboriginal Cultural Tours	• various tours from one-day cultural experience to 2-day camp-outs and 5-day tours from Darwin • award-winning enterprise • caravan-park and cabin facilities
Nitmiluk National Park (30 km N)	Travel North	• 2½ hour Aboriginal-guided bush tour • learn bush skills, food gathering and bush medicine
IN CENTRAL AUSTRALIA		
	Spencer Tours	• range of short and extended tours • specialises in personally-designed private tours
	Desert Tracks	• tours vary from 1 to 8 days • specialise in small groups visiting Aboriginal land and learning from local people
	Rod Steinert Tours	• visit to bush campsite • learn boomerang and spear-throwing, bush tucker, bush survival skills • purchase art and craft
	Vast Visual Arts and Specialist Tours	• personally-designed art, culture and nature tours
ALICE SPRINGS Strehlow Research Centre	Strehlow Research Centre	• display revolves around Arrernte people and their association with Strehlow and the European community
Pitchi Richi Sanctuary (3 km SW)	Pitchi Richi Cultural Experience	• Ricketts' collection of Aboriginal clay sculptures • billy tea and damper, boomerang-throwing, whip-cracking and storytelling
Hermannsburg (123 km SW)	Hermannsburg Tour	• first Aboriginal mission in NT
Wallace Rockhole (west)	Rockhole Tour	• historical artworks • camping facilities
Oak Valley (100 km S)	Oak Valley Tours	• day tour • ancient rock art • learn culture and lifestyle
Uluru-Kata Tjuta National Park	Anangu Tours	• local Aboriginal (Anangu) guides offer insights into their history, knowledge and lifestyle

National Parks

Ghost gum in West MacDonnell National Park

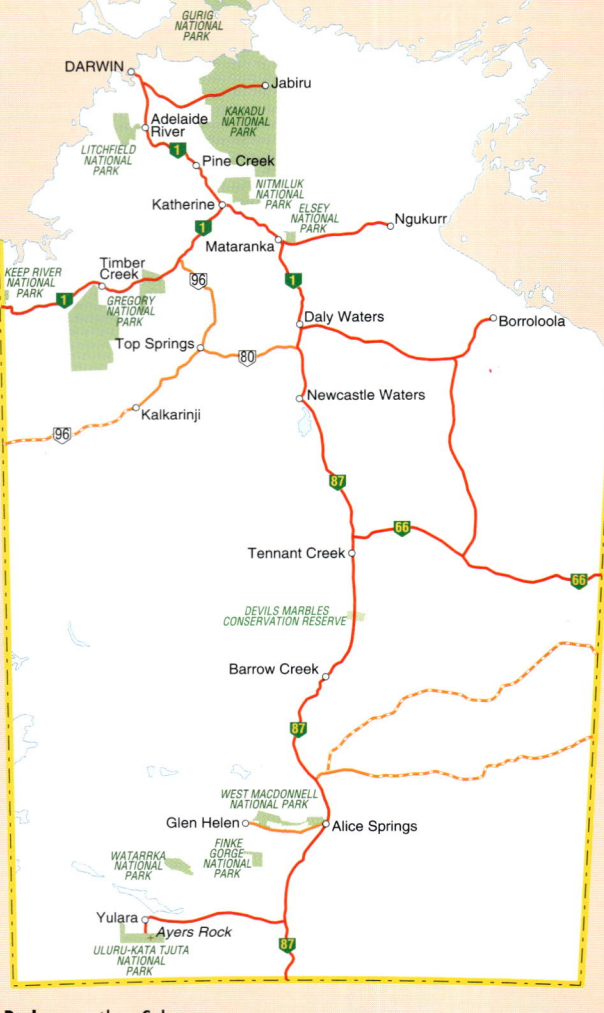

There are more than 90 parks, reserves and protected areas in the Northern Territory. The major ones are grouped in two sections: one group is at the Top End, the second in Central Australia from Tennant Creek through to Yulara.

At the Top End

At the Top End of the Territory are several impressive national parks, including the splendid **Kakadu National Park**, leased by the traditional Aboriginal owners to the Australian Nature Conservation Agency. Here the visitor can see Aboriginal rock-art and the magnificent scenery of Arnhem Land, go bushwalking or take a boat cruise through wetlands. On the way to this park, do not miss the Territory Wildlife Park, where you can see native fauna in a bush setting.

The popular **Litchfield National Park** is only 100 kilometres south of Darwin. Waterfalls cascade from the sandstone plateau of Tabletop Range and create beautiful swimming holes for year-round swimming. Monsoonal rainforests contrast with treeless, black-soil plains where magnetic termite mounds dot the landscape. Tjaynera Falls (Sandy Creek) and the Lost City with its fascinating sandstone formation, are on 4WD tracks. Swimming, photography, wildlife observation and bushwalking are all popular activities.

Gurig National Park, on the Cobourg Peninsula, is Aboriginal land managed by agreement with the Parks and Wildlife Commission of the Northern Territory, hence a permit is necessary. The park can be reached by 4WD but road access is only available between May and October. This isolated park is rich in Aboriginal culture as well as containing lonely ruins of early European attempts at settlement. A wilderness lodge, Seven Spirit Bay (not in the park), overlooks Coral Bay and can only be reached from Darwin by air or sea. The complex offers a true wilderness experience. Fishing, sailing, a trip to historic ruins at Victoria Settlement, and exploration of the area's natural environment are available.

Located 29 kilometres north-east of Katherine is **Nitmiluk (Katherine Gorge) National Park**. This fascinating river canyon, with its abundant wildlife and Aboriginal rock paintings, can be seen from a walking track, canoe or tour boat. When the river flows peacefully in the dry season (May–October), anglers make good catches of barramundi and other fish in the gorge's deep pools. **Elsey National Park**, 100 kilometres southeast of Katherine, and located alongside the Roper River, includes Mataranka Hot Springs, a refreshing swimming area believed to have therapeutic powers.

On the Victoria Highway to the west of Katherine lie **Gregory National Park**, one of the largest parks in the Territory, and **Keep River National Park**. Both feature tropical and semiarid plant life, and spectacular range and gorge scenery. Significant Aboriginal sites and evidence of early European settlement and pastoral history are also features. Boat tours can be arranged at Victoria River Wayside Inn and Timber Creek, both on the Victoria River.

In Central Australia

South of Tennant Creek is **Devils Marbles Conservation Reserve**. The spherical boulders in the park were formed by the weathering of granite outcrops on a wide quartz plain. According to Aboriginal legend, they are eggs laid by the

Rainbow Serpent. Devils Marbles are particularly attractive at sunset, when they glow a deep red. There are no marked walking tracks in the reserve, but the flatness of the plain and the sparse vegetation a low easy walking.

Best-known of all the parks in the Centre is World Heritage-listed **Uluru-Kata Tjuta National Park**, which contains the monolith Uluru (Ayers Rock) and Kata Tjuta (The Olgas) rising abruptly from the surrounding plains. The area is of vital cultural and religious significance to the Anangu (the traditional owners), whose ancestors have lived in the area for at least 30 000 years.

An easy way to explore Uluru's attractions is either by undertaking the Circuit Walk or joining a guided coach tour around the 9-kilometre rock base to see significant traditional sites, such as the Mutitjulu Cave containing elaborate Aboriginal paintings, and Kantju Gorge. The climb to the 348-metre summit is strictly for those with a good head for heights. It should not be attempted by anyone who is unfit or unwell, or in hot weather; casualties are common. The traditional owners, the Anangu community, encourage visitors to seek alternatives to the climb.

Further west, the great domes of Kata Tjuta are separated by deep clefts, many of which hold sweet water and support abundant wildlife. The name Kata Tjuta means 'many heads'. There are several walks such as Valley of the Winds, and Olga

Gorge which take from one to four hours to complete. Keep to the marked tracks.

In the **West MacDonnell National Park** lie the MacDonnell Ranges, the land of the Arrernte Aboriginal people and a paradise for photographers and artists. Cutting through the ranges are spectacular gorges offering some of the finest scenery in Australia: crimson and ochre rock walls bordering deep blue pools, and slopes covered with spring wildflowers. In this park are a number of highlights. Close to Alice Springs is Simpsons Gap, only 18 kilometres west and best seen on foot. There are several walking tracks as well as ranger-guided tours, through rocky gaps and along steep-sided ridges overlooking huge gums and timbered creek flats. A bicycle path linking Alice Springs to Simpsons Gap provides a different way to see this part of the MacDonnell Ranges. Other well-known scenic spots include Ormiston Gorge and Pound, where fish bury themselves in the mud as a string of waterholes shrink to puddles, then wait for the rains to fill them again. The deepest part of Ormiston Creek is a magnificent permanent pool the Arrernte believe to be linked to the Emu Dreaming story (Kwartetweme). At the far end of the gorge, the walls are curtained by a variety of ferns and plants, including the lovely Sturt's desert rose and the relic *Macrozamia*.

Finke Gorge National Park, a scenic wilderness straddling the Finke River, includes the picturesque

Palm Valley. This valley is a refuge for cycad palms and the rare red cabbage palm *Livistona mariae*, estimated to be about 5000 years old. The park is particularly rugged and visitors who do not join tours are advised to use a 4WD.

Between Finke and Uluru lies **Watarrka National Park**, its main attraction being the beautiful Kings Canyon. Waterholes, rock formations and abundant wildlife provide excellent photographic and bushwalking opportunities.

Note: In national parks, reserves and other areas, it is essential to heed local advice on the dangers of swimming. Both salt water and freshwater crocodiles are found throughout waterways in the Top End. The saltwater crocodile is particularly dangerous and can be found in both salt water (including the sea) and fresh water. Heed local warning advice and warning signs.

For more information about the Territory's parks and reserves, contact the Parks and Wildlife Commission of the Northern Territory, PO Box 496, Palmerston NT 0830, (08) 8999 5511. For Kakadu and Uluru, contact the Australian Nature Conservation Agency (ANCA), GPO Box 636, Canberra ACT 2601, (06) 250 0200, or PO Box 1260, Darwin NT 0801, (08) 8981 5299. **See also:** The Top End. **Note** detailed map of Kakadu National Park on page 413.

Jim Jim Falls, accessible only by 4WD, in Kakadu National Park

NORTHERN TERRITORY

Wildlife-Watching

A visit to the Territory without wildlife-spotting would be incomplete. Mary River crocodiles attract attention from wildlife lovers, as do the bird-friendly billabongs of Kakadu. Further south, Central Australia is home to dingoes, kangaroos, thorny devils and a host of other reptiles.

In Darwin

Aquascene, at **Doctors Gully**, attracts hundreds of fish to its shallow waters for a free meal each high tide. Milkfish, catfish, batfish and many other species compete for offerings. There is no need to bring snorkel and mask as these wild fish can be hand-fed as you wade amongst them.

At the Top End

It is tempting to head straight for Kakadu, but those who stop along the way will have some wonderful wildlife-watching experiences. **Fogg Dam** was constructed east of Darwin in the 1950s for an ill-fated rice-growing scheme, and was an unexpected gift to the Territory's bird population. It is now a peaceful conservation reserve with a bird-viewing platform. You are likely to encounter comb-crested jacanas as they step nimbly over waterlilies, as well as pairs of green pygmy-geese amongst the reeds. Harmless water pythons and wallabies are often seen in the evenings.

Further east is **Mary River**, a fascinating mix of salt and freshwater habitats. There is definitely no shortage of saltwater crocodiles here, and a river cruise provides the best way to see them. A close-up view of these oversized reptiles explains why there are no 'swim-with-the-croc' tours on offer. Boat tours operate regularly through both the freshwater and saltwater sections.

For bird-watchers, the Mary River is also home to a large population of sea eagles and egrets. Pelicans, jabirus, jacanas, spoonbills and kingfishers are often seen as well.

Kakadu National Park is world-renowned for its ecological and cultural significance. It is either the temporary or permanent home to one-third of Australian bird species so it makes good sense to begin with a bird checklist. This can be obtained from the Bowali Visitor Centre.

Two of the best bird-watching sites within the park are Mamukala and Yellow Water. Towards the end of the dry season between August and October, these and other billabongs become welcome oases for many of Kakadu's birds. Large flocks of magpie geese, plumed whistling-ducks and many other waterbirds crowd in as the surrounding country dries out. The opportunity to see this wonderful parade of birds should not be missed. Bring your binoculars to the bird hide at Mamukala, or enjoy the spectacle from the raised croc-proof boardwalk at Yellow Water. Regular boat cruises through Yellow Water provide an opportunity to spot saltwater crocodiles as well as birds.

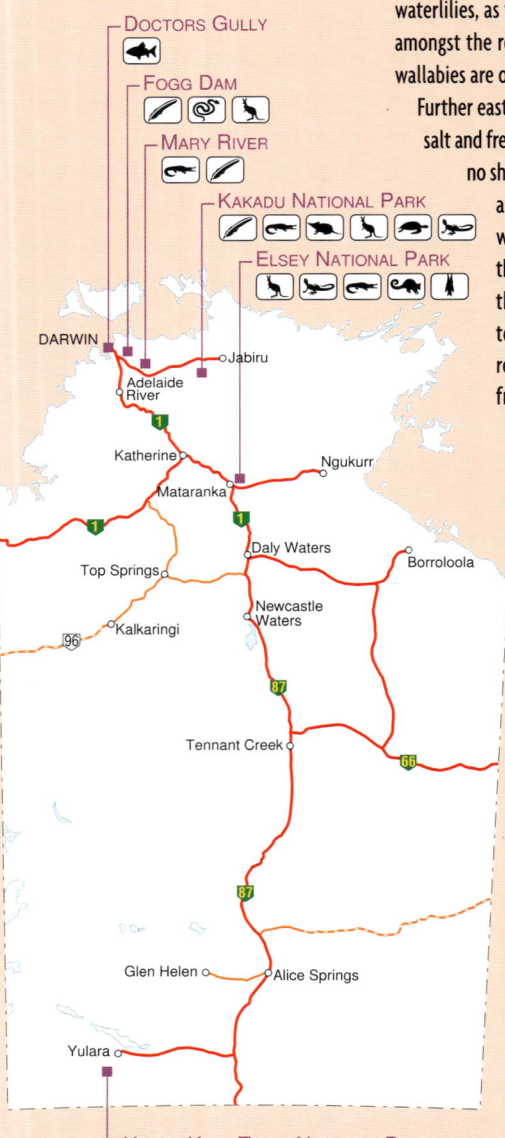

The magpie goose, a resident of the Top End wetlands

The thorny devil, one of the more unusual creatures found in Central Australia

If you are camping, you may see brown bandicoots at night, and wallabies and wallaroos in the park's open grassy areas. Northern short-necked turtles can sometimes be seen resting on logs at the water's edge, and many kinds of monitor lizards can be spotted around billabongs and on road verges.

South of Kakadu is **Elsey National Park**, famous for its rejuvenating thermal pool. When the sun is high overhead the pool is the best place to be – save your energy for wildlife-spotting in the early morning and late afternoon. At these cooler times of the day the park's animals are at their most active. Wallabies and goannas can be seen, as well as water monitors and occasional freshwater crocodiles along the river – treat the latter with the same respect as their notorious saltwater cousins. Evening is a good time to glimpse a possum or flying fox in the trees.

In Central Australia

Much of Central Australia's wildlife is right at your feet. Larger animals are less common, though insects and lizards flourish in the harsh desert environment. Their tiny tracks criss-cross the sand and tell a fascinating tale of the previous night's adventures and activities.

In **Uluru-Kata Tjuta National Park** birds are always a welcome sight against the deep-blue skies of Uluru. Cockatoos, ringneck parrots and budgerigars share the air, keeping an eye out for birds of prey such as kestrels and whistling kites. Honeyeaters are at home in the park, and flocks of tiny zebra finches make the most of precious water puddles.

The Territory Wildlife Park south of Darwin brings together the Territory's wildlife at one location. Barrumundi and turtles swim overhead at the walk-through aquarium tunnel, and eleven aviaries cover different habitats. For a close-up view of Central Australian wildlife the Alice Springs Desert Park should not be missed. The park showcases a range of both common and rare Central Australian animals. In its desert nocturnal house tiny mammals, bats, birds and insects go about their business oblivious of curious visitors. For more information on wildlife-watching in national parks and reserves, contact the Parks and Wildlife Commission of the Northern Territory, PO Box 496, Palmerston NT 0830; (08) 8999 5511. For more information on bird-watching contact the Bird Observers Club of Australia, 183 Springvale Rd, Nunawading, Victoria 3131; (03) 9877 5342. **See also:** National Parks, The Top End.

Remains of gold-mining town in Arltunga Historical Reserve, near Ross River

NORTHERN TERRITORY

Renner Springs
Pop. 19

MAP REF. 421 J8

A roadside stop on the Stuart Hwy, Renner Springs is 161 km N of Tennant Creek. The water source for the springs is unknown. Picnic/barbecue facilities available. **Accommodation:** 1 hotel/ motel, 1 cara./camp. park.

Ross River
Pop. 30

MAP REF. 417 O2, 423 K8

At Ross River is Ross River Homestead, a ranch-style outback resort with cabins and backpacker accommodation, 85 km E of Alice Springs. The homestead is renowned for its outback activities ranging from billy tea and damper to overnight safaris. **In the area:** Scenic walking tracks at Trephina Gorge Nature Park, 17 km NW. N'Dhala Gorge Nature Park (4WD access only), 11 km SW, features Aboriginal rock engravings and ancient fossil deposits. Corroboree Rock Reserve, 33 km SW, has signposted walk explaining significance of rock to Eastern Arrernte people. Arltunga Historical Reserve (4WD access only), 25 km E, old gold-mining town with stone ruins, scattered workings and gravestones; police station and gaol have been restored and Visitor Centre displays local history. Nearby, gold panning and metal detecting opportunities in declared fossicking area; fossicking permits available at Arltunga hotel. Further east, Ruby Gap Gorge (4WD access only) on the intermittent Hale River. **Tourist information:** Ross River Homestead, Ross Hwy; (08) 8956 9711. **Accommodation:** 1 hostel, 1 cara./camp park.

Tennant Creek
Pop. 3480

MAP REF. 421 K10

According to legend, the town of Tennant Creek was founded when a beer wagon carrying building supplies broke down at the site. The town is 507 km N of Alice Springs, on the Stuart Hwy. Gold and copper deposits account for its development today. The town is a thriving centre for the Barkly Tablelands. **Of interest:** Civic Centre, Peko Rd, houses art, gem and mineral collection. National Trust Museum in historic Tuxworth Fullwood House, Schmidt St, features photographic collection and displays of early mine buildings and equipment (open May– Sept., check times). Travellers Rest Area in Purkiss Reserve, Ambrose St, has picnic area and swimming pool nearby. Tours of goldmining areas including night-time tours of old mines; scenic drives; heritage walk; information available from Tourist information. May: Cup Day (horseracing); Go-Kart Grand Prix. July: Agricultural Show. Sept.: Desert Harmony Festival with local artists, craftspeople, musicians and performers. **In the area:** Gold fossicking, contact Tourist information. Gold Stamp Battery and Museum, Peko Rd, 1 km E, features one of the two 10-stamp batteries still operational in Australia (tours daily). Just past the Battery, Ben Allen lookout offers views of town and surrounding area. Juno Horse Centre, 10 km E, for horseriding. Nobles Nob, 16 km E, once richest open-cut goldmine of its size in world. Mary Ann Dam, 5 km NE, for water sports. Three Ways Roadhouse and Hotel, junction of Stuart and Barkly hwys, 25 km N; nearby, John Flynn Memorial. Attack Creek Historical Reserve, 73 km N, site of encounter between John McDouall Stuart and local Aborigines. The Pebbles, 16 km NW, miniatures of Devil's Marbles (huge 'balancing rocks' found 103 km S). **Tourist information:** Battery Hill Regional Centre, Peko Rd; (08) 8962 3388. **Accommodation:** 1 hotel/motel, 3 motels, 2 hostels, 2 cara./ camp. parks.

Ti Tree
Pop. 50

MAP REF. 422 I5

A rest stop on the Stuart Hwy, Ti Tree is 194 km N of Alice Springs. **Of interest:** Ti Tree Park, with picnic area and playground. **In the area:** Central Mt Stuart Historical Reserve, 8 km N, includes monument at base of mountain marking the spot as the centre of Australia. **Tourist information:** Roadhouse, Stuart Hwy; (08) 8956 9741. **Accommodation:** 1 motel, 1 cara./camp. park.

Timber Creek
Pop. 100

MAP REF. 418 D13, 420 D2

Timber Creek is located 290 km SW of Katherine on the Victoria Hwy. **Of interest:** National Trust Museum, off hwy, has displays of historical artifacts (open Apr.–Aug.). Boat tours, cruises, fishing tours and scenic flights available; inquire at Tourist information for details. Conservation Commission Headquarters, Victoria Hwy, provides road and park information for visitors travelling into Gregory or Keep River national parks. May: Rodeo. Sept.: Timber Creek Races (horseracing). **In the area:** Gregory National Park, 15 km W, features Limestone Gorge, Aboriginal and European heritage sites and boab trees. Keep River National Park, 175 km W, features rugged scenery,

Fishing for barramundi on the lower Daly River, south of Darwin

Fishing in the Territory

Whether you are fishing in salt or freshwater, the Territory provides some of the best fishing in Australia. The coast has sheltered bays, estuaries, mangrove-lined creeks, offshore reefs and islands, and much of the fishing is easily reached from population centres. The inland has huge areas of wetlands, with rivers, billabongs and flood plains to be explored. In these outback environments the barramundi is king. Many visitors go on an inland camping and fishing tour with an experienced guide so that they can enjoy the camping life and get to the fishing spots with someone who knows where to go. Note that it is an unwritten rule of the north that you retain fish only for the table, and catch and release the others.

Some of the best blue-water fishing in Australia is available straight out of Darwin. You can fish from the shore or wharves of the city; explore the coastal estuaries, mangroves and sandbars; venture along the coast or to the offshore reefs by boat; or organise a charter to go game fishing. The fishing on the east coast of Arnhem Land, based on the Gove Peninsula and Groote Eylandt, is legendary, but as access is difficult these great tropical waters remain scarcely touched. Nhulunbuy on the Gove Peninsula is the starting point. The popular fish are giant trevally, queenfish (leatherskin), mackerel, cobia and tuna. Black jewfish and fingermark (golden snapper) are taken from the harbour wharves, and sweetlip, coral trout and stripey are around the reefs.

Essentially, freshwater fishing in the Territory is best just after the wet, and at the end of the dry when the receding waters and increasing water temperatures mobilise the fish into an aggressive feeding pattern. The freshwater fishing around Darwin is both easily reached and varied, with dams and lakes adding to the possibilities. In Darwin itself there are many operators of guided fishing tours. To the east of Darwin lies Kakadu National Park which contains several major angling rivers. Fishing is prohibited in parts of the park, however the areas where anglers are welcome fish well. The Mary and Adelaide rivers' wetlands, the McArthur River at Borroloola and the Victoria River west of Katherine are popular places for catching barramundi. Fishing in inland waters away from major population centres is not for the inexperienced. Much of the Territory is rugged and during the wet season the country can only be traversed on the few sealed highways and all-weather gravel roads.

Anglers should watch out for crocodiles in the tidal estuary waters and inland waters, and observe basic safety measures. Cleaning fish close to the waterline or wading in the water for long periods are not advised.

For further information on fishing in the Territory, contact the Darwin Region Tourism Association, Beagle House, cnr Mitchell and Knuckey sts, Darwin; (08) 8981 4300.

Aboriginal rock art and wildlife; most trails are accessible by 4WD only. For both parks, check with Conservation Commission for details regarding access. Jasper Gorge, 48 km SW, a scenic gorge with permanent waterhole. **Tourist information:** Timber Creek Hotel, Victoria Hwy; (08) 8975 0722. **Accommodation:** 2 hotels/motels, 2 cara./camp. parks. **See also:** National Parks

Victoria River   Pop. 6

MAP REF. 418 E12, 420 E2

Victoria River is a rest stop located where the Victoria Hwy crosses the mighty Victoria River. Scenic bushwalks in area, particularly Joe's Creek Walk, 10 km W. **Tourist information:** Wayside Inn, Victoria Hwy; (08) 8975 0744. **Accommodation:** 1 hotel/motel, 1 cara./camp. park.

Wauchope   Pop. 7

MAP REF. 421 K13, 423 K2

Wauchope is on the Stuart Hwy, 113 km S of Tennant Creek. The historic hotel once served the old Wolfram Mines. **In the area:** Devil's Marbles, 8 km N, a collection of large, precariously-balanced granite boulders. **Tourist information:** Wauchope Hotel, Stuart Hwy; (08) 8964 1963. **Accommodation:** 1 hotel/motel, 1 cara./camp. park.

Devil's Marbles, north of Wauchope

Yulara   Pop. 2169

MAP REF. 416 E10, 422 E11

Situated on the outskirts of Uluru-Kata Tjuta National Park, this town is the location for the world-class Ayers Rock Resort, offering full visitor facilities and comfortable air-conditioned accommodation in all price brackets (advance bookings are essential). **Of interest:** Visitors Centre has displays and information on national park. Tours available include Aboriginal Desert Culture Tour; Uluru Experience Night Sky Show, which offers night-sky viewing and narration of Aboriginal and European legends relating to the night sky; book tours at Tourist information or reception in accommodation areas. **In the area:** On approach road to Uluru, Uluru-Kata Tjuta Cultural Centre, designed in shape of two snakes, has displays and sales of Aboriginal culture and arts. Uluru (Ayers Rock), 20 km SE, Australia's famous sandstone monolith, has Aboriginal rock-art sites; spectacular at sunrise and sunset; guided tours available around base of Uluru highlighting its Aboriginal significance. Kata Tjuta (The Olgas), 50 km W, the Centre's other famous landmark; highlights are Valley of Winds walk, views, and flora and fauna. **Tourist information:** Visitors Centre; (08) 8956 2240. **Accommodation:** 3 hotels, hostel units, apartments, cara./camp. ground. **See also:** The Red Centre.

The Victoria River flows through the spectacular Gregory National Park

Location
Map

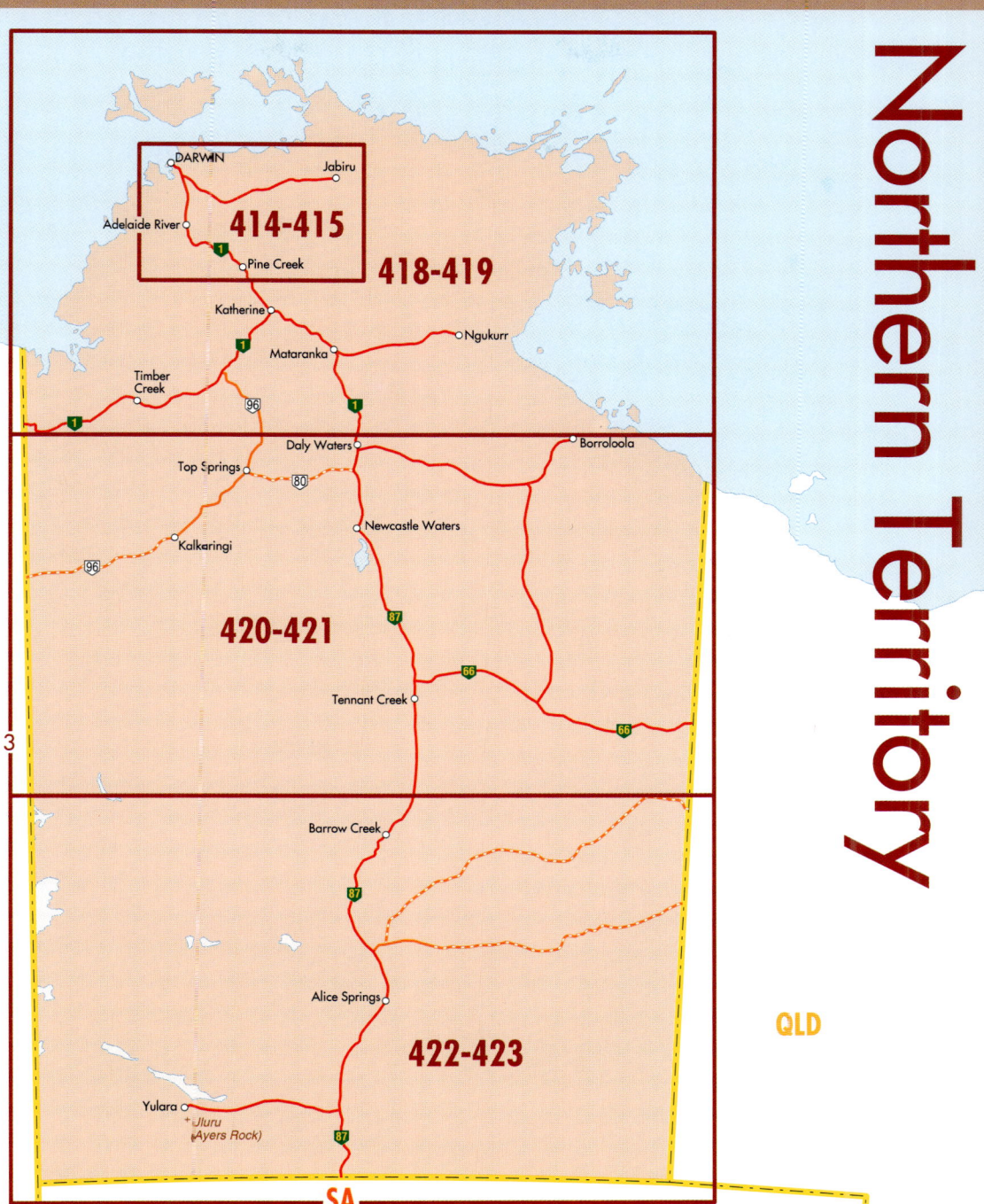

414-415

418-419

420-421

422-423

DARWIN
Jabiru

Adelaide River

Pine Creek

Katherine

Mataranka
Ngukurr

Timber
Creek

Top Springs
Daly Waters
Borroloola

Newcastle Waters

Kalkaringi

Tennant Creek

Barrow Creek

Alice Springs

Yulara
+ Uluru
(Ayers Rock)

Northern Territory

Other Map Coverage

Central Darwin 410
Darwin & Northern
  Suburbs 411
North Eastern
  Suburbs, Darwin 412
Kakadu National Park 413
The Red Centre 416

WA

QLD

SA

410 Central Darwin

0 — 250 — 500 m

Accommodation Only a sample range is listed;
inclusion is not necessarily a recommendation.

0 0.25 0.5 0.75 1 km

DARWIN AIRPORT

Ludmilla

BAGOT ABORIGINAL RESERVE

RAAF Base

The Narrows

Dwyer Park

Winnellie

East Point

East Point Military Museum

East Point Reserve

Dudley Point

Lake Alexander

Rocks

Mangroves

Ludmilla Creek

Fannie Bay Racecourse

Richardson Park

Waratah Sports Club

Kurringal

Ross Smith Memorial

Fannie Bay Gaol Museum

Trailer Boat Club
Boat Ramp
Sailing Club

Vesteys Beach

Skiing and Yachting Area

Boat Ramp

Water Ski Club
Boat Ramp

Parap

Olympic Pool
Waterslide
Primary School

FANNIE BAY

Fannie Bay

Darwin Bowling Club

Museum and Art Gallery of the Northern Territory

Darwin High School

Bullocky Point

Cliffs

The Gardens

Sacred Heart College

St Johns College

Botanic Gardens

Mindil Beach Sunset Markets (May to October)

Mindil Beach

Mindil Beach Reserve

Gardens Oval NTFL

MGM Grand Darwin

Tennis Courts

Old Cemetery

Amphitheatre

Gardens Park

Golf Course

Myilly Point
Rocks

Emery Point
Cliffs

Cullen Bay Marina

Larrakeyah

MILITARY AREA

Aquascene

Doctors Gully

Lyons Cottage Museum

Old Admiralty House

Lameroo Beach

Parliament House

Government House

Overland Telegraph Memorial

Fort Hill

DARWIN

Daly Bridge

Chinese Temple

Chinese Cemetery
Boat Ramp

Stuart Park

Dinah Oval

Dinah Beach

Small Boat Harbour

Deckchair Cinema

Indo Pacific Marine/Australian Pearling Exhibition

Stokes Hill

FRANCES BAY

For more detail on Central Darwin see page 410

Darwin Harbour

Stokes Hill Wharf

Fort Hill Wharf

Land Backed Wharf

Iron Ore Wharf

PORT DARWIN

Patrol Boat Harbour

Slipway

Elliott Point
Rocks

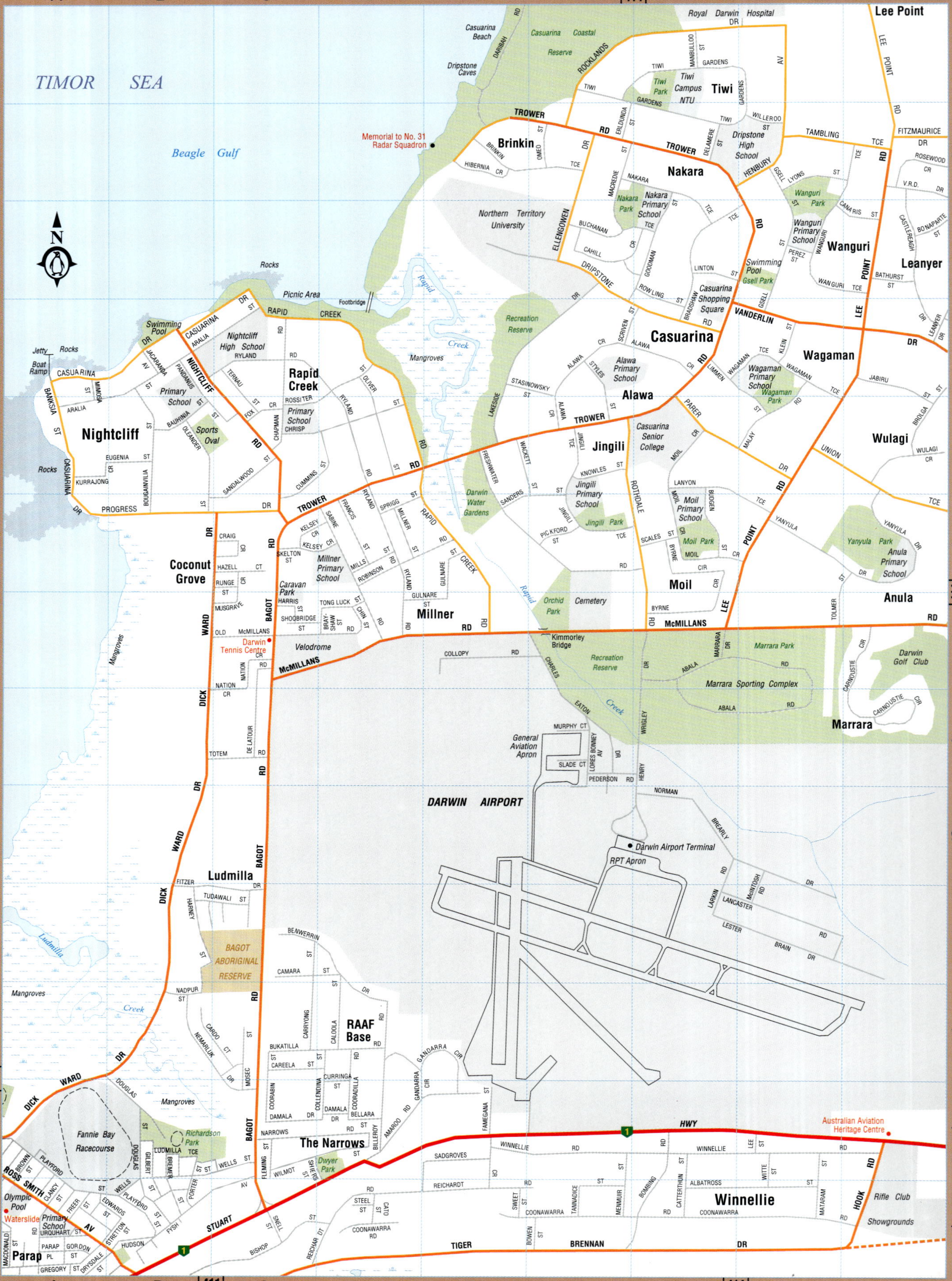

0   0.25   0.5   0.75   1 km

A B C D E F G H I

TIMOR SEA

Beagle Gulf

Lee Point

Royal Darwin Hospital

Casuarina Beach

Dripstone Caves

Casuarina Coastal Reserve

Memorial to No. 31 Radar Squadron

Brinkin

Tiwi

Tiwi Park

Tiwi Campus NTU

Nakara

Dripstone High School

Henbury

Nakara Park

Nakara Primary School

Northern Territory University

Wanguri Park

Wanguri Primary School

Wanguri

Leanyer

Rapid Creek

Rocks

Picnic Area

Footbridge

Casuarina

Wagaman Primary School

Wagaman Park

Wagaman

Mangroves

Recreation Reserve

Alawa Primary School

Alawa

Wulagi

Swimming Pool

Nightcliff High School

Rapid Creek Primary School

Casuarina Shopping Square

Casuarina Senior College

Nightcliff

Primary School

Sports Oval

Jingili

Jingili Primary School

Jingili Park

Moil Primary School

Moil Park

Yanyula Park

Anula Primary School

Jetty Boat Ramp

Rocks

Darwin Water Gardens

Moil

Anula

Coconut Grove

Caravan Park

Millner Primary School

Millner

Orchid Park

Cemetery

McMillans

Marrara Park

Darwin Golf Club

Darwin Tennis Centre

Velodrome

Kimmorley Bridge

Recreation Reserve

Marrara Sporting Complex

Marrara

General Aviation Apron

DARWIN AIRPORT

Ludmilla

Bagot Aboriginal Reserve

Darwin Airport Terminal

RPT Apron

RAAF Base

Fannie Bay Racecourse

Richardson Park

The Narrows

Australian Aviation Heritage Centre

HWY

Winnellie

Ross Smith

Olympic Pool

Waterslide

Primary School

Rifle Club Showgrounds

Parap

TIGER

BRENNAN DR

A B C D E F G H I

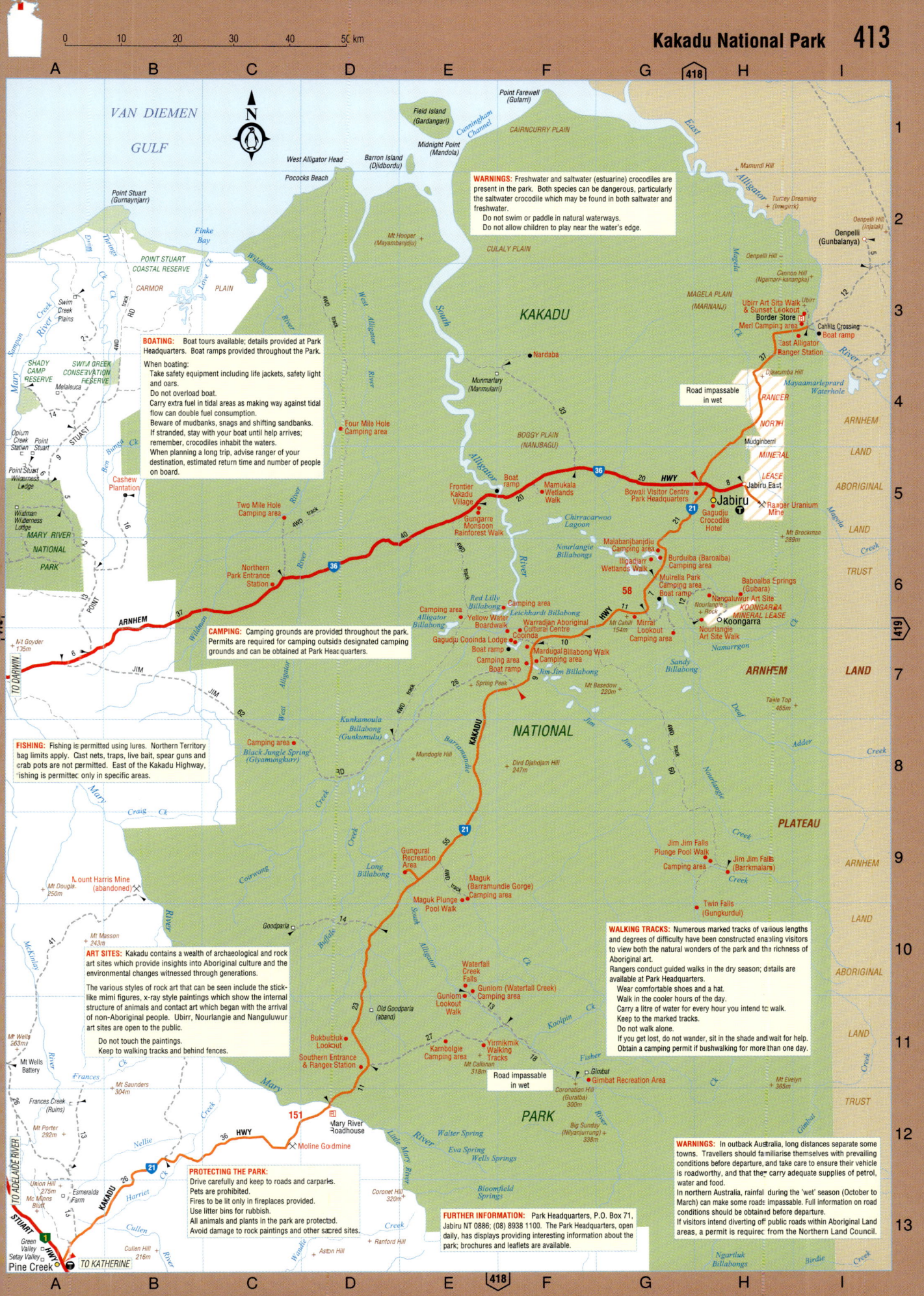

VAN DIEMEN GULF

KAKADU

KAKADU NATIONAL PARK

CAIRNCURRY PLAIN

CULALY PLAIN

BOGGY PLAIN (NANJBAGU)

MAGELA PLAIN (MARNANJ)

ARNHEM LAND ABORIGINAL LAND TRUST

ARNHEM LAND PLATEAU

ARNHEM LAND ABORIGINAL LAND TRUST

Point Farewell (Gularri)
Field Island (Gardangari)
Midnight Point (Mandola)
West Alligator Head
Pococks Beach
Point Stuart (Gurnanjarr)
Finke Bay
Barron Island (Djidbordu)
Mt Hooper (Mayambanjidju)

SHADY CAMP RESERVE
SWIM CREEK CONSERVATION RESERVE
Point Stuart Coastal Reserve
CARMOR PLAIN
Swim Creek Plains
Melaleuca
Point Stuart Wilderness Lodge
Cashew Plantation
Wildman Wilderness Lodge

MARY RIVER NATIONAL PARK

Opium Creek Station

Nardaba
Munmarlary (Manmularri)

Oenpelli (Gunbalanya)
Oenpelli Hill (Injalak)
Cannon Hill (Nganarri-kanangka)
Turkey Dreaming (Irregirrk)
Manurdi Hill

BOATING: Boat tours available; details provided at Park Headquarters. Boat ramps provided throughout the Park.
When boating:
Take safety equipment including life jackets, safety light and oars.
Do not overload boat.
Carry extra fuel in tidal areas as making way against tidal flow can double fuel consumption.
Beware of mudbanks, snags and shifting sandbanks.
If stranded, stay with your boat until help arrives; remember, crocodiles inhabit the waters.
When planning a long trip, advise ranger of your destination, estimated return time and number of people on board.

WARNINGS: Freshwater and saltwater (estuarine) crocodiles are present in the park. Both species can be dangerous, particularly the saltwater crocodile which may be found in both saltwater and freshwater.
Do not swim or paddle in natural waterways.
Do not allow children to play near the water's edge.

Four Mile Hole Camping area
Two Mile Hole Camping area
Frontier Kakadu Village
Boat ramp
Gungarre Monsoon Rainforest Walk
Mamukala Wetlands Walk
Chirracarwoo Lagoon
Bowali Visitor Centre Park Headquarters
Gagudju Crocodile Hotel
Jabiru
Jabiru East
Ranger Uranium Mine
Mt Brockman 289m

Northern Park Entrance Station

RANGER NORTH MINERAL LEASE

Mudginberri
Dawumba Hill
Mayaamarleprard Waterhole

Ubirr Art Site Walk & Sunset Lookout
Border Store
Meri Camping area
East Alligator Ranger Station
Cahills Crossing Boat ramp

ARNHEM

CAMPING: Camping grounds are provided throughout the park. Permits are required for camping outside designated camping grounds and can be obtained at Park Headquarters.

Red Lilly Billabong
Yellow Water Boardwalk
Warradjan Aboriginal Cultural Centre
Gagudju Cooinda Lodge
Boat ramp
Camping area Boat ramp
Camping area Alligator Billabong
Leichhardt Billabong
Nourlangie Billabongs
Malabanbanjdju Camping area
Iligadjarr Wetlands Walk
Burdulba (Baroalba) Camping area
Muirella Park Camping area Boat ramp
Mirrai Lookout Camping area
Nourlangie Rock
Nourlangie Art Site Walk
Mardugal Billabong Walk Camping area
Mt Cahill 154m
Mt Basedow 220m
Jim Jim Billabong
Sandy Billabong
Namarrgon
Nangaluwur Art Site
Baboalba Springs (Gubara)
KOONGARRA
Koongarra
KOONGARRA MINERAL LEASE

58

NATIONAL

ARNHEM LAND

Spring Peak
Kunkamoula Billabong (Gunkumulu)
Black Jungle Spring (Giyamengkurr)
Camping area
Mundogie Hill
RD
Dird Djahdjam Hill 247m
Table Top 465m
Adder Creek
Dead Creek

FISHING: Fishing is permitted using lures. Northern Territory bag limits apply. Cast nets, traps, live bait, spear guns and crab pots are not permitted. East of the Kakadu Highway, fishing is permitted only in specific areas.

Mount Harris Mine (abandoned)
Mt Dougla 250m

PLATEAU

Long Billabong
Gungural Recreation Area
Maguk (Barramundie Gorge) Camping area
Maguk Plunge Pool Walk

Jim Jim Falls Plunge Pool Walk
Camping area
Jim Jim Falls (Barrkmalam)
Twin Falls (Gungkurdul)

ARNHEM LAND

Goodparla
Old Goodparla (aband)

ART SITES: Kakadu contains a wealth of archaeological and rock art sites which provide insights into Aboriginal culture and the environmental changes witnessed through generations.
The various styles of rock art that can be seen include the stick-like mimi figures, x-ray style paintings which show the internal structure of animals and contact art which began with the arrival of non-Aboriginal people. Ubirr, Nourlangie and Nanguluwur art sites are open to the public.
Do not touch the paintings.
Keep to walking tracks and behind fences.

Waterfall Creek Falls
Gunlom (Waterfall Creek) Camping area
Gunlom Lookout Walk
Bukbukluk Lookout
Southern Entrance & Ranger Station
Kambolgie Camping area
Yirmikmik Walking Tracks
Gimbat
Gimbat Recreation Area
Coronation Hill (Guratba) 300m
Big Sunday (Nilyanturrung) 538m
Mt Evelyn 385m
Mt Callanan 318m

Mt Wells 263m
Mt Wells Battery
Frances Creek (Ruins)
Mt Saunders 304m
Mt Porter 292m

PARK

WALKING TRACKS: Numerous marked tracks of various lengths and degrees of difficulty have been constructed enabling visitors to view both the natural wonders of the park and the richness of Aboriginal art.
Rangers conduct guided walks in the dry season; details are available at Park Headquarters.
Wear comfortable shoes and a hat.
Walk in the cooler hours of the day.
Carry a litre of water for every hour you intend to walk.
Keep to the marked tracks.
Do not walk alone.
If you get lost, do not wander, sit in the shade and wait for help.
Obtain a camping permit if bushwalking for more than one day.

Road impassable in wet

PROTECTING THE PARK:
Drive carefully and keep to roads and carparks.
Pets are prohibited.
Fires to be lit only in fireplaces provided.
Use litter bins for rubbish.
All animals and plants in the park are protected.
Avoid damage to rock paintings and other sacred sites.

FURTHER INFORMATION: Park Headquarters, P.O. Box 71, Jabiru NT 0886; (08) 8938 1100. The Park Headquarters, open daily, has displays providing interesting information about the park; brochures and leaflets are available.

WARNINGS: In outback Australia, long distances separate some towns. Travellers should familiarise themselves with prevailing conditions before departure, and take care to ensure their vehicle is roadworthy, and that they carry adequate supplies of petrol, water and food.
In northern Australia, rainfall during the 'wet' season (October to March) can make some roads impassable. Full information on road conditions should be obtained before departure.
If visitors intend diverting off public roads within Aboriginal Land areas, a permit is required from the Northern Land Council.

Mary River Roadhouse
Moline Goldmine

TO DARWIN
TO ADELAIDE RIVER
TO KATHERINE
STUART HWY
Pine Creek
Green Valley
Setay Valley
Nellie Ck
Cullen Hill 216m
Cullen
Woandi
Aston Hill
Ranford Hill
Coronet Hill 320m
Esmeralda Farm
Union Hill 275m
Mc Minns Bluff

Walter Spring
Eva Spring
Wells Springs
Bloomfield Springs
Ngarluk Billabongs
Birdie Creek

PRICE

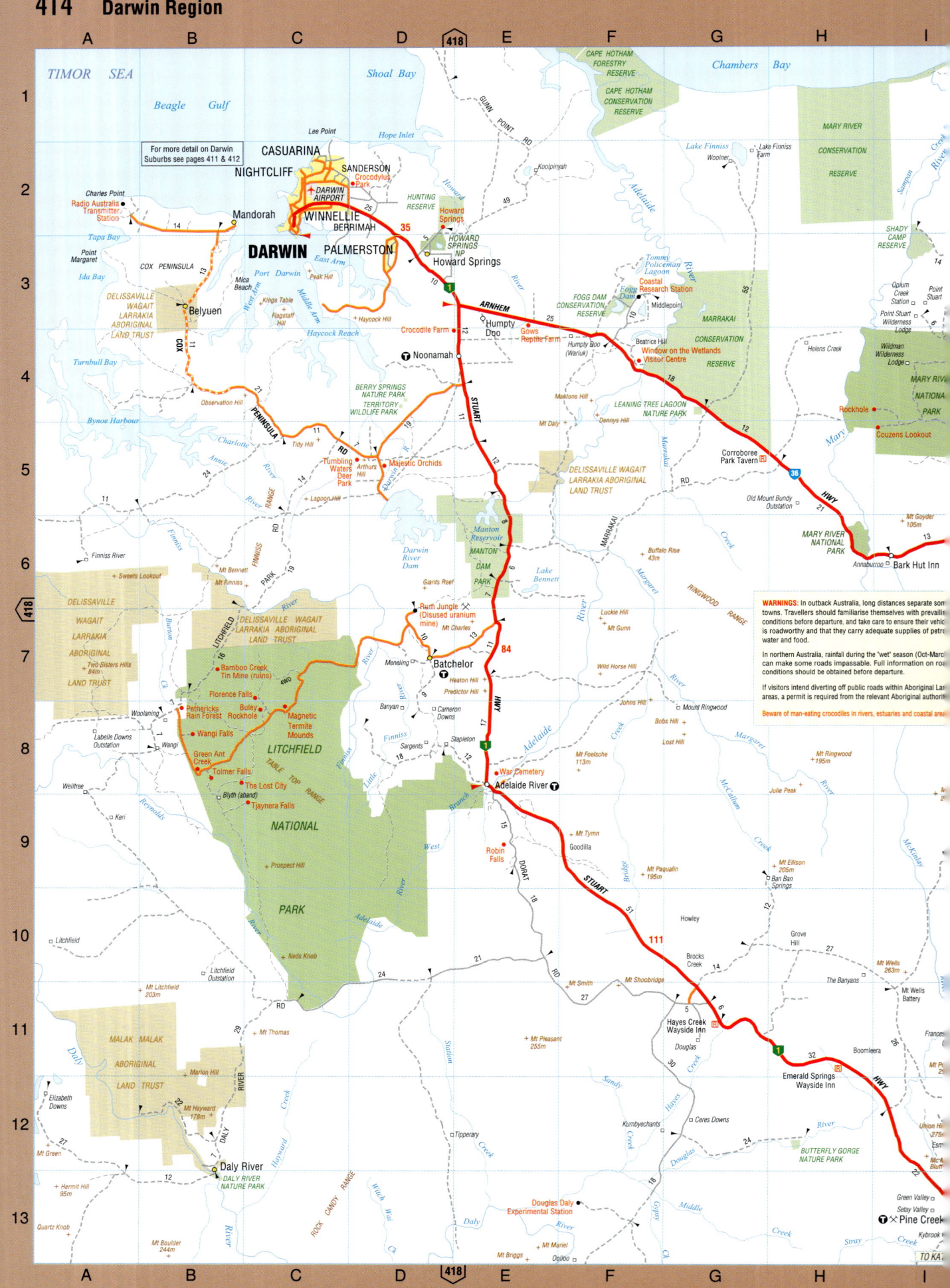

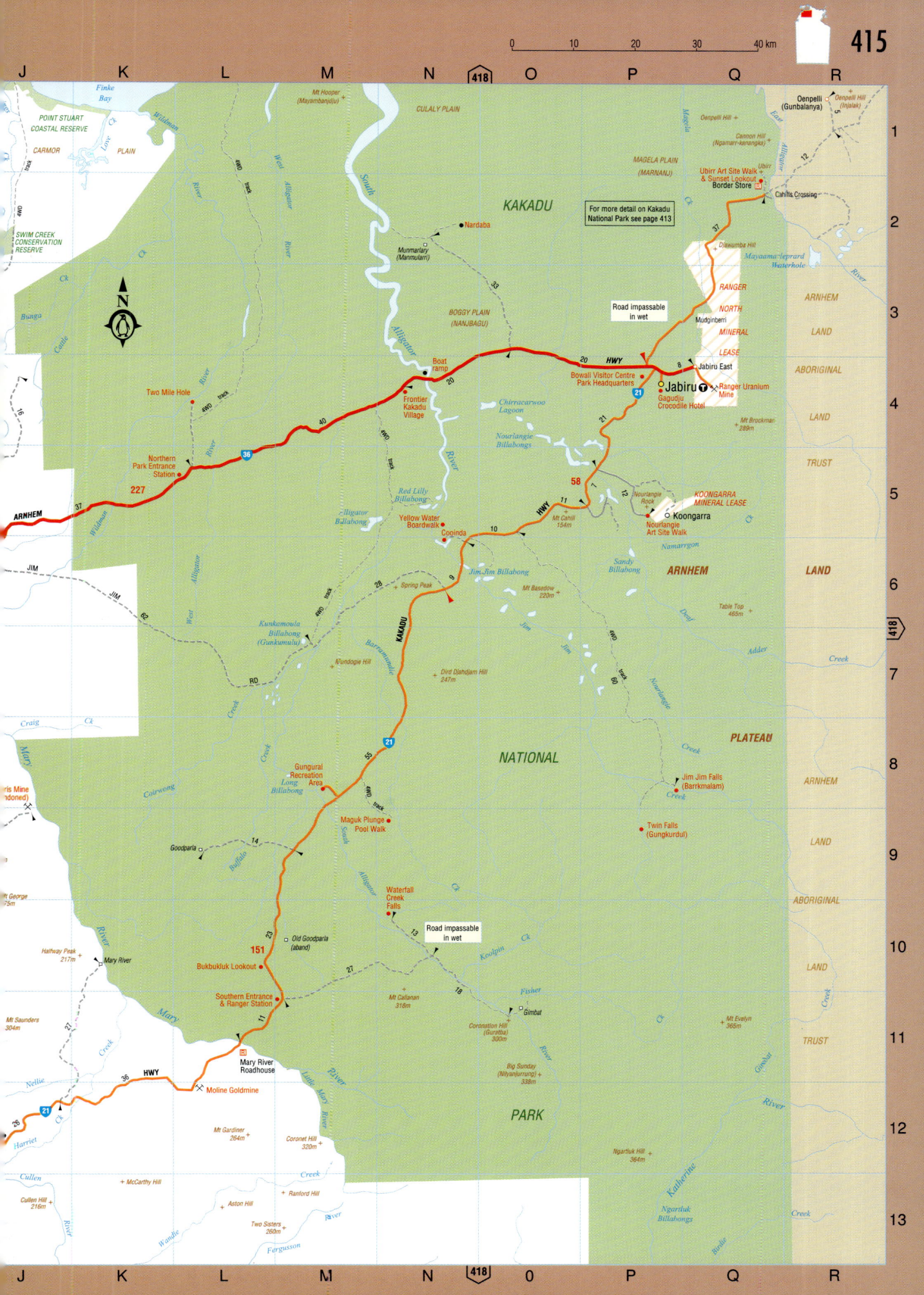

For more detail on Kakadu
National Park see page 413

Mt Liebig 1524m

Ulambaura

422

Mt Chapple 1166m

Milton Park

Haasts Bluff 1125m

Dashwood

Creek

10

Glen Helen

Mt Zell 1510m

TROPIC OF CAPRICORN

Haasts Bluff

14

HAASTS BLUFF

45

The Ck

Arumbera Ck

Mt Razorback 1231m

Redbank Gorge

Mt Sonder 1380m

WEST MACDONNELL

Redbank Creek

Ormiston Creek

NATIONAL PARK

MEREENIE

VALLEY

17

20

Ormiston Gorge

Mt Giles

Davenport Ck

HEAVITREE

Glen Helen

3

18

Glen Helen Gorge

NAMATJIRA

Ochre Pits

Serp Gor

HAASTS BLUFF

ABORIGINAL LAND TRUST

HERMANNSBURG

MACDONNELL

85

TNORALA (GOSSE BLUFF) CONSERVATION RESERVE

Gosse Bluff

50

Creek

Finke

WARNING: Visitors planning to travel along Larapinta Drive through Aboriginal Land require a permit.

LARAPINTA
(MEREENIE

124

MISSIONARY PLAIN

47

Gilbert

DR

Tjuwanpa Resource Centre

LARAP

DR

LOOP)

LARAPINTA

ABORIGINAL LAND TRUST

24

Namatjira Monument

Lookout

Katapata Pass

19

Ipolera

Hermannsburg

Mt Hermannsburg

4WD track

Palm

Ck

Palm Valley

Finke River Gorge

KRICHAUFF RANGE

Areyonga

PALM VALLEY: With its rock pools, cycad palms and *Livistona* palms unique to the area, Palm Valley is yet another of the incredible sights of the Centre. The valley's plant life has such a "prehistoric" appearance, to enter the area seems like taking a trip back in time.

JAMES RANGES

FINKE GORGE NATIONAL PARK

4WD

Boggy Hole Police Camp (ruins)

422

LARAPINTA

WATARRKA

NATIONAL

DR

Illara

McMinn

River

track

PARK

Ulpanyali

Kings Canyon

Kings Canyon Resort

Lilla

Walker

Creek

ILLAMURTA SPRINGS CONSERVATION RESERVE

4WD track

35

MIDDLE RANGE

Mt Lewis 808m

PETERMANN HILLS

Creek

Tempe Downs

4WD track

KINGS CANYON: One of the most interesting and scenic areas of the Centre. Spectacular views can be obtained by crossing the wooden staircase bridge to the north wall. The Lost City and the Garden of Eden are of particular note.

Kings Creek Station (Camping ground)

LURITJA

Petermann

Creek

LEVI RANGE

63

ERNEST

51

Ayers Lookout 572m

47

Palmer

GILES

STONE PLAIN

BACON

RD

37

Mt Ormerod 561m

SEYMOUR

88

INSET: ULURU - KATA TJUTA NATIONAL PARK

To Connellan Airport

LASSETER HWY

KATITI ABORIGINAL LAND TRUST

Yulara
Ayers Rock Resort

To Erldunda

Desert Oak Hill 624m

To Docker River

KATA TJUTA (THE OLGAS)

Car Park

Valley of the Winds Walk

Park Entrance Station

Sunset Viewing Area

Car Park

Olga Gorge Walk

ULURU - KATA TJUTA

NATIONAL PARK

Angas Hill 611m

Sunset Viewing Area (Coaches)

Sunset Viewing Area (Cars)

ULURU (AYERS ROCK)

Mt Ebenezer 702m

KATA TJUTA

DR

Cairn 863m

Imanpa Community

Cultural Centre

Ranger Station

0 2 4 6 8 10 km

TO ULURU

LASSETER

LASSETER

51

Mt Ebenezer Roadhouse

Karinga Ck

HWY

4

HWY

55

HWY

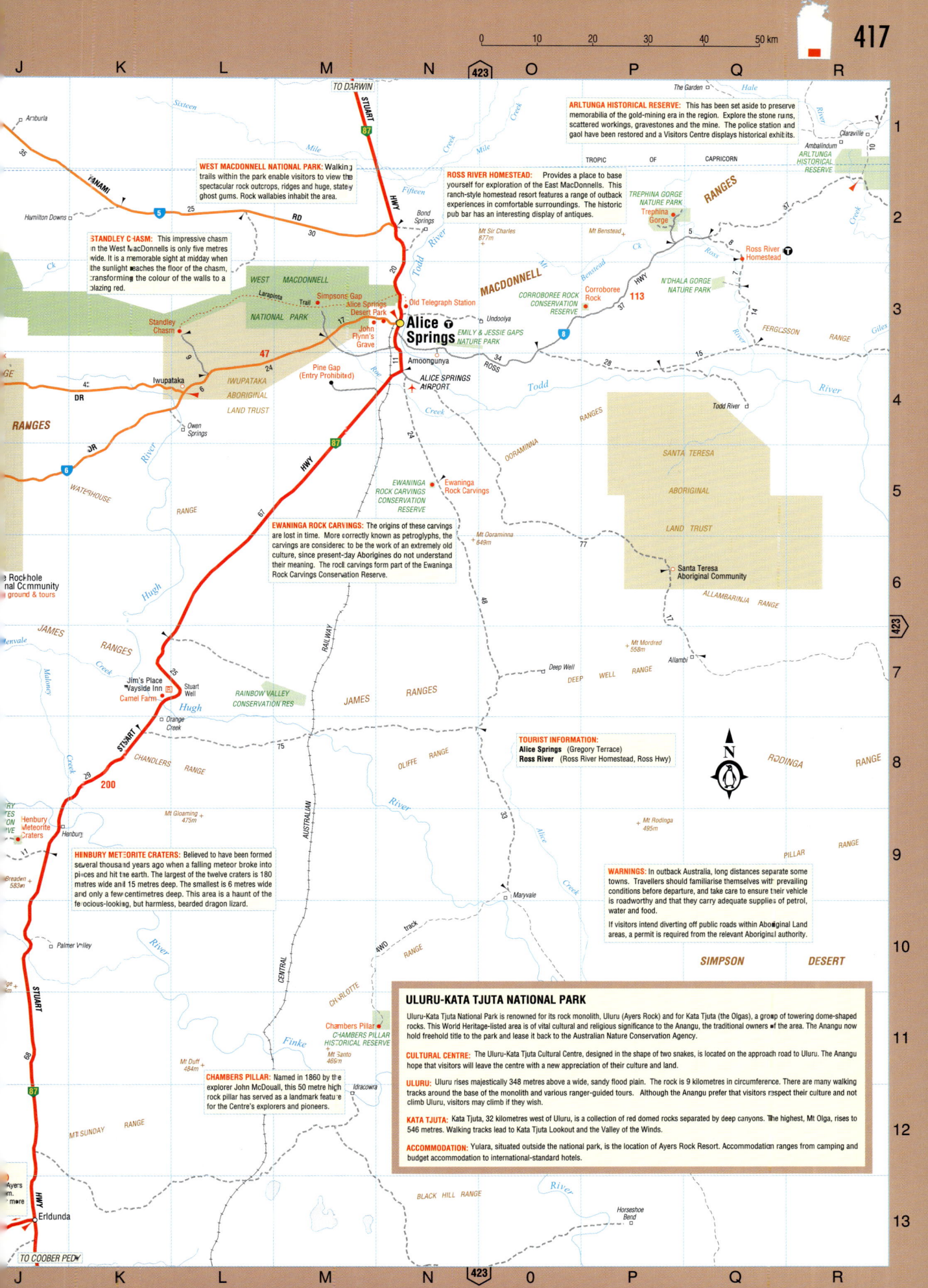

ARLTUNGA HISTORICAL RESERVE: This has been set aside to preserve memorabilia of the gold-mining era in the region. Explore the stone ruins, scattered workings, gravestones and the mine. The police station and gaol have been restored and a Visitors Centre displays historical exhibits.

WEST MACDONNELL NATIONAL PARK: Walking trails within the park enable visitors to view the spectacular rock outcrops, ridges and huge, stately ghost gums. Rock wallabies inhabit the area.

ROSS RIVER HOMESTEAD: Provides a place to base yourself for exploration of the East MacDonnells. This ranch-style homestead resort features a range of outback experiences in comfortable surroundings. The historic pub bar has an interesting display of antiques.

STANDLEY CHASM: This impressive chasm in the West MacDonnells is only five metres wide. It is a memorable sight at midday when the sunlight reaches the floor of the chasm, transforming the colour of the walls to a blazing red.

EWANINGA ROCK CARVINGS: The origins of these carvings are lost in time. More correctly known as petroglyphs, the carvings are considered to be the work of an extremely old culture, since present-day Aborigines do not understand their meaning. The rock carvings form part of the Ewaninga Rock Carvings Conservation Reserve.

HENBURY METEORITE CRATERS: Believed to have been formed several thousand years ago when a falling meteor broke into pieces and hit the earth. The largest of the twelve craters is 180 metres wide and 15 metres deep. The smallest is 6 metres wide and only a few centimetres deep. This area is a haunt of the ferocious-looking, but harmless, bearded dragon lizard.

CHAMBERS PILLAR: Named in 1860 by the explorer John McDouall, this 50 metre high rock pillar has served as a landmark feature for the Centre's explorers and pioneers.

WARNINGS: In outback Australia, long distances separate some towns. Travellers should familiarise themselves with prevailing conditions before departure, and take care to ensure their vehicle is roadworthy and that they carry adequate supplies of petrol, water and food.

If visitors intend diverting off public roads within Aboriginal Land areas, a permit is required from the relevant Aboriginal authority.

TOURIST INFORMATION:
Alice Springs (Gregory Terrace)
Ross River (Ross River Homestead, Ross Hwy)

ULURU-KATA TJUTA NATIONAL PARK

Uluru-Kata Tjuta National Park is renowned for its rock monolith, Uluru (Ayers Rock) and for Kata Tjuta (the Olgas), a group of towering dome-shaped rocks. This World Heritage-listed area is of vital cultural and religious significance to the Anangu, the traditional owners of the area. The Anangu now hold freehold title to the park and lease it back to the Australian Nature Conservation Agency.

CULTURAL CENTRE: The Uluru-Kata Tjuta Cultural Centre, designed in the shape of two snakes, is located on the approach road to Uluru. The Anangu hope that visitors will leave the centre with a new appreciation of their culture and land.

ULURU: Uluru rises majestically 348 metres above a wide, sandy flood plain. The rock is 9 kilometres in circumference. There are many walking tracks around the base of the monolith and various ranger-guided tours. Although the Anangu prefer that visitors respect their culture and not climb Uluru, visitors may climb if they wish.

KATA TJUTA: Kata Tjuta, 32 kilometres west of Uluru, is a collection of red domed rocks separated by deep canyons. The highest, Mt Olga, rises to 546 metres. Walking tracks lead to Kata Tjuta Lookout and the Valley of the Winds.

ACCOMMODATION: Yulara, situated outside the national park, is the location of Ayers Rock Resort. Accommodation ranges from camping and budget accommodation to international-standard hotels.

A B C D E F G H I

TIMOR

SEA

N

1

2

MELVILLE ISLAND

Cape Van Diemen

Deception Point

Pularumpi
Milikapiti

BATHURST ISLAND

TIWI ABORIGINAL LAND TRUST

Nguiu
Paru
Pickertaramoor

Conder Point

3

Point Jahleel

Vashon Head
Smith Pt
Danger Pt
Minjilang
Lingi Pt

COBOURG PENINSULA

GURIG NATIONAL PARK

COBOURG

Greenhill Island
Morse Island
MARINE
Endyalgout Island
PARK
Field Island

Cape Keith

Cape Croker
McCluer Island
Grant Island

CROKER ISLAND

Cape Cockburn

Murgenella Settlement

Warru

Cape Gambier

VAN DIEMEN

GULF

For more detail on Kakadu National Park see page 413

Mt Permain 220m
Cooper

East

4

Beagle Gulf

Clarence Strait

Cape Hotham
CAPE HOTHAM FORESTRY RES

Point Stuart (Gurnaynjarr)

SwimCreek Plains

KAKADU

Oenpelli (Gunbalanya)

Ubirr Art Site Walk & Sunset Lookout
Ubirr
Border Store

Cahills Crossing

Mt Howship = 368m

5

Gunn Point

For more detail on Darwin Region see pages 414 & 415

DARWIN

Radio Australia Transmitter Station

Mandorah
Belyuen

Howard Springs

Koolpinyah
L Finniss
Woolner

MARY RIVER CONSERVATION RESERVE

Mary River

Melaleuca

Field Island

Munmarlary (Marmukarr)

Mt Cahill 289m

Jabiru East

58

Jabiru

Mt Brockman 289m

Nourlangie Rock
Nourlangie Art Site Walk

6

JOSEPH

BONAPARTE

GULF

Dundee Beach

Fog Bay

Point Blaze

Finniss River

DELISSAVILLE WAGAIT LARRAKIA ABORIGINAL LAND TRUST

Noonamah

Humpty Doo (Warluk)

ARNHEM

35

10

HWY

49

45

MARRAKAI CON RES

18

MARY RIVER NP

Helens Creek

Point Stuart

12

Mary

39

37

40

Two Mile Hole

227

Frontier Kakadu Village

Cooinda

75

101

78

151

KAKADU

HWY

20

21

HWY

Mt Cahill 154m

ARNHEM

LAND

NATIONAL

PLATEAU

Jim Jim Falls (Barrkmalam)

Twin Falls (Gungkurdul)

Mt Evelyn 365m

7

North Peron Island

South Peron Island

Anson Bay

Cape Ford

Reynolds

Darwin River Dam

Rum Jungle

Batchelor

Wangi Falls

Banyan

Wangi

Welltree

Keri

84

13

28

33

57

27

38

LITCHFIELD NATIONAL PARK

Litchfield Outstation

War Cemetery
Adelaide River

Mount Ringwood

Ban Ban Springs

McKinlay

Mt Masson 243m
Mt George 275m

Goodparla

STUART

111

24

21

Douglas Hot Springs

The Banyans

19

Mary River

73

Mary River Roadhouse

PARK

Katherine

Ginbar Creek

8

Litchfield

Daly

MALAK MALAK ABORIGINAL LAND TRUST

Douglas
Elizabeth Downs

27

12

Daly River

Tipperary

Douglas Daly Experimental Station

Hayes Creek Wayside Inn

BUTTERFLY GORGE NP

80

Setay Valley

19

Oolloo

Bonalbo

Jindare

Emerald Springs Wayside Inn

Esmeralda Farm

Bonrook

UMBRAWARRA GORGE NATURE PARK

Umbrawarra Gorge

Pine Creek

22

River

Horseshoe Creek

NITMILUK NATIONAL PARK

Mt Lambell 317m

Katherine

Grace Ck

Funny Ck

BESWICK

9

DALY RIVER

PORT KEATS

Peppimenarti

Cape Dombey

Moyle

River

WINGATE

MOUNTAINS

RANGE

Fish River

FISH RIVER FORESTRY RESERVE

Claravale Station

Claravale

Florina

Edith River

Morrisons

Marilyum

Helling

36

42

28

26

90

HWY

58

Edith Falls

Katherine Gorge

Mt Felix 332m

Manyallaluk

O'Sullivans House

ABORIGINAL LAND TRUST

Beswick

10

Pearce Point

Treachery Bay

Swamp Point

Turtle Point

Wadeye Community

ABORIGINAL

RANGE

MACADAM

LAND TRUST

Dorisvale

Flora Yards

Wombungi

90

30

76

Katherine

Tindal

RAAF Base

Manbulloo

Cutta Cutta Caves Nature Park

29

Mt Shepherd 232m

Maranboy

Barunga

23

19

112

Roper

61

Beswick

CEN

11

NORTHERN TERRITORY
WESTERN AUSTRALIA

KEEP RIVER NATIONAL PARK

1

Mt Hensman 384m

Legune

Kneebone

Bradshaw

Fitzmaurice River

YAMBARRAN RANGE

Mt Thymanan 304m

Innesvale

Willeroo

66

1

125

HWY

Dry River

52

King River

Mataranka

Thermal Po
ELSEY NP

We of the Na Graves

12

38

PINKERTON

RANGE

Newry

Auvergne

Bulla

58

77

40

Kneebone

Victoria

Angalarri

Bulla

River

GREGORY NATIONAL PARK

Coolibah

Fitzroy

24

Gregory

Delamere

BUNTINE

14

96

HWY

86

STUART

Gorrie

75

13

20

198

Limestone Gorge

Jasper Gorge

73

GREGORY NATIONAL PARK

Barra Barra

BUCHANAN

Police Station & Store

Timber Creek

27

63

VICTORIA

80

HWY

Victoria River Wayside Inn

Old Delamere

131

23

Western Creek

Sunday Creek

HWY

44

168

Larrimah

Gilnockie

NOTE: Borroloola and Timber Creek, while located on Aboriginal Land, are open towns. No entry permit is required.

A B C D E F G H

ARAFURA   SEA

Cape Wessel ★

WESSEL

ISLANDS

Marchinbar
Island

Guluwuru
Island

Drysdale Island

ELCHO
ISLAND

Point Wilberforce

Bremer Island

Braithwaite Point

132

Maningrida

Cape Stewart

Mooroongga Is

Milingimbi

HOWARD
ISLAND

Galiwinku

Point Napier

Nangalala

Castlereagh
Bay

35

81

Ramingining

Gapuwiyak
Landing Ground

Arnhem
Bay

Nhulunbuy ⊕

79

Yirrkala

27

Cape Arnhem

ARNHEM LAND

112

Old Arafura

Gapuwiyak

GOVE
PENINSULA

Gapuwiyak

Mirrngadja
Village

River

FREDERICK   HILLS

172

Camburinga

Point Alexander

ABORIGINAL

ARNHEM

160

RANGE

Maitunga

Gulbuwangay

RD

Gondar

MITCHELL

Koolatong

Cape Grey

LAND

CENTRAL

83

Creek

RANGE

River

BATH   RANGE

River

Cape Shield

Annie

Walker

Isle Woodah

GULF

Willton

Mawn

PARSONS   RANGE

River

Harris

Creek

Cape Barrow

Bulman

116   RD

↑ Mt Marumba

Milyakburra

Cape Beatrice

OF

Mountain
Valley

Mainoru

Jalboi

DOWNERS

Phelp

Ck

Bickerton
Island

Angurugu

Alyangula

Umbakumba

GROOTE

EYLANDT

CARPENTARIA

Mt Furner
168m↑

RANGE

River

TRUST

River

Lake
Allen

Roper River
Bar

COLLERA   MTNS

Creek

Numbulwar

Tasman Point

HWY

63   198

Roper River
Store

24

Ngukurr

Urapunga

Cape Beatrice

Roper

47

Roper Valley

87

PORT   ROPER   RD

Limmen
Bight

Maria Island

Mt Harriet
938m

39

Hodgson Downs

Towns

NATHAN

MARRA ABORIGINAL
LAND TRUST

St Vidgeon (ruins)

SIR EDWARD PELLEW GROUP

West Island

North Island

BARRANYI (NORTH ISLAND)
NATIONAL PARK

Maryfield
(ruins)

128

Hodgson
River

ALAWA
ABORIGINAL
LAND
TRUST

River

Arnold

RIVER

Nathan River

Bight

River

Rosie

Creek

Bing Bong

SW
Is

Centre Island

Vanderlin
Island

18

Nutwood
Downs

Minamia

Cox

Hodgson

Lorella
Springs

RD

54

Yako   Creek

31

⊕ Borroloola

18

Manangoora

WARNINGS: In outback Australia, long distances separate some
towns. Travellers should familiarise themselves with prevailing
conditions before departure, and take care to ensure their vehicle
is roadworthy and that they carry adequate supplies of petrol,
water and food.

In northern Australia, rainfall during the "wet" season (Oct–March)
can make some roads impassable. Full information on road
conditions should be obtained from local authorities before departure.

If visitors intend diverting off public roads within Aboriginal Land
areas, a permit is required from the relevant Aboriginal authority.

Beware of man-eating crocodiles in rivers, estuaries and coastal areas.

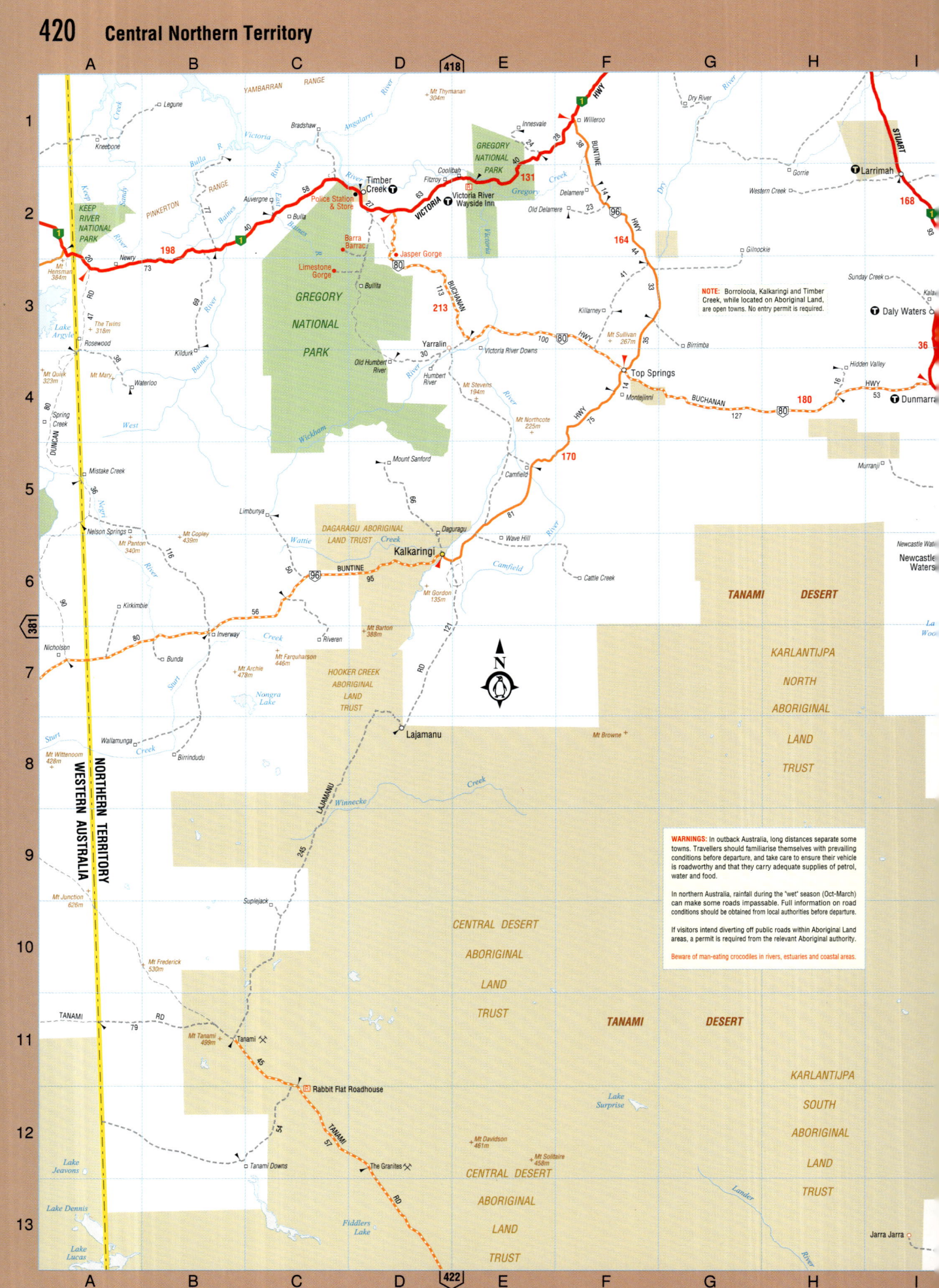

NOTE: Borroloola, Kalkaringi and Timber Creek, while located on Aboriginal Land, are open towns. No entry permit is required.

WARNINGS: In outback Australia, long distances separate some towns. Travellers should familiarise themselves with prevailing conditions before departure, and take care to ensure their vehicle is roadworthy and that they carry adequate supplies of petrol, water and food.

In northern Australia, rainfall during the 'wet' season (Oct-March) can make some roads impassable. Full information on road conditions should be obtained from local authorities before departure.

If visitors intend diverting off public roads within Aboriginal Land areas, a permit is required from the relevant Aboriginal authority.

Beware of man-eating crocodiles in rivers, estuaries and coastal areas.

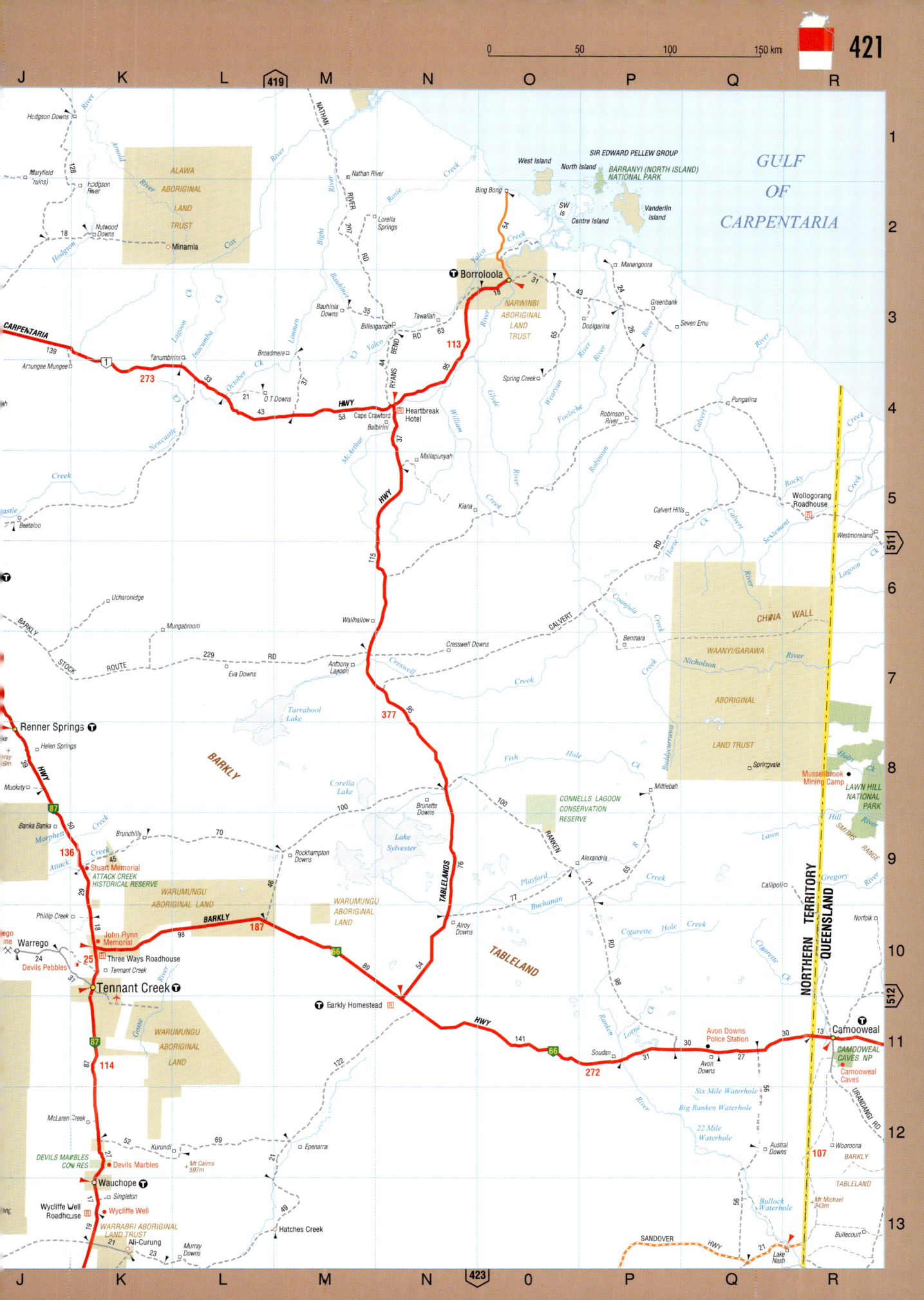

420

379

A B C D E F G H I

1

KARLANTIJPA

Rabbit Flat Roadhouse

TANAMI

Lake Surprise

SOUTH

ABORIGINAL

Lake Jeavons

TANAMI DESERT

2

Lake Dennis

Lander River

LAND

Tanami Downs

The Granites

Mt Davidson 461m

CENTRAL DESERT

TRUST

Lake Lucas

Fiddlers Lake

Mt Solitaire 458m

Jarra Jarra

3

Lake Hazlett

ABORIGINAL

LAND

Willowra

Mt Theo 583m

TRUST

MALA

Mt Patricia 577m

Mt Peaks 568m

Mount Barkly

Old Mount Peake

4

LAKE MACKAY

ABORIGINAL

LAND

Mt Campbell 628m

Mt Leichhardt 1139m

Mount Esther

ABORIGINAL

TRUST

Anningie

Mount

Cent Mou Hist Res

LAND

Hanson

5

Mt Farewell 603m

Mt Singleton 808m

Mount Doreen

Mt Hardy 840m

YUENDUMU ABORIGINAL LAND TRUST

MOUNT DENISON

Coniston

Coniston (ruins)

Mt Stafford 1049m

Ti Tree Store & Police Station

TRUST

31

28

38

Mount Denison

Mt Gardiner 999m

178

RD

Mt Finniss 978m

12

Vaughan Springs

77

Yuendumu

26

Star

Yuelamu

YALPIRAKINU ABORIGINAL LAND TRUST

Mt Boothby 886m

Aile

Lake Mackay

Mt Nicker 632m

YUNKANJINI ABORIGINAL LAND TRUST

61

Napperby

TANAMI

Mt Harris 721m

6

Nyirripi

Mt Cockburn 846m

Gurner

Newhaven

Central Mount Wedge

29

Tilmouth Well Roadhouse

Mt Hammond 750m

CSIRO Experimental Station

Lake Bennett

118

Mount Wedge

Lake Lewis

92

268

7

Mt Tietkens 546m

Ininti

Pinpirnga

Derwent

Narwietooma

23

Mt Chapple 1166m

39

Amburla

23

Kintore

Tinki

Papunya

51

31

Milton Park

Mt Hay 1252m

Hamilton Downs

Mt Leisler 901m

Ilpilla

Warren Creek Bore

Mt Liebig

273

Mt Liebig 1524m

Ulambaura

44

Mt Zeil 1510m

Haasts Bluff 1125m

8

Lake Macdonald

TROPIC

OF

CAPRICORN

HAASTS BLUFF

Haasts Bluff

14

45

Redbank Gorge

37

Mt Sonder 1380m

Ormiston Gorge

WEST MACDONNELL NATIONAL PARK

Standl Chas

Ualki

ABORIGINAL

HAASTS BLUFF RD

Serpentine Gorge

132

Mt Forbes 762m

LAND

TNORALA (GOSSE BLUFF) CON RES

Gosse Bluff

HERMANNSBURG ABORIGINAL LAND TRUST

Glen Helen

NAMATJIRA

Iwupata

WARNING: Visitors planning to travel along Larapinta Drive through Aboriginal Land require a permit.

50

24

127

9

Lake Hopkins

TRUST

124

LARAPINTA (LOOP)

Ipolera

41

Tjuwanpa Resource Centre

LARAPINTA

86

DR

Hermannsburg

Wallace Rockhol Aboriginal Community

LARAPINTA (MEREENIE)

19

Areyonga

Palm Valley

Lake Neale

Mt Murray

WATARRKA NATIONAL PARK

FINKE

10

Mt Harris 1067m

Ulpanyali

Kings Canyon

Mt Lewis 808m

GORGE NATIONAL PARK

ILLAMURTA SPRINGS CONSERVATION RES

Jim's Place Wayside Inn

Mt Taylor 1001m

Docker River Community

Kings Canyon Resort

Lila

35

Tempe Downs

4WD track

47

Henbury Meteorite Craters

29

199

PETERMANN

Lake Amadeus

Kings Creek Station (Camping ground)

63

LURITJA RD

ERNEST

GILES

RD

48

Palmer Valley

51

ABORIGINAL

Desert Oak Hill 624m

11

GUNBARREL

76

ABORIGINAL

LAND

183

231

KATITI ABORIGINAL LAND TRUST

LASSETER

RD

KERNOT RANGE

LURITJA RD

50

LIDDLE

HILLS

BASEDOW RANGE

Imanpa Community

242

18

HWY

Erldunda

TRUST

Mt Olga 1069m

Yulara

Ayers Rock Resort

84

41

Curtin Springs

41

51

Mt Ebenezer Roadhouse

4

55

STUART

74

12

105

HWY

PETERMANN RANGES

Kata Tjuta (The Olgas)

41

ULURU-KATA TJUTA NATIONAL PARK

Uluru (Ayers Rock) 863m

11

Mygoora Lake

Mt Connor 863m

Mt Connor (ruins)

Lyndvale

87

Stevensons Pk 1319m

68

Kulgera

Mt Gosse 885m

Butlers Dome 1111m

Feltham Hill 863m

Alpara

63

Mulga Park

Mount Cavenagh

13

Mt Aloysius 1085m

Surveyor Generals Corner

Mt Cockburn 1138m

NORTHERN TERRITORY

SOUTH AUSTRALIA

165

19

Victory Downs

Kalka

Mt Edwin 1193m

Mt Whinham 1231m

Mt Woodward 1227m

MANN

RANGES

Ayliffe Hill (Thg) 1044m

Mt Cuthbert 1035m

Sentinel Hill 910m

Pipalyatjara

Mt Davies 1058m

Aparawatatja

Kanypi

213

Amata

Mt Morris 1288m

Mt Davenport 1139m

Marryat

Creek

A B C D E F G H

308

309

NORTHERN TERRITORY WESTERN AUSTRALIA

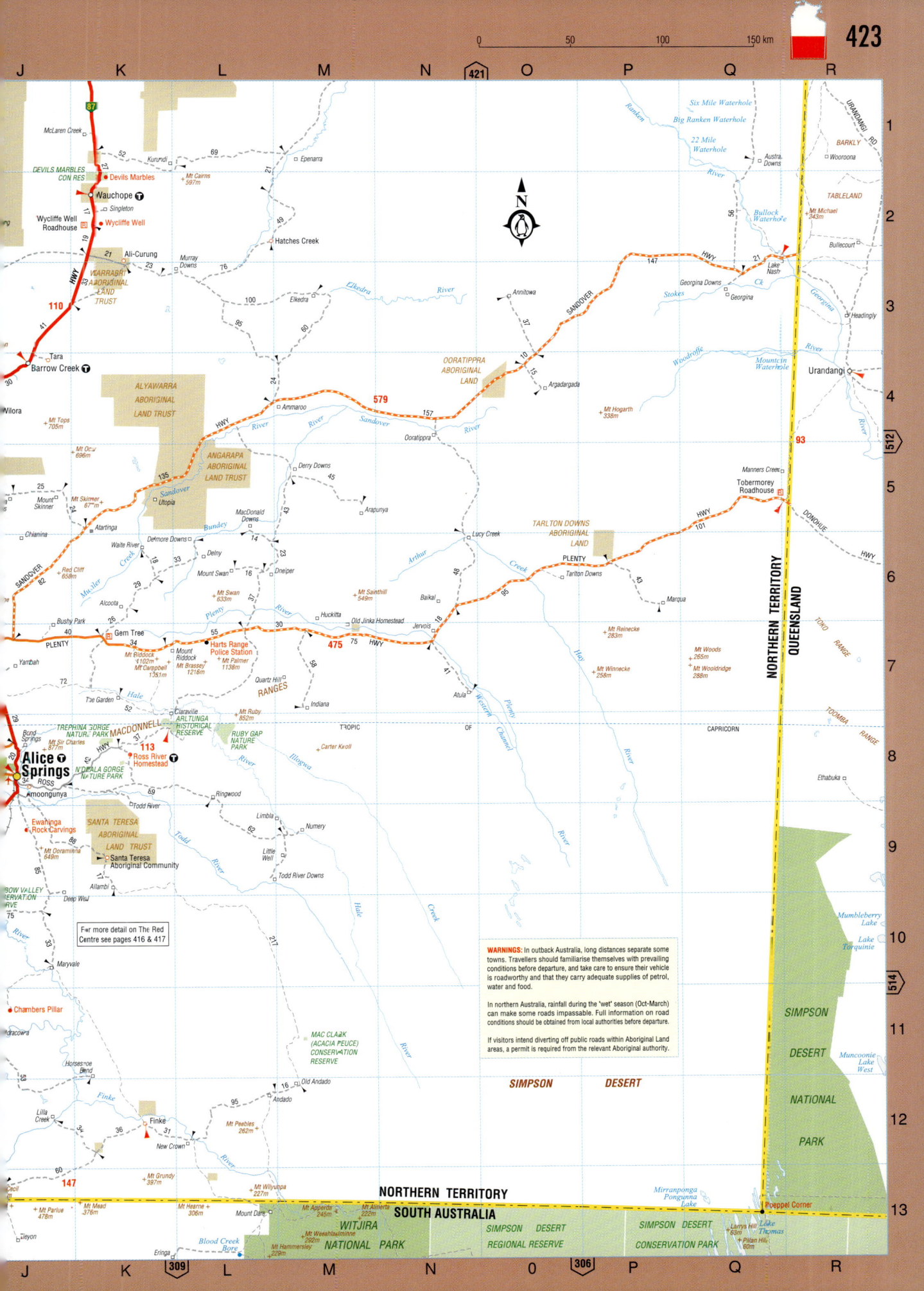

0   50   100   150 km

J   K   L   M   N   O   P   Q   R

421

WARNINGS: In outback Australia, long distances separate some towns. Travellers should familiarise themselves with prevailing conditions before departure, and take care to ensure their vehicle is roadworthy and that they carry adequate supplies of petrol, water and food.

In northern Australia, rainfall during the 'wet' season (Oct-March) can make some roads impassable. Full information on road conditions should be obtained from local authorities before departure.

If visitors intend diverting off public roads within Aboriginal Land areas, a permit is required from the relevant Aboriginal authority.

For more detail on The Red Centre see pages 416 & 417

NORTHERN TERRITORY
SOUTH AUSTRALIA

NORTHERN TERRITORY
QUEENSLAND

J   K   L   M   N   O   P   Q   R

309   306

Queensland

Sunshine State

To visitors from other States, as well as to many Queenslanders, the Sunshine State is holiday country, evoking dreams of long, golden days, tropical islands set in jewel-blue seas and the chance to relax outdoors. The first settlers in the tropical north, however, were there for grimly practical reasons.

In 1821 Sir Thomas Brisbane, then Governor of New South Wales, sent John Oxley, his Surveyor-General, to explore the almost unknown country north of the Liverpool Plains. Oxley's task was to find a suitable site for a penal settlement and he decided on Moreton Bay. In 1824 troops and convicts arrived at Redcliffe, but a lack of fresh water and the hostility of the Aborigines persuaded them to move south and they decided to settle at the present site of Brisbane. By 1859 the settlement was well established and the free settlers were urging separation from New South Wales; on 10 December of that year, the State of Queensland was proclaimed.

Having gained legislative independence, the population of just 23 000 then set about achieving economic independence. Fortunately the new State was well endowed with excellent farming land, and wool and beef production were soon established on the western plains and tablelands. It was not long before sugar production, worked by 'kanaka' labour from the Pacific Islands, became much more important, and it is still significant.

As well as being blessed with fertile land that produces grain, sugar, dairy produce, wool, mutton, beef, cotton, peanuts and timber, Queensland has immensely rich mineral deposits, and the vast Mount Isa mining complex in the west produces copper, lead and zinc in enormous quantities.

Over the years, Queensland has been developing another, very different, form of industry – tourism. Its attraction as a holiday destination is very much due to its climate.

In the west, the climate is similar to that of the arid Red Centre, with fierce daytime heat, but on the coast the temperature rarely exceeds 38°C and for seven months or so of the year the weather is extremely pleasant. If you are unused to high humidity, however, the period from December to April can be uncomfortably damp.

Four geographic and climatic regions run north to south, neatly dividing the State. In the west is the Great Artesian Basin, flat and hot. Parched and bare during drought, it becomes grassy after rain, thanks to a complex system of boreholes that distribute water through channels and allow grazing. The tablelands to the east are undulating and sparsely timbered, broken up by slow, meandering rivers. The backbone of Queensland is the Great Dividing Range – most spectacular in its extreme north and south, where it comes closest to the coast. Although the coastal region is the area most popular with visitors, Queensland's hinterland is lushly beautiful and its national parks, with many species of flora and fauna unique to the State, total more than one million hectares.

The State's highway and road system is good in the south-east and in areas close to the larger northern towns, but in more remote areas

NOT TO BE MISSED
in Queensland

	Map Ref.
• **Carnarvon National Park** – beautiful park with magnificent gorge and Aboriginal art	504 F2
• **Darling Downs** – an area of beauty and prosperity – rural Australia at its best	496 A6
• **Gemfield towns of Anakie, Rubyvale and Sapphire** – for fossicking (with a licence!)	506 H11
• **Gold Coast hinterland** – spectacular scenery in Numinbah Valley and at Springbrook	499 B12
• **Great Barrier Reef** – best seen by boat; your own, a charter boat or a cruise boat	507 M3
• **The *Gulflander* train** – ride between Normanton and old gold-mining town of Croydon	508 C8
• **Kuranda Scenic Railway** – spectacular train ride from Cairns to Kuranda; return via Skyrail Rainforest Cableway	509 M6
• **Noosa National Park** – beautiful coastal park offering memorable views and walks	500 H2
• **Scenic drive through Mapleton, Flaxton, Montville and Maleny** – one of the best in south-east Queensland	500 C8
• **Theme parks on the Gold Coast** – Dreamworld, Movie World and Seaworld – fun for all the family	499 C1, C3, F4

The rich marine life of the Great Barrier Reef

Coastal edge of Daintree National Park in northern Queensland

roads can be narrow and poorly graded, and conditions deteriorate during drought or heavy rain.

The two main towns of the tropical northern region are Townsville and Cairns. The more northerly Cairns is a fashionable holiday centre and makes an excellent base for deep-sea fishing and for exploring the region, with its lush sugar plantations, mountainous jungle country and the wilds of the Cape York Peninsula. The Atherton Tableland is a rich volcanic area west of Cairns, with superb lakes, waterfalls and fern valleys. Stretching along this coastline are some of Queensland's famed islands including Lizard (north of Cooktown), Green, Fitzroy, Dunk, Bedarra, Hinchinbrook, Orpheus and Magnetic. Further south are the beautiful Whitsunday Islands and Great Keppel, North West, Heron, Lady Musgrave, Lady Elliot, and Fraser islands. If you are planning an island holiday, make sure your choice fits in with your idea of a tropical paradise. Many islands are extensively developed for tourism; others remain relatively untouched. Beyond, and

QUEENSLAND

CALENDAR OF EVENTS

Note: The information given here was accurate at the time of printing. However, as the timing of events held annually is subject to change and some events may extend into the following month, it is best to check with the local tourism authority or event organisers to confirm the details. The calendar is not exhaustive. Most towns and regions throughout the State hold sporting competitions; regattas and rodeos; art, craft, and trade exhibitions; agricultural and flower shows; music festivals and other events annually. Details of these events are available from local tourism outlets.

JANUARY
Public holidays: New Year's Day; Australia Day. **Coominya:** Watermelon Festival. **Georgetown:** Race Meeting.

Pittsworth: Crimson Flash Shield (footrace). **Redcliffe:** Blessing of the Fleet. **Warwick:** Antique and Collectables Fair (sometimes held in Feb.). **Yeppoon:** Australia Day Celebrations.

FEBRUARY
Chinchilla: Melon Festival (biennial, odd-numbered years). **Killarney:** Agricultural Show. **Redcliffe:** Seafood Festival. **Yeppoon:** Surf Lifesaving Championships.

MARCH
Dalby: Queensland Cotton Week. **Gin Gin:** Wild Scotchman Festival. **Stanthorpe:** Apple and Grape Harvest Festival (biennial, even-numbered years); Rodeo.

EASTER
Public holidays: Good Friday; Easter Monday. **Brisbane:** Brisbane–Gladstone Yacht Race.

Airlie Beach: Whitsunday Masters Games. **Bundaberg:** Country Music Roundup. **Burketown:** World Barramundi Handline-rod Fishing Championships. **Cannonvale:** Great Whitsunday Boating Regatta. **Charters Towers:** Rodeo. **Emerald:** Sunflower Festival. **Eromanga:** Rodeo. **Gladstone:** Harbour Festival (includes finish of Brisbane–Gladstone Yacht Race). **Gold Coast:** IndyCar Australia Racing Spectacular (at Surfers Paradise). **Mundubbera:** Citrus Festival (even-numbered years). **Roma:** Easter in the Country. **Tin Can Bay:** Easter Festival. **Warwick:** Rock Swap.

APRIL
Public holiday: Anzac Day. **Allora:** 500 Endurance Motor Race. **Ipswich:** Heritage Festival. **Kilkivan:** Great Horse Ride. **Kingaroy:** Peanut Festival

(biennial, odd-numbered years). **Laidley:** Clydesdale Heavy Horse Show. **Mooloolaba:** Finish of Sydney–Mooloolaba Yacht Race; Triathlon. **Mount Isa:** Country Music Festival. **Rockhampton:** Good Earth Expo. **Winton:** Waltzing Matilda Festival.

MAY
Public holiday: Labour Day. **Brisbane:** Winter Racing Carnival begins. **Beaudesert:** Rodeo. **Cardwell:** Country and Western Music Festival. **Charters Towers:** Country Music Festival. **Childers:** Agricultural Show. **Chinchilla:** Rotary May Day Carnival. **Eromanga:** Race Day. **Fraser Island:** Fishing Expo. **Gatton:** Heavy Horse Field Day. **Ingham:** Australian-Italian Festival. **Julia Creek:** Dirt and Dust Triathlon; Campdraft. **Kuranda:** Folk Festival. **Mareeba:** Dimbulah Festival. **Maryborough:** Best of Brass.

Moranbah: May Day Union Parade. **Mount Morgan:** Golden Mount Festival. **Proserpine:** Rodeo. **Richmond:** Rodeo. **Seventeen Seventy:** 1770 Commemorative Festival. **Stanthorpe:** Opera at Sunset. **Strathpine:** Pine Rivers Heritage Festival. **Taroom:** Agricultural Show. **Thursday Island:** Cultural Festival.

JUNE
Public holiday: Queen's Birthday. **Allora:** Allora Apex Auction. **Biloela:** Country and Western Muster. **Blackall:** Race Meeting. **Caboolture:** Agricultural Show; Medieval Festival. **Cardwell:** Coral Sea Memorial. **Charters Towers:** Annual Vintage Car Restorers' Swap Meet. **Cloncurry:** Agricultural Show. **Cooktown:** Endeavour Festival. **Coolangatta:** Wintersun Festival. **Croydon:** Rodeo. **Emerald:** Wheelbarrow

Derby (odd-numbered years). **Gayndah:** Orange Festival (biennial, odd-numbered years). **Georgetown:** Race Meeting. **Hamilton Island:** Cup (outrigger canoes). **Jundah:** Bronco Branding. **Landsborough:** William Landsborough Day. **Longreach:** Hall of Fame Race Meeting. **Malanda:** Agricultural Show. **Monto:** Dairy Festival (biennial, even-numbered years). **Mossman:** Bavarian Festival. **Muttaburra:** Landsborough Flock Ewe Show. **Nindigully:** 5-Hour Enduro (for motor bikes). **Noosa:** Aqueous Festival of Arts. **Normanton:** Show, Rodeo and Gymkhana. **Quilpie:** Diggers Races. **Taldora Station:** Saxby Roundup. **Tin Can Bay:** Seafood and Leisure Festival. **Yungaburra:** Yuletide.

JULY
Airlie Beach: Festival (for the start of whale

protecting them from the South Pacific, is the outer Great Barrier Reef, the world's largest and most famous coral formation.

South of the Reef is the Sunshine Coast. This scenic coastal region, with its leisurely pace and its wide variety of natural attractions and sporting facilities, offers an alternative to the more commercialised Gold Coast. Bribie Island and the Glass House Mountains are nearby.

Brisbane, Australia's third-largest capital city, is built on both sides of the Brisbane River. The city is easygoing, and its parks and gardens are lush with subtropical plants. It has a year-round average of 7½ hours of sunshine a day. The Gold Coast, 75 kilometres to the south, is the heart of holiday country. Luxuriously developed, it offers a wide range of accommodation, glittering nightlife, golden beaches and constant sun. Inland is rich agriculturally, mainly sugarcane and dairy farming, its setting a sharp contrast with the tropical north or the mining areas of Mount Isa.

The Sunshine State is a diverse place indeed.

CLIMATE GUIDE

BRISBANE

	J	F	M	A	M	J	J	A	S	O	N	D
Maximum °C	29	29	28	27	24	21	21	22	24	26	27	29
Minimum °C	21	21	20	17	14	11	10	10	13	16	18	20
Rainfall mm	169	177	152	86	84	82	66	45	34	102	95	123
Raindays	14	14	15	11	10	8	7	7	7	10	10	11

COOLANGATTA REGION

	J	F	M	A	M	J	J	A	S	O	N	D
Maximum °C	28	28	27	25	23	21	20	21	22	24	26	26
Minimum °C	20	20	19	17	13	11	9	10	12	15	17	19
Rainfall mm	184	181	213	114	124	122	96	103	49	108	137	166
Raindays	14	15	16	14	10	9	7	9	9	11	11	13

MACKAY VALLEY

	J	F	M	A	M	J	J	A	S	O	N	D
Maximum °C	30	29	28	27	24	22	21	22	25	27	29	30
Minimum °C	23	23	22	20	17	14	13	14	16	20	22	23
Rainfall mm	293	311	303	134	104	59	47	30	15	38	87	175
Raindays	16	17	17	15	13	7	7	6	5	7	9	12

CAIRNS REGION

	J	F	M	A	M	J	J	A	S	O	N	D
Maximum °C	31	31	30	29	28	26	26	27	28	29	31	31
Minimum °C	24	24	23	22	20	18	17	18	19	21	22	23
Rainfall mm	413	435	442	191	94	49	28	27	36	38	90	175
Raindays	18	19	20	17	14	10	9	8	8	8	10	13

---

watching season). **Burketown:** Rodeo and Races. **Caboolture:** St Peters Arts and Crafts Festival. **Cairns:** Agricultural Show. **Childers:** Multicultural Food and Wine Festival. **Chinchilla:** Polocrosse Carnival. **Cleveland:** Flinders Day. **Cooktown:** Laura-Cape York Aboriginal Dance Festival (biennial, odd-numbered years). **Emu Park:** Service of Remembrance. **Esk:** Picnic Races. **Hughenden:** Dinosaur Festival (biennial, even-numbered years). **Innisfail:** Agricultural Show. **Ipswich:** Medieval Fair. **Karumba:** Karumba Kapers. **Longreach:** Diamond Shears. **Mackay:** Festival of the Arts. **Mareeba:** Rodeo. **Mission Beach:** Banana Festival. **Nebo:** Rodeo. **Pomona:** King of the Mountain Festival. **Rainbow Beach:** Fishing Classic. **Rockhampton:** Bauhinia Arts Festival.

Sarina: Visual Arts Festival. **Texas:** Agricultural Show. **Townsville:** Australian Festival of Chamber Music. **Yungaburra:** Jazz Festival.

AUGUST
Public holiday: Brisbane Show Day. **Brisbane:** Brisbane International Film Festival; Royal Brisbane National Show ('the Ekka'); Spring Hill Fair. **Atherton:** Maize Festival. **Boulia:** Rodeo and Gymkhana. **Bowen:** Art, Craft and Orchid Expo. **Buderim:** Buderim Festival. **Caboolture:** Caboolture Air Display (odd-numbered years). **Charters Towers:** Great Gold Rush. **Cloncurry:** Merry Muster Rodeo. **Emerald:** Gemfest. **Gympie:** National Country Music Muster. **Hamilton Island:** Race Week (sailing). **Hervey Bay:** Whale Festival. **Mount Isa:** Rodeo. **Quilpie:** Diggers Races. **Rockhampton:** Rocky

Round Up. **Sarina:** Agricultural Show. **Taroom:** Leichhardt Festival. **Yeppoon:** World Cooeeing Festival.

SEPTEMBER
Brisbane: Brisbane Festival. **Airlie Beach:** Whitsunday Fun Race. **Beaudesert:** Mini Royal Agricultural Show. **Birdsville:** Races. **Bundaberg:** Bundy in Bloom Festival. **Caloundra:** Art and Craft Show. **Cardwell:** Festival of Sport. **Clermont:** Rodeo. **Coominya:** Boss Camel Races. **Cunnamulla:** Opal Festival. **Emerald:** Music Spectacular. **Eulo:** World Lizard Racing Championships. **Herberton:** Tin Festival. **Kabar:** Fassifern German Festival. **Kynuna:** 'Surf' Carnival. **Laidley:** Chelsea Festival Week. **Longreach:** Starlight Stampede (biennial, even-numbered years). **Mackay:** Sugartime Festival. **Maryborough:** Heritage City Festival.

Miles: Back to the Bush (includes Wildflower Festival). **Noosa:** Jazz Party. **Port Douglas:** Yachting Regatta. **Quilpie:** Agricultural Show; Kangaranga Do Street Party; Get-your-rocks-off Competition. **Redcliffe:** First Settlement Festival; Bomboora-The Redcliffe Festival. **Redland Bay:** Strawberry Festival. **St George:** Fishing Competition. **Strathpine:** Camp Oven Bush Poets Festival. **Surfers Paradise:** International Aquathon. **Tambo:** Spring Flower Festival. **Texas:** Roundup (even-numbered years). **Thangool:** Lucerne Festival. **Toowoomba:** Carnival of Flowers. **Winton:** Outback Festival (biennial, odd-numbered years). **Yeppoon:** Pineapple Festival.

OCTOBER
Brisbane: Colonial George Street Festival. **Ayr:** Water Festival. **Biggenden:** Rose Festival (biennial, odd-

numbered years). **Bowen:** Coral Coast Festival. **Bundaberg:** Bundaberg Arts Festival. **Cairns:** The Reef Festival. **Charleville:** Booga Woongaroo (mulga tree) Festival. **Crows Nest:** Crows Nest Day; Worm Races. **Dalby:** Quilts and Craft Show. **Emu Park:** Octoberfest. **Gatton:** Potato Festival. **Georgetown:** Race Meeting. **Goondiwindi:** Spring Festival. **Gympie:** Gold Rush Festival. **Hervey Bay:** Hervey Bay to Fraser Island Sailboard Marathon. **Ingham:** Maraka Festival. **Innisfail:** Harvest Festival. **Ipswich:** Jacaranda Festival. **Jundah:** Race Carnival. **Laidley:** Festival of Performing Arts. **Logan:** Street Parade. **Mapleton:** Yarn Festival. **Maryborough:** Master Games. **Mission Beach:** Aquatic Festival; Sailing Regatta. **Murgon:** Fishing Carnival. **Nanango:** Pioneer Festival. **Noosa:** Beach Car Classic.

Proserpine: Harvest Festival (including World Championship Cane Cutting). **Ravenswood:** Halloween Ball. **Warwick:** Rose and Rodeo City Festival. **Yandina:** Spring Flower and Ginger Festival. **Yungaburra:** Folk Festival.

NOVEMBER
Georgetown: Race Meeting. **Goondiwindi:** Rodeo. **Home Hill:** Harvest Festival; Country Music Festival. **Killarney:** Rodeo. **Kynuna:** Rodeo. **Noosa:** Triathlon.

DECEMBER
Public holidays: Christmas Day; Boxing Day. **Karumba:** Fisherman's Ball. **Surfers Paradise:** New Year's Eve Fireworks. **Tin Can Bay:** Robert Pryde Memorial Surf Classic. **Woodford:** Folk Festival.

BRISBANE

A Subtropical City

The Brisbane River winds its way through the city

The best place from which to see the layout of Brisbane is the lookout on **Mount Coot-tha**, located 8 kilometres south-west of the city centre and easily distinguished by its television towers. Brisbane sprawls over the series of small hills below, with the Brisbane River wandering lazily through the suburbs and city, and out into **Moreton Bay**, 32 kilometres downstream. Surprisingly little use is made of the river for public transport, and most riverside houses back on to rather than face it. **Moreton and Stradbroke islands** look like a protective mountain range against the Pacific Ocean, far to the east. On a good day, you can see the rugged mountains behind the Gold Coast to the south, and northward, the strange **Glass House Mountains** just south of the Sunshine Coast. Brisbane's best-known building, the **City Hall**, is now lost among the cluster of high-rise office buildings that dominate the skyline.

Although Brisbane is an international tourist destination, the city still does not bustle like the larger southern capitals. The architecture in many suburbs is predominantly the traditional galvanised iron-roofed timber house on stumps which residents think sensible and visitors find quaint. While some of these houses may be lacking in paint, this is more than made up for by colourful subtropical trees and shrubbery.

The city started inauspiciously as a convict settlement as far removed from Britain, and even from Sydney, as possible. In 1799 Matthew Flinders sailed into Moreton Bay on the sloop *Norfolk*. In 1823 John Oxley, then Surveyor-General, on board the cutter *Mermaid* sailed up the river that flowed into the bay and called it 'the Brisbane', after the Governor of New South Wales, Sir Thomas Brisbane. The first troops and

NOT TO BE MISSED

in Brisbane

	Map Ref.
• **City Botanic Gardens** – lush tropical vegetation in a riverside setting	490 G8
• **City Hall** – architecturally interesting building with an 85-metre clocktower	490 D5
• **City Sights tour** – for a scenic round-up of the major attractions from tram-style coaches	490 D5
• **Earlystreet Historical Village** – fine collection of early-Queensland buildings	494 I1
• **Lone Pine Koala Sanctuary** – take a ferry ride to this famous koala sanctuary	494 E4
• **Mt Coot-tha Lookout** – for superb views of Brisbane and surrounding area	492 D13
• **Newstead House** – Brisbane's premier historic house with period furnishings and exhibits	492 H10
• **Queensland Cultural Centre** – museum, art gallery, library and theatres; all in one building	490 B7
• **South Bank Parklands** – beach, cruise ships, rainforest and butterfly house – in the city	490 C9
• **Sunday markets at Riverside Centre and at South Bank Parklands** – art and craft	490 C9, G4

convicts arrived in 1824 on the brig *Amity*. Soon, the original settlement at Redcliffe was abandoned, mainly because of a lack of fresh water, and barracks were built on the present site of the city centre, previously investigated by Oxley. The penal settlement was closed in 1839 and the region was opened for free settlement in 1842.

Today Brisbane is a busy city with a modern and extensive public transport system a wide selection of restaurants, beautiful entertainment and nightlife; parks and gardens which thrive in the subtropical climate; and a population of over 1.3 million.

Among several interesting historic buildings is the **Old Windmill** on Wickham Terrace, overlooking the city. Built in 1828, the mill proved unworkable, so convicts were pressed into service to crush the grain on a treadmill. In 1934 a picture of the mill was the first television image transmitted in Australia; it was sent to Ipswich, 33 kilometres away.

The restored **Commissariat Stores**, at North Quay below the old **State Library** building, were built by convicts in 1829. The **Treasury Building** at the top of Queen Street, an impressive Italian Renaissance-style structure built of local grey sandstone, was commenced in 1838 and is now the site for the **Conrad Treasury Casino**. The nearby **Lands Administration Building** is a boutique hotel. **Newstead House**, a charming building overlooking the river at Breakfast Creek, was built in 1846 by Patrick Leslie, the first settler on the Darling Downs. He sold it to his brother-in-law Captain John Wickham, RN, resident of the Moreton Bay colony, and it was the centre of official and social life in Brisbane until the first Government House was built in 1862. Newstead House is Brisbane's oldest house and has been restored. With its spacious verandahs, formal gardens and lawns right down to the river, it is the quintessential Australian homestead. **Old Government House**, a classic colonial building with additions made between 1882 and 1895, was also the original University. It now forms part of the **Queensland University of Technology** complex at the bottom of George Street and is the home of the National Trust of Queensland. Nearby, is **Parliament House** designed by Charles Tiffin in a French Renaissance-style and opened in 1868. The

Parliament House Annexe (irreverently called the Taj Mahal) is a modern tower block behind Parliament House overlooking the river. The exclusive **Queensland Club** is diagonally opposite Parliament House and was built during the 1880s.

The **General Post Office** in Queen Street was built between 1871 and 1879 on the site of the female convict barracks. The small church behind the Post Office in Elizabeth Street and beside **St Stephen's Catholic Cathedral** is the third oldest building in Brisbane, having been dedicated in 1850. The **Customs House** at Petrie Bight at the bottom of Queen Street was built in 1884; recently refurbished, it includes an art gallery, bookshop and cafe. The **Deanery**, built in 1849, behind **St John's Anglican Cathedral** in Ann Street, became a temporary residence for the first Governor of Queensland, Sir George Bowen. The proclamation announcing Queensland as a separate colony was read from its balcony on 10 December, 1859. It became the residence of the Dean of Brisbane in 1910. Further south along Ann Street is **All Saints' Church**, which dates from 1861.

Earlystreet Historical Village is a fine collection of Queensland buildings located at 75 McIlwraith Avenue, Norman Park, east of the city centre. Among the buildings are reconstructions of Stromness, one of the first houses at Kangaroo Point, and the ballroom and billiard-room of Auchenflower House. The village is open daily.

To the north of the city in Bowen Hills, another building open to the public is **Miegunyah**, a traditional Queensland house with verandahs and ironwork. Located in Jordan Terrace, it is home to the Queensland Women's Historical Society.

There are very few terrace houses in Brisbane, but a row at the **Normanby Junction** has been lovingly restored and incorporates two restaurants. A similar development has occurred on **Coronation Drive**. Brisbane's more impressive houses, including the famous old 'Queenslanders', are scattered throughout the inner-city suburbs. Many small cottages in the **Spring Hill**, **Paddington** and **Red Hill** areas are being restored. The **Regatta Hotel** on the river at Coronation Drive is worth a visit, and the famous **Breakfast Creek Hotel** has a popular outdoor area serving excellent steaks and beer 'off-the-wood' (straight from the keg).

The main city department stores are located in **Queen Street**, which, between Edward and George streets, is a mall containing four large shopping complexes, boutiques, entertainment centres, the major department stores, restaurants and taverns. Most shops in the city are open seven days a week and for late-night shopping on Fridays. Three of the city's most popular markets are the kilometre-long stretch of Sunday craft markets at the **Riverside Centre** in Eagle Street; the **South Bank Markets**, held on Friday nights, Saturdays and Sundays; and the Saturday markets in **Brunswick Street**, Fortitude Valley.

For the sports enthusiast, Brisbane's famous 'Gabba' ground at Woolloongabba hosts cricket and AFL football matches. There are horseracing venues

ACCOMMODATION

HOTELS
Brisbane International Hilton
190 Elizabeth St, Brisbane
(07) 3234 2000

Conrad International
130 William St, Brisbane
(07) 3306 8888

Hotel Grand Chancellor
cnr Leichhardt St and
Wickham Tce, Spring Hill
(07) 3831 4055

Novotel Brisbane
200 Creek St, Brisbane
(07) 3309 3309

The Heritage Hotel
cnr Edward and Margaret sts,
Brisbane
(07) 3221 1999

ITT Sheraton Brisbane Hotel and Towers
249 Turbot St, Brisbane
(07) 3835 3535

FAMILY AND BUDGET
Albert Park Hotel
551 Wickham Tce, Spring Hill
(07) 3831 3111

Kingsford Hall Private Hotel
114 Kingsford Smith Dr., Hamilton
(07) 3862 1317

Queensland Countrywomen's Association Club
89–95 Gregory Tce, Spring Hill
(07) 3831 8188

South Bank Backpackers
73 Melbourne St, South Brisbane
(07) 3844 0022

Story Bridge Motor Inn
321 Main St, Kangaroo Point
(07) 3393 1433

MOTEL GROUPS: BOOKINGS
Best Western 1800 22 2166
Flag 13 2400
Travelodge, Centra and Parkroyal 1300 363 300

This list is for information only; inclusion is not necessarily a recommendation.

at Doomben and Eagle Farm. Albion Park is the venue for trotting and greyhound racing. The **ANZ Stadium** at Nathan and the Chandler aquatic centre, indoor sports hall and velodrome were all built for the 1982 Commonwealth Games. The ANZ Stadium is now the home of the rugby-league premiers, the Brisbane Broncos. Rugby-union headquarters are at the **Ballymore Stadium** at Herston. The Brisbane Entertainment Centre at Boondal is the basketball venue.

The **King George Square** facing the **City Hall** is a popular spot for watching the world go by. The **Anzac Memorial** and **Eternal Flame** is located opposite **Central Railway Station** with its towering backdrop, the ITT Sheraton Brisbane Hotel and Towers.

Across Victoria Bridge lies **South Bank Parklands**, 16 hectares of redeveloped and landscaped parklands with walking and bicycle paths, a constructed beach, a series of canals where the South Ships cruise, and several restaurants. The Gondwana Rainforest Sanctuary, the Butterfly and Insect House and Our World Environment Display are special features within the parklands.

For the art lover, the **Queensland Art Gallery** is in the **Queensland Cultural Centre** at South Bank. This impressive gallery includes significant Australian, British and European collections. The Cultural Centre also houses an auditorium, the award-winning **Queensland Performing Arts Complex** with three theatres, along with the **State Library of Queensland** and the **Queensland Museum**. The **Brisbane City Gallery** in the City Hall, the **Museum of Contemporary Art** at Petrie Terrace and the University of Queensland Art Gallery in the Queensland Cultural Centre at South Bank are

excellent. Private galleries include the Philip Bacon Galleries at New Farm; the Red Hill Gallery at Red Hill and the Victor Mace Fine Art Gallery in Milton. Galleries in the central city include the Australian Perspectives Fine Art Gallery in Mary Street and Queensland Aboriginal Creations in George Street. In Fortitude Valley, Fusions Gallery has ceramics and glasswork by local artists for sale and the Fire-Works Gallery in Ann Street features Aboriginal art. The **Leichhardt Street** area of Spring Hill has developed as a centre for arts and crafts enthusiasts.

The annual Brisbane Festival, a feast of art, craft and cultural activities, occurs in late September and draws large crowds to the city. Also held annually are the Royal Brisbane National Show (known as 'The Ekka') held at the RNA Showgrounds in August and the Spring Hill Fair (usually on the second weekend in September) in the streets of Spring Hill. The Brisbane International Film Festival is held in August and the Queensland Winter Racing Carnival – sport, racing, and visual and performing arts – spans May and June. The **Brisbane Convention and Exhibition Centre** located on the corner of Glenelg and Merivale streets in South Brisbane is also the venue for a variety of exhibitions.

Queensland University is on a superb site on the river at St Lucia. It is built mainly from Helidon freestone. A second university, **Griffith**, is in beautiful bush country in the southern suburb of Nathan. The **Queensland University of Technology** is located on several campuses throughout Brisbane.

The present **Government House** at Bardon was built in 1865 for Johann Heussler, who brought German farmworkers to the State; it became the official residence for the State Governor in 1920.

The Queensland Museum, adjacent to the Art Gallery in the Queensland Cultural Centre at South Bank, features a natural history collection and displays explaining Brisbane's and Queensland's folk history. Popular exhibits are the life-size dinosaurs and the world of Queensland's marine turtles. The **Science Centre** in George Street has hands-on interactive displays. The main Post Office in Queen Street has a museum of telegraphic material. The **Queensland Maritime Museum** in Stanley Street, South Brisbane, incorporates the old South Brisbane dry dock containing the World War II frigate HMAS *Diamantina*. Nearby are the popular **Riverside Esplanade walking and bicycle paths** leading to Kangaroo Point, with access to picnic areas.

The **City Botanic Gardens** next to Parliament House are magnificent. **New Farm Park**, which is close to the city via Fortitude Valley, has 12 000 rose bushes, jacaranda trees that blossom in October and November, and poinciana trees flowering in November and December.

Brisbane is famous for its seafood, and several good restaurants allow you the opportunity to come to grips with the awesome Queensland mudcrab, Moreton Bay bugs, tiger prawns, delicious reef fish and barramundi. Popular riverside venues include the Eagle Street Pier precinct and Bretts Wharf in Hamilton. **Chinatown** in Fortitude Valley offers distinctive shopping and dining.

Because of Brisbane's vast size (the Brisbane City Council controls an area of 12 200 hectares), the city's public transport network is extensive. Council buses take most of the load, while modern electric air-conditioned trains run to many areas. Timetables and brochures are available from Brisbane Transport; (07) 3403 3880. **City Sights** tours operate narrated tours of the major attractions in colourful tram-style coaches collecting passengers at city sights stops every 40 minutes. There is also a daily City Heights service departing from the City Hall and stopping at attractions along the route to Mount Coot-tha lookout and botanical gardens. In the evenings there is a City Nights tour, offering spectacular views of the city lights. The City Cat vessels, operated by the Brisbane City Council, criss-cross the river, travelling downstream to Breakfast Creek and upstream to Queensland University. Small ferries supplement this new service, operating from the city to Kangaroo

BRISBANE ON FOOT

A series of self-guide heritage trails has been prepared by the Brisbane City Council. In addition to the central business district, heritage trails exist for Brisbane's riverfront, Fortitude Valley, Toowong Cemetery and some of the older residential suburbs including Hamilton, New Farm, Paddington, Windsor and Wynnum-Manly. Pamphlets are available from the Brisbane Visitors and Convention Bureau information centres or Brisbane City Council.

- **Step into the Past:** 2½-hour historic walking tour, daily; bookings essential.

For further information contact the Brisbane Visitors and Convention Bureau, City Hall, King George Square; (07) 3221 8411.

Point, Thornton Street, New Farm Park and South Bank. Golden Mile operates river and bay cruises from North Quay, and Mirimar Cruises goes to Lone Pine Koala Sanctuary. Tours also operate from Breakfast Creek to the historic penal settlement on Helena Island. The paddlewheeler *Kookaburra Queen* cruises the river daily.

Several of Brisbane's attractions lie just outside the city area. There are good views from the surrounding hills particularly from **Bartley's Hill Lookout** at Hamilton. The **Historical Observation Tower** at Breakfast Creek Walk in Newstead, a 33-metre tower, affords outstanding views of the city.

The *Southern Cross*, Sir Charles Kingsford Smith's Fokker tri-motor aircraft, is on display at Brisbane Airport in Airport Drive. Just across the river is **Fort Lytton**, a garrison built in 1880 and opened to visitors in 1989. Brisbane's **Lone Pine Koala Sanctuary**, is 11 kilometres away at Fig Tree Pocket. **Amazons Aquatic Adventureland** at Jindalee, 12 kilometres from the city, has family water-slide entertainment and picnic areas. **Brisbane Forest Park** at The Gap, 12 kilometres from the city, provides 'bushranger' and wildlife tours in its 25 000 hectares of bushland. Tours of the Castlemaine Perkins brewery are available.

The **Australian Woolshed**, 14 kilometres north-west of the city, features trained rams, sheep-shearing demonstrations and tame koalas and kangaroos. At Kallangur, north of Brisbane, **Alma Park Zoo** exhibits native and exotic species of fauna, and has beautiful gardens.

For further information on Brisbane, contact the Brisbane Visitors and Convention Bureau, City Hall, King George Square; (07) 3221 8411, or visit the BVCB Information Booth in the Queen Street Mall.

Mount Coot-tha

View from the summit of Mount Coot-tha

Located only 8 kilometres from Brisbane's city centre, Mount Coot-tha offers city dwellers an attractive breathing space. Brisbane's newest botanic gardens are in the foothills of Mount Coot-tha. The tropical display house, in the form of a futuristic-looking dome, has a superb display of tropical plants and is open daily. The arid-zone garden and cactus house are nearby. The gardens also include a lagoon and pond, a demonstration garden, ornamental trees and shrubs, areas of Australian and tropical rainforest, and a large collection of Australian native plants.

Situated in the Botanic Gardens is the Sir Thomas Brisbane Planetarium. The largest planetarium in the country, it accommodates 144 people and was named after the 'founder of organised science in Australia'. When Sir Thomas was Governor of New South Wales, he set up an astronomical observatory in 1821 at Parramatta. His observations resulted in the publication of *The Brisbane Catalog of Stars*. Various programmes are shown at the Planetarium's Star Theatre. A representation of the night sky is projected on to the interior of the dome and the movements of the sun, moon and stars are described as they occur. Additional projectors are used to produce special effects in order to demonstrate more unusual phenomena in the sky. Programmes are shown in both the afternoon and evening, Wednesday to Sunday, with an additional afternoon show at weekends. Children under six are not admitted. The planetarium complex also contains an observatory that is used by members of the public, by prior arrangement, to view the day or night sky.

There are many picnic and barbecue areas at Mount Coot-tha, including a particularly attractive spot for walks at the J.C. Slaughter Falls. The Mount Coot-tha Summit Restaurant on Sir Samuel Griffith Drive is open daily for lunch and dinner. The Kuta Café and Craft Shop serves morning and afternoon teas and lunches. The view from the summit is superb, across the city and Moreton Bay, and sometimes as far as the Lamington Plateau in the south and the Glass House Mountains in the north.

Perhaps the best view of all from Mount Coot-tha is at night when the lights of the city of Brisbane are spread out before you – a breath-taking sight. Even if you have only one evening in Brisbane, it is worth making the short trip to the lookout to take in this memorable scene.

For further information, contact the Brisbane Visitors and Convention Bureau, City Hall, King George Square; (07) 3221 8411. **Map references:** 492 D13, 494 D1.

TOURS from Brisbane

Spring Bluff station at Toowoomba, 127 kilometres west of Brisbane

QUEENSLAND

There is a variety of things to see and do around Brisbane. Most tours can be done in one day, but some are more suited to an overnight stop.

The Brisbane forest parks concept is being developed as breathing space for the city, and many new national parks have been declared in the surrounding area. As well as visiting the beaches, take advantage of these parks – they are well worth a visit.

Wynnum-Manly and Redland Bay

40 km from Brisbane via Wynnum

You will not have to drive far to enjoy the bayside suburbs of Wynnum and Manly, south-east of Brisbane on the shores of Moreton Bay. Manly has a marina and is the headquarters of the Royal Queensland Yacht Squadron. Continue on to Redland Bay, a peaceful holiday town. The area is famed for its market gardens and the Strawberry Festival (at the Cleveland Showground on the first weekend in September). Wayside stalls sell fruit and flowers at weekends. Boats can be hired all along this coast, so that you can do your own exploring, go fishing or visit the islands of Moreton Bay. **See also:** Entry for Redland Bay in A–Z listing.

Redcliffe

41 km from Brisbane via Gympie Road

Drive to Redcliffe via Petrie and a detour to the North Pine Dam. The Redcliffe Peninsula is almost completely surrounded by the waters of Moreton Bay. The sandy beaches are safe for swimming and the fishing is good. High on the volcanic red cliffs there are spectacular views far across Moreton Bay to Moreton and Stradbroke islands, famous for their natural surroundings and mountainous sand dunes. **See also:** Entry for Redcliffe in A–Z listing.

Bribie Island

69 km from Brisbane via Bruce Highway

See: Fraser and Moreton Bay islands.

Mount Glorious

45 km from Brisbane via Waterworks Road

One of the more interesting short drives from Brisbane is through mountainous country due west of the city to Mount Glorious, via Mount Nebo, and then back via Samford. From Mount Glorious it is possible to extend this drive to take in the delights of Lake Wivenhoe, only 15 kilometres further on. There are spectacular views of the mountainous Brisbane Forest Park. Stop at McPhee's and Jolly's lookouts before arriving at the pretty town of Mount Nebo. Hear bellbirds and whipbirds in the Manorina section of D'Aguilar National Park. At Mount Glorious, in the Maiala section of the same park, there are many long and short self-guide walks through the lush rainforest. Local Aboriginal history is recorded on a bush trail at Bellbird Grove in Brisbane Forest Park. At the information centre for the park (60 Mount Nebo Rd, The Gap; (07) 3300 4855), you can see exhibits of Queensland's native freshwater fish and other animals at the Walkabout Creek aquatic study centre, and then dine in the restaurant upstairs.

The Gold Coast

70 km from Brisbane via the Pacific and Gold Coast highways

See: The Gold Coast.

Gold Coast Hinterland

70 km from Brisbane via the Pacific Highway and Nerang

The McPherson Ranges just west of the Gold Coast have some of Australia's finest scenery.

Mount Tamborine

75 km from Brisbane via the Pacific Highway

Mount Tamborine, some 30 kilometres from Oxenford, is a retreat from the bustle of Brisbane. Here walking tracks lead through the rainforest – where palms, staghorns, elkhorns, ferns and orchids grow in profusion – to waterfalls and lookouts. There are picnic and barbecue facilities here and in the nearby Tamborine National Park. **See also:** National Parks.

The Big Pineapple Complex

96 km from Brisbane via the Bruce Highway

Six kilometres south of Nambour, the Big Pineapple complex is the largest and most popular tourist attraction on the Sunshine Coast. The Big Pineapple itself is a 16-metre replica of a pineapple, with a top-floor observation deck offering views of the plantation of tropical fruit below. A restaurant, fruit market and large art and craft shop are nearby. A sugarcane train travels through more than 40 hectares of pineapple, mango, avocado and sugar cane plantations and visits an attractive animal farm. The Nutmobile takes visitors to the Magic Macadamia, a giant nut replica. Here the complete process, from cracking the nut to the final product, is revealed. The Harvest Boatride offers an entertaining and educational tour of agricultural/horticultural history and visions of the future.

Lamington National Park

112 km from Brisbane via the Mt Lindesay or Pacific highways, and Canungra

Lamington National Park is one of the wildest and finest in Queensland. On a plateau in the Green Mountain section of the park is O'Reilly's Rainforest Guest House, and it is worth making this a full weekend's trip, though an advance booking should be made. A maze of walking tracks and an elevated treetop walkway allow you to see the area's many attractions. But if walking is not for you, you can just sit in the sun, breathe in the refreshing mountain air and admire the superb scenery or feed the birds. The subtropical rainforest has an abundance of wildlife, which has been protected for many years. You can walk from O'Reilly's to Binna Burra Mountain Lodge, a distance of 22 kilometres. It is a much longer trip by road. Binna Burra Mountain Lodge is a good base from which to enjoy the great variety of walks in the area, but a sensible pair of shoes is a must. Bring a jumper

too – it can get cold even in summer. If you plan to spend a weekend wilderness camping in the mountains, a permit is necessary and can be obtained from the national park office at Binna Burra or Green Mountain. Information is available at Canungra information centre about the many walks and places of interest on the way. Those who prefer more comfort can stay overnight at the Binna Burra Mountain Lodge, but book in advance. **See also:** National Parks.

Toowoomba

127 km from Brisbane via the Warrego Highway

A comfortable distance from Brisbane for a day trip, this drive takes you past some small towns and old farmhouses. Stop at Marburg on the way to admire the old timber pub with its wrought iron and lattice verandah largely unaltered since it was built in the 1880s. Toowoomba's most popular tourist attraction is its parks and gardens with their magnificent deciduous trees including oaks, elms, plane trees and poplars. The gardens are best seen during September when the city has its Carnival of Flowers. The carnival is usually held during the last week of September, and includes a procession, dancing and entertainment in the streets. A tourist drive around the city, laid out by the city council with floral direction markers, is a must for visitors. You could return to Brisbane via the New England and Cunningham highways. **See also:** Entry for Toowoomba in A–Z listing.

The Jondaryan Woolshed Historical Museum and Park

176 km from Brisbane via the Warrego Highway

The Jondaryan Woolshed, between Oakey and Bowenville, was built in 1859, with space for 88 blade shearers to handle some 200 000 sheep a season. Now ideal for an outing for all the family, it has been developed as a working memorial to the early pastoral pioneers. As well as the woolshed, you can visit the blacksmith's shop, the one-roomed schoolhouse and the dairy. There is also a fascinating collection of old agricultural machinery. Open every day except Good Friday and Christmas Day; conducted tours operate daily.

The Bunya Mountains

250 km from Brisbane via Brisbane Valley and D'Aguilar highways

This three-hour drive is often spectacular, but hairpin bends make the journey unsuitable for cars towing caravans or trailers. Because there is so much to see along the way, it would be wise to stay overnight either camping or at a hotel. On the way, Savages Crossing is a good place for a picnic. Bellevue Homestead at Coominya is worth a detour as it is a major National Trust project, the homestead having been moved from its original site, rebuilt and restored. Further on, stop to see the Koomba Falls at Maidenwell. There are many more places to visit on the way to the mountains, all of which are fully signposted. Most of the area is set aside as the Bunya Mountains National Park; there are two major camping sites in the park and bushwalkers will enjoy the excellent graded tracks. If you have time and do not want to camp, continue on to Kingaroy, the peanut-growing area, where there is plenty of accommodation. **See also:** National Parks.

The Sunshine Coast

100 km from Brisbane to its nearest point via the Bruce Highway

See: The Sunshine Coast.

Beerwah and Buderim past the Glass House Mountains

100 km from Brisbane via the Bruce Highway and the Glass House Mountains Tourist Road

When travelling past the Glass House Mountains, you will see the ten spectacular trachyte peaks named by Captain Cook as he sailed up the coast in 1770. The sun shining on the rockfaces reminded him of glasshouses in his native Yorkshire. Further north from Beerwah is the Queensland Reptile and Fauna Park, where venomous snakes, including taipans, and lizards of all sizes, can be seen. Continue on through Landsborough to Buderim. Visit the Pioneer Cottage, one of Buderim's earliest houses (it contains many of its original furnishings from last century), the art galleries and the festive markets. **See also:** Entries for Buderim and Landsborough in A–Z listing.

The Gold Coast

The Gold Coast, Australia's premier holiday destination, consists of 70 kilometres of coastline boasting 42 kilometres of golden, unpolluted beaches stretching from South Stradbroke Island in the north to Coolangatta in the south, with a lush subtropical backdrop in the Gold Coast hinterland – the 'green behind the gold'.

Only one hour's drive south of Brisbane, this international resort city offers a multitude of constructed and natural attractions, and, of course, superb surfing beaches – Main Beach, Surfers Paradise, Broadbeach, Mermaid Beach, Miami, Burleigh Heads, Tallebudgera, Palm Beach, Currumbin, Tugun, Kirra and Coolangatta.

With almost 300 days of sunshine each year – an average winter maximum of 21°C and an average summer maximum of 28°C – the Gold Coast region is the country's holiday playground, attracting almost four million visitors annually.

Accommodation caters for all budgets, ranging from international five-star-plus hotels and resorts to hotels, motels, apartments, guest houses, caravan parks, camping grounds and backpackers' hostels. It is estimated there are more than 35 000 rooms with more than 55 000 beds available on the Gold Coast. A variety of theme parks, sporting facilities, restaurants, shops, nightlife and entertainment, guarantee to satisfy all tastes. The Gold Coast is said to have the largest number of restaurants per square kilometre in Australia.

With its towering skyline, beachfront esplanade, glitz and glamour, Surfers Paradise is the hub of the central Gold Coast region, while the Gold Coast hinterland is a subtropical hideaway with numerous national parks and reserves complete with massive trees, spectacular views, cascading waterfalls and bush walks only 30 minutes from the hustle and bustle of the city.

Moving west from the coastline into the hinterland, the terrain climbs steadily to 1000 metres and breathtaking scenery in the Numinbah Valley and at Springbrook. Highlights here include Canyon Lookout; the 190-metre Purlingbrook Falls; Wunburra Lookout; and the Hinze Dam.

In the Numinbah Valley is the Natural Arch, a spectacular waterfall which plummets through a stone archway into a rock pool below. This picturesque area is excellent for picnics, barbecues and bush walks.

Tamborine Mountain's rainforests and Lamington National Park provide the backdrop to Beaudesert Shire. The more adventurous are easily tempted into tackling the rugged ranges and gorges of Lamington National Park, the largest preserved natural subtropical rainforest in Australia, with 160 kilometres of walking tracks.

At **Oxenford:** Warner Bros Movie World, based on the famous Hollywood movie set, is a theme park and part of a fully operational movie set. Close by is Wet 'n' Wild, Australia's largest aquatic fun park.

At **Coomera:** To the north is Dreamworld, a theme park with 12 'themed worlds' including Tiger Island, and the Tower of Terror. Nearby is the exclusive

Monorail at Sea World, a major attraction on the Gold Coast

The Gold Coast Highway separates the high-rise buildings and the beach at Surfers Paradise

Sanctuary Cove residential resort, which incorporates the Hyatt Regency Hotel, two golf courses and a marina. Just south is Cable Sports World and Pine Ridge Environmental Park at Coombabah.

At Main Beach: Sea World, on The Spit, is the largest marine park in the southern hemisphere. Its world-class attractions include performing dolphins, a monorail, a skyway, water-ski ballet, helicopter rides, a replica of the *Endeavour*, the Old Fort, a corkscrew roller-coaster, and for a journey into the unknown, board a 'lifeboat' and enter the Bermuda Triangle. It adjoins the Sea World Nara Resort. Also on The Spit overlooking the Broadwater is Fisherman's Wharf, a complex of specialty shops, outdoor cafes and restaurants. The Gold Coast's major cruise boats operate from its jetties. Mariner's Cove is also along the Broadwater with its marina, shopping and restaurants, and Marina Mirage, an upmarket shopping and boating complex, is opposite the Sheraton Mirage Hotel. Visitors can enjoy a variety of water sports on the Broadwater.

At Surfers Paradise: Attractions include Ripleys Believe It or Not Museum, Funtasia family entertainment centre, resort shopping, restaurants, many international hotels, numerous nightclubs and the sport of 'people watching'. The Gold Coast Arts Centre is near Surfers Paradise at Bundall.

At Broadbeach: Pacific Fair shopping resort is on the Nerang River. Conrad Jupiters hotel and casino, is linked by monorail to the Oasis Shopping Resort and the Pan Pacific Hotel. Cascade Park and Gardens on the Nerang River is ideal for picnicking. View the area by an open-cockpit flight in a Tiger Moth plane.

At Mermaid Beach: A huge cinema complex is located near family restaurants and a variety of specialty restaurants.

At Burleigh Heads: Burleigh Knoll Conservation Park, Burleigh Head National Park and Fleay's Wildlife Park are all worth a visit.

Inland at **Mudgeeraba** are the Gold Coast War Museum with indoor and outdoor displays of army memorabilia, Skirmish, Movie Militaria and Balloon Down Under for balloon rides over the Gold Coast.

At Robina: Robina Town Centre, one of Queensland's largest shopping complexes, and Balloon Walk, Australia's only permanently moored hot-air balloon offers 360°-views of the Gold Coast.

At **Tallebudgera:** Playroom rock venue.

At **Currumbin:** Feed the thousands of lorikeets that flock to the Currumbin Sanctuary daily. The Chocolate Expo Factory is opposite. Visit Olson's Bird Gardens, the Currumbin Rock Pool. and the Cougal section of Springbrook National Park. On the way, visit Schusters Lookout and further south-west Arthur Freeman Lookout – both offer superb views over Currumbin Valley.

At **Coolangatta:** Beach House Plaza links the main street with the beachfront; and the lighthouse at Point Danger.

At **Tweed Heads:** Across the border from Coolangatta, visit the Minjungbal Aboriginal Culture Centre. It is also home to some of Australia's largest sports and entertainment clubs.

For further information contact the Gold Coast Tourism Bureau, 64 Ferry Ave, Surfers Paradise; (07) 5592 2699. There are information centres at Cavill Mall, Surfers Paradise, (07) 5538 4419, and Beach House, Marine Pde, Coolangatta, (07) 5536 7765. **See also:** entries for Coolangatta, Currumbin, Southport and Tweed Heads in A–Z listing. **Map references:** 497 O13, 499, 505 R10.

QUEENSLAND from A to Z

Airlie Beach, on the beautiful Whitsunday coast

Airlie Beach

Pop. 2524

MAP REF. 507 K3

Airlie Beach is the centre of the thriving Whitsunday coast. Located 20 km from the Bruce Hwy at Proserpine, Airlie overlooks the Whitsunday Passage and islands, and has its own beach and marina. From Airlie and Shute Harbour passengers can travel to the outer reef and reef-fringed islands. It is a holiday town offering several major resorts with all facilities, top-grade holiday accommodation and a large range of activities and services for visitors. **Of interest:** Vic Hislop's Shark Show, 13 Waterson Rd. Community market each Sat. on foreshore. Easter: Whitsunday Masters Games. July: Festival (for start of whale-watching season). Sept.: Whitsunday Fun Race. **In the area:** Neighbouring Shute Harbour and islands of Whitsunday Passage. Fishing trips to nearby coastal wetlands and crocodile safaris available. Conway National Park, 5 km SE, renowned for its natural beauty and habitat of the rock wallaby and many species of butterfly. **Tourist information:** Beach Plaza, The Esplanade; (079) 46 6673. **Accommodation:** 1 hotel, 4 motels, 4 apartment complexes, 7 hostels, 6 cara./camp. parks.

Allora

Pop. 950

MAP REF. 496 E12, 505 N10

North of Warwick just off the Toowoomba road, the picturesque town of Allora is in a prime agricultural area. **Of interest:** Historical museum, Drayton St. Apr.: 500 Endurance Motor Race. June: Allora Apex Auction. **In the area:** Historic National Trust-classified Talgai Homestead (c. 1860), 6 km W, offers meals and accommodation. Historic Glengallan Homestead, 15 km N on the New England Hwy, (open 4th Sun. each month except Dec. or by appt; contact Tourist information). Goomburra State Forest, 35 km E, in the western foothills of the Great Dividing Range. Main Range National Park, 50 km E, part of the Scenic Rim – a crescent of national parks and mountains around Brisbane – has extensive walking tracks through dense rainforest, camping and picnic areas. **Tourist information:** 49 Albion St (New England Hwy), Warwick; (076) 61 3122. **Accommodation:** Limited.

Aramac

Pop. 326

MAP REF. 506 C10, 513 Q10

This small pastoral town is 67 km N of Barcaldine. Originally called Marathon, it was renamed by explorer William Landsborough as an acronym of Sir Robert Ramsay Mackenzie, Colonial Secretary in 1866 and Premier of Qld (1867–8). **Of interest:** Tramway Museum housing old engines and rolling stock, McWhannell St. **In the area:** Lake Dunn, 68 km NE, for swimming, fishing and birdwatching. **Tourist information:** Post Office, Gordon St; (076) 51 3147. **Accommodation:** 1 hotel, 1 cara./camp. park.

Atherton

Pop. 5206

MAP REF. 503 C12, 509 M7

Atherton is the agricultural hub of the Atherton Tableland. This farming town is 100 km SW of Cairns on the Kennedy Hwy and is surrounded by a patchwork of dense rainforest that abounds in varied birdlife and tropical vegetation. The fertile basalt soil, the gently undulating terrain and abundant rainfall have made the region the centre of the dairy and grain-growing industries that are still the major income-earners. The area bounded by the towns of Atherton, Kairi and Tolga is particularly suited to growing tomatoes, avocados, potatoes, peanuts, maize and other grains.

Of interest: Chinese Joss House and Old Post Office Gallery, Herberton Rd. Fascinating Facets and the Crystal Caves mineral museum, Main St, has a constructed underground attraction comprising tunnels and chambers, and displays of minerals and gemstones. **In the area:** Picturesque Atherton Tableland (surrounding area), one of oldest land masses in Australia, features rainforest-fringed volcanic crater lakes, spectacular waterfalls and fertile farmlands. Bushwalking at Halloran Hill, 3 km E; Baldy Mountain, 10 km SW; Wongabel State Forest, 8 km SE. At Tolga, 5 km N: woodworks, peanut factory and craft. At Herberton, 19 km SW: Foster's Winery; Historical Village with more than 30 restored buildings. Mt Hypipamee National Park, 26 km S, includes sheer-sided explosion crater 124 m deep. At Malanda, 25 km SE: market, in 19th century Majestic Theatre, 3rd Sat. each month; Agricultural Show in June. Signposted rainforest walks and the Jungle Interpretive Centre at Malanda Falls Conservation Park on the edge of town. McHugh Road Lookout, 20 km S of Malanda. Beautiful crater lakes, lakes Eacham and Barrine, in Crater Lakes National Park, 25 km E; cruises available on Lake Barrine. Historic Yungaburra, 13 km E. The Curtain Fig Tree, 2.5 km SW of Yungaburra, renowned for its spectacular aerial roots in curtain formation. Lake Tinaroo, 15 km NE, for swimming, fishing, water-skiing and sailing; houseboats available for hire. **Tourist information:** cnr Mabel and Vernon sts; (070) 91 4222. **Accommodation:** 4 motels, 1 hostel, 3 cara./camp. parks. **See also:** Atherton Tableland; The Far North.

Ayr   Pop. 8637

MAP REF. 506 H1, 509 Q13

This busy sugar town on the north side of the Burdekin delta is surrounded by intensively irrigated sugarcane fields, the most productive in Australia. The Burdekin River Irrigation Scheme, the lifeblood of the area, is the largest land and water conservation scheme in the State. **Of interest:** Ayr Nature Display, Wilmington St, fine collection of emu egg carvings, butterflies and beetles. Burdekin Cultural Complex, Queen St, includes 530-seat theatre, library and activities centre; distinctive 'Living Lagoon' in theatre forecourt. ESA

markets, Plantation Creek Park, 3rd Sun. each month. Oct.: Water Festival. **In the area:** Alva Beach, 18 km N, for beach walks, birdwatching, swimming and fishing; market 1st Sun. each month. Australian Institute of Marine Science at Cape Bowling Green, 20 km N. Hutchings Lagoon, 5 km NW, for watersports and on-shore picnics. Scenic drives in area, contact Tourist information. **Tourist information:** 161 Queen St; (077) 83 2888 or Tourist Hut, Plantation Creek Park, Queen St; (077) 83 5988. **Accommodation:** 6 hotels, 7 motels, 3 cara./camp. parks.

Babinda   Pop. 1268

MAP REF. 503 H13, 509 N7

A small sugar town, 57 km S of Cairns in the Wooroonooran National Park. In the park are the State's two highest mountains, Mt Bartle Frere (1615 m) and Mt Bellenden Ker (1582 m), and the Josephine Falls. **Of interest:** Deeral Cooperative, Nelson Rd, makes footwear and Aboriginal artifacts. **In the area:** The Boulders Wildland Park, 10 km W, offers excellent bushwalking along Babinda Creek below Mt Bartle Frere. Deeral, 14 km N, departure point for cruises through rainforest and the saltwater-crocodile haunts of the Mulgrave and Russell rivers. **Tourist information:** Far North Qld Promotion Bureau, cnr Grafton and Hartley sts, Cairns; (070) 51 3588. **Accommodation:** Limited.

Barcaldine   Pop. 1530

MAP REF. 506 C11, 513 Q11

A pastoral and rail town, Barcaldine is 108 km E of Longreach. All the streets are named after trees. **Of interest:** Mad Mick's Hoppers and Huts Funny Farm, cnr Pine and Bauhinia sts, features 8 settlers' buildings (including woolskin buyer's residence housing large doll collection and Cobb & Co. office now studio and art gallery), old shearing sheds with plant and press, and hand-reared wildlife. Historical Folk Museum, cnr Gidyes and Beech sts. 'Tree of Knowledge', ghost gum in Oak St, the meeting-place for 1891 shearers' strike, which resulted in the formation of the Australian Labor Party. Australian Workers' Heritage Centre, Ash St, features buildings containing tributes to Australia's workers in landscaped oasis around Burnsy's

Billabong. National Trust-classified buildings: masonic lodge, Beech St; Anglican Church, Elm St; Shire Hall, Ash St. During months Mar.–Oct., mini steam-train rides last Sun. each month; market at Tourist information, Oak St, 1st Sun. each month. **In the area:** Marraroo Gallery, 1 km W, unique Qld colonial and Aboriginal contemporary works. Wondae Deer Farm, 1 km W, a walk-through park with hand-feeding of animals and Kiddies Corner. Botanical walk, 9 km S, through variety of bushland. North Delta Station, 32 km E, outback station at work, also prolific birdlife and bushwalking; accommodation available. Red Mountain scenic drive from Richmond Hills station 55 km E. **Tourist information:** Oak St; (076) 51 1724. **Accommodation:** 6 hotels, 4 motels, 2 cara./camp. parks.

Bargara   Pop. 2703

MAP REF. 505 O2

This popular surf beach, 13 km E of Bundaberg, is patrolled by one of Qld's top surf clubs. Nearby beaches include Neilson Park and Kelly's. **In the area:** Mon Repos Conservation Park, 3 km N, largest and most accessible mainland loggerhead turtle rookery in Australia; giant sea turtles come ashore to lay their eggs, and babies hatch Nov.–Mar. In 1912 Bert Hinkler, engineering apprentice, flew to a height of 9 m in his home-made glider off Mon Repos Beach, marking the start of his distinguished career in aviation. **Tourist information:** cnr Bourbong and Mulgrave sts, Bundaberg; (071) 52 2333. **Accommodation:** 2 resorts, 1 hotel/motel, 5 motels, 12 apartment complexes.

Beaudesert   Pop. 4028

MAP REF. 497 L12, 505 P10

Beaudesert is a major market town on the Mt Lindesay Hwy, 66 km SW of Brisbane, near the NSW border. A road west leads to the Cunningham Hwy, and the road east leads to the Gold Coast via Tamborine. The district is noted for dairying, agriculture and beef cattle. **Of interest:** Historical Museum, Brisbane St. Popular Beaudesert race meetings. May: Rodeo. Sept.: Mini Royal Agricultural Show. **In the area:** Woollahra Farmworld, 8 km N at Gleneagle. Bigriggen Park, 30 km SW and Darlington Park, 12 km S, both

The hotel at Birdsville provides a resting place for travellers

recreation areas with picnic/barbecue facilities. Lamington National Park, 40 km S, subtropical rainforest with excellent graded walking tracks. At Tamrookum, 24 km SW, fine example of a timber church; guided tours by appt, contact Tourist information. Mt Barney National Park, 55 km SW, good hiking and camping. Unique flora and good views of Gold Coast at Tamborine Mountain, 35 km E. Nearby, dig for your own thunder eggs at Thunderbird Park, Cedar Creek. **Tourist information:** Historical Museum, 54 Brisbane St; (07) 5541 1284. **Accommodation:** 3 hotels, 3 motels, 1 cara. park.

Beenleigh   Pop. 16 388

MAP REF. 495 P13, 497 M10, 505 Q9
Midway between Brisbane and the Gold Coast, Beenleigh is now almost a satellite town of Brisbane. The Beenleigh Distillery on the Albert River has been producing rum from local sugar since 1884. Rocky Point Sugar Mill, 20 km E, is Australia's only privately-owned mill. **In the area:** Windaroo Golf Course, 2 km SW. At Yatala, 4 km S on Pacific Hwy, the Carlton Brewhouse has regular tours. Wolfdene, 10 km S, has one of the world's largest model railways. Coomera, 20 km S, has several family attractions including Dreamworld

family fun park. At Oxenford, 22 km S, Movie World theme park and Wet 'n' Wild aquatic fun park. **Tourist information:** Beenleigh Chamber of Commerce, 96 George St; (07) 3807 8077. **Accommodation:** 2 motels, 3 cara./camp. parks.

Biggenden   Pop. 686

MAP REF. 505 N4
This agricultural centre is near Mt Walsh National Park and The Bluff, 100 km SE of Bundaberg. Oct.: Rose Festival (odd-numbered years). **In the area:** Mt Walsh National Park, 8 km S, wilderness park popular with experienced bushwalkers. Coalstoun Lakes National Park, 20 km SW, protects two volcanic crater lakes. Coongara Rock (4WD access only), 20 km S, a volcanic core surrounded by rainforest. Mt Woowoonga, 10 km NW, forestry reserve with bushwalking and picnic/ barbecue facilities. Chowey Bridge (1905), 20 km NW, concrete arch railway bridge (one of two surviving in Aust.); picnic facilities nearby. Silver Bell Novelty Farm, 2 km N on Old Coach Rd, has buildings and collections; open by appt. **Tourist information:** Addy's Place, 26 Edward St; (071) 27 1440. **Accommodation:** 1 hotel, 1 hotel/ motel, 1 cara./camp. park.

Biloela   Pop. 6200

MAP REF. 505 K1, 507 N13
This modern, thriving town in the fertile Callide Valley is at the crossroads of the Burnett and Dawson hwys, 142 km S of Rockhampton. The name is Aboriginal for 'white cockatoo'. Underground water provides irrigation for lucerne, cotton, sorghum, wheat and sunflower crops. **Of interest:** Greycliffe Homestead, Gladstone Rd, open by appt; inquire at Tourist information. The Silo, Primary Industries Exhibition, Dawson Hwy, theme park combining display of hi-tech farming techniques with scenes of rural life. Bus tours of town on weekdays; inquire at Tourist information. June: Country and Western Muster. **In the area:** Callide Dam, 5 km NE, for good boating, fishing and swimming. Nearby, Callide open-cut coal mine and power station, tours available, inquire at Tourist information. Cotton Ginnery, 2 km N, tours Mar.–July. Lyle Semgreen Gems at Jambin, 32 km NW, open by appt. At Wowan, 75 km NW, Scrub Turkey Museum housed in old butter factory. Baralaba Historical Village, 100 km NW. Mt Scoria, 14 km S, solidified volcano core. Thangool, 10 km SE, renowned for its race days; Lucerne Festival held in Sept. **Tourist information:** Callide St; (079) 92 2405. **Accommodation:** 2 hotels, 4 motels, 4 cara./camp. parks. **See also:** Capricorn Region.

Birdsville   Pop. 102

MAP REF. 514 E5
The well-known Birdsville Track starts here on its long path into and across SA. In the 1870s the first settlers arrived in Birdsville, nearly 2000 km by road west of Brisbane, and at the turn of the century it was a thriving settlement with three hotels, three stores, several offices and a doctor. When the toll on cattle crossing the border near the town was abolished after Federation in 1901, prosperity declined and the population diminished. **Of interest:** Museum, McDonald St, features Australiana, domestic artifacts and working farm equipment. In Adelaide St: ruins of Royal Hotel, reminder of Birdsville's boom days; Birdsville Hotel, a hive of activity during Birdsville Races (held first weekend in Sept.) as population swells to about 5000. Hotel is an important overnight stop for tourists

travelling down the Track, west across the Simpson Desert (4WD country), north to Mount Isa or east to Brisbane. *Travel in this area can be hazardous, especially in the wet season (approx. Oct.–Mar.). Supplies of food and water should always be carried, as well as petrol, oil and spare parts. Motorists are advised to ring the Northern Roads Condition Hotline on (08) 11633 for information before departing down the Track, and to advise police if heading west to the Simpson Desert National Park; motorists should also read section on Outback Motoring.* The famous Flynn of the Inland founded the first Australian Inland Mission at Birdsville; there is still a well-equipped medical outpost, Adelaide St. Birdsville's water comes from a 1219-m-deep artesian bore; water emerges almost at boiling point and four cooling ponds bring it to a safe temperature. Electricity is supplied by two diesel-run generators. **In the area:** Waddi trees, 14 km N. Big Red, a huge sand dune, 35 km W. **Tourist information:** Brooklands Store, Adelaide St; (076) 56 3241. **Accommodation:** 1 hotel/motel, 1 cara./camp. park. **See also:** Channel Country.

Blackall   Pop. 1578

MAP REF. 506 D13, 513 R13, 515 R1

Centre of some of the most productive sheep and cattle country in central Qld, Blackall has many sheep and cattle studs in its vicinity. In 1892 the legendary Jackie Howe set the almost unbeliev-

The Simpson Desert, near the Birdsville Track

able record of shearing 321 sheep with blade shears in less than 8 hours, at Alice Downs Station, 25 km N. Blackall sank the first artesian bore in Qld in 1885. **Of interest:** Jackie Howe statue, at junction of Short and Shamrock sts. Also in Shamrock St: petrified tree stump, millions of years old; Major Mitchell Memorial clock. Behind the school in Thistle St is a replica of the Black Stump, a key reference point used by Thomas Frazer when he surveyed the area in 1886. Self-guide historic walk; property tours to view shearing; contact Tourist information for more details. June: Race Meeting. **In the area:** Steam-driven Blackall Wool Scour (1906), 4 km N on Clematis St; guided tours daily (Apr.–Nov.) or by appt, contact Tourist information for details. Idalia National Park, 100 km SW, renowned as habitat of the yellow-footed rock wallaby. **Tourist information:** Short St; (076) 57 4637. **Accommodation:** 4 hotels, 2 motels, 1 cara./camp. park.

Blackwater   Pop. 6760

MAP REF. 507 K11

This major mining town is 190 km W of Rockhampton on the Capricorn Hwy. The name comes from the discolouration of the local waterholes caused by ti-trees. Coal mined in the area is railed to Gladstone. The town's population is made up of workers of many nationalities and it displays what is claimed to be

the most varied collection of national flags this side of the United Nations. Cattle rearing is the traditional industry. **In the area:** Utah coal mine, 35 km S, tours available; bookings necessary. Expedition Range (732 m), 139 km SW near Springsure, discovered by Ludwig Leichhardt. At Comet, 30 km E, show and camp draft each Sept. Rainbow Falls in Blackdown Tableland National Park, 50 km SE, also picnic/barbecue facilities at Horseshoe Lookout and Mimosa Creek camping area. **Tourist information:** Clermont St, Emerald; (079) 82 4142. **Accommodation:** 3 motels, 2 cara./camp. parks. **See also:** Capricorn Region.

Boonah   Pop. 2100

MAP REF. 497 J12, 505 P10

Eighty-six km SW of Brisbane between Warwick and Ipswich, Boonah is the main town in the Fassifern district, a highly productive agricultural and pastoral area. Its location was noted as a 'beautiful vale' by the explorer and colonial administrator Captain Logan in 1827, and by the explorer Allan Cunningham in 1828. Boonah Country Markets in Springleigh Park, 2nd and 4th Sat. each month. **In the area:** Kabar, 10 km N, holds the popular Fassifern German Festival in Sept. At Templin, 5 km W, Historical Village; open Sun.–Thurs. Moogerah Peaks National Park, 12 km W. Lake Moogerah, 20 km SW, for water sports. In Main Range National Park, Cunninghams Gap lookout, 35 km W; walking tracks from lookout. Park is part of the Scenic Rim, a ring of mountains and national parks around Brisbane offering scenic drives (brochure available), bushwalking, trail-riding, rock-climbing, skydiving, water sports, picnic spots, recreation facilities, camping and accommodation. Coochin Coochin historic homestead, 14 km S; not open to public. **Tourist information:** Shire Offices, High St; (07) 5463 1599. **Accommodation:** 2 hotels, 1 motel, 1 cara./camp. park.

Boulia   Pop. 281

MAP REF. 512 F9

Near the Burke River, 360 km W of Winton, 295 km S of Mt Isa and 242 km E of the NT border, Boulia is the capital of the Channel Country. **Of interest:** Town's oldest house, Stone Cottage

Mystery craters, south-west of Bundaberg

(1880s), now a museum displaying Aboriginal artifacts and historic relics of region; Pituri St. In Herbert St: The Red Stump, warning travellers of dangers of Simpson Desert; artificial 'Min Min' light. Tree, near Boulia State School, thought to be last known corroboree tree of Pitta Pitta community. Varied birdlife around river. Aug.: Rodeo and Gymkhana. **In the area:** Mysterious Min Min light, first reportedly sighted near ruins of Min Min Hotel (130 km E). Cawnpore Hills, 140 km E, offer good views from summit. Ruins of police barracks, 19 km NE. The Burke and Wills tree, 110 km NE on the west bank of the Burke River. Diamantina Gates National Park, 150 km SE. *Travel by road in wet season can be difficult.* **See:** Outback Motoring. **Tourist information:** Herbert St; (077) 46 3386. **Accommodation:** 1 hotel, 1 cara./camp park. **See also:** Channel Country.

Bowen   Pop. 8312

MAP REF. 507 J2

A relaxed town exactly halfway between Mackay and Townsville, Bowen was named after the State's first Governor. The town was established in 1861 on the shores of Port Denison and was the first settlement in north Qld. It boasts an excellent climate with an average of 8 hours' sunshine daily. Bowen region is famous for its tomatoes, and particularly for its mangoes (in season Nov.–Jan.). **Of interest:** Signposted Golden Arrow tourist route starts at Salt Works, Don St. Twelve historical murals in central city area. Historical Museum, Gordon St. Aug.: Art, Craft and Orchid Expo. Oct. or Nov.: Coral Coast Festival. **In the area:** Excellent small bays (within 7 km of town and connected by walking tracks) for fishing, snorkelling and swimming. Collinsville coal mines, 82 km SW. **Tourist information:** Shire Offices, Herbert St; (077) 86 1866. **Accommodation:** 3 hotels, 5 motels, 3 hostels, 7 cara./camp. parks.

Buderim   Pop. 7499

MAP REF. 597 N1, 500 G9, 505 Q7

Buderim is a delightful town just inland from the Sunshine Coast, high on the fertile red soil of Buderim Mountain, and between the Bruce Hwy and Mooloolaba on the coast. It is a popular residential and retirement area. **Of interest:** In Burnett St: Blue Marble and Fine Art Images galleries; Buderim Festive Markets, in Old Ginger Factory (open daily; entertainment on weekends). Pioneer timber cottage (1876), one of Buderim's earliest houses, faithfully restored and retaining many original furnishings; Ballinger Rd. Historic town walk: brochure from pioneer cottage. Late Aug.–early Sept.: Buderim Festival. **In the area:** Buderim Forest Park, Quorn Close (just north of town) features waterfalls and walking tracks; wheelchair access to lower end, entry from Lindsay Rd. Rainforest walks at Foote Sanctuary, north-eastern end of town. Self-guide Forest Glen–Tanawah Tourist Drive includes Super Bee honey factory; Forest Glen Sanctuary (deer and native fauna); Moonshine Valley Winery, wines made from local tropical fruits. **Tourist information:** cnr Aerodrome Rd and Sixth Ave, Maroochydore; (07) 5479 1566. **Accommodation:** 2 motels, 2 cara./camp. parks.

Bundaberg   Pop. 38 074

MAP REF. 505 O2

Bundaberg, 368 km N of Brisbane, is the southernmost access point to the Great Barrier Reef and an important provincial city in the centre of the fertile Burnett River plains. The district is known for its sugar (the area's main crop), timber, beef production and, in more recent years, tomatoes, avocados and small crops. Sugar has been grown in the area since 1866. Raw sugar is exported from an extensive storage and bulk terminal facility at Port Bundaberg, 16 km NE. Industry sidelines include the distilling of the world famous Bundaberg Rum, refined sugar production, and the manufacture and export of advanced Austoft cane-harvester equipment. Bundaberg is a city of parks and botanical gardens; its wide streets lined with majestic figs, poincianas and bauhinias provide a brilliant display in spring and summer. The Burnett River flows through the city dividing it in two. Several famous Australians have called Bundy home: aviator Bert Hinkler, the first man to fly solo from England to Australia in 1928; singer Gladys Moncrieff; cricketer Don Tallon; and rugby league star Mal Meninga. **Of interest:** Alexandra Park and Zoo on river bank, Quay St: free zoo, historic band rotunda, cactus garden and children's playground. In Bourbong St: Whaling Wall, a 6-storey-high whale mural; Boyd's Antiquatorium, considered best Edison Gramophone collection in Australia. In East Bundaberg: Bundaberg Rum Distillery, Avenue St, offers guided tours daily to see Famous Aussie Spirit being

The Sunshine Coast

A chain of sundrenched beaches bathed by the cobalt-blue Pacific stretches from Rainbow Beach southward to the tip of Bribie Island to form Queensland's Sunshine Coast. This scenic coastal region, with its average winter temperature of 25°C, its leisurely pace and its wide variety of natural attractions and sporting facilities, offers an attractive alternative to the more commercialised Gold Coast.

While huge waves thunder onto white sand beaches to provide year-round surfing, the calmer waters of protected beaches ensure safe swimming, boating and water-skiing. Rivers and streams alive with fish lure the angler, and the foreshores of forest-fringed lakes become perfect picnic spots for the family.

The Sunshine Coast is blessed with many wonders of nature. The coloured sands of Teewah in the Cooloola section of **Great Sandy National Park**, between Tewantin and Rainbow Beach, rise in multi-coloured cliffs to over 200 metres. Geologists consider that these sandcliffs are over 40 000 years old and claim the main colouring is either the result of oxidisation or the dye of vegetation decay. However, an Aboriginal legend relates that the colours come from a rainbow serpent killed by a boomerang when it came to the rescue of a young woman. Another marvel of nature, the Glass House Mountains, were formed by giant cores of long-extinct volcanoes.

The **Noosa** area, at the northern end of the region, has facilities for fishing, boating and golf. Poised on the edge of Laguna Bay is the resort area of Noosa Heads, with its 2280-hectare Noosa National Park. This coastal park contains a network of walking tracks some winding through rainforests, others giving spectacular ocean views of such unusual rock formations as Hell's Gates, Paradise Caves, Lion's Rock, Devil's Kitchen and Witches' Cauldron. The park also houses an animal sanctuary and there are coastal lakes inhabited by elegant black swans, pelicans, ducks and cranes.

The southernmost town of the Sunshine Coast is **Caloundra**, meaning 'the beautiful place', where Aborigines once came down from the hills to feast on seafood.

The hinterland of the Sunshine Coast is like a huge cultivated garden, covered with pineapples,

The Big Pineapple complex, south of Nambour

sugarcane, ginger and citrus; dotted with dairy farms and enclosing within its folds cascading waterfalls, lush rainforests and bubbling streams. Looming majestically behind this garden of plenty is the Blackall Range, a world apart, with art and craft galleries, Devonshire-tea places, comfortable hotels and a feeling of 'olde England'. The scenic drive through the towns of Mapleton, Flaxton, Montville and Maleny is one of the best in south-east Queensland. The **Blackall Range National Park** is a must for nature lovers. The park includes the 80-metre Kondalilla Falls which drop into a valley of rainforest. The Mapleton Hotel offers authentic country-pub hospitality and panoramas from the traditional Queensland verandah. Visit the miniature English village with its castles, churches, thatched cottages and inns. A number of art and craft cottages surround Montville's Village Green. Take in the view from the picture window at the De'Lisle Gallery while being surrounded by works of art from the Sunshine Coast's best artists. Mary

Cairncross Park, at the southern end of the range, gives breathtaking views of the coast and the Glass House Mountains. **Nambour** is conveniently located, just off the Bruce Highway, for trips to the mountains of the Blackall Range or to the beach.

Just 7 kilometres south of Nambour is the Big Pineapple complex, a working plantation of pineapples and macadamia nuts, and home of the Big Pineapple.

The Sunshine Coast has accommodation to suit all tastes and budgets, from beachfront caravan parks through to luxury 5-star international hotels; and if you enjoy dining out, there are dozens of fine restaurants in the area.

For more information on the Sunshine Coast, contact Maroochy Shire Tourism, cnr Sixth Ave and Aerodrome Rd, Maroochydore; (07) 5479 1566. **See also:** National Parks and individual town entries for those parks and towns indicated by bold type. **Map references:** 497 N1, 500, 505 Q7.

Turtle Bay, a beautiful beach east of Cairns

QUEENSLAND

made. Schmeider's Cooperage and Craft Centre, demonstrations of ancient art of barrel-making; Alexandra St. Across the river in North Bundaberg: Botanical Gardens (Mt Perry Rd) include Hinkler House Memorial Museum (repository of aviation history), railway (steam-train rides around lakes), Bundaberg Historical Museum, and Sugar Museum in Fairymead House; Tropical Wines and Sunny Soft Drinks (unique tropical-fruit wine) also Mt Perry Rd; Baldwin Swamp Environmental Wetlands, Steindal St, East Bundaberg: boardwalks and pathways, waterlily lagoons, abundant birdlife and native fauna. Shalom College Markets, Fitzgerald St, West Bundaberg (each Sun. a.m.). West School Craft Markets, George St, West Bundaberg (2nd Sun. each month). Easter: Country Music Roundup. Sept.: Bundy in Bloom Festival. Oct.: Bundaberg Arts Festival. **In the area:** Cane fires, sugarcane harvesting season (July–Nov.). Moore Park (21 km NW) and Elliott Heads (18 km SE); fishing at Burnett Heads, Elliott Heads and Moore Park. Hummock Lookout, 7 km NE, for excellent views over city, cane-fields and coast. Bauers Gerbera Nursery, 10 km NE on road to Hummock Lookout. Tours to see migrating humpback whales, mid-Aug.–mid-Oct. At Burnett Heads, Poseidon Seashells, Rickets Rd, displays and sales of coral, seashells and local

shellcraft. Meadowvale Nature Park, 10 km W, features rainforest and walkway to Splitters Creek. Sharon Gorge, 12 km SW, features rainforest and walkway to Burnett River. Unexplained mystery, 25 km SW: 35 strange craters said to be 25 million years old. Dreamtime Reptile Reserve, 8 km S on Childers Rd. Avocado Grove, 10 km S, subtropical gardens. Near Childers, 45 km S, Isis Central Sugar Mill tours (July–Nov.). Cruises to Lady Musgrave Island, a true coral cay, on either MV *Lady Musgrave* (departs Bundaberg Port) or by seaplane with Bundaberg Seaplane Tours. Flights available to Lady Elliot Island resort. **Tourist information:** cnr Mulgrave and Bourbong sts; (071) 52 2333. **Accommodation:** Many hotels, 33 motels, 2 B&B, 8 cara./camp. parks.

Burketown   Pop. 200

MAP REF. 511 E8

The centre of rich beef country, Burketown is 230 km W of Normanton. The Gulf of Carpentaria is accessible by boat from Burketown. The town is near the Albert River and on the dividing line between the wetlands to the north and the beginning of the Gulf Savannah grass plains to the south. In Sept. and Oct. visitors can witness the unusual meteorological phenomenon locally known as Morning Glory – a tube-like

cloud formation that rolls across the sky. **Of interest:** 100-year-old bore, which issues boiling water. Burketown Hotel (1860s), originally customs house, oldest building in the Gulf. Burketown to Normanton telegraph line. Original post office. Easter: World Barramundi Handline-rod Fishing Championships. July: Rodeo and Races. **In the area:** Original Gulf meatworks just north of town. Cemetery, 2 km N, for insights into town's historic past. Nicholson River wetlands, 17 km W, breeding grounds for crocodiles, and variety of fish and birdlife. Escott Lodge, 17 km W, operating cattle station; camping and accommodation available. Lawn Hill National Park, 180 km SW, renowned for its rare vegetation, contains World Heritage-listed Riversleigh Fossil Field, an outstanding paleontological area. Landsborough Tree, 5 km E, blazed by explorer in 1862 when searching for Burke and Wills. Leichhardt Falls, 71 km SE: picturesque area, walks and flowing falls in rainy months. **Tourist information:** Burke Shire Council; (077) 45 5100. **Accommodation:** 1 hotel/motel, 1 motel (cabin-style), 1 cara./camp. park. **See also:** Gulf Savannah.

Burrum Heads   Pop. 770

MAP REF. 505 P3

This pleasant holiday resort on the foreshore of Hervey Bay, 45 km N of Maryborough off Bruce Hwy, offers excellent fishing. Easter: Burrum Heads Hotel/Motel Amateur Fishing Classic. **In the area:** Fishing villages of Buxton and Walkers Point on north side of Burrum River. Magnificent ocean beach at Woodgate, 90 km N (5 km N by boat). Nearby, Burrum Coast National Park, accessible from Woodgate, features walking tracks (including boardwalk), prolific birdlife, picnic spots and camping areas. **Tourist information:** Phillips Travel, 45 Burrum St; (071) 29 5211. **Accommodation:** 1 hotel/motel, 2 cara./camp. parks.

Caboolture   Pop. 12 716

MAP REF. 497 M4, 505 P8

Just off the Bruce Hwy, 46 km N of Brisbane, Caboolture is a developing commercial centre surrounded by subtropical fruit farms. Market at showground each Sun. June: Agricultural Show. July: St Peters Arts and Crafts Festival. Aug.: Caboolture Air Display (odd-numbered years). **In the area:** Caboolture Historical Village, faithfully restored; 2 km N on Beerburrum Rd. Glass House Mountains, 22 km N. Popular fishing towns of Donnybrook and Toorbul (20 and 22 km NE), and Beachmere (13 km SE). Woodford, 22 km NW, has a Folk Festival each Dec. Abbey Museum, 9 km E just off road to Bribie Island, traces growth of Western civilisation; Medieval Festival held in June. War Plane Museum, 2 km E, features restored fighter planes. Bribie Island, 23 km E, for family day-trips, picnic areas, fishing and safe swimming. **Tourist information:** 55 King St; (07) 5495 3122. **Accommodation:** 2 hotel/motels, 1 motel, 1 cara./camp. park.

Cairns   Pop. 64 463

MAP REF. 502, 503 F8, 509 N6

This modern, colourful, coastal city is capital of the tropical Far North. The cosmopolitan Esplanade traces the bay foreshore, and parks and gardens abound with colour and tropical trees and plants. Cairns' location is superb: the Great Barrier Reef to the east, the mountain rainforests and plains of the Atherton Tableland to the west, and palm-fringed beaches to the north and south. Cairns is one of the great black-marlin fishing locations and offers easy access to the Great Barrier Reef for anglers, snorkelling enthusiasts, scuba divers and visitors wishing to see the coral from glass-bottomed boats. **Of interest:** Cairns Red Explorer bus from Lake St, 9 stops at attractions in and around city. National Trust-listed Regional Gallery, cnr Shields and Abbott sts. Cairns Museum, cnr Lake and Shields sts, displays of Aboriginal, gold-rush, timber and sugarcane history. The McLeod Street Pioneer Cemetery honours local pioneers. Game-fishing boats moor at Marlin Marina, Marlin Jetty, Trinity Wharf and The Pier, end of Spence St. Reef Hotel Casino complex, Wharf St. Historical complex Freshwater Connection, 34 km NW, is also departure point for 100-year-old Kuranda Scenic Railway trip through Barron Gorge to rainforest village of Kuranda. Wetland areas including The Esplanade; opportunities for birdwatching. Flecker Botanic Gardens, Collins Ave, features plants used by Aborigines, exotic trees and shrubs, and 200 varieties of palm.

Walking track links gardens to Centenary Lakes Parkland. Tanks Centre, near Botanic Gardens, multi-purpose centre in revamped World War II oil storage tanks. Jack Barnes Bicentennial Mangrove Boardwalk, Airport Ave. Rainforest walk to top of Mt Whitfield, in park opposite airport. Royal Flying Doctor Service Visitor Centre, Junction St, Edge Hill. Doll and Bear Museum, Mayers St, Manunda. Rusty's Bazaar, Grafton and Sheridan sts: markets with local craft, home-made produce, plants, and new and secondhand goods (open Fri. p.m., Sat. and Sun. a.m.). Markets at the Pier, Sat. and Sun. July: Agricultural Show. Oct.: The Reef Festival. **In the area:** Bulk sugar terminal, Cook St, Portsmith, south of city centre, has guided tours during crushing season (June–Dec.). Marlin Coast, 26 km of spectacular coastline, extends from Machans Beach (10 km N) to Ellis Beach. Holloways Beach, 11 km N, popular seaside spot. Wild World and Outback Opal Mine, 22 km NW. Skyrail Rainforest Cableway, spectacular gondola ride through rainforest to Kuranda; departs from Caravonica Lakes Station, Smithfield, 11 km NE (return via Scenic Railway or vice versa). Award-winning Tjapukai Aboriginal Dance Theatre, adjacent to Caravonica Lakes Station, performs daily. Bushwalking, hiking, whitewater rafting and camping in delightful rural settings of Barron and Freshwater valleys, north and south of Cairns; attractions include the Crystal Cascades, Barron Gorge hydro-electric power station and Copperlode Dam (Lake Morris). Reef and islands can be explored by private charters, daily cruises and by air (seaplane and helicopter). Longer cruises to resort islands and reef on catamarans *Coral Princess*, *Reef Escape* and *Kangaroo Explorer*. Access to nearby Green, Fitzroy and Frankland islands on cruise vessels. Cairns also offers easy access to wilderness areas of Atherton Tableland, Daintree, Cape Tribulation, Cape York and Gulf Savannah regions. Safaris (4WD) to Cape York and Gulf Savannah. **Tourist information:** cnr Ring Road and The Esplanade; (070) 51 3588. **Accommodation:** Many hotels and motels from 5-star, international-standard to family and budget, 12 cara./camp. parks. **See also:** The Far North; Cape York.

Caloundra   Pop. 22 094

MAP REF. 497 N2, 500 I13, 505 Q7

This popular holiday spot on the Sunshine Coast is 96 km N of Brisbane via a turnoff from the Bruce Hwy. The main beaches are Kings, Shelly, Moffat, Dicky, Golden and Bulcock. The main shipping channel to Brisbane is just offshore. Pumicestone Passage (State Marine Park) to the south, between Bribie Island and the mainland, has sheltered waters for fishing, boating, water-skiing and sailboarding. **Of interest:** Queensland Air Museum at airport, Pathfinder Dr. (open Wed., Sat., Sun. and school holidays). Scenic flights available from airport. Market each Sun. at Caloundra Hospital grounds, West Terrace. Sept.: Art and Craft Show. **In the area:** Scenic drives: north along coastal strip; west to Blackall Range; south-west to Glass House Mountains. Wreck of SS *Dicky* (1893), Dicky Beach, 3 km N. Currimundi Lake Conservation Park, 4 km N. Pt Cartwright Lookout, 15 km N. Opals Down Under and House of Herbs, Bruce Hwy, 15 km NW. Aussie World incorporating Ettamogah Pub, Bruce Hwy, 16 km NW. **Tourist information:** 7 Caloundra Rd; (07) 5491 0202. **Accommodation:** 2 hotels, 13 motels, 12 cara./camp. parks. **See also:** The Sunshine Coast.

Camooweal   Pop. 234

MAP REF. 421 R11, 512 B2

On the Barkly Hwy, 188 km NW of Mount Isa, Camooweal is the last Qld town before crossing the NT border, 13 km W. **Of interest:** On Barkly Hwy: Shire Hall (1922–3) and Freckleton's Store, both National Trust-classified. Ellen Finlay Park, Morrison St. **In the area:** Cemetery, 1 km E on hwy, headstones tell local history. Caves in Camooweal Caves National Park, 25 km S; challenge to experienced potholers. **Tourist information:** Post Office, Barkly Hwy; (077) 48 2110. **Accommodation:** 1 hotel, 1 motel, 1 cara. park.

Cannonvale   Pop. 2402

MAP REF. 507 K3

Cannonvale is the first of three seaside resorts along the Shute Harbour Rd from the Proserpine turnoff, and is a suburb of the town of Whitsunday. Located 3 km from Airlie Beach,

City Hall in Charters Towers, with its classic Australian architecture

Cannonvale is fast becoming a vital centre for service and manufacturing businesses in the region. **Of interest:** Wildlife Park, Shute Harbour Rd, with bungy-jumping and go-kart racing adjacent. Easter: Great Whitsunday Boating Regatta. **In the area:** Airlie Beach and Shute Harbour, neighbouring resorts to south. Conway National Park, 10 km S. Tours to Whitsunday Islands. **Tourist information:** Beach Plaza, The Esplanade, Airlie Beach; (079) 46 6673. **Accommodation:** 1 hotel, 1 motel, 2 apartment complexes, 1 hostel, 3 cara./camp. parks.

Cardwell   Pop. 1294

MAP REF. 509 N10
From Cardwell, 58 km N of Ingham, there are beautiful views of Rockingham Bay and Great Barrier Reef islands in region. Local fishing and snorkelling is excellent. Channel is sheltered area for houseboats. **Of interest:** Museum (part of library), Victoria St. In Marine Pde: departure point for cruises to nearby islands including Hinchinbrook Island (4-day walk available); houseboat and yacht hire, bookings at Tourist information. National Parks Office, Victoria St, information about local national parks and Great Barrier Reef Marine Park. Market on Cardwell Esplanade (1st Sat.

each month). May: Country and Western Music Festival. June: Coral Sea Memorial. Sept.: Festival of Sport. **In the area:** Scenic drives in Cardwell Forest (spectacular coastal scenery), and Kirrama Range, 9–10 km N, on Kennedy Rd. Murray Falls in State Forest Park, 20 km NW; also camping and picnic areas. Dalrymple Gap walking track (10 km) 20 km S, between Damper Creek Bridge on Bruce Hwy and Abergowrie State Forest; permission required from Cardwell or Ingham Forestry offices. Blencoe Falls, 71 km E. **Tourist information:** Hinchinbrook Island Ferries, 135 Bruce Hwy; (070) 66 8539. **Accommodation:** 1 hotel, 6 motels, 2 hostels, 5 cara./camp. parks.

Charleville   Pop. 3513

MAP REF. 504 B6
Charleville marks the terminus of the Westlander rail service and is at the centre of a rich pastoral district carrying some 800 000 sheep and 100 000 cattle. Charleville's river, the Warrego, was explored by Edmund Bourke in 1847, and in 1862 William Landsborough camped nearby when searching for Burke and Wills. By the late 1890s Charleville was a frontier town with its own brewery, 10 hotels and 500 registered bullock teams. Cobb & Co.

had a coach-building factory here in 1893. The last coach on Australian roads ran to Surat in 1923. A monument 19 km N of the town marks the spot where Ross and Keith Smith landed with engine trouble on the first flight from London to Sydney in 1919. Amy Johnson also landed here in 1920. Qantas started flights from Charleville in 1922. The town is the heart of Mulga Country; the mulga ('the life-giving trees') provide welcome shade and in times of drought are cut down for sheep fodder. **Of interest:** In Alfred St: Historic House Museum in restored Qld National Bank building (1880), features amazing 5-m-long 'vortex gun' used in unsuccessful rainmaking experiments in 1902; Cobb & Co. coach and craft shop. Outback Queensland Skywatch at Meteorological Bureau at airport, features powerful telescopes outside and guided 'Adventure Through the Night Sky' in the evenings. 'Weary Willie' swagman statue, Wills St. National Parks and Wildlife Service Research Centre, Park St. Royal Flying Doctor Base and Visitors Centre, southern end of town. Nature walk on banks of Warrego River, northern end of town. Market, Historic House Museum, 1st Sun. each month. Oct.: Booga Woongaroo (mulga tree) Festival. **Tourist information:** Town Hall Building, Wills St; (076) 54 3057. **Accommodation:** 2 hotels, 2 hotel/motels, 4 motels, 2 cara./camp. parks.

Charters Towers   Pop. 9016

MAP REF. 506 E2
This peaceful and historic city once had a gold-rush population of some 30 000. Between 1872 and 1916, Charters Towers produced ore worth 25 million pounds ($50m). On 25 December 1871 an Aboriginal boy named Jupiter made the first strike while looking for horses that had bolted during a thunderstorm. He brought some gold-laden quartz back to his employer, Hugh Mosman, who rode to Ravenswood to register his claim, and the gold rush was on. The Government rewarded Mosman, who adopted and educated Jupiter. Charters Towers is 135 km inland from Townsville in hot, dry country, on the road and rail line to Mount Isa. Mining and cattle-raising are the main industries in the area; four large goldmines are operating, the result of another gold boom. **Of interest:** Much classic

QUEENSLAND

Fraser and Moreton Bay Islands

Wreck of the *Maheno,* on Fraser Island

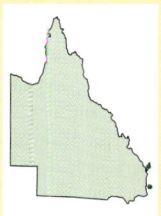

Fraser Island

If you like sand, sea, fishing and plenty of peace and quiet, World Heritage-listed Fraser Island is your ideal holiday destination. Fraser is the largest sand island in the world, 123 kilometres long, and the largest island off Australia's east coast. It acts as a breakwater, protecting the coast from Bundaberg to well south of Maryborough, and forms the eastern shores of Hervey Bay. The sandy straits between Fraser Island and the mainland are ideal for sailing and also attract hundreds of anglers each year for the tailor season.

Fraser's remote and abundant beaches are particularly attractive to those with 4WD vehicles, but the island is large enough to prevent them becoming intrusive. Apart from its long stretches of beautiful beach, Fraser Island has a unique area of fresh water lakes and tangled rainforests. There are over 40 lakes on the island, all of them above sea level, and the dense forests surrounding them attract a wide range of bird and animal life. Surf beaches extend along the entire east coast – a rarity on Queensland islands, as those further north are sheltered from the surf by the Barrier Reef.

An odd feature of the island is its ever-shifting creeks, which may run parallel to the ocean for several kilometres, then spill through a dune, carving a new course through the sand to the sea.

The island is accessible by air from Brisbane or Hervey Bay, or by barge from Hervey Bay, Inskip Point (Rainbow Beach) and Mary River Heads.

Kingfisher Bay Resort and Village is at North White Cliffs, on the western side of the island opposite Mary River Heads. The following accommodation is on the ocean side of Fraser Island: Happy Valley, Eurong, Dilli Village and Cathedral Beach Camping Park. Korawinga Lodge at Eurong has time-share units. All these holiday centres offer family accommodation. Day tours leave daily from Hervey Bay and Rainbow Beach. Camping and vehicle permits are required. For further information on Fraser Island, contact Department of Environment Information Centre, Eurong; (071) 27 9128. **Map reference:** 505 Q3.

Moreton Bay Islands

Bribie Island is a largely residential island, 69 kilometres north of Brisbane, reached via a turnoff on the Bruce Highway and a 1-kilometre bridge across Pumicestone Passage. Bribie is about 31 kilometres long, the northern tip being opposite Caloundra on the Sunshine Coast. Matthew Flinders landed on the southern tip in 1799. Part of the island is a national park. There are three townships: Bellara and Bongaree on the mainland side and Woorim on the surf side. The island offers excellent fishing, boating, crabbing and bushwalking. Accommodation available includes 2 hotel/motels, 2 motels and 6 cara./camp. parks. For further information on Bribie Island, contact the Bribie Island Information Centre; (07) 3408 9026. **Map references:** 497 N4, 500 I13.

Moreton Island, predominantly national park, is a remarkable wilderness island only 35 kilometres east of Brisbane. Apart from rocky headlands, the island is mostly huge sandhills, native scrub and banksias, and freshwater lakes, which attract over 125 species of sea, wetland and forest birds. A lighthouse at the northern tip, built in 1857, still guides ships into Brisbane. There are very few roads on the island, but cars (mostly 4WD) use the tracks and the magnificent 40-kilometre beach. Mt Tempest (286 m) is probably the highest permanent sandhill in the world. The resort of Tangalooma is on the leeward side and nearby, wild dolphins come to be fed each night as soon as the tide is high enough. Other activities include water sports, fishing and bushwalking. There are five campsites in the park (permit required). The island is reached by charter plane from Brisbane or more commonly, by barge from Brisbane or Redcliffe. For further information on Moreton Island, contact the Moreton Island office of the Department of Environment; (07) 3408 2710. **Map references:** 497 P5, 505 Q8.

North Stradbroke Island, or 'Straddie', is a 32-kilometre-long unspoiled island east of Brisbane across Moreton Bay, noted for being the home of the Aboriginal poet and activist Oodgeroo Noonuccal (Kath Walker), who died in 1993. It is popular for fishing, surfing, horseriding, canoeing, kayaking, snorkelling, diving, bike riding, 4WD tours and weekend stays. The small settlements of Dunwich, with its historic cemetery nearby, and Amity Point are on the leeward side, and Point Lookout is the vantage-point for watching the annual migration of whales, beginning in June. Point Lookout has the only hotel on the island. Nearby, the Captain Cook Memorial is near the beginning of the North Gorge Scenic Walk along the headland. Dunwich started as a quarantine station for Brisbane in 1828. The Goompi Trail, a 1½-hour walking tour of Dunwich, is led by a local Aboriginal guide. Straddie is a sanctuary for many unique species of flora and fauna. The 500-hectare Blue Lake National Park offers scenic walks through coastal woodland, and a variety of wildlife. Take a vehicular ferry or water taxi from Cleveland; the ferry journey takes an hour, while a water taxi takes about 30 minutes. Accommodation includes 5 resorts/hotels, 4 hostels and 10 cara./camp. parks. For further information on North Stradbroke Island, contact the Information Centre; (07) 3409 9555. **Map references:** 497 P9, 505 R9.

South Stradbroke Island was separated from North Stradbroke Island by a cyclone in 1896, and the channel between them is called Jumpinpin. South Stradbroke stretches south to Southport on the Gold Coast, the protected Broadwater being a well-used boating playground. The island, a natural reserve, is almost uninhabited and there are no vehicles on the island. Day cruises operate from Southport and a ferry operates from Runaway Bay. Accommodation is limited to one resort. For further information, contact South Stradbroke Island Resort; (07) 5577 3311. **Map references:** 497 O11, 499 F1, 505 Q10.

Australian architecture with verandahs and lacework still remains, particularly facades in Mosman and Gill sts. Historic homes: Ay-Ot-Lookout (1886), Hodgkinson St; Pfeiffer House (1880), Paull St. In Mosman St: Zara Clark Museum, for local history; souvenir centre in restored Stock Exchange. Venus Gold Battery, Millchester Rd, offers guided tours. Buckland's Hill lookout, Fraser St. Country Markets, cnr Mary and Show sts, 2nd Sun. each month. National Trust Markets, Stock Exchange, 1st and 3rd Sun. each month. Easter: Rodeo. May: Country Music Festival. June: Annual Vintage Car Restorers' Swap Meet. Aug.: Great Charters Towers Gold Rush. **In the area:** Towers Hill, 1.5 km W along Mosman St, has old mine shafts and ammunition bunkers from World War II. Mt Leyshon goldmine, 30 km S. Burdekin Falls Dam, 150 km SE, nearby, camping and accommodation. Big Bend, 40 km NW, contains fossilised coral (part of ancient reef). Great Basalt Wall, 80 km NW, 4 million year-old solidified lava wall extending 100 km. **Tourist information:** 74 Mosman St; (077) 87 1280. **Accommodation:** 5 hotels, 3 hotel/motels, 6 motels,1 hostel, 3 cara./camp. parks. **See also:** The Far North.

Childers
Pop. 1473

MAP REF. 505 O3

Childers is a picturesque sugar town, 53 km S of Bundaberg. Much of it was destroyed by fire in 1902; today it is a National Trust town. **Of interest:** Historic Childers, self-guide town walk taking in many historic buildings including: Old Butcher's Shop (1896), North St; Grand Hotel and Federal Hotel, Churchill St; also in Churchill St, Gaydon's Building (1894), now a Pharmaceutical Museum, art gallery and tourist centre; Royal Hotel, Randall St. Historic Complex, Taylor St, includes school, cottage and locomotive. May: Agricultural Show. July: Multicultural Food and Wine Festival. **In the area:** Burrum Coast National Park, 40 km E. Isis Central Sugar Mill, Cordalba, 10 km N; tours July–Nov. **Tourist information:** Pharmaceutical Museum, Churchill St; (071) 26 1994. **Accommodation:** 4 hotels, 4 motels, 1 hostel, 2 cara./camp. parks.

Chillagoe
Pop. 502

MAP REF. 509 K7

Chillagoe, once a thriving town where copper, silver, lead, gold and wolfram were mined, is now a small outback town where the recent development of tourism, international-standard marble mines and the Red Dome goldmine have returned the town to some of its former glory. **Of interest:** Local museum, for history of town including display of relics from old mining days. May: Annual Races, Concert and Rodeo. **In the area:** Rugged limestone outcrops and magnificent caves in Chillagoe-Mungana Caves National Park, via Donna and Trezkin caves, 1½ km S or Royal Arch Cave, 7 km S; guided tours available. **Tourist information:** Post Office and Department of Environment office, cnr Queen and Cathedral sts; (070) 94 7163. **Accommodation:** 1 hotel, 1 hotel/ motel, 1 motel, 3 cara./camp. parks.

Chinchilla
Pop. 3152

MAP REF. 505 K7

Chinchilla is a prosperous town in the western Darling Downs, 335 km NW of Brisbane on the Warrego Hwy. Ludwig Leichhardt named the area in 1844 from Jinchilla, the local Aboriginal name for cypress pines. Grain-growing is the traditional industry, as well as cattle, sheep, pigs, timber and, more recently, grapes, cotton and watermelons. **Of interest:** Historical Museum, Villiers St, features working steam engines and slab cottage (1880s). Newman's Collection of Petrified Wood, Boyd St. Fishing on Charley's Creek and Condamine River. Feb.: Melon Festival (odd-numbered years). May: Rotary May Day Carnival. July: Polocrosse Carnival. **In the area:** Cactoblastis Memorial Hall, at Boonarga, 8 km E, dedicated to the insect introduced to eradicate the prickly pear cactus. Fossicking for petrified wood, treefern and agate at 3 district properties; contact Chinchilla Tourist information. **Tourist information:** Warrego Hwy; (076) 68 9564. **Accommodation:** 1 hotel/motel, 4 motels, 3 cara./camp. parks.

Clermont
Pop. 2727

MAP REF. 506 H9

Centre of a fertile region which breeds cattle and sheep, and grows wheat, sorghum, cotton, safflower and sunflower as well as hardwood timber, Clermont is 274 km SW of Mackay, just off the Gregory Hwy. The town, which takes its name from Clermont in France, was established over 130 years ago (one of the first inland settlements in the tropics) after the discovery of gold. At first the settlement was at Hoods Lagoon, but was moved to the present site on higher ground after a major flood in 1916 in which 60 people died. Remnants of the gold rushes can still be seen. **Of interest:** Hoods Lagoon, Lime St on northern edge of town: Mary MacKillop Grotto; boardwalk and walking track; birdlife. Sept.: Rodeo. **In the area:** Clermont and District Historical Museum, 4 km NW on road to Charters Towers. Blair Athol open-cut mine, 23 km NW, largest seam of steaming coal in the world, mine tours (Tues. and Fri.); inquire at Tourist information. Wildlife sanctuary at mine. Copperfield Store museum, 7 km S, in original shop from copper-mining era. Copperfield Chimney, 8 km SW, chimney from copper-mining days. Copperfield Cemetery 10 km SW, 19th century graves of copper mines; monument to those who died in the 1916 flood. Theresa Creek Dam, 17 km SW; water-skiing and fishing, picnic areas and bush walks nearby. **Tourist information:** Capella St; (079) 83 1406. **Accommodation:** 1 hotel, 3 hotel/motels, 2 motels, 1 cara./camp. park.

Cleveland
Pop. 9270

MAP REF. 497 O8, 505 Q9

Centre of the Redland region, 35 km SE of Brisbane, Cleveland was nearly the capital for the new colony of Qld; however, when Governor Gipps and his official party arrived for an inspection, the tide was out and the trudge over the mudflats created a less than favourable impression. **Of interest:** Cleveland Point Heritage Trail (brochure available from Tourist information) includes: court house (1853) in Paxton St, built by Francis Bigge for timber-getters, became first police station and court house, now restaurant; lighthouse (1864) in Shore St, wooden structure restored and relocated, and holder of Australian record for length of tenancy by one attendant (50 years by James Froy); restored Grand View Hotel (1849) in North St, built by Francis Bigge in anticipation of influx of

QUEENSLAND

Captain Cook statue overlooking Endeavour River, Cooktown

holidaymakers when Cleveland was named capital of Qld, later known as Bigge's Folly (main bar exhibits murals depicting historic events). Redlands Museum, at Showgrounds in Smith St, has Cobb & Co. coach, maritime exhibits and blacksmith's forge on display, open Fri.–Sun. Old School House Gallery in William Ross Park, Queen St. Cleveland is departure point for barges and water taxis to North Stradbroke Island. Bayside markets each Fri. night and Sun. July: Flinders Day. **In the area:** Ormiston House (1862) open Sun. p.m. Mar.–Nov., overlooking bay at Ormiston 5 km NW; its builder, Captain Louis Hope, pioneered the State's sugar industry at this location. Whepstead Manor (1874), at Wellington Point 7 km N, historic Queenslander-style home in beautifully-landscaped grounds; now operates as a restaurant and function centre. **Tourist information:** 152 Shore St West; (07) 3821 0057. **Accommodation:** 3 hotel/motels, 4 motels.

Clifton   Pop. 805

MAP REF. 496 E11, 505 N10

Located between Toowoomba and Warwick, Clifton is the centre of a rich grain-growing and dairying area. **Of interest:** Historic buildings: Club Hotel (1889), King St; Church of St James and St John (1890s), cnr Tooth St and Meara Pl. **In the area:** Tours of peanut factory, 5 km E. Arthur Hoey Davis (Steele Rudd), author of *On Our Selection*, grew

up at East Greenmount, 10 km N. At Nobby, 8 km N: Burial site of Sister Kenny, renowned for her unorthodox method of treating poliomyelitis; Rudd's Pub (1893), where Arthur Hoey Davis used to write, has a museum in part of hotel's dining room. Tourist drive through 'Steele Rudd country', inquire at Tourist information. **Tourist information:** Shire Offices, King St; (076) 97 3299. **Accommodation:** Limited.

Cloncurry   Pop. 2309

MAP REF. 512 G4

Located in the Gulf Savannah region, Cloncurry is an important mining town, 124 km E of Mount Isa, with an interesting history and on the brink of another mining boom. In 1861, John McKinlay of Adelaide, leading an expedition to search for Burke and Wills, reported distinctive traces of copper in the area. Six years later, pioneer pastoralist Ernest Henry discovered the first copper lodes. A rail link to Townsville was built in 1908. During World War I, Cloncurry was the centre of a copper boom and in 1916 it was the largest source of copper in Australia, with four smelters operating. Following the war, copper prices slumped and the burgeoning pastoral industry, which had developed in the surrounding area, took its place. In 1920 a new Qantas air service linked Cloncurry to Winton. In 1928 the town became the first base for the famous Royal Flying Doctor Service (RFDS). In 1979 a rare type of pure 22-carat gold,

resembling crystallised straw, was discovered, and is now used for making jewellery. The region is mainly cattle country, and Cloncurry is a major railhead for transporting stock. **Of interest:** John Flynn Place, Daintree St, includes Fred McKay Art Gallery and RFDS Museum, cultural centre, outdoor theatre and Cloncurry Gardens. Cloncurry-Mary Kathleen Memorial Park, McIlwraith St, features four buildings from abandoned uranium mining town of Mary Kathleen, re-erected and used to display items of historic interest including Robert O'Hara Burke's water bottle as well as one of Australia's most comprehensive rock, mineral and gem collections. Cloister of Plaques (RFDS memorial), Uhr St. Court house (1884), Shaeffe St. Afghan Cemetery, Henry St. Chinese Cemetery, Flinders Hwy. In Sir Hudson Fyshe Dr.: old Qantas hangar at aerodrome; cattleholding yards Market, 1st Sat. each month at Florence Park. June: Agricultural Show. Aug.: Merry Muster Rodeo. **In the area:** Rotary Lookout, 2 km W near Normanton Rd turnoff, Mt Isa Hwy; for views. Burke and Wills cairn near Corella River, 43 km W. Great Australia Copper Mine, 2 km S, tours available; inquire at Tourist information. Kuridala ghost town, 88 km SE; amethyst fossicking a further 8 km, signposted. Walkabout Creek Hotel at McKinlay, 105 km SE, location for film *Crocodile Dundee*. Ruins of old goldmining town of Mount Cuthbert, 10 km from Kajabbi (77 km NW). Ernest Henry Copper and Gold Mine, another working mine, 29 km NE; inquire about tours at Tourist information. **Tourist information:** Cloncurry-Mary Kathleen Memorial Park, McIlwraith St; (077) 42 1361. **Accommodation:** 4 hotels, 6 motels, 1 cara. park. **See also:** Gulf Savannah.

Cooktown   Pop. 1342

MAP REF. 509 L3

Captain James Cook beached the *Endeavour* here in 1770 to repair damage after running aground on a coral reef. Gold was discovered at the Palmer River in 1872 and by 1877 Cooktown was a booming, brawling gold-rush port with 37 busy hotels and a transient population of some 18 000 people a year, including 6000 Chinese. Cooktown today has three hotels and the town's main industry is tourism. Located 240 km NW of Cairns, it is the departure point for Cape

York Peninsula. The surrounding district is good agriculturally and the town is also supported by prawning, fishing and tin mining. **Of interest:** Cemetery, with graves of tutor, early immigrant and heroine Mrs Mary Watson, and the nearby Chinese Shrine to the many who died on the goldfields. Grassy Hill offers views across the reef, township and hinterland. James Cook Historical Museum has collection tracing town's two centuries of history, and an anchor from the *Endeavour*. Cooktown Museum, featuring maritime history of area; also shell collection. Endeavour River Gallery, Sovereign Resort Complex, Charlotte St. Cooktown Botanic Gardens, Walker St. Markets at Endeavour Lions Park, each Sat. June: Cooktown Endeavour Festival (long weekend), with re-enactment of Cook's landing. July: Laura-Cape York Aboriginal Dance Festival (odd-numbered years). **In the area:** Snorkelling and diving tours to Outer Reef with Cooktown and Cape York Dive and Reef Centre, Charlotte St. Walking trails to Cherry Tree Bay and Finch Bay start at Botanic Gardens. Brochures on other local walks from Tourist information. Bicentennial National Trail (5000 km) for walkers and horse riders, runs from Cooktown to Healesville in Vic. Endeavour River National Park, just north of town. Lakefield National Park, 58 km NW; rivers, lagoons and swamps provide habitat for a great variety of wildlife and are crucial areas for crocodile conservation. Offshore, Lizard Island, 90 km NE, offers resort, national park and secluded beaches; access by seaplane. Beautiful sandstone escarpments at Split Rock rock-art site, 12 km S of Laura (166 km W of Cooktown), perhaps the largest Aboriginal art site in Australia; guided tours of hundreds of cave paintings. **Tourist information:** Cooktown and Cape York Visitors Centre, Charlotte St; (070) 69 6100. **Accommodation:** 1 resort, 1 hotel, 4 motels, 2 B&B, 2 hostels, 3 cara./camp. parks. **See also:** Atherton Tableland.

Coolangatta   Pop. part of Gold Coast

MAP REF. 499 H10, 505 Q11
Coolangatta is the most southerly of Qld's coastal towns, with its twin town of Tweed Heads across the border in NSW. June: Wintersun Festival. **In the area:** Coolangatta Airport, Bilinga, services Gold Coast for domestic flights, charters, joy flights and tandem skydiving. Captain Cook Memorial Lighthouse, North Head. Tom Beaston Outlook (Razorback Lookout), behind Tweed Heads, for excellent views. **Tourist information:** Beach House, Marine Pde; (07) 5536 7765. **Accommodation:** Low and high-rise resorts, hotels and motels, numerous apartment complexes. **See also:** The Gold Coast.

Crows Nest   Pop. 1154

MAP REF. 496 F5, 505 N8
This small town, 45 km N of Toowoomba, acquired its name from Jim Crow, an Aborigine from the Kabi-Kabi community who once made his home in a hollow tree near what is now the police station. A memorial in Centenary Park commemorates this. **Of interest:** John French VC Memorial Library, William St. In Thallon St: Carbethon Folk Museum and Pioneer Village; Salts Antiques, open weekends. Oct.: Crows Nest Day; Worm Races. **In the area:** Several local host farms, inquire at Tourist information. Crows Nest National Park, 6 km E (look for sign to Valley of Diamonds), walking tracks to falls, picnic and camping facilities. Ravensbourne National Park, 25 km SE. **Tourist information:** Toowoomba information centre, cnr James and Kitchener sts, Toowoomba; (076) 39 3797. **Accommodation:** 1 motel, 2 B&B, 1 cara./camp. park.

Croydon   Pop. 220

MAP REF. 508 F10
This Gulf town, 561 km SW of Cairns, is the eastern terminus for the Gulflander train service which leaves each Thurs. for Normanton. In town, many original buildings (1887–97), classified by National Trust and Australian Heritage Commission, have been restored to their former splendour. **Of interest:** In Samwell St: Hospital Museum in old police station, old gaol, courthouse with original furniture, Town Hall with hanging murals and gas lamps on the footpath. Also Outdoor Museum, featuring a display of mining machinery from the age of steam. In Brown St: old butcher shop and hospital ward (now a gym). In Sircom St: General Store/Museum. Self-guide and guided walking tours of town, contact Tourist information. June: Rodeo. **In the area:** Working Mine Museum including battery stamper, 1 km N. Old cemetery, 1 km W, has historic graves. Birdwatching areas, inquire at Tourist information. **Tourist information:** Shire Offices; (077) 45 6185. **Accommodation:** 1 hotel, 1 roadhouse, 1 cara./camp. park. **See also:** Gulf Savannah.

Cunnamulla   Pop. 1683

MAP REF. 504 A10, 515 R10
A western sheep town known for its friendliness and hospitality, Cunnamulla is near the Warrego River, 118 km N of the NSW border. It is the biggest wool-loading station on the Qld railway network, with some 2 million sheep in the area, plus beef cattle. Explorers Sir Thomas Mitchell and Edmund Kennedy were the first European visitors in 1846 and 1847 respectively, and by 1879 it had become a town with regular Cobb & Co. services. In 1880 a daring but disorganised villain, Joseph Wells, held up the local bank and tried to escape with the loot, but could not find his horse. Irate locals bailed him up in a tree (known as 'The Robbers' Tree'), demanding justice and their money back. The tree, in Stockyard St, is still a landmark. **Of interest:** Historical Society display in Bicentennial Museum, John St. Yupunyah Tree planted by Princess Anne, cnr Louise and Stockyard sts. Centenary Park, Jane St, has picnic/barbecue facilities. Outback Botanic Gardens and Herbarium (in early stages of development), tours available, inquire at Tourist information for details. Sept.: Opal Festival. **In the area:** Wildflowers in spring; varied wetland birdlife, particularly black swans, brolgas, pelicans and eagles. Noorama Sports Centre, 110 km SE; Noorama Picnic Races in Apr. **Tourist information:** Centenary Park; (076) 55 2481. **Accommodation:** 2 hotels, 3 hotel/motels, 1 motel, 1 cara./camp. park.

Currumbin   Pop. part of Gold Coast

MAP REF. 499 G10, 505 Q10
Situated at the mouth of the Currumbin Creek, this part of the Gold Coast has many attractions for visitors. **Of interest:** Currumbin Sanctuary, 20-ha reserve owned by National Trust, features free-ranging animals in open areas, lorikeet feeding (twice-daily),

QUEENSLAND

Great Barrier Reef

The Great Barrier Reef is a living phenomenon. Its coloured coral branches sit upon banks of limestone polyps that have been built up slowly over thousands of years from the seabed. The banks of coral are separated by channels of water, shaded from the delicate green of the shallows to the deepest blue. The reef area is over 1200 kilometres long, stretching from near the coast of western Papua New Guinea to north of Breaksea Spit, east of Bundaberg on the central Queensland coast. It is only between 15 and 20 kilometres wide in the north, but south of Cairns the reef area can extend up to 325 kilometres out to sea. The Great Barrier Reef was proclaimed a marine park in 1979 and a management programme was undertaken to balance the interests of scientists, tourists and fishing enthusiasts, and to preserve the reef for future generations. With over 700 islands scattered through the tropical sea, and the banks of reefs darkening the water, this sun-drenched, tropical paradise attracts thousands of visitors each year.

The coral presents an incredibly beautiful picture. Visitors can see it from semi-submersible vessels, which allow occupants to go underwater without getting wet, or from glass-bottomed boats; or, even better, they can swim around using snorkels or diving gear. The colours of purple, pink, yellow, white and red are intermixed and made more startling by the spectacular shapes of the coral. There are more than 340 varieties of identified coral, the most common being the staghorns, brain corals, mushroom corals, organ pipes and black corals. Spread among these are waving fields of soft coral, colourful anemones, sea urchins and sea slugs. Shellfish of all kinds, ranging from great clams to tiny cowries, cling to the reef while shoals of brightly coloured tropical fish – among them red emperors, coral trout, sweetlip, angel-fish, parrot-fish and demoiselles – glide and dart through the coral gardens. Multitudes of seabirds nest on the islands of the reef through spring and summer.

Three island resorts, Green Island, Lizard Island and Lady Elliot Island, are coral cays – actually part of the reef – and at low tide it is possible to walk on the coral ledges that surround them. Other resort islands are continental islands, having once been part of the mainland, and are generally more wooded and mountainous.

The Great Barrier Reef is Australia's most beautiful tourist attraction, and the best way to see

it is by boat. If you do not have your own yacht, and the holiday budget will not stretch to chartering one, there are many excellent cruises available through the reef and its islands. Charter boats, scuba diving and fishing trips are also available.

The resort islands off the reef and the Queensland coast offer different styles of living to suit various tastes in holidays and entertainment. The common denominator is their beautiful setting and a consistency of climate, broken only

by the sudden and short-lived downpours of the monsoonal period from December to February. The period from June to November is considered the best time to visit.

For further information on the islands of the Great Barrier Reef, contact the Queensland Government Travel Centre, cnr Adelaide and Edward sts, Brisbane; 13 1801.

QUEENSLAND

Island	Features	Activities	Access	Accommodation
SOUTHERN REEF ISLANDS	The Southern Reef extends offshore from Bundaberg to Rockhampton.			
LADY ELLIOT ISLAND 80 km NE of Bundaberg	• small, sand covered coral cay • 19 major dive areas to view coral and marine life • significant bird rookeries • turtle nesting site	Birdwatching, turtle watching (turtles come ashore to lay eggs Nov.–Mar.; hatching can be seen late Feb.–May), humpback whale migration (late June to Late Oct.), diving, snorkelling, reef walking, reef fishing, island walking.	From Bundaberg, by plane. From Hervey Bay, by plane.	Low-key resort ranging from budget to deluxe. Max. 100 people.
LADY MUSGRAVE ISLAND 105 km NNE of Bundaberg	• superb coral cay with navigable lagoon • underwater observatory • glass-bottomed boats • floating pontoon • semi-submersible submarine • prolific birdlife • turtle nesting site	Birdwatching, turtle watching (turtles come ashore to lay eggs Nov.–Mar.; hatching can be seen late Dec.–May), snorkelling, island walking.	From Bundaberg, by seaplane, catamaran or trimaran. From Gold Coast, by seaplane. From Seventeen Seventy, by boat.	Camping only; permit required (contact Gladstone office of Dept of Environment; (079) 72 6055). Max. 50 people.
HERON ISLAND 72 km NE of Gladstone	• small coral cay • entire island is a national park • prolific flora and fauna • turtle nesting site	Birdwatching, turtle watching (turtles come ashore to lay eggs Nov.–Mar.; hatching can be seen late Dec.–May), diving, snorkelling, reef walk.	From Gladstone, by catamaran or charter helicopter.	Resort. Max. 280 people.
NORTH WEST ISLAND 75 km NE of Gladstone	• uninhabited • second largest coral cay on reef • turtle nesting site • breeding site of common noddy and wedgetailed shearwater	Birdwatching, turtle watching (turtles come ashore to lay eggs Nov.–Mar.; hatching can be seen late Dec.–May).	From Gladstone, by charter boat. From Bundaberg, by catamaran or trimaran. From Town of Seventeen-Seventy, by boat.	Camping only; permit required (contact Gladstone office of Dept of Environment; (079) 72 6055). Max. 150 people.
GREAT KEPPEL ISLAND 48 km NE of Rockhampton	• 30 km of white, sandy beaches • unspoiled tropical island scenery	Tennis, water-skiing, skindiving, parasailing, coral viewing, island cruises, golf. 'Kids Klub' operates during school holidays.	From Rockhampton, by light plane. From Rosslyn Bay, by launch.	Wide range from cabins and tents to lodge or resort. Max. 650 people.
WHITSUNDAY ISLANDS	There are more than 80 islands in the magnificent Whitsunday Passage, most are uninhabited.			
BRAMPTON ISLAND 32 km NE of Mackay	• national park and wildlife sanctuary • fine, white beaches • snorkelling trail	Water sports, reef cruises, snorkelling trail (with waterproof map), bushwalking, archery.	From Mackay, by light plane or launch.	Resort. Max. 280 people.
LINDEMAN ISLAND 67 km N of Mackay	• Club Med resort • national park • prolific birds and butterflies • secluded sandy beaches • picturesque golf course • superb views from summit of Mt Oldfield	Water sports, bird and butterfly watching, tennis, golf, excercise in the gym or pool, bushwalking.	From Proserpine, by light plane. From Shute Harbour, Mackay or Hamilton Island, by plane or launch.	Club Med resort. Max. 460 people.

Island	Features	Activities	Access	Accommodation
HAMILTON ISLAND 16 km SE of Shute Harbour	• most complex island resort • extensive facilities including jet airport, school, bank, post office, 24 shops and boutiques • 200-berth marina • fauna park • waterside village	Wide range of activities and entertainment including windsurfing, sailing, fishing, scuba diving, parasailing, tennis and squash; catamaran cruises.	Direct flight from Melbourne, Sydney, Brisbane, Cairns, Proserpine and Mackay. Also from Mackay and Shute Harbour, by launch.	Hotel resort offering wide range of accommodation. Max. 750 people.
LONG ISLAND 9 km from Shute Harbour	• part of Conway National Park • excellent walking tracks leading to scenic lookouts • friendly scrub turkeys • fresh oysters	Bushwalking, water sports, fishing, resort activities.	From Shute Harbour or Hamilton Island, by launch or helicopter. From Proserpine or Hamilton by seaplane.	3 resorts: Club Crocodile, family resort (max. 400 people); Palm Bay Hideaway for relaxation (max. 50 people); South Long Island Wilderness Lodge for a tranquil eco-experience (max. 16 people).
SOUTH MOLLE ISLAND 8 km from Shute Harbour	• small, lightly timbered island with numerous inlets • splendid scenery and views of Whitsunday Passage from island's peaks • golf course	Bushwalking, snorkelling, scuba diving, windsurfing, golf, squash.	From Shute Harbour, by launch. From Hamilton Island, by water taxi.	Resort. Max. 520 people.
DAYDREAM ISLAND 5 km from Shute Harbour	• luxurious resort on this small island of volcanic rock and coral • dense tropical foliage • shopping arcade	Resort activities and facilities including 'Kids Only' Club, tennis, gymnasium, water sports centre, diving, trips to outer reef and other islands.	From Shute Harbour, by launch or helicopter. From Hamilton Island, by launch or helicopter.	Resort. Max. 1000 people.
WHITSUNDAY ISLAND 25 km E of Shute Harbour	• uninhabited • entire island is a national park • beautiful white silica beach, Whitehaven Beach • Hill Inlet mangrove system (marine 'nursery')	Bush and beach walking.	From Shute Harbour or Able Point Marina, by boat.	Camping only, permit required (contact Airlie Beach office of Dept of Environment; (079) 46 7022). Max. 20 people.
HOOK ISLAND 20 km NE of Shute Harbour	• small low-key resort • underwater observatory	Snorkelling, scuba diving, fishing, reef trips.	From Shute Harbour, by launch.	Wilderness Lodge with cabins and campsites. Max. 70 people.
HAYMAN ISLAND 25 km NE of Shute Harbour	• luxury resort • prolific birdlife • northernmost island in Whitsundays; close to outer reef • shopping arcade	Fishing, sightseeing trips, scenic flights, diving, water sports 'Kidz Club', and whale-watching excursions in season (July–early Sept.).	From major Australian cities, direct flight to Hamilton Island, then by launch to Hayman Island. From Airlie Beach, by water taxi.	Luxury resort. Max. 450 people.

Island	Features	Activities	Access	Accommodation
TROPICAL NORTH ISLANDS	This group of islands is located off the north coast of Queensland between Townsville and Cooktown. Generally speaking, the reef in this section is closer to the mainland than it is further south.			
■ **MAGNETIC ISLAND** 8 km NE of Townsville	• permanent population • national park • excellent walking tracks • beautiful beaches • buses and taxis available	Horseriding, snorkelling, parasailing, swimming, fishing, sea kayaking, reef excursions; Harley tours.	From Townsville, by vehicular ferry, catamaran or water taxi.	Wide variety of hotels and accommodation from budget to deluxe.
■ **ORPHEUS ISLAND** 80 km N of Townsville	• small island surrounded by coral reefs • island is a national park • prolific birdlife	Birdwatching, water sports, coral viewing in glass-bottomed boat, island walks, fishing.	From Townsville or Cairns, by sea plane.	5-star resort (max. 74 people) or camping (max. 54 people) (camping permit required, contact Ingham office of Dept of Environment; (070) 68 8601).
■ **HINCHINBROOK ISLAND** 5 km E of Cardwell	• small, low-key resort • island is a national park • mountains, tropical vegetation and waterfalls • sandy beaches and secluded coves on eastern side	Snorkelling, swimming, fishing.	From Cardwell, by launch.	Resort. Max. 50 people.
■ **BEDARRA ISLAND** 35 km NE of Cardwell	• exclusive resort • untouched tropical beauty • no day visitors	Bushwalking, snorkelling, fishing, swimming, wind-surfing, sailing, tennis and gourmet picnics in a dinghy.	From Dunk Island, by launch.	One exclusive resort. Max. 32 people.
■ **DUNK ISLAND** 5 km SE of Mission Beach	• popular resort • island is a national park • extensive walking tracks through superb rainforest • prolific birdlife, butterflies and wild orchids	Bushwalking, birdwatching, nightwalks, parasailing, water-skiing, sailing, clay target shooting.	From Townsville or Cairns, by plane. From Clump Point near Mission Beach, by launch. From Wongaling Beach and South Mission Beach, by water taxi.	Resort. Max. 360 people.
■ **FITZROY ISLAND** 30 km SE of Cairns	• low-key resort • magnificent flora and fauna • secluded sandy beaches • 360° views from lighthouse	Bushwalking, diving, snorkelling.	From Cairns, by catamaran.	Resort offering bunkhouses and cabins (max. 160 people). Also camping (max. 60 people).
■ **GREEN ISLAND** 27 km NE of Cairns	• popular with day-trippers • true coral cay • thick tropical vegetation • glass-bottomed boats • underwater observatory • theatrette with films on reef life	Reef viewing, bushwalking.	From Cairns, by catamaran.	Resort. Max. 90 people.
■ **LIZARD ISLAND** 95 km NE of Cooktown	• small, luxurious resort • national park • excellent reefs surround island • game-fishing offshore, especially marlin in season (Sept.–Nov.)	Reef viewing, fishing, island walks.	From Cairns, by plane.	Bungalow-style resort (max. 80 people) or camping (max. 20 people). Permit required, contact Cairns office of Dept of Environment; (070) 52 3096.

QUEENSLAND

walk-through rainforest aviary with pools and waterfalls, and rides through sanctuary on miniature railway. Opposite, Chocolate Expo Factory. **In the area:** Olson's Bird Gardens, 9 km W in Currumbin Valley, has large land-scaped aviaries in subtropical setting. Section of Springbrook National Park, 22 km SW at end of Currumbin Creek Rd, scenic rainforest area ideal for bush-walking and picnicking. **Tourist information:** Beach House, Marine Pde, Coolangatta; (07) 5536 7765. **Accommodation:** 5 apartment complexes. **See also:** The Gold Coast.

Daintree   Pop. 200

MAP REF. 503 A1, 509 M5

This unspoilt township, 115 km NW of Cairns, lies in the heart of the Daintree River catchment basin surrounded by the McDowall Ranges. The area has abundant native plant life, birds and tropical butterflies. Australia's prehistoric reptile, the estuarine crocodile, can be seen in the mangrove-lined creeks and tributaries of the Daintree River. **Of interest:** Daintree Timber Museum. Local art and craft. A truly old-time local store. River cruises; vehicular ferry, one of last cable ferries in Australia. **In the area:** Wonga-Belle Orchid Garden, 17 km SE, 3½ ha of lush gardens. Daintree Rainforest Environmental Centre, 11 km N via ferry, has a boardwalk through rainforest. Cape Tribulation, 35 km NE, where rainforest meets reef, features crystal-clear creeks, forests festooned with creepers and vines, palm trees, orchids, butterflies, cassowaries and bushwalks. Bloomfield Falls, 85 km N, via Cape Tribulation. **Tourist information:** Douglas Shire Tourism Assoc.; (070) 99 4588; or Port Douglas and Cooktown Tourist Information Centre, 23 Macrossan St, Port Douglas; (070) 99 5599. **Accommodation:** 5 B&B, 1 cara./camp. park.

Dalby   Pop. 9385

MAP REF. 496 A4, 505 M8

Dalby, 84 km NW of Toowoomba on the Darling Downs, is a pleasant, well-planned country town at the crossroads of the Warrego, Bunya and Moonie hwys. It is the centre of Australia's richest grain and cotton-growing area. Cattle, pigs, sheep and coal add wealth to the district. **Of interest:** Pioneer Park Museum, Black St: historic buildings,

Rainbow lorikeets feeding at Currumbin Sanctuary

displays of household and agricultural items, and craft shop. Obelisk at crossing in Edward St marks spot where explorer Henry Dennis camped in 1841. Memorial cairn in Myall Creek picnic area pays homage to the cactoblastis, the Argentinian caterpillar that eradicated the dreaded prickly pear cactus in the 1920s. Cultural and Administration Centre, Drayton St, includes theatre, cinema, art gallery and restaurant. Self-guide heritage walk and self-guide drive tour available, contact Tourist information. Walkway along banks of Myall Creek, bird habitat. Mar.: Queensland Cotton Week. Oct.: Dalby Quilts and Craft Show. **In the area:** Lake Broad-water Conservation Park, 29 km SW: boating and water-skiing on lake when full, 3-km walk, tower for birdwatching, picnic/barbecue facilities and camping. Historic Jimbour House, 27 km N, grounds open daily except in wet weather. Bunya Mountains National Park, 60 km NE. **Tourist information:** Thomas Jack Park, cnr Drayton and Condamine sts; (076) 62 1066. **Accommodation:** 3 hotels, 2 hotel/motels, 5 motels, 2 cara./camp. parks. **See also:** Darling Downs.

Eidsvold   Pop. 587

MAP REF. 505 M3

The Eidsvold goldfield was extremely productive for 12 years from 1888 and still remains attractive to fossickers. The district is the State's best producer of quality beef cattle. **Of interest:**

Historical Museum, features Knock-break Homestead (1850s), George Schafer and Eric Schultz Collection of rocks and minerals, Noel Duncan Bottle Collection and local history displays, especially of goldmining. **In the area:** Waruma Dam, 48 km N via Burnett Hwy, for swimming, sailing and water-skiing. **Tourist information:** Historical Museum, Mt Rose St; (071) 65 1277. **Accommodation:** 1 hotel/motel, 1 motel, 1 cara./camp. park.

Emerald   Pop. 6557

MAP REF. 506 I11

An attractive town, 263 km W of Rockhampton at the junction of the Capricorn and Gregory hwys. Emerald is the hub of the Central Highlands. The largest sapphire fields in the southern hemisphere are nearby. As well as the cattle industry, grain, oilseeds, soybeans and cotton are important. **Of interest:** Shady Moreton Bay fig trees line Clermont and Egerton sts. National Trust-classified railway station (1901), Clermont St. Pioneer Cottage and Museum, Harris St. Pastoral College, Capricorn Hwy. Easter: Sunflower Festival. June: Wheelbarrow Derby (odd-numbered years). Aug.: Gemfest. Sept.: Music Spectacular. **In the area:** For farmstays and day tours of local cattle stations, inquire at Tourist information. Fossicking for gems, licence required. At Rubyvale, 60 km NE: Miner's Heritage Walk-in Mine, tours

Great Keppel Island

of underground sapphire mine and gemcutting displays; Bobby Dazzler Walk-in Mine, also has museum and shop; various gem outlets; 4WD tours of Tomahawk Creek and other local gemfields available. Gregory coalfields, 60 km N. At Capella, 51 km NW: Capella Pioneer Village, home to first settlement in area, Peak Downs Homestead. Capella Pioneer Village Arts and Crafts Fair in Apr. Lake Maraboon/Fairbairn Dam, 19 km S, for fishing and water sports; cruises of lake available. Tour historic schoolhouse, storehouse and slab homestead at Old Rainworth Fort, Springsure; 66 km S. **Tourist information:** Clermont St; (079) 82 4142. **Accommodation:** 3 hotels, 6 motels, 6 cara./camp. parks. **See also:** Capricorn Region.

Emu Park
Pop. 1919

MAP REF. 507 O10

This seaside resort, 45 km NE of Rockhampton, has excellent picnic spots and a safe beach. **Of interest:** Historical Museum, Hill St, features King O'Malley Memorial. Unusual 'singing ship' memorial to Captain Cook, who discovered the bay on voyage up east coast in May 1770 (sea breezes cause hidden organ pipes to make sounds). Bell Park, on beach. Markets, 4th Sun. each month at Bell Park. July: Service of Remembrance (memorial to American

troops). Oct.: Octoberfest. **In the area:** Great Keppel Island and nearby underwater observatory; tours daily. Other islands in Keppel group offer limited facilities including camping and day trips (permit required); contact Tourist information. Coral Life Marineland, 3 km NE at Kinka Beach; open weekends and school holidays. Koorana Crocodile Farm, 19 km SW, off the Emu Park–Rockhampton Rd. **Tourist information:** Ross Creek Roundabout, Yeppoon; (079) 39 4888. **Accommodation:** 2 motels, 1 cara./ camp. park.

Eromanga
Pop. 90

MAP REF. 515 M7

A centre for extensive oil exploration, 103 km W of Quilpie, Eromanga has a refinery producing around 1.5 million barrels of oil a year. Named from an Aboriginal word meaning 'hot windy plain', Eromanga is reputedly the furthest town from the sea in Australia. **Of interest:** Royal Hotel, Webber St, once Cobb & Co. staging post. Some original 19th-century buildings. Easter: Rodeo. May: Race Day. **In the area:** Opal fields; some leaseholders permit visitors, contact Mining Warden at Quilpie or police at Eromanga. **Tourist information:** Quilpie Shire Offices, Brolga St, Quilpie; (076) 56 1133. **Accommodation:** 1 hotel, 1 cara./camp. park.

Esk
Pop. 882

MAP REF. 496 I5, 505 O8

Esk, in the Upper Brisbane Valley, is 99 km NW of Brisbane. The Upper Brisbane Valley is renowned for its beautiful lakes and dams. **Of interest:** Numerous antique and local craft shops. July: Picnic Races. **In the area:** Lakes and dams: Lake Somerset (25 km NE) and Lake Wivenhoe (25 km E), the source of Brisbane's main water supply, and Atkinson Dam (30 km SE); all are popular swimming, fishing and boating spots. Lake Wivenhoe is State's main centre for championship rowing. At Coominya, 22 km SE: historic Bellevue Homestead; Watermelon Festival in Jan. Boss camel races in Sept. Prenzlau, 44 km SE near Lowood, has its Clydesdale Bush Carnival in Oct. Further north, some of the finest grazing country in Brisbane Valley; this is deer country, where progeny of a small herd of deer presented to the State by Queen Victoria in 1873 still roam. Caboonbah Homestead (1890), 19 km NE, is headquarters of Brisbane Valley Historical Society. **Tourist information:** Shire Offices, 2 Redbank St; (07) 5424 1200. **Accommodation:** 2 hotels, 3 motels, 1 cara./camp. park.

Eulo
Pop. 42

MAP REF. 515 Q11

Once the centre for opal mining in the area, Eulo is on the banks of the Paroo River, 68 km W of Cunnamulla. **Of interest:** Eulo Queen Hotel, Leo St, owes its name to Isobel Robinson (nee Richardson) who ran the hotel and virtually reigned over the opal fields at turn of century. Eulo Date Farm, western outskirts of town (open Aug.–Sept.). Sept.: World Lizard Racing Championships, at Paroo Lizard Race Track, next to hotel. Destructo Cockroach Monument commemorates death of a champion racing cockroach. **In the area:** Fossicking area for visitors at Yowah, 87 km NW. Mud Springs, 7 km W, natural pressure valve to artesian basin, currently inactive. Birdwatching at Lake Bindegolly, 100 km W. Thargomindah, 130 km W; inquire at Tourist information for mud map to Burke and Wills Dig Tree site. Good fishing at Noccundra water hole on Wilson River, 260 km W. Currawinya National Park, 60 km SW, for birdwatching and fishing. **Tourist information:** Centenary Park,

QUEENSLAND

Curnamulla; (076) 55 2481. **Accommodation:** 1 hotel, 1 cara./ camp. park.

Gatton   Pop. 5098

MAP REF. 496 H8, 505 O9

First settled in the 1840s, this agricultural town in the Lockyer Valley is midway between Ipswich and Toowoomba, and 96 km W of Brisbane via the Warrego Hwy. Saw-milling, pecan farming, dairy cattle, small-crop farming and raising of beef cattle, pigs and calves, are the main activities of the area. May: Heavy Horse Field Day. Oct.: Potato Festival. **In the area:** Agricultural College, 5 km E, opened 1897. Helidon, 14 km W, noted for its freestone, used in many Brisbane buildings, and for its spa water. Grantham, 7 km SW, known for fresh fruit and vegetables; many roadside stalls offer local produce. Tourist drive (82-km circuit) through surrounding countryside including visits to local farms, inquire at Tourist information. **Tourist information:** Lake Apex Dr.; (07) 5462 3430. **Accommodation:** 3 hotels, 1 hotel/ motel, 1 motel, 3 cara./camp. parks. **See also:** Darling Downs.

Gayndah   Pop. 1750

MAP REF. 505 N4

Gayndah claims to be Qld's oldest town, having been founded in 1848. It is on the Burnett Hwy near the Burnett River, just over 100 km W of Maryborough in a significant citrus-growing area. **Of interest:** Original school (1863), still in use. Several homesteads in district built in 1850s. Historical Museum, Simon St, includes Ban Ban Springs Homestead. June: Orange Festival (odd-numbered years). **In the area:** Claude Warton Weir Recreation Area, 3 km W, for fishing and picnics. Natural springs at Ban Ban Springs, 26 km S, a popular picnic area. **Tourist information:** Grand Hotel, 2 Meson St; (071) 61 1200. **Accommodation:** 1 hotel, 2 motels, 2 cara./camp. parks.

Georgetown   Pop. 310

MAP REF. 508 I10

Georgetown is a small town on the Gulf Developmental Rd to Croydon and Normanton. It was once one of many small goldmining towns on the Etheridge Goldfield. The area is now noted for its gemstones, especially agate

and gold nuggets. New Year's Day, June, Oct. and Nov.: Race Meetings. **In the area:** Cobbold Gorge, 75 km S, boat tours on river through gorge, inquire at Tourist information. Gemfields at Agate Creek, 95 km S, and O'Briens Creek, 129 km NE. Tallaroo hot springs, lava tubes, 55 km E, open Apr.–Sept.; tours essential, inquire at Tourist information for details. Undara Volcanic National Park, 129 km E, variety of birdlife. **Tourist information:** Etheridge Shire Offices, St George St; (070) 62 1233. **Accommodation:** 1 hotel, 1 motel, 2 cara./camp. parks. **See also:** Gulf Savannah.

Gin Gin   Pop. 907

MAP REF. 505 N2

Some of Qld's oldest cattle properties are in the area around this pastoral town on the Bruce Hwy, 52 km SW of Bundaberg. The district is known as Wild Scotchman Country, after James McPherson, Qld's only authentic bushranger. **Of interest:** The Residence, Mulgrave St, former police sergeant's house now displaying district's pioneering memorabilia, also 'The Bunyip', old cane locomotive, part of historic railway display. March: Wild Scotchman Festival. **In the area:** Mystery Craters, 17 km NE on the Bundaberg Rd, curious formation of 35 craters, about 25 million years old. Lake Monduran, 24 km NW, held back by Fred Haigh Dam (Qld's second largest), ideal for boating and picnics. Boolboonda Tunnel, 17 km W, longest artificial non-supported tunnel in southern hemisphere; now part of scenic tourist drive; brochure available from Tourist information. Moonora Craft Spinning, 25 km W, daily demonstrations of spinning process. Wonbah Estate Winery, 25 km W, tours available. Currajong Gardens, 9 km S, indoor and outdoor plants featuring exotic and rare cacti (by appt; (071) 57 6103. **Tourist information:** Mulgrave St; (071) 57 2133. **Accommodation:** 3 motels, 1 cara./ camp. park.

Gladstone   Pop. 23 462

MAP REF. 507 P12

Matthew Flinders discovered Port Curtis, Gladstone's impressive deepwater harbour, in 1802, but it was not until the 1960s that its potential began to be utilised. As an outlet for central Qld's mineral and agricultural wealth,

Gladstone, 550 km NW of Brisbane, is now one of Australia's most prosperous seaboard cities. Its harbour is one of Australia's busiest, handling more shipping tonnage per annum than Sydney. One reason for this growth is the opening up of the almost inexhaustible coal supplies in the hinterland. Another is that the world's largest single alumina plant is at Parsons Point where millions of tonnes of bauxite from Weipa on the Gulf of Carpentaria are processed annually into millions of tonnes of alumina, the halfway stage of aluminium. Comalco has built an aluminium smelter at Boyne Island. A large power station has been built in Gladstone to supply power to the refinery and smelter, as well as feeding into the State's electricity grid. Chemical processing is a new regional industry. Gladstone's most important tourist advantage is its proximity to the southern section of the Great Barrier Reef. The city is known for its mud crabs and prawns, and has won the State Tidy Towns Competition eight times in 12 years. **Of interest:** In Goondoon St: historic Kullaroo House (1911); Radar Hill Lookout. Gladstone Regional Art Gallery and Museum, cnr Goondoon and Bramston sts. Potter's Place, Dawson Hwy, art and craft gallery. In Glenlyon St: Tondoon Botanic Gardens has only native species (tours available at weekends); Reg Tanna Park including Railway Dam. Barney Point Beach and Friend Park, Barney St. Waterfall, end Auckland St, is floodlit at night. Views of harbour and islands from Auckland Hill Lookout. Round Hill Lookout, Boles St, West Gladstone. Auckland Inlet offers anchorage alongside James Cook Park; finishing-line for annual Brisbane to Gladstone yacht race, highlight of 10-day Harbour Festival held Easter. Marina, departure point for daily Barrier Reef cruises and harbour cruises. **In the area:** Tours of Gladstone Power Station, north of town. Curtis Island, also north, in Gladstone Harbour, is a family recreation area. Spectacular views from Mt Larcom summit, 33 km W. Port Curtis Historical Village, 26 km SW at Calliope River. Lake Awoonga, 30 km S, offers picnic and camping areas, water-based recreation, walking trail and varied wildlife. Historic town of Many Peaks, 80 km SE. Nearby towns of Boyne Island and Tannum Sands are linked by bridge; Boyne Island renowned for its beautiful foreshore

Rainbow Beach, near Gympie, famous for its coloured sands

parks, also Boyne Smelter on island has visitor information centre and guided tours; Tannum Sands offers long stretches of sandy beaches with year-round swimming. Various national parks in region, contact Tourist information for details. **Tourist information:** 56 Goondoon St; (079) 72 9922. **Accommodation:** 19 motels, 5 hotel/motels, 10 cara./camp. parks.

Goondiwindi   Pop. 4331

MAP REF. 122 H2, 505 K11

This country town at the junction of five highways is near the picturesque MacIntyre River, which was discovered by explorer Allan Cunningham in 1827 and forms the State border. The Aboriginal word *goonawinna* means 'resting place of the birds'. The district's thriving economy is based on cotton, wheat, beef and wool, and a growing manufacturing sector. **Of interest:** Botanic Gardens of Western Woodlands (25 ha), access from Brennans Rd, 1 km W. Statue of famous racehorse Gunsynd, the 'Goondiwindi Grey', in Apex Park, MacIntyre St. Customs House Museum, opposite park. Historic Victoria Hotel, Marshall St. Tours of Bulk Grains depot and cotton gin (by appt, in season). Walking track along riverbank, brochure available at Tourist information. Oct.: Spring Festival (coincides with flowering of jacarandas and silky oaks). Nov.: Rodeo. **In the area:**

Boobera Lagoon, 20 km SW into NSW, wildlife sanctuary. **Tourist information:** Watertower, McLean St; (076) 71 2653. **Accommodation:** 2 hotels, 2 hotel/motels, 7 motels, 3 cara./camp. parks. **See also:** Darling Downs.

Gordonvale   Pop. 2658

MAP REF. 503 F10, 509 N7

This town is 24 km S of Cairns. **In the area:** Gillies Hwy, with 295 bends, leads west to Atherton. Goldsborough Valley State Forest, 6 km W (15 km off Gillies Hwy), for walking, swimming, canoeing and picnicking. Wooroonooran National Park, 10 km S, spectacular views from summit of Walsh's Pyramid. Orchid Valley Nursery and Gardens, 15 km SW, tropical gardens and coffee shop; tours available. The Mulgrave Rambler, 15-km steam-train ride along cane railway system through canefields and rainforest; charter only. Hambledon Sugar Mill at Edmonton, 16 km N. **Tourist information:** Far North Queensland Promotion Bureau, cnr Ring Road and The Esplanade, Cairns; (070) 51 3588. **Accommodation:** 4 hotels, 1 cara./ camp. park.

Gympie   Pop. 10 791

MAP REF. 505 P6

The city of Gympie started with the 'Great Australian Gold Rush' in 1867, following the discovery of gold by James

Nash. The field proved extremely rich, and some 4 million ounces had been found by the time the gold petered out in the 1920s. By then dairying and agriculture were well established and Gympie continued to prosper. Near the Mary River and 166 km N of Brisbane via the Bruce Hwy, Gympie is the major provincial city servicing the Cooloola region. It is an attractive city with its jacarandas, flowering silky oaks, cassias, poincianas and flame trees. **Of interest:** Woodworks Forestry and Timber Museum, Fraser Rd. Gympie Golden Gem, Bruce Hwy, gem display and sales. Self-guide heritage walk, contact Tourist information for details. Market, 2nd and 4th Sun. each month at Gympie South State School. Aug.: National Country Music Muster. Oct.: Gold Rush Festival. **In the area:** Gold Mining Museum, Brisbane Rd, 5 km S; nearby, cottage of Andrew Fisher, first Queenslander to become Prime Minister (1908). Cooloola Rocks and Minerals, Bruce Hwy, 15 km S. Kenilworth State Forest, 50 km S: 1.3-km Fig Tree walk, north of Little Yabba Creek bridge on the Kenilworth–Maleny Rd. Rock pools and excellent views at Mothar Mountain, 20 km SE. Cooloola section of Great Sandy National Park, 50 km E. Part of the Bicentennial National Trail (a 5000-km trail for walkers and horse riders) runs through Kilkivan, 50 km NW; Great Horse Ride held here each April. Goomeri, 25 km further W, known as 'clock town' because of unique memorial clock in town centre. Nearby, Imbil Forest Drive through scenic pine-forest plantations. Mary Valley Scenic Way runs south between Gympie and Maleny, via Kenilworth. Mary Valley Heritage Railway operates between Gympie and Imbil. **Tourist information:** Bruce Hwy, Lake Alford; (07) 5482 5444. **Accommodation:** 12 hotels, 7 motels, 4 cara./camp. parks.

Hervey Bay   Pop. 22 205

MAP REF. 505 P3

Hervey (pronounced Harvey) Bay is the large area of water between Maryborough and Bundaberg that is protected by Fraser Island. It is also the name of a thriving city on its shore that comprises the pleasant strip of seaside spots along its southern shore, some 34 km NE of Maryborough. An ideal climate makes the area popular, and during the winter months there is an influx of visitors from the south. Hervey Bay is actively promoted as 'Australia's family aquatic playground'. As there is no surf, swimming is safe even for children. Fishing is the main recreation. Boats may be hired and yabbies caught for bait. **Of interest:** In Pialba: Village Pottery, Old Maryborough Rd, open for tour of manufacturing process; Hervey Bay Tourist and Visitors Centre, Old Maryborough Rd, displays model village and ships, and woodwork; paintings at Wide Bay Gallery, Main St; Nature World Wildlife Park, features koalas, other marsupials, lorikeets, crocodiles and other reptiles. In Scarness: Hervey Bay Historical Society Museum, Zephyr St, recalls pioneer days. In Torquay: Golf 'n' Games, Cypress St, with 18-hole mini-golf and 120-m water-slide. At Urangan: cairn in Pulgul St at Dayman Point commemorates landing by Matthew Flinders in 1799 and the Z-Force commandoes who trained there on the *Krait* in World War II; 1-km long pier, off The Esplanade, used by anglers; Neptune's Aquarium, Pulgul St, has performing seals and sharks; Vic Hislop's Shark Show. Humpback whales visit Hervey Bay early Aug.–mid-Oct. on their annual migration; viewing cruises available, contact Tourist information for details. Day trips to Fraser Island. Sun. markets at Urangan and Nikenbar. Aug.: Whale Festival. Oct.: Hervey Bay to Fraser Island Sailboard Marathon. **In the area:** Hervey Bay Marine Park, 40 km N. Quiet seaside resorts at Toogoom and Burrum Heads, 15 km NW. Go-kart track, 2 km W. Historic Brooklyn House at Howard, 25 km W. **Tourist information:** 63 Old Maryborough Rd, Pialba; (071) 24 4050. **Accommodation:** 4 hotel/motels, 18 motels, 1 B&B, many apartments, 6 hostels, 20 cara. parks.

Home Hill   Pop. 3197

MAP REF. 506 H1, 509 Q13
Sister town to Ayr, Home Hill is on the south side of the Burdekin River, 98 km SE of Townsville. The towns are joined by a high-level bridge as the river is liable to flood. **Of interest:** Tours (Mon.–Fri.) of Inkerman Sugar Mill, Seventh Ave, during crushing season (June–Nov.). Ashworths, Eighth Ave, rock shop, museum, and art and craft. Nov. Harvest Festival; Country Music Festival. **In the area:** Groper Creek, 16 km W, for fishing and catching giant

mud crabs; nearby, camping, caravan and picnic areas. Lookout on summit of Mt Inkerman at Inkerman, 15 km SE. **Tourist information:** Ashworths, Eighth Ave; (077) 82 1177. **Accommodation:** 3 hotels, 1 motel, 2 cara./camp. parks.

Hughenden   Pop. 1592

MAP REF. 506 A4, 513 O4
The first recorded Europeans to pass this spot on the Flinders River were members of the expedition led by Frederick Walker in 1861. Walker's party was searching for the lost Burke and Wills expedition. Two years later Ernest Henry visited this area to select a cattle station, and Hughenden came into existence. The town is on the Townsville–Mount Isa rail line and the Flinders Hwy, 243 km SW of Charters Towers. The major regional industries are beef cattle and merino wool. **Of interest:** Explorers' Tree, Stansfield St East, on east bank of Station Creek, a coolibah tree blazed by Walker in 1861, and again by William Landsborough in 1862 when he passed through the area also searching for the lost Burke and Wills expedition. Dinosaur Display Centre, Gray St, houses 14-m replica of *Muttaburrasaurus langdoni*. July: Dinosaur Festival (even-numbered years). **In the area:** At Prairie, 44 km E on Flinders Hwy: mini-museum; historical relics at Cobb & Co. Yards; Hamilton Butchery. Torrens Creek, 88 km E: World War II airstrip near hotel; Exchange Hotel, home of 'dinosaur steaks'. Porcupine National Park, 62 km N, features mini 'Grand Canyon'. Gemstone fossicking at Cheviot Hills, 200 km N, contact Tourist information. **Tourist information:** Shire Offices, 34 Gray St; (077) 41 1288. **Accommodation:** 1 hotel, 2 hotel/motels, 2 motels, 2 cara./camp. parks.

Ilfracombe   Pop. 350

MAP REF. 506 A11, 513 P11
This town, 27 km E of Longreach on the Matilda Hwy, was developed in 1891 as a transport nucleus for Wellshot Station, the largest sheep station in the world (in terms of stock numbers) at that time; the head station was itself the size of a town. The first Qld motorised mail service departed from Ilfracombe in 1910. **Of interest:** Folk Museum, on hwy, includes Oakhampton Craft Cottage (local crafts on display in historic

cottage). Opposite, historic Wellshot Hotel. Langenbaker House, Mitchell St, an early settler's house and rare example of outback living conditions of the era. Extensive range of historical machinery displayed along the highway through the town. **Tourist information:** Shire Offices, Devon St; (076) 58 2233. **Accommodation:** 1 hotel, 1 cara./camp. park.

Ingham   Pop. 5075

MAP REF. 509 N11
A major sugar and sightseeing town near the waterways of the Hinchinbrook Channel, Ingham is on the Bruce Hwy, 110 km NW of Townsville. The town has a strong Italian and Spanish Basque cultural background. **Of interest:** Macknade Mill, Halifax Rd, oldest sugar mill still operating on original site. Victoria Sugar Mill, Forrest Beach Rd, largest in southern hemisphere; guided tours in crushing season, July–Nov. Raintree market, 1st Sun. each month. May: Australian-Italian Festival. Oct.: Maraka Festival. **In the area:** Cemetery, 5 km E, interesting Italian mausoleums. Forrest Beach, 20 km E, 16 km of sandy beach overlooking Palm Group of islands, stinger net swimming enclosures installed in summer. Taylor's Beach, 24 km NE, popular family seaside spot. Hinchinbrook and Orpheus resort islands offshore. Lucinda, 27 km NE on banks of Herbert River, excellent base for fishing holidays. Lumholtz National Park, 50 km NW, features 305-m Wallaman Falls, spectacular scenery, and excellent camping, swimming and picnic spots. Broadwater State Forest Park, 45 km W, in the Herbert River Valley; popular camping and picnic area, includes 1.6-km circuit rainforest walk. Mt Fox, extinct volcano, 65 km SW. Jourama Falls in Paluma Range National Park, 25 km S. Spectacular view from McClelland's Lookout, 48 km S off Bruce Hwy. **Tourist information:** Bruce Hwy; (077) 76 5211. **Accommodation:** 7 hotels, 2 motels, 1 B&B, 1 hostel, 1 cara./camp. park.

Inglewood   Pop. 1007

MAP REF. 123 K1, 505 L11
An early hostelry called Brown's Inn grew into the town of Inglewood, in the south-western corner of the Darling Downs, 108 km SW of Warwick. In the surrounding area beef cattle and sheep

The Johnstone River at Innisfail

are raised, and lucerne, grain and fodder crops are irrigated from Coolmunda Dam, 20 km E, which attracts boating enthusiasts as well as many pelicans and swans. **Tourist information:** cnr Albert and Elizabeth sts; (076) 52 1444. **Accommodation:** 2 motels, 3 cara./ camp. parks.

Innisfail

Pop. 8520

MAP REF. 509 N8

Innisfail is a prosperous, colourful town on the banks of the North and South Johnstone rivers, 88 km SE of Cairns. Sugar has been grown here since the early 1880s and its contribution to the area is celebrated with a Harvest Festival held early Oct. Besides the growing of sugarcane, bananas, pawpaws and other tropical and rare fruit, beef cattle are raised, and the town has a prawn and reef fishing fleet. **Of interest:** Local history museum, Edith St. Chinese Joss House, Owen St. Cane Cutter Monument, Fitzgerald Espl. Warrina Lakes and Botanical Gardens, Charles St. Historic town walk, brochure from Tourist information. Several lovely parks with riverside picnic facilities.

Market, Anzac Memorial Park, 3rd Sat. each month. July: Agricultural Show. Oct.: Harvest Festival. **In the area:** Flying Fish Point and Ella Bay, 5 km N, for swimming and camping. Bramston Beach, palm-fringed shoreline, 23 km N. Eubenangee Swamp National Park 29 km N via Miriwinni, birdwatching. Johnstone River Crocodile Farm, 8 km NE. Qld's highest peak Mt Bartle Frere (1611 m), 25 km NW; track to summit; Josephine Falls at base. Johnstone River Gorge, via Palmerston Hwy, 18 km W, has walking tracks to several waterfalls. Crawfords Lookout, 38 km W, off the Palmerston Hwy, spectacular views of Johnstone River. Wooroonooran National Park, 30 km W; road leads to Atherton Tableland. Australian Sugar Museum at Mourilyan, 7 km S. Etty Bay, 15 km S, beach and picnic area. Innisfail is excellent base for exploration of quieter lagoons and islands (including Dunk) of Great Barrier Reef. Scenic tourist drives, brochure from Tourist information. **Tourist information:** Cassowary Coast Development Bureau, River Ave; (070) 61 6448. **Accommodation:** 4 hotels, 7 motels, 3 hostels, 4 cara./camp. parks.

Ipswich

Pop. 65 346

MAP REF. 497 K9, 505 P9

In 1827 a convict settlement was established alongside the Bremer River to quarry limestone and convey it down the river to Brisbane for building. In 1842 the settlement, called Limestone, opened to free settlers and in 1843 it was renamed Ipswich. The town is a major industrial centre, with railways, coalmining, sawmills, and foundries. Australia's largest RAAF base is in the suburb of Amberley. **Of interest:** Numerous heritage buildings including St Pauls Anglican Church (1859), Brisbane St; St Mary's Catholic Church (1904), Elizabeth St; Claremont (1858), Milford St; Gooloowan (1864), Quarry St; Ginn Cottage, Ginn St; and Ipswich Grammar School (1863), Burnett St. Regional Art Gallery, cnr Limestone St and D'Arcy Doyle Pl. Self-guide historic walks, contact Tourist information. Showground market each Sun. Redbank Woollen Mills markets, each Sat. and Sun. Country markets, 1st Sun. each month. Apr.: Heritage Festival. July: Medieval Fair. Oct.: Jacaranda Festival. **In the area:** North-east: College's Crossing (7 km), Mt Crosby (12 km)

and Lake Manchester (22 km) – all popular swimming and picnic spots. Outback Emu Farm, 6 km N. At Rosewood, 20 km W: St Brigid's Church, largest wooden church in South Pacific; steam-train rides, 4 km N of Rosewood, last Sun. each month. At Swanbank Power Station, 12 km SE, steam trains run by Qld Pioneer Steam Railway Co-op; check times with Tourist information. Restored historic homestead Wolston House at Wacol, 16 km E. **Tourist information:** cnr Brisbane St and D'Arcy Doyle Pl.; (07) 3281 0555. **Accommodation:** 3 hotel/motels, 6 motels, 4 B&B, 1 hostel, 4 cara./camp. parks.

Isisford

Pop. 150

MAP REF. 506 A13, 513 P13, 515 O1

Established in 1877 by travelling hawkers William and James Whitman, Isisford is 116 km S of Longreach. First called Wittown, the town was renamed in 1880 to recall the ford in the nearby Barcoo River and the proximity of Isis Downs Station Homestead. **Of interest:** Bicentennial Museum, Centenary Dr. **In the area:** Huge (largest in Australia) semicircular, prefabricated shearing shed, (1913), at Isis Downs Station, 20 km E; visits by appt; (076) 58 8203. Oma Waterhole, 16 km W, popular spot for fishing and water sports. **Tourist information:** Shire Offices, St Marys St; (076) 58 8277. **Accommodation:** 2 hotels, 1 cara./camp. park.

Julia Creek

Pop. 572

MAP REF. 513 J4

A small cattle and rail township named after the niece of Donald MacIntyre, the first European settler in the area. Located on the Flinders Hwy, Julia Creek is 134 km E of Cloncurry. A sealed road runs north to Normanton in the Gulf Savannah. The town is an important cattle-trucking centre. **Of interest:** McIntyre Museum, Burke St. May: Julia Creek Dirt and Dust Triathlon; Campdraft. **In the area:** Saxby Roundup held each June at Taldora Station, an isolated area 230 km N; access via Julia Creek. **Tourist information:** Shire Offices, Julia St; (077) 46 7166. **Accommodation:** 1 hotel, 1 hotel/motel, 1 motel, 1 cara./camp. park. **See also:** Gulf Savannah.

QUEENSLAND

Jundah
Pop. 100

MAP REF. 515 M2

Jundah (an Aboriginal word for 'women'), 219 km SW of Longreach, was gazetted as a town in 1880. For 20 years the area was important for opal mining, but lack of water eventually caused the mines to close. **Of interest:** Barcoo Historical Museum, Perkins St. June: Bronco Branding. Oct.: Race Carnival. **In the area:** Jundah Opal Fields, 27 km NW. Welford National Park, 20 km S. **Tourist information:** Shire Offices, Dickson St; (076) 58 6133. **Accommodation:** 1 hotel, 1 cara./camp. park.

Karumba
Pop. 708

MAP REF. 508 B8, 511 H8, 515 O1

Karumba, 69 km NW of Normanton, is at the mouth of the Norman River and is the centre of the prawning industry in the Gulf of Carpentaria. A barramundi fishing industry and live-cattle industry also operate from the town. **Of interest:** Slipway once used by the Sydney-to-England Empire Flying Boats Service. Boat hire and accommodation at Karumba Point. Barramundi display at the Barra Restocking Ponds, Riverview Dr.; feeding at 4.45pm daily. Old cemetery, 2 km NW, on road to Karumba Point, a small settlement 6 km NW. July: Karumba Kapers. Dec.: Fishermen's Ball. **In the area:** Town is surrounded by flat wetlands extending 30 km inland, habitat of saltwater crocodiles and several species of birds, including brolgas and cranes. Karumba is easiest point of access to the Gulf. Charter vessels for fishing and exploration of the Gulf and Norman River. *The Ferryman*, cruises on Norman River. **Tourist information:** Shire Offices, Haig St, Normanton; (077) 45 1166. **Accommodation:** 1 hotel./motel, 3 cara./camp. parks. **See also:** Gulf Savannah.

Kenilworth
Pop. 257

MAP REF. 505 P7

West of the Blackall Range, through the Obi Obi Valley, is Kenilworth. The town is famous for its Kenilworth Country Foods hand-crafted cheeses. This enterprise began when the local cheese factory closed and six employees mortgaged their homes to start the venture. Lasting Impressions Gallery of Fine Art, 6 Elizabeth St. **Of interest:**

Kev Franzi's Photo Workshop and Movie Museum, Eumundi Rd. **In the area:** Kenilworth Bluff, 6 km N, steep walking track to lookout point. Little Yabba Creek, 8 km S, is a good picnic spot where bellbirds are often heard. Lake Borumba 32 km NW, for picnics and water sports. Nearby, Imbil Forest Drive through scenic forests and farmlands to Gympie. **Tourist information:** cnr Sixth Ave and Aerodrome Rd, Maroochydore; (07) 5479 1566. **Accommodation:** 1 hotel, 1 motel, camping facilities.

Killarney
Pop. 827

MAP REF. 123 N1, 505 O11

This attractive small town is on the banks of the Condamine River, 34 km SE of Warwick, and very close to the NSW border. Feb.: Agricultural Show. Nov.: Rodeo. **In the area:** Noteworthy mountain scenery. Dagg's and Brown's waterfalls, 1–2 km S. Cherrabah Homestead Resort, 7 km S, offers horseriding, golf, sailing and excellent bushwalking. Carrs Lookout, 12 km E. Queen Mary Falls in Main Range National Park, 15 km E; native birds fed daily at kiosk. **Tourist information:** 49 Albion St (New England Hwy), Warwick; (076) 61 3122. **Accommodation:** 1 cara./camp. park, 1 resort.

Kingaroy
Pop. 6672

MAP REF. 505 N6

This prosperous agricultural town is known for its peanuts and is the home of Sir Johannes (Joh) Bjelke-Petersen, the former Premier of Qld. Peanuts, maize, wheat, stonefruit and grapes, soy and navy beans are grown, and specialised agricultural equipment is manufactured. Kingaroy is 233 km NW of Brisbane and its giant peanut silos are a distinctive landmark. Kingaroy claims the title 'Peanut Capital of Australia', and also 'Baked Bean Capital of Australia', with 75 per cent of Australia's navy beans grown in the district. **Of interest:** In Haly St: Kingaroy Bicentennial Heritage Museum; Tourist Information Centre, with videos on peanut and navy-bean industries; Garden of Rocks, landscaping with semi-precious stones and petrified wood. Apr.: Peanut Festival (odd-numbered years). **In the area:** Farmstays and scenic drives available, inquire at Tourist information. Mt Wooroolin scenic lookout, 3 km W.

Bunya Mountains National Park, 56 km SW. **Tourist information:** Haly St (opp. silos); (071) 62 3199. **Accommodation:** 5 hotels, 6 motels, 2 cara./camp. parks.

Kuranda
Pop. 616

MAP REF. 503 E7, 509 M6

This village in the rainforest at the top of the Macalister Range is best known to tourists who have taken the 34-km trip from Cairns on the 100-year-old Scenic Railway or the more recent Skyrail cableway. **Of interest:** Railway station with platforms adorned by lush ferns and orchids. Skyrail Rainforest Cableway, spectacular gondola ride through rainforest to Cairns; return via Scenic Railway, or vice versa. Wildlife Noctarium, displays rainforest animals normally active only at night. Australian Butterfly Sanctuary, over 2000 butterflies in forest setting; guided tours available. Heritage markets and Bird Sanctuary in rainforest setting. Guided tours of river and rainforest depart from riverbank below railway station. Markets Wed.–Fri. and Sun. May: Folk Festival. **In the area:** Paradise in the Rainforest, offers scenic rides on tractor train. Wrights Lookout, 7 km SE, offers views of the Barron Falls, spectacular after heavy rain. **Tourist information:** Far North Queensland Promotion Bureau, cnr Ring Rd and The Esplanade, Cairns; (070) 51 3588. **Accommodation:** 2 hotels, 3 motels, 1 cara./camp. park. **See also:** Atherton Tableland; The Far North.

Kynuna
Pop. 18

MAP REF. 513 J6

On the Matilda Hwy, 161 km NW of Winton, Kynuna was established in the 1860s and was a staging point for Cobb & Co. coaches. **Of interest:** Kynuna's only hotel is the famous Blue Heeler with its 1-m high, illuminated blue heeler statue on roof. Waltzing Matilda Exhibition, open Apr.–Sept., in tent opposite hotel. Sept.: 'Surf' Carnival (inland version of Iron Man contest). Nov.: Rodeo. **In the area:** Combo Waterhole, 24 km SE on western side of old Winton–Kynuna Rd, scene of the events described in 'Waltzing Matilda', Banjo Paterson's famous song. **Tourist information:** Blue Heeler Hotel, Matilda Hwy; (077) 46 8650. **Accommodation:** 1 hotel/motel, 2 cara./camp. parks.

The Far North

Elinjaa Falls, near Millaa Millaa on the Atherton Tableland

Sitting in a lush, tropical garden through dusk and into evening, and dining superbly on king prawns and Queensland mud crabs, you will find it hard to believe you are at 'the end of the line' – **Port Douglas** is the most northerly of the easily accessible coastal towns of Queensland. Such a Port Douglas scene typifies the beauty of coastal Queensland; a restaurant looking down from a forest-covered hill that looms over the small town and the 7 kilometres of ocean beach. By day the dense tropical forest is revealed in showers of coloured flowers against the intense green. The lavish rainforest and the rush of sparkling mountain streams are lasting impressions for the traveller in the north – a region larger than most European countries and considered by many to be the most diversely beautiful and exciting part of Australia.

Cairns, 1832 kilometres from Brisbane, is the stepping-stone to a variety of sightseeing excursions. A major city for tourism, Cairns is often known as the 'capital of Far North Queensland'. Nestling beside Trinity Bay, this scenic city is an ideal base for visiting the surrounding tourist attractions. From Cairns you can relax on a launch cruise that takes you to see the wonders of the Great Barrier Reef or explore uninhabited islands. Aerial tours from Cairns take you over the Great Plateau, with its lush tablelands and spectacular waterfalls.

The pleasant climate in winter and early spring is one of the main attractions of this city. Visitors can enjoy snorkelling or other water sports, while anglers flock to Cairns from September to December to catch the big black marlin. Cairns itself is a picturesque city. Delicate ferns, tropical shrubs and fragrant flowers thrive in the Botanical Gardens, where a walking track joins the Centenary Lakes Parkland, created in 1976 to mark the city's hundredth anniversary. Two lakes, one saltwater and the other freshwater, provide a haven for wildlife among native trees and shrubs. You can also see orchids, which form the basis of one of Cairns' important export industries, growing to perfection in orchid nurseries.

There are dozens of places around Cairns, all within easy driving distance on good roads, that will claim the traveller's attention. Port Douglas is only one of them. The 60-kilometre journey north from Cairns passes through a magnificent stretch of coastal scenery as the Cook Highway winds past white coral beaches, through archways of tropical forest and past the islands that dot the blue northern waters. Despite its increasing popularity with tourists, Port Douglas still retains some of its fishing-village atmosphere.

Just north of Port Douglas (and remember to stop at the cemetery that contains the graves of many pioneer settlers who were lured north by the Palmer River gold rush) is the sugar town of **Mossman**. From July to October, sugarcane farmers once created raging fires to prepare the cane for harvesting; nowadays, however, cane is more often harvested green. These days the cane cutter is seldom seen, having exchanged a machete for a seat on an ingenious machine that cuts the cane and throws it, in a shower of short sticks, into the hopper that trails behind. Sugar-growing is a major industry of the north, and the waving fields of cane wind through the mountains for hundreds of kilometres down the lush coastal plain.

Near Mossman is one of those perfect places that seem so plentiful in the north, the Mossman River Gorge. A short walk under the dense green canopy of the rainforest leads to the boulder-strewn river, which rushes in a series of cascades through the jungle-sided gorge. It is a place to picnic, to swim or simply to bask in the rays of the North Queensland sun.

There are many such places, particularly on the edge of the Atherton Tableland, where the mountains have thrown up fascinating geological oddities and where waterfalls spill. For example, near **Atherton** township there are two volcanic lakes, Barrine and Eacham, where walking tracks through the rainforest give beautiful water views and a chance to see the abundant wildlife, including parrots, waterfowl, turtles, platypuses, goannas and many marsupials. Nearby is Tinaburra, a popular tourist settlement alongside Tinaroo Dam. On the Yungaburra–Malanda road is the amazing and much-photographed Curtain Fig Tree which has resulted from a strangling fig taking over its host tree, climbing higher and higher and throwing down showers of roots to support its massive structure. The rich dairy country around Malanda, 14 kilometres south-east of Atherton, supplies milk for what is known as the longest milk run in the world: to Weipa, Mount Isa, Darwin, and into Western Australia. At Malanda Falls, just west of town, water cascades over a fern-swathed precipice into a delightful swimming pool.

South-west of Malanda is Mount Hypipamee National Park, where visitors can walk beneath huge rainforest trees, past staghorn ferns and orchics, along Dinner Creek to the falls and up to the crater, a funnel of sheer granite walls that fall away into dark and forbidding water. There are dozens of other waterfalls in this area. Near **Millaa Millaa** is Falls Circuit, where the Millaa Millaa, Zillie, Mungalli and Elinjaa waterfalls are sited amid a magnificent panorama of rainforest mountains and plains.

There are four main highways linking the tablelands with the coast; all are magnificent scenic routes. Undoubtedly, however, the most novel and popular way of getting up to the tableland is by the scenic railway to **Kuranda**, built to serve the Herberton tin mine in the 1890s and now regarded as one of the most difficult feats of engineering in Queensland. The track climbs 300 metres in 20 kilometres to traverse the Barron Gorge, and part of it runs over a viaduct along the edge of a 200-metre precipice. The lovely old carriages of the train have rear platforms with decorative iron railings where travellers can stand and take in the superb view uninterrupted. The Kuranda railway station, festooned in tropical plants, ferns and orchids, is a much-photographed stop before the descent to Cairns. More recently the Skyrail Rainforest Cableway has been constructed between Smithfield, near Cairns, and Kuranda providing visitors an alternative: a spectacular gondola ride through the rainforest.

The Atherton and Evelyn tablelands are areas of volcanic land at altitudes between 600 and 1000 metres, mild in climate and supporting dairying, maize and tea tree (for oil). Gradually the tablelands change to dry, rough country, where tin, copper, lead and zinc were once mined. Beyond the main tableland settlement of Atherton is the fascinating mining town of Herberton, with its Historical Village, Tin Festival each September, local museum called the Tin Pannikan and old houses proclaiming its boom days of the late nineteenth century. Ravenshoe, on the Kennedy Highway, is noted for its gemstones and fine timbers grown and milled in the area (the Torimba forest festival is held each October); and further west, Mount Garnet, an old mining town where tourists can pan the tailings.

Four-wheel drive tours of the region with an Aboriginal guide are available. Visitors are educated on the local Aboriginal sites, Dreamtime legends and native flora; details are available at Port Douglas Dive Centre. Near Mission Beach, join the Giramay Walkabout where members of the Giramay Aboriginal group share with visitors the beauty of the Murray Falls area, as well as their knowledge of the environment.

For further information on the Far North, contact the Far North Qld Promotion Bureau Ltd, cnr Grafton & Hartley sts, Cairns; (070) 51 3588. For more information on the Atherton Tableland, contact the Atherton Tableland Promotion Bureau, cnr Mabel and Vernon sts, Atherton; (070) 91 4222. **See also:** individual entries in A–Z listing for those towns indicated by bold type. **Map references:** 503, 509.

Atherton Tableland – its European history

A century ago the Atherton Tableland was unknown to Europeans until an aptly named prospector, James Venture Mulligan, led several expeditions south-west from Cooktown between 1874 and 1876, having previously discovered the spectacular Palmer River goldfields in 1873. The northern Aboriginal groups bitterly resented the miners' intrusion, and during the 1860s and 1870s there were many skirmishes between new settlers and Aborigines, and several massacres.

In 1874 Mulligan named the Hodgkinson and St George rivers, and Mount Mulligan, north of the tobacco town of Dimbulah. He returned in 1875 and found a beautiful river flowing north. This was the Barron River, which eventually flows east to the Pacific coast. Mulligan travelled up the Barron and camped at Granite Creek, where Mareeba now stands. He travelled over rich basaltic plains, now the tobacco fields on the Kuranda road, until stopped by dense, impenetrable forest near what is now Tolga. He marvelled at huge cedar and kauri trees, but skirted the forest and camped near the site of Atherton. Nearby he discovered the Wild River and traces of tin. However, as the nearest ports were Cooktown and Cardwell, some 500 kilometres away, Mulligan considered the area too isolated for tin mining.

Mulligan later found extensive gold strikes as he prospected the valley. The Hodgkinson gold rush started as soon as Mulligan reported his find, most of the diggers coming from Cooktown and the Palmer River. The towns of Kingsborough and Thornborough quickly sprang up in 1876 between Mount Mulligan and Mareeba, and in two years the population was approximately 10 000.

This caused an unusual situation, the interior being opened up before a direct route to the coast had been discovered and a port founded. During 1876 several difficult tracks were cut down the steep, densely jungled coastal ranges towards Port Douglas and Trinity Bay. The latter eventually became Cairns. Some epic hauls up the range were recorded: in 1881, 80 bullocks hauled up the complete battery for the Great Northern tin mine at Herberton. An impressive monument at the foot of the Cairns–Kuranda road, the Kennedy Highway, commemorates the trailblazers.

The railway line from Cairns to Kuranda, on the edge of the Tableland, is only 34 kilometres long but took four years to build, cost 20 workers their lives, and has 15 tunnels. It was completed in 1888, and the prosperity of the Atherton Tableland, and Cairns, was assured.

In April 1877 John Atherton settled at the junction of Emerald Creek and the Barron River, and formed Emerald End station. When he found alluvial tin in the headwaters of the creek, he reputedly yelled 'Tin-hurroo' to his mate – hence the name of the area, Tinaroo. Atherton led others to major tin lodes on the Wild River, discovered by Mulligan four years earlier. Mining commenced and the town of Herberton came into existence. The Tate River field was also an important find, and tin proved to be more influential in the development of the area than the short-term excitement of gold.

In 1880 Atherton built a wide-verandahed shanty at Granite Creek, a popular camping spot halfway between Port Douglas and Herberton, which was used by men flocking to the new field. This became Mareeba. Eventually the railway linked Herberton and Ravenshoe with Cairns.

Stockman's Hall of Fame and Outback Heritage Centre, Longreach

QUEENSLAND

Laidley
Pop. 2315

MAP REF. 496 H9, 505 O9

Laidley, 75 km from Brisbane, is between Ipswich and Gatton, in the Lockyer Valley. It is the principal town in a rural area of the Greater Brisbane Region regarded as 'Queensland's country garden'. **Of interest:** Das Neumann Haus (1893), William St, an historic house with tourist centre and art gallery. Regular country markets 2nd and last Sat. each month. Apr.: Clydesdale Heavy Horse Show. Sept.: Chelsea Festival Week. Oct.: Festival of Performing Arts. **In the area:** Laidley Pioneer Village, 1 km S, features original buildings from old township. Adjacent, Narda Lagoon, flora and fauna sanctuary; longest suspension footbridge in southern hemisphere crosses over lagoon. Lake Dyer, 1 km W; water-skiing and fishing, picnic/barbecue facilities nearby. Lake Clarendon, 17 km NW, birdwatching and picnicking. Scenic drives; leaflets from Tourist information. **Tourist information:** cnr William and Patrick sts; (07) 5465 3241. **Accommodation:** 2 hotels, 1 motel, 1 B&B.

Landsborough
Pop. 1150

MAP REF. 497 M2, 500 E13, 505 P7

Landsborough is just off Glass House Mountains Tourist Dr., 9 km SW of the Caloundra turnoff from the Bruce Hwy. **Of interest:** In Maleny St: Historical museum; De Maine Pottery. Collectorama, Glass House Mountains Tourist Dr., a bottle, gemstone and shell museum. June: William Landsborough Day. **In the area:** Queensland Reptile and Fauna Park, 4 km S. Dularcha National Park, 1 km NE; 'Dularcha' is the Aboriginal word for Blackbutt country. Big Kart Track, 5 km N, unsealed road suitable for conventional vehicles (except after heavy rain). **Tourist information:** Museum, Maleny St; (07) 5494 1755. **Accommodation:** 1 motel, 2 cara./camp. parks.

Longreach
Pop. 3607

MAP REF. 506 A11, 513 O11

Longreach has a small population, but there are 800 000 sheep and 20 000 beef cattle in the area. It is the most important and prosperous town in the central west of the State. On the Thomson River, this friendly, modern town is some 700 km by road or rail west of Rockhampton. It was here in 1870 that Harry Redford, better known as Captain Starlight, with four mates rounded up 1000 head of cattle and drove them 2400 km into SA over wild unmapped country that only 10 years before had been the downfall of Burke and Wills. There Starlight sold the cattle. Since they did not belong to him, he was arrested in Adelaide and brought back to Qld to be put on trial at Roma. Despite the evidence, the jury found him not guilty, probably because of the pioneer philosophy that if you are daring enough to carry out that sort of deed, you deserve to get away with it! The events were the basis for Rolf Boldrewood's novel *Robbery Under Arms*. Although Qantas (**Q**ueensland **An**d **N**orthern **T**erritory **A**erial **S**ervice) actually started in Winton, it soon moved its base to Longreach and began regular operations. The same hangar used then became Australia's first aircraft factory and the first of 6 DH-50 biplanes was assembled in 1926. The world's first Flying Surgeon Service started from Longreach in 1959. **Of interest:** Broad streets and several historic buildings. On Galah St: Uniting Church (1892), built for Grazier's Association; court house (1892). Post office (1902), cnr Duck and Eagle sts. Railway station (1916), Sir Hudson Fysh Dr. Old machinery displayed at Powerhouse Museum, Swan St; open Mar.–Oct. Arts and Crafts, Ibis St; open p.m. Mar.–Oct. On Matilda Hwy: Stockman's Hall of Fame and Outback Heritage Centre, featuring exhibition hall, theatre with audiovisuals, library and resource centre; nearby, Banjo's Outback Theatre and Pioneer Shearing Shed (open Mar.–Oct.); School of Distance Education (tours on weekdays during term); Longreach Pastoral College (tours, inquire at Tourist information). Qantas Park, Eagle St, replica of original Qantas booking office which now houses Tourist information. Qantas Founders Outback Museum at airport, Matilda Hwy. Jackson's Weapon Museum, Cassowary St. Pamela's Doll Display and Syd's Outback Collection Corner, Quail St. Cobb & Co. coach rides around town. *Yellowbelly Express* and Billabong Boat Cruises, for cruises on Thomson River. Tourist Promotion Assoc. Markets, 2nd Sun. Apr.–Sept. June: Hall of Fame Race Meeting. July: Diamond Shears (Australia's premier shearing competition). Sept.: Starlight Stampede (even-numbered years). **In the area:** Oakley Station, 15 km N; tours available of this sheep and cattle station. Group tours available to quarter-horse stud at Longway Station, 16 km N. Folk Museum at Ilfracombe,

27 km E. Toobrack Station, 68 km S, 100-year-old homestead; open daily, also offers accommodation and camping. **Tourist information:** Qantas Park, Eagle St; (076) 58 3555. **Accommodation:** 3 hotels, 2 hotel/motels, 5 motels, 2 B&B, 2 cara./camp. parks.

Lucinda Pop. 784

MAP REF. 509 O11

Lucinda, the port for Ingham's sugar, has the world's longest offshore sugar-loading jetty. The conveyor belt, 5.76 km long, loads 2000 tonnes of sugar an hour. Charter boats leave the Dungeness harbour for fishing, cruising and trips to the islands. **In the area:** Unique Italian cemetery, 3 km N. Wallaman Falls, 305-m-high single fall, 80 km S in Lumholtz National Park. **Tourist information:** Bruce Hwy, Ingham; (077) 76 5211. **Accommodation:** 1 hotel/motel, 1 cara./camp. park.

Mackay Pop. 40 250

MAP REF. 507 L5

Mackay, often called the sugar capital of Australia, produces one-third of the nation's sugar crop. Five mills operate in the area, and the bulk-sugar loading terminal is the world's largest. Sugar was first grown in 1866, a mill was built, and in the same year Mackay became a town. It became a major port in 1939 when a breakwater was built, making it one of Australia's largest artificial harbours. The nearby Hay Point coal-loading terminals handle the output from the Central Qld coalfields. Gazetted in 1918, Mackay is now a progressive tropical city. Besides sugar and coal, the town's economy depends on beef cattle, dairying, timber, grain, seafood and the growing of tropical fruit. Tourism is a growth industry, with the islands of Brampton, Lindeman and Hamilton, and the Great Barrier Reef accessible from Mackay. **Of interest:** Self-guide heritage walk of historic buildings includes: Commonwealth and National banks, town hall, court house, police station and customs house. Queens Park and Orchid House, Goldsmith St. Entertainment Centre, Gordon St. Replica of old Richmond sugar mill, Nebo Rd, houses Tourist information. Just north of town: Mt Bassett Weather Station and lookout; Mt Pleasant Reservoir and lookout. Numerous beaches: Harbour, Town, Blacks,

Bucasia, Illawong, Lamberts and Shoal Point. Cruises, fishing charters and scenic flights available. July: Festival of the Arts. Sept.: Sugartime Festival. **In the area:** Farleigh sugar mill, 15 km N; tours available during crushing season (July–Oct.). Cape Hillsborough National Park, 40 km N. Various lookouts off road to Eungella township. Eungella National Park, 84 km NW. Polstone Sugar Cane Farm, 15 km W; tours from July–Oct. Historic Greenmount Homestead, 20 km W, near Walkerston. Kinchant Dam, 20 km W of Walkerston. At Mirani, 30 km W, Juipera Walkabout, an educational walk with Aboriginal guide explaining use of plants; contact Mirani museum in Victoria St. Nebo, 100 km SW of Mackay on Peak Downs Hwy: Nebo Museum, Reynolds St, and a rodeo in July. Orchidways, orchid farm on Homebush Rd, 25 km S; closed Thurs. At Homebush: craft and art gallery; self-drive tour through historic Homebush area (pamphlet available at Tourist information). Lookout at Hay Point coal-loading terminal, 30 km S. Cape Palmerston National Park, 80 km S; 4WD access only. **Tourist information:** The Mill, Nebo Rd; (079) 52 2677. **Accommodation:** 19 hotels, 29 motels, 10 cara./camp. parks.

Main Beach Pop. part of Gold Coast

MAP REF. 497 O12, 499 F5, 505 Q10

Towards the northern end of the Gold Coast strip, Main Beach is packed with attractions. **In the area:** At Main Beach on The Spit: Sea World, famous marine park; Marina Mirage, Mariner's Cove and Fisherman's Wharf – tourist complexes with specialty shops, restaurants, outdoor cafes and weekend entertainment. **Tourist information:** Cavill Mall, Surfers Paradise; (07) 5538 4419. **Accommodation:** Low and high-rise hotels and motels, self-contained apartments, 1 cara./camp. park. **See also:** The Gold Coast.

Maleny Pop. 789

MAP REF. 497 L2, 500 B11, 505 P7

A steep road climbs from the coast west to Maleny, 50 km SW of Maroochydore. The surrounding area is excellent dairy country. From Mary Cairncross Park, an area of thick rainforest south-east of town, there is a fine view of the Glass House Mountains to the south These 10 spectacular trachyte peaks were named by Captain Cook as he sailed up the coast in 1770, for the sun shining on the rockfaces reminded him of glass-houses in his native Yorkshire. **Of interest:** Art and craft galleries. **In the area:** 28-km scenic drive north-east from Maleny through Montville and Flaxton to Mapleton (one of the best in south-east Qld), offering views of Sunshine Coast, Moreton Island, and nearby pineapple and sugarcane fields; museums, antique shops, fruit stalls, tea

Customs house, Mackay

The Herb Garden at Montville, near Maleny

rooms and tourist attractions along the way. Montville, 17 km NE, has excellent potteries and art and craft galleries. At Flaxton, 3 km further N, miniature English village and clock museum. Kondalilla and Mapleton Falls national parks, off to E between Montville and Mapleton. Lookout with 360° views at Howell's Knob, 4 km W. Rainforest walks and spectacular views at Mary Cairncross Park, 7 km SE. **Tourist information:** 23 Maple St; (07) 5499 9033. **Accommodation:** 1 hotel, 3 motels, 12 B&B, 1 cara./camp. park. **See also:** The Sunshine Coast.

Mareeba   Pop. 6795

MAP REF. 503 C9, 509 M7

Tobacco-growing is being phased out and replaced with mango, tea-tree oil, coffee and sugarcane crops. Farms in the Mareeba-Dimbulah area are irrigated from Lake Tinaroo. Mining and cattle are also important industries. **Of interest:** Bicentennial Lakes, a park with plantings to encourage wildlife; Mason St. Mareeloa Heritage Museum and Tourist Information Centre: local history exhibits, Centenary Park, Byrnes St. May: Dimbulah Festival. July: Rodeo. **In the area:** Pinevale Ranch, 10 km E, offers day-horseriding. Aviation and Military Museum (The

Beck Collection), 5 km S, Kennedy Hwy. Granite Gorge, 12 km SW, off Chewko Rd. Mareeba Coffee Estates, 7 km W on Mareeba–Dimbulah road. Mainly sealed road via Dimbulah (only 20 km dirt) crosses Great Dividing Range to Chillagoe (145 km W), old mining town with fine limestone caves nearby. The new Wetlands Project, 22 km N at end of Fabis Rd, extends for 5000 ha and backs onto the Hann Tablelands. Several cattle station farmstays in Mareeba area; inquire at Tourist information. **Tourist information:** Centenary Park, Byrnes St; (070) 92 5674. **Accommodation:** 4 hotels, 2 motels, 3 cara./camp. parks. **See also:** Atherton Tableland; Cape York.

Maroochydore   Pop. 28 509

MAP REF. 497 N1, 500 H9, 505 Q7

A well-established and popular beach resort, Maroochydore, 112 km N of Brisbane, is the business centre of the Sunshine Coast. **Of interest:** Famous surfing beaches. Maroochy River, with pelicans and swans, offers safe swimming. Cotton Tree, at river mouth, popular camping area. Replica of Captain Cook's ship *Endeavour*, David Low Way. **In the area:** River cruises up Maroochy River to Dunethin Rock through sugarcane fields. Bli Bli Castle,

10 km NE, a 'medieval' castle with dungeon torture chamber and doll museum. Nostalgia Town, 11 km NE, emphasises humour in history. **Tourist information:** cnr Sixth Ave and Aerodrome Rd; (07) 5479 1566. **Accommodation:** 2 hotels, 11 motels, several apartment complexes, 4 cara./ camp. parks. **See also:** The Sunshine Coast.

Maryborough   Pop. 20 790

MAP REF. 505 P4

Maryborough is a well-planned, attractive, provincial city, 3 hours' drive north of Brisbane and on the banks of the Mary River. It was discovered in 1842. In 1847 a wool store was established near the original town site. A village and port soon grew to handle the wool being produced inland. The settlement was officially proclaimed a port in 1859 and a municipality in 1861. Maryborough is promoted as the Heritage City and visitors are encouraged to take the Heritage Walk and drive through the suburbs to see the excellent architecture of a bygone era. The climate is dry subtropical with warm moist summers and mild winters, and several seaside resorts are nearby. **Of interest:** Fine examples of early colonial architecture: St Paul's bell tower (1887), Lennox St, with one of the last sets of pealing bells in Qld; Brennan & Geraghty's Store, also in Lennox St, property of National Trust. Historic displays at Bond Store Museum, Wharf St. Croydon Foundry Office, Ferry St, includes museum and tourist information centre. Fruit Salad Cottage Heritage Museum, Banana St. Pioneer gravesites and original township site in Alice St, Baddow; historic time gun outside city hall. Several parks: in Sussex St, Queen's Park, unusual domed fernery and waterfall; in Kent St, Elizabeth Park, rose gardens; on cnr Cheapside and Alice sts, Anzac Park; Ululah Lagoon, near the golf links, off Lions Dr., a scenic waterbird sanctuary where black swans, wild geese, ducks and waterhens may be hand-fed. Maryborough Heritage Walk and Drive, brochure from Tourist information. Houseboat hire available at 102 Steindl St, Granville. Heritage City Market each Thurs., Adelaide and Kent sts. Ebenezer's Lamplight Bazaar, Wharf St, every Fri. 4 p.m. till late; stallholders dress in 1870s costume. May: Best of Brass. Sept.: Heritage City Festival. Oct.: Maryborough Master

Cape York

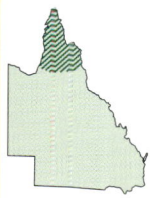

The Cape York Peninsula is a vast area as large as Victoria. There are more than 10 000 people living on the Cape. About half live in Weipa and the rest in Aboriginal and Islander communities, isolated townships and on scattered pastoral stations. Many of these are along the telegraph line which runs to the northern tip.

The first European exploration of Cape York was in the 1840s and the 1860s by the Jardine brothers, John Bradford, Robert Jack, and the ill-fated Edmund Kennedy and his famous Aboriginal guide Jacky Jacky. Vegetation varies from gums and anthills in the south to swamps and rainforests in the north. Many areas of the Cape are traditional Aboriginal lands, national parks and a sanctuary for much of Australia's unique flora and fauna.

There are two distinct seasons: the wet and the dry. During the wet virtually all road transport stops as there are almost no sealed roads or bridges in the area. Movement during this season is limited to regular flights with Flight West, Sunstate and Trans Pacific airlines; all run scheduled daily flights to Cape York Airport. There is also sea access (year round) on the *Kangaroo Explorer* departing weekly from Cairns. Some 50 kilometres further along, a dirt track leads to the northernmost area of Cape York. The local Aboriginal place name for this area is Pajinka.

Situated 400 metres from the very tip of the peninsula, on traditional Aboriginal land, is the comfortable Pajinka Wilderness Lodge providing cabin-style rooms with private amenities. Adjacent to the lodge is the Pajinka camping ground. Both are owned and operated by the Injinoo Aboriginal Community. Permits are required to enter the Injinoo area north of the Dulhunty River; these can be obtained on board the Jardine River ferry, or by contacting the Injinoo Community Council on (070) 69 3252.

All Aboriginal and Islander communities are self-sufficient and may be visited, but *it is essential that a permit be obtained in writing beforehand.* The main communities are Lockhart River on the east coast; Injinoo and Pajinka at the tip; and Edward River, Weipa South and Aurukun on the Gulf. The Ang-Gnarra Aboriginal Corporations at Laura offer a guide and ranger service to visitors. Details at the caravan park.

The Cape is the ideal place to go exploring. A reliable and well-equipped 4WD vehicle, preferably with a winch, is essential for this area. It is possible to drive north from Cairns or Mareeba to Bamaga through Laura and Coen. The Royal Automobile Club of Queensland provides an excellent map and information sheet both of which are essential reading before an expedition north is planned. *Conditions on the track are often unpredictable and the RACQ or police at Cairns should be contacted before heading north.*

June to November are the recommended travel months. At the peak of the season over one hundred vehicles travel northern Cape roads daily. The narrow, rough and blind roads are difficult, and a motorist travelling fast has no chance of avoiding an oncoming car. There are many accidents in this area each year. Drivers are advised to travel slowly and exercise particular care. The Laura, Kennedy, Stewart, Archer, Wenlock and Dulhunty rivers must be forded. The Jardine River provides the main source of water for the local communities. In order to maintain this natural asset, it is requested that motorists do not attempt to cross the river at any point other than the ferry crossing. During good, dry conditions it is possible to take a conventional car, with care, north to Coen and west to Weipa.

Weipa, on the Gulf of Carpentaria, has the world's largest deposits of bauxite. Comalco offers conducted tours of the bauxite mining operation. Direct access to Weipa is by regular Ansett flights from Cairns.

Further information on the national parks in the area and permits for camping may be obtained from the Department of Environment, McLeod St, Cairns; (070) 52 3096.

For further information on Cape York, contact the Far North Qld Promotion Bureau Ltd, cnr Grafton & Hartley sts, Cairns; (070) 51 3588. **See also:** Entry for Weipa in A–Z listing. **Map references:** 508 F2, 510.

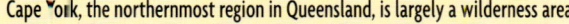
Cape York, the northernmost region in Queensland, is largely a wilderness area

Games. **In the area:** Hervey Bay, Rainbow Beach, Tin Can Bay, Burrum Heads and Woodgate seaside resorts. Also at Hervey Bay, tours to see humpback whale migration. Fraser Island, just off coast, World Heritage-listed sand island. Pioneer museum at Brooweena, 49 km W on Biggenden Rd. Teddington Weir, 15 km S. Tuan Forest, 24 km SE. **Tourist information:** 30 Ferry St; (071) 21 4111. **Accommodation:** 5 hotel/motels, 8 motels, 6 cara./camp. parks.

Miles   Pop. 1260

MAP REF. 505 K7

Ludwig Leichhardt passed through the Miles district (340 km W of Brisbane) on three separate expeditions. He named the place Dogwood Crossing, after the shrub that grows on the banks of the creek. In 1878 the western railway line reached Dogwood Crossing, and Cobb & Co. continued the journey to Roma. The town was renamed Miles after a local member of parliament. The area has always been good sheep country, but today the emphasis is on cattle, mainly Herefords, and wheat; tall silos dominate the surrounding plains. After the spring rains the wildflowers are magnificent. **Of interest:** Historical village, Warrego Hwy, 'pioneer settlement' with all types of early buildings, a war museum, and vehicles and implements on display. Sept.: Back to the Bush (includes Wildflower Festival). **In the area:** Gorges, walks, wildlife and fishing. For overnight visitors only, Possum Park, 21 km N; caravans and camping available, and ex-airforce ammunition store with underground bunkers converted for accommodation. Myall Park Botanical Gardens at Glenmorgan, 100 km SW. Wildflower tourist drive in Sept.; brochure from Tourist information. **Tourist information:** Historical village, Warrego Hwy; (076) 27 1492. **Accommodation:** 3 hotels, 4 motels, 2 cara./camp. parks.

Millaa Millaa   Pop. 325

MAP REF. 509 M8

Located 75 km inland from Innisfail, Millaa Millaa is noted for the many spectacular waterfalls in the area. The town's main industry is dairying. **Of interest:** Eacham Historical Society Museum. **In the area:** Millaa Millaa Falls, Zillie Falls and Elinjaa Falls – all seen from 15-km gravel road that leaves

and rejoins Palmerston Hwy east of town. Millstream Falls, 40 km SW. White-water rafting on Tully River, south of town. Lookout to west of town for excellent views of district. **Tourist information:** Rainforest Holiday Park, Palmerston Hwy; (070) 97 2290. **Accommodation:** 1 hotel, 1 cara./camp. park. **See also:** Atherton Tableland; The Far North.

Millmerran   Pop. 1159

MAP REF. 495 A10, 505 M10

This town on the Condamine River produces eggs, cotton, grain, vegetables, cattle and wool. **Of interest:** Historical Society Museum, Charlotte St. **In the area:** Ned's Corner, 27 km N, offers camp-oven meals, Australiana, yarns and poetry; open by appt. **Tourist information:** Toowoomba Information Centre, cnr James and Kitchener sts, Toowoomba; (076) 39 3797. **Accommodation:** 1 hotel, 1 motel, 1 cara./camp. park.

Miriam Vale   Pop. 447

MAP REF. 505 M1, 507 Q13

Situated on the Bruce Hwy, 150 km N of Bundaberg, this town is renowned for its mud-crab sandwiches. Watch for the Giant Crab. The hinterland is ideal for bushwalking, four-wheel driving and horseriding. **In the area:** The twin towns of Seventeen Seventy and Agnes Water (the most northerly surfing beach in Qld) lie 25 km E. Captain Cook, while on his voyage of discovery in Australian waters, made his first landing in Qld at the town of Seventeen Seventy. Estuary and beaches provide ideal spots to get away from it all. Fishing is excellent. Commemorative Festival held in May, in honour of Captain Cook's first Qld landing. **Tourist information:** Discovery Coast Information Centre, Bruce Hwy; (079) 74 5428. **Accommodation:** 1 hotel, 1 motel, 1 cara./camp. park.

Mission Beach   Pop. 814

MAP REF. 509 N9

This quiet 14-km-long beach with magnificent golden sand, close to Tully, is fringed by coconut palms and World Heritage wet tropics rainforest. The Great Barrier Reef is closest to shore here. Day cruises and sailing trips to Dunk and surrounding islands can be

taken from the jetty at Clump Point. A cairn at South Mission Beach Esplanade commemorates the ill-fated 1848 Cape York expedition of Edmund Kennedy. Many artists, potters, sculptors, jewellers, tapestry artists and cane weavers have settled in the area, attracted by the beautiful rainforest and relaxed lifestyle. Monster markets, last Sun. each month (Easter–Nov.). July: Banana Festival. Oct.: Aquatic Festival; Sailing Regatta. **In the area:** Art and craft galleries. Horseriding, boat, catamaran and jetski hire, tandem parachuting, game and island reef fishing. Water taxis to Dunk Island. Spectacular walking trails to Bicton Hill and Cuttens Lookout commence at base of Bicton Hill, off Misson Beach to Bingil Bay road. Guided and self-guide rainforest walks; scenic drives; calm water, guided, canoe and kayak trips; gamefishing; croc-spotting tours on Hull River – contact Tourist information. Giramay Walkabout and Clump Mountain Walk, Aboriginal cultural experiences; half or full-day. **Tourist information:** Porters Promenade; (070) 68 7099. **Accommodation:** 5 resorts, 2 motels, 8 apartment complexes, 4 B&B, 2 hostels, 8 cara./camp. parks.

Mitchell   Pop. 1101

MAP REF. 504 F6

This town, on the banks of the Maranoa River, lies on the Warrego Hwy between Roma and Charleville, and was named after Sir Thomas Mitchell, explorer and Surveyor-General of NSW, who visited the region in 1846. **Of interest:** Kenniff Court House and Visitor Information Centre, Cambridge St, features exhibition on bushrangers, local art and craft and video of local points of interest; landscaped court house grounds incorporate community mosaic, operating artesian windmill and small billabong. Also in Cambridge St, Nalingu Aboriginal Corporation for guided tours of local Aboriginal community's cultural and heritage centre at Yumba, 3 km E. **In the area:** *There are no facilities north of town. For all tours north, sufficient petrol and supplies must be carried for return trip; read section on Outback Motoring.* This region was former stronghold of local turn-of-century bushrangers, the Kenniff brothers; monument and statues erected 7 km S at the site of their last stand. Carnarvon National Park, 256 km N; camping, walking tracks, two major Aboriginal art sites

QUEENSLAND

and views of impressive sandstone rock formations. Bird sanctuary and picnic/barbecue facilities near Neil Turner Weir, 3.5 km NW. Maranoa River Nature Walk (a 1.8-km circuit) commences at Fishermans Rest, 1.7 km W. **Tourist information:** Cambridge St; (076) 23 1133. **Accommodation:** 5 hotels, 2 motels, 2 cara./ camp. parks.

Monto
Pop. 1339

MAP REF. 505 M2

Monto, on the Burnett Hwy, 250 km inland from Bundaberg, is the centre of a rich dairying, beef cattle and agricultural district. Monto History Centre, cnr Kelvin and Lister sts, local history displays and videos. June: Dairy Festival (even-numbered years). **In the area:** Cania Gorge National Park, 25 km N. Wattle Dale Ostrich Farm, 28 km SW. The Bonnie View Collection, 2 km S, includes over 1000 dolls. **Tourist information:** Three Moon Motel, 4 Flinders St; (071) 66 1777. **Accommodation:** 2 motels, 1 cara./camp. park.

Mooloolaba
Pop. part of Maroochydore

MAP REF. 497 N1, 500 I9, 505 Q7

Because of its excellent beach and variety of restaurants and nightlife,

Mooloolaba is popular for both family and young people's holidays. The Mooloolaba Esplanade, offering beachside resort shopping, rises to the bluff at Alexandra Headland. From the headland there are sweeping views up the beach to the Maroochy River and Mudjimba Island, with Mt Coolum creating an impressive backdrop. Alexandra Headland beach is a popular board-riding location. One of the safest anchorages on the eastern coast is at Mooloolaba Harbour. **Of interest:** Underwater World complex, on The Spit, includes the Oceanarium with its 80-m transparent tunnel for viewing three separate marine environments; the Wharf, and many restaurants and specialty shops. Harbour: finishing point for the annual Sydney-to-Mooloolaba Yacht Race in Apr.; also base for Sunshine Coast's main prawning and fishing fleet; and for pilot vessels guiding ships into Port of Brisbane. Yachting and game-fishing trips to near offshore reefs available. Paraflying off Mooloolaba Beach. Apr.: Triathlon. **Tourist information:** cnr Aerodrome Rd and Sixth Ave, Maroochydore; (07) 5479 1566. **Accommodation:** 2 hotels, 10 motels, 13 apartment complexes, 3 cara./camp. parks.

Moranbah
Pop. 6525

MAP REF. 506 I7

Just off the Peak Downs Hwy, 182 km SW of Mackay, this modern mining town established in 1971 services the huge open-cut coal mines of the expanding Bowen Coal Basin. Coking coal is railed to the Hay Point export terminal just south of Mackay. **Of interest:** Tours to BHP's Peak Downs Mine leave town square each Thurs. 10 a.m; phone (079) 41 7222. May: May Day Union Parade and Fireworks. **Tourist information:** Shire Offices, Griffin St; (079) 41 7254. **Accommodation:** 1 hotel/motel, 1 motel, 2 cara./camp. parks.

Mossman
Pop. 1771

MAP REF. 503 B3, 509 M5

Mossman, the sugar town of the north, 78 km NW of Cairns on the Captain Cook Hwy, is surrounded by green mountains and fields of green sugarcane. **Of interest:** Saturday markets a.m. each week. **In the area:** Mt Demi (1159 m) towers over town. Popular beaches: Cooya, Newell and Wonga. Mossman Gorge, 9 km S, short walk through rainforest to picturesque cascades, regular guided walks by Kuku Yulanji people whose ancestors were

Thursday Island

Situated 35 kilometres north-west off the tip of Cape York Peninsula in the Torres Strait, Thursday Island is a colourful outpost. Its population of around 2900 is made up of islanders, a minority of Europeans, Malays, Polynesians, Chinese and Japanese. At Rosie's Shop, at the corner of Douglas and Blackall streets, a range of Torres Strait Islander and Aboriginal artifacts are available for purchase. The Harbours and Marine Department's Torres Strait Pilot Service operates from its harbour, once the base for 150 pearling luggers. Ferry and day cruises depart from the harbour and operate

View towards Thursday Island

between Bamaga, Horn Island, Punsand Bay and Pajinka Wilderness Lodge. A cultural festival is held each May.

For more information contact Far North Qld Promotion Bureau Ltd, cnr Ring Rd and The Esplanade, Cairns; (070) 51 3588. **Map reference:** 510 B2.

National Parks

The diverse landscapes of Queensland's national parks lure visitors by the million each year. They are drawn not only to the endless stretches of sandy beaches and the magnificent Great Barrier Reef cays and islands off the coast, but also to the cooler mountains of the southern ranges, the inland plains and semi-arid areas, and the wilderness of Cape York.

Many parks and reserves are accessible by conventional vehicle, some require a 4WD. Their major attraction is the climate – beautiful one day, perfect the next! Daytime temperatures in the north and west can reach a searing 40°C or more in summer, and the northern wet season (November to March) brings the occasional cyclone and rainfall that can be measured in metres, but other than these extremes, the climate is ideal for a variety of activities such as bushwalking, camping and watersports.

Great Sandy National Park on Fraser Island

In the south-east of the State

Around Brisbane, the crescent of national parks, or Scenic Rim, includes **Main Range**, **Mount Barney**, **Lamington** and **Springbrook** national parks. These offer Brisbane residents and visitors panoramic views, extensive walking tracks, picnic facilities and a range of recreational opportunities. Lamington attracts visitors by the thousands to its cool rainforest, rich in elkhorn and staghorn ferns and over 700 plant species, including orchids.

Tamborine National Park, in the Gold Coast hinterland, attracts many day visitors from Brisbane and the Gold Coast to its varied rainforests, waterfalls and scenic lookouts. **Girraween National Park**, the 'Place of Flowers', south of Stanthorpe and close to the New South Wales border, offers

visitors the best floral displays in the State. This area is a photographer's paradise, while the park's massive granite outcrops provide quite a challenge for walkers.

Offshore in Moreton Bay, **Moreton Island National Park** is predominantly a wilderness area with vast tracts of sand dunes including Mt Tempest (280 m), which is probably the tallest permanent sand dune in the world. On the leeward side near the resort, wild dolphins make regular visits to be fed by visitors.

Bunya Mountains National Park, 250 kilometres north-west of Brisbane, was established to preserve the last remaining large community of bunya pine rainforest. It was here that Aborigines used to gather about every third year to feast on bunya nuts. Further east lie the **Glass House Mountains**, eroded volcanic plugs that rise suddenly from the landscape. First sighted by Captain Cook in 1770, four of these mountains – Coonoorwin, Tibrogargan, Ngungun, and Beerwah – are in the national park.

Noosa National Park, 160 kilometres north of Brisbane, offers the visitor a wide variety of coastal scenery. Walking tracks lead to lookouts from which can be seen such unusual rock formations as Hell's Gates, Boiling Pot and Fairy Pool. Located further north off Hervey Bay is the world's largest sand island, Fraser Island. The northern third of the island is part of **Great Sandy National Park**. This and its Cooloola section on the mainland are largely 4WD territory; the Cooloola section offers excellent boating opportunities, particularly on the Noosa River.

QUEENSLAND

Map of Queensland showing national parks and towns:

JARDINE RIVER NATIONAL PARK

IRON RANGE NATIONAL PARK

Weipa

MUNGKAN KANDJU NATIONAL PARK

LAKEFIELD NATIONAL PARK

Cooktown

DAINTREE NATIONAL PARK

BARRON GORGE NATIONAL PARK

CHILLAGOE-MUNGANA CAVES NATIONAL PARK

MT HYPIPAMEE & MILLSTREAM FALLS NP

Mareeba — Cairns

WOOROONOORAN NATIONAL PARK

Innisfail

CRATER LAKES NATIONAL PARK

Normanton

HINCHINBROOK ISLAND NATIONAL PARK

Georgetown

LUMHOLTZ NP

LAWN HILL NATIONAL PARK

Townsville

Bowen

Charters Towers

EUNGELLA NATIONAL PARK

CAPE HILLSBOROUGH NATIONAL PARK

Mackay

Mt Isa

Julia Creek

Cloncurry

Hughenden

Winton

Clermont

Boulia

Barcaldine

Emerald

Rockhampton

Longreach

Gladstone

LADY MUSGRAVE NP

EURIMBULA NP

Biloela

MON REPOS CONSERVATION PARK

CANIA GORGE NATIONAL PARK

Bundaberg

GREAT SANDY NATIONAL PARK

CARNARVON NATIONAL PARK

BURRUM COAST NP & BALDWIN SWAMP CP

Taroom

Maryborough

GREAT SANDY NATIONAL PARK

AUBURN RIVER NATIONAL PARK

Gympie

NOOSA NP

Charleville

Roma

BUNYA MOUNTAINS NP

Kingaroy

GLASSHOUSE MOUNTAINS NP

Miles

MORETON IS NP

Dalby

BRISBANE

TAMBORINE NATIONAL PARK

Toowoomba

MAIN RANGE NP

Coolangatta

Cunnamulla

St George

MOUNT BARNEY NR

SPRINGBROOK NATIONAL PARK

Goondiwindi

LAMINGTON NATIONAL PARK

GIRRAWEEN NATIONAL PARK

Birdsville

Launches and charter vessels from several central Queensland ports will take visitors to Heron, Masthead, North West and Lady Musgrave islands, all rich in coral and marine life and a paradise for snorkellers and scuba divers. The Southern Reef islands are outstanding rookeries of the loggerhead and green turtles, and the summer nesting-grounds for thousands of wedgetailed shearwaters and white-capped noddies. **Lady Musgrave Island** is a charming coral cay reached from Bundaberg and Seventeen Seventy. Around the cay's edge, exposed to wind and salt spray, grows a vegetation fringe of casuarina and pandanus, which protects the shady pisonia forest on the inner part of the island. The sheltered lagoon is popular for sailing, snorkelling and reef-viewing in glass-bottomed boats.

Coastal parks around Bundaberg include Burrum Coast National Park, and Baldwin Swamp and Mon Repos conservation parks. **Burrum Coast National Park**, south of Bundaberg, covers 21 300 hectares and provides an essential habitat for wildlife; plant communities in the park include mangroves lining the Gregory and Burrum rivers, wallum heathland, eucalypt and angophora forests, ti-tree swamps and small pockets of palm forest. Roads within the park are gravel or sand, and 4WD vehicles are recommended, although at times conventional vehicle access is possible. Situated only 3 kilometres east of Bundaberg and covering 40 hectares is the Baldwin Wetlands, containing the **Baldwin Swamp Conservation Park**. Walking tracks and a boardwalk allow observation of the park's wildlife. **Mon Repos Conservation Park**, 14 kilometres east of Bundaberg, is eastern Australia's largest mainland turtle rookery. The turtle season extends from November to March. Visitors to the information centre gain some basic knowledge of sea turtles and acceptable human interaction with them. This ensures that a visit to the rookery is an enlightening and enjoyable experience.

Eurimbula National Park is south-east of Gladstone, near the twin communities of Agnes Water and Seventeen Seventy. Over 200 years ago Captain Cook and his crew chose this picturesque stretch of coast, with its broad sandy beaches between small rocky headlands, for their first landing in what is now Queensland. Botanically this is a key coastal area, preserving a complex array of vegetation, including some plants common in southern areas and others found in northern forests. Inland parks in this area include Auburn River and Cania Gorge national parks. **Auburn River National Park**, south-west of Mundubbera,

Lush rainforest and crystal-clear creeks, a feature of Daintree National Park

protects an area of open eucalypt forest and dry scrub. The Auburn River flows through this 390-hectare park over a jumbled mass of pink granitic boulders. Over time, water erosion has sculptured the river's rock pools and cataracts. Vegetation along the river banks includes stunted figs, and bottle trees are common. Dry rainforest species occur in some areas and small lizards can be seen sunbaking on rocks near the water. North-west of Monto, **Cania Gorge National Park** features prominent sandstone cliffs up to 70 metres high, cave formations, dry rainforest on sheltered slopes and open eucalypt forest. This park protects a valuable scenic resource and provides an important wildlife habitat.

In the north-east of the State

Queensland's central and northern coastal islands range from large, steep continental types to coral cays, many of them lying between the mainland and the outer Great Barrier Reef. Several national park islands have been developed for tourism; these include **Hinchinbrook**, one of the world's largest national park islands with 39 900 hectares of wilderness and quiet beaches. More than 90 per cent of the 100 islands in the Whitsunday Group are national parks and six also have resorts. Sail-yourself yachts are a novel way to visit some of the more isolated spots.

Two well-known parks around Mackay are Eungella and Cape Hillsborough national parks. **Eungella National Park**, 83 kilometres west of Mackay, is the Aboriginal 'Land of the Clouds'. It is one of Queensland's wildest and most majestic parks, and the freshness under the canopy of rainforest makes it a perfect destination for a day trip. Many visitors, however, choose to camp by the Broken River, where the normally shy platypus

Causeway and mangroves at Cape Hillsborough National Park

QUEENSLAND

can be seen swimming casually in the creek waters. **Cape Hillsborough National Park**, 50 kilometres north-west of Mackay, often referred to as 'the island you can drive to', combines the beauty of an island with the accessibility of the mainland. Wildlife includes kangaroos, wallabies, possums, echidnas and numerous bird species.

Within a several-hundred-kilometre radius of Cairns are scores of national parks catering for all tastes. About 50 kilometres from Cairns is the Atherton Tableland, on which lie several national parks. Here visitors can follow walking tracks through spectacular rainforest at **Mt Hypipamee**, or visit the 65-metre-wide **Millstream Falls**, or the famous crater lakes of Eacham and Barrine in **Crater Lakes National Park**.

A north Queensland visit would not be complete without a train trip to Kuranda via **Barron Gorge National Park**, or a visit to the **Wooroonooran**, **Lumholtz** and **Daintree** national parks. This undeveloped mountainous country, with its scenic waterfalls and lush rainforest, should not be missed. **Chillagoe-Mungana Caves National Park,** three hours' drive from Cairns, is dominated by weird limestone outcrops, castle-like pinnacles that house a wonderland of colourful caves. Guided tours are conducted daily. Once Queensland's leading mineral producing area, it is still popular with fossickers.

Today Cape York Peninsula is like a magnet to tourists, even though the only aim of thousands of visitors may be simply to stand at its tip. The peninsula's vast and monotonous country is interspersed with surprising pockets of forest, broad vegetation-fringed rivers and occasional waterfalls – all the home of a wide variety of wildlife. **Jardine River, Mungkan Kandju** and **Iron Range** national parks are destinations for keen and experienced wilderness explorers. However, a growing number of visitors divert to **Lakefield**. Its fringing rainforest, paperbark woodland, open grassy plains, swamps and coastal mudflats leading to mangroves along Princess Charlotte Bay all offer a variety of attractions for the most demanding visitor. Basic campsites are located along many watercourses.

Central Queensland

One of the most breathtakingly beautiful scenic reserves in Australia is **Carnarvon National Park**, 720 kilometres by road north-west of Brisbane. The Carnarvon Gorge section of this park, a dramatic, twisting chasm of soft sandstone gouged from vertical white cliffs, is a popular destination for campers. Formed walking tracks lead through forests of eucalypt, she-oaks, tall cabbage palms and relic macrozamia palms. Two major Aboriginal art sites, the Art Gallery and Cathedral Cave,

contain rock paintings of great significance. Limits on campground visitor numbers protect the ecology of the park.

In the north-west of the State

In the remote north-west of Queensland, **Lawn Hill National Park** is an oasis on the edge of the Barkly Tableland. The road into the park is very rough in places, so 4WD travel is recommended, especially for caravanners. Lawn Hill Gorge has colourful cliffs rising 60 metres to the surrounding plateau. On the gorge walls are Aboriginal rock paintings, and middens also remain. Visitors can see these from the boardwalk and viewing platforms. The creek has permanent water and offers a habitat for tropical vegetation including cabbage tree palms and Leichhardt pines. The water attracts various bird species and reptiles, including freshwater crocodiles, tortoises and water monitors. There are over 20 kilometres of walking tracks in the park. World Heritage-listed Riversleigh Fosssil Field, site of unique fossil finds of previously unknown animals, is an extension to the park.

For more information about Queensland's national parks, including the requirement for camping permits, contact the Naturally Queensland Information Centre, 160 Ann St, Brisbane (PO Box 155, Brisbane Albert St 4002); (07) 3227 8185.

original inhabitants; inquire at Tourist information. Hartleys Creek Wildlife Reserve, 35 km S, features crocodiles and other native fauna. Tropical fruit and restaurant in rainforest setting at High Falls Farm, Miallo, 15 km N. Wonga Belle Orchid Garden, 20 km N. Exotic jungle river cruises on Daintree River, 25 km N. Daintree National Park, 64 km NE, largest tract of tropical rainforest in Australia. **Tourist information:** Douglas Shire Tourism Assoc.; (070) 99 4588 or Port Douglas and Cooktown Tourist Information Centre, 23 Macrossan St, Port Douglas; (070) 99 5599. **Accommodation:** 2 hotels, 2 motels, 1 cara./ camp. park. **See also:** The Far North.

Mount Isa Pop. 23 667

MAP REF. 512 E4

In 1923, John Campbell Miles discovered a rich silver-lead deposit on the western edge of the Cloncurry field. Today the progressive city of Mount Isa is the most important industrial, commercial and administrative centre in north-west Qld. The city is a company town, with Mount Isa Mines operating one of the largest silver-lead mines in the world. Copper and zinc are also mined and processed. Ore trains run 900 km E to Townsville for shipment. The city is an oasis of civilisation with excellent amenities and facilities in the otherwise hot and monotonous spinifex and cattle country. **Of interest:** Surface and underground mine tours, advance bookings essential. Lead smelter stack, Australia's tallest free-standing structure (265 m). Riversleigh Interpretive Centre, Centenary Park, features displays of fossil discoveries in Riversleigh area and of early Aboriginal occupation. In Church St: John Middlin Mining Display and Visitors Centre; Frank Aston Underground Museum, opp. KMart. National Trust Tent House, Fourth Ave. Kalkadoon Tribal Centre and Cultural Keeping Place, Marian St. Mt Isa Potters Gallery, Alma St. Flying Doctor Service base, Barkly Hwy. School of Distance Education, Kalkadoon High School, Abel Smith Pde; open schooldays, tours a.m. City Lookout, Hilary St. Donaldson Memorial lookout and walking track, off Marian St. Apr.: Country Music Festival. Aug.: Rodeo (largest in Australia, attracts rough-riders from all over Qld; population almost doubles at this time). **In the area:** Artificial Lake Moondarra, 15 km N, a wildlife sanctuary offering swimming, water sports and picnic/barbecue facilities nearby. West Leichhardt Station, 30 km NE, 280 000-acre cattle property; inquire at Tourist information for day or overnight visits. Lake Julius and surrounds 100 km NE, features Aboriginal cave paintings, fishing, water-skiing, nature trails and abandoned goldmine. Air-charter companies provide flights to excellent barramundi fishing grounds near Birri Fishing Lodge at Birri Beach on Mornington Island and Sweers Island in Gulf of Carpentaria. Gunpowder Resort, 140 km NW, offers several activities ranging from bull-catching to water-skiing. Tours of World Heritage-listed Riversleigh Fossil Site, 200 km NW, an extension of Lawn Hill National Park, 500 km NW. Malbonvale Holiday Station, 40 km S, 180 000-acre cattle property; inquire at Tourist information for day or overnight visits. Mount Frosty, 53 km E, old limestone mine and swimming-hole (not recommended for children as hole is some 9 metres deep with no shallow areas); popular area for fossickers; Burke and Wills memorial cairn near Corella River, 90 km E. **Tourist information:** Riversleigh Interpretive Centre, Centenary Park, Marian St; (077) 49 1555. **Accommodation:** 4 hotels, 13 motels, 2 hostels, 8 cara. parks.

Mount Morgan Pop. 2782

MAP REF. 507 N11

Located 32 km SW of Rockhampton, the crater of the Mount Morgan open-cut gold, silver and copper mine is the largest excavation in the southern hemisphere, measuring some 800 m across and 185 m deep. In the golden heyday of the mine, around 1910, the town had 14 000 people. Mine tours leave town 1 p.m. daily; bookings essential, contact Tourist information for details. **Of interest:** Museum, Morgan St. Court house and other historic buildings have National Trust classifications. At Railway Station, Burnett Hwy: tearooms and rail museum; restored 1904 steam engine operates Fri.–Mon.; fettler's trolley rides along 4-km track operates Tues.–Thurs. May: Golden Mount Festival. **In the area:** The Big Dam, 2.7 km N via William St, for good boating and fishing. **Tourist information:** Railway Station, Burnett Hwy; (079) 38 2312. **Accommodation:** 3 hotels, 1 hotel/motel, 2 cara./camp. parks. **See also:** Capricorn Region.

Mourilyan Pop. 446

MAP REF. 509 N8

Mourilyan, located 7 km S of Innisfail, is the bulk-sugar outlet for sugar produced in the Innisfail area. **Of interest:** Australian Sugar Museum, Bruce Hwy. **In the area:** South-west on Old Bruce Hwy: tours of South Johnstone Sugar Mill (8 km) in season, July–Oct.; National Trust-classified Paronella Park (14 km), ruins of Spanish castle set in rainforest; suspension bridge, waterfall, and picnic and camping areas nearby. Etty Bay, 8 km E, quiet tropical beach with cara./camp. park. **Tourist information:** Australian Sugar Museum, Bruce Hwy; (070) 63 2306. **Accommodation:** 1 hotel.

Mundubbera Pop. 1118

MAP REF. 505 M4

The citrus capital of the State, Mundubbera is on the Burnett Hwy, 410 km NW of Brisbane. Jones Weir, Bauer St. Easter: Citrus Festival (even-numbered years). **In the area:** Golden Mile Orchard, 13 km W, open Apr.–Sept.; tours of packing sheds. Rare *Neoceratodus* (lungfish) found in Burnett River. Auburn River National Park, 40 km SW. Peanut, maize and bean crops on Gurgeena and Binjour plateaus, to north-east. **Tourist information:** Big Mandarin Information Centre, Dalby–Durong Hwy; (071) 65 4549. **Accommodation:** 2 hotels, 2 motels, 1 cara./ camp. park.

Murgon Pop. 2210

MAP REF. 505 N6

Murgon, known as the beef capital of the Burnett, is one of the most attractive towns in southern Qld. Settlement dates back to 1853 and the name comes from an Aboriginal word meaning 'lily pond'. Beef, dairying, pigs and mixed crops are the main industries. A local wine industry is being established. The town is 101 km inland from Gympie and 46 km N of Kingaroy. **Of interest:** Queensland Dairy Museum, Gayndah Rd. Adjacent, relocated Trinity Homestead, one of district's original buildings. Oct.: Fishing Carnival (water levels permitting, at Bjelke-Petersen Dam). **In the** area: Cherbourg Emu Farm at Cherbourg Aboriginal Community, 5 km SW, has walk-through enclosures, educational displays and sales of emu products and Aboriginal artifacts. Bjelke-Petersen Dam, 15 km SE, for water sports and fishing. Scenic tourist drives, brochures available from Tourist information. Nature walk and scenic views in Jack Smith Scrub Conservation Park, 15 km NE; adjacent, Boat Mountain Conservation Park. **Tourist information:** 118 Lamb St; (071) 68 1984. **Accommodation:** 1 hotel, 1 hotel/motel, 1 motel, 2 cara. parks.

Muttaburra   Pop. 195

MAP REF. 506 A9, 513 P9

Muttaburra, 119 km N of Longreach, was developed as a town in the late 1870s, the name being derived from an Aboriginal word meaning 'meeting of the waters'. **Of interest:** Joe Arratta Memorial Museum, in old hospital, Sword St; tours by appt, contact Tourist information. Behind museum, site of Shearers' Strike 1891. Replica of dinosaur, Edkins St. June: Landsborough Flock Ewe Show. **In the area:** The area has many fossil remains as it was formerly part of an inland sea. The name *Muttaburrasaurus* was given to a previously unknown dinosaur, the fossilised bones of which were discovered here. Fishing and water-skiing in Landsborough River, 6 km S, bush-camping on riverbanks. Agate fossicking, 5 km W. **Tourist information:** Post Office, Sword St; (076) 58 7147. **Accommodation:** 1 hotel, 1 cara./camp. park (rest area).

Nambour   Pop. 10 355

MAP REF. 497 M1, 500 E8, 505 P7

Nambour is a busy provincial town, 106 km N of Brisbane, just off the Bruce Hwy. The district was settled in the 1860s, mainly by disappointed miners from the Gympie goldfields, and sugar has been the main crop since the 1890s. Small locomotives pulling trucks of sugarcane trundle across the main street to Moreton Central Mill during the crushing season (July–Oct.). Pineapples and other tropical fruit are grown extensively. Nambour is the Aboriginal name for the red-flowering ti-tree that grows locally. **In the area:** Spectacular Glass House Mountains to south, and scenic Blackall Range to west. The Big

Pineapple complex, home of the Big Pineapple and Macfarms macadamia nut factory, 7 km S. Moonshine Valley Winery, Forest Glen deer sanctuary and Super Bee honey factory, 10 km further S on Forest Glen–Tanawah Tourist Dr. Beach resorts of Maroochydore and Mooloolaba, 20 km E. Mapleton, 13 km W, has a Yarn Festival in Oct. **Tourist information:** The Big Pineapple complex, Bruce Hwy, Woombye; (07) 5442 1333. **Accommodation:** 12 hotels, 8 motels, 2 cara./camp. parks. **See also:** The Sunshine Coast.

Nanango   Pop. 2571

MAP REF. 505 N7

Gold was mined here from 1850 to 1900, but the area, 24 km SE of Kingaroy, now relies on beef cattle, beans and grain. The 1400-megawatt Tarong power station and Meandu coal mine, 18 km SW, are also of economic importance to the area. **Of interest:** Ringsfield Museum (1908), originally a house, became a maternity hospital in 1912; restored 1993, now a local history museum. Market, 1st Sat. a.m. each month. Oct.: Pioneer Festival. **In the area:** Berlin's Gem and Historical Museum, 17 km SW. Coomba Falls, near Maidenwell, 28 km SW. Bunya Mountains National Park, 84 km SW. Seven Mile Diggings, 11 km SE, gold and gem fossicking area; inquire at Tourist information. Forest drive from Benarkin, 40 km SE. Tipperary Flat, 2 km E, park with replica of old gold-mining camp; picnic facilities. **Tourist information:** Shire Offices, 48 Drayton St; (071) 63 1307. **Accommodation:** 3 hotels, 4 motels, 2 cara./camp. parks.

Nerang   Pop. 10 174

MAP REF. 497 N12, 499 C5, 505 Q10

This town in the Gold Coast hinterland is 10 km from Southport. **In the area:** At Carrara, 5 km SE, weekend Hinterland country market. Hinze Dam on Advancetown Lake, 8 km SW, good for swimming and sailing. Spectacular scenery in Numinbah Valley area, 15 km SW near Beechmont. Towards Springbrook, 42 km SW: Wunburra Lookout on Springbrook Plateau; Best of All View, off Repeater Station Rd; Purlingbrook Falls in Springbrook National Park. Natural Bridge section of Springbrook National Park, 38 km SW, popular picnic spot, walking tracks

through scenic rainforest, lookout nearby, glow-worms in cave under bridge. Paradise Country, 2 km W, small working farm. Historic River Mill (1910), 10 km W, arrowroot mill. Lookout near Mt Tamborine, 20 km NE, offers spectacular views to Gold Coast and north to South Stradbroke Island. **Tourist information:** Cavill Mall, Surfers Paradise; (07) 5538 4419. **Accommodation:** 3 motels.

Noosa   Pop. 17 776

MAP REF. 500 H1, 505 Q6

Noosa extends from Tewantin to Sunshine Beach and includes Noosa Heads and the commercial area Noosa Junction. The most northerly of the Sunshine Coast resorts, it is noted for its natural scenery. A combination of the Noosa National Park, a protected main beach facing north, the Noosa River and lakes system, and Qld sunshine has made a fashionable, relaxed resort with temperate weather and safe year-round swimming. Wildlife abounds in the area. There are excellent restaurants and accommodation without Gold Coast-style high-rise development. Tewantin, 6 km up river, was first settled in the 1870s as a base for timber-cutters. Noosaville, on the river between Tewantin and Noosa Heads, is a family-style resort. **Of interest:** At Tewantin: Noosa Regional Gallery, Pelican St; Big Shell, Gympie St; House of Bottles, Myles St. Selina Antiques, Sunshine Beach Rd, at Noosa Junction. Noosa National Park, between Noosa Heads and Sunshine Beach, features walks, surfing beach, rocky headlands, Cook's monument, Devils Kitchen (blowhole), sandy coves, patches of rainforest and views of river and lakes from Laguna Lookout. June: Aqueous Festival of Arts. Sept.: Jazz Party. Oct.: Beach Car Classic. Nov.: Triathlon. **In the area:** Camel rides on Noosa's north-shore beach. Horseriding through the bush. Within 20–40 km N: Stranded freighter *Cherry Venture* (accessible by 4WD); Noosa River Everglades (part accessible by car) – both accessible via boat tours from Noosaville; Cooloola section of Great Sandy National Park (accessible by 4WD). Coloured sands of Teewah in Cooloola section: multi-coloured sand cliffs that rise to over 200 metres, considered to be over 40 000 years old. Noosa Lakes system, navigable for 50 km into Great Sandy National Park,

QUEENSLAND

Tea Tree Bay, near Noosa off Queensland's Sunshine Coast

ideal for boating, sailing and windsurfing; houseboat hire available. Boreen Point holiday and sailing centre near Lake Cootharaba, 21 km N of Tewantin. At Eumundi, 16 km SW, markets held each Sat. Dig for volcanic rocks at Thunder Egg Farm, 30 km SW. **Tourist information:** Hastings St roundabout, Noosa Heads; (07) 5447 4988. **Accommodation:** 47 hotels/ motels, 3 cara./ camp. parks. **See also:** The Sunshine Coast.

Normanton   Pop. 1189

MAP REF. 508 C8, 511 I8

Normanton, 151 km from Croydon, is the central town of the Gulf Savannah and is on a high, gravel ridge on the edge of the savannah grasslands that extend to the west and the wetlands that extend to the north. The town is also the terminus of the historic Normanton to Croydon railway, and the Normanton railway station is the home of the award-winning *Gulflander* tourist train. **Of interest:** Penitentiary, Haig St. Restored Bank of NSW building, Little Brown St. Town well, Landsborough St; no longer in use. In Shire Office Gardens, Haig St: life-size replica of Krys the Savannah King, 8.6-metre saltwater crocodile. Self-guide walk and drive, brochure from Tourist information. Giant barramundi, outside Gulfland Motel in Landsborough St. June: Show, Rodeo and Gymkhana. **In the area:** Fishing and camping at Walkers Creek, 32 km NW, and Norman River at Glenore, 23 km S. Lakes on outskirts of Normanton attract jabirus, brolgas, herons and other birds.

Shady Lagoons, 18 km E, for bush camping, birdwatching and wildlife. Dorunda Station, 170 km NE, cattle station offering barramundi and saratoga fishing in lake and rivers, and accommodation. Burke and Wills Cairn, 40 km SW. Bang Bang Jump Up rock formation, 106 km SW: a solitary hill on the surrounding flat plains, road goes over top, excellent views. **Tourist information:** Shire Offices, Haig St; (077) 45 1166. **Accommodation:** 3 hotel/motels, 1 motel, 1 cara./camp. park. **See also:** Cape York; Gulf Savannah.

Oakey   Pop. 3425

MAP REF. 496 D6, 505 N9

On the Warrego Hwy, 29 km NW of Toowoomba, this town, the base for Australian Army Aviation, is surrounded by beautiful rolling hills and dark soil plains. **Of interest:** Bronze statue of racehorse Bernborough in front of Community Centre, Campbell St. Oakey Historical Museum, Warrego Hwy. Flypast Museum of Australian Army Flying, at army base, via Kelvinaugh St, has large collection of original and replica aircraft (some in flying condition), and aviation memorabilia. **In the area:** Acland Coal Mine Museum, 18 km N; open Mar.–Jan., Sat.–Wed. or by appt; (076) 91 5703. Jondaryan Woolshed (1859), off Warrego Hwy, 22 km NW: memorial to pioneers of wool industry, includes huge woolshed and other buildings, shearing demonstrations, sheep dogs, billy tea and damper, and sales of goods at wool store; Australian heritage festival, at

Woolshed in Aug. **Tourist information:** Library, 64 Campbell St; (076) 91 1388. **Accommodation:** 4 hotels, 3 motels, 2 cara./ camp. parks.

Palm Cove   Pop. 2800

MAP REF. 503 E7, 509 M6

Serene Palm Cove, 27 km NW of Cairns, offers visitors an inviting selection of world-class accommodation with an equally splendid range of boutiques, art galleries and souvenir shops – all set on a tropical beach. Dive and tour bookings to the Great Barrier Reef are available, as are pick-up services for a host of day tours to the Atherton Tableland and surrounding areas. There is also convenient access to Mossman and Port Douglas. **In the area:** On Captain Cook Hwy at Clifton Beach, 7 km S: Wild World, Australian Wildlife Showpark, features exotic range of flora and fauna; Outback Opal Mine, simulated mine with displays of Australia's most famous stone. Bungy tower in rainforest, McGregor Rd, Smithfield, 14 km S. **Tourist information:** cnr Ring Road and The Esplanade, Cairns; (070) 51 3588. **Accommodation:** 12 motels, 3 resorts, 2 cara./ camp. parks.

Pittsworth   Pop. 2110

MAP REF. 496 C9, 505 N9

Pittsworth is a typical Darling Downs town, situated 40 km SW of Toowoomba on the road to Millmerran. It is the centre of a rich grain and dairying district. Cotton is grown with the help of irrigation. The jacarandas and silky oaks in and around the town are a spectacular sight when they flower in late spring. **Of interest:** Some buildings listed by National Trust. Folk Museum, Pioneer Way, includes pioneer cottage, blacksmith's shop and early school. Jan.: Crimson Flash Shield (footrace), Australia Day. **Tourist information:** Sunkist Cafe, Yandilla St; (076) 93 1246. **Accommodation:** 1 hotel, 1 hotel/ motel, 1 motel, 1 cara./camp. park.

Pomona   Pop. 885

MAP REF. 500 B1

This small farming centre is in the northern hinterland of the Sunshine Coast, 33 km S of Gympie. Mt Cooroora (439 m) dominates the town. **Of interest:** Majestic Theatre, cinema museum and location for annual film festival. July: King of the Mountain Festival (race attracting mountain runners from around world). **In the area:** Water sports at Lake Cootharaba, 18 km NE, a large, shallow saltwater lake on Noosa River near where Mrs Eliza Fraser spent time with Aborigines after wreck of *Stirling Castle* on Fraser Island in 1836. **Tourist information:** Noosa Information Centre, Hastings St roundabout, Noosa Heads; (07) 5447 4988. **Accommodation:** 1 hotel.

Port Douglas   Pop. 3660

MAP REF. 503 C4, 509 M5

Just 65 km NW of Cairns, along one of the most scenic coastal drives in Australia, Port Douglas offers the contrast of cosmopolitanism in a tropical, tree-covered mountain setting beside the Coral Sea. Once a small village, Port Douglas has become an international tourist destination. The town, off the main highway, is surrounded by lush vegetation and pristine rainforests. This setting, along with its proximity to the Great Barrier Reef, makes it an ideal holiday destination. **Of interest:** Ben Cropp's Shipwreck Museum, end of Macrossan St, in Anzac Park. Rainforest Habitat, Port Douglas Rd, displays flora and fauna in natural setting. Flagstaff Hill, end Murphy St, commands excellent views of Four Mile Beach and Low Isles. Tours available from town include: horse trail-riding, rainforest tours, 4WD safaris, coach tours to Cape Tribulation, Kuranda and Cooktown, reef tours to Outer Barrier Reef and Low Isles, and the *Lady Douglas* paddlewheel cruise. Market, each Sun. at Anzac Park. Sept.: Yachting Regatta. **In the area:** Daintree River rainforest cruises begin further 26 km NW. Rex Lookout, 21 km S, for stunning coastal views. **Tourist information:** Douglas Shire Tourism Assoc.; (070) 99 4588 or Port Douglas and Cooktown Information Centre, 23 Macrossan St; (070) 99 5599. **Accommodation:** 5 resorts, 3 motels, 2 hostels, 29 apartment complexes, 3 cara./camp. parks. **See also:** The Far North.

Proserpine   Pop. 3034

MAP REF. 507 J3

A sugar town, Proserpine is close to Airlie Beach, Shute Harbour and the islands of Whitsunday Passage. **Of interest:** Proserpine Historical

Museum, 3 Main St, limited opening hours, inquire at Tourist information. May: Rodeo. Oct.: Harvest Festival (includes World Championship Cane Cutting). **In the area:** Conway National Park, 10 km SE, views across islands of Whitsunday Passage from vantage points within park. Lake Proserpine at Peter Faust Dam, 20 km W, offers boat hire, water-skiing, fishing and swimming. **Tourist information:** Bruce Hwy; (079) 45 3711. **Accommodation:** 5 hotels, 5 motels, 1 cara./camp. park.

Quilpie   Pop. 624

MAP REF. 515 O7

Quilpie, 217 km W of Charleville, was established as a centre for the large sheep and cattle properties in the area, but is better known as a boulder opal town. It takes its name from the Aboriginal word *quilpeta*, meaning 'stone curlew'. **Of interest:** Quilpie Museum, Brolga St. Sales of opals at various outlets in town. Altar, font and lectern of St Finbarr's Catholic Church, Buln Buln St, made from opal-bearing rock. June and Aug.: Diggers Races. Late Aug.–early Sept.: Kangaranga Do Street Party; Get-your-rocks-off (rock throwing) Competition, (Wed. prior to Birdsville Races). Sept.: Agricultural Show. **In the area**: Opal workings just outside town. Lake Houdraman, 6 km NE on river road to Adavale, popular recreation area. Designated opal-fossicking area near Toompine Roadhouse 76 km S; inquire at Tourist information. **Tourist information:** Quilpie Museum, Brolga St; (076) 56 1133. **Accommodation:** 1 hotel/motel, 1 motel, 1 cara./camp. park. **See also:** Channel Country.

Ravenswood   Pop. 120

MAP REF. 506 G2

Ravenswood, friendly and 'not quite a ghost town', is 88 km E of Charters Towers via Mingela. One hundred years ago it was the classic gold-rush town. Visitors will find interesting old workings and perhaps a little gold along with the nostalgia. **Of interest:** Several restored historic buildings in town, including court house, shops and current ambulance centre. Oct.: Halloween Ball. **In the area:** Burdekin Dam, 80 km SE, popular recreational area. **Tourist information:** Court House, Barton St; (077) 70 2047. **Accommodation:** 2

hotels, 1 motel/camping park, camping in showgrounds.

Redcliffe   Pop. 39 073

MAP REF. 497 N6, 505 Q8

Redcliffe was the first European settlement in Qld. Matthew Flinders landed here in 1799 while exploring Moreton Bay and the spot was named for what he found: red cliffs. In 1824 John Oxley and Commandant Miller arrived with convicts and troops to set up the Moreton Bay penal colony, which was abandoned the following year in favour of Brisbane. The Aborigines called the place Humpybong, meaning 'dead houses', and the name is still used for the Redcliffe Peninsula, which comprises the towns of Woody Point, Margate, Clontarf, Scarborough and Redcliffe. The City of Redcliffe, 35 km N of Brisbane, was proclaimed in 1959 and is a fast-growing area and a satellite city of Brisbane. The 2.6-km bridge, which links the two cities, is known as the Houghton Hwy; the old Hornibrook Bridge which runs parallel is a favourite spot for local anglers. Fishing and boating are popular pastimes. **Of interest:** Historical museum, Marine Pde. Self-guide heritage walks and drives of city; pamphlets available from Tourist information. Seawater lagoon at Redcliffe Point. Craft markets on beach each Sun. Jan.: Blessing of the Fleet. Feb.: Seafood Festival. Sept.: First Settlement Festival; Bomboora-The Redcliffe Festival. **In the area:** Scarborough is departure point for vehicular ferry to Moreton Island, where sand dunes are reputed to be highest in world; dolphin feeding at Tangalooma resort on western side of island. **Tourist information:** Shire Offices; (07) 3283 0283. **Accommodation:** 6 hotels, 3 motels, 7 cara./camp. parks. **See also:** Tours from Brisbane.

Redland Bay   Pop. 2576

MAP REF. 497 O9, 505 Q9

Some 40 km SE of Brisbane on the shores of Moreton Bay, the famous red soil of this area grows excellent vegetables and strawberries, mainly for the Brisbane market. It is a popular Sunday afternoon drive from the city. Redland Bay is departure point for boats to Russell, Lamb, Macleay and Karragarra islands. Cleveland is the main centre of the Redland area, and beaches at

QUEENSLAND

Wellington Point, Victoria Point and Redland Bay offer safe swimming and boating. **In the area:** Roseworld, 2 km S, exhibition gardens showing most varieties of roses. Koala Bushland National Park, Mt Cotton, 12 km SW, a fauna sanctuary with walking tracks and picnic/barbecue area. King Country Nursery at Thornlands, 10 km NW, in rainforest setting with picnic facilities. Off Victoria Point, 6 km N, Coochiemudlo Island is quiet but popular. Islands are all excellent places to picnic, swim and explore; full range of facilities and services. **Tourist information:** Redlands Tourism, 152 Shore St West, Cleveland; (07) 3821 0057. **Accommodation:** 1 hotel/motel, 2 cara./camp. parks. **See also:** Tours from Brisbane.

Richmond
Pop. 631

MAP REF. 513 M4

This small town on the Flinders Hwy ('the Dinosaur Hwy'), 500 km SW of Townsville, serves the surrounding sheep and cattle properties. **Of interest:** In Goldring St: restored Cobb & Co. coach; Marine Fossil Museum in the Old Strand Theatre; display of moon rocks (spherical fossil rocks of various sizes, feature of local landscape) in Lions Park. Pioneer Cemetery, Flinders Hwy, on western edge of town. **In the area:** The area is rich in fossils. **Tourist information:** Shire Offices, Goldring St; (077) 41 3277 or Marine Fossil Museum, cnr Goldring and Larsen sts; (077) 41 3429. **Accommodation:** 1 hotel, 1 hotel/motel, 2 motels, 1 hostel, 1 cara. park.

Rockhampton
Pop. 55 768

MAP REF. 507 N11

Rockhampton is called the beef capital of Australia, with some 2.5 million cattle in the region. Gold was discovered at Canoona, 60 km NW of Rockhampton, in 1858; however, cattle became the major industry, with Herefords the main breed, since cross-bred with more exotic breeds to produce disease-resistant herds. Rockhampton straddles the Tropic of Capricorn. It is a prosperous city on the banks of the Fitzroy River and has considerable architectural charm. Many of the original stone buildings and churches remain, set off by flowering bauhinia and brilliant bougainvilleas. The city has several well-established secondary industries, including two of Australia's largest meat processing and exporting factories. **Of interest:** In Quay St, alongside river, National Trust-classified buildings: ANZ Bank (1864); Customs House (1901). Heritage walk around city centre, contact Tourist information. Scattered around city are old Queensland houses carefully preserved. Botanic Gardens on Athelstane Range, via Spencer St, contain fine tropical displays, an orchid and fern house, a Japanese-style garden, monkeys, koala park and walk-in aviary.

Fishing in Queensland

The tropical climate, breathtaking scenery and variety of fishing combine to make the State a wonderful destination for the angler. The coast is the chief attraction with Cairns being world famous as a location for black marlin and other game-fishing. The Great Barrier Reef is closest to the coast north of Cairns and is easily fished on day trips either in your own boat or from a charter boat. Coral trout, red emperor and nannygai are here and, for those with an inclination for sportfishing, Spanish mackerel, giant trevally and marlin. Cairns is a major centre for charter boats going out to the Great Barrier Reef and deepwater game-fishing. Further north the remote regions of Cape York provide a frontier experience for those seeking barramundi, queenfish and giant trevally.

Around Brisbane the warm tropical currents provide a mix of temperate fish, such as bream, whiting and flathead and tropical fish species including snapper, sweet lips and reef cod. Estuary, beach, reef and offshore fishing are possible. Further north, the tailor at Hervey Bay are legendary, and the nearby Great Sandy Strait has a large variety of estuary species in the mangrove

Heading out of Fitzroy Island for some light-tackle sportfishing

channels. Around Townsville the mangrove estuaries on the coastline are renowned for barramundi and mangrove jack. Just off the coast are the wonders of the Whitsundays surrounded by waters teeming with mackerel, queenfish, trevally and other species.

Inland fishing areas, particularly in the north, are vast distances from population centres. In the south-east the stocking of impoundments has improved inland fishing; anglers can now fish for golden and silver perch and Murray cod.

Carnarvon Gorge in Carnarvon National Park

Cliff Kershaw Gardens, Bruce Hwy, features Braille Trail. Fitzroy River Barrage, Savage St, separates tidal salt-water from upstream freshwater. The Capricorn Spire (14 m) at Curtis Park, Gladstone Rd, marks the line of Tropic of Capricorn. Rocky markets, Sat. and Sun. in Denison St. Apr.: Good Earth Expo. July: Bauhinia Arts Festival. Aug.: Rocky Round Up. **In the area:** Capricorn Scenic Loop tourist drive, inquire at Tourist information. Dreamtime Cultural Centre, north on Bruce Hwy, largest Aboriginal and Torres Strait Islander Cultural Centre in Australia, features culture of the Darumbal language group. Old Glenmore historic homestead, 5 km N, has displays and historic buildings. Rockhampton Heritage Village, Gangalook, 20 km N: heritage buildings with hall of clocks and pioneering tools, also steam engine; tours daily, special events last Sun. in month. St Christopher's Chapel, 20 km N, on Emu Park Rd, built by American servicemen. Olsen's Capricorn Caverns and Cammoo Caves, both limestone cave systems, 23 km N; tours daily. Thunderegg fossicking at Mt Hay Gemstone Tourist Park, 41 km W on Capricorn Hwy. Pleasant drive to top of Mt Archer, 6 km E. **Tourist information:** The Spire, Gladstone Rd; (079) 27 2055. **Accommodation:** 18 hotels, 8 hotel/motels, 32 motels, 1 hostel, 9 cara./camp. parks. **See also:** Capricorn Region.

Roma
Pop. 5669

MAP REF. 504 H6

Roma is 261 km W of Dalby at the junction of the Warrego and the Carnarvon hwys. It was named after the wife of Sir George Bowen, Qld's first Governor, and was first surveyed in 1862. The Mt Abundance cattle station was established in 1847, and sheep and cattle have been the area's economic mainstay ever since. The famous trial of Harry Redford, alias Captain Starlight, was held in Roma in 1872. In 1863 Samuel Symons Bassett brought vine cuttings to Roma and Qld's first wine-making enterprise began. Australia's first natural gas strike was made at Hospital Hill in 1900 (inquire at Tourist information about tourist drive around the area), and the gas from this source was used, in 1906, to light the town. Further deposits were found periodically, and 'oil' (actually gas and condensate) caused excitement in the area in the late 1920s. Roma has supplied Brisbane with gas via a 450-km pipeline since 1969, but a major pipeline is now being constructed to bring gas from far western Qld to supplement the Roma area's depleting gas reserves. **Of interest:** Oil rig, named Big Rig by locals, erected as landmark at eastern entrance to town on Warrego Hwy. Romavilla Winery, Injune Rd. Cultural Centre, cnr Bungil and Injune rds, includes mural by local artists. Roma Bottle Trees in Heroes' Ave, planted to commemorate local soldiers who died in World War I. Adjacent park has picnic facilities. Markets at Big Rig site, 2nd and 4th Sun. each month. Market, 3rd Sun. each month at Roma Fair Arcade, Wyndham St. Easter: Easter in the Country. **In the area:** Largest inland cattle market in Australia, 4 km E on Warrego Hwy. Meadowbank Museum, 15 km W on Warrego Hwy. Carnarvon National Park, 251 km NW, features Carnarvon Gorge, Aboriginal cave paintings, varied scenery and walks; guided tours and accommodation available. Injune, 89 km N, is the southern gateway to Carnarvon National Park. **Tourist information:** Big Rig site, Lower McDowall St; (076) 22 4355. **Accommodation:** 7 hotels, 7 motels, 3 cara./camp. parks.

St George
Pop. 2512

MAP REF. 504 G10

Situated at a major road junction, St George is in the centre of a rich grape, peanut and cotton-growing district. It is on the Balonne River, 118 km NW of Mungindi on the Carnarvon Hwy, and 286 km SW of Dalby on the Moonie Hwy. It is often referred to as the inland fishing capital of Qld as there are many fishing spots yielding Murray cod and yellowbelly, particularly in the Balonne River. As St George has a rainfall of only 500 mm a year, extensive irrigation is carried out by means of a dam and three weirs. Cotton-growing and harvesting is completely mechanised; planting Oct. to Nov., harvesting Apr. to June. Wheat, barley, oats and sunflowers are also irrigated, and sheep and cattle are raised. **Of interest:** Kajarabi Craft Co-op, 101 Victoria St, for local craft. Riversands Winery, Whytes Rd. Carved, illuminated emu eggs displayed at Balonne Sports store, Victoria St. Sept.: Fishing Competition. **In the area:** Ostrich farming at Burra Boogie, 3 km W, off Balonne Hwy; open a.m. by appt only. Rosehill Aviaries, 64 km W, one of Australia's largest private collections of Australian parrots. At Bollon, 112 km W, large koala population in trees along Wallan Creek; Heritage and craft centre, George St, local history exhibits. Cotton Ginnery, 20 km S; open by appt from Mar.–July. Thallon, 76 km S: swimming and fishing at Barney's Beach on Moonie River; nearby old Bullamon Homestead (1860) with original shingle roof and canvas ceilings; tours by appt only, inquire at Tourist information. Historic hotel (1863) at Nindigully, 44 km SE; motorbike riders arrive each June to tackle the Nindigully 5-hour Enduro. Native flowers including Geraldton Wax at Gillebri flower farm, 24 km E; flower tours Aug.–Oct., by appt only; watch rockmelons being prepared and packed Nov.–Mar. Further 3 km, restored vintage tractor collection; open by appt. Ancient rockwell, 37 km E, hand hewn by Aborigines possibly thousands of years ago. Beardmore Dam, 20 km N, for fishing and water sports; scenic picnic spots in surrounding parklands. Pastoral township, Dirranbandi, 97 km SW near the NSW border: Railway Park, Railway St; Cubbie Station, 33 km further west, largest privately-owned cotton property in State (tours available, contact Tourist information). **Tourist information:** Shire Offices, Victoria St; (076) 25 3222 and Kamarooka Caravan Park, 56 Victoria St; (076) 25 3120. **Accommodation:** 1 hotel, 3 hotel/motels, 2 motels, 4 cara./camp. parks.

Sarina   Pop. 3094

MAP REF. 507 L6

In the sugar belt, Sarina lies 37 km S of Mackay on the Bruce Hwy. The area has many fine beaches, including Sarina, Campwin, Grasstree, Salonika, Halftide, and, to the south, Armstrong. Sarina produces molasses and ethyl alcohol as byproducts of the sugar industry. Sarina is also the location for the Plane Creek

Shute Harbour, main departure point for the Whitsunday Islands

Central Sugar Mill and the CSR Distillery, Bruce Hwy, which produces Dundah, fertiliser for local sugarcane crops. **Of interest:** Rosegardens, in Broad St and around Railway Sq. Railway Sq.: Old Court house (1901); Sarina Tourist Art and Craft Centre, with local arts and craft and information on local industry. Flea market, last Thurs. each month in Broad St. July: Visual Arts Festival. Aug.: Agricultural Show. **In the area:** To the north: tours of Campwin Beach Prawn Farm (8.5 km); Prawn and Crab Hatchery at Grasstree, 13 km NE, sells local seafood direct to public; cafe. Viewing gallery at Hay Point and Dalrymple Bay coal terminal complex (12 km N). **Tourist information:** Sarina Tourist Art and Craft Centre, Railway Sq.; (079) 56 2251. **Accommodation:** 3 hotels, 2 motels, 2 cara./camp. parks.

Shute Harbour   Pop. 200

MAP REF. 507 K3

Shute Harbour, 36 km NE of Proserpine, has one of the largest marine passenger terminals in Australia, second only to Sydney's Circular Quay. **Of interest:** Jetty at Shute Harbour, best place to start exploring the 80 or more tropical islands in the beautiful Whitsunday waters including well-known Hayman, Daydream, South Molle, Hamilton and Lindeman islands; variety of cruise boats depart daily; booking offices, souvenir and food outlets on main jetty. Boom-net riding available daily. Seaplane ride to Hardy's Lagoon on the outer Great Barrier Reef for snorkelling among the coral. Ex-America's Cup challenger *Gretel* takes day trips through the Whitsunday islands. Day trips to the pontoon at Hardy Reef for swimming, scuba diving and snorkelling. Sail and power vessels, varying sizes and classes, can be hired. Lions Lookout, Whitsunday Dr., for spectacular views. June: Hamilton Island Cup (outrigger canoes). Aug.: Hamilton Island Race Week (sailing). **In the area:** Conway National Park, 15 km S. Great Barrier Reef and Whitsunday islands. **Tourist information:** Beach Plaza, The Esplanade, Airlie Beach; (079) 46 6673. **Accommodation:** 4 motels, 3 cara./camp. parks.

Stanthorpe   Pop. 4187

MAP REF. 123 M2, 505 N12

The main town in the Granite Belt and in the mountain ranges along the border between Qld and NSW, Stanthorpe, 225 km SW of Brisbane, came into being after the discovery of tin at Quartpot Creek in 1872. Silver and lead were discovered in 1880, but the minerals boom did not last. The area has produced excellent wool for more than a century, but is best known for its large-scale growing of apples, pears, plums, peaches and grapes. Stanthorpe is 915 m above sea level and is often the coolest part of the State. Spring is particularly beautiful with fruit trees and wattles in bloom. There are 90 varieties of wild orchids found in the area. **Of interest:** Museum, High St. Art Gallery and Library Complex, Weeroona Park, Marsh St. Mar.: Apple and Grape Harvest Festival (even-numbered years); Rodeo. May: Opera at Sunset. **In the area:** Granite Belt wineries, most open for tastings and cellar-door sales: Old Caves, just north of town; Castle Glen at Summit, 10 km N; Heritage Wines at Cottonvale, 12 km NW; Granite Cellars, Granite Country Estate, Stone Ridge, Felsberg, Mountview and Kominos, near Glen Alpin, 11 km S; Rumbalara at Fletcher and the Bramble Patch berry gardens and winery, 14 km S; Ballandean Estate Golden Grove, Winewood, Bungawarra and Robinson's Family Winery, near Ballandean, 19 km S; Bald Mountain at Wallangarra, 30 km S. Girraween National Park, 32 km S, for camping, bushwalking, rock climbing and spectacular wildflowers in spring. Sundown National Park, 79 km SW, wilderness area; camping on Severn River in south-west of park. Sunworld

Park at Eukey, 13 km SE, has displays of sun and wind-powered instruments. Storm King Dam, 26 km SE, for canoeing and water-skiing. Falls in Boonoo Boonoo National Park, 60 km SE. Mt Marlay, 2 km E, for excellent views. **Tourist information:** 61 Marsh St; (076) 81 2057. **Accommodation:** 5 hotels, 7 motels, 12 B&B, 1 hostel, 3 cara./camp. parks.

Strathpine   Pop. 10 108

MAP REF. 492 C3, 497 L6

Immediately behind Brisbane and to the north is the Pine Rivers region, a peaceful rural district that includes the forested areas and national parks closest to Brisbane. Taking advantage of this rural setting so close to the city are a number of art and craft industries. Each Sunday the oldest and largest country market is held at North Pine Country Park, Whiteside, 6 km NW of Strathpine; local artworks, food and produce are sold while buskers entertain and craft demonstrations are given. May: Pine Rivers Heritage Festival.

Sept.: Camp Oven Bush Poets Festival. **In the area:** Alma Park Zoo at Dakabin, 14 km N, features native and exotic animals, and a Friendship Farm for children. Lakeside Racing Circuit, 14 km N, venue for major events. Bunya Park Wildlife Sanctuary, Eatons Hill, 8 km SW, native animals in bush setting. Australian Woolshed at Ferny Hills, 16 km SW, for demonstrations of shearing, spinning and sheepdogs working; also bush dances with bush band. Brisbane Forest Park, via Ferny Hills. Mountains and national parks that form scenic rim around Brisbane. **Tourist information:** Shire Offices, 220 Gympie Rd; (07) 3205 0555. **Accommodation:** 2 hotels, 2 motels, 3 hostels, 1 cara./camp. park, 1 overnight camp. ground.

Surfers Paradise   Pop. part of Gold Coast

MAP REF. 497 O13, 499 F6, 505 Q10

Over the past 50 years, Surfers Paradise has become famous as Australia's most popular holiday destination. With world-famous surf beaches, international standard accommodation and

Darling Downs

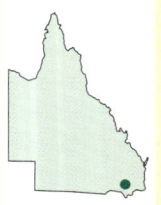

The 72 500 square kilometres of black volcanic soil on the Darling Downs produce 90 per cent of the State's wheat, 50 per cent of its maize, 90 per cent of its oilseeds, two-thirds of its fruit and one-third of its tobacco, as well as oats, sorghum, millet, cotton, soybeans and navy beans. It is a major sheep, cattle and dairying area and the home of several famous bloodstock studs.

Allan Cunningham was the first European to ride across these fertile plains in 1827. The Darling Downs is rural Australia at its best, with a touch of England in the oaks, elms, plane trees and poplars of **Toowoomba's** parks, and the rose gardens of **Warwick** in the south. The climate is cooler and more bracing than in the rest of the State. The Downs with its neat strips of grainfields, lush pastures, patches of forest and national parks, and well-established homesteads, give the visitor a lasting impression of beauty and quiet prosperity.

The Warrego Highway leads north-west from Toowoomba to the wheatfields and silos of **Dalby**.

Paddock patterns are an attractive sight in the Darling Downs

The New England Highway, the main Sydney to Brisbane inland route, turns into the Cunningham Highway at Warwick, and descends from the Downs towards the coast through Cunninghams Gap. Main Range National Park has lovely rainforest, palms and native wildlife. An alternative inland route between Brisbane and Melbourne is the Newell Highway, running west from Warwick to **Goondiwindi** and south into New South Wales. A less-used but scenic

route is the Heifer Creek Way through the Lockyer Valley from near Greenmount East to **Gatton**.

For further information on the Darling Downs, contact the Southern Downs Tourist Association, 49 Albion St (New England Hwy), Warwick; (076) 61 3122. **See also:** individual entries in A–Z listing for those towns indicated by bold type. **Map reference:** 496 A6

Wildlife-Watching

In keeping with the State's reputation for showmanship, there are plenty of 'star performers' on Queensland's wildlife billing: friendly dolphins, humpback whales, turtles and tropical fish, just to name a few. However, visitors who make the effort will also enjoy the thrill of glimpsing a flash of blue as a Ulysses butterfly disappears into the rainforest, or the anticipation of waiting for a platypus to surface in a mountain stream.

Around Brisbane

Do not let the busy cityscape and bustling seaside shopping plazas fool you – there are many wildlife-watching opportunities in and around Brisbane.

Some favourite wildlife-watching destinations in the hinterland area include **Daisy Hill State Forest** and **Brisbane Forest Park**. Daisy Hill State Forest, a bushy pocket in the outskirts of Brisbane's southern suburbs, supports a variety of animals including a colony of koalas. The Daisy Hill Koala Centre in the park provides a wealth of information on these animals and their habitat. Visitors can climb the treetop tower to scan the surrounding canopy for wild koalas. Brisbane Forest Park, which abuts the eastern suburbs of the city, features Walk-about Creek, a simulated creek environment with perspex windows. Brisbane Forest Park is also home to a colourful array of forest birdlife and nocturnal animals such as possums and gliders; inquire on (07) 3300 4855 for guided spotlight tours.

Wildlife-watching opportunities also abound along the coast. In particular, the waters around **Moreton Island**, only 35 km east of Brisbane, are a haven for a variety of marine mammals including dolphins, whales and dugongs.

Dolphins can be seen frolicking in the warm shallow waters surrounding Moreton Island on the bay and surf sides. Tangalooma Resort has developed a wild dolphin care and hand-feeding programme. A diet chart has been developed and care is taken to feed the dolphins only one third of their daily food needs. Participants are asked not to touch or handle the dolphins in any way, although it is not uncommon for the animals to give a friendly nudge as they approach humans.

Humpback whales can also be spotted passing the island between June and October; whale-watch cruises operate in season. There is some irony in this new attraction, given that Tangalooma was a

The cobalt-blue Ulysses butterfly

whaling station from 1952 to 1962, when an estimated 600 whales were slaughtered per year.

Another marine mammal common to these waters is the dugong, which grazes on the seagrass beds fringing the island's western shores. These elusive creatures can sometimes be seen surfacing for air near the shores of the island.

With its variety of habitat types, ranging from inter-tidal wetlands to swamps, heathlands and open forests, Moreton Island also supports nearly one hundred species of sea and shore birds, as well as over eighty species of land birds. Prime bird-watching sites include Mirrapool and the tidal flats on the south western side of the island, where thousands of migratory birds feed and roost from September to April.

In the Great Barrier Reef

The **Great Barrier Reef** brims with life: iridescent blue starfish; pink sponge baubles; bright green turtle weed; fragile needle coral; brain coral; mushroom coral; slender yellow trumpet fish; vivid parrot fish with beak-like jaws; schools of delicate blue pillars; butterfly fish and angel fish... This maze of coral reefs and coral cays, extending over 2000 kilometres along the Queensland coast, supports the most diverse collection of marine life to be found anywhere in the world.

The Great Barrier Reef can be viewed on one of the many day cruises operating from mainland ports including Cairns, Port Douglas and Mission Beach. The cruise companies offer a variety of packages and generally include expert guides and use of snorkelling equipment. Alternatively, you might choose to base yourself on one of the islands on or near the reef. If you go reef walking, remember to walk gently, following marked trails where available. Take care not to break the fragile coral, wear strong-soled shoes for your own protection and keep an eye on the tides. Enjoy nature's display, but refrain from collecting or disturbing the marine life.

In the Mackay Region

80 kilometres west of Mackay, in the enchanting rainforest setting of **Eungella National Park**, there runs a clear mountain stream which is home to one of nature's great mysteries, the platypus. This egg-laying mammal with webbed feet, a flat paddle-like tail and a duck-shaped bill is frequently spotted swimming below the special viewing platform on the banks of the Broken River.

Platypuses are generally sighted at dusk and in the early morning. It is important to keep quiet because they have sensitive hearing and are easily disturbed. Concentric rings on the water surface indicate that platypuses are active below. They feed on creatures such as insect larvae and freshwater shrimps found at the bottom of pools and creeks. The platypuses store their food in their cheeks and can be seen returning to the surface at intervals to chew and swallow.

As darkness closes in, the forest floor and treetops rustle with nocturnal life. An evening walk by torchlight will reveal a large number of busy animals including birds such as tawny frogmouths, curlews and boobook owls, as well as gliders and both northern and southern species of bandicoots and brushtail possums.

Eungella is also known as the southernmost location of the spectacular cobalt-blue Ulysses butterfly, often sighted in the wind tunnels created by gullies and roads. The Ulysses grubs feed on the euodia trees in the park. It is not unusual to see the magical 'flashing of the blue' on a visit to Eungella, but do not expect to see these butterflies in large numbers.

On the Fraser Coast

Whale-watching is fast becoming a not-to-be-missed activity for visitors to Queensland coastal destinations from Stradbroke Island to the Whitsundays. Every year humpback whales leave the cold Antarctic waters in April and migrate along Australia's eastern shoreline, past Fraser Island and on to their breeding grounds in the Great Barrier Reef.

An estimated 200–400 humpback whales travel through **Hervey Bay** (between Fraser Island and the mainland) between August and October each season, making this one of the prime whale-watching spots in Queensland. The humpbacks provide great entertainment for their human audience. To see a 30–40 tonne whale exhale then arch its expansive back and roll forward, tail in air, is to bear witness to one of nature's greatest spectacles. Other antics include the 'spy hop', 'pec slapping' and 'tail slapping'. Numerous whale-watching cruises operate in the area. Contact the Whale Watch Tourist Centre at Urangan for information and bookings; (071) 28 9800.

Mon Repos Conservation Park near Bundaberg features the largest mainland turtle rookery in eastern Australia. It is the hatching ground for loggerhead, green and Australian flatback turtles that nest between mid-November and February. Hatchlings emerge from January to March. A ranger is present during the turtle season to provide information and ensure visitors do not disturb the turtles. Visitor numbers are strictly limited to minimise impact on breeding. Successful breeding

QUEENSLAND

A humpback whale tail-slaps as it passes the Queensland coast

here is critical to the survival of the turtles, particularly the endangered loggerhead species.

The best time of day to view nesting turtles is after dark near high tide, whereas hatchlings are best viewed between 8 p.m. and midnight. It is recommended that you phone the Mon Repos Information Centre on (071) 53 8620 to check times. Remember that turtles are wild marine animals, so there are occasions when they choose not to arrive.

During nesting time, visitors watch as the large female loggerheads haul themselves onto the beach and scoop a nest in the sand with their rear flippers, then fill it with eggs. Later in the season, young turtles provide another great spectacle as they emerge from the sand and scurry into the sea.

On the Atherton Tableland

Seven species of possum inhabit the dense rainforest surrounding an extinct volcanic crater in **Mount Hypipamee National Park**. This small pocket of dense vegetation surrounded by farmland on the Atherton Tableland in Northern Queensland, really comes alive at night. Day visitors can expect to see the usual gang of brush turkeys scavenging

WILDLIFE-WATCHING ETHICS

- Do not disturb wildlife or wildlife habitats. Keep the impact of your presence to a minimum. Use available cover or hides wherever possible.
- Do not feed wildlife, even in urban areas. (Note: supervised feeding is allowed at some locations)
- Be careful not to introduce exotic plants and animals – definitely no pets.
- Stay on defined trails.

for scraps around the main picnic area. However, visitors who stay until dusk and wait quietly as the sun sets, will enjoy a more exciting wildlife-watching experience. Leaves rustle on the forest floor; geckoes, bandicoots and pademellons start to emerge. Branches crack and tree-tops shudder under the weight of heavy possums.

Most of the possum species at Mount Hypipamee can be seen by torchlight within the short distance between the main picnic area and the road leading into the park. The most common is the coppery brushtail. Other species include: the green ringtail possum with green-tinged fur and

the lemuroid possum, which leaps through the air from branch to branch.

Another nocturnal mammal, the Lumholtz tree kangaroo, is often found here and in other pockets of forest on the Atherton Tableland. These animals spend the day asleep in a crouched sitting position in the crown of a tree or on a branch. As evening approaches, they unfold their powerful limbs and display their remarkable climbing skills. They are the only kangaroos that are able to move their hind legs independently of each other

For a good introduction to Queensland's wildlife, visit Fleays Wildlife Park, on the Gold Coast. Features include the Nocturnal House and 'creature feature' wildlife demonstrations. For more information on wildlife-watching in Queensland's national parks, contact the Department of Environment's Naturally Queensland Information Centre, 160 Ann St, Brisbane (PO Box 155, Brisbane Albert St 4002); (07) 3227 8185. For more information on bird-watching, contact the Bird Observers Club of Australia, 183 Springvale Rd, Nunawading, Victoria, 3131; (03) 9877 5342. **See also:** National Parks; Great Barrier Reef.

The Botanic Gardens at Toowoomba in full bloom

exciting attractions, Surfers Paradise appeals to a wide range of holiday-makers from Australia and around the world. It has earned a reputation as a great destination for families, young adults and those seeking a luxury experience. During the winter months, the sunny sub-tropical climate and year-round festive atmosphere make Surfers Paradise particularly attractive to southerners. **Of interest:** Attractions in Surfers Paradise include: Cavill Mall, regular free entertainment; Orchid Avenue, just off Cavill Mall, European designer fashions and outdoor cafes; art and craft markets, beachfront markets, Friday evenings in Cavill Mall; Timezone Funtasia, family fun centre, Paradise Centre, just off Cavill Mall; beach volleyball area near Cavill Mall, year-round action; GP Go Karting, Ferny Ave; Flycoaster and Bungee Rocket thrill rides, Cypress Ave; Gold Coast City Art Gallery and riverside Evandale sculpture walk, 135 Bundall Rd. Apr.: IndyCar Australia Race. Sept.: Surfers Paradise International Aquathon. Dec.: New Year's Eve Fireworks. **Tourist information:** Cavill Mall; (07) 5538 4419. **Accommodation:** Low and high-rise hotels and motels, numerous apartment complexes. **See also:** The Gold Coast.

Tambo   Pop. 351

MAP REF. 504 B2

Tambo, 101 km SE of Blackall on the Matilda Hwy, was established in the mid-1860s. From a point where the town now stands, explorer Thomas Mitchell first saw the Barcoo River in 1846. **Of interest:** Old Post Office Museum; also produces Tambo Teddies, all-wool teddy bears. Court house (1888), now library. Sept.: Spring Flower Festival (includes ram racing). **In the area:** Ivanhoe Hills, just east of town, the highest point on the hwy west of Toowoomba. Salvator Rosa section of Carnarvon National Park, 120 km E; the area was named by Major Mitchell, who was reminded of landscapes painted by 17th-century artist; access to park via Dawson Development Rd and Cungelella Station (4WD recommended); permission to camp must be obtained from Department of Environment; (079) 84 1716. **Tourist information:** Shire Offices, Arthur St; (076) 54 6133. **Accommodation:** 1 hotel, 1 hotel/motel, 1 motel, 1 cara./camp. park.

Taroom   Pop. 705

MAP REF. 505 J4

Taroom is on the banks of the Dawson River almost 300 km due W of Maryborough. Cattle-raising is the main industry. **Of interest:** Coolibah tree in main street, marked 'L.L.' by Ludwig Leichhardt on his 1844 trip from Jimbour House near Dalby to Port Essington (Darwin). Museum, Kelman St, features old telephone-exchange equipment, farm machinery and items of local history, by appt only; phone Cattle Camp Motel (076) 27 3412. May: Agricultural Show. Aug.: Leichhardt Festival. **In the area:** Scenic/historic tourist drives, brochure available from Tourist information or local service stations. Rare Livistona palms near Leichhardt Hwy, 15 km N. Glebe Weir, 40 km N, off Leichhardt Hwy, water-skiing and fishing. Isla Gorge National Park, 55 km N. Robinson Gorge, 108 km NW. **Tourist information:** Shire Offices, Yaldwyn St; (076) 27 3211. **Accommodation:** 1 hotel/motel, 1 motel, 1 cara./ camp. park.

Texas   Pop. 816

MAP REF. 123 K3, 505 M12

Quite the opposite in size to its American namesake, Texas lies alongside the Dumaresq River and the Qld-NSW border, 55 km SE of Inglewood. **Of interest:** Historical Museum in old police station (1893), by appt or every Sat.; inquire at Tourist information. Old Texas, on river off Swanky St, remains of original town. July: Agricultural Show. Sept.: Texas Roundup (even-numbered years). **In the area:** Beacon Lookout, 3 km SE, on Stanthorpe Rd. Good fishing along the river and in Glenlyon Dam, 45 km SE. Whyalla Feedlot, eastern side of Texas–Yelarbon Rd, largest cattle feedlot in Australia. Cunningham Weir, 31 km W off Texas–Yelarbon Rd, site where Allan Cunningham crossed the Dumaresq River in 1827. **Tourist information:** Ridgways, 40 High St; (076) 53 1245. **Accommodation:** 1 hotel/motel, 1 motel, 1 cara./camp. park.

Theodore   Pop. 502

MAP REF. 505 J2

Grain and cotton are the main crops on the irrigated land around this town on the Leichhardt Hwy, 220 km N of Miles. Timber milling and cattle grazing are also significant. Theodore was named after Edward Theodore, who became Premier of Qld in 1919, and designed by Walter Burley Griffin. **Of interest:** Theodore Hotel, The Boulevard; only cooperative hotel in Qld. Dawson Folk Museum, Second Ave. **In the area:** Irrigation area: birdwatching, cotton picking (Mar.–May); inquire at Tourist information. Fishing on Theodore Weir, on southern outskirts of town. Isla Gorge National Park, 35 km SW. Cracow, 49 km SE, where gold was produced from famous Golden Plateau mine 1932–76. **Tourist information:** Theodore Hotel, The Boulevard; (079) 93 1244. **Accommodation:** 1 hotel, 1 motel, 1 cara./camp. park.

Tin Can Bay   Pop. 1355

MAP REF. 505 P5

Half an hour's drive north-east of Gympie takes travellers to Tin Can Bay and nearby Rainbow Beach. These two hamlets are popular fishing, prawning and crabbing areas; the quiet waters of Tin Can Bay are ideal for boating and fishing, while Rainbow Beach has good surfing. **Of interest:** Market, 3rd Sat. each month. Easter: Festival. June: Seafood and Leisure Festival. Dec.: Robert Pryde Memorial Surf Classic. **In the area:** Fishing Classic at Rainbow Beach in July. Road south from Rainbow Beach (4WD) leads to coloured sands and beaches of Cooloola section of Great Sandy National Park. North, at Inskip Point, ferry to Fraser Island. At Carlo Point, 3 km E, cruising, fishing, swimming; houseboats and yachts for hire. **Tourist information:** 4 Gympie Rd; (07) 5486 4333. **Accommodation:** 1 hotel, 3 motels, 4 cara./camp. parks.

Toowoomba   Pop. 75 990

MAP REF. 496 F8, 505 N9

The garden city of Toowoomba has a distinctive charm and graciousness in its wide, tree-lined streets, colonial architecture and many fine parks and gardens. Toowoomba is 127 km W of Brisbane, on the rim of the Great Dividing Range. It began in 1849 as a village near an important staging post for teamsters and travellers, and was known as The Swamp. Aborigines pronounced the name 'T'wamp-bah'; this became 'Toowoomba'. Today it is the commercial centre for the fertile Darling Downs, with butter and cheese factories, sawmills, flour mills, tanneries, engineering and railway workshops, a modern iron foundry, clothing and shoe factories. It has an active cultural and artistic life. **Of interest:** Self-guide Russell St heritage walk. Cobb & Co. Museum, Lindsay St, traces history of horse-drawn vehicles. St Patrick's Cathedral (1880s), James St. St Luke's Anglican Church (1897), cnr Herries and Ruthven sts. Parks include Lake Annand, MacKenzie St, for birdlovers; Laurel Bank, scented gardens; Botanic Gardens and adjacent Queens Park, Lindsay St; Waterbird Habitat, MacKenzie St. Royal Bull's Head Inn (1847), Brisbane St, fully restored by National Trust. Toowoomba Art Gallery and Linton Gallery in Ruthven St; Downs Gallery, Margaret St. Willow Springs Adventure Park, Spring St. Antique and craft shops. Tourist Drive with floral markers; brochure from Tourist information. Markets, Queens Park, 3rd Sun. each month. Sept.: Carnival of Flowers. **In the area:** Self-guide scenic drives of varying lengths (brochure from Tourist information): 48-km circuit to Spring Bluff (old railway station at Spring Bluff has superb gardens) and Murphy's Creek; 100-km circuit to Heifer Creek, known as Valley of the Sun, provides spectacular scenery; 255-km circuit takes in Bernborough Centre, Jondaryan Woolshed, Cecil Plains Cotton Ginnery, Millmerran Museum and Pittsworth Folk Museum. Picnic Point, 5 km E, offers mountain views and waterfall; restaurant, coffee shop and take-away food available. At Highfields, 15 km N: Orchid Park; Danish Flower Art; Pioneer Museum. At Cabarlah, 20 km N: Telopea Gallery; Black Forest Hill Cuckoo Clock Centre; Country Markets last Sun. each month. **Tourist information:** cnr James and Kitchener sts; (076) 39 3797 **Accommodation:** 35 motels, 5 B&B, 1 hostel, 5 cara./camp. parks. **See also:** Tours from Brisbane; Darling Downs.

Townsville   Pop. 75 990

MAP REF. 501, 509 P12

In 1864 a sea captain named Robert Towns commissioned James Melton Black to build a wharf and establish a settlement on Cleveland Bay to service the new cattle industry inland. Townsville was gazetted in 1865 and declared a city in 1903. Today it is Australia's largest tropical city. There are many handsome historic buildings, particularly in the waterfront park area around Cleveland Bay. The city's busy port handles minerals from Mount Isa and Cloncurry; beef and wool from the western plains; sugar and timber from the rich coastal region; and its own manufacturing and processing industries. Townsville is the administrative, commercial, education and manufacturing capital of northern Qld. It is becoming a renowned centre for research into marine life and is the headquarters for the Great Barrier Reef Marine Park Authority. **Of interest:** The Strand with its tropical parks, waterfall and overhanging bougainvillea gardens. At the end of The Strand is the Rockpool, which provides year-round swimming. Sheraton Breakwater Casino-Hotel, Sir Leslie Thiess Dr. Great Barrier Reef Wonderland, Flinders St East: aquarium with touch-tank and walk-through transparent underwater viewing-tunnel, Omnimax theatre and Museum of Tropical Queensland; the complex is also a ferry terminal for services to Magnetic Island and for day cruises to the Great Barrier Reef. Billabong Sanctuary, entry from Muntalunga Dr., features koala feeding and crocodile shows. Perc Tucker Regional Art Gallery, Flinders Mall. Jezzine Military Museum, end of The Strand. Queen's Gardens, cnr Paxton and Gregory sts. Anzac Memorial Park, The Strand. Botanic Gardens, Anderson Park, Kings Rd. Historic Flinders Street East. Castle Hill Lookout, off Stanley St. Town Common and Environmental Park, Pallarenda Rd, a coastline park with prolific birdlife. Maritime Museum, Palmer St, South Townsville. Contact Tourist information for information on: cruises to Cairns via resort islands and reef on luxury catamaran *Coral Princess*; reef day-trips and dive cruises; day sailing around Magnetic Island; daily connections to resort islands of Magnetic, Orpheus, Hinchinbrook and Dunk; day outback tours, rainforest and white-water rafting tours. Cotters Market, each Sun. at Flinders Mall. July: Australian Festival of Chamber Music. **In the area:** Bowling Green Bay National Park, 25 km S, off Bruce Hwy. Pangola Park (32 km S) at Spring Creek. Near Giru, 50 km SE: waterfalls, bush walks, swimming and picnic and camping facilities. Internationally-recognised Australian Institute of Marine Science, 30 km E at Cape Ferguson. Offshore, Magnetic Island with a resident population of more than 2000; two-thirds of

White-water rafting on the Tully River

QUEENSLAND

island is national park featuring beaches, walks and wildlife. **Tourist information:** Flinders Mall; (077) 21 3660. **Accommodation:** 40 hotel/motels, 1 hostel, 11 cara./camp. parks. **See also:** The Far North.

Tully
Pop. 2715

MAP REF. 509 N9

Situated at the foot of Mt Tyson, Tully receives one of the highest annual rainfalls in Australia, averaging around 4200 mm annually. Major industries are sugarcane, bananas, tropical fruit, cattle and timber. **Of interest:** Beautiful railway station, with its profusion of tropical plants; Bruce Hwy. Tully Sugar Mill tours (June–Nov.), bookings essential; inquire at Tourist information. Market, 2nd Sat. each month. **In the area:** White-water rafting, canoeing, and reef and island cruising. Popular picnic spot on Tully River near Cardstone, 44 km W. Fishing at Tully Heads, 22 km SE and at Cardwell, 45 km S. Spectacular rainforests at Tully River Gorge (44 km W) and Murray Falls (40 km SW). White-water rafting and kayaking on Tully River, beginning at Tully Gorge; also superb scenery and swimming in the top reaches of the river. **Tourist information:** Bruce Hwy; (070) 68 2288. **Accommodation:** 1 motel, 1 hostel, 1 cara./camp. park.

Warwick
Pop. 10 393

MAP REF. 123 M1, 496 F13, 505 N11

An attractive city on the Darling Downs, Warwick is 162 km SW of Brisbane on the Cunningham Hwy, and 86 km S of Toowoomba on the New England Hwy. The area was first explored by Allan Cunningham in 1827; in 1840 the Leslie brothers arrived from the south and established a sheep station at Canning Downs; other pastoralists followed. The NSW government asked Patrick Leslie to select a site for a township, and in 1849 Warwick was surveyed and established. It was the first town, after Brisbane, in what became Qld. The railway line from Ipswich was opened in 1871 and Warwick became a city in 1936. In what seemed to be a minor incident in 1917, Prime Minister Billy Hughes was hit by an egg while addressing a crowd on the controversial conscription issue of the day. He asked a local policeman to arrest the man responsible but the policeman refused. The result was the formation of the Federal Police Force. Warwick is alongside the willow-shaded Condamine River, 458 m above sea level, and calls itself 'the Rose and Rodeo city'. The surrounding rich pastures support famous horse and cattle studs, and produce some of Australia's finest wool and grain. Fruit, vegetables and timber grow well, and the area is noted for its dairy products and bacon. **Of interest:** Self-guide walk around historic buildings; map available from Tourist information. Pringle Cottage (1870), Dragon St, houses large historical photo collection, vehicles and machinery. Leslie Park in Palmerin St. Jubilee Gardens, cnr Alice and Helene sts, features displays of roses. Warwick Regional Art Gallery, Albion St. Emus R Us, Old Stanthorpe Rd, emu farm open to the public. In Jan. or Feb.: Antique and Collectables Fair. Easter: Warwick Rock Swap. Oct.: Rose and Rodeo City Festival. **In the area:** Leslie Dam, 15 km W, for water sports. Sheep and emu farm at Mirambeena, 15 km E, along Yangan Rd and right at Wieman. Main Range National Park, 45 km E via Killarney, and Carr's Lookout, a further 14 km. Goomburra State Forest, east of Allora, 26 km N. **Tourist information:** 49 Albion St (New England Hwy); (076) 61 3122. **Accommodation:** 13 hotels, 10 motels, 1 B&B, 3 cara./camp. parks. **See also:** Darling Downs.

Weipa
Pop. 2510

MAP REF. 510 B7

Located on the west coast of Cape York, the township of Weipa is the home of the world's largest bauxite mine. This small mining town provides a comprehensive range of services and facilities for travellers. **Of interest:** Guided tours

Capricorn Region

This rich and varied slice of Queensland stretches inland from Rockhampton and the Capricorn Coast out to Jericho, and straddles the Tropic of Capricorn. The area includes the Capricorn Coast, Rockhampton city and surrounds, the central highlands and the rural hinterlands, and is drained by the Fitzroy, Mackenzie, Comet, Nogoa and Dawson rivers. The district was first opened up by gold and copper mining around **Emerald** in the 1860s, and the discovery of sapphires around Anakie. The original owners of the land have left their heritage in superb and mysterious rock paintings on the silent stone walls of the Carnarvon Ranges to the south. Cattle have been the economic mainstay of the region since European settlement, but vast tracts of brigalow scrub were cleared after World War II to grow wheat, maize, sorghum and safflower. These days coal is dominant, with mainly American companies gouging out enormous deposits for local and Japanese markets. On a smaller scale, professional and amateur fossickers still find gems in the region with a great deal of enjoyment.

For a pleasurable tour of the region, drive west from **Rockhampton**, the commercial and manufacturing capital, along the Capricorn Highway. Detour to Blackdown Tableland National Park where there are waterfalls, rock pools and camping areas; the turnoff is between Dingo and Blackwater. (If camping in the park, you will need a permit – available on arrival at park except during busy school holiday periods when it is necessary to obtain a permit from the regional office of the Department of Environment (079) 86 1964.) At Emerald turn south to Springsure, then east to **Biloela** on the Dawson Highway. Continue north on the Burnett Highway via **Mount Morgan** back to Rockhampton.

Mount Hay Gemstone Tourist Park, 41 kilometres west of Rockhampton, allows visitors to fossick for thunder eggs and rhyolite, which may be cut and polished at the factory in the park. Utah's Blackwater coalmine produces 4 million tonnes of coking coal and almost 3 million tonnes of steaming coal annually. Tours can be arranged.

Emerald is the main town in the central-highlands region, with the central-western railway continuing much further west to **Longreach** and

Fossicking for sapphires near Emerald

the Channel Country. Clermont and the Blair Athol coalfields are 106 kilometres to the north-west. The gemfields of Anakie, Rubyvale, Sapphire, The Willows and Tomahawk Creek are west of Emerald, and are popular with tourists seeking a different holiday. (A fossicker's licence is necessary.)

Springsure, 66 kilometres south of Emerald, is one of Queensland's oldest towns, having been surveyed in 1854. It produces beef and grain. Nearby is the Old Rainworth Fort at Burnside, a fascinating piece of Australiana, where early farm equipment, wool presses and the like, are on display. It was built in 1853 from local stone.

Rolleston, 70 kilometres to the south-east, is the turnoff to the magnificent **Carnarvon National Park**, 103 kilometres further south. The park covers 28 000 hectares of rugged mountains, forests, caves and deep gorges, some of which are Australia's earliest art galleries. There are countless Aboriginal paintings and engravings, which in

places extend in a colourful frieze for more than 50 metres.

The Callide open-cut mine is near Biloela, the principal town in the Callide Valley. The nearby Callide Power Station supplies the Rockhampton, Moura and Blackwater districts as well as Biloela.

What are known as the 'Snowy Mounts' are actually huge piles of salt in the Fitzroy River delta between Bajool and Port Alma. Underground salty water is pumped to the surface into pools called crystallisers, and the salt is harvested during October and November after solar evaporation.

For further information on the Capricorn Region, contact the Capricorn Information Centre, The Spire, Gladstone Rd, Rockhampton; (079) 27 2055. **See also:** National Parks and individual entries in A–Z listing for those parks and towns indicated by bold type. **Map reference:** 506–9.

of bauxite mine provide excellent coverage of whole mining process at Weipa. **In the area:** Tours of local areas, such as Rocky Point, Trunding, Nanum and Evans Landing, give insight into town's development and lifestyle. Number of fishing and camping areas near the town developed for well-equipped tourist. **Tourist information:** cnr Ring Road and The Esplanade, Cairns; (070) 51 3588. **Accommodation:** Limited. **See also:** Cape York.

Winton   Pop. 1156

MAP REF. 513 M8

Banjo Paterson wrote Australia's most famous song, 'Waltzing Matilda', on Dagworth Station near Winton in 1895. Combo Waterhole was then part of Dagworth, and the ballad had its first public airing in Winton on 6 April, 1895. The town is 174 km NW of Longreach on the Matilda Hwy. A major sheep area, Winton is also a large trucking centre for the giant road trains bringing cattle from the Channel

Channel Country

The remote Channel Country is an endless horizon of sweeping plains in the far west and south-west corner of the State. It seldom rains here, but after the northern monsoons the Georgina, Hamilton and Diamantina rivers and Cooper Creek take over as they flood through hundreds of channels in their efforts to reach Lake Eyre. After the 'wet without rain', the enormous quantities of water usually vanish into waterholes, salt pans and desert sands; grass, wildflowers and bird and animal life miraculously appear, and cattle are moved in for fattening.

The region is sparsely populated except for large pastoral holdings and scattered settlements linked by essential beef-roads. The Diamantina Developmental Road runs south from Mount Isa through Dajarra and Boulia to Bedourie, then swings east across the many channels of the Diamantina River and Cooper Creek through Windorah to the railhead at Quilpie, then on to Charleville, a journey of some 1335 kilometres.

Boulia, proclaimed the capital of the Channel Country, was first settled by Europeans in 1877. It is 295 kilometres south of Mount Isa and 360 kilometres west of Winton. A friendly, relaxed town on the Burke River, its name comes from an Aboriginal word meaning 'clear water'. Burke and Wills filled their water-bags here.

Bedourie, 191 kilometres further south, is the administrative centre for the Diamantina region, and has a store, school, police station, Flying Doctor medical clinic, roadhouse, motel and caravan park. It has ample artesian water, without the usual pungent smell, and swimming is popular.

South of Bedourie the Diamantina Developmental Road swings east for the partly sealed drive to Windorah. The name means 'place of large fish'. During drought the area is a dustbowl, during the

Boulia, a town within the remote Channel Country

monsoonal period, a lake. There is a good hotel in town and sheep-raising is the only industry.

A good but narrow sealed road leads 237 kilometres east to **Quilpie**, the eastern gateway to the Channel Country. Cattle, sheep and wool are transported by rail to the coast from here. Opals have been found here since 1880. Although the town is near the Bulloo River, its water supply is from a near-boiling artesian bore.

Thargomindah, 193 kilometres south of Quilpie, is a small settlement on the eastern fringe of the Channel Country, 198 kilometres from Cunnamulla. Noccundra, 122 kilometres even further west, has a permanent population of three, but can put you up at the hotel and sell you fuel.

The Kennedy Developmental Road from Winton to Boulia is sealed for most of its 256 kilometres. A welcome stop is the remote bush hotel at Middleton. Visitors are sure to be told about the Min Min light, an unexplained phenomenon that often appears at night near the old Min Min hotel, some 130 kilometres from Boulia.

The Eyre Developmental Road starts south of Bedourie and leads to **Birdsville**, the most isolated

settlement in Queensland, and 11 kilometres from the South Australian border, with the Simpson Desert to the west. It is at the top end of the Birdsville Track to Marree in South Australia. The Birdsville Developmental Road runs north-east to join the Diamantina Developmental Road and east to Windorah. Betoota is the only stop on the lonely 394-kilometre drive from Birdsville to Windorah. Betoota has one building (a hotel) that basks in the centre of a very large, virtually featureless gibber plain. The hotel is open every day and sells fuel.

Whilst summer in the Channel Country can become extremely hot, most accommodation, pubs etc. are now airconditioned and all services operate as usual. The best time to visit is between April and October. The wildflowers in here usually bloom around late August.

For further information on the Channel Country, contact the Outback Qld Tourism Authority, Library Building, Shamrock St, Blackall; (076) 57 4255. **See also:** individual entries for those towns indicated by bold type in A–Z listing. **Map reference:** 512 O11.

QUEENSLAND

Country to the railhead. In 1920 the first office of a company called Qantas was registered in Winton. The town's water supply comes out of deep artesian bores at a temperature of 83°C. **Of interest:** In Elderslie St: Historic Royal Theatre, open-air movie theatre and museum, one of the oldest still operating in Australia; swagman statue near swimming pool; Gift and Gem Shop with 'Opal Walk' set up inside; Qantilda Pioneer Place, a complex of seven buildings includes re-creation of the lounge room where Banjo Paterson finalised 'Waltzing Matilda' after he arrived from Dagworth Station, Qantas Room, old telephone exchange, radio display, Aboriginal artifacts, steam locomotive and railway carriage, vintage vehicles, and collection of 4000 bottles. Arno's Wall, Bindex St opposite Shire Offices, ongoing concrete-wall creation containing 'every item imaginable'. Apr. Waltzing Matilda Festival. Sept.: Outback Festival (odd-numbered years). **In the area:** Bladensburg National Park, 2 km S, self-drive tour of park; inquire at Tourist information. Aboriginal paintings and bora ceremonial grounds at Skull Hole, 40 km S. Opalton, 115 km S, historic ghost town; gemfields nearby. Combo Waterhole, 150 km NW via Matilda Hwy. Carisbrooke Station, 85 km SW, a working sheep station; Aboriginal cave paintings and scenic drives in surrounds; day tours and accommodation available. Lark Quarry Conservation Park, 110 km SW, features preserved tracks of dinosaur 'stampede'. **Tourist information:** Qantilda Pioneer Place, Elderslie St; (076) 57 1618. **Accommodation:** 4 hotels, 3 motels, 2 cara./camp. parks.

Wondai   Pop. 1156

MAP REF. 505 N6

This typical small country town in the South Burnett region is 15 km S of Murgon and 31 km N of Kingaroy. The surrounding area produces peanuts and a variety of grains; other industries include dairying, beef and pork production, timber milling and dolomite mining. **Of interest:** Museum with local history displays, Mackenzie St. Country market, 2nd Sat. each month. **In the area:** Gem-fossicking areas surround district; inquire at Tourist information. Boondooma Dam, 50 km NW near Proston, for water sports. **Tourist information:** Shire Offices, Scott St;

(071) 68 5155. **Accommodation:** 2 hotels, 1 hotel/motel, 1 motel, 1 cara./camp. park.

Yandina   Pop. 707

MAP REF. 500 E6

Yandina lies 10 km N of Nambour on the Bruce Hwy and is the home of the world-famous Ginger Factory and Gingertown, where visitors may enjoy ginger goodies. The processing of the crop can be observed from the tower platform at the factory and the *Ginger Bell* paddlesteamer offers river cruises from the factory to a working ginger farm. Bunya Park Wildlife Sanctuary, in grounds of Ginger Factory. **Of interest:** Carinya, historic homestead on Bruce Hwy at northern edge of town. The Queenslander, sells antiques and bric-a-brac. Oct.: Spring Flower and Ginger Festival. **In the area:** Wappa Dam, just west of town. At Eumundi, 8 km N: Country Fair selling fresh produce each Wed.; markets each Sat. a.m., selling goods ranging from locally-grown fruit and vegetables to art and craft; old and impressive Imperial Hotel, near markets. **Tourist information:** cnr Aerodrome Rd and Sixth Ave, Maroochydore; (07) 5479 1566. **Accommodation:** 1 hotel, 1 cara./camp. park.

Yeppoon   Pop. 7542

MAP REF. 507 O10

This popular coastal resort, 40 km NE of Rockhampton, lies on the shores of Keppel Bay. Yeppoon and the strip of beaches to its south – Cooee Bay, Rosslyn Bay, Causeway Lake, Emu Park and Keppel Sands – are known as the Capricorn Coast. Great Keppel Island Resort is 13 km offshore. Market, 1st Sun. each month. Fig Tree markets, next to Tourist information, 3rd Sun. each month. Jan.: Australia Day Celebrations. Feb.: Surf Lifesaving Championships. Aug.: World Cooeeing Festival. Sept.: Pineapple Festival. **In the area:** Scenic drives and adventure tours, contact Tourist information. Wetland Tour at Capricorn International Resort, 8 km N. Cooberrie Park, 15 km N, a noted flora and fauna reserve. Further 17 km N, Byfield State Forest, home of extremely rare Byfield fern, boardwalk along Waterpark Creek; rainforest cabins nearby. Keppel Bay Marina at Rosslyn Bay Harbour,

7 km S; bareboat and fishing charters available. Blow Hole at Double Head, 7 km S. Capricorn Hearts Flower and Tea Garden on Tanby Rd, 8 km S, exotic teas and heart-shaped flowers. Waterpark Creek. Coral Life Marineland, 13 km S at Kinka Beach, unique living displays of coral and marine life; open weekends and school holidays. Catamaran service daily to Great Keppel Island and nearby underwater observatory. Water taxi to Pumpkin Island. **Tourist information:** Ross Creek Roundabout; (079) 39 4888. **Accommodation:** 2 resorts, 3 hotels, 5 motels, 17 apartment complexes, 1 hostel, 7 cara./camp. parks.

Yungaburra   Pop. 807

MAP REF. 503 D12, 509 M7

On the edge of the Atherton Tableland, 13 km from Atherton and inland from Cairns, the town is known for its National Trust Historic Precinct listing. **Of interest:** Self-guide Historic Precinct Buildings Walk, inquire at Tourist information. Lake Eacham Hotel, Cedar St. Artists Galleries, cnr Gillies Hwy and Cedar St. Various gem and craft shops, inquire at Tourist information. Produce and craft markets, 4th Sat. each month on Gillies Hwy. June: Yuletide. July: Jazz Festival. Oct.: Folk Festival. **In the area:** Curtain Fig Tree, 2.5 km SW, spectacular example of strangler fig. The Seven Sisters, seven rolling hills, 2 km W. Tinaburra, 3 km N on the shores of Lake Tinaroo. Across the lake, The Chimneys, two chimneys from timber-milling days. Views of lake from Tinaroo Falls dam outlet, 23 km NW. Spectacular views over Gillies Range from Heales Outlook Lookout, 16 km NE. Lakes Eacham (5 km E) and Barrine (10 km E), volcanic crater lakes. **Tourist information:** Nick's Swiss-Italian Restaurant, Gillies Hwy; (070) 95 3330. **Accommodation:** 1 hotel, 4 motels.

Gulf Savannah

The Gulf Savannah is a vast, remote, thinly populated region stretching east to the Undara Volcanic National Park, north from **Mount Isa** and **Cloncurry** to the mangrove-covered shores of the Gulf of Carpentaria, and west to the Queensland-Northern Territory border. The unfortunate Burke and Wills were the first European visitors, although the waters of the Gulf itself were first charted by Dutch navigators almost 400 years ago. The country is flat and open, and has more rivers than roads. April to October is the recommended time to see the Gulf country. During the wet season, generally November to March, rain may close the dirt roads in this area. However, bird-migration patterns make this the best time for observing the spectacular birdlife. Motorists should realise that this is not 'Sunday-driving' country, although main roads have been upgraded, and should plan accordingly. An alternative way to travel is to fly in from Cairns, Mount Isa or Karumba. The Gulf Savannah is, however, an ideal corner of Australia if you want to get away from it all.

The wide expanses of the Gulf Savannah region divide themselves into separate areas. The Eastern Savannah is easily reached via the Great Top Road (Gulf Developmental Road), which winds up the eastern face of the Dividing Range, passing above Cairns. As an alternative route to Georgetown, or for travellers with only limited time to explore the outback, the Undara Loop is a leisurely 3–5 day round trip from Cairns through the Lynd Junction, Einasleigh and Forsayth to Georgetown.

Georgetown, 411 kilometres from Cairns, is the centre of the Etheridge Goldfield, where nuggets can still be found. Completing the loop back to Cairns takes the traveller to Tallaroo Hot Springs, Mt Surprise and Undara Volcanic National Park, where you can see the lava tubes, a geological phenomenon. The *Savannahlander* train operates twice weekly between Mt Surprise and Forsayth.

From Georgetown the traveller can head west 150 kilometres to **Croydon**, terminus of the railway from Normanton, an historic link established to service Croydon, a rich goldmining town of the last century. The railway between the two towns is not connected to any other system.

Lawn Hill National Park is close to the Northern Territory border

It is used once a week by the *Gulflander*, the award-winning tourist train, which leaves Normanton every Wednesday and Croydon every Thursday. Many of Croydon's buildings have been classified by the National Trust and the Australian Heritage Commission.

Normanton is the central town of the whole Gulf Savannah, with a population of 1189, although in the gold days of 1891 it had a population of about 3000 people.

Karumba, 71 kilometres north-west of Normanton on the mouth of the Norman River, is the centre of the Gulf prawning industry and home to the barramundi fishing industry. Keen anglers from all over Australia come to Karumba to try their skills.

The Western Savannah has endless flat grassed plains stretching as far as the eye can see, while the wetlands around Karumba stretch across the top of the Western Savannah above Burketown and beyond to the border. Here rivers some 8 kilometres apart overflow their banks during the monsoons and form an unbroken sheet of water.

The town of **Burketown**, close to the Gulf, can be isolated for long periods during the wet. Explorer John Stokes termed the surrounding area the 'Plains of Promise', and today, like most of the Gulf region, it is cattle country. Barramundi fishing and birdwatching attract adventurers; a well-equipped 4WD vehicle is advisable in some areas, but is not essential for a visit to the majority of locations.

Lawn Hill National Park, includes the World Heritage-listed Riversleigh Fossil Field Section.

The park is located to the west of the Gregory Downs Hotel, a welcome watering-hole for the traveller. Within the park, 60-metre sheer sandstone walls form Lawn Hill Gorge with emerald green water at their base. The National Parks Service has established 20 kilometres of walking tracks to enable visitors to see this beautiful country safely.

The Gulf Savannah is a new frontier in Australia that is opening up to those in search of interesting but authentic educational and adventure experiences. To assist visitors, an organisation of Savannah Guides has been formed. These guides are professional interpreters who have lived in the Gulf Savannah for many years and are able to offer a wide range of knowledge concerning the wilderness environment. There are guide stations at: Tallaroo (at Tallaroo Station); Hells Gate (at Hells Gate Roadhouse); Undara Volcanic National Park (at Lava Lodge, Undara); Borroloola, NT (at McArthur River Caravan Park); Lawn Hill National Park (at Adels Grove); and Cape Crawford, NT (at Heartbreak Hotel).

For further information on the area, including road reports and free birdwatching guidebooks, contact Gulf Savannah Tourist Organisation, 55 McLeod St, Cairns; (070) 51 4658. **See also:** Lawn Hill National Park entry in National Parks; individual entries in A–Z listing for those towns indicated by bold type. **Map references:** 508 C12, 511 H12.

Location Map

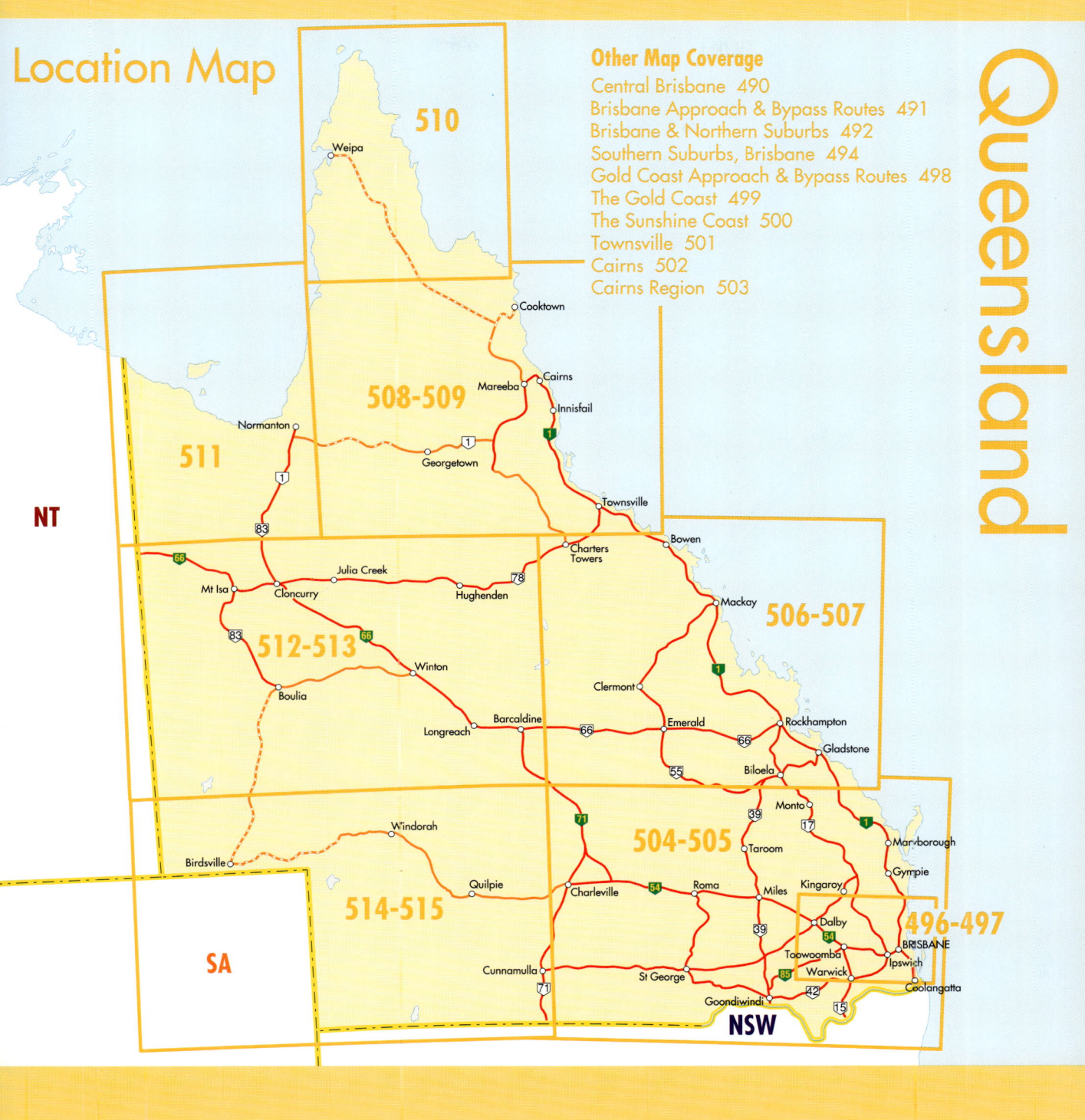

Queensland

510

Weipa

Other Map Coverage
Central Brisbane 490
Brisbane Approach & Bypass Routes 491
Brisbane & Northern Suburbs 492
Southern Suburbs, Brisbane 494
Gold Coast Approach & Bypass Routes 498
The Gold Coast 499
The Sunshine Coast 500
Townsville 501
Cairns 502
Cairns Region 503

Cooktown

508-509

Mareeba   Cairns
                Innisfail

Normanton

Georgetown

511

Townsville

Charters
Towers   Bowen

Julia Creek   Mackay   506-507

Mt Isa   Cloncurry   Hughenden

512-513   Winton

Boulia   Clermont

Longreach   Barcaldine   Emerald   Rockhampton
                                                         Gladstone

                                            Biloela

NT   Monto   Maryborough

Windorah   Taroom   17
                          504-505   Gympie

Birdsville   Kingaroy
            Quilpie   Charleville   Roma   Miles

514-515   Dalby   496-497
                                                    Toowoomba   BRISBANE
            Cunnamulla   St George   Warwick   Ipswich

SA   Goondiwindi   Coolangatta

                                              NSW

Spring Hill

Petrie Terrace

Albert Park

Victoria Barracks

Roma St

Brisbane Transit Centre

Observatory

King Edward Park

Jacobs Ladder

Central

Anzac Square

Post Office Square

King George Square

City Hall

BRISBANE

Conrad Treasury Casino

Queens Gardens

Riverside Centre

Riverside Ferry Terminal

Eagle Street Ferry Terminal

Watertront Place

Eagle Street Ferry Terminal

Edward Street Ferry Terminal

BRISBANE RIVER

Petrie Bight

Kangaroo Point

Capt John Burke Park

James Warner Park

CT White Park

Thornton Street Ferry Terminal

Dockside

Queensland Art Gallery

Museum

Cultural Centre

Performing Arts Centre

Brisbane Convention & Exhibition Centre

South Brisbane

Musgrave Park

Entertainment Piazza

South Bank

Brisbane Institute of TAFE South Bank Campus

Brisbane State High School

Stanley Street Plaza

Victoria Bridge

North Quay Ferry Terminal

Queens Wharf

Sciencentre

Parliament House

Heliport

South Bank 1 & 2 Ferry Terminal

QUT Gardens Point Ferry Terminal

Gardens Gate

Queensland University of Technology Gardens Point Campus

South Bank Institute Conservatorium of Music

City Botanic Gardens

Information Pavilion

Kiosk

Brisbane River Stage

Domain Car Park

Gardens Point

Mt Olivet Hospital

St Marys Anglican Church

Kangaroo Point

South Bank Institute of TAFE Kangaroo Point Campus

Raymond Park

Kangaroo Point Cliffs Lookout

Queensland Maritime Museum

Dry Dock

River Plaza Hotel Ferry Terminal

South Bank 3 Ferry Terminal

Memorial Park

Sommerville House Girls School

St Laurences School

Mater Misericordiae Hospital

Woolloongabba

Brisbane Cricket Ground (The Gabba)

TO CABOOLTURE
TO GOLD COAST
TO IPSWICH

Legend

Accommodation
Bellevue Hotel 1 E7
Brisbane City Travel Lodge 2 B4
Brisbane International Hilton 3 E5
Brisbane Parkroyal 4 F7
Conrad International 5 E7
Country Comfort Lennons Hotel 6 D6
Gazebo Hotel 7 C3
The Heritage Hotel 8 G6
Hotel Grand Chancellor 9 C2
ITT Sheraton Brisbane Hotel 10 E3
Mercure Hotel Brisbane 11 C5
Novotel Brisbane 12 F2
Story Bridge Motor Inn 13 I6
Radisson North Quay 14 A4
Ridge Hotel 15 E2
Rydges South Bank 16 C9

General Information
Ansett Australia 17 D6
Brisbane Transit Centre 18 B4
Central Railway Station 19 E3
General Post Office 20 F4
Motoring Organisation (RACQ) 21 F4

Police Headquarters 22 B4
Qantas Travel Centre 23 F4
Roma Street Station 24 B3
Tourist Information 25 D5, E5

Places of Interest
Anzac War Memorial 26 E4
Brisbane Cricket Ground 27 I13
City Botanic Gardens 28 G8
City Hall 29 D5
City Plaza 30 D5
Commissariat Stores 31 D7
Conrad Treasury Casino 32 D6
Customs House 33 G3
Deanery 34 G3
Observatory (Old Windmill) 35 D3
Old Government House 36 F9
Parliament House 37 E8
Qld Art Gallery 38 B7
Qld Cultural Centre 39 B8
Qld Maritime Museum 40 E11
Qld Museum 41 B7
Qld University of Technology 42 F9
State Library of Qld 43 B6

Accommodation Only a sample range is listed; inclusion is not necessarily a recommendation.

Thick roads represent recommended approach and bypass routes.

Griffin · **Petrie** · **Joyner** · **Lawnton** · **Bray Park** · **Strathpine** · **Warner** · **Cashmere** · **Clear Mountain** · **Branch Creek** · **Bunya** · **Eatons Hill** · **Albany Creek** · **Brendale** · **Bald Hills** · **Bridgeman Downs** · **Carseldine** · **Fitzgibbon** · **Taigum** · **Boondall** · **Bracken Ridge** · **Brighton** · **Sandgate** · **Shorncliffe** · **Deagon** · **Zillmere** · **Geebung** · **Aspley** · **McDowall** · **Chermside West** · **Chermside** · **Wavell Heights** · **Virginia** · **Banyo** · **Northgate** · **Nundah** · **Toombul** · **Everton Hills** · **Everton Park** · **Stafford Heights** · **Kalinga** · **Kedron** · **Arana Hills** · **Oxford Park** · **Grovely** · **Keperra** · **Ferny Hills** · **Ferny Grove** · **Upper Kedron** · **Mitchelton** · **Gaythorne** · **Stafford** · **Grange** · **Alderley** · **Lutwyche** · **Wooloowin** · **Clayfield** · **Hendra** · **Ascot** · **Hamilton** · **Eagle Junction** · **Enoggera** · **Newmarket** · **Windsor** · **Wilston** · **Albion** · **Breakfast Creek** · **Kingsford** · **Mayne** · **Bowen Hills** · **Newstead** · **Dorrington** · **Ashgrove** · **Herston** · **Kelvin Grove** · **Spring Hill** · **Fortitude Valley** · **New Farm** · **Bulimba** · **Balmoral** · **The Gap** · **Red Hill** · **Paddington** · **Milton** · **BRISBANE** · **Kangaroo Point** · **Hawthorne** · **Norman Park** · **Bardon** · **Rainworth** · **Jubilee** · **Auchenflower** · **Toowong** · **West End** · **South Brisbane** · **Highgate Hill** · **East Brisbane** · **Woolloongabba**

Bramble Bay · Pine River · Samsonvale · Lake Samsonvale · State Forest · Brisbane Forest Park · Samford State Forest · Bunyaville State Forest · Enoggera Military Camp · Enoggera Reservoir · Mount Coot-tha Park · Botanical Gardens · Planetarium · Mt Coot-tha 244m · One Tree Hill Lookout

Bruce Hwy · Gateway · Gympie Rd · South Pine Rd · Western Freeway · Sir Samuel Griffith Dr · Waterworks Rd · Mt Nebo Rd

0 1 2 3 4 5 km

J K L M N O P Q R

MORETON

BAY

MUD
ISLAND

For more detail on Central
Brisbane see page 490

Vehicular Ferry

Vehicular Ferry

Juno Point

CHANNEL

Jubilee Ck

Port of Brisbane

ST HELENA
ISLAND

ST HELENA
ISLAND
NATIONAL
PARK

Luggage
Point

FISHERMAN
ISLANDS

Myrtletown

Oil Refinery

Bulwer
Island

Boat Passage

Whyte
Island

Crab

Green
Island

Domestic
Terminal

BRISBANE
AIRPORT

FORT LYTTON
NATIONAL PARK

Lytton

Oil Refinery

International
Terminal

Pinkenba

LOMANDRA

Meeandah

Pinkenba

Wynnum North

Elanora
Park

Oyster Point

Wynnum
North

Eagle Farm

Eagle Farm

Royal
Queensland
Golf Club

Gateway
Bridge

Aquarium

Gibson Island

Sibley

Lindum

Wynnum
Golf Course

Wynnum

Darling Point

King Island

CONSERVATION
PARK

Quarries Reach

Crawfords

Memorial
Park

Mountjoy

Manly
Boat Harbour

Wellington Point

Hemmant

NEW
LINDUM RD

Preston

Manly

Queensport

Doboy

Hemmant
Park

Wynnum
West

Manly
West

Lota

Fig Tree Point

Erobin

Geoff Skinner
Reserve

Waterloo

Bay

Mooroondu Point

Murarrie

Murarrie
Recreation Reserve

Carmichael
Park

Cemetery

Villanova
College Sports
Ground

Thorneside

Wellington
Point

Historic
Ormiston House

Cannon
Hill

Tingalpa

Kianawah
Park

Wakerley

Rickertt

Ransome

Birkdale

Hills

Gumdale

Howeston Golf Course

Tingalpa
Creek Reserve

Ormiston

Carina

Meadowlands
Picnic Ground

The Plantation

Carindale

Belmont
Hospital

Belmont
Rifle Range

Cannon
Hill Rifle Range

Chandler
(Sleeman)
Sports
Complex

Chandler

J K L M N O P Q R

Grid columns: A B C D E F G H I
Grid rows: 1–13

N (compass, Penguin logo)

Gap Creek Reserve · BRISBANE FOREST PARK · Gap Creek · Moggill Ck

The Summit 285m+ · SIR SAMUEL · GRIFFITH · PARK · MOUNT COOT-THA PARK · The Pinnacle · SIR SAMUEL GRIFFITH DR · GRIFFITH DR · MT COOT-THA GEN CEMETERY · Birdwood TCE · Birdwood · MILTON RD · Botanic Gardens · South Brisbane · LYTTON · Heath Park · Bennetts RD · Norman · Res

Constitution Hill 258m · Planetarium · Brisbane Botanic Gardens · FREDERICK ST · MISKIN ST · Auchenflower · SYLVAN RD · West End · Highgate Hill · MAIN · WELLINGTON · East Brisbane · VULTURE ST EAST · Griffin Park · CAVENDISH · Cambley Park

Mt Coot-tha 244m · One Tree Hill Lookout · WESTERN FWY · Toowong · SHERWOOD RD · Toowong Park · JEPHSON ST · SYLVAN ST · GALEY RD · South Brisbane · STEPHENS · HARDGRAVE · DORNOCH · VULTURE · STANLEY ST · Woolloongabba · OLD · CLEVELAND · Stones Corner · PEMBROKE · CHA

Taringa · STANLEY TCE · WAVERLEY · SWANN · MOGGILL · St Lucia · SIR FRED SCHONELL · Sports Ground · The Elbow · Cornwall · Dutton Park · IPSWICH · F3 · JULIETTE · Greenslopes · 41

Kenmore Hills · BOSCOMBE RD · Indooroopilly · GAILEY RD · HARTS RD · Queensland University · St Lucia Reach · ANNERLEY · Fairfield · SEXTON · Anneley · 3

Cemetery Showground · BROOKFIELD RD · Chapel Hill · CHAPEL HILL RD · RUSSELL · Moore Park · COHAN ST · LAMBERT · Indooroopilly Golf Course · St Lucia Reach · HAWKEN · IRONSIDE · HYDE · VENNER · WATERTON · C.B. Mott Park · 3

Brookfield · BROOKFIELD RD · Creekside Park · Moggill Ck · Reserve · Kenmore · MOGGILL RD · FIG TREE · Chelmer · OXLEY · LEYBOURNE · Indooroopilly Golf Course Indooroopilly Island · Yeronga · Yeronga Park · SCHOOL · CRACKNELL · Ekibin · ESHER · WELLER · 11

MOGGILL RD · Reserve · MARSHALL LA · Cubberla Creek Reserve · Marist Bros Rosalie Sportsground · HONOUR AV · Graceville · GRACEVILLE AV · Long Pocket · Tennyson · GREEN GOW · CLIFTON · Tarragindi · TOOHEY · MONASH · 11

Kenmore · Fig Tree Pocket · Graceville Memorial Park · LONG ST EAST · Yeerongpilly · FAIRFIELD · WEIR · PRIOR · MARSHALL · 11

War Veterans Home · Kenmore Repatriation Hospital · Centenary Bridge · Sherwood · Sherwood Forest Park · SHERWOOD RD · Brisbane Golf Course · Moorooka · MAYFIELD · Toohey Forest Park · Toohey Mountain Reserve · 4

Pullenvale · MT CROSBY RD · Mosquito Is · BURRENDAH · Amazons Aquatic Adventureland · Lone Pine Koala Sanctuary · KENNY ST · BOTTICELLI ST · DEWAR · Corinda · GRAY AV · Animal Husbandry Research Farm · Rocklea · Salisbury · Griffith University · KESSELS · Na

Anstead · MT CROSBY RD · 37 · Jindalee Park · Jindalee · Jindalee Golf Course · WESTLAKE · Seventeen Mile Rocks · SEVENTEEN · MILE · ROCKS RD · Oxley · OXLEY STATION RD · Reserve · Showground · Kookaburra Park · FAIRLIE · LILLIAN · ORANGE GROVE RD · RIAWENA · Rob

Pinjarra Hills · Brisbane River · McLeod Country Golf Club · ARRABRI · Sinnamon Park · Oxley · IPSWICH RD · GRANARD RD · MUSGRAVE · Coopers Plains · McC

Bellbowrie · MOGGILL RD · Reserve · Westlake · HORIZON · Mount Ommaney · DANDENONG · Darra · ATTHOWS PARK · WESTCOMBE ST · MONIER · CARDIFF · STATION RD · DOUGLAS ST · Archerfield · ARCHERFIELD AERODROME · BOUNDARY RD · BEAUDESERT RD · MORTIMER · BANOON · 11 · Sunny · LIST

Moggill · Moggill Cemetery · SUMMERS RD · Middle Park · RIVERHILLS RD · Jamboree Heights · HARCOURT · Archerfield International Astrodome · BEATTY · Acacia Ridge · BRADMAN · 11 · CHILTE

Riverhills · Moggill Country Club · WACOL STATION RD · Sumner · WANDU RD · The Centenary Highway Park · IPSWICH RD · GARDEN RD · Greenfield Park · KELLNER · FREEMAN · ARCHERFIELD RD · Oxley Golf Course · FREEMAN · GLENALA · Delbridge Park · Inala · Durack · KING · Algester · JACKSON · MT LINDESAY

Wacol Prison · Wolston House · GRINDLE · Department of Primary Industries · Cockatoo Island · PROGRESS RD · Caravan Park · McEwen Park · AZALEA · LAVENDER · LILAC ST · Kev Hooper Mem Park · Inala · Caravan Park · ROSELLA · Willawong · PARADISE · RIDGEWOOD · Col Bennett Park · Calamva

Redbank · Steam Locomotive Museum · IPSWICH BRISBANE MWY · 15 · Wolston Park Hospital · Gailes Golf Course · Wolston Park Golf Course · WILRUNA · Gailes · Richlands · GOVERNMENT RD · BOSS · TAMARIND ST · Doolandella · Pallara · SPORTING COMPLEX

Priors Pocket · Richardson Park TCE · Leslie Park · Goodna · WATERFORD · Carole Park · CLENDON · Ellen Grove · Forest Lake · BLUNDER RD · Larapinta · Parkinso

Redbank · DUNCAN ST · SMITH ST · Rifle Range · Cemetery · ALICE ST · QUEEN ST · CHURCH ST · MILL ST · BERTHA ST · OLD LOGAN RD · COBALT · JULIE · ROXWELL · Forest Lake · WADEVILLE ST · Heathwood · STAPYLTON · LOGAN MWY · Larapinta · 40 · LOGAN · Parkinso

Banjo Paterson Park · KRUGER PDE · STUART · JONES · ROSEMARY · Camira · SHIMEAL · ADDISON · MOSS · BROWNS PLAINS RD · LOGAN MWY · JOHNSON · PARADISE · JOHNSON · BUSHMILLS · PEVERELL

REDBANK PLAINS RD · PLAINS · JONES · KERTES · OLD LOGAN RD · GREENBANK MILITARY CAMP · Forestdale · FORESTDALE RD · ABBEY · CONIFER · LINDESAY

Redbank Plains Recreation Park · Wongaroo Ck · Opposum Ck · GOODNA - OXLEY CREEK RD · OLD LOGAN RD · Oxley Ck · Boronia Heights · CORONATION RD · MACKELLAR DR · FEDRICK ST · MIDDLE · SHORT · CREST · Boronia Bushland Reserve · Win Par

Wongaroo Ck · Mountain Ck · GOODNA - OXLEY CREEK RD · OLD LOGAN RD

0 1 2 3 4 5 km

493

497

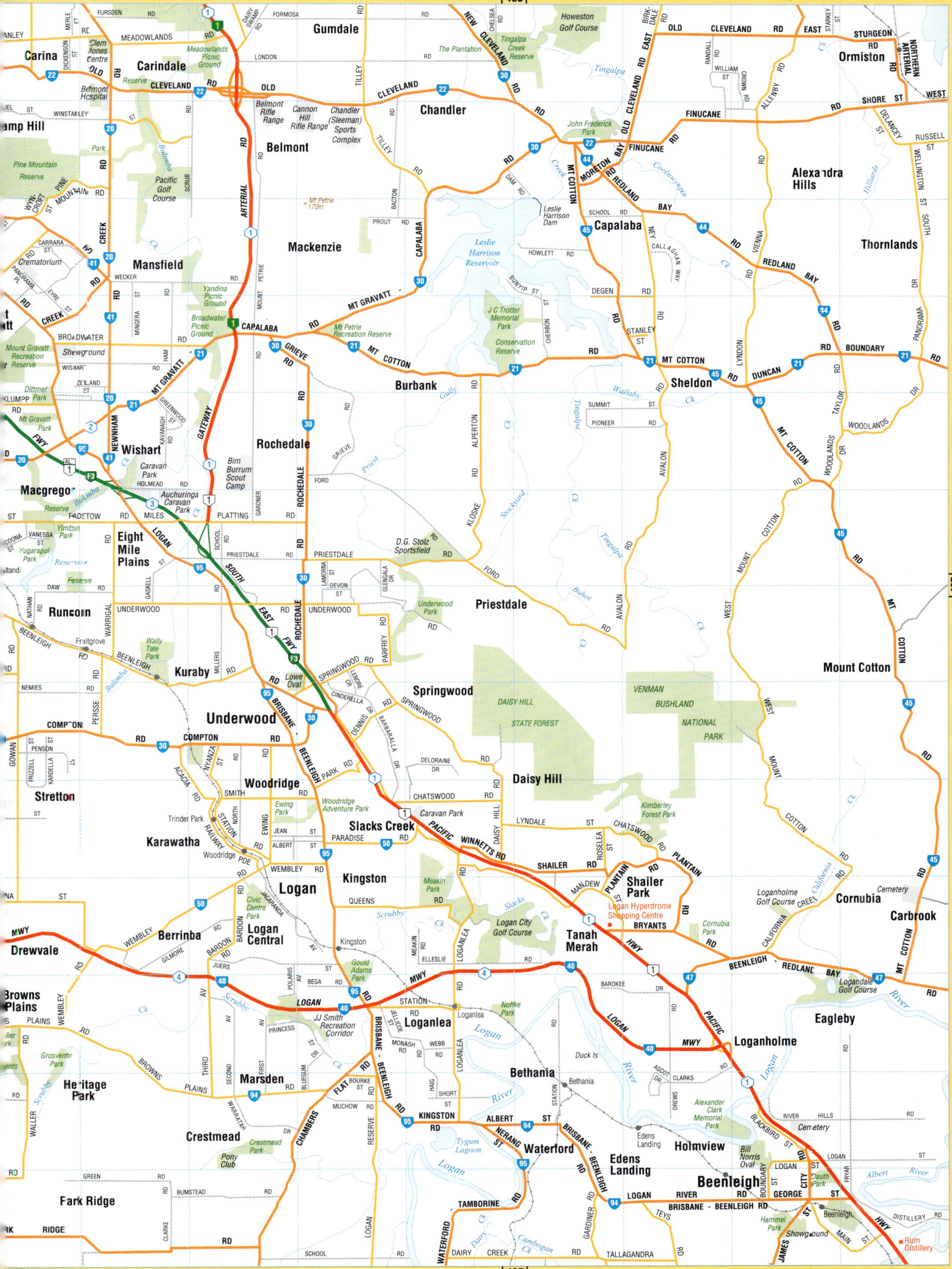

Carina
Carindale
Gumdale
Camp Hill
Belmont Hospital
Belmont
Chandler
Mackenzie
Mansfield
Capalaba
Alexandra Hills
Thornlands
Ormiston
Pacific Golf Course
Pine Mountain Reserve
Crematorium
Leslie Harrison Reservoir
Leslie Harrison Dam
Sheldon
Mt Gravatt Recreation Reserve
Wishart
Newnham
Burbank
J C Trotter Memorial Park
Macgregor
Rochedale
Eight Mile Plains
Runcorn
Underwood
Priestdale
Mount Cotton
Kuraby
Springwood
Stretton
Woodridge
Daisy Hill
Venman Bushland National Park
Karawatha
Slacks Creek
Kingston
Shailer Park
Cornubia
Logan
Carbrook
Drewvale
Berrinba
Logan Central
Tanah Merah
Loganholme
Eagleby
Browns Plains
Heritage Park
Loganlea
Bethania
Marsden
Holmview
Crestmead
Waterford
Edens Landing
Park Ridge
Beenleigh

TO KINGAROY

BUNYA MOUNTAINS NATIONAL PARK

Mt Kiangarow 1146m
Haly Mtn 956m
Mt Mowbullan 1106m

Jimbour
Bell
Kogandah
Warmga
Woodlawn
Squaretop
Yamsion
Kaimkillenbun

TO KINGAROY
Brooklands
Tarong
Meandu Creek
Buckland
South Nanango
Tarong Power Station
Rocky Hill
Neumgna
Yarraman
Blackbutt
Benarkin
Moore
Linville
Avoca Vale
Mt Spencer 445m
Nurinda
Colinton
Harlin
Yimbun
Ivory Creek
Toogoolawah
Ottaba
Caboc
Biarra
Esk

Ellesmere
Maidenwell
Wengenville
Pimpimbudgee
Upper Yarraman
Kooralgin
THE PALMS NP
Cooyar
Nutgrove
Thornville
St Aubyn
Djuan
Googa Googa

Moola
MacLagan
Woodleighton
Malling
Narko
Coalbank
Cookes Hill 737m
Mt Sheni 631m
Andiramba
Queen Mab Mtn 527m
Mt Japheth 664m
Virginia
Bluff Mtn 520m
The Bluff
Barnes Hill 733m
Mt Tin Tin 390m
Mt Deongwat 548m

Quinalow
Peranga
Evergreen
Mount Darry
Doctors Creek
Jones Gully
Pinelands
Kipper

Kulpi
Brymaroo
Plain View
Haden
Neuve
Bald Hill No2 762m
Crows Nest
CROWS NEST NATIONAL PARK
Cressbrook Dam
Mt Hallen
Buaraba

Bowenville
Muldu
Acland
Coal Mine Museum
Goombungee
Sabine
Greenwood
Nara
Douglas
Whichello
Pechey
RANGE
Lake Perseverance
Ravensbourne
Mt Hallen 308m
Goomi

Jondaryan
Woolshed
Devon Park
Kelvinhaugh
Boodua
Munigaheen
Groomsville
Hampton
RAVENSBOURNE NP
Geham
Perseverance
Mt Perseverance 807m
Mt Cross 625m
Buaraba Creek
Yellow Gully 410m
Buaraba

Oakey
Tangkam
Yargullen
Yalangur
Meringandan
Cabarlah
Murphys Creek
Byars Hill
Lake Clarendon
Buaraba Creek
Atkinson's Dam
Mt Tarampa

Norwin
Mount Tyson
Aubigny
Kingsthorpe
Gowrie
Highfields
Spring Bluff
Ballard
Postmans Ridge
Lockyer
Brightview

DOWNS
Bongeen
Norillee
Biddeston
Wellcamp
Irongate
Rossvale
Linthorpe
Beauaraba
Athol
Bunkers Hill
Westbrook
Vale View
WITHCOTT
TOOWOOMBA
Helidon
Grantham
Gatton
Carpendale
Lilydale
Winwill
Tenthill
Forest Hill
Plainland
Hatto Vale
Glenore Grove
Summer

Springside
Wallingford
Umbiram
Wyreema
Shepperd
Preston
Stockyard
Flagstone Creek
Ma Ma Creek
Woodlands
Ropeley
Blenheim
La dley

Southbrook
Cambooya
Hodgson Vale
Mt Campbell 719m
Sugarloaf
Ramsay
Mount Whitestone
Upper Tenthill
Mount Berryman
Mount Sylvia
Ingoldsby
Mount Cooper 712m
Thornton
Hidden Vale
Rosevale

Brookstead
Pampas
Yarranlea
Pittsworth
Mt Rubieslaw
Greenmount East
Greenmount
Emu Creek
Budgee Gap 714m
West Haldon
Junction View
Mt Beau Brummel 700m

Milmeran
Yandilla
Felton East
Mt Perkins 673m
Felton
Mt Kent 602m
Mount Sibley
Budgee
West Haldon
East Haldon
Mt Haldon 906m
Mt Zahel 871m
MAIN RANGE NATIONAL PARK

Tummaville
Leslies Bridge
Felton South
Back Plains
Nobby
Nevilton
Pilton
Hirstglen
Mt Lowe 958m
Mt Cooper
Grass Tree Knob 805m

Rocky Creek
Mount Emlyn
Ellangowan
Ryford
Kings Creek
Spring Creek Upper
Mt Mistake 1092m
Mt Castle 1137m
Kangaroo Mtn 770m

Leyburn
Clifton
Elphinstone
Spring Creek
Tarome
Aratula

Talgai
Allora
Kital
Berat
Spring Creek Upper
RANGE
Dalrymple Creek
Mount Edwards
MOOGERAH PEAKS NP

Pratten
Thanes Creek
Bony Mountain
Cunningham
Mt Marshall
Willowvale
Clintonvale
Freestone
Upper Freestone
Mt Cordeaux 1135m
Cunninghams Gap Lookout
Mt Mitchell 1167m
Clumber
Lake Moogerah
Spicers Peak 1219m
Mt Huntley 1266m
Mt Asplenium 1280m

Karara
Greymare
Truck 'n' Travel Roadhouse
Yangan
Warwick

TO GOONDIWINDI
CUNNINGHAM HWY
Leslie Dam

DARLING DOWNS

GREAT DIVIDING RANGE

WARREGO HWY

NEW ENGLAND HWY

GORE HWY

CUNNINGHAM HWY

TO STANTHORPE

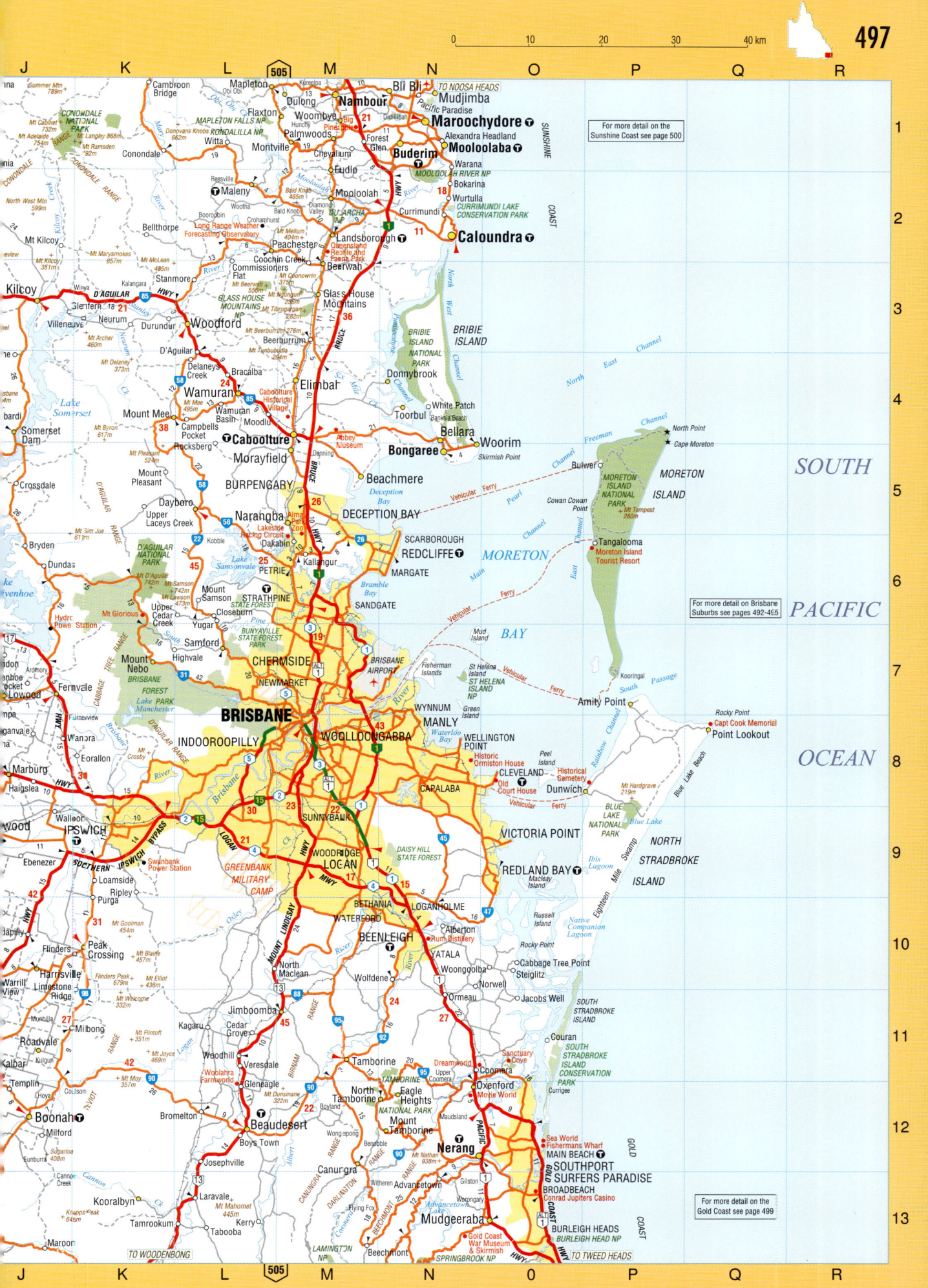

0 2 4 6 8 km

A | **B** | 497 | **C** | **D** | **E** | 505 | **F** | **G** | **H** | **I**

TO BRISBANE

Coomera

Oxenford

Helensvale

Coombabah

Paradise Point

HOPE ISLAND

Coomera Island

SOUTH STRADBROKE ISLAND CONSERVATION PARK

SOUTH

SOUTH STRADBROKE ISLAND

Runaway Bay

SOUTHPORT RD

BROADWATER AV

OXENFORD RD

TAMBOURINE – OXENFORD RD

Saltwater Creek

Coomera River

Coombabah Lake

BAYVIEW ST

OXLEY AV

The Broadwater

PACIFIC

Gaven

GAVEN WAY

PACIFIC WAY

Coombabah Ck

Arundel

Parkwood

Molendinar

Nerang

GOLD COAST

12

Labrador

SMITH

OLSEN AV

CURRUMBURRA RD

ASHMORE RD

NERANG RD

SOUTHPORT RD

Porpoise Point
Nerang Head

THE SPIT

PACIFIC

Main Beach

Narrow Neck

5

Southport

Bundall

Benowa

ROSS ST

BROADBEACH RD

NERANG RD

NIELSENS RD

Nerang River

BEAUDESERT RD

NERANG RD

GILSTON RD

Nerang Creek

GOLD COAST HWY

Carrara

Merrimac

Worongary

Robina

Mudgeeraba

GILSTON (WORONGARY) RD

MUDGEERABA RD

Worongary Ck

Advancetown Lake

SPRINGBROOK RD

Mudgeeraba Creek

Wallaby Ck

SURFERS PARADISE

Surfers Paradise

Broadbeach

3

Mermaid Waters

Mermaid Beach

6.5

Miami

BURLEIGH RD

SOUTHPORT ST

SUNSHINE BLVD

ROBINA PKWY

COTTESLOE DR

SPRINGBROOK RD

GOLD COAST –

BERMUDA ST

Burleigh Waters

REEDY CREEK

Reedy Ck

PACIFIC

99

5

5

GOLD COAST

PACIFIC HWY

Burleigh Heads

Burleigh Head
BURLEIGH HEAD NP

4.5

Palm Beach

Currumbin Point

Currumbin

Tugun

Bilinga

Elanora

4

Tallebudgera

Currumbin Waters

TALLEBUDGERA CREEK

CONNECTION RD

GUINEAS CREEK RD

Tallebudgera Creek

Tallebudgera Dam

5

3

5

GOLD COAST HWY

Coolangatta

Coolangatta Airport

NORTH HEADS

TWEED

North Head

Tweed Heads

SPRINGBROOK NATIONAL PARK

Bonogin Ck

Bilambil Ck

NICOLL SCRUB NP

NEW SOUTH WALES

QUEENSLAND

98

CURRUMBIN CREEK RD

Cobaki Broadwater

Piggabeen

Cobaki

TOMEWIN RD

BILAMBIL RD

Terranora Broadwater

Banora Point

TWEED HEADS BYPASS

TO MURWILLUMBAH

PACIFIC OCEAN

Thick roads represent recommended approach and bypass routes.

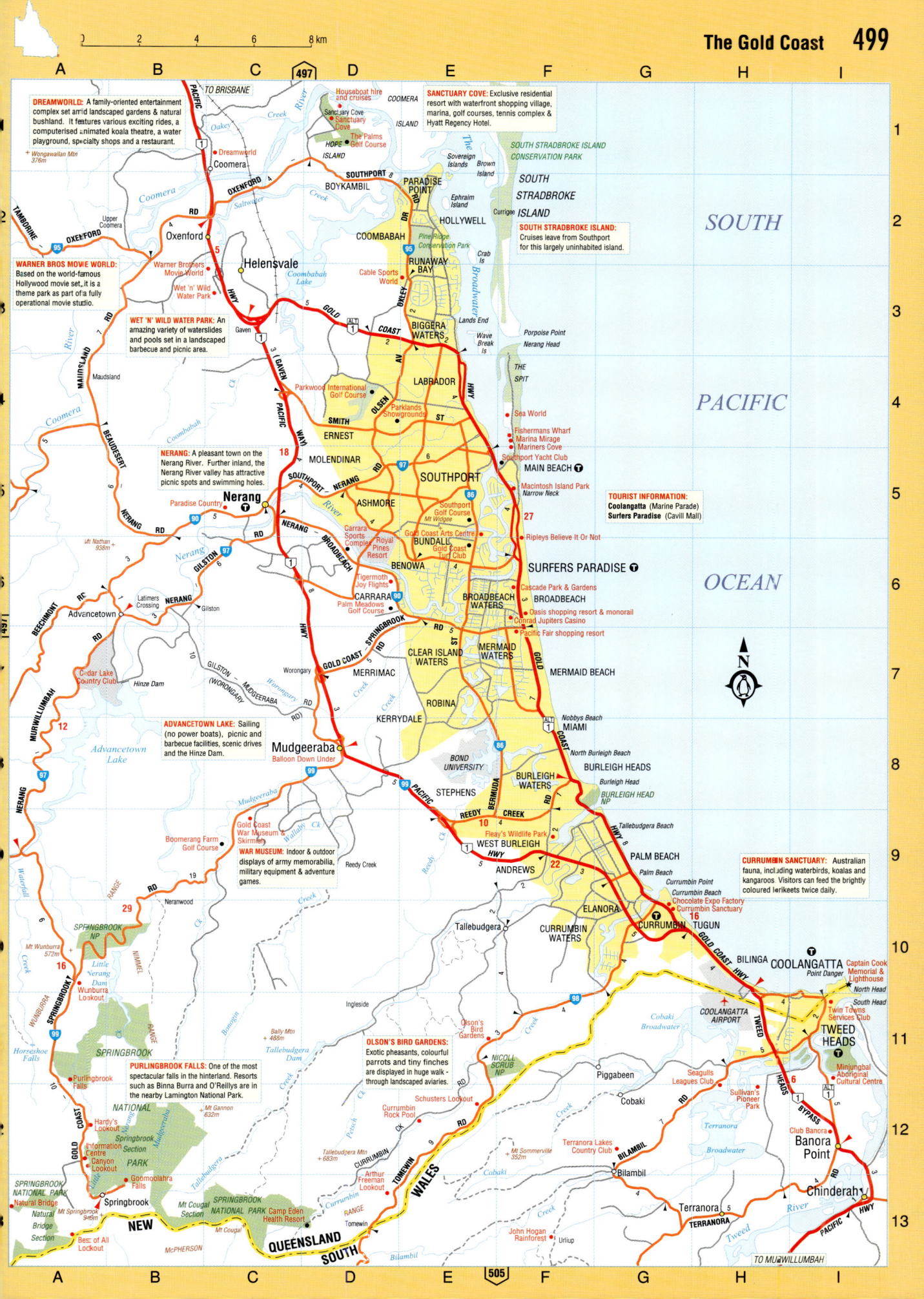

DREAMWORLD: A family-oriented entertainment complex set amid landscaped gardens & natural bushland. It features various exciting rides, a computerised animated koala theatre, a water playground, specialty shops and a restaurant.

WARNER BROS MOVIE WORLD: Based on the world-famous Hollywood movie set, it is a theme park as part of a fully operational movie studio.

WET 'N' WILD WATER PARK: An amazing variety of waterslides and pools set in a landscaped barbecue and picnic area.

NERANG: A pleasant town on the Nerang River. Further inland, the Nerang River valley has attractive picnic spots and swimming holes.

SANCTUARY COVE: Exclusive residential resort with waterfront shopping village, marina, golf courses, tennis complex & Hyatt Regency Hotel.

SOUTH STRADBROKE ISLAND: Cruises leave from Southport for this largely uninhabited island.

TOURIST INFORMATION:
Coolangatta (Marine Parade)
Surfers Paradise (Cavill Mall)

ADVANCETOWN LAKE: Sailing (no power boats), picnic and barbecue facilities, scenic drives and the Hinze Dam.

WAR MUSEUM: Indoor & outdoor displays of army memorabilia, military equipment & adventure games.

CURRUMBIN SANCTUARY: Australian fauna, including waterbirds, koalas and kangaroos. Visitors can feed the brightly coloured lorikeets twice daily.

PURLINGBROOK FALLS: One of the most spectacular falls in the hinterland. Resorts such as Binna Burra and O'Reillys are in the nearby Lamington National Park.

OLSON'S BIRD GARDENS: Exotic pheasants, colourful parrots and tiny finches are displayed in huge walk-through landscaped aviaries.

0   2   4   6   8   10 km

NOOSA: A highly developed tourist infrastructure of restaurants, boutiques, apartment-style accommodation & resorts have not impacted on the area's great natural beauty. Drive up Viewland Drive to Laguna Lookout for a spectacular view of the area.

NOOSA NATIONAL PARK: This coastal park contains a network of walking tracks that wind through rainforest, giving spectacular views of the ocean and several unusual rock formations.

TOURIST INFORMATION:
Caloundra (Caloundra Rd)
Maroochydore (Cnr Aerodrome Rd & Sixth Ave)
Nambour (Big Pineapple, Bruce Hwy, Woombye)
Noosa Heads (Hastings St)

HINTERLAND: The inland towns including Mapleton, Flaxton, Montville, Maleny and Palmwoods are renowned for their galleries, antique shops, craft shops, inns, guesthouses and tea shops. The surrounding area is particularly scenic and ideal for bushwalking and picnicking. Note that the road linking Palmwoods and Montville is steep and winding.

THE BIG PINEAPPLE: This 16 m high fibreglass replica of a pineapple is one of the best-known landmarks on the Sunshine Coast and is situated on a 112-hectare subtropical plantation.

MARY CAIRNCROSS PARK: Considered the best vantage point in the Blackall Range for spectacular views that extend back to the coast. The park also features walking tracks through the rainforest.

GLASS HOUSE MOUNTAINS: A group of 13 volcanic peaks that dominate the landscape 10 km south of Landsborough. Formed by giant cores of long-extinct volcanoes they were first sighted by Captain Cook in 1770, four of them - Mounts Coonoowrin, Beerwah, Tibrogargan and Ngungun - are national parks.

TO BRISBANE

0   0.5   1   1.5   2 km

Rowes Bay

Belgian Gardens

North Ward

CLEVELAND BAY

TOWNSVILLE

Castle Hill
Castle Hill Lookout 284m
22

Garbutt

West End

TOWNSVILLE INTERNATIONAL AIRPORT

Domestic Terminal

International Terminal

South Townsville

Currajong

Hyde Park

Hermit Park

Railway Estate

Ross Island

Gulliver

Pimlico

Mysterton

Rosslea

Townsville Golf Course

Oonoonba

Aitkenvale

Mundingburra

Animal Health Station

Idalia

Ross River Bridge

Murray Sporting Complex

Cluden

Wulguru

Cluden Park Racecourse

Mains Road Depot

LAVARACK BARRACKS

N

Accommodation ■
Aquarius on the Beach 1 F2
Hi Roller Motel 2 D9
Reef Lodge 3 G3
Seagulls Holiday Inn 4 D2
South Bank Motor Inn 5 G4
Townsville Plaza Hotel 6 F4
Townsville Travelodge 7 G4
YHA 8 G3

General Information ■
Ansett Australia 9 G4
Hospital 10 F3
Motoring Organisation (RACQ) 11 F5
Police Station 12 F4
Post Office 13 G4
Qantas Travel Centre 14 G4

Accommodation Only a sample range is listed; inclusion is not necessarily a recommendation.

Tourist Information 15 G4
Town Hall 16 F4
Townsville Railway Station 17 F4
Townsville Transit Centre 18 G4
Vehicular Ferry 19 H3

Places of Interest ■
Art Gallery 20 G4
Botanic Gardens 21 C8
Castle Hill Lookout 22 E4
Civic Theatre 23 F6
Flinders Mall 24 G4
Great Barrier Reef
  Wonderland 25 G4
Jimmy's Lookout 26 B1
Old Fort & Museum 27 E1
St James Cathedral 28 G3
Sheraton Breakwater Casino 29 H3
Townsville Breakwater
  Entertainment Centre 30 H3

0   0,5   1   1,5   2 km

0 5 10 15 20 km

509

A B C D E F G H I

DAINTREE NATIONAL PARK: A stunning combination of rainforest, reef and beach. The park encompasses the largest and one of the oldest tracts of tropical rainforest in Australia.

THE GREAT BARRIER REEF: The world's largest coral reef system is a living phenomenon that has World Heritage status. Despite its name, The Great Barrier Reef is not one reef but a complex of some 2500 reefs and 1000 islands, including 71 coral cays, that stretch from near the coast of western Papua to Breaksea Spit east of Gladstone. While most of the islands are uninhabited, a number have been developed as tourist resorts and they attract thousands of visitors each year.

GREAT BARRIER REEF

CORAL SEA

MOSSMAN RIVER GORGE: A short walk under a dense green canopy of rainforest leads to the boulder-strewn Mossman River which rushes in a series of cascades through the gorge an ideal location for picnicking and swimming.

GREEN ISLAND: A coral cay surrounded by beautiful patches of reef and crested with thick tropical vegetation. Visitors from Cairns frequent the island daily to view the Reef through glass-bottomed boats and to visit the underwater observatory. Accommodation is available.

TOURIST INFORMATION:
Atherton (cnr Mabel & Vernon sts)
Cairns (cnr Ring Rd & The Esplanade)
Port Douglas (23 Macrossan St)

FITZROY ISLAND: This island offers magnificent native flora and fauna and secluded sandy beaches. Accommodation ranging from villa-style to bunk-style, with communal amenities is available.

CURTAIN FIG TREE: This extraordinary tree is one of the most-frequently visited spots on the Tablelands. Located within a state forest park, the Curtain Fig Tree has resulted from a strangling Fig taking over its host tree, climbing higher and higher and throwing down showers of roots to support its massive structure. Rainforest birds and animals frequent the park.

WOOROONOORAN NATIONAL PARK: Seventy-nine thousand five hundred hectares of dense rainforest make this park a haven for a variety of reptiles and birds. Mt Bartle Frere and Mt Bellenden - the two highest mountains in the State - are within the park boundaries.

509

A B C D 506 E F G 507 H I

1 Blackall ⊤
Allandale
Birkhead
DAWSON Castlevale DEVELOPMENTAL RD
208
Spring Creek
Mt Catherine 627m
Rolleston
55 DAWSON
Mt Hope 352m
Bauhinia
74 302 19 FITZROY DEV RD
RANGE

LANDSBOROUGH (MATILDA)
101 Barcoo River
42 Barcoo River
Sumnersvale
RANGE
BUCKLAND TABLELAND
Consuelo
2 217 ⊤ Tambo
Mt Playfair
Mt Hutton 699m
Mt Faraday 790m
CARNARVON NP
Mt Hornet 920m
Mt Acland 975m
69 Camel River
Nuga Nuga NP
Mt Nicholson 769m
Fairfield
Mt Boordomen 330m

WARREGO RANGE River
Milray Woolga
75 HWY
Caldervale
River
GREAT
CARNARVON NATIONAL PARK
Carnarvon Gorge
41 Lake Nuga Nuga
EXPEDITION NATIONAL PARK
Mt Round 460m
Broadmere

3 Milray Woolga
71
116
Mt King 807m
MURPHY TABLELAND
DIVIDING
103
110 CARNARVON
Mt Weldon 660m
EXPEDITION NATIONAL PARK
Mt Roe
LYND RANGE

4 SCRUBBY CREEK RECREATION RESERVE
Langlo Downs
Langlo Downs
87
Mt Ogilby 700m
101
Injune
Mt Hutton 914m
RANGE
Durham Downs
53
Muggleton
Mt Combarla 354m

ADAVALE
Langlo Crossing
Box Creek
CHARLEVILLE RD
CHESTERTON RANGE
Mt Boyd 614m
Mt Hotspur 696m
Gunnewin
Bymount
71 DEVELOPMENTAL RD
89

5 84 90 54
Augathella
CHESTERTON RANGE NATIONAL PARK
71
Moranui
Amby
82

6 515 3
Cooladdi Roadhouse
Charleville ⊤
Royal Flying Doctor Base & Visitors Centre
Sommariva
71 89 14
Morven
WARREGO 44
176 54 Womalilla
Mungallala 45
Mitchell ⊤
HWY
18 Roma ⊤ 41 44 Yuleba
Muckadilla 87
Wallumbilla 54
Jack

7 Coolabah
Guesting
99 73
Boatman Bore
Bonus Downs
206 Creek
55 45
HWY 33

8 HWY (MATILDA)
199 71
Wyandra
49
210
Albany Downs
Surat
194 SURAT
87 Glenr
Coalf

9 Koroit Opal Field
Coongoola
Clifton
87
Begonia
Lake Kajarabie
116 CARNARVON
Bindia
Rocky Crossing
Flinton

10 MITCHELL (MATILDA) 54
Glendilla
134 BALONNE
45 HWY
112 Boolba
49 St George
St George Irrigation Area
CARNARVON
114
Alton
182 MOR
ALTON NATIONAL PARK

Cunnamulla ⊤
49
291
Bollon
66
49
44
80

11 118
Charlotte Plains
WARREGO
71
Wallum Creek
HWY
77
55 River
Nindigully
BARWON
65 16
200 Talwood
Bu

12 Noorama Sports Centre
CULGOA FLOODPLAIN NATIONAL PARK
Tinpenburra
Culgoa River
Dirranbandi
Ngondoo
20 44
162
73
118
Thallon
Daymar
55 42 HWY
Gradule
Caloona
41

13 QUEENSLAND
Barringun
NEW SOUTH WALES
Sharoon
Jobs Gate
38
Goodooga
47
Hebel
New Angledool
19 20 31
Lake Bokhara
Angledool Lake
Mungindi
49
Neeworra
30
Weemelah
18 42
125 B C 122 H

Grid columns: A B C 515 509 D E F 504 G H I

Grid rows: 1 2 3 4 5 6 7 8 9 10 11 12 13

Towns, features and labels

KENNEDY DEVELOPMENTAL

260 167

Big Ben 899m
Bobs Mtn 755m
Craigie
Kings Knob 925m
Mt Dick 899m
Mt Courtney 820m
Cargoon
Mt Emu 975m
Allensleigh
Spring Creek
Mt Louisa 671m
Starbright
Dotswood
Marlow
Southwick
Somerset
Fern Spring
Burdekin Downs
Woodstock
Mt Flagstone 590m
Mt Sugarloaf 539m
BOWLING GREEN BAY NP Mt Ellie 1234m
Giru
Brandon
Alva
Ayr
Home Hill
Inkerman
Clare
Gumlu
CAPE UPSTART NATIONAL PARK
Abbot Bay
Upstart Bay
Guthalungra
Meri

78 HWY 135 202
Burdekin River Irrigation Area
Mingela
Sellheim
Macrossan
Charters Towers
Balfes Creek
Tuckers Mtn 562m
Ravenswood
Millaroo
Edinburgh Castle 533m
Mt Louisa 488m
1 BRUCE

GREAT BASALT WALL NATIONAL PARK
Toomba Lake
Daintrees Lookout 823m
Wall
LOLWORTH
Mt Stewart 1000m
Homestead
243
Lake Powlathanga
Brittania
Mt Sunrise 500m
Dalbeg
Mt Cooper 500m
Mt Glenroy 573m
LEICHHARDT
Burdekin Falls Dam
Mt Constance 573m
Mt Wickham 554m
Scottville
Collinsville
BOWEN PETER DEL
Binbee

PORCUPINE NATIONAL PARK
WHITE MOUNTAINS NATIONAL PARK
GREAT DIVIDING RANGE
Pentland
Helensleigh
Campaspe
Mt Redan 437m
Braceborough
Mt Janet 518m
Mt Bellevue 274m
204
Mt Stone 311m
Mt Tindale 426m
RANGE

Mt Agnes 479m
Hughenden
Mt Walker 479m
Prairie
FLINDERS 44
Torrens Creek
78 50
Lake Moocha
Corea Plains
Native
Dog
Crooked Ck
Cape
Mt Helena 305m
Mt Loudon 418m
Mt Patterson 408m
DEVELOPMENTAL
Newlands Coal Mine
Glender

Arrara
Barenya
RANGE
Webb Lake
Bullock
MOORRINYA NATIONAL PARK
232
Nunkumbil
Lake Buchanan
DARKIES RANGE
Mt Bingeringo 518m
BLACKWOOD NATIONAL PARK
Mt Douglas
BOWEN 48 COLLINSVILLE
Mt Manamon 360m
Police
Suttor
Mt Coolon
Eaglefield
72
358 513

WARNINGS: In northern Australia, long distances separate some towns. Travellers should familiarise themselves with prevailing conditions before departure, and take care to ensure their vehicle is roadworthy and that they carry adequate supplies of petrol, water and food.
Rainfall during the wet season (Oct-March) can make roads impassable. Full information on road conditions should be obtained from local authorities before departure.
If visitors intend diverting off public roads within Aboriginal Land areas, a permit is required from the relevant Aboriginal authority.

Tangorin
Ronlow Park
Carmichael
Corinda
Bygana
Mt Donnybrook 502m
MAZEPPA NP
Mt Wilkin 315m
Moranbah
366
128
DOWNS
PEAK

Inverness
Levuka
FOREST DEN NATIONAL PARK
Lake Huffer
Lake Galilee
Glenavon
Lake Barcoorah
Lake Mueller
Lake Dunn
Police Mtn 546m
Blair Athol
Mt McLaren 466m
Mt Pollux 678m
Mt Donald 770m
GREGORY
Muttaburra
Rankin
Aramac
Ambo
22
NARRIEN RANGE NATIONAL PARK
Campoven Mtn 759m
Clermont
Capella
106 55
35

Maranthona
119 116
Darr
Longreach
Ilfracombe
Dartmouth
Brixton
66 CAPRICORN
Barcaldine
Lochnagar
Busthinia
Jericho
53
Alpha
HWY 72 66
Pine Hill
Bogantungan
Mt Chantrey 676m
Withersfield
Willows
Rubyvale
Sapphire Mines
Sapphire
Anakie
Emera
Tomahawk Creek Gemfields
Mt Leura 579m
Mt Tabletop 823m
Fairbairn Dam
27 81 101
TROPIC OF CAPRICORN

Mt Mica 418m

Elton
Coleraine
Sandy
184
GREAT DIVIDING RANGE
CAPRICORN
Mt Craven 515m
79 44 45

Patrick
LANDSBOROUGH (MATILDA)
107
70
Yalleroi
JERICHO RD
Beta
304
44
Mt Portview 748m
Willows Gemfields
Lockington
SNAKE RANGE NP
Mt Hall 462m
Gemstones Area
Lake Maraboon
Fernlee
Gino
DRUMMOND RANGE
MINERVA HILLS NP
Springsure
Mt Alexander 597m

BLACKALL 79
71
Isisford
Blackall
Allandale
Birkhead
DAWSON
Castlevale
DEVELOPMENTAL
CARNARVON NP
Spring Creek

Barcoo
515 ISISFORD RD 44

0   25   50   75   100 km

J K L M N O P Q R

CORAL

SEA

1

SOUTH

PACIFIC

2

OCEAN

N

3

THE WHITSUNDAYS

Gloucester Island
Dingo
Beach
Earlando
Hayman Island
Hook Island
en
Cannonvale Airlie Beach
Whitsunday Island
WHITSUNDAY ISLANDS NP
roserpine
Shute
Harbour
CONWAY
NP
Hamilton Island
Lindeman
Island
Shaw Island
4
GREAT

190
Midge Point
Bloomsbury
SMITH ISLANDS
NATIONAL PARK
Elaroc
Mt Crompton
792m
Yalboroo
Brampton Island
SOUTH CUMBERLAND ISLANDS
NATIONAL PARK
Scawfell Island
Hibiscus Coast
BARRIER
Seaforth
Ball Bay
Cape Hillsborough
Keswick
Island
St Bees
Island
Calen
Mount
Ossa
Kuttabul
Shoal Point
Bucasia
EUNGELLA
NATIONAL
PARK
Mount
Charlton
Fanleigh
Slade Point
Eungella
Walkerston
Mackay
5
Finch
Hatton
Miraini
Marian
Eton
Bakers Creek
Half Tide
Grasstree
Sarina Beach
Armstrong Beach
HOMEVALE
NATIONAL
PARK
Sarina
Homevale
Hall Creek
6
Koumala
CAPE PALMERSTON
NATIONAL PARK
Nebo
Mt White
594m
Ilbilbie
Middle Island
South Island
REEF
50
Blue Mtn
625m
Mt Fort Cooper
528m
Mt Scott
852m
57
274
Coppabella
Mt Orange
530m
Carmila
Flaggy Rock
WEST HILL NP
7
MtCoxendean
490m
Saltbush Park
334
Clairview
Quail Island
Stanage
CAPRICORN
Dysart
FITZROY River
St Lawrence
Broad
Sound
Mt Edward
171m
Mt Price
164m
Townshend Is
8
Mt Joss
421m
Ogmore
Mt Phillip
395m
Mt Wellington
528m
Mt Westall
560m
Middlemount
Mt Bora
350m
Glenprairie
Mt Mulgrave
655m
Mt Atherton
438m
9
Manly
Marlborough
Mt Magog
575m
MILITARY
TRAINING
AREA
Junee
Clifton
Kunwarara
BRUCE
HWY
eri
Mt Gardiner
450m
Royles
Apis Creek
Merimal
Glen
Geddes
BYFIELD
NATIONAL
PARK
Oaky Creek
Mine
Arizona
Burkan
Farnborough
Yeppoon
KEPPEL ISLANDS
NATIONAL PARK
10
Fairhill
Telson
Yaamba
Milman
The Caves
Mulambin
Great Keppel Island
Ensham
Mine
South Yaamba
Kinka
Emu Park
Ridgelands
Parkhurst
TROPIC
OF
Round Mtn
746m
ROCKHAMPTON
Tungamull
Keppel Sands
Joskeleigh
CAPRICORN
Gracemere
Dalma
Kabra
11
Bluff
Midgee
Port
Alma
Heron Island
Comet
CAPRICORN
Wycarbah
Stanwell
Boulercombe
Marmor
CURTIS
ISLAND NP
Blackwater
Blackwater
Mine
Dingo
270
Duaringa
Westwood
Gogango
17
Mt Battery
486m
Mount
Morgan
Raglan
Mt Barker
161m
CAPRICORN CAYS
NATIONAL PARK
South Blackwater
Mine
Wallaroo
Coomooboolaroo
Dulula
Mt Hope
458m
107
Ambrose
Mt Larcom
Gladstone
12
Mt Dawson
317m
Wowan
145
Cedric Mtn
699m
Yarwun
Boyne Island
Tannum Sands
Benaraby
EURIMBULA NP
Lady Musgrave Island
WOORABINDA
ABORIGINAL
COMMUNITY
Vimy
Lancefield
102
Calliope
Turkey
Beach
Baralaba
Rannes
Mt Redshirt
597m
DAWSON
HWY
Barmundu
Seventeen Seventy
Agnes Water
Goovigen
Jambin
Argoon
Specimen Hill
671m
Bororen
Bustard
Bay
13
DAWSON
46
Banana
Bilqela
Thangool
Callide
Callide Coal Mine
Power Station
Callide Dam
KROOMBIT TOPS
NATIONAL PARK
Nagoorin
Ubobo
Mt Graarbi
800m
Miriam
Vale
Mt Diemedar
477m
DEEPWATER
NATIONAL PARK
Rolleston

J K L M N O P Q R

504   505

A B C D E **510** F G H I

1

WARNINGS: In northern Australia, long distances separate some towns. Travellers should familiarise themselves with prevailing conditions before departure, and take care to ensure their vehicle is roadworthy and that they carry adequate supplies of petrol, water and food.

Rainfall during the wet season (Oct-March) can make roads impassable. Full information on road conditions should be obtained from local authorities before departure.

If visitors intend diverting off public roads within Aboriginal Land areas, a permit is required from the relevant Aboriginal authority.

Beware of man-eating crocodiles in rivers and estuaries.

Edward River

New Strathgordon 227
Strathmay
Strathaven
River

Musgrave Station

Hann River Roadhouse & Camping

307

Pormpuraaw Aboriginal Community

ABORIGINAL

Coleman

Creek

New Dixie

CAPE

Wallaby Island

LAND

Mottle

Oroners Outstation

81 Killaraey

2

Alice

Mitchell

YORK

Kimba

Pinnacles

King R

44

King Junction

Palme

Kowanyama Aboriginal Community

MITCHELL-ALICE RIVERS NATIONAL PARK

Magnificent

River

PENINSULA

GULF

Rutland Plains

Alice

Koolatah

3

Creek

105

Nassau

River

Dunbar

Mitchell

BURKE

Drumduff

Strathleven

OF

48

Windermere Lagoon

Purumu Lagoon

Mosquito Lagoon

Rosser

90

4

Inkerman

River

Creek

Kingfish Lagoon

DEVELOPMENTAL

Twelve Mile Lagoon

CARPENTARIA

Staaten

86

Geddes Creek

Clark

Creek

STAATEN RIVER NATIONAL PARK

Highbury Lagoon

Longreach Lagoon

Dinner Camp Lagoon

Wa

5

Waukanaka Lagoon

Wyaaba

Dorunda

River

Back River

Byrnes

Lynd

Bulimbe

6

Point Burrowes

Delta Downs

Middle

Gilbert

DEVELOPMENTAL

Vanrook

Pelican

Ponds

Creek

Staaten

Pandanus

River

Smithburne R

Creek

BULL NAT PA

7

Fitzmaurice Point

ABORIGINAL

Snake Ck

Fitzmaurice

176

River

Red

Pelican

Torwol

LAND

Creek

Miranda Downs

Sandy

Creek

River

Barge Service Karumba to Weipa

BURKE

Walker

Fish

Hole

Fourteen Mile

Creek

Abingdon Downs

River

8

Karumba

41

30

Wills Creek

Mutton Hole

Rocky

Creek

Einasleigh

Etheridge

Middle Point

Normanton

Shady Lagoon

Carron

Strathmore

Jampot

Gilbert

Mt Campbell 366m

Vanlee

Dagworth

9

Rocky Lake

Manrika Lake

Burke & Wills Cairn

Magowra

Glenore Crossing

25

Twelve Mile Lagoon

68

Carron

GULF

River

69

Huonfels

Chadshunt

51

Gilbert River

73

DEVELOPMENTAL

Tallaroo Hotl

NEWCASTLE

Inverleigh

83

Norman

The Lakes

Clarina

60

Croydon

Inorunie

1

Kutchera

577

10

Alexandra

Macalister

195

RD HWY

134

River

The Forty Mile Waterhole

132

Belmore

Creek

Hole

Coralie

75

Alehvale

Little

River

Langdon

Georgetown

40 Delaney R

67

Forsayth

11

511

Neumayer Valley

Punchbowl Creek

Bang Bang Jump Up Rock Formation

1

Donors Hill

Bang Bang

Wondoola

Flinders

Sandy

Jumble

Racecourse Lagoon

Clara

Claraville

162

Muggera Lagoon

Yappar

Mittagong

114

River

Templeton

Esmeralda

Glenora

GREGORY

Malacura

RANGE

Goldsmiths

Robin Ho

Cobbold Gorge

Agate Creek Gemfields

12

Clancurry

DEVELOPMENTAL (MATILDA)

61

GULF

SAVANNAH

Iffley

Forrest

Norman

River

Clara

Nara

Bairds Table Mounta 914m

13

WILLS

Burke & Wills Roadhouse

DEVELOPMENTAL

95

Boomarra

Canobie

Lyrian Waterhole

Taldora

Twelve Mile Ck

Boorabin

Pelham

Victoria Vale

Norman

Perry Vale

Gorge

BURKE

RD

A B **512** C D E F **513** G H

0   25   50   75   100 km

TORRES   STRAIT

BADU ISLAND
Mulgrave Hill 209m +
+ Mt Augustus 399m
MOA ISLAND
Mount Earnest Island

Thursday Island
Horn Is
PRINCE OF WALES ISLAND
Cape York Pajinka
Wilderness Lodge

Seisia
Injinoo
Bamaga
Newcastle Bay
Endeavour Strait

Parslow Point
SHADWELL RESOURCE RESERVE

Vehicle Ferry
Jardine River
JARDINE RIVER NATIONAL PARK
Orford Bay

Vrilya Point

GULF

OF

CARPENTARIA

ABORIGINAL LAND
RICHARDSON RANGE
Puddingpan Hill 123m
Cridland Hill 112m
Helby Hill + 150m
HEATHLAND RESOURCE RESERVE
Captain Billy Landing

Jackson River
Dulhunty River
410
River
250
Messum Hill 87m
Shelburne Bay

Mapoon Aboriginal Community
Port Musgrave
Ducie River
Palm Creek
Conical Hill + 86m
Cape Grenville

Bramwell
Briscoe Hill + 147m

Bertiehaugh
GREAT
Glennie 299m +
Temple Bay

Wenlock River
Old Moreton Telegraph Station
Huxley Hill + 283m
Kennedy Hill + 518m
Weymouth Bay

Mission River
Batavia Downs
Barret Hill + 368m
IRON RANGE NP
Portland Roads
Cape Weymouth

Duyfken Point
Albatross Bay
Weipa
Barge Service Weipa to Karumba
85
PENINSULA
40
Mt Dobson 495m
Bowden 345m
Mt Tozer 545m
Lockhart River Aboriginal Community
Iron Range
Cape Direction
Direction Hill + 148m

CORAL

GREAT

Pera Head
Coconut Ck
EMBLEY RANGE
48
70
247
Iguana Mtn 244m +
Jacks Knob 411m +
Mt Carter + 671m
Night Island

Ward River
Watson River
Lagoon Creek
Merkunga
GEKIE RANGE
Piccaninny
Creek
DIVIDING
Bald Hill + 441m
Gekie Creek
Table Mtn 458m
Cape Sidmouth

SEA

Aurukun Aboriginal Community
MUNGKAN KANDJU NATIONAL PARK
Archer River
Archer River Roadhouse
MUNGKAN KANDJU NATIONAL PARK
Birthday Mtn + 438m
McILWRAITH RANGE
Whale Hill + 306m
Round Mtn + 321m

BARRIER

Archer River
Coen River
112
Double Hill + 411m
Claremont Isles

Meripah
CAPE
ABORIGINAL LAND
Mt Croll 488m +
Coen
Mt White 449m +
Silver Plains
Port Stewart

YORK
53
FLINDERS GROUP NP
Flinders Island
Pipon Island
Cape Melville + St Pauls Hill 418m
CAPE MELVILLE NP
Barrow Point

REEF

Kendall River
LAND
Holroyd River
45
Kintore + 405m
Yarraden
Mt Ryan + 518m
RANGE
63
Princess Charlotte Bay
Bathurst Bay
Bay Hill 432m
CAPE MELVILLE NP

Christmas Ck
PENINSULA
Strathburn
Lily Vale
Marina Plains
Wakooka
Howick Island

Pormpuraaw Aboriginal Community
Edward River
227
New Strathgordon
Strathmay
Strathaven
Coleman River
Musgrave Station
87
Hann Crossing
LAKEFIELD NATIONAL PARK
North Kennedy River
Normanby River
Flat Top Hill + 107m
Saddle Hill + 508m
Mt Stuckey (Numbanguline) + 479m
STARCKE NP
RD
307

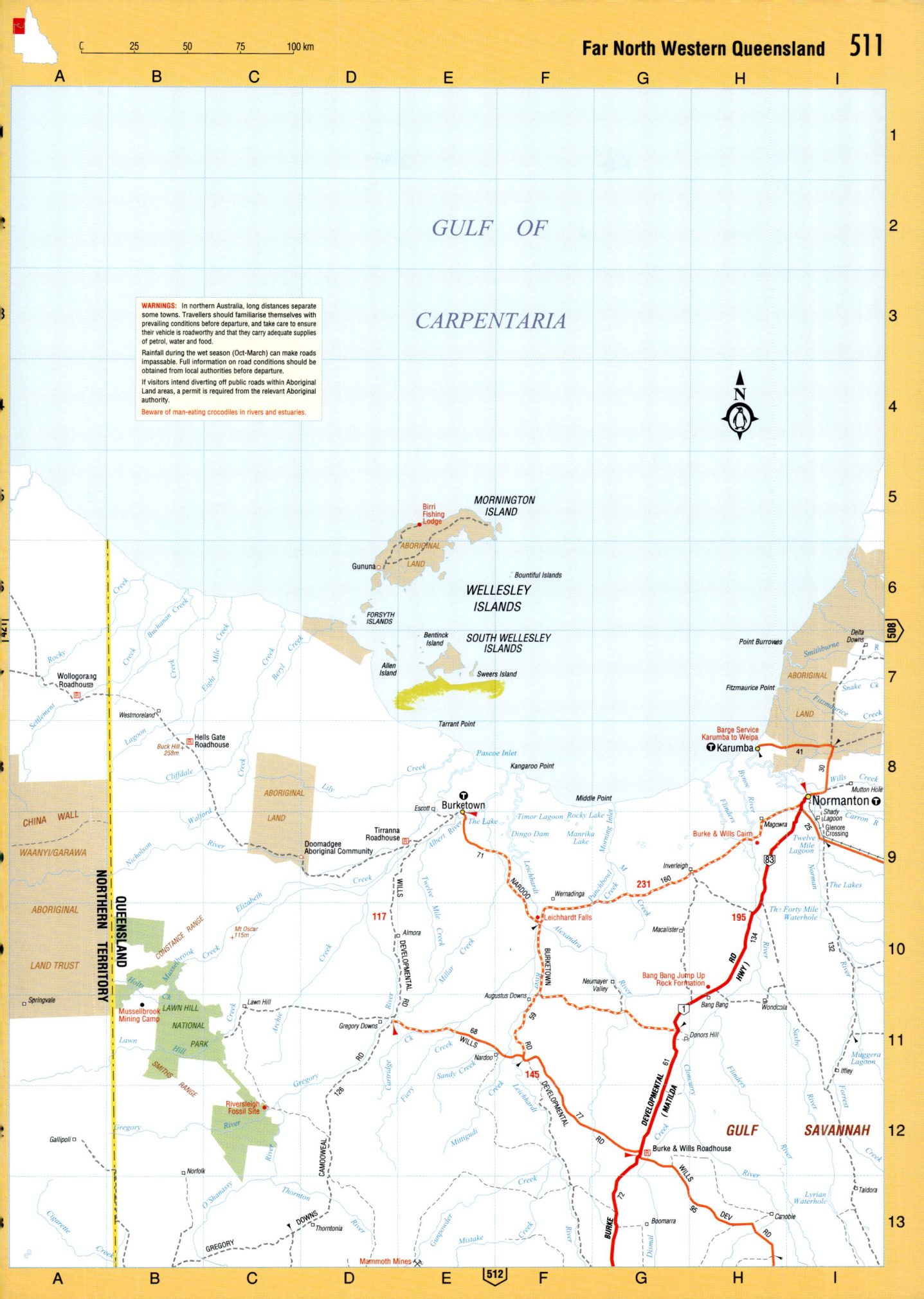

GULF OF CARPENTARIA

MORNINGTON ISLAND

Birri Fishing Lodge

Gununa

ABORIGINAL LAND

WELLESLEY ISLANDS

Bountiful Islands

FORSYTH ISLANDS

Bentinck Island

SOUTH WELLESLEY ISLANDS

Allen Island

Sweers Island

Tarrant Point

Point Burrowes

Delta Downs

ABORIGINAL LAND

Fitzmaurice Point

Smithburne R

Snake Ck

Rocky Creek

Wollogorang Roadhouse

Westmoreland

Buchanan Creek

Eight Mile Creek

Beryl Creek

Lily Creek

Pascoe Inlet

Kangaroo Point

Barge Service Karumba to Weipa

Karumba

41

Wills Creek

Mutton Hole

CHINA WALL

WAANYI/GARAWA

Hells Gate Roadhouse

Buck Hill 258m

ABORIGINAL LAND

Cliffdale Creek

Nicholson River

Walford River

Doomadgee Aboriginal Community

Escott

Burketown

The Lake

Timor Lagoon

Middle Point

Rocky Lake

30

25

Magowra

Normanton

Shady Lagoon

Glenore Crossing

Carron R

QUEENSLAND

NORTHERN TERRITORY

ABORIGINAL LAND TRUST

Springvale

Musselbrook Mining Camp

CONSTANCE RANGE

Mt Oscar +115m

Tirranna Roadhouse

Dingo Dam

Manrika Lake

Morning Inlet

Burke & Wills Cairn

Twelve Mile Lagoon

83

The Forty Mile Waterhole

117

Almora

71

Leichhardt Falls

Wernadinga

Punchbowl Creek

231

160

Inverleigh

Macalister

195

134

132

Norman River

The Lakes

NARDOO

Alexandra

Augustus Downs

Neumayer Valley

Bang Bang Jump Up Rock Formation

RD

Lawn Hill

LAWN HILL NATIONAL PARK

SMITHS RANGE

Musselbrook Creek

Holroyd Creek

Elizabeth Creek

Millar Creek

DEVELOPMENTAL RD

BURKETOWN RD

95

Donors Hill

Bang Bang

1

Wondola

Iffley

Muggera Lagoon

Gallipoli

Norfolk

Riversleigh Fossil Site

Gregory River

Lawn Hill Creek

Archie Creek

Gregory Downs

68

WILLS

Nardoo

Sandy Creek

145

Leichhardt River

DEVELOPMENTAL RD

61

DEVELOPMENTAL (MATILDA) HWY

Burke & Wills Roadhouse

Cloncurry River

Flinders River

Saxby River

GULF SAVANNAH

128

Currijinga Ck

Fiery Creek

Mittiguди Creek

77

72

95

DEV RD

Boomarra

Canobie

Taldora

Cigarette Creek

O'Shanassy River

Thornton Creek

Gunpowder Creek

Mistake Creek

BURKE

Dismal Creek

Lyrian Waterhole

Gregory River

Thorntonia

GREGORY DOWNS

Mammoth Mines

CAMOOWEAL

508

511

508

419

421

A B C D E F G H I

1

2

3

4

5

6

7

8

9

10

11

12

13

Cigarette Creek

Thorntonia

CAMOOWEAL RD

DOWNS
91

Mammoth Mines

Gunpowder

Mistake Creek

Leichhardt River

BURKE

Boomarra

Canoble

Sandy

72

Alcala

Dobbyn

Brinard

Barkly
30

13

GREGORY

BARKLY

Camooweal

Microwave Repeater Station

URANDANGI

YELVERTOFT

58

71

CAMOOWEAL CAVES NP
Camooweal Caves

WAGGABOONYAH RANGE

Calton Hills

Lake Julius

Leichhardt

83

66

188

73

OGILVIE RANGE

PILPAH RANGE

107

Wooroona

RD

Austral Downs

56

Mt Michael 243m

HWY

44

HWY

Moondarra Lake

Cordilla

Mt McKeon 311m

Gereta

Kajabbi

Granada

Clonagh

Mt Crusader 299m

Belliman

47

Spoonbill

Dalgonally McI

DEVELOPMENTAL (MATILDA RD HWY)

62

83

177

124

Zingari

Williams

Quamby

Mt Margaret

River

Eastern

DEVELOPMENTAL

35

Cloncurry

FLINDERS

78

112

Gill

Oorindi

Mount Isa

Royal Flying Doctor Service Base & Visitors Centre

66

118

Burke & Wills Memorial

Mt Frosty

Mary Kathleen (former uranium mining town)

83

56

Cloncurry

LANDSBOROUGH (MATILDA

66

Baenfields

105

McKinlay

McKinlay HWY

Bullock Waterhole

56

Lake Nash

21

HWY

SANDOVER
Georgina Downs

Georgina

BARKLY

TABLELAND

Conkerberry Dam

Bullecourt

Sheila Outstation

83

73

Rifle Creek Reservoir

91

Black Mtn 568m

Malbon

Devoncourt

Kuridala

69

GILL

McKinlay RANGE

Georgina

Headingly

Georgina River

RD

98

DIAMANTINA

78

Duchess

18

56

SELWYN RANGE

Mt Wills or Imbi 335m

Beaudesert

Woodroffe

Mountain Waterhole

Urandangi

URANDANGI

Ardmore

Binyeah Outstation

295

Dajarra

The Monument

Mt Birnie 450m

66

STANDISH RANGES

Cannington

Chatsworth

Toolebuc

FINUCANE RANGE

Denbigh Downs

River

Carandotta

MANGANESE RIDGE

53

58

36

Burke and Wills Tree

Digby Peaks 306m

Manners Creek

93

DEVELOPMENTAL

144

131

Mt Unbunmaroo + (Black Mtn) 392m

Middl

Tobermorey Roadhouse

HWY

DONOHUE

116

HWY

Alderley

Burke

115

DEVELOPM

PLENTY

Georgina

83

Police Barracks (ruins)

Elrose

Min Min Hotel (ruins)

360

Cawnpore Lookout

Chill

MACARTNEY

242

Glenormiston

61

Badalia

65

Boulia

KENNEDY

77

Slashers Creek

Pollygammon

RANGES

Mt Macartn 14

TOKO RANGE

Mt Idamea 184m

Herbert Downs

Paravituari Waterhole

Georgina

Warra

Mt Woods + 265m

Mt Wooldridge 288m

TOOMBA RANGE

Cravens Peak

Carlo

Mt Whelan 184m

OF

Ck

Marion Downs

Loma Downs

CAPRICORN

Springvale

DIAMANTINA

Gum

Gun

TROPIC

191

Windmill

RD

Coorabulka

Springvale

Creek

River

NATIONAL

SIMPSON

Ethabuka

Lake Wongitta

Sylvester

Pulchera Lake

Breadalbane

CHANNEL

COUNTRY

ASTREBLA DOWNS NATIONAL PARK

PARK

DIAMANTINA

SIMPSON

DESERT

Mumbleberry Lake

DESERT

NATIONAL

PARK

DIAMANTINA DEVELOPMENTAL

Lake Phillipi

Kamaran Downs

Bedourie

23

Daverport Downs

Cluny

Diamantina

NORTHERN TERRITORY

QUEENSLAND

514

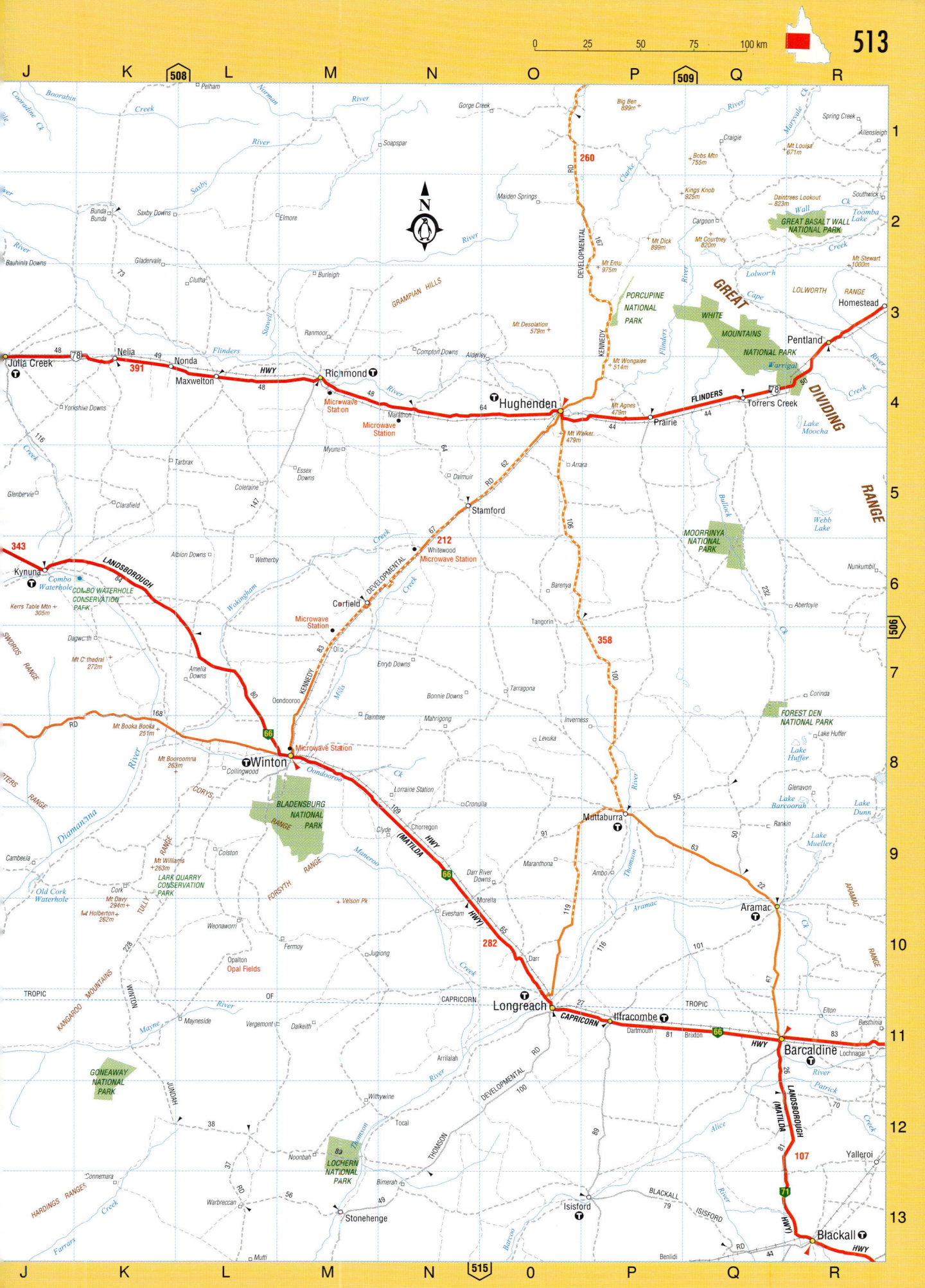

A B C D E F G H I

1

2

3

4

5

6

7

8

9

10

11

12

13

NORTHERN TERRITORY

QUEENSLAND

SIMPSON DESERT NATIONAL PARK

ASTREBLA DOWNS NATIONAL PARK

Kamaran Downs
Lake Phillipi
Mumbleberry Lake
Lake Torquinie
Muncoonie Lake West

Bedourie
Cluny
23
Lake Machattie
Glengyle
56
Bilpa Morea Claypan
Diamantina River
215
Monkira
DIAMANTINA
400

191
RD
32
Cacoory (ruins)
Currawilla
53
Mooraberee
92

DEVELOPMENTAL
80
Mt Collins 260m+
51

SIMPSON DESERT

EYRE

Durrie
Betoota
114
DEVELOPMENTAL
RD
51
50
Lake Cuddapan

Mt Lewis 100m
Birdsville
BIRDSVILLE
Shallow Lake
Moonda Lake
Frew Hill 123m
Haddon Corner

Mirranponga Pongunna Lake

Poeppel Corner
QUEENSLAND
SOUTH AUSTRALIA
Lake Cooninnie
Cadelga (ruins)

SIMPSON DESERT CONSERVATION PARK
Larrys Hill 63m
Lake Thomas
Pillan Hill 60m

Diamantina River
Pandie Pandie
Lake Short
Lake Etamunbanie
Lake Moorayepe
STRZELECKI
Stony Point 195m+
Lake Yamma Yamma

SIMPSON DESERT

The West Lake

REGIONAL RESERVE

WARNING: Visitors planning to enter Desert Parks are required to contact the National Parks and Wildlife Service. A Desert Pass is necessary.

New Alton Downs
Lake Uloowaranie
DESERT
Pulcara Hill 170m+
Cordillo Downs

Pcolowanna Lake
Beale Hill 53m
Perra Perra Poolanna Lake
Ephemeral Lakes

INSIDE
Goyder Lagoon
Dickinna Hill 87m+
Arrabury
Cooks Outstation
Lake Pure

SIMPSON DESERT
Apawyilarranie Lake
Koomarinna Lake
BIRDSVILLE (Not
Recommended)
TRACK
Coongie Lakes
Leap Year Bore
Lake Pu

REGIONAL
Umaroona Lake
Creek
Clifton Hills
312
BIRDSVILLE
OUTSIDE
INNAMINCKA
Coongie
Mulga Bore
SOUTH AUSTRALIA
QUEENSLAND

RESERVE
Willawilannina Lake
STURT
STONY
DESERT
Cooper
Creek
REGIONAL
Patchawara Bore
Nappa Merrie

Pantoowarinna Lake
Pathraootara Lake
Lake Koodnanie
516
RESERVE
Gidgealpa
Aboriginal Rock Carvings
Burke and Wills Dig Tree

Peeramudlayeppa Lake
Pompapillinna Lake
Cowarie
Lake Howitt
Mirra Mitta Bore
44
Innamincka

Warburton
Koolkootinnie Lake
Kalamurina
Lake Miamiana
Kalamurra Lake
BIRDSVILLE
Cooper
Creek
47

LAKE EYRE NATIONAL PARK
Lake Ngapakaldi
Lake Kittakittaooloo
Mungerannie
Mungerannie Roadhouse
Winthekarrinna Waterhole
Moomba Gasfield
60
Tickalara Oil Field

Lake Eyre North
Lake Mulapula
Lake Puntawolona
Mulka
Cooper
Lake Walpayapeninna
Lake Warrakalanna
STRZELECKI
50
Big Lake Moomba
Munro Oil Field

Lake Killamperpunna
Flood by-pass ferry
Lake Hope
TRACK
Lake Murteree
120

ELLIOT PRICE CONSERVATION PARK
Lake Palankarinna
Eladunna
Flood by-pass track
Lake Kopperekoppinna
REGIONAL
Merty Merty
Bollards Lagoon
Corner Store
Cameron Corner

Lake Frances
Lake Ellen
Lake Florence
Dulkaninna
Lake Gregory
RESERVE
STRZELECKI
Strzelecki Crossing
STURT
NATIONAL
Explorers Tree
Lake Frome

Mulloorina
Lake Blanche
Waka

307 124

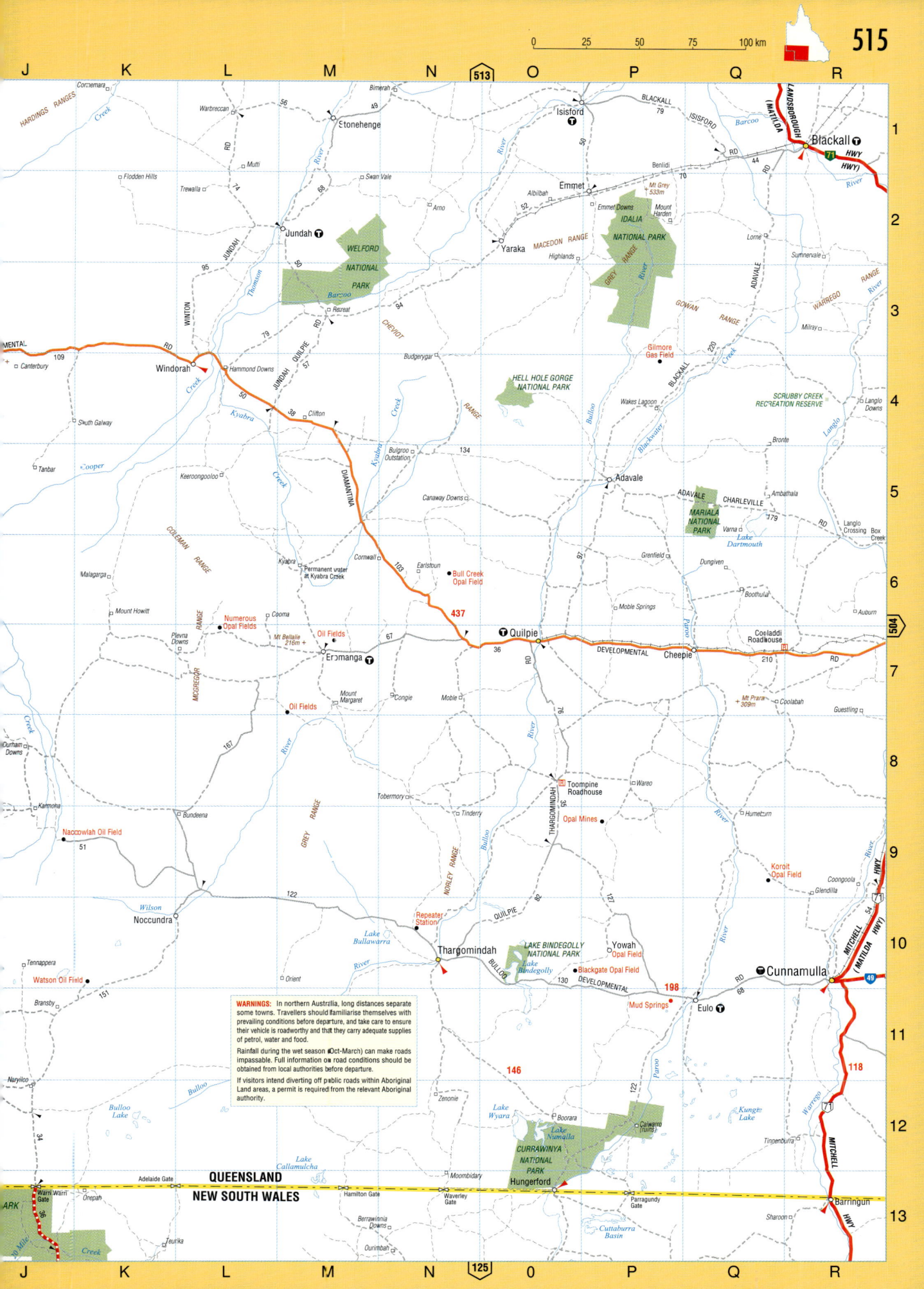

J K L M N O P Q R

QUEENSLAND
NEW SOUTH WALES

J K L M N O P Q R

Tasmania

Heritage Island

TASMANIA

Tasmania has certainly won many more hearts than it can claim square kilometres. It has only 68 000 of the latter, but it crams into them its rugged west, a central plateau broken by steep mountains and narrow river valleys, and an eastern coastal region offering a soft pastoral beauty.

Tasmania's diverse charms have made it a popular tourist attraction for Australians from 'the mainland' for many years.

This dramatically beautiful island, however, has a far from beautiful early history. The first European to sight the island was Abel Tasman in 1642; it was later claimed by Captain Cook for the English and the British settlement dates from 1803. For the next fifty years it was maintained primarily as a penal colony, although prosperous settlements developed around Hobart and New Norfolk. The convicts did the hard labour and lived in brutal conditions at Port Arthur. The Tasmanian Aborigines, who resisted the takeover of their land, were treated even more harshly than the convicts.

Political separation from New South Wales was granted in 1825 and transportation of convicts ceased in 1853. Today the ruins of Port Arthur have taken on a mellow charm and Tasmania is an infinitely more hospitable place.

Tasmania was first called Van Diemen's Land; these days it is known as the 'heritage island', 'treasure island' or the 'apple isle'. Its economy is basically agricultural with the major growth area being in quality specialised food products. The Tasmanian hydro-electric system has a greater output than that of the Snowy Mountains Scheme; Tasmania's high rainfall helps this. The climate offers mild summers and cool winters, with much of the mountain regions receiving heavy winter snowfall. Mid-December to late January is very popular with tourists; late spring or autumn are also pleasant. Even the winter months offer good touring.

When planning a trip to Tasmania note the heavy booking for the *Spirit of Tasmania* ferry service between Melbourne and Devonport from December to March. Either book well in advance or consider a fly/drive holiday, which can be a relaxing and economic alternative. Tasmania's roads are well suited to relaxed meandering, many of them being winding and narrow. In a fortnight, however, you can happily complete what is virtually a round tour of the island.

Hobart, the capital of Tasmania, is built on either side of the Derwent River, and is dominated by Mount Wellington. The Wrest Point Hotel-Casino, Australia's first casino, with its lavish entertainment and International Convention Centre, is now competing for first place as the city's best-known landmark, towering over Hobart's many colonial buildings. Within easy reach are Port Arthur, Richmond with its beautiful bridge (the oldest in Australia) and the settlements of Bothwell and New Norfolk.

The Derwent Valley with its hop fields and apple orchards, lovely in blossom-time and in autumn, lies to the west. Further west is Lake Pedder;

NOT TO BE MISSED

in Tasmania

	Map Ref.
Bicheno – old sealing and whaling town, now home port for crayfishing boats	559 Q2
Cataract Gorge – Launceston's own piece of wilderness	557 N10
Clarendon House – one of the finest Georgian homes in the country	557 P13
Cradle Mountain-Lake St Clair National Park – for excellent bushwalking in this famous mountain wilderness	558 F10
Don River Railway – a scenic train trip along the banks of the river	556 D5
Freycinet Peninsula – features magnificent rocky coastline	559 Q4
Gordon River – enjoy its beauty from a cruise boat	558 E5
Port Arthur – said to be Australia's most significant heritage site	555 N10
Richmond – delightful, well-preserved Georgian village	559 M7
Stanley – quiet historic township nestled under The Nut	560 D3
Strahan Wharf Centre – for fascinating history in a unique hands-on museum	558 D3

Early morning view of Ben Lomond in north-east Tasmania

Dove Lake, Cradle Mountain-Lake St Clair National Park

the flooding of this area was a source of great controversy when it was made part of the hydro-electric scheme. The surrounding country makes up the Southwest National Park, Tasmania's largest and one which has been given World Heritage status. The Lyell Highway leads to Cradle Mountain-Lake St Clair National Park. Queenstown, surrounded by stark ochre-coloured mountains, is the largest settlement in this

CALENDAR OF EVENTS

Note: The information given here was accurate at the time of printing. However, as the timing of events held annually is subject to change and some events may extend into the following month, it is best to check with the local tourism authority or event organisers to confirm the details. The calendar is not exhaustive. Most towns and regions hold sporting competitions, art, craft, and trade exhibitions, agricultural and flower shows, music festivals and other events annually. Details of these events are available from local tourism outlets.

JANUARY
Public holidays: New Year's Day; Australia Day. **Hobart:** Summer Festival; Hobart Cup; Taste of Tasmania. **Burnie:** New Year's Day Athletic Carnival. **Cygnet:** Huon Folk Festival. **George Town:** Folk Festival. **Latrobe:** Australia Day Carnival; Henley-on-the-Mersey. **Latrobe-Port Sorell:** Summer Festival. **Queenstown:** Mt Lyell Picnic. **Strahan:** Mt Lyell Picnic. **Triabunna:** Spring Bay Crayfish Derby.

FEBRUARY
Hobart: Royal Hobart Regatta; ANZ Symphony Under the Stars. **Devonport:** Food and Wine Festival. **Evandale:** Village Fair and National Penny Farthing Championships. **Golconda:** Tasmanian Circus Festival. **Latrobe-Port Sorell:** Summer Festival (contd). **Launceston:** Country Music Festival. **Oatlands:** Rodeo. **Richmond:** Country Music Festival; St Andrews Pipe Band Competition. **Waratah:** Axemen's Carnival.

MARCH
Public holiday: Eight Hours Day. **Hobart:** Garden Week and Fine Food Fair. **Campbell Town:** Highland Games. **Cygnet:** Port Cygnet Fishing Carnival. **Devonport:** Harbours Festival. **Fingal:** Fingal Valley Festival. **Kingston:** Kingborough Festival. **Launceston:** A Night in the Gorge. **Longford:** Blessing of the Harvest Festival. **New Norfolk:** Hop Harvest Festival. **St Helens:** Tasmanian Game-Fishing Classic. **Sheffield:** Steam Fest. **Strahan:** Piners' Festival. **Westbury:** Maypole Festival; St Patrick's Day Festival.

EASTER
Public holidays: Good Friday; Easter Monday; Easter Tuesday. **Beauty Point:** Three Peaks Yacht Race. **Deloraine:** Grand National Steeplechase.

APRIL
Public holiday: Anzac Day. **Hobart:** Targa Tasmania (exotic car rally).

MAY
Hobart: City to Casino Fun Run (Glenorchy to Sandy Bay). **Carrick:** Agfest. **Richmond:** Harvest Festival. **Sheffield:** Mt Roland Folk Festival.

JUNE
Public holiday: Queen's Birthday. **Hobart:** Tasmanian Celtic Winterfest. **Campbell Town:** Show. **St Helens:** Suncoast Jazz Festival. **Scottsdale:** Arts and Crafts Exhibition.

JULY
Hobart: Brighton Craft Fair.

AUGUST
New Norfolk: Winter Challenge.

SEPTEMBER
Hobart: Tasmanian Football League Grand Final (sometimes Oct.); Tasmanian Tulip Festival. **Burnie:** Festival. **Sheffield:** Daffodil Festival.

OCTOBER
Public holidays: Hobart Show Day (southern Tas. only); Launceston Show Day (northern Tas. only); Flinders Island Show Day (Flinders Island only); Burnie Show Day (Burnie only). **Hobart:** Royal Hobart Agricultural Show. **Burnie:** Rhododendron Festival. **Derby:** Derby River Derby. **Kingston:** Olie Bollen Festival. **Launceston:** Garden Festival; Launceston Royal National Show; Tasmanian Poetry Festival. **New Norfolk:** Spring in the Valley. **Richmond:** Village fair. **Ringarooma:** Agricultural Show. **Ulverstone:** Show. **Wynyard:** Tulip Festival.

NOVEMBER
Public holiday: Recreation Day (northern Tas. only). **Hobart:** North Hobart Fiesta. **Brighton:** Agricultural Show. **Deloraine:** Tasmanian Craft Fair; Tasmanian Trout Fishing Championships. **Evandale:** Railex. **Longford:** Village Green Garden Festival. **Scottsdale:** Agricultural Show. **Sorell:** Taste of Sorell. **Stanley:** Tasmania Day. **Westbury:** Steam Spectacular.

DECEMBER
Public holidays: Christmas Day; Boxing Day. **Hobart:** Christmas Pageant (sometimes Nov.); Summer Festival; Sydney–Hobart/Melbourne–Hobart Yacht Race. **Latrobe:** Latrobe Wheel Race and Latrobe Gift. **Port Arthur:** Boxing Day Woodchop; Absconders Run. **Stanley:** Agricultural Show. **Ulverstone:** Christmas Mardi Gras. **Zeehan:** King of the Mountain Fun Run.

TASMANIA

wild, forested region. Nearby coastal Strahan, once a mining boom-town is now the departure-point of the Gordon River cruises and scenic flights over the Franklin-Gordon Wild Rivers National Park. North of Queenstown, the town of Zeehan is currently enjoying a mining revival with the reopening of the Renison Bell Tin Mine.

The north coast is yet another contrasting area. Burnie is one of the larger towns and Stanley is a classified historic town situated beneath The Nut, an unusual peninsula. East of Burnie, the Bass Highway hugs the coast as far as Devonport, the terminal of the Bass Strait passenger/vehicle ferry *Spirit of Tasmania* and the centre of an apple-growing area. Inland is Launceston, Tasmania's second largest city, situated on the Tamar River. Only minutes from the city centre is the beautiful Cataract Gorge. The nearby colonial villages of Evandale, Hagley, Westbury, Carrick, Perth, Longford and Hadspen are well worth a visit.

A mild climate, good surfing beaches and sheltered seaside towns add to the attraction of the east-coast region. St Helens, 160 kilometres east of Launceston, is the principal resort town. Try not to miss Bicheno, a picturesque old port and one-time whaling town. Further south, the Hazards, a red granite mountain range, towers up behind Coles Bay, at the entrance to the Freycinet National Park. Nearby Swansea offers top-class ocean and freshwater fishing.

A sense of Tasmania's history can be gained from studying graveyards and headstones: in St David's Park, in the centre of Hobart; on Maria Island; on the Isle of the Dead off Port Arthur; King Island; Flinders Island and Sarah Island in Macquarie Harbour; at National Trust properties; and in towns like Stanley, Richmond, Ross, Evandale and Corinna.

Whether you complete a round trip or only explore parts of this island State, it is very likely that, by the time you come to leave, Tasmania will have won yet another heart.

CLIMATE GUIDE

HOBART

	J	F	M	A	M	J	J	A	S	O	N	D
Maximum °C	22	22	21	18	15	13	12	13	15	17	19	20
Minimum °C	12	12	11	9	6	5	4	5	6	7	9	11
Rainfall mm	37	38	40	49	41	29	49	49	42	48	48	59
Raindays	9	8	10	11	13	11	13	15	14	13	14	13

LAUNCESTON REGION

	J	F	M	A	M	J	J	A	S	O	N	D
Maximum °C	23	23	21	17	14	11	11	12	14	16	19	21
Minimum °C	10	10	9	7	5	3	2	3	4	6	7	9
Rainfall mm	40	43	43	58	63	61	81	80	65	63	51	53
Raindays	8	7	9	11	13	13	16	16	13	13	11	10

CRADLE MOUNTAIN REGION

	J	F	M	A	M	J	J	A	S	O	N	D
Maximum °C	17	18	14	11	8	5	5	5	7	10	12	14
Minimum °C	6	7	6	4	2	0	0	0	-1	2	3	4
Rainfall mm	147	131	158	228	288	276	329	309	277	249	216	192
Raindays	16	14	18	20	21	21	24	23	22	21	19	19

BICHENO REGION

	J	F	M	A	M	J	J	A	S	O	N	D
Maximum °C	21	21	20	19	16	14	14	14	16	18	18	19
Minimum °C	12	13	12	10	9	7	6	6	8	8	10	11
Rainfall mm	47	61	60	63	63	66	54	51	43	56	55	70
Raindays	7	7	7	9	9	9	9	9	7	9	9	9

Richmond Bridge, the oldest bridge in Australia

HOBART

An Historic City

The city's skyline viewed from Mt Nelson

Hobart is Australia's second oldest and most southerly city. It is an enchanting city built around a beautiful harbour and under the spell of nearby majestic Mount Wellington. A strong seafaring flavour and sense of the past give Hobart an almost European air.

This feeling is heightened in winter when Mount Wellington is snow-capped and temperatures drop to a crisp 4°C. The rest of the year Hobart has plenty of days with sparkling blue skies, but temperatures rarely exceed 25°C. It is Australia's second driest capital city.

Many of Hobart's beautiful colonial sandstone buildings were erected by the unfortunate convicts who formed the majority of the European settlers in the early 19th century. Yet, in spite of its convict troubles, the small colony flourished. Hobart's deepwater harbour on the broad estuary of the Derwent River soon became a thriving seaport and by 1842 Hobart was proclaimed a city. The harbour is still Hobart's lifeblood and the port is always busy with yachts. The suburbs nestle right up to the lower slopes of **Mount Wellington** and the city's population of 217 900 spreads on both sides of the graceful **Tasman Bridge**.

From the bridge you will see **Government House** and the **Royal Tasmanian Botanical Gardens** set in the **Queen's Domain**, a large parkland with sporting facilities. In the lovely old Botanical Gardens are a Japanese garden and a restaurant that serves lunch and teas. Further along the Tasman Highway towards the city is the **Gasworks Shopping Village** with shops and restaurants in restored 19th century buildings near Sullivans Cove. Australia's only commercial whisky distillery is located here and is open daily for tours.

In a matter of minutes you are in the heart of Hobart, which has escaped the usual pressures of modern city life. Parking is no problem. Visitors should note that most of the city streets are one-way.

Hobart's waterfront retains much of its early character and it is not hard to imagine it in the early whaling days when Hobart Town was a lusty, brawling seaport known to sailors all round the world. Foreign ships tie up almost in the centre of town, battered whalers are now replaced by fishing-trawlers at Victoria Dock. Wander around to **Constitution Dock**, a haven for the yachts during the annual Sydney to Hobart Yacht Race; here you can buy live seafood.

Just round the corner in Macquarie Street is the **Tasmanian Museum and Art Gallery**, which has a fine collection of Aboriginal artifacts, early prints and

TASMANIA

NOT TO BE MISSED	
in Hobart	Map Ref.
• **Battery Point** – former mariners' village with fascinating tiny houses	551 F11
• **Cadbury Cruise** – take a sweet cruise to the chocolate factory	551 F8
• **Cascade Brewery** – Australia's oldest brewery	552 E9
• **Constitution Dock** – for watching the bustle of fishing boats and larger vessels	551 F6
• **Derwent River ferry ride** – a pleasant means to see the city at a different angle	551 F8
• **Ghost tour** – a spooky way to see the Penitentiary Chapel	551 B2
• **Mount Wellington** – stunning views of the city and surrounds from summit	552 A9
• **Royal Tasmanian Botanical Gardens** – the horticultural jewel of the State	552 G6
• **Salamanca Place** – for art galleries and restaurants in old merchant warehouses	551 D9
• **Theatre Royal** – Australia's oldest operating theatre	551 E4

paintings, and convict relics. From here it is only a short stroll to the **Theatre Royal**, which was built in 1837 and is the oldest operating theatre in Australia. It is worth going inside to glimpse its charming small-scale Georgian interior. Dame Sybil Thorndike rated it as the finest theatre she had played in outside of London. Not far from the Theatre Royal are the **Criminal Courts** and **Penitentiary Chapel**, both operated by the National Trust; guided tours are conducted daily.

Heading back towards the centre of the city, you will see Hobart's sandstone Italianate-style **Town Hall**, built on the site of the original **Government House**, on the corner of Macquarie and Elizabeth streets.

Hobart has a wealth of beautiful Georgian buildings, mostly concentrated in **Macquarie and Davey streets**. More than ninety of them have a National Trust classification. Built around 1846, the **Anglesea Barracks**, in Davey Street, is the oldest military establishment in Australia still used by the army. The **Cascade Brewery** in South Hobart, is over a century and a half old and offers conducted tours on weekdays (bookings essential).

Several modern complexes blend in with the older buildings without destroying the overall scale and atmosphere. The largest landmark is the tower of Australia's first hotel-casino, **Wrest Point**, built on a promontory in the suburb of Sandy Bay, just out of town. Back towards the waterfront is the famous **Salamanca Place**, which displays the finest row of early merchant warehouses in Australia. Dating back to the whaling days of the 1830s, the whole area has been sympathetically restored and the warehouses are now used as art and craft galleries, restaurants and a puppet theatre. A colourful open-air craft market, where almost anything is sold for almost any price, is held here each Saturday.

The steep **Kelly's Steps**, wedged between two old warehouses in Salamanca Place, lead to the heart of unique **Battery Point**, a former mariners' village, which has retained its nineteenth-century character. Battery Point has several quaint cottage tea-rooms and many excellent restaurants offering a variety of different cuisines.

This area is also Hobart's mecca for antique-hunters. Just round the corner is the **Van Diemen's Land Folk Museum**, with its interesting collection of colonial relics housed in Narryna, a gracious old town house, complete with a shady garden and an ornamental fountain. A short walk from here is the graceful old **St George's Anglican Church**, which was built between 1836 and 1847 and designed by two of Tasmania's most prominent colonial architects, John Lee Archer and James Blackburn. The **Tasmanian Maritime Museum**, in Secheron Road, has a collection of old seafaring relics and documents.

Back towards the city, **St David's Park**, with its beautiful old trees, is an ideal place for a rest. One side of this park was Hobart Town's first colonial burial ground; the pioneer gravestones, which date from 1804, make fascinating reading. Across the road, in Murray Street, is **Parliament House**, one of the oldest buildings in Hobart. Originally used as the Customs House, it was built by convicts between 1835 and 1841. Visitors may ask to see the tiny **Legislative Council Chamber**, which is exactly as it was when it was inaugurated. The ceiling has been painstakingly repainted in its original ornate pastel patterns and the benches refurbished in plush red velvet. The building was designed by the colonial architect John Lee Archer.

The **Allport Library and Museum of Fine Arts**, a library of rare books and a collection of antique furniture, china and silver, is also in Murray Street, in the **State Library**.

The main shopping area of Hobart is centred round the **Elizabeth Street Mall**, between Collins and Liverpool streets. The **Cat and Fiddle Arcade and Square** is located between the Mall and Murray Street. Shoppers can relax in the modern square with its fountain and an animated mural which 'performs' on the hour. In the Mall, in addition to the hourly antics of the Cat and Fiddle Clock, entertainment is also provided by strolling buskers. Further along Elizabeth Street, in **Franklin Square**, you can play giant chess.

Hobart offers a sophisticated nightlife with the Wrest Point Hotel-Casino with its casino and revolving restaurant, and a range of licensed restaurants – from Japanese and Mexican to colonial-style. For a touch of old-world class you can sip cocktails in the drawing-room of **Lenna**, an Italianate former mansion (now a distinctive hotel-motel) in Battery Point, before dining in the lavishly decorated restaurant. Fresh seafood is a specialty of many of the city's restaurants. **Mures Fish Centre**, at Victoria Dock, offers a range of fish delights from takeaway to fisherman's basket (brimming with such delicacies as crayfish, mussels, squid and scallops). Hobart also has several interesting old pubs with a nautical flavour; a good example is the **Customs House Hotel** on the corner of Murray and Morrison streets.

The suburbs of Hobart have much to offer the visitor. Nearby Sandy Bay is the site of both the **University of Tasmania** and the **Model Tudor Village**. Beyond this, just out of Taroona, is the convict-built **Shot Tower**, from which you can get a superb view of the Derwent estuary. As well as the original owner's house, built in 1835, the Shot Tower complex includes a small museum and tearooms, both housed in an 1855 building. **North Hobart**, only a few minutes from the centre of the city, is the gourmet's suburb, where a concentration of excellent restaurants and delicatessens have proliferated to the delight of residents and visitors alike. Slightly further north, in the suburb of New Town, is **Runnymede**, a National Trust homestead. Beautifully restored, it commands

ACCOMMODATION

HOTELS

Hotel Grand Chancellor
1 Davey St, Hobart
(03) 6235 4535 or 1800 625138

Lenna of Hobart
20 Runnymede St, Battery Point
(03) 6232 3900 or 1800 030633

Wrest Point Hotel-Casino
410 Sandy Bay Rd, Sandy Bay
(03) 6225 0112 or 1800 030611

FAMILY AND BUDGET

Hobart Pacific Hotel/Motel
Kirby Crt, West Hobart
(03) 6234 6733

Hobart Tower Motel
300 Park St, New Town
(03) 6228 0166

Taroona Hotel
178 Channel Hwy, Taroona
(03) 6227 8748

MOTEL GROUPS: BOOKINGS

Best Western 13 1779

Flag 13 2400

Innkeepers 1800 030111

The above list is for information only; inclusion is not necessarily a recommendation.

an attractive view over New Town Bay and Risdon, where Hobart's first European settlement began. Further north, in the suburb of Goodwood, the **Derwent Entertainment Centre** stands beside the river and **Elwick Racecourse**. **Bellerive**, the ruins of an old fort at Kangaroo Bluff, was built to guard Hobart against a feared Russian invasion late last century. Some of Hobart's best beaches, including **Lauderdale**, **Cremorne** and **Seven Mile Beach**, are in this area. For surfers there is a wild ocean beach at **Clifton**.

There are dozens of scenic drives and lookouts around Hobart, with spectacular views from the pinnacle of **Mount Wellington** and from the old **Signal Station** on top of **Mount Nelson**. The **Waterworks Reserve** is an attractive picnic area close to town.

The hundreds of yachts moored near the prestigious **Royal Yacht Club** in Sandy Bay are evidence of one of Hobart's most popular sports. Other sports are well catered for with a public golf course at Rosny Park, racing and trotting at Glenorchy, and public squash courts at Sandy Bay, New Town and Bellerive. The Southern Tasmanian Tennis Association Courts are in Queen's Domain. Tasmania's cricket headquarters is at Bellerive.

Hobart offers a complete range of accommodation, from the modern Hotel Grand Chancellor or the Wrest Point Hotel-Casino to tiny Georgian cottage guest houses at Battery Point. Between these two extremes there are many hotels, motels and numerous guest houses, as well as caravan parks, holiday flats and cottages.

As a result of the popularity of colonial accommodation over the last few years, there are now over 150 properties, including host farms and colonial cottages, available for visitors. Host farms provide a wide variety of standard and type of service, and offer guests the opportunity to observe farm life or become involved in it. Colonial accommodation is provided in buildings or cottages established on their present sites before 1901. Although concessions are made to allow modern facilities to be incorporated, interiors are presented in colonial style by the use of genuine or reproduction furniture and other decoration.

Hobart offers the visitor an impressive State capital, rich in history, and only minutes away from a wide variety of natural attractions.

For further information, contact the Tasmanian Travel and Information Centre, 20 Davey St; (03) 6230 8233.

HOBART ON FOOT

There are many walking tours around Hobart, including:

- **Battery Point:** National Trust guided walk; leaves Franklin Square each Sat. morning; bookings essential

- **Battery Point and Sullivans Cove:** Self-guide walk; brochure available; small donation required

- **Old Penitentiary Chapel and Criminal Courts:** Guided ghost tours; bookings essential

- **Sullivans Cove:** Guided walk, departs Visitor Centre, Davey St; bookings essential

Brochures are available for the self-guide walk. For further information, contact the Tasmanian Travel and Information Centre, 20 Davey Street, Hobart; (03) 6230 8233.

Battery Point

Arthurs Circus

A most delightful part of Hobart is the former maritime village **Battery Point,** perched between the city docks and Sandy Bay. Battery Point dates back to the early days of Hobart Town, when it became a lively mariners' village with fishermen's cottages, shops, churches, a village green and a riot of pubs with such evocative names as the Whalers' Return and the Neptune Inn. Miraculously, it has hardly changed since those days. To anyone strolling through its narrow, hilly streets – with enchanting glimpses of the harbour, yachts and mountains at every turn – it looks almost like a Cornish fishing village.

Quaint **Arthurs Circus** is built around the former village green, now a children's playground. A profusion of old-fashioned flowers – sweet william, honeysuckle, daisies and geraniums – grow in pocket-sized gardens.

Pubs such as the Knopwood's Retreat and the Shipwright's Arms add to the feeling that time has stood still. Knopwood Street and Kelly's Steps are reminders of two pioneer settlers: the Reverend Bobby Knopwood, Battery Point's first landowner, and the adventurer James Kelly, who owned a whaling fleet and undertook a daring voyage around Van Diemen's Land.

Battery Point gets its name from a battery of guns set up on the promontory in front of a small guardhouse in 1818. This soon became a signalling station and is now the oldest building in Battery Point.

Today the Point has many inviting restaurants and tearooms, and several antique shops to explore, but it is still mainly a residential area. Most of the houses are tiny dormer-windowed fishermen's cottages, with a few grander houses such as Secheron, Stowell, Narryna and Lenna. An attractive leaflet with a detailed map, *Let's Talk About Battery Point*, is available from the Tasmanian Travel and Information Centre, and the National Trust organises walking tours of the area, departing from the Wishing Well, Franklin Square, each Saturday morning.

For further information, contact the Tasmanian Travel and Information Centre, 20 Davey St, Hobart; (03) 6230 8233.

TASMANIA

TOURS from Hobart

The charming town of Richmond has many historic buildings

A marvellous range of tourist attractions is within easy reach of Hobart. To appreciate its superb natural setting it is worth going on a scenic flight over the city and its surroundings, taking in the beautiful Derwent estuary, the patchwork fields of the Midlands, the Tasman Peninsula, and the spectacular lakes and mountains of central and south-western Tasmania. Flight bookings can be made at the Tasmanian Travel and Information Centre, Hobart, which can also arrange half-day and full-day coach tours.

Mount Wellington

22 km from Hobart via the Huon Road

The most popular short trip from Hobart is to the pinnacle of Mount Wellington, 1271 metres above the city, which commands panoramic views of both the D'Entrecasteaux Channel to the south and the Derwent Valley to the north. A novel way to see the views is the half-day tour 'Mount Wellington Downhill': transport to the summit and a thrilling bike ride back down.

Richmond

26 km from Hobart via the Eastern Outlet Road

See: Entry for Richmond in A–Z listing.

Cadbury's Chocolate Factory, Claremont

14 km from Hobart on the Brooker Highway

A visit to this beautifully sited model factory, the biggest chocolate and cocoa factory in Australia, is another popular short trip. Privately-run coach tours leave Tuesday to Thursday and self-drive tours may be made Monday to Friday. A Cadbury Cruise operates Monday to Friday. Reservations are essential; book well in advance for the holiday season. The chocolate factory is usually closed for two weeks in September and from the end of December to mid-January when reduced tours are available subject to demand. Contact the Tasmanian Travel and Information Centre, Hobart, for information and bookings.

New Norfolk

32 km from Hobart on the Lyell Highway

See: Entry for New Norfolk in A–Z listing.

Huonville

37 km from Hobart via Huon Road and the Huon Highway

Huonville, just south-west of Hobart, is the centre of Tasmania's picturesque apple-growing district. You can take the scenic route from Hobart via the shoulder of Mount Wellington on the Huon Highway, returning via the

Channel Highway and passing through the small town of Cygnet. The Channel Highway commands spectacular vistas of the coastline and rugged Bruny Island. **See:** Entry for Huonville in A–Z listing.

Mount Field National Park and Russell Falls

72 km from Hobart via the Lyell Highway and Gordon River Road

The road from New Norfolk to Mount Field passes through some of the loveliest parts of the Derwent Valley. A nature walk leads to the magnificent Russell Falls, cascades that drop 32 metres into a gorge of rainforest and tree ferns, from near the park entrance. This large scenic wildlife reserve shelters many native birds and animals, including the elusive Tasmanian devil. **See also:** National Parks.

Tasman Peninsula and Port Arthur

100 km from Hobart via the Arthur Highway

There is so much to see on this fascinating trip that it would be well worth staying overnight at the narrow isthmus of Eaglehawk Neck, at Port Arthur or at Nubeena. Once guarded by a line of tethered dogs to prevent convicts escaping, Eaglehawk Neck is now a base for game-fishing charter boats. There are four unique coastal formations in the area: the spectacular Devil's Kitchen, the Blowhole, Tasman's Arch and the Tessellated Pavement. The old penal settlement of Port Arthur is Tasmania's number one tourist attraction. Other attractions in the area include Bush Hill, Remarkable Cave and Safety Cove. **See also:** A Convict Past; and entries for Port Arthur and Eaglehawk Neck in A–Z listing.

Hastings Caves

110 km from Hobart via the Huon Road and Huon Highway

These caves, 13 km from the small township of Hastings, are another popular attraction. There are regular guided tours of the only illuminated cave, Newdegate Cave, regarded as one of the most beautiful limestone caves in Australia. A natural thermal swimming-pool with an average temperature of 27°C is nearby. Motorists are warned that Dover is the last place to buy petrol when travelling south towards Recherche Bay. The Ida Bay Scenic Railway is another popular tourist attraction near Hastings. **See also:** Entry for Hastings in A–Z listing.

Lake Pedder and Lake Gordon

170 km from Hobart via the Lyell Highway and Gordon River Road

In clear weather, the road from Mount Field National Park to the township of Strathgordon is probably the most spectacular stretch of mountain highway in Australia. Unfortunately (from the visitor's point of view), there is very high rainfall in the area, which of course results in its unique natural topography. Motorists are advised to cancel trips on overcast days and to take note that Maydena is the last place to buy petrol when heading west on the Gordon River Road. Constructed lakes Pedder and Gordon, part of the Hydro-Electric Commission's giant Gordon River power development, are liberally stocked with trout. The underground power station at the Gordon Dam can be inspected on regular tours. You can hire boats and fishing tackle from Strathgordon, where a chalet is available for overnight accommodation. Inquiries should be directed to the Tasmanian Travel and Information Centre in Hobart. **See also:** National Parks.

Lake Pedder, Southwest National Park, is renowned for its trout fishing

TASMANIA from A to Z

Old mine building, one of many brick ruins at Beaconsfield

Beaconsfield   Pop. 1088

MAP REF. 557 J5, 561 K7

The ruins of several impressive brick buildings with Romanesque arches dominate this quiet town on the West Tamar Hwy, 46 km NW of Launceston. Formerly a thriving gold township (called Cabbage Tree Hill), the ruins are the remains of several buildings erected at the pithead of the Tasmanian Gold Mine in 1904. When the mine closed 10 years later after water seepage, more than 6 million dollars' worth of ore had been won from the reef. In 1804 a party of officers established a settlement north of the town, called York Town. **Of interest:** Grubb Shaft Museum, West St, in one of old mine buildings, features working mining models, mining relics and interactive displays; restored miner's cottage and original Flowery Gully School opposite museum. Van Dieman's Gallery, Weld St, has local art and craft. **In the area:** York Town monument, 9 km N on Kelso–Greens Beach Rd. At Rowella, 15 km E, Holm Oak Vineyards. Auld Kirk (1843) historic church at Sidmouth, 9 km SE; nearby, Batman Bridge, with its A-frame reaching 100 m above Tamar River. **Tourist information:** Tamar Visitor Centre, Main Rd, Exeter; (03) 6394 4454. **Accommodation:** 2 hotels, 1 motel, 1 B&B.

Beauty Point   Pop. 1137

MAP REF. 557 K5, 561 K6

This popular fishing and yachting centre on the West Tamar Hwy, 48 km NW of Launceston, is the oldest deepwater port in the area and was constructed to serve the Beaconsfield goldmine. Today the town is home to the Australian Maritime College. Cargo is loaded at Bell Bay across the river. **Of interest:** Nearby Sandy Beach for safe swimming. Easter: Three Peaks Yacht Race (to Hobart). **In the area:** Two northern holiday towns: Kelso, 15 km NW, dates back to early York Town settlement; Greens Beach, 20 km NW, at mouth of Tamar River. Asbestos Range National Park, 25 km NW, panoramic views of coastline and walks ranging from 10 minutes to the 5-hour walking trail from Badger Head to Bakers Beach. Marion's Vineyard, Foreshore Dr., Deviot, 12 km SE. **Tourist information:** Tamar Visitor Centre, Main Rd, Exeter; (03) 6394 4454. **Accommodation:** 2 hotels, 2 motels, 3 B&B, 2 cara./camp. parks.

Bicheno   Pop. 705

MAP REF. 559 Q2, 561 Q12

A fishing port and holiday destination on the east coast, 195 km from Hobart, Bicheno offers surf, rock, sea and estuary fishing. The town's mild climate, outstanding fishing, fine sandy beaches nearby and its picturesque setting make it one of Tasmania's most popular holiday resorts. Licensed seafood restaurants and a range of accommodation add to its appeal. Originally a sealing and whaling town from about 1803, it later became a coal-mining port in 1854. Today crayfishing is the main local industry. **Of interest:** On Tasman Hwy: Sea Life Centre, with small aquarium and seafood restaurant; Dive Centre, offering diving instruction and charters. Foreshore walkway, from Redbill Point north of town, south to Blowhole. Lookouts at top of town's twin hills: Whalers Lookout, off Foster St, and National Park Lookout, off Morrison St; rock orchids, unique to east coast, spectacular sight here in Oct. and Nov. Grave of Aboriginal heroine Waubedebar, Lions Park, Burgess St. Historic tours of town; inquire at Tourist information. Fishing charters and glass - bottomed boat rides to view underwater life in Governor Island Marine Reserve; inquire at Tourist information. Adventure tours available, including scuba diving and mountain-bike riding. **In the area:** Little (fairy) Penguin Rookery, 6 km N; guided nightly tours only in season, contact Tourist information. East Coast Bird Life and Animal Park, 8 km N, exhibits Tasmanian devils and other native fauna. Douglas Aspley Vineyard, 11 km N. Lookout in Douglas Apsley National Park, 14 km NW. Freycinet Vineyard and the adjacent Springbrook Vineyard, 18 km SW on Tasman Hwy. Freycinet National Park, 40 km S. **Tourist information:** Bicheno Penguin Adventure Tours, Tasman Hwy; (03) 6375 1333. **Accommodation:** 8 hotel/motels, 2 hostels, 2 cara./camp. parks.

Boat Harbour   Pop. 109

MAP REF. 560 F5

The clear water and rocky points of this attractive town make it an ideal spot for skindiving and spear fishing. Situated on the north-west coast, 31 km W of Burnie, it adjoins one of the richest agricultural areas in the State. **Of interest:** Shannondoah Cottage, Bass Hwy, for local craft, lunches and Devonshire teas. **In the area:** Boat Harbour Beach, 3 km N, offers safe swimming, marine life in pools at low tide, fishing, water-skiing and bushwalking. Sisters Beach, 8 km NW, for good fishing and swimming. Nearby, Birdland Native Gardens and Aboriginal caves in Rocky Cape National Park, 19 km NW. **Tourist information:** Seaside Garden Motel, The Esplanade; (03) 6445 1111. **Accommodation:** 2 motels, 1 hostel, 1 cara./camp. park.

Bothwell   Pop. 396

MAP REF. 559 K5

This peaceful old country town in the beautiful Clyde River valley, 74 km NW of Hobart, has been proclaimed an historic village. It has 52 buildings either classified or recorded by the National Trust. Surveyed in 1824 and named by Lieutenant-Governor Arthur after the Scottish town, it is now the centre of sheep and cattle country. It is possible that the first golf in Australia was played at the nearby homestead of Ratho in the 1830s. This course still exists and is open to visitors with golf-club membership elsewhere. **Of interest:** Bothwell Grange (c. 1836), Alexander St, a guest house with tearooms and art gallery. Australasian Golf Museum, Market Place. Lamont Weaving Studio, Patrick St, has demonstrations and a sales room. Peter Muere Woodturning, Queens St. St Luke's Church (1830), Dennistoun Rd. In High St: Georgian brick Slate Cottage (1836), restored and furnished in style of day; Old bootmaker's Shop; tours by appt (inquire at Tourist information). **In the area:** Steppe Stones, 20 km N, a collection of 13 monoliths by sculptor Steven Walker, each representing an aspect of area's history and character. Excellent trout fishing at Arthurs Lake, 51 km N, Penstock Lagoon, 45 km NW, Great Lake, 56 km N, and Lake Echo, 48 km NW; all via Lakes Hwy. **Tourist information:** Australasian Golf Museum, Market Pl.; (03) 6259 4033. **Accommodation:** 1 cara./camp. park.

Bridgewater   Pop. 8684

MAP REF. 554 H4, 559 L7

This town, only 19 km N of Hobart, is situated on the bank at the main northern crossing of the Derwent River. The causeway was built in the early 1830s by 200 convicts, who barrowed 2 million tonnes of stone and clay from the site. The original bridge was opened in 1849; the present one dates from 1946. **In the area:** At Granton, 1 km S across bridge: Old Watch House (1838), now a petrol station, was built by convicts to guard the causeway and has the smallest cell in Australia (50 cm square, 2 m high); Black Snake Inn (1833), also convict-built. Risdon Cove Historic Site, 15 km SE, site of original Hobart Town settlement. **Tourist information:** Council Offices, Tivoli Rd, Gagebrook; (03) 6263 0333. **Accommodation:** None.

Bridport   Pop. 1165

MAP REF. 557 R2, 561 N6

Bridport is a popular holiday and fishing town on the north-east coast, 85 km NE of Launceston. **Of interest:** Fine beaches, excellent river, sea and lake fishing. '2000 Plus' Information Centre, Main St. **In the area:** Bowood (1839), 8 km W, historic homestead near town; open Sun. or by appt. Views from Waterhouse Point and Ranson's Beach. Winegrowing at Piper's Brook, 18 km SW. **Tourist information:** '2000 Plus' Information Centre, Main St; or Motor Inn, Main St; (03) 6356 1238. **Accommodation:** 1 hotel, 1 hotel/ motel, 1 motel, 1 hostel, 1 cara./camp. park.

Bruny Island   Pop. 520

MAP REF. 559 L11

Almost two islands, separated by a narrow isthmus, Bruny was named after the French Admiral Bruni D'Entrecasteaux, who surveyed the channel between the island and the mainland of Tasmania in 1792; the Aboriginal name for the island was Lunawannaaloona. Abel Tasman saw the island in 1642 but did not land. Other European visitors in the 18th century included Furneaux (1773), James Cook (1777) and William Bligh (1788, 1792). The first apple trees in Tasmania are said to have been planted here by a botanist with the Bligh expedition. **Of interest:** Bruny Island ferry departs from Kettering, on the mainland, several times daily. On isthmus between North and South Bruny: memorial to Truganini, Tasmania's last full-blood Aborigine who died in 1876; lookout, views of spectacular coastal scenery; boardwalk; and little (fairy) penguin and short-tailed shearwater (muttonbird) viewing. *On South Bruny:* Bligh Museum, exhibits island's recorded history; Captain Cook's Landing Place, has model of Cook's ship; Mavista Falls, in scenic reserve; lookouts at Adventure and Cloudy bays; lighthouse (1836) at Cape Bruny, second oldest in Australia; walking tracks to Mt Mangana and Mt Bruny. *On North Bruny:* Dennes Point beach, D'Entrecasteaux Channel, has picnic/ barbecue facilities; at Variety Bay, remains of convict-built church on private property near airstrip, conducted tours available; at Barnes Bay, vault of William Lawrence (1839). Fishing. Camel tours. **Tourist information:** Bruny D'Entrecasteaux Visitor Centre, Ferry Rd, Kettering; (03) 6267 4494. **Accommodation:** 1 hotel, approx. 30 holiday cottages, 2 cara./ camp. parks.

Buckland   Pop. 228

MAP REF. 555 M2, 559 N7

A stained-glass window depicting the life of John the Baptist and dating back to the 14th century is in the church in this tiny township, 64 km NE of Hobart. History links the window with Battle Abbey, England. The abbey was sacked by Oliver Cromwell in the 17th century, but the window was hidden before it could be destroyed. Two centuries later it was given to Rev. T.H. Fox, Buckland's first rector, by the Marquis of Salisbury. It is now set into the east wall of the Church of St John the Baptist (1846), on the Tasman Hwy. Although the window has been damaged and restored several times in its long life, the original figure-work is intact. Also of interest is Ye Olde Buckland Inn, in Kent St, a 19th-century tavern and restaurant. **Tourist information:** Ye Olde Buckland Inn, Kent St; (03) 6257 5114. **Accommodation:** None.

Burnie   Pop. 20 505

MAP REF. 560 G6

The rapid expansion of Burnie, now Tasmania's fourth largest city, is based on one of the State's largest industrial enterprises, Australian Paper. Situated on the banks of Emu Bay, 148 km NW of Launceston, Burnie has a deepwater port, which serves the west coast mining centres. Other important industries include the manufacture of mining equipment and production of dried milk, chocolate products and cheese. **Of interest:** Lactos

TASMANIA

The Hazards at Freycinet National Park, near Coles Bay

cheese factory, Old Surrey Rd, has educational facility and sales outlet. Tours of Amcor (Mon.–Fri.), a paper mill, Marine Tce. Pioneer Village Museum, High St, includes reconstruction of Burnie's small tradesmen's shops c. 1900. Restored Burnie Inn, town's oldest remaining building, re-erected in Burnie Park. Glen Osborne, Aileen Cres., historic building, now a B&B. New Year's Day: Athletic Carnival. Sept.: Festival. Oct.: Rhododendron Festival. **In the area:** Views from Round Hill, 5 km E. Fern Glade, off Old Surrey Rd, 5 km W, for riverside walks and picnics. Emu Valley Rhododendron Gardens, off Cascade Rd, 6 km S. Annsleigh Gardens, 9 km S on Mount Rd. Guide Falls near Ridgley, 17 km S. Upper Natone Forest Reserve, 20 km S, for picnics. Scenic drive southwest via Somerset through Elliott to Yolla. Day tours available to Cradle Mountain, Gunns Plains, Leven Canyon and Fossil Cliffs. Pieman and Arthur river cruises, contact Tourist information. **Tourist information:** Pioneer Village Museum, Civic Centre Precinct, Little Alexander St; (03) 6434 6111. **Accommodation:** 4 hotels, 3 hotel/motels, 5 motels, 2 B&B, 2 cara./camp. parks.

Campbell Town   Pop. 820

MAP REF. 559 M2, 561 N12
Campbell Town, on the Midland Hwy, 66 km SE of Launceston, is a national centre for selling stud sheep. The area's links with the wool industry go back to the early 1820s, when Saxon merinos were introduced to the Macquarie Valley, west of the town. Timber and stud beef are also important primary industries. The town and the Elizabeth River were named by Governor Macquarie for his wife, the former Elizabeth Campbell. **Of interest:** National Trust-classified buildings: St Michael's Church (1857) and Wesleyan Chapel (1846), no longer operational, King St; Balmoral Cottage (1840s), Bridge St; St Luke's Church (1839), The Grange (1847), now colonial accommodation, Campbell Town Inn (1840), Fox Hunters Return (1830s), now colonial accommodation, Kean's Brewery (1840), now an antique emporium, and convict-built Red Bridge (1837) – all in High St. Memorial to locally-born Harold Gatty, first round-the-world flight navigator, High St. Mar.: Highland Games. June: Show (oldest continuous Show in Australia). **In the area:** Trout fishing in local rivers and lakes, particularly Lake Leake, 30 km SE. Evansville Game Park, 30 km E. **Tourist information:** 103 High St; (03) 6381 1283. **Accommodation:** 1 hotel, 3 B&B.

Coles Bay   Pop. 120

MAP REF. 559 Q4, 561 Q13
This beautiful unspoiled bay, 42 km S of Bicheno on the Freycinet Peninsula, is a good base for visitors to the 70 000-ha Freycinet National Park. **In the area:** At Freycinet National Park: pleasant beaches, clear waters and heathland; ideal for swimming, fishing and bushwalking including the scenic walk to Wineglass Bay; abundant birdlife; variety of wildflowers, including 60 varieties of small ground orchid; rock climbing on 'The Hazards', spectacular granite peaks rising to 620 m, and nearby cliffs; waterskiing, scuba-diving, canoeing and sailing; charter boat trips to Schouten Island available. **Tourist information:** Park Ranger; (03) 6257 0107. **Accommodation:** 1 lodge, 2 cara./camp parks, basic camping ground in park. **See also:** National Parks.

Cygnet   Pop. 924

MAP REF. 554 F10, 559 K10
The centre of a fruit-growing district, 52 km SW of Hobart, the town was originally named Port de Cygne Noir (meaning Black Swan Port) by the French Admiral Bruni D'Entrecasteaux because of the number of swans in the bay. **Of interest:** Art and Craft shops. Jan.: Huon Folk Festival. Mar.: Port Cygnet Fishing Carnival. **In the area:** Boating, fishing, bushwalking, gem fossicking. Nine Pin Point Marine Nature Reserve, 18 km S, near Verona Sands. Good beaches and boat-launching facilities at Randalls Bay, 14 km S, nearby Verona Sands, and Egg and Bacon Bay, 15 km S. Panorama Vineyard, 9 km N. Unique Lymington lace agate sometimes found at Drip Beach, Lymington, 7.5 km SW. Lymington Geological Trail (car tour); brochure available from Tourist information. Pelvereta Falls, 10 km N on Sandfly Rd. The Deepings, woodturners' workshop and sales, 10 km E at Nicholls Rivulet. Talune Wildlife Park and Koala Gardens, 6 km SE at Gardners Bay, has cabin accommodation, good picnic/barbecue facilities and sells local cider and fruit wine. Hartzview Vineyard and Wine Centre, 10 km SE. **Tourist information:** Talune Wildlife Park, Gardners Bay; (03) 6295 1775. **Accommodation:** 3 hotels, 1 hostel, 1 cara./camp. park.

Deloraine   Pop. 2098

MAP REF. 556 I11, 561 J9
Scenic Deloraine, with Bass Strait to the north and the Great Western Tiers to the south, is an ideal base for exploring the many attractions of northern Tasmania. The surrounding countryside is used mainly for dairying and mixed farming. **Of interest:** Walk along river bank, through parkland. Gallery 9, West

Touring Tasmania

Wineglass Bay, one of many pretty coves in Freycinet National Park

Tasmania is small, but its sights are grand. Nurtured by the temperate climate, the trees are taller here than on the mainland (Tasmania has the world's tallest hardwood trees, some exceeding 90 metres); mountains vault to the skies from wild forest land. The great inland lakes in the mountains feed savage rivers, some of which are harnessed for the State's hydro-electric schemes. The hills and valleys are harshly carved by the weather and become gentle only in the rolling pastoral lands of the Midlands and the north.

In this romantic landscape, more reminiscent of Scotland than Australia, are set the remnants of a rich past of convict and colonial life – the prisons, churches, cottages and court houses, the barracks, mansions and homesteads from the earliest days of European settlement.

Most travellers start their Tasmanian holiday in the north, where they have either taken their car off the ferry or have hired a car or mobile home for the journey south. The Scenic Circle Route is a popular tour that covers some of the State's best scenic and historical attractions. A shorter route, the Heritage Highway, links Launceston and Hobart. Travellers can choose between these two routes or combine sections of each to suit their interests.

Scenic Circle Route

This magnificent touring route will take you through some of the most fascinating country that Australia has to offer: the incomparable wilderness of the west coast, the lavish orchard country around Launceston and the Huon Valley, and the snug beaches, bays and villages of the east coast.

From **Devonport** the coast road to the west runs with the northern railway along the sea's edge. Along this road are the thriving towns of **Ulverstone, Burnie, Wynyard** and **Stanley,** and the striking headlands of Table Cape, Rocky Cape and The Nut. They are worth a special trip, as is a detour down the side road from **Penguin** to the peaceful mountain farmland of Gunns Plains and the Gunns Plains caves. The road from Forth into the vast wilderness areas of the magnificent **Cradle Mountain-Lake St Clair National Park** is also well worth a visit, but the turnoff to follow the Scenic Circle Route is at Somerset, and from there you head south down the Murchison Highway through the rich farmlands towards the increasingly mountainous country of the west coast. An interesting diversion leads to Corinna, once a thriving town but now virtually abandoned, on the beautiful Pieman River, not far from its mouth. A launch trip from Corinna travels through deeply-cut river gorges west to the Indian Ocean.

Back on the main road, the mountain scenery is unique and quite spectacular. The towns here developed as a result of their mineral wealth. **Zeehan** now has only a small population, but at the turn of the century there were more than 10 000 inhabitants when silver, lead and zinc mining was at its height. Many buildings of those early days still stand. The larger town of **Queenstown** has grown up around the Mount Lyell copper mine, in a valley beneath bare, bleached hills, streaked and stained with the hues of minerals – chrome, purple, grey and pink. Nearby is **Strahan** on Macquarie Harbour, the only coastal town in the west. The harbour can be reached only by shallow-draught vessels through the notorious passage called Hell's Gates. Cruises are available through wilderness country along the Gordon River, past the ruins of the remote convict settlement on Sarah Island, or take a sea-plane flight over the **Franklin-Gordon Wild Rivers National Park**.

The road turns inland from these towns, avoiding the almost inaccessible south-west, and travels through the Franklin-Gordon Wild Rivers National Park, across the central highlands past Lake St Clair and down the Derwent River valley through the town of **New Norfolk,** centre of the Tasmanian hop-growing industry. This valley, beautiful in spring and brilliantly coloured with foliage in autumn, is of both scenic and historical interest. It was settled by Europeans in 1808, the site having been chosen by Governor Macquarie.

A detour from the Hobart road leads to the old town of **Richmond,** probably the best example of a Tasmanian historic town, with its old Georgian houses and cottages clustered together and its bridge, convict-built and the oldest freestone bridge still in use in Australia. The gaol pre-dates Port Arthur as a penal settlement; two churches, a court house, a schoolhouse, a rectory, the hotel granary a general store and a flour mill were all built in the 1820s and 1830s.

Hobart, Australia's second oldest and most southerly city, is attractively sited on the Derwent River, with Mount Wellington looming behind. The port area at Salamanca Place, where the old bond stores and warehouses are located, is a reminder of the days when the whaling fleet and the timber ships tied up at the wharf and sailors went out on the town. Battery Point with its barracks, workers' cottages and Arthurs Circus – its Georgian-style houses built around a circular green – is part of Hobart's beginnings.

The grim but beautiful penal settlement of **Port Arthur** is not far from Hobart, on the Tasman Peninsula. Here, within the forbidding sandstone walls, visitors will feel some of the hopelessness and isolation of the thousands of convicts who passed through this settlement during its 47 years of existence.

South of Hobart is the scenic Huon Valley, particularly spectacular when the apple trees are in blossom. At the southern end of the route is Cockle Creek on Recherche Bay, where the South Coast walking track begins.

North on the Scenic Circle Route from Hobart, the Tasman Highway traverses the east coast, a region enjoying a generally mild and equable climate. Many attractive seaside towns are set on sheltered inlets but within easy reach of surf beaches and fishing grounds: towns like **Orford**, **Triabunna**, **Swansea**, **Bicheno**, **Scamander** and **St Helens**.

Off the Tasman Highway near Bicheno is the **Freycinet National Park** on the Freycinet Peninsula. There are many walking tracks through this park, which is dominated by the Hazards, a red-granite mountain range.

The road cuts across the less developed farming country of the north and goes west to **Launceston**, the northern capital of Tasmania, 64 kilometres from the north coast at the junction of the North Esk, South Esk and Tamar rivers. It is a smaller, more provincial city than Hobart, set in hilly countryside, and makes an excellent base from which to explore the rich coastal plain of the Tamar Valley and the mountain country to the north. Cataract Gorge, historic Franklin House and Entally House are all within easy distance of Launceston.

The Heritage Highway

The first Europeans to travel between Launceston and Hobart made the journey by foot in 1807, after which a regular stage coach service was established. Today visitors can take a similar route along the Midland Highway through the gentle pastoral landscape of the Midlands, stopping at some of the most beautiful and historic towns in Australia. Colonial bed and breakfast accommodation abounds, as does a wonderful variety of antique shops and galleries housed in historic buildings.

Just south of Launceston are the finely preserved Georgian-period townships of **Evandale** and **Longford**. Christ Church (1839) at Longford has an outstanding stained-glass window and pioneer graveyard. A little further on from the town is Brumbys Creek at Cressy, one of the State's premier fly-fishing locations. February is a good time to visit Evandale for the annual Village Fair and Pennyfarthing Championships, while garden-lovers will enjoy the extensive formal gardens at nearby Clarendon mansion.

Further south, short detours lead to the former garrison towns of **Ross** and **Campbell Town**. Ross is set amongst some of Australia's finest merino wool country, and the Tasmanian Wool Centre in town highlights its rural history. The bridge at Ross is one of Australia's finest historical bridges — its arches contain 184 stones depicting Celtic symbols, interspersed with images of notable personalities and animals. So fine was the stonework that the two convict stonemasons received pardons for their efforts.

Several other historic towns feature along the Heritage Highway, including Tunbridge, **Oatlands**, and **Pontville**. A side trip south of Oatlands leads to peaceful Bothwell on the Clyde River, with over 50 National Trust-classified buildings and the oldest golf club in Australia. Quarries near Pontville provided quality stone for many of the State's oldest buildings.

For further information, contact the Tasmanian Travel and Information Centre, 20 Davey St, Hobart; (03) 6230 8233. **See also:** National Parks and individual town entries for those parks and towns indicated by bold type.

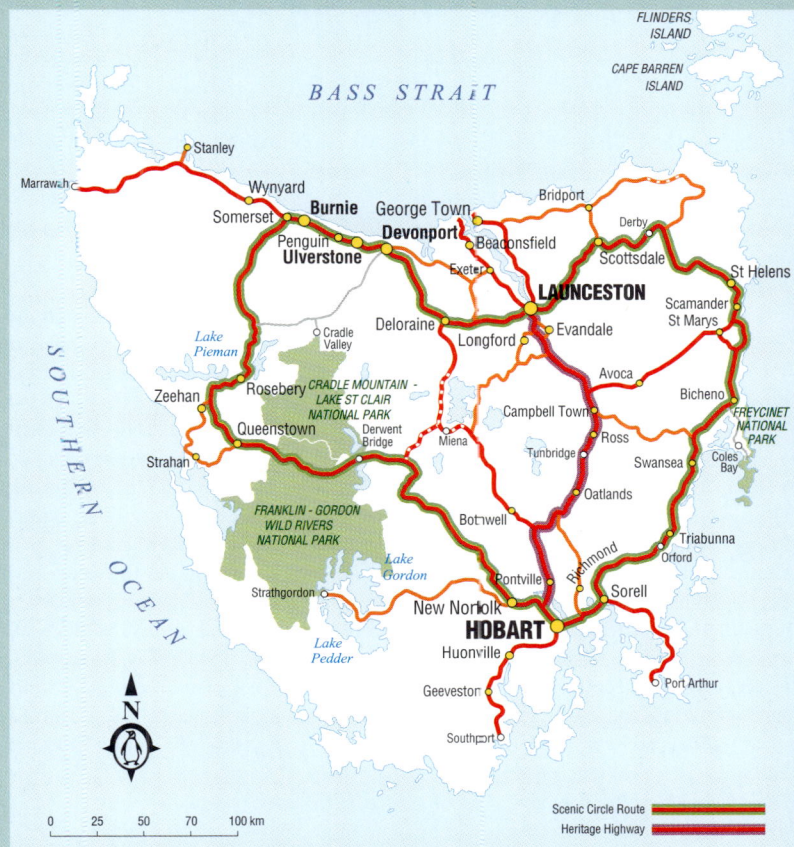

Scenic Circle Route
Heritage Highway

Lighthouse on Mersey Bluff, Devonport

Barrack St. 'Yarns', large multi-panelled artwork in silk, Community Complex, Alverston Dr., Mon.–Wed. or by appt; inquire at Tourist information. Markets, 1st Sat. each month. Easter: Grand National Steeplechase. Nov.: Tasmanian Craft Fair; Tasmanian Trout Fishing Championships. **In the area:** Ashgrove Farm, Elizabeth Town, 10 km NW, sells English-style cheeses. Lobster Falls, 15 km W, 2-hour return walk from roadside; Westmorland Falls, further 10 km SW at Caveside. Trowunna Wildlife Park, 18 km W on Mole Creek Rd, has specially designed noctarium for displaying nocturnal animals. Montana Falls, 9 km SW, small but pretty falls; 5–10 min. approach walk. Meander Falls in Meander Forest Reserve, 22 km SW, 5-hour return walk from carpark (not accessible if heavy snow); other walking tracks in reserve. Quamby Bluff, 20 km S, solitary mountain behind town; walking track to summit (6-hour return, medium difficulty) starts near Lake Hwy. Liffey Falls, 29 km S, 45 min. return walk from carpark. Scenic drive south to Central Highlands, through Golden Valley, to Great Lake, one of the largest high-water lakes in Australia. Dry's Bluff, 40 km SE, part of Great Western Tiers. Excellent trout fishing on lake and in Mersey and Meander rivers. Heidi Cheese Farm, 6 km E at Exton, sells Swiss-style cheeses. **Tourist information:** 29 West Church St; (03) 6362 2046. **Accommodation:** 3 hotels, 1 motel, 6 B&B, 2 hostels. **See also:** Stately Homes.

Derby   Pop. 200

MAP REF. 561 O7

Derby is a former mining town on the Tasman Hwy, 34 km E of Scottsdale in the north-east. In its heyday, tin mining was a flourishing industry, but there has been a gradual swing to rural production, although tin is still worked in the area. **Of interest:** Derby Tin Mine Museum, in old school (1897), has displays of local history, gemstones, minerals and tin panning. Cottage Craft, outside the museum. Reconstructed Shanty Town, surrounding museum, has original buildings from area: miner's cottage, newspaper office, mining assay office, butcher's shop, general store, blacksmith's shop and two cells from old Derby gaol. In Main St: Wallaby's Woodcraft, woodturning; Bank House Antiques and Craft, in old bank. Oct.: Derby River Derby. **In the area:** At Moorina, 8 km NE: gemstone fossicking park on Tasman Hwy; cemetery has graves of Chinese miners. Former tin-mining town of Branxholm, 12 km SW. Near Ringarooma, 24 km SW, lookouts at Mathinna Hill and Mt Victoria; scenic drives; Ringarooma Agricultural Show held in Oct. **Tourist information:** Tin Mine Museum, Main St; (03) 6354 2262. **Accommodation:** 1 hotel, 1 camp. area.

Devonport   Pop. 22 660

MAP REF. 556 E5, 560 I6

As the terminal for the vehicular ferry *Spirit of Tasmania* from Melbourne, Devonport has become a busy industrial and agricultural-export town, as well as a major tourist centre. Devonport has its own airport, and is ideally suited as a visitor base for seeing scenic northern Tasmania. **Of interest:** Tiagarra, Tasmanian Aboriginal Culture and Art Centre, Bluff Rd, Mersey Bluff; Tasmanian Aboriginal rock engravings outside display area. Maritime Museum, Victoria Pde. National Trust-classified Home Hill, Middle Rd, home of former Prime Minister Joseph Lyons and Dame Enid Lyons; tours available. Scenic flights available, contact Tourist information. Historic cottage accommodation. Feb.: Food and Wine Festival. Mar.: Harbours Festival. **In the area:** Walking and cycling track from town to Don, 6 km W, via Mersey Bluff lighthouse, for excellent coastal views. At Don, Don River Railway and Museum, scenic train rides; vintage trains run on weekdays and steam trains on weekends.

Braddon's Lookout, 9 km W near Forth, has panoramic view of coastline. Tasmanian Aboretum (45 ha), 10 km S at Eugenana; also picnic area and walking tracks. **Tourist information:** Tasmanian Travel and Information, Devonport Showcase, 5 Best St; (03) 6424 4466. **Accommodation:** 5 hotels, 3 motels, 6 B&B, 3 hostels, 5 cara./camp. parks.

Dover   Pop. 521

MAP REF. 554 E12, 559 K11

This attractive fishing port, south-west of Hobart, was once a convict station. The original Commandant's Office still stands, but the cells, which are underground just up from the wharf, can no longer be seen. From the late 1850s several large sawmills were built, with a large output of first-class timber. The main industries today are fruit-growing, fishing and Atlantic salmon fish-farming. Quaint old cottages and English trees give the town an old-world atmosphere. The three islands in the bay are called Faith, Hope and Charity. **Of interest:** Chartered fishing trips, Atlantic salmon cruises and twilight and adventure cruises on *Olive May*, depart end Jetty Rd; inquire at Tourist information. **In the area:** Attractive scenery and unspoiled beaches, ideal for bushwalking and swimming. Several old graves on Faith Island. **Tourist information:** Church St, Geeveston; (03) 6297 1836. **Accommodation:** 1 hotel/motel, 1 B&B, 1 hostel, 1 cara./camp. park.

Dunalley   Pop. 306

MAP REF. 555 M6, 559 N9

This small fishing village borders on the narrow isthmus connecting the Forestier Peninsula to the rest of Tasmania. The Denison Canal, spanned by a swing bridge, provides access to the east coast for small vessels. **Of interest:** Tasman Memorial, Imlay St, marks first landing by Europeans on 2 Dec. 1642; actual landing occurred to the north-east, near Cape Paul Lamanon. **In the area:** Just east, Bangor Farm, on Arthur Hwy, a conservation and sheep and cattle farm, once home of Oyster Bay Aborigines, also site of Abel Tasman's landing; tours available, bookings essential; (03) 6253 5233. Collection of memorabilia in museum at Copping, 11 km N. **Tourist information:** Dunalley Hotel, 210 Arthur Hwy; (03) 6253 5101. **Accommodation:** 2 B&B.

A Convict Past

The infamous Port Arthur settlement ruins are the greatest historic tourist attraction in Tasmania. The fact that they were a place of incarceration for more than 12 000 prisoners has been blurred by time but it is still possible, particularly in bleak weather, for the ruins to create something of the atmosphere of hopelessness and misery that existed there about 160 years ago.

Port Arthur is on the Tasman Peninsula, which extends from the Forestier Peninsula south-east of Hobart, screening Pitt Water and the Derwent estuary from the Tasman Sea. Both peninsulas are very beautiful, with sweeping pastures, timbered areas, sheltered bays and towering cliffs.

Eaglehawk Neck is the isthmus between the two peninsulas. In the days of the penal colony, dogs were tethered in a tight line across the Neck to prevent escapes. The line was continually patrolled and guard posts were established in the nearby hills. No prisoner ever broke through this barrier, although some did swim or sail to freedom. A major Port Arthur conservation project was completed in 1986. Among the ruins still standing are the church, penitentiary, guard tower, hospital and model prison. Buildings that have been restored include the home of exiled Irish rebel William Smith O'Brien, the Commandant's House and the Junior Medical Officer's House. The restored former lunatic asylum is a museum and gift shop. Introductory walking tours of the site are conducted all year round, between 9.30 a.m. and 4 p.m.

The settlement was established by Governor Arthur in 1830 and, although transportation ceased in 1853, it was not abandoned until 1877. Many buildings were demolished by contractors and others were badly damaged by bushfires in 1895 and 1897. Today, nocturnal historical 'ghost tours' through the settlement are an unforgettable experience; they begin at 8.30 p.m. in winter and 9.30 p.m. during daylight saving. The site is open daily; an entrance fee allows visitors access to over 40 hectares of ruins and sites.

In Port Arthur Bay stands the Island of the Dead, with its 1100 convict, free settler, prison staff and military graves. As well as harbour cruises, a ferry makes regular trips to this unique island cemetery from Port Arthur.

For further information, contact Port Arthur Historic Site, Clougha, Port Arthur 7182; (03) 6250 2363. **See also:** Entries for Port Arthur and Eaglehawk Neck in A–Z listing.

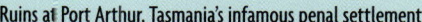

Ruins at Port Arthur, Tasmania's infamous penal settlement

Evandale, an historic village near Launceston

Eaglehawk Neck   Pop. 150

MAP REF. 555 N8, 559 O9

In convict days this narrow isthmus, which separates the Tasman from the Forestier Peninsula, was guarded by a line of ferocious tethered dogs. Soldiers and constables also stood guard, to ensure that no convicts escaped from the notorious convict settlement at Port Arthur. The only prisoners to escape did so by swimming or by boat. The town today, in complete contrast, is a pleasant fishing destination. A charter tuna-fishing fleet operates from Pirate's Bay. **Of interest:** Restored historic officers' quarters, next to Officers Mess, off Arthur Hwy. **In the area:** Tessellated Pavement, 1 km N. Unusual natural features 4 km E in Tasman Arch State Reserve, off Arthur Hwy: Tasman's Arch, Devil's Kitchen and Tasman Blowhole. Tasmanian Devil Park, a wildlife refuge centre, 12 km S. Fortescue Forest Reserve, south along coast from Waterfall Bay to Munro Bight, for water sports and picnics; coastal walking track from Waterfall Bay to Fortescue Bay. Good sailing in Eaglehawk Neck Bay. Port Arthur Convict Settlement, 21 km SW. **Tourist information:** Officers Mess, off Arthur Hwy; (03) 6250 3635. **Accommodation:** 1 hotel, 1 motel, 1 B&B. **See also:** A Convict Past; Tours from Hobart.

Evandale   Pop. 772

MAP REF. 557 P12, 561 M9

This little township, 20 km from Launceston, has been proclaimed an historic village. Founded in 1829, some of its buildings date from 1809. Originally it was named Morven but was renamed in 1836 in honour of Tasmania's first Surveyor-General, G. W. Evans. Streetscapes remain unspoiled by progress and there are many buildings of historical and architectural significance. **Of interest:** Self-guide Heritage Walk from Tourism and History Centre, High St; brochure available. Also in High St: Solomon House (1836), now a cafe, also has accommodation; St Andrew's Anglican (1871) and Uniting (1839) churches; Blenheim (1840s), now workshop with antiques and sales of stained glass. Clarendon Arms Hotel, Russell St, has mural depicting early history of area. Cornwall Cottage, Scone St, has variety of unusual bicycles for hire. Market, each Sun. a.m. at Falls Park, Russell St. Feb.: Village Fair and National Penny Farthing Championships. Nov.: Railex (model train exhibition). **In the area:** Clarendon (1836), 8 km S near Nile, a Georgian mansion designed in grand manner set in extensive formal gardens. At Deddington, 24 km SE, chapel (1840), on private land, designed by artist John Glover who bought land where town now stands; Glover's grave beside chapel.

Tourist information: 18 High St; (03) 6391 8128. **Accommodation:** 2 hotels, 5 B&B. **See also:** Stately Homes.

Exeter   Pop. 394

MAP REF. 557 L7, 561 L7

Exeter, once a busy shipyard town 24 km NW of Launceston, now serves a large fruit-growing area. **In the area:** To the north-east, former river towns of Gravelly Beach (5 km E) and Paper Beach (9 km E). Walking track (5 km return) from Paper Beach to Supply River; near mouth of Supply River, 10 km N off Gravelly Beach Rd, ruins of first water-driven flour mill in Tasmania, built 1825. Five wineries in West Tamar area; Wine Centre in Tamar Court Restaurant, in Main Rd; Tasmanian Wine Route, brochure available from Tourist information. Notley Fern Gorge, Notley Hills, 11 km S, a 10-ha rainforest reserve with picnic/barbecue areas. Brady's Lookout, 5 km SE in State Reserve, a rocky outcrop used by notorious bushranger Matthew Brady. On Rosevears Dr. which begins just south of Exeter: historic Rosevears Hotel, first licensed 1831; Waterbird Haven, a wetlands habitat with treetop hide; Clever Hands Crafts; monument to John Batman's locally-built ship *Rebecca*, in which he crossed Bass Strait to Yarra River; St Matthias Vineyard; Strathlynn Wine Centre. Grindelwald Swiss Village, 10 km SE, a Swiss-architectural style village. At Robigana, 4 km SE, Artisan Gallery and Robigana Appleshed Crafts. **Tourist information:** Tamar Visitor Centre, Main Rd; (03) 6394 4454. **Accommodation:** 3 B&B.

Fingal   Pop. 428

MAP REF. 559 P1, 561 P10

In the Esk Valley, 21 km inland from St Marys on the South Esk River, Fingal is the headquarters of the State's coal industry. The first payable gold in Tasmania was found in 1852 at The Nook, near Fingal. **Of interest:** Historic buildings: St Joseph's Church, Grey St; Masonic Lodge, Brown St. In Talbot St: St Peter's Church; Holder Bros. General Store; Fingal Hotel, with its collection of over 340 brands of Scotch whisky. Fingal History Room, by appt only; inquire at Tourist information. On eastern outskirts, view coal-washing process at Cornwell Coal Company washery. Mar.: Fingal Valley Festival (incorporating World Coal Shovelling Championships and Roof Bolting Championships). **In the area:** Evercreech Forest Reserve, 30 km N, on road to Mathinna, features an 89-m white gum; also picnic/barbecue area and walking tracks. Mathinna Falls, 36 km N near Mathinna; picnic/barbecue area nearby. At Avoca, 27 km NE, historic buildings; town located in foothills of Ben Lomond. **Tourist information:** Old Tasmanian Hotel Community Centre, Talbot St; (03) 6374 2344. **Accommodation:** 1 hotel. **See also:** Stately Homes.

Franklin   Pop. 462

MAP REF. 554 E9, 559 K10

This timber milling town, 45 km SW of Hobart, was the site of the first European settlement in the Huon district in 1804. It was named after Governor Sir John Franklin, who took up 259 ha on the banks of the Huon River. Timber milling has been an important local industry since the very early years. Orcharding and dairy farming are the other main industries. **Of interest:** On Main Rd: Franklin Tea Gardens by the river with cottage gardens, craft and curios and tasty local produce; Franklin Lodge, one of the State's most established colonial accommodation places. **Tourist information:** Huon River Jet Boats, Esplanade, Huonville; (03) 6264 1838. **Accommodation:** Limited.

Geeveston   Pop. 826

MAP REF. 554 D10, 559 J10

This important timber town is the gateway to Tasmania's south-west World Heritage Area. **Of interest:** Forest and Heritage Centre, Church St, a tourist complex featuring an interpretive 'forest room' and Hartz Gallery (wilderness art and craft). **In the area:** Arve Valley west of town contains world's tallest (87 m) hardwood trees. Hartz Mountains National Park, 23 km SW off Arve Rd, self-guide brochure available at Tourist information; bird-watching, waratah and other wildflowers in spring and summer; short walks to waterfalls and glacial tarns. Arve Road Forest Drive, includes Arve River Picnic Area (10 km W); Big Tree Lookout (15 km W); Keoghs Creek Walk (15 km W); and Tahune Forest Reserve (27 km W); where camping, fishing and rafting allowed. Cruises on Huon River available from Port Huon, 4 km NE. **Tourist information:** Forest and Heritage Centre, Church St; (03) 6297 1836. **Accommodation:** 1 B&B.

George Town   Pop. 5026

MAP REF. 557 K4, 561 K6

Situated at the mouth of the Tamar River, George Town (Australia's third settled town, after Sydney and Hobart) was settled by Europeans in 1811, when it was named for King George III. Today it is a commercial centre, mainly as a result of the Comalco plant at Bell Bay and other industrial developments. **Of interest:** Self-guide Discovery Trail of region, brochure available at Tourist information. Monument on Esplanade commemorates an unintentional landing in 1804, when Lieut.-Col. William Paterson and his crew in HMS *Buffalo* ran aground during a storm. The Grove (c. 1838), cnr Elizabeth and Cimitiere sts, now serves Devonshire teas and lunches. Market, 2nd Sat. each month. Jan.: Folk Festival. **In the area:** Comalco and BHP Temco plants, Bell Bay, 6 km S; tours available, inquire at Tourist information. At Hillwood, 24 km SE, apple orchards and a pick-your-own strawberry farm. Lefroy, 10 km E, ghost town of goldmining settlement with ruins, old diggings and cemetery. Several wineries in Pipers Brook region to the east, including Rochecombe, Delamere, Pipers Brook, Heemskerk, Dalrymple and Brook Eden; open for tastings and cellar-door sales (check times). Tasmanian Wine Route, brochure from Tourist information. Historic maritime village Low Head, 5 km N, has surf and river beaches; Maritime Museum in Australia's oldest continuously used pilot station, opened 1803; nearby, lighthouse and little (fairy) penguin colony, viewed via guided tours at dusk, contact Tourist information. Cruises to fur seal colony at mouth of Tamar River, inquire at Tourist information. **Tourist information:** Main Rd; (03) 6382 1700. **Accommodation:** 2 hotels, 1 hotel/ motel, 2 motels, 3 B&B, 1 hostel, 1 cara./camp. park. **See also**: Stately Homes.

Gladstone   Pop. 200

MAP REF. 561 P6

The small town of Gladstone is a service centre for surrounding dairy, sheep and cattle farms. The district was once a thriving tin and goldmining area, with a colourful early history. Now many of these once substantial townships are ghost towns or nearly so. **Of interest:** Chinese graves at Gladstone Cemetery, eastern outskirts of town. **In the area:** Geological formations south-west in area between Gladstone and South Mount Cameron. At South Mount Cameron, 8 km S, Blue Lake, a disused tin mine filled with brilliant blue water coloured by pyrites. Mt William National Park, 25 km E, has prolific flora and fauna, and excellent beaches. Historic lighthouse at Eddystone Point, 35 km E. **Tourist information:** Gladstone Hotel, Chaffey St; (03) 6357 2143. **Accommodation:** 1 hotel.

Hadspen   Pop. 1334

MAP REF. 557 N11, 561 L9

The township of Hadspen, which was first settled in the early 1820s, has many historic buildings some of which offer accommodation and/or meals. **Of interest:** Row of Georgian buildings, Main Rd: Red Feather Inn (c. 1844); old coaching station; Hadspen Gaol (c. 1840); Church of the Good Shepherd, building of church commenced in 1858, funded by Thomas Reibey, who withdrew his support after a dispute with the bishop; church was completed in 1961, almost 50 years after Reibey's death. **In the area:** Entally House (1819), 1 km W on banks of South Esk River, one of Tasmania's most famous historic homes; magnificent collection of Regency furniture and fine silverware. Carrick, 5 km SW, fine examples of Georgian and Victorian buildings; Agfest held each May. **Tourist information:** Tasmanian Travel and Information Centre, cnr St John and Paterson sts, Launceston; (03) 6336 3133. **Accommodation:** 1 hotel/motel, 1 cara./camp. park. **See also:** Stately Homes.

Hamilton   Pop. 150

MAP REF. 554 D1, 559 J6

A classified historic town in a rural setting, Hamilton has retained many of its colonial buildings. **Of interest:** Old School House (1858), Lyell Hwy, B&B accommodation and antique shop in grounds. Glen Clyde House (c. 1840), Grace St, now craft gallery with works representing over 100 craft artists and tearooms. **In the area:** Meadowbank Lake, 10 km NW, a popular venue for picnics, boating, water-skiing and trout fishing. Sheep Centre, 4 km W, has sheep shearing and mustering demonstrations; pre-bookings only, contact Tourist information. Old MacDonalds Tourist Farm, 28 km SW, a children's adventure farm. **Tourist information:** Council Offices,

National Parks

Tasmania packs an incredible variety into a remarkably compact area. Even in a few days you can experience a surprising cross-section of the natural and cultural heritage that help make Tasmania unique. But the best of the island State, from wild rivers and deep forests to grand mountains and ancient cave shelters, is to be found in its national parks. The island's landscape is shaped by ice as much as by isolation. In the national parks you can find mountains, tarns and lakes carved out during the past Ice ages, and a unique flora and fauna that survives from ancient times. The rainforests are clothed in trees that trace their origins back to the supercontinent of Gondwana. Nowhere else in Australia is there such rich and unusual flora and fauna.

The Parks and Wildlife Service of Tasmania manages the State's 15 national parks and also the many State reserves with their Aboriginal sites, caves, gorges, waterfalls, rivers and European historic sites that date back as far as 1803, when Europeans first arrived.

All parks are accessible year round, and a park entry fee applies in all national parks. Some tourists believe the highland parks are best seen in summer and autumn, when the weather is more reliable, when wildflowers bloom in profusion and when flowering trees and shrubs attract birdlife. Bushwalking in the parks is popular, however in the highland parks, there can be sudden storms even in summer. Bushwalkers are advised to be prepared for sudden changes in the weather.

In the south-west of the State

Mount Field National Park, just 80 kilometres north-west of Hobart, is a popular tourist venue, offering a diversity of activities ranging from picnicking to overnight bushwalking. It also has the only developed skiing area in southern Tasmania. There are several waterfalls in the park, the best-known being Russell Falls, first seen by Europeans in 1856. Here the cascading water plunges in two stages into a forested valley where tree ferns filter sunlight and create a mosaic effect. The forest includes large myrtles, giant 250-year-old gum trees, sassafras, huge tree ferns, the unique horizontal scrub and a variety of mosses, ferns, lichens and fungi. There are many walks, including the aptly named Tall Trees Walk and a circuit walk that takes in Russell, Horseshoe and Lady Barron falls.

A 1½-hour drive from Hobart, through Geeveston to the south-west, brings visitors to the **Hartz Mountains National Park**. Most of the area is over 600 metres in altitude with Hartz Peak being 1255 metres high. There are basic facilities for the day visitor and no camping facilities, although camping is permitted. Bushwalking is popular with visitors to the park.

Tasmania's largest national park is **Southwest National Park**, which has 605 213 hectares of mainly remote wilderness country. Here there are dolerite- and quartzite-capped mountains, sharp ridges and steep valleys left by glaciers. The dense forests are made up of eucalypts, myrtles, sassafras and leatherwood, often covered with mosses, ferns and lichens, and tangled with pink-flowered climbing heath and bauera. Climbers will find a challenge in Federation Peak, Mount Anne and Precipitous Bluff, while anglers will be kept busy with trout fishing at lakes Pedder and Gordon. A specially-built bird hide at Melaleuca can be used in summer to observe the rare and endangered orange-bellied parrot.

The 440 000-hectare **Franklin-Gordon Wild Rivers National Park** forms the central portion of Tasmania's World Heritage Area. The Franklin attracts wilderness adventurers from around the world to test its challenging rapids. Along the slightly more placid lower Gordon River are stands of 2000-year-old Huon pine. Unusual buttongrass vegetation, growing right to the edge of the water, stains it the colour of tea. The Lyell Highway, the road link between Hobart and the west coast, runs through the park. A number of excellent short walks lead off the highway to rainforests, waterfalls and spectacular lookouts.

In the central north of the State

Covering some of Tasmania's highest country is **Cradle Mountain-Lake St Clair National Park**. There is a visitor centre near the park entrance at Cradle Mountain, and a nature walk into the nearby rainforest. Cradle Mountain has a variety of fine bushwalks, including one of Australia's best-known walking routes, the 85-kilometre Overland Track, through forests of deciduous beech, Tasmanian 'myrtle', pandanus, King Billy pine and a wealth of wildflowers. Cradle Mountain Wilderness Lodge lies on the northern boundary of the national park. At the other end of the park, there is a new visitor centre with displays on the

Bushwalking in Cradle Mountain-Lake St Clair National Park

TASMANIA

history of the area. The tranquil Lake St Clair, with a depth of over 200 metres, occupies a basin gouged out by glaciers more than 20 000 years ago. The Lake St Clair Park Centre features a hologram of the thylacine (Tasmanian tiger) and a life-size model of its ancient predecessor the thylacoleo. Cruises operate daily, and a 5–8 day trek traverses the park, taking in Mt Ossa (Tasmania's highest mountain) and a range of highland lakes and waterfalls. There are several campsites and cabins, and luxury accommodation nearby.

Steep, jagged mountains create a natural amphitheatre at the **Walls of Jerusalem National Park** (51 800 hectares), and ancient forests of pencil pines ring tiny glacially-formed lakes, making the park very popular with bushwalkers. The park is not accessible for day trips.

In the north of the State

The central north coastal strip of **Asbestos Range National Park** is an important refuge for a wide variety of birds, as well as wombats, kangaroos and wallabies. Its islands off Port Sorell provide an important breeding area for little (fairy) penguins, and the tidal and mud flats are ideal feeding grounds for a variety of migratory seabirds. On the unspoiled beaches, white sands come to life with thousands of soldier crabs.

Further west along the coast, **Rocky Cape National Park** (3064 hectares) encompasses rugged coastline with small sheltered beaches backed by heath-covered hills. It is known for its rock shelters used for over 8000 years by Tasmanian Aborigines.

In the north central region, the new **Mole Creek Karst National Park** is in the forested hills below the impressive Western Tiers. Underground streams have made caves with splendid calcite formations. Guided tours of King Solomons and Marakoopa caves are available.

In the east of the State

Many of Tasmania's national parks are important wildlife reserves. One such park, the 13 899-hectare **Mount William National Park**, is a sanctuary for native animals, including the Forester kangaroo (Tasmania's only kangaroo), echidna, wombat, pademelon, Bennett's wallaby and Tasmanian

devil. Spring brings a carpet of wildflowers to this park: red and white heaths, golden wattle and guinea flower. At Lookout Point, thousands of colourful rock orchids cover the granite rocks. Sheltered bays and beaches complete this little-known but beautiful park.

Fifty kilometres south-east of Launceston is **Ben Lomond National Park**, one of Tasmania's two main ski fields offering both downhill and cross country skiing, with an alpine village, ski-tows, ski hire, a tavern with accommodation, and a public shelter.

A short distance north of Freycinet National Park is **Douglas-Apsley** (16 080 hectares). Proclaimed in 1990, this park contains the State's last large dry sclerophyll forest and can be traversed along a 3-day north-south walking track. Here lightly forested ridges contrast with patches of rainforest and river gorges. Waterfalls and spectacular coastal views add to the grandeur of the area.

Freycinet National Park offers wide stretches of white sands, rocky headlands, granite peaks, quiet beaches and small coves, and an excellent choice of short and long walking tracks. Freycinet

National Park also includes Schouten Island, separated from the Freycinet Peninsula by a kilometre-wide passage, and reached only by boat. Near the park is Coles Bay, a fishing and swimming destination with delightful coastal scenery and a range of accommodation.

Maria Island, off the east coast, is well worth a visit. You can get there either by light aircraft or by passenger ferry from Louisville. On arrival, it seems as if you have stepped into another world, for on Maria Island no tourist vehicles are permitted. This island national park embraces magnificently coloured sandstone cliffs and is a refuge for over 80 species of birds. Forester kangaroos, emus and Cape Barren geese roam freely in this unspoiled landscape. Its intriguing history and historic buildings date back to the convict era which began in 1825.

For further information on Tasmania's national parks, contact the Parks and Wildlife Service, 134 Macquarie Street, Hobart (GPO Box 44A, Hobart 7001); (03) 6233 6191.

Tarleton St; (03) 6286 3202. **Accommodation:** 1 hotel, 1 B&B.

Hastings
Pop. 20

MAP REF. 554 D13, 559 J12

This tiny town, about 100 km SW of Hobart on the Huon Hwy, attracts many tourists to its famous dolomite caves, local gemstones and nearby scenic railway. **In the area:** Hastings Forest Tour, self-drive with cassette guide available from Tourist information and other outlets, begins off Hastings Rd and heads north-west to Esperance River. Hastings Caves, 13 km NW, tours of illuminated Newdgate Cave, swimming in thermal springs pool, streamside walks and picnic/barbecue facilities. Lune River, 2 km S, a haven for gem collectors. Beyond river, 2 km further S, Ida Bay Scenic Railway, originally built to carry dolomite, now carries passengers 7 km to Deep Hole and back; picnic facilities at both ends of track (check departure times at Tourist information). Cockle Creek, 41 km S, in Southwest National Park at the start of extended South Coast Walking Track, offers fishing, boating and bushwalking. Southport, 6 km SE, originally a fishing port in days of sealers and whalers, offers good fishing, swimming, surfing and bushwalking. **Tourist information:** Church St, Geeveston; (03) 6297 1836. **Accommodation:** None. **See also:** Tours from Hobart.

Huonville
Pop. 1524

MAP REF. 554 F8, 559 K9

Huonville is a busy commercial centre serving the nearby townships, and is also the centre for the surrounding apple-producing area. As well as producing apples, the nearby Huon Valley is the State's cherry-growing centre and in summer roadside stalls and pick-your-own orchards sell cherries. Other stone fruits are also grown in the area. The valuable softwood now known as Huon pine was discovered in this district. **Of interest:** Model Train World, Main Rd. Horseback Wilderness Tours, Sale St. Pedal boat and aqua bike hire, Esplanade. **In the area:** River jet-boat rides over rapids to Glen Huon. Apple and Heritage Museum just out of Grove, 6 km NE. Possum's Country Market, 4 km N on Huon Hwy, for craft. Antique Motor Museum near Ranelagh, 5 km NW. Snowy Range Trout Fishery, Little Dennison River, 25 km NW. Scenic

drives: west to Glen Huon, Judbury and Ranelagh; south east to Cygnet. Model Miniature Village and apple carvings at Glen Huon, 8 km W. At holiday town of Port Huon, 10 km SW, river cruises visit salmon farms on river. **Tourist information:** Huon River Jet Boats, Esplanade; (03) 6264 1838. **Accommodation:** 1 hotel. **See also:** Tours from Hobart.

Kettering
Pop. 295

MAP REF. 554 H9, 559 L10

This town on the Channel Hwy south of Hobart serves a large fruit-growing district. **Of interest:** Bruny Island ferry, leaves several times daily from Ferry Rd terminal; extra services during holidays. Oyster Cove Inn and marina, Ferry Rd. Variety of boats for hire; skippered cruises available. **In the area:** Bruny Island. Channel Historical and Folk Museum, 5 km N, open Nov.–Apr., inquire at Tourist information. At Snug, 8 km N: Mother's Favourites, for seafood; holiday cottages; pleasant walks in Snug Falls Track area. Nearby, Coningham Beach, for good swimming and boating. Woodbridge Hill Hand-weaving Studio, 4 km S on Woodbridge Hill Rd. Monument to French explorer Admiral Bruni D'Entrecasteaux, 21 km S at Gordon. **Tourist information:** Bruny D'Entrecasteaux Visitor Centre, Ferry Rd; (03) 6267 4494. **Accommodation:** 1 hotel/motel, 1 cara./camp. park.

Kingston
Pop. 12 907

MAP REF. 554 H7, 559 L9

Kingston, 12 km S of Hobart, is the administrative centre for the nearby area. **Of interest:** Display at Federal Government's Antarctic research headquarters, southern outskirts on Channel Hwy; open Mon.–Fri. Mar.: Kingborough Festival. Oct.: Olie Bollen Festival (relates to Dutch community). **In the area:** Scenic drives south through Blackmans Bay, Tinderbox and Howden; magnificent views of Droughty Point and Bruny Island from Piersons Point. Small blowhole at Blackmans Bay, 7 km S at reserve on Blowhole Rd; spectacular in stormy weather. Boronia Hill Flora Trail (2 km) follows ridgeline between Kingston and Blackmans Bay through remnant bush. Old shot tower, 7 km NE near Taroona; wonderful views of Derwent River estuary from top of tower. **Tourist information:** Tasmanian Travel and Information Centre, 20 Davey St,

Hobart; (03) 6230 8233. **Accommodation:** 2 hotel/motels, numerous B&B.

Latrobe
Pop. 2551

MAP REF. 556 E6, 560 I7

This historic township is situated on the Mersey River, 9 km SE of Devonport. Once a busy shipyard town, today it is the site of one of the biggest cycling carnivals in Australia, held at Christmas. **Of interest:** Many early buildings and shopfronts dating from 1840s, some National Trust-classified; self-guide walk, leaflet available from Tourist information. Court House Museum, Gilbert St, for local history. Bells Parade, off Gilbert St along riverbank, has picturesque reserve and picnic areas. Also on Bells Parade, Sherwood Hall is an historic timber structure. Markets, each Sun. at Gilbert St and James St. Jan.: Latrobe-Port Sorell Summer Festival (continues into Feb.); Australia Day Carnival; Henley-on-the-Mersey. Dec.: Latrobe Wheel Race and Latrobe Gift. **In the area:** Myrtle Hole, 3 km S, for picnics and water sports. Henry Somerset Orchard Reserve, 7 km S, has native orchids and other rare flora. **Tourist information:** Shop 1, 70 Gilbert St; (03) 6426 2693. **Accommodation:** 2 hotels, 1 motel, 2 B&B.

Launceston
Pop. 66 747

MAP REF. 557 N10, 561 L8

Although it is Tasmania's second-largest city and a busy tourist centre, Launceston manages to retain a relaxed, friendly atmosphere. Nestling in hilly country where the Tamar, North Esk and South Esk rivers meet, Launceston is also at the junction of three main highways and has direct air links with Melbourne and Hobart. It is sometimes known as the Garden City because of its beautiful parks and gardens. **Of interest:** Yorktown Square, The Avenue, Quadrant Mall, Civic Square, and Prince's Square with its magnificent baroque-style fountain and fine surrounding buildings. Main shopping area around the Mall. Old Umbrella Shop, George St, a unique 1860s shop preserved by National Trust. Penny Royal World, Paterson St, a collection of buildings originally sited at Barton, near Cressy, and moved stone by stone to Launceston; includes tavern, museum, working water mill, corn mill, graceful windmill, Mole Hill Fantasy (an ever-popular mole diorama), accommodation and restaurants; linked by restored tramway to Penny Royal Gunpowder Mill at old Cataract quarry site; boat trips available on artificial lake and paddlesteamer cruise on *Lady Stelfox* along the Tamar River and Cataract Gorge. Parks include 5-ha City Park with Monkey Island and conservatory (Design Centre of Tasmania nearby displays contemporary art and craft), end of Cameron St; Royal Park, formal civic park on South Esk River; Zig Zag Reserve, leading to Cataract Gorge area. Queen Victoria Museum and Art Gallery, in Royal Park off Wellington St, with displays of Aboriginal and convict relics, Tasmania's mineral wealth, flora and fauna, early china and glassware, and colonial and modern art. Boags Brewery, William St, has guided tours. Self-guide and guided walking tours, contact Tourist information. Feb.: Country Music Festival. Mar.: A Night in the Gorge. Oct.: Garden Festival; Royal National Show; Tasmanian Poetry Festival. **In the area:** One of Launceston's outstanding natural attractions, spectacular Cataract Gorge, 2 km W of city centre. Historic Kings Bridge (1867) spans the Tamar River at the gorge entrance. Cataract Cliff Grounds Reserve, on north side of gorge, a formal park with lawns, European trees, peacocks and restaurant. Area linked to swimming pool and kiosk on south side by scenic chairlift and suspension bridge. Walks on both sides of gorge. Trevallyn Dam, 6 km W, an attractive picnic spot. Nearby, Australia's only cable hang-gliding simulator. Launceston Federal Country Club Casino, 7 km SW. Punchbowl Reserve and Rhododendron Gardens, 5 km SW, has native and European fauna in natural surroundings. Waverley Woollen Mills, 5 km E, offers tours which include historic collection of plant machinery used to create the industry for which Launceston earned national reputation. Alpine Village in Ben Lomond National Park, 60 km SE; open during ski season. St Matthias' Church, Windermere, 15 km N. Tasmanian Wine Route, Pipers Brook and Tamar Valley regions, brochure from Tourist information. Guided tours throughout northern Tasmania; details from Tourist information. Three National Trust historic houses: Entally House, 13 km SW at Hadspen; Franklin House, 6 km S; Clarendon, near Nile, 28 km SE. **Tourist information:** cnr St John and Paterson sts; (03) 6336 3133. **Accommodation:** 17 hotels, 12 motels,

Kings Bridge, Launceston

1 cara./camp. park. **See also:** Anglers Paradise; Stately Homes.

Lilydale
Pop. 333

MAP REF. 557 P6, 561 M7

At the foot of Mt Arthur, 27 km from Launceston, the town of Lilydale has many nearby bush tracks and picnic spots. **In the area:** Tasmanian Wine Route, brochure available from Tourist information. Lilydale Falls Reserve, 3 km N, has two oak trees grown from acorns from Windsor Great Park, planted here on coronation day of British King George IV, 12 May 1937. Scenic walks to top of Mt Arthur (1187 m). Clover Hill Vineyards, 12 km N. At Lalla, 4 km W, Walker Rhododendron Reserve; Appleshed, for local art and craft; Providence Vineyards. Ash tree plantation at Hollybank Forest Reserve, Underwood, 5 km S; picnic/ barbecue areas. Brook Eden Vineyard, 15 km NE. **Tourist information:** Tasmanian Travel and Tourist Information Centre, cnr St John and Paterson sts, Launceston; (03) 6336 3133. **Accommodation:** 1 B&B.

Longford
Pop. 2601

MAP REF. 557 N13, 561 L9

Longford, 22 km S of Launceston, was established in 1813 when former settlers of Norfolk Island were given land grants in the area. Since then it has had two name changes; its previous names were Norfolk Plains and Latour. Now classified as an historic town, it serves a rich agricultural district. **Of interest:** Many historic buildings, including some convict-built and many now converted to self-contained colonial cottage and B&B accommodation. In Wellington St: Christ Church (1839), has outstanding stained-glass window and pioneer gravestones; 'Car in window' and Grand Prix memorabilia at Country Club Hotel. Walking track along South Esk River, inquire at Tourist information. Heritage and Headstones Tour, inquire at Tourist information. The Village Green, cnr Wellington and Archer sts, orginally the town market, now a picnic/barbecue spot. Mar.: Blessing of the Harvest Festival; Brickendon and Woolmers Hunt. Nov.: Longford Village Green Garden Festival. **In the area:** Brickendon (1824), 2 km S, a homestead built by William Archer and still owned by descendants; tours by appt. Cressy, 10 km S, renowned for its fly-fishing at Brumbys Creek, especially in Nov. when mayflies hatch. Woolmers Estate (c. 1816), 5 km SE, working farm, colonial cottages and guided tours of main house and gardens. At Perth, 5 km NE, historic buildings: Eskleigh; Jolly Farmer Inn; Old Crown Inn and Leather Bottell Inn. Longford Wildlife Park, 5 km N, a conservation area for fallow deer and Australian fauna and flora; also has picnic/barbecue areas and constructed lake. Bowthorpe Farm and Gardens, 11 km N, pastoral estate set on South Esk River; Georgian farmhouse, cottage garden and tearooms. **Tourist information:** Council Offices, Smith St; (03) 6391 1303. **Accommodation:** 3 hotels, 3 B&B, 1 cara./camp. park. **See also:** Stately Homes.

Wildlife-Watching

Tasmania's isolation from the Australian mainland ensures some truly unique wildlife-watching experiences. Pademelons, spotted-tailed quolls and eastern quolls are now rare or extinct on the mainland, but are still plentiful in Tasmania. This is largely due to the absence of both foxes and dingoes in this scenic island State. Tasmania is also a haven for a wide variety of birdlife including little (fairy) penguins. Its coastline is home to many of the popular marine mammals.

CRADLE MOUNTAIN - LAKE ST CLAIR NATIONAL PARK

STRAHAN

ASBESTOS RANGE NATIONAL PARK

LOW HEAD

TENTH ISLAND

MOUNT WILLIAM NATIONAL PARK

FREYCINET PENINSULA

MARIA ISLAND NATIONAL PARK

SORELL

HOBART

Smithton • A2 • Burnie • Devonport • George Town • Scottsdale • Gladstone • St Helens • Deloraine • Launceston • St Marys • Rosebery • Zeehan • Queenstown • Campbell Town • Swansea • Strahan • Triabunna • Strathgordon • Sorell • HOBART • Huonville • Port Arthur • Southport
A10 A5 A8 A3 A4 A5 A3 A6 A3 A10

In and around Hobart

Hobart is one of the most accessible places in Australia to view wild peregrine falcons. Visitors who venture down to the Tasman Bridge at dusk in winter might be lucky enough to see these birds of prey in action. Peregrines swoop down on the flocks of starlings returning to roost under the bridge. Keep your binoculars ready to see the peregrines catch their prey in mid-air.

The Thylacine (Tasmanian Tiger)

Along with its smaller relative, the Tasmanian devil, the thylacine (Tasmanian tiger) would have to be one the State's best-known native animals. This is despite the fact that the last recorded thylacine was captured in 1933 and died in 1936. Like a mythical beast, the thylacine has lived on in the popular imagination, sustained by well-publicised but unsubstantiated sightings.

Referred to as the Tasmanian tiger because of the stripes on its back and rump, this lean-bodied marsupial with a large head and short legs is more like a dog in overall appearance.

In recent years, most reported sightings of the thylacine have occurred in the north of the State. However, if you are keen to come face-to-face with this mysterious creature, your best opportunity is to visit the life-size hologram at Lake St Clair Park Centre in Cradle Mountain-Lake St Clair National Park.

For a more tranquil bird-watching experience, visit Orielton Lagoon at **Sorell**, north-east of Hobart. This wetland area is protected by the international Ramsar Convention because of its significance as a habitat for migratory birds. Birds seen wading here at low tide have travelled many thousands of kilometres along the East Asian-Australasian Flyway from as far afield as Siberia. Waders, such as plovers and oystercatchers, feed on the mud flats as the tide is falling and when the tide is almost high they seek a safe roosting place. Tide times are published in The Mercury newspaper; Sorell's low tide is 2.5 hours later than Hobart's. There are a number of access points to the lagoon: from the Sorell Causeway, from Henry Street on the east side of the lagoon and from Shark Point Road. You will need patience, a good field guide, binoculars and, after rain, a pair of gumboots.

On the East Coast

Maria Island National Park, a short ferry-ride from Triabunna on the east coast, is a natural showcase for Tasmania's unique bird species. It is the only national park where all of the State's 11 endemic species can be spotted. Some of these include the yellow wattlebird, Tasmanian thornbill, yellow-throated honeyeater and the dusky robin. This range of birdlife is due to the incredibly diverse habitats on this small island, ranging from ocean, swamp, cleared-grazing and dry sclerophyll, to moist gully environments.

The grasslands of Darlington at the northern end of the island are active with wildlife throughout the day. Bennett's wallabies and pademelons (also a type of wallaby) graze here, as does Tasmania's only kangaroo, the Forester kangaroo. Flocks of Cape Barren geese regularly graze and breed in this area. They pair off to mate in autumn and lay eggs in grassland tussocks. The fluffy goslings develop rapidly in winter and are ready to fly by late spring.

Freycinet Peninsula, roughly mid-way between Hobart and Launceston, offers a range of wildlife-watching opportunities. Bennett's wallabies and pademelons tend to congregate in the Freycinet National Park carpark throughout the day and in

TASMANIA

Tasmanian devils are renowned for their spine-chilling screeches

the grassland by the beaches at dusk. Nocturnal mammals include Tasmanian devils, common brushtail possums and common wombats.

Freycinet Sea Charters operate regular wildlife cruises featuring seasonal sightings of bottlenose and common dolphins, Australian fur seals, white-bellied sea-eagles and southern right and humpback whales.

Moulting Lagoon Game Reserve, located at the beginning of Freycinet Peninsula, is another wetland of international significance protected by the Ramsar Convention. Birds commonly seen here include the migratory waders, as well as black swans, wild ducks, egrets, cormorants, pelicans and birds of prey.

In the North-East of the State

Mount William National Park was originally established as a national park in order to protect its substantial Forester kangaroo population. Forester Kangaroo Drive passes through the pasture area in the northern section of the park, where Bennett's wallabies can also be seen, especially at dawn or dusk. As darkness falls, a whole cast of nocturnal wildlife appears – common wombats, possums, pademelons and eastern quolls are just some of the characters you might expect to see.

Asbestos Range National Park, which has the advantage of being slightly closer to the main ports of Devonport and Launceston, has a similar array of wildlife. These parks are probably the best places in the State to view healthy examples of the icon of Tasmanian wildlife, the Tasmanian devil. This squat little meat-eater, renowned for its spine-chilling screeches, is active after dark, when it roams in search of carcasses.

Bird-watching is a popular activity in the two north-eastern parks. Gulls, oystercatchers, terns, dotterels, pelicans and albatrosses can all be sighted along the coastline. Musselroe Point and Campsite 4 in Mount William National Park and the bird hide behind Bakers Beach in Asbestos Range National Park are prime birdwatching locations.

Also in the north-east is George Town, the jumping off point for cruises to see the Australian fur seal colony at **Tenth Island**. These seals with their endearing whiskered faces can be seen year-round. As the boat approaches, the playful pups swim towards it and dive underneath, while the large bull seals look on from the rocks about 100 metres away. Pelicans, black swans and dolphins are a common sight enroute to the island.

At **Low Head** near George Town, little (fairy) penguins can be viewed at dusk during the breeding period (July to April). Access is by tour only. Inquire at George Town tourist information for cruise and tour details; (03) 6382 1700.

In the West of the State

Cradle Mountain-Lake St Clair National Park is one of the State's best-known wildlife-watching destinations. Visitors are guaranteed to see a range of nocturnal marsupials such as Bennett's wallabies, pademelons, wombats and possums around the camping and accommodation areas, especially in the evenings. Platypuses live in the lakes and streams, but are far more elusive. Tasmanian devils are generally spotted at night on the edges of roadways, ripping apart the carcasses of animals killed by cars.

Strahan is probably best-known as the jumping-off point for cruises along the Gordon River. However, many visitors have discovered another more low-key attraction during the summer months. Every year in late September, the first of thousands of short-tailed shearwaters (muttonbirds) reach their rookery on Ocean Beach, having travelled 15 000 kilometres from the Arctic region. Throughout summer, the sky fills with shearwaters every evening as they return with food for their young.

For more information on wildlife-watching in Tasmania's national parks, contact the Parks and Wildlife Service, 134 Macquarie Street, Hobart (GPO Box 44A, Hobart 7001); (03) 6233 6191. For more information on bird-watching, contact the Bird Observers Club of Australia, 183 Springvale Rd, Nunawading, Victoria 3131; (03) 9877 5342.

WILDLIFE-WATCHING ETHICS

- Do not disturb wildlife or wildlife habitats. Keep the impact of your presence to a minimum. Use available cover or hides wherever possible.
- Do not feed wildlife, even in urban areas. (Note: supervised feeding is allowed at some locations)
- Be careful not to introduce exotic plants and animals – definitely no pets.
- Stay on defined trails.

Mole Creek
Pop. 249

MAP REF. 556 E12, 560 I9

This town, 74 km S of Devonport, serves an important farming and forestry district. It was named after the creek which curiously 'burrows' underground. The unique Tasmanian leatherwood honey from the blossom of the leatherwood tree, which grows only in the rainforests of the west coast of Tasmania, is processed here. Each summer, apiarists transport hives to the nearby leatherwood forests. **Of interest:** Honey Factory, Pioneer Dr., provides viewing of extraction and processing of honey; open Mon.–Fri. **In the area:** Guided tours of fine limestone caves in the new Mole Creek Karst National Park: Marakoopa, 8 km W, also has glow worm display; and smaller but still spectacular King Solomons Cave further 8 km W. Trowunna Wildlife Park, 4 km E. Devils Gullet, 40 km SE, a natural lookout overlooking Fisher River Valley, in World Heritage area; reached by walking track (30-min. return). Popular day bushwalk in Walls of Jerusalem National Park, starts 45 km S. **Tourist information:** Mole Creek Guest House, Pioneer Dr.; (03) 6363 1399. **Accommodation:** 1 hotel, 1 B&B, 1 cara./camp. park.

New Norfolk
Pop. 5822

MAP REF. 554 F4, 559 K8

Colonial buildings set among English trees and hop fields dotted with oast houses give this classified historic town a decidedly English look; the countryside has often been compared to that of Kent in England. On the Derwent River, 33 km NW of Hobart, the town owes its name to the fact that displaced European settlers from the abandoned Norfolk Island settlement were granted land in this area. Although the New Norfolk district produces a majority of the hops used by Australian breweries, the chief industry today is paper manufacture. **Of interest:** River walk from Esplanade to Tynwald Park Wetlands Conservation Area. At Historical Centre in Council Chambers, Circle St: genealogical and other records; also self-guide historic walk leaflets. Scenic lookouts: Peppermint Hill, off Blair St; Pulpit Rock and Four Winds Display Gardens, off Rocks Rd. Old Colony Inn (1835), Montague St, now museum with large antique dolls' house and original

kitchen. On Lyell Hwy: Oast House, Tynwald Park, a hop museum, Hop House Cafe, and art gallery; Bush Inn (1815), claims oldest licence in Commonwealth, although contested by Launceston Hotel. Jet boat rides on Derwent River rapids leave from Bush Inn. St Matthew's Church (1823), Bathurst St, reputedly oldest church still standing in Tasmania; craft centre in adjoining Close. Mar.: Hop Harvest Festival. Aug.: Winter Challenge. Oct.: Spring in the Valley (including open gardens). **In the area:** Tours of Australian Newsprint Mill, 5 km E at Boyer; 24-hrs notice required. Famous Salmon Ponds, 11 km NW at Plenty, hatchery where first brown and rainbow trout in southern hemisphere were bred in 1864; restaurant; museum. Meadowbank Vineyard, 20 km NW. Mt Field National Park, 40 km NW, features impressive Russell Falls. **Tourist information:** Oast House, Tynwald Park (Wed.–Sun.); (03) 6261 1030 or Council Offices, Circle St; (03) 6261 2777. **Accommodation:** 3 hotels, 1 motel, 3 B&B, 1 cara./camp. park. **See also:** Stately Homes; Tours from Hobart.

Oatlands
Pop. 522

MAP REF. 559 M5

This classified historic town on the shores of Lake Dulverton, 84 km N of Hobart, attracts both anglers (lake dries up in times of drought) and lovers of history. It was designated as a garrison town by Governor Macquarie in 1821 and surveyed in 1832. Many of the town's unique sandstone buildings were constructed in the 1830s and it is said that most residents live in historic houses. **Of interest:** Convict-built court house (1829), Campbell St. Holyrood House (1840), High St, has historic gardens. St Peter's Church (c. 1838), William St. Callington Flour Mill (1836), Mill Lane. Lake Dulverton Wildlife Sanctuary, Esplanade. Historic self-guide walks around town and on lake foreshore; brochures from Tourist information. Fielding's Ghost Tours, inquire at Tourist information. Feb.: Rodeo. **In the area:** Convict-built mud walls, 13 km S on Jericho Rd. Trout fishing on Lake Sorell, 29 km NW, and adjoining Lake Crescent. **Tourist information:** Council Offices, 71 High St; (03) 6254 0011. **Accommodation:** 2 hotels, 5 B&B, 1 hostel.

Orford
Pop. 502

MAP REF. 555 N2, 559 O6

Views from this popular holiday town at the estuary of the Prosser River, on the Tasman Hwy, are dominated by Maria Island National Park, 20 km offshore. **Of interest:** Walk along Old Convict Rd follows northern bank of river; starts adjacent to Tourist information. **In the area:** River and sea fishing, and scuba diving. The Thumbs Lookout, 2 km S, overlooks Maria Island. Daily ferry service to Maria Island from Eastcoaster Resort, 4 km NE on Louisville Rd. On Maria Island, historic settlement of Darlington has dormitory-style accommodation and camping; walking trails across island. Wielangta Relic Rainforest Walk, 20 km S, a boardwalk through ancient pocket of rainforest. **Tourist information:** Riverside Villas, Old Convict Rd; (03) 6257 1372. **Accommodation:** 1 hotel/motel, 1 motel, 1 cara./camp. park.

Penguin
Pop. 2876

MAP REF. 556 A4, 560 H6

The Dial Range rises over this quiet town, named after little (fairy) penguins still found in rookeries nearby. **Of interest:** In Main St: St Stephen's Church and Uniting Church, both National Trust-classified. Hiscutt Park, off Crescent St, has working Dutch windmill and tulips in season. The Big Penguin, Main St, is popular for souvenir photographs. Penguin rookeries on eastern outskirts, tours available Dec.–early Mar. East Penguin Flower Gardens, on Old Coast Rd to Ulverstone, are tended by community volunteers. Old School Market, King Edward St, 2nd and 4th Sun. each month. **In the area:** Mt Montgomery, 5 km S, has magnificent view from summit. Mason's Fuschia Fantasy, 6 km S on West Pine Rd, with 750 varieties; open p.m. and Sat. Ferndene Wildlife Reserve, 6 km S, has scenic picnic spot and good walking tracks. Pioneer Park, 10 km SW at Riana, with gardens, walks and picnic facilities. Pindari Deer Farm, 15 km SW, has deer-handling demonstrations. Beyond South Riana (20 km SW), lies Gunns Plains, caves and hop fields. Scenic drive south-east to Ulverstone via coast road. **Tourist information:** Main St; (03) 6437 1421. **Accommodation:** 1 hotel, 2 B&B, 1 cara. park.

TASMANIA

Pontville
Pop. 1125

MAP REF. 554 H3, 559 L7

Much of the freestone used in Tasmania's old buildings was quarried near this classified historic town. On the Midland Hwy, 27 km N of Hobart, Pontville was founded in 1830 and many of its early buildings remain. **Of interest:** Historic buildings on or adjacent to Midland Hwy include: St Mark's Church (1841); The Sheiling (built 1819, restored 1953), behind church; old post office; Crown Inn; and 'The Row', thought to have been built in 1824 as soldiers' quarters, now restored. **In the area:** Towns nearby with interesting historic buildings: Bagdad, 8 km N; Kempton, 11 km further N; Broadmarsh, 10 km W; Tea Tree, 5 km E. Brighton, 3 km S, an important military post; Agricultural Show held each Nov. Bonorong Park Wildlife Centre, 5 km S. **Tourist information:** Council Offices, Tivoli Rd, Gagebrook; (03) 6263 0333. **Accommodation:** None.

Port Arthur
Pop. 190

MAP REF. 555 N10, 559 N10

This historic settlement on the scenic Tasman Peninsula was one of Australia's most infamous penal settlements from the 1830s to the 1870s. Today it is still possible to sense the incredible hardships endured by the early convict population.

The Gourmet Island

Tasmania has a growing reputation for fresh produce and wine, and there is a wide variety of gourmet options available to the traveller.

For an overview of gourmet Tasmania, visit The Taste of Tasmania festival in Hobart, held at Princes Wharf each January. The best of the island's food and wine is on show, from chargrilled seafood to delicious relishes, smoked quail, pink-eye potatoes and Tasmanian wines.

Try to be in Hobart on Saturday to explore the famous Salamanca Market where you will find some of Tasmania's most innovative food producers. The Wursthaus Kitchen, in Montpellier Retreat just off Salamanca Place, is open daily and offers a wonderful range of Tasmanian delicatessan products.

Cascade Premium Lager, with its distinctive Tasmanian tiger label, has become a highly-prized beer in recent years. Tours of the historic brewery in South Hobart are held on weekdays.

The Huon Valley is Tasmania's apple and cherry-growing centre. During the summer months roadside stalls and pick-your-own orchards offer a variety of stone fruits to passing travellers. Fresh apricots are a particular favourite.

Central Tasmania is famous for its trout fishing. Near Miena is the 'Land of Three Thousand Lakes', which provides the angler with the chance to catch fresh trout. For the less dedicated, there are a number of outlets in Tasmania which sell smoked trout. Besides trout, atlantic salmon is one of Tasmania's finest fish. A significant salmon-farming industry has developed on the south coast, and salmon can be purchased across the State. Salmon roe is also popular. Boat tours of the Huon River salmon farms leave daily from Port Huon.

Between Launceston and Hobart are a number of small food producers, including Butlers Butchery in Campbell Town, which specialises in large 'stag snags' (venison sausages).

An unusual place to sample Tasmanian beers is the Pub in the Paddock at Pyengana, near St Helens. It is precisely that: a hotel in the middle of a large empty paddock, where drinkers can share their Premium Lagers with the resident pig.

In the north of the island, travel the Tasmanian Wine Route from Launceston across the Tamar River to Bridport, returning via Lilydale. The highlight of this drive is the Pipers Brook wine region, noted for its good rieslings and, more recently, for its chardonnays and pinot noirs. Like all Tasmanian wine-growing areas, it is relatively new. In less than three decades it has become the State's premier wine region, and is now responsible for half of Tasmania's wine production. Most of the wineries in this region, including Heemskerk, Delamere and Pipers Brook, encourage cellar-door sales.

Strathlynn, a wine-centre and cafe at Rosevears on the west bank of the Tamar, is a pleasant lunch or afternoon tea stop.

West of Launceston is some of the finest dairy country in Australia. Heidi Cheese Farm at Exton, on the highway to Deloraine, specialises in nutty Gruyere, Heidi Barrel and Reblechon.

Off the north-western coast is King Island which has built a strong reputation for its pure cream and double brie. The Island has some great cheeses which visitors can taste at the King Island Dairy, and has also gained a reputation for its crayfish and smoked meats.

Vineyards and fresh food producers are dotted across the island. Take a basket, and stop at roadside stalls and farms to buy the best food and wine that Tasmania has to offer.

Historic Cascade Brewery, famous for its Premium Lager

Of interest: Port Arthur Historic Site: stabilised and restored ruins of the convict settlement, period houses, museum, and Heritage Nursery and Gallery; self-guide and guided walks available. Ghost Tours depart nightly from the Visitor Information Office. Dec.: Boxing Day Woodchop; Absconders Run. **In the area:** Daily cruises on harbour and to Isle of the Dead (1100 convict, military and civil graves). Historic and nature walk to nearby Stewarts Bay, brochures available from Tourist information. Steam-train rides available at the re-created milling settlement of Bush Mill, 1km N. Coal Mines Historic Site, 30 km NW, Tasmania's first operational mine. Palmers Lookout, 3 km S, views of harbour and surrounding coastline. Remarkable Cave, 6 km S on coast, formed by wave action; check tides. **Tourist information:** Visitor Information Office, Historic Site, Arthur Hwy; (03) 6250 2363. **Accommodation:** 2 hotel/motels, 1 hostel, 1 B&B, 1 cara./camp. park. **See also:** A Convict Past.

Port Sorell   Pop. 1494

MAP REF. 556 G5, 561 J6
Sheltered by hills, this well-established holiday town at the estuary of the Rubicon River near Devonport enjoys a mild climate. Named after Governor Sorell and established in 1822, it is the oldest township on the north-west coast. Unfortunately many of its oldest buildings were destroyed by bushfires early this century. **Of interest:** Swimming, fishing, boating and bushwalking. Views from Watch House Hill, off Meredith St, once site of old gaol, now bowling green. Asbestos Range National Park across estuary, with numerous isolated beaches. Jan.-Feb.: Latrobe-Port Sorell Summer Festival. **In the area:** Walking track (3 km one way) from Port Sorell (beach end of Rice St) to Hawley Beach (6 km return), excellent views of Asbestos Ranges and coastline. At Hawley Beach: safe swimming and good fishing; historic Hawley House (1878) offers meals and accommodation. **Tourist information:** Shop 1, 70 Gilbert St, Latrobe; (03) 6426 2693. **Accommodation:** 2 cara./camp. parks. **See also:** National Parks.

Queenstown   Pop. 3368

MAP REF. 558 E3, 560 E12
The discovery of gold and mineral resources in the Mt Lyell field in the

1880s led to the almost overnight emergence of Queenstown. It is a town carved out of the mountains that tower starkly around it. Mining was continuous in Queenstown from 1893 to 1994, and the field produced more than 670 000 tonnes of copper, 510 000 kg of silver and 20 000 kg of gold. Copper Mines of Tasmania resumed mining for copper, silver and gold at the end of 1995; tours of the mine are available. The town has modern shops and facilities, but its wide streets, remaining historic buildings and unique setting give it an old mining-town flavour. In certain lights, multi-coloured boulders on the bare hillsides surrounding the town reflect the sun's rays and turn to amazing shades of pink and gold. **Of interest:** Spion Kop lookout, off Bowes St in town centre. Famous gravel football oval, Bachelor St. Penghana, former mine manager's residence (c. 1898), off Preston St, now a B&B. Guided tours of Mt Lyell Mine depart from Tourist information; surface tours by minibus (1 hr 15 min) and underground mine tours (3½ hrs). Galley Museum, cnr Sticht and Driffield sts, displays history of west coast, photographs and memorabilia. Chairlift, from Penghana Rd, to old silica and limestone quarries; magnificent views, particularly at sunset. Jan.: Mt Lyell Picnic at Lake Bunbury. **In the area:** Scenic flights from Queenstown Airport, Oct.–Apr.; inquire at Tourist information. Spectacular views from Lyell Hwy as it climbs steeply out of town. Original Iron Blow goldmine (1833), off Lyell Hwy at Gormanston, 6 km E. Ghost town of Linda, 9 km E. Mt Jukes Rd lookout, 7 km S; road leads to old mining settlement of Lynchford, and Crotty Dam. Lake Burbury, 25 km S, offers excellent brown and rainbow trout fishing. Lake Margaret Power Station, 12 km N, can be reached on a 4-hr return walk uphill along Penstock Pipe. Lyell Tours, offers 4WD day or half-day tours south to Bird River rainforest area and Mt McCall. **Tourist information:** Mt Lyell Mine Tour Office, 1 Driffield St; (03) 6471 2388. **Accommodation:** 2 hotels, 2 hotel/motels, 3 motels, 1 B&B, 1 hostel, 1 cara./camp. park. **See also:** The West Coast.

Richmond   Pop. 754

MAP REF. 555 J4, 559 M7
Richmond, 26 km from Hobart, is

the most important historic town in Tasmania. The much-photographed Richmond Bridge is the oldest surviving bridge in Australia (1823–25) and many of the town's buildings were constructed in the 1830s or even earlier. Some of these structures, including the bridge, were built by convicts under appallingly harsh conditions. Legend has it that the ghost of an overseer who was murdered by convicts still haunts the bridge. **Of interest:** Self-guide leaflet of town and area, contact Tourist information. Old Richmond Gaol (1825), Bathurst St, one of Australia's best-preserved convict prisons; guided tours available. St John's (1837), St John's Circle, oldest Catholic church in Australia still in use. St Luke's Church (1834–36), Torrens St, has fine timber ceiling. General store and former post office (1832), Bridge St, oldest postal building in Australia. Also in Bridge St: galleries featuring local art and craft, including Saddler's Court (c. 1848) and Peppercorn Gallery (c. 1850); restored Bridge Inn, one of town's oldest buildings, housing complex of shops; Old Hobart Town, a model of Hobart in early 1800s; Toy Museum; The Maze; Village Store (1836), one of oldest general stores still operating in Tasmania. Georgian mansion, Prospect House (1830s) off Hobart Rd, haunted by ghost of Mrs Buscombe; offers meals and colonial accommodation. Feb.: Country Music Festival; St Andrews Pipe Band Competition. May: Harvest Festival. Oct.: Village Fair. **In the area:** Scenic drive north through Campania (7 km) and Colebrook (19 km). Stoney Vineyard, 6 km N, on Colebrook Rd. Crosswinds Vineyard, 10 km NW. **Tourist information:** Saddler's Court Gallery, 48 Bridge St; (03) 6260 2132. **Accommodation:** 1 hotel, 17 B&B, 1 cara./camp park. **See also:** Stately Homes; Tours from Hobart.

Rokeby   Pop. 3495

MAP REF. 553 O10, 555 J6, 559 M8
This old town on the eastern shore of the Derwent River was first settled in 1809. The first apples to be exported from Tasmania were grown here, as was the first wheat ever produced in Tasmania. Rokeby's rural character is now rapidly changing as housing developments occupy the farmland. **Of interest:** Historic cemetery, Rokeby Rd, contains graves of many First

Fleeters. Historic buildings include Rokeby Court and Rokeby House, in Hawthorn Pl. Historic St Matthew's Church (1843), North Pde, some chairs in chancel were carved from wood from ship in Nelson's fleet; church's organ, brought from England in 1825 and first installed in what is now St David's Cathedral, Hobart, is still in use. **In the area**: Historic buildings at Bellerive, 8 km NW. Historic Centre at Rosny, 10 km NW. To the south, excellent surfing at Clifton Beach (9 km); boating and swimming at South Arm (22 km). **Tourist information:** Council Offices, 38 Bligh St, Rosny Park; (03) 6244 0600. **Accommodation:** Limited.

Rosebery
Pop. 1637

MAP REF. 558 E1, 560 E10

Gold was discovered at Rosebery in 1893 in what is now called Rosebery Creek. Huge deposits of lead and zinc were also discovered in the area. Goldmining has long since been abandoned and the town now owes its existence to the zinc mining company Pasminco-EZ; surface tours of mine, inquire at Tourist information. **In the area:** Accommodation available in old miners' cottages. Trout fishing and 4WD tours, inquire at Tourist information. Montezuma Falls, highest waterfall in State, 5 km SW; accessible by 4WD or walking track. Picturesque lake near Tullah, 12 km NE; nearby, historical Wee Georgie Wood Railway, check operating times. **Tourist information:** West Coast Pioneers Museum, Main St, Zeehan; (03) 6471 6225. **Accommodation:** 2 hotels, 1 cara./camp. park. **See also:** The West Coast.

Ross
Pop. 282

MAP REF. 559 M3, 561 N12

One of the oldest and most beautiful bridges in Australia spans the Macquarie River at this classified historic township. The bridge, completed in 1836, was designed by colonial architect John Lee

Stately Homes

One of Tasmania's attractions is its wealth of beautiful stately homes with a distinctly English air. You can dine in style in some, such as **Prospect House** in the historic town of Richmond, and stay in others.

Several of Tasmania's grand old mansions, such as **Malahide** and **Killymoon**, both on the Esk Highway near Fingal, are privately-owned and cannot be inspected, but many of the State's finest homesteads are open daily to the public.

Clarendon, via Evandale, 27 kilometres from Launceston, is probably Australia's grandest Georgian mansion. Completed in 1838 for wool-grower James Cox and given to the National Trust in 1962, it has been meticulously restored.

Three other stately homesteads within reach of Launceston are Franklin House, just 6 kilometres south. Entally House at Hadspen, 18 kilometres from Launceston; and Brickendon in Longford.

Franklin House, an elegant Georgian mansion now owned by the National Trust, was built in 1838 for Mr Britton Jones, a Launceston brewer and innkeeper. In 1842 it became the W.K. Hawkes School for Boys.

Charming **Entally House**, the most historic of the Trust houses, was built in 1819. Set in superb grounds, Entally has a greenhouse, chapel and coach-house. It was opened to the public in 1950.

At Longford, the privately-owned two-storeyed, shuttered **Brickendon**, with its graceful metal front porch, looks French, but long stretches of hawthorn hedges and many old chestnuts, oaks, ash and junipers make it seem part of an English landscape.

Prospect House, Richmond

The Grove in George Town, north of Launceston, is another privately-owned historic house open to visitors. Built in the 1820s, it has been painstakingly restored by the present owners, who dress in period costume to serve lunch and teas.

Home Hill in Middle Road, Devonport, the home of former Prime Minister Joseph Lyons and Dame Enid Lyons, was built by them in 1916. Now open to the public, the house and grounds are owned by the City of Devonport. The contents of the house are owned by the National Trust.

Privately-owned but operated by the Trust, the **White House**, in Westbury, near Deloraine, was built c. 1841 as a corner shop and residence. It stands on a corner of the town's Village Green and houses a unique and varied display of the results of a lifetime of collecting by the owner.

Hobart has two historic houses open for inspection: the National Trust property **Runnymede**, in the suburb of New Town, and **Narryna** in Battery Point. Graceful Runnymede, built c. 1836, has been restored and furnished by the Trust. Narryna, a Georgian sandstone and brick townhouse with a walled courtyard, is set in an old-world garden shaded by elm trees. Also known as the Van Diemen's Land Memorial Folk Museum, it houses a significant collection of colonial artifacts and is owned and operated by the State government.

The misleadingly named **Old Colony Inn** (1835) in New Norfolk was never used as an inn. It serves light lunches and Devonshire teas. Three rooms are set aside for antique objects, including an antique dolls' house. This beautiful old building, set in delightful grounds, has become one of Tasmania's most photographed tourist attractions.

For further information on National Trust properties, contact the National Trust of Australia (Tasmania), 413 Hobart Rd, Franklin Village 7249; (03) 6344 6233.

The West Coast

The beautiful but inhospitable west coast, with its wild mountain ranges, lakes, rivers, eerie valleys and dense rainforests, is one of Tasmania's most fascinating regions. The majestic, untamed beauty of this coast is in complete contrast to the State's pretty pastures. The whole area has vast mineral wealth and a colourful mining history, reflected in its towns. The discovery of tin and copper in 1871 and 1883 started a rush to the west coast, booming at the turn of the century. **Queenstown,** the largest town, and the other main towns – **Zeehan, Rosebery** and **Strahan** – largely owe their existence to mining.

It was not until 1932 that a rough road was pushed through the mountainous country between Queenstown and Hobart. Fortunately, modern road-making techniques have improved the situation and today west coast towns are linked by the Murchison, Zeehan and Waratah highways, and the Lyell Highway (the original road to Hobart) has been brought up to modern standards. In fact, the flooding of Lake Burbury has resulted in the re-routing of the highway, which now takes motorists across the lake itself, enhancing the spectacular entry to Queenstown. Driving round the west coast road circuit and seeing the scenery and towns of the area is an unforgettable experience. The only drawback is that the area is subject to heavy rainfall, even in summer and autumn.

The little township of Zeehan, south-west of Rosebery, typifies the changing fortunes of mining towns. Following the rich silver-lead ore discoveries in 1882, its population swelled to 10 000 and the town boasted 26 hotels and the Gaiety Theatre, with seating for over 10 000, where Dame Nellie Melba sang. Many of these fine buildings from the boom period can still be seen, including the Gaiety Theatre at the Grand Hotel. Zeehan's West Coast Pioneers Memorial Museum, housed in the former School of Mines, is a popular tourist attraction.

One of the most spectacular views on any highway in Australia can be seen as you drive into Queenstown. As the narrow road winds down the steep slopes of Mt Owen, you can see the amazingly bare hills – tinged with pale pinks, purples, golds and greys – that surround the town. At the turn of the century, bushfires combined with logging of trees for fuel for copper smelters denuded the hills. Pollution from the copper smelters in the valley prevented the vegetation from recovering and the high rainfall eroded remaining topsoil, revealing the strangely hued rocks beneath. The copper smelters closed in 1969, and today the hills are slowly recovering.

The first European settlement on the west coast was established in 1821, when the most unruly convicts from Hobart were dispatched to establish a penitentiary on Sarah Island (Settlement Island) in Macquarie Harbour and to work the valuable Huon pine forests around the Gordon and King rivers.

Sarah Island soon became a notorious prison and most of the unfortunate convicts who managed to escape died in the magnificent but unyielding surrounding bush. The horrors of that time are echoed in the name of the entrance to the harbour – Hell's Gates. Today the port of Strahan on Macquarie Harbour has thousands of visitors each year, many attracted to the spectacular Gordon River, one of Tasmania's largest and most remote wild rivers. Cruise boats make regular trips to Heritage Landing at the mouth of the river. On the return trip they stop along the way to allow visitors to see the old convict ruins on Sarah Island. Scenic flights departing from Strahan enable visitors to take in the beauty of more inaccessible areas. Another interesting trip from Strahan is to Ocean Beach, 6 kilometres from the town. This long, lonely stretch of beach, lashed by spectacular breakers, somehow typifies the magnificent wild west coast.

The magnificent scenic wilderness in Tasmania's remote south-west can be reached only by plane or boat. Flights with Par Avion leave Cambridge Airport near Hobart daily. Good fishing, hiking and sailing are offered in this incredibly rugged area of Tasmania; also, sightings of the rare and endangered orange-bellied parrot are becoming more frequent.

See also: individual entries in A–Z listing for those towns indicated by bold type.

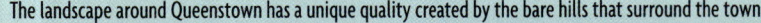

The landscape around Queenstown has a unique quality created by the bare hills that surround the town

TASMANIA

Archer and built by convicts. The convict stonemason Daniel Herbert received a free pardon in recognition for his 186 fine carvings on the bridge. Herbert's grave is in the old burial ground in Park St. Ross was established in 1812 as a military post for the protection of travellers who once stopped there to change coaches. Today it is still an important stopping-place on the Midland Hwy between Launceston and Hobart and has a range of accommodation including self-contained colonial cottages. The district is famous for its superfine wool. **Of interest:** Self-guide leaflet on town and area, contact Tourist information. Ruins of women's prison, off Bond St. In Church St: Tasmanian Wool Centre highlights area's links with wool industry; avenue of English elms complements historic sandstone buildings, including Scotch Thistle Inn and Coach House, former coaching stop; old Ross General Store and Tea Room, now selling Tasmanian crafts and Devonshire teas; Uniting Church (1885) prominent on hill overlooking town; Orderly Rooms, weatherboard building, original headquarters of 50th Ordinance Corps in early 1830s, moved two doors south in 1836 to what is now known as the Memorial Library, Billiard and Recreation Room. In Bridge St, old barracks building, restored by local National Trust; street leads to Ross Bridge (floodlit at night). The four corners of the intersection of Church and Bridge sts at the centre of town are said to represent temptation (hotel), recreation (Town Hall), salvation (church) and damnation (gaol, now a residence). **In the area:** World-class fly-fishing for brown trout in Macquarie River. Some of State's best trout-fishing lakes – Sorell, Crescent, Tooms and Leake – are within an hour's drive of town. **Tourist information:** Tasmanian Wool Centre, Church St; (03) 6381 5466. **Accommodation:** 1 hotel, 1 B&B, 1 cara./camp. park.

St Helens   Pop. 1145

MAP REF. 561 Q8

This popular resort on the shores of Georges Bay is renowned for its crayfish and scalefish. Three fish-processing plants in or near the settlement handle the catch of the fishing fleet based in its harbour. **Of interest:** Bay beaches ideal for swimming, coastal beaches for surfing. Charter boats for deep-sea fishing, and dinghy hire for bay fishing, Tasman

Hwy. Excellent fishing for bream and trout on Scamander River. Many local restaurants specialise in fish dishes. Mar.: Tasmanian Game-Fishing Classic. June: Suncoast Jazz Festival. **In the area:** Bushwalks to view birdlife and wildflowers. Binalong Bay, 11 km NE, has good surf and rock fishing. At Pyengana, 28 km NW: St Columba Falls; Healey's Cheese Factory; the 'Pub in the Paddock', hotel in middle of empty paddock. Several coastal reserves in Bay of Fires district offer camping and good beach fishing. **Tourist information:** St Helens Secretariat, 20 Cecilia St; (03) 6376 1329. **Accommodation:** 2 hotel/motels, 1 motel, 5 B&B, 2 cara./camp. parks.

St Marys   Pop. 629

MAP REF. 561 Q10

The position of this small town, at the junction of the Tasman Hwy and the Esk Main Rd, makes it a busy thoroughfare. At the headwaters of the South Esk River system, St Marys is about 10 km inland. **In the area:** Small coastal township of Falmouth, 14 km NE, an early settlement of historical interest, with several convict-built structures, fine beaches, attractive rocky headlands and good fishing. Spectacular mountain and coast views to south through Elephant Pass, 4 km S. **Tourist information:** St Marys Coach House Restaurant, 34 Main St; (03) 6372 2529. **Accommodation:** 1 hotel.

Scamander   Pop. 407

MAP REF. 561 Q9

This well-developed holiday town, midway between St Marys and St Helens, offers excellent sea and river fishing, and has good swimming beaches. **In the area:** Scenic walks and drives via forestry roads through plantations south of town. Scamander River, noted for bream fishing, trout in upper reaches. Beaches and lagoons at Beaumaris, 5 km N. Trout Creek Reserve, 10 km W, has fishing landing stage and picnic/barbecue facilities. **Tourist information:** St Helens Secretariat, 20 Cecilia St, St Helens; (03) 6376 1329. **Accommodation:** 1 hotel/motel, 1 cara./camp. park.

Scottsdale   Pop. 2020

MAP REF. 561 N7

Scottsdale, the major town in Tasmania's north-east, serves some of the richest

agricultural and forestry country on the island. The town's main industry is food-processing, specialising in the deep-freezing of locally-grown vegetables. **Of interest:** Lyric Theatre Gift Shop & Visitor Information Centre, 29–31 King St, operated as a theatre from 1924–1972, being re-developed to include museum. June: Arts and Crafts Exhibition. Nov.: Agricultural Show. **In the area:** Bridestowe Lavender Farm near Nabowla, 13 km W, for sales of lavender products and tours in flowering season, Dec.–Jan. Sideling Lookout, 16 km W. Golconda, 20 km W, holds Tasmanian Circus Festival each Feb. South Springfield Forest Park, 20 km S. Mt Maurice Forest Reserve, 30 km S. **Tourist information:** Lyric Theatre Gift Shop & Visitor Information Centre, 29–31 King St; (03) 6352 3095. **Accommodation:** 2 hotels, 1 motel, 2 B&B, 1 cara./camp. park.

Sheffield   Pop. 992

MAP REF. 556 D9, 560 I8

This town, 30 km S of Devonport, is located in the foothills of Mt Roland, in one of the most scenically attractive areas of the State. The town's economy is based on farming. **Of interest:** 36 murals on various buildings depict area's history; video explanation of murals, at Diversity, Main St. Kentish Museum, Main St, has local history and hydro-electric exhibits. Red Water Creek and Heritage Society runs steam train 1st weekend of month (departs cnr Spring and Main sts) and daily around New Year; check times with Tourist information. Claude Road Hall markets, 3rd weekend in Mar., June, Sept. and Dec. Mar.: Steam Fest. May: Mt Roland Folk Festival. Sept.: Daffodil Festival. **In the area:** Lakes and dams of Mersey-Forth Power Development Scheme, 10 km W. Lake Barrington, created by scheme, a major recreation area; international rowing venue, 14 km SW. Lake Barrington Estate Vineyard, 10 km W, for tastings and sales. Devil's Gate Dam, 13 km NW, with unique semi-circular dam wall; spectacular scenery from viewing areas. Stoodley Forest Reserve, 7 km NE, between Sheffield and Railton; walking tracks and picnic/barbecue areas. Cradle Mountain-Lake St Clair National Park, 61 km SW for bushwalking, spectacular rainforest and mountain scenery, and flora and fauna. **Tourist information:** Kentish

The Nut, Stanley

Museum, 93 Main St; (03) 6491 1861. **Accommodation:** 1 hotel, 2 motels, 2 B&B, 1 hostel, 1 cara./camp. park. **See also:** National Parks.

Smithton   Pop. 3495

MAP REF. 560 C4

This substantial township is the administrative centre of Circular Head, which is renowned for its unique blackwood swamp forests and was the first European settlement in the far north-west. Smithton serves the most productive dairying and vegetable-growing area in the State, and is also the centre of one of Tasmania's most important forestry areas, with several large sawmills. Fishing is another important industry. **Of interest:** Lookout tower, Tier Hill, end of Massey St. Western Esplanade Community Park, centre of town overlooking the mouth of Duck River; fishing, walking and picnic spot. **In the area:** Forestry Tasmania reserves throughout district offer wide range of recreational activities. Duck River and Duck Bay, 2 km N, for fishing and boating. Lacrum Dairy Farm, Mella, 6 km W, has milking demonstrations during summer, afternoon teas, cheese tastings and sales. Nearby, Wombat Tarn has picnic/barbecue area, lookout, bush-walks and playground. At Marrawah, 50 km SW, excellent surfing. Sumac Lookout, 4 km S on Sumac Rd, for views

over Arthur River and surrounding eucalypt forest. Allendale Gardens, 13 km S at Edith Creek, offers rainforest walks and Devonshire teas. Seasonal scenic cruises on Arthur River, 70 km S; closed mid-June–1 Aug. **Tourist information:** Council Offices, Goldie St; (03) 6452 1265. **Accommodation:** 2 motels, 1 B&B.

Sorell   Pop. 3199

MAP REF. 555 K5, 559 M8

Named after Governor Sorell, this town is 23 km NE of Hobart. Founded in 1821, it played an important part in early colonial history by providing most of the grain for the State from 1816–60. It also supplied grain to the colony of NSW for more than 20 years. The area is still an important agricultural district, specialising in sheep farming and forestry. **Of interest:** In Somerville St, Historic Blue Bell Inn. Pioneer Park, Parsonage Pl., has picnic/barbecue facilities. Orielton Lagoon, internationally-significant bird sanctuary, on western shore of town. Nov.: Taste of Sorell. **In the area:** Orani Vineyard, 3 km E. Bream Creek Vineyard, 22 km E. Popular beach areas around Dodges Ferry and Carlton Beach, 18 km S. **Tourist information:** Council Offices, Somerville St; (03) 6265 2201. **Accommodation:** 4 B&B.

Stanley   Pop. 576

MAP REF. 560 D3

This quaint little village, steeped in history, nestles under an ancient rocky outcrop called The Nut, which rises to 152 m sheer on three sides. It was the site for the headquarters of the Van Diemen's Land (VDL) Company, set up in 1825 to establish a high-quality merino wool industry. Then its wharf handled whalers and sailing ships. Today these are replaced by a strong fleet of cray and other fishing boats, but little else has changed. The birthplace of Australia's only Tasmanian prime minister, the Hon. J. A. (Joe) Lyons, Stanley has been declared an historic town and for 5 of the last 7 years has won the State's Premier Tourist Town award. **Of interest:** Historic buildings in wharf area: bluestone bond store, Wharf Rd; former VDL Co. store, in Marine Park, designed by colonial architect John Lee Archer, who lived in township. Archer's own home, now Poet's Cottage, Alexander Tce, at base of The Nut; not

open to public. Also in Alexander Tce, Lyons Cottage, birthplace of J. A. Lyons. Other historic buildings in Church St include: still-licensed Union Hotel (1849), with its nest of cellars and narrow stairways; Commercial Hotel (1842), now private residence; Stanley Craft Centre with fine Tasmanian craft. Next door, Discovery Centre Folk Museum. Chairlift, from Browns Rd to top of The Nut (152 m). Graves in burial ground on Browns Rd, dating from 1828, include those of John Lee Archer and explorer Henry Hellyer. Small colonies of little (fairy) penguins near wharf and cemetery, and on Scenic Drive. Nov.: Tasmania Day. Dec.: Agricultural Show. **In the area:** Highfield Historic Site (1835), headquarters of VDL Co., 2 km N on Scenic Dr; homestead, chapel, schoolhouse, barn, stables, workers' cottages and remains of barracks nearby; two arched gates remain of former deer park. Dip Falls, 40 km SE off hwy, via Mawbanna; nearby, Big Tree (giant eucalypt) and picnic area. Pelletising plant of Savage River Mines, Port Latta, 20 km SE, where ore is moved by conveyor to jetty for loading onto bulk ore ships. **Tourist information:** The Nut Chairlift, Browns Rd; (03) 6458 1286. **Accommodation:** 1 hotel, 2 motels, 10 B&B, 1 hostel, 1 cara./camp. park.

Strahan   Pop. 597

MAP REF. 558 D3, 560 D12

This pretty little port on Macquarie Harbour on Tasmania's forbidding west coast is best known as the departure point for cruises to the Franklin-Gordon Wild Rivers National Park. Originally a Huon pine timber-milling town, its growth was boosted by the copper boom at the Mt Lyell mine. When the Strahan–Zeehan railway opened in 1892, it became a busy port. Today it is a popular holiday town with a variety of accommodation, including holiday units and cabins. It is also used as a base by crayfish, abalone and shark-fishing operators, but the harbour is limited by the formidable bar at Hell's Gates, its mouth. **Of interest:** Award-winning Wharf Centre, The Esplanade, has historical display of Tasmania's south-west, from Aboriginal times to present. Adjacent, Morrison's Mill, one of three remaining Huon pine sawmills. Tuts Whittle Wonders, Reid St, features carvings from driftwood. Excellent views of township and harbour from Water Tower Hill. Mineral and gemstone museum, Innes St. Jan.: Mt Lyell Picnic. Mar.: Piners' Festival. **In the area:** Ocean Beach, Tasmania's longest beach, 6 km W, offers area for trail rides, and beach fishing; also has a muttonbird rookery. Teepookana Forest Reserve, 15 km S, features Huon pines, walking tracks, viewing platform and historic bridge. At Henty Dunes, 12 km N on Strahan–Zeehan Hwy, spectacular, vast sand dunes, lagoon and picnic/barbecue areas. Cruises available include upstream along the Gordon River to Heritage Landing and infamous Sarah (or Settlement) Island, Tasmania's first and most brutal penal establishment; and across Macquarie Harbour to Hell's Gates. Seaplane flights over Gordon River and Frenchmans Cap, landing at Sir John's Falls or at Heritage Landing for a steamboat ride; depart from The Esplanade. Wild River jet-boat rides; West Coast Yacht Charters, overnight to Gordon River and evening or fishing cruises; South West Coast Adventure 4WD tours, including fishing tour; Huon pine forestry tour; Henty Dunes Tour; Strahan Trail Rides; contact Tourist information. **Tourist information:** Wharf Centre, The Esplanade; (03) 6471 7488. **Accommodation:** 1 hotel, 1 motel, 13 B&B, 1 hostel, 1 cara./camp. park. **See also:** The West Coast.

Swansea   Pop. 418

MAP REF. 559 P4, 561 P13

Swansea is a small town of historical interest on scenic Great Oyster Bay, in the centre of Tasmania's east coast. **Of interest:** Self-guide leaflet on town and area, contact Tourist information. Original council chambers (c. 1860), Noyes St, still in use. On Tasman Hwy: Bark Mill and Yesteryear Museum (c. 1885); restored wattlebark mill machinery; Wine and Wool Centre; tearooms. In Franklin St: Morris' General Store (1838), run by Morris family for over 100 years; Community Centre (c. 1860), has museum with unusually large slate billiard table made for 1880 World Exhibition. Schouten House (c. 1846), Bridge St, once Swansea Inn, now restaurant and colonial accommodation. Meredith House (c. 1853), Noyes St, two-storeyed Georgian house, now offering colonial accommodation. Redcliffe House (c. 1835), on northern edge of town, convict-built farm cottage now offering colonial accommodation. Many colonial accommodation places (some self-contained cottages, some B&B) in and around town. Waterloo Point, at edge of golfcourse near town centre, little (fairy) penguin and short-tailed shearwater (muttonbird) viewing at dusk. Coswell Beach, 1 km S along coast from Waterloo Point, little (fairy) penguin viewing at dusk. **In the area:** Splendid views from Duncombes Lookout, 3 km S. Spikey Beach, 7 km S, with picnic area and excellent rock fishing. Kabuki, Japanese restaurant, on clifftop 12 km S. Mayfield Beach, 14 km S, for safe swimming, fishing and walking (track from camping area to Three Arch Bridge). Meetus and Lost falls, 50 km NW. Springvale and Craigie Knowe vineyards, 15 km N, cellar-door sales (weekends and holidays). **Tourist information:** Wine and Wool Centre, 96 Tasman Hwy; (03) 6257 8677. **Accommodation:**

The Bass Strait Islands

King Island and Flinders Island, Tasmania's two main Bass Strait islands, are ideal holiday spots for the adventurous. You can fish, swim, go bushwalking or scuba-dive among the wrecks of the many ships that foundered off their shores last century. Birdwatching is also popular and each spring millions of short-tailed shearwaters (muttonbirds) make a spectacular sight as they fly in to nest in coastal rookeries on the islands.

King Island, at the western end of the strait, is a picturesque, rugged island with an unspoiled coastline of beautiful sandy beaches on the east and north coasts, contrasting with the forbidding cliffs of Seal Rocks and the lonely coast to the south. The island is only accessible by air. The lighthouse at Cape Wickham is the largest in Australia. There is a penguin colony on the breakwater at Grassy Port which can be visited at dusk. Once famous for its seal population and now almost extinct sea lions, the island's main industries today are dairy and beef products, kelp harvesting, fishing and sheep farming. King Island dairy and beef products have earned a reputation for their high quality. The King Island Dairy, on North Rd, is open Sunday to Friday. The main town is Currie, which has a kelp factory. Accommodation includes a hotel, several motels, numerous guest houses, holiday flats, host farms and a caravan/camping park.

Flinders Island is renowned for its excellent fishing, its magnificent granite mountains and its gemstone, the Killiecrankie 'diamond', actually a kind of topaz. The island produces fine woollen products, hand-made chocolates and gourmet fare. Strzelecki National Park, near the civic centre, Whitemark, provides challenging rock climbing. From Whitemark, 4WD tours are available to hills and remote beaches. The island is also popular with scuba divers, naturalists and photographers. Accommodation on the island includes 1 hotel, 1 lodge, host farms and several holiday houses. Flinders is one of more than 50 islands in the Furneaux Group that were once part of the land bridge linking Tasmania with the mainland.

In the 1830s the few surviving Tasmanian Aborigines were settled near Emita in an attempt to save them from extinction. All that remains of the settlement today is the graveyard and the chapel, Wybalenna, which has been restored by the National Trust. Nearby, there are historic displays relating to the Furneaux Islands in the museum.

Fishing is the main industry of the tiny community of Lady Barron to the south, a port village overlooking Franklin Sound and **Cape Barren Island**.

For further information on King Island contact The Trend, Main St, Currie, King Island (for brochures); or for pre-arrival information, contact the King Island Tourist Development Association; 1800 64 5014. For information on Flinders Island, contact Council Offices, Davey St, Flinders Island; (03) 6359 2131 or write to Flinders Island Tourism Assoc., PO Box 143, Whitemark 7255. For information on Cape Barren Island, contact the Cape Barren Island Community Assoc.; (03) 6359 3533. For general information and holiday bookings, contact the Tasmanian Travel and Information Centre, 20 Davey St, Hobart; (03) 6230 8233.

1 hotel/motel, 4 B&B, 2 cara./camp. parks.

Triabunna   Pop. 831

MAP REF. 555 O1, 559 O6

When Maria Island was a penal settlement, Triabunna, 86 km NE of Hobart, was a garrison town and whaling base. Today it is a centre for the scallop and abalone industries, with an important export wood-chipping mill just south of the town. **Of interest:** On The Esplanade: Bicentennial Park, with picnic/barbecue areas; National Trust-run Pioneer Park, featuring machinery exhibits. Jan.: Spring Bay Crayfish Derby. **In the area:** Daily ferry from Eastcoaster Resort at Louisville Point, 7 km S, to historic settlement of Darlington in Maria Island National Park. Local beaches for swimming, water-skiing and fishing. Working Horse Museum, 25 km N. **Tourist information:** Council Offices, cnr Vicary and Henry sts; (03) 6257 3113. **Accommodation:** 1 hotel, 1 hotel/motel, 1 cara./camp. park. **See also:** National Parks.

Ulverstone   Pop. 9923

MAP REF. 556 B5, 560 H6

Situated 19 km W of Devonport, near the mouth of the Leven River, Ulverstone is a well-equipped tourist centre that was established as a town in 1852. Dairying, furniture making, and poultry and vegetable farming are the main industries of the area. **Of interest:** Shrine of Remembrance Clock Tower (1953), Reibey St. History Museum, Main St. On Beach Rd: Riverside Anzac Park, with children's playground and picnic/barbecue areas; Fairway Park, a wildfowl reserve, with giant water-slide. Footpath inscribed with excerpts of 75-year history of Royal Australian Navy leads from town centre to HMAS *Shropshire* Naval Memorial Park, Dial St. Numerous antique, and art and craft shops. Glencraft Puppets, 3 The Quadrant, manufactures Australian wildlife hand puppets and soft toys. Legion Park, Esplanade at West Ulverstone, has magnificent coastal position. Tobruk Park, Hobbs Pde. Boer War Memorial, Queens Gardens, Kings Pde. Weeda Copper, Eastland Dr., for hand-made local copperware. Lookout, eastern end of Upper Maud St. Apex House Market, Grove St, 1st and 3rd

Sun. each month (9 a.m. to 2 p.m.). Oct.: Show. Dec.: Christmas Mardi Gras. **In the area:** Extensive beaches east and west of town, safe swimming for children. Good beach, river and estuary fishing. Miniature railway, 2 km E, check times. Goat Island Sanctuary, 5 km W; walking access to island at low tide only. Scenic views at Preston Falls, 19 km S. Castra Falls, 30 km S. Near Gunns Plains, 24 km SW: hop farm, with visitor centre and tours during harvest time (mid Mar.–mid Apr.); Gunderman Trail Rides, Wings Farm Park; Creative Wood and Floral Designs; Gunns Plains Store; caves featuring underground river and glow worms (guided tours). Walking tracks to viewing platform with spectacular views at Leven Canyon, 41 km SW; beyond, south-west of South Nietta, Winterbrook Rainforest Walk and Falls. **Tourist information:** Car Park Lane, (behind PO); (03) 6425 2839. **Accommodation:** 2 hotels, 3 motels, 3 B&B, 2 cara./camp. parks.

Waratah   Pop. 360

MAP REF. 560 E8

This picturesque little settlement, set in mountain heathland 100 km N of Queenstown, was the site of the first mining boom in Tasmania. In 1900 it had a population of 2000 and Mount Bischoff was the richest tin mine in the world. The deposits were discovered in 1871 by James 'Philosopher' Smith, a colourful local character, and the mine closed in 1947, with dividends totalling 200 pounds for every one pound of original investment. Today the town is experiencing a revival of mining activity at nearby Hellyer Mine, operated by Aberfoyle. **Of interest:** Self-drive tour of town, leaflet available at Tourist information. In Smith St: Waratah Museum and Gift Shop; adjacent, Philosopher Smith's Hut, replica of miner's hut; Atheneum Hall (c. 1887), has portrait of Smith; St James' Anglican Church (1880), first church in Tasmania to be lit by hydro power. Feb.: Axemen's Carnival. **In the area:** River and lake trout fishing. At Corinna, 66 km SW, a fascinating former goldmining town, cruises on Pieman River. **Tourist information:** Fossey River Information Bay, 8 km S on Murchison Hwy; or Council Offices, Smith St; (03) 6439 1231. **Accommodation:** 1 hotel, 1 B&B, 1 cara./camp. park. **See also:** The West Coast.

Westbury   Pop. 1292

MAP REF. 557 K11, 561 K9

A village green, said to be unique in Australia, gives this town, 35 km SW of Launceston, a decidedly English air. Situated on the Bass Hwy, Westbury was first surveyed in 1823 and laid out in 1828; it has several fine old colonial buildings. **Of interest:** Self-guide leaflet on town and area, leaflet available from Tourist information. In Village Green, King St: White House (c. 1841), comprising extensive colonial museum, house, bakery, coachhouse, courtyard and stable complex; former police barracks (c. 1832), now an RSL Club; St Andrews Church. Antique shops and colonial accommodation. On Bass Hwy: Hedge maze; Pearn's Steam World, a large collection of working steam traction engines. Tractor Shed, Veterans Row, a museum of old tractors and farm machinery; also scale-model tractor exhibition. Market, 2nd Sun. each month at St Andrews Church. Mar.: Maypole Festival (includes Morris dancing on Village Green); St Patrick's Day Festival. Nov.: Steam Spectacular. **In the area:** At Hagley, 5 km E, St Mary's Anglican Church, noted for fine east window donated by Lady Dry, wife of Sir Richard Dry, first Tasmanian-born premier. Culzean, open garden, William St, 5 km N, open Sept.–May. Trout fishing at Bushy Lagoon, 15 km NW, and Four Springs, 15 km NE. **Tourist information:** Old Bakehouse, 52 William St; (03) 6393 1140. **Accommodation:** 1 hotel, 3 B&B. **See also:** Stately Homes.

Wynyard   Pop. 4679

MAP REF. 560 F5

Within a short driving distance of many varied attractions, this small centre at the mouth of the Inglis River, west of Burnie, has become a well-developed tourist centre, offering a range of accommodation and sporting facilities. There are daily flights between nearby Burnie-Wynyard airport and Melbourne. The Waratah–Wynyard region is a prosperous dairying and mixed-farming district and the town has a large, modern dairy factory. **Of interest:** Table Cape Tulip Farm; open in season. Oct.: Tulip Festival. **In the area:** 'Scenic Walks of Wynyard and Surrounding Districts' brochure available from Tourist information; network of nature walks, including boardwalk along Inglis

TASMANIA

River. Excellent fly-fishing for trout and sea fishing. Table Cape Lookout, 5 km N, for coastal and inland views. Oldest marsupial fossil in Australia found at Fossil Bluff, 7 km N; displayed at the Hobart Museum. **Tourist information:** cnr Hogg and Goldie sts; (03) 6442 4143. **Accommodation:** 2 hotels, 1 hotel/motel, 1 motel, 4 B&B, 3 hostels, 2 cara./camp. parks. **See also:** National Parks.

Zeehan   Pop. 1132

MAP REF. 558 D1, 560 D11

Named after one of Abel Tasman's ships, this former mining town, 36 km NW of Queenstown, has had a chequered history and is now a National Trust-classified historic town. Silver-lead deposits were discovered here in 1882. By 1901, Zeehan had 26 hotels and a population of 10 000, making it Tasmania's third largest town. Just 7 years later mining began to decline and Zeehan became almost a ghost town. In the boom period between 1893 and 1908, 8 million dollars' worth of ore had been recovered. Now the town is again on an upward swing with the reopening of the Renison Bell tin mine. **Of interest:** Self-guide scenic drives of town and surrounding area, brochures available at Tourist information. Many 'boom' buildings in Main St, including Gaiety Theatre at the Grand Hotel, ANZ Bank, St Luke's Church, post office and court house. Four old miners' cottages in Main St available as accommodation. West Coast Pioneers Memorial Museum, in School of Mines building (1894), Main St, has mineral, historical, geological and biological collections. Beside museum, display of steam locomotives and rail carriages used on west coast. Frank Long Memorial Park, Dodd St; Long discovered silver-lead deposit here. Pioneer cemetery, southern outskirts of town. Dec.: King of the Mountain Fun Run. **In the area:** Old mine workings at Dundas, 13 km E. Trial Harbour, 20 km W, a popular fishing area. Unsealed roads to both areas often in poor condition; check before departure. Corinna, 48 km NW, once a bustling gold-mining town, now a base for gold panning, trout fishing, bushwalking and Pieman River cruises. Fishing and boating on Lake Pieman, 50 km NW. Trout fishing on Henty River, 25 km S. **Tourist information:** West Coast Pioneers Memorial Museum, Main St; (03) 6471 6225. **Accommodation:** 2 hotels, 1 hotel/motel, 1 cara./camp. park. **See also:** The West Coast.

Angler's Paradise

Fish are biting all year round in Tasmania, which is why it is an angler's paradise by any standards. Tasmania is famous for three species of fish: trout in fresh water, bream in the estuaries and tuna on the east coast.

One area alone contains hundreds of lakes and lagoons stocked with **trout** of world-class size. This is the undeveloped region known as the 'Land of Three Thousand Lakes'. You are more likely, however, to choose from the huge range of developed areas brimming with trout in the central highlands region, reputed to offer some of the best trout fishing in Australia. Top spots include Great Lake, Bronte Lagoon, Arthurs Lake, Brumbys Creek and Macquarie River.

Tasmania is well known world-wide for its 'sighted' fishing, that is fly-fishing to individual fish. Early in the season in particular, when lake levels are high, brown trout move into shallow water in the weedy lake margins, in search of food. Their tails are often visible above the water providing exciting fly-fishing at close range. In summer, especially in the Land of Three Thousand Lakes, it is possible for the angler wearing polarised glasses to spot individual fish in bright light conditions and present flies to them.

Around March, game fish begin to move down the mild east coast and anglers start hauling in the

Trout fishing at Brumbys Creek, near Cressy

big ones: **bluefin tuna**, often weighing over 45 kilograms. Then, as the bluefin leave in the mid-winter months, large **Australian salmon** schools return to the estuaries and along the shoreline.

In spring, one of the great sport fish of Tasmania, the tasty **silver bream**, arrives in the river estuaries. Anglers regard this as one of the best fighting fish for its size.

January and February are peak months for inland trout-fishing, and from February to March schools of Australian salmon swim close to the shoreline of Tasmania's many river estuaries, providing exciting fishing for the angler from the beach or rocks.

For further information on licence requirements, fees, bag limits, seasons and regulations for freshwater fishing contact the Inland Fisheries Commission, 127 Davey St, Hobart 7000; (03) 6223 6622. For more information on sea fishing, contact the department of Primary Industries and Fisheries, Marine Resources Division, 1 Franklin Wharf, Hobart 7000; (03) 6233 6234.

Location Map

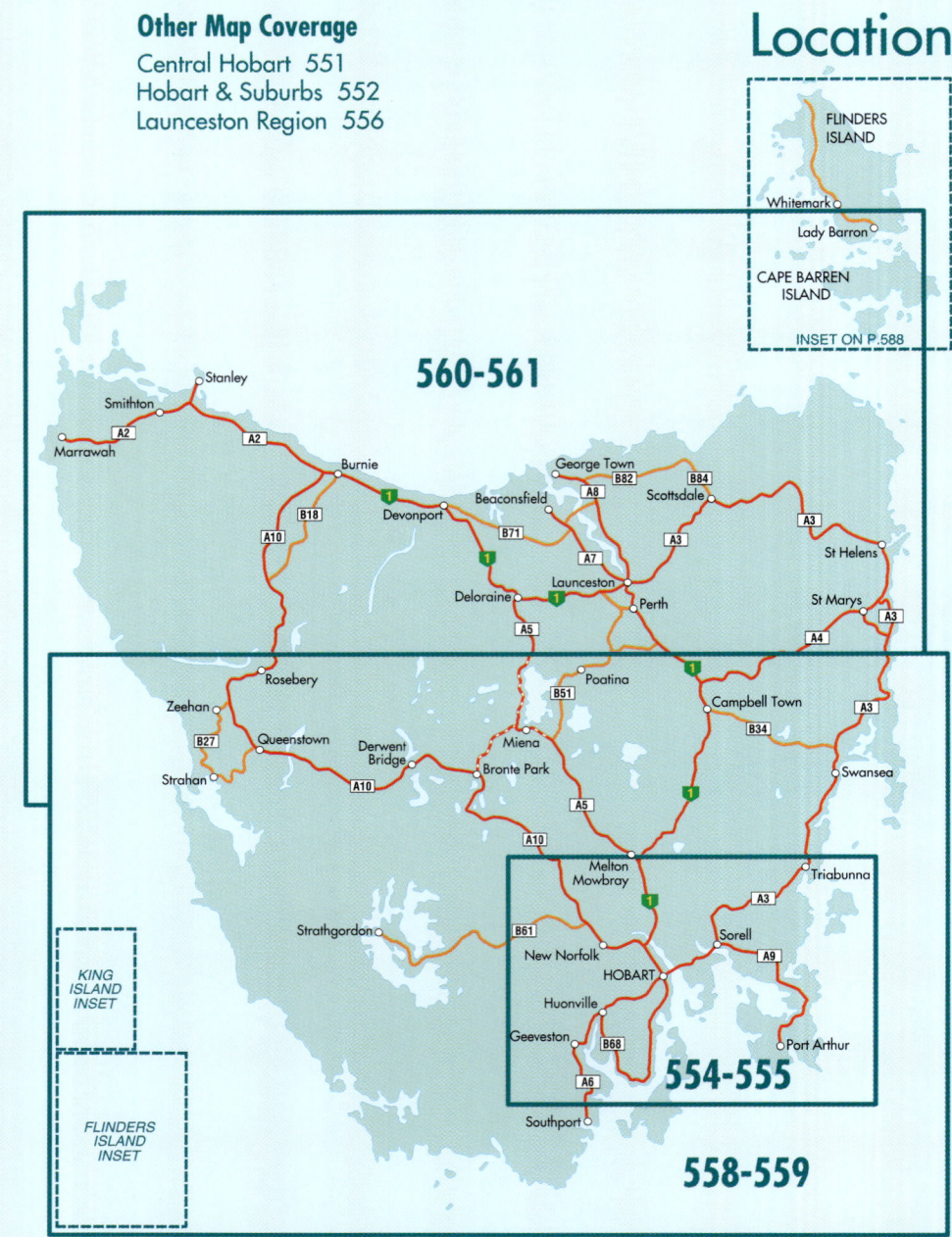

Tasmania

Other Map Coverage

Central Hobart 551
Hobart & Suburbs 552
Launceston Region 556

KING ISLAND
Currie
Grassy
INSET ON P.588

FLINDERS ISLAND
Whitemark
Lady Barron

CAPE BARREN ISLAND
INSET ON P.588

560-561

Stanley
Smithton
A2
Marrawah
A2
Burnie
George Town
B82
Scottsdale
B84
A8
Beaconsfield
A3
Devonport
B18
B71
St Helens
A10
Deloraine
A7
A3
St Marys
Launceston
Perth
A4
A3
A5

Rosebery
Poatina
Campbell Town
A3
Zeehan
B51
B34
Queenstown
Derwent Bridge
Miena
Strahan
B27
Bronte Park
Swansea
A10
A5
A10
Strathgordon
Melton Mowbray
Triabunna
A3
B61
New Norfolk
Sorell
HOBART
A9
Huonville
Port Arthur
Geeveston
B68
554-555
A6
Southport

KING ISLAND INSET

FLINDERS ISLAND INSET

558-559

0   0.25   0.5   0.75   1 km

A B C D E 552 F G H I

Glebe

TO TASMAN BRIDGE
TO HOBART AIRPORT

Queens
Domain

27

Tattersalls Hobart
Aquatic Centre

BROOKER   AV

CAMPBELL   ST

SHORT   ST

GLEBE   ST

ABERDEEN   ST

EDWARD   ST

DAVIES   AV

A3

CENOTAPH   AV

Cenotaph

18

Rose
Garden

LIVERPOOL   ST

A3

TASMAN   HWY

Railway
Roundabout
Fountain

26
Penitentiary Chapel
& Courts
(National Trust HQ)

PATRICK   ST

ARGYLE   ST

TAFE
Technical
College

Ambulance
HQ

Fire Brigade

ABC Radio, Television
& Administration

BROOKER   AV

A6

Railway
Goods
Yard

BRISBANE   ST

BRISBANE   LA

Steps

TAFE
Technical
College

Magistrates
Court

15   Tigerline
Terminal

MISTRAL   PL

SACKVILLE   ST

SUN   ST

Wapping
Residential
Neighbourhood

A6

Gasworks
Shopping
Village

21

Railway
Freight
Terminal

ELIZABETH

MELVILLE   ST

Police
Headquarters

13

CAMPBELL   ST

Theatre
Royal

32

Royal Hobart Hospital

MARKET   ST

City Hall

Car Park

EVANS   ST

MELVILLE   ST

Multi Storey
Car Park

Bathurst Street
Post Office

BATHURST   ST

Queen Alexandra
Maternity Hospital

Multi Storey
Car Park

KEMP   ST

PL

Hotel
Grand
Chancellor

5

HUNTER   ST

Victoria
Dock

Swing
Bridge

Centre for
the Arts

MURRAY   ST

BATHURST   ST

30   State Library
& Museum of
Fine Arts

MATHERS   LA

CRITERION   ST

Arcade

LIVERPOOL   ST

Bank   Arcade

WELLINGTON   CT

14

8   Ansett
Australia

Elizabeth
St Mall

HOBART

ELIZABETH   ST

LORDS   PL

GPO   10

31

Tasmanian
Museum
& Art Gallery

Car Park

A6

Fishermans
Market

19   Constitution
Dock

Wharf

Lift
Bridge

SULLIVANS

Ferry

552

WATCHORN   ST

HARRINGTON   LA

12

Metro City Bus
Terminus

33   Town Hall

MACQUARIE

Wharf

COVE

HARRINGTON   ST

Cat & Fiddle   Arcade

17

COLLINS   CT

St Davids
Cathedral

Franklin
Square   20

16   Tourist
Information

A6

Franklin   St

Passenger   Bellerive

Multi Storey
Car Park

LIVERPOOL   ST

VICTORIA   ST

MURRAY   PL

Centrepoint   Arcade

TRAFALGAR   CT

Country
Comfort
Hadleys
Hotel

3

COLLINS   ST

Government
Offices

DAVEY   ST

Hobart
City Council
Customer Service
Centre

BROOKE   ST

MORRISON   ST

Elizabeth Street Pier

Franklin Wharf
Cruise Centre

Brooke Street
Pier

Cadbury Cruise & Derwent River
ferry departure point

9

Watermans Dock

Murray Street Pier

Princes   Wharf

CSIRO

COLLINS   ST

VICTORIA   ST

Hobart
Macquarie

4

Commonwealth
Government
Centre

Commonwealth
Law Courts

SALAMANCA   PL

Parliament
House

25

Parliament
Square

MORRISON   ST

CASTRAY   ESPLANADE

ESPLANADE

BARRACK   ST

11

MACQUARIE   ST

A6

St Helens
Hospital

DAVEY   ST

SANDY   BAY   RD

HEATHFIELD   AV

WILMOT   ST

28

St Davids
Park

Supreme
Court

National Trust
Shop   24

29

SALAMANCA
Salamanca
Market

Salamanca
Arts Centre

22

Kellys
Steps

PL

RUNNYMEDE   ST

6   Lenna
of Hobart

Princes
Park

BATTERY   SQ

BATTERY   ST

A6

7
Salamanca
Inn

RETREAT

McGREGOR   ST

ARTHUR   ST

Battery   Point

KNOPWOOD   ST

KELLY   ST

SOUTH   ST

SECHERON   RD

FRANCIS   ST

FINLAY   ST

CLARKE   ST

Tourist
Information
Signboard

GLADSTONE   ST

KIRKSWAY   PL

B68

MONTPELIER   ST

JAMES   ST

34

STOWELL   AV

ARTHURS   CIRCUS

CASTRAY   ST

MONA   ST

23
Maritime
Museum

HAMPDEN   RD

ELLERSLIE   RD

DE   WITT   ST

NEWCASTLE   ST

LOGAN   RD

Barton
Cottage

1

WATERLOO   CR

COLVILLE   ST

Colville
Cottage

TO WREST POINT HOTEL-CASINO

Accommodation ■
Barton Cottage 1 F13
Colville Cottage 2 H13
Country Comfort Hadleys Hotel 3 C7
Hobart Macquarie 4 B9
Hotel Grand Chancellor 5 F5
Lenna of Hobart 6 H11
Salamanca Inn 7 E10

General Information ■
Ansett Australia 8 C6
Derwent River Cruises 9 F8
General Post Office 10 E6
Hobart Transit Centre 11 A10
Metro City Bus Terminus 12 D6
Police Headquarters 13 D4
Qantas Travel Centre 14 C6
Tigerline Terminal 15 E3
Tourist Information 16 E7

Accommodation Only a sample
range is listed; inclusion is not
necessarily a recommendation.

Places of Interest ■
Cat and Fiddle Arcade 17 C6/7
Cenotaph 18 H3
Constitution Dock 19 F6
Franklin Square 20 E7
Gasworks Shopping Village 21 G4
Kellys Steps 22 G10
Maritime Museum 23 I13
National Trust Shop 24 E10
Parliament House 25 E9
Penitentiary Chapel & Courts
  (National Trust HQ) 26 C2
Queens Domain 27 E1
St Davids Park 28 D9
Salamanca Place 29 F10
State Library/Allport Library
  and Museum of Fine Arts 30 A6
Tasmanian Museum & Art Gallery 31 E6
Theatre Royal 32 E4
Town Hall 33 E6
Van Diemen's Land
  Folk Museum (Narryna) 34 E12

A B C D E F G H I

1 Chigwell
Moonila Wine Centre
Elliss Point
Berriedale Bay
Derwent Haven
B32 EAST HWY
C324
Risdon Vale Historic Site
Risdon Prison
Risdon Va
River

2 Berriedale
Rosetta
Elwick Bay
Derwent Entertainment Centre
Elwick Racecourse
B35
Goodwood
Risdon Cove
Porter Bay
East Risdon Nature Reserve
Risdon
Sugarloaf
Sugarloaf Hill

3 Montrose
Glenorchy
Transport Museum
Royal Showgrounds
Derwent Park
Prince of Wales Bay
Lutana
Zinc Works
Golf Course
Shag Bay
Recreation Reserve
Faggs Gully
Geilston Bay

4 West Moonah
Moonah
Derwent Park
RAC Escort
Albert
Selfs Point
New Town Bay
Cemetery
Limekiln Point
Lindisfarne Recreation Reserve

5 Merton
Springfield
Lower Glenorchy Reservoir
Barrier
New Town Creek
Runnymede
Bellevue
B36
Cornelian Bay
Lindisfarne Point
Rose Bay
Ros

6 Knights Creek Reservoir
Limekiln Gully Reservoir
WELLINGTON PARK
Lenah Valley
New Town
Lady Franklin Museum
New Town
North Hobart
Upper Domain
Royal Tasmanian Botanic Gardens
Pavilion Point
Government House
HWY
Montagu Bay
Lookout
Rosny Hill
Montag
Rosny

7 Mount Stuart
Lookout
Fossil Hill 340m
Brushy Hill 400m
New Town
Knocklofty
North Hobart
Glebe
HOBART
Rose Garden
Cenotaph
Macquarie Point
Rosny Point
Ferry

8 WELLINGTON PARK
Knocklofty Park
West Hobart
Constitution Dock
Sullivans Cove
Salamanca Place
Kelly's Steps
Van Diemens Museum
Battery Point
Secheron Point

9 Cascade Brewery
Cascades
Cascade
South Hobart
Battery Point Historic Area
Sandy Bay
Royal Yacht Club of Tasmania
Derwent Sailing Squadron
For more detail on Central Hobart see page 551

10 Lookout
Mt Wellington 1270m
O'Gradys Falls
Lower Reservoir
Upper Reservoir
WATERWORKS
Dynnyrne
University of Tasmania
A6
Wrest Point
Wrest Point Hotel-Casino
B68
Sandy Bay

11 The Springs Lookout
RIDGEWAY PARK
Ridgeway Reservoir
Skyline Reserve
Hobart College Mt Nelson Campus
Lower Sandy Bay
Lookout
Skyline Reserve

12 Silver Falls
Fern Tree
Chimney Pot Hill
RIDGEWAY PARK
Ridgeway
Recreation Reserve
Mount Nelson
Mount Nelson Signal Station Reserve
Lookout
Pierces Reserve
Tudor Court Model Village
Truganini Reserve

13 HUON
MENUGGANA
Badger Hill
The Lea Conservation Area
Taroona
TO SHOT TOWER

A B C D E F G H I

0 1 2 3 km

J K L M N O P Q R

Pitt Water

Barilla Bay

Railway Point

MEEHAN RANGE STATE RECREATION AREA

Creek

555 RD

COLEBROOK

HANSLOW

Richmond Golf Course

Mile Beach

A3

CAMBRIDGE AERODROME

HOBART AIRPORT

MEEHAN

RANGE

COLEBROOK RD

KENNEDY

HOLYMAN AV

TASMAN HWY

Flagstaff Gully Reservoir

STATE RECREATION

C330

ACTON RD

MEEHAN RANGE

RD

B31

CAMBRIDGE

A3

Cambridge

istarne

AREA

FLAGSTAFF GULLY

Observatory

Canopus Hill

ACTON RD

Flagstaff Gully

GORDONS HILL RD

KANDOLA RD

FLAGSTAFF GULLY LINK

RD

Tunnel Hill

C329

C328

MT RUMNEY

RD

Lookout

SEVEN MILE BEACH RD

HELENS ST

RD

TASMAN HWY

CAMBRIDGE

Mt Rumney 378m

C330

Seven Mile Beach

NS HILL REC EA

Rosny Park

A3

C329

BLIGH ST

ST

Mornington

RD

PASS

MEEHAN

ACTON RD

TASMAN HWY

ny

Kangaroo Bay

BLIGH

RD

Warrane

JINALONG

RD

B33

C329

Knopwood Hill

Clarence Plains

RANGE

Bay

Bellerive

Waverley Park

KNOPWOOD HILL STATE RECREATION AREA

Mornington Hill

ACTON DR

Roches Beach

HILL RD

CAMBRIDGE

WAVERLEY

HILL

ST

SOUTH

NINABAH

TILANBI ST

NORMA ST

Howrah

PASS

TARA DR

CLARENCE

QUEEN ST

DENNISON ST

ST

Bellerive Oval

Beach

Bellerive Beach

WENTWORTH ST

Wentworth Park

HOWRAH RD

ARM

Glebe Hill

RD

GOODWINS

TARA DR

ROCHES BEACH

Kangaroo Bluff Historic Site

Second Bluff

Howrah Point

MINERVA ST

OCEANA DR

ST

ROKEBY

RD

ROCKINGHAM DR

Clarendon Vale

RD

ACTON RD

C330

Howrah Beach

HWY

TRANMERE

RD

MARSTON ST

Lauderdale

ST

CARELLA ST

B33

MOCKRIDGE RD

Rokeby

B33

ROCHES BEACH RD

BANGALEE ST

Tranmere

TOLLARD DR

DR

Clarence Plains Rivulet

DROUGHTY POINT

RD

SOUTH

RD

SOUTH

Frederick Henry Bay

Derwent

N

DUNTROON

ARM

Tasmania Police Academy

RALPHS BAY COASTAL RESERVE

BAYVIEW

ARM

RD

ROKEBY HILLS

Rokeby Beach

Mill Point

Droughty Hill 153m

Gibsons Point

Ralphs Bay

Mt Mather 175m

Sandford

Trywork Point

Droughty Point

J K L M N O 555 P Q R

1
2
3
4
5
555
6
7
8
9
10
11
12
13

TO QUEENSTOWN Hamilton · Glen Clyde House · Sheep Centre · [559] · [A10]

Meadowbank Lake · Meadowbank Power Station · Mt Spode 521m · Peckham Vale · Pelham · Windsor Park · Kempton · **TO LAUNCESTON** · Quoin Mtn 900m · Colebrook · Pleasant Mount · Fair View

Ellendale · Old MacDonalds Tourist Farm · Mt Bethune 508m · Norton Mandeville · Allanvale · Taylors Tier 639m · Elderslie Park · Huntington Tier 545m · Constitution Hill · Dysart · Chauncy Vale

MOUNT FIELD NATIONAL PARK · Lake Webster · Mt Field East 1269m · Lake Nicholls · Russell Falls · Fentonbury · Clarendon · Jordan River · Elderslie · Bagdad · **28** · Mangalore Farm · Mangalore

Lake Seal · Lake Fenton · Florentine Peak · Mt Mawson · Westerway · Karanja · Gretna · Broadmarsh · Woodlands · Pontville · Tea Tree

National Park · B61 · **37** · Glenora · Rosegarland · Mt Belmont 456m · Mt Dromedary 989m · Broadmarsh · Brighton · Bonorong Park Wildlife Centre · Gove Hill 239m

Tyenna · B62 · Bushy Park · Macquarie Plains · Kinvarra · Black Hills · Dromedary · B10 · Bridgewater · Gagebrook · Grasstree Hill 544m · Risdon Vale

Fitzgerald · GORDON RIVER · Maydena · TO LAKE PEDDER · Plenty · Salmon Ponds · Hayes · Magra · Australian Newsprint Mill · Boyer · Jet Boat Rides · Granton · A10 · Claremont · Motor Racing Circuit · Old Beach · Grasstree Hill · Risdon Cove Historic Site

Uxbridge · Moogara · Feilton · New Norfolk · Old Colony Inn · Oast House · Malbina · Molesworth · Alpenrail · Cadbury's Chocolate Factory · Berriedale · Glenlusk · Mt Direction 448m

Mt Styx 1080m · Glenfern · Mount Lloyd · Lachlan · Collins Cap · Collinsvale · Glenorchy · Moonah · North Hobart · **HOBART**

SOUTHWEST NATIONAL PARK · Mt Weld 1338m · Lonnavale · WELLINGTON PARK · Trestle Mtn · Collins Bonnet 1259m · Mt Wellington 1270m · Lookout · Rosny Park · Battery Point · Sandy Bay · Wrest Point Hotel-Casino

[558] · Part of World Heritage Area · Blue Hill · Mt Montagu 1058m · Mountain River · Fern Tree · Ridgeway · Lookout · Tudor Court Model Village · B68

Crabtree · Apple & Heritage Museum · Grove · HUON HWY · Longley · Neika · Leslie Vale · Taroona · Shot Tower

Judbury · Lucaston · A6 · Sandfly · SOUTHERN · Kingston · Kingston Beach · Opossum Bay

Ranelagh · Motor Museum · Model Train World · Grove · Kaoota · Allens Rivulet · Howden · Margate · Blackmans Bay · South Arm

Glen Huon · Apple Carver & Model Village · Huonville · Jet Boat Rides · B68 · Pelverata · Nierinna · Electrona · Snug · Tinderbox · Cape Direction · Iron Pot

Woodstock · Upper Woodstock · Grey Mountain 831m · Snug Falls · Coningham · Dennes Point · North West Bay

Franklin · Egg Island · Glaziers Bay · Cradoc · CHANNEL HWY · Oyster Cove · Killora · B66 · Lowes Hill 212m · Barnes Bay

Castle Forbes Bay · Port Huon · **44** · Cruises · Wattle Grove · Cygnet · The Deepings (Woodturners Workshop) · Kettering · Passenger & Vehicular Ferry · Oyster Cove

Geeveston · Forest and Heritage Centre · Cairns Bay · Petcheys Bay · Nicholls Rivulet · Hartzview Vineyard · Woodbridge · Roberts Hill 206m

Waratah Lookout · HARTZ MOUNTAINS NATIONAL PARK · Hartz Peak 1255m · Waterloo · Lymington · Talune Wildlife Park · Gardners Bay · Birchs Bay · Great Bay

Big Tree Lookout · Mt Picton 1327m · Lake Picton · Lake Riveaux · Glendevie · Police Point · Gardens Bay · Garden Island Creek · Flowerpot · BRUNY ISLAND

Surges Bay · Hideaway Bay · Simpsons Point · Middleton · D'Entrecasteaux Monument · Gordon · **48** · Simpsons Bay

SOUTHWEST NATIONAL PARK · Mt Esperance 462m · Verona Sands · Huon Island · SOUTH BRUNY ISLAND · Adventure Bay · Alonnah · B66

Francistown · Surveyors Bay · Satellite Island · Little Taylors Bay · Lunawanna · Mt Mangana 571m

Part of World Heritage Area · Raminea · Strathblane · Dover · Port Esperance · Adamsons Peak 1226m

Hastings Cave · Thermal Springs Pool · Hastings · A6 · **TO SOUTHPORT** · [559] · Captain Cook's Landing Place · Cookville · Fluted Cape · Bligh Museum

N

BASS **STRAIT**

SPIRIT OF TASMANIA: Ferries passengers and cars across Bass Strait between Melbourne and Devonport. This powerful sea voyager offers all the facilities of an ocean cruise-liner, accommodating passengers seeking luxury to the budget-conscious backpacker.

ASBESTOS RANGE NATIONAL PARK: Lying between Greens Beach and Port Sorell, this scenic northern coastal park has numerous isolated beaches, sand dunes and grasslands covered in wildflowers. Mineral asbestos was mined last century at the northern point.

West Head

Badger Head

Spirit of Tasmania Ferry
Devonport to Melbourne

TO BURNIE
Sulphur Creek
Penguin
B17
1
12
13
Ferndene

Point Sorell
ASBESTOS RANGE
NATIONAL PARK
C721

Ulverstone
Turners Beach
Leith
10
22
Gawler
Braeside
4
6
B15
Forth
C145
B19
Don
Don River Railway
6
Devonport
Searoad Terminal
DEVONPORT AIRPORT
BASS

Hawley Beach
Shearwater
Port Sorell
Bakers Beach
Bubicon Estate
C741

North Motton
B17
C124
Abbotsham
B16
8
Quoiba
11
B71
B74
Wesley Vale
19
Northdown
Squeaking Point
York Town

C125
Spalford
15
Kindred
10
Spreyton
6
Thirlstane
3
Moriarty
C740
Browns
Creek

Sprent
3
Melrose
Eugenana
C145
C704
8
Harford
FRANKFORD
65
Saxons

Gunns Plains
Preston
Paloona
Power Station
5
Latrobe
18
Sassafras East
Franklin
19

Caves
Warringa
C132
Lower Barrington
C150
31
B13
Sassafras
Robin Hood
West Frankf
B71

C125
Upper Castra
C133
12
Lake Paloona
Barrington
B14
Nook
Railton
Mersey
C153
Rosslyn

Nietta
B15
10
Devils Gate Dam & Power Station
C143
C150
Stoodley Forest Reserve
Murals
Sheffield
B14
Merseylea
Sunnyside
50
BASS
HWY
22
Parkham

Leven Canyon
South Nietta
Wilmot
Narrawa
C132
West Kentish
Roland
STATE RECREATION AREA
Paradise
Stoodley
C156
Kimberley
C160
C711

Winterbrook Falls
Rainforest Walk
Rowling
C136
Claude Road
Beulah
Beaula
C159
Moltema
B13
1
Elizabeth Town
C710
Reedy Marsh
Weetah

Moina
Erriba
C140
Staverton
Mt Roland +1234m
Lower Beulah
Weegena
C161
Dunorlan
C163
Wattle Bank

Lake Gairdner
Wilmot Power Station
Cethana Power Station
Gowrie Park
GOG
RANGE
Lemana
BASS
HWY
8
Red Hills
Deloraine
C503

Daisy Dell
Lorinna
C138
Mersey
Mayfield
Trowunna Wildlife Park
B12
24
Needles
C164
Montana
A5

Lemonthyme Power Station
C139
Liena
King Solomons Cave
B12
15
Mayberry
Marakoopa Cave
Mole Creek
Chudleigh
C168
C166
C167
Quamby Brook
C504

CRADLE MOUNTAIN-
LAKE ST CLAIR
NATIONAL PARK
C171
MOLE CREEK KARST NATIONAL PARK
Caveside
C169
Mountleigh
C166
TO HOBART

CENTRAL PLATEAU CONSERVATION AREA & PROTECTED AREA

560

WINERIES: ❶
Brook Eden Vineyard 1 P4
Clover Hill Vineyards 2 P5
Dalrymple Vineyard 3 O3
Delamere Vineyard 4 O3
Heemskerk Vineyards 5 O3
Holm Oak Vineyards 6 L5
Marion's Vineyard 7 L6
Pipers Brook Vineyard 8 O3
Providence Vineyards 9 P6
Rochecombe Vineyard 10 N4
St Matthias Vineyard 11 M8
Strathlynn Wine Centre 12 M8

DOUBLE SANDY POINT
COASTAL RESERVE

West Sandy Cape   East Sandy Cape

GRANITE POINT
COASTAL RESERVE

Anderson
Bay

Bridport

TASMANIAN WINE ROUTE: Pipers Brook
and the Tamar Valley are referred to as
the centre of northern Tasmania's grape-
growing area. Vineyards in the district
are open to visitors for tours and tastings.

Lavender Farm

TO SCOTTSDALE
561

TOURIST INFORMATION:
Deloraine (23 West Church St)
Devonport (5 Best St)
Evandale (18 High St)
Exeter (Tamar Visitor Centre, Main Rd)
George Town (Main Rd)
Latrobe (70 Gilbert St)
Launceston (cnr St John and Paterson sts)
Longford (Council Offices, Smith St)
Scottsdale (The Lyric Theatre, 29-31 King St)
Ulverstone (Car Park La, behind P.O.)
Westbury (Old Bakehouse, 52 William St)

TAMAR RIVER: This magnificent broad river
was the passageway of the first European
settlement and exploration in northern Tasmania.
Batman Bridge, one of the world's first cable-
stayed truss bridges, is 30 km from Launceston
and links the east and west banks.

LAUNCESTON

560

SOUTHWEST CONSERVATION AREA

CRADLE MOUNTAIN – LAKE ST CLAIR NATIONAL PARK

Rosebery
Renison Bell
Melba Flats
Williamsford
Montezuma Falls
Dundas
Zeehan
Pioneers Memorial Museum
Trial Harbour
Remine

Anthony Power Station
Mt Murchison 1275m
Mt Dundas 1458m
Lake Margaret

WALLS OF JERUSALEM NATIONAL PARK
Mt Jerusalem 1458m
PROTECTED

Mt Lyell Mine
Gormanston
Queenstown
Linda
Lynchford
King River PS
Strahan
Strahan Wharf Centre
Renatta Point
King River Forest Drive
Ocean Beach
Cape Sorell
Point Hibbs

Mt Owen 1146m
Mt Jukes 1168m
Mt Darwin 1031m
Darwin Dam
Mt Sorell 1144m
Pillinger

LAKE ST CLAIR
Mt Ossa 1617m
Mt Gould 1491m
Mt Olympus 1447m
Mt Hugel 1307m
Mt Rufus 1402m
Mt Gell 1439m
Mt Arrowsmith 981m

Derwent Bridge
Lake King William
Clark Dam
Butlers Gorge PS
Butlers Gorge
Tarraleah
Dee Lagoon
Liapootah PS
Wayatinah
Wayatinah PS

FRANKLIN – GORDON WILD RIVERS NATIONAL PARK
Frenchmans Cap 1443m
Mt King William I 1324m
Mt King William II 1359m
Mt King William III 1158m
Mt Seal 878m
Mt Curly 1039m
Mt Humboldt 1079m
Mt Wright 1119m
Mt Field West 1439m

SOUTHERN OCEAN

SOUTHWEST CONSERVATION AREA

Sloop Point
Gorge Point
Birthday Bay
Hibbs Bay
Point Hibbs
Spero Bay
Endeavour Bay
Wanderer River
High Rocky Point
Low Rocky Point
Elliott Bay
Nye Bay
Wreck Bay
Point St Vincent
Port Davey
Stephens Bay
Island Bay
Window Pane Bay
South West Cape
Karama Bay

Mt Discovery 680m
Mt Lee 734m
Mt Osmund 369m
Hardwood Hill 412m
Elliott Hill 209m
Frederick Hill 518m
Mt Sprent 1058m
Mt Gaffney 588m
Mt Hean 747m
Mt Rugby 771m
Mt Bowes 957m
Mt Wedge 1146m
Mt Giblin 878m
Mt Orion 1119m
Mt Braddon 729m
Mt Counsel 800m
Mt Melaleuca 595m

Gordon PS Dam
Strathgordon
Lookout
Serpentine Dam
Forest Walk
Maydena
Mt Mueller 1234m
MOUNT FIELD NATIONAL PARK
Adamsfield
Clear Hill 1198m

SOUTHWEST NATIONAL PARK
Lake Pedder
Lake Gordon
Scotts Peak Dam
Edgar Dam
Lookout
Mt Anne 1425m
Mt Eliza

Part of World Heritage Area
Bathurst Harbour
New Harbour
Cox Bight
Louisa Bay
De Witt Island
Ile Du Golfe
MAATSUYKER GROUP
Maatsuyker Island
Surprise Bay
Prion Bay
New River Lagoon

KING ISLAND

Cape Wickham
Cape Farewell
Phoques Bay
New Year Is
Christmas Is
Whistler Point
Egg Lagoon
Lavinia Point
LAVINIA NATURE RESERVE
Yambacoona
Reekara
Loorana
Dairy Factory
Sea Elephant
Currie
Pegarah
Lymwood
Pearshape
Naracoopa
Parenna
Yarra Creek
Bold Head
Grassy
Seal Point
Cataraqui Point
Surprise Point
Surprise Bay
Stokes Point

BASS STRAIT
Sea Elephant Bay
Fitzmaurice Bay

0 10 20 km

King Island   Flinders Island
Launceston
HOBART

FLINDERS ISLAND

Inner Sister Island
Stanley Point
Blyth Pt
Palana
Killiecrankie Bay
Killiecrankie
Cape Frankland
Marshall Bay
Emita
Lughrata
Museum
Memana
Babel Is
Sellars Lagoon
Whitemark
Long Point
Parry's Bay
Ranga
Loccota
Lady Barron
Mt Chappell Is
Trousers Pt
Anderson Is
Vansittart Is
Puncheon Pt
Cape Barren Island
Mt Munro 716m
CAPE BARREN ISLAND
Sloping Pt
Kent Bay
Mt Kerford 499m
Cape Barren
Preservation Is
Clarke Is
Lookout Heads
Moriarty Point

Prime Seal Island
Arthur Bay
FURNEAUX GROUP
Cameron Inlet
FRANKLIN SOUND
STRZELECKI NP
Badger Is
Long Is

BASS STRAIT
Passage Is
Forsyth Is

SOUTHERN OCEAN
BANKS STRAIT

OCEAN

BASS

SOUTHERN

OCEAN

Cuvier Bay
Hope Channel
Three Hummock Island
Cape Adansan
Hunter Island
Trefoil Island
Cape Grim
Valley Bay
Studland Bay
Woolnorth
Robbins Island
Cape Elie
Robbins Passage
Perkins Island
Walker Island
Walker Channel
Hunter Passage
Ransonnet Bay
North Point
West Point
Half Moon Bay
Highfield Point
Stanley
The Nut
Circular Head
Sawyer Bay
Perkins Bay
Brickmakers Bay
West Montagu
Montagu
Mt Cameron West 168m
West Point
Marrawah
ARTHUR PIEMAN PROTECTED AREA
Redpa
Togari
Mella
Mowbray Park
Fonthill
Christmas Hills
Smithton
Forest
South Forest
Wiltshire Junction
Black River
Port Latta
Crayfish Creek
Edgcumbe Beach
Hellyer
Rocky Cape
ROCKY CAPE NATIONAL PARK
Detention River
Sisters Beach
Birdland Native Gardens
Boat Harbour Beach
Boat Harbour
Table Cape
Table Cape Lookout
Brittons Swamp
Irishtown
Mengha
Alcomie
Lileah
Edith Creek
Nabageena
Trowutta
Roger River
Roger River West
Arthur River
Cruise
Seymour Hill 134m
Montumana
Mawbanna
Sisters Creek
Myalla
Milabena
Moorleah
Wynyard
Somerset
Camdale
Cooee
Burnie
Wivenhoe
Heybridge
Howth
Sulphur Creek
Penguin
Ulverstone
Turners Beach
Devon
Preolenna
Calder
Oldina
Lower Mount Hicks
Upper Mount Hicks
Mooreville
Yolla
Elliott
Stowport
Upper Stowport
Cuprona
Mount Hicks
Kellatier
Meunna
Takone
East Yolla
West Yolla
West Ridgley
Ridgley
Natone
Upper Natone
Ferndene
Camena
Riana
West Pine
North Motton
Gawler
Forth
Quoiba
Spreyton
Melrose
Paloona
Latrobe
West Takone
Henrietta
Highclere
Tewkesbury
South Riana
Gunns Plains
Spalford
Kindred
Preston
Central Castra
Lower Barrington
Barrington
Hampshire
Heka
Loyetea
Warringa
Peak Hill Farm
Upper Castra
Nietta
Loongana
Narrawa
Wilmot
Sheffield
Stoodley
Paradise
Beulah
Moina
Loorana
Daisy Dell
Lorinna
Liena
Mayberry
Caveside
Devils Gate Dam & PS
Wilmot PS
Cethana PS
Gowrie Park
King Solomons Cave
Marakoopa Cave
Devils Gullet Lookout
MOLE CREEK KARST NP
Mole Creek
Rowallan PS
Fisher PS
Cradle Mountain Lodge
Lemonthyme Power Station
Waldheim Historic Site
Cradle Valley
CRADLE MOUNTAIN - LAKE ST CLAIR NATIONAL PARK
WALLS OF JERUSALEM NATIONAL PARK
SOUTHWEST CONSERVATION AREA
Temma
Temma Harbour
Nelson Bay
Couta Rocks
Balfour
Mt Frankland 433m
Mt Hazelton 671m
ARTHUR
PIEMAN
PROTECTED AREA
Sandy Cape
Mt Norfolk 759m
Mt Hadmar 762m
Rupert Point
Pieman Head
Hardwick Bay
Corinna
Cruise
Reece Power Station Dam
PIEMAN RIVER STATE RESERVE
Mt Livingstone 782m
Granville Harbour
Lake Pieman
Renison Bell
Melba Flats
Rosebery
Williamsford
Tullah
Bastyan PS Dam
Mackintosh Power Station
Lake Mackintosh
Mt Murchison 1275m
Anthony Power Station
Lake Plimsoll
Ahrberg Bay
Pioneers Memorial Museum
Dundas
Zeehan
Montezuma Falls
Mt Dundas 1158m
Mt Agnew 846m
Trial Harbour
Remine
Lake Rosebery
Lake Rolleston
LAKE ST CLAIR
Mt Ossa 1617m
Mt Pelion East 1451m
Mt Oakleigh 1000m
Lake Margaret
Mt Lyell Mine
Gormanston
Queenstown
Linda
Lynchford
King River PS
Strahan
Strahan Wharf Centre
Regatta Point
King River Forest Drive
Cape Sorell
Point Hibbs
Mt Owen 1146m
Mt Jukes 1168m
Mt Darwin 1031m
Darwin Dam
Mt Sorell 1144m
Franklin - Gordon Wild Rivers National Park
Frenchmans Cap 1443m
Mt Gell 1439m
Mt Arrowsmith 981m
Mt King William I 1324m
Derwent Bridge
Butlers Gorge PS
Clark Dam
Butlers Gorge
Lake King William
Lake Burbury
Collingwood River
Franklin River
Mt Gould 1481m
Mt Ida 1158m
Mt Hugel 1397m
Mt Rufus 1402m
Mt Olympus 1447m
Lake St Clair
SOUTHWEST CONSERVATION AREA
Sloop Point
Ocean Beach
Macquarie Harbour
Spirit of Tasmania Ferry Devonport to Melbourne

Index of Place Names

Place names that appear in this gazetteer are followed by a map page number and grid reference, and/or the text page number on which that place name occurs. A page number set in bold type indicates the main text entry for that place name.
Bairnsdale Vic. 242 F13, **161**, 187, 194
Bairnsdale – Place name
Vic. – State
242 F13 – Bairnsdale appears on this map page
161 – Main entry for Bairnsdale
187, 194 – Bairnsdale is mentioned on these pages

The alphabetical order followed in the index is that of 'word-by-word', where all entries under one word are grouped together. Where a place name consists of more than one word, the order is governed by the first and then the second word. For example:
Green Bay
Green River
Greenbank
Greens Beach
Greenwood Forest
Greg Greg
Gregafell

Names beginning with Mc are indexed as Mac and those beginning with St, as Saint.
The following abbreviations and contractions are used in the index:
ACT – Australian Capital Territory
JBT – Jervis Bay Territory
NSW – New South Wales
NT – Northern Territory
Qld – Queensland
SA – South Australia
St – Saint
Tas. – Tasmania
Vic. – Victoria
WA – Western Australia

Dreeite Vic. 218 A9, 223 F5, 235 N8

Drewvale Qld 495 J10

Drik Drik Vic. 234 C7

Drillham Qld 505 J7

Dripstone NSW 120 F4

Dromana Vic. 219 J11, 220 I7, 232 D8, 158, 190, 199

Dromedary Tas. 554 G3, 559 L7

Dropmore Vic. 240 I10, 210

Drouin Vic. 219 P9, 232 H6

Drouin South Vic. 219 P10, 232 H6

Drouin West Vic. 207

Drumborg Vic. 234 D7

Drumcondra Vic. 224 D2

Drummartin Vic. 237 R7, 240 D6

Drummond Vic. 218 F1, 229 Q7, 235 Q1, 237 Q12, 240 C11

Drummoyne NSW 99 J9

Drung Drung Vic. 236 H9

Drung Drung South Vic. 236 H10

Dry Creek SA 294 H10

Dry Creek Vic. 241 K9

Dryander National Park Qld 507 J2

Drysdale Vic. 218 H9, 225 H7, 232 B6, **173**

Drysdale River National Park WA 373 K1, 381 O3

Duaringa Qld 507 M11

Dubbo NSW 120 E2, 31, **57**

Dubelling WA 374 G4

Dublin SA 303 K7

Duchess Qld 512 F5

Duckenfield NSW 112 D6

Duckmaloi NSW 104 E7

Duddo Vic. 238 C10

Dudley Vic. 232 G10

Dudley Park SA 292 H2

Duffholme Vic. 236 E9

Duffy ACT 140 B13, 141 A3

Duffys Forest NSW 101 K7, 41

Dulacca Qld 505 J7

Dularcha National Park Qld 497 M2, 500 E12

Dullah NSW 120 A11, 127 Q9

Dulong Qld 497 M1, 500 C8

Dululu Qld 507 N12

Dulwich SA 293 K7

Dulwich Hill NSW 99 J12, 103 L2

Dumbalk Vic. 219 Q13, 232 I9

Dumberning WA 374 F7

Dumbleyung WA 374 H8, 376 E10, **333**

Dumosa Vic. 126 G13, 237 L4

Dunach Vic. 218 B1, 229 L7, 235 O1, 237 O12

Dunalley Tas. 555 M6, 559 N9, **530**

Dunbogan NSW 109 G10, 123 O12, 72

Duncraig WA 364 C5

Dundas NSW 98 E6

Dundas Qld 497 J6

Dundas Tas. 558 D1, 560 E11, 549

Dundas Valley NSW 98 E5

Dundee NSW 123 M5

Dundee Beach NT 418 C6

Dundinin WA 376 E9

Dundonnell Vic. 223 B1, 235 K6

Dundurrabin NSW 123 O7

Dunedoo NSW 120 G1

Dungog NSW 112 A1, 121 N3, **58**

Dungowan NSW 123 K11

Dunk Island Qld 509 O9, 426, 452, 466

Dunkeld NSW 104 B4, 120 H6

Dunkeld Vic. 234 H4, **173**

Dunlop ACT 140 A3

Dunluce Vic. 229 K3

Dunmarra NT 420 I4, **397**

Dunmore NSW 116 G9, 120 C4

Dunmore Vic. 234 G7

Dunneworthy Vic. 228 E6, 235 K1, 237 K12

Dunnstown Vic. 218 D4, 229 N11, 235 P3, 240 B13, 166

Dunolly Vic. 229 L3, 237 O10, **173**

Dunorlan Tas. 556 G11, 561 J8

Dunrobin Vic. 234 C4

Duns Creek NSW 112 C5

Dunsborough WA 367 C7, 369 C2, 374 B9, 376 B10, **333**

Duntroon ACT 140 I10, 141 G1, 129, 134

Dunwich Qld 497 P8, 505 Q9, 445

Durack Qld 494 F8

Dural NSW 100 B8

Duranillin WA 374 F8, 376 D10

Durdidwarrah Vic. 218 E6, 225 C2, 235 Q5

Durham Lead Vic. 218 C5, 229 M13, 235 O4

Durham Ox Vic. 126 I13, 237 P5, 240 A4

Duri NSW 123 J11

Durong Qld 505 M6

Durran Durra NSW 119 G5, 120 I12, 143 L3

Durras NSW 119 H7, 143 O6

Durundur Qld 497 K3

Dutson Vic. 233 N7

Dutton SA 296 H3, 303 M7

Dutton Park Qld 494 G2

Duverney Vic. 218 B8, 223 F3, 235 N6

Dwarda WA 366 H11, 374 E6

Dwellingup WA 366 D11, 374 D6, 376 C9, **334**

Dwyer Vic. 230 F4

Dwyers NSW 125 O6

Dynnyrne Tas. 552 G10

Dysart Qld 507 J9

Dysart Tas. 554 H1

Eagle Bay WA 367 B6, 369 C1, 374 A8, 333

Eagle Farm Qld 493 J9, 430

Eagle Heights Qld 497 N12

Eagle Junction Qld 492 G9

Eagle On The Hill SA 293 M10

Eagle Point Vic. 233 Q5

Eagleby Qld 495 Q11

Eaglehawk Vic. 229 Q1, 237 Q9, 240 B8, 164

Eaglehawk Neck Tas. 555 N8, 559 O9, 524, 531, **532**

Earlando Qld 507 J2

Earlston Vic. 241 J7

Earlville Qld 502 D12

Earlwood NSW 98 I13, 103 K3

East Boyd NSW 117 G11, 119 G12, 243 Q8

East Brisbane Qld 492 H12, 494 H1

East Cannington WA 363 N7

East Fremantle WA 362 C10

East Greenmount Qld 447

East Gresford NSW 121 M3

East Haldon Qld 496 G10

East Hills NSW 102 E6

East Jindabyne NSW 118 G11, 142 D12

East Kurrajong NSW 105 L5

East Lynne NSW 143 O6

East Melbourne Vic. 212 I6, 155

East Perth WA 360 H5, 362 I3, 316

East Point NT 411 C2, 386, 388

East Sydney NSW 96 G9

East Victoria Park NSW 363 J6

East Yolla Tas. 560 F6

Eastbourne NSW 118 G7

Eastern Creek NSW 43

Eastern View Vic. 218 E12, 225 B12, 235 P10

Eastlakes NSW 103 O4

Eastville Vic. 229 N3

Eastwood NSW 98 G5

Eastwood SA 290 I13, 293 J7, 250

Eaton WA 367 G4, 374 C8

Eatons Hill Qld 492 C5, 478

Eatonsville NSW 123 O6, 61

Eba SA 303 N6

Ebden Vic. 241 Q4, 242 C2

Ebenezer NSW 105 L5, 82, 92

Ebenezer Qld 497 J9

Ebor NSW 123 N8, 57

Eccleston NSW 121 M2

Echuca Vic. 127 K13, 240 E4, 147, **173**, 199, 205

Echuca Village Vic. 127 K13, 240 F4

Echunga SA 296 D12, 297 I3, 253

Ecklin South Vic. 223 A7

Eddington Vic. 229 M3, 237 O10, 240 A9

Eddystone Point Tas. 561 R6, 533

Eden NSW 117 F11, 119 G11, 243 Q8, **58**, 59

Eden Hill WA 365 M10

Eden Hills SA 292 H13

Eden Park Vic. 219 K3

Eden Valley SA 296 G6, 303 M8

Edenhope Vic. 236 C11, **174**

Edens Landing Qld 495 O12

Edgcumbe Beach Tas. 560 E4

Edge Hill Qld 502 E6

Edgecliff NSW 99 O11, 103 Q1

Edgecombe Vic. 218 G1

Edgeroi NSW 122 G7

Edgewater WA 364 D1

Edi Vic. 230 F4, 241 N7

Edi Upper Vic. 230 G5, 241 N8

Edillilie SA 302 D7

Edith NSW 104 E8, 120 I7

Edith Creek Tas. 560 C5, 546

Edith River NT 418 F9

Edithburgh SA 302 I10, **261**

Edithvale Vic. 217 D7

Edmonton Qld 503 F10, 509 N7, 456

Edmund Kennedy National Park Qld 509 N9

Edward River Qld 465

Edwardstown SA 292 G11

Eganstown Vic. 229 O8

Egg Lagoon Tas. 558 A8

Eidsvold Qld 505 M3, **453**

Eight Mile Plains Qld 495 K6

Eildon Vic. 219 P2, 230 A12, 241 K11, 145, 146, 160, **174**, 189

Einasleigh Qld 509 J10, 488

Ejanding WA 374 F1

Ekibin Qld 494 H3

El Arish Qld 509 N9

Elaine Vic. 218 D6, 225 B1, 235 P5

Elands NSW 109 A10, 123 N12

Elanora Qld 499 F10

Elanora Heights NSW 101 O9, 105 O7

Elaroo Qld 507 J4

Elbow Hill SA 302 G5

Elcombe NSW 122 I6

Elderslie Tas. 554 F1, 559 K7

Eldon Tas. 559 M6

Eldorado Vic. 241 N5, 242 A3, 206

Electrona Tas. 554 H8

Elermore Vale NSW 112 F8

Elimbah Qld 497 M4, 505 P8

Elingamite Vic. 223 B7

Elizabeth SA 295 M1, 296 B7, 301 C1, 303 L8

Elizabeth Bay NSW 99 N10, 39, 40

Elizabeth Beach NSW 121 P2

Elizabeth East SA 295 N1

Elizabeth Grove SA 295 M2

Elizabeth Town Tas. 556 G10, 561 J8, 530

Elizabeth Vale SA 295 M3

Ellalong NSW 112 C11, 121 L4

Ellam Vic. 126 D13, 236 G5

Ellangowan Qld 496 D11

Ellen Grove Qld 494 E9

Ellenborough NSW 109 C8, 123 N12

Ellendale Tas. 554 B2, 559 J7

Ellerslie Vic. 235 J8

Ellerston NSW 121 L1, 123 K13

Ellesmere Qld 496 E1

Elliminyt Vic. 218 B11, 223 G7, 235 N9

Ellinbank Vic. 219 P10, 232 H7

Elliott NT 421 J6, **397**

Elliott Tas. 560 F6, 527

Elliott Heads Qld 505 O2, 442

Ellis Beach Qld 503 E6, 509 M6, 443

Elliston SA 302 A5, **261**, 262

Elmhurst Vic. 228 G6, 235 L1, 237 L12, 161

Elmore Vic. 240 E6

Elong Elong NSW 120 F2

Elphinstone Qld 496 E11

Elphinstone Vic. 229 R6, 237 R12, 240 C10

Elsey National Park NT 418 I11, 395, 398, 400, 402, 405

Elsinore NSW 125 L10

Elsmore NSW 123 K6

Elsternwick Vic. 215 L12, 154

Eltham NSW 123 Q3, 505 Q12

Eltham Vic. 215 Q4

Elwomple SA 301 E3, 303 N10

Elwood Vic. 215 K11

Embleton WA 365 K10

Emerald Qld 506 I11, **453**, 485

Emerald Vic. 219 M7, 222 C13, 232 F5, 159, **174**

Emerald Beach NSW 123 P7

Emerald Hill NSW 122 H10

Emerald Springs Wayside Inn NT 414 H11, 418 F8

Emita Tas. 558 A11, 547

Emmaville NSW 123 L5, 60

Emmdale Roadhouse NSW 125 J10

Emmet Qld 515 P2

Empire Bay NSW 108 G8

Empire Vale NSW 123 Q3, 505 Q13

Emu Vic. 228 I1, 237 M9

Emu Bay SA 302 H11

Emu Creek Qld 496 E10

Emu Creek Vic. 229 R2

Emu Downs SA 303 M5

Emu Junction SA 309 J10

Emu Park Qld 507 O10, **454**

Emu Plains NSW 43

Emu Point Vic. 164

Endeavour Hills Vic. 217 I4, 219 L8

Endeavour River National Park Qld 509 L3

Eneabba WA 376 B5, 333, 355

Enfield NSW 98 H11, 103 J1

Enfield SA 295 J12, 296 B9

Enfield Vic. 218 C6, 229 L13, 235 O5, 163

Engadine NSW 102 F12

Englefield Vic. 234 E2, 236 E13

English Town Tas. 561 N9

Enmore NSW 99 K12, 103 M2, 123 M9

Enngonia NSW 125 N2

Enoch Point Vic. 219 R3

Enoggera Qld 492 E10

Ensay Vic. 119 B12, 233 R1, 242 G10

Ensay South Vic. 119 A13, 233 Q1, 242 G10

Jim's Place Wayside Inn NT 417 K7, 422 I9
Jindabyne NSW 118 G11, 119 D9, 142 C12, 243 K4, **67**
Jindalee Qld 494 C5, 431
Jindera NSW 127 P13, 241 P3, 242 B1, 57
Jindivick Vic. 219 P8, 232 H5
Jindong WA 367 D8, 369 E4
Jingalup WA 370 I3, 374 F10
Jingellic NSW 119 A8, 242 F1, 205
Jingili NT 412 F5
Jitarning WA 374 I6, 376 F9
Joadja NSW 116 A6, 119 H2, 121 J10
Joanna SA 234 A1, 236 A12, 301 I9
Joel Joel Vic. 228 E4, 237 K11
Joel South Vic. 228 E5
Johanna Vic. 223 E12, 235 M12
John Forrest National Park WA 366 D3, 313, 319, 325, 330, 338, 348
Johnburgh SA 299 E12, 305 K11
Johns River NSW 109 E11, 123 O13
Johnsonville Vic. 233 Q4, 242 G13
Jolimont WA 362 E2
Jondaryan Qld 496 C6, 505 M8, 473, 483
Jones Gully Vic. 496 F5
Joondalup WA 366 B1, 338
Joondanna WA 364 G11
Josbury WA 374 F7
Josephville Qld 497 L12
Joskeleigh Qld 507 O11
Joyces Creek Vic. 229 N5
Joyner Qld 492 B1
Jubilee Qld 492 E11
Jubuck WA 374 H5
Judbury Tas. 554 D7, 559 K9, 536
Jugiong NSW 119 C4, 120 E11, 62
Julatten Qld 503 B5, 509 M6
Julia SA 303 M6
Julia Creek Qld 513 J4, **458**
Jumbuk Vic. 233 K8
Jumbunna Vic. 219 O12, 232 G9
Junction Hill NSW 123 P6
Junction View Qld 496 G10
Jundah Qld 515 M2, **459**
Junee NSW 119 A4, 120 C11, 127 R9, **68**
Junee Reefs NSW 119 A3, 120 C11
Jung Vic. 236 H8
Junortoun Vic. 229 R2, 237 R10, 240 C8
Jupiter Creek SA 297 H3
Jura WA 374 I3
Jurien WA 376 B6, **337**
Jurunjung Vic. 218 H4

Kaarimba Vic. 240 H4
Kabra Qld 507 N11
Kadina SA 302 I6, 245, 246, 254, 261, **263**, 271
Kadnook Vic. 234 C1, 236 C12
Kadungle NSW 120 C4
Kagaru Qld 497 L11
Kaglan WA 371 O11, 374 I12
Kaimkillenbun Qld 496 B3, 505 M8
Kain NSW 119 F7, 143 J6
Kainton SA 303 J6
Kairi Qld 503 D12, 509 M7, 436
Kajabbi Qld 512 F2, 447
Kakadu National Park NT 413 F3, 415 O2, 418 G5, 383, 384, 390, 395, 396, 397, 398, 400, 402, 404, 407
Kalamunda WA 348
Kalamunda National Park WA 366 D5, 330
Kalangadoo SA 301 H11
Kalangara Qld 497 K3
Kalannie WA 376 D6

Kalaru NSW 117 G8, 119 G10, 243 Q6
Kalbar Qld 497 J11, 505 P10, 439
Kalbarri WA 375 C13, 376 A2, 332, **340**
Kalbarri National Park WA 375 C13, 376 A1, 314, 325, 331, 340
Kaleen ACT 140 F5
Kaleentha Loop NSW 126 F1
Kalgoorlie-Boulder WA 376 I6, 313, 314, 316, **340**, 343, 346
Kalimna West Vic. 233 R4, 242 G13
Kalinga Qld 492 G8
Kalka SA 308 A1, 379 R11, 422 B13
Kalkallo Vic. 219 J4, 232 C2, 240 F13
Kalkaringi NT 420 D6
Kalkee Vic. 236 G8
Kalkite NSW 118 G10, 142 D12
Kallangur Qld 497 M6, 431
Kallaroo WA 364 A2
Kallista Vic. 216 G12
Kaloorup WA 369 E4
Kalorama Vic. 216 G9, 222 B10, 194
Kalpienung Vic. 237 M3
Kalpowar Qld 505 M2
Kalumburu WA 381 N2
Kalunga Qld 509 M8
Kalyan SA 301 F1, 303 O9
Kamarah NSW 120 A9, 127 P7
Kamarooka Vic. 237 R8, 240 D6
Kambah ACT 141 B7
Kambalda WA 377 J7, 314, **341**, 346
Kamballup WA 371 O8, 374 I11
Kamber NSW 122 D12
Kambul Qld 503 C8
Kameruka NSW 117 E8, 243 P6
Kamma Qld 503 F10
Kamona Tas. 561 O7
Kanangra Boyd National Park NSW 104 F9, 119 H1, 120 I8
Kanawalla Vic. 234 G4
Kancoona Vic. 231 M2, 241 P7, 242 C5
Kancoona South Vic. 231 M3
Kandos NSW 120 I4, 84
Kangaloon NSW 116 D7
Kangarilla SA 296 C12, 297 G3, 298 I5, 301 B2, 303 L10
Kangaroo Flat NSW 123 M11
Kangaroo Flat SA 296 C5
Kangaroo Flat Vic. 229 Q2
Kangaroo Ground Vic. 215 R2, 216 A3
Kangaroo Island SA 297 A11, 302 F11, 245, 264, 265, 272, **277**
Kangaroo Point Qld 490 H8, 492 H12, 430
Kangaroo Valley NSW 116 D10, 119 I3, 80, 84
Kangarooby NSW 120 E7
Kangawall Vic. 236 D10
Kangiara NSW 119 D3, 120 F10
Kaniva Vic. 236 C7, **184**
Kanmantoo SA 296 F11
Kanumbra Vic. 241 J10
Kanya Vic. 228 E1, 237 K10
Kanyapella Vic. 127 K13, 240 F4
Kanypi SA 308 D2, 422 C13
Kaoota Tas. 554 G8, 559 L9
Kapinnie SA 302 C6
Kapooka NSW 120 B12, 127 R10
Kapunda SA 296 E3, 303 L7, 252, **263**
Karabeal Vic. 234 G4
Karadoc Vic. 126 E7, 238 H4
Karalundi WA 378 C11
Karanja Tas. 554 D3
Karara Qld 123 L1, 496 B13, 505 M11
Karatta SA 302 G13

Karawara WA 363 J7
Karawatha Qld 495 K9
Karawinna Vic. 126 C8, 238 E4
Kardinya WA 362 E11
Kareela NSW 102 I9
Kariah Vic. 223 C5, 235 L8
Karijini (Hamersley Range) National Park WA 375 I5, 378 B5, 313, 315, 331, 349, 355
Karingal Vic. 217 F12
Kariong NSW 108 E7
Karkoo SA 302 D6
Karlgarin WA 376 F9
Karlo Creek Vic. 119 F13, 243 O11
Karn Vic. 230 B4, 241 L7
Karnak Vic. 236 D10
Karnup WA 344, 355
Karonie WA 377 K6
Karoola Tas. 557 O6, 561 M7
Karoonda SA 301 F2, 303 O10
Karoonda Roadhouse Vic. 119 C12, 242 I9
Karrakatta WA 362 D5
Karratha WA 375 G1, **341**, 349
Karratha Roadhouse WA 375 G1
Karridale WA 367 C12, 369 C11, 374 B10
Karrinyup WA 364 C8
Kars Springs NSW 121 J1, 122 I13
Karte SA 301 H2, 303 Q10
Karuah NSW 112 F2, 121 N3
Karumba Qld 508 B8, 511 H8, **459**, 488
Karween Vic. 126 B8, 238 C4
Karyrie Vic. 237 K4
Katamatite Vic. 127 M13, 241 J4, 210
Katandra Vic. 240 I5
Katanning WA 371 L1, 374 H9, 376 E10, 327, **341**
Kata Tjuta NT 416 B11, 422 D11
Katherine NT 418 G10, 384, 395, 396, **398**, 401, 402, 407
Katoomba NSW 104 H7, 106 E9, 121 J7, 29, 42, 43, **68**
Kattyong Vic. 238 F9
Katunga Vic. 127 M13, 240 I3, 194
Katyil Vic. 236 G7
Kawarren Vic. 218 B12, 223 F8, 235 N10
Kayena Tas. 557 L5, 561 K7
Kealba Vic. 214 F5
Kedron Qld 492 G8
Keep River National Park NT 373 Q2, 381 R5, 418 A13, 420 A2, 402, 406
Keera NSW 123 J7
Keilor Vic. 214 G4, 151
Keilor Downs Vic. 214 F4
Keilor East Vic. 214 H5
Keilor Park Vic. 214 H4
Keiraville NSW 114 B9
Keith SA 301 G6, 303 P13, **264**
Kelfeera Vic. 230 C3
Kellalac Vic. 236 H7
Kellatier Tas. 560 F6
Kellerberrin WA 374 H3, 376 E7, 347
Kellevie Tas. 555 N5, 559 N8
Kelmscott WA 366 D6
Kelso NSW 104 B4
Kelso Tas. 557 J4, 561 K6, 525
Kelvin NSW 122 I10
Kelvin Grove Qld 492 F11
Kelvin View Vic. 241 J9
Kelvinhaugh Qld 496 D6
Kempsey NSW 109 G3, 123 O11, **69**
Kempton Tas. 554 H1, 559 L6, 541
Kendall NSW 109 E10, 123 O12, 72
Kendenup WA 371 M8, 374 H11, 348
Kenebri NSW 122 E9

Kenilworth Qld 505 P7, 456, **459**
Kenley Vic. 239 M7
Kenmare Vic. 126 D13, 236 G4
Kenmore NSW 119 G3, 120 H10
Kenmore Qld 494 C3
Kenmore Hills Qld 494 B2
Kennedy Qld 509 N10
Kennedy Range National Park WA 375 D8, 336
Kennedys Creek Vic. 223 C10, 235 L11
Kennett River Vic. 223 I11, 235 O11
Kennys Creek NSW 119 D2, 120 F10
Kensington NSW 99 N12, 103 P2
Kensington SA 293 L6
Kensington WA 363 J5
Kensington Gardens SA 293 L5
Kent Town SA 290 H8, 293 J6
Kentbruck Vic. 234 C8
Kenthurst NSW 100 A6
Kentlyn NSW 116 G1
Kentucky NSW 123 L9
Kenwick WA 363 P8
Keperra Qld 492 C9
Keppel Islands National Park Qld 507 P10
Keppel Sands Qld 507 O10
Keppoch SA 301 H8
Kerang Vic. 126 I12, 237 P3, 239 P13, 240 A2, 46, **184**, 205
Kerang East Vic. 237 P3, 240 B2
Kerang South Vic. 126 I12, 237 P3, 240 A2
Kergunyah Vic. 241 Q5, 242 C3
Kergunyah South Vic. 241 P6, 242 C4
Kernot Vic. 219 N12, 232 G8
Kerrabee NSW 121 J3
Kerrie Vic. 218 I2
Kerrisdale Vic. 219 L1, 240 H11, 210
Kerrs Creek NSW 120 G5
Kerry Qld 497 L13
Kerrydale Qld 499 D8
Kersbrook SA 296 E8, 301 C1, 303 L9, 266, 283
Keswick SA 292 H7
Kettering Tas. 554 H9, 559 L10, 526, **536**
Kevington Vic. 219 R3, 232 I1, 241 L12
Kew NSW 109 E10, 123 O12
Kew Vic. 215 M8
Kewarra Beach Qld 503 E7
Kewdale WA 363 M5
Kewell Vic. 236 H8
Keyneton SA 296 H5, 303 M8
Keysborough Vic. 217 F4
Keysbrook WA 366 C9, 374 D5
Khancoban NSW 118 A9, 119 B9, 242 H3, 69, 89
Ki Ki SA 301 F4, 303 O11
Kiah NSW 117 F12, 119 G12, 243 Q9
Kialla NSW 119 F3, 120 H10, 201
Kialla West Vic. 240 H6
Kiama NSW 116 H9, 121 K10, 55, **69**
Kiamba Qld 500 C6
Kiamil Vic. 126 E10, 238 H8
Kiana SA 302 C8, 261
Kiandra NSW 118 D3, 119 C7, 142 C7, 89
Kianga NSW 117 I2, 143 N11
Kiara WA 365 L9
Kiata Vic. 236 E7, 172
Kidaman Creek Qld 500 A8
Kidman Park SA 292 D5
Kidston Qld 509 J11
Kielpa SA 302 E4
Kies Hill SA 300 C10
Kiewa Vic. 241 Q5, 242 C3
Kikoira NSW 127 P5

Mulgrave Vic. 215 R13, 217 G1
Mullaley NSW 122 H11
Mullalco WA 364 A1, 366 A3
Mullalyup WA 367 I8, 370 B2, 374 D9
Mullaway NSW 123 P7
Mullenderee NSW 143 N8
Mullengandra NSW 127 Q13, 241 Q3
Mullengudgery NSW 122 A13, 125 R11
Mullewa WA 376 B3, **348**
Mulli Mulli NSW 123 O2, 505 P11
Mullindolingong Vic. 231 N4, 241 Q8, 242 C5
Mullion Creek NSW 120 G5
Mullumbimby NSW 123 Q2, 505 Q12, **76**
Mulpata SA 301 G2, 303 P10
Mulwala NSW 127 N13, 241 L3, **76**, 210
Mumballup WA 374 D8
Mumbannar Vic. 234 B6, 301 I12
Mumbel Vic. 237 M2, 239 M12
Mumbil NSW 120 F4
Mumblin Vic. 223 A7, 235 K9
Mummulgum NSW 123 O3, 505 P12
Munbilla Qld 497 J11
Mundaring WA 366 E4, 374 D3, 376 C8, **348**
Mundijong WA 366 D7, 374 D5, 353
Mundingburra Qld 501 B9
Mundoona Vic. 240 H4
Mundoora SA 303 J4
Mundrabilla Roadhouse WA 377 Q8, **348**
Mundubbera Qld 505 M4, **471**
Mundulla SA 301 H7, 257
Munetta SA 297 F5, 298 F13
Mungala SA 311 L4
Mungallala Qld 504 E6
Mungana Qld 509 J7
Mungar Qld 505 P4
Mungerannie Roadhouse SA 307 K8, 514 C 0, 267
Mungeribar NSW 120 D2
Mungery NSW 120 D3
Mungindi NSW 122 E3, 504 H13
Mungkan Kandju National Park Qld 510 D_0, 470
Munglinup WA 376 I10
Mungo National Park NSW 126 G5, 46, 66, 91
Mungungo Qld 505 M2
Muniganeen Qld 496 E6
Munjina Roadhouse WA 378 C4
Munro Vic. 233 N5, 201
Munster WA 366 B6
Muntadgin WA 376 F7
Muradup WA 370 I2, 374 F9
Murarrie Qld 493 K11
Murchison Vic. 240 H7, 193, 200, 201
Murchison WA 375 E12, 376 C1
Murchison East Vic. 240 H7
Murdinga SA 302 D5
Murdoch WA 362 G12
Murdunna Tas. 555 N7, 559 O9
Murga NSW 120 E6
Murgenella Settlement NT 418 H3
Murgheboluc Vic. 218 E9, 225 C6
Murgon Qld 505 N6, **471**
Murninnie Beach SA 302 H3
Murphys Creek Qld 496 F7, 505 N9, 483
Murphys Creek Vic. 229 L1, 237 O9
Murra Warra Vic. 236 G7
Murrabit Vic. 126 I11, 237 P1, 239 P12, 46, 184
Murramarang National Park NSW 143 O7, 47
Murrawal NSW 122 F12

Murray Bridge SA 296 I12, 301 D2, 303 M10, 205, **274**
Murray River NSW 31, 46, 56, 76, 88, 91, 145, 147, 173, 178, 190, 194, 198, 199, 203, **205**, 208, 210
Murray River SA 205, 246, 257, 262, 263, 267, 271, 274, 282, 283, 284, 285
Murray River National Park SA 126 A7, 303 Q7, 257
Murray Town SA 303 K2, 305 J12, 267
Murray-Sunset National Park Vic. 126 B9, 238 C7, 301 I1, 303 R8, 178, 196, 205
Murrayville Vic. 126 B11, 238 B10, 303 R10, 193
Murrindal Vic. 119 C13, 242 I10
Murrindindi Vic. 219 N2, 232 F1, 240 I12
Murringo NSW 119 C2, 120 E9, 94
Murroon Vic. 218 C12, 223 H8, 235 O10
Murrumba Qld 496 I5
Murrumbateman NSW 119 E4, 120 F11, 94, 135
Murrumbeena Vic. 215 N12
Murrumburrah NSW 119 C3, 120 E10, **76**
Murrungowar Vic. 119 D13, 243 K12
Murrurundi NSW 123 J13, **76**
Murtoa Vic. 236 I9, **192**
Murwillumbah NSW 123 Q1, 505 Q11, 73, **76**
Musgrave Station Qld 508 H1, 510 F13
Musk Vic. 218 E2, 229 P9
Musk Vale Vic. 218 E2, 229 P9
Muskerry East Vic. 240 D8
Musselboro Tas. 561 N9
Mussleroe Bay Tas. 561 Q4
Muston SA 302 I12
Muswellbrook NSW 121 K2, **78**
Mutarnee Qld 509 O12
Mutdapilly Qld 497 J10
Muttaburra Qld 506 B9, 513 P9, **472**
Muttama NSW 119 B4, 120 D11
Myall Vic. 237 P2, 239 P12
Myall Lakes National Park NSW 121 O3, 52, 65
Myall Mundi NSW 120 C1
Myall Plains NSW 127 N11
Myalla Tas. 560 E5
Myalup WA 367 G2, 374 C7, 337
Myamyn Vic. 234 E7
Myaree WA 362 F10
Myaring Vic. 234 B5
Myers Flat Vic. 229 Q1
Mylestom NSW 123 P8
Mylor SA 296 D11, 297 H2, 253
Myola Qld 503 D7
Myola Vic. 240 E8
Mypolonga SA 301 D2, 303 N9
Myponga SA 297 E6, 301 B3, 303 K11, 255
Myponga Beach SA 297 D6
Myrla SA 303 P7
Myrniong Vic. 218 F4, 229 R12, 235 R4, 240 C13, 166
Myrrhee Vic. 230 E5, 241 M8
Myrtle Bank SA 293 K9
Myrtle Bank Tas. 557 Q7, 561 M7
Myrtle Creek Vic. 237 R11, 240 D10
Myrtle Scrub NSW 123 M11
Myrtleford Vic. 231 J2, 241 O7, 242 B5, **193**
Myrtletown Qld 493 L6
Myrtleville NSW 119 G3, 120 I10
Mysia Vic. 237 O6
Mysterton Qld 501 C8
Mystic Park Vic. 126 H11, 237 O2, 239 O12, 203

Mywee Vic. 240 I2
Mywybilla Qld 496 B7

Nabageena Tas. 560 C5
Nabawa WA 376 B3
Nabiac NSW 121 O2
Nabowla Tas. 557 R5, 561 N7, 545
Nackara SA 303 M2, 305 M12
Nadda SA 126 A8, 303 Q8
Nagambie Vic. 240 G8, **193**, 199, 201
Nagoorin Qld 505 M1, 507 P13
Nailsworth SA 293 J3
Nairne SA 296 E11, 253
Nakara NT 412 G2
Nala Tas. 559 M5
Nalangil Vic. 223 F6
Nalinga Vic. 241 J6
Nallama NSW 88
Nalya WA 374 G5
Namadgi National Park ACT 118 I1, 119 D6, 120 F13, 139 B7, 142 E4, 136, 177
Nambour Qld 497 M1, 500 E8, 505 P7, 441, **472**
Nambrok Vic. 233 M6
Nambucca Heads NSW 123 P9, **78**
Nambung National Park WA 376 B6, 313, 330, 340, 344
Nana Glen NSW 123 P7
Nanango Qld 505 N7, **472**
Nanarup WA 371 P12, 374 I13, 321
Nandaly Vic. 126 F11, 239 J10
Nandi Qld 505 M8
Nanga WA 366 D12, 374 D6
Nangalala NT 419 L5
Nangana Vic. 219 N7, 222 E11, 232 F4
Nangar National Park NSW 120 E6
Nangari SA 126 A8, 238 A5, 303 R8
Nangeenan WA 374 I2
Nangiloc Vic. 126 E8, 238 H5
Nangkita SA 297 H5, 301 C3, 303 L10
Nangus NSW 119 B5, 120 C12
Nangwarry SA 301 H11
Nanneella Vic. 240 F5
Nannup WA 367 G10, 370 A4, 374 C10, 376 C11, **348**
Nanson WA 376 A3
Nantabibbie SA 303 M2, 305 L12
Nantawarra SA 303 K6
Nanutarra Roadhouse WA 375 E4
Napoleons Vic. 218 C5, 229 L12, 235 O4
Napperby SA 303 J3, 305 J13
Nar Nar Goon Vic. 219 N9, 232 F6
Nara Qld 496 E6
Naracoopa Tas. 558 B9
Naracoorte SA 301 H9, **275**
Naracoorte Caves Conservation Park SA 301 H9, 268, 272
Naradhan NSW 127 O5
Naraling WA 376 B3
Narangba Qld 497 M5
Narara NSW 105 P3, 108 E5
Narbethong Vic. 219 N4, 222 G4, 232 G2, 241 J13
Nareen Vic. 234 D3
Narellan NSW 105 K10, 116 F1, 53
Narembeen WA 376 F8
Naremburn NSW 99 M6
Naretha WA 377 M6
Nariel Vic. 119 B9, 242 G4
Naringal Vic. 235 J9
Narioka Vic. 240 G4
Narko Qld 496 D4
Narnu Bay SA 297 I8

Naroghid Vic. 223 A6
Narooma NSW 117 I2, 119 H9, 143 N11, 243 R2, 59, 70, **78**
Narrabarba NSW 117 E13, 119 G12, 243 P9
Narrabeen NSW 101 P10, 105 P7
Narrabri NSW 122 G8, **78**
Narrabri West NSW 122 G8
Narrabundah ACT 140 H13, 141 F4
Narracan Vic. 219 R11, 233 J7
Narrandera NSW 127 P9, **78**, 83
Narraport SA 237 K5
Narrawa NSW 119 E2, 120 G10
Narrawa Tas. 556 B9, 560 H8
Narrawallee NSW 143 P3, 89
Narraweena NSW 99 P2, 101 N12
Narrawong Vic. 234 E8
Narre Warren Vic. 219 L8
Narrewillock Vic. 237 M5
Narridy SA 303 K4
Narrien Range National Park Qld 506 G9
Narrikup WA 371 M10, 374 H12
Narrogin WA 374 G6, 376 E9, 325, **350**
Narromine NSW 120 D2, **79**
Narrung SA 301 D3, 303 M11, 271
Narrung Vic. 239 L7
Narwee NSW 102 I5
Nashdale NSW 120 F6
Nathalia Vic. 127 L13, 240 H4, 194
Nathan Qld 494 I5, 430
Natimuk Vic. 236 F9, **193**
National Park Tas. 554 C2, 559 J7
Native Dog Flat Vic. 119 B11, 242 I7
Natone Tas. 560 G6
Nattai NSW 104 I11, 116 C1, 121 J8
Nattai National Park NSW 104 I12, 116 B3, 119 H2, 121 J9
Natte Yallock Vic. 228 I3, 237 M11
Natural Arch National Park see Springbrook National Park
Natya Vic. 126 G9, 239 L8
Naval Base WA 366 A6
Navarre Vic. 228 F3, 237 L10
Navigators Vic. 218 D4, 229 N11, 235 P4, 240 A13
Nayook Vic. 219 P7, 207
Neale Junction WA 377 N2
Neales Flat SA 296 H1, 303 M7
Neath NSW 112 C9, 113 G11
Nebo Qld 507 K6, 463
Nectar Brook SA 299 B13, 303 J1, 304 I11
Nedlands WA 362 E6
Neds Corner Vic. 238 C3
Needles Tas. 556 G12, 561 J9
Neerabup National Park WA 366 A2, 374 C3, 376 E8
Neerdie Qld 505 P5
Neerim Vic. 219 P8, 232 H5
Neerim East Vic. 219 Q8
Neerim Junction Vic. 219 P7
Neerim South Vic. 219 P8, 232 H5, 207
Neeworra NSW 122 E4, 504 H13
Neika Tas. 554 H7, 559 L9
Neilborough Vic. 237 Q8, 240 C7
Neilborough East Vic. 237 Q8, 240 C7
Neilmongle NSW 125 Q2, 504 D13
Neilrex NSW 122 F13
Nelia Qld 513 K4
Nelligen NSW 119 H6, 143 N6, 47
Nelly Bay Qld 509 P12
Nelshaby SA 303 J3, 305 J13
Nelson NSW 105 M6
Nelson Vic. 234 A7, 301 I13, 198, 274
Nelson Bay NSW 112 H2, 121 O4, 51, 70, **79**

Nyora Vic. 219 O11, 232 G8, 185
Nypo Vic. 236 F3, 238 F13

O'Connell NSW 104 C5, 47
O'Connor ACT 140 G8
O'Connor WA 362 D11
O'Halloran Hill SA 298 D2
O'Malley ACT 141 E4
O'Malley SA 310 G4
O'Sullivan Beach SA 298 A4
Oak Beach Qld 503 D5, 509 M6
Oak Forest Qld 503 D7
Oak Park Vic. 214 I4
Oakbank SA 296 D10, 297 I1, 253, 254
Oakdale NSW 105 J11, 116 D1, 119 I1,
  121 J3
Oakden SA 295 L11
Oakey Qld 496 D6, 505 N9, 433, 473
Oakey Creek NSW 122 G12
Oaklands NSW 127 O11
Oaklands SA 302 I9
Oaklands Park SA 292 F12
Oakleigh Vic. 215 O12, 217 D1, 232 D4
Oakleigh East Vic. 215 O12
Oaks Tas. 557 L13, 561 L9
Oakvale Vic. 237 N4
Oakwood Tas. 555 N10, 559 N10
Oasis Roadhouse Qld 509 K11
Oatlands Tas. 559 M5, 529, 540
Oatley NSW 102 I7
Ob Flat SA 301 H12
Oberne NSW 119 A6, 120 C13
Oberon NSW 104 E7, 120 I7
Obi Obi Qld 497 L1, 500 A8
Obley NSW 120 E4
OBX Creek NSW 123 O6
Ocean Grove Vic. 218 G10, 225 G9, 232 A7,
  235 R3, 194
Ocean Shores NSW 123 Q2, 505 Q12
Ockley WA 374 G6
Oenpelli (Gunbalanya) NT 413 I2, 415 R1,
  418 I5
Officer Vic. 219 M9
Ogilvie WA 376 A3
Ogmore Qld 507 M9
Olangalah Vic. 223 G10
Olary SA 305 P10
Old Adaminaby NSW 118 G5, 119 D8,
  142 D9, 243 K1, 44
Old Bar NSW 121 P1
Old Beach Tas. 554 H4, 559 L8
Old Bonalbo NSW 123 O2, 505 P12
Old Junee NSW 119 A4, 120 C11, 127 R9
Old Noarlunga SA 296 A12, 297 F3, 298 C7,
  301 B2, 303 K10, 266, 275
Old Talangatta Vic. 241 R4, 242 D2
Old Toongabbie NSW 98 B5
Old Warrah NSW 122 I12
Oldina Tas. 560 F6
Olgas, The see Kata Tjuta
Olinda NSW 120 I4
Olinda Vic. 216 F11, 219 M7, 222 B11,
  232 E4, 159, 194
Olio Qld 513 M7
Olympic Dam Village SA 304 F4
Ombersley Vic. 218 C10, 223 I5, 235 O8
Omega NSW 116 G10
Omeo Vic. 119 A12, 242 F8, 187, 194, 195
Ondit Vic. 218 B10, 223 G6
One Arm Point WA 380 I6
One Tree NSW 127 K7
One Tree Hill SA 295 R1
Ongerup WA 371 R3, 376 F11

Onkaparinga Hills SA 298 E4
Onslow WA 375 D3, 349, 352
Oodla Wirra SA 303 M2, 305 L12
Oodnadatta SA 306 B6, 267, 275, 287
Ooldea SA 310 I4
Ooma Creek NSW 120 D7
Ooma North NSW 120 D7
Oonah Tas. 560 F7
Oondooroo Qld 513 L7
Oonoonba Qld 501 G9
Oorindi Qld 512 H4
Ootann Qld 509 K8
Ootha NSW 120 B5, 127 R3
Opalton Qld 513 L10
Ophir NSW 120 G5
Opossum Bay Tas. 554 I8, 559 M9
Ora Banda WA 376 I5, 341
Orange NSW 120 G6, 81
Orange Grove WA 363 Q8
Orangeville NSW 105 J10, 116 D1
Oranmeir NSW 119 F7, 143 K6
Orbost Vic. 243 J12, 194, 196
Orchid Beach Qld 505 Q2
Orford Tas. 555 N1, 559 O6, 529, 540
Orford Vic. 234 G8
Organ Pipes National Park Vic. 214 E1,
  218 I5, 232 C3, 176
Orielton Tas. 555 K4, 559 M7
Orient Point NSW 116 F12
Ormeau Qld 497 N11
Ormiston Qld 493 R13, 495 R1, 447
Ormiston Gorge National Park see West
  MacDonnell National Park
Ormond Vic. 215 M12, 217 B1
Orpheus Island National Park Qld
  509 O11, 426, 452, 457
Orroroo SA 299 E13, 303 L1, 305 K12, 276
Orrvale Vic. 240 I6
Orton Park NSW 104 B4
Osborne SA 294 D7
Osborne Park WA 364 F11
Osbornes Flat Vic. 241 P5, 242 B3
Osbourne NSW 120 A13, 127 P11
Osmaston Tas. 557 J12, 561 K9
Osmington WA 367 D9, 369 E7, 374 B9
Osterley Tas. 559 J5
Otford NSW 105 M12, 116 I3
Ottaba Qld 496 I5
Ottoway SA 294 F11
Otway National Park Vic. 223 F12,
  235 N12, 160, 177
Oura NSW 119 A5, 120 C12, 127 R10
Ourimbah NSW 105 P3, 108 E4, 121 M6,
  61
Ournie NSW 119 B8, 242 G1
Ouse Tas. 559 J5
Outer Harbor SA 294 C5, 296 A7
Outtrim Vic. 219 O13, 232 G9
Ouyen Vic. 126 E10, 238 H9, 196
Ovens Vic. 231 J3, 241 O7, 242 B5
Overland Corner SA 303 P6
Overlander Roadhouse WA 375 C11
Ovingham SA 290 B3
Owanyilla Qld 505 P4
Owen SA 296 A1, 303 K7
Owens Gap NSW 121 K1
Oxenford Qld 497 N12, 499 C2, 505 Q10,
  434, 438
Oxford Falls NSW 99 O1, 101 N11
Oxford Park Qld 492 D9
Oxley ACT 141 C9
Oxley NSW 126 I7, 239 Q3, 63
Oxley Qld 494 E6

Oxley Vic. 230 F1, 241 M6, 189
Oxley Wild Rivers National Park NSW
  123 M10, 45, 90
Oyster Bay NSW 102 I9
Oyster Cove Tas. 554 G9, 559 L10
Ozenkadnook Vic. 236 C10
Paaratte Vic. 223 A9, 235 K10
Pacific Palms NSW 121 P2
Pacific Paradise Qld 497 N1, 500 H8
Packsaddle Roadhouse NSW 124 C7
Padbury WA 364 B3
Paddington NSW 99 N11, 103 P1, 105 O8,
  38, 40
Paddington Qld 492 F12, 430
Paddys River NSW 119 H3, 120 I10
Padstow NSW 102 G6
Padthaway SA 301 H7, 257
Page ACT 140 C6
Pages Flat SA 297 F5
Pagewood NSW 103 P5
Paignie Vic. 238 G9
Painswick Vic. 229 L2
Pajinka Wilderness Lodge Qld 510 C2, 465
Pakenham Vic. 219 M9, 232 F6, 184
Palana Tas. 558 A10
Palgarup WA 370 D5, 374 D10
Pallamallawa NSW 122 H5
Pallara Qld 494 G9
Pallarang Vic. 238 C9
Pallarenda Qld 509 P12
Pallarup WA 376 H10, 342
Palm Beach NSW 101 Q2, 105 P5, 108 H11,
  35, 40, 41
Palm Beach Qld 499 G9, 434
Palm Cove Qld 503 E7, 509 M6, 473
Palm Dale NSW 105 P3, 108 E3
Palm Grove NSW 105 P3, 108 D4
Palm Valley see Finke Gorge National Park
Palm View Qld 500 G11
Palmer SA 296 H9, 301 D1, 303 M9
Palmer River Roadhouse Qld 509 K4
Palmers Island NSW 123 Q5
Palmers Oakey NSW 104 D2, 120 I5
Palmerston ACT 140 G3
Palmerston NT 414 D3, 388
Palmerville Qld 509 J4
Palmwoods Qld 497 M1, 500 E9
Palmyra WA 362 D10
Paloona Tas. 556 D7, 560 I7
Paluma Range National Park Qld 509 N11,
  457
Pambula NSW 117 F10, 119 G11, 243 Q7,
  59, 75
Pambula Beach NSW 117 F10, 119 G11,
  243 Q7
Pampas Qld 496 B9, 505 M10
Panania NSW 102 E5
Panitya Vic. 238 A10, 301 I2, 303 R10
Panmure Vic. 235 J9
Pannawonica WA 375 F3, 357
Panorama SA 293 J11
Pantapin WA 374 H3
Panton Hill Vic. 216 C1, 219 L5, 232 E3
Paper Beach Tas. 557 L6, 532
Pappinbarra NSW 109 C7, 123 N12
Papunya NT 422 G7
Para Hills SA 295 M8
Para Vista SA 295 M9
Paraburdoo WA 375 H5, 378 A6, 349
Parachilna SA 299 D6, 305 J6, 257
Paradise SA 293 M2, 295 N13
Paradise Tas. 556 D10, 560 I8
Paradise Vic. 228 F2, 237 K10

Paradise Vic. 223 G12, 235 N12
Paradise Beach Vic. 233 O7, 201
Paradise Point Qld 499 E2
Parafield SA 295 K8
Parafield Gardens SA 295 J6
Paralowie SA 295 J4
Parap NT 411 E6, 412 A13, 396
Paraparap Vic. 225 D9
Parattah Tas. 559 M5
Pardoo Roadhouse WA 380 D12
Parenna Tas. 558 A9
Parilla SA 301 H3, 303 Q10
Paringa SA 126 A7, 303 Q6, 280
Paris Creek SA 296 D13, 297 I4
Park Holme SA 292 F11
Park Orchards Vic. 215 R7, 216 A7
Park Ridge Qld 495 J13
Parkers Corner Vic. 233 J5
Parkes ACT 138 D9, 140 G11, 141 F1
Parkes NSW 120 D5, 81
Parkham Tas. 556 H9, 561 J8
Parkhurst Qld 507 N10
Parkinson Qld 494 I10
Parkside SA 290 H13, 293 J8
Parkside Tas. 561 Q8
Parkville NSW 121 K1
Parkville Vic. 215 K7, 155
Parkwood Vic. 234 E4
Parndana SA 302 H12, 277
Parnella Tas. 561 R8
Parrakie SA 301 G3, 303 P11
Parramatta NSW 98 C6, 105 M8, 121 L7,
  39, 43, 431
Parramatta Park Qld 502 F9
Parrawe Tas. 560 E7
Paru NT 418 D4
Paruna SA 125 A9, 301 H1, 303 Q8
Parwan Vic. 218 G5, 229 R13, 232 A3,
  235 R4
Pasadena SA 292 H12
Paschendale Vic. 234 D4
Pascoe Vale Vic. 215 J4
Paskeville SA 303 J6, 263
Pastoria Vic. 218 H1
Pata SA 303 Q8
Patchewollock Vic. 126 D11, 238 G11, 196
Pateena Tas. 557 N12, 561 L9
Paterson NSW 112 B5, 121 M3, 74
Patersonia Tas. 557 Q8, 561 M8
Patho Vic. 240 D3
Patonga NSW 105 O5, 108 F10
Patrick Estate Qld 497 J7
Patterson Lakes Vic. 217 E9
Patyah Vic. 236 C10
Paupong NSW 118 H13, 119 D10, 243 K5
Pawleena Tas. 555 K4, 559 N7
Pawtella Tas. 559 M5
Paxton NSW 112 B11, 121 L4
Payneham SA 293 L4
Paynes Crossing NSW 121 L4
Paynes Find WA 376 E4
Paynesville Vic. 233 Q5, 195, 196, 201
Paytens Bridge NSW 120 D7
Peaceful Bay WA 370 I12, 374 F13, 376 D12
Peachester Qld 497 L2, 500 C13
Peak Charles National Park WA 376 I9,
  331
Peak Crossing Qld 497 K10, 505 P10
Peak Downs Qld 506 I8, 467
Peak Hill NSW 120 D4, 81
Peak Hill WA 378 C10
Peak Range National Park Qld 506 I9
Peak View NSW 119 F8, 142 I10, 243 O1

Peake SA 301 F3, 303 O11
Peakhurst NSW 102 H6, 105 N9
Pearce ACT 141 C5
Pearcedale Vic. 219 L10, 221 O3, 232 E7
Pearl Beach NSW 108 F10
Pearshape Tas. 558 A9
Peats Ridge NSW 105 O3, 108 B4, 121 L6
Pebbly Beach NSW 119 H6, 143 O6
Pebbly Beach Qld 503 D5
Pechey Qld 496 F6
Peebinga SA 126 A9, 238 A8, 301 I1, 303 R9
Peechelba Vic. 241 M4
Peechelba East Vic. 241 M4
Peel NSW 104 C3, 120 H6
Peelhurst WA 366 B9, 374 C5
Peelwood NSW 104 A11, 119 F1, 120 G8, 57
Peep Hill SA 303 M6
Pegarah Tas. 558 A9
Pekina SA 303 K2, 305 K12
Pelaw Main NSW 112 D9
Pelham Tas. 554 E1, 559 K6
Pella Vic. 236 F4, 198
Pelverata Vic. 554 F8, 559 K9
Pemberton WA 370 C7, 374 D11, 376 C11, 327, **352**
Pemberton National Park WA 327
Pembroke NSW 109 F7, 123 O12
Penarie NSW 126 H7, 239 N4
Penderlea NSW 118 E12
Pendle Hill NSW 98 A6
Penguin Tas. 556 A4, 560 H6, 528, **540**
Penna Tas. 555 K4, 559 M8
Pennant Hills NSW 98 G1, 100 E11
Penneshaw SA 303 J12, 264, 277
Pennington SA 292 E1, 294 E12
Pennyroyal Vic. 218 C12, 223 I8
Penola SA 234 A3, 301 I10, **275**
Penong SA 311 M9, 258, 343
Penrice SA 300 H5
Penrith NSW 105 K7, 121 K7, 43
Penrose NSW 119 H3, 121 J10
Penshurst NSW 102 I7
Penshurst Vic. 234 H6
Pentland Qld 506 C3, 513 R3
Penwortham SA 303 L6, 259
Penzance Tas. 555 O9
Peppermint Grove WA 362 C7
Peppers Plains Vic. 236 G6
Peppimenarti NT 418 C9
Peranga Qld 496 D4
Percydale Vic. 228 I5
Peregian Beach Qld 500 H4, 505 Q6
Perekerten NSW 126 I9, 239 P8
Perenjori WA 376 C4, **352**
Perenna Vic. 236 E5
Pericoe NSW 117 C11, 119 F12, 243 P8
Perisher NSW 118 E11, 119 C9, 142 B12, 243 J4, 68, 77, 87
Perkins Reef Vic. 229 O5
Peronne Vic. 236 C9
Perponda SA 301 F2, 303 O9
Perroomba SA 303 K2, 305 J12
Perry Bridge Vic. 233 O6
Perseverance Qld 496 G6
Perth Tas. 557 O12, 561 L9, 519, 537
Perth WA 360, 366 B4, 374 C3, 376 B8, 313, **316–19**, 325, 330, 338
Perthville NSW 104 B5, 120 H6
Petal Point Tas. 561 P5
Petcheys Bay Tas. 554 E10
Peterborough SA 303 L2, 305 L13, **276**, 281
Peterborough Vic. 223 A10, 235 K11
Peterhead SA 294 C10

Petersham NSW 99 J11, 103 L1
Petersville SA 302 I7
Petford Qld 509 L7
Petrie Qld 492 C1, 497 L6
Petrie Terrace Qld 490 A2
Pewsey Vale SA 300 F10
Pheasant Creek Vic. 219 L3, 232 E1, 240 H13
Phillip ACT 140 F13, 141 D4
Phillip Bay NSW 103 Q7
Phillip Island Vic. 219 L13, 221 N12, 232 E9, 145, **171**, 182
Phils Creek NSW 119 E2, 120 F9
Pialba Qld 457
Piallaway NSW 122 I11
Pialligo ACT 141 H2
Piambie Vic. 239 M7
Piangil Vic. 126 G10, 239 M9
Piawaning WA 376 D6, 350
Piccadilly SA 293 Q10
Pickertaramoor NT 418 D4
Picnic Bay Qld 509 P12
Picnic Point NSW 102 E7
Picola Vic. 127 L13, 240 G3
Picola North Vic. 127 L13, 240 G3
Picton NSW 105 J11, 116 E2, 119 I2, 121 K9, **81**
Picton WA 367 G4, 324
Pier Millan Vic. 126 F10, 239 J10
Piesseville WA 374 G7
Pigeon Ponds Vic. 234 E2, 236 E13
Piggabeen NSW 499 G11
Piggoreet Vic. 218 B5, 229 K13, 235 N4
Pikedale Qld 123 L2, 505 M12
Pilbara, The WA 375 I3, 378 B4
Pilcherra Bore SA 301 G2, 303 P10
Pilchers Bridge Vic. 229 R3
Pile Siding Vic. 223 E10
Pillar Valley NSW 123 P6
Pilliga NSW 122 E8
Pillinger Tas. 558 E4
Pilot Hill NSW 142 A5
Pilton Qld 496 F10
Pimba SA 304 F6, 287
Pimlico Qld 501 C7
Pimpimbudgee Qld 496 D2
Pimpinio Vic. 236 G8
Pinaroo SA 238 A10
Pindar WA 376 C3
Pine Creek NT 413 A13, 414 I13, 418 F8, **400**
Pine Hill Qld 506 G11
Pine Lodge Vic. 240 I5
Pine Point SA 302 I8
Pine Ridge NSW 122 I12
Pinelands Qld 496 F5
Pinery SA 296 A2, 303 K7
Pingaring WA 376 F9
Pingelly WA 374 F5, 376 D9, **352**
Pingrup WA 376 F10
Pinjarra WA 366 C10, 374 C6, 376 C9, 327, **353**
Pinjarra Hills Qld 494 B5
Pinkenba Qld 493 K8
Pinnaroo SA 126 A11, 301 I3, 303 R10, **276**
Pioneer Tas. 561 P6
Pioneer Bend SA 302 H12
Pipalyatjara SA 308 B2, 379 R11, 422 B13
Pipers Brook Tas. 557 O3, 561 M6, 526, 533, 537, 541
Pipers Creek Vic. 218 G2
Pipers Flat NSW 104 E3
Pipers River Tas. 557 N4, 561 L6

Pira Vic. 126 G10, 239 M10
Piries Vic. 219 R1, 230 D11, 241 L11
Pirlta Vic. 238 F4
Pirron Yallock Vic. 218 A11, 223 E7, 235 M9
Pithara WA 376 D6
Pitt Town NSW 105 L6, 46, **82**
Pittong Vic. 218 A5, 228 I12, 235 M4
Pittsworth Qld 496 C9, 505 N9, **473**, 483
Pittwater NSW 46
Plain View Qld 496 D5
Plainland Qld 496 I8
Platts NSW 117 A11, 119 F12, 243 N8
Pleasant Hills NSW 120 A13, 127 P11
Pleasure Point NSW 102 D6
Plenty Tas. 554 E3, 559 K7, 540
Plenty Vic. 215 O2
Plush Corner SA 300 H4
Plympton SA 292 F8
Plympton Park SA 292 F10
Poatina Tas. 559 K1, 561 K11
Point Clare NSW 105 P4, 108 F7
Point Cook Vic. 214 D13
Point Leo Vic. 219 K12, 221 K10, 175
Point Lonsdale Vic. 218 H11, 220 A6, 225 H9, 232 B7, 156, 198
Point Lookout Qld 497 Q8, 505 R9
Point Pass SA 303 M6
Point Piper NSW 99 P10
Point Samson WA 375 G1, 378 A1, **353**, 355
Point Turton SA 302 H9
Pokataroo NSW 122 D5
Pokolbin NSW 112 A10, 113 A9, 83
Police Point Tas. 554 E11, 559 K11
Policemans Point SA 301 E5, 303 N13
Polkemmet Vic. 236 F9
Pomborneit Vic. 223 D6, 235 M9
Pomborneit East Vic. 223 E6
Pomborneit North Vic. 223 D6
Pomona Qld 500 B1, 505 P6, **473**
Pomonal Vic. 228 A6, 234 I1, 236 I12
Pompapiel Vic. 237 Q7, 240 B6
Pompoota SA 296 I10
Ponde SA 296 I10
Pondooma SA 302 G4
Pontville Tas. 554 H3, 559 L7, 529, **541**
Pontypool Tas. 559 O5
Poochera SA 302 A1, 304 A12, 311 R12
Pooginagoric SA 301 H7
Poolaijelo Vic. 234 B2, 236 B13, 301 I10
Poona National Park Qld 505 P4
Pooncarie NSW 126 E4
Poonindie SA 302 D8, 278
Pooraka SA 295 K9
Pootilla Vic. 218 D3, 229 N10
Pootnoura SA 309 P9
Poowong Vic. 219 O11, 232 G8
Poowong East Vic. 219 P11
Popanyinning WA 374 F6
Porcupine Flat Vic. 229 O4
Porcupine National Park Qld 506 A3, 513 P3, 457
Porcupine Ridge Vic. 218 E2, 229 P7, 235 Q1, 237 Q13, 240 C11
Porepunkah Vic. 231 L5, 241 P8, 242 C6, 167
Pormpuraaw Aboriginal Community Qld 508 D1, 510 A13
Porongurup WA 371 O9, 374 H12
Porongurup National Park WA 371 N9, 374 H12, 321, 331, 348
Port Adelaide SA 294 D11, 296 A8, 301 A1, 303 K9, 250, 251

Port Albert Vic. 233 L10, **196**, 210
Port Alma Qld 507 O11, 485
Port Arthur Tas. 555 N10, 559 N10, 517, 519, 524, 529, 531, 532, **541**
Port Augusta SA 299 A12, 304 I11, 245, **276**, 281, 287, 343, 392
Port Bonython SA 302 I2, 304 I12
Port Broughton SA 303 J4, **276**
Port Campbell Vic. 223 A10, 235 K11, 168, 182, 191, **197**
Port Campbell National Park Vic. 223 B11, 235 K11, 146, 177, 191, 197, 207
Port Clinton SA 303 J7
Port Davis SA 302 I3, 303 I3, 304 I13
Port Denison WA 376 B4, 333
Port Douglas Qld 503 C4, 509 M5, 460, 461, **474**
Port Elliot SA 297 H8, 301 C3, 303 L11, **278**, 284
Port Fairy Vic. 234 G9, 191, **197**, 207
Port Franklin Vic. 233 J10, 175
Port Gawler SA 296 A6, 303 K8
Port Germein SA 303 J2, 304 I13, 279
Port Gibbon SA 302 G5
Port Gregory WA 351
Port Hacking NSW 103 K13
Port Hedland WA 378 C1, 380 B13, 349, 350, **353**
Port Hughes SA 302 I6
Port Huon Tas. 554 E10, 559 K10, 536, 541
Port Julia SA 302 I8
Port Kembla NSW 116 H6, 121 K10, 29
Port Kenny SA 302 A3, 311 Q13, 262, 282
Port Latta Tas. 560 E4, 546
Port Lincoln SA 302 D8, 245, 246, 254, 262, 265, **278**
Port MacDonnell SA 301 H13, **278**
Port Macquarie NSW 109 G7, 123 P12, 30, **82**
Port Melbourne Vic. 215 J10, 154
Port Minlacowie SA 302 H9
Port Neill SA 302 E6, 262, 283
Port Noarlunga SA 298 B5, 301 A2, 303 J10, 252, 275
Port Noarlunga South SA 298 A6
Port Pirie SA 303 J3, 304 I13, **279**
Port Rickaby SA 302 H8, 271
Port Sorell Tas. 556 G5, 561 J6, **542**
Port Stephens NSW 112 G2, 121 N4, **51**, 70
Port Victoria SA 302 H7, 261, **279**
Port Vincent SA 302 I9, 271
Port Wakefield SA 303 J6, 256
Port Welshpool Vic. 233 K10, 208
Port Willunga SA 296 A13, 297 E4, 298 B10, 255
Portarlington Vic. 218 H9, 225 I7, 232 B6, 173
Porters Retreat NSW 104 D10, 119 G1, 120 H8
Portland NSW 104 E3, 120 I6
Portland Vic. 234 D9, 170, **197**
Portland Roads Qld 510 F7
Portsea Vic. 218 I11, 220 C7, 225 I10, 232 B8, 158, 202
Portsmith Qld 502 G13, 443
Postmans Ridge Qld 496 F7
Potato Point NSW 117 I1, 143 N10
Pothana NSW 113 C1
Potts Point NSW 99 N10
Pottsville NSW 123 Q1, 505 R11, 89
Pound Creek Vic. 232 H10
Powelltown Vic. 219 O7, 222 H11, 232 G4, 206

Tarcowie SA 303 K2, 305 K12
Tarcutta NSW 119 A5, 120 C13
Tardun WA 376 C3, 348
Taree NSW 109 C13, 121 P1, 123 N13, **85**
Taren Point NSW 103 K10
Targa Tas. 557 R7, 561 M8
Tarilta Vic. 218 E1, 229 P6
Taringa Qld 494 E2
Tarlee SA 296 D1, 303 L7, 264
Tarlo NSW 119 G3, 120 I10
Tarlo River National Park NSW 119 G3, 120 I10
Tarnagulla Vic. 229 M2, 237 O10, 240 A8, 173
Tarneit Vic. 214 B9, 218 H6, 225 I2, 232 B4
Tarnma SA 303 L6
Tarnook Vic. 241 K7
Tarome Qld 496 I12
Tarong Qld 496 E1
Taroom Qld 505 J4, **482**
Taroona Tas. 552 H13, 554 I7, 559 L9, 521, 536
Tarpeena SA 301 H11
Tarra-Bulga National Park Vic. 233 K8, 147, 191, 204, 210
Tarragal Vic. 234 C9
Tarragindi Qld 494 H4
Tarraleah Tas. 558 I4
Tarranginnie Vic. 236 D7
Tarrango Vic. 238 E5
Tarranyurk Vic. 236 F6
Tarraville Vic. 233 L10, 196, 210
Tarrawanna NSW 114 D3
Tarrawingee Vic. 241 N6
Tarrayoukyan Vic. 234 D2, 236 D13
Tarrenlea Vic. 234 E5
Tarrington Vic. 234 G5
Tarrion NSW 125 Q5
Tarwin Vic. 232 H10
Tarwin Lower Vic. 232 H10, 209
Tarwin Meadows Vic. 232 H10
Tarwonga WA 374 F7
Tascott NSW 108 F7
Tasman Peninsula Tas. 555 M10, 559 O10
Tatham NSW 123 P3
Tathra NSW 117 G8, 119 G10, 243 R6, 48, **86**
Tathra National Park WA 376 C5, 326
Tatong Vic. 230 C5, 241 L8
Tatura Vic. 240 H6, 201
Tatyoon Vic. 228 D11, 235 K3
Tawonga Vic. 231 N4, 241 Q8, 242 D6, 203
Tawonga South Vic. 231 N5, 241 Q8, 242 D6
Tayene Tas. 561 N8
Taylors Arm NSW 123 O9
Taylors Beach Qld 509 O11, 457
Taylors Flat NSW 119 E2, 120 F9
Taylors Lakes Vic. 214 E3
Taylorville SA 303 O6
Tea Gardens NSW 112 H1, 121 O4
Tea Tree Tas. 554 I3, 541
Tea Tree Gully SA 295 Q9
Teal Flat SA 301 E1, 303 N9
Teal Point Vic. 237 P2, 239 P13, 240 B1
Tecoma Vic. 216 F13
Teddywaddy Vic. 237 M6
Teesdale Vic. 218 D8, 225 B5, 235 P7
Teeval Qld 441
Telegraph Point NSW 109 F6, 123 O11
Telford Vic. 241 K4
Telita Tas. 561 O7
Telopea NSW 98 D5

Telopea Downs Vic. 236 B5, 301 I6, 303 R13
Temma Tas. 560 B6
Temora NSW 119 A2, 120 C10, 127 R8, **86**
Tempe NSW 99 K13, 103 M3
Templers SA 296 D4, 303 L7
Templestowe Vic. 215 Q6, 219 K6
Templin Qld 497 J12, 439
Tempy Vic. 126 E11, 238 H11
Ten Mile Vic. 219 R3
Ten Mile Hollow NSW 105 N3
Tenandra NSW 122 D11
Tennant Creek NT 421 K10, 384, 396, **406**
Tennyson NSW 98 I8
Tennyson Qld 494 F4
Tennyson SA 292 B3
Tennyson Vic. 237 R7, 240 D5
Tenterden WA 371 L7, 374 H11
Tenterfield NSW 123 M4, 505 N13, 79, **86**
Tenth Island Tas. 561 L5, 539
Tenthill Qld 496 G8
Tepko SA 296 H10, 301 D2, 303 M9
Terang Vic. 223 A6, 235 K8, **203**
Teridgerie NSW 122 E10
Teringie SA 293 O5
Terip Terip Vic. 240 I10
Terka SA 303 J1, 305 J12
Termeil NSW 119 H6, 121 J13, 143 O5
Terowie NSW 120 C3
Terowie SA 303 L3, 305 L13, 276
Terranora NSW 499 H13
Terrey Hills NSW 101 L8, 105 O6
Terrick Terrick Vic. 237 Q5, 240 C4
Terrigal NSW 105 Q4, 108 H5, 121 M6, **86**
Terry Hie Hie NSW 122 H6
Tesbury Vic. 223 C6
Tewantin Qld 500 G2, 505 Q6, 441, 472
Tewinga NSW 123 O9
Tewkesbury Tas. 560 F6
Texas Qld 123 K3, 505 M12, **482**
Thalaba NSW 104 B13, 119 F2, 120 G9
Thalia Vic. 237 L5
Thallon Qld 122 E2, 504 H12, 477
Thanes Creek Qld 496 C12
Thangool Qld 505 K1, 507 N13
Tharbogang NSW 127 N7
Thargomindah Qld 515 N10, 454, 486
Tharwa ACT 139 E7, 142 G4, 136
The Anchorage NSW 143 N9
The Basin Vic. 216 E11
The Bluff Qld 496 G5
The Brothers Vic. 119 A11, 242 G7
The Cascade Vic. 241 R5, 242 E3
The Caves Qld 507 N10
The Channon NSW 123 Q2, 80
The Cove Vic. 235 J10
The Entrance NSW 105 Q3, 108 H2, 121 M6, **86**
The Entrance North NSW 105 Q3, 108 H2
The Gap NSW 40
The Gap Qld 492 C11
The Gap Vic. 218 H4
The Gardens NT 410 C3, 411 D8
The Gardens Tas. 561 R7
The Glen Tas. 557 N5, 561 L7
The Granites NT 420 D12, 422 D2
The Gulf NSW 123 L4, 505 M13
The Gums Qld 505 K8
The Gurdies Vic. 219 N11, 232 G8
The Heart Vic. 233 N6
The Highlands Vic. 218 G5, 229 R12
The Hill NSW 110 F8
The Junction NSW 110 C9
The Lagoon NSW 104 B5

The Lakes National Park Vic. 233 Q5, 177, 195, 196, 201
The Levels SA 295 J8
The Lynd Qld 509 K11
The Monument Qld 512 F6
The Narrows NT 411 H5, 412 C12
The Oaks NSW 105 J11, 116 D1, 119 I1, 121 J8, 53
The Palms National Park Qld 496 F2
The Patch Vic. 216 H12, 219 M7, 222 B12
The Pines SA 302 H9
The Range SA 298 H10
The Risk NSW 123 P2, 505 P11
The Rock NSW 120 B13, 127 Q11, 90
The Rocks NSW 96 D3, 33, 34, 36, 38, 41
The Sisters Vic. 235 J8
The Spit NSW 99 O6
The Summit Qld 123 M2, 505 N12, 478
The Vale NSW 126 H5, 239 O1
Thebarton SA 292 G5, 250, 251
Theodore ACT 141 E11
Theodore Qld 505 J2, **482**
Theresa Park NSW 105 K10
Thevenard SA 311 N10, 258
Thirlmere NSW 105 J12, 116 D3, 119 I2, 121 J9, 82
Thirlmere Lakes National Park NSW 105 J12, 116 D3, 75, 82
Thirlstane Tas. 556 G6, 561 J7
Thirroul NSW 105 M13, 116 H5, 121 K9
Thomas Plains SA 303 J6
Thomastown Vic. 215 M2, 219 K5, 232 D3
Thomson Vic. 224 H10
Thoona Vic. 241 L5
Thora NSW 123 O8, 48
Thornborough Qld 509 L6, 461
Thornbury Vic. 215 L6
Thorneside Qld 493 O11
Thorngate SA 290 D1
Thornlands Qld 495 R3, 475
Thornleigh NSW 98 F1, 100 E11
Thornlie WA 363 N11
Thornton NSW 112 D7
Thornton Qld 496 H10, 505 O10
Thornton Vic. 219 P2, 241 K11, 174
Thornville Qld 496 E3
Thorpdale Vic. 219 R11, 232 I7, 207
Thowgla Vic. 119 B8, 242 H3
Thowgla Upper Vic. 119 B9, 242 H3
Thredbo NSW 118 C13, 119 C10, 142 A13, 242 I5, 68, 77, **87**, 136
Three Bridges Vic. 219 O7, 222 G11, 232 G4
Three Springs WA 376 C4, **355**
Three Ways Roadhouse NT 421 K10, 406
Thrington SA 302 I6
Thrushton National Park Qld 504 E9
Thuddungra NSW 119 B1, 120 D9
Thulimbah Qld 123 M2, 505 N12
Thulloo NSW 120 A7, 127 P5
Thuringowa Qld 509 O13
Thurla Vic. 238 G4
Thursday Island Qld 510 B2, **467**
Thuruna SA 283
Ti Tree NT 422 I5, **406**
Ti Tree Store & Police Station NT 422 I5
Tia NSW 123 M11
Tiaro Qld 505 P4
Tibbuc NSW 121 N1, 123 M13
Tiberias Tas. 559 M6
Tibooburra NSW 124 D3, **88**
Tichborne NSW 120 D5
Tickera SA 302 I5

Tidal River Vic. 233 J12, 177, 183, 192
Tiega Vic. 238 G9
Tieri Qld 507 J10
Tighes Hill NSW 110 B3
Tilba Tilba NSW 117 H3, 119 H9, 143 M12, 243 R3
Tilmouth Well Roadhouse NT 422 H6
Tilpa NSW 125 J8, 92
Timbarra Vic. 119 B12, 242 H10
Timber Creek NT 418 D13, 420 D2, 402, **406**
Timberoo Vic. 238 G9
Timberoo South Vic. 238 G10
Timbertown NSW 82, 91
Timbillica NSW 119 G13, 243 P10
Timboon Vic. 223 A8, 235 K10, 168, 197
Timmering Vic. 240 F6
Timor Vic. 229 L4, 237 O11, 189
Timor West Vic. 229 K4, 237 N11
Tin Can Bay Qld 505 P5, **483**
Tinaburra Qld 503 D12, 509 M7, 460, 487
Tinamba Vic. 233 M5
Tinaroo Falls Qld 503 D11, 509 M7, 461
Tinbeerwah Qld 500 E2
Tincurrin WA 374 H7
Tindal NT 418 G10
Tinderbox Tas. 554 I8, 559 L9, 536
Tingalpa Qld 493 L12
Tingaringy NSW 119 D11, 243 K7
Tingha NSW 123 K7, 79, **88**
Tingoora Qld 505 N6
Tinonee NSW 109 B13, 121 O1, 123 N13
Tintaldra Vic. 119 B8, 242 H1, 170
Tintinara SA 301 F5, 303 O12, 260
Tiparra West SA 302 I7, 302 I7
Tipton Qld 496 A6, 505 M8
Tirranaville NSW 119 G4, 120 H11
Tirranna Roadhouse Qld 511 E9
Tittybong Vic. 237 M3, 239 M13
Tiwi NT 412 G1
Tjukayirla Roadhouse WA 377 M1, 379 L12, 344
Tjuwanpa Resource Centre NT 416 H5, 422 H9
Tobermorey Roadhouse NT 423 Q5, 512 B8
Tocal NSW 74
Tocal Qld 513 N12
Tocumwal NSW 127 M12, 240 I2, **88**, 169, 205
Togari Tas. 560 B4
Toggannoggera NSW 119 F6, 143 K6
Toiberry Tas. 557 M13, 561 L9
Tolga Qld 503 C12, 509 M7, 436, 437
Tolmie Vic. 230 E8, 241 M9, 188
Tom Groggin NSW 118 B13, 88
Tom Price WA 375 H4, 378 B5, 349, **355**
Tomago NSW 79
Tomahawk Tas. 561 O5
Tomahawk Creek Vic. 223 E8
Tomakin NSW 143 N8
Tomalla NSW 121 M1, 123 L13
Tomaree National Park NSW 112 I2, 121 O4, 79
Tombong NSW 119 E11, 243 M7
Tomboye NSW 119 G5, 120 I12, 143 M2
Tomerong NSW 143 Q1
Tomewin Qld 499 D13
Tomingley NSW 120 D3
Tongala Vic. 240 F5
Tonganah Tas. 561 N7
Tonghi Creek Vic. 119 E13, 243 M12
Tongio Vic. 119 A12, 242 G9

Tongio West Vic. 119 A12, 242 F9
Tonimbuk Vic. 219 O8, 232 G5
Tooan Vic. 236 E10
Toobanna Qld 509 N11
Toobeah Qld 122 G1, 505 J11
Tooborac Vic. 240 F10
Toodyay WA 366 G1, 374 E2, 376 D7, **356**
Toogong NSW 120 E6
Toogoolawah Qld 496 I4, 505 O8
Toogoom Qld 505 P3
Tookayerta SA 303 P8
Toolamba Vic. 240 H7
Toolangi Vic. 219 M4, 222 D3, 232 F2, 240 I13, 180
Toolern Vale Vic. 218 H4, 232 B2, 240 E13
Tooleybuc NSW 126 G10, 239 M9, 203
Toolibin WA 374 H6
Tooligie SA 302 D5
Toolleen Vic. 240 E8
Toolondo Vic. 236 F11
Toolong Vic. 234 G9
Tooloom NSW 123 N2, 505 O12
Tooloon NSW 122 C10
Tooma NSW 119 B8, 242 H1, 89
Toombul Qld 492 H8
Toombullup Vic. 230 E8, 241 M9
Toompine Roadhouse Qld 515 O8, 474
Toongabbie Vic. 233 L6
Toongi NSW 120 E3
Toonumbar NSW 123 O2, 505 P12
Tooperang SA 297 H6
Toora Vic. 233 J10, 208
Tooradin Vic. 219 M10, 221 R3, 232 F7, 184
Toorak Vic. 215 M10, 149, 154
Toorak Gardens SA 293 K6
Tooraweenah NSW 122 E12
Toorbul Qld 497 N4, 443
Toorongo Vic. 219 Q6
Tootgarook Vic. 218 I11, 220 F8
Tootool NSW 120 A12, 127 Q10
Toowong Qld 492 E13, 494 E2, 430
Toowoomba Qld 496 F8, 505 N9, 433, 478, **483**
Toowoon Bay NSW 105 Q3, 108 H3
Top End, The NT **395**, 396, 401, 402, 403, 404
Top Springs NT 420 F4
Topaz Qld 509 M8
Torbanlea Qld 505 P3
Torndirrup National Park WA 371 N13, 374 I13, 376 F12, 321, 325, 331
Toronto NSW 112 F10
Torquay Qld 457
Torquay Vic. 218 F11, 225 E10, 235 Q9, 160, 191, **204**, 208
Torrens ACT 141 D6
Torrens Creek Qld 506 B4, 513 Q4
Torrens Park SA 293 J10
Torrensville SA 292 G6
Torrington NSW 123 L4, 505 N13, 60
Torrita Vic. 126 D10, 238 F9
Torrumbarry Vic. 127 J13, 240 D3
Tostaree Vic. 242 I13
Tottenham NSW 120 B2, 125 R12
Tottenham Vic. 214 G8
Tottington Vic. 228 F1
Toukley NSW 105 Q2, 112 H13, 121 M6, **88**
Tourello Vic. 218 C2, 229 L8
Towallum NSW 123 O7
Towamba NSW 117 D11, 119 F12, 243 P8
Towan Vic. 239 L9
Towaninny Vic. 237 M3
Tower Hill Tas. 561 P9

Tower Hill Vic. 234 H9
Towitta SA 296 I5
Townsville Qld 501, 509 P12, 426, 475, **483**
Towong Vic. 119 B8, 242 H2, 170
Towradgi NSW 114 F5, 116 H5
Towrang NSW 119 G3, 120 I10
Tracy SA 303 M4
Trafalgar Vic. 219 R10, 232 I7, 207
Tragowel Vic. 237 P3, 240 B2
Trangie NSW 120 C1
Tranmere SA 293 M4
Tranmere Tas. 553 M9
Traralgon Vic. 233 K7, **204**
Traralgon South Vic. 233 K7
Trawalla Vic. 218 A3, 228 I9, 235 M3
Trawool Vic. 240 H10, 201
Trayning WA 374 H1, 376 E7
Traynors Lagoon Vic. 237 K8
Treasures Homestead Vic. 231 O11
Trebonne Qld 509 N11
Treeton WA 367 C9, 369 D6, 374 B9
Tremont Vic. 216 E12
Trenah Tas. 561 O8
Trentham Vic. 218 F3, 229 Q9, 235 R2, 237 R13, 240 C12, 172, 185, 209
Trentham East Vic. 218 G3, 229 R9, 209
Tresco Vic. 126 H11, 237 O1, 239 O12
Tresco West Vic. 237 N1, 239 N12
Trevallyn NSW 121 M3
Trevallyn Tas. 557 N10, 561 L8
Trewalla Vic. 234 D9
Trewilga NSW 120 D4
Triabunna Tas. 555 O1, 559 O6, 529, **548**
Trida NSW 127 L3
Trida Vic. 219 P11
Trinita Vic. 238 H8
Trigg WA 364 B9, 318
Trinity Beach Qld 503 E7
Trinity Gardens SA 293 L5
Trinity Park Qld 503 E7
Trowutta Tas. 560 C5
Truck 'n' Travel Roadhouse Qld 123 M1, 496 F13
Truganina Vic. 214 D9
Trundle NSW 120 C4
Trunkey NSW 104 A8, 120 G7
Trunkey Creek NSW 47
Truro SA 296 G3, 303 M7
Tuan Qld 505 P4
Tuart Forest National Park WA 367 F6, 369 H1
Tuart Hill WA 364 F10
Tubbul NSW 119 B2, 120 D9
Tubbut Vic. 119 D11, 243 K8
Tucklan NSW 120 G2
Tuena NSW 104 A10, 119 F1, 120 G8, 57
Tuggerah NSW 105 P3, 108 F2, 94
Tuggeranong ACT 139 E5, 141 B9, 142 G3
Tugun Qld 499 H10, 434
Tulendeena Tas. 561 O7
Tulkara Vic. 228 E3, 237 K11
Tullah Tas. 560 F10, 543
Tullamarine Vic. 214 H3
Tullamore NSW 120 B3, 127 R1
Tullibigeal NSW 127 P4
Tulloh Vic. 218 B12, 223 G7
Tully Qld 509 N9, **484**
Tully Heads Qld 509 N9, 484
Tumbarumba NSW 119 B7, **89**
Tumbi Umbi NSW 105 P3, 108 G3
Tumblong NSW 119 B5, 120 D12
Tumbulgum NSW 123 Q1, 505 Q11
Tumby Bay SA 302 E7, 262, 278, **283**

Tummaville Qld 496 B10
Tumorrama NSW 119 C5, 120 E12, 142 B1
Tumoulin Qld 509 M8
Tumut NSW 119 C5, 120 D12, 142 A2, **89**
Tunart Vic. 126 B8, 238 C5
Tunbridge Tas. 559 M4, 561 M13, 529
Tuncurry NSW 121 P2, 59
Tungamah Vic. 127 N13, 241 K4
Tungamull Qld 507 O10
Tungkillo SA 296 G8, 301 D1, 303 M9
Tunnack Tas. 559 M6
Tunnel Tas. 557 O5, 561 M7
Tunnel Creek National Park WA 372 F9, 381 L8, 331, 332, 335
Tura Beach NSW 117 G9, 119 G11, 243 Q7
Turallin Qld 505 M10
Turill NSW 120 I2
Turkey Creek Roadhouse WA 373 O6, 381 Q7
Turlinjah NSW 143 M9
Turner ACT 140 G8
Turners Beach Tas. 556 C5, 560 H6
Turners Marsh Tas. 557 O7, 561 L7
Turondale NSW 104 B1, 120 H5
Tuross Head NSW 117 I1, 119 H8, 143 N10
Turramurra NSW 98 I1, 100 G11
Turrawan NSW 122 G8
Turrella NSW 103 L4
Turriff Vic. 126 E11, 236 I1, 238 I11, 181
Turriff East Vic. 236 I1, 238 I11
Turriff West Vic. 236 H1, 238 H11
Turtons Creek Vic. 219 R13, 175
Tusmore SA 293 L7
Tutunup WA 367 F7, 369 I3, 374 C9
Tutye Vic. 238 D10
Tweed Heads NSW 123 Q1, 499 I11, 505 Q11, **89**, 435, 448
Twelve Mile NSW 120 G3
Two Mile Flat NSW 120 G3
Two Rocks WA 374 C2
Two Wells SA 296 A5, 303 K8
Tyaak Vic. 219 K1, 240 G11
Tyabb Vic. 219 L10, 221 N5, 232 E7, 190
Tyagarah NSW 123 Q2, 505 Q12, 76
Tyagong NSW 119 C1, 120 E8
Tyalgum NSW 123 P1, 505 Q11
Tyalla Vic. 238 D10
Tycannah NSW 122 G6
Tyenna Tas. 554 B3, 559 J7
Tyers Vic. 233 K6
Tyers Junction Vic. 233 J5
Tylden Vic. 218 G2, 229 R8, 232 A1, 235 R2, 237 R13, 240 D12, 209
Tyndale NSW 123 P5
Tynong Vic. 219 N9, 232 G6, 184, 207
Tyntynder Central Vic. 239 N10
Tyntynder South Vic. 239 N10
Typo Vic. 230 H7, 241 N9, 242 A7
Tyrendarra Vic. 234 E8
Tyrendarra East Vic. 234 F8
Tyringham NSW 123 N8
Tyrrell Downs Vic. 239 K11

Uarbry NSW 120 H1
Ubobo Qld 505 M1, 507 P13
Ucolta SA 303 M2, 305 L12
Uki NSW 123 Q1, 505 Q11
Ulamambri NSW 122 F11
Ulan NSW 120 H2
Ulinda NSW 122 F12
Ulladulla NSW 119 I6, 121 J13, 143 P4, 55, **89**
Ullina Vic. 218 D2, 229 M7, 235 O1, 237 O13, 240 A11

Ullswater Vic. 236 C11
Ulmarra NSW 123 P6, 61
Ulong NSW 123 P8
Ulooloo SA 303 L3
Ultima Vic. 126 G11, 237 L1, 239 M12
Ultimo NSW 96 B13, 99 M11, 103 O1
Ulupna Vic. 127 M13, 240 I3
Uluru NT 416 F12, 422 E12, 344, 383, 385, 391, 392, 394, 403, 405
Uluru-Kata Tjuta National Park NT 416 C11, 422 E12, 385, 392, 393, 401, 405, 408
Ulva WA 374 I2
Ulverstone Tas. 556 C5, 560 H6, 528, 540, **548**
Umbakumba NT 419 P9
Umbiram Qld 496 D8
Umina NSW 105 P5, 108 F9
Unanderra NSW 116 G6
Undalya SA 303 L6
Undara Volcanic National Park Qld 509 K10, 455, 488
Undera Vic. 240 H5
Undera North Vic. 240 H5
Underbool Vic. 126 C10, 238 E10
Undercliffe NSW 103 L4
Underdale SA 292 F5
Underwood Qld 495 L8
Underwood Tas. 557 P7, 561 M7, 537
Ungarie NSW 120 A7, 127 Q5
Ungarra SA 302 E6
Unley SA 290 E13, 292 I8
Unley Park SA 293 J9
Upper Beaconsfield Vic. 219 M8, 232 F5
Upper Bingara NSW 122 I7, 49
Upper Blessington Tas. 561 N9
Upper Bowman NSW 121 M1, 123 L13
Upper Castra Tas. 556 B8, 560 H7
Upper Cedar Creek Qld 497 L6
Upper Colo NSW 105 K4
Upper Coomera Qld 497 N11, 499 A2
Upper Esk Tas. 561 O9
Upper Ferntree Gully Vic. 216 F13, 222 A12
Upper Freestone Qld 496 G13
Upper Gellibrand Vic. 218 B13, 223 G9
Upper Horton NSW 122 I7
Upper Kedron Qld 492 B10
Upper Kinchela NSW 109 H2, 123 P10
Upper Koondah Qld 496 C2
Upper Laceys Creek Qld 497 K5
Upper McDonald NSW 105 L2
Upper Mangrove NSW 105 N2
Upper Mangrove Creek NSW 105 N2
Upper Manilla NSW 122 I9
Upper Mount Hicks Tas. 560 F6
Upper Myall NSW 121 O2
Upper Natone Tas. 560 G7
Upper Pappinbarra NSW 109 B5, 123 N11
Upper Plenty Vic. 219 K3, 232 D1, 240 G12
Upper Scamander Tas. 561 Q9
Upper Sturt SA 293 N13
Upper Swan WA 365 P1, 366 C3
Upper Tenthill Qld 496 G9
Upper Widgee Qld 505 O5
Upper Woodstock Tas. 554 F9
Upper Yarra Dam Vic. 219 P5
Upper Yarraman Qld 496 F2
Upwey Vic. 216 E13, 219 L7
Uraidla SA 293 Q8, 296 C10, 297 H1
Uralla NSW 123 L9, 79, **89**
Urana NSW 127 O11
Urandangi Qld 423 R4, 512 B6

SUGGESTION FORM

This 16th edition of EXPLORE AUSTRALIA is updated from information supplied by consultants, tourist organisations and the general public. We would welcome suggestions from you. Please use the form below to supply us with any information you feel is relevant.

SUGGESTIONS FOR IMPROVEMENT

Text: ....
....
....

Maps: ....
....
....

SUGGESTED AMENDMENT OR ADDITION

TEXT

Town Name	Amendment/Addition

MAPS

Page no.	Grid	Amendment/Addition

Have you purchased a copy of EXPLORE AUSTRALIA before? ....

If so what edition? ....

OPTIONAL

Name: ....

Address: ....

Please cut out and send to:
 Managing Editor
 Penguin Cartographic
 A division of Penguin Books Australia Ltd
 487 Maroondah Hwy
 Ringwood Vic. 3134

ACCIDENT ACTION

Simple first aid can save a life.

When you approach the scene of an accident, remember to follow the DRABC action plan:

D	DANGER
R	RESPONSE
A	AIRWAY
B	BREATHING
C	CIRCULATION

1. Check for DANGER –
to yourself and others.

- Do not touch occupants or vehicle if live wires are in contact with car.

- Turn off ignition of crashed car.

- If power lines are causing sparks nearby but not touching car, remove people quickly in case spilt petrol is set alight.

- Ensure no one is smoking.

- Station people to warn oncoming cars and people of the danger ahead.

- At night, light up area and use flashing indicators on vehicles as additional warning.

- Where possible, people, vehicles and debris should be cleared from roadway.

- Only move victim when unconscious or in danger (e.g. from fire, traffic or burns from hot roadway) or when victim's position makes it impossible to carry out essential treatment (such as stopping bleeding).

- If you do have to move victim, get three or four people to help if possible. Avoid bending or twisting neck or back – keep them straight. Support any injured limbs.

REMEMBER: Most casualties will be suffering some degree of shock. One of the best ways of treating this is by reassuring them – but never give alcohol. Keep casualties calm and protect them from uncomfortable weather conditions, particularly hot sun.

2. Check for RESPONSE –
see if the casualty is conscious.

- Gently shake and ask 'Can you hear me?'.

- If conscious, check for bleeding (see Stopping Bleeding on opposite page).

3. Check and clear AIRWAY –
if unconscious, ensure airway is not blocked.

- Remove any obstructions, such as blood, vomit, loose teeth or broken dentures and teeth.

- Lie victim on side and tilt head back to clear airway.

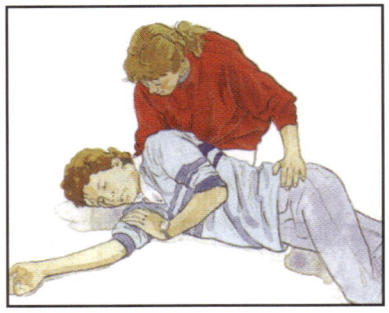

- Quickly clear mouth, using fingers if necessary. If breathing, leave on side.

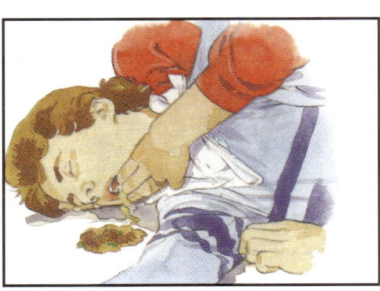

- If victim is trapped in car, tilt head back and support jaw to clear airway.

4. Check BREATHING –
see if casualty is breathing.

- Look, listen and feel for breathing.

- If breathing, leave on side and check for other injuries.

- If not breathing, turn on to back and commence Expired Air Resuscitation (see opposite page).

5. Check CIRCULATION –
check for pulse.

- Feel for pulse by placing end of your finger in groove behind the Adam's apple, on either side of neck.

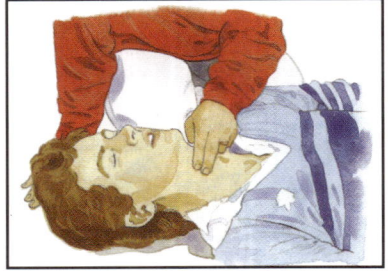

- If no pulse, perform cardiopulmonary resuscitation, if you have been taught this procedure (15 compressions to 2 breaths in 15 seconds).

LEARN BASIC FIRST AID

There are several organisations including St John Ambulance Australia that teach cardiopulmonary resuscitation and how to handle emergencies.